"There can be no doubt that this is the best text of the history of philosophy now available in English."

—*The Historical Bulletin*

"Father Copleston continues to write with the assured air of a teacher in complete mastery of his material."

—*The Catholic Messenger*

"Not only is the treatment as impartial, as judicious in emphasis and in scale, as accurate and as well illustrated as in the previous volumes, but it also brings into the ken of those who need general piloting an orientation in philosophy of a sphere of thinkers who are as great as they are strange, and as worth knowing as they are hard to know."

—*Heythrop's*

"This latest contribution to a series which is already a requisite for any philosophical library should be indispensable to both scholars and students of French philosophy and culture."

—*Religious Media Today*

" . . . stands as a clear-sighted, intelligent, and thought-provoking achievement — an unrivalled reference book for every serious student of philosophy, and an abiding monument to the richness and variety of the thought of men."

—*Catholic Herald*

" . . . a masterpiece [that] will remain for a very long time an unsurpassed work of philosophical reference."

—*The* (London) *Tablet*

A
HISTORY OF PHILOSOPHY

VOLUME VII:
FICHTE TO NIETZSCHE

VOLUME VIII:
BENTHAM TO RUSSELL

VOLUME IX:
MAINE DE BIRAN TO SARTRE

by
Frederick Copleston, S.J.

IMAGE BOOKS
DOUBLEDAY
NEW YORK LONDON TORONTO SYDNEY AUCKLAND

AN IMAGE BOOK
PUBLISHED BY DOUBLEDAY
a division of Bantam Doubleday Dell Publishing Group, Inc.
666 Fifth Avenue, New York, New York 10103

IMAGE, DOUBLEDAY, and the portrayal of a deer drinking
from a stream are trademarks of Doubleday, a division of
Bantam Doubleday Dell Publishing Group, Inc.

Image Books editions of Volumes VII, VIII, IX of A HISTORY OF
PHILOSOPHY first published 1965, 1967, 1977 by special arrangement
with The Newman Press.

This Image edition, published April 1985, consists of Volumes VII, VIII
and IX in one book.

VOL. VII
DE LICENTIA SUPERIORUM ORDINIS:
John Coventry, S.J., Praep. Prov. Angliae

NIHIL OBSTAT:
T. Gornall, S.J., Censor Deputatus

IMPRIMATUR:
✠ Franciscus, Archiepiscopus Birmingamiensis
Birmingamiae die 26a Julii 1962

VOL. VIII
DE LICENTIA SUPERIORUM ORDINIS:
J. Corbishley, S.J.
Vice-Praep. Prov. Angliae Soc. Jesu

NIHIL OBSTAT:
T. Gornall, S.J.
Censor Deputatus

IMPRIMATUR:
✠ Joseph Cleary
Episcopus Cresimensis
Vic. Cap.
Birmingamiae die 25a Junii 1965

The *Nihil obstat* and *Imprimatur* are a declaration that a book or pamphlet is
considered to be free from doctrinal or moral error. It is not implied that
those who have granted the *Nihil obstat* and *Imprimatur* agree with the
contents, opinions or statements expressed.

ISBN 0-385-23033-8
Library of Congress Catalog Card Number
All Rights Reserved
Printed in the United States of America

8   10   9

CONTENTS

v

PART II

THE REACTION AGAINST METAPHYSICAL IDEALISM

PREFACE

As Volume VI of this *History of Philosophy* ended with Kant, the natural procedure was to open the present volume with a discussion of post-Kantian German idealism. I might then have turned to the philosophy of the first part of the nineteenth century in France and Great Britain. But on reflection it seemed to me that nineteenth-century German philosophy could reasonably be treated on its own, and that this would confer on the volume a greater unity than would otherwise be possible. And in point of fact the only non-German-speaking philosopher considered in the book is Kierkegaard, who wrote in Danish.

The volume has been entitled *Fichte to Nietzsche*, as Nietzsche is the last world-famous philosopher who is considered at any length. It might indeed have been called *Fichte to Heidegger*. For not only have a good many philosophers been mentioned who were chronologically posterior to Nietzsche, but also in the last chapter a glance has been taken at German philosophy in the first half of the twentieth century. But I decided that to call the volume *Fichte to Heidegger* would tend to mislead prospective readers. For it would suggest that twentieth-century philosophers such as Husserl, N. Hartmann, Jaspers and Heidegger are treated, so to speak, for their own sake, in the same way as Fichte, Schelling and Hegel, whereas in fact they are discussed briefly as illustrating different ideas of the nature and scope of philosophy.

In the present work there are one or two variations from the pattern generally followed in preceding volumes. The introductory chapter deals only with the idealist movement, and it has therefore been placed within Part I, not before it. And though in the final chapter there are some retrospective reflections, there is also, as already indicated, a preview of thought in the first half of the twentieth century. Hence I have called this chapter 'Retrospect and Prospect' rather than 'Concluding Review'. Apart from the reasons given in the text for referring to twentieth-century thought there is the reason that I do not propose to include within this *History* any full-scale treatment of the philosophy of the present century. At the same time I did not wish to end the volume abruptly without any reference at all to later developments. The result is, of course, that one lays oneself open to the comment that it would be better to say nothing about these developments than to make some sketchy and inadequate remarks. However, I decided to risk this criticism.

To economize on space I have confined the Bibliography at the end of the book to general works and to works by and on the major figures. As for minor philosophers, many of their writings are mentioned at the appropriate places in the text. In view of the number both of nineteenth-century philosophers and of their publications, and in view of the vast literature on some of the major figures, anything like a full bibliography is out of the question. In the case of the twentieth-century thinkers mentioned in the final chapter, some books are referred to in the text or in footnotes, but no explicit bibliography has been given. Apart from the problem of space I felt that it would be inappropriate to supply, for example, a bibliography on Heidegger when he is only briefly mentioned.

The present writer hopes to devote a further volume, the eighth in this *History*, to some aspects of French and British thought in the nineteenth century. But he does not propose to spread his net any farther. Instead he plans, circumstances permitting, to turn in a supplementary volume to what may be called the philosophy of the history of philosophy, that is, to reflection on the development of philosophical thought rather than to telling the story of this development.

A final remark. A friendly critic observed that this work would be more appropriately called *A History of Western Philosophy* or *A History of European Philosophy* than *A History of Philosophy* without addition. For there is no mention, for instance, of Indian philosophy. The critic was, of course, quite right. But I should like to remark that the omission of Oriental philosophy is neither an oversight nor due to any prejudice on the author's part. The composition of a history of Oriental philosophy is a work for a specialist and requires a knowledge of the relevant languages which the present writer does not possess. Bréhier included a volume on Oriental philosophy in his *Histoire de la philosophie*, but it was not written by Bréhier.

Finally I have pleasure in expressing my gratitude to the Oxford University Press for their kind permission to quote from Kierkegaard's *The Point of View* and *Fear and Trembling* according to the English translations published by them, and to the Princeton University Press for similar permission to quote from Kierkegaard's

Sickness unto Death, Concluding Unscientific Postscript and *The Concept of Dread.* In the case of quotations from philosophers other than Kierkegaard I have translated the passages myself. But I have frequently given page-references to existing English translations for the benefit of readers who wish to consult a translation rather than the original. In the case of minor figures, however, I have generally omitted references to translations.

PART I

POST-KANTIAN IDEALIST SYSTEMS

CHAPTER I

INTRODUCTION

Preliminary remarks—Kant's philosophy and idealist meta-physics—The meaning of idealism, its insistence on system and its confidence in the power and scope of philosophy—The idealists and theology—The romantic movement and German idealism—The difficulty in fulfilling the idealist programme—The anthropomorphic element in German idealism—Idealist philosophies of man.

1. In the German philosophical world during the early part of the nineteenth century we find one of the most remarkable flowerings of metaphysical speculation which have occurred in the long history of western philosophy. We are presented with a succession of systems, of original interpretations of reality and of human life and history, which possess a grandeur that can hardly be called in question and which are still capable of exercising on some minds at least a peculiar power of fascination. For each of the leading philosophers of the period professes to solve the riddle of the world, to reveal the secret of the universe and the meaning of human existence.

True, before the death of Schelling in 1854 Auguste Comte in France had already published his *Course of Positive Philosophy* in which metaphysics was represented as a passing stage in the history of human thought. And Germany was to have its own positivist and materialist movements which, while not killing metaphysics, would force metaphysicians to reflect on and define more closely the relation between philosophy and the particular sciences. But in the early decades of the nineteenth century the shadow of positivism had not yet fallen across the scene and speculative philosophy enjoyed a period of uninhibited and luxuriant growth. With the great German idealists we find a superb confidence in the power of the human reason and in the scope of philosophy. Looking on reality as the self-manifestation of infinite reason, they thought that the life of self-expression of this reason could be retraced in philosophical reflection. They were not nervous men looking over their shoulders to see if critics were whispering that they were producing poetic effusions under the thin disguise of theoretical philosophy, or that their profundity and obscure language were a mask for lack of clarity of thought. On the contrary, they were convinced that the human spirit had at last come into its own and that the nature of reality was at last clearly revealed to human consciousness. And each set out his vision of the Universe with a splendid confidence in its objective truth.

It can, of course, hardly be denied that German idealism makes on most people today the impression of belonging to another world, to another climate of thought. And we can say that the death of Hegel in 1831 marked the end of an epoch. For it was followed by the collapse of absolute idealism[1] and the emergence of other lines of thought. Even metaphysics took a different turn. And the superb confidence in the power and range of speculative philosophy which was characteristic of Hegel in particular has never been regained. But though German idealism sped through the sky like a rocket and after a comparatively short space of time disintegrated and fell to earth, its flight was extremely impressive. Whatever its shortcomings, it represented one of the most sustained attempts which the history of thought has known to achieve a unified conceptual mastery of reality and experience as a whole. And even if the presuppositions of idealism are rejected, the idealist systems can still retain the power of stimulating the natural impulse of the reflective mind to strive after a unified conceptual synthesis.

Some are indeed convinced that the elaboration of an overall view of reality is not the proper task of scientific philosophy. And even those who do not share this conviction may well think that the achievement of a final systematic synthesis lies beyond the capacity of any one man and is more of an ideal goal than a practical possibility. But we should be prepared to recognize intellectual stature when we meet it. Hegel in particular towers up in impressive grandeur above the vast majority of those who have tried to belittle him. And we can always learn from an outstanding philosopher, even if it is only by reflecting on our reasons for disagreeing with him. The historical collapse of metaphysical idealism does not necessarily entail the conclusion that the great idealists

[1] The fact that there were later idealist movements in Britain, America, Italy and elsewhere does not alter the fact that after Hegel metaphysical idealism in Germany suffered an eclipse.

have nothing of value to offer. German idealism has its fantastic aspects, but the writings of the leading idealists are very far from being all fantasy.

2. The point which we have to consider here is not, however, the collapse of German idealism but its rise. And this indeed stands in need of some explanation. On the one hand the immediate philosophical background of the idealist movement was provided by the critical philosophy of Immanuel Kant, who had attacked the claims of metaphysicians to provide theoretical knowledge of reality. On the other hand the German idealists looked on themselves as the true spiritual successors of Kant and not as simply reacting against his ideas. What we have to explain, therefore, is how metaphysical idealism could develop out of the system of a thinker whose name is for ever associated with scepticism about metaphysics' claim to provide us with theoretical knowledge about reality as a whole or indeed about any reality other than the *a priori* structure of human knowledge and experience.[1]

The most convenient starting-point for an explanation of the development of metaphysical idealism out of the critical philosophy is the Kantian notion of the thing-in-itself.[2] In Fichte's view Kant had placed himself in an impossible position by steadfastly refusing to abandon this notion. On the one hand, if Kant had asserted the existence of the thing-in-itself as cause of the given or material element in sensation, he would have been guilty of an obvious inconsistency. For according to his own philosophy the concept of cause cannot be used to extend our knowledge beyond the phenomenal sphere. On the other hand, if Kant retained the idea of the thing-in-itself simply as a problematical and limiting notion, this was tantamount to retaining a ghostly relic of the very dogmatism which it was the mission of the critical philosophy to overcome. Kant's Copernican revolution was a great step forward, and for Fichte there could be no question of moving backwards to a pre-Kantian position. If one had any understanding of the development of philosophy and of the demands of modern thought, one could only go forward and complete Kant's work. And this meant eliminating the thing-in-itself. For, given Kant's premises, there was no room for an unknowable occult entity supposed to be independent of mind. In other words, the critical philosophy had to

---

[1] I say 'could develop' because reflection on Kant's philosophy can lead to different lines of thought, according to the aspects which one emphasizes. See Vol. VI, pp. 433-4.

[2] See Vol. VI, pp. 268-72, 384-6.

be transformed into a consistent idealism; and this meant that things had to be regarded in their entirety as products of thought.

Now, it is immediately obvious that what we think of as the extramental world cannot be interpreted as the product of conscious creative activity by the human mind. As far as ordinary consciousness is concerned, I find myself in a world of objects which affect me in various ways and which I spontaneously think of as existing independently of my thought and will. Hence the idealist philosopher must go behind consciousness, as it were, and retrace the process of the unconscious activity which grounds it.

But we must go further than this and recognize that the production of the world cannot be attributed to the individual self at all, even to its unconscious activity. For if it were attributed to the individual finite self as such, it would be very difficult, if not impossible, to avoid solipsism, a position which can hardly be seriously maintained. Idealism is thus compelled to go behind the finite subject to a supra-individual intelligence, an absolute subject.

The word 'subject', however, is not really appropriate, except as indicating that the ultimate productive principle lies, so to speak, on the side of thought and not on the side of the sensible thing. For the words 'subject' and 'object' are correlative. And the ultimate principle is, considered in itself, without object. It grounds the subject-object relationship and, in itself, transcends the relationship. It is subject and object in identity, the infinite activity from which both proceed.

Post-Kantian idealism was thus necessarily a metaphysics. Fichte, starting from the position of Kant and developing it into idealism, not unnaturally began by calling his first principle the ego, turning Kant's transcendental ego into a metaphysical or ontological principle. But he explained that he meant by this the absolute ego, not the individual finite ego. But with the other idealists (and with Fichte himself in his later philosophy) the word 'ego' is not used in this context. With Hegel the ultimate principle is infinite reason, infinite spirit. And we can say that for metaphysical idealism in general reality is the process of the self-expression or self-manifestation of infinite thought or reason.

This does not mean, of course, that the world is reduced to a process of thinking in the ordinary sense. Absolute thought or reason is regarded as an activity, as productive reason which posits or expresses itself in the world. And the world retains all the reality which we see it to possess. Metaphysical idealism does not involve the thesis that empirical reality consists of subjective ideas; but it involves the vision of the world and human history as the objective expression of creative reason. This vision was fundamental in the outlook of the German idealist: he could not avoid it. For he accepted the necessity of transforming the critical philosophy into idealism. And this transformation meant that the world in its entirety had to be regarded as the product of creative thought or reason. If, therefore, we look on the need for transforming the philosophy of Kant into idealism as a premiss, we can say that this premiss determined the basic vision of the post-Kantian idealists. But when it comes to explaining what is meant by saying that reality is a process of creative thought, there is room for different interpretations, for the several particular visions of the different idealist philosophers.

The direct influence of Kant's thought was naturally felt more strongly by Fichte than by Schelling or Hegel. For Schelling's philosophizing presupposed the earlier stages of Fichte's thought, and Hegel's absolute idealism presupposed the earlier phases of the philosophies of both Fichte and Schelling. But this does not alter the fact that the movement of German idealism as a whole presupposed the critical philosophy. And in his account of the history of modern philosophy Hegel depicted the Kantian system as representing an advance on preceding stages of thought and as demanding to be itself developed and surpassed in succeeding stages.

In this section reference has been made so far only to the process of eliminating the thing-in-itself and transferring Kant's philosophy into metaphysical idealism. But it was certainly not my intention to suggest that the post-Kantian idealists were influenced only by the idea that the thing-in-itself had to be eliminated. They were also influenced by other aspects of the critical philosophy. For example, Kant's doctrine of the primacy of the practical reason had a powerful appeal for Fichte's strongly-marked ethical outlook. And we find him interpreting the absolute ego as an infinite practical reason or moral will which posits Nature as a field and instrument for moral activity. In his philosophy the concepts of action, of duty and of moral vocation are extremely prominent. And we are perhaps entitled to say that Fichte turned Kant's second *Critique* into a metaphysics, employing his development of the first *Critique* as a means of doing so. With Schelling, however, the prominence given to the philosophy of art, to the role of genius and to the metaphysical significance of aesthetic intuition and artistic creation links him with the third *Critique* rather than with the first or second.

But instead of dwelling at length on the particular ways in which different parts or aspects of Kant's philosophy influenced this or that idealist, it will be more appropriate in our introductory chapter if we take a broader and more general view of the relation between the critical philosophy and metaphysical idealism.

The desire to form a coherent and unified interpretation of reality is natural to the reflective mind. But the actual task to be performed presents itself in different ways at different times. For example, the development of physical science in the post-mediaeval world meant that the philosopher who wished to construct an overall interpretation had to grapple with the problem of reconciling the scientific view of the world as a mechanical system with the demands of the moral and religious consciousness. Descartes was faced with this problem. And so was Kant.[1] But though Kant rejected the ways of dealing with this problem which were characteristic of his philosophical predecessors and offered his own original solution, it is arguable that in the long run he left us with 'a bifurcated reality'.[2] On the one hand we have the phenomenal world, the world of Newtonian science, governed by necessary causal laws.[3] On the other hand there is the supersensuous world of the free moral agent and of God. There is no valid reason for asserting that the phenomenal world is the only reality.[4] But at the same time there is no theoretical proof of the existence of a supersensuous reality. It is a matter of practical faith, resting on the moral consciousness. It is true that in the third *Critique* Kant endeavoured to bridge the gulf between the two worlds to the extent in which he considered this to be possible for the human mind.[5] But it is understandable if other philosophers were not satisfied with his performance. And the German idealists were able to proceed beyond Kant by means of their development and transformation of his philosophy. For if reality is the unified

[1] See Vol. IV, pp. 55–6 and Vol. VI, pp. 233–4; 428–9.
[2] Vol. IV, p. 60.
[3] Necessity and causality are for Kant *a priori* categories. But he does not deny, indeed he affirms, that the world of science is 'phenomenally real'.
[4] This is true at least if we refrain from pressing Kant's doctrine of the restricted field of application of the categories to an extent which would exclude any meaningful talk about supersensuous reality, even in the context of moral faith.
[5] See Vol. VI, ch. 15.

process by which absolute thought or reason manifests itself, it is intelligible. And it is intelligible by the human mind, provided that this mind can be regarded as the vehicle, as it were, of absolute thought reflecting on itself.

This condition possesses an obvious importance if there is to be any continuity between Kant's idea of the only possible scientific metaphysics of the future and the idealists' conception of metaphysics. For Kant the metaphysics of the future is a transcendental critique of human experience and knowledge. We can say in fact that it is the human mind's reflective awareness of its own spontaneous formative activity. In metaphysical idealism, however, the activity in question is productive in the fullest sense (the thing-in-itself having been eliminated); and this activity is attributed, not to the finite human mind as such, but to absolute thought or reason. Hence philosophy, which is reflection by the human mind, cannot be regarded as absolute thought's reflective awareness of itself unless the human mind is capable of rising to the absolute point of view and becoming the vehicle, as it were, of absolute thought or reason's reflective awareness of its own activity. If this condition is fulfilled, there is a certain continuity between Kant's idea of the only possible scientific type of metaphysics and the idealist conception of metaphysics. There is also, of course, an obvious inflation, so to speak. That is to say, the Kantian theory of knowledge is inflated into a metaphysics of reality. But the process of inflation retains a certain measure of continuity. While going far beyond anything that Kant himself envisaged, it is not a simple reversion to a pre-Kantian conception of metaphysics.

The transformation of the Kantian theory of knowledge into a metaphysics of reality carries with it, of course, certain important changes. For example, if with the elimination of the thing-in-itself the world becomes the self-manifestation of thought or reason, the Kantian distinction between the *a priori* and the *a posteriori* loses its absolute character. And the categories, instead of being subjective forms or conceptual moulds of the human understanding, become categories of reality; they regain an objective status. Again, the teleological judgment is no longer subjective, as with Kant. For in metaphysical idealism the idea of purposiveness in Nature cannot be simply a heuristic or regulative principle of the human mind, a principle which performs a useful function but the objectivity of which cannot be theoretically proved. If Nature is the expression and manifestation of thought or reason in its movement towards a goal, the process of Nature must be teleological in character.

It cannot indeed be denied that there is a very great difference between Kant's modest idea of the scope and power of metaphysics and the idealists' notion of what metaphysical philosophy is capable of achieving. Kant himself repudiated Fichte's demand for the transformation of the critical philosophy into pure idealism by the elimination of the thing-in-itself. And it is easy to understand the attitude of the neo-Kantians who, later in the century, announced that they had had enough of the airy metaphysical speculations of the idealists and that it was time to return to the spirit of Kant himself. At the same time the development of Kant's system into metaphysical idealism is not unintelligible, and the remarks in this section may have helped to explain how the idealists were able to look on themselves as Kant's legitimate spiritual successors.

3. It will be clear from what has been said about the development of metaphysical idealism that the post-Kantian idealists were not subjective idealists in the sense of holding that the human mind knows only its own ideas as distinct from extramentally existing things. Nor were they subjective idealists in the sense of holding that all objects of knowledge are the products of the finite human subject. True, Fichte's use of the word 'ego' in his earlier writings tended to give the impression that this was precisely what he did hold. But the impression was mistaken. For Fichte insisted that the productive subject was not the finite ego as such but the absolute ego, a transcendental and supra-individual principle. And as for Schelling and Hegel, any reduction of things to products of the individual finite mind was entirely foreign to their thought.

But though it is easily understood that post-Kantian idealism did not involve subjective idealism in either of the senses alluded to in the last paragraph, it is not so easy to give a general description of the movement which will apply to all the leading idealist systems. For they differ in important respects. Moreover, the thought of Schelling in particular moved through successive phases. At the same time there is, of course, a family likeness between the different systems. And this fact justifies one in venturing on some generalizations.

Inasmuch as reality is looked on as the self-expression or self-unfolding of absolute thought or reason, there is a marked tendency in German idealism to assimilate the causal relation to the logical relation of implication. For example, the empirical world is conceived by Fichte and by Schelling (in at any rate the earlier phases of the latter's thought) as standing to the ultimate productive principle in the relation of consequent to antecedent. And this means, of course, that the world follows necessarily from the first productive principle, the priority of which is logical and not temporal. Obviously, there is not and cannot be any question of external compulsion. But the Absolute spontaneously and inevitably manifests itself in the world. And there is really no place for the idea of creation in time, in the sense of there being an ideally assignable first moment of time.[1]

This notion of reality as the self-unfolding of absolute reason helps to explain the idealists' insistence on system. For if philosophy is the reflective reconstruction of the structure of a dynamic rational process, it should be systematic, in the sense that it should begin with the first principle and exhibit the essential rational structure of reality as flowing from it. True, the idea of a purely theoretical deduction does not in practice occupy such an important place in metaphysical idealism as the foreground dialectical process of Fichte and above all Hegel tends to suggest. For idealist philosophy is the conceptual reconstruction of a dynamic activity, a self-unfolding infinite life, rather than a strict analysis of the meaning and implications of one or more initial basic propositions. But the general world-view is embryonically contained in the initial idea of the world as the process of absolute reason's self-manifestation. And it is the business of philosophy to give systematic articulation to this idea, reliving the process, as it were, on the plane of reflective awareness. Hence, though it would be possible to start from the empirical manifestations of absolute reason and work backwards, metaphysical idealism naturally follows a deductive form of exposition, in the sense that it systematically retraces a teleological movement.

Now, if we assume that reality is a rational process and that its essential dynamic structure is penetrable by the philosopher, this assumption is naturally accompanied by a confidence in the power and scope of metaphysics which contrasts sharply with Kant's modest estimate of what it can achieve. And this contrast is

---

[1] Hegel admits the idea of free creation on the level of the language of the religious consciousness. But this language is for him pictorial or figurative.

obvious enough if one compares the critical philosophy with Hegel's system of absolute idealism. Indeed, it is probably true to say that Hegel's confidence in the power and reach of philosophy was unequalled by any previous philosopher of note. At the same time we have seen in the last section that there was a certain continuity between Kant's philosophy and metaphysical idealism. And we can even say, though it is a paradoxical statement, that the closer idealism kept to Kant's idea of the only possible form of scientific metaphysics, the greater was its confidence in the power and scope of philosophy. For if we assume that philosophy is thought's reflective awareness of its own spontaneous activity, and if we substitute a context of idealist metaphysics for the context of Kant's theory of human knowledge and experience, we then have the idea of the rational process, which is reality, becoming aware of itself in and through man's philosophical reflection. In this case the history of philosophy is the history of absolute reason's self-reflection. In other words, the Universe knows itself in and through the mind of man. And philosophy can be interpreted as the self-knowledge of the Absolute.

True, this conception of philosophy is characteristic more of Hegel than of the other leading idealists. Fichte ended by insisting on a divine Absolute which in itself transcends the reach of human thought, and in his later philosophy of religion Schelling emphasized the idea of a personal God who reveals himself to man. It is with Hegel that the idea of the philosopher's conceptual mastery of all reality and the interpretation of this mastery as the self-reflection of the Absolute become most prominent. But to say this is simply to say that it is in Hegelianism, the greatest achievement of metaphysical idealism, that the faith in the power and scope of speculative philosophy which inspired the idealist movement finds its purest and most grandiose expression.

4. Mention has just been made of Fichte's later doctrine of the Absolute and of Schelling's philosophy of religion. And it is appropriate to say something here of the relations between German idealism and theology. For it is important to understand that the idealist movement was not simply the result of a transformation of the critical philosophy into metaphysics. All three of the leading idealists started as students of theology, Fichte at Jena, Schelling and Hegel at Tübingen. And though it is true that they turned very quickly to philosophy, theological themes played a conspicuous role in the development of German idealism. Nietzsche's

statement that the philosophers in question were concealed theologians was misleading in some respects, but it was not altogether without foundation.

The importance of the role played by theological themes in German idealism can be illustrated by the following contrast. Though not a professional scientist Kant was always interested in science. His first writings were mainly concerned with scientific topics,[1] and one of his primary questions was about the conditions which render scientific knowledge possible. Hegel, however, came to philosophy from theology. His first writings were largely theological in character, and he was later to declare that the subject-matter of philosophy is God and nothing but God. Whether the term 'God', as here used, is to be understood in anything approaching a theistic sense is not a question which need detain us at present. The point to be made is that Hegel's point of departure was the theme of the relation between the infinite and the finite, between God and creatures. His mind could not remain satisfied with a sharp distinction between the infinite Being on the one hand and finite beings on the other, and he tried to bring them together, seeing the infinite in the finite and the finite in the infinite. In the theological phase of his development he was inclined to think that the elevation of the finite to the infinite could take place only in the life of love, and he then drew the conclusion that philosophy must in the long run yield to religion. As a philosopher, he tried to exhibit the relation between the infinite and the finite conceptually, in thought, and tended to depict philosophical reflection as a higher form of understanding than the way of thinking which is characteristic of the religious consciousness. But the general theme of the relation between the infinite and the finite which runs through his philosophical system was taken over, as it were, from his early theological reflections.

It is not, however, simply a question of Hegel. In Fichte's earlier philosophy the theme of the relation between the infinite and the finite is not indeed conspicuous, for he was primarily concerned with the completion, as he saw it, of Kant's deduction of consciousness. But in his later thought the idea of one infinite divine Life comes to the fore, and the religious aspects of his philosophy were developed. As for Schelling, he did not hesitate to say that the relation between the divine infinite and the finite is the chief problem of philosophy. And his later thought was profoundly

[1] See Vol. VI, pp. 181–2, 185–7.

religious in character, the ideas of man's alienation from and return to God playing a prominent role.

Being philosophers, the idealists tried, of course, to understand the relation between the infinite and the finite. And they tended to view it according to the analogy of logical implication. Further, if we make the necessary exception for Schelling's later religious philosophy, we can say that the idea of a personal God who is both infinite and fully transcendent seemed to the idealists to be both illogical and unduly anthropomorphic. Hence we find a tendency to transform the idea of God into the idea of the Absolute, in the sense of the all-comprehensive totality. At the same time the idealists had no intention of denying the reality of the finite. Hence the problem which faced them was that of including, as it were, the finite within the life of the infinite without depriving the former of its reality. And the difficulty of solving this problem is responsible for a good deal of the ambiguity in metaphysical idealism when it is a question of defining its relation to theism on the one hand and pantheism on the other. But in any case it is clear that a central theological theme, namely the relation between God and the world, looms large in the speculations of the German idealists.

It has been said above that Nietzsche's description of the German idealists as concealed theologians is misleading in some respects. For it suggests that the idealists were concerned with reintroducing orthodox Christianity by the backdoor, whereas in point of fact we find a marked tendency to substitute metaphysics for faith and to rationalize the revealed mysteries of Christianity, bringing them within the scope of the speculative reason. To use a modern term, we find a tendency to demythologize Christian dogmas, turning them in the process into a speculative philosophy. Hence we may be inclined to smile at J. H. Stirling's picture of Hegel as the great philosophical champion of Christianity. We may be more inclined to accept McTaggart's view, and also Kierkegaard's, that the Hegelian philosophy undermined Christianity from within as it were, by professing to lay bare the rational content of the Christian doctrines in their traditional form. And we may feel that the connection which Fichte sought to establish between his later philosophy of the Absolute and the first chapter of St. John's Gospel was somewhat tenuous.

At the same time there is no cogent reason for supposing, for instance, that Hegel had his tongue in his cheek when he referred to St. Anselm and to the process of faith seeking understanding.

His early essays showed marked hostility to positive Christianity; but he came to change his attitude and to take the Christian faith under his wing, so to speak. It would be absurd to claim that Hegel was in fact an orthodox Christian. But he was doubtless sincere when he represented the relation of Christianity to Hegelianism as being that of the absolute religion to the absolute philosophy, two different ways of apprehending and expressing the same truth-content. From an orthodox theological standpoint Hegel must be judged to have substituted reason for faith, philosophy for revelation, and to have defended Christianity by rationalizing it and turning it, to borrow a phrase from McTaggart, into exoteric Hegelianism. But this does not alter the fact that Hegel thought of himself as having demonstrated the truth of the Christian religion. Nietzsche's statement, therefore, was not altogether wide of the mark, especially if one takes into account the development in the religious aspects of Fichte's thought and the later phases of Schelling's philosophy. And in any case the German idealists certainly attributed significance and value to the religious consciousness and found a place for it in their systems. They may have turned from theology to philosophy, but they were very far from being irreligious men or rationalists in a modern sense.

5. But there is another aspect of metaphysical idealism which must also be mentioned, namely its relation to the romantic movement in Germany. The description of German idealism as the philosophy of romanticism is indeed open to serious objection. In the first place it suggests the idea of a one-way influence. That is to say, it suggests that the great idealist systems were simply the ideological expression of the romantic spirit, whereas in point of fact the philosophies of Fichte and Schelling exercised a considerable influence on some of the romantics. In the second place, the leading idealist philosophers stood in somewhat different relations to the romantics. We can say indeed that Schelling gave notable expression to the spirit of the romantic movement. But Fichte indulged in some sharp criticism of the romantics, even if the latter had derived inspiration from certain of his ideas. And Hegel had scant sympathy with some aspects of romanticism. In the third place it is arguable that the term 'philosophy of romanticism' would be better applied to the speculative ideas developed by romantics such as Friedrich Schlegel (1772–1829) and Novalis (1772–1801) than to the great idealist systems. At the same time there was undoubtedly some spiritual affinity between

the idealist and romantic movements. The romantic spirit as such was indeed an attitude towards life and the universe rather than a systematic philosophy. One may perhaps borrow Rudolf Carnap's terms and speak of it as a *Lebensgefühl* or *Lebenseinstellung*.[1] And it is perfectly understandable that Hegel saw a considerable difference between systematic philosophical reflection and the utterances of the romantics. But when we look back on the German scene in the first part of the nineteenth century, we are naturally struck by affinities as well as by differences. After all, metaphysical idealism and romanticism were more or less contemporary German cultural phenomena, and an underlying spiritual affinity is only what one might expect to find.

The romantic spirit is notoriously difficult to define. Nor indeed should one expect to be able to define it. But one can, of course, mention some of its characteristic traits. For example, as against the Enlightenment's concentration on the critical, analytic and scientific understanding the romantics exalted the power of the creative imagination and the role of feeling and intuition.[2] The artistic genius took the place of *le philosophe*. But the emphasis which was laid on the creative imagination and on artistic genius formed part of a general emphasis on the free and full development of the human personality, on man's creative powers and on enjoyment of the wealth of possible human experience. In other words, stress was laid on the originality of each human person rather than on what is common to all men. And this insistence on the creative personality was sometimes associated with a tendency to ethical subjectivism. That is to say, there was a tendency to depreciate fixed universal moral laws or rules in favour of the free development of the self in accordance with values rooted in and corresponding to the individual personality. I do not mean to imply by this that the romantics had no concern for morality and moral values. But there was a tendency, with F. Schlegel for example, to emphasize the free pursuit by the individual of his own moral ideal (the fulfilment of his own 'Idea') rather than obedience to universal laws dictated by the impersonal practical reason.

[1] According to Rudolf Carnap, metaphysical systems express a feeling for or attitude towards life. But such terms are much more applicable to the romantic spirit than, say, to Hegel's dialectical system.

[2] Two comments are appropriate here. First, I do not mean to imply that the romantic movement proper followed immediately upon the Enlightenment. But I pass over the intervening phases. Secondly, the generalization in the text should not be interpreted as meaning that the men of the Enlightenment had no understanding at all of the importance of feeling in human life. See, for example, Vol. VI, pp. 24-7.

In developing their ideas of the creative personality some of the romantics derived inspiration and stimulus from Fichte's early thought. This is true of both F. Schlegel and Novalis. But it does not follow, of course, that the use which they made of Fichte's ideas always corresponded with the philosopher's intentions. An example will make this clear. As we have seen, in his transformation of the Kantian philosophy into pure idealism Fichte took as his ultimate creative principle the transcendental ego, considered as unlimited activity. And in his systematic deduction or reconstruction of consciousness he made copious use of the idea of the productive imagination. Novalis seized on these ideas and represented Fichte as opening up to view the wonders of the creative self. But he made an important change. Fichte was concerned with explaining on idealist principles the situation in which the finite subject finds itself in a world of objects which are given to it and which affect it in various ways, as in sensation. He therefore represented the activity of the so-called productive imagination, when it posits the object as affecting the finite self, as taking place below the level of consciousness. By transcendental reflection the philosopher can be aware *that* this activity takes place, but neither he nor anyone else is aware of it *as* taking place. For the positing of the object is logically prior to all awareness or consciousness. And this activity of the productive imagination is certainly not modifiable at the will of the finite self. Novalis, however, depicted the activity of the productive imagination as modifiable by the will. Just as the artist creates works of art, so is man a creative power not only in the moral sphere but also, in principle at least, in the natural sphere. Fichte's transcendental idealism was thus turned into Novalis's 'magical idealism'. In other words, Novalis seized on some of Fichte's philosophical theories and used them in the service of a poetic and romantic extravaganza, to exalt the creative self.

Further, the romantics' emphasis on the creative genius links them with Schelling much more than with Fichte. As will be seen in due course, it was the former and not the latter who laid stress on the metaphysical significance of art and on the role of artistic genius. When Friedrich Schlegel asserted that there is no greater world than the world of art and that the artist exhibits the Idea in finite form, and when Novalis asserted that the poet is the true 'magician', the embodiment of the creative power of the human self, they were speaking in ways which were more in tune with the thought of Schelling than with the strongly ethical outlook of Fichte.

Emphasis on the creative self was, however, only one aspect of romanticism. Another important aspect was the romantics' conception of Nature. Instead of conceiving Nature simply as a mechanical system, so that they would be forced to make a sharp contrast (as in Cartesianism) between man and Nature, the romantics tended to look on Nature as a living organic whole which is in some way akin to spirit and which is clothed in beauty and mystery. And some of them showed a marked sympathy with Spinoza, that is, a romanticized Spinoza.

This view of Nature as an organic totality akin to spirit again links the romantics with Schelling. The philosopher's idea of Nature below man as slumbering spirit and the human spirit as the organ of Nature's consciousness of herself was thoroughly romantic in tone. It is significant that the poet Hölderlin (1770–1843) was a friend of Schelling when they were fellow-students at Tübingen. And the poet's view of Nature as a living comprehensive whole seems to have exercised some influence on the philosopher. In turn Schelling's philosophy of Nature exercised a powerful stimulative influence on some of the romantics. As for the romantics' sympathy with Spinoza, this was shared by the theologian and philosopher Schleiermacher. But it was certainly not shared by Fichte who had a profound dislike for anything approaching a divinization of Nature, which he looked on simply as a field and instrument for free moral activity. In this respect he was anti-romantic in his outlook.

The romantics' attachment to the idea of Nature as an organic living totality does not mean, however, that they emphasized Nature to the detriment, so to speak, of man. We have seen that they also stressed the free creative personality. In the human spirit Nature reaches, as it were, its culmination. Hence the romantic idea of Nature could be and was allied with a marked appreciation of the continuity of historical and cultural development and of the significance of past cultural periods for the unfolding of the potentialities of the human spirit. Hölderlin, for example, had a romantic enthusiasm for the genius of ancient Greece,[1] an enthusiasm which was shared by Hegel in his student days. But special attention can be drawn here to the reawakened interest in

---

[1] It is a mistake to suppose that Hölderlin's attachment to Greece necessarily makes of him a classicist as opposed to a romantic.

the Middle Ages. The man of the Enlightenment had tended to see in the mediaeval period a dark night which preceded the dawn of the Renaissance and the subsequent emergence of *les philosophes*. But for Novalis the Middle Ages represented, even if imperfectly, an ideal of the organic unity of faith and culture, an ideal which should be recovered. Further, the romantics showed a strong attachment to the idea of the spirit of a people (*Volksgeist*) and an interest in the cultural manifestation of this spirit, such as language. In this respect they continued the thought of Herder[1] and other predecessors.

The idealist philosophers not unnaturally shared this appreciation of historical continuity and development. For history was for them the working-out in time of a spiritual Idea, a *telos* or end. Each of the great idealists had his philosophy of history, that of Hegel being particularly notable. As Fichte looked on Nature primarily as an instrument for moral activity, he naturally laid more emphasis on the sphere of the human spirit and on history as a movement towards the realization of an ideal moral world-order. In Schelling's philosophy of religion history appears as the story of the return to God of fallen humanity, of man alienated from the true centre of his being. With Hegel the idea of the dialectic of national spirits plays a prominent role, though this is accompanied by an insistence on the part played by so-called world-historical individuals. And the movement of history as a whole is depicted as a movement towards the realization of spiritual freedom. In general, we can say, the great idealists regarded their epoch as a time in which the human spirit had become conscious of the significance of its activity in history and of the meaning or direction of the whole historical process.

Above all perhaps romanticism was characterized by a feeling for and longing for the infinite. And the ideas of Nature and of human history were brought together in the conception of them as manifestations of one infinite Life, as aspects of a kind of divine poem. Thus the notion of infinite Life served as a unifying factor in the romantic world-outlook. At first sight perhaps the romantics' attachment to the idea of the *Volksgeist* may appear to be at variance with their emphasis on the free development of the individual personality. But there was really no radical incompatibility. For the infinite totality was conceived, generally speaking, as infinite Life which manifested itself in and through finite beings

[1] See Vol. VI, pp. 138–46, 172–9.

but not as annihilating them or as reducing them to mere mechanical instruments. And the spirits of peoples were conceived as manifestations of the same infinite Life, as relative totalities which required for their full development the free expression of the individual personalities which were the bearers, so to speak, of these spirits. And the same can be said of the State, considered as the political embodiment of the spirit of a people.

The typical romantic was inclined to conceive the infinite totality aesthetically, as an organic whole with which man felt himself to be one, the means of apprehending this unity being intuition and feeling rather than conceptual thought. For conceptual thought tends to fix and perpetuate defined limits and boundaries, whereas romanticism tends to dissolve limits and boundaries in the infinite flow of Life. In other words, romantic feeling for the infinite was not infrequently a feeling for the indefinite. And this trait can be seen as well in the tendency to obscure the boundary between the infinite and the finite as in the tendency to confuse philosophy with poetry or, within the artistic sphere itself, to intermingle the arts.

Partly, of course, it was a question of seeing affinities and of synthesizing different types of human experience. Thus F. Schlegel regarded philosophy as akin to religion on the ground that both are concerned with the infinite and that every relation of man to the infinite can be said to belong to religion. Indeed art too is religious in character, for the creative artist sees the infinite in the finite, in the form of beauty. At the same time the romantics' repugnance to definite limits and clear-cut form was one of the reasons which led Goethe to make his famous statement that the classical is the healthy and the romantic the diseased. For the matter of that, some of the romantics themselves came to feel the need for giving definite shape to their intuitive and rather hazy visions of life and reality and for combining the nostalgia for the infinite and for the free expression of the individual personality with a recognition of definite limits. And certain representatives of the movement, such as F. Schlegel, found in Catholicism a fulfilment of this need.

The feeling for the infinite obviously constitutes common ground for romanticism and idealism. The idea of the infinite Absolute, conceived as infinite Life, comes to the fore in Fichte's later philosophy, and the Absolute is a central theme in the philosophies of Schelling, Schleiermacher and Hegel. Further, we can say that the German idealists tend to conceive the infinite not as something set over against the finite but as infinite life or activity which expresses itself in and through the finite. With Hegel especially there is a deliberate attempt to mediate between the finite and the infinite, to bring them together without either identifying the infinite with the finite or dismissing the latter as unreal or illusory. The totality lives in and through its particular manifestations, whether it is a question of the infinite totality, the Absolute, or of a relative totality such as the State.

The spiritual affinity between the romantic and idealist movements is thus unquestionable. And it can be illustrated by many examples. For instance, when Hegel depicts art, religion and philosophy as concerned with the Absolute, though in different ways, we can see an affinity between his view and the ideas of F. Schlegel to which reference was made in the last paragraph. At the same time it is necessary to emphasize an important contrast between the great idealist philosophers and the romantics, a contrast which can be illustrated in the following manner.

Friedrich Schlegel assimilated philosophy to poetry and dreamed of their becoming one. In his view philosophizing was primarily a matter of intuitive insights, not of deductive reasoning or of proof. For every proof is a proof of something, and the intuitive grasp of the truth to be proved precedes all argument, which is a purely secondary affair.[1] As Schlegel put it, Leibniz asserted and Wolff proved. Evidently, this remark was not intended as a compliment to Wolff. Further, philosophy is concerned with the Universe, the totality. And we cannot prove the totality: it is apprehended only in intuition. Nor can we describe it in the same way in which we can describe a particular thing and its relations to other particular things. The totality can in a sense be displayed or shown, as in poetry, but to say precisely what it is transcends our power. The philosopher, therefore, is concerned with attempting to say what cannot be said. And for this reason philosophy and the philosopher himself are for the true philosopher a matter for ironic wit.

When, however, we turn from Friedrich Schlegel, the romantic, to Hegel, the absolute idealist, we find a resolute insistence on systematic conceptual thought and a determined rejection of appeals to mystical intention and feeling. Hegel is indeed concerned with the totality, the Absolute, but he is concerned with

[1] Schlegel's view can be compared with the view advanced by some modern writers on metaphysics, that what really matters in a metaphysical system is the 'vision' and that arguments are persuasive devices to commend or put across a vision.

thinking it, with expressing the life of the infinite and its relation to the finite in conceptual thought. It is true that he interprets art, including poetry, as having the same subject-matter as philosophy, namely absolute Spirit. But he also insists on a difference of form which it is essential to preserve. Poetry and philosophy are distinct, and they should not be confused.

It may be objected that the contrast between the romantics' idea of philosophy and that of the great idealists is not nearly so great as a comparison between the views of F. Schlegel and Hegel tends to suggest. Fichte postulated a basic intellectual intuition of the pure or absolute ego an idea which was exploited by some of the romantics. Schelling insisted, at least in one stage of his philosophizing, that the Absolute can be apprehended in itself only in mystical intuition. And he also emphasized an aesthetic intuition through which the nature of the Absolute is apprehended not in itself but in symbolic form. For the matter of that, romantic traits can be discerned even within the Hegelian dialectical logic, which is a logic of movement, designed to exhibit the inner life of the Spirit and to overcome the conceptual antitheses which ordinary logic tends to render fixed and permanent. Indeed, the way in which Hegel depicts the human spirit as passing successively through a variety of attitudes and as restlessly moving from position to position can reasonably be regarded as an expression of the romantic outlook. Hegel's logical apparatus itself is alien to the romantic spirit, but this apparatus belongs to the foreground of his system. Underneath we can see a profound spiritual affinity with the romantic movement.

It is not, however, a question of denying the existence of a spiritual affinity between metaphysical idealism and romanticism. We have already argued that there is such an affinity. It is a question of pointing out that, in general, the idealist philosophers were concerned with systematic thought whereas the romantics were inclined to emphasize the role of intuition and feeling and to assimilate philosophy to poetry. Schelling and Schleiermacher stood indeed closer to the romantic spirit than did Fichte or Hegel. It is true that Fichte postulated a basic intellectual intuition of the pure or absolute ego; but he did not think of this as some sort of privileged mystical insight. For him it was an intuitive grasp of an activity which manifests itself to the reflective consciousness. What is required is not some mystical or poetic capacity but transcendental reflection, which is open in principle to all. And in his attack on the romantics Fichte insisted that his philosophy, though demanding this basic intellectual intuition of the ego as activity, was a matter of logical thought which yielded science, in the sense of certain knowledge. Philosophy is the knowledge of knowledge, the basic science; it is not an attempt to say what cannot be said. As for Hegel, it is doubtless true that we, looking back, can discern romantic traits even within his dialectic. But this does not alter the fact that he insisted that philosophy is not a matter of apocalyptic utterances or poetic rhapsodies or mystical intuitions but of systematic logical thought which thinks its subject-matter conceptually and makes it plain to view. The philosopher's business is to understand reality and to make others understand it, not to edify or to suggest meaning by the use of poetic images.

6. As we have seen, the initial transformation of Kant's philosophy into pure idealism meant that reality had to be looked on as a process of productive thought or reason. In other words, being had to be identified with thought. And the natural programme of idealism was to exhibit the truth of this identification by means of a deductive reconstruction of the essential dynamic structure of the life of absolute thought or reason. Further, if the Kantian conception of philosophy as thought's reflective awareness of its own spontaneous activity was to be retained, philosophical reflection had to be represented as the self-awareness or self-consciousness of absolute reason in and through the human mind. Hence it pertained also to the natural programme of idealism to exhibit the truth of this interpretation of philosophical reflection.

When, however, we turn to the actual history of the idealist movement, we see the difficulty encountered by the idealists in completely fulfilling this programme. Or, to put the matter in another way, we see marked divergences from the pattern suggested by the initial transformation of the critical philosophy into transcendental idealism. For example, Fichte starts with the determination not to go beyond consciousness, in the sense of postulating as his first principle a being which transcends consciousness. He thus takes as his first principle the pure ego as manifested in consciousness, not as a thing but as an activity. But the demands of his transcendental idealism force him to push back, as it were, the ultimate reality behind consciousness. And in the later form of his philosophy we find him postulating absolute infinite Being which transcends thought.

With Schelling the process is in a sense reversed. That is to say, while at one stage of his philosophical pilgrimage he asserts the existence of an Absolute which transcends human thought and conceptualization, in his subsequent religious philosophy he attempts to reconstruct reflectively the essence and inner life of the personal Deity. At the same time, however, he abandons the idea of deducing in a *a priori* manner the existence and structure of empirical reality and emphasizes the idea of God's free self-revelation. He does not entirely abandon the idealist tendency to look on the finite as though it were a logical consequence of the infinite; but once he has introduced the idea of a free personal God his thought necessarily departs to a large extent from the original pattern of metaphysical idealism.

Needless to say, the fact that both Fichte and Schelling, especially the latter, developed and changed their initial positions does not by itself constitute any proof that the developments and changes were unjustified. My point is rather that these illustrate the difficulty in carrying through to completion what I have called the idealist programme. One can say that neither with Fichte nor with Schelling is being in the long run reduced to thought.

It is with Hegel that we find by far the most sustained attempt to fulfil the idealist programme. He has no doubt that the rational is the real and the real the rational. And in his view it is quite wrong to speak of the human mind as merely finite and on this ground to question its power to understand the self-unfolding life of the infinite Absolute. The mind has indeed its finite aspects, but it is also infinite, in the sense that it is capable of rising to the level of absolute thought, at which level the Absolute's knowledge of itself and man's knowledge of the Absolute are one. And Hegel makes what is undoubtedly a most impressive attempt to show in a systematic and detailed way how reality is the life of absolute reason in its movement towards the goal of self-knowledge, thus becoming in actual existence what it always is in essence, namely self-thinking thought.

Clearly, the more Hegel identifies the Absolute's knowledge of itself with man's knowledge of the Absolute, the more completely does he fulfil the demand of the idealist programme that philosophy should be represented as the self-reflection of absolute thought or reason. If the Absolute were a personal God, eternally enjoying perfect self-awareness quite independently of the human spirit, man's knowledge of God would be an outside view, so to speak. If, however, the Absolute is all reality, the Universe, interpreted as the self-unfolding of absolute thought which attains self-reflection in and through the human spirit, man's knowledge of the Absolute is the Absolute's knowledge of itself. And philosophy is productive thought thinking itself.

But what is then meant by productive thought? It is arguable at any rate that it can hardly mean anything else but the Universe considered teleologically, that is, as a process moving towards self-knowledge, this self-knowledge being in effect nothing but man's developing knowledge of Nature, of himself and of his history. And in this case there is nothing behind the Universe, as it were, no thought or reason which expresses itself in Nature and human history in the way that an efficient cause expresses itself in its effect. Thought is teleologically prior, in the sense that man's knowledge of the world-process is represented as the goal of the process and as giving it its significance. But that which is actually or historically prior is Being in the form of objective Nature. And in this case the whole pattern of idealism, as suggested by the initial transformation of Kant's philosophy, is changed. For this transformation inevitably suggests the picture of an activity of infinite thought which produces or creates the objective world, whereas the picture described above is simply the picture of the actual world of experience interpreted as a teleological process. The *telos* or goal of the process is indeed depicted as the world's self-reflection in and through the human mind. But this goal or end is an ideal which is never complete at any given moment of time. Hence the identification of being and thought is never actually achieved.

7. Another aspect of the divergences from the natural pattern of post-Kantian idealism can be expressed in this way. F. H. Bradley, the English absolute idealist, maintained that the concept of God inevitably passes into the concept of the Absolute. That is to say, if the mind tries to think the infinite in a consistent manner, it must in the end acknowledge that the infinite cannot be anything else but the universe of being, reality as a whole, the totality. And with this transformation of God into the Absolute religion disappears. 'Short of the Absolute God cannot rest, and, having reached that goal, he is lost and religion with him.'[1] A similar view was expressed by R. G. Collingwood. 'God and the absolute are not identical but irretrievably distinct. And yet they are identical

---

[1] *Appearance and Reality* (2nd edition), p. 447.

in this sense: God is the imaginative or intuitive form in which the absolute reveals itself to the religious consciousness.'[2] If we preserve speculative metaphysics, we must admit in the long run that theism is a half-way house between the frank anthropomorphism of polytheism on the one hand and the idea of the all-inclusive Absolute on the other.

It is indeed obvious that in the absence of any clear idea of the analogy of being the notion of a finite being which is ontologically distinct from the infinite cannot stand. But let us pass over this point, important as it is, and note instead that post-Kantian idealism in what one might call its natural form is thoroughly anthropomorphic. For the pattern of human consciousness is transferred to reality as a whole. Let us suppose that the human ego comes to self-consciousness only indirectly. That is to say, attention is first directed to the not-self. The not-self has to be posited by the ego or subject, not in the sense that the not-self must be ontologically created by the self but in the sense that it must be recognized as an object if consciousness is to arise at all. The ego can then turn back upon itself and become reflectively aware of itself in its activity. In post-Kantian idealism this process of human consciousness is used as a key-idea for the interpretation of reality as a whole. The absolute ego or absolute reason or whatever it may be called is regarded as positing (in an ontological sense) the objective world of Nature as a necessary condition for returning to itself in and through the human spirit.

This general scheme follows naturally enough from the transformation of the Kantian philosophy into metaphysical idealism. But inasmuch as Kant was concerned with human knowledge and consciousness, the inflation of his theory of knowledge into cosmic metaphysics inevitably involves interpreting the process of reality as a whole according to the pattern of human consciousness. And in this sense post-Kantian idealism contains a marked element of anthropomorphism, a fact which it is just as well to notice in view of the not uncommon notion that absolute idealism is much less anthropomorphic than theism. Of course, we cannot conceive God other than analogically; and we cannot conceive the divine consciousness except according to an analogy with human consciousness. But we can endeavour to eliminate in thought the aspects of consciousness which are bound up with finitude. And it is arguable, to put it mildly, that to attribute to the infinite a

[2] *Speculum Mentis*, p. 151.

process of becoming self-conscious is an evident expression of anthropomorphic thinking.

Now, if there is a spiritual reality which is at any rate logically prior to Nature and which becomes self-conscious in and through man, how are we to conceive it? If we conceive it as an unlimited activity which is not itself conscious but grounds consciousness, we have more or less Fichte's theory of the so-called absolute ego.

But the concept of an ultimate reality which is at the same time spiritual and unconscious is not easily understood. Nor, of course, does it bear much resemblance to the Christian concept of God. If, however, we maintain with Schelling in his later religious philosophy that the spiritual reality which lies behind Nature is a personal Being, the pattern of the idealist scheme is inevitably changed. For it cannot then be maintained that the ultimate spiritual reality becomes self-conscious in and through the cosmic process. And inasmuch as Schelling outlived Hegel by more than twenty years we can say that the idealist movement which immediately followed the critical philosophy of Kant ended, chronologically speaking, in a reapproximation to philosophical theism. As we have seen, Bradley maintained that the concept of God is required by the religious consciousness but that, from the philosophical point of view, it must be transformed into the concept of the Absolute. Schelling would have accepted the first contention but rejected the second, at least as understood by Bradley. For in his later years Schelling's philosophy was pretty well a philosophy of the religious consciousness. And he believed that the religious consciousness demanded the transformation of his own former idea of the Absolute into the idea of a personal God. In his theosophical speculations he undoubtedly introduced obvious anthropomorphic elements, as will be seen later. But at the same time the movement of his mind towards theism represented a departure from the peculiar brand of anthropomorphism which was characteristic of post-Kantian idealism.

There is, however, a third possibility. We can eliminate the idea of a spiritual reality, whether unconscious or conscious, which produces Nature, and we can at the same time retain the idea of the Absolute becoming self-conscious. The Absolute then means the world, in the sense of the universe. And we have the picture of man's knowledge of the world and of his own history as the self-knowledge of the Absolute. In this picture, which represents the general line of one of the main interpretations of Hegel's absolute idealism,[1] nothing is added, as it were, to the empirical world except a teleological account of the world-process. That is to say, no existent transcendent Being is postulated; but the universe is interpreted as a process moving towards an ideal goal, namely complete self-reflection in and through the human spirit.

This interpretation can hardly be taken as merely equivalent to the empirical statements that in the course of the world's history man has as a matter of fact appeared and that as a matter of fact he is capable of knowing and of increasing his knowledge of himself, his history and his environment. For presumably none of us, whether materialists or idealists, whether theists, pantheists or atheists, would hesitate to accept these statements. At the very least the interpretation is meant to suggest a teleological pattern, a movement towards human knowledge of the universe, considered as the universe's knowledge of itself. But unless we are prepared to admit that this is only one possible way of regarding the world-process and thus to lay ourselves open to the objection that our choice of this particular pattern is determined by an intellectualist prejudice in favour of knowledge for the sake of knowledge (that is, by a particular valuational judgment), we must claim, it appears, that the world moves by some inner necessity towards the goal of self-knowledge in and through man. But what ground have we for making this claim unless we believe either that Nature itself is unconscious mind (or, as Schelling put it, slumbering Spirit) which strives towards consciousness or that behind Nature there is unconscious mind or reason which spontaneously posits Nature as a necessary precondition for attaining consciousness in and through the human spirit? And if we accept either of these positions, we transfer to the universe as a whole the pattern of the development of human consciousness. This procedure may indeed be demanded by the transformation of the critical philosophy into metaphysical idealism; but it is certainly not less anthropomorphic in character than philosophical theism.

8. In this chapter we have been mainly concerned with German idealism as a theory, or rather set of theories, about reality as a whole, the self-manifesting Absolute. But a philosophy of man is also a prominent feature of the idealist movement. And this is indeed only what one would expect if one considers the metaphysical premises of the several philosophers. According to

[1] The adequacy of this interpretation of Hegel is highly disputable. But this is a question which need not detain us here.

Fichte, the absolute ego is an unlimited activity which can be represented as striving towards consciousness of its own freedom. But consciousness exists only in the form of individual consciousness. Hence the absolute ego necessarily expresses itself in a community of finite subjects or selves, each of which strives towards the attainment of true freedom. And the theme of moral activity inevitably comes to the fore. Fichte's philosophy is essentially a dynamic ethical idealism. Again, for Hegel the Absolute is definable as Spirit or as self-thinking Thought. Hence it is more adequately revealed in the human spirit and its life than in Nature. And more emphasis must be placed on the reflective understanding of man's spiritual life (the life of man as a rational being) than on the philosophy of Nature. As for Schelling, when he comes to assert the existence of a personal and free God, he occupies himself concurrently with the problem of freedom in man and with man's fall from and return to God.

In the idealist philosophies of man and society insistence on freedom is a conspicuous feature. But it does not follow, of course, that the word 'freedom' is used throughout in the same sense. With Fichte the emphasis is on individual freedom as manifested in action. And we can doubtless see in this emphasis a reflection of the philosopher's own dynamic and energetic temperament. For Fichte man is from one point of view a system of natural drives, instincts and impulses; and if he is looked at simply from this point of view, it is idle to talk about freedom. But as spirit man is not tied, so to speak, to the automatic satisfaction of one desire after another: he can direct his activity to an ideal goal and act in accordance with the idea of duty. As with Kant, freedom tends to mean rising above the life of sensual impulse and acting as a rational, moral being. And Fichte is inclined to speak as though activity were its own end, emphasizing free action for the sake of free action.

But though Fichte's primary emphasis is on the individual's activity and on his rising above the slavery of natural drive and impulse to a life of action in accordance with duty, he sees, of course, that some content has to be given to the idea of free moral action. And he does this by stressing the concept of moral vocation. A man's vocation, the series of actions which he ought to perform in the world, is largely determined by his social situation, by his position, for example, as the father of a family. And in the end we have the vision of a multiplicity of moral vocations converging towards a common ideal end, the establishment of a moral world-order.

As a young man Fichte was an enthusiastic supporter of the French Revolution which he regarded as liberating men from forms of social and political life which hindered their free moral development. But then the question arose, what form of social, economic and political organization is best fitted to favour man's moral development? And Fichte found himself compelled to lay increasing emphasis on the positive role of political society as a morally educative power. But though in his later years reflection on contemporary political events, namely the Napoleonic domination and the war of liberation, was partly responsible for the growth in his mind of a nationalistic outlook and for a strong emphasis on the cultural mission of a unified German State in which alone the Germans could find true freedom, his more characteristic idea was that the State is a necessary instrument to preserve the system of rights as long as man has not attained his full moral development. If man as a moral being were fully developed, the State would wither away.

When we turn to Hegel, however, we find a different attitude. Hegel too was influenced in his youth by the ferment of the French Revolution and the drive to freedom. And the term 'freedom' plays a conspicuous role in his philosophy. As will be seen in due course, he represents human history as a movement towards the fuller realization of freedom. But he distinguishes sharply between negative freedom, as mere absence of restraint, and positive freedom. As Kant saw, moral freedom involves obeying only that law which one gives oneself as a rational being. But the rational is the universal. And positive freedom involves identifying oneself with ends that transcend one's desires as a particular individual. It is attained, above all, by identifying one's particular will with Rousseau's General Will which finds expression in the State. Morality is essentially social morality. The formal moral law receives its content and field of application in social life, especially in the State.

Both Fichte and Hegel, therefore, attempt to overcome the formalism of the Kantian ethic by placing morality in a social setting. But there is a difference of emphasis. Fichte places the emphasis on individual freedom and action in accordance with duty mediated by the personal conscience. We have to add as a corrective that the individual's moral vocation is seen as a member of a system of moral vocations, and so in a social setting. But in Fichte's ethics the emphasis is placed on the individual's struggle to overcome himself, to bring his lower self, as it were, into tune with the free will which aims at complete freedom. Hegel, however, places the emphasis on man as a member of political society and on the social aspects of ethics. Positive freedom is something to be attained through membership in a greater organic whole. As a corrective or counterweight to this emphasis we must add that for Hegel no State can be fully rational unless it recognizes the value of and finds room for subjective or individual freedom. When at Berlin Hegel lectured on political theory and described the State in highfaluting terms, he was concerned with making his hearers socially and politically conscious and with overcoming what he regarded as an unfortunate one-sided emphasis on the inwardness of morality rather than with turning them into totalitarians. Further, political institutions constitute, according to Hegel, the necessary basis for man's higher spiritual activities, art, religion and philosophy, in which the freedom of the spirit reaches its supreme expression.

What one misses, however, in both Fichte and Hegel is perhaps a clear theory of absolute moral values. If we talk with Fichte about action for action's sake, freedom for the sake of freedom, we may show an awareness of the unique character of each human being's moral vocation. But at the same time we run the risk of emphasizing the creative personality and the uniqueness of its moral vocation at the expense of the universality of the moral law. If, however, we socialize morality with Hegel, we give it concrete content and avoid the formalism of the Kantian ethic, but at the same time we run the risk of implying that moral values and standards are simply relative to different societies and cultural periods. Obviously, some would maintain that this is in fact the case. But if we do not agree, we require a clearer and more adequate theory of absolute values than Hegel actually provides.

Schelling's outlook was rather different from that either of Fichte or of Hegel. At one period of his philosophical development he utilized a good many of the former's ideas and represented the moral activity of man as tending to create a second Nature, a moral world-order, a moral world within the physical world. But the difference between his attitude and Fichte's showed itself in the fact that he proceeded to add a philosophy of art and of aesthetic intuition to which he attributed a great metaphysical significance.

With Fichte the emphasis was placed on the moral struggle and on free moral action, with Schelling it was placed on aesthetic intuition as a key to the ultimate nature of reality, and he exalted the artistic genius rather than the moral hero. When, however, theological problems came to absorb his interest, his philosophy of man naturally took on a marked religious colouring. Freedom, he thought, is the power to choose between good and bad. And personality is something to be won by the birth of light out of darkness, that is, by a sublimation of man's lower nature and its subordination to the rational will. But these themes are treated in a metaphysical setting. For example, the views on freedom and personality to which allusion has just been made lead Schelling into theosophical speculation about the nature of God. In turn, his theories about the divine nature react on his view of man.

To return to Hegel, the greatest of the German idealists. His analysis of human society and his philosophy of history are certainly very impressive. Many of those who listened to his lectures on history must have felt that the significance of the past and the meaning of the movement of history were being revealed to them. Moreover, Hegel was not exclusively concerned with understanding the past. As has already been remarked, he wished to make his students socially, politically and ethically conscious. And he doubtless thought that his analysis of the rational State could furnish standards and aims in political life, especially in German political life. But the emphasis is placed on understanding. Hegel is the author of the famous saying that the owl of Minerva spreads her wings only with the falling of the dusk, and that when philosophy spreads her grey on grey, then has a shape of life grown cold. He had a vivid realization of the fact that political philosophy is apt to canonize, as it were, the social and political forms of a society or culture which is about to pass away. When a culture or society has become mature and ripe, or even over-ripe, it becomes conscious of itself in and through philosophical reflection, just at the moment when the movement of life is demanding and bringing forth new societies or new social and political forms.

With Karl Marx we find a different attitude. The business of the philosopher is to understand the movement of history in order to change existing institutions and forms of social organization in accordance with the demands of the teleological movement of history. Marx does not, of course, deny the necessity and value of understanding, but he emphasizes the revolutionary function of understanding. In a sense Hegel looks backward, Marx forward. Whether Marx's idea of the philosopher's function is tenable or not is a question which we need not discuss here. It is sufficient to note the difference between the attitudes of the great idealist and the social revolutionary. If we wish to find among the idealist philosophers something comparable to Marx's missionary zeal, we have to turn to Fichte rather than to Hegel. As will be seen in the relevant chapters, Fichte had a passionate belief in the saving mission of his own philosophy for human society. But Hegel felt, as it were, the weight and burden of all history on his shoulders. And looking back on the history of the world, his primary aim was to understand it. Further, though he certainly did not imagine that history had stopped with the coming of the nineteenth century, he was too historically minded to have much faith in the finality of any philosophical Utopia.

CHAPTER II

FICHTE (1)

Life and writings—On looking for the fundamental principle of philosophy; the choice between idealism and dogmatism—The pure ego and intellectual intuition—Comments on the theory of the pure ego; phenomenology of consciousness and idealist metaphysics—The three fundamental principles of philosophy— Explanatory comments on Fichte's dialectical method—The theory of science and formal logic—The general idea of the two deductions of consciousness—The theoretical deduction—The practical deduction—Comments on Fichte's deduction of consciousness.

1. JOHANN GOTTLIEB FICHTE was born in 1762 at Rammenau in Saxony. He came of a poor family, and in the ordinary course of events he could hardly have enjoyed facilities for pursuing advanced studies. But as a small boy he aroused the interest of a local nobleman, the Baron von Miltitz, who undertook to provide for his education. At the appropriate age Fichte was sent to the famous school at Pforta where Nietzsche was later to study. And in 1780 he enrolled as a student of theology in the University of Jena, moving later to Wittenberg and subsequently to Leipzig.

During his studies Fichte came to accept the theory of determinism. To remedy this sad state of affairs a good clergyman recommended to him an edition of Spinoza's *Ethics* which was furnished with a refutation by Wolff. But as the refutation seemed to Fichte to be extremely weak, the effect of the work was the very opposite of that intended by the pastor. Determinism, however, was not really in tune with Fichte's active and energetic character or with his strong ethical interests, and it was soon replaced by an insistence on moral freedom. He was later to show himself a vigorous opponent of Spinozism, but it always represented for him one of the great alternatives in philosophy.

For financial reasons Fichte found himself compelled to take a post as tutor in a family at Zürich where he read Rousseau and Montesquieu and welcomed the news of the French Revolution with its message of liberty. His interest in Kant was aroused when a student's request for the explanation of the critical philosophy led him to study it for the first time. And in 1791, when returning to Germany from Warsaw, where he had a brief and rather humiliating experience as tutor in a nobleman's family, he visited Kant at Königsberg. But he was not received with any enthusiasm. And he therefore attempted to win the great man's favour by writing an essay to develop Kant's justification of faith in the name of the practical reason. The resulting *Essay towards a Critique of all Revelation* (*Versuch einer Kritik aller Offenbarung*) pleased Kant, and after some difficulties with the theological censorship it was published in 1792. As the name of the author was not given, some reviewers concluded that the essay had been written by Kant. And when Kant proceeded to correct this error and to praise the real author, Fichte's name became at once widely known.

In 1793 Fichte published his *Contributions designed to correct the Judgment of the Public on the French Revolution*. This work won for him the reputation of being a democrat and Jacobin, a politically dangerous figure. In spite of this, however, he was appointed professor of philosophy at Jena in 1794, partly owing to a warm recommendation by Goethe. In addition to his more professional courses of lectures Fichte gave a series of conferences on the dignity of man and the vocation of the scholar, which were published in the year of his appointment to the chair. He was always something of a missionary or preacher. But the chief publication of 1794 was the *Basis of the Entire Theory of Science* (*Grundlage der gesammten Wissenschaftslehre*) in which he presented his idealist development of the critical philosophy of Kant. His predecessor in the chair of philosophy at Jena, K. L. Reinhold (1758–1823), who had accepted an invitation to Kiel, had already demanded that the Kantian criticism should be turned into a system, that is to say, that it should be derived systematically from one fundamental principle. And in his theory of science Fichte undertook to fulfil this task more successfully than Reinhold had done.[1] The theory of science was conceived as exhibiting the systematic development from one ultimate principle of the fundamental propositions which lie at the basis of and make possible all particular sciences or ways of knowing. But to exhibit this development is at the same time to portray the development of creative thought. Hence the theory of science is not only epistemology but also metaphysics.

[1] From about 1797 Reinhold accepted and defended the philosophy of Fichte. But he was a restless spirit, and after a few years he turned to other lines of thought.

But Fichte was very far from concentrating exclusively on the theoretical deduction of consciousness. He laid great stress on the moral end of the development of consciousness or, in more concrete terms, on the moral purpose of human existence. And we find him publishing in 1796 the *Basis of Natural Right* (*Grundlage des Naturrechts*) and in 1798 *The System of Ethics* (*Das System der Sittenlehre*). Both subjects are said to be treated 'according to the principles of the theory of science'. And so no doubt they are. But the works are much more than mere appendages to the *Wissenschaftslehre*. For they display the true character of Fichte's philosophy, that is, as a system of ethical idealism.

Complaints have often been made, and not without reason, of the obscurity of the metaphysical idealists. But a prominent feature of Fichte's literary activity was his unremitting efforts to clarify the ideas and principles of the theory of science.[1] For instance, in 1797 he published two introductions to the *Wissenschaftslehre* and in 1801 his *Sonnenklarer Bericht, A Report, Clear as the Sun, for the General Public on the Real Essence of the Latest Philosophy: An Attempt to compel the Reader to Understand*. The title may have been over-optimistic, but at any rate it bore witness to the author's efforts to make his meaning clear. Moreover, in the period 1801–13 Fichte composed, for his lecture courses, several revised versions of the *Wissenschaftslehre*. In 1810 he published *The Theory of Science in its General Lines* (*Die Wissenschaftslehre in ihrem allgemeinen Umrisse*) and the *Facts of Consciousness* (*Tatsachen des Bewusstseins*, second edition, 1813).

In 1799 Fichte's career at Jena came to an abrupt end. He had already aroused some antagonism in the university by his plans to reform the students' societies and by his Sunday discourses which seemed to the clergy to constitute an act of trespass on their preserves. But his crowning offence was the publication in 1798 of an essay *On the Ground of our Belief in a Divine World-Order* (*Ueber den Grund unseres Glaubens an eine göttliche Weltregierung*). The appearance of this essay led to a charge of atheism, on the ground that Fichte identified God with a moral world-order to be created and sustained by the human will. The philosopher tried to defend himself, but without success. And in 1799 he had to leave Jena and went to Berlin.

In 1800 Fichte published *The Vocation of Man* (*Die Bestimmung*

---

[1] It is perhaps needless to say that the word 'science' must be understood in the sense of 'knowledge' rather than according to the narrower modern use of the term.

des Menschen). The work belongs to his so-called popular writings, addressed to the general educated public rather than to professional philosophers; and it is a manifesto in favour of the author's idealist system as contrasted with the romantics' attitude to Nature and to religion. Fichte's exalted language may indeed easily suggest a romantic pantheism, but the significance of the work was understood well enough by the romantics themselves. Schleiermacher, for example, saw that Fichte was concerned with repudiating any attempt to achieve a fusion of Spinozism and idealism, and in a sharply critical review he maintained that Fichte's hostile reaction to the idea of the universal necessity of Nature was really caused by his predominating interest in man as a finite, independent being who had at all costs to be exalted above Nature. In Schleiermacher's opinion Fichte should have sought for a higher synthesis which would include the truth in Spinozism while not denying moral freedom, instead of simply opposing man to Nature.

In the same year, 1800, Fichte published his work on *The Closed Commercial State* (*Der geschlossene Handelsstaat*) in which he proposed a kind of State socialism. It has already been remarked that Fichte was something of a missionary. He regarded his system not only as the philosophical truth in an abstract, academic sense, but also as the saving truth, in the sense that the proper application of its principles would lead to the reform of society. In this respect at least he resembles Plato. Fichte had once hoped that Free-masonry might prove an apt instrument for promoting moral and social reform by taking up and applying the principles of the *Wissenschaftslehre*. But he was disappointed in this hope and turned instead to the Prussian government. And his work was really a programme offered to the government for implementation.

In 1804 Fichte accepted the offer of a chair at Erlangen. But he was not actually nominated professor until April 1805, and he employed the interval by lecturing at Berlin on the *Characteristics of the Present Age* (*Grundzüge des gegenwärtigen Zeitalters*). In these lectures he attacked the view of romantics such as Novalis, Tieck and the two Schlegels. Tieck introduced Novalis to Boehme's writings, and some of the romantics were enthusiastic admirers of the mystical shoemaker of Görlitz. But their enthusiasm was not shared by Fichte. Nor had he any sympathy with Novalis's dream of the restoration of a theocratic Catholic culture. His lectures were also directed against the philosophy of Nature which had been developed by Schelling, his former disciple. But these polemics are in a sense incidental to the general philosophy of history which is sketched in the lectures. Fichte's 'present age' represents one of the epochs in the development of man towards the goal of history described as the ordering of all human relations with freedom according to reason. The lectures were published in 1806.

At Erlangen Fichte lectured in 1805 *On the Nature of the Scholar* (*Ueber das Wesen des Gelehrten*). And in the winter of 1805-6 he gave a course of lectures at Berlin on *The Way to the Blessed Life or The Doctrine of Religion* (*Die Anweisung zum seligen Leben, oder auch die Religionslehre*). At first sight at least this work on religion seems to show a radical change from the philosophy expounded in Fichte's early writings. We hear less about the ego and much more about the Absolute and life in God. Indeed, Schelling accused Fichte of plagiarism, that is, of borrowing ideas from Schelling's theory of the Absolute and trying to graft them on to the *Wissenschaftslehre*, oblivious of the incompatibility between the two elements. Fichte, however, refused to admit that his religious ideas, as set forth in *The Doctrine of Religion*, were in any way inconsistent with his original philosophy.

When Napoleon invaded Prussia in 1806, Fichte offered to accompany the Prussian troops as a lay preacher or orator. But he was informed that the King considered it a time for speaking by acts rather than by words, and that oratory would be better suited for celebrating victory. When events took a menacing turn Fichte left Berlin; but he returned in 1807, and in the winter of 1807-8 he delivered his *Addresses to the German Nation* (*Reden an die deutsche Nation*). These discourses, in which the philosopher speaks in exalted and glowing terms of the cultural mission of the German people,[1] have lent themselves to subsequent exploitation in an extreme nationalist sense. But in justice to him we should remember the circumstances in which they were delivered, namely the period of Napoleonic domination.

The year 1810 saw the foundation of the University of Berlin, and Fichte was appointed dean of the philosophical faculty. From 1811 to 1812 he was rector of the university. At the beginning of 1814 he caught typhus from his wife who had contracted the disease while nursing the sick, and on January 29th of that year he died.

---

[1] A. G. Schlegel had already spoken in a not dissimilar vein of Germany's cultural mission in a course of lectures given in 1803-4.

2. Fichte's initial conception of philosophy has little in common with the romantic idea of the kinship between it and poetry. Philosophy is, or at least ought to be, a science. In the first place, that is to say, it should be a body of propositions which form a systematic whole of such a kind that each proposition occupies its proper place in a logical order. And in the second there must be a fundamental or logically prior proposition. 'Every science must have a fundamental proposition [*Grundsatz*]. . . . And it cannot have more than one fundamental proposition. For otherwise it would be not one but several sciences.'[1] We might indeed wish to question the statement that every science must have one, and only one basic proposition; but this is at any rate part of what Fichte means by a science.

This idea of science is obviously inspired by a mathematical model. Indeed, Fichte takes geometry as an example of a science. But it is, of course, a particular science, whereas philosophy is for Fichte the science of science, that is, the knowledge of knowledge or doctrine of knowledge (*Wissenschaftslehre*). In other words, philosophy is the basic science. Hence the fundamental proposition of philosophy must be indemonstrable and self-evidently true. 'All other propositions will possess only a mediate certainty, derived from it, whereas it must be immediately certain.'[2] For if its fundamental proposition were demonstrable in another science, philosophy would not be the basic science.

As will be seen in the course of the exposition of his thought, Fichte does not actually adhere to the programme suggested by this concept of philosophy. That is to say, his philosophy is not in practice a strict logical deduction such as could in principle be performed by a machine. But this point must be left aside for the moment. The immediate question is, what is the basic proposition of philosophy?

But before we can answer this question we must decide in what direction we are going to look for the proposition which we are seeking. And here, according to Fichte, one is faced with an initial option, one's choice depending on what kind of a man one is. A man of one type will be inclined to look in one direction and a man of another type in another direction. But this idea of an initial option stands in need of some explanation. And the explanation

---

[1] *F*, I, pp. 41–2; *M*, I, p. 170. In this and similar references to Fichte's writings *F* and *M* signify respectively the editions of his *Works* by his son, I. H. Fichte, and F. Medicus.

[2] *F*, I, p. 48; *M*, I, p. 177.

throws light on Fichte's conception of the task of philosophy and of the issue with which contemporary thought is faced.

In his *First Introduction to the Theory of Science* Fichte tells us that philosophy is called upon to make clear the ground of all experience (*Erfahrung*). But the word experience is here used in a somewhat restricted sense. If we consider the contents of consciousness, we see that they are of two kinds. 'We can say in brief: some of our presentations [*Vorstellungen*] are accompanied by the feeling of freedom, while others are accompanied by the feeling of necessity.'[1] If I construct in imagination a griffin or a golden mountain, or if I make up my mind to go to Paris rather than to Brussels, such presentations seem to depend on myself. And, as depending on the subject's choice, they are said to be accompanied by the feeling of freedom. If we ask why they are what they are, the answer is that the subject makes them what they are. But if I take a walk along a London street, it does not depend simply on myself what I see or hear. And such presentations are said to be accompanied by the feeling of necessity. That is to say, they appear to be imposed upon me. The whole system of these presentations is called by Fichte 'experience' even if he does not always use the term in this limited sense. And we can ask, what is the ground of experience? How are we to explain the obvious fact that a very large class of presentations seem to be imposed on the subject? 'To answer this question is the task of philosophy.'[2]

Now, two possibilities lie open to us. Actual experience is always experience of something by an experiencer: consciousness is always consciousness of an object by a subject or, as Fichte sometimes puts it, intelligence. But by a process which Fichte calls abstraction the philosopher can isolate conceptually the two factors which in actual consciousness are always conjoined. He can thus form the concepts of intelligence-in-itself and thing-in-itself. And two paths lie before him. Either he can try to explain experience (in the sense described in the last paragraph) as the product of intelligence-in-itself, that is, of creative thought. Or he can try to explain experience as the effect of the thing-in-itself. The first path is obviously that of idealism. The second is that of 'dogmatism'. And in the long run dogmatism spells materialism and determinism. If the thing, the object, is taken as the fundamental principle of explanation, intelligence will ultimately be reduced to a mere epiphenomenon.

[1] *F*, I, p. 423; *M*, III, p. 7.   [2] *Ibid.*

This uncompromising Either-Or attitude is characteristic of Fichte. There is for him a clear-cut option between two opposed and mutually exclusive positions. True, some philosophers, notably Kant, have endeavoured to effect a compromise, to find, that is to say, a middle path between pure idealism and a dogmatism which ends in deterministic materialism. But Fichte has no use for such compromises. If a philosopher wishes to avoid dogmatism with all its consequences, and if he is prepared to be consistent, he must eliminate the thing-in-itself as a factor in the explanation of experience. The presentations which are accompanied by a feeling of necessity, by the feeling of being imposed upon or affected by an object existing independently of mind or thought, must be accounted for without any recourse to the Kantian idea of the thing-in-itself.

But on what principle is the philosopher to make his choice between the two possibilities which lie open to him? He cannot appeal to any basic theoretical principle. For we are assuming that he has not yet found such a principle but has to decide in what direction he is going to look for it. The issue must, therefore, be decided 'by inclination and interest'.[1] That is to say, the choice which the philosopher makes depends on what kind of a man he is. Needless to say, Fichte is convinced that the superiority of idealism to dogmatism as an explanation of experience becomes evident in the process of working out the two systems. But they have not yet been worked out. And in looking for the first principle of philosophy we cannot appeal to the theoretical superiority of a system which has not yet been constructed.

What Fichte means is that the philosopher who is maturely conscious of his freedom as revealed in moral experience will be inclined to idealism, while the philosopher who lacks this mature moral consciousness will be inclined to dogmatism. The 'interest' in question is thus interest in and for the self, which Fichte regards as the highest interest. The dogmatist, lacking this interest, emphasizes the thing, the not-self. But the thinker who has a genuine interest in and for the free moral subject will turn for his basic philosophical principle to intelligence, the self or ego, rather than to the not-self.

Fichte's preoccupation with the free and morally active self is thus made clear from the start. Underlying and inspiring his theoretical inquiry into the ground of experience there is a profound

[1] *F*, I, p. 433; *M*, III, p. 17.

conviction of the primary significance of man's free moral activity. He continues Kant's insistence on the primacy of the practical reason, the moral will. But he is convinced that to maintain this primacy one has to take the path to pure idealism. For behind Kant's apparently innocent retention of the thing-in-itself Fichte sees the lurking spectre of Spinozism, the exaltation of Nature and the disappearance of freedom. If we are to exorcize this spectre, compromise must be rejected.

We can, of course, detach Fichte's idea of the influence exercised by 'inclination and interest' from his historically-conditioned picture of the initial option with which philosophers are faced. And the idea can then be seen as opening up fascinating vistas in the field of what Karl Jaspers calls 'the psychology of world-views'. But in a book of this kind one must resist the temptation to embark on a discussion of this attractive topic.

3. Assuming that we have chosen the path of idealism, we must turn for the first principle of philosophy to intelligence-in-itself. But it is better to drop this cumbersome term and to speak, as Fichte proceeds to do, of the *I* or ego. We are committed, therefore, to explaining the genesis of experience from the side, so to speak, of the self. In reality Fichte is concerned with deriving consciousness in general from the ego. But in speaking of experience, in the restricted sense explained above, he lays his finger on the crucial difficulty which pure idealism has to face, namely the evident fact that the self finds itself in a world of objects which affect it in various ways. If idealism is incapable of accounting adequately for this fact, it is evidently untenable.

But what is the ego which is the foundation of philosophy? To answer this question we obviously have to go behind the objectifiable self, the ego as object of introspection or of empirical psychology, to the pure ego. Fichte once said to his students: 'Gentlemen, think the wall.' He then proceeded: 'Gentlemen, think him who thought the wall.' Clearly, we could proceed indefinitely in this fashion. 'Gentlemen, think him who thought him who thought the wall', and so on. In other words, however hard we may try to objectify the self, that is, to turn it into an object of consciousness, there always remains an *I* or ego which transcends objectification and is itself the condition of all objectifiability and the condition of the unity of consciousness. And it is this pure or transcendental ego which is the first principle of philosophy.

It is clearly idle to object against Fichte that we cannot find a pure or transcendental ego by peering about. For it is precisely Fichte's contention that the pure ego cannot be found in this way, though it is the necessary condition of our being able to do any peering about. But for this very reason it may appear that Fichte has gone beyond the range of experience (in a wide sense) or consciousness and has failed to observe his own self-imposed limitations. That is to say, having reaffirmed the Kantian view that our theoretical knowledge cannot extend beyond experience, he now seems to have transgressed this limit.

But this, Fichte insists, is not the case. For we can enjoy an intellectual intuition of the pure ego. This is not, however, a mystical experience reserved for the privileged few. Nor is it an intuition of the pure ego as an entity existing behind or beyond consciousness. Rather is it an awareness of the pure ego or *I* principle as an activity within consciousness. And this awareness is a component element in all self-consciousness. 'I cannot take a pace, I cannot move hand or foot, without the intellectual intuition of my self-consciousness in these actions. It is only through intuition that I know that I perform the action. . . . Everyone who ascribes activity to himself appeals to this intuition. In it is the foundation of life, and without it is death.'[1] In other words, anyone who is conscious of an action as his own is aware of himself acting. In this sense he has an intuition of the self as activity. But it does not follow that he is reflectively aware of this intuition as a component element in consciousness. It is only the philosopher who is reflectively aware of it, for the simple reason that transcendental reflection, by which the attention is reflected onto the pure ego, is a philosophical act. But this reflection is directed, so to speak, to ordinary consciousness, not to a privileged mystical experience. Hence, if the philosopher wishes to convince anyone of the reality of this intuition, he can only draw the man's attention to the data of consciousness and invite him to reflect for himself. He cannot show the man the intuition existing in a pure state, unmixed with any component elements; for it does not exist in this state. Nor can he convince the other man by means of some abstract proof. He can only invite the man to reflect on his own self-consciousness and to see that it includes an intuition of the pure ego, not as a thing, but as an activity. 'That there is such a power of intellectual intuition cannot be demonstrated through concepts, nor can its

[1] *F*, I, p. 463; *M*, III, p. 47.

nature be developed by means of concepts. Everyone must find it immediately in himself or he will never be able to know it.'[1]

Fichte's thesis can be clarified in this way. The pure ego cannot be turned into an object of consciousness in the same way that a desire, for example, can be objectified. It would be absurd to say that through introspection I see a desire, an image and a pure ego. For every act of objectification presupposes the pure ego. And for this reason it can be called the transcendental ego. But it does not follow that the pure ego is an inferred occult entity. For it manifests itself in the activity of objectification. When I say, 'I am walking', I objectify the action, in the sense that I make it object-for-a-subject. And the pure *I* reveals itself to reflection in this activity of objectification. An activity is intuited, but no entity behind consciousness is inferred. Hence Fichte concludes that the pure ego is not something which acts but simply an activity or doing. 'For idealism the intelligence is a doing [*Thun*] and absolutely nothing else; one should not even call it an active thing [*ein Tätiges*].'[2]

At first sight at least Fichte appears to contradict Kant's denial that the human mind possesses any faculty of intellectual intuition. In particular, he seems to be turning into an object of intuition the transcendental ego which for Kant was simply a logical condition of the unity of consciousness and could be neither intuited nor proved to exist as a spiritual substance. But Fichte insists that his contradiction of Kant is really only verbal. For when Kant denied that the human mind possesses any faculty of intellectual intuition, he meant that we do not enjoy any intellectual intuition of supersensible entities transcending experience. And the *Wissenschaftslehre* does not really affirm what Kant denied. For it is not claimed that we intuit the pure ego as a spiritual substance or entity transcending consciousness but simply as an activity within consciousness, which reveals itself to reflection. Further, apart from the fact that Kant's doctrine of pure apperception[3] gives us at any rate a hint of intellectual intuition, we can easily indicate the place, Fichte claims, at which Kant ought to have spoken of and admitted this intuition. For he asserted that we are conscious of a categorical imperative; and if he had considered the matter thoroughly, he should have seen that this consciousness involves the intellectual intuition of the pure ego as activity.

---

[1] *F*, I, p. 463; *M*, III, p. 47.   [2] *F*, I, p. 440; *M*, III, p. 24.
[3] See Vol. VI, pp. 253–6, 282–6, 391–2.

Indeed, Fichte goes on to suggest a specifically moral approach to the topic. 'In the consciousness of this law . . . is grounded the intuition of self-activity and freedom. . . . It is only through the medium of the moral law that I apprehend *myself*. And if I apprehend myself in this way, I necessarily apprehend myself as self-active. . . .'[1] Once again, therefore, the strongly ethical bent of Fichte's mind finds clear expression.

4. If we look at the matter from the point of view of phenomenology of consciousness, Fichte is, in the opinion of the present writer, perfectly justified in affirming the I-subject or transcendental ego. Hume, looking into his mind, so to speak, and finding only psychical phenomena, tried to reduce the self to the succession of these phenomena.[2] And it is understandable that he acted in this way. For part of his programme was to apply to man the empirical method, as he conceived it, which had proved so successful in 'experimental philosophy' or natural science. But the direction of his attention to the objects or data of introspection led him to slur over the fact, all-important for the philosopher, that psychical phenomena become phenomena (appearing to a subject) only through the objectifying activity of a subject which transcends objectification in the same sense. Obviously, there is no question of reducing the human being to a transcendental or metaphysical ego. And the problem of the relation between the self as pure subject and other aspects of the self is one that cannot be evaded. But this does not alter the fact that a recognition of the transcendental ego is essential to an adequate phenomenology of consciousness. And in regard to this point Fichte shows a degree of insight which Hume lacked.

But Fichte is not, of course, simply concerned with the phenomenology of consciousness, that is, with a descriptive analysis of consciousness. He is concerned also with developing a system of idealist metaphysics. And this point has an important bearing on his theory of the transcendental ego. From a purely phenomenological point of view talk about 'the transcendental ego' no more commits us to saying that there is one and only one such ego than a medical writer's generalizations about 'the stomach' commit him to holding that there is one and only one stomach. But if we propose to derive the whole sphere of the objective, including Nature and all selves in so far as they are objects for a subject, from the transcendental ego, we must either

---

[1] *F*, I, p. 466; *M*, III, p. 50.   [2] See Vol. V, pp. 300–5.

embrace solipsism or interpret the transcendental ego as a supra-individual productive activity which manifests itself in all finite consciousnesses. As, therefore, Fichte has no intention of defending solipsism, he is bound to interpret the pure ego as a supra-individual absolute ego.

To be sure, Fichte's use of the term *I* or *ego* not unnaturally suggested to many of his readers that he was talking about the individual self or ego. And this interpretation was facilitated by the fact that the more metaphysical aspects of his thought were comparatively inconspicuous in his earlier writings. But the interpretation, Fichte insisted, was erroneous. Lecturing in the winter of 1810–11 and looking back at the criticism that had been levelled against the *Wissenschaftslehre* he protested that he had never intended to say that the creative ego is the individual finite self. 'People have generally understood the theory of science as attributing to the individual effects which could certainly not be ascribed to it, such as the production of the whole material world. . . . They have been completely mistaken: it is not the individual but the one immediate spiritual Life which is the creator of all phenomena, including phenomenal individuals.'[1]

It will be noticed that in this passage the word 'Life' is used instead of 'ego'. Starting, as he did, from the position of Kant and being concerned with transforming it into pure idealism, he not unnaturally began by talking about the pure or absolute ego. But in the course of time he saw that it was inappropriate to describe the infinite activity which grounds consciousness, including the finite self, as itself an ego or subject. However, we need not dwell at present on this point. It is sufficient to note Fichte's protest against what he considered to be a fundamental misinterpretation of his theory. The absolute ego is not the individual finite self but an infinite (better, unlimited) activity.

Fichte's *Wissenschaftslehre* is thus both a phenomenology of consciousness and an idealist metaphysics. And to a certain extent at any rate the two aspects can be separated. Hence it is possible to attach some value to a good deal of what Fichte has to say without committing oneself to his metaphysical idealism. We have already indicated this in regard to the theory of the trans-cendental ego. But the distinction has a wider field of application.

5. In the second section of this chapter it was remarked that philosophy, according to Fichte, must have a fundamental and

---

[1] *F*, II, p. 607 (not included in *M*).

indemonstrable proposition. And the thought may have occurred to the reader that whatever else the ego may be, it is not a proposition. This is, of course, true. We have still to ascertain what is the basic proposition of philosophy. But we know at any rate that it must be the expression of the original activity of the pure ego.

Now, we can distinguish between the spontaneous activity of the pure ego on the one hand and the philosopher's philosophical reconstruction or thinking of this activity on the other. The spontaneous activity of the pure ego in grounding consciousness is not, of course, itself conscious. As spontaneous activity the pure ego does not exist 'for itself'. It comes to exist for itself, as an ego, only in the intellectual intuition by which the philosopher in transcendental reflection apprehends the ego's spontaneous activity. It is through the act of the philosopher, 'through an activity directed towards an activity . . . that the ego first comes to be *originally* [*ursprünglich*] for itself'.[1] In intellectual intuition, therefore, the pure ego is said to posit itself (*sich setzen*). And the fundamental proposition of philosophy is that 'the ego simply posits in an original way its own being'.[2] In transcendental reflection the philosopher goes back, as it were, to the ultimate ground of consciousness. And in his intellectual intuition the pure ego affirms itself. It is not demonstrated as a conclusion from premises: it is seen as affirming itself and so as existing. 'To *posit itself* and to *be* are, as said of the ego, completely the same.'[3]

But though by means of what Fichte calls an activity directed towards an activity[4] the pure ego is, so to speak, made to affirm itself, the ego's original spontaneous activity is not in itself conscious. Rather is it the ultimate ground of consciousness, that is, of ordinary consciousness, one's natural awareness of oneself in a world. But this consciousness cannot arise unless the non-ego is opposed to the ego. Hence the second basic proposition of philosophy is that 'a non-ego is simply opposed to the ego'.[5] This oppositing must, of course, be done by the ego itself. Otherwise pure idealism would have to be abandoned.

Now, the non-ego of which the second proposition speaks is unlimited, in the sense that it is objectivity in general rather than

---

[1] *F*, I, p. 459; *M*, III, p. 43.   [2] *F*, I, p. 98; *M*, I, p. 292.   [3] *Ibid.*
[4] *Durch ein Handeln auf ein Handeln.* The philosopher's reflection is an activity, a doing. It makes the spontaneous activity of the pure ego relive itself, so to speak, for consciousness.
[5] *F*, I, p. 104; *M*, I, p. 298.

a definite object or set of finite objects. And this unlimited non-ego is opposed to the ego within the ego. For we are engaged in the systematic reconstruction of consciousness; and consciousness is a unity, comprising both ego and non-ego. Hence the unlimited activity which constitutes the pure or absolute ego must posit the non-ego within itself. But if both are unlimited, each will tend, as it were, to fill all reality to the exclusion of the other. They will tend to cancel one another out, to annihilate one another. And consciousness will be rendered impossible. Hence, if consciousness is to arise, there must be reciprocal limitation of ego and non-ego. Each must cancel the other out, but only in part. In this sense both ego and non-ego must be 'divisible' (*theilbar*). And in his *Basis of the Entire Theory of Science* Fichte offers the following formulation of the third basic proposition of philosophy. 'I posit in the ego a divisible non-ego as opposed to a divisible ego.'[1] That is to say, the absolute ego posits within itself a finite ego and a finite non-ego as reciprocally limiting and determining one another. Fichte obviously does not mean that there can be only one of each. Indeed, as will be seen later, he maintains that for self-consciousness the existence of the Other (and so of a plurality of finite selves) is required. His point is that there can be no consciousness unless the absolute ego, considered as unlimited activity, produces within itself the finite ego and the finite non-ego.

6. If we mean by consciousness, as Fichte means by it, human consciousness, the assertion that the non-ego is a necessary condition of consciousness is not difficult to understand. To be sure, the finite ego can reflect on itself, but this reflection is for Fichte a bending back of the attention from the not-self. Hence the non-ego is a necessary condition even of self-consciousness.[2] But we can very well ask why there should be consciousness at all. Or, to put the question in another way, how can the second basic proposition of philosophy be deduced from the first?

Fichte answers that no purely theoretical deduction is possible. We must have recourse to a practical deduction. That is to say, we must see the pure or absolute ego as an unlimited activity striving towards consciousness of its own freedom through moral self-realization. And we must see the positing of the non-ego as a

---

[1] *F*, I, p. 110; *M*, I, p. 305.

[2] We can notice again the distinction between phenomenology and idealist metaphysics. It is one thing to say that the positing (recognition) of the non-ego is a condition of human consciousness. It is another thing to say that the non-ego is posited (produced or created) by the pure or absolute ego.

necessary means to the attainment of this end. True, the absolute ego in its spontaneous activity does not act consciously for any end at all. But the philosopher consciously rethinking this activity sees the total movement as directed towards a certain goal. And he sees that self-consciousness demands the non-ego, from which the otherwise unlimited activity of the ego, comparable to a straight line stretching out indefinitely, can recoil, as it were, onto itself. He sees too that moral activity requires an objective field, a world, in which actions can be performed.

Now, the second basic proposition of philosophy stands to the first as antithesis to thesis. And we have seen that the ego and non-ego tend to cancel one another out, if both are unlimited. It is this fact that drives the philosopher to enunciate the third basic proposition, which stands to the first and second propositions as synthesis to thesis and antithesis. But Fichte does not mean to imply that the non-ego ever exists in such a way that it annihilates the pure ego or threatens to do so. It is because this annihilation would take place if an unlimited non-ego were posited within the ego that we are compelled to proceed to the third proposition. In other words, the synthesis shows what the antithesis must mean if the contradiction between an unlimited ego and an unlimited non-ego is not to arise. If we assume that consciousness is to arise at all, the activity which grounds consciousness must produce the situation in which an ego and a non-ego limit one another.

Looked at under one aspect, therefore, Fichte's dialectic of thesis, antithesis and synthesis[1] takes the form of a progressive determination of the meanings of the initial propositions. And the contradictions which arise are resolved in the sense that they are shown to be only apparent. 'All contradictions are reconciled by determining more closely the contradictory propositions.'[2] Speaking, for example, of the statements that the ego posits itself as infinite and that it posits itself as finite, Fichte remarks that 'were it posited as both infinite and finite in one and the same sense, the contradictions could not be resolved. . . .'[3] The apparent contradiction is resolved by so defining the meanings of the two statements that their mutual compatibility becomes evident. In the case in question we have to see the one infinite activity expressing itself in and through finite selves.

---

[1] On the hint of a dialectical method in the philosophy of Kant see Vol. VI, pp. 251–2. Kant's antithetical development of the antinomies (pp. 287 f.) is also relevant.

[2] *F*, 1, p. 255; *M*, 1, p. 448.　　　　　[3] *Ibid.*

Yet it would not be accurate to say that in actual fact Fichte's dialectic consists simply in the progressive determination or clarification of meanings. For he introduces by the way ideas which cannot be obtained through strict analysis of the initial proposition or propositions. For instance, in order to proceed from the second basic proposition to the third Fichte postulates a limiting activity on the part of the ego, though the idea of limitation cannot be obtained simply through logical analysis of either the first or the second proposition.

This procedure was criticized by Hegel as being insufficiently speculative, that is, philosophical. In Hegel's opinion it was unworthy of a philosopher to offer a deduction which was admittedly no strict theoretical deduction[1] and to introduce, like a *deus ex machina*, undeduced activities of the ego to make possible the transition from one proposition to another.

It can hardly be denied, I think, that Fichte's actual procedure does not square very well with his initial account of the nature of philosophy as a deductive science. At the same time we must remember that for him the philosopher is engaged in consciously reconstructing, as it were, an active process, namely the grounding of consciousness, which in itself takes place unconsciously. In doing so the philosopher has his point of departure, the self-positing of the absolute ego, and his point of arrival, human consciousness as we know it. And if it is impossible to proceed from one step to another in the reconstruction of the productive activity of the ego without attributing to the ego a certain function or mode of activity, then this must be done. Thus even if the concept of limitation is not obtained through strict logical analysis of the first two basic propositions, it is none the less required, from Fichte's point of view, to clarify their meaning.

7. When outlining Fichte's theory of the three basic propositions of philosophy I omitted the logical apparatus which is employed in the *Basis of the Entire Theory of Science* and which figures prominently in some accounts of his philosophy. For this apparatus is not really necessary, as is shown by the fact that Fichte himself omits it in some of the expositions of his system. At the same time something ought to be said about it because it serves to clarify Fichte's idea of the relations between philosophy and formal logic.

In the *Basis of the Entire Theory of Science* Fichte approaches

---

[1] We have noted Fichte's frank admission that no purely theoretical deduction of the second basic proposition is possible.

the first fundamental proposition of philosophy by reflecting on an indemonstrable logical proposition, the truth of which would be admitted by all. This is the principle of identity, stated in the form A is A or $A = A$. Nothing is said about the content of A; nor is it asserted that A exists. What is asserted is a necessary relation between A and itself. If there is an A, it is necessarily self-identical. And this necessary relation between A as subject and A as predicate is referred to by Fichte as X.

This judgment is asserted or posited only in and through the I or ego. Thus the existence of the ego is affirmed in its activity of judging, even if no value has been assigned to A. 'If the proposition $A = A$ is certain, so also must the proposition I am be certain.'[1] In affirming the principle of identity the ego affirms or posits itself as self-identical.

While, therefore, the formal principle of identity is used by Fichte as a means or device for arriving at the first basic proposition of philosophy, the principle of identity is not itself this proposition. Indeed, it is sufficiently obvious that one would not get very far with a deduction or reconstruction of consciousness if one proposed to use the formal principle of identity as a starting-point or foundation.

At the same time the relation between the formal principle of identity and the first basic proposition of philosophy is closer, according to Fichte, than the description of the former as a means or device for arriving at the latter tends to suggest. For the principle of identity is, so to speak, the first basic proposition of philosophy with variables substituted for definite values or content. That is to say, if we took the first basic proposition of philosophy and rendered it purely formal, we would obtain the principle of identity. And in this sense the latter is grounded in the former and derivable from it.

Similarly, what Fichte calls the formal axiom of opposition, $Not-A$ $not = A$, is used to arrive at the second basic proposition. For the positing of Not $-A$ presupposes the positing of A and is thus an oppositing to A. And this oppositing takes place only in and through the ego. At the same time the formal axiom of opposition is said to be grounded in the second proposition of philosophy which affirms the ego's oppositing to itself of the non-ego in general. Again, the logical proposition which Fichte calls the axiom of the ground or of sufficient reason, A in part $= -A$, and

[1] F, 1, p. 95; M, 1, p. 289.

conversely, is said to be grounded in the third basic proposition of philosophy, in the sense that the former is derived by abstracting definite content from the latter and substituting variables instead.

In brief, therefore, Fichte's view is that formal logic is dependent on and derived from the *Wissenschaftslehre*, and not the other way round. This view of the relation between formal logic and basic philosophy is indeed somewhat obscured by the fact that in the *Basis of the Entire Theory of Science* Fichte starts by reflecting on the principle of identity. But in his subsequent discussion he proceeds to make his view of the derivative character of formal logic quite clear. And this view is in any case entailed by his insistence that the *Wissenschaftslehre* is the fundamental science.

We may add that in his deduction of the fundamental propositions of philosophy Fichte begins to deduce the categories. In his opinion Kant's deduction was insufficiently systematic. If, however, we start with the self-positing of the ego, we can deduce them successively in the course of the reconstruction of consciousness. Thus the first basic proposition gives us the category of reality. For 'that which is posited through the mere positing of a thing . . . is its reality, its essence [*Wesen*]'.[1] The second proposition obviously gives us the category of negation and the third that of limitation or determination.

8. The idea of reciprocal limitation provides the basis for the twofold deduction of consciousness which Fichte considers necessary. Take the statement that the absolute ego posits within itself a finite ego and a finite non-ego as reciprocally limiting or determining one another. This implies two propositions. One is that the absolute ego posits itself as limited by the non-ego. The other is that the absolute ego posits (within itself) the non-ego as limited or determined by the (finite) ego. And these two propositions are respectively the basic propositions of the theoretical and practical deductions of consciousness. If we consider the ego as affected by the non-ego, we can proceed to the theoretical deduction of consciousness which considers what Fichte calls the 'real' series of acts, that is, the acts of the ego as determined by the non-ego. Sensation, for example, belongs to this class of acts. If, however, we consider the ego as affecting the non-ego, we can proceed to the practical deduction of consciousness which considers the 'ideal' series of acts, including, for instance, desire and free action.

[1] *F*, I, p. 99; *M*, I, p. 293.

The two deductions are, of course, complementary, forming together the total philosophical deduction or reconstruction of consciousness. At the same time the theoretical deduction is subordinated to the practical. For the absolute ego is an infinite striving towards self-realization through free moral activity, and the non-ego, the world of Nature, is a means or instrument for the attainment of this end. The practical deduction gives us the reason why the absolute ego posits the non-ego as limiting and affecting the finite ego; and it leads us to the confines of ethics. Indeed, Fichte's theories of rights and of morals are a continuation of the practical deduction as contained in the *Wissenschaftslehre* proper. As already mentioned, Fichte's philosophy is essentially a dynamic ethical idealism.

It is not possible to discuss here all the stages of Fichte's deduction of consciousness. And even if it were possible, it would scarcely be desirable. But in the next two sections some features of the theoretical and practical deductions will be mentioned, to give the reader some idea of Fichte's line of thought.

9. In Fichte's idealist system all activity must be referred ultimately to the ego itself, that is, to the absolute ego, and the non-ego must exist only for consciousness. For to admit the idea of a non-ego which exists quite independently of all consciousness and which affects the ego would be to readmit the idea of the thing-in-itself and to abandon idealism. At the same time it is obvious that from the point of view of ordinary consciousness there is a distinction between presentation (*Vorstellung*) and thing. We have the spontaneous belief that we are acted upon by things which exist independently of the ego. And to all appearances this belief is fully justified. Hence it is incumbent on Fichte to show, in a manner consistent with the idealist position, how the point of view of ordinary consciousness arises, and how from this point of view our spontaneous belief in an objective Nature is in a sense justified. For the aim of idealist philosophy is to explain the facts of consciousness on idealist principles, not to deny them.

Obviously, Fichte must attribute to the ego the power of producing the idea of an independently existing non-ego when in point of fact it is dependent on the ego, so that the non-ego's activity is ultimately the activity of the ego itself. Equally obviously, this power must be attributed to the absolute ego rather than to the individual self, and it must work spontaneously, inevitably and without consciousness. To put the matter crudely, when consciousness comes on the scene the work must be already done. It must take place below the level of consciousness. Otherwise it would be impossible to explain our spontaneous belief in a Nature existing independently of the ego. In other words, for empirical consciousness Nature must be something given. It is only the philosopher who in transcendental reflection retraces with consciousness the productive activity of the absolute ego, which in itself takes place without consciousness. For the non-philosopher, and for the empirical consciousness of the philosopher himself, the natural world is something given, a situation in which the finite ego finds itself.

This power is called by Fichte the power of imagination or, more appropriately, the productive power of imagination or power of productive imagination. The power of imagination was prominent in the philosophy of Kant, where it served as an indispensable link between sensibility and understanding.[1] But with Fichte it assumes an all-important role in grounding ordinary or empirical consciousness. It is not, of course, a kind of third force in addition to the ego and non-ego: it is the activity of the ego itself, that is, the absolute ego. In his earlier writings Fichte may sometimes give the impression that he is talking about the activity of the individual self, but when he reviews the development of his thought he protests that he never meant this.

In what he calls a pragmatic history of consciousness[2] Fichte pictures the ego as spontaneously limiting its own activity and thus positing itself as passive, as affected. Its state is then that of sensation (*Empfindung*). But the ego's activity reasserts itself, as it were, and objectifies sensation. That is to say, in the outwardly-directed activity of intuition the ego spontaneously refers sensation to a non-ego. And this act grounds the distinction between representation or image (*Bild*) and thing. In empirical consciousness, the finite self regards the distinction between image and thing as a distinction between a subjective modification and an object which exists independently of its own activity. For it is ignorant of the fact that the projection of the non-ego was the work of the productive imagination functioning on an infra-conscious level.

Now, consciousness requires not simply an indeterminate non-

---

[1] See Vol. VI, pp. 256–60.
[2] This is given in the *Basis of the Entire Theory of Science*. A more detailed analysis of some of the stages is given in the *Outline of the Essence of the Theory of Science*.

ego but definite and distinct objects. And if there are to be distinguishable objects, there must be a common sphere in which and in relation to which objects mutually exclude one another. Hence the power of imagination produces space, extended, continuous and indefinitely divisible, as a form of intuition.

Similarly, there must be an irreversible time series of such a kind that successive acts of intuition are possible and that if a particular act of intuition occurs at any moment, every other possibility is excluded as far as this moment is concerned. Hence the productive imagination conveniently posits time as a second form of intuition. Needless to say, the forms of space and time are produced spontaneously by the activity of the pure or absolute ego: they are not consciously and deliberately posited.

The development of consciousness, however, requires that the product of the creative imagination should be rendered more determinate. And this is effected by means of the powers of understanding and judgment. At the level of understanding the ego 'fixes' (*fixiert*) presentations as concepts, while the power of judgment is said to turn these concepts into *thought* objects, in the sense that they come to exist not only *in* but also *for* the understanding. Both understanding and judgment, therefore, are required for understanding in the full sense. 'Nothing in the understanding, no power of judgment: no power of judgment, nothing in the understanding *for the understanding*. . . .'[1] Sensible intuition is riveted, as it were, to particular objects; but at the level of understanding and judgment we find abstraction from particular objects and the making of universal judgments. Thus in the pragmatic history of consciousness we have seen the ego rising above the unconscious activity of the productive imagination and acquiring, so to speak, a certain freedom of movement.

Self-consciousness, however, requires more than the power to abstract from particular objects in favour of the universal. It presupposes the power to abstract from the object in general, in order to achieve reflection on the subject. And this power of absolute abstraction, as Fichte calls it, is reason (*Vernunft*). When reason abstracts from the sphere of the non-ego, the ego remains, and we have self-consciousness. But one cannot totally eliminate the ego-object and identify oneself in consciousness with the ego-subject. That is to say, pure self-consciousness, in which the I-subject would be completely transparent to itself, is an ideal which

[1] *F*, 1, p. 242; *M*, 1, p. 435.

can never be actually achieved, but to which one can only approximate. 'The more a determinate individual can think himself (as object) away, the closer does his empirical self-consciousness approximate to pure self-consciousness.'[1]

It is, of course, the power of reason which enables the philosopher to apprehend the pure ego and to retrace, in transcendental reflection, its productive activity in the movement towards self-consciousness. But we have seen that the intellectual intuition of the absolute ego is never unmixed with other elements. Not even the philosopher can achieve the ideal of what Fichte calls pure self-consciousness.

10. The practical deduction of consciousness goes behind, as it were, the work of the productive imagination and reveals its ground in the nature of the absolute ego as an infinite striving (*ein unendliches Streben*). True, if we speak of striving, we naturally tend to think of striving after something. That is to say, we presuppose the existence of the non-ego. But if we start with the absolute ego as infinite striving, we obviously cannot presuppose the existence of the non-ego. For to do this would be to reintroduce the Kantian thing-in-itself. At the same time striving, Fichte insists, demands a counter-movement, a counter-striving, a check or obstacle. For if it met with no resistance, no obstacle or check, it would be satisfied and would cease to be a striving. But the absolute ego cannot cease to be a striving. Hence the very nature of the absolute ego necessitates the positing of the non-ego by the productive imagination, that is, by the absolute ego in its 'real' activity.

The matter can be expressed in this way. The absolute ego is to be conceived as activity. And this activity is fundamentally an infinite striving. But striving, according to Fichte, implies overcoming, and overcoming requires an obstacle to overcome. Hence the ego must posit the non-ego, Nature, as an obstacle to be overcome, as a check to be transcended. In other words, Nature is a necessary means or instrument to the moral self-realization of the ego. It is a field for action.

Fichte does not, however, proceed directly from the idea of the ego as striving to the positing of the non-ego. He argues first that striving takes the determinate form of infra-conscious impulse or drive (*Trieb*) and that this impulse exists 'for the ego' in the form of feeling (*Gefühl*). Now, impulse or drive aims, as Fichte puts it, at

---

[1] *F*, I, p. 244; *M*, I, p. 437.

being causality, at effecting something outside itself. Yet it cannot, considered simply as impulse, effect anything. Hence the feeling of impulse or drive is a feeling of constraint, of not-being-able, of being hindered. And the feeling ego is compelled to posit the non-ego as a felt I-know-not-what, a felt obstacle or check. And impulse can then become 'impulse *towards the object*'.[1]

It is worth noting that for Fichte feeling is the basis of all belief in reality. The ego feels impulse or drive as power or force (*Kraft*) which is hindered. The feeling of force and the feeling of hindrance go together. And the total feeling is the foundation of belief in reality. 'Here lies the ground of all reality. Only through the relation of feeling to the ego . . . is reality possible for the ego, whether of the ego or of the non-ego.'[2] Belief in reality is based ultimately on feeling, not on any theoretical argument.

Now, the feeling of impulse as force represents a rudimentary grade of reflection. For the ego is itself the impulse which is felt. Hence the feeling is self-feeling. And in successive sections of the practical deduction of consciousness Fichte traces the development of this reflection. We see, for instance, impulse or drive as such becoming more determinate in the form of distinct impulses and desires, and we see the development in the ego of distinct feelings of satisfaction. But inasmuch as the ego is infinite striving, it is unable to rest in any particular satisfaction or group of satisfactions. And we see it as reaching out towards an ideal goal through its free activity. Yet this goal always recedes. Indeed, it must do so, if the ego is infinite or endless striving. In the end, therefore, we have action for the sake of action, though in his ethical theory Fichte shows how the infinite striving of the absolute ego after complete freedom and self-possession is fulfilled, so far as it can be, through the series of determinate moral actions in the world which it has posited, through, that is to say, the convergence of the determinate moral vocations of finite subjects towards an ideal goal.

In its detailed development Fichte's practical deduction of consciousness is notoriously difficult to follow. But it is clear enough that for him the ego is from the start the morally active ego. That is to say, it is potentially this. And it is the actualization of the ego's potential nature which demands the positing of the non-ego and the whole work of the productive imagination. Behind, as it were, the theoretical activity of the ego lies its nature as striving, as impulse or drive. For example, the production

[1] *F*, I, p. 291; *M*, I, p. 483.   [2] *F*, I, p. 301; *M*, I, p. 492.

of the presentation (*Vorstellung*) is the work of the theoretical power, not of the practical power or impulse as such. But the production presupposes the drive to presentation (*der Vorstellungstrieb*). Conversely, the positing of the sensible world is necessary in order that the fundamental striving or drive can take the determinate form of free moral activity directed towards an ideal goal. Thus the two deductions are complementary, though the theoretical deduction finds its ultimate explanation in the practical. In this sense Fichte endeavours to satisfy in his own way the demands of Kant's doctrine of the primacy of the practical reason.

We can also say that in his practical deduction of consciousness Fichte tries to overcome the dichotomy, present in the Kantian philosophy, between the higher and lower nature of man, between man as a moral agent and man as a complex of instincts and impulses. For it is the self-same fundamental drive which is represented as assuming different forms up to that of free moral activity. In other words, Fichte sees the moral life as a development out of the life of instinct and impulse rather than as a counterblast to it. And he even finds a prefiguring of the categorical imperative on the level of physical longing (*Sehnen*) and desire. In his ethics he has, of course, to allow for the fact that there may be, and often is, a conflict between the voice of duty and the claims of sensual desire. But he tries to resolve the problem within the framework of a unified view of the ego's activity in general.

11. From one point of view Fichte's deduction of consciousness can be regarded as a systematic exhibition of the conditions of consciousness as we know it. And if it is regarded simply in this way, questions about the temporal or historical relations between the different conditions are irrelevant. For example, Fichte takes it that the subject-object relationship is essential to consciousness. And in this case there must be both subject and object, ego and non-ego, if there is to be consciousness. The historical order in which these conditions appear is irrelevant to the validity of this statement.

But, as we have seen, the deduction of consciousness is also idealist metaphysics, and the pure ego has to be interpreted as a supra-individual and transfinite activity, the so-called absolute ego. Hence it is understandable if the student of Fichte asks whether the philosopher regards the absolute ego as positing the sensible world before the finite ego or simultaneously with it or through it.

At first sight at least this may seem to be a silly question. The temporal, historical point of view, it may be said, presupposes for Fichte the constitution of empirical consciousness. Hence the transcendental deduction of empirical consciousness necessarily transcends the temporal and historical order and possesses the timelessness of a logical deduction. After all, the time-series is itself deduced. Fichte has no intention of denying the point of view of empirical consciousness, for which Nature precedes finite selves. He is concerned with grounding it, not with denying it.

But the matter is not quite so simple. In the Kantian philosophy it is the human mind which exercises a constitutive activity in giving its *a priori* form to phenomenal reality. True, in this activity the mind acts spontaneously and unconsciously, and it acts as mind as such, as the subject as such, rather than as the mind of Tom or John. But it is none the less the human mind, not the divine mind, which is said to exercise this activity. And if we eliminate the thing-in-itself and hypostatize Kant's transcendental ego as the metaphysical absolute ego, it is quite natural to ask whether the absolute ego posits Nature immediately or through the infra-conscious levels, as it were, of the human being. After all, Fichte's deduction of consciousness not infrequently suggests the second of these alternatives. And if this is what the philosopher really means, he is faced with an obvious difficulty.

Happily, Fichte answers the question in explicit terms. At the beginning of the practical deduction of consciousness he draws attention to an apparent contradiction. On the one hand the ego as intelligence is dependent on the non-ego. On the other hand the ego is said to determine the non-ego and must thus be independent of it. The contradiction is resolved (that is, shown to be only apparent) when we understand that the absolute ego determines immediately the non-ego which enters into representation (*das vorzustellende Nicht-Ich*), whereas it determines the ego as intelligence (the ego as representing, *das vorstellende Ich*) *mediately*, that is, by means of the non-ego. In other words, the absolute ego does not posit the world through the finite ego, but immediately. And the same thing is clearly stated in a passage of the lectures on *The Facts of Consciousness*, to which allusion has already been made. 'The material world has been deduced earlier on as an absolute limitation of the productive power of imagination. But we have not yet stated clearly and explicitly whether the productive power in this function is the self-manifestation of the one Life as such or whether it is the manifestation of individual life; whether, that is to say, a material world is posited through one self-identical Life or through the individual as such. . . . It is not the individual as such but the one Life which intuits the objects of the material world.'[1]

The development of this point of view obviously requires that Fichte should move away from his Kantian point of departure, and that the pure ego, a concept arrived at through reflection on human consciousness, should become absolute Being which manifests itself in the world. And this is indeed the path which Fichte takes in the later philosophy, to which the lectures on *The Facts of Consciousness* belong. But, as will be seen later, he never really succeeds in kicking away the ladder by which he has climbed up to metaphysical idealism. And though he clearly thinks of Nature as being posited by the Absolute as a field for moral activity, he maintains to the end that the world exists only in and for consciousness. Apart, therefore, from the explicit denial that material things are posited 'through the individual as such', his position remains ambiguous. For though consciousness is said to be the Absolute's consciousness, the Absolute is also said to be conscious through man, and not in itself considered apart from man.

---

[1] *F*, II, p. 614 (not included in *M*).

CHAPTER III

FICHTE (2)

Introductory remarks—The common moral consciousness and the science of ethics—Man's moral nature—The supreme principle of morality and the formal condition of the morality of actions—Conscience as an unerring guide—The philosophical application of the formal moral law—The idea of moral vocation and Fichte's general vision of reality—A community of selves in a world as a condition of self-consciousness—The principle or rule of right—The deduction and nature of the State—The closed commercial State—Fichte and nationalism.

1. IN the section on Fichte's life and writings we saw that he published the *Basis of Natural Right* in 1796, two years before the publication of *The System of Ethics*. In his opinion the theory of rights and of political society could be, and ought to be, deduced independently of the deduction of the principles of morality. This does not mean that Fichte thought of the two branches of philosophy as having no connection at all with each other. For one thing the two deductions possess a common root in the concept of the self as striving and as free activity. For another thing the system of rights and political society provides a field of application for the moral law. But it was Fichte's opinion that his field is external to morality, in the sense that it is not a deduction from the fundamental ethical principle but a framework within which, and in regard to which, the moral law can be applied. For example, man can have moral duties towards the State and the State should bring about those conditions in which the moral life can develop. But the State itself is deduced as a hypothetically necessary contrivance or means to guard and protect the system of rights. If man's moral nature were fully developed, the State would wither away. Again, though the right of private property receives from ethics what Fichte calls a further sanction, its initial deduction is supposed to be independent of ethics.

One main reason why Fichte makes this distinction between the theory of rights and political theory on the one hand and ethics on the other is that he looks on ethics as concerned with interior morality, with conscience and the formal principle of morality, whereas the theory of rights and of political society is concerned with the external relations between human beings. Further, if the comment is made that the doctrine of rights can be regarded as applied ethics, in the sense that it is deducible as an application of the moral law, Fichte refuses to admit the truth of this contention. The fact that I have a right does not necessarily mean that I am under an obligation to exercise it. And the common good may demand on occasion a curtailment of or limitation on the exercise of rights. But the moral law is categorical: it simply says, 'Do this' or 'Do not do that'. Hence the system of rights is not deducible from the moral law, though we are, of course, morally obliged to respect the system of rights as established in a community. In this sense the moral law adds a further sanction to rights, but it is not their initial source.

In Hegel's opinion Fichte did not really succeed in overcoming the formalism of the Kantian ethics, even if he provided some of the material for doing so. And it was indeed Hegel rather than Fichte who synthesized the concepts of right, interior morality and society in the general concept of man's ethical life. But the chief reason why I have dwelt in the first section of this chapter on Fichte's distinction between the doctrine of rights and ethical theory is that I propose to treat of the philosopher's moral theory before outlining his theory of rights and of the State. And this procedure might otherwise give the erroneous impression that Fichte regarded the theory of rights as a deduction from the moral law.

2. A man can have knowledge, Fichte says, of his moral nature, of his subjection to a moral imperative, in two ways. In the first place he can possess this knowledge on the level of common moral consciousness. That is to say, he can be aware through his conscience of a moral imperative telling him to do this or not to do that. And this immediate awareness is quite sufficient for a knowledge of one's duties and for moral behaviour. In the second place a man can assume the ordinary moral consciousness as something given and inquire into its grounds. And a systematic deduction of the moral consciousness from its roots in the ego is the science of ethics and provides 'learned knowledge'.[1] In one sense, of course, this learned knowledge leaves everything as it was before. It does not create obligation, nor does it substitute a new set of duties for those of which one is already aware through conscience. It will not

[1] *F*, IV, p. 122; *M*, II, p. 516.

give a man a moral nature. But it can enable him to understand his moral nature.

3. What is meant by man's moral nature? Fichte tells us that there is in man an impulsion to perform certain actions simply for the sake of performing them, without regard to external purposes or ends, and to leave undone other actions simply for the sake of leaving them undone, again without regard to external purposes or ends. And the nature of man in so far as this impulsion necessarily manifests itself within him is his 'moral or ethical nature'.[1] To understand the grounds of this moral nature is the task of ethics.

The ego is activity, striving. And as we saw when considering the practical deduction of consciousness, the basic form taken by the striving which constitutes the ego is infra-conscious impulse or drive. Hence from one point of view man is a system of impulses, the impulse which can be ascribed to the system as a whole being that of self-preservation. Considered in this light, man can be described as an organized product of Nature. And as conscious of myself as a system of impulses I can say, 'I find myself as an organized product of Nature.'[2] That is to say, I posit or affirm myself as being this when I consider myself as object.

But man is also intelligence, a subject of consciousness. And as subject of consciousness the ego necessarily tends or is impelled to determine itself through itself alone; that is, it is a striving after complete freedom and independence. Inasmuch, therefore, as the natural impulses and desires which belong to man as a product of Nature aim at satisfaction through some relation to a determinate natural object and consequently appear to depend on the object, we understandably contrast these impulses with the spiritual impulse of the ego as intelligence, the impulse, that is to say, to complete self-determination. We speak of lower and higher desires, of the sphere of necessity and the sphere of freedom, and introduce a dichotomy into human nature.

Fichte does not deny, of course, that such distinctions have, so to speak, a cash value. For one can look at man from two points of view, as object and as subject. As we have seen, I can be conscious of myself as an object in Nature, as an organized product of Nature, and I can be aware of myself as a subject for whose consciousness Nature, including myself as object, exists. To this

<hr />

[1] *F*, IV, p. 13; *M*, II, p. 407.
[2] *F*, IV, p. 122; *M*, II, p. 516.

extent Kant's distinction between the phenomenal and noumenal aspects of man is justified.

At the same time Fichte insists that this distinction is not ultimate. For instance, the natural impulse which aims at satisfaction and the spiritual impulse which aims at complete freedom and independence are from the transcendental or phenomenal point of view one impulse. It is a great mistake to suppose that man as an organized product of Nature is the sphere of mere mechanism. As Fichte puts it, 'I do not hunger because food exists for me, but a certain object becomes food for me because I am hungry.'[1] The organism asserts itself: it tends to activity. And it is fundamentally the same impulse to self-activity which reappears in the form of the spiritual impulse to the realization of complete freedom. For this basic impulse cannot be stilled and brought to quiescence by temporary sense satisfaction, but reaches out, as it were, to infinity. It is true, of course, that the basic impulse or striving could not take the form of the higher spiritual impulse without consciousness. Consciousness is indeed a dividing-line between man as an organized product of Nature and man as a rational ego, as spirit. But from the philosophical point of view there is ultimately only one impulse, and man is subject and object in one. 'My impulse as a being of Nature and my tendency as pure spirit: are they two different impulses? No, from the transcendental point of view both are one and the same original impulse which constitutes my being: it is only regarded from two different sides. That is to say, I am subject-object, and in the identity and inseparability of both consists my true being. If I regard myself as an *object*, completely determined through the laws of sense intuition and discursive thinking, then that which is actually my one impulse becomes for me a natural impulse, because from this point of view I myself am Nature. If I regard myself as subject, the impulse becomes for me a purely spiritual impulse or the law of self-determination. All the phenomena of the ego rest simply on the reciprocity of these two impulses, and this is really the reciprocal relation *of one and the same impulse to itself*.'[2]

This theory of the unity of man in terms of one impulse has an important bearing on ethics. Fichte makes a distinction between formal and material freedom. Formal freedom requires only the presence of consciousness. Even if a man always followed his natural impulses as directed to pleasure, he would do so freely,

---

[1] *F*, IV, p. 124; *M*, II, p. 518.   [2] *F*, IV, p. 130; *M*, II, p. 524.

provided that he did so consciously and deliberately.[1] Material freedom, however, is expressed in a series of acts tending to the realization of the ego's complete independence. And these are moral acts. Now, if we pressed this distinction, we should be faced with the difficulty of giving any content to the moral act. For we should have on the one hand actions performed in accordance with natural impulse, which are rendered determinate by their reference to particular objects, and on the other actions which exclude all determination by particular objects and are performed solely in accordance with the idea of freedom for freedom's sake. And this second class of actions would appear to be completely indeterminate. But Fichte answers that we have to effect a synthesis which is demanded by the fact that the impulse or tendency which constitutes man's nature is ultimately one impulse. The lower impulse or lower form of the one impulse must sacrifice its end, namely pleasure, while the higher impulse or form of the one impulse must sacrifice its purity, that is, its lack of determination by any object.

Expressed in this abstract way Fichte's idea of a synthesis may seem extremely obscure. But the fundamental notion is clear enough. For example, it is clearly not demanded of the moral agent that he should cease to perform all those actions to which natural impulse prompts him, such as eating and drinking. It is not demanded of him that he should try to live as a disembodied spirit. What is demanded is that his actions should not be performed simply for the sake of immediate satisfaction, but that they should be members of a series converging towards the ideal end which man sets before himself as a spiritual subject. In so far as he fulfils this demand man realizes his moral nature.

This suggests, of course, that the moral life involves substituting one end for another, a spiritual ideal for natural satisfaction and pleasure. And this idea may seem to be at variance with Fichte's picture of morality as demanding the performance of certain actions simply for the sake of performing them and the non-performance of other actions simply for the sake of not performing them. But the spiritual ideal in question is for Fichte self-activity, action determined through the ego alone. And his point is that such action must take the form of a series of determinate actions in the

---

[1] There are activities in man, the circulation of the blood for example, of which he is not immediately, but only mediately, conscious. And he cannot be said to control them. But when I am immediately conscious of an impulse or desire, I am free, Fichte takes it, to satisfy or not to satisfy it.

world, though at the same time they must be determined by the ego itself and express its freedom rather than subjection to the natural world. This means in effect that the actions should be performed for the sake of performing them.

One can say, therefore, that Fichte makes a resolute attempt to exhibit the unity of human nature and to show that there is continuity between the life of man as a natural organism and the life of man as spiritual subject of consciousness. At the same time the influence of the Kantian formalism is strongly marked. And it shows itself clearly in Fichte's account of the supreme principle of morality.

4. Speaking of the ego when it is thought only as *object* Fichte asserts that 'the essential character of the ego, by which it is distinguished from everything external to itself, consists in a tendency to self-activity [*Selbstthätigkeit*] for the sake of self-activity; and it is this tendency which is thought when the ego is thought in and for itself without relation to anything outside it'.[1] But it is the ego as subject, as intelligence, which thinks itself as object. And when it thinks itself as a tendency to self-activity for the sake of self-activity, it necessarily thinks itself as free, as able to realize absolute self-activity, as a power of self-determination. Further, the ego cannot conceive itself in this way without conceiving itself as subject to law, the law of determining itself in accordance with the concept of self-determination. That is to say, if I conceive my objective essence as a power of self-determination, the power of realizing absolute self-activity, I must also conceive myself as obliged to actualize this essence.

We have, therefore, the two ideas of freedom and law. But just as the ego as subject and the ego as object, though distinguished in consciousness, are inseparable and ultimately one, so are the ideas of freedom and law inseparable and ultimately one. 'When you think yourself as free, you are compelled to think your freedom as falling under a law; and when you think this law, you are compelled to think yourself as free. Freedom does not follow from the law any more than the law follows from freedom. They are not two ideas, of which the one can be thought as dependent on the other, but they are one and the same idea; it is a complete synthesis.'[2]

---

[1] *F*, iv, p. 29; *M*, ii, p. 423.

[2] *F*, iv, p. 53; *M*, ii, p. 447. Kant, Fichte remarks, did not mean that the *thought* of freedom is derived from the thought of law. He meant that faith in the objective validity of the thought of freedom is derived from consciousness of the moral law.

By this somewhat tortuous route Fichte deduces the fundamental principle of morality, 'the necessary idea of the intelligence that it ought to determine its freedom purely and without exception in accordance with the concept of independence [*Selbständigkeit*]'.[1] The free being ought to bring its freedom under a law, namely the law of complete self-determination or absolute independence (absence of determination through any external object). And this law should admit of no exception because it expresses the very nature of the free being.

Now, a finite rational being cannot ascribe freedom to itself without conceiving the possibility of a series of determinate free actions, caused by a will which is capable of exercising real causal activity. But the realization of this possibility demands an objective world in which the rational being can tend towards its goal through a series of particular actions. The natural world, the sphere of the non-ego, can thus be regarded as the material or instrument for the fulfilment of our duty, sensible things appearing as so many occasions for specifying the pure ought. We have already seen that according to Fichte the absolute ego posits the world as an obstacle or check which renders possible the recoil of the ego onto itself in self-consciousness. And we now see the positing of the world in a more specifically ethical context. It is the necessary condition for the rational being's fulfilment of its moral vocation. Without the world it could not give content, as it were, to the pure ought.

To be a moral action, each of these particular actions must fulfil a certain formal condition. '*Act always according to your best conviction of your duty* or *Act according to your conscience*. This is the formal condition of the morality of our actions. . . .'[2] The will which so acts is the good will. Fichte is obviously writing under the influence of Kant.

5. 'Act according to your conscience.' Fichte defines conscience as 'the immediate consciousness of our determinate duty'.[3] That is to say, conscience is the immediate awareness of a particular obligation. And from this definition it obviously follows that conscience never errs and cannot err. For if conscience is defined as an immediate awareness of one's duty, it would be contradictory to say that it can be a non-awareness of one's duty.

It is clear that Fichte wishes to find an absolute criterion of right and wrong. It is also clear that he wishes, like Kant, to avoid

---

[1] *F*, IV, p. 59; *M*, II, p. 453.   [2] *F*, IV, p. 173; *M*, II, p. 567.
[3] *F*, IV, pp. 173–4; *M*, II, pp. 567–8.

heteronomy. No external authority can be the required criterion. Further, the criterion must be at the disposal of all, unlearned as well as learned. Fichte fixes, therefore, upon conscience and describes it as an immediate feeling (*Gefühl*). For inasmuch as the practical power has priority over the theoretical power, it is the former which must be the source of conscience. And as the practical power does not judge, conscience must be a feeling.

Fichte's description of conscience as an immediate feeling does indeed fit in with the way in which the ordinary man is accustomed to speak about his moral convictions. A man might say, for example, 'I feel that this is the right thing to do. I feel that any other course of action would be wrong.' And he may very well feel certain about it. At the same time one might wish to comment that feeling is scarcely an unerring criterion of duty. Fichte, however, argues that the immediate feeling in question expresses the agreement or harmony between 'our empirical ego and the pure ego. And the pure ego is our only true being; it is all possible being and all possible truth.'[1] Hence the feeling which constitutes conscience can never be erroneous or deceptive.

To understand Fichte's theory we must understand that he is not excluding from man's moral life all activity by the theoretical power. The ego's fundamental tendency to complete freedom and independence stimulates this power to look for the determinate content of duty. After all, we can and do reflect about what we ought to do in this or that set of circumstances. But any theoretical judgment which we make may be mistaken. The function of argument is to draw attention to the different aspects of the situation under discussion and so to facilitate the attunement, so to speak, of the empirical ego with the pure ego. This attunement expresses itself in a feeling, the immediate consciousness of one's duty. And this immediate awareness puts a stop to theoretical inquiry and argument which might otherwise be prolonged indefinitely.

Fichte will not admit that anyone who has an immediate consciousness of his duty can resolve not to do his duty precisely because it is his duty. 'Such a maxim would be diabolical; but the concept of the devil is self-contradictory.'[2] At the same time 'no man, indeed no finite being so far as we know, is confirmed in good'.[3] Conscience as such cannot err, but it can be obscured or even

---

[1] *F*, IV, p. 169; *M*, II, p. 563.   [2] *F*, IV, p. 191; *M*, II, p. 585.
[3] *F*, IV, p. 193; *M*, II, p. 587.

vanish. Thus the concept of duty may remain, though the consciousness of its connection with some particular action may be obscured. To put the matter crudely, I may not give my empirical ego the chance to click with the pure ego.[1] Further, the consciousness of duty may practically vanish, in which case 'we then act either according to the maxim of self-advantage or according to the blind impulse to assert everywhere our lawless will'.[2] Thus even if the possibility of diabolical evil is excluded, the doctrine of infallibility of conscience does not exclude the possibility of acting wrongly. For I may be accountable for allowing my conscience to become obscured or even to vanish altogether.

According to Fichte, therefore, the ordinary man has at his disposal, if he chooses to make use of it, an infallible criterion for assessing his particular duties, which does not depend on any knowledge of the science of ethics. But the philosopher can inquire into the grounds of this criterion. And we have seen that Fichte offers a metaphysical explanation.

6. Conscience is thus the supreme judge in the practical moral life. But its dictates are not arbitrary and capricious. For the 'feeling' of which Fichte speaks is really the expression of our implicit awareness that a particular action falls inside or outside the series of actions which fulfil the fundamental impulse of the pure ego. Hence even if conscience is a sufficient guide for moral conduct, there is no reason why the philosopher should be unable to show theoretically that actions of a certain type belong or do not belong to the class of actions which lead to the ego's moral goal. He cannot deduce the particular obligations of particular individuals. This is a matter for conscience. But a philosophical application of the fundamental principle of morality is possible, within the limits of general principles or rules.

To take an example. I am under an obligation to act, for only through action can I fulfil the moral law. And the body is a necessary instrument for action. On the one hand, therefore, I ought not to treat my body as if it were itself my final end. On the other hand I ought to preserve and foster the body as a necessary instrument for action. Hence self-mutilation, for example, would be wrong unless it were required for the preservation of the body as a whole. Whether in this or that particular instance self-mutilation is justified is, however, a matter for conscience rather

[1] This happens, for example, if I do not really size up the situation but look exclusively at one partial aspect.
[2] *F*, IV, p. 194; *M*, II, p. 588.

than for the philosopher. I can only consider the situation under its different aspects and then act according to my immediate consciousness of my duty, confident, according to Fichte, that this immediate 'feeling' cannot err.

Similarly, one can formulate general rules in regard to the use of the cognitive powers. Fichte's profound respect for the vocation of the scholar is expressed in his insistence on the need for combining complete freedom of thought and research with the conviction that 'knowledge of my duty must be the final end of all my knowledge, all my thought and research'.[1] The synthesizing rule is that the scholar should pursue his researches in a spirit of devotion to duty and not out of mere curiosity or to have something to do.

7. The philosopher, therefore, can lay down certain general rules of conduct as applications of the fundamental principle of morality. But an individual's moral vocation is made up of countless particular obligations, in regard to which conscience is the unerring guide. Thus each single individual has his own real moral vocation, his own personal contribution to make to converging series of actions which tend to realize a moral world-order, the perfect rule of reason in the world. The attainment of this ideal goal requires, as it were, a division of moral labour. And we can reformulate the fundamental principle of morality in this way: 'Always fulfil your moral vocation.'[2]

The general outlines of Fichte's vision of reality should now be clear. The ultimate reality, which can be described, according to our point of view, as the absolute ego or as infinite Will, strives spontaneously towards perfect consciousness of itself as free, towards perfect self-possession. But self-consciousness, in Fichte's view, must take the form of finite self-consciousness, and the infinite Will's self-realization can take place only through the self-realization of finite wills. Hence the infinite activity spontaneously expresses itself in a multiplicity of finite selves or rational and free beings. But self-consciousness is not possible without a non-ego, from which the finite ego can recoil onto itself. And the realization of the finite free will through action requires a world in and through which action is possible. Hence the absolute ego or infinite Will must posit the world, Nature, if it is to become conscious of its own freedom through finite selves. And the moral vocations of finite selves in a common goal can be seen as the way in which the absolute ego or infinite Will moves towards its goal. Nature is

[1] F, IV, p. 300; M, II, p. 694.   [2] F, IV, p. 150; M, II, p. 544

simply the condition, though a necessary condition, for the expression of the moral will. The really significant feature in empirical reality is the moral activity of human beings, which is itself the expression of the infinite Will, the form which the infinite Will, an activity or doing rather than a being which acts, spontaneously and necessarily assumes.

8. We can turn now to the theory of right and the deduction of the State, to a consideration, that is to say, of the framework within which man's moral life is developed. But the theory of right and political theory, treating, as they do, of relations between human beings, presupposes a plurality of selves. Hence it is appropriate to begin by saying a little more about Fichte's deduction of this plurality.

As we have seen, the absolute ego must limit itself in the form of the finite ego if self-consciousness is to arise. But 'no free being becomes conscious of itself without at the same time becoming conscious of other similar beings'.[1] It is only by distinguishing myself from other beings which I recognize as rational and free that I can become conscious of myself as a determinate free individual. Intersubjectivity is a condition of self-consciousness. A community of selves is thus required if self-consciousness is to arise. Intelligence, as existing, is a manifold. In fact it is 'a closed manifold, that is, a *system* of rational beings'.[2] For they are all limitations of the one absolute ego, the one infinite activity.

This recognition of oneself as a member of a community or system of rational beings requires in turn, as a precondition, the sensible world. For I perceive my freedom as manifested in actions which interlock, so to speak, with the actions of others. And for such a system of actions to be possible there must be a common sensible world in which distinct rational beings can express themselves.

9. Now, if I cannot become conscious of myself as free without regarding myself as a member of a community of free rational beings, it follows that I cannot ascribe to myself alone the totality of infinite freedom. 'I limit myself in my appropriation of freedom by the fact that I also recognize the freedom of others.'[3] At the same time I must also conceive each member of the community as limiting the external expression of his freedom in such a way that all other members can express their freedom.

This idea of each member of the community of rational beings limiting the expression of his freedom in such a way that all other

---

[1] *F*, II, p. 143; *M*, IV, p. 143.   [2] *Ibid.*   [3] *F*, III, p. 8; *M*, II, p. 12.

members can also express their freedom is the concept of right. And the principle or rule of right (*Rechtsregel*) is stated by Fichte in this way: 'Limit your freedom through the concept of the freedom of all other persons with whom you come into relation.'[1] The concept of right for Fichte is essentially a social concept. It arises together with the idea of other rational beings who are capable of interfering with one's own activity, and with whose activities one is oneself capable of interfering. If I think away all other rational beings save myself, I have *powers*, and I may have a moral duty to exercise them or some of them. But it is inappropriate in this context to speak of my having a *right* to exercise them. For instance, I have the power of free speech. But if I think away all other rational beings, it is absurd, according to Fichte, to speak of my having a right to free speech. For the concept makes no sense unless I conceive the existence of other beings capable of interfering with my exercise of the power to speak my mind freely. Similarly, it makes no sense to speak of a right to private property except in a social context. True, if I were the only rational being I should have a duty to act and to use material things, expressing my freedom in and through them. I should have possessions. But the concept of the right of private property in the strict sense arises only when I conceive other human beings to whom I have to ascribe similar rights. What can private property mean outside a social context?

Now, though the existence of a community of free selves demands that each member should take the rule of right as the operative principle of his conduct, no individual will is necessarily governed by the rule. Fichte argues, however, that the union of many wills into one can produce a will constantly directed by the rule. 'If a million men are together, it may well be that each one wills for himself as much freedom as possible. But if we unite the will of all in one concept as one will, this will divides the sum of possible freedom into equal parts. It aims at all being free in such a way that the freedom of each individual is limited by the freedom of all the rest.'[2] This union expresses itself in mutual recognition of rights. And it is this mutual recognition which gives rise to the right of private property, considered as the right to exclusive possession of certain things.[3] 'The right of exclusive possession is

---

[1] *F*, III, p. 10; *M*, II, p. 14.   [2] *F*, III, p. 106; *M*, II, p. 110.
[3] It is worth noting that for Fichte rightful ownership of a thing is really the exclusive right to perform certain actions in regard to it. For instance, a farmer's property right in regard to a field is an exclusive right to sow it, plough it, graze cattle on it, and so on.

brought into being *through mutual recognition*: and it does not exist without this condition. All property is grounded on the union of many wills into one will.'[1]

10. If the stability of rights rests on sustained common recognition, reciprocal loyalty and trust are required in the persons concerned. But these are moral conditions on which one cannot count with certainty. Hence there must be some power which can enforce respect for rights. Further, this power must be the expression of the freedom of the human person: it must be established freely. We thus require a compact or contract whereby the contracting parties agree that anyone who infringes the rights of another should be treated in accordance with coercive law. But such a contract can be effective only when it takes the form of the social contract whereby the State is established,[2] furnished with the requisite power to secure the attainment of the end desired by the general will, namely the stability of the system of rights and the protection of the freedom of all. The union of all wills into one thus takes the form of the General Will as embodied in the State.

The influence of Rousseau[3] is obvious, both in Fichte's theory of the General Will and in his idea of the social contract. But the ideas are not introduced simply out of reverence for the name of the French philosopher. For Fichte's deduction of the State consists in a progressive argument showing that the State is a necessary condition for maintaining relations of right without which a community of free persons cannot be conceived. And this community is itself depicted as a necessary condition for the self-realization of the absolute ego as infinite freedom. The State must thus be interpreted as the expression of freedom. And Rousseau's theories of the Social Contract and General Will lend themselves for this purpose.

Fichte does indeed speak of the State as a totality, and he compares it with an organized product of Nature. We cannot say, therefore, that the organic theory of the State is absent from Fichte's political thought. At the same time he emphasizes the fact that the State not only expresses freedom but also exists to create a state of affairs in which each citizen can exercise his personal freedom so far as this is consistent with the freedom of

---

[1] *F*, III, p. 129; *M*, II, p. 133.
[2] Fichte distinguishes various stages of the social contract, culminating in what he calls the union-compact, whereby the members of political society become an organized totality.
[3] See Vol. VI, chapters 3 and 4.

others. Further, the State, considered as a coercive power, is only hypothetically necessary. That is to say, it is necessary on the hypothesis that man's moral development has not reached a point at which each member of society respects the rights and liberties of others from moral motives alone. If this condition were fulfilled, the State, as a coercive power, would no longer be necessary. Indeed, as one of the functions of the State is to facilitate man's moral development, we can say that for Fichte the State should endeavour to bring about the conditions for its own demise. To use Marxist language, Fichte looks forward to the withering away of the State, at least as an ideal possibility. He cannot, therefore, regard it as an end in itself.

Given these premisses, Fichte naturally rejects despotism. What may seem surprising in a sympathizer with the French Revolution is that he also rejects democracy. 'No State may be ruled either *despotically* or *democratically*.'[1] But by democracy he understands direct rule by the whole people. And his objection to it is that in a literal democracy there would be no authority to compel the multitude to observe its own laws. Even if many citizens were individually well disposed, there would be no power capable of preventing the degeneration of the community into an irresponsible and capricious mob. Provided, however, that the two extremes of unqualified despotism and democracy are avoided, we cannot say what form of constitution is the best. It is a matter of politics, not of philosophy.

At the same time reflection on the possibility of abuse of power by the civil authority led Fichte to lay great stress on the desirability of establishing a kind of supreme court or tribunal, the 'Ephorate'. This would possess no legislative, executive or judicial power in the ordinary sense. Its function would be to watch over the observance of the laws and constitution, and in the event of a serious abuse of power by the civil authority the Ephors would be entitled to suspend it from the exercise of its functions by means of a State interdict. Recourse would then be had to a referendum to ascertain the people's will concerning a change in the constitution, the law or the government, as the case might be.

That Fichte shows no inclination to deify the State is clear enough. But his political theory, as so far outlined, may suggest that he is committed to minimizing the functions of the State by defending a purely *laissez-faire* policy. But this conclusion does not

[1] *F*, III, p. 160; *M*, II, p. 164.

represent his mind. He does indeed maintain that the purpose of
the State is to maintain public security and the system of rights.
And from this it follows that interference with the freedom of the
individual should be limited to what is required for the fulfilment
of this purpose. But the establishment and maintenance of a
system of rights and its adjustment to the common good may
require a very considerable amount of State activity. It is idle, for
example, to insist that everyone has a right to live by his labour if
conditions are such that many people cannot do so. Further,
though the State is not the fount of the moral law, it is its business
to promote the conditions which facilitate the moral development
without which there is no true freedom. In particular it should
attend to the matter of education.

11. Hence it is not really so astonishing if in his *Closed Commercial State* we find Fichte envisaging a planned economy. He
presupposes that all human beings have a right not simply to live
but to live a decent human life. And the question then arises how
this right can be most effectively realized. In the first place, as
Plato recognized centuries ago, there must be division of labour,
giving rise to the main economic classes.[1] And in the second place
a state of harmony or balance must be maintained. If one economic
class grows disproportionately large, the whole economy may be
upset. In *The System of Ethics* Fichte emphasized the individual's
duty to choose his profession in accordance with his talents and
circumstances. In *The Closed Commercial State* he is concerned
rather with the common good, and he stresses the State's need to
watch over and regulate the division of labour for the good of the
community. True, changing circumstances will demand changes in
the State's regulations. But supervision and planning are in any
case indispensable.

In Fichte's opinion a balanced economy, once established, cannot
be maintained unless the State has the power to prevent its being
upset by any individual or set of individuals. And he draws the
conclusion that all commercial relations with foreign countries
should be in the hands of the State or subject to strict State control.
'In the rational State immediate trade with a foreign subject
cannot be permitted to the individual citizen.'[2] Fichte's ideal is

---

[1] Fichte assumes that there will be three main economic classes. First, the
producers of the raw materials required for human life. Secondly, those who
transform these raw materials into goods such as clothes, shoes, flour and so on.
Thirdly, the merchants.

[2] *F*, III, p. 421; *M*, III, p. 451.

that of a closed economy in the sense of a self-sufficient economic community.[1] But if there has to be trade with foreign countries, it should not be left to the private initiative and judgment of individuals.

What Fichte envisages, therefore, is a form of national socialism. And he thinks of a planned economy as calculated to provide the material conditions required for the higher intellectual and moral development of the people. In fact, by 'the rational State' (*der Vernunftstaat*) he really means a State directed according to the principles of his own philosophy. We may not feel particularly optimistic about the results of State patronage of a particular philosophical system. But in Fichte's opinion rulers who were really conversant with the principles of transcendental idealism would never abuse their power by restricting private freedom more than was required for the attainment of an end which is itself the expression of freedom.

12. Regarded from the economic point of view, Fichte can be spoken of as one of Germany's first socialist writers. Politically speaking, however, he moved from an earlier cosmopolitan attitude towards German nationalism. In the *Basis of Natural Right* he interpreted the idea of the General Will as leading to the idea of the union of all human wills in a universal community, and he looked forward to a confederation of nations. The system of rights, he thought, could be rendered really stable only through the establishment of a world-wide community. And to a certain extent he always retained this wide outlook. For his ideal was always that of the advance of all men to spiritual freedom. But he came to think that the ideals of the French Revolution, which had aroused his youthful enthusiasm, had been betrayed by Napoleon and that the Germans were better qualified than the French for leading mankind towards its goal. After all, were not the Germans best suited for understanding the principles of the *Wissenschaftslehre* and so for enlightening mankind and teaching it by example what the saving truth could effect? In other words, he thought of Germany as having a cultural mission. And he was convinced that this mission could not be effectively fulfilled without the political unity of the German people. Cultural and linguistic unity go together, and no culture can be unified and lasting without the backbone of

---

[1] Fichte's advocacy of a 'closed' commercial State is not based entirely on economic reasons. Like Plato before him, he believes that unrestricted intercourse with foreign countries would hamper the education of the citizens according to the principles of the true philosophy.

political unity. Hence Fichte looked forward to the formation of one German *Reich* which would put an end to the existing division of the Germans into a multiplicity of States. And he hoped for the emergence of a leader who would achieve this political unification of the Germans into one 'rational State'.

If we look back on Fichte's hopes and dreams in the light of Germany's history in the first half of the twentieth century, they obviously tend to appear as sinister and ominous. But, as has already been remarked, we should bear in mind the historical circumstances of his own time. In any case further reflections on this matter can be left to the reader.

FICHTE (3)

Fichte's early ideas on religion—God in the first version of the theory of science—The charge of atheism and Fichte's reply— The infinite Will in The Vocation of Man*—The development of the philosophy of Being, 1801–5—The Doctrine of Religion— Later writings—Explanatory and critical comments on Fichte's philosophy of Being.*

1. IN 1790 Fichte wrote some notes or *Aphorisms on Religion and Deism* (*Aphorismen über Religion und Deismus*) which express clearly enough a sense of tension between simple Christian piety and speculative philosophy or, to use a rather hackneyed phrase, between the God of religion and the God of the philosophers. 'The Christian religion seems to be designed more for the heart than for the understanding.'[1] The heart seeks a God who can respond to prayer, who can feel compassion and love; and Christianity fulfils this need. But the understanding, as represented by what Fichte calls deism, presents us with the concept of a changeless necessary Being who is the ultimate cause of all that happens in the world. Christianity offers us the picture of an anthropomorphic Deity, and this picture is well adapted to religious feeling and its exigencies. Speculative philosophy offers us the idea of a changeless first cause and of a system of finite beings which is governed by determinism. And this idea of the understanding does not meet the needs of the heart. True, the two are compatible, in the sense that speculative philosophy leaves untouched the subjective validity of religion. And for the pious Christian who knows little or nothing of philosophy there is no problem. But what of the man whose heart desires a God conceived in human terms but who is at the same time so constituted that the inclination to philosophical reflection is part of his nature? It is all very well to say that he should set limits to philosophical reflection. 'But can he do so, even if he wishes?'

Fichte's own reflection, however, led him in the direction of the Kantian conception of God and of religion rather than in that of deism, which belonged to the pre-Kantian era. And in his *Essay*

[1] *F*, v, p. 5 (not contained in *M*).   [2] *F*, v, p. 8.

towards a Critique of All Revelation (Versuch einer Kritik aller Offenbarung, 1792) he attempted to develop Kant's point of view. In particular he made a distinction between 'theology' and religion. The idea of the possibility of a moral law demands belief in God not only as the Power which dominates Nature and is able to synthesize virtue and happiness but also as the complete embodiment of the moral ideal, as the all-holy Being and supreme Good. But assent to propositions about God (such as 'God is holy and just') is not the same thing as religion which 'according to the meaning of the word [*religio*] should be something which *binds* us, and indeed binds us *more strongly* than we would otherwise be bound'.[1] And this binding is derived from the acceptance of the rational moral law as God's law, as the expression of the divine will.

Needless to say, Fichte does not mean that the content of the moral law is arbitrarily determined by the divine will, so that it cannot be known without revelation. Nor does he propose to substitute the concept of heteronomy, of an authoritarian ethics, for the Kantian concept of the autonomy of the practical reason. To justify his position, therefore, he has recourse to the idea of a radical evil in man, that is, to the idea of the ingrained possibility of evil, owing to the strength of natural impulse and passion, and to the idea of the consequent obscuring of man's knowledge of the moral law. The concept of God as the moral legislator and of obedience to the all-holy will of God helps man to fulfil the moral law and grounds the additional element of binding which is peculiar to religion. Further, as the knowledge of God and his law can be obscured, God's revelation of himself as moral legislator is desirable if it is possible.

This may sound as though Fichte is going well beyond Kant. But the difference is much less than may appear at first. Fichte does not decide where revelation is to be found. But he gives general criteria for deciding whether an alleged revelation is really what it claims to be. For example, no alleged revelation can possibly be what it is claimed to be if it contradicts the moral law. And any alleged revelation which goes beyond the idea of the moral law as the expression of the divine will is not revelation. Hence Fichte does not really transcend the limits of Kant's conception of religion. And the sympathy which he was later to show for Christian dogmas is absent at this stage of his thought.

[1] *F*, v, p. 43; *M*, I, p. 12.

Obviously, it can be objected against Fichte's position that to decide whether revelation really is revelation or not we have first to know the moral law. Hence revelation adds nothing except the idea of fulfilling the moral law as the expression of the all-holy will of God. True, this additional element constitutes what is peculiar to religion. But it seems to follow, on Fichte's premisses, that religion is, as it were, a concession to human weakness. For it is precisely human weakness which needs strengthening through the concept of obedience to the divine legislator. Hence if Fichte is not prepared to abandon the Kantian idea of the autonomy of the practical reason and if at the same time he wishes to retain and support the idea of religion, he must revise his concept of God. And as will be seen presently, his own system of transcendental idealism, in its first form at least, left him no option but to do this.

2. In Fichte's first exposition and explanations of the *Wissenschaftslehre* there is very little mention of God. Nor indeed is there much occasion for mentioning God. For Fichte is concerned with the deduction or reconstruction of consciousness from a first principle which is immanent in consciousness. As we have seen, the pure ego is not a being which lies behind consciousness but an activity which is immanent in consciousness and grounds it. And the intellectual intuition by which the pure ego is apprehended is not a mystical apprehension of the Deity but an intuitive grasping of the pure I-principle revealing itself as an activity or doing (*Thun*). Hence if we emphasize the phenomenological aspect of Fichte's theory of science or knowledge, there is no more reason for describing his pure ego as God than there is for so describing Kant's transcendental ego.

The phenomenological aspect is not indeed the only aspect. In virtue of his elimination of the thing-in-itself and his transformation of the critical philosophy into idealism Fichte is bound to attribute to the pure ego an ontological status and function which was not attributed by Kant to the transcendental ego as logical condition of the unity of consciousness. If the thing-in-itself is to be eliminated, sensible being must be derived, in all the reality which it possesses, from the ultimate principle on the side of the subject; that is, from the absolute ego. But the word 'absolute' must be understood as referring in the first place to that which is fundamental in the transcendental deduction of consciousness from a principle which is immanent in consciousness, not as referring to a Being beyond

all consciousness. To postulate such a Being in a system of transcendental idealism would be to abandon the attempt to reduce
being to thought.

It is true, of course, that the more the metaphysical implications
of the theory of the absolute ego are developed, the more does it
take on, as it were, the character of the divine. For it then appears
as the infinite activity which produces within itself the world of
Nature and of finite selves. But while Fichte is primarily engaged in
transforming the system of Kant into idealism and in deducing
experience from the transcendental ego, it would hardly occur to
him to describe this ego as God. For, as the very use of the word
'ego' shows, the notion of the pure, transcendental or absolute ego
is so entangled, as it were, with human consciousness that such a
description necessarily appears as extremely inappropriate.

Further, the term 'God' signifies for Fichte a personal self-
conscious Being. But the absolute ego is not a self-conscious being.
The activity which grounds consciousness and is a striving towards
self-consciousness cannot itself be conscious. The absolute ego,
therefore, cannot be identified with God. What is more, we cannot
even think the idea of God. The concept of consciousness involves
a distinction between subject and object, ego and non-ego. And
self-consciousness presupposes the positing of the non-ego and
itself involves a distinction between the I-subject and the me-
object. But the idea of God is the idea of a Being in which there is
no such distinction and which is perfectly self-luminous quite
independently of the existence of a world. And we are unable to
think such an idea. We can *talk* about it, of course; but we cannot
be said to *conceive* it. For once we try to *think* what is said, we
necessarily introduce the distinctions which are verbally denied.
The idea of a subject to which nothing is opposed is thus 'the
unthinkable idea of the Godhead'.[1]

It should be noted that Fichte does not say that God is
impossible. When Jean-Paul Sartre says that self-consciousness
necessarily involves a distinction and that the idea of an infinite
self-consciousness in which there is perfect coincidence of subject
and object without any distinction is a contradictory idea, he
intends this as a proof of atheism, if, that is to say, theism is
understood as implying the idea which is alleged to be contradictory.
But Fichte carefully avoids saying that it is impossible that there
should be a God. He appears to leave open the possibility of a

[1] *F*, I, p. 254; *M*, I, p. 448.

Being which transcends the range of human thought and conception. In any case Fichte does not assert atheism.

At the same time it is easily understandable that Fichte was accused of atheism. And we can turn to a brief consideration of the famous atheism controversy which resulted in the philosopher having to abandon his chair at Jena.

3. In his paper *On the Basis of Our Belief in a Divine Providence* (1798) Fichte gave an explicit account of his idea of God. Let us assume first of all that we are looking at the world from the point of view of ordinary consciousness, which is also that of empirical science. From this point of view, that is, for empirical consciousness, we find ourselves as being in the world, the universe, and we cannot transcend it by means of any metaphysical proof of the existence of a supernatural Being. 'The world is, simply because it is; and it is what it is, simply because it is what it is. From this point of view we start with an absolute being, and this absolute being is the world: the two concepts are identical.'[1] To explain the world as the creation of a divine intelligence is, from the scientific point of view, 'simply nonsense' (*totaler Unsinn*). The world is a self-organizing whole which contains in itself the ground of all the phenomena which occur in it.

Now let us look at the world from the point of view of transcendental idealism. The world is then seen as existing only for consciousness and as posited by the pure ego. But in this case the question of finding a cause of the world apart from the ego does not arise. Therefore neither from the scientific nor from the transcendental point of view can we prove the existence of a transcendent divine Creator.

There is, however, a third point of view, the moral. And when looked at from this point of view the world is seen to be 'the sensible material for (the performance of) our duty'.[2] And the ego is seen to belong to a supersensible moral order. It is this moral order which is God. The 'living and operative moral order is itself God. We need no other God, and we cannot conceive any other.'[3] 'This is the true faith; this moral order is the *divine*. . . . It is constructed by right action.'[4] To speak of God as substance or as

---

[1] *F*, v, p. 179; *M*, iii, p. 123.
[2] *F*, v, p. 185; *M*, iii, p. 129.   [3] *F*, v, p. 186; *M*, iii, p. 130.
[4] *F*, v, p. 185; *M*, iii, p. 129. It is important to notice the original German text: *Dies ist der wahre Glaube; diese moralische Ordnung ist das Göttliche, das wir annehmen. Er wird construirt durch das Rechtthun.* Grammatically, *Er* (It) should refer to *der wahre Glaube* (the true faith) and cannot refer to *diese moralische Ordnung* (this moral order). Unless, therefore, we are prepared to say that Fichte

personal or as exercising with foresight a benevolent providence
is so much nonsense. Belief in divine providence is the belief that
moral action always has good results and that evil actions can
never have good results.

That such statements led to a charge of atheism is not altogether
surprising. For to most of Fichte's readers God seemed to have
been reduced to a moral ideal. And this is not what is generally
meant by theism. After all, there are atheists with moral ideals.
Fichte, however, was indignant at the accusation and answered it
at considerable length. His replies did not achieve the desired
result of clearing his name in the eyes of his opponents; but this is
irrelevant for our purposes. We are concerned only with what he
said.

In the first place Fichte explained that he could not describe
God as personal or as substance because personality was for him
something essentially finite and substance meant something
extended in space and time, a material thing. In fact, none of the
attributes of things or beings could be predicated of God. 'Speaking
in a purely philosophical manner one would have to say of God:
He is . . . not a being but a *pure activity*, the life and principle of a
supersensible world-order.'[1]

In the second place Fichte maintained that his critics had misunderstood what he meant by a moral world-order. They had
interpreted him as saying that God is a moral order in a sense
analogous to the order created by a housewife when she arranges
the furniture and other objects in a room. But what he had really
meant was that God is an active ordering, an *ordo ordinans*, a living
and active moral order, not an *ordo ordinatus*, something merely
constructed by human effort. God is *ein tätiges Ordnen*, an active
ordering, rather than an *Ordnung*, an order constructed by man.[2]
And the finite ego, considered as acting in accordance with duty, is
'a member of that supersensible world-order'.[3]

In Fichte's idea of God as the moral world-order we can perhaps
see the fusion of two lines of thought. First there is the concept of
the dynamic unity of all rational beings. In the *Basis of the Entire
Theory of Science* Fichte had not much occasion for dwelling on the
plurality of selves. For he was primarily concerned with an abstract

has simply neglected grammatical propriety, we must recognize that he is *not*
saying that God, identified with the moral order, is no more than a creation or
construction of man.
[1] *F*, v, p. 261. (Fichte's *Gerichtliche Verantwortungsschrift* is not printed in *M*.)
[2] *F*, v, p. 382; *M*, III, p. 246.   [3] *F*, v, p. 261.

deduction of 'experience' in the sense already explained. But in the *Basis of Natural Right* he insisted, as we have seen, on the necessity of a plurality of rational beings. 'Man becomes man only amongst men; and as he can be nothing else but man and would not exist at all if he were not man, *there must be a plurality of men if there is to be man at all.*'[1] Hence Fichte was naturally impelled to reflect on the bond of union between men. In *The Science of Ethics* he was primarily concerned with the moral law as such and with personal morality; but he expressed his conviction that all rational beings have a common moral end, and he spoke of the moral law as using the individual as a tool or instrument for its self-realization in the sensible world. And from this notion there is an easy transition to the idea of a moral world-order which fulfils itself in and through rational beings and unites them in itself.

The second line of thought is Fichte's strongly moralistic conception of religion. At the time when he wrote the essay which occasioned the atheism-controversy he tended, like Kant before him, to equate religion with morality. Not prayer but the performance of one's duty is true religion. True, Fichte allowed that the moral life has a distinguishable religious aspect, namely the belief that whatever appearances may suggest performance of one's duty always produces a good result because it forms part, as it were, of a self-realizing moral order. But, given Fichte's moralistic interpretation of religion, faith in this moral world-order would naturally count for him as faith in God, especially as on his premisses he could not think of God as a personal transcendent Being.

This moralistic conception of religion finds clear expression in an essay to which the title *From a Private Paper* (1800) has been given. The place or locus of religion, Fichte asserts, is found in obedience to the moral law. And religious faith is faith in a moral order. In action considered from a purely natural and non-moral point of view man reckons on the natural order, that is, on the stability and uniformity of Nature. In moral action he reckons on a supersensible moral order in which his action has a part to play and which ensures its moral fruitfulness. 'Every belief in a divine being *which contains more* than this concept of the moral order is to that extent imagination and superstition.'[2]

Obviously, those who described Fichte as an atheist were from one point of view quite justified. For he refused to assert what

---

[1] *F*, III, p. 39; *M*, II, p. 43.   [2] *F*, V, pp. 394-5; *M*, III, p. 258.

theism was generally taken to mean. At the same time his indignant repudiation of the charge of atheism is understandable. For he did not assert that nothing exists except finite selves and the sensible world. There is, at least as an object of practical faith, a supersensible moral world-order which fulfils itself in and through man.

4. But if the moral world-order is really an *ordo ordinans*, a truly active ordering, it must obviously possess an ontological status. And in *The Vocation of Man* (1800) it appears as the eternal and infinite Will. 'This Will binds me in union with itself: it also binds me in union with all finite beings like myself and is the common mediator between us all.'[1] It is infinite Reason. But dynamic creative Reason is Will. Fichte also describes it as creative Life.

If we took some of Fichte's expressions literally, we should probably be inclined to interpret his doctrine of the infinite Will in a theistic sense. He even addresses the 'sublime and living Will, named by no name and compassed by no concept'.[2] But he still maintains that personality is something limited and finite and cannot be applied to God. The infinite differs from the finite in nature and not merely in degree. Further, the philosopher repeats that true religion consists in the fulfilment of one's moral vocation. At the same time this idea of doing one's duty and so fulfilling one's moral vocation is undoubtedly infused with a spirit of devout abandonment to and trust in the divine Will.

To appreciate the role of *The Vocation of Man* in the development of Fichte's later philosophy it is important to understand that the doctrine of the infinite Will is described as a matter of faith. This somewhat strange and turgid work, which is introduced by the remarks that it is not intended for professional philosophers and that the *I* of the dialogue portions should not be taken without more ado to represent the author himself, is divided into three parts, entitled respectively *Doubt*, *Knowledge* and *Faith*. In the second part idealism is interpreted as meaning that not only external objects but also one's own self, so far as one can have any idea of it, exist only for consciousness. And the conclusion is drawn that everything is reduced to images or pictures (*Bilder*) without there being any reality which is pictured. 'All reality is transformed into a wonderful dream, without a life which is dreamed of and without a mind which dreams it, into a dream which consists of a dream of itself. *Intuition* is the dream; *thought*—the source of all the being

---

[1] *F*, II, p. 299; *M*, III, p. 395.   [2] *F*, II, p. 303; *M*, III, p. 399.

and all the reality which I imagine to myself, of *my* being, my power, my purpose—is the dream of that dream.'[1] In other words, subjective idealism reduces everything to presentations without there being anything which does the presenting or to which the presentations are made. For when I try to grasp the self for whose consciousness the presentations exist, this self necessarily becomes one of the presentations. Knowledge, therefore, that is, idealist philosophy, can find nothing abiding, no being. But the mind cannot rest in such a position. And practical or moral faith, based on consciousness of myself as a moral will subject to the moral imperative, asserts the infinite Will which underlies the finite self and creates the world in the only way in which it can do so, 'in the finite reason'.[2]

Fichte thus retains idealism but at the same time goes beyond the ego-philosophy to postulate the infinite underlying and all-comprehensive Will. And with this postulate the atmosphere, so to speak, of his original philosophy changes dramatically. I do not mean to imply that there is no connection. For the theory of the Will can be regarded as implicit in the practical deduction of consciousness in the original *Wissenschaftslehre*. At the same time the ego retreats from the foreground and an infinite reality, which is no longer described as the absolute ego, takes its place. 'Only Reason exists; the infinite in itself, the finite in it and through it. Only in our minds does He create a world, at least that *from which* and that *by which* we unfold it: the voice of duty, and harmonious feelings, intuition and laws of thought.'[3]

As already mentioned, this dynamic panentheistic idealism is for Fichte a matter of practical faith, not of knowledge. To fulfil properly our moral vocations, we require faith in a living and active moral order which can only be interpreted as infinite dynamic Reason, that is, as infinite Will. This is the one true Being behind the sphere of presentation, creating and sustaining it through finite selves which themselves exist only as manifestations of the infinite Will. The development of Fichte's later philosophy is largely conditioned by the need to *think* this concept of absolute Being, to give it philosophical form. In *The Vocation of Man* it remains within the sphere of moral faith.

5. In the *Exposition of the Theory of Science*[4] which he composed in 1801 Fichte clearly states that 'all knowledge presupposes . . .

---

[1] *F*, II, p. 245; *M*, III, p. 341.   [2] *F*, II, p. 303; *M*, III, p. 399.
[3] *Ibid.*   [4] *Darstellung der Wissenschaftslehre.*

its own being'.[1] For knowledge is 'a being *for itself* and *in itself*':[2] it is being's 'self-penetration'[3] and is thus the expression of Freedom. Absolute knowledge, therefore, presupposes absolute Being: the former is the latter's self-penetration.

Here we have a clear reversal of the position adopted by Fichte in the earlier form of his doctrine of knowledge. At first he maintained that all being is being for consciousness. Hence it was not possible for him to admit the idea of an absolute divine Being behind or beyond consciousness. For the very fact of conceiving such a Being made it conditioned and dependent. In other words, the idea of absolute Being was for him contradictory. Now, however, he asserts the primacy of Being. Absolute Being comes to exist 'for itself' in absolute knowledge. Hence the latter must presuppose the former. And this absolute Being is the divine.

It does not follow, of course, that absolute Being is for Fichte a personal God. Being 'penetrates itself', comes to knowledge or consciousness of itself, in and through human knowledge of reality. In other words, absolute Being expresses itself in and bears within itself all finite rational beings, and their knowledge of Being is Being's knowledge of itself. At the same time Fichte insists that absolute Being can never be wholly understood or comprehended by the finite mind. In this sense God transcends the human mind.

Evidently, there is some difficulty here. On the one hand absolute Being is said to penetrate itself in absolute knowledge. On the other hand absolute knowledge seems to be ruled out. If, therefore, we exclude Christian theism, according to which God enjoys perfect self-knowledge independently of the human spirit, it appears that Fichte should logically adopt the Hegelian conception of philosophical knowledge as penetrating the inner essence of the Absolute and as being the Absolute's absolute knowledge of itself. But in point of fact Fichte does not do this. To the very end he maintains that absolute Being in itself transcends the reach of the human mind. We know images, pictures, rather than the reality in itself.

In the lectures on the *Wissenschaftslehre* which he delivered in 1804 Fichte emphasizes the idea of absolute Being as Light,[4] an idea which goes back to Plato and the Platonic tradition in metaphysics. This living Light in its radiation is said to divide itself into

---

[1] *F*, II, p. 68; *M*, IV, p. 68.   [2] *F*, II, p. 19; *M*, IV, p. 19.   [3] *Ibid.*
[4] This idea had already been mentioned in the *Wissenschaftslehre* of 1801.

Being and Thought (*Denken*). But conceptual thought, Fichte insists, can never grasp absolute Being in itself, which is incomprehensible. And this incomprehensibility is 'the negation of the concept'.[1] One might expect Fichte to draw the conclusion that the human mind can approach the Absolute only by way of negation. But in point of fact he makes a good many positive statements, telling us, for example, that Being and Life and *esse* are one, and that the Absolute *in itself* can never be subject to division.[2] It is only in its appearance, in the radiation of Light, that division is introduced.

In *The Nature of the Scholar* (1806), the published version of lectures delivered at Erlangen in 1805, we are again told that the one divine Being is Life and that this Life is itself changeless and eternal. But it externalizes itself in the life of the human race throughout time, 'an endlessly self-developing life which always advances towards a higher self-realization in a never-ending stream of time'.[3] In other words, this external life of God advances towards the realization of an ideal which can be described, in anthropomorphic language, as 'the Idea and fundamental notion of God in the production of the world, God's purpose and plan for the world'.[4] In this sense the divine Idea is 'the ultimate and absolute foundation of all appearances'.[5]

6. These speculations were worked out more at length in *The Way to the Blessed Life or the Doctrine of Religion* (1806), which comprises a series of lectures delivered at Berlin. God is absolute Being. And to say this is to say that God is infinite Life. For 'Being and Life are one and the same'.[6] In itself this Life is one, indivisible and unchanging. But it expresses or manifests itself externally. And the only way in which it can do this is through consciousness which is the ex-istence (*Dasein*) of God. 'Being ex-ists [*ist da*] and the ex-istence of Being is necessarily consciousness or reflection.'[7] In this external manifestation distinction or division appears. For consciousness involves the subject-object relation.

The subject in question is obviously the limited or finite subject, namely the human spirit. But what is the object? It is indeed Being. For consciousness, the divine *Dasein*, is consciousness of Being. But Being in itself, the immediate infinite Life, transcends the comprehension of the human mind. Hence the object of

---

[1] *F*, x, p. 117; *M*, iv, p. 195.   [2] *F*, x, p. 206; *M*, iv, p. 284.
[3] *F*, vi, p. 362; *M*, v, p. 17.   [4] *F*, vi, p. 367; *M*, v, p. 22.
[5] *F*, vi, p. 361; *M*, v, p. 15.   [6] *F*, v, p. 403; *M*, v, p. 115.
[7] *F*, v, p. 539; *M*, v, p. 251.

consciousness must be the image or picture or *schema* of the
Absolute. And this is the world. 'What does this consciousness
contain? I think that each of you will answer: the world and
nothing but the world. . . . In consciousness the divine Life is
inevitably transformed into an abiding world.'[1] In other words,
Being is objectified for consciousness in the form of the world.

Although Fichte insists that the Absolute transcends the grasp
of the human mind, he says a good deal about it. And even if the
finite spirit cannot know the infinite Life as it is in itself, it can at
least know that the world of consciousness is the image or *schema*
of the Absolute. Hence there are two main forms of life which lie
open to man. It is possible for him to immerse himself in apparent
life (*das Scheinleben*), life in the finite and changeable, life directed
towards the gratification of natural impulse. But because of its
unity with the infinite divine Life the human spirit can never be
satisfied with love of the finite and sensible. Indeed, the endless
seeking for successive finite sources of satisfaction shows that even
apparent life is informed or carried along, as it were, by the
longing for the infinite and eternal which is 'the innermost root of
all finite existence'.[2] Hence man is capable of rising to true life
(*das wahrhaftige Leben*) which is characterized by love of God. For
love, as Fichte puts it, is the heart of life.

If it is asked in what this true life precisely consists, Fichte's
reply is still given primarily in terms of morality. That is to say,
true life consists primarily in a man's fulfilling his moral vocation,
by which he is liberated from the servitude of the sensible world
and in which he strives after the attainment of ideal ends. At the
same time the markedly moralistic atmosphere of Fichte's earlier
accounts of religion tends to disappear or at any rate to diminish.
The religious point of view is not simply identical with the moral
point of view. For it involves the fundamental conviction that
God alone is, that God is the one true reality. True, God as he is in
himself is hidden from the finite mind. But the religious man
knows that the infinite divine Life is immanent in himself, and his
moral vocation is for him a divine vocation. In the creative
realization of ideals or values through action[3] he sees the image or
schema of the divine Life.

[1] *F*, v, p. 457; *M*, v, p. 169.   [2] *F*, v, p. 407; *M*, v, p. 119.
[3] In what Fichte calls the higher morality man is creative, seeking actively to
realize ideal values. He does not content himself, as in the lower morality, with
the mere fulfilment of the successive duties of his state of life. Religion adds belief
in God as the one reality and a sense of divine vocation. The life of higher morality
is seen as the expression of the one infinite divine Life.

But though *The Doctrine of Religion* is permeated with a religious atmosphere, there is a marked tendency to subordinate the religious point of view to the philosophical. Thus, according to Fichte, while the religious point of view involves belief in the Absolute as the foundation of all plurality and finite existence, philosophy turns this belief into knowledge. And it is in accordance with this attitude that Fichte attempts to show the identity between Christian dogmas and his own system. To be sure, this attempt can be regarded as the expression of a growth in sympathy with Christian theology; but it can also be regarded as an essay in 'demythologization'. For instance, in the sixth lecture Fichte refers to the prologue to St. John's Gospel and argues that the doctrine of the divine Word, when translated into the language of philosophy, is identical with his own theory of the divine ex-istence or *Dasein*. And the statement of St. John that all things were made in and through the Word means, from the speculative point of view, that the world and all that is in it exist only in the sphere of consciousness as the ex-istence of the Absolute.

However, with the development of the philosophy of Being there goes a development in Fichte's understanding of religion. From the religious point of view moral activity is love of God and fulfilment of his will, and it is sustained by faith and trust in God. We exist only in and through God, infinite Life, and the feeling of this union is essential to the religious or blessed life (*das selige Leben*).

7. *The Way to the Blessed Life* is a series of popular lectures, in the sense that it is not a work for professional philosophers. And Fichte is obviously concerned with edifying and uplifting his hearers, as well as with reassuring them that his philosophy is not at variance with the Christian religion. But the fundamental theories are common to Fichte's later writings: they are certainly not put forward simply for the sake of edification. Thus in *The Facts of Consciousness* (1810) we are told that 'knowledge is certainly not merely knowledge of itself . . . it is knowledge of a *Being*, namely of the one Being which truly is, God'.[1] But this object of knowledge is not grasped in itself; it is splintered, as it were, into forms of knowledge. And 'the demonstration of the necessity of these forms is precisely philosophy or the *Wissenschaftslehre*'.[2] Similarly, in *The Theory of Science in its General Outline* (1810) we read that 'only one Being exists purely through

---

[1] *F*, II, p. 685 (not included in *M*)   [2] *Ibid.*

itself, God. . . . And neither within him nor outside him can a new being arise.'[1] The only thing which can be external to God is the *schema* or picture of Being itself, which is 'God's Being outside his Being',[2] the divine self-externalization in consciousness. Thus the whole of the productive activity which is reconstructed or deduced in the theory of science is the schematizing or picturing of God, the spontaneous self-externalization of the divine life.

In the *System of Ethics* of 1812 we find Fichte saying that while from the scientific point of view the world is primary and the concept a secondary reflection or picture, from the ethical point of view the Concept is primary. In fact 'the Concept is ground of the world or of Being'.[3] And this assertion, if taken out of its context, appears to contradict the doctrine which we have been considering, namely that Being is primary. But Fichte explains that 'the proposition in question, namely that the Concept is ground of Being, can be expressed in this way: Reason or the Concept is practical'.[4] He further explains that though the Concept or Reason is in fact itself the picture of a higher Being, the picture of God, 'ethics can and should know nothing of this. . . . Ethics must know nothing of God, but take the Concept itself as the Absolute.'[5] In other words, the doctrine of absolute Being, as expounded in the *Wissenschaftslehre*, transcends the sphere of ethics which deals with the causality of the Concept, the self-realizing Idea or Ideal.

8. Fichte's later philosophy has sometimes been represented as being to all intents and purposes a new system which involved a break with the earlier philosophy of the ego. Fichte himself, however, maintained that it was nothing of the kind. In his view the philosophy of Being constituted a development of his earlier thought rather than a break with it. If he had originally meant, as most of his critics took him to mean, that the world is the creation of the finite self as such, his later theory of absolute Being would indeed have involved a radical change of view. But he had never meant this. The finite subject and its object, the two poles of consciousness, had always been for him the expression of an unlimited or infinite principle. And his later doctrine of the sphere of consciousness as the ex-istence of infinite Life or Being was a development, not a contradiction, of his earlier thought. In other words, the philosophy of Being supplemented the *Wissenschaftslehre* rather than took its place.

[1] F, II, p. 696; M, v, p. 615.   [2] *Ibid.*   [3] F, XI, p. 5; M, VI, p. 5.
[4] F, XI, p. 7; M, VI, p. 7.   [5] F, XI, p. 4; M, VI, p. 4.

It is indeed arguable that unless Fichte was prepared to defend a subjective idealism which it would have been difficult to dissociate from a solipsistic implication, he was bound in the long run to transgress his initial self-imposed limits, to go behind consciousness and to find its ground in absolute Being. Further, he explicitly admitted that the absolute ego, as transcending the subject-object relationship which it grounds, must be the identity of subjectivity and objectivity. Hence it is not unnatural that in proportion as he developed the metaphysical aspect of his philosophy he should tend to discard the word 'ego' as an appropriate descriptive term for his ultimate principle. For this word is too closely associated with the idea of the subject as distinct from the object. In this sense his later philosophy was a development of his earlier thought.

At the same time it is also arguable that the philosophy of Being is superimposed on the *Wissenschaftslehre* in such a way that the two do not really fit together. According to the *Wissenschaftslehre* the world exists only for consciousness. And this thesis really depends on the premiss that being must be reduced to thought or consciousness. Fichte's philosophy of absolute Being, however, clearly implies the logical priority of being to thought. True, in his later philosophy Fichte does not deny his former thesis that the world has reality only within the sphere of consciousness. On the contrary, he reaffirms it. What he does is to depict the whole sphere of consciousness as the externalization of absolute Being in itself. But it is very difficult to understand this idea of externalization. If we take seriously the statement that absolute Being is and eternally remains one and immutable, we can hardly interpret Fichte as meaning that Being *becomes* conscious. And if the sphere of consciousness is an eternal reflection of God, if it is the divine self-consciousness eternally proceeding from God as the Plotinian *Nous* emanates eternally from the One, it seems to follow that there must always have been a human spirit.

Fichte could, of course, depict absolute Being as an infinite activity moving towards self-consciousness in and through the human spirit. But then it would be natural to conceive the infinite Life as expressing itself immediately in objective Nature as a necessary condition for the life of the human spirit. In other words, it would be natural to proceed in the direction of Hegel's absolute idealism. But this would involve a greater change in the *Wissenschaftslehre* than Fichte was prepared to make. He does indeed say that it is the one Life, and not the individual as such, which 'intuits' the material world. But he maintains to the end that the world, as the image or *schema* of God, has reality only within the sphere of consciousness. And as absolute Being in itself is not conscious, this can only mean human consciousness. Until this element of subjective idealism is abandoned, the transition to the absolute idealism of Hegel is not possible.

There is indeed another possibility, namely that of conceiving absolute Being as eternally self-conscious. But Fichte can hardly take the path of traditional theism. For his idea of what self-consciousness essentially involves prevents him from attributing it to the One. Hence consciousness must be derivative. And this is human consciousness. But there can be no being apart from God. Hence human consciousness must be in some sense the Absolute's consciousness of itself. But in what sense? It does not seem to me that any clear answer is forthcoming. And the reason is that Fichte's later philosophy of Being could not be simply superimposed on the *Wissenschaftslehre*. A much greater measure of revision was required.

It may be objected that to interpret Fichte's philosophy as demanding revision either in the direction of Hegel's absolute idealism or in that of theism is to fail to do justice to its intrinsic character. And this is true in a sense. For Fichte has his own ethical vision of reality, to which attention has been drawn in these chapters. We have seen the infinite Will expressing itself in finite selves for which Nature forms the scene and material for the fulfilment of their several moral vocations. And we have seen these vocations converging towards the realization of a universal moral order, the goal, as it were, of the infinite Will itself. And the grandeur of this vision of reality, of Fichte's dynamic ethical idealism in its main lines, is not in question. But Fichte did not offer his philosophy simply as an impressionistic vision or as poetry, but as the truth about reality. Hence criticism of his theories is quite in place. After all, it is not the vision of the realization of a universal ideal, a moral world-order, which has been subjected to adverse criticism. This vision may well possess an abiding value. And it can serve as a corrective to an interpretation of reality simply in terms of empirical science. One can certainly derive stimulus and inspiration from Fichte. But to draw profit from him one has to discard a good deal of the theoretical framework of the vision.

It has been stated above that Fichte could hardly take the path of traditional theism. But some writers have maintained that his later philosophy is in fact a form of theism. And in support of this contention they can appeal to certain statements which represent the philosopher's firm convictions and are not simply *obiter dicta* or remarks calculated to reassure his more orthodox readers or hearers. For example, Fichte constantly maintains that absolute Being is unchangeable and that it can suffer no self-diremption. It is the eternal immutable One; not a static lifeless One but the fullness of infinite Life. True, creation is free only in the sense that it is spontaneous; but creation does not effect any change in God. To be sure, Fichte refuses to predicate personality of God, even if he frequently employs Christian language and speaks of God as 'He'. But as he regards personality as necessarily finite, he obviously cannot attribute it to infinite Being. But this does not mean that he looks on God as infra-personal. God is supra-personal, not less than personal. In Scholastic language, Fichte has no analogical concept of personality, and this prevents him from using theistic terms. At the same time the concept of absolute Being which transcends the sphere of the distinctions which necessarily exist between finite beings is clearly a move in the direction of theism. The ego no longer occupies the central position in Fichte's picture of reality: its place is taken by infinite Life which in itself suffers no change or self-diremption.

This is all very well as far as it goes. And it is true that Fichte's refusal to predicate personality of God is due to the fact that personality for him involves finitude. God transcends the sphere of personality rather than falls short of it. But it is also the absence of any clear idea of analogy which involves Fichte's thought in a radical ambiguity. God is infinite Being. Therefore there can arise no being apart from God. If there were such a being, God would not be infinite. The Absolute is the sole Being. This line of thought clearly points in the direction of pantheism. At the same time Fichte is determined to maintain that the sphere of consciousness, with its distinction, between the finite ego and the world, is in some sense outside God. But in what sense? It is all very well for Fichte to say that the distinction between the divine Being and the divine ex-istence arises only for consciousness. The question inevitably suggests itself, are finite selves beings or are they not? If they are not, monism results. And it is then impossible to explain how consciousness, with the distinctions which it introduces, arises. If, however, finite selves are beings, how are we to reconcile this with the statement that God is the only Being unless we have recourse to a theory of analogy? Fichte wishes to have things both ways. That is, he wishes to say at the same time that the sphere of consciousness, with its distinction between the finite self and its object, is external to God and that God is the only Being. Hence his position in regard to the issue between theism and pantheism inevitably remains ambiguous. This is not to deny, of course, that the development of Fichte's philosophy of Being conferred on his thought a much greater resemblance to theism than would be suggested by his earlier writings. But it seems to me that if a writer who admires Fichte for his use of the transcendental method of reflection or for his ethical idealism proceeds to interpret his later philosophy as a clear statement of theism, he is going beyond the historical evidence.

If, finally, it is asked whether in his philosophy of Being Fichte abandons idealism, the answer should be clear from what has been already said. Fichte does not repudiate the *Wissenschaftslehre*, and in this sense he retains idealism. When he says that it is the one Life, and not the individual subject, which 'intuits' (and so produces) the material world, he is obviously accounting for the fact that the material world appears to the finite subject as something given, as an already constituted object. But he had proclaimed from the beginning that this is the crucial fact which idealism has to explain, and not to deny. At the same time the assertion of the primacy of Being and of the derivative character of consciousness and knowledge is a move away from idealism. Hence we can say that in so far as this assertion proceeded from the exigencies of his own thought, idealism with Fichte tended to overcome itself. But this is not to say that the philosopher ever made a clear and explicit break with idealism. In any case we may well feel that though in recent times there has been a tendency to emphasize Fichte's later thought, his impressive vision of reality is his system of ethical idealism rather than his obscure utterances about absolute Being and the divine *Dasein*.

CHAPTER V

SCHELLING (I)

*Life and writings—The successive phases in Schelling's thought
—Early writings and the influence of Fichte.*

1. FRIEDRICH WILHELM JOSEPH VON SCHELLING, son of a learned
Lutheran pastor, was born in 1775 at Leonberg in Württemberg.
A precocious boy, he was admitted at the age of fifteen to the
Protestant theological foundation at the University of Tübingen
where he became a friend of Hegel and Hölderlin, both of whom
were five years older than himself. At the age of seventeen he wrote
a dissertation on the third chapter of Genesis, and in 1793 he
published an essay *On Myths* (*Ueber Mythen*). This was followed in
1794 by a paper *On the Possibility of a Form of Philosophy in
General* (*Ueber die Möglichkeit einer Form der Philosophie überhaupt*).
At this time Schelling was more or less a disciple of Fichte, a
fact which is apparent in the title of a work published in 1795, *On
the Ego as Principle of Philosophy* (*Vom Ich als Prinzip der
Philosophie*). In the same year there appeared his *Philosophical
Letters on Dogmatism and Criticism* (*Philosophische Briefe über
Dogmatismus und Kritizismus*), dogmatism being represented by
Spinoza and criticism by Fichte.

But though Fichte's thought formed a point of departure for his
reflections, Schelling very soon showed the independence of his
mind. In particular, he was dissatisfied with Fichte's view of
Nature as being simply an instrument for moral action. And his
own view of Nature as an immediate manifestation of the Absolute,
as a self-organizing dynamic and teleological system which moves
upwards, as it were, to the emergence of consciousness and to
Nature's knowledge of herself in and through man, found expression in a series of works on the philosophy of Nature. Thus in 1797
he published *Ideas towards a Philosophy of Nature* (*Ideen zu einer
Philosophie der Natur*), in 1798 *On the World-Soul* (*Von der
Weltseele*), and in 1799 a *First Sketch of a System of the Philosophy
of Nature* (*Erster Entwurf eines Systems der Naturphilosophie*) and
an *Introduction to the Sketch of a System of the Philosophy of Nature,
or On the Concept of Speculative Physics* (*Einleitung zu dem Entwurf*

94

eines Systems der Naturphilosophie oder über den Begriff der spekulativen Physik).

It will be noted that the title of the last work refers to speculative physics. And a similar term occurs in the full title of the work *On the World-Soul*, the world-soul being said to be an hypothesis of 'the higher physics'. One can hardly imagine Fichte giving much attention to speculative physics. Yet the series of publications on the philosophy of Nature does not indicate a complete break with Fichte's thought. For in 1800 Schelling published his *System of Transcendental Idealism (System des transzendentalen Idealismus)* in which the influence of Fichte's *Wissenschaftslehre* is obvious. Whereas in his writings on the philosophy of Nature Schelling moved from the objective to the subjective, from the lowest grades of Nature up to the organic sphere as a preparation for consciousness, in the *System of Transcendental Idealism* he began with the ego and proceeded to trace the process of its self-objectification. He regarded the two points of view as complementary, as is shown by the fact that in 1800 he also published a *General Deduction of the Dynamic Process (Allgemeine Deduktion des dynamischen Prozesses),* which was followed in 1801 by a short piece *On the True Concept of the Philosophy of Nature (Ueber den wahren Begriff der Naturphilosophie).* In the same year he also published *An Exposition of my System of Philosophy (Darstellung meines Systems der Philosophie).*

In 1798 Schelling was appointed to a chair in the University of Jena. He was only twenty-three, but his writings had won him the commendation not only of Goethe but also of Fichte. From 1802 to 1803 he collaborated with Hegel in editing the *Critical Journal of Philosophy.* And during the period of his professorship at Jena he was in friendly relations with the circle of the romantics, such as the two Schlegels and Novalis. In 1802 Schelling published, *Bruno, or On the Divine and Natural Principle of Things (Bruno, oder über das göttliche und natürliche Prinzip der Dinge)* and also a series of *Lectures on the Method of Academic Study (Vorlesungen über die Methode des akademischen Studiums)* in which he discussed the unity of the sciences and the place of philosophy in academic life.

It has been mentioned that in his *System of Transcendental Idealism* Schelling started with the ego and utilized ideas taken from Fichte's *Wissenschaftslehre* in his reconstruction of the ego's self-objectification, for example in morals. But this work culminated in a philosophy of art, to which Schelling attached great importance.

And in the winter of 1802-3 he lectured at Jena on the philosophy of art. At this time he looked on art as the key to the nature of reality. And this fact alone is sufficient to show the marked difference between Schelling's outlook and that of Fichte. In 1803 Schelling married Caroline Schlegel after the legal dissolution of her marriage with A. W. Schlegel, and the pair went to Würzburg, where Schelling lectured for a period in the University. About this time he began to devote his attention to problems of religion and to the theosophical utterances of the mystical shoe-maker of Görlitz, Jakob Boehme.[1] And in 1804 he published *Philosophy and Religion* (*Philosophie und Religion*).

Schelling left Würzburg for Munich in 1806. His reflections on freedom and on the relation between human freedom and the Absolute found expression in *Philosophical Inquiries into the Nature of Human Freedom* (*Philosophische Untersuchungen über das Wesen der menschlichen Freiheit*), a work which was published in 1809. But by this time his star had begun to grow dim. We have seen that he collaborated with Hegel for a short period in editing a philosophical journal. But in 1807 Hegel, who had previously been little known, published his first great work, *The Phenomenology of Spirit*. And this work not only formed the first stage in its author's rise to fame as Germany's leading philosopher but also represented his intellectual break with Schelling. In particular, Hegel gave a somewhat caustic expression to his opinion of Schelling's doctrine of the Absolute. And Schelling, who was the very opposite of thick-skinned, took this betrayal, as he saw it, very much to heart. In the years that followed, as he witnessed the growing reputation of his rival, he became obsessed by the thought that his former friend had foisted on a gullible public an inferior system of philosophy. Indeed, his bitter disappointment at Hegel's rise to a pre-eminent position in the philosophical world of Germany probably helps to explain why, after a remarkable burst of literary activity, he published comparatively little.

Schelling continued, however, to lecture. Thus a course of lectures which he gave at Stuttgart in 1810 is printed in his collected *Works*. In 1811 he wrote *The Ages of the World* (*Die Zeitalter*), but the work remained unfinished and was not published during his lifetime.

During the period 1821-6 Schelling lectured at Erlangen. In 1827 he returned to Munich to occupy the chair of philosophy and

---

[1] For Jakob Boehme (1575-1624) see Vol. III, pp. 270-3.

zestfully set about the congenial task of undermining the influence of Hegel. He had become convinced that a distinction must be made between negative philosophy, which is a purely abstract conceptual construction, and positive philosophy, which treats of concrete existence. The Hegelian system, needless to say, was declared to be an example of the first type.

The death of Schelling's great rival[1] in 1831 should have facilitated his task. And ten years later, in 1841, he was appointed professor of philosophy at Berlin with the mission of combating the influence of Hegelianism by expounding his own religious system. In the Prussian capital Schelling began lecturing as a prophet, as one announcing the advent of a new era. And he had among his audience professors, statesmen and a number of hearers whose names were to become famous, such as Sören Kierkegaard, Jakob Burckhardt, Friedrich Engels and Bakunin. But the lectures were not as successful as Schelling hoped that they would be, and the audience started to diminish. In 1846 he abandoned lecturing, except for occasional discourses at the Berlin Academy. Later he retired to Munich and busied himself with preparing manuscripts for publication. He died in 1854 at Ragaz in Switzerland. His *Philosophy of Revelation* (*Philosophie der Offenbarung*) and *Philosophy of Mythology* (*Philosophie der Mythologie*) were published posthumously.

2. There is no one closely-knit system which we can call Schelling's system of philosophy. For his thought passed through a succession of phases from the early period when he stood very much under the influence of Fichte up to the final period which is represented by the posthumously published lectures on the philosophy of revelation and mythology. There has been no general agreement among historians about the precise number of phases which should be distinguished. One or two have contented themselves with Schelling's own distinction between negative and positive philosophy; but this distinction fails to take account of the variety of phases in his thought before he set about expounding his final philosophy of religion. Hence it has been customary to make further divisions. But though there certainly are distinct phases in Schelling's thought, it would be a mistake to regard these phases as so many independent systems. For there is a visible continuity.

---

[1] Hegel himself does not seem to have been much concerned with personal rivalries as such; he was absorbed in ideas and in the exposition of what he believed to be the truth. But Schelling took Hegel's criticism of his own ideas as a personal affront.

That is to say, reflection on a position already adopted led Schelling to raise further problems, the solution of which required fresh moves on his part. True, in his later years he emphasized the distinction between negative and positive philosophy. But though he regarded a good deal of his own previous thought as negative philosophy, he stressed the distinction in the course of his polemic against Hegel; and what he desired was not so much a complete rejection of so-called negative philosophy as its incorporation into and subordination to positive philosophy. Further, he claimed that some inkling at least of positive philosophy could be found in his early *Philosophical Letters on Dogmatism and Criticism*, and that even in his first philosophical essays his inclination towards the concrete and historical had manifested itself.

In 1796, when Schelling was twenty-one, he drew up for himself a programme for a system of philosophy. The projected system would proceed from the idea of the ego or self as an absolutely free being by way of the positing of the non-ego to the sphere of speculative physics. It would then proceed to the sphere of the human spirit. The principles of historical development would have to be laid down, and the ideas of a moral world, of God and of the freedom of all spiritual beings would have to be developed. Further, the central importance of the idea of beauty would have to be shown, and the aesthetic character of the highest act of reason. Finally, there would have to be a new mythology, uniting philosophy and religion.

This programme is illuminating. On the one hand it illustrates the element of discontinuity in Schelling's thought. For the fact that he proposes to start from the ego reveals the influence of Fichte, an influence which grew progressively less as time went on. On the other hand the programme illustrates the element of continuity in Schelling's philosophizing. For it envisages the development of a philosophy of Nature, a philosophy of history, a philosophy of art, a philosophy of freedom and a philosophy of religion and mythology, themes which were to occupy his attention in turn. In other words, though Schelling at first gave the impression of being a disciple of Fichte, his interests and bent of mind were already apparent at the beginning of his career.

The upshot of all this is that time spent on discussing exactly how many phases or 'systems' there are in Schelling's philosophizing is time wasted. There certainly are distinct phases, but a genetic account of his thought can do justice to these distinctions without its being implied that Schelling jumped from one self-enclosed system to another. In fine, the philosophy of Schelling is a philosophizing rather than a finished system or succession of finished systems. In a sense the beginning and the end of his pilgrimage coincide. We have seen that in 1793 he published an essay *On Myths*. In his old age he returned to this subject and lectured on it at length. But in between we find a restless process of reflection moving from the ego-philosophy of Fichte through the philosophy of Nature and of art to the philosophy of the religious consciousness and a form of speculative theism, the whole being linked together by the theme of the relation between the finite and the infinite.

3. In his essay *On the Possibility of a Form of Philosophy in General* (1794) Schelling follows Fichte in asserting that philosophy, being a science, must be a logically unified system of propositions, developed from one fundamental proposition which gives expression to the unconditioned. This unconditioned is the self-positing ego. Hence 'the fundamental proposition can only be this: I is I'.[1] In the work *On the Ego as Principle of Philosophy* (1795) this proposition is formulated in the less peculiar form, '*I am I* or *I am*'.[2] And from this proposition Schelling proceeds to the positing of the non-ego and argues that ego and non-ego mutually condition one another. There is no subject without an object and no object without a subject. Hence there must be a mediating factor, a common product which links them together; and this is representation (*Vorstellung*). We thus have the form of the fundamental triad of all science or knowledge, namely subject, object and representation.

The influence of Fichte is obvious enough. But it is worth noting that from the very start Schelling emphasizes the difference between the absolute and the empirical ego. 'The completed system of science starts with the absolute ego.'[3] This is not a thing but infinite freedom. It is indeed one, but the unity which is predicated of it transcends the unity which is predicated of the individual member of a class. The absolute ego is not and cannot be a member of any class: it transcends the concept of class. Further, it transcends the grasp of conceptual thought and can be apprehended only in intellectual intuition.

[1] *W*, 1, p. 57. References to Schelling's writings are given according to volume and page of the edition of his *Works* by Manfred Schröter (Munich, 1927–8).

Schelling prefers '*I is I*' (*Ich ist Ich*) to 'the ego is the ego' (*das Ich ist das Ich*) on the ground that the ego is given only as *I*.

[2] *W*, 1, p. 103.   [3] *W*, 1, p. 100.

None of this contradicts Fichte; but the point is that Schelling's metaphysical interests are revealed from the beginning of his career. Whereas Fichte, starting from the philosophy of Kant, gave so little prominence at first to the metaphysical implications of his idealism that he was widely thought to be taking the individual ego as his point of departure, Schelling emphasizes at once the idea of the Absolute, even if, under Fichte's influence, he describes it as the absolute ego.

It will be noted that in the essay *On the Possibility of a Form of Philosophy in General* Schelling follows Fichte in deducing the presentation or representation. But his real interest is ontological. In the early *Wissenschaftslehre* Fichte declared that the task of philosophy is to explain experience in the sense of the system of presentations which are accompanied by a feeling of necessity. And he did so by showing how the ego gives rise to these presentations through the activity of the productive imagination which works unconsciously, so that for empirical consciousness the world inevitably possesses an appearance of independence. But in his *Philosophical Letters on Dogmatism and Criticism* (1795) Schelling roundly declares that the 'chief business of all philosophy consists in solving the problem of the existence of the world'.[1] In one sense, of course, the two statements come to the same thing. But there is a considerable difference in emphasis between saying that the business of philosophy is to explain the system of presentations which are accompanied by a feeling of necessity and saying that the business of philosophy is to explain the existence of the world. And with the help of a little hindsight at any rate we can discern beneath all the Fichtean trappings of Schelling's early thought the same metaphysical bent of mind which led him to say at a later stage that the task of philosophy is to answer the question, why there is something rather than nothing. True, Fichte himself came to develop the metaphysical implications of his philosophy. But when he did so, Schelling accused him of plagiarism.

Schelling's *Philosophical Letters* is an illuminating work. It is in a sense a defence of Fichte. For Schelling contrasts criticism, represented by Fichte, with dogmatism, represented chiefly by Spinoza. And he comes down on the side of Fichte. At the same time the work reveals the author's profound sympathy with Spinoza and an at any rate latent dissatisfaction with Fichte.

---

[1] *W*, I, p. 237. This work will be referred to in future simply as *Philosophical Letters*.

Dogmatism, says Schelling, involves in the long run the absolutization of the non-ego. Man is reduced to a mere modification of the infinite Object, Spinoza's substance, and freedom is excluded. It is true that Spinozism, which aims at the attainment of peace and tranquillity of soul through 'quiet self-surrender to the absolute Object',[1] possesses an aesthetic appeal and can exercise a powerful attraction on some minds. But ultimately it means the annihilation of the human being as a free moral agent. Dogmatism has no room for freedom.

But it does not follow that dogmatism can be theoretically refuted. The philosophy of Kant 'has only weak weapons against dogmatism',[2] and can achieve nothing more than a negative refutation. For example, Kant shows that it is impossible to disprove freedom in the noumenal sphere, but he admits himself that he can give no positive theoretical proof of freedom. Yet 'even the completed system of criticism cannot refute dogmatism *theoretically*',[3] even if it can deliver some shrewd blows. And this is not at all surprising. For as long as we remain on the theoretical plane dogmatism and criticism lead, Schelling maintains, to much the same conclusion.

In the first place both systems try to make the transition from the infinite to the finite. But 'philosophy cannot proceed from the infinite to the finite'.[4] We can, of course, invent reasons why the infinite must manifest itself in the finite, but they are simply ways of covering up an inability to bridge the gulf. It appears, therefore, that we must proceed the other way round. But how is this to be done when the traditional *a posteriori* demonstrations have been discredited? Obviously what is required is the suppression of the problem. That is to say, if the finite can be seen in the infinite and the infinite in the finite, the problem of bridging the gulf between them by means of a theoretical argument or demonstration no longer arises.

This need is fulfilled by intellectual intuition, which is an intuition of the identity of the intuiting with the intuited self. But it is interpreted in different ways by dogmatism and criticism. Dogmatism interprets it as an intuition of the self as identical with the Absolute conceived as absolute Object. Criticism interprets it as revealing the identity of the self with the Absolute as absolute Subject, conceived as pure free activity.

[1] *W*, I, p. 208.   [2] *W*, I, p. 214.
[3] *W*, I, p. 220. The reference is, of course, to Fichte's idealism.
[4] *W*, I, p. 238.

Though, however, dogmatism and criticism interpret intellectual intuition in different ways, the two interpretations lead to much the same theoretical conclusion. In dogmatism the subject is ultimately reduced to the object, and with this reduction one of the necessary conditions of consciousness is cancelled out. In criticism the object is ultimately reduced to the subject, and with this reduction the other necessary condition of consciousness is cancelled out. In other words, both dogmatism and criticism point to the theoretical annihilation of the finite self or subject. Spinoza reduces the finite self to the absolute Object: Fichte reduces it to the absolute Subject or, more precisely (since the absolute ego is not properly a subject), to infinite activity or striving. In both cases the self is swamped, so to speak, in the Absolute.

But though from the purely theoretical point of view the two systems lead by different routes to much the same conclusion, their practical or moral demands are different. They express different ideas of man's moral vocation. Dogmatism demands of the finite self that it should surrender itself to the absolute causality of the divine substance and renounce its own freedom that the divine may be all in all. Thus in the philosophy of Spinoza the self is called on to recognize an already existing ontological situation, namely its position as a modification of infinite substance, and to surrender itself. Criticism, however, demands that man shall realize the Absolute in himself through constant free activity. For Fichte, that is to say, the identity of the finite self with the Absolute is not simply an existing ontological situation which has only to be recognized. It is a goal to be achieved through moral effort. Moreover, it is an always receding goal. Hence even if the philosophy of Fichte points to the identification of the self with the Absolute as a theoretical ideal, on the practical plane it demands unceasing free moral activity, unceasing fidelity to one's personal moral vocation.

In a sense, therefore, the choice between dogmatism and criticism is for the finite self a choice between non-being and being. That is to say, it is a choice between the ideal of self-surrender, of absorption in the impersonal Absolute, of renunciation of personal freedom as illusion, and the ideal of constant free activity in accordance with one's vocation, of becoming more and more the moral agent who rises free and triumphant over the mere object. 'Be! is the highest demand of criticism.'[1] With Spinoza the

1 *W*, I, p. 259.

absolute Object carries all before it: with Fichte Nature is reduced to a mere instrument for the free moral agent.

Obviously, if a man accepts the demand of criticism, he is thereby committed to rejecting dogmatism. But it is also true that dogmatism cannot be refuted, even on the moral or practical plane, in the eyes of the man 'who can tolerate the idea of working at his own annihilation, of annulling in himself all free causality, and of being the modification of an object in the infinity of which he sooner of later finds his moral destruction'.[1]

This account of the issue between dogmatism and criticism obviously echoes Fichte's view that the sort of philosophy which a man chooses depends on the sort of man that one is. Further, we can, if we wish, link up Schelling's contention that neither dogmatism nor criticism is theoretically refutable and that the choice between them must be made on the practical plane with the view which has sometimes been advanced in much more recent times that we cannot decide between metaphysical systems on the purely theoretical plane but that moral criteria can be used to judge between them when they serve as backgrounds for and tend to promote different patterns of conduct. But for our present purpose it is more relevant to note that though the *Philosophical Letters* was written in support of Fichte and though Schelling comes down ostensibly on his side, the work implies the unspoken, but none the less clear, criticism that both the philosophy of Spinoza and the transcendental idealism of Fichte are one-sided exaggerations. For Spinoza is depicted as absolutizing the object and Fichte as absolutizing the subject. And the implication is that the Absolute must transcend the distinction between subjectivity and objectivity and be subject and object in identity.[2]

In other words, the implication is that some sort of synthesis must be effected which will reconcile the conflicting attitudes of Spinoza and Fichte. Indeed, we can see in the *Philosophical Letters* evidence of a degree of sympathy with Spinoza which was alien to Fichte's mind. And it is in no way surprising if we find Schelling very soon devoting himself to the publication of works on the philosophy of Nature. For the Spinozistic element in the fore-shadowed synthesis will be the attribution to Nature as an organic

---

[1] *W*, 1, p. 263.
[2] Fichte himself came to assert that the absolute ego is the identity of subject and object. But he did so partly under the influence of Schelling's criticism. And in any case Fichte's idealism was always characterized, in Schelling's opinion, by an over-emphasis on the subject and on subjectivity.

totality of an ontological status which was denied it by Fichte. Nature will be shown as the immediate objective manifestation of the Absolute. At the same time the synthesis, if it is to be a synthesis at all, must depict Nature as the expression and manifestation of Spirit. A synthesis must be idealism, if it is not to represent a return to pre-Kantian thought. But it must not be a subjective idealism in which Nature is depicted as no more than an obstacle posited by the ego in order that it may have something to overcome.

These remarks may perhaps seem to go beyond what the early writings of Schelling entitle one to say. But we have already seen that in the programme which Schelling drew up for himself in 1796, very shortly after the writing of *Philosophical Letters*, he explicitly envisaged the development of a speculative physics or philosophy of Nature. And it is quite evident that dissatisfaction with Fichte's one-sided attitude to Nature was already felt by Schelling within the period of his so-called Fichtean phase.

CHAPTER VI

SCHELLING (2)

The possibility and metaphysical grounds of a philosophy of Nature—The general outlines of Schelling's philosophy of Nature—The system of transcendental idealism—The philosophy of art—The Absolute as identity.

1. IT is the growth of reflection, Schelling maintains, that has introduced a rift between the subjective and the objective, the ideal and the real. If we think away the work of reflection, we must conceive man as one with Nature. That is to say, we must conceive him as experiencing this unity with Nature on the level of the immediacy of feeling. But through reflection he has distinguished between the external object and its subjective representation, and he has become an object for himself. In general, reflection has grounded and perpetuated the distinction between the objective external world of Nature and the subjective inner life of representation and self-consciousness, the distinction between Nature and Spirit. Nature thus becomes externality, the opposite of Spirit, and man, as a self-conscious reflective being, is alienated from Nature.

If reflection is made an end in itself, it becomes 'a spiritual malady'.[1] For man is born for action, and the more he is turned in on himself in self-reflection, the less active he is. At the same time it is the capacity for reflection which distinguishes man from the animal. And the rift which has been introduced between the objective and the subjective, the real and the ideal, Nature and Spirit, cannot be overcome by a return to the immediacy of feeling, to the childhood, as it were, of the human race. If the divided factors are to be reunited and the original unity restored, this must be achieved on a higher plane than feeling. That is to say, it must be achieved by reflection itself in the form of philosophy. After all, it is reflection which raises the problem. At the level of ordinary commonsense there is no problem of the relation between the real and the ideal order, between the thing and its mental representation. It is reflection which raises the problem, and it is reflection which must solve it.

[1] *W*, I, p. 663.

One's first impulse is to solve the problem in terms of causal activity. Things exist independently of the mind and cause representations of themselves: the subjective is causally dependent on the objective. But by saying this one simply gives rise to a further problem. For if I assert that external things exist independently and cause representations of themselves in me, I necessarily set myself above thing and representation. And I thus implicitly affirm myself as spirit. And the question at once arises, how can external things exercise a determining causal activity on spirit?

We can indeed attempt to tackle the problem from the other side. Instead of saying that things cause representations of themselves we can say with Kant that the subject imposes its cognitive forms on some given matter of experience and so creates phenomenal reality. But we are then left with the thing-in-itself. And this is inconceivable. For what can a thing possibly be apart from the forms which the subject is said to impose?

There have been, however, two notable attempts to solve the problem of the correspondence between the subjective and the objective, the ideal and the real, without having recourse to the idea of causal activity. Spinoza explained the correspondence by means of the theory of parallel modifications of different attributes of one infinite substance, while Leibniz had recourse to the theory of a pre-established harmony. But neither theory was a genuine explanation. For Spinoza left the modifications of Substance unexplained, while Leibniz, in Schelling's opinion, simply postulated a pre-established harmony.

At the same time both Spinoza and Leibniz had an inkling of the truth that the ideal and the real are ultimately one. And it is this truth which the philosopher is called upon to exhibit. He must show that Nature is 'visible Spirit' and Spirit 'invisible Nature'.[1] That is to say, the philosopher must show how objective Nature is ideal through and through in the sense that it is a unified dynamic and teleological system which develops upwards, so to speak, to the point at which it returns upon itself in and through the human spirit. For, given this picture of Nature, we can see that the life of representation is not something which is simply set over against and alien to the objective world, so that there arises the problem of correspondence between the subjective and the objective, the ideal and the real. The life of representation is Nature's knowledge of

[1] *W*, 1, p. 706.

itself; it is the actualization of Nature's potentiality, whereby
slumbering Spirit awakens to consciousness.

But can we show that Nature is in fact a teleological system,
exhibiting finality? We cannot indeed accept as adequate the
purely mechanistic interpretation of the world. For when we
consider the organism, we are driven to introduce the idea of
finality. Nor can the mind remain content with a dichotomy
between two sharply divided spheres, namely those of mechanism
and teleology. It is driven on to regard Nature as a self-organizing
totality in which we can distinguish various levels. But the
question arises whether we are not then simply reading teleology
into Nature, first into the organism and then into Nature as a
whole. After all, Kant admitted that we cannot help thinking of
Nature as if it were a teleological system. For we have a regulative
Idea of purpose in Nature, an Idea which gives rise to certain
heuristic maxims of judgment. But Kant would not allow that this
subjective Idea proves anything about Nature in itself.

Schelling is convinced that all scientific inquiry presupposes the
intelligibility of Nature. Every experiment, he insists, involves
putting a question to Nature which Nature is forced to answer.
And this procedure presupposes the belief that Nature conforms to
the demands of reason, that it is intelligible and in this sense ideal.
This belief is justified if we once assume the general view of the
world which has been outlined above. For the idea of Nature as
an intelligible teleological system then appears as Nature's self-
reflection, as Nature knowing itself in and through man.

But we can obviously ask for a justification of this general view
of Nature. And the ultimate justification is for Schelling a metaphysical theory about the Absolute. 'The first step towards
philosophy and the indispensable condition for even arriving at it
is to understand that the Absolute in the ideal order is also the
Absolute in the real order.'[1] The Absolute is the 'pure identity'[2] of
subjectivity and objectivity. And this identity is reflected in the
mutual interpenetration of Nature and Nature's knowledge of
itself in and through man.

In itself the Absolute is one eternal act of knowledge in which
there is no temporal succession. At the same time we can distinguish three moments or phases in this one act, provided that we do
not look on them as succeeding one another temporally. In the
first moment the Absolute objectifies itself in ideal Nature, in the

[1] *W*, I, p. 708.   [2] *W*, I, p. 712.

universal pattern, as it were, of Nature, for which Schelling uses Spinoza's term *Natura naturans*. In the second moment the Absolute as objectivity is transformed into the Absolute as subjectivity. And the third moment is the synthesis 'in which these two absolutenesses (absolute objectivity and absolute subjectivity) are again one absoluteness'.[1] The Absolute is thus an eternal act of self-knowledge.

The first moment in the inner life of the Absolute is expressed or manifested in *Natura naturata*, Nature as a system of particular things. This is the symbol or appearance of *Natura naturans*, and as such it is said to be 'outside the Absolute'.[2] The second moment in the inner life of the Absolute, the transformation of objectivity into subjectivity, is expressed externally in the world of representation, the ideal world of human knowledge whereby *Natura naturata* is represented in and through the human mind and the particular is taken up, as it were, into the universal, that is, on the conceptual level. We have, therefore, two unities, as Schelling calls them, objective Nature and the ideal world of representation. The third unity, correlated with the third moment in the inner life of the Absolute, is the apprehended interpenetration of the real and the ideal.

It can hardly be claimed, I think, that Schelling makes the relation between the infinite and the finite, between the Absolute in itself and its self-manifestation, crystal clear. We have seen indeed that *Natura naturata*, considered as the symbol or appearance of *Natura naturans*, is said to be outside the Absolute. But Schelling also speaks of the Absolute as expanding itself into the particular. Clearly, Schelling wishes to make a distinction between the unchanging Absolute in itself and the world of finite particular things. But at the same time he wishes to maintain that the Absolute is the all-comprehensive reality. But we shall have to return later to this topic. For the moment we can content ourselves with the general picture of the Absolute as eternal essence or Idea objectifying itself in Nature, returning to itself as subjectivity in the world of representation and then knowing itself, in and through philosophical reflection, as the identity of the real and the ideal, of Nature and Spirit.[3]

[1] *W*, I, p. 714. I have used 'absoluteness' to render *Absoluthheit*.

[2] *W*, I, p. 717.

[3] Schelling's picture of the metaphysical basis of a philosophy of Nature exercised a powerful influence on the thought of Hegel. But it would be inappropriate to discuss this matter here.

Schelling's justification of the possibility of a philosophy of Nature or of the so-called higher physics is thus admittedly metaphysical in character. Nature (that is, *Natura naturata*) must be ideal through and through. For it is the symbol or appearance of *Natura naturans*, ideal Nature: it is the 'external' objectification of the Absolute. And as the Absolute is always one, the identity of objectivity and subjectivity, *Natura naturata*, must also be subjectivity. This truth is manifested in the process by which Nature passes, as it were, into the world of representation. And the culmination of this process is the insight by which it is seen that human knowledge of Nature is Nature's knowledge of itself. There is really no rift between the objective and the subjective. From the transcendental point of view they are one. Slumbering Spirit becomes awakened Spirit. The distinguishable moments in the supra-temporal life of the Absolute as pure essence are manifested in the temporal order, which stands to the Absolute in itself as consequent to antecedent.

2. To develop a philosophy of Nature is to develop a systematic ideal construction of Nature. In the *Timaeus* Plato sketched a theoretical construction of bodies out of fundamental qualities. And Schelling is concerned with the same sort of thing. A purely experimental physics would not deserve the name of science. It would be 'nothing but a collection of facts, of reports on what has been observed, of what has happened either under natural or under artificially-produced conditions'.[1] Schelling admits indeed that physics as we know it is not purely experimental or empirical in this sense. 'In what is now called physics empiricism [*Empirie*] and science are mixed up.'[2] But there is room, in Schelling's opinion, for a purely theoretical construction or deduction of matter and of the fundamental types of bodies, the inorganic and the organic. Moreover, this speculative physics will not simply assume natural forces, such as gravitation, as something given. It will construct them from first principles.

According to Schelling's intentions at least this construction does not involve producing a fanciful and arbitrary deduction of the fundamental levels of Nature. Rather does it mean letting Nature construct itself before the watchful attention of the mind. Speculative or higher physics cannot indeed explain the basic productive activity which gives rise to Nature. This is a matter for metaphysics rather than for the philosophy of Nature proper. But

[1] *W*, ii, p. 283.   [2] *Ibid.*

if the development of the natural system is the necessary progressive self-expression of ideal Nature, *Natura naturans*, it must
be possible to retrace systematically the stages of the process by
which ideal Nature expresses itself in *Natura naturata*. And to do
this is the task of speculative physics. Schelling is obviously well
aware that it is through experience that we become acquainted
with the existence of natural forces and of inorganic and organic
things. And it is not the philosopher's task to tell us the empirical
facts for the first time, so to speak, or to work out *a priori* a natural
history which can be developed only on the basis of empirical
investigation. He is concerned with exhibiting the fundamental
and necessary teleological pattern in Nature, in Nature, that is to
say, as known in the first instance by experience and empirical
inquiry. One might say that he is concerned with explaining to us
the why and wherefore of the facts.

To exhibit Nature as a teleological system, as the necessary
self-unfolding of the eternal Idea, involves showing that the
explanation of the lower is always to be found in the higher. For
instance, even if from the temporal point of view the inorganic is
prior to the organic, from the philosophical point of view the latter
is logically prior to the former. That is to say, the lower level exists
as a foundation for the higher level. And this is true throughout
Nature. The materialist tends to reduce the higher to the lower.
For example, he tries to explain organic life in terms of mechanical
causality, without introducing the concept of finality. But he has
the wrong point of view. It is not, as he is inclined to imagine, a
question of denying the laws of mechanics or of regarding them as
suspended in the organic sphere, if one introduces the concept of
finality. Rather is it a question of seeing the sphere of mechanics
as the necessary setting for the realization of the ends of Nature in
the production of the organism. There is continuity. For the lower
is the necessary foundation for the higher, and the latter subsumes
the former in itself. But there is also the emergence of something
new, and this new level explains the level which it presupposes.

When we understand this, we see that 'the opposition between
mechanism and the organic sphere disappears'.[1] For we see the
production of the organism as that at which Nature unconsciously
aims through the development of the inorganic sphere, with the
laws of mechanics. And it is thus truer to say that the inorganic is
the organic *minus* than that the organic is the inorganic *plus*. Yet

[1] *W*, I, p. 416.

even this way of speaking can be misleading. For the opposition between mechanism and the organic sphere is overcome not so much by the theory that the former exists for the latter as by the theory that Nature as a whole is an organic unity.

Now, the activity which lies at the basis of Nature and which 'expands' itself in the phenomenal world is infinite or unlimited. For Nature is, as we have seen, the self-objectification of the infinite Absolute which, as an eternal *act*, is activity or willing. But if there is to be any objective system of Nature at all, this unlimited activity must be checked. That is to say, there must be a checking or limiting force. And it is the interaction between the unlimited activity and the checking force which gives rise to the lowest level of Nature, the general structure of the world and the series of bodies,[1] which Schelling calls the first potency (*Potenz*) of Nature. Thus if we think of the force of attraction as corresponding to the checking force and the force of repulsion as corresponding to the unlimited activity, the synthesis of the two is matter in so far as this is simply mass.

But the drive of the unlimited activity reasserts itself, only to be checked at another point. And the second unity or potency in the construction of Nature is universal mechanism, under which heading Schelling deduces light and the dynamic process or the dynamic laws of bodies. 'The dynamic process is nothing else but the second construction of matter.'[2] That is to say, the original construction of matter is repeated, as it were, at a higher level. On the lower level we have the elementary operation of the forces of attraction and repulsion and their synthesis in matter as mass. At the higher level we find the same forces showing themselves in the phenomena of magnetism, electricity and chemical process or the chemical properties of bodies.

The third unity or potency of Nature is the organism. And on this level we find the same forces further actualizing their potentialities in the phenomena of sensibility, irritability and reproduction. This unity or level of Nature is represented as the synthesis of the two others. Hence it cannot be said that at any level Nature is simply lifeless. It is a living organic unity which actualizes its potentialities at ascending levels until it expresses itself in the organism. We must add, however, that there are obviously distinguishable levels within the organic sphere itself. On the lower levels

[1] *Der allgemeine Weltbau und die Körperreihe; W*, I, p. 718.
[2] *W*, II, p. 320.

reproductivity is particularly conspicuous whereas sensibility is comparatively undeveloped. The individual organisms are lost, as it were, in the species. On the higher levels the life of the senses is more developed, and the individual organism is, so to speak, more of an individual and less a mere particular member of an indefinite class. The culminating point is reached in the human organism, which most clearly manifests the ideality of Nature and forms the point of transition to the world of representation or subjectivity, Nature's reflection on itself.

Throughout his construction of Nature Schelling employs the idea of the polarity of forces. But 'these two conflicting forces . . . lead to the idea of an *organizing principle* which makes the world a system'.[1] And to this principle we can conveniently give the time-hallowed name of world-soul. It cannot indeed be discovered by empirical investigation. Nor can it be described in terms of the qualities of phenomena. It is a postulate, 'an hypothesis of the higher physics for explaining the universal organism'.[2] This so-called world-soul is not in itself a conscious intelligence. It is the organizing principle which manifests itself in Nature and which attains consciousness in and through the human ego. And unless we postulated it, we could not look on Nature as a unified, self-developing super-organism.

It may have occurred to the reader to wonder how Schelling's theory of Nature stands to the theory of evolution in the sense of the transformation of forms or the emergence of higher from lower forms. And it is clearly arguable not only that a theory of emergent evolution would fit in very well with Schelling's interpretation but that it is demanded by his view of the world as a self-developing organic unity. Indeed, he explicitly refers to the possibility of evolution. He observes, for instance, that even if man's experience does not reveal any case of the transformation of one species into another, lack of empirical evidence does not prove that such a transformation is impossible. For it may well be that such changes can take place only in a much longer period of time than that covered by man's experience. At the same time Schelling goes on to remark, 'however, let us pass over these possibilities'.[3] In other words, while he allows for the possibility of emergent evolution, he is primarily concerned not with a genetic history of Nature but with an ideal or theoretical construction.

This construction is indeed rich in ideas. It echoes much past

[1] *W*, I, p. 449.   [2] *W*, I, p. 413.   [3] *W*, I, p. 417.

speculation about the world. For instance, the pervasive idea of the polarity of forces recalls Greek speculation about Nature, while the theory of Nature as slumbering Spirit recalls certain aspects of Leibniz's philosophy. Schelling's interpretation of Nature also looks forward to later speculation. For example, there is some family resemblance between Schelling's philosophy of Nature and Bergson's picture of inorganic things as representing, as it were, the extinguished sparks thrown off by the *élan vital* in its upward flight.

At the same time Schelling's construction of Nature inevitably appears so fanciful and arbitrary to the scientific mentality that there does not seem to be any justification for devoting space here to further detailed treatment of it.[1] It is not that the philosopher fails to incorporate into his philosophy of Nature theories and hypotheses taken from science as he knows it. On the contrary, he borrows and utilizes ideas taken from contemporary physics, electrodynamics, chemistry and biology. But these ideas are fitted into a dialectical scheme, and they are often held together by the application of analogies which, however ingenious and perhaps sometimes suggestive, tend to appear fanciful and far-fetched. Hence discussion of the details is more a matter for a specialized treatment of Schelling and of his relations to scientists such as Newton and to contemporary writers such as Goethe than for a general history of philosophy.

To say this is not, however, to deny the importance of Schelling's philosophy of Nature in its general outlines. For it shows clearly that German idealism does not involve subjectivism in the ordinary sense. Nature is the immediate and objective manifestation of the Absolute. It is indeed ideal through and through. But this does not mean that Nature is in any sense the creation of the human ego. It is ideal because it expresses the eternal Idea and because it is orientated towards self-reflection in and through the human mind. Schelling's view of the Absolute as the identity of objectivity and subjectivity demands, of course, that the Absolute's self-objectification, namely Nature, should reveal this identity. But the identity is revealed through the teleological pattern of Nature, not through its reduction to human ideas. Nature's representation in and through the human mind presupposes the objectivity of the world, though at the same time it presupposes the

---

[1] The details of Schelling's construction of Nature vary somewhat in his different writings on the subject.

intelligibility of the world and its intrinsic orientation to self-reflection.

Further, if we prescind from Schelling's rather fanciful speculations about magnetism, electricity and so on, that is, from the details of his theoretical construction of Nature, the general view of Nature as an objective manifestation of the Absolute and as a teleological system possesses an abiding value. It is obviously a metaphysical interpretation, and as such it can hardly commend itself to those who reject all metaphysics. But the general picture of Nature is not unreasonable. And if we once accept with Schelling, and afterwards with Hegel, the idea of a spiritual Absolute, we should expect to find in Nature a teleological pattern, though it does not necessarily follow that we can deduce the forces and phenomena of Nature in the way that Schelling thought that speculative physics is capable of doing.

3. In view of the fact that Schelling's philosophy of Nature represents his divergence from Fichte and his own original contribution to the development of German idealism it is at first sight surprising to find him publishing in 1800 a *System of Transcendental Idealism* in which he starts from the ego and proceeds to elaborate 'the continuous history of self-consciousness'.[1] For it looks as though he is adding to the philosophy of Nature an incompatible system inspired by the influence of Fichte. In Schelling's opinion, however, transcendental idealism forms a necessary complement to the philosophy of Nature. In knowledge itself subject and object are united: they are one. But if we wish to explain this identity, we have first to think it away. And then we are faced with two possibilities. Either we can start with the objective and proceed towards the subjective, asking how unconscious Nature comes to be represented. Or we can start with the subjective and proceed towards the objective, asking how an object comes to exist for the subject. In the first case we develop the philosophy of Nature, showing how Nature develops the conditions for its own self-reflection on the subjective level. In the second case we develop the system of transcendental idealism, showing how the ultimate immanent principle of consciousness produces the objective world as the condition of its attainment of self-consciousness. And the two lines of reflection are and must be complementary. For if the Absolute is the identity of subjectivity and objectivity, it must be possible to start from either pole and to develop a philosophy in

[1] *W*, II, p. 331.

harmony with the philosophy developed by starting from the other pole. In other words, it is Schelling's conviction that the mutually complementary characters of the philosophy of Nature and the system of transcendental idealism manifest the nature of the Absolute as identity of subject and object, of the ideal and the real.

As transcendental idealism is described as the science of knowledge, it prescinds from the question whether there is an ontological reality behind the whole sphere of knowledge. Hence its first principle must be immanent within this sphere. And if we are to proceed from the subjective to the objective by transcendental deduction, we must start with the original identity of subject and object. This identity within the sphere of knowledge is self-consciousness, wherein subject and object are the same. And self-consciousness is described by Schelling as the ego. But the term 'ego' does not signify the individual self. It signifies 'the act of *self-consciousness in general*'.[1] 'The self-consciousness which is our point of departure is *one absolute act*.'[2] And this absolute act is a production of itself as object. 'The ego is nothing else but a producing which becomes its own object.'[3] It is in fact 'an intellectual intuition'.[4] For the ego exists through knowing itself, and this self-knowledge is the act of intellectual intuition, which is 'the organ of all transcendental thought'[5] and freely produces as its object what is otherwise no object. Intellectual intuition and the production of the object of transcendental thought are one and the same. Hence a system of transcendental idealism must take the form of a production or construction of self-consciousness.

Schelling makes a wider use than Fichte had made of the idea of intellectual intuition. But the general pattern of his transcendental idealism is obviously based on Fichte's thought. The ego is in itself an unlimited act or activity. But to become its own object it must limit this activity by setting something over against itself, namely the non-ego. And it must do so unconsciously. For it is impossible to explain the givenness of the non-ego within the framework of idealism unless we assume that the production of the non-ego is an unconscious and necessary production. The non-ego is a necessary condition of self-consciousness. And in this sense the limitation of the infinite or unlimited activity which constitutes the ego must always remain. But in another sense the limitation must

---

[1] *W*, II, p. 374.   [2] *W*, II, p. 388.   [3] *W*, II, p. 370.
[4] *Ibid.*   [5] *W*, II, p. 369.

be transcended. That is to say, the ego must be able to abstract from the non-ego and recoil, as it were, on to itself. Self-consciousness, in other words, will take the form of human self-consciousness which presupposes Nature, the non-ego.

In the first part of the system of transcendental idealism, which corresponds to Fichte's theoretical deduction of consciousness in the *Wissenschaftslehre*, Schelling traces the history of consciousness in three main epochs or stages. Many of Fichte's themes reappear, but Schelling is naturally at pains to correlate his history of consciousness with the philosophy of Nature. The first epoch ranges from primitive sensation up to productive intuition. And it is correlated with the construction of matter in the philosophy of Nature. In other words, we see the production of the material world as the unconscious activity of Spirit. The second epoch ranges from productive intuition up to reflection. The ego is here conscious on the level of sense. That is to say, the sensible object appears as distinct from the act of productive intuition. And Schelling deduces the categories of space, time and causality. A universe begins to exist for the ego. Schelling also occupies himself with the deduction of the organism as a necessary condition for the ego's return on itself. This takes place in the third epoch which culminates in the act of absolute abstraction by which the ego reflectively differentiates itself from the object or non-ego as such and recognizes itself as intelligence. It has become object to itself.

The act of absolute abstraction is explicable only as an act of the self-determining will. And we thus pass to the idea of the ego or intelligence as an active and free power, and so to the second or practical part of the system of transcendental idealism. After treating of the part played by the consciousness of other selves, other free wills, in the development of self-consciousness Schelling goes on to discuss the distinction between natural impulse and the will considered as an idealizing activity (*eine idealisierende Tätigkeit*), that is, as seeking to modify or change the objective in accordance with an ideal. The ideal belongs to the side of the subjective: it is in fact the ego itself. Hence in seeking to actualize the ideal in the objective world the ego also realizes itself.

This idea sets the stage for a discussion of morality. How, asks Schelling, can the will, namely the ego as self-determining or self-realizing activity, become objectified for the ego as intelligence? That is to say, how can the ego become conscious of itself as will?

The answer is, through a demand, the demand that the ego should will nothing else but self-determination. 'This demand is nothing else but the categorical imperative or the moral law which Kant expresses in this way: you ought to will only that which other intelligences can will. But that which all intelligences can will is only pure self-determination, pure conformity to law. Through the law of morality, therefore, pure self-determination . . . becomes an object for the ego.'[1]

But self-determination or self-realization can be achieved only through concrete action in the world. And Schelling proceeds to deduce the system of rights and the State as conditions for moral action. The State is, of course, an edifice built by human hands, by the activity of the Spirit. But it is a necessary condition for the harmonious realization of freedom by a plurality of individuals. And though it is an edifice built by human hands, it should become a second Nature. In all our actions we count on the uniformity of Nature, on the reign of natural laws. And in our moral activity we ought to be able to count on the rule of rational law in society. That is to say, we ought to be able to count on the rational State, the characteristic of which is the rule of law.

Yet even the best-ordered State is exposed to the capricious and egoistic wills of other States. And the question arises, how can political society be rescued, as far as this is possible, from this condition of instability and insecurity? The answer can be found only in 'an organization which transcends the individual State, namely a federation of all States',[2] which will do away with conflicts between nations. Only in this way can political society become a second Nature, something on which we can count.

For this end to be attained, however, two conditions are required. First, the fundamental principles of a truly rational constitution must be generally acknowledged, so that all individual States will have a common interest in guaranteeing and protecting one another's law and rights. Secondly, individual States must submit themselves to a common fundamental law in the same way that individual citizens submit themselves to the law of their own State. And this means in effect that the federation will have to be a 'State of States',[3] in ideal at least a world-organization with sovereign power. If this ideal could be realized, political society would become a secure setting for the full actualization of a universal moral order.

[1] *W*, II, pp. 573-4.   [2] *W*, II, p. 586.   [3] *W*, II, p. 587.

Now, if this ideal is to be realized at all, it must obviously be realized within history. And the question arises whether we can discern in human history any necessary tendency towards the attainment of this goal. In Schelling's opinion 'there lies in the concept of history the concept of endless *progress*'.[1] Obviously, if this statement meant that the word 'history', as ordinarily used, necessarily includes as part of its meaning the concept of endless progress towards a predetermined goal, its truth would be open to question. But Schelling is looking on history in the light of his theory of the Absolute. 'History as a whole is a continual revelation of the Absolute, a revelation which gradually discloses itself.'[2] As the Absolute is the pure identity of the ideal and the real, history must be a movement towards the creation of a second Nature, a perfect moral world-order in the framework of a rationally-organized political society. And as the Absolute is infinite, this movement of progress must be endless. If the Absolute were perfectly revealed in its true nature, the point of view of human consciousness, which presupposes a distinction between subject and object, would no longer exist. Hence the revelation of the Absolute in human history must be in principle endless.

But are we not then faced with a dilemma? If on the one hand we assert that the human will is free, must we not admit that man can thwart the ends of history and that there is no necessary progress towards an ideal goal? If on the other hand we assert that history necessarily moves in a certain direction, must we not deny human freedom and explain away the psychological feeling of freedom?

In dealing with this problem Schelling has recourse to the idea of an absolute synthesis, as he puts it, of free actions. Individuals act freely. And any given individual may act for some purely private and selfish end. But there is at the same time a hidden necessity which achieves a synthesis of the apparently unconnected and often conflicting actions of human beings. Even if a man acts from purely selfish motives, he will none the less unconsciously contribute, even though against his will, to the fulfilment of the common end of human history.[3]

Up to this point we have been considering briefly the parts of

---

[1] *W*, II, p. 592.   [2] *W*, II, p. 603.
[3] We can call this a doctrine of divine providence if we like. But at this stage at any rate of Schelling's thought we should not think of the Absolute as a personal Deity. The working out of the absolute synthesis is the necessary expression of the Absolute's nature as pure identity of the ideal and the real.

the system of transcendental idealism which cover more or less the ground covered by Fichte in his theoretical and practical deductions of consciousness and in his works on the theory of rights and on ethics, though Schelling makes, of course, some changes and introduces and develops ideas of his own. But Schelling adds a third part which is his own peculiar contribution to transcendental idealism and which serves to underline the difference between his general outlook and that of Fichte. The philosophy of Nature deals with slumbering or unconscious Spirit. In the system of transcendental idealism as hitherto outlined we see conscious Spirit objectifying itself in moral action and in the creation of a moral world-order, a second Nature. But we have yet to find an intuition in which the identity of the unconscious and of the conscious, of the real and of the ideal, is presented in a concrete manner to the ego itself. And in the third part of the system of transcendental idealism Schelling locates what he is seeking in aesthetic intuition. Thus transcendental idealism culminates in a philosophy of art, to which Schelling attaches great importance. And provided that the statement is not taken as implying that the philosopher sets out to minimize the significance of moral activity, we can say that with Schelling, as contrasted with Fichte, the emphasis shifts from ethics to aesthetics, from the moral life to artistic creation, from action for the sake of action to aesthetic contemplation.

From one point of view it would be desirable to treat first of Schelling's philosophy of art as given in the third part of the *System of Transcendental Idealism* and later of his aesthetic ideas as expressed in his lectures on *The Philosophy of Art*. For in the meantime he had developed his theory of the Absolute, and this fact is reflected in the lectures. But it is more convenient to outline his ideas on art in one section, though I shall draw attention to their historical development.

4. In the *System of Transcendental Idealism* we read that 'the objective world is only the original, still unconscious poetry of the Spirit: the universal organon of philosophy—and the keystone of the whole arch—is *the philosophy of art*'.[1] But the view that the philosophy of art is 'the true organon of philosophy'[2] stands in need of some explanation.

In the first place art is grounded on the power of productive intuition which is the indispensable organ or instrument of transcendental idealism. As we have seen, transcendental idealism

[1] *W*, II, p. 349.   [2] *W*, II, p. 351.

comprises a history of consciousness. But the stages of this history are not present from the start to the ego's vision as so many already constituted objects at which it only needs to look. The ego or intelligence has to produce them, in the sense that it has to re-create or, to use a Platonic term, re-collect them in a systematic manner. And this task of re-creation or re-collection is performed by the power of productive intuition. Aesthetic intuition is an activity of the same power, though there it is directed outwards, as it were, rather than inwards.

In the second place aesthetic intuition manifests the basic truth of the unity of the unconscious and the conscious, of the real and the ideal. If we consider aesthetic intuition from the side of the creative artist, the genius, we can see that in a real sense he knows what he is doing: he acts consciously and deliberately. When Michelangelo made the statue of Moses, he knew what he was about. At the same time, however, we can equally well say that the genius acts unconsciously. Genius is not reducible to a technical proficiency which can be imparted by instruction: the creative artist is, as it were, the vehicle of a power which acts through him. And for Schelling this is the same power which operates in Nature. In other words, the same power which acts without consciousness in producing Nature, the unconscious poetry of the Spirit, acts with consciousness in producing the work of art. That is to say, it acts through the consciousness of the artist. And this illustrates the ultimate unity of the unconscious and the conscious, of the real and the ideal.

The matter can be considered from another point of view. We can ask why it is that contemplation of a work of art is accompanied by 'the feeling of infinite satisfaction',[1] why it is that 'every impulse to produce is stilled with the completion of the product, that all contradictions are reconciled and all riddles solved'.[2] In other words, why is it that in contemplating a work of art the mind, whether of the artist himself or of someone else, enjoys a feeling of finality, the feeling that nothing should be added or subtracted, the feeling that a problem is solved, even if the problem cannot be stated? In Schelling's opinion the answer is that the completed work of art is the intelligence's supreme objectification of itself to itself, that is, as the identity of the unconscious and the conscious, the real and the ideal, the objective and the subjective. But as the intelligence or ego does not know this reflectively, it

---

[1] *W*, II, p. 615.   [2] *Ibid.*

simply feels a boundless satisfaction, as though some unstated mystery had been revealed, and ascribes the production of the work of art to some power which acts through it.

The philosophy of art is thus the culmination of the *System of Transcendental Idealism*. It will be remembered that transcendental idealism starts with the idea of the so-called ego or intelligence considered as an absolute act of self-consciousness in which subject and object are one. But this absolute act is a producing: it has to produce its object. And the supreme objectification is the work of art. True, the organism, as considered in the philosophy of Nature, is a partial manifestation of the identity of the real and the ideal. But it is ascribed to an unconscious productive power which does not work with freedom, whereas the work of art is the expression of freedom: it is the free ego's manifestation of itself to itself.

Transcendental idealism, as was remarked in the last section, starts with the first immanent principle within the sphere of knowledge, namely with the absolute act which becomes an object for itself, and prescinds from the question whether there is a reality behind, as it were, this absolute act or ego.[1] But by the time (1802–3) that Schelling came to deliver the lectures which were eventually published as the *Philosophy of Art* he had developed his theory of the Absolute, and we find him emphasizing the metaphysical significance of the work of art as the finite manifestation of the infinite Absolute. The Absolute is the 'indifference' (that is to say, the ultimate identity) of the ideal and the real, and 'the indifference of the ideal and the real, as indifference, is expressed in the ideal world through art'.[2] Schelling is not contradicting what he has previously said about art. But in the lectures he transcends the self-imposed Fichtean limitations of the *System of Transcendental Idealism* and adopts the frankly metaphysical point of view which is really characteristic of his thought.

In *Bruno* (1802) Schelling introduced the notion of divine ideas and asserted that things are beautiful in virtue of their participation in these ideas. And this theory reappears in the lectures on art. Thus we are told that 'beauty exists where the particular (the real) is so in accord with its idea that this idea itself, as infinite, enters into the finite and is intuited *in concreto*'.[3] Aesthetic intuition is thus the intuition of the infinite in a finite product of

[1] Similarly, the philosophy of Nature starts with the postulated infinite activity which manifests itself in Nature.
[2] *W*, III, p. 400.   [3] *W*, III, p. 402.

intelligence. Further, the conformity of a thing with its eternal idea is its truth. Hence beauty and truth[1] are ultimately one.

Now, if the creative genius exhibits in the work of art an eternal idea, he must be akin to the philosopher. But it does not follow that he is a philosopher. For he does not apprehend the eternal ideas in an abstract form but only through a symbolic medium. Artistic creation requires the presence of a symbolic world, a world of 'poetic existence'[2] which mediates between the universal and the particular. The symbol represents neither the universal as such nor the particular as such, but both in unity. We must distinguish, therefore, between the symbol and the image. For the image is always concrete and particular.

This symbolic world of poetic existence is provided by mythology which is 'the necessary condition and primary matter [*Stoff*] of all art'.[3] Schelling dwells at length on Greek mythology, but he does not confine the symbolic world which in his view forms the material for artistic creation to the mythology of the Greeks. He includes, for instance, what he calls Jewish and Christian mythology. The Christian mind has constructed its own symbolic world which has proved a fruitful source of material for the artist.

This emphasis on mythology in Schelling's account of the symbolic world of poetic existence may well appear too narrow. But it illustrates Schelling's constant interest in myths as being at the same time imaginative constructions and intimations or expressions of the divine. In his later years he makes a distinction between myth and revelation. But his interest in the significance of mythology is a lasting element in his thought. And we shall have to return to the subject in connection with his later philosophy of religion.

In this outline of Schelling's aesthetic philosophy the terms 'art' and 'artist' have been used in a wider sense than is customary in ordinary English. But it would not, I think, be very profitable to devote space here to Schelling's discussion of the particular fine arts which he divides into those belonging to the real series, such as painting and sculpture, and those belonging to the ideal series, such as poetry.[4] For general purposes it is sufficient to understand how Schelling makes aesthetic theory an integral part of his

---

[1] The reference is obviously to what the Scholastics called ontological truth, as distinct from logical truth.
[2] *W*, III, p. 419.   [3] *W*, III, p. 425.
[4] The reader who is interested in this subject can consult the third part of Schelling's *Philosophy of Art* or, for example, Bernard Bosanquet's *History of Aesthetic*.

philosophy. In the third *Critique* Kant had indeed discussed the aesthetic judgment, and he can be said to have made aesthetics an integral part of the critical philosophy. But the nature of Kant's system made it impossible for him to develop a metaphysics of art in the way that Schelling does. Kant allowed, it is true, that from the subjective point of view we can see a hint of noumenal reality, of the so-called supersensible substrate. But with Schelling the product of artistic genius becomes a clear revelation of the nature of the Absolute. And in his exaltation of the genius, in his partial assimilation of the artistic genius to the philosopher and his insistence on the metaphysical significance of aesthetic intuition we can see clear evidence of his romantic affiliations.

5. In the foregoing sections reference has frequently been made to Schelling's theory of the Absolute as the pure identity of subjectivity and objectivity, of the ideal and the real. In a sense these references were premature. For in the preface to his *Exposition of My System of Philosophy* (1801) Schelling speaks of expounding 'the system of absolute identity'.[1] And this way of speaking shows that he does not regard himself as simply repeating what he has already said. At the same time the so-called system of identity can be looked on as an inquiry into and exposition of the metaphysical implications of the conviction that the philosophy of Nature and the system of transcendental idealism are mutually complementary.

'The standpoint of philosophy,' says Schelling, 'is the standpoint of Reason.'[2] That is to say, philosophical knowledge of things is knowledge of them as they are in Reason. 'I give the name of Reason [*Vernunft*] to the absolute Reason or to Reason in so far as it is conceived as the total indifference of the subjective and objective.'[3] In other words, philosophy is knowledge of the relation between things and the Absolute or, as the Absolute is infinite, between the finite and the infinite. And the Absolute is to be conceived as the pure identity or indifference (lack of all difference) of subjectivity and objectivity.

In attempting to describe the relation between the finite and the infinite Schelling is in a very difficult position. On the one hand there can be nothing outside the Absolute. For it is infinite reality and must contain all reality within itself. Hence it cannot be the external cause of the universe. 'The absolute identity is not the cause of the universe but the universe itself. For everything which exists is the absolute identity itself. And the universe is everything

---

[1] *W*, III, p. 9.   [2] *W*, III, p. 11.   [3] *W*, III, p. 10.

which is.'[1] On the other hand, if the Absolute is pure identity, all distinctions must be outside it. 'Quantitative difference is possible only outside the absolute totality.'[2] Hence finite things must be external to the Absolute.

Schelling cannot say that the Absolute somehow proceeds outside itself. For he maintains that 'the fundamental error of all philosophy is the proposition that the absolute identity has really gone out of itself. . . .'[3] Hence he is forced to say that it is only from the point of view of empirical consciousness that there is a distinction between subject and object and that there are subsistent finite things. But this really will not do. For the emergence of the point of view of empirical consciousness and its ontological status remain unexplained. It is all very well for Schelling to say that quantitative difference is posited 'only in appearance'[4] and that the Absolute is 'in no way affected by the opposition between subjectivity and objectivity'.[5] If appearance is anything at all, it must, on Schelling's premises, be within the Absolute. And if it is not within the Absolute, the Absolute must be transcendent and unidentifiable with the universe.

In *Bruno* (1802) Schelling makes play with the theory of divine Ideas, taken over from the Platonic and Neo-Platonic traditions. Considered from one point of view at least, the Absolute is the Idea of ideas, and finite things have eternal existence in the divine Ideas. But even if we are prepared to admit that this theory of divine Ideas is compatible with the view of the Absolute as pure identity, a view which is reaffirmed in *Bruno*, there is still the temporal status of finite things and their quantitative differentiation to be explained. In the dialogue Bruno tells Lucian that individual finite things are separate 'only for you'[6] and that for a stone nothing proceeds out of the darkness of absolute identity. But we can very well ask how empirical consciousness, with the distinctions which it involves, can arise either within the Absolute, if it is pure identity, or outside it, if it is the totality.

Schelling's general point of view is that absolute Reason, as the identity of subjectivity and objectivity, is self-consciousness, the absolute act in which subject and object are one. But Reason is not itself actually self-conscious: it is simply the 'indifference' or lack of difference between subject and object, the ideal and the real. It attains actual self-consciousness only in and through human

[1] *W*, III, p. 25.   [2] *W*, III, p. 21.   [3] *W*, III, p. 16.
[4] *W*, III, p. 23.   [5] *Ibid*.   [6] *W*, III, p. 155.

consciousness, the immediate object of which is the world. In other words, the Absolute manifests itself or appears in two series of 'potencies', the real series, which is considered in the philosophy of Nature, and the ideal series, which is considered in transcendental idealism. And from the standpoint of empirical consciousness the two series are distinct. We have subjectivity on the one hand and objectivity on the other. And the two together constitute 'the universe', which, as everything that is, is the Absolute. If, however, we try to transcend the standpoint of empirical consciousness, for which distinctions exist, and to grasp the Absolute as it is in itself rather than in its appearance, we can conceive it only as the indifference or vanishing-point of all difference and distinctions. True, the concept has then no positive content. But this simply shows that by conceptual thought we can apprehend only the appearance of the Absolute, the absolute identity as it appears in its 'external' being, and not as it is in itself.

In Schelling's opinion the theory of identity enables him to transcend all disputes between realism and idealism. For such controversy assumes that the distinction made by empirical consciousness between the real and the ideal can be overcome only by subordinating or even reducing the one to the other. But once we understand that the real and the ideal are one in the Absolute, the controversy loses its point. And the system of identity can thus be called real-idealism (*Realidealismus*).

But though Schelling himself was pleased with the system of identity, there were others who were not so appreciative. And the philosopher set himself to explain his position in such a way as to meet what he regarded as the misunderstandings of his critics. Further, his own reflections on his position drove him to develop fresh lines of thought. Maintaining, as he did, that the relation between the finite and the infinite or the problem of the existence of the world of things is the fundamental problem of metaphysics, he could hardly rest content with the system of identity. For it seemed to imply that the universe is the actualization of the Absolute, while it also asserted that the distinction between potentiality and act falls outside the Absolute in itself. Some more satisfactory account of the relation between the finite and the infinite was obviously required. But a sketch of Schelling's further philosophical journeying is best reserved for the next chapter.

CHAPTER VII

SCHELLING (3)

The idea of the cosmic Fall—Personality and freedom in man and God; good and evil—The distinction between negative and positive philosophy—Mythology and revelation—General remarks on Schelling—Notes on Schelling's influence and on some kindred thinkers.

1. IN his work on *Philosophy and Religion* (1804) Schelling explains that the description of the Absolute as pure identity does not mean either that it is a formless stuff, composed of all phenomena fused together, or that it is a vacuous nonentity. The Absolute is pure identity in the sense that it is an absolutely simple infinity. We can approach it in conceptual thought only by thinking away and denying of it the attributes of finite things; but it does not follow that it is in itself empty of all reality. What follows is that it can be apprehended only by intuition. 'The nature of the Absolute *itself*, which as ideal is also immediately real, cannot be known by explanations, but only through intuition. For it is only the composite which can be known by description. The simple must be intuited.'[1] This intuition cannot be imparted by instruction. But the negative approach to the Absolute facilitates the act of intuition of which the soul is capable through its fundamental unity with the divine reality.

The Absolute as ideal manifests or expresses itself immediately in the eternal ideas. Strictly speaking, indeed, there is only one Idea, the immediate eternal reflection of the Absolute which proceeds from it as the light flows from the sun. 'All ideas are one Idea.'[2] But we can speak of a plurality of ideas inasmuch as Nature with all its grades is eternally present in the one Idea. This eternal Idea can be described as the divine self-knowledge. 'But this self-knowledge must not be conceived as a mere accident or attribute of the Absolute-ideal but as itself a subsistent Absolute. For the Absolute cannot be the ideal ground of anything which is not like itself, absolute.'[3]

In developing this theory of the divine Idea, which, as we have

[1] *W*, IV, pp. 15–16.   [2] *W*, IV, pp. 23–4.   [3] *W*, IV, p. 21.

seen, was first expounded in *Bruno*, Schelling draws attention to its origins in Greek philosophy. No doubt he has also at the back of his mind the Christian doctrine of the divine Word; but the description of the eternal Idea as a second Absolute is more akin to the Plotinian theory of *Nous* than to the Christian doctrine of the second Person of the Trinity. Further, the ideas of the negative approach to the Absolute and of intuitive apprehension of the supreme Godhead also go back to Neo-Platonism, though the first idea at any rate reappears in Scholasticism, as well, of course, as the theory of divine ideas.

However, in spite of its venerable history Schelling's theory of the eternal Idea cannot by itself explain the existence of finite things. For Nature as present in the eternal Idea is *Natura naturans* rather than *Natura naturata*. And from ideas, Schelling sensibly maintains, we can derive by deduction only other ideas. He therefore has recourse to the speculations of Jakob Boehme and introduces the notion of a cosmic Fall. The origin of the world is to be found in a falling-away or breaking-away (*Abbrechen*) from God, which can also be described as a leap (*Sprung*). 'From the Absolute to the real there is no continuous transition; the origin of the sensible world is thinkable only as a complete breaking-away from Absoluteness by means of a leap.'[1]

Schelling does not mean that a part of the Absolute breaks away or splits off. The Fall consists in the emergence of a dim image of an image, resembling the shadow which accompanies the body. All things have their eternal ideal existence in the Idea or divine ideas. Hence the centre and true reality of any finite thing is in the divine Idea, and the essence of the finite thing may thus be said to be infinite rather than finite. Considered, however, precisely as a finite thing, it is the image of an image (that is, an image of the ideal essence which is itself a reflection of the Absolute). And its existence as a distinct finite thing is an alienation from its true centre, a negation of infinity. True, finite things are not simply nothing. They are, as Plato said, a mixture of being and not-being. But particularity and finitude represent the negative element. Hence the emergence of *Natura naturata*, the system of particular finite things, is a Fall from the Absolute.

It must not be thought, however, that the cosmic Fall, the emergence of an image of an image, is an event in time. It is 'as eternal (outside all time) as the Absolute itself and the world of

[1] *W*, IV, p. 28.

Ideas'.[1] The Idea is an eternal image of God. And the sensible
world is an indefinite succession of shadows, images of images,
without any assignable beginning. This means that no finite thing
can be referred to God as its immediate cause. The origin of any
given finite thing, a man for instance, is explicable in terms of
finite causes. The thing, in other words, is a member in the endless
chain of causes and effects which constitutes the sensible world.
And this is why it is psychologically possible for a human being to
look upon the world as the one reality. For it possesses a relative
independence and self-subsistence. But this point of view is
precisely the point of view of a fallen creature. From the metaphysical and religious standpoints we must see in the world's
relative independence a clear sign of its fallen nature, of its
alienation from the Absolute.

Now, if creation is not an event in time, the natural conclusion is
that it is a necessary external self-expression of the eternal Idea.
And in this case it should be in principle deducible, even if the
finite mind is unable actually to perform the deduction. But we
have seen that Schelling refuses to allow that the world is deducible
even in principle from the Absolute. 'The Fall cannot be, as they
say, explained.'[2] Hence the origin of the world must be ascribed to
freedom. 'The ground of the possibility of the Fall lies in freedom.'[3]
But in what sense? On the one hand this freedom cannot be
exercised by the world itself. Schelling may sometimes speak as
though the world broke away from the Absolute. But as it is the
very existence and origin of the world which are in question, we
can hardly conceive it as freely leaping away, as it were, from the
Absolute. For *ex hypothesi* it does not yet exist. On the other hand,
if we ascribe the timeless origination of the world to a free creative
act of God, in a theistic sense, there is no very obvious reason for
speaking about a cosmic Fall.

In treating of this problem Schelling appears to connect the
Fall with a kind of double-life led by the eternal Idea considered
as 'another Absolute'.[4] Regarded precisely as the eternal reflection
of the Absolute, as the eternal Idea, its true life is in the Absolute
itself. But regarded as 'real', as a second Absolute, as Soul, it
strives to produce, and it can produce only phenomena, images of
images, 'the nothingness of sensible things'.[5] It is, however, only
the *possibility* of finite things which can be 'explained', that is,

[1] *W*, IV, p. 31.　　　[2] *W*, IV, p. 32.　　　[3] *W*, IV, p. 30.
[4] *W*, IV, p. 31.　　　[5] *W*, IV, p. 30.

deduced from the second Absolute. Their actual existence is due to freedom, to a spontaneous movement which is at the same time a lapse.

Creation is thus a Fall in the sense that it is a centrifugal movement. The absolute identity becomes differentiated or splintered on the phenomenal level, though not in itself. But there is also a centripetal movement, the return to God. This does not mean that particular finite material things as such return to the divine Idea. We have seen that no particular sensible thing has God for its immediate cause. Similarly, no particular sensible thing, considered precisely as such, returns immediately to God. Its return is mediate, by means of the transformation of the real into the ideal, of objectivity into subjectivity, in and through the human ego or reason which is capable of seeing the infinite in the finite and referring all images to the divine exemplar. As for the finite ego itself, it represents from one point of view 'the point of furthest alienation from God'.[1] For the apparent independence of the phenomenal image of the Absolute reaches its culminating-point in the ego's conscious self-possession and self-assertion. At the same time the ego is one in essence with infinite Reason, and it can rise above its egoistic point of view, returning to its true centre from which it has been alienated.

This point of view determines Schelling's general conception of history, which is well illustrated by the following oft-quoted passage. 'History is an epic composed in the mind of God. Its two main parts are: first, that which depicts the departure of humanity from its centre up to its furthest point of alienation from this centre, and, secondly, that which depicts the return. The first part is the *Iliad*, the second the *Odyssey* of history. In the first the movement was centrifugal, in the second it is centripetal.'[2]

In grappling with the problem of the One and the Many or of the relation between the infinite and the finite Schelling is obviously concerned with allowing for the possibility of evil. The idea of the Fall and of alienation allows for this possibility. For the human self is a fallen self, entangled, as it were, in particularity; and this entanglement, this alienation from the self's true centre, renders possible selfishness, sensuality and so on. But how can man be really free if the Absolute is the totality? And if there is a real possibility of evil, must it not have a ground in the Absolute itself? If so, what conclusions must we draw about the nature of the

[1] *W*, iv, p. 32.   [2] *W*, iv, p. 47.

Absolute or God? In the next section we can consider Schelling's reflections on these problems.

2. In the Preface to his *Philosophical Inquiries into the Nature of Human Freedom* (1809) Schelling frankly admits that *Philosophy and Religion* was deficient in clarity. He intends, therefore, to give another exposition of his thought in the light of the idea of human freedom.[1] This is especially desirable, he says, in view of the accusation that his system is pantheistic and that there is accordingly no room in it for the concept of human freedom.

As for the charge of pantheism, this is, Schelling remarks, an ambiguous term. On the one hand it might be used to describe the theory that the visible world, *Natura naturata*, is identical with God. On the other hand it might be understood as referring to the theory that finite things do not exist at all but that there is only the simple indifferentiated unity of the Godhead. But in neither sense is Schelling's philosophy pantheistic. For he neither identifies the visible world with God nor teaches acosmism, the theory of the non-existence of the world. Nature is a consequence of the first principle, not the first principle itself. But it is a real consequence. God is the God of the living, not of the dead: the divine Being manifests itself and the manifestation is real. If, however, pantheism is interpreted as meaning that all things are immanent in God, Schelling is quite prepared to be called a pantheist. But he proceeds to point out that St. Paul himself declared that in God we live and move and have our being.

To clarify his position, Schelling reinterprets the principle of identity. 'The profound logic of the ancients distinguished subject and predicate as antecedent and consequent [*antecedens et consequens*] and thereby expressed the real meaning of the principle of identity.'[2] God and the world are identical; but to say this is to say that God is the ground or antecedent and the world the consequent. The unity which is asserted is a creative unity. God is self-revealing or self-manifesting life. And though the manifestation is immanent in God, it is yet distinguishable from him. The consequent is dependent on the antecedent, but it is not identical with it in the sense that there is no distinction between them.

This theory, Schelling insists, in no way involves the denial of human freedom. For by itself it says nothing about the nature of

---

[1] The revised system is also expounded in the Stuttgart lectures (1810), which are printed together with *Philosophical Inquiries* in the fourth volume of his *Works*.

[2] *W*, IV, p. 234.

the consequent. If God is free, the human spirit, which is his image, is free. If God is not free, the human spirit is not free.

Now, in Schelling's view the human spirit is certainly free. For 'the real and living concept [of freedom] is that it is a power of good and evil'.[1] And it is evident that man possesses this power. But if this power is present in man, the consequent, must it not also be present in God, the antecedent? And the question then arises, whether we are forced to draw the conclusion that God can do evil.

To answer this question, let us first look more closely at the human being. We talk about human beings as persons, but personality, Schelling maintains, is not something given from the start, it is something to be won. 'All birth is birth out of darkness into light',[2] and this general proposition is true of the birth of human personality. There is in man a dark foundation, as it were, the unconscious and the life or urge and natural impulse. And it is on this foundation that personality is built. Man is capable of following sensual desire and dark impulse rather than reason: he is able to affirm himself as a particular finite being to the exclusion of the moral law. But he also has the power of subordinating selfish desire and impulse to the rational will and of developing his true human personality. He can do this, however, only by strife, conflict and sublimation. For the dark foundation of personality always remains, though it can be progressively sublimated and integrated in the movement from darkness to light.

As far as man is concerned, what Schelling has to say on this subject obviously contains a great deal of truth. But stimulated by the writings of Boehme and impelled by the exigencies of his theory of the relation between the human spirit and God, he applies this notion of personality to God himself. There is in God a ground of his personal existence,[3] which is itself impersonal. It can be called will, but it is a 'will in which there is no understanding'.[4] It can be conceived as an unconscious desire or yearning for personal existence. And the personal divine existence must be conceived as rational will. The irrational or unconscious will can be called 'the egoism in God'.[5] And if there were only this will in God, there would be no creation. But the rational will is the will of love, and as such it is 'expansive',[6] self-communicating.

[1] *W*, IV, p. 244.   [2] *W*, IV, p. 252.
[3] It should be noted that the divine Being is now for Schelling a personal Deity and no longer an impersonal Absolute.
[4] *W*, IV, p. 251.   [5] *W*, IV, p. 330.   [6] *W*, IV, p. 331.

The inner life of God is thus conceived by Schelling as a dynamic process of self-creation. In the ultimate dark abyss of the divine Being, the primal ground or *Urgrund*, there is no differentiation but only pure identity. But this absolutely undifferentiated identity does not exist as such. 'A division, a difference must be posited, that is, if we wish to pass from essence to existence.'[1] God first posits himself as object, as the unconscious will. But he cannot do this without at the same time positing himself as subject, as the rational will of love.

There is, therefore, a likeness between the divine and the human conquest of personality. And we can even say that 'God makes himself.'[2] But there is also a great difference. And an understanding of this difference shows that the answer to the question whether God can do evil is that he cannot.

In God the conquest of personality is not a temporal process. We can distinguish different 'potencies' in God, different moments in the divine life, but there is no temporal succession. Thus if we say that God first posits himself as unconscious will and then as rational will, there is no question of temporally successive acts. 'Both acts are one act, and both are absolutely simultaneous.'[3] For Schelling the unconscious will in God is no more temporally prior to the rational will than the Father is temporally prior to the Son in the Christian theology of the Trinity. Hence, though we can distinguish different moments in the 'becoming' of the divine personality, one moment being logically prior to another, there is no becoming at all in the temporal sense. God is eternally love, and 'in love there can never be the will to evil'.[4] Hence it is metaphysically impossible for God to do evil.

But in God's external manifestation the two principles, the lower and the higher wills, are and must be separable. 'If the identity of the two principles were as indissoluble in the human spirit as in God, there would be no distinction (that is, between God and the human spirit); that is to say, God would not manifest himself. Therefore the unity which is indissoluble in God must be dissoluble in man. And this is the possibility of good and evil.'[5] This possibility has its ground in God, but as a realized possibility it is present only in man. Perhaps one can express the matter by saying that whereas God is necessarily an integrated personality, man need not be. For the basic elements are separable in man.

[1] *W*, IV, p. 316.   [2] *W*, IV, p. 324.   [3] *W*, IV, p. 326.
[4] *W*, IV, p. 267.   [5] *W*, IV, p. 256.

It would, however, be erroneous to conclude that Schelling attributes to man a complete liberty of indifference. He is too fond of the idea of antecedent and consequent to admit the concept of freedom as 'a completely indeterminate power of willing one or other of two contradictory things without determining grounds and simply because it is willed'.[1] Schelling rejects this concept and finds the determining ground of a man's successive choices in his intelligible essence or character which stands to his particular acts as antecedent to consequent. At the same time he does not wish to say that it is God who predetermines a man's acts by conceiving him in the eternal Idea. Hence he is forced to depict a man's intelligible character as due to an original self-positing of the ego, as the result of an original choice by the ego itself. He can thus say both that a man's actions are in principle predictable and that they are free. They are necessary; but this necessity is an inner necessity, imposed by the ego's original choice, not a necessity externally imposed by God. 'This inner necessity is itself freedom, the essence of man is essentially *his own act*; necessity and freedom are mutually immanent, as one reality which appears as one or the other only when looked at from different sides. . . .'[2] Thus Judas's betrayal of Christ was necessary and inevitable, given the historical circumstances; but at the same time he betrayed Christ 'willingly and with complete freedom'.[3] Similarly it was inevitable both that Peter would deny Christ and that he would repent of this denial; yet both the denial and the repentance, being Peter's own acts, were free.

If the theory of an intelligible character is given a purely psychological interpretation, it can be made at any rate very plausible. On the one hand we not infrequently say of a given man that he could not act in this or that manner, meaning that such a way of acting would be quite contrary to his character. And if after all he does act in this way, we are inclined to say that his character was not what we supposed. On the other hand we come to know not only other people's characters but also our own through their and our acts. And we might wish to draw the conclusion that in each man there is, as it were, a hidden character which manifests itself progressively in his acts, so that his acts stand to his character in a relation analogous to that between consequent and ground or antecedent. The objection can indeed be made that this presupposes that character is something fixed and settled from the start (by heredity, environment, very early experiences and so on), and that

[1] *W*, IV, p. 274.   [2] *W*, IV, p. 277.   [3] *W*, IV, p. 278.

this presupposition is false. But as long as the theory is presented as a psychological theory, it is a matter for empirical investigation. And it is clear that some empirical data count in its favour, even if others tell against it. It is a question of weighing, interpreting and co-ordinating the available evidence.

But Schelling does not present his theory simply as an empirical hypothesis. It is a metaphysical theory. At least it depends in part on metaphysical theories. For example, the theory of identity is influential. The Absolute is the identity of necessity and freedom, and this identity is reflected in man. His acts are both necessary and free. And Schelling draws the conclusion that a man's intelligible essence, which determines his particular acts, must itself have, as it were, an aspect of freedom, in that it is the result of the ego's self-positing. But this original choice of itself by the ego is neither a conscious act nor an act in time. According to Schelling, it is outside time and determines all consciousness, though a man's acts are free inasmuch as they issue from his own essence or self. But it is extremely difficult to see what this primeval act of will can possibly be. Schelling's theory bears some resemblance to M. Sartre's interpretation of freedom in his existentialist philosophy; but the setting is much more meta-physical. Schelling develops Kant's distinction between the intelligible and phenomenal spheres in the light of his theory of identity and of his preoccupation with the idea of ground and consequent, and the resulting theory is extremely obscure. It is indeed clear that Schelling wishes to avoid the Calvinist doctrine of divine predestination on the one hand and the theory of liberty of indifference on the other, while at the same time he wishes to allow for the truths which find expression in these positions. But it can hardly be claimed that the conclusion of his reflections is crystal clear. True, Schelling did not claim that everything in philosophy could be made crystal clear. But the trouble is that it is difficult to assess the truth of what is said unless one understands what is being said.

As for the nature of evil, Schelling experienced considerable difficulty in finding a satisfactory descriptive formula. As he did not look on himself as a pantheist in the sense of one who denies any distinction between the world and God, he felt that he could affirm the positive reality of evil without committing himself to the conclusion that there is evil in the divine Being itself. At the same time his account of the relation between the world and God as being that of consequent or ground to antecedent implies that if evil is a positive reality it must have its ground in God. And the conclusion might be thought to follow that 'in order that evil should not be, God would have not to be himself'.[1] In the Stuttgart lectures Schelling attempts to steer a middle course between asserting and denying the positive reality of evil by saying that it is 'from one point of view nothing, from another point of view an extremely real being'.[2] Perhaps we can say that he was feeling after the Scholastic formula which describes evil as a privation, though a real privation.

In any case evil is certainly present in the world, whatever its precise nature may be. Hence the return to God in human history must take the form of the progressive triumph of good over evil. 'The good must be brought out of darkness into actuality that it may live everlastingly with God; and evil must be separated from the good that it may be cast into not-being. For this is the final end of creation.'[3] In other words, the complete triumph of the rational will over the lower will or urge, which is eternally accomplished in God, is the ideal goal of human history In God the sublimation of the lower will is eternal and necessary. In man it is a temporal process.

3. We have already had occasion to note Schelling's insistence that from ideas we can deduce only ideas. It is not surprising, therefore, if in his later years we find him emphasizing the distinction, to which allusion was made in the section on his life and writings, between negative philosophy, which is confined to the world of concepts and essences, and positive philosophy, which stresses existence.

All philosophy worthy of the name, Schelling maintains, is concerned with the first or ultimate principle of reality. Negative philosophy, however, discovers this principle only as a supreme essence, as the absolute Idea. And from a supreme essence we can deduce only other essences, from the Idea only other ideas. From a *What* we cannot deduce a *That*. In other words, negative philosophy is quite incapable of explaining the existent world. Its deduction of the world is not a deduction of existents but only of what things must be if they exist. Of being outside God the negative philosopher can only say that '*if* it exists, it can exist only in this way and only as such and such'.[4] His thought moves

[1] *W*, IV, p. 295.   [2] *W*, IV, p. 296.
[3] *W*, IV, p. 296.   [4] *W*, V, p. 558.

within the realm of the hypothetical. And this is especially clear in the case of the Hegelian system which, according to Schelling, by-passes the existential order.

Positive philosophy, however, does not start simply with God as Idea, as a *What* or essence, but rather with God 'as a pure That',[1] as pure act or being in an existential sense. And from this supreme existential act it passes to the concept or nature of God, showing that he is not an impersonal Idea or essence but a creative personal Being, the existing 'Lord of being',[2] where 'being' means the world. Schelling thus connects positive philosophy with the concept of God as a personal Being.

Schelling does not mean to imply that he is the first to discover positive philosophy. On the contrary, the whole history of philosophy manifests the 'combat between negative and positive philosophy'.[3] But the use of the word 'combat' must not be misunderstood. It is a question of emphasis and priority rather than of a fight to the death between two completely irreconcilable lines of thought. For negative philosophy cannot be simply rejected. No system can be constructed without concepts. And even if the positive philosopher places the emphasis on existence, he obviously does not and cannot disdain all consideration of what exists. Hence we have 'to assert the connection, yes the unity, between the two',[4] that is, between positive and negative philosophy.[5]

But how, Schelling asks, are we to make the transition from negative to positive philosophy? It cannot be made merely by thinking. For conceptual thought is concerned with essences and logical deductions. Hence we must have recourse to the will, 'a will which demands with inner necessity that God should not be a mere idea'.[6] In other words, the initial affirmation of the divine existence is based on an act of faith demanded by the will. The ego is conscious of its fallen condition, of its state of alienation, and it is aware that this alienation can be overcome only by God's activity. It demands, therefore, that God should be not simply a transmundane ideal but an actually existing personal God through whom man can be redeemed. Fichte's ideal moral order will not satisfy man's religious needs. The faith which lies at the basis of

[1] *als reines Dass*; W, v, p. 746.   [2] *Ibid.*   [3] *Ibid.*   [4] W, v, p. 746.
[5] Schelling's distinction is similar in certain respects to the distinction made by some modern writers, notably Professor Gilson, between essentialist and existential philosophy, the latter term meaning, not 'existentialism', but philosophy which lays its fundamental emphasis on being in the sense of existence (*esse*) rather than on being in the sense of essence. But the extent of the similarity is limited.   [6] W, v, p. 746.

positive philosophy is faith in a personal creative and redeeming God, not in Fichte's ideal moral order, nor in Hegel's absolute Idea.

At first sight at least Schelling may appear to be repeating Kant's theory of practical or moral faith. But Schelling makes it clear that he regards the critical philosophy as an example of negative philosophizing. Kant does indeed affirm God on faith, but simply as a postulate, that is, as a possibility. Further, Kant affirms God as an instrument, as it were, for synthesizing virtue and happiness. In his religion within the limits of bare reason there is no room for genuine religion. The truly religious man is conscious of his profound need of God, and he is brought by this consciousness and by his longing for God to a personal Deity. 'For the person seeks a person.'[1] The truly religious man does not affirm God simply as an instrument for apportioning happiness to virtue: he seeks God for himself. The ego 'demands God himself. *Him, him*, will it have, the God who acts, who exercises providence, who, as being himself real, can meet the reality of the Fall. . . . In this God alone does the ego see the *real* supreme good.'[2]

The distinction between positive and negative philosophy thus turns out to be a distinction between philosophy which is truly religious and philosophy which cannot assimilate the religious consciousness and its demands. Schelling says this quite explicitly with an evident reference to Kant. 'The longing for the real God and for redemption through him is, as you see, nothing else but the expression of the need of *religion*. . . . Without an active God . . . there can be no religion, for religion presupposes an actual, real relationship of man to God. Nor can there be any history in which God is providence. . . . At the end of negative philosophy I have only possible and not actual religion, religion only "within the limits of bare reason". . . . It is with the transition to positive philosophy that we first enter the sphere of religion.'[3]

Now, if positive philosophy affirms the existence of God as a first principle, and if the transition to positive philosophy cannot be made by thinking but only by an act of the will issuing in faith, Schelling obviously cannot turn negative into positive philosophy by supplementing the former by a natural theology in the traditional sense. At the same time there can be what we may call an empirical proof of the rationality of the will's act. For the demand of the religious man is for a God who reveals himself and accomplishes man's redemption. And the proof, if one may so put

[1] *W*, v, p. 748.   [2] *Ibid.*   [3] *W*, v, p. 750.

it, of God's existence will take the form of showing the historical development of the religious consciousness, the history of man's demand for God and of God's answer to this demand. 'Positive philosophy is historical philosophy.'[1] And this is the reason why in his later writings Schelling devotes himself to the study of mythology and revelation. He is trying to exhibit God's progressive self-revelation to man and the progressive work of divine redemption.

This is not to say that Schelling abandons all his earlier speculations in favour of an empirical study of the history of mythology and revelation. As we have seen, his thesis is that negative and positive philosophy must be combined. And his earlier religious speculations are not jettisoned. For example, in the essay entitled *Another Deduction of the Principles of Positive Philosophy* (1841) he takes as his point of departure 'the unconditioned existent'[2] and proceeds to deduce the moments or phases of God's inner life. He does indeed lay emphasis on the primacy of being in the sense of existence, but the general scheme of his earlier philosophy of religion, with the ideas of the moments in the divine life, of the cosmic Fall and of the return to God, is retained. And though in his lectures on mythology and religion he concerns himself with the empirical confirmation, as it were, of his religious philosophy, he never really frees himself from the idealist tendency to interpret the relation between God and the world as a relation of ground or antecedent to consequent.

The reader may be inclined to share Kierkegaard's disappointment that after making his distinction between negative and positive philosophy Schelling proceeds to concentrate on the study of mythology and revelation instead of radically rethinking his philosophy in the light of this distinction. At the same time we can understand the philosopher's point of view. The philosophy of religion has come to occupy the central position in his thought. And the self-manifesting impersonal Absolute has become the self-revealing personal God. Schelling is anxious, therefore, to show that man's faith in God is historically justified and that the history of the religious consciousness is also the history of the divine self-revelation to man.

4. If, however, we speak of Schelling's philosophy of mythology and revelation as an empirical study, the word 'empirical' must be understood in a relative sense. Schelling has not abandoned deductive metaphysics for pure empiricism. Far from it. For

example, the deduction of three 'potencies' in the one God is pre-supposed. It is also presupposed that if there is a self-manifesting God, this necessary nature of an absolute Being will be progressively revealed. Hence when Schelling turns to the study of mythology and revelation, he already possesses the scheme, as it were, of what he will find. The study is empirical in the sense that its matter is provided by the actual history of religion as known through empirical investigation. But the framework of interpretation is provided by the supposedly necessary deductions of metaphysics. In other words, Schelling sets out to find in the history of religion the self-revelation of one personal God, whose unity does not exclude three distinguishable potencies or moments. And he has, of course, no difficulty in discovering expressions of this conception of the Deity in the development of religious beliefs from the ancient mythologies of East and West up to the Christian dogma of the Trinity. Similarly, he has no difficulty in finding expressions of the ideas of a Fall and of a return to God.

If Schelling's premises are once assumed, this procedure is, of course, justified. For, as we have seen, he never intended to jettison metaphysics, the abstract philosophy of reason, which, to use modern jargon, shows us what must be the case if anything is the case. Hence from Schelling's point of view metaphysical presuppositions are quite in order. For philosophy as a whole is a combination of negative and positive philosophy. At the same time Schelling's procedure is doubtless one reason why his philosophy of mythology and revelation exercised comparatively little influence on the development of the study of the history of religion. This is not to say that metaphysical presuppositions are illegitimate. Whether one thinks that they are legitimate or illegitimate obviously depends on one's view of the cognitive value of metaphysics. But it is easy to understand that Schelling's *philosophy* of mythology and revelation was looked at askance by those who wished to free the study of the history of religion from the presuppositions of idealist metaphysics.

A distinction is drawn by Schelling between mythology on the one hand and revelation on the other. 'Everything has its time. Mythological religion had to come first. In mythological religion we have blind (because produced by a necessary process), *unfree* and *unspiritual* religion.'[1] Myths are not simply arbitrary and capricious products of the imagination. But neither are they

[1] *W*, v, p. 437.

revelation, in the sense of a freely-imparted knowledge of God. They can, of course, be consciously elaborated, but fundamentally they are the product of an unconscious and necessary process, successive forms in which an apprehension of the divine imposes itself on the religious consciousness. In other words, mythology corresponds to the dark or lower principle in God, and it has its roots in the sphere of the unconscious. When, however, we pass from mythology to revelation, we pass 'into a completely different sphere'.[1] In mythology the mind 'had to do with a necessary process, here with something which exists only as the result of an absolutely free will'.[2] For the concept of revelation presupposes an act whereby God 'freely gives or has given himself to mankind'.[3]

Inasmuch as mythological religion and revealed religion are both religion, it must be possible, Schelling insists, to subsume them under a common idea. And in fact the whole history of the religious consciousness is a second theogony or birth of God, in the sense that the eternal and timeless becoming or birth of God in himself[4] is represented in time in the history of religion. Mythology, as rooted in the unconscious, represents a moment in the divine life. It logically precedes revelation and is a preparation for it. But it is not itself revelation. For revelation is essentially God's free manifestation of himself as infinite, personal and free creator and lord of being. And, as a free act on God's part, it is not simply a logical consequence of mythology. At the same time revelation can be described as the truth of mythology. For mythology is, as it were, the exoteric element which veils the revealed truth. And in paganism the philosopher can find mythological representations or antcipiations of the truth.

In other words, Schelling wishes to represent the whole history of the religious consciousness as God's revelation of himself, while at the same time he wishes to leave room for a specifically Christian concept of revelation. On the one hand revelation, in what we might perhaps call a weak sense of the term, runs through the whole history of religion. For it is the inner truth of mythology. On the other hand revelation in a strong sense of the term is found in Christianity. For it is in the Christian religion that this inner truth first comes to the clear light of day. Christianity thus gives the truth of mythology, and it can be described as the culmination of historical religion. But it does not follow that Christianity is an

---

[1] *W*, VI, p. 396.   [2] *Ibid*.   [3] *W*, VI, p. 395.
[4] The reference is to the logically distinguishable 'potencies' in God's inner life.

automatic consequence of mythology. Mythology as such is, as we have seen, a necessary process. But in and through Christ the personal God freely reveals himself. Obviously, if Schelling wishes to represent the whole history of religion as the temporal representation of the divine life, it is very difficult for him to avoid asserting a necessary connection between pagan mythology and Christianity. The former would represent God as unconscious will, while the latter would represent God as free will, the will of love. At the same time Schelling tries to preserve an essential distinction between mythology and revelation by insisting that the concept of revelation is the concept of a free act on God's part. Revelation is the truth of mythology in the sense that it is that at which mythology aims and that which underlies the exoteric clothing of myth. But it is in and through Christ that the truth is clearly revealed, and it is revealed freely. Its truth could not be known simply by logical deduction from the pagan myths.

But though Schelling certainly tries to allow for a distinction between mythology and revelation, there is a further important point to make. If we mean by revelation Christianity simply as a fact which stands over against the fact of paganism, there is room for a higher standpoint, namely that of reason understanding both mythology and revelation. And this higher standpoint is positive philosophy. But Schelling is careful to explain that he is not referring to a rationalistic interpretation of religion from outside. He is referring to the activity of the religious consciousness whereby it understands itself from within. The philosophy of religion is thus for Schelling not only philosophy but also religion. It presupposes Christianity and cannot exist without it. It arises within Christianity, not outside it. 'Philosophical religion is therefore *historically* mediated through revealed religion.'[1] But it cannot be simply identified with Christian belief and life as facts. For it takes these facts as subject-matter for free reflective understanding. In contrast, therefore, with the simple acceptance of the original Christian revelation on authority philosophical religion can be called 'free' religion. 'The free religion is only *mediated* through Christianity; it is not immediately *posited* by it.'[2] But this does not mean that philosophical religion rejects revelation. Faith seeks understanding; but understanding from within does not annul what is understood.

This process of understanding, of free reflection, has its own

1 *W*, v, p. 437.   2 *W*, v, p. 440.

history, ranging through Scholastic theology and metaphysics, up to Schelling's own later religious philosophy. And in this philosophy we can discern Schelling's hankering after a higher wisdom. There was always something of the Gnostic in his mental make-up. Just as he was not content with ordinary physics but expounded a speculative or higher physics, so in later years he expounded an esoteric or higher knowledge of God's nature and of his self-revelation.

It is not surprising, therefore, to find Schelling giving an interpretation of the history of Christianity which in certain respects is reminiscent of the theories of the twelfth-century Abbot Joachim of Flores. According to Schelling there are three main periods in the development of Christianity. The first is the Petrine, characterized by the dominating ideas of law and authority and correlated with the ultimate ground of being in God, which is itself identified with the Father of Trinitarian theology. The second period, the Pauline, starts with the Protestant Reformation. It is characterized by the idea of freedom and correlated with the ideal principle in God, identified with the Son. And Schelling looks forward to a third period, the Johannine, which will be a higher synthesis of the first two periods and unite together law and freedom in the one Christian community. This third period is correlated with the Holy Spirit, the divine love, interpreted as a synthesis of the first two moments in God's inner life.

5. If we look at Schelling's philosophical pilgrimage as a whole, there is obviously a very great difference between its point of departure and its point of arrival. At the same time there is a certain continuity. For we can see how fresh problems arise for him out of positions already adopted, and how his solutions to these problems demand the adoption of new positions which involve modifications in the old or display them in a new light. Further, there are certain pervasive fundamental problems which serve to confer a certain unity on his philosophizing in spite of all changes.

There can be no reasonable objection to this process of development as such, unless we are prepared to defend as reasonable the thesis that a philosopher should expound a rigid closed system and never change it. Indeed, it is arguable that Schelling did not make sufficient changes. For he showed a tendency to retain ideas already employed even when the adoption of a new idea or set of ideas might well have suggested the advisability of discarding them. This characteristic may not be peculiar to Schelling: it is likely to be found in any philosopher whose thought passed through a variety of distinct phases. But it leads to a certain difficulty in assessing Schelling's precise position at a given moment. For instance, in his later thought he emphasizes the personal nature of God and the freedom of God's creative act. And it is natural to describe the evolution of his thought in its theological aspects as being a movement from pantheism to speculative theism. At the same time his insistence on the divine freedom is accompanied by a retention of the idea of the cosmic Fall and by a persistent inclination to look on the relation between the world and God as analogous to that between consequent and antecedent. Hence, though it seems to me more appropriate to describe his later thought in terms of the ideas which are new rather than in terms of those which are retained for the past, he provides material for those who maintain that even in the last phase of his philosophizing he was a dynamic pantheist rather than a theist. It is, of course, a question partly of emphasis and partly of terminology. But the point is that Schelling himself is largely responsible for the difficulty in finding the precise appropriate descriptive term. However, perhaps one ought not to expect anything else in the case of a philosopher who was so anxious to synthesize apparently conflicting points of view and to show that they were really complementary.

It scarcely needs saying that Schelling was not a systematizer in the sense of one who leaves to posterity a closed and rigid system of the take-it-or-leave-it type. But it does not necessarily follow that he was not a systematic thinker. True, his mind was notably open to stimulus and inspiration from a variety of thinkers whom he found in some respects congenial. For example, Plato, the Neo-Platonists, Giordano Bruno,[1] Jakob Boehme, Spinoza and Leibniz, not to speak of Kant and Fichte, were all used as sources of inspiration. But this openness to the reception of ideas from a variety of sources was not accompanied by any very pronounced ability to weld them all together into one consistent whole. Further, we have seen that in his later years he showed a strong inclination to take flight into the cloudy realm of theosophy and gnosticism. And it is understandable that a man who drew heavily on the speculations of Jakob Boehme can exercise only a very limited appeal among philosophers. At the same time it is

[1] Schelling's theory of the Absolute as pure identity can be regarded as a continuation of Bruno's idea of the infinite as the *coincidentia oppositorum*, an idea which was itself derived from Nicholas of Cusa.

necessary, as Hegel remarks, to make a distinction between Schelling's philosophy and the imitations of it which consist in a farrago of words about the Absolute or in the substitution for sustained thought of vague analogies based on alleged intuitive insights. For though Schelling was not a systematizer in the sense that Hegel was, he none the less thought systematically. That is to say, he made a real and sustained effort to understand his material and to think through the problems which he raised. It was always systematic understanding at which he aimed and which he tried to communicate. Whether he succeeded or not, is another question.

Schelling's later thought has been comparatively neglected by historians. And this is understandable. For one thing, as was remarked in the introductory chapter, Schelling's philosophy of Nature, system of transcendental idealism and theory of the Absolute as pure identity are the important phases of his thought if we choose to regard him primarily as a link between Fichte and Hegel in the development of German idealism. For another thing, his philosophy of mythology and revelation, which in any case belonged to a period when the impetus of metaphysical idealism was already spent, has seemed to many not only to represent a flight beyond anything which can be regarded as rational philosophy but also to be hardly worth considering in view of the actual development of the history of religion in subsequent times.

But though this neglect is understandable, it is also perhaps regrettable. At least it is regrettable if one thinks that there is room for a philosophy of religion as well as for a purely historical and sociological study of religions or a purely psychological study of the religious consciousness. It is not so much a question of looking to Schelling for solutions to problems as of finding stimulus and inspiration in his thought, points of departure for independent reflection. And possibly this is a characteristic of Schelling's philosophizing as a whole. Its value may be primarily suggestive and stimulative. But it can, of course, exercise this function only for those who have a certain initial sympathy with his mentality and an appreciation of the problems which he raised. In the absence of this sympathy and appreciation there is a natural tendency to write him off as a poet who chose the wrong medium for the expression of his visions of the world.

6. In the introductory chapter some mention was made of Schelling's relations with the romantic movement as represented by F. Schlegel, Novalis, Hölderlin and so on. And I do not propose

either to repeat or to develop what was then said. But some remarks may be appropriate in this last section of the present chapter on Schelling's influence on some other thinkers both inside and outside Germany.

Schelling's philosophy of Nature exercised some influence on Lorenz Oken (1779–1851). Oken was a professor of medicine at Jena, Munich and Zürich successively; but he was deeply interested in philosophy and published several philosophical works, such as *On the Universe (Ueber das Universum)*, 1808. In his view the philosophy of Nature is the doctrine of the eternal transformation of God into the world. God is the totality, and the world is the eternal appearance of God. That is to say, the world cannot have had a beginning because it is the expressed divine thought. And for the same reason it can have no end. But there can be and is evolution in the world.

Schelling's judgment of Oken's philosophy was not particularly favourable, though he made use of some of Oken's ideas in his lectures. In his turn Oken refused to follow Schelling into the paths of his later religious philosophy.

The influence of Schelling's philosophy of Nature was also felt by Johann Joseph von Görres (1776–1848), a leading Catholic philosopher of Munich.[1] But Görres is chiefly known as a religious thinker. At first somewhat inclined to the pantheism of Schelling's system of identity, he later expounded a theistic philosophy, as in the four volumes of his *Christian Mysticism (Christliche Mystik*, 1836–42), though, like Schelling himself, he was strongly attracted to theosophical speculation. Görres also wrote on art and on political questions. Indeed he took an active part in political life and interested himself in the problem of the relations between Church and State.

Görres's abandonment of the standpoint represented by Schelling's system of identity was not shared by Karl Gustav Carus (1789–1860), a doctor and philosopher who defended pantheism throughout his career. He is of some importance for his work on the soul (*Psyche*, 1846) in which he maintains that the key to the conscious life of the soul is to be found in the sphere of the unconscious.

Turning to Franz von Baader (1765–1841) who, like Görres, was an important member of the circle of Catholic thinkers and writers at Munich, we find a clear case of reciprocal influence. That is to say,

[1] Schelling's influence was felt in southern rather than in northern Germany.

though Baader was influenced by Schelling, he in turn influenced the latter. For it was Baader who introduced Schelling to the writings of Boehme and so helped to determine the direction taken by his thought.

It was Baader's conviction that since the time of Francis Bacon and Descartes philosophy had tended to become more and more divorced from religion, whereas true philosophy should have its foundations in faith. And in working out his own philosophy Baader drew on the speculations of thinkers such as Eckhart and Boehme. In God himself we can distinguish higher and lower principles, and though the sensible world is to be regarded as a divine self-manifestation it none the less represents a Fall. Again, just as in God there is the eternal victory of the higher principle over the lower, of light over darkness, so in man there should be a process of spiritualization whereby the world would return to God. It is evident that Baader and Schelling were kindred souls who drank from the same spiritual fountain.

Baader's social and political writings are of some interest. In them he expresses a resolute opposition to the theory of the State as a result of a social compact or contract between individuals. On the contrary, the State is a natural institution in the sense that it is grounded in and proceeds from the nature of man: it is not the product of a convention. At the same time Baader strongly attacks the notion that the State is the ultimate sovereign power. The ultimate sovereign is God alone, and reverence for God and the universal moral law, together with respect for the human person as the image of God, are the only real safeguards against tyranny. If these safeguards are neglected, tyranny and intolerance will result, no matter whether sovereignty is regarded as residing with the monarch or with the people. To the atheistic or secular power-State Baader opposes the ideal of the Christian State. The concentration of power which is characteristic of the secular or the atheistic national State and which leads to injustice at home and to war abroad can be overcome only if religion and morality penetrate the whole of human society.

One can hardly call Karl Christian Friedrich Krause (1781–1832) a disciple of Schelling. For he professed to be the true spiritual successor of Kant, and his relations with Schelling, when at Munich, were far from friendly. However, he was wont to say that the approach to his own philosophy must be by way of Schelling, and some of his ideas were akin to those of Schelling. The body, he maintained, belongs to the realm of Nature, while the spirit or ego belongs to the spiritual sphere, the realm of 'reason'. This idea echoes indeed Kant's distinction between the phenomenal and noumenal spheres. But Krause argued that as Spirit and Nature, though distinct and in one sense opposed, react on one another, we must look for the ground of both in a perfect essence, God or the Absolute. Krause also expounded a 'synthetic' order, proceeding from God or the Absolute to the derived essences, Spirit and Nature, and to finite things. He insisted on the unity of all humanity as the goal of history, and after abandoning his hope of this end being attained through Freemasonry, issued a manifesto proclaiming a League of Humanity (*Menschheitsbund*). In Germany his philosophy was overshadowed by the systems of the three great idealists, but it exercised, perhaps somewhat surprisingly, a wide influence in Spain where 'Krausism' became a fashionable system of thought.

In Russia Schelling appealed to the pan-Slavist group, whereas the westernizers were influenced more by Hegel. For instance, in the early part of the nineteenth century Schelling's philosophy of Nature was expounded at Moscow by M. G. Pavlov (1773–1840), while the later religious thought of Schelling exercised some influence on the famous Russian philosopher Vladimir Soloviev (1853–1900). It would certainly not be accurate to call Soloviev a disciple of Schelling. Apart from the fact that he was influenced by other non-Russian thinkers, he was in any case an original philosopher and not the 'disciple' of anyone. But in his tendency to theosophical speculation[1] he showed a marked affinity of spirit with Schelling, and certain aspects of his profoundly religious thought are very similar to positions adopted by the German philosopher.

In Great Britain the influence of Schelling has been negligible. Coleridge, the poet, remarks in his *Biographia Literaria* that in Schelling's philosophy of Nature and system of transcendental idealism he found 'a genial coincidence' with much that he had worked out for himself, and he praises Schelling at the expense of Fichte, whom he caricatures. But it can hardly be said that professional philosophers in this country have shown any enthusiasm for Schelling.

In recent times there has been a certain renewal of interest in

---

[1] Soloviev made great play with the idea of Wisdom or *Sophia*, as found in the Bible and also, for instance, in the writings of Boehme.

Schelling's philosophy of religion. For instance, it acted as a stimulus in the development of the thought of the Protestant theologian Paul Tillich. And in spite of Kierkegaard's attitude there has been a tendency to see in Schelling's distinction between negative and positive philosophy, in his insistence on freedom and in his emphasis on existence, an anticipation of some themes of existentialism. But though this interpretation has some limited justification, the desire to find anticipations of later ideas in illustrious minds of the past should not blind us to the great differences in atmosphere between the idealist and existentialist movements. In any case Schelling is perhaps most notable for his transformation of the impersonal Absolute of metaphysical idealism into the personal God who reveals himself to the religious consciousness.

CHAPTER VIII

SCHLEIERMACHER

Life and writings—The basic religious experience and its interpretation—The moral and religious life of man—Final remarks.

1. CONCERNED as they were with the Absolute, with the relation between the infinite and the finite and with the life of the spirit, the three great German idealists naturally devoted attention to religion as an expression of the finite spirit's relation to the divine reality. And as all three were professors of philosophy and constructors of philosophical systems, it was also natural that they should interpret religion in the light of the fundamental principles of these systems. Thus in accordance with the spirit of his ethical idealism Fichte tended to reduce religion to ethics,[1] while Hegel tended to depict it as a form of knowledge. Even Schelling, whose thought, as we have seen, became more and more a philosophy of the religious consciousness and who laid emphasis on man's need of a personal God, tended to interpret the development of the religious consciousness as the development of a higher knowledge. With Schleiermacher, however, we find an approach to the philosophy of religion from the point of view of a theologian and preacher, a man who in spite of his strongly-marked philosophical interests retained the imprint of his pietistic upbringing and who was concerned with making a sharp distinction between the religious consciousness on the one hand and metaphysics and ethics on the other.

Friedrich Daniel Ernst Schleiermacher was born at Breslau on November 21st, 1768. His school education was entrusted by his parents to the Moravian Brotherhood. In spite of a loss of faith in some fundamental Christian doctrines he then proceeded to Halle for the study of theology, though during his first two years at the university he interested himself in Spinoza and Kant more than in purely theological subjects. In 1790 he passed his examinations at Berlin and then took a post as tutor in a family. From 1794 until the end of 1795 he acted as pastor at Landsberg near Frankfurt on

---

[1] As was mentioned in the account of Fichte's philosophy, the strength of this tendency was considerably weaker in his later thought.

the Oder, and from 1796 until 1802 he held an ecclesiastical position at Berlin.

During this period at Berlin Schleiermacher was in relation with the circle of the romantics, particularly with Friedrich Schlegel. He shared the general romantic concern with the totality, and he had a profound sympathy with Spinoza. At the same time he had been attracted from an early age by Plato's view of the world as the visible image of the ideal realm of true being. And Spinoza's Nature was conceived by him as the reality which reveals itself in the phenomenal world. But as an admirer of Spinoza he was faced with the task of reconciling his philosophical outlook with the religion which he was commissioned to teach. Nor was this simply a matter of satisfying his professional conscience as a Protestant clergyman. For he was a sincerely religious man who, as already remarked, retained the lasting imprint of the piety of his family and of his early teachers. He had therefore to think out the intellectual framework for the religious consciousness as he conceived it. And in 1799 he published his *Discourses on Religion* (*Reden über die Religion*), of which there were several subsequent editions.

This work was followed in 1800 by *Monologues* (*Monologen*) treating of problems connected with the relation between the individual and society, and in 1801 by Schleiermacher's first collection of sermons. Schleiermacher was not, however, what would generally be considered an orthodox Protestant theologian, and the years 1802–4 were passed in retirement. In 1803 he published *Outlines of a Critique of the Doctrine of Morals up to Present* (*Grundlinien einer Kritik der bisherigen Sittenlehre*). He also occupied himself with translating into German the dialogues of Plato, furnished with introductions and notes. The first part appeared in 1804, the second in 1809 and the third in 1828.

In 1804 Schleiermacher accepted a chair at the University of Halle. And when Napoleon closed the university, he remained in the town as a preacher. In 1807, however, he returned to Berlin where he took part in political life and collaborated in the foundation of the new university. In 1810 he was appointed professor of theology in the university and he held this post until his death in 1834. In 1821–2 he published his *Christian Faith according to the Principles of the Evangelical Church* (*Der christliche Glaube nach den Grundsätzen der evangelischen Kirche*), a second edition of which appeared in 1830–1. He also published further collections of sermons. His lecture-courses at the university, which covered not only theological but also philosophical and educational themes, were published after his death.

2. Thought and being, Schleiermacher maintains, are correlative. But there are two ways in which thought can be related to being. In the first place thought can conform itself to being, as in scientific or theoretical knowledge. And the being which corresponds to the totality of our scientific concepts and judgments is called Nature. In the second place thought can seek to conform being to itself. And this is verified in the thinking which lies at the basis of our moral activity. For through moral action we seek to realize our ethical ideals and purposes, endeavouring in this way to conform being to our ideas rather than the other way round. 'Thought which aims at knowledge relates itself to a being which it presupposes; the thought which lies at the root of our actions relates itself to a being which is to come about through us.'[1] And the totality of that which expresses itself in thought-directed action is called Spirit.

We are thus presented, at first sight at least, with a dualism. On the one hand we have Nature, on the other Spirit. But though Spirit and Nature, thought and being, subject and object, are distinct and different notions for conceptual thinking, which is unable to transcend all distinction and oppositions, the dualism is not absolute. The ultimate reality is the identity of Spirit and Nature in the Universe or God. Conceptual thought cannot apprehend this identity. But the identity can be felt. And this feeling is linked by Schleiermacher with self-consciousness. It is not indeed reflective self-awareness, which apprehends the identity of the ego in the diversity of its moments or phases. But at the basis of reflective self-awareness there lies an 'immediate self-consciousness, which equals feeling'.[2] In other words, there is a fundamental immediacy of feeling, at which level the distinctions and oppositions of conceptual thought have not yet emerged. We can speak of it as an intuition. But if we do, we must understand that it is never a clear intellectual intuition. Rather is it the feeling-basis, so to speak, in self-consciousness, and it cannot be separated from consciousness of the self. That is to say, the self does not enjoy any intellectual intuition of the divine totality as

---

[1] W., III, p. 59. References to Schleiermacher's writing are given according to volume and page of the edition of his Works by O. Braun and J. Bauer (4 vols., Leipzig, 1911–13). This edition consists of selections.

[2] W, III, p. 71.

direct and sole object, but it feels itself as dependent on the totality which transcends all oppositions.

This feeling of dependence (*Abhängigkeitsgefühl*) is the 'religious side'[1] of self-consciousness: it is in fact 'the religious feeling'.[2] For the essence of religion is 'neither thought nor action but intuition and feeling. It seeks to intuit the Universe. . . .'[3] And the Universe, as Schleiermacher uses the term, is the infinite divine reality. Hence religion is for him essentially or fundamentally the feeling of dependence on the infinite.

In this case it is obviously necessary to make a sharp distinction between religion on the one hand and metaphysics and ethics on the other. True, metaphysics and ethics have 'the same subject-matter as religion, namely the Universe and man's relation to it'.[4] But their approaches are quite different. Metaphysics, says Schleiermacher with an obvious reference to Fichte's idealism, 'spins out of itself the reality of the world and its laws'.[5] Ethics 'develops out of the nature of man and his relation to the Universe a system of duties; it commands and prohibits actions. . . .'[6] But religion is not concerned with metaphysical deduction, nor is it concerned with using the Universe to derive a code of duties. It is neither knowledge nor morality: it is feeling.

We can say, therefore, that Schleiermacher turns his back on the tendency shown by Kant and Fichte to reduce religion to morals, just as he rejects any attempt to exhibit the essence of religion as a form of theoretical knowledge, and that he follows Jacobi in finding the basis of faith in feeling. But there is an important difference between Schleiermacher and Jacobi. For while Jacobi grounded all knowledge on faith, Schleiermacher wishes to differentiate between theoretical knowledge and religious faith and finds in feeling the specific basis of the latter. We can add that though for Schleiermacher the religious consciousness stands closer to the aesthetic consciousness than to theoretical knowledge, the feeling on which the religious consciousness is based, namely the feeling of dependence on the infinite, is peculiar to it. Hence Schleiermacher avoids the romantic tendency to confuse the religious with the aesthetic consciousness.

It must not be concluded from what has been said that in Schleiermacher's view there is no connection at all between religion on the one hand and metaphysics and ethics on the other. On the

[1] *W*, III, p. 72.   [2] *Ibid*.   [3] *W*, IV, p. 240.
[4] *W*, IV, p. 235.   [5] *W*, IV, p. 236.   [6] *Ibid*.

contrary, there is a sense in which both metaphysics and ethics stand in need of religion. Without the fundamental religious intuition of the infinite totality metaphysics would be left hanging in the air, as a purely conceptual construction. And ethics without religion would give us a very inadequate idea of man. For from the purely ethical point of view man appears as the free and autonomous master of his fate, whereas religious intuition reveals to him his dependence on the infinite Totality, on God.

Now, when Schleiermacher asserts that religious faith is grounded on the feeling of dependence on the infinite, the word 'feeling' must obviously be understood as signifying the immediacy of this consciousness of dependence rather than as excluding any intellectual act. For, as we have seen, he also talks about 'intuition'. But this intuition is not an apprehension of God as a clearly-conceived object: it is a consciousness of self as essentially dependent on infinite being in an indeterminate and unconceptualized sense. Hence the feeling of dependence stands in need of interpretation on the conceptual level. And this is the task of philosophical theology. It is arguable, of course, that Schleiermacher's account of the basic religious experience already comprises a conspicuous element of interpretation. For turning away from the moralism of Kant and the metaphysical speculation of Fichte and inspired by the thought of 'the holy, rejected Spinoza'[1] he identifies that on which the self is felt to depend with the infinite totality, the divine Universe. 'Religion is feeling and taste for the infinite';[2] and of Spinoza we can say that 'the infinite was his beginning and end; the Universe was his only and eternal love. . . .'[3] Thus the basic religious feeling of dependence is initially described in a manner inspired by a romanticized Spinoza. At the same time the influence of Spinoza should not be overestimated. For whereas Spinoza set the 'intellectual love of God' at the summit of the mind's ascent, Schleiermacher finds the feeling of dependence on the infinite at the basis of the religious view of the world. And the question arises, how are we to think or conceive this immediate consciousness of dependence?

A difficulty immediately arises. The basic religious feeling is one of dependence on an infinite in which there are no oppositions, the self-identical totality. But conceptual thought at once introduces distinctions and oppositions: the infinite unity falls apart into the ideas of God and the world. The world is thought of as the totality

[1] *W*, IV, p. 243.   [2] *W*, IV, p. 242.   [3] *W*, IV, p. 243.

of all oppositions and differences, while God is conceived a simple unity, as the existing negation of all opposition and distinction. As conceptual thought cannot do away altogether with the distinction to which it necessarily gives rise, it must conceive God and the world as correlates. That is to say, it must conceive the relation between God and the world as one of mutual implication and not as one of mere compresence, nor even as a one-way relation of dependence, that is, of the world's dependence on God. 'No God without the world, and no world without God.'[1] At the same time the two ideas, namely of God and the world, must not be identified: 'therefore neither complete identification nor complete separation of the two ideas'.[2] In other words, as conceptual thought necessarily conceives the Universe through two ideas, it should not confuse them. The unity of the Universe of being must be conceived in terms of their correlation rather than of their identification.

At first sight at least this suggests that for Schleiermacher the distinction between God and the world exists only for human reflection, and that in reality there is no distinction. In point of fact, however, Schleiermacher wishes to avoid both the reduction of the world to God and the reduction of God to the world. On the one hand an acosmistic theory which simply denied any reality to the finite would be unfaithful to the basic religious consciousness. For this would inevitably be misinterpreted by a theory which left nothing at all of which it could be said that it was dependent. On the other hand a simple identification of God with the spatio-temporal system of finite things would leave no room for an underlying undifferentiated unity. Hence the distinction between God and the world must be something more than the expression of a defect in conceptual thought. True, conceptual thought is quite unable to attain an adequate understanding of the totality, the divine Universe. But it can and should correct its tendency to separate completely the ideas of God and the world by conceiving them as correlates and seeing the world as standing to God in the relation of consequent to antecedent, as the necessary self-manifestation of an undifferentiated unity, or, to use Spinoza's terms, as *Natura naturata* in relation to *Natura naturans*. This is, as it were, the best that conceptual thought can do, avoiding, that is to say, both complete separation and complete identification. The divine reality in itself transcends the reach of our concepts.

[1] *W*, III, p. 81.   [2] *W*, III, p. 86.

The really interesting and significant feature in Schleiermacher's philosophy of religion is the fact that it is for him the explicitation of a fundamental religious experience. In interpreting this experience he is obviously influenced by Spinoza. And, like Spinoza, he insists that God transcends all human categories. As God is the unity without differentiation or opposition, none of the categories of human thought, such as personality, can really apply to him. For they are bound up with finitude. At the same time God is not to be conceived as static Substance but as infinite Life which reveals itself necessarily in the world. In this respect Schleiermacher stands closer to Fichte's later philosophy than to the system of Spinoza, while the theory of God or the Absolute as the undifferentiated self-identity to which the world stands as consequent to antecedent resembles the speculations of Schelling. But Schelling's later gnosticism would hardly have met with Schleiermacher's full approval. Religion for Schleiermacher really consists in the appropriation of the basic feeling of dependence on the infinite. It is an affair of the heart rather than of the understanding, of faith rather than knowledge.

3. Though he refuses to ascribe personality to God, except in a symbolic sense, Schleiermacher lays great stress on the value of the individual personality when he is considering human beings as moral agents. The totality, the universal, is indeed immanent in all finite individuals. And for this reason sheer egoism, involving the deification of one finite self, cannot possibly be the moral ideal for man. At the same time every individual is a particular manifestation of God, and he has his own special gifts, his own particularity (*Eigentümlichkeit*). It is thus his duty to develop his individual talents. And education should be directed to the formation of fully developed and harmoniously integrated individual personalities. Man combines in himself Spirit and Nature, and his moral development requires their harmonization. From the metaphysical point of view Spirit and Nature are ultimately one. Hence the human personality cannot be properly developed if we make so sharp a distinction between, say, reason and natural impulse as to imply that morality consists in disregarding or opposing all natural impulses. The moral ideal is not conflict but harmonization and integration. In other words, Schleiermacher has little sympathy with the rigoristic morality of Kant and with his tendency to assert an antithesis between reason and inclination or impulse. If God is the positive negation, so to speak, of all differences and

oppositions, man's moral vocation involves expressing the divine nature in finite form through the harmonization in an integrated personality of reason, will and impulse.

But though Schleiermacher stresses the development of the individual personality, he also insists that individual and society are not contradictory concepts. For particularity 'exists only in relation to others'.[1] On the one hand a man's element of uniqueness, that which distinguishes him from other men, presupposes human society. On the other hand society, being a community of distinct individuals, presupposes individual differences. Hence individual and society imply one another. And self-expression or self-development demands not only the development of one's individual gifts but also respect for other personalities. In other words, every human being has a unique moral vocation, but this vocation can be fulfilled only within society, that is, by man as member of a community.

If we ask what is the relation between morality as depicted by the philosopher and specifically Christian morality, the answer is that they differ in form but not in content. The content of Christian morality cannot contradict the content of 'philosophical' morality, but it has its own form, this form being furnished by the elements in the Christian consciousness which mark it off from the religious consciousness in general. And the specific note of the Christian consciousness is that 'all community with God is regarded as conditioned by Christ's redemptive act'.[2]

As regards historical religions, Schleiermacher's attitude is somewhat complex. On the one hand he rejects the idea of a universal natural religion which should be substituted for historical religions. For there are only the latter; the former is a fiction. On the other hand Schleiermacher sees in the series of historical religions the progressive revelation of an ideal which can never be grasped in its entirety. Dogmas are necessary in one sense, namely as concrete symbolic expressions of the religious consciousness. But they can at the same time become fetters preventing the free movement of the spirit. An historical religion such as Christianity owes its origin and impetus to a religious genius, analogous to an artistic genius; and its life is perpetuated by its adherents steeping themselves in the spirit of the genius and in the vital movement which stems from him rather than by subscription to a certain set of dogmas. It is true that as time went on Schleiermacher came to

[1] *W*, II, p. 92.   [2] *W*, III, p. 128.

lay more stress on the idea of the Church and on specifically Christian belief; but he was and remained what is sometimes called a liberal theologian. And as such he has exercised a very considerable influence in German Protestant circles, though this influence has been sharply challenged in recent times by the revival of Protestant orthodoxy.

4. In his attempt to interpret what he regarded as the basic religious consciousness Schleiermacher certainly attempted to develop a systematic philosophy, a coherent whole. But it can hardly be claimed that this philosophy is free from internal strains and stresses. The influence of a romanticized Spinoza, the man possessed by a passion for the infinite, impelled him in the direction of pantheism. At the same time the very nature of the fundamental feeling or intuition which he wished to interpret militated against sheer monism and demanded some distinction between God and the world. For unless we postulate some distinction, how can we sensibly speak of the finite self as conscious of its dependence on the infinite? Again, whereas the pantheistic aspects of Schleiermacher's thought were unfavourable to the admission of personal freedom, in his moral theory and in his account of the relations between human beings he needed and used the idea of freedom. In other words, the pantheistic elements in his metaphysics were offset by his emphasis on the individual in his theories of moral conduct and of society. There was no question of the theory of the divine Universe being reflected in political totalitarianism. On the contrary, quite apart from his admission of the Church as a society distinct from the State, he emphasized the concept of the 'free society', the social organization which gives free play to the expression of the unique character of each individual personality.

The strains in Schleiermacher's philosophy were not, however, peculiar to it. For any philosophy which tried to combine the idea of the divine totality with personal freedom and the idea of an ultimate identity with a full recognition of the value of the distinct finite particular was bound to find itself involved in similar difficulties. But Schleiermacher could hardly evade the problem by saying that the universal exists only in and through the particulars. For he was determined to justify the feeling of dependence on a reality which was not identifiable with the spatio-temporal world. There had to be something 'behind' the world. Yet the world could not be something outside God. Hence he was driven in the same direction taken by Schelling. Perhaps we can say that Schleiermacher had a profound quasi-mystical conscious-ness of the One as underlying and expressing itself in the Many, and that this was the foundation of his philosophy. The difficulties arose when he tried to give theoretical expression to this conscious-ness. But, to do him justice, he readily admitted that no adequate theoretical account was possible. God is the object of 'feeling' and faith rather than of knowledge. Religion is neither metaphysics nor morals. And theology is symbolical. Schleiermacher had indeed obvious affinities with the great idealists, but he was certainly not a rationalist. Religion was for him the basic element in man's spiritual life; and religion, he insisted, is grounded on the immediate intuitive feeling of dependence. This feeling of absolute dependence was for him the food, as it were, of philosophical reflection. And this is not, of course, a view which can be summarily dismissed as the amiable prejudice of a man who attributed to the pious feelings of the heart a cosmic significance which the reflective reason denies them. For it is at any rate arguable that speculative metaphysics is, in part at least, a reflective explicitation of a preliminary apprehension of the dependence of the Many on the One, an apprehension which for want of a better word can be described as intuitive.

CHAPTER IX

HEGEL (1)

*Life and writings—Early theological writings—Hegel's relations
to Fichte and Schelling—The life of the Absolute and the nature
of philosophy—The phenomenology of consciousness.*

1. GEORG WILHELM FRIEDRICH HEGEL, greatest of German
idealists and one of the most outstanding of western philosophers,
was born at Stuttgart on August 27th, 1770.[1] His father was a
civil servant. In his school years at Stuttgart the future philosopher
did not distinguish himself in any particular way, but it was at this
period that he first felt the attraction of the Greek genius, being
especially impressed by the plays of Sophocles, above all by the
Antigone.

In 1788 Hegel enrolled as a student in the Protestant theological
foundation of the University of Tübingen where he formed
relations of friendship with Schelling and Hölderlin. The friends
studied Rousseau together and shared a common enthusiasm for
the ideals of the French Revolution. But, as at school, Hegel gave
no impression of exceptional ability. And when he left the university
in 1793, his certificate mentioned his good character, his fair
knowledge of theology and philology and his inadequate grasp of
philosophy. Hegel's mind was not precocious like Schelling's: it
needed more time to mature. There is, however, another side to the
picture. He had already begun to turn his attention to the relation
between philosophy and theology, but he did not show his jottings
or notes to his professors, who do not appear to have been remarkable in any way and in whom he doubtless did not feel much
confidence.

After leaving the university Hegel gained his livelihood as a
family tutor, first at Berne in Switzerland (1793–6) and then at
Frankfurt (1797–1800). Though outwardly uneventful these years
constituted an important period in his philosophical development.
The essays which he wrote at the time were published for the first
time in 1907 by Hermann Nohl under the title *Hegel's Early
Theological Writings* (*Hegels theologische Jugendschriften*), and

[1] This was the year of Kant's inaugural dissertation. It was also the year of
birth of Hölderlin in Germany and of Bentham and Wordsworth in England.

159

something will be said about their content in the next section. True, if we possessed only these essays we should not have any idea of the philosophical system which he subsequently developed, and there would be no good reason for devoting space to him in a history of philosophy. In this sense the essays are of minor importance. But when we look back on Hegel's early writings in the light of our knowledge of his developed system, we can discern a certain continuity in his problematics and understand better how he arrived at his system and what was his leading idea. As we have seen, the early writings have been described as 'theological'. And though it is true that Hegel became a philosopher rather than a theologian, his philosophy was always theology in the sense that its subject-matter was, as he himself insisted, the same as the subject-matter of theology, namely the Absolute or, in religious language, God and the relation of the finite to the infinite.

In 1801 Hegel obtained a post in the University of Jena, and his first published work, on the *Difference between the Philosophical Systems of Fichte and Schelling* (*Differenz des Fichteschen und Schellingschen Systems*) appeared in the same year. This work gave the impression that he was to all intents and purposes a disciple of Schelling. And the impression was strengthened by his collaboration with Schelling in editing the *Critical Journal of Philosophy* (1802-3). But Hegel's lectures at Jena, which were not published before the present century, show that he was already working out an independent position of his own. And his divergence from Schelling was made clear to the public in his first great work, *The Phenomenology of Spirit* (*Die Phänomenologie des Geistes*), which appeared in 1807. Further reference to this remarkable book will be made in the fifth section of this chapter.

After the Battle of Jena, which brought the life of the university to a close, Hegel found himself practically destitute; and from 1807 to 1808 he edited a newspaper at Bamberg. He was appointed rector of the *Gymnasium* at Nuremberg, a post which he held until 1816. (In 1811 he married.) As rector of the *Gymnasium* Hegel promoted classical studies, though not, we are told, to the detriment of study of the students' mother tongue. He also gave instruction to his pupils in the rudiments of philosophy, though more, it appears, out of deference to the wish of his patron Niethammer than from any personal enthusiasm for the policy of introducing philosophy into the school curriculum. And one imagines that most of the pupils must have experienced great difficulty in understanding Hegel's meaning. At the same time the philosopher pursued his own studies and reflections, and it was during his sojourn at Nuremberg that he produced one of his main works, the *Science of Logic* (*Wissenschaft der Logik*, 1812–16).

In the year in which the second and final volume of this work appeared Hegel received three invitations to accept a chair of philosophy, from Erlangen, Heidelberg and Berlin. He accepted the one from Heidelberg. His influence on the general body of the students does not seem to have been very great, but his reputation as a philosopher was steadily rising. And it was enhanced by the publication in 1817 of the *Encyclopaedia of the Philosophical Sciences in Outline* (*Enzyklopädie der philosophischen Wissenschaften im Grundriss*) in which he gave a conspectus of his system according to its three main divisions, logic, philosophy of Nature and philosophy of Spirit. We may also note that it was at Heidelberg that Hegel first lectured on aesthetics.

In 1818 Hegel accepted a renewed invitation to Berlin, and he occupied the chair of philosophy in the university until his death from cholera on November 14th, 1831. During this period he attained an unrivalled position in the philosophical world not only of Berlin but also of Germany as a whole. To some extent he was looked on as a kind of official philosopher. But his influence as a teacher was certainly not due to his connections with the government. Nor was it due to any outstanding gift of eloquence. As an orator he was inferior to Schelling. His influence was due rather to his evident and uncompromising devotion to pure thought, coupled with his remarkable ability for comprising a vast field within the scope and sweep of his dialectic. And his disciples felt that under his tuition the inner nature and process of reality, including the history of man, his political life and spiritual achievements, were being revealed to their understanding.

During his tenure of the chair of philosophy at Berlin Hegel published comparatively little. His *Outlines of the Philosophy of Right* (*Grundlinien der Philosophie des Rechts*) appeared in 1821, and new editions of the *Encyclopaedia* were published in 1827 and 1830. At the time of his death Hegel was revising *The Phenomenology of Spirit*. But he was, of course, lecturing during the whole of this period. And the texts of his courses, partly based on the collated notes of students, were published posthumously. In their English translations the lectures on the philosophy of art comprise four volumes, those on the philosophy of religion and on the history of philosophy three volumes each, and those on the philosophy of history one volume.

In Hölderlin's opinion Hegel was a man of calm prosaic understanding. In ordinary life at least he never gave the impression of exuberant genius. Painstaking, methodical, conscientious, sociable, he was from one point of view very much the honest *bourgeois* university professor, the worthy son of a good civil servant. At the same time he was inspired by a profound vision of the movement and significance of cosmic and human history, to the expression of which he gave his life. This is not to say that he was what is usually meant by a visionary. Appeals to mystical intuitions and to feelings were abhorrent to him, so far as philosophy at any rate was concerned. He was a firm believer in the unity of form and content. The content, truth, exists for philosophy, he was convinced, only in its systematic conceptual form. The real is the rational and the rational the real; and reality can be apprehended only in its rational reconstruction. But though Hegel had little use for philosophies which took short-cuts, as it were, by appealing to mystical insights or for philosophies which, in his opinion, aimed at edification rather than at systematic understanding, the fact remains that he presented mankind with one of the most grandiose and impressive pictures of the Universe which are to be met with in the history of philosophy. And in this sense he was a great visionary.

2. We have seen that Hegel was attracted by the Greek genius while he was still at school. And at the university this attraction exercised a marked influence on his attitude towards the Christian religion. The theology which he heard from his professors at Tübingen was for the most part Christianity adapted to the ideas of the Enlightenment, that is to say, rationalistic theism with a certain infusion of or tincture of Biblical supernaturalism. But this religion of the understanding, as Hegel described it, seemed to him to be not only arid and barren but also divorced from the spirit and needs of his generation. And he contrasted it unfavourably with Greek religion which was rooted in the spirit of the Greek people and formed an integral part of their culture. Christianity is, he thought, a book-religion, and the book in question, namely the Bible, is the product of an alien race and out of harmony with the Germanic soul. Hegel was not, of course, proposing a literal substitute of Greek religion for Christianity. His point was that Greek religion was a *Volksreligion*, a religion

intimately related to the spirit and genius of the people and forming an element of this people's culture, whereas Christianity, at least as presented to him by his professors, was something imposed from without. Moreover, Christianity was, he thought, hostile to human happiness and liberty and indifferent to beauty.

This expression of Hegel's early enthusiasm for the Greek genius and culture was soon modified by his study of Kant. While not abandoning his admiration for the Greek spirit, he came to regard it as lacking in moral profundity. In his opinion this element of moral profundity and earnestness had been supplied by Kant who had at the same time expounded an ethical religion which was free from the burdens of dogma and Bible-worship. Obviously, Hegel did not mean to imply that mankind had to wait till the time of Kant for the appearance of moral profundity. On the contrary, he attributed a Kantian-like emphasis on morality to the Founder of Christianity. And in his *Life of Jesus* (*Das Leben Jesu*, 1795), which was written while he was a family tutor at Berne, he depicted Christ as being exclusively a moral teacher and almost as an expounder of the Kantian ethics. True, Christ insisted on his personal mission; but according to Hegel he was forced to do so simply because the Jews were accustomed to think of all religions and moral insights as revealed, as coming from a divine source. Hence to persuade the Jews to listen to him at all Christ had to represent himself as the legate or messenger of God. But it was not really his intention either to make himself the unique mediator between God and man or to impose revealed dogmas.

How, then, did Christianity become transformed into an authoritarian, ecclesiastical and dogmatic system? Hegel considered this question in *The Positivity of the Christian Religion* (*Die Positivität der christlichen Religion*), the first two parts of which were composed in 1795-6 and the third somewhat later, in 1798-9. As one would expect, the transformation of Christianity is attributed in large part to the apostles and other disciples of Christ. And the result of the transformation is depicted as the alienation of man from his true self. Through the imposition of dogmas liberty of thought was lost, and through the idea of a moral law imposed from without moral liberty perished. Further, man was regarded as alienated from God. He could be reconciled only by faith and, in Catholicism at least, by the sacraments of the Church.

During his Frankfurt period, however, Hegel's attitude towards

Christianity underwent a certain change, which found expression in *The Spirit of Christianity and Its Fate* (*Der Geist des Christentums und sein Schicksal*, 1800). In this essay Judaism with its legalistic morality becomes the villain of the piece. For the Jew God was the master and man the slave who had to carry out his master's will. For Christ God is love, living in man; and the alienation of man from God, as of man from man, is overcome by the union and life of love. Kant's insistence on law and duty and the emphasis which he lays on the overcoming of passion and impulse seem now to Hegel to express an inadequate notion of morality and to smack in their own way of the master-slave relationship which was characteristic of the Jewish outlook. Christ, however, rises above both Jewish legalism and Kantian moralism. He recognizes, of course, the moral struggle, but his ideal is that morality should cease to be a matter of obedience to law and should become the spontaneous expression of a life which is itself a participation in the infinite divine life. Christ does not abrogate morality in regard to its content, but he strips it of its legal form, substituting the motive of love for that of obedience to law.

It will be noted that Hegel's attention is already directed to the themes of alienation and to the recovery of a lost unity. At the time when he was contrasting Christianity with Greek religion to the detriment of the former he was already dissatisfied with any view of the divine reality as a remote and purely transcendent being. In the poem entitled *Eleusis* which he wrote at the end of his sojourn at Berne and which he dedicated to Holderlin he expressed his feeling for the infinite Totality. And at Frankfurt he represented Christ as preaching the overcoming of the gulf between man and God, the infinite and the finite, by the life of love. The Absolute is infinite life, and love is the consciousness of the unity of this life, of unity with the infinite life itself and of unity with other men through this life.

In 1800, while still at Frankfurt, Hegel wrote some notes to which Hermann Nohl gave the title *Fragment of a System* (*System-fragment*). For on the strength of an allusion in a letter from Hegel to Schelling, Nohl and Dilthey thought that the extant notes represented the sketch of a completed system. This conclusion seems to be based on somewhat insufficient evidence, at least if the word 'system' is understood in terms of Hegel's developed philosophy. At the same time the notes are of considerable interest, and deserve some mention.

Hegel is grappling with the problem of overcoming oppositions or antitheses, above all the opposition between the finite and the infinite. If we put ourselves in the position of spectators, the movement of life appears to us an infinite organized multiplicity of finite individuals, that is, as Nature. Indeed, Nature can well be described as life posited for reflection or understanding. But the individual things, the organization of which is Nature, are transitory and perishing. Thought, therefore, which is itself a form of life, thinks the unity between things as an infinite, creative life which is free from the mortality which affects finite individuals. And this creative life, which is conceived as bearing the manifold within itself and not as a mere conceptual abstraction, is called God. It must also be defined as Spirit (*Geist*). For it is neither an external link between finite things nor the purely abstract concept of life, an abstract universal. Infinite life unites all finite things from within, as it were, but without annihilating them. It is the living unity of the manifold.

Hegel thus introduces a term, namely Spirit, which is of great importance in his developed philosophy. But the question arises whether we are able by conceptual thought so to unify the infinite and the finite that neither term is dissolved in the other while at the same time they are truly united. And in the so-called *Fragment of a System* Hegel maintains that it is not possible. That is to say, in denying the gulf between finite and infinite conceptual thought inevitably tends to merge them without distinction or to reduce the one to the other, while if it affirms their unity it inevitably tends to deny their distinction. We can see the necessity for a synthesis in which unity does not exclude distinction, but we cannot really think it. The unification of the Many within the One without the former's dissolution can be achieved only by living it, that is, by man's self-elevation from finite to infinite life. And this living process is religion.

It follows from this that philosophy stops short of religion, and that in this sense it is subordinate to religion. Philosophy shows us what is demanded if the opposition between finite and infinite is to be overcome, but it cannot itself fulfil this demand. For its fulfilment we have to turn to religion, that is, to the Christian religion. The Jews objectified God as a being set over above and outside the finite. And this is the wrong idea of the infinite, a 'bad' infinity. Christ, however, discovered the infinite life within himself as source of his thought and action. And this is the right idea of the

infinite, namely as immanent in the finite and as comprising the
finite within itself. But this synthesis can only be lived as Christ
lived it: it is the life of love. The organ of mediation between
finite and infinite is love, not reflection. True, there is a passage
where Hegel foreshadows his later dialectical method, but he
asserts at the same time that the complete synthesis transcends
reflection.

Yet if it is presupposed that philosophy demands the overcoming of the oppositions which it posits, it is only to be expected
that philosophy will itself try to fulfil this demand. And even if we
say that the life of love, the religious life, fulfils the demand,
philosophy will attempt to understand what religion does and how
it does it. It is thus not surprising if Hegel soon tries to accomplish
by reflection what he had previously declared to be impossible.
And what he requires for the fulfilment of this task is a new form
of logic, a logic which is able to follow the movement of life and
does not leave opposed concepts in irremediable opposition. The
adoption of this new logic signifies the transition from Hegel the
theologian to Hegel the philosopher or, better, from the view that
religion is supreme and that philosophy stops short of it to the view
that speculative philosophy is the supreme truth. But the problem
remains the same, namely the relation of the finite to the infinite.
And so does the idea of the infinite as Spirit.

3. Some six months after his arrival at Jena Hegel published his
work on the *Difference between the Philosophical Systems of Fichte
and Schelling* (1801). Its immediate aim was twofold; first to show
that these systems really were different and not, as some people
supposed, the same, and secondly to show that the system of
Schelling represented an advance on that of Fichte. But Hegel's
discussion of these topics naturally leads him into general reflections
on the nature and purpose of philosophy.

The fundamental purpose of philosophy, Hegel maintains, is
that of overcoming oppositions and divisions. 'Division [*Entz-
weiung*] is the source of *the need of philosophy*.'[1] In the world of
experience the mind finds differences, oppositions, apparent
contradictions, and it seeks to construct a unified whole, to overcome the splintered harmony, as Hegel puts it. True, division and
opposition present themselves to the mind in different forms in
different cultural epochs. And this helps to explain the peculiar

[1] *W*, I, p. 44. Unless otherwise stated, references to Hegel's writings will be given
according to volume and page of the jubilee edition of his *Works* by Hermann
Glockner (26 vols., Stuttgart, 1928).

characteristics of different systems. At one time the mind is confronted, for instance, with the problem of the division and opposition between soul and body, while at another time the same sort of problem presents itself as that of the relation between subject and object, intelligence and Nature. But in whatever particular way or ways the problem may present itself, the fundamental interest of reason (*Vernunft*) is the same, namely to attain a unified synthesis.

This means in effect that 'the Absolute is to be constructed for consciousness; such is the task of philosophy'.[1] For the synthesis must in the long run involve reality as a whole. And it must overcome the basic opposition between the finite and the infinite, not by denying all reality to the finite, not by reducing the infinite to the multiplicity of finite particulars as such, but by integrating, as it were, the finite into the infinite.

But a difficulty at once arises. If the life of the Absolute is to be constructed by philosophy, the instrument will be reflection. Left to itself, however, reflection tends to function as understanding (*Verstand*) and thus to posit and perpetuate oppositions. It must therefore be united with transcendental intuition which discovers the interpenetration of the ideal and the real, idea and being, subject and object. Reflection is then raised to the level of reason (*Vernunft*), and we have a speculative knowledge which 'must be conceived as identity of reflection and intuition'.[2] Hegel is evidently writing under the influence of Schelling's ideas.

Now, in the Kantian system, as Hegel sees it, we are repeatedly confronted with unreconciled dualisms or oppositions, between phenomena and noumena, sensibility and understanding, and so on. Hegel shows therefore a lively sympathy with Fichte's attempt to remedy this state of affairs. He entirely agrees, for instance, with Fichte's elimination of the unknowable thing-in-itself, and regards his system as an important essay in genuine philosophizing. 'The absolute principle, the one real foundation and firm standpoint of philosophy is, in the philosophy of Fichte as in that of Schelling, intellectual intuition or, in the language of reflection, the identity of subject and object. In science this intuition becomes the object of reflection, and philosophical reflection is thus itself transcendental intuition which makes itself its own object and is one with it. Hence it is speculation. Fichte's philosophy, therefore, is a genuine product of speculation.'[3]

---

[1] *W*, I, p. 50.   [2] *W*, I, p. 69.   [3] *W*, I, pp. 143–4.

But though Fichte sees that the presupposition of speculative philosophy is an ultimate unity and starts with the principle of identity, 'the principle of identity is not the principle of the system: directly the construction of the system begins, identity disappears'.[1] In the theoretical deduction of consciousness it is only the idea of the objective world which is deduced, not the world itself. We are left simply with subjectivity. In the practical deduction we are indeed presented with a real world, but Nature is posited only as the opposite of the ego. In other words, we are left with an unresolved dualism.

With Schelling, however, the situation is very different. For 'the principle of identity is the absolute principle of the *whole* system of Schelling. Philosophy and system coincide: identity is not lost in the parts, and much less in the result.'[2] That is to say, Schelling starts with the idea of the Absolute as the identity of subjectivity and objectivity, and it persists as the guiding-idea of the parts of the system. In the philosophy of Nature Schelling shows that Nature is not simply the opposite of the ideal but that, though real, it is also ideal through and through: it is visible Spirit. In the system of transcendental idealism he shows how subjectivity objectifies itself, how the ideal is also the real. The principle of identity is thus maintained throughout the whole system.

In his works on the systems of Fichte and Schelling there are indeed signs of Hegel's divergence from Schelling. For instance, it is clear that intellectual intuition does not mean for him a mystical intuition of a dark and impenetrable abyss, the vanishing-point of all differences, but rather reason's insight into antitheses as moments in the one all-comprehensive life of the Absolute. But as the work is designed to illustrate the superiority of Schelling's system to that of Fichte, Hegel naturally does not make explicit his points of divergence from the former's thought. The independence of his own standpoint is, however, clearly revealed in the lectures of his Jena period.

In the Jena lectures Hegel argues, for example, that if finite and infinite are set over against one another as opposed concepts, there is no passage from one to the other. A synthesis is impossible. But in point of fact we cannot think the finite without thinking the infinite: the concept of the finite is not a self-contained and isolated concept. The finite is limited by what is other than itself. In Hegel's language, it is affected by negation. But the finite is not

---

[1] *W*, I, p. 122.   [2] *Ibid.*

simply negation. Hence we must negate the negation. And in doing so we affirm that the finite is more than finite. That is to say, it is a moment in the life of the infinite. And from this it follows that to construct the life of the Absolute, which is the task of philosophy, is to construct it in and through the finite, showing how the Absolute necessarily expresses itself as Spirit, as self-consciousness, in and through the human mind. For the human mind, though finite, is at the same time more than finite and can attain the standpoint at which it is the vehicle, as it were, of the Absolute's knowledge of itself.

To a certain extent, of course, this is in harmony with Schelling's philosophy. But there is also a major difference. For Schelling the Absolute in itself transcends conceptual thought, and we must approach the absolute identity by the *via negativa*, thinking away the attributes and distinctions of the finite.[1] For Hegel the Absolute is not an identity about which nothing further can be said: it is the total process of its self-expression or self-manifestation in and through the finite. It is not surprising, therefore, to find in the Preface to *The Phenomenology of Spirit* a sharp rejection of Schelling's view of the Absolute. True, Schelling is not mentioned by name, but the reference is clear enough. It was clear to Schelling himself, who felt deeply wounded. Hegel speaks of a monotonous formalism and abstract universality which are said to constitute the Absolute. All the emphasis is placed on the universal in the bare form of identity. 'And we see speculative contemplation identified with the dissolution of the distinct and determinate, or rather with hurling it down, without more ado and without justification, into the abyss of vacuity.'[2] To consider a thing as in the Absolute is taken to mean considering it as dissolved in an undifferentiated self-identical unity. But 'to pit this one piece of knowledge, namely that in the Absolute all is one, against determinate and complete knowledge or knowledge which at least seeks and demands completion—to proclaim the *Absolute* as the night in which, as we say, all cows are black—this is the naïvety of empty knowledge'.[3] It is not by plunging ourselves into a mystical

---

[1] Needless to say, the reference is to Schelling's philosophical ideas in the first years of the nineteenth century.

[2] *W*, II, p. 21; *B*, p. 79. In references, as here, to *The Phenomenology of Spirit* *B* signifies the English translation of this work by J. B. Baillie. But it does not necessarily follow that the present writer has followed this translation. The like holds good of other such references to standard English translations, which are included for the convenience of readers.

[3] *W*, II, p. 22; *B*, p. 79.

night that we can come to know the Absolute. We come to know it only by understanding a determinate content, the self-developing life of the Absolute in Nature and Spirit. True, in his philosophy of Nature and in his system of transcendental idealism Schelling considered determinate contents, and in regard to these contents he attempted a systematic demonstration of the identity of the ideal and the real. But he conceived the Absolute in itself as being, for conceptual thought at least, a blank identity, a vanishing-point of all differences, whereas for Hegel the Absolute is not an impenetrable reality existing, as it were, above and behind its determinate manifestations: it *is* its self-manifestation.

4. This point is of great importance for understanding Hegel. The subject-matter of philosophy is indeed the Absolute. But the Absolute is the Totality, reality as a whole, the universe. 'Philosophy is concerned with the true and the true is the whole.'[1] Further, this totality or whole is infinite life, a process of self-development. The Absolute is 'the process of its own becoming, the circle which presupposes its end as its purpose and has its end as its beginning. It becomes concrete or actual only by its development and through its end.'[2] In other words, reality is a teleological process; and the ideal term presupposes the whole process and gives to it its significance. Indeed we can say that the Absolute is 'essentially a result'.[3] For if we look on the whole process as the self-unfolding of an essence, the actualization of an eternal Idea, we can see that it is the term or end of the process which reveals what the Absolute really is. True, the whole process is the Absolute; but in a teleological process it is the *telos* or end which shows its nature, its meaning. And philosophy must take the form of a systematic understanding of this teleological process. 'The true form in which truth exists can only be the scientific system of the same.'[4]

Now, if we say that the Absolute is the whole of reality, the Universe, it may seem that we are committed to Spinozism, to the statement that the Absolute is infinite Substance. But this is for Hegel a very inadequate description of the Absolute. 'In my view —a view which can be justified only through the exposition of the system itself—everything depends on grasping the true not merely as *Substance* but as *Subject* as well.'[5] But if the Absolute is subject, what is its object? The only possible answer is that its object is itself. In this case it is Thought which thinks itself, self-thinking

[1] *W*, II, p. 24; *B*, p. 81.   [2] *W*, II, p. 23; *B*, p. 81.
[3] *W*, II, p. 24; *B*, p. 81.   [4] *W*, II, p. 14; *B*, p. 70.
[5] *W*, II, p. 22; *B*, p. 80.

Thought. And to say this is to say that the Absolute is Spirit, the infinite self-luminous or self-conscious subject. The statement that the Absolute is Spirit is for Hegel its supreme definition.

In saying that the Absolute is self-thinking Thought Hegel is obviously repeating Aristotle's definition of God, a fact of which he is, of course, well aware. But it would be a great mistake to assume that Hegel is thinking of a transcendent Deity. The Absolute is, as we have seen, the Totality, the whole of reality; and this totality is a process. In other words, the Absolute is a process of self-reflection: reality comes to know itself. And it does so in and through the human spirit. Nature is a necessary precondition of human consciousness in general: it provides the sphere of the objective without which the sphere of the subjective cannot exist. But both are moments in the life of the Absolute. In Nature the Absolute goes over into, as it were, or expresses itself in objectivity. There is no question with Hegel of Nature being unreal or merely idea in a subjectivist sense. In the sphere of human consciousness the Absolute returns to itself, that is, as Spirit. And the philosophical reflection of humanity is the Absolute's self-knowledge. That is to say, the history of philosophy is the process by which the Absolute, reality as a whole, comes to think itself. Philosophical reason comes to see the whole history of the cosmos and the whole history of man as the self-unfolding of the Absolute. And this insight is the Absolute's knowledge of itself.

One can put the matter in this way. Hegel agrees with Aristotle that God is self-thinking Thought,[1] and that this self-thinking Thought is the *telos* or end which draws the world as its final cause. But whereas the self-thinking Thought of Aristotle is, so to speak, an already constituted self-consciousness which does not depend on the world, the self-thinking Thought of Hegel is not a transcendent reality but rather the universe's knowledge of itself. The whole process of reality is a teleological movement towards the actualization of self-thinking Thought; and in this sense the Thought which thinks itself is the *telos* or end of the universe. But it is an end which is immanent within the process. The Absolute, the universe or totality, is indeed definable as self-thinking Thought. But it is Thought which comes to think itself. And in this sense we can say, as Hegel says, that the Absolute is essentially a result.

To say, therefore, that the Absolute is self-thinking Thought is

---

[1] Hegel frequently speaks of the Absolute as 'God'. But it does not necessarily follow from his use of religious language that he looks on the Absolute as a personal Deity in the theistic sense. This question will be discussed later.

to affirm the identity of the ideal and the real, of subjectivity and objectivity. But this is an identity-in-difference, not a blank undifferentiated identity. Spirit sees itself in Nature: it sees Nature as the objective manifestation of the Absolute, a manifestation which is a necessary condition for its own existence. In other words, the Absolute knows itself as the Totality, as the whole process of its becoming; but at the same time it sees the distinctions between the phases of its own life. It knows itself as an identity-in-difference, as the unity which comprises distinguishable phases within itself.

As we have seen, the task of philosophy is to construct the life of the Absolute. That is to say, it must exhibit systematically the rational dynamic structure, the teleological process or movement of the cosmic Reason, in Nature and the sphere of the human spirit, which culminates in the Absolute's knowledge of itself. It is not, of course, a question of philosophy trying to do over again, or to do better, the work accomplished by empirical science or by history. Such knowledge is presupposed. Rather is it philosophy's task to make clear the basic teleological process which is immanent in the material known in other ways, the process which gives to this material its metaphysical significance. In other words, philosophy has to exhibit systematically the self-realization of infinite Reason in and through the finite.

Now if, as Hegel believes, the rational is the real and the real the rational, in the sense that reality is the necessary process by which infinite Reason, the self-thinking Thought, actualizes itself, we can say that Nature and the sphere of the human spirit are the field in which an eternal Idea or an eternal essence manifests itself. That is to say, we can make a distinction between the Idea or essence which is actualized and the field of its actualization. We then have the picture of the eternal Idea or *Logos* manifesting itself in Nature and in Spirit. In Nature the *Logos* goes over, as it were, into objectivity, into the material world, which is its antithesis. In Spirit (the sphere of the human spirit) the *Logos* returns to itself, in the sense that it manifests itself as what it essentially is. The life of the Absolute thus comprises three main phases: the logical Idea or Concept or Notion,[1] Nature and Spirit. And the system of philosophy will fall into three main parts: logic,

---

[1] The word 'Idea' can have different shades of meaning with Hegel. It may refer to the logical Idea, otherwise called the Concept (*Begriff*) or Notion. It may refer to the whole process of reality, as the actualization of the Idea. Or it may refer primarily to the term of the process.

which for Hegel is metaphysics in the sense that it studies the nature of the Absolute 'in itself', the philosophy of Nature and the philosophy of Spirit. These three parts together form the philosophical construction of the life of the Absolute.

Obviously, if we talk about the eternal Idea 'manifesting itself' in Nature and Spirit, we imply that the *Logos* possesses an ontological status of its own, independently of things. And when Hegel uses, as he so frequently does, the language of religion and speaks of the logical Idea as God-in-himself, he inevitably tends to give the impression that the *Logos* is for him a transcendent reality which manifests itself externally in Nature. But such use of religious language does not necessarily justify this conclusion about his meaning. However, I do not wish to discuss this disputed problem here. For the moment we can leave undecided the question whether or not the self-thinking Thought which forms the culminating category of Hegel's logic can properly be said to exist, that is, independently of the finite. It is sufficient to have noticed the three main parts of philosophy, each of which is concerned with the Absolute. Logic studies the Absolute 'in itself'; the philosophy of Nature studies the Absolute 'for itself'; and the philosophy of Spirit studies the Absolute 'in and for itself'. Together they constitute the complete construction of the life of the Absolute.

Philosophy must, of course, exhibit this life in conceptual form. There is no other form in which it can present it. And if the life of the Absolute is a necessary process of self-actualization, this necessity must be reflected in the philosophical system. That is to say, it must be shown that concept *A* gives rise to concept *B*. And if the Absolute is the Totality, philosophy must be a self-contained system, exhibiting the fact that the Absolute is both Alpha and Omega. A truly adequate philosophy would be the total system of truth, the whole truth, the perfect conceptual reflection of the life of the Absolute. It would in fact be the Absolute's knowledge of itself in and through the human mind; it would be the self-mediation of the Totality. Hence, on Hegelian principles, there would be no question of comparing the absolute philosophy with the Absolute, as though the former were a purely external account of the latter, so that we had to compare them to see whether the philosophy fitted the reality which it described. For the absolute philosophy would *be* the Absolute's knowledge of itself.

But if we say that philosophy must exhibit the life of the Absolute

in conceptual form, a difficulty at once arises. The Absolute is, as
we have seen, identity-in-difference. For instance, it is the
identity-in-difference of the infinite and the finite, of the One and
the Many. But the concepts of infinite and finite, as of the One
and the Many, seem to be mutually exclusive. If, therefore,
philosophy operates with clearly-defined concepts, how can it
possibly construct the life of the Absolute? And if it operates with
vague, ill-defined concepts, how can it be an apt instrument for
understanding anything? Would it not be better to say with
Schelling that the Absolute transcends conceptual thought?

In Hegel's view this difficulty does indeed arise on the level of
understanding (*Verstand*). For understanding posits and perpetu-
ates fixed static concepts of such a kind that it cannot itself
overcome the oppositions which it posits. To take the same example
which has already been given, for understanding the concepts of
the finite and the infinite are irrevocably opposed. If finite, then
not infinite: if infinite, then not finite. But the conclusion to be
drawn is that understanding is an inadequate instrument for the
development of speculative philosophy, not that philosophy is
impossible. Obviously, if the term 'understanding' is taken in a
wide sense, philosophy is understanding. But if the term is taken
in the narrow sense of *Verstand*, the mind, functioning in this way,
is unable to produce the understanding (in the wide sense) which
is, or ought to be, characteristic of philosophy.

Hegel has, of course, no intention of denying that understanding,
in the sense of the mind operating as *Verstand*, has its uses in
human life. For practical purposes it is often important to maintain
clear-cut concepts and oppositions. The opposition between the
real and the apparent might be a case in point. Moreover, a great
deal of scientific work, such as mathematics, is based on *Verstand*.
But it is a different matter when the mind is trying to grasp the
life of the Absolute, the identity-in-difference. It cannot then
remain content with the level of understanding, which for Hegel is
a superficial level. It must penetrate deeper into the concepts
which are categories of reality, and it will then see how a given
concept tends to pass over into or to call forth its opposite. For
example, if the mind really thinks through, so to speak, the concept
of the infinite, it sees it losing its rigid self-containedness and the
concept of the infinite emerging. Similarly, if the mind really
thinks through the concept of reality as opposed to appearance, it
will see the absurd or 'contradictory' character of a reality which

in no way at all appears or manifests itself. Again, for common sense and practical life one thing is distinct from all other things; it is self-identical and negates all other things. And so long as we are not concerned with thinking what this really means, the idea has its practical uses. But once we really try to think it, we see the absurdity of the notion of a completely isolated thing, and we are forced to negate the original negation.

Thus in speculative philosophy the mind must elevate itself from the level of understanding in the narrow sense to the level of dialectical thinking which overcomes the rigidity of the concepts of the understanding and sees one concept as generating or passing into its opposite. Only so can it hope to grasp the life of the Absolute in which one moment or phase passes necessarily into another. But this is obviously not enough. If for the understanding concepts *A* and *B* are irrevocably opposed whereas for the deeper penetration of dialectical thought *A* passes into *B* and *B* into *A*, there must be a higher unity or synthesis which unites them without annulling their difference. And it is the function of reason (*Vernunft*) to grasp this moment of identity-in-difference. Hence philosophy demands the elevation of understanding through dialectical thinking to the level of reason or speculative thought which is capable of apprehending identity-in-difference.[1]

It is perhaps unnecessary to add that from Hegel's point of view it is not a question of producing a new species of logic out of the hat to enable him to establish an arbitrarily preconceived view of reality. For he sincerely believes that dialectical thought gives a deeper penetration of the nature of reality than understanding in the narrow sense can possibly do. For example, it is not for Hegel a question of insisting that the concept of the finite must pass over into or call forth the concept of the infinite simply because of a preconceived belief that the infinite exists in and through the finite. For it is his conviction that we cannot really think the finite without relating it to the infinite. It is not we who do something to the concept, juggling about with it, as it were: it is the concept itself which loses its rigidity and breaks up before the mind's attentive gaze. And this fact reveals to us the nature of the finite: it has a metaphysical significance.

---

[1] The terms 'understanding' and 'reason' are not used in precisely the same ways by Kant and Hegel. This fact apart, however, the contrast between Kant's mistrust of the flights of reason, coupled with his admission of its practical function, and Hegel's depreciation of understanding, coupled with a recognition of its practical use, well illustrates their respective attitudes to speculative metaphysics.

In his account of dialectical thinking Hegel makes a rather disconcerting use of the word 'contradiction'. Through what he calls the power of the negative a concept of the understanding is said to give rise to a contradiction. That is to say, the contradiction implicit in the concept becomes explicit when the concept loses its rigidity and self-containedness and passes into its opposite. Further, Hegel does not hesitate to speak as though contradictions are present not only in conceptual thought or discourse about the world but in things themselves. And indeed this must be so in some sense if the dialectic mirrors the life of the Absolute. Moreover, this insistence on the role of contradiction is not simply incidental to Hegel's thought. For the emergence of contradiction is the motive force, as it were, of the dialectical movement. The conflict of opposed concepts and the resolution of the conflict in a synthesis which itself gives rise to another contradiction is the feature which drives the mind restlessly onwards towards an ideal term, an all-embracing synthesis, the complete system of truth. And, as we have noted, this does not mean that contradiction and conflict are confined to discourse about reality. When philosophy considers, for example, the history of man, it discovers a dialectical movement at work.

This use of the word 'contradiction' has led some critics of Hegel to accuse him of denying the logical principle of non-contradiction by saying that contradictory notions or propositions can stand together. And in refutation of this charge it has often been pointed out that for Hegel it is precisely the impossibility of being satisfied with a sheer contradiction which forces the mind onwards to a synthesis in which the contradiction is overcome. This answer, however, lays itself open to the retort that Hegel does not share Fichte's tendency to argue that the contradictions or antinomies which arise in the course of dialectical thinking are merely apparent. On the contrary, he insists on their reality. And in the syntheses the so-called contradictory concepts are preserved. In turn, however, it can be replied that though the concepts are preserved, they are not preserved in a relation of mutual exclusiveness. For they are shown to be essential and complementary moments in a higher unity. And in this sense the contradiction is resolved. Hence the simple assertion that Hegel denies the principle of non-contradiction gives a quite inaccurate view of the situation. What Hegel does is to give a dynamic interpretation of the principle in place of the static interpretation which is characteristic of the level of understanding. The principle operates in dialectical thinking, but it operates as a principle of movement.

This discussion might be prolonged. But it would be pointless to do so without first inquiring in what sense Hegel actually understands the term 'contradiction' when he is engaged in working out his dialectical philosophy rather than in talking abstractly about dialectical thought. And it is a notorious fact that the result of such an inquiry is to show that there is no single precise and invariable sense in which Hegel uses the term. Occasionally indeed we find a verbal contradiction. Thus the concept of Being is said to give rise to and pass into the concept of Not-being, while the concept of Not-being passes into the concept of Being. And this dialectical oscillation gives rise to the concept of Becoming which synthesizes Being and Not-being. But, as will be seen in the section on Hegel's logic in the next chapter, the meaning of this dialectical performance is easily intelligible, whether we agree or not with what Hegel has to say. In any case Hegel's so-called contradictions are much more often contraries than contradictions. And the idea is that one contrary demands the other, an idea which, whether true or false, does not amount to a denial of the principle of non-contradiction. Again, the so-called contradictory or opposed concepts may be simply complementary concepts. A one-sided abstraction evokes another one-sided abstraction. And the one-sidedness of each is overcome in the synthesis. Further, the statement that every thing is contradictory sometimes bears the meaning that a thing in a state of complete isolation, apart from its essential relations, would be impossible and 'contradictory'. Reason cannot remain in the idea of a completely isolated finite thing. Here again there is no question of denying the principle of non-contradiction.

We have used the word 'synthesis' for the moment of identity-in-difference in the dialectical advance. But in point of fact the terms 'thesis', 'antithesis' and 'synthesis' are more characteristic of Fichte than of Hegel, who seldom uses them. At the same time the most cursory inspection of the Hegelian system reveals his preoccupation with triads. Thus there are three main phases in the construction of the life of the Absolute: the logical Idea, Nature and Spirit. And each phase is divided and subdivided into triads. Moreover, the whole system is, or aims at, a necessary development. That is to say, for philosophical reflection one stage reveals itself as demanding the next by an inner necessity. Thus, in theory at least, if we start with the first category of the *Logic*, the inner necessity of dialectical development forces the mind to proceed not simply to the final category of the *Logic* but also to the ultimate phase of the philosophy of Spirit.

As for Hegel's preoccupation with triadic development, we may think that it is unnecessary and that it sometimes produces highly artificial results, but we obviously have to accept it as a fact. But though it is a fact that he develops his system according to this pattern, it obviously does not follow that the development always possesses the character of necessity which Hegel implies that it ought to have. And if it does not, this is easily understandable. For when Hegel is concerned, for example, with the life of the Spirit in art or in religion, he is faced with a multitude of historical data which he takes over, as it were, from the relevant sources and which he then interprets according to a dialectical pattern. And it is clear that there might be various possible ways of grouping and interpreting the data, no one of which was strictly necessary. The discovery of the best way will be a matter of reflection and insight rather than of strict deduction. To say this is not necessarily to condemn Hegel's practice. For in point of fact his interpretations of vast masses of data can sometimes be illuminating and are often stimulating even when we do not agree with them. At the same time the transitions between the stages of his dialectic are by no means always of the logical type suggested by his claim that philosophy is a necessary deductive system, even if the persistent observance of the same external pattern, namely the triadic arrangement, tends to obscure the underlying complexity.

Of course, when Hegel claims that philosophy is or ought to be a necessary deductive system, he does not really mean that it is the sort of deductive system which could be worked out by a machine. If it were, then it would belong to the sphere of understanding rather than to that of reason. Philosophy is concerned with the life of absolute Spirit, and to discern the unfolding of this life in, say, human history, *a priori* deduction is obviously not enough. The empirical material cannot be supplied by philosophy, though philosophy discerns the teleological pattern which works itself out in this material. At the same time the whole dialectical movement of the Hegelian system should, in theory at least, impose itself on the mind by its own inner necessity. Otherwise the system could hardly be, as Hegel claims that it is, its own justification. Yet it is clear that Hegel comes to philosophy with certain basic convictions; that the rational is the real and the real the rational, that reality is the self-manifestation of infinite reason, and that infinite reason is self-thinking Thought which actualizes itself in the historical process. True, it is Hegel's contention that the truth of these convictions is demonstrated in the system. But it is arguable that the system really depends upon them, and that this is one of the main reasons why those who do not share, or at least are not sympathetically disposed towards, Hegel's initial convictions are not much impressed by what we may call his empirical confirmation of his general metaphysical scheme. For it seems to them that his interpretations of the material are governed by a preconceived scheme, and that even if the system is a remarkable intellectual *tour de force*, it demonstrates at best only on what lines we must interpret the various aspects of reality if we have already made up our minds that reality as a whole is of a certain nature. This criticism would indeed be invalidated if the system really showed that Hegel's interpretation of the process of reality was the only interpretation which satisfied the demands of reason. But it may well be doubted whether this can be shown without giving to the word 'reason' a meaning which would beg the whole question.

One might perhaps neglect or pass over Hegel's theory of the necessity inherent in the dialectical development of the system and view his philosophy simply as one of the possible ways of satisfying the mind's impulse to obtain conceptual mastery over the whole wealth of empirical data or to interpret the world as a whole and man's relation to it. And we could then compare it with other large-scale interpretations or visions of the universe and try to find criteria for judging between them. But though this procedure may seem eminently reasonable to many people, it does not square with Hegel's own estimation of his own philosophy. For even if he did not think that his presentation of the system of philosophy was the whole truth in its final form, he certainly thought that it represented the highest stage which the Absolute's developing knowledge of itself had reached up to date.

This may seem to be an extremely bizarre notion. But we have to bear in mind Hegel's view of the Absolute as identity-in-difference. The infinite exists in and through the finite, and infinite Reason or Spirit knows itself in and through the finite spirit or mind. But it is not every sort of thinking by the finite mind which can be said to form a moment in the developing self-knowledge of the infinite Absolute. It is man's knowledge of the Absolute which is the Absolute's knowledge of itself. Yet we cannot say of any finite mind's knowledge of the Absolute that it is identical with the Absolute's knowledge of itself. For the latter transcends any given finite mind or set of finite minds. Plato and Aristotle, for example, are dead. But according to Hegel's interpretation of the history of philosophy the essential elements in their respective apprehensions of reality were taken up into and persist in the total dialectical movement of philosophy through the centuries. And it is this developing movement which is the Absolute's developing knowledge of itself. It does not exist apart from all finite minds, but it is obviously not confined to any given mind or set of minds.[1]

5. We can speak, therefore, of the human mind rising to a participation in the self-knowledge of the Absolute. Some writers have interpreted Hegel on more or less theistic lines. That is to say, they have understood him to mean that God is perfectly luminous to himself quite independently of man, though man is capable of participating in this self-knowledge. But I have interpreted him here as meaning that man's knowledge of the Absolute and the Absolute's knowledge of itself are two aspects of the same reality. Even, however, on this interpretation we can still speak of the finite mind rising to a participation in the divine self-knowledge. For, as we have seen, it is not every sort of idea and thought in man's mind which can be regarded as a moment in the Absolute's self-knowledge. It is not every level of consciousness which is a participation in the divine self-consciousness. To achieve this participation the finite mind has to rise to the level of what Hegel calls absolute knowledge.

In this case it is possible to trace the successive stages of consciousness from the lowest to the highest levels. And this is what Hegel does in *The Phenomenology of Spirit*, which can be described as a history of consciousness. If we consider the mind and its activity in themselves, without relation to an object, we are concerned with psychology. If, however, we consider mind as essentially related to an object, external or internal, we are concerned with consciousness. And phenomenology is the science of consciousness in this sense. Hegel begins with the natural unscientific consciousness and proceeds to trace the dialectical development of this consciousness, showing how the lower levels

[1] I do not mean to imply that for Hegel philosophy is the only way of apprehending the Absolute. There are also art and religion. But in the present context we are concerned only with philosophy.

are subsumed in the higher according to a more adequate point of view, until we reach the level of absolute knowledge.

In a certain sense *The Phenomenology* can be regarded as an introduction to philosophy. That is to say, it systematically traces the development of consciousness up to the level of what we might call the properly philosophical consciousness. But it is certainly not an introduction to philosophy in the sense of being an external preparation for philosophizing. Hegel did not believe that an introduction in this sense was possible. And in any case the work is itself an outstanding example of sustained philosophical reflection. It is, we may say, the philosophical consciousness reflecting on the phenomenology of its own genesis. Moreover, even if the work is in some sense an introduction to the point of view required by the Hegelian system, there is an overlapping. The system itself finds a place for the phenomenology of consciousness, and *The Phenomenology* contains an outline of a certain amount of material which is later treated by Hegel at greater length. The religious consciousness is a case in point. Lastly, by no stretch of the imagination can *The Phenomenology* be described as an introduction to philosophy in the sense of a work of philosophy-without-tears. On the contrary, it is a profound work and often extremely difficult to understand.

The Phenomenology falls into three main parts, corresponding with the three main phases of consciousness. The first of these phases is consciousness of the object as a sensible thing standing over against the subject. And it is to this phase that Hegel appropriates the name 'consciousness' (*Bewusstsein*). The second phase is that of self-consciousness (*Selbstbewusstsein*). And here Hegel has a lot to say about social consciousness. The third phase is that of Reason (*Vernunft*), which is represented as the synthesis or unity of the preceding phases on a higher level. In other words, Reason is the synthesis of objectivity and subjectivity. Needless to say, each of these main divisions of the work has its subdivisions. And Hegel's general procedure is first to describe the spontaneous attitude of consciousness at a given level and then to institute an analysis of it. The result of the analysis is that the mind is compelled to proceed to the next level, considered as a more adequate attitude or point of view.

Hegel begins with what he calls sense-certainty, the uncritical apprehension by the senses of particular objects, which to the naïve consciousness appears to be not only the most certain and basic form of knowledge but also the richest. Analysis, he argues, shows that it is in fact a peculiarly empty and abstract form of knowledge. The naïve consciousness feels certain that it is directly acquainted through sense-apprehension with a particular thing. But when we try to say what it is that we know, that is, to describe the particular object with which we claim to be immediately acquainted, we find that we can describe it only in universal terms which are applicable to other things as well. We can, of course, attempt to pin the object down, as it were, by using words such as 'this', 'here', and 'now', accompanying them perhaps with an ostensive gesture. But a moment later the same words apply to another object. Indeed, it is impossible, Hegel argues, to give even to words like 'this' a genuinely particular significance, however much we may wish and try to do so.

We might wish to say that Hegel is simply calling attention to a feature of language. And he is, of course, perfectly well aware that he is saying something about language. But his main concern is epistemological. He wishes to show that the claim of 'sense-certainty' to be knowledge *par excellence* is a bogus claim. And he draws the conclusion that this level of consciousness, on the path towards becoming genuine knowledge, must pass into the level of perception for which the object is a thing conceived as the centre of distinct properties and qualities. But analysis of this level of consciousness shows that it is not possible, as long as we remain simply on the level of sense, to reconcile in any satisfactory manner the elements of unity and multiplicity which are postulated by this view of the object. And the mind passes, therefore, by various stages to the level of scientific understanding which invokes metaphenomenal or unobservable entities to explain sense-phenomena.

For instance, the mind sees sense-phenomena as the manifestations of hidden forces. But, Hegel maintains, the mind cannot rest here and proceeds instead to the idea of laws. Yet natural laws are ways of ordering and describing phenomena; they are not explicative. Hence they cannot perform the function for which they have been invoked, namely to explain sense-phenomena. Hegel obviously does not mean to deny that the concept of natural laws has a useful function to perform at the appropriate level. But it does not give the sort of knowledge which, in his opinion, the mind is seeking.

In the end the mind sees that the whole realm of the metaphenomenal which has been invoked to explain sense-phenomena is the product of the understanding itself. Consciousness is thus turned back on itself as the reality behind the veil of phenomena and becomes self-consciousness.

Hegel begins with self-consciousness in the form of desire (*Begierde*). The self is still concerned with the external object, but it is characteristic of the attitude of desire that the self subordinates the object to itself, seeking to make it minister to its satisfaction, to appropriate it, even to consume it. And this attitude can be shown, of course, in regard to living and non-living things. But when the self is confronted with another self, this attitude breaks down. For the presence of the Other is for Hegel essential to self-consciousness. Developed self-consciousness can arise only when the self recognizes selfhood in itself and others. It must take the form, therefore, of a truly social or we-consciousness, the recognition at the level of self-consciousness of identity-in-difference. But in the dialectical evolution of this phase of consciousness developed self-consciousness is not attained immediately. And Hegel's study of the successive stages forms one of the most interesting and influential parts of *The Phenomenology*.

The existence of another self is, we have mentioned, a condition of self-consciousness. But the first spontaneous reaction of a self confronted with another self is to assert its own existence as a self in face of the other. The one self desires to cancel out or annihilate the other self as a means to the triumphant assertion of its own selfhood. But a literal destruction would defeat its own purpose. For consciousness of one's own selfhood demands as a condition the recognition of this selfhood by another self. There thus arises the master-slave relationship. The master is the one who succeeds in obtaining recognition from the other, in the sense that he imposes himself as the other's value. The slave is the one who sees his own true self in the other.

Paradoxically, however, the original situation changes. And it must do so because of the contradictions concealed in it. On the one hand, by not recognizing the slave as a real person the master deprives himself of that recognition of his own freedom which he originally demanded and which is required for the development of self-consciousness. He thus debases himself to an infra-human condition. On the other hand, by carrying out his master's will the slave objectifies himself through labour which transforms material things. He thus forms himself and rises to the level of true existence.[1]

It is obvious that the concept of the master-slave relationship has two aspects. It can be considered as a stage in the abstract dialectical development of consciousness. And it can also be considered in relation to history. But the two aspects are by no means incompatible. For human history itself reveals the development of Spirit, the travail of the Spirit on the way to its goal. Hence we need not be surprised if from the master-slave relationship in its primary form Hegel passes to an attitude or state of consciousness to which he gives a name with explicit historical associations, namely the Stoic consciousness.

In the Stoic consciousness the contradictions inherent in the slave relationship are not really overcome: they are overcome only to the extent that both master (typified by Marcus Aurelius) and slave (typified by Epictetus) take flight into interiority and exalt the idea of true interior freedom, internal self-sufficiency, leaving concrete relationships unchanged. Hence, according to Hegel, this negative attitude towards the concrete and external passes easily into the Sceptical consciousness for which the self alone abides while all else is subjected to doubt and negation.

But the Sceptical consciousness contains an implicit contradiction. For it is impossible for the sceptic to eliminate the natural consciousness; and affirmation and negation coexist in the same attitude. And when this contradiction becomes explicit, as it must do, we pass to what Hegel calls 'the unhappy consciousness' (*das unglückliche Bewusstsein*), which is a divided consciousness. At this level the master-slave relationship, which has not been successfully overcome by either the Stoic or the Sceptical consciousness, returns in another form. In the master-slave relationship proper the elements of true self-consciousness, recognition of selfhood and freedom both in oneself and in the Other, were divided between two individual consciousnesses. The master recognized selfhood and freedom only in himself, not in the slave, while the slave recognized them only in the master, not in himself. In the so-called unhappy consciousness, however, the division occurs in the same self. For example, the self is conscious of a gulf between a changing, inconsistent, fickle self and a changeless, ideal self. The first appears as in some sense a false self, something

[1] For obvious reasons Hegel's profound analysis of the master-slave relationship contained lines of reflection which found favour with Karl Marx.

to be denied, while the second appears as the true self which is not yet attained. And this ideal self can be projected into an other-worldly sphere and identified with absolute perfection, God considered as existing apart from the world and the finite self.[1] The human consciousness is then divided, self-alienated, 'unhappy'.

The contradictions or divisions implicit in self-consciousness are overcome in the third phase of *The Phenomenology* when the finite subject rises to universal self-consciousness. At this level self-consciousness no longer takes the form of the one-sided awareness of oneself as an individual subject threatened by and in conflict with other self-conscious beings. Rather is there a full recognition of selfhood in oneself and in others; and this recognition is at least an implicit awareness of the life of the universal, the infinite Spirit, in and through finite selves, binding them together yet not annulling them. Present implicitly and imperfectly in the developed moral consciousness, for which the one rational will expresses itself in a multiplicity of concrete moral vocations in the social order, this awareness of the identity-in-difference which is characteristic of the life of the Spirit attains a higher and more explicit expression in the developed religious consciousness, for which the one divine life is immanent in all selves, bearing them in itself while yet maintaining their distinctness. In the idea of a living union with God the division within the unhappy or divided consciousness is overcome. The true self is no longer conceived as an ideal from which the actual self is hopelessly alienated, but rather as the living core, so to speak, of the actual self, which expresses itself in and through its finite manifestations.

This third phase of the phenomenological history of conscious-ness, to which, as we have seen, Hegel gives the general name of Reason, is represented as the synthesis of consciousness and self-consciousness, that is, of the first two phases. In consciousness in the narrow sense (*Bewusstsein*) the subject is aware of the sensible object as something external and heterogeneous to itself. In self-consciousness (*Selbstbewusstsein*) the subject's attention is turned back on itself as a finite self. At the level of Reason it sees Nature as the objective expression of infinite Spirit with which it is itself united. But this awareness can take different forms. In the developed religious consciousness the subject sees Nature as the creation and self-manifestation of God, with whom it is united in

[1] Hegel, the Lutheran, tended to associate the unhappy or divided conscious-ness, in a somewhat polemical way, with mediaeval Catholicism, especially with its ascetic ideals.

the depth of its being and through whom it is united with other selves. And this religious vision of reality is true. But at the level of the religious consciousness truth finds expression in the form of figurative or pictorial thought (*Vorstellung*), whereas at the supreme level of 'absolute knowledge' (*das absolute Wissen*) the same truth is reflectively apprehended in philosophical form. The finite subject is explicitly aware of its inmost self as a moment in the life of the infinite and universal Spirit, as a moment in absolute Thought. And, as such, it sees Nature as its own objectification and as the precondition of its own life as actually existing Spirit. This does not mean, of course, that the finite subject considered precisely as such sees Nature as its own product. Rather does it mean that the finite subject, aware of itself as more than finite, as a moment in the innermost life of absolute Spirit, sees Nature as a necessary stage in the onward march of Spirit in its process of self-actualization. In other words, absolute knowledge is the level at which the finite subject participates in the life of self-thinking Thought, the Absolute. Or, to put the matter in another way, it is the level at which the Absolute, the Totality, thinks itself as identity-in-difference in and through the finite mind of the philosopher.

As in the previous main phases of the phenomenology of consciousness Hegel develops the third phase, that of Reason, through a series of dialectical stages. He treats first of observing Reason which is seen as obtaining some glimpse at any rate of its own reflection in Nature (through the idea of finality, for example), then as turning inwards in the study of formal logic and of empirical psychology, and finally as manifesting itself in a series of practical ethical attitudes, ranging from the pursuit of happiness up to that criticism of the universal moral laws dictated by the practical reason which follows from recognition of the fact that a universal law stands in need of so many qualifications that it tends to lose all definite meaning. This sets the stage for the transition to concrete moral life in society. Here Hegel moves from the unreflective ethical life in which human beings simply follow the customs and traditions of their community to the form of culture in which individuals are estranged from this unreflective background and pass judgments about it. The two moments are synthesized in the developed moral consciousness for which the rational general will is not something over and above individuals in society but a common life binding them together as free persons.

In the first moment, we can say, Spirit is unreflective, as in the ancient Greek morality before the time of the so-called Sophists. In the second moment Spirit is reflective but at the same time estranged from actual society and its traditions, on which it passes judgment. In the extreme case, as in the Jacobin Terror, it annihilates actual persons in the name of abstract freedom. In the third moment, however, Spirit is said to be ethically sure of itself. It takes the form of a community of free persons embodying the general will as a living unity.

This living unity, however, in which each member of the community is for the others a free self demands an explicit recognition of the idea of identity-in-difference, of a life which is present in all as their inner bond of unity though it does not annihilate them as individuals. It demands, that is to say, an explicit recognition of the idea of the concrete universal which differentiates itself into or manifests itself in its particulars while uniting them within itself. In other words, morality passes dialectically into religion, the moral into the religious consciousness, for which this living unity is explicitly recognized in the form of God.

In religion, therefore, we see absolute Spirit becoming explicitly conscious of itself. But religion, of course, has its history; and in this history we see earlier phases of the dialectic being repeated. Thus Hegel moves from what he calls 'natural religion', in which the divine is seen under the form of perceptual objects or of Nature, to the religion of art or of beauty, in which, as in Greek religion, the divine is seen as the self-conscious associated with the physical. The statue, for example, represents the anthropomorphic deity. Finally, in the absolute religion, Christianity, absolute Spirit is recognized for what it is, namely Spirit; Nature is seen as a divine creation, the expression of the Word; and the Holy Spirit is seen as immanent in and uniting together finite selves.

But the religious consciousness expresses itself, as we have seen, in pictorial forms. And it demands to be transmuted into the pure conceptual form of philosophy which at the same time expresses the transition from faith to knowledge or science. That is to say, the pictorial idea of the transcendent personal Deity who saves man by a unique Incarnation and the power of grace passes into the concept of absolute Spirit, the infinite self-thinking Thought which knows itself in Nature (as its objectification and as the condition for its own actualization) and recognizes in the history of

human culture, with its successive forms and levels, its own
Odyssey. Hegel is not saying that religion is untrue. On the
contrary, the absolute religion, Christianity, is the absolute truth.
But it is expressed in the imaginative or pictorial form which is
correlative to the religious consciousness. In philosophy this truth
becomes absolute knowledge which is 'Spirit knowing itself in the
form of Spirit.'[1] The Absolute, the Totality, comes to know itself
in and through the human spirit, in so far, that is to say, as the
human spirit rises above its finitude and identifies itself with pure
Thought. God cannot be equated with man. For God is Being, the
Totality, and man is not. But the Totality comes actually to know
itself in and through the spirit of man; on the level of pictorial
thought in the evolution of the religious consciousness, on the level
of science or pure conceptual knowledge in the history of philosophy which has as its ideal term the complete truth about reality
in the form of the Absolute's knowledge of itself.

In *The Phenomenology*, therefore, Hegel starts with the lowest
levels of human consciousness and works dialectically upwards to
the level at which the human mind attains the absolute point of
view and becomes the vehicle, as it were, of infinite self-conscious
Spirit. The connections between one level and the next are often
very loose, logically speaking. And some of the stages are obviously
suggested not so much by the demands of a dialectical development as by Hegel's reflections on the spirits and attitudes of
different cultural phases and epochs. Further, some of the topics of
which Hegel treats strike the modern reader as somewhat odd.
There is, for example, a critical treatment of phrenology. At the
same time, as a study of the Odyssey of the human spirit, of the
movement from one attitude or outlook, which proves to be one-
sided and inadequate, to another, the work is both impressive and
fascinating. And the correlations between stages of the dialectic of
consciousness and historically-manifested attitudes (the spirit of
the Enlightenment, the romantic spirit, and so on) add to its
interest. One may be suspicious of Hegel's summaries and interpretations of the spirits of epochs and cultures, and his exaltation
of philosophical knowledge may strike one as having a comical
aspect; but in spite of all reservations and disagreements the
reader who really tries to penetrate into Hegel's thought can
hardly come to any other conclusion than that *The Phenomenology*
is one of the great works of speculative philosophy.

[1] *W*, II, p. 610; *B*, p. 798.

CHAPTER X

HEGEL (2)

*The logic of Hegel—The ontological status of the Idea or Absolute
in itself and the transition to Nature—The philosophy of Nature
—The Absolute as Spirit; subjective Spirit—The concept of right
—Morality—The family and civil society—The State—
Explanatory comments on Hegel's idea of political philosophy—
The function of war—Philosophy of history—Some comments on
Hegel's philosophy of history.*

1. As we have seen, Hegel rejected the view, advanced by
Schelling in his so-called system of identity, that the Absolute in
itself is for conceptual thought the vanishing-point of all differences,
an absolute self-identity which cannot properly be described except
in negative terms and which can be positively apprehended only,
if at all, in mystical intuition. Hegel was convinced that the
speculative reason can penetrate the inner essence of the Absolute,
the essence which manifests itself in Nature and in the history of
the human spirit.

The part of philosophy which is concerned with laying bare the
inner essence of the Absolute is for Hegel logic. To anyone who is
accustomed to regard logic as a purely formal science, entirely
dissociated from metaphysics, this must seem an extraordinary
and even absurd point of view. But we have to bear in mind the
fact that for Hegel the Absolute is pure Thought. This Thought can
be considered in itself, apart from its externalization or self-
manifestation. And the science of pure Thought in itself is logic.
Further, inasmuch as pure Thought is the substance, as it were, of
reality, logic necessarily coincides with metaphysics, that is, with
metaphysics as concerned with the Absolute in itself.

The matter can be made clearer by relating Hegel's conception
of logic to Kant's view of transcendental logic. In the philosophy
of Kant the categories which give shape and form to phenomena
are *a priori* categories of human thought. The human mind does
not create things-in-themselves, but it determines the basic
character of the phenomenal world, the world of appearance. On
Kant's premises, therefore, we have no warrant for assuming that
the categories of the human mind apply to reality in itself; their

cognitive function is limited to the phenomenal world. But, as was explained in the introductory chapter, with the elimination of the unknowable thing-in-itself and the transformation of the critical philosophy into pure idealism the categories become the categories of creative thought in the full sense. And if a subjectivist position, threatening to lead to solipsism, is to be avoided, creative thought must be interpreted as absolute Thought. The categories, therefore, become the categories of absolute Thought, the categories of reality. And logic, which studies them, becomes metaphysics. It discloses the essence or nature of the absolute Thought which manifests itself in Nature and history.

Now, Hegel speaks of the Absolute in itself as God in himself. The subject-matter of logic is 'the truth as it is without husk and for itself. One can therefore express the matter by saying that its content is the presentation of God as he is in his eternal essence before the creation of Nature and of a finite spirit.'[1] And this manner of speaking tends to suggest the very odd picture of the logician penetrating the inner essence of a transcendent Deity and describing it in terms of a system of categories. But Hegel's use of religious language can be misleading. We have to remember that though his Absolute is certainly transcendent in the sense that it cannot be identified with any particular finite entity or set of entities, it is not transcendent in the sense in which the God of Christianity is said to transcend the created universe. Hegel's Absolute is the Totality, and this Totality is depicted as coming to know itself in and through the finite spirit, in so far as the finite spirit attains the level of 'absolute knowledge'. Logic, therefore, is the Absolute's knowledge of itself in itself, in abstraction from its concrete self-manifestation in Nature and history. That is to say, logic is absolute Thought's knowledge of its own essence, the essence which exists concretely in the process of reality.

If we use the word 'category' in a somewhat wider sense than that in which it is used by Hegel himself, we can say, therefore, that his logic is the system of categories. But if we say this, it is essential to understand that the whole system of categories is a progressive definition of the Absolute in itself. Hegel starts with the concept of being because it is for him the most indeterminate and the logically prior concept. And he then proceeds to show how this concept passes necessarily into successive concepts until we

---

[1] *W*, IV, p. 46; *J-S*, I, p. 60. The letters *J-S* signify the English translation of the *Science of Logic* by W. H. Johnston and L. G. Struthers.

reach the absolute Idea, the concept or category of self-knowledge or self-consciousness, self-thinking Thought. But the Absolute is not, of course, a string or chain of categories or concepts. If we ask what the Absolute is, we can answer that it is being. And if we ask what being is, we shall in the end be forced to answer that being is self-thinking Thought or Spirit. The process of showing that this is the case, as worked out by the logician, is obviously a temporal process. But the Absolute in itself does not, to put the matter crudely, start as being at seven in the morning and end as self-thinking Thought at seven in the evening. To say that the Absolute is being is to say that it is self-thinking Thought. But the logician's demonstration of the fact, his systematic dialectical elucidation of the meaning of being, is a temporal process. It is his business to show that the whole system of categories turns in on itself, so to speak. The beginning is the end, and the end is the beginning. That is to say, the first category or concept contains all the others implicitly, and the last is the final explicitation of the first: it gives its true meaning.

The point is easily understood if we employ the religious or theological language which Hegel not infrequently uses. God is being, he is also self-thinking Thought. But the word 'also' is really inappropriate. For to say that God is being is to say that he is self-thinking Thought. The systematic exhibition of this fact by the philosopher is a temporal process. But this temporality obviously does not affect the divine essence in itself. There is, of course, a great difference between Hegel's Absolute and the God of Christian theology. But though Hegel's Absolute is said to be the process of its own becoming, we are not concerned in logic with this actual process, the actualization of the *Logos*: we are concerned with the Absolute 'in itself', with the logical Idea. And this is not a temporal process.

The dialectical movement of Hegel's logic can be illustrated by means of the first three categories. The logically prior concept of the Absolute is the concept of being. But the concept or category of pure being (*reines Sein*) is wholly indeterminate. And the concept of wholly indeterminate being passes into the concept of not-being. That is to say, if we try to think being without any determination at all, we find that we are thinking nothing. The mind passes from being to not-being and from not-being back to being: it can rest in neither, and each disappears, as it were, in its opposite. 'Their truth is thus this *movement* of the immediate disappearing of the one into the other.'[1] And this movement from being to not-being and from not-being to being is becoming. Becoming is thus the synthesis of being and not-being; it is their unity and truth. Being must therefore be conceived as becoming. In other words, the concept of the Absolute as being is the concept of the Absolute as becoming, as a process of self-development.[2]

According to our ordinary way of looking at things a contradiction brings us to a full stop. Being and not-being are mutually exclusive. But we think in this way because we conceive being as determinate being and not-being as the not-being of this determination. Pure being, however, is for Hegel indeterminate, empty or vacuous; and it is for this reason that it is said to pass into its opposite. But contradiction is for Hegel a positive force which reveals both thesis and antithesis as abstract moments in a higher unity or synthesis. And this unity of the concepts of being and not-being is the concept of becoming. But the unity gives rise in turn to a 'contradiction', so that the mind is driven onwards in its search for the meaning of being, for the nature or essence of the Absolute in itself.

Being, not-being or nothing and becoming form the first triad of the first part of Hegel's logic, the so-called logic of being (*die Logik des Seins*). This part is concerned with the categories of being-in-itself, as distinct from the categories of relation. And the three main classes of categories in this part of logic are those of quality, which include the above-mentioned triad, quantity and measure. Measure is described as the synthesis of quality and quantity. For it is the concept of a specific quantum determined by the nature of the object, that is, by its quality.

In the second main part of the *Logic*, the logic of essence (*die Logik des Wesens*), Hegel deduces pairs of related categories, such as essence and existence, force and expression, substance and accident, cause and effect, action and reaction. These categories are called categories of reflection because they correspond with the reflective consciousness which penetrates beneath the surface, as it were, of being in its immediacy. Essence, for example, is conceived as lying behind appearance, and force is conceived as the reality displayed in its expression. In other words, for the reflective

---

[1] *W*, iv, p. 89; *J-S*, i, p. 95.

[2] This statement does not contradict what has been said about the non-temporal nature of the logical Absolute. For we are not concerned here with the actual process of the Absolute's self-actualization.

consciousness being-in-itself undergoes self-diremption, breaking up into related categories.

But the logic of essence does not leave us with the division of being into inner essence and outward phenomenal existence. For the last main subdivision is devoted to the category of actuality (*die Wirklichkeit*) which is described as 'the unity of essence and existence'.[1] That is to say, the actual is the inner essence which ex-ists, the force which has found complete expression. If we identify being with appearance, with its external manifestation, this is a one-sided abstraction. But so is the identification of being with a hidden essence underlying appearance. Being as actuality is the unity of the inner and the outer; it is essence manifesting itself. And it must manifest itself.

It is under the general heading of the category of actuality that Hegel deduces the categories of substance and accident, cause and effect, and action and reaction or reciprocal action. And as we have said that his logic is a progressive definition or determination of the nature of the Absolute in itself, the impression may be given that for him there is only one substance and one cause, namely the Absolute. In other words the impression may be given that Hegel embraces Spinozism. But this would be an incorrect interpretation of his meaning. The deduction of the categories of substance and cause is not intended to imply, for example, that there can be no such thing as a finite cause. For the Absolute as actuality is essence manifesting itself; and the manifestation is the universe as we know it. The Absolute is not simply the One. It is the One, but it is also the Many: it is identity-in-difference.

From the logic of essence Hegel passes to the logic of the Concept (*die Logik des Begriffs*) which is the third main part of his work. In the logic of being each category is at first sight independent, standing on its own feet, as it were, even if the dialectical movement of thought breaks down this apparent self-contained-ness. In the logic of essence we are concerned with obviously related categories, such as cause and effect or substance and accident. We are thus in the sphere of mediation. But each member of a pair of related categories is conceived as mediated 'by another', that is, by something different from itself. The cause, for example, is constituted as a cause by passing into its opposite, namely the effect, which is conceived as something different from the cause. Similarly, the effect is constituted as an

---

[1] *W*, IV, p. 662; *J-S*, II, p. 160.

effect by its relation to something different from itself, namely the cause. The synthesis of the spheres of immediacy and of mediation by another will be the sphere of self-mediation. A being is said to be self-mediating when it is conceived as passing into its opposite and yet as remaining identical with itself even in this self-opposition. And the self-mediating is what Hegel calls the Concept or the Notion.[1]

Needless to say, the logic of the Notion has three main subdivisions. In the first Hegel considers the Notion as 'subjectivity', as thought in its formal aspects. And this part corresponds more or less with logic in the ordinary sense. Hegel tries to show how the general idea of being going out from itself and then returning to itself at a higher level is verified in a formal manner in the movement of logical thought. Thus the unity of the universal concept is divided in the judgment and is re-established at a higher level in the syllogism.

Having considered the Notion as subjectivity, Hegel goes on to consider it as objectivity. And as in the first phase or part of the logic of the Notion he finds three moments, the universal concept, the judgment and syllogistic inference, so in this second phase or part he finds three moments, namely mechanism, chemism and teleology. He thus anticipates the main ideas of the philosophy of Nature. But he is concerned here with the thought or concept of the objective rather than with Nature considered as an empirically-given existing reality. The nature of the Absolute is such that it comprises the concept of self-objectification.

Given the character of the Hegelian dialectic, the third phase of the logic of the Notion will obviously be the synthesis or unity on a higher plane of subjectivity and objectivity. As such the Notion is called the Idea. In the Idea the one-sided factors of the formal and the material, the subjective and the objective, are brought together. But the Idea too has its phases or moments. And in the final subdivision of the logic of the Notion Hegel considers in turn life, knowledge and their unity in the absolute Idea which is, as it were, the union of subjectivity and objectivity enriched with rational life. In other words, the absolute Idea is the concept or category of self-consciousness, personality, self-thinking Thought which knows itself in its object and its object as itself. It is thus the category of Spirit. In religious language, it is the concept of God in and for himself, knowing himself as the totality.

[1] As the word 'concept' has too restricted a meaning in English, Hegel's *Begriff* is frequently rendered as 'Notion'.

After a long dialectical wandering, therefore, being has at length revealed itself as the absolute Idea, as self-thinking Thought. The Absolute is being, and the meaning of this statement has now been made explicit. 'The absolute Idea alone is *being*, eternal *life*, *self-knowing truth*, and it is *all truth*. It is the one subject-matter and content of philosophy.'[1] Hegel does not mean, of course, that the logical Idea, considered precisely as such, is the one subject-matter of philosophy. But philosophy is concerned with reality as a whole, with the Absolute. And reality, in the sense of Nature and the sphere of the human spirit, is the process by which the logical Idea or *Logos* actualizes itself. Hence philosophy is always concerned with the Idea.

2. Now, if we speak of the logical Idea or *Logos* as manifesting or expressing itself in Nature and in the sphere of the human spirit, we are obviously faced with the question, what is the ontological status of the logical Idea or the Absolute in itself? Is it a reality which exists independently of the world and which manifests itself in the world, or is it not? If it is, how can there be a subsistent Idea? If it is not, how can we speak of the Idea as manifesting or actualizing itself?

At the end of the *Logic* in the *Encyclopaedia of the Philosophical Sciences*[2] Hegel asserts that the Idea 'in its absolute freedom . . . *resolves* to let its moment of particularity . . . the immediate Idea as its reflected image, go forth freely out of itself as Nature'.[3] In this passage, therefore, Hegel seems to imply not only that Nature is ontologically derived from the Idea but also that the Idea freely posits Nature. And if this implication were taken literally, we should clearly have to interpret the Idea as a name for the personal creative Deity. For it would be preposterous to speak of an Idea in any other sense as 'resolving' to do something.

But consideration of the Hegelian system as a whole suggests that this passage represents an intrusion, as it were, of the way of speaking which is characteristic of the Christian religious consciousness, and that its implications should not be pressed. It seems to be clear enough that according to Hegel the doctrine of

[1] *W*, v, p. 328; *J-S*, ii, p. 466.
[2] The *Logic* contained in the *Encyclopaedia* is known as the *Lesser* or *Shorter Logic*, in distinction from the *Greater Logic*, that is, Hegel's *Science of Logic*. Quotations in the last section were from the latter work.
[3] *W*, vi, p. 144; *E*, 191. The letter *E* stands for *Encyclopaedia*. As this work is divided into numbered sections, no reference to particular translations is required. A glance at the number of the relevant volume in the reference to *W* will show whether it is the Heidelberg edition (*W*, vi) or the Berlin edition (*W*, viii–x) which is being referred to.

free creation by God belongs to the figurative or pictorial language of the religious consciousness. It expresses indeed a truth, but it does not do so in the idiom of pure philosophy. From the strictly philosophical point of view the Absolute in itself manifests itself necessarily in Nature. Obviously, it is not constrained to do so by anything external to itself. The necessity is an inner necessity of nature. The only freedom in the *Logos'* self-manifestation is the freedom of spontaneity. And from this it follows that from the philosophical point of view there is no sense in speaking of the Absolute in itself as existing 'before' creation. If Nature is derived ontologically from the Idea, the latter is not temporally prior to the former.[1] Further, though some writers have interpreted Hegel in a theistic sense, as holding, that is to say, that the Absolute in itself is a personal Being, existing independently of Nature and of the sphere of the human spirit, it does not seem to me that this interpretation is correct. True, there are passages which can be cited in support of it. But these passages can equally well be interpreted as expressions of the religious consciousness, as pictorial or figurative statements of the truth. And the nature of the system as a whole clearly suggests that the Absolute attains actual self-consciousness only in and through the human spirit. As has already been explained, this does not mean that human consciousness can be identified without more ado with the divine self-consciousness. For the Absolute is said to know itself in and through the human mind in so far as this mind rises above mere finitude and particularity and reaches the level of absolute knowledge. But the point is that if the Absolute becomes actually existent only in and through the human spirit, the Absolute in itself, the logical Idea, cannot properly be said to 'resolve' to posit Nature, which is the objective precondition for the existence of the sphere of Spirit. If such language is used, it is a concession, as it were, to the mode of thought which is characteristic of the religious consciousness.

If, however, we exclude the theistic interpretation of the Absolute in itself,[2] how are we to conceive the transition from the logical Idea to Nature? If we conceive it as a real ontological transition, that is to say, if we conceive a subsistent Idea as manifesting itself necessarily in Nature, we are obviously attributing

---

[1] Cf., for example, *W*, IX, pp. 51–4; *E*, 247.
[2] The theistic view is certainly admitted by Hegel as far as the religious consciousness and its own characteristic expression are concerned. But we are treating here of the strictly philosophical point of view.

to Hegel a thesis which, to put it mildly, is somewhat odd. We expose him at once to the criticism made by Schelling in his polemic against 'negative philosophy', that from ideas we can deduce only other ideas, and that it is quite impossible to deduce an existing world from an Idea.

It is understandable, therefore, that some writers have endeavoured to exclude altogether the concept of an ontological derivation of Nature from the Idea. The Absolute is the totality, the universe. And this totality is a teleological process, the actualization of self-thinking Thought. The essential nature of this process can be considered in abstraction. It then takes the form of the logical Idea. But it does not exist as a subsistent reality which is logically prior to Nature and which is the efficient cause of Nature. The Idea reflects the goal or result of the process rather than a subsistent reality which stands at its beginning. Hence there is no question of an ontological derivation of Nature from the logical Idea as efficient cause. And the so-called deduction of Nature from the Idea is really an exhibition of the fact, or alleged fact, that Nature is a necessary precondition for the realization of the goal of the total process of reality, the universe's knowledge of itself in and through the human spirit.

It seems to the present writer that the foregoing line of interpretation must be accepted in so far as it denies the separate existence of the logical Idea as a reality quite distinct from the world or as an external efficient cause of the world. For Hegel the infinite exists in and through the finite; the universal lives and has its being, as it were, in and through the particulars. Hence there is no room in his system for an efficient cause which transcends the world in the sense that it exists quite independently of it. At the same time, even though the infinite exists in and through the finite, it is obvious that finite things arise and perish. They are, so to speak, transitory manifestations of an infinite Life. And Hegel certainly tends to speak of the *Logos* as though it were pulsating Life, dynamic Reason or Thought. It exists, it is true, only in and through its manifestations. But inasmuch as it is a continuous Life, Being actualizing itself as what it potentially is, namely Spirit, it is quite natural to look on the passing manifestations as ontologically dependent on the one immanent Life, as an 'outside' in relation to an 'inside'. And Hegel can thus speak of the *Logos* spontaneously expressing itself in or going over into Nature. For Being, the Absolute, the infinite Totality, is not a mere collection of finite things, but one infinite Life, self-actualizing Spirit. It is the universal of universals; and even though it exists only in and through the particulars, it itself persists whereas the particulars do not. Hence it is perfectly reasonable to speak of the *Logos* as expressing or manifesting itself in finite things. And inasmuch as it is absolute Spirit which comes to exist as such through the process of its own self-development, material Nature is naturally conceived as its opposite, the opposite which is a precondition for the attainment of the end or *telos* of the process.

This line of interpretation may seem to be an attempt to have things both ways. On the one hand it is admitted that the logical Idea does not exist as a subsistent reality which creates Nature from outside, as it were. On the other hand, it is claimed that the logical Idea, in the sense of the essential structure or meaning of Being as grasped by the metaphysician, represents a metaphysical reality which, though it exists only in and through its self-manifestation, is in a certain sense logically prior to its manifestation. But I do not think that we can exclude metaphysics from Hegelianism or eliminate altogether a certain element of transcendence. The attempt to do this seems to me to make nonsense of Hegel's doctrine of the infinite Absolute. The Absolute is indeed the totality, the universe, considered as the process of its own self-development; but in my opinion we cannot escape making a distinction between inner and outer, between, that is to say, the one infinite Life, self-actualizing Spirit, and the finite manifestations in and through which it lives and has its being. And in this case we can equally well say that the finite manifestations derive their reality from the one Life which expresses itself in them. If there is a certain element of ambiguity in Hegel's position, this is scarcely surprising. For if there were no such element, his philosophy would hardly have given rise to divergent interpretations.

3. 'Nature,' says Hegel, 'is *in itself*, in the Idea, divine. . . . But as it exists, its being does not correspond with its concept.'[1] In the language of religion, the idea of Nature in the divine mind is divine, but the objectification of this idea in existing Nature cannot be called divine. For the fact that the idea is expressed in the material world, in that which is most unlike God, means that it is only inadequately expressed. God cannot be adequately manifested in the material world. In the language of philosophy, the Absolute is defined as Spirit. Hence it can manifest itself adequately

[1] *W*, VI, p. 147; *E*, 193.

only in the sphere of Spirit. Nature is a precondition of the existence of this sphere, but it is not in itself Spirit, though in its rational structure it bears the imprint of Spirit. One might say with Schelling that it is slumbering Spirit or visible Spirit; but it is not Spirit prop*, Spirit as awoken to consciousness of itself.

Spirit is freedom: Nature is the sphere of necessity rather than of freedom. It is also the sphere of contingency (*Zufälligkeit*). For example, it does not exhibit in any uniformly clear-cut way the distinctions postulated by a purely rational pattern. There are, for instance, 'monsters' in Nature which do not conform clearly to any one specific type. And there are even natural species which seem to be due to a kind of Bacchic dance or revel on Nature's part, and not to any rational necessity. Nature appears to run riot as much in the wealth of forms which she produces as in the number of individual members of given species. They elude all logical deduction. Obviously, an empirical explanation of any natural object can be given in terms of physical causality. But to give an empirical explanation in terms of physical causality is not the same thing as to give a logical deduction.

Obviously, Nature cannot exist without particular things. Immanent teleology, for instance, cannot exist without particular organisms. The universal exists only in and through its particulars. But it does not follow that any given individual is logically deducible from the concept of its specific type or from any more general concept. It is not simply a question of its being very difficult or practically impossible for the finite mind to deduce particulars which could in principle be deduced by an infinite mind. For Hegel seems to say that particular objects in Nature are not deducible even in principle, even though they are physically explicable. To put the matter somewhat paradoxically, contingency in Nature is necessary. For without it there could be no Nature. But contingency is none the less real, in the sense that it is a factor in Nature which the philosopher is unable to eliminate. And Hegel ascribes it to 'the *impotence* of Nature'[1] to remain faithful to the determination of the Notion. He is speaking here about the way in which Nature mixes specific types, producing intermediate forms. But the main point is that contingency is ascribed to the impotence of Nature itself and not to the finite mind's incapability of giving a purely rational account of Nature. Whether on his

[1] *W*, IX, pp. 63–4; *E*, 250.

principles Hegel ought to have admitted contingency in Nature is disputable, but the fact that he did so is not open to doubt. And this is why he sometimes speaks of Nature as a Fall (*Abfall*) from the Idea. In other words, contingency represents the externality of Nature in relation to the Idea. And it follows that Nature 'is not to be deified'.[1] Indeed, it is a mistake, Hegel says, to regard natural phenomena such as the heavenly bodies as works of God in a higher sense than the creations of the human spirit, such as works of art or the State. Hegel certainly followed Schelling in attributing to Nature a status which it did not enjoy in the philosophy of Fichte. At the same time he shows no inclination to share the romantic divinization of Nature.

But though Hegel rejects any deification of existing Nature, the fact remains that if Nature is real it must be a moment in the life of the Absolute. For the Absolute is the totality. Hegel is thus placed in a difficult position. On the one hand he has no wish to deny that there is an objective Nature. Indeed, it is essential to his system to maintain that there is. For the Absolute is the identity-in-difference of subjectivity and objectivity. And if there is real subjectivity, there must be real objectivity. On the other hand it is not easy for him to explain how contingency can have any place in a system of absolute idealism. And it is understandable if we can discern a marked tendency to adopt a Platonic position by distinguishing between the inside, as it were, of Nature, its rational structure or reflection of the Idea, and its outside, its contingent aspect, and by relegating the latter to the sphere of the irrational and unreal. There must indeed be an objective Nature. For the Idea must take the form of objectivity. And there cannot be an objective Nature without contingency. But the philosopher cannot cope with this element, beyond registering the fact that it is there and must be there. And what Professor Hegel cannot cope with he tends to dismiss as irrational and so as unreal. For the rational is the real and the real the rational. Obviously, once contingency has been admitted Hegel is driven either to admit some kind of dualism or to slide over the contingent element in Nature as though it were not 'really real'.

However this may be, Nature, in so far as it can be treated by the philosopher, 'is to be considered as a system of stages, of which one proceeds necessarily from the other'.[2] But it must be clearly understood that this system of stages or levels in Nature is a

---

[1] *W*, vi, p. 147; *E*, 193.   [2] *W*, vi, p. 149; *E*, 194.

dialectical development of concepts and not an empirical history of Nature. It is indeed somewhat amusing to find Hegel dismissing the evolutionary hypothesis in a cavalier manner.[1] But a physical hypothesis of this kind is in any case irrelevant to the philosophy of Nature as expounded by Hegel. For it introduces the idea of temporal succession which has no place in the dialectical deduction of the levels of Nature. And if Hegel had lived to a time when the evolutionary hypothesis had won wide acceptance, it would have been open to him to say: 'Well, I dare say that I was wrong about evolution. But in any case it is an empirical hypothesis, and its acceptance or rejection does not affect the validity of my dialectic.'

As one would expect, the main divisions of Hegel's philosophy of Nature are three in number. In the *Encyclopaedia* they are given as mathematics, physics and organic physics, while in the lectures on the philosophy of Nature they are given as mechanics, physics and organics. In both cases, however, Hegel starts with space, with what is most removed from mind or Spirit, and works dialectically up to the animal organism which of all levels of Nature is the closest to Spirit. Space is sheer externality: in the organism we find internality. Subjectivity can be said to make its appearance in the animal organism, though not in the form of self-consciousness. Nature brings us to the threshold of Spirit, but only to the threshold.

It is hardly worth while following Hegel into the details of his philosophy of Nature. But attention should be drawn to the fact that he is not trying to do the work of the scientist all over again by some peculiar philosophical method of his own. He is concerned rather with finding in Nature as known through observation and science the exemplification of a dynamic rational pattern. This may sometimes lead to bizarre attempts to show that natural phenomena are what they are, or what Hegel believes that they are, because it is rational and, so to speak, for the best that they should be what they are. And we may well feel somewhat sceptical about the value of this kind of speculative or higher physics, as well as amused at the philosopher's tendency to look down on empirical science from a superior position. But it is as well to understand that Hegel takes empirical science for granted, even if he sometimes takes sides, and not always to the advantage of his reputation, in controversial issues. It is more a question of fitting

[1] *W*, ix, pp. 59–62; *E*, 249.

the facts into a conceptual scheme than of pretending to deduce the facts in a purely *a priori* manner.

4. 'The Absolute is Spirit: this is the highest definition of the Absolute. To find this definition and to understand its content was, one may say, the final motive of all culture and philosophy. All religion and science have striven to reach this point.'[1] The Absolute in itself is Spirit, but it is potential rather than actual Spirit.[2] The Absolute for itself, Nature, is Spirit, but it is 'self-alienated Spirit',[3] in religious language it is, as Hegel puts it, God in his otherness. Spirit begins to exist as such only when we come to the human spirit, which is studied by Hegel in the third main part of his system, the philosophy of Spirit.

The philosophy of Spirit, needless to say, has three main parts or subdivisions. 'The two first parts of the doctrine of Spirit treat of the finite spirit',[4] while the third part deals with absolute Spirit, the *Logos* in its concrete existence as self-thinking Thought. In this section we shall be concerned only with the first part, to which Hegel gives the title 'subjective Spirit'.

This first part of the philosophy of Spirit is subdivided, according to Hegel's pervasive dialectical scheme, into three subordinate parts. Under the heading of anthropology he treats of the soul (*Seele*) as sensing and feeling subject. The soul is, as it were, a point of transition from Nature to Spirit. On the one hand it reveals the ideality of Nature, while on the other hand it is 'only the *sleep* of the Spirit'.[5] That is to say, it enjoys self-feeling (*Selbstgefühl*) but not reflective self-consciousness. It is sunk in the particularity of its feelings. And it is actual precisely as embodied, the body being the externality of the soul. In the human organism soul and body are its inner and outer aspects.

From the concept of the soul in this restricted sense Hegel passes to the phenomenology of consciousness, resuming some of the themes already treated in *The Phenomenology of Spirit*. The soul of the section on anthropology was subjective spirit considered on its lowest level, as a yet undifferentiated unity. On the level of consciousness, however, subjective spirit is confronted by an object, first by an object regarded as external to and independent of the subject, then, in self-consciousness, by itself. Finally, the subject

---

[1] *W*, vi, p. 228; *E*, 302.
[2] The logical Idea, considered precisely as such, is the category of Spirit, of self-thinking Thought, rather than potential Spirit.
[3] *W*, ix, p. 50; *E*, 247.   [4] *W*, vi, p. 229; *E*, 305.
[5] *W*, vi, p. 232; *E*, 309.

is depicted as rising to universal self-consciousness in which it recognizes other selves as both distinct from and one with itself. Here, therefore, consciousness (consciousness, that is, of something external to the subject) and self-consciousness are unified on a higher level.

The third section of the philosophy of subjective Spirit is entitled 'mind' or 'spirit' (*Geist*), and it considers the powers or general modes of activity of the finite spirit as such. We are no longer concerned simply with slumbering spirit, the 'soul' of the section on anthropology, nor, as in phenomenology, with the ego or subject in relation to an object. We have returned from the finite spirit as term of a relation to spirit in itself but at a higher level than that of soul. In a sense we are concerned with psychology rather than with the phenomenology of consciousness. But the psychology in question is not empirical psychology but a dialectical deduction of the concepts of the logically successive stages in the activity of the finite spirit in itself.

Hegel studies the activity of the finite spirit or mind in both its theoretical and its practical aspects. Under the theoretical aspect he treats, for instance, of intuition, memory, imagination and thought, while under the practical aspect he considers feeling, impulse and will. And his conclusion is that 'the actual free will is the unity of the theoretical and practical spirit; *free will which exists for itself as free will*'.[1] He is speaking, of course, of the will as conscious of its freedom. And this is '*will* as free *intelligence*'.[2] We can say, therefore, that the concept of Spirit in itself is the concept of the rational will (*der vernünftige Wille*).

But 'whole regions of the world, Africa and the East, have never had this idea and do not yet have it. The Greeks and the Romans, Plato and Aristotle, also the Stoics, did not have it. On the contrary, they knew only that man is actually free by birth (as a citizen of Athens or Sparta and so on) or through strength of character, education or philosophy (the wise man is free even when he is a slave and in chains). This idea entered the world through Christianity, according to which the individual *as such* possesses an *infinite* value, . . . that is, that man *in himself* is destined to the highest freedom.'[3] This idea of the realization of freedom is a key-idea in Hegel's philosophy of history.

5. We have seen that the Absolute in itself objectifies or expresses itself in Nature. So also does Spirit in itself objectify or

<hr>

[1] *W*, x, p. 379; *E*, 481.   [2] *Ibid.*   [3] *W*, x, p. 380; *E*, 482.

express itself, issuing, as it were, out of its state of immediacy. Thus we come to the sphere of 'objective Spirit', the second main part of the philosophy of Spirit as a whole.

The first phase of objective Spirit is the sphere of right (*das Recht*). The person, the individual subject conscious of his freedom, must give external expression to his nature as free spirit; he must 'give himself an external sphere of freedom'.[1] And he does this by expressing his will in the realm of material things. That is to say, he expresses his free will by effectively appropriating and using material things. Personality confers the capacity for having and exercising rights such as that of property. A material thing, precisely because it is material and not spiritual, can have no rights: it is an instrument for the expression of rational will. By its being taken possession of and used a thing's non-personal nature is actually revealed and its destiny fulfilled. Indeed, it is in a sense elevated by being thus set in relation to a rational will.

A person becomes the owner of a thing not by a merely internal act of will but by effective appropriation, by embodying his will in it, as it were.[2] But he can also withdraw his will from the thing, thereby alienating it. And this is possible because the thing is external to him. A man can relinquish his right, for example, to a house. He can also relinquish his right to his labour for a limited time and for a specified purpose. For his labour can then be looked upon as something external. But he cannot alienate his total freedom by handing himself over as a slave. For his total freedom is not and cannot properly be regarded as something external to himself. Nor can his moral conscience or his religion be regarded as an external thing.[3]

In Hegel's somewhat odd dialectical progression the concept of alienation of property leads us to the concept of contract (*Vertrag*). True, alienation of property might take the form of withdrawing one's will, as it were, from a thing and leaving it ownerless. I might alienate an umbrella in this way. But we then remain within the sphere of the abstract concept of property. We advance beyond

---

[1] *W*, VII, p. 94; *R*, 41. The letter *R* signifies *The Philosophy of Right*. The following number refers to the section. In references to *R* the word 'addition' refers to the additions made by Hegel to the original text. In Professor T. M. Knox's translation these additions are printed after the version of the original text.

[2] Hegel is speaking of the right of property in the abstract. Needless to say, once the concept of society has been introduced the range of legitimate appropriation is restricted.

[3] This refers to religion as something internal. In a state of organized society a man cannot claim inviolability for the external expression of his religious beliefs when such expression is socially harmful.

this sphere by introducing the concept of the unity of two or more individual wills in respect of property, that is, by developing the concept of contract. When a man gives, sells or exchanges by agreement, two wills come together. But he can also agree with one or more persons to possess and use certain property in common for a common end. And here the union of wills, mediated by an external thing, is more evident.

But though contract rests on a union of wills, there is obviously no guarantee that the particular wills of the contracting parties will remain in union. In this sense the union of wills into a common will is contingent. And it comprises within itself the possibility of its own negation. This negation is actualized in wrong. The concept of wrong, however, passes through several phases; and Hegel considers in turn civil wrong (which is the result of incorrect interpretation rather than of evil intent or disrespect of other persons' rights), fraud and crime and violence. The notion of crime brings him to the subject of punishment, which he interprets as a cancellation of wrong, a cancellation which is said to be demanded even by the implicit will of the criminal himself. A criminal, according to Hegel, is not to be treated like an animal which has to be deterred or reformed. As a rational free being, he implicitly consents to and even demands the annulment of his crime through punishment.

Now, it is easy to see how Hegel is led from the concept of contract to that of wrong. For contract, as a free act, involves the possibility of its violation. But it is not so easy to see how the concept of wrong can reasonably be regarded as the unity on a higher plane of the concepts of property and contract. However, it is obvious that Hegel's dialectic is often a process of rational reflection in which one idea leads more or less naturally to another than a process of strictly necessary deduction. And even though he persists in observing his uniform triadic scheme, there is not much point in pressing it.

6. In wrong there is an opposition between the particular will and the universal will, the principle of rightness, which is implicit in the common will expressed in contract. This is true at least of wrong in the form of crime. The particular will negates right, and in doing so it negates the conception or notion of the will, which is universal, the rational free will as such. As we have seen, punishment is the negation of this negation. But punishment is external, in the sense that it is inflicted by an external authority. The

opposition or negation can be adequately overcome only when the particular will is in harmony with the universal will, that is, when it becomes what it ought to be, namely in accord with the concept of the will as raised above mere particularity and selfishness. Such a will is the moral will. We are thus led to make the transition from the concept of right to that of morality (*Moralität*).

It is important to note that the term 'morality' is used by Hegel in a much more restricted sense than it bears in ordinary usage. True, the term can be used in a variety of ways in ordinary language. But when we think of morality, we generally think of the fulfilment of positive duties, especially in a social setting, whereas Hegel abstracts from particular duties, towards the family, for example, or the State, and uses the term for what he calls 'a determination of the will [*Willensbestimmtheit*], so far as it is in the interior of the will in general'.[1] The moral will is free will which has returned on itself, that is, which is conscious of itself as free and which recognizes only itself, and no external authority, as the principle of its actions. As such the will is said to be 'infinite' or universal not only in itself but also for itself. 'The moral standpoint is the standpoint of the will in so far as it is *infinite* not simply *in itself* but *for itself*.'[2] It is the will as conscious of itself as the source of its own principle of action in an unrestricted way. Hegel does indeed introduce in passing the topic of obligation or ought (*Sollen*). For the will considered as a particular finite will may not be in accordance with the will considered as universal; and what is willed by the latter thus appears to the former as a demand or obligation. And, as will be seen presently, he discusses action from the point of view of the responsibility of the subject for its action. But in his treatment of morality he is concerned with the autonomous free will in its subjective aspect, that is, with the purely formal aspect of morality (in the wider sense of the term).

This purely formal treatment of morality is, of course, an unfortunate legacy from the Kantian philosophy. It is all the more important, therefore, to understand that morality, as Hegel uses the term, is a one-sided concept in which the mind cannot rest. It is certainly not his intention to imply that morality consists simply of 'interiority'. On the contrary, it is his intention to show that the purely formal concept of morality is inadequate. And we can say, therefore, that he treats the Kantian ethic as a one-sided

[1] *W*, x, p. 392; *E*, 503.   [2] *W*, vii, p. 164; *R*, 105.

moment in the dialectical development of the full moral conscious-ness. If, then, we use the term 'morality' to mean the whole ethical life of man, it would be quite incorrect to say that Hegel makes it entirely formal and 'interior' or subjective. For he does nothing of the kind. At the same time it is arguable that in the transition from morality in the restricted sense (*Moralität*) to the concrete ethical life (*Sittlichkeit*) some important elements in the moral conscious-ness are omitted or at least slurred over.

The subjective will externalizes itself in action. But the free will, as self-determined, has the right to regard as its own action, for which it can be held accountable, only those acts which stand in certain relations to it. We can say, therefore, that Hegel raises the question, for what actions can a person rightly be held accountable? Or, what are, properly speaking, the actions of a person? But it must be remembered that Hegel is thinking of the general formal characteristics of actions, and that he is not concerned at this stage with indicating where a person's concrete moral duties lie. For the matter of that, a person can be accountable for bad as well as for good actions. Hegel is, as it were, going behind the moral distinction between good and bad to the characteristics of action which make it possible for us to say that a person has acted morally or immorally.

In the first place any change or alteration in the world which the subject brings about can be called his 'deed' (*Handlung*). But he has the right to recognize as his 'action' (*That*) only that deed which was the purpose (*Vorsatz*) of his will. The external world is the sphere of contingency, and I cannot hold myself responsible for the unforeseeable consequences of my action. It does not follow, of course, that I can disavow all its consequences. For some consequences are simply the outward shape which my acting necessarily assumes, and they must be counted as comprised within my purpose. But it would be contrary to the idea of the self-determining free will to hold myself responsible for the unforeseeable consequences or alterations in the world which are in some sense my deed but which were certainly not comprised within my purpose.

Purpose is thus the first phase of morality. The second is intention (*Absicht*) or, more accurately, intention and welfare or well-being (*das Wohl*). It seems true to say that we generally use the words 'purpose' and 'intention' synonymously. But Hegel distinguishes between them. If I apply a lighted match to inflammable material in the grate, the natural and foreseen consequence of my action is the ensuing fire. My purpose was to light the fire. But I should not perform this action except in view of an intended end, such as warming myself or drying the room. And my intention is relevant to the moral character of the action. It is not, of course, the only relevant factor. Hegel is far from saying that any sort of action is justified by a good intention. But intention is none the less a moment or relevant factor in morality.

Hegel assumes that intentions are directed to welfare or well-being. And he insists that the moral agent has a right to seek his own welfare, the satisfaction of his needs as a human being. He is not suggesting, of course, that egoism is the norm or morality. But at present we are considering morality apart from its social framework and expression. And when Hegel insists that a man has a right to seek his own welfare, he is saying that the satisfaction of one's needs as a human being belongs to morality and is not opposed to it. In other words, he is defending a point of view comprised in Greek ethics as represented by Aristotle and rejecting the Kantian notion that an act loses its moral value if performed from inclination. In his opinion it is quite wrong to suppose that morality consists in a constant warfare against inclinations and natural impulses.

But though the individual is entitled to seek his own welfare, morality certainly does not consist in the particular will seeking its particular good. At the same time this idea has to be preserved and not simply negated. Hence we must proceed to the idea of the particular will identifying itself with the rational and so universal will and aiming at universal welfare. And the unity of the particular will with the concept of the will in itself (that is, with the rational will as such) is the good (*das Gute*), which can be described as 'the realization of freedom, the absolute final purpose of the world'.[1]

The rational will as such is a man's true will, his will as a rational, free being. And the need for conforming his particular will, his will as this or that particular individual, to the rational will (to his true self, one might say) presents itself as duty or obligation. Inasmuch, therefore, as morality abstracts from all concrete positive duties, we can say that duty should be done for duty's sake. A man ought to conform his particular will to the universal will, which is his true or real will; and he ought to do so

[1] *W*, vii, p. 188; *R*, 129.

simply because it is his duty. But this, of course, tells us nothing about what a man ought to will in particular. We can only say that the good will is determined by the subject's inward certainty, which is conscience (*Gewissen*). 'Conscience expresses the absolute right of subjective self-consciousness to know *in itself* and *through itself* what is right and duty, and to recognize nothing as good other than what it knows to be good, at the same time asserting that what it knows and wills as good is in truth right and duty.'[1]

Hegel thus incorporates into his account of morality what we may perhaps call the Protestant insistence on inwardness and on the absolute authority of conscience. But pure subjectivism and inwardness are really abhorrent to him. And he proceeds immediately to argue that to rely on a purely subjective conscience is to be potentially evil. If he had contented himself with saying that a person's conscience can err and that some objective norm or standard is required, he would have been expounding a familiar and easily intelligible position. But he gives the impression of trying to establish a connection between undiluted moral inwardness and wickedness, at least as a possible conjunction. Exaggeration apart, however, his main point is that we cannot give a definite content to morality on the level of pure moral inwardness. To do so, we have to turn to the idea of organized society.

The concepts of abstract right and of morality are thus for Hegel one-sided notions which have to be unified on a higher level in the concept of ethical life (*die Sittlichkeit*). That is to say, in the dialectical development of the sphere of objective Spirit they reveal themselves as moments or phases in the development of the concept of concrete ethics, phases which have at the same time to be negated, preserved and elevated.

Concrete ethics is for Hegel social ethics. It is one's position in society which specifies one's duties. Hence social ethics is the synthesis or unity at a higher level of the one-sided concepts of right and morality.

7. Hegel's way of dealing with the concrete life is to deduce the three moments of what he calls 'the ethical substance' (*die sittliche Substanz*). These are the family, civil society and the State. One might perhaps expect him to consider man's concrete duties in this social setting. But what he actually does is to study the essential natures of the family, civil society and the State and to

[1] *W*, VII, pp. 196–7; *R*, 137.

show how one concept leads to another. It is not necessary, he remarks, to add that a man has these or those duties towards his family or towards the State. For this will be sufficiently evident from a study of the natures or essences of these societies. In any case it cannot properly be expected of the philosopher that he should draw up a code of particular duties. He is concerned with the universal, with the dialectical development of concepts, rather than with moralizing.

The family, the first moment in 'the ethical substance' or union of moral subjectivity and objectivity, is said to be 'the immediate or natural ethical spirit'.[1] In the social sphere the human spirit, issuing, as it were, out of its inwardness, objectifies itself first of all in the family. This is not to say that in Hegel's opinion the family is a transitory institution which passes away when other types of society have reached their full development. It is to say that the family is the logically prior society inasmuch as it represents the universal in its logically first moment of immediacy. The members of the family are considered as one, united primarily by the bond of feeling, that is, by love.[2] The family is what one might call a feeling-totality. It is, as it were, one person whose will is expressed in property, the common property of the family.

But if we consider the family in this way, we must add that it contains within itself the seeds of its own dissolution. Within the family, considered as a feeling-totality and as representing the moment of universality, the children exist simply as members. They are, of course, individual persons, but they are such *in* themselves rather than *for* themselves. In the course of time, however, they pass out of the unity of family life into the condition of individual persons, each of whom possesses his own plans in life and so on. It is as though the particulars emerge out of the universality of family life and assert themselves as particulars.

The notion of the comparatively undifferentiated unity of the family breaking up through the emergence of particularity is not in itself, of course, the notion of a society. Rather is it the notion of the dissolution or negation of a society. But this negation is itself negated or overcome in what Hegel calls 'civil society' (*die bürgerliche Gesellschaft*) which represents the second moment in the development of social ethics.

[1] W, vii, p. 237; R, 157.
[2] Obviously, Hegel is not so foolish as to maintain that as a matter of empirical fact every family is united by love. He is talking about the concept or ideal essence of the family, what it ought to be.

To understand what Hegel means by civil society we can first picture a plurality of individuals, each of whom seeks his own ends and endeavours to satisfy his own needs. We must then conceive them as united in a form of economic organization for the better furtherance of their ends. This will involve specialization of labour and the development of economic classes and corporations. Further, an economic organization of this kind requires for its stability the institution of law and the machinery of law-enforcements, namely law-courts, a judiciary and police.

Inasmuch as Hegel considers the political constitution and government under the heading of the State and not under that of civil society, we may be inclined to comment that the latter could never exist. For how can there be laws and the administration of justice except in a State? The answer is, of course, that there cannot. But Hegel is not concerned with maintaining that civil society ever existed in the precise form in which he describes it. For the concept of civil society is for him a one-sided and inadequate concept of the State itself. It is the State 'as external State'.[1] That is to say, it is the State with the latter's essential nature omitted.

In other words, Hegel is concerned with the dialectical development of the concept of the State. And he does so by taking two one-sided concepts of society and showing that both represent ideas which are united on a higher plane in the concept of the State. The family, of course, persists in the State. So does civil society. For it represents an aspect of the State, even though it is only a partial aspect. But it does not follow that this aspect, taken in isolation and called 'civil society', ever actually existed precisely as such. The dialectical development of the concept of the State is a conceptual development. It is not equivalent to the statement that, historically speaking, the family existed first, then civil society, then the State, as though these concepts were all mutually exclusive. If we interpret Hegel in this way, we shall probably be inclined to think that he is concerned with expounding a thoroughly totalitarian theory of the State as against, for example, the sort of theory advanced by Herbert Spencer which more or less corresponds, though with certain important qualifications, to the concept of civil society. But though Hegel would doubtless have regarded Spencer's theory of society as very inadequate, he thought of the moment of particularity, represented by the concept of civil

[1] *W*, x, p. 401; *E*, 523.

society, as being preserved, and not simply cancelled out, in the State.

8. The family represents the moment of universality in the sense of undifferentiated unity. Civil society represents the moment of particularity. The State represents the unity of the universal and the particular. Instead of undifferentiated unity we find in the State differentiated universality, that is, unity in difference. And instead of sheer particularity[1] we find the identification of the particular with the universal will. To put the matter in another way, in the State self-consciousness has risen to the level of universal self-consciousness. The individual is conscious of himself as being a member of the totality in such a way that his selfhood is not annulled but fulfilled. The State is not an abstract universal standing over against its members: it exists in and through them. At the same time by participation in the life of the State the members are elevated above their sheer particularity. In other words, the State is an organic unity. It is a concrete universal, existing in and through particulars which are distinct and one at the same time.

The State is said to be 'the self-conscious ethical substance'.[2] It is 'ethical mind as substantial will manifest and clear to itself, which thinks and knows itself and accomplishes what it knows in so far as it knows it'.[3] The State is the actuality of the rational will when this has been raised to the plane of universal self-consciousness. It is thus the highest expression of objective Spirit. And the preceding moments of this sphere are resumed and synthesized in it. For instance, rights are established and maintained as the expression of the universal rational will. And morality obtains its content. That is to say, a man's duties are determined by his position in the social organism. This does not mean, of course, that a man has duties only to the State and none to his family. For the family is not annulled in the State: it is an essential, if subordinate, moment in the State's life. Nor does Hegel mean to imply that a man's duties are determined once and for all by an unchangeable social position. For though he insists that the welfare of the whole

---

[1] To speak of civil society as representing 'sheer particularity' is from one point of view to be guilty of exaggeration. For within civil society itself the antagonisms consequent on the emergence and self-assertion of the particulars are partly overcome through the corporations on which Hegel lays stress. But the union of wills among members of a corporation in seeking a common end has also a limited universality and prepares the way for the transition to the concept of the State.

[2] *W*, x, p. 409; *E*, 535.   [3] *W*, vii, p. 328; *R*, 257.

social organism is paramount, he also insists that the principle of individual freedom and personal decision is not annihilated in the State but preserved. The theory of 'my station and its duties', to use Bradley's famous phrase, does not imply acceptance of some sort of caste system.

It is indeed undeniable that Hegel speaks of the State in the most exalted terms. He even describes it, for instance, as 'this actual God'.[1] But there are several points to be borne in mind. In the first place the State, as objective Spirit, is necessarily 'divine' in some sense. And just as the Absolute itself is identity-in-difference, so is the State, though on a more restricted scale. In the second place it is essential to remember that Hegel is speaking throughout of the concept of the State, its ideal essence. He has no intention of suggesting that historical States are immune from criticism. Indeed, he makes this point quite clear. 'The State is no work of art; it stands in the world, and so in the sphere of caprice, contingency and error; it can be disfigured by evil conduct in many respects. But the ugliest human being, the criminal, the diseased and the cripple, each is still a living man. The positive element, life, remains in spite of the privation; and it is with this positive element that we have to do here.'[2]

In the third place we must bear in mind Hegel's insistence on the fact that the mature or well-developed State preserves the principle of private liberty in the ordinary sense. He maintains indeed that the will of the State must prevail over the particular will when there is a clash between them. And inasmuch as the will of the State, the universal or general will, is for him in some sense the 'real' will of the individual, it follows that the individual's identification of his interests with those of the State is the actualization of freedom. For the free will is potentially universal, and, as universal, it wills the general good. There is a strong dose of Rousseau's doctrines in Hegel's political theory. At the same time it is unjust to Hegel to draw from the highfaluting way in which he speaks of the majesty and divinity of the State the conclusion that his ideal is a totalitarian State in which private freedom and initiative are reduced to a minimum. On the contrary, a mature State is for Hegel one which ensures the maximum development of personal liberty which is compatible with the sovereign rights of the universal will. Thus he insists that while the stability of the State requires that its members should make

[1] *W*, VII, p. 336; *R*, 258, addition.   [2] *Ibid.*

the universal end their end[1] according to their several positions and capacities, it also requires that the State should be in a real sense the means to the satisfaction of their subjective aims.[2] As already remarked, the concept of civil society is not simply cancelled out in the concept of the State.

In his treatment of the State Hegel discusses first the political constitution. And he represents constitutional monarchy as being the most rational form. But he regards a corporative State as more rational than democracy after the English model. That is to say, he maintains that the citizens should participate in the affairs of the State as members of subordinate wholes, corporations or Estates, rather than as individuals. Or, more accurately, representatives should represent corporations or Estates rather than the individual citizens precisely as such. And this view seems to be required by Hegel's dialectical scheme. For the concept of civil society, which is preserved in that of the State, culminates in the idea of the corporation.

It has frequently been said that by deducing constitutional monarchy as the most rational form of political organization Hegel canonized the Prussian State of his time. But though he may, like Fichte, have come to regard Prussia as the most promising instrument for educating the Germans to political self-consciousness, his historical sense was far too strong to allow him to suppose that one particular type of constitution could be profitably adopted by any given nation without regard to its history, traditions and spirit. He may have talked a good deal about the rational State, but he was far too reasonable himself to think that a constitution could be imposed on all nations simply because it corresponded best with the demands of abstract reason. 'A constitution *develops* out of the spirit of a nation *only* in identity with this spirit's own development; and it runs through, together with this spirit, the grades of formation and the alterations required by its spirit. It is the indwelling spirit and the history of the nation (and, indeed, the history is simply the history of this spirit) by which constitutions have been and are made.'[3] Again, 'Napoleon wished to give the Spaniards, for example, a constitution *a priori*, but the attempt fared badly enough. For a constitution is no mere artificial product; it is the work of centuries, the idea and the consciousness of the rational in so far as it has been developed in a

---

[1] It should be remembered that Hegel was partly concerned with educating the Germans to political self-consciousness.

[2] Cf. *W*, VII, p. 344; *R*, 265, addition.   [3] *W*, x, p. 416; *E*, 540.

people. . . . What Napoleon gave the Spaniards was more rational than what they had before, and yet they rejected it as something alien to them.'[1]

Hegel further observes that from one point of view it is idle to ask whether monarchy or democracy is the best form of government. The fact of the matter is that any constitution is one-sided and inadequate unless it embodies the principle of subjectivity (that is, the principle of personal freedom) and answers to the demands of 'mature reason'.[2] In other words, a more rational constitution means a more liberal constitution, at least in the sense that it must explicitly allow for the free development of individual personality and respect the rights of individuals. Hegel was by no means so reactionary as has sometimes been supposed. He did not hanker after the *ancien régime*.

9. It is worth drawing attention to Hegel's general idea of political theory. His insistence that the philosopher is concerned with the concept or ideal essence of the State may suggest that in his opinion it is the philosopher's business to show politicians and statesmen what they should aim at, by portraying more or less in detail a supposedly ideal State, subsisting in some Platonic world of essences. But if we look at the Preface to *The Philosophy of Right* we find Hegel denying in explicit terms that it is the philosopher's business to do anything of the kind. The philosopher is concerned with understanding the actual rather than with offering political schemes and panaceas. And in a sense the actual is the past. For political philosophy appears in the period of a culture's maturity, and when the philosopher attempts to understand the actual, it is already passing into the past and giving place to new forms. In Hegel's famous words, 'when philosophy paints its grey on grey, then has a shape of life grown old. And by this grey on grey it can only be understood, not rejuvenated. The owl of Minerva spreads its wings only with the falling of the dusk.'[3]

Some thinkers, of course, have supposed that they were delineating an eternal pattern, a changeless ideal essence. But in Hegel's opinion they were mistaken. 'Even the Platonic *Republic*, which passes proverbially as an *empty ideal*, was in essence nothing but an interpretation of Greek ethical life.'[4] After all, 'every individual is a son of his time [and] it is just as foolish to suppose

[1] *W*, VII, p. 376; *R*, 274, addition.   [2] *W*, VII, p. 376; *R*, 273, addition.
[3] *W*, VII, pp. 36–7; *R*, preface. Marx's equally famous retort was that it is the philosopher's business to change the world, not simply to understand it.
[4] *W*, VII, p. 33; *R*, preface.

that a philosophy can transcend its contemporary world as it is to suppose that an individual can overleap his own time. . . .'[1]

The clear expression of this view obviously constitutes an answer to those who take too seriously Hegel's apparent canonization of the Prussian State. For it is difficult to suppose that a man who understood very well that Aristotle, for example, canonized the Greek *polis* or City-State at a time when its vigorous life was already on the decline really supposed that the contemporary State of his own period represented the final and culminating form of political development. And even if Hegel did think this, there is nothing in his philosophy as such to warrant his prejudice. On the contrary, one would expect the sphere of objective Spirit to undergo further developments as long as history lasts.

Given this interpretation of political philosophy, the natural conclusion to draw is that the philosopher is concerned with making explicit what we may call the operative ideal of the culture or nation to which he belongs. He is an interpreter of the spirit of his time (*die Zeitgeist*). In and through him the political ideals of a society are raised to the level of reflective consciousness. And a society becomes self-conscious in this way only when it has reached maturity and looks back, as it were, on itself, at a time, that is to say, when a form of life has already actualized itself and is ready to pass into or give way to another.

No doubt, this is partly what Hegel means. His remarks about Plato's *Republic* show that it is. But in this case, it may be asked, how can he at the same time speak of the political philosopher as being concerned with the concept or essence of the State?

The answer to this question must be given, I think, in terms of Hegel's metaphysics. The historical process is the self-actualization of Spirit or Reason. 'What is rational is real and what is real is rational.'[2] And the concept of Spirit is the concept of identity-in-difference at the level of rational life. Objective Spirit, therefore, which culminates in the State tends towards the manifestation of identity-in-difference in political life. And this means that a mature or rational State will unite in itself the moments of universality and difference. It will embody universal self-consciousness or the self-conscious General Will. But this is embodied only in and through distinct finite spirits, each of which, as spirit, possesses 'infinite' value. Hence no State can be fully mature or rational (it cannot accord with the concept of the

---

[1] *W*, VII, p. 35; *R*, preface.   [2] *W*, VII, p. 33; *R*, preface.

State) unless it reconciles the conception of the State as an organic totality with the principle of individual freedom. And the philosopher, reflecting on the past and present political organizations, can discern how far they approximate to the requirements of the State as such. But this State as such is not a subsistent essence, existing in a celestial world. It is the *telos* or end of the movement of Spirit or Reason in man's social life. The philosopher can discern this *telos* in its essential outline, because he understands the nature of reality. But it does not follow that he is in a better position, as a philosopher, than is anyone else to prophesy the future or to tell statesmen and politicians what they ought to do. 'Philosophy always comes too late on the scene to do so.'[1] Plato may indeed have told contemporary Greeks how they ought, in his opinion, to organize the City-State. But he was in any case too late. For the shape of life which he dreamed of reorganizing was growing cold and would before long be ripe for decay. Utopian schemes are defeated by the movement of history.

10. Each State is in relation to other States a sovereign individual and demands recognition as such. The mutual relations between States are indeed partly regulated by treaties and by international law, which presuppose acceptance by the States concerned. But if this acceptance is refused or withdrawn, the ultimate arbiter in any dispute is war. For there is no sovereign power above individual States.

Now, if Hegel was simply registering an obvious empirical fact in the international life of his time, there would be no reason for adverse comment. But he goes on to justify war, as though it were an essential feature of human history. True, he admits that war can bring with it much injustice, cruelty and waste. But he argues that it has an ethical aspect and that it should not be regarded as 'an absolute evil and as a mere external contingent fact'.[2] On the contrary, it is a rational necessity. 'It is *necessary* that the finite, property and life, should be *posited* as contingent. . . .'[3] And this is precisely what war does. It is 'the condition in which we have to take seriously the vanity of temporal goods and things, which otherwise is usually only an edifying phrase'.[4]

It should be noted that Hegel is not simply saying that in war a man's moral qualities can be displayed on an heroic scale, which is obviously true. Nor is he saying merely that war brings home to

---

[1] *W*, VII, p. 36; *R*, preface.
[3] *Ibid.*
[2] *W*, VII, p. 434; *R*, 324.
[4] *Ibid.*

us the transitory character of the finite. He is asserting that war is a necessary rational phenomenon. It is in fact for him the means by which the dialectic of history gets, so to speak, a move on. It prevents stagnation and preserves, as he puts it, the ethical health of nations. It is the chief means by which a people's spirit acquires renewed vigour or a decayed political organism is swept aside and gives place to a more vigorous manifestation of the Spirit. Hegel rejects, therefore, Kant's ideal of perpetual peace.[1]

Obviously, Hegel had no experience of what we call total war. And he doubtless had the Napoleonic Wars and Prussia's struggle for independence fresh in his mind. But when one reads the passages in which he speaks of war and dismisses Kant's ideal of perpetual peace it is difficult to avoid the impression, partly comical and partly unpleasant, of a university professor romanticizing a dark feature of human history and decking it out with metaphysical trappings.[2]

11. Mention of international relations and of war as an instrument by which the historical dialectic progresses brings us to the subject of Hegel's concept of world-history.

Hegel distinguishes three main types of history or, rather, historiography. First there is 'original history', that is to say, descriptions of deeds and events and states of society which the historian had before his eyes. Thucydides' history represents this type. Secondly there is 'reflective history'. A general history, extending beyond the limits of the historian's experience, belongs to this type. So, for instance, does didactic history. Thirdly, there is 'philosophical history' or the philosophy of history. This term, says Hegel, signifies 'nothing else but the thoughtful consideration of history'.[3] But it can hardly be claimed that this description, taken by itself, is very enlightening. And, as Hegel explicitly admits, something more must be said by way of elucidation.

To say that the philosophy of history is the thoughtful consideration of history is to say that a thought is brought to this consideration. But the thought in question, Hegel insists, is not a preconceived plan or scheme into which the facts have somehow to be fitted. 'The only idea which philosophy brings with it [that is, to the contemplation of history] is the simple idea of reason,

---

[1] See Vol. VI, pp. 185 and 209.

[2] In justice to Hegel we can recall that he himself had felt the effect of war, its exhibition of the transitoriness of the finite, when he lost his position and belongings at Jena as a result of Napoleon's victorious campaign.

[3] W, XI, p. 34; S, p. 8. The letter S signifies J. Sibree's translation of Hegel's lectures on the philosophy of history.

that reason dominates the world and that world-history is thus a rational process.'[1] As far as philosophy is concerned, this truth is provided in metaphysics. But in history as such it is an hypothesis. Hence the truth that world-history is the self-unfolding of Spirit must be exhibited as the result of reflection on history. In our reflection history 'must be taken as it is; we must proceed historically, empirically'.[2]

The obvious comment on this is that even if Hegel disclaims any desire to force history into a preconceived mould, the thought or idea which the philosopher brings to the study of history must obviously exercise a great influence on his interpretation of events. Even if the idea is professedly proposed as an empirically verifiable hypothesis, the philosopher who, like Hegel himself, believes that its truth has been demonstrated in metaphysics will undoubtedly be prone to emphasize those aspects of history which seem to offer support for the hypothesis. Moreover, for the Hegelian the hypothesis is really no hypothesis at all but a demonstrated truth.

Hegel remarks, however, that even the would-be 'impartial' historians bring their own categories to the study of history. Absolute impartiality is a myth. And there cannot be a better principle of interpretation than a proven philosophical truth. Evidently, Hegel's general idea is more or less this. As the philosopher knows that reality is the self-unfolding of infinite reason, he knows that reason must operate in human history. At the same time we cannot tell in advance how it operates. To discover this, we have to study the course of events as depicted by historians in the ordinary sense and try to discern the significant rational process in the mass of contingent material. In theological language, we know in advance that divine providence operates in history. But to see how it operates we must study the historical data.

Now, world-history is the process whereby Spirit comes to actual consciousness of itself as freedom. Hence 'world-history is progress in the consciousness of freedom'.[3] This consciousness is attained, of course, only in and through the mind of man. And the divine Spirit, as manifested in history through the consciousness of man, is the World-Spirit (*der Weltgeist*). History, therefore, is the process whereby the World-Spirit comes to explicit consciousness of itself as free.

But though the *Weltgeist* attains consciousness of itself as free

---

[1] *W*, XI, p. 34; *S*, p. 9.   [2] *W*, XI, p. 36; *S*, p. 10.
[3] *W*, XI, p. 46; *S*, p. 19.

only in and through the human mind, the historian is concerned with nations rather than with individuals. Hence the unit, so to speak, in the concrete development of the World-Spirit is the national spirit or the spirit of a people (*der Volksgeist*). And by this Hegel means in part a people's culture as manifested not only in its political constitution and traditions but also in its morality, art, religion and philosophy. But a national spirit is not, of course, resident simply in legal forms, works of art and so on. It is a living totality, the spirit of a people as living in and through that people. And the individual is a bearer of the *Weltgeist* in so far as he participates in this more limited totality, the *Volksgeist*, which is itself a phase or moment in the life of the World-Spirit.

Hegel does indeed assert that 'in world-history the individuals with whom we have to do are peoples, the totalities which are States'.[1] But he can use the terms 'State' and 'national spirit' more or less interchangeably because the first term signifies for him something much more than the juridical State. He understands by the State in this context a totality which exists in and through its members, though it is not identical with any given set of citizens existing here and now, and which gives concrete form to the spirit and culture of a people or nation.

It should be noted, however, that one important reason why Hegel insists that world-history is concerned with States is that in his view a national spirit exists for itself (that is, as conscious of itself) only in and through the State. Hence those peoples which do not constitute national States are practically excluded from consideration in world-history. For their spirits are only implicit: they do not exist 'for themselves'.

Each national spirit, therefore, embodied in a State, is a phase or moment in the life of the *Weltgeist*. Indeed, this World-Spirit is really a *result* of the interplay of national spirits. They are, so to speak, the moments in its actualization. National spirits are limited, finite 'and their fates and deeds in their relations to one another reveal the dialectic of the finitude of these spirits. Out of this dialectic there arises the *Universal Spirit*, the unlimited *World-Spirit* which pronounces its judgment—and its judgment is the highest—upon the finite national spirits. It does so within *world-history* which is the *world's court of* judgment.'[2] The judgment of the nations is for Hegel immanent in history. The actual fate of each nation constitutes its judgment.

---

[1] *W*, XI, p. 40; *S*, p. 14.   [2] *W*, VIII, p. 446; *R*, 340.

Spirit, therefore, in its progress towards full and explicit self-consciousness takes the form of limited and one-sided manifestations of itself, the several national spirits. And Hegel assumes that in any given epoch one particular nation represents in a special way the development of the World-Spirit. 'This people is the dominant people in world-history for this epoch—*and it is only once that it can make its hour strike.*'[1] Its national spirit develops, reaches its zenith and then declines, after which the nation is relegated to the background of the historical stage. Hegel is doubtless thinking of the way in which Spain, for instance, developed into a great empire, with a peculiar stamp and culture of its own, and then declined. But he assumes without more ado that a nation cannot occupy the centre of the stage more than once. And this assumption is perhaps disputable, unless, of course, we choose to make it necessarily true by maintaining that a nation which enjoys a second period of outstanding importance is really a different nation with a different spirit. In any case Hegel's desire to find a particular world-historical nation for each epoch has a narrowing effect on his conception of history.

To say this is not, however, to deny that in his lectures on the philosophy of history Hegel covers a wide field. As he is dealing with world-history, this is obviously bound to be the case. The first part of his work is devoted to the Oriental world, including China, India, Persia, Asia Minor, Palestine and Egypt. In the second part he treats of the Greek world, and in the third of the Roman world, including the rise of Christianity to the position of an historical power (*eine geschichtliche Macht*). The fourth part is devoted to what Hegel calls the Germanic world. The period covered stretches from the Byzantine Empire up to the French Revolution and the Napoleonic Wars inclusively. Mohammedanism receives a brief treatment in this fourth part.

The Orientals, according to Hegel, did not know that man as such is free. And in the absence of this knowledge they were not free. They knew only that *one* man, the despot, was free. 'But for this very reason such freedom is only caprice, ferocity or brutal passion—or a mildness and tameness in the passions which is itself only an accident of Nature or caprice. This *one* is, therefore, only a despot, he is not a free man, a true human being.'[2]

In the Greco-Roman world there arises the consciousness of freedom. But the Greeks and Romans of classical times knew only

<hr>

[1] *W*, VII, p. 449; *R*, 347.   [2] *W*, XI, p. 45; *S*, p. 18.

that *some* men are free, namely the free men as opposed to the slaves. Even Plato and Aristotle exemplify this inadequate phase in the growth of the consciousness of freedom.

In Hegel's view it was the 'Germanic' peoples who under the influence of Christianity first arrived at the conscious awareness that man as such is free. But though this principle was recognized from the start in Christianity, it does not follow that it immediately found expression in laws, government and political organization and institutions. The awareness of the freedom of the spirit arose first in religion, but a long process of development was required for it to attain explicit practical recognition as the basis of the State. And this process of development is studied in history. The inner consciousness of the freedom of the spirit had to give itself explicit objectification, and here Hegel attributes a leading role to the so-called Germanic peoples.

Now, we have seen that the units to which primary consideration is given in world-history are national States. But it is a notorious fact that Hegel emphasizes the role of what he calls the world-historical individuals (*die weltgeschichtlichen Individuen*), men such as Alexander the Great, Julius Caesar and Napoleon. And this may seem to involve him in some inconsistency. But national spirits and the World-Spirit which arises out of their dialectic exist and live and operate only in and through human beings. And Hegel's point of view is that the World-Spirit has used certain individuals as its instruments in a signal way. In theological language, they were the special instruments of divine providence. They had, of course, their subjective passions and private motives. Napoleon, for example, may have been dominated to a great extent by personal ambition and megalomania. But though the private motives, conscious and unconscious, of a Caesar or a Napoleon are of interest to the biographer and the psychologist, they are not of much importance or relevance for the philosopher of history who is interested in such men for what they accomplished as instruments of the World-Spirit. Nothing great, Hegel remarks, is accomplished in this world without passion. But the passions of the great figures of history are used as instruments by the World-Spirit and exhibit 'the cunning of Reason'. Whatever motives Julius Caesar may have had for crossing the Rubicon his action had an historical importance which probably far transcended anything that he understood. Whatever his private interests may have been, the cosmic Reason or Spirit in its 'cunning' used these interests to transform the Republic into the Empire and to bring the Roman genius and spirit to the peak of its development.

If we abstract from all questionable metaphysics, Hegel is obviously saying something quite sensible. It is certainly not absurd to claim, for example, that the historian is or ought to be more interested in what Stalin actually accomplished for Russia than in the psychology of that unpleasing tyrant. But Hegel's teleological view of history implies in addition, of course, that what Stalin accomplished *had* to be accomplished, and that the Russian dictator, with all his unpleasant characteristics, was an instrument in the hands of the World-Spirit.[1]

12. In view of the already somewhat inordinate length of this chapter I have no wish either to repeat or to amplify the general remarks about the philosophy of history which I made in the preceding volume.[2] But one or two comments relating to Hegel's concept of world-history may be appropriate.

In the first place, if history is a rational process in the sense of being a teleological process, a movement towards a goal which is determined by the nature of the Absolute rather than by human choice, it may appear that all that occurs is justified by the very fact that it occurs. And if the history of the world is itself the highest court of judgment, the judgment of the nations, it may appear to follow that might is right. For example, if one nation succeeds in conquering another, it seems to follow that its action is justified by its success.

Now, the saying 'might is right' is perhaps generally understood as being an expression of that type of cynical outlook which is manifested by Callicles in Plato's *Gorgias*. For this outlook the notion of a universally obligatory and fundamentally unchanging moral law is the creation of a self-defensive instinct on the part of the weak who try by this means to enslave the strong and free. The really free and strong man sees through this notion of morality and rejects it. He sees that the only right is might. In his judgment the weak, nature's slaves, implicitly admit the truth of this judgment, though they are not consciously aware of the fact. For, individually weak, they try to exercise a collective might by imposing on the strong an ethical code which is of advantage to themselves.

[1] Hegel's answer to any theologically-minded critic is that the theory of the cunning of Reason is in accord with Christianity. For Christianity maintains that God brings good out of evil, using, for instance, Judas's betrayal of Christ in the accomplishment of the Redemption.
[2] See Vol. VI, pp. 422–7.

But Hegel was no cynic. As we have seen, he was convinced of the value of the human person as such, not merely of the value of some human beings. And it can be reasonably claimed that with him it is not so much a question of the cynical view that might is right as of the exaggeratedly optimistic view that in history right, in the form of the rational, is the necessarily dominant factor.

Yet it is arguable, of course, that in the long run it comes more or less to the same thing, even if there is a difference of attitude between Hegel and the cynic. If right always prevails in history, then successful might is justified. It is justified because it is right rather than because it is might; but it is none the less justified. Hegel does indeed allow, for example, that moral judgments can be passed on what he calls world-historical individuals. But he also makes it clear that such judgments possess for him only a purely formal rectitude, as he puts it. From the point of view of a given system of social ethics a great revolutionary, for example, may be a bad man. But from the point of view of world-history his deeds are justified, for he accomplishes what the universal Spirit requires. And if one nation conquers another, its action is justified inasmuch as it is a moment in the dialectic of world-history, whatever moral judgments are passed on the actions of the individuals involved when they are considered, so to speak, in their private capacities. Indeed, world-history is not interested in this second aspect of the situation.

We can say, therefore, that it is Hegel's metaphysical views rather than any cynical outlook which involve him in justifying all the events in which the world-historian or philosopher of history is interested. Hegel argues indeed that he is simply taking seriously and applying to history as a whole the Christian doctrine of divine providence. But there are obvious differences. Once the transcendent God has been transformed into the Hegelian Absolute and judgment has been made purely immanent in history itself, no escape is left from the conclusion that from the world-historical point of view all the events and actions which form moments in the self-manifestation of the Absolute are justified. And moral questions which possess importance from the Christian point of view become practically irrelevant. I do not mean to imply, of course, that this shows of itself that Hegel's point of view is false. Nor do I mean to imply that a Christian historian is committed to moralizing. But Hegel's philosophy of history is much more than what historians generally understand by history. It is a meta-physical interpretation of history. And my point is that Hegel's metaphysics drives him to conclusions to which the Christian theologian is not committed. True, Hegel thought that he was giving the philosophical essence, as it were, of the Christian doctrine of providence. But in point of fact this 'demythologization' was a transformation.

Mention of Hegel's metaphysics suggests another comment. If, as Hegel maintains, world-history is the process by which the universal Spirit actualizes itself in time, it is difficult to understand why the goal of the process should not be a universal world-State or world-society in which personal freedom would be perfectly realized within an all-embracing unity. Even if Hegel wishes to insist that the universal is manifested in its particulars and that the particulars in question are national spirits, it would seem that the ideal end of the whole movement should be a world-federation, representing the concrete universal.

Hegel did not, however, adopt this point of view. World-history is for him essentially the dialectic of national spirits, of States, which are the determinate shape which Spirit assumes in history. If we consider Spirit as rising above these particular finite forms, we enter the sphere of absolute Spirit, which will be the theme of the next chapter.

CHAPTER XI

HEGEL (3)

The sphere of absolute Spirit—The philosophy of art—The philosophy of religion—The relation between religion and philosophy—Hegel's philosophy of the history of philosophy— The influence of Hegel and the division between right-wing and left-wing Hegelians.

1. As we have seen, difficulties arise directly we begin to probe beneath the surface of the outlines of Hegel's system. For example, when we start to inquire into the ontological reference of the logical Idea and the precise relation between the *Logos* and Nature, several possible lines of interpretation present themselves to the mind. But this does not alter the fact that a preliminary statement of the outline of the system can be easily made. The Absolute is Being. Being, considered first (though not in a temporal sense) as the Idea, objectifies itself in Nature, the material world. As the objectification of the Idea, Nature manifests the Idea. At the same time it cannot do so adequately. For Being, the Absolute, is defined as Spirit, as Thought which thinks itself. And it must come to exist as such. It cannot do so in Nature, though Nature is a condition for its doing so. Being comes to exist as Spirit and thus to manifest its essence adequately only in and through the human spirit. But Being as Spirit can be conceived in different ways. It can be conceived 'in itself', in the form of the finite spirit in its inwardness or subjectivity. This is the sphere of subjective Spirit. It can be conceived as issuing out of itself and objectifying itself in the institutions, above all the State, which it posits or creates. This is the sphere of objective Spirit. And it can be conceived as rising above finitude and knowing itself as Being, the totality. And this is the sphere of absolute Spirit. Absolute Spirit exists only in and through the human spirit, but it does so at the level at which the individual human spirit is no longer a finite mind, enclosed in its own private thoughts, emotions, interests and purposes, but has become a moment in the life of the infinite as an identity-in-difference which knows itself as such. In other words, absolute Spirit is Spirit at the level of that absolute knowledge of

which Hegel wrote in *The Phenomenology of Spirit*. And we can thus say that man's knowledge of the Absolute and the Absolute's knowledge of itself are two aspects of the same reality. For Being actualizes itself as concretely existing self-thinking Thought through the human spirit.

For the sake of clarity the following point must be made clear. I am conscious of myself as a finite being: I have, so to speak, my own self-consciousness which is quite different from the self-consciousness of any other human being. But though, like anything else, this subjective self-consciousness must be within the Absolute, it is not at all what Hegel means by absolute knowledge. This arises when I am aware, not simply of myself as a finite individual standing over against other finite persons and things, but rather of the Absolute as the ultimate and all-embracing reality. My knowledge, if I attain it, of Nature as the objective manifestation of the Absolute and of the Absolute as returning to itself as subjectivity in the form of Spirit, existing in and through the spiritual life of man in history, is a moment in absolute self-consciousness, that is, in the self-knowledge of Being or the Absolute.

The matter can be put in this way. We have seen that according to Hegel the World-Spirit arises out of the dialectic of national spirits. And in the comments at the end of the last chapter it was remarked that this view might reasonably be expected to involve the conclusion that the end or goal of history is a universal society, a world-State or at least a world-federation of States. But this was not Hegel's point of view. National spirits are limited and finite. And when the World-Spirit is conceived as rising above this finitude and limitation and existing as infinite Spirit, it must be conceived as knowledge, as self-thinking Thought. We thus pass out of the political sphere. The State is indeed described by Hegel as the self-conscious ethical substance, in the sense that it conceives its own ends and consciously pursues them. But it cannot be described as self-thinking Thought or as personality. Self-thinking Thought is Spirit knowing itself as Spirit and Nature as its objectification and as the condition for its own concrete existence as Spirit. It is the Absolute knowing itself as the Totality, that is, as identity-in-difference: it is infinite Being reflectively conscious of the distinct phases or moments in its own life. It is Spirit set free, as it were, from the limitations of the finitude which characterizes the national spirit.

Absolute Spirit is thus the synthesis or unity of subjective

Spirit and objective Spirit on a higher plane. It is subjectivity and objectivity in one. For it is Spirit knowing itself. But whereas in the spheres of subjective Spirit and objective Spirit we are concerned with the finite Spirit, first in its inwardness, then in its self-manifestation in objective institutions, such as the family and the State, in the sphere of absolute Spirit we are concerned with infinite Spirit knowing itself as infinite. This does not mean that infinite Spirit is something set over against, opposed to and existing entirely apart from the finite spirit. The infinite exists in and through the finite. But in the sphere of absolute Spirit the infinite is reflectively conscious of itself as such. Hence absolute Spirit is not a repetition, so to speak, of subjective Spirit. It is Spirit's return to itself at a higher level, a level at which subjectivity and objectivity are united in one infinite act.

To speak, however, of one infinite act can be misleading. For it suggests the idea of an eternally changeless self-intuition on the part of the Absolute, whereas for Hegel absolute Spirit is the life of the Absolute's developing self-knowledge. It is the process whereby the Absolute actualizes itself precisely as self-thinking Thought. And it does so at three main levels, those of art, religion and philosophy.

What Hegel means by this can most easily be understood if we approach the matter from the point of view of man's knowledge of the Absolute. First, the Absolute can be apprehended under the sensuous form of beauty as manifested in Nature or, more adequately, in the work of art. Hegel thus accepts Schelling's theory of the metaphysical significance of art. Secondly, the Absolute can be apprehended in the form of pictorial or figurative thought which finds expression in the language of religion. Thirdly, the Absolute can be apprehended purely conceptually, that is, in speculative philosophy. Art, religion and philosophy are thus all concerned with the Absolute. The infinite divine Being is, as it were, the content or subject-matter of all three spiritual activities. But though the content is the same, the form is different. That is to say, the Absolute is apprehended in different ways in these activities. As having the same content or subject-matter, art, religion and philosophy all belong to the sphere of absolute Spirit. But the differences in form show that they are distinct phases in the life of absolute Spirit.

The philosophy of absolute Spirit, therefore, consists of three main parts, the philosophy of art, the philosophy of religion and

what we may call the philosophy of philosophy. And as Hegel
proceeds dialectically, showing how art passes into or demands the
transition to religion and how religion in turn demands the
transition to philosophy, it is important to understand in what
sense the time element enters into this dialectic and in what sense
it does not.

In his philosophy of art Hegel does not confine himself to a
purely abstract account of the essence of the aesthetic consciousness. He surveys the historical development of art and tries to
show a development in the aesthetic consciousness up to the point
at which it demands the transition to the religious consciousness.
Similarly, in his philosophy of religion he does not confine himself
to delineating the essential features or moments of the religious
consciousness: he surveys the history of religion from primitive
religion up to the absolute religion, Christianity, and endeavours
to make clear a dialectical pattern of development in the religious
consciousness up to the point at which it demands a transition to
the standpoint of speculative philosophy. There is, therefore, a
mixture of the temporal and the non-temporal. On the one hand
the actual historical developments of art, religion and philosophy
are all temporal processes. This is sufficiently obvious. For
instance, classical Greek art temporally preceded Christian art, and
Greek religion temporally preceded the Christian religion. On the
other hand Hegel is not so foolish as to suppose that art ran
through all its forms before religion appeared on the scene or that
there was no philosophy before the appearance of the absolute
religion. He is as well aware as anyone else that Greek temples
were associated with Greek religion, and that there were Greek
philosophers. The dialectical transition from the concept of art to
the concept of religion and from the concept of religion to that of
philosophy is in itself timeless. That is to say, it is in essence a
conceptual, and not a temporal or historical, progression.

The point can be expressed in this way. Hegel might have
confined himself to a purely conceptual movement, in which the
only priority involved would be logical, not temporal. But the
life of the Spirit is an historical development in which one form of
art succeeds another, one stage in the evolution of the religious
consciousness succeeds another stage, and one philosophical
system succeeds another philosophical system. And Hegel is
anxious to show the dialectical patterns exhibited in the history of
art, the history of religion and the history of philosophy. Hence the

philosophy of absolute Spirit, as he expounds it, cannot abstract from all temporal succession. And it has, therefore, two aspects. It may not indeed be always a simple matter to sort them out. But in any case we only make nonsense of Hegel's doctrine if we take him to mean, for example, that religion started only when art stopped. And whatever some writers may think that Hegel ought to have said, in my opinion he looked on art, religion and philosophy as permanent activities of the human spirit. He may have thought that philosophy is the highest of these activities. But it does not follow that he imagined that man would ever become pure thought.

By way of conclusion to this section it is worth drawing attention to the following point. It is a mistake to think that according to Hegel the State is the highest of all realities and political life the highest activity of man. For, as we have seen, the sphere of objective Spirit leads on to the sphere of absolute Spirit. And while organized society in some form is for Hegel a condition for art, religion and philosophy, these three activities are the highest expression of Spirit. Hegel doubtless exalted the State, but he exalted philosophy still more.

2. Dialectically or logically speaking, the Absolute is manifested first of all in the form of immediacy, under the guise, that is to say, of objects of sense. As such, it is apprehended as beauty, which is 'the sensuous semblance [*Scheinen*] of the Idea'.[1] And this sensuous appearance of the Idea, this shining of the Absolute through the veils of sense, is called the Ideal. Looked at from one point of view the Idea as beauty is, of course, identical with the Idea as truth. For it is the same Absolute which is apprehended as beauty by the aesthetic consciousness and as truth in philosophy. But the forms or modes of apprehension are distinct. Aesthetic intuition and philosophy are not the same thing. Hence the Idea as beauty is termed the Ideal.

While not denying that there can be such a thing as beauty in Nature, Hegel insists that beauty in art is far superior. For artistic beauty is the immediate creation of Spirit; it is Spirit's manifestation of itself to itself. And Spirit and its products are superior to Nature and its phenomena. Hegel confines his attention, therefore, to beauty in art. It may indeed be regrettable that he underestimates natural beauty as a manifestation of the divine. But,

---

[1] *W*, XII, p. 160; *O*, I, p. 154. In references to Hegel's lectures on *The Philosophy of Fine Art* the letter *O* signifies the English translation by F. P. B. Osmaston.

given the construction of his system, he can hardly do anything else but concentrate on artistic beauty. For he has left the philosophy of Nature behind him and is concerned with the philosophy of Spirit.

But, we may ask, if artistic beauty is said to be the sensuous semblance or appearance of the Idea, what does this proposition mean? Is it anything more than a high-sounding but vague statement? The answer is fairly simple. The Idea is the unity of subjectivity and objectivity. And in the beautiful work of art this unity is expressed or represented in the union of spiritual content with external or material embodiment. Spirit and matter, subjectivity and objectivity, are fused together in a harmonious unity or synthesis. 'Art has the task of presenting the Idea to immediate intuition in sensuous form, and not in the form of thought or pure spirituality. And the value and dignity of this presentation lie in the correspondence and unity of the two aspects of ideal content and its embodiment, so that the perfection and excellence of art and the conformity of its products with its essential concept depend on the degree of inner harmony and unity with which the ideal content and sensuous form are made to interpenetrate.'[1]

Obviously, Hegel does not mean to imply that the artist is consciously aware of the fact that his product is a manifestation of the nature of the Absolute. Nor does he mean to imply that a man is unable to appreciate the beauty of a work of art unless he has this conscious awareness. Both the artist and the beholder may feel that the product is, so to speak, just right or perfect, in the sense that to add or subtract anything would be to impair or disfigure the work of art. Both may feel that spiritual content and sensuous embodiment are perfectly fused. And they may both feel that the product is in some undefined sense a manifestation of 'truth'. But it by no means follows that either of them can state the metaphysical significance of the work of art, whether to himself or to anyone else. Nor does this indicate any defect in the aesthetic consciousness. For it is philosophy, and not the aesthetic consciousness, which explicitly or reflectively apprehends the metaphysical significance of art. In other words, this apprehension arises from philosophical reflection *about* art. And this is something very different from artistic creation. A great artist may be a very bad philosopher or no philosopher at all. And a great philosopher may well be incapable of painting a beautiful picture or composing a symphony.

[1] *W*, XII, p. 110; *O*, I, p. 98.

In the perfect work of art, therefore, there is complete harmony between ideal content and its sensuous form or embodiment. The two elements interpenetrate and are fused into one. But this artistic ideal is not always attained. And the different possible types of relation between the two elements give us the fundamental types of art.

First we have the type of art in which the sensuous element predominates over the spiritual or ideal content, in the sense that the latter has not mastered its medium of expression and does not shine through the veils of sense. In other words, the artist suggests rather than expresses his meaning. There is ambiguity and an air of mystery. And this type of art is *symbolic* art. It can be found, for example, among the ancient Egyptians. 'It is in *Egypt* that we have to look for the perfect exemplification of the symbolic mode of expression, in regard both to its peculiar content and to its form. Egypt is the land of symbol which sets itself the spiritual task of the self-interpretation of Spirit, without really being able to fulfil it.'[1] And Hegel finds in the Sphinx 'the symbol of the symbolic itself'.[2] It is 'the objective riddle'.[3]

Hegel subdivides symbolic art into subordinate phases and discusses the difference between Hindu and Egyptian art and the religious poetry of the Hebrews. But we cannot follow him into details. It is sufficient to notice that according to him symbolic art is best suited to the early ages of humanity when the world and man itself, Nature and Spirit, are felt as mysterious and enigmatic.

Secondly we have the type of art in which spiritual or ideal content are fused into a harmonious unity. This is *classical* art. Whereas in symbolic art the Absolute is conceived as a mysterious, formless One which is suggested rather than expressed in the work of art, in classical art Spirit is conceived in concrete form as the self-conscious individual spirit, whose sensuous embodiment is the human body. This type of art, therefore, is predominantly anthropomorphic. The gods are simply glorified human beings. And the leading classical art is thus *sculpture*, which presents Spirit as the finite embodied spirit.

Just as Hegel associates symbolic art with the Hindus and Egyptians, so he associates classical art with the ancient Greeks. In the great works of Greek sculpture we find the perfect marriage, as it were, of Spirit and matter. The spiritual content shines through the veils of sense: it is expressed, not merely suggested

---

[1] *W*, xii, p. 472; *O*, ii, p. 74. [2] *W*, xii, p. 480; *O*, ii, p. 83. [3] *Ibid.*

in symbolic form. For the human body, as represented by a Praxiteles, is the clear expression of Spirit.

Yet 'classical art and its religion of beauty do not satisfy wholly the depths of the Spirit'.[1] And we have the third main type of art, namely *romantic* art, in which Spirit, felt as infinite, tends to overflow, as it were, its sensuous embodiment and to abandon the veils of sense. In classical art there is a perfect fusion of ideal content and sensuous form. But Spirit is not merely the particular finite spirit, united with a particular body: it is the divine infinite. And in romantic art, which is to all intents and purposes the art of Christendom, no sensuous embodiment is felt to be adequate to the spiritual content. It is not, as in symbolic art, a case of the spiritual content having to be suggested rather than expressed because Spirit has not yet been conceived as such and remains enigmatic, a riddle or problem. Rather is it that Spirit has been conceived as what it is, namely infinite spiritual Life as God, and therefore as overflowing any finite sensuous embodiment.

Romantic art, according to Hegel, is concerned with the life of the Spirit, which is movement, action, conflict. Spirit must, as it were, die to live. That is to say, it must go over into what is not itself that it may rise again to become itself, a truth which is expressed in Christianity, in the doctrine of self-sacrifice and resurrection, exemplified above all in the life, death and resurrection of Christ. The typical romantic arts, therefore, will be those which are best adapted to expressing movement, action and conflict. And these are painting, music and poetry. Architecture is least adapted for expressing the inner life of the Spirit and is the typical form of symbolic art. Sculpture, the typical form of classical art, is better adapted than architecture for this purpose, but it concentrates on the external, on the body, and its expression of movement and life is very limited. In poetry, however, the medium consists of words, that is, of sensuous images expressed in language; and it is best suited for expressing the life of the Spirit.

This asscoiation of particular arts with definite general types of art must not, however, be understood in an exclusive sense. Architecture, for example, is particularly associated with symbolic art because, while capable of expressing mystery, it is of all the fine arts the least fitted for expressing the life of the Spirit. But

[1] *W*, XIII, p. 14; *O*, II, p. 180. Note that Hegel here associates a particular type of art with a particular type of religion.

to say this is not to deny that there are forms of architecture which are characteristic of classical and romantic art. Thus the Greek temple, the perfect house for the anthropomorphic deity, is an obvious example of classical architecture, while the Gothic, an example of romantic architecture, expresses the feeling that the divine transcends the sphere of finitude and of matter. In contrast with the Greek temple we can see how 'the romantic character of Christian churches consists in the way in which they arise out of the soil and soar into the heights'.[1]

Similarly, sculpture is not confined to classical art, even if it is the characteristic classical art-form. Nor are painting, music and poetry confined to romantic art. But we cannot follow Hegel any further into his lengthy discussion of the particular fine arts.

Now, if we are considering art simply in itself, we must say that the highest type of art is that in which spiritual content and sensuous embodiment are in perfect harmonious accord. And this is classical art, the leading characteristic form of which is sculpture. But if we are considering the aesthetic consciousness as a stage in the self-manifestation of God or as a level in man's developing knowledge of God, we must say that romantic art is the highest type. For, as we have seen, in romantic art infinite Spirit tends to drop the veils of sense, a fact which becomes most evident in poetry. Of course, as long as we remain in the sphere of art at all, the veils of sense are never completely abandoned. But romantic art provides the point of transition from the aesthetic to the religious consciousness. That is to say, when the mind perceives that no material embodiment is adequate to the expression of Spirit, it passes from the sphere of art to that of religion.[2] Art cannot satisfy the Spirit as a means of apprehending its own nature.

3. If the Absolute is Spirit, Reason, self-thinking Thought, it can be adequately apprehended as such only by thought itself. And we might perhaps expect Hegel to make a direct transition from art to philosophy, whereas in point of fact he makes the transition to philosophy by way of an intermediate mode of apprehending the Absolute, namely religion. 'The sphere of conscious life which is nearest in ascending order to the realm of art is religion.'[3] Obviously, Hegel is not simply concerned with completing a triad, so that the sphere of absolute Spirit may

---

[1] *W*, XIII, p. 334; *O*, III, p. 91.
[2] To repeat, this transition is dialectical rather than temporal. The Egyptians and the Hindus, for instance, had their own religions as well as their own forms of art.   [3] *W*, XII, p. 151; *O*, I, p. 142.

conform to the general pattern of the system. Nor is it simply that he sees the need for a philosophy of religion in view of the importance of religion in the history of mankind, and of the obvious fact that it is concerned with the divine. The insertion of religion between art and philosophy is due above all to Hegel's conviction that the religious consciousness exemplifies an intermediate way of apprehending the Absolute. Religion in general is or essentially involves the self-manifestation of the Absolute in the form of *Vorstellung*, a word which can be translated in this context as figurative or pictorial thought. On the one hand the religious consciousness differs from the aesthetic in that it *thinks* the Absolute. On the other hand the thought which is characteristic of religion is not pure conceptual thought as found in philosophy. It is thought clothed, as it were, in imagery: it is, one may say, the product of a marriage between imagination and thought. A *Vorstellung* is a concept, but it is not the pure concept of the philosopher. Rather is it a pictorial or imaginative concept.

For example, the truth that the logical Idea, the *Logos*, is objectified in Nature is apprehended by the religious consciousness (at least in Judaism, Christianity and Mohammedanism) in the form of the imaginative or pictorial concept of the free creation of the world by a transcendent Deity. Again, the truth that the finite spirit is in essence a moment in the life of infinite Spirit is apprehended by the Christian consciousness in the form of the doctrine of the Incarnation and of man's union with God through Christ. For Hegel the truths are the same in content, but the modes of apprehension and expression are different in religion and in philosophy. For instance, the idea of God in the Christian consciousness and the concept of the Absolute have for Hegel exactly the same content: they refer to or mean the same reality. But this reality is apprehended and described in different ways.

As for the existence of God, there is an obvious sense in which Hegel needs no proof, no proof, that is to say, in addition to his system itself. For God is Being, and the nature of Being is demonstrated in logic or abstract metaphysics. At the same time Hegel devotes a good deal of attention to traditional proofs of God's existence. Nowadays, he remarks, these proofs have fallen into discredit. They are regarded not only as completely antiquated from a philosophical point of view but also, from a religious standpoint, as irreligious and practically impious. For there is a strong tendency to substitute unreasoned faith and pious feelings of the heart for any attempt to give faith a rational foundation. Indeed, so unfashionable has this business of proof become that 'the proofs are here and there hardly even known as historical data; and even by theologians, people, that is to say, who profess to have a scientific knowledge of religious truths, they are sometimes unknown'.[1] Yet the proofs do not merit this contempt. For they arose 'out of the need to satisfy thought, reason',[2] and they represent the elevation of the human mind to God, making explicit the immediate movement of faith.

Speaking of the cosmological proof, Hegel remarks that its essential defect in its traditional forms is that it posits the finite as something existing on its own and then tries to make a transition to the infinite as something different from the finite. But this defect can be remedied if we once understand that 'Being is to be defined not only as finite but also as infinite.'[3] In other words, we have to show that 'the being of the finite is not only its being but also the being of the infinite'.[4] Conversely, of course, it has to be shown that infinite Being unfolds itself in and through the finite. The objections against making the transition from the finite to the infinite or from the infinite to the finite can be met only by a true philosophy of Being which shows that the supposed gulf between the finite and the infinite does not exist. Kant's criticism of the proofs then falls to the ground.

This amounts to saying that the true proof of the existence of God is, as was remarked above, the Hegelian system itself. And to expound this system is obviously a philosophical task. Hence the philosophy of religion proper is concerned more with the religious consciousness and its mode or modes of apprehending God than with proving God's existence.

Considered abstractly, the religious consciousness comprises three main moments or phases. The first, as the normal scheme of the Hegelian dialectic would lead one to expect, is the moment of universality. God is conceived as the undifferentiated universal, as the infinite and only true reality. The second moment is that of particularity. In conceiving God I distinguish between myself and him, between the infinite and the finite. He becomes for me an object over against me. And my consciousness of God as 'outside' me or over against me involves the consciousness of myself as

---

[1] W, XVI, p. 361; SS, III, p. 156. In references to Hegel's *Lectures on The Philosophy of Religion SS* signifies the English translation by E. B. Speirs and J. Burdon Sanderson.   [2] W, XVI, p. 361; SS, III, p. 157.
[3] W, XVI, p. 457; SS, III, p. 259.   [4] W, XVI, p. 456; SS, III, p. 259.

separated or alienated from him, as a sinner. Finally, the third moment is that of individuality, of the return of the particular to the universal, of the finite to the infinite. Separation and alienation are overcome. For the religious consciousness this is accomplished in worship and in the way of salvation, that is, by the variety of means by which man conceives himself as entering into union with God.

The mind thus moves from the bare abstract thought of God to the consciousness of itself and God in separation, and thence to awareness of itself as one with God. And this movement is the essential movement of the religious consciousness. Its three moments or phases, one may note, correspond with the three moments of the Idea.

But religion is not, of course, simply religion in the abstract. It takes the form of definite religions. And in his lectures on the philosophy of religion Hegel traces the development of the religious consciousness through different types of religion. He is primarily concerned with exhibiting a logical or conceptual sequence; but this sequence is developed through reflection on the historical religions of mankind, the existence and nature of which is obviously known by other means than *a priori* deduction. Hegel's concern is to exhibit the dialectical pattern exemplified in the empirical or historical data.

The first main phase of definite or determinate religion is called by Hegel the religion of Nature (*die Naturreligion*), this phrase being used to cover any religion in which God is conceived as less than Spirit. It is subdivided into three phases. First there is immediate religion or magic. Secondly there is the religion of substance, under which heading Hegel considers in turn Chinese religion, Hinduism and Buddhism. Thirdly there are the religions of Persia, Syria and Egypt in which there can be found some glimmering of the idea of spirituality. Thus while in Hinduism Brahman is the purely abstract undifferentiated One, in the Persian religion of Zoroastrianism God is conceived as the Good.

The religion of Nature can be said to correspond with the first moment of the religious consciousness as described above. In the characteristic *Naturreligion*, namely the religion of substance, God is conceived as the undifferentiated universal. This is pantheism in the sense that the finite being is regarded as swallowed up by or as purely accidental to the divine Being. At the same time, though in Hinduism Brahman is conceived in a way corresponding to the first moment of the religious consciousness, this does not mean that the other moments are altogether absent.

The second main phase of definite religion is the religion of spiritual individuality. Here God is conceived as Spirit, but in the form of an individual person or of individual persons. The inevitable triad comprises the Jewish, Greek and Roman religions, entitled respectively the religions of sublimity, beauty and utility. Thus Jupiter Capitolinus has as his function the preservation of the safety and sovereignty of Rome.[1]

These three types of religion correspond to the second moment of the religious consciousness. The divine is conceived as being over against or apart from the human. In Jewish religion, for example, God is exalted above the world and man in transcendent sublimity. At the same time the other moments of the religious consciousness are also represented. Thus in Judaism there is the idea of man's reconciliation with God through sacrifice and obedience to the divine law.

The third main phase of definite religion is absolute religion, namely Christianity. In Christianity God is conceived as what he really is, infinite Spirit which is not only transcendent but also immanent. And man is conceived as united with God by participating in the divine life through the grace received from Christ, the God-man. Hence the Christian religion corresponds above all with the third moment of the religious consciousness, which is the synthesis or unity of the first two moments. God is not looked on as an undifferentiated unity, but as the Trinity of Persons, as infinite spiritual Life. And the infinite and finite are not regarded as set over against one another, but as united without confusion. As St. Paul says, in him we live and move and have our being.

To say that Christianity is the absolute religion is to say that it is the absolute truth. And Hegel fulminates against preachers and theologians who pass lightly over the Christian dogmas or who whittle them down to suit the outlook of a supposedly enlightened age. But we must add that Christianity expresses the absolute truth under the form of *Vorstellung*. There arises, therefore, the demand for a transition to philosophy which thinks the content of religion in pure conceptual form. The attempt to do so is, according

---

[1] Evidently, the third member of the triad, the religion of utility, is from one point of view a degradation of religion. For it practically reduces God to an instrument. At the same time it demands the transition to a higher form of religion. For example, the admission by Rome of all deities into its pantheon reduces polytheism to an absurdity and demands the transition to monotheism.

to Hegel, the continuation of the pioneer work of men such as St. Anselm who consciously set out to understand and justify by necessary reasons the content of faith.

4. As we have seen, the transition from religion to philosophy is in no way a transition from one subject-matter to another. The subject-matter is in both cases the same, '*the eternal truth* in its objectivity, God and nothing but God and the unfolding [*die Explication*] of God'.[1] In this sense, therefore, 'religion and philosophy come to the same thing'.[2] 'Philosophy unfolds only itself when it unfolds religion; and when it unfolds itself, it unfolds religion.'[3]

The distinction between them lies in the different ways in which they conceive God, 'in the peculiar ways in which they occupy themselves with God'.[4] For example, the change from *Vorstellung* to pure thought involves the replacement of the form of contingency by that of logical sequence. Thus the theological concept of divine creation as a contingent event, in the sense that it might or might not have taken place, becomes in philosophy the doctrine that the *Logos* is necessarily objectified in Nature, not because the Absolute is subject to compulsion but because it is what it is. Speculative philosophy, in other words, strips away the imaginative or pictorial element which is characteristic of religious thought and expresses the truth, the same truth, in purely conceptual form.

It does not follow, however, that philosophy is irreligious. In Hegel's opinion the notion that philosophy and religion are incompatible or that the former is hostile or dangerous to the latter rests on a misconception of their respective natures. Both treat of God and both are religion. 'What they have in common is that both are religion; what distinguishes them lies only in the kind and manner of religion which we find in each.'[5] It is indeed this difference in their respective ways of apprehending and expressing the truth which gives rise to the idea that philosophy threatens religion. But philosophy would be a threat to religion only if it professed to substitute truth for falsity. And this is not the case. The truth is the same, though the religious consciousness demands a mode of expression which must be distinguished from that of philosophy.

One may be inclined to comment that Hegel uses the term

[1] *W*, xv, p. 37; *SS*, I, p. 19. [2] *W*, xv, p. 37; *SS*, I, p. 20.
[3] *W*, xv, p. 37; *SS*, I, p. 19. [4] *W*, xv, p. 38; *SS*, I, p. 20.
[5] *Ibid.*

'religion' ambiguously. For he uses it to cover not only religious experience, faith and cult but also theology. And while a plausible case can be made out for saying that philosophy is not hostile to religious experience as such, or even to pure faith, it must necessarily be hostile to religion if religion is taken to mean or include theology and if philosophy proposes to reveal the un-varnished truth, as it were, which is contained in the doctrines which theologians believe to be the best possible expression of the truth in human language.

As regards the first point, Hegel insists that '*knowledge* is an essential part of the Christian religion itself'.[1] Christianity strives to understand its own faith. And speculative philosophy is a continuation of this attempt. The difference lies in the fact that philosophy substitutes the form of pure thought for the form of *Vorstellung*, pictorial or figurative thought. But this does not mean that speculative philosophy takes the place of Christianity in the sense that the latter is simply discarded in favour of the former. Christianity is the absolute religion and absolute idealism is the absolute philosophy. Both are true, and their truth is the same. The forms of conception and expression may differ, but it does not follow that Christianity is superseded by absolute idealism. For the human being is not simply pure thought: he is by no means only a philosopher, even if he is a philosopher at all. And for the religious consciousness Christian theology is the perfect expression of the truth. This is why preachers, who are addressing themselves to the religious consciousness, have no business to tamper with Christian dogmas. For Christianity is the revealed religion, in the sense that it is the perfect self-manifestation of God to the religious consciousness.

It is not my intention to imply that Hegel's attitude is consistent with the standpoint of Christian orthodoxy. For I am convinced that it is not. I agree with McTaggart, who was not himself a Christian believer, when he points out that as an ally of Christianity Hegelianism is 'an enemy in disguise—the least evident but the most dangerous. The doctrines which have been protected from external refutation are found to be transforming themselves till they are on the point of melting away. . . .'[2] Thus Hegel gives philosophical proofs of such doctrines as the Trinity, the Fall and the Incarnation. But when he has finished with stating them in the

---

[1] *W*, xv, p. 35; *SS*, I, p. 17.
[2] *Studies in Hegelian Cosmology* (1901 edition), p. 250.

form of pure thought, they are obviously something very different from the doctrines which the Church believes to be the correct statement of the truth in human language. In other words, Hegel makes speculative philosophy the final arbiter of the inner meaning of Christian revelation. Absolute idealism is presented as esoteric Christianity and Christianity as exoteric Hegelianism; and the mystery insisted on by theology is subordinated to a philosophical clarification which amounts in fact to a transformation.

At the same time there is, in my opinion at least, no cogent reason for accusing Hegel of personal insincerity. I do not believe that when he posed as a champion of orthodoxy he had his tongue in his cheek. As was noted in the introductory chapter, Benedetto Croce argued that there could be no valid reason for retaining an inferior form of thought, namely religion, along with science, art and philosophy. If philosophy really gives the inner meaning of religious beliefs, then religion must give place to philosophy. That is to say, the two cannot coexist in the same mind. A man may think in the categories of religion or he may think in the categories of philosophy. But he cannot think in both. But while Croce's comments are by no means without point, it does not necessarily follow that they represent Hegel's real, though concealed, opinion. After all, Croce, though not a believing Catholic, was accustomed to the idea of ecclesiastical authority as the final arbiter of religious truth and its statement. And it is perfectly obvious that Hegel's theory of the relation of speculative philosophy to Christianity is incompatible with *this* idea. But Hegel was a Lutheran. And though the superiority of speculative philosophy to faith is very far from being a Lutheran idea, it was much easier for him than it would have been for Croce to be sincerely convinced that his view of the relation between the absolute philosophy and the absolute religion was acceptable from the Christian standpoint. He doubtless thought of himself as continuing the work of the theologians who in their accounts of the Christian dogmas endeavoured to avoid the crudely imaginative forms in which these dogmas were pictured by the theologically uneducated religious consciousness.

5. But the absolute philosophy is no more the only manifestation of the speculative reason than is the absolute religion the only manifestation of the religious consciousness. Just as art and religion have their history, so has philosophy. And this history is a dialectical process. From one point of view it is the process by

which infinite Thought comes to think itself explicitly, moving from one inadequate conception of itself to another and then uniting them in a higher unity. From another point of view it is the process by which the human mind moves dialectically towards an adequate conception of the ultimate reality, the Absolute. But these two points of view represent simply different aspects of one process. For Spirit, self-thinking Thought, becomes explicit in and through the reflection of the human mind on the level of absolute knowledge.

This means, of course, that the different one-sided and inadequate concepts of reality which emerge at different stages of the history of philosophy are taken up and preserved in the succeeding higher stages. 'The last philosophy is the result of all earlier ones: nothing is lost, all principles are preserved.'[1] 'The general result of the history of philosophy is this. First, throughout all time there has been only one philosophy, the contemporary differences of which represent the necessary aspects of the one principle. Secondly, the succession of philosophical systems is no matter of chance but exhibits the necessary succession of stages in the development of this science. Thirdly, the final philosophy of a period is the result of this development and is truth in the highest form which the self-consciousness of Spirit affords. The final philosophy, therefore, contains the ones which went before; it embraces in itself all their stages; it is the product and result of all the philosophies which preceded it.'[2]

Now, if the history of philosophy is the development of the divine self-knowledge, of absolute self-consciousness, the successive stages in this history will tend to correspond with the successive phases or moments in the Notion or logical Idea. We find, therefore, that Hegel represents Parmenides as the first genuine philosopher, the man who apprehended the Absolute as Being, while Heraclitus affirms the Absolute as Becoming. If this is taken as a statement of chronological sequence, it is open to criticism. But it illustrates Hegel's general procedure. Like Aristotle before him, he looks on his predecessors as bringing to light aspects of truth which are preserved, elevated and integrated with complementary aspects in his own system. Needless to say, the explicit and adequate recognition of the category of Spirit is reserved for German idealism.

[1] W, xix, p. 685; HS, iii, p. 546. In references to Hegel's Lectures on the History of Philosophy HS signifies the English translation by E. S. Haldane and F. H. Simson.
[2] W, xix, pp. 690–1; HS, iii, pp. 552–3.

And the philosophies of Fichte and Schelling are treated as moments in the development of absolute idealism. Hegel's history of philosophy is thus an integral part of his system. It is not simply an account of what philosophers have held, of the factors which influenced their thought and led them to think in the ways that they did, and of their influence on their successors and perhaps on society at large. It is a sustained attempt to exhibit a necessary dialectical advance, a teleological development, in the data of the history of philosophy. And this enterprise is obviously carried out in the light of a general philosophy. It is the work of a philosopher looking back on the past from the vantage-point of a system which he believes to be the highest expression of the truth up to date and seeing this system as the culmination of a process of reflection which, in spite of all contingent elements, has been in its essential outlines a necessary movement of Thought coming to think itself. Hegel's history of philosophy is thus a philosophy of the history of philosophy. If it is objected that the selection of the essential elements in a given system is governed by philosophical preconceptions or principles, Hegel can, of course, answer that any history of philosophy worthy of the name necessarily involves not only interpretation but also a separation of the essential from the unessential in the light of beliefs about what is philosophically important and what is not. But such an answer, though reasonable enough, would not be adequate in the context. For just as Hegel approaches the philosophy of history with the belief that the history of mankind is a rational teleological process, so does he approach the history of philosophy with the conviction that this history is 'the temple of self-conscious reason',[1] the dialectically continuous and progressive determination of the Idea, 'a logical progress impelled by an inherent necessity',[2] the one true philosophy developing itself in time, the dynamic process of self-thinking Thought.

Does this conception of the history of philosophy imply the conclusion that for Hegel his philosophy is the final system, the system to end all systems? He has sometimes been represented as thinking precisely this. But it seems to me that this picture is a caricature. He does indeed depict German idealism in general, and his own system in particular, as the highest stage yet reached in the historical development of philosophy. In view of his interpretation of the history of philosophy he cannot do anything else. And

[1] W, XVII, p. 65; HS, I, p. 35.   [2] W, XVII, p. 66; HS, I, p. 36.

he makes remarks which lend themselves for use by those who wish to ascribe to him the absurd idea that with Hegelianism philosophy comes to an end. 'A new epoch has arisen in the world. It seems that the World-Spirit has now succeeded in freeing itself from all alien objective existence and in apprehending itself at last as absolute Spirit. . . . The strife between the finite self-consciousness and the absolute self-consciousness, which seemed to finite self-consciousness to lie outside it, now ceases. Finite self-consciousness has ceased to be finite, and thereby absolute self-consciousness on the other hand has attained the reality which it formerly lacked.'[1] But though this passage clearly states that absolute idealism is the culmination of all preceding philosophy, Hegel goes on to speak of 'the whole history of the World in general and of the history of philosophy in particular up to the present'.[2] And is it probable that a man who stated roundly that 'philosophy is *its own time expressed in thoughts*'[3] and that it is just as foolish to suppose that a philosophy can transcend its contemporary world as it is to suppose that an individual can overleap his own time seriously thought that philosophy had come to an end with himself? Obviously, on Hegel's principles subsequent philosophy would have to incorporate absolute idealism, even if his system revealed itself as a one-sided moment in a higher synthesis. But to say this is not the same as to deny that there could be or would be any subsequent philosophy.

There is, however, this point. If Christianity is the absolute religion, Hegelianism, as esoteric Christianity, must be the absolute philosophy. And if we take the word 'absolute' in this context as meaning truth in the highest form which it has yet attained rather than as meaning the final or terminal statement of the truth, Christianity is no more the final religion than is Hegelianism the final philosophy. On Hegel's own principles Christianity and absolute idealism stand or fall together. And if we wish to say that Christianity cannot be surpassed whereas Hegelianism can, we cannot at the same time accept Hegel's account of the relation between the two.

6. In view of the comprehensive character of Hegel's system and of the commanding position which he came to occupy in the German philosophical world it is not surprising that his influence was felt in a variety of fields. As one would expect in the case of a man whose thought centred round the Absolute and who appeared,

---

[1] *W*, XIX, pp. 689–90; *HS*, III, p. 551.
[2] *W*, XIX, p. 690; *HS*, III, p. 551.   [3] *W*, VII, p. 35; *R*, preface.

to the not too critical or too orthodox observer, to have provided a rational justification of Christianity in terms of the most up-to-date philosophy, his sphere of influence included the theological field. For example, Karl Daub (1765–1836), professor of theology at Heidelberg, abandoned the ideas of Schelling and endeavoured to use the dialectical method of Hegel in the service of Protestant theology. Another eminent theologian who was converted or seduced, according as one chooses to regard the matter, by the attraction of Hegel was Philipp Konrad Marheineke (1780–1846) who became a professor of theology at Berlin and who helped to edit the first general edition of Hegel's works. In his posthumously published *System of Christian Dogmatics* Marheineke attempted to translate Hegelianism into the terms of Christian theology and at the same time to interpret the content of Christian dogma in the Hegelian manner. For instance, he represented the Absolute as attaining full consciousness of itself in the Church, which was for him the concrete actualization of Spirit, this Spirit being interpreted as the Third Person of the Trinity.

The history of ethical systems was studied from an Hegelian point of view by Leopold von Henning (1791–1866) who followed Hegel's courses at Berlin and became one of his most fervent admirers. In the field of law Hegel's influence was considerable. Prominent among his disciples was the celebrated jurist Eduard Gans (1798–1839) who obtained a chair of law at Berlin and published a well-known work on the right of inheritance.[1] In the field of aesthetics Heinrich Theodor Rötscher (1803–71) may be mentioned as one of those who derived inspiration from Hegel. In the history of philosophy Hegel's influence was felt by such eminent historians as Johann Eduard Erdmann (1805–92), Eduard Zeller (1814–1908) and Kuno Fischer (1824–1907). Whatever one may think of absolute idealism, one cannot deny Hegel's stimulating effect on scholars in a variety of fields.

To return to the theological field. We have noted that the Hegelian system left room for dispute about its precise relation to Christian theism. And in point of fact controversy arose on this topic even before Hegel's death, though this event naturally gave it fresh impetus. Some writers, who are generally classified as belonging to the Hegelian right wing, maintained that absolute idealism could be legitimately interpreted in a sense compatible with Christianity. While Hegel was still alive Karl Friedrich

[1] *Das Erbrecht in weltgeschichtlicher Entwicklung* (1824–35).

Göschel (1784–1861) tried to interpret the philosopher's theory of the relation between the form of thought peculiar to the religious consciousness and pure thought or knowledge in such a way as not to imply that religion is inferior to philosophy. And this defence of Hegel met with a warm response from the philosopher. After Hegel's death Göschel published writings designed to show that Hegelianism was compatible with the doctrines of a personal God and of personal immortality. Mention can also be made of Karl Ludwig Michelet (1801–93), a Berlin professor, who identified the Hegelian triad with the Persons of the Trinity (as indeed Hegel himself had done) and tried to show that there was no incompatibility between Hegelianism and Christian theology.

The left wing was represented, for example, by David Friedrich Strauss (1808–74), author of the celebrated *Life of Jesus* (1835). According to Strauss the Gospel stories were myths, and he explicitly connected this view with Hegel's theory of *Vorstellung* and represented his own dissolution of historic Christianity as a genuine development of Hegel's thought. He thus provided valuable ammunition for the Christian writers who refused to accept the contention of the right-wing Hegelians that Hegelianism and Christianity were compatible.

The centre of the Hegelian movement can be represented by the name of Johann Karl Friedrich Rosenkranz (1805–79), biographer of Hegel and a professor at Königsberg. As a pupil of both Schleiermacher and Hegel he tried to mediate between them in his development of the Hegelian system. In his *Encyclopaedia of the Theological Sciences* (1831) he distinguished between speculative, historical and practical theology. Speculative theology exhibits the absolute religion, Christianity, in an *a priori* form. Historical theology deals with the temporal objectification of this Idea or concept of the absolute religion. In his evaluation of historic Christianity Rosenkranz was more restrained than Strauss, who looked on him as belonging to the centre of the Hegelian school. Later on Rosenkranz attempted to develop Hegel's logic, though his efforts in this direction were not much appreciated by other Hegelians.

We can say, therefore, that the split between right- and left-wing Hegelians concerned first of all the interpretation, evaluation and development of Hegel's position in regard to religious and theological problems. The right wing interpreted Hegel in a sense more or less compatible with Christianity, which meant that God had to be represented as a personal, self-conscious Being in his own right, so to speak. The left wing maintained a pantheistic interpretation and denied personal immortality.

The left wing, however, soon went beyond pantheism to naturalism and atheism. And at the hands of Marx and Engels the Hegelian theories of society and history were revolutionized. The left wing is thus of much greater historical importance than the right wing. But the radical thinkers of the former group must be accorded separate treatment and not treated as disciples of Hegel, who would scarcely have recognized them as such.

Under the heading of the influence of Hegel we might refer, of course, to the British idealism of the second half of the nineteenth century and of the first two decades of the present century, to Italian philosophers such as Benedetto Croce (1866–1952) and Giovanni Gentile (1875–1944) and to recent French works on Hegel, not to mention other examples of the philosopher's long-term influence. But these topics would take us outside the scope of the present volume. Instead we can turn to consideration of the reaction against metaphysical idealism and of the emergence of other lines of thought in the German philosophical world of the nineteenth century.

PART II

THE REACTION AGAINST METAPHYSICAL IDEALISM

CHAPTER XII

EARLIER OPPONENTS AND CRITICS

Fries and his disciples—The realism of Herbart—Beneke and psychology as the fundamental science—The logic of Bolzano— Weisse and I. H. Fichte as critics of Hegel.

1. THE development of idealism at the hands of Fichte, Schelling and Hegel was regarded as a great mistake by Jakob Friedrich Fries (1773–1843). In his view the proper and profitable task for philosophy was to carry on the work of Kant without turning the Kantian philosophy into a system of metaphysics. True, Fries himself made use of the word 'metaphysics', and in 1824 he published a *System of Metaphysics* (*System der Metaphysik*). But this word meant for him a critique of human knowledge, not a science of the Absolute. To this extent, therefore, he walked in the footsteps of Kant. Yet at the same time he turned Kant's transcendental critique of knowledge into a psychological investigation, a process of psychological self-observation. Although, therefore, Fries starts with Kant and tries to correct and develop his position, the fact that this correction takes the form of psychologizing the Kantian critique results in a certain measure of affinity with the attitude of Locke. For according to Fries we must investigate the nature and laws and scope of knowledge before we can tackle problems about the object of knowledge. And the method of pursuing this investigation is empirical observation.

Fries did not by any means confine his activities to the theory of knowledge. In 1803 he published a *Philosophical Theory of Right* (*Philosophische Rechtslehre*) and in 1818 an *Ethics* (*Ethik*). His political ideas were liberal, and in 1819 he was deprived of his chair at Jena. Some years later, however, he was nominated to a chair of mathematics and physics in the same university. He had already published some works on natural philosophy and physics, and he tried to unite the mathematical physics of Newton with the Kantian philosophy as he interpreted it.

In 1832 Fries published a *Handbook of the Philosophy of Religion and of Philosophical Aesthetics (Handbuch der Religionsphilosophie und der philosophischen Aesthetik)*. As a boy he had been educated in the traditions of pietism, and he maintained to the end an insistence on religious feeling and interior piety. On the one hand we have mathematical and scientific knowledge; on the other hand we have the presage of religious and aesthetic feeling, its witness to the Being which lies behind the sphere of phenomena. Practical or moral faith relates us to noumenal reality, but religious and aesthetic feeling gives us a further assurance that the reality behind phenomena is that which moral faith conceives it to be. Fries thus added to Kant's doctrine of practical faith an insistence on the value of religious emotion.

Fries was not without influence. Prominent among his disciples was E. F. Apelt (1812–59), who defended his master's psychological interpretation of Kant and insisted on the need for a close union between philosophy and science.[1] And it is worth mentioning that the celebrated philosopher of religion Rudolf Otto (1869–1937) was influenced by Fries's insistence on the fundamental importance of feeling in religion, though it would be quite incorrect to call Otto a disciple of Fries.

In the early part of the present century the so-called Neo-Friesian School was founded by Leonard Nelson (1882–1927).

2. Among the contemporary opponents of post-Kantian idealism the name of Fries is much less widely known than that of Johann Friedrich Herbart (1776–1841). In 1809 Herbart was nominated to the chair at Königsberg which had once been held by Kant, and he occupied it until 1833 when he went to Göttingen. While in Switzerland (1797–1800) he had known Pestalozzi, and he took a great interest in and wrote on educational subjects. Among his main philosophical works are his *Introduction to Philosophy (Einleitung in die Philosophie*, 1813), *Psychology as a Science (Psychologie als Wissenschaft*, 1824–5) and *General Metaphysics (Allgemeine Metaphysik*, 1828–9).

Herbart once remarked that he was a Kantian of the year 1828. He meant, of course, that though he paid tribute to the work of the great thinker whose chair he then occupied, a good deal of water

---

[1] Modern logicians rightly look with disfavour on the psychologizing of logic. But the tendency to do this was connected, however mistakenly, with the notion that it was the expression of a scientific attitude.

had flowed under the bridge in the meantime, and that he did not simply accept the Kantian system as it came from the hands of the master. Indeed, Herbart cannot be called a Kantian in any ordinary sense. To be sure, he rejected post-Kantian idealism. But to regard post-Kantian idealism as a perversion of the thought of Kant is not necessarily the same as to be a Kantian. And in some respects Herbart's affinities are with the pre-Kantian philosophers rather than with Kant himself.

When considered under one aspect at least, Herbart's account of philosophy has an extremely modern flavour. For he describes philosophy as the elaboration (*Bearbeitung*) of concepts. An obvious objection to this description is that no indication is given of the peculiar subject-matter of philosophy. Any science might be described in this way. But it is Herbart's contention that philosophy does not possess a peculiar subject-matter of its own alongside the subject-matters of the various particular sciences. Or, more accurately, we cannot say from the start that philosophy has a particular field of reality as its peculiar subject-matter. We must first describe it as the activity of elaborating and clarifying concepts.

It is in the course of this activity that the different branches of philosophy arise. For example, if we concern ourselves with working out the theory of distinct concepts and their combination and the principles of the clarification of concepts, we are engaged in logic. If, however, we apply logical principles to the clarification of concepts furnished by experience, we are engaged in metaphysics.

In Herbart's opinion this work of clarification is essential. For when the fundamental concepts derived from experience are submitted to logical analysis, they show themselves to be riddled with contradictions. Take, for example, the concept of a thing. If it can properly be called a thing, it must be one, a unity. But if we try to describe it, it is resolved into a plurality of qualities. It is one and many, one and not-one, at the same time. We are thus faced with a contradiction, and we cannot rest content with it. It is not, however, a question of simply rejecting the concept derived from experience. For if we sever the link between thought and experience, we cut ourselves off from reality. What is required is a clarification and elaboration of the concept in such a way that the contradiction disappears.

Herbart assumes, therefore, that the principle of non-contradiction is fundamental. He will have nothing to do with the dialectical logic of Hegel which in his opinion blurs this principle. Reality must be without contradiction. That is to say, it must be of such a kind that a true world-view or account of the world would be a harmonious system of mutually consistent and intrinsically non-contradictory concepts. Raw experience, so to speak, does not present us with such a world-view. It belongs to philosophy to construct it by clarifying, modifying and rendering consistent the concepts derived from experience and used in the sciences.

A better way of expressing Herbart's point of view would be to say that reality is of such a kind that a complete account of it would take the form of a comprehensive system of mutually consistent non-contradictory propositions. It is indeed arguable that Hegel himself had a similar ideal of truth, and that he should not be interpreted as having denied the principle of non-contradiction. After all, Herbart too allows contradictions to emerge from our ordinary ways of regarding things and then tries to resolve them. But Hegel speaks as though contradictions were a feature of the process of reality itself, of the life of the Absolute, whereas for Herbart contradictions emerge only from our inadequate ways of conceiving reality: they are not a feature of reality itself. Hence Herbart's view bears more resemblance to that of F. H. Bradley than it does to that of Hegel. And in point of fact Bradley was considerably influenced by Herbart.[1]

Now, let us assume that our ordinary view of things contains or gives rise to contradictions. We regard a rose as one thing and a lump of sugar as another thing. Each seems to be a unity. But when we try to describe them, each dissolves into a plurality of qualities. The rose is red, fragrant and soft; the sugar is white, sweet and hard. In each case we attribute the qualities to a uniting substance or thing. But what is it? If we try to say anything about it, the unity dissolves once more into a plurality. Or, if we say that it underlies the qualities, it seems to be a different thing. We can no longer say that the rose *is* red, fragrant and soft.

According to Herbart, the solution of this problem lies in postulating a plurality of simple and unchangeable entities or substances which he calls 'reals' (*Realen*). They enter into different relations with one another, and phenomenal qualities and changes

---

[1] I am speaking, of course, simply of Bradley's view that our ordinary ways of conceiving and describing things give rise to contradictions, whereas reality itself is a harmonious whole without any contradiction. On the issue between pluralism and monism there is a great difference between Herbart and the British absolute idealist.

correspond to these relations. For instance, the lump of sugar, which appears to us as a unit, is composed of a plurality of unextended and changeless entities. And the various phenomenal qualities of the sugar correspond to the relations in which these entities stand to one another, while the phenomenal changes in the sugar correspond to the changing relations between the entities. We are thus able to harmonize unity and multiplicity, constancy and change.

After having proposed, therefore, a view of philosophy which has been recently fashionable in this country, namely that philosophy consists in the clarification of concepts or in conceptual analysis, Herbart goes on to raise a problem to which Bradley subsequently gave a good deal of attention in *Appearance and Reality*. But whereas Bradley, in accordance with the spirit of post-Kantian idealism, finds the solution in terms of a One which 'appears' as a multiplicity of things, Herbart has recourse to a pluralistic metaphysics which calls to mind the atoms of Democritus and the monads of Leibniz. His 'reals' are indeed different from Democritus's atoms in that they are said to possess qualities, though these, being metaphenomenal, are unknowable. Further, though each 'real' is simply and essentially unchanging, they do not seem to be, like Leibniz's monads, 'windowless'. For each 'real' is said to preserve its self-identity in the face of disturbances (*Störungen*) from other such entities, so that there appears to be some reciprocal influence. At the same time Herbart's theory obviously has affinity with pre-Kantian metaphysics.

The theory of disturbances, each of which calls forth a self-preservative reaction on the part of the disturbed entity, gives rise to some difficulty. For it is not easy to reconcile it with the idea that space, time and causal interaction are phenomenal. To be sure, Herbart assumes that phenomenal occurrences are grounded on and explicable by the behaviour of the 'reals'. And the world of the 'reals' is not taken to be the static reality of Parmenides. But it seems arguable that so far as the postulated relations between 'reals' are thought at all, they are inevitably brought into the phenomenal sphere. For they can hardly be thought except in terms of relations which are said to be phenomenal.

In any case it is on this metaphysical basis that Herbart constructs his psychology. The soul is a simple and unextended substance or 'real'. It is not, however, to be identified with the pure subject or ego of consciousness. The soul, considered simply as such, is not conscious at all. Nor is it furnished with any Kantian apparatus of *a priori* forms and categories. All psychical activities are secondary and derived. That is to say, the soul strives to preserve itself in face of disturbances occasioned by other 'reals', and the self-preservative reactions are expressed in sensations and ideas. And mental life is constituted by the relations and inter-actions between sensations and ideas. The idea of distinct faculties can be thrown overboard. For instance, an idea which meets with hindrance can be called a desire, while an idea which is accompanied by a supposition of success can be called a volition. There is no need to postulate appetitive and volitional faculties. The relevant psychical phenomena can be explained in terms of ideas which are themselves explicable in terms of stimuli directly or indirectly caused by the soul's self-preservative reactions to disturbances.

An interesting feature of Herbart's psychology is his theory of the subconscious. Ideas may be associated with one another, but they may also be mutually opposed. In this case a state of tension is set up, and some idea or ideas are forced below the level of consciousness. They then turn into impulses, though they can return to consciousness as ideas. We may also note Herbart's insistence not only that on the conscious level consciousness of objects other than the self precedes self-consciousness but also that self-consciousness is always empirical self-consciousness, conscious-ness of the me-object. There are ego-ideas, but there is no such thing as pure self-consciousness.

Though, however, Herbart's theory of the subconscious is not without historical importance, the salient feature of his psychology is perhaps his attempt to make it a science by mathematicizing it. Thus he assumes that ideas have varying degrees of intensity, and that the relations between them can be expressed in mathematical formulas. When, for example, an idea has been inhibited and forced below the level of consciousness, its return to consciousness will involve the return, according to a mathematically determinable sequence, of associated ideas. And if we possessed sufficient empirical evidence, we could predict the cause of such events. In principle at any rate psychology is capable of being turned into an exact science, the statics and dynamics of the mental life of presentations.

Psychology, therefore, like metaphysics, is concerned with the real. Aesthetics and ethics are concerned with values. The more fundamental of these two is aesthetics. For the ethical judgment is a subdivision of the aesthetic judgment, the judgment of taste which expresses approval or disapproval. But this is not to say that the ethical judgment has no objective reference. For approval and disapproval are grounded in certain relations, and in the case of ethics these are relations of the will, of which Herbart discovers five. In the first place experience shows that we express approval of the relation in which the will is in agreement with a person's inner conviction. That is to say, we express approval in accordance with the ideal of inner freedom.[1] Secondly our approval is given to a relation of harmony between the different tendencies or strivings of the individual will. And our approval is then elicited in accordance with the ideal of perfection. Thirdly we approve the relation in which one will takes as its object the satisfaction of another will. And here it is the ideal of benevolence which informs our judgment. Fourthly approval or disapproval is elicited in accordance with the idea of justice. We disapprove a relation of conflict or disharmony between several wills, while we approve a relation in which each will allows the others to limit it. Fifthly we disapprove a relation in which deliberate good and evil acts are unrecompensed. Here the idea of retribution is operative.

It is in the light of this theory of values that Herbart criticizes the Kantian ethics. We cannot take the categorical imperative as an ultimate moral fact. For we can always ask whence the practical reason or will derives its authority. Behind a command and obedience to it there must be something which warrants respect for the command. And this is found in the recognition of values, the morally beautiful and pleasing.

We cannot enter here into Herbart's educational theory. But it is worth noting that it involves a combination of his ethics with his psychology. Ethics, with its theory of values, provides the end or aim of education, namely character-development. The goal of the moral life is the perfect conformity of the will with moral ideals or values. And this is virtue. But to estimate how this aim is to be pedagogically attained we have to take account of psychology and utilize its laws and principles. The main end of education is moral, but the educator has to build upon the two masses of presentations derived from experience of the world and from social intercourse

[1] Given the psychology outlined above, Herbart does not accept the theory of liberty of indifference. Indeed, he regards the theory as incompatible with the idea of a stable and firm character, the development of which is one of the principal aims of education. But he recognizes, of course, a psychological difference between choosing in accordance with conviction or conscience and being led by impulse or desire to act in a manner contrary to one's conscience.

and environment. The first basis has to be developed into knowledge, the second into benevolence towards and sympathy with others.

Herbart's philosophy clearly lacked the romantic appeal of the great idealist systems. In one sense it was out of date. That is to say, it looked back behind Kant, and its author was out of sympathy with the contemporary prevailing movement in Germany. But in another sense it was very much up to date. For it demanded a closer integration of philosophy and science and looked forward to some of the systems which followed the collapse of idealism and demanded precisely this integration. The most significant features of Herbart's philosophy were probably his psychology and his educational theory. In the second field he helped to provide a theoretical background for the practical ideas of Pestalozzi. In the field of psychology he exercised a stimulative influence. But in view of his idea of psychology as the mechanics of the mental life of sensations and ideas it is as well to remind oneself that he was no materialist. Matter was for him phenomenal. Further, he accepted a form of the argument from design, pointing to a divine supersensible Being.

3. The importance of psychology was even more strongly emphasized by Friedrich Eduard Beneke (1798–1854). Beneke was considerably influenced by the writings of Herbart, but he was certainly not a disciple. He was also influenced by Fries, but above all he derived inspiration from British thought and had a high regard for Locke. He was quite out of sympathy with the dominant idealist philosophy and encountered great difficulties in his academic career. In the end he appears to have committed suicide, an event which elicited some remarks in thoroughly bad taste from Arthur Schopenhauer.

In Beneke's view psychology is the fundamental science and the basis of philosophy. It should not be grounded, as with Herbart, on metaphysics. On the contrary, it is or ought to be grounded on interior experience which reveals to us the fundamental psychical processes. Mathematics is no help and is not required. Beneke was indeed influenced by the associationist psychology, but he did not share Herbart's notion of turning psychology into an exact science by mathematicizing it. He looked rather to the introspective method of the English empiricists.

As for the soul, it is, as Locke rightly claimed, devoid of innate ideas. There are also, as Herbart saw, no distinct faculties in the traditional sense. But we can discover a number of predispositions or impulses which can be called faculties if we wish to do so. And the unity of the self results from the harmonization of these impulses. Further, pedagogy and ethics, which are both applied psychology, show how the impulses and predispositions are to be developed and harmonized in view of a hierarchy of goods or values determined by a consideration of actions and their effects.

Beneke's philosophy is doubtless very small beer compared with the grandiose systems of German idealism. At the same time we can see perhaps in the emphasis which he lays upon impulses as the fundamental elements in the psychical life and in his tendency to stress the practical rather than the theoretical some affinity with the shift towards voluntarism which was given large-scale expression in the metaphysical system of Schopenhauer, the very man who made caustic remarks about Beneke's suicide. For the matter of that, Fichte had already emphasized the fundamental role of impulse and drive.

4. Chronological reasons justify the inclusion in this chapter of some brief reference to Bernhard Bolzano (1781–1848), even if his rediscovery as a forerunner in certain respects of modern logical developments tends to make one think of him as a more recent writer than he actually was.

Bolzano was born in Prague of an Italian father and German mother. In 1805 he was ordained priest and soon afterwards he was appointed to the chair of philosophy of religion in the University of Prague. But at the end of 1819 he was deprived of his post, not, as has sometimes been stated, by his ecclesiastical superiors, but by order of the Emperor in Vienna. The imperial decree made special mention of Bolzano's objectionable doctrines on war, social rank and civic disobedience. In point of fact Bolzano had told the students that war would one day be regarded with the same abhorrence as duelling, that social differences would in time be reduced to proper limits, and that obedience to the civil power was limited by the moral conscience and by the norms of the legitimate exercise of sovereignty. And though these views may have been objectionable in the eyes of the Holy Roman Emperor, they were far from being theologically heretical. Indeed, the ecclesiastical authorities at Prague, when instructed by Vienna to investigate the case of Bolzano, declared that he was an orthodox Catholic. However, Bolzano had to abandon teaching and he devoted himself to a life of study and writing, though he had some difficulties about publication, at any rate in the Austrian dominions.

In 1827 Bolzano published anonymously a work, commonly called *Athanasia*, on the grounds of belief in the immortality of the soul. His chief work, *Theory of Science: an Essay towards a Detailed and for the most part New Exposition of Logic (Wissenschaftslehre: Versuch einer ausführlichen und grösstenteils neuen Darstellung der Logik)* appeared in four volumes in 1837. The *Paradoxes of the Infinite (Paradoxen des Unendlichen)* was published posthumously in 1851. In addition he wrote a considerable number of papers on logical, mathematical, physical, aesthetic and political themes, many of them for the Bohemian Society of the Sciences of which he was an active member.

In a short account which he wrote of his intellectual development Bolzano remarked that at no time had he felt inclined to recognize any given philosophical system as the one true philosophy. Referring to Kant, whose first *Critique* he had begun to study in his eighteenth year, he admitted that he found much to approve of in the critical philosophy. At the same time he found much to disagree with and much that was lacking. For example, while he welcomed the distinction between analytic and synthetic propositions, he could not agree with Kant's explanation of the distinction. Nor could he accept the view of mathematical propositions as synthetic propositions based on *a priori* intuitions. For he had himself succeeded in deducing some geometrical truths by analysis of concepts. Mathematics, he thought, is purely conceptual in character, and it should be constructed by a rigorous process of analysis.

This insistence on conceptual analysis and on logical rigour was indeed characteristic of Bolzano. Not only did he find fault with leading philosophers for failing to define their terms,[1] for slovenly conceptual analysis and for lack of consistency in their use of terms, but he also made it clear that in his opinion nobody could be a good philosopher unless he was a good mathematician. Obviously, he was not disposed to regard with a particularly kindly eye the goings-on of the metaphysical idealists.

Further, the tendency of Bolzano's mind was to de-psychologize logic, to formalize it and to set it free from any intrinsic connection with the subject or ego or productive imagination or any other

[1] For instance, he blames Kant for introducing the term 'experience' at the beginning of the first *Critique* without any adequate and unambiguous explanation of the meaning which he attaches to it.

subjective factor. And this tendency shows itself in his theory of the proposition in itself (*der Satz an sich*). A proposition in itself is defined as 'a statement that something is or is not, irrespective of whether this statement is true or false, irrespective of whether anyone has ever formulated it in words, and even irrespective of whether it has ever been present in any mind as a thought'.[1] The idea of propositions in themselves may give rise to some difficulties; but it is clear that for Bolzano the primary element in a proposition is its objective content or meaning. Its being thought or posited by a subject is a secondary factor, irrelevant to the objective meaning.

Bolzano also speaks of the presentation in itself (*die Vorstellung an sich*). This is described as whatever can be a component part in a proposition but which does not by itself constitute a proposition. Hence no presentation or concept can be in itself true or false. For truth and falsity are predicated only of propositions, not of their component parts taken singly. But the meaning or content of a presentation in itself can be analysed; and this can be done without reference to any subject. Logically speaking, the subject is irrelevant. For example, if idea *X* is conceived by *A*, *B* and *C*, there are three ideas from the psychological point of view but only one from the point of view of the logical analyst who is interested simply in the content of the concept. It seems to me disputable whether the range of meaning of a concept can be analysed in abstraction from the propositions in which it is employed. For meaning is determined by use. But in any case Bolzano's concern with de-psychologizing logic is clear enough.

In the third place Bolzano speaks of the judgment in itself (*das Urteil an sich*). Every judgment expresses and affirms a proposition.

Now, if there are propositions in themselves, there must also be truths in themselves (*Wahrheiten an sich*), namely those propositions which are in fact true. Their truth does not, however, depend in any way on their being expressed and affirmed in judgments by thinking subjects. And this holds good not only of finite subjects but also of God. Truths in themselves are not true because God posits them; God thinks them because they are true. Bolzano does not mean that it is false to say that God makes true factual propositions about the world to be true in the sense that God is creator and thus responsible for there being a world at all. He is looking at the matter from the logician's point of view and

---

[1] *Theory of Science* (2nd edition, Leipzig, 1929), p. 77.

maintaining that the truth of a proposition does not depend on its being thought by a subject, whether finite or infinite. The truth of a mathematical proposition, for example, depends on the meanings of the terms, not on whether it is thought by a mathematician, human or divine.

As a philosopher, Bolzano rejected Kant's condemnation of metaphysics and maintained that important truths about God and about the spirituality and immortality of the soul could be proved. In his general metaphysical outlook he was influenced by Leibniz. Bolzano did not indeed accept Leibniz's theory of 'windowless' monads; but he shared his conviction that every substance is an active being, its activity being expressed in some form of representation or, as Leibniz puts it, perception. But Bolzano's significance does not lie in his metaphysics but in his work as logician and mathematician. It was his status as a mathematician which first met with recognition, but in modern times tribute has been paid to him as a logician, notably by Edmund Husserl.

5. In the foregoing sections of this chapter we have been concerned with thinkers who stood apart from the movement of post-Kantian metaphysical idealism and followed other lines of thought. We can now consider briefly two philosophers who belonged to the idealist movement but who both developed a critical attitude towards absolute idealism.

(a) Christian Hermann Weisse (1801–66), who was a professor in the University of Leipzig, stood at one time fairly close to Hegel, though he considered that Hegel had exaggerated the role of logic, particularly by trying (according to Weisse's interpretation) to deduce reality from the abstract forms of Being. We require the idea of a personal creative God to make the system tenable.

In his development of a speculative theism Weisse was stimulated by the later religious philosophy of Schelling. And in the *Philosophical Problem of Today* (*Das philosophische Problem der Gegenwart*, 1842) he maintained that Hegel had developed in his logic the negative side of philosophy. The Hegelian dialectic provides us with the idea of the possible Godhead. The logical Absolute is· not the real God, but it is the necessary logical foundation of his reality. Hegel, of course, might have agreed. For the logical Idea as such was not for him the existing divine Being. But what Weisse was concerned to defend was the idea of a personal and free God, whose existence cannot be deduced from the absolute Idea, though it presupposes the validity of the Idea.

That is to say, the divine Being, if there is one, must be self-thinking Thought, a personal and self-conscious Being. But that there is such a Being must be shown in some other way than by a *priori* logical deduction. Further, Weisse tried to show that God cannot be *a* Person, and that we must accept the Christian doctrine of the Trinity.

(*b*) Weisse's criticism of Hegel seemed to be only half-hearted in the eyes of Immanuel Hermann Fichte (1796–1879), son of the famous idealist. The younger Fichte laid emphasis on the individual human personality, and he was strongly opposed to what he regarded as Hegel's tendency to merge the individual in the universal. In Hegelianism as he interpreted it the human person was presented as being no more than a transitory moment in the life of universal Spirit, whereas in his own view the development of personality was the end of creation and man was assured of personal immortality.

The thought of the younger Fichte passed through several stages, from a period when the influence of his father and of Kant was strong to his later concentration on a philosophical anthropology, accompanied by a marked interest in the preconscious aspects of man and in parapsychological phenomena. But the general framework of his philosophy was provided by a speculative theism in which he tried to combine idealist themes with theism and with an emphasis on the human personality. In his *Speculative Theology or General Doctrine of Religion* (*Die spekulative Theologie oder allgemeine Religionslehre*, 1846), which forms the third volume of his trilogy on speculative theism, God is represented as the supreme personal unity of the ideal and the real. The ideal aspect of God is his infinite self-consciousness, while the real aspect is formed by the monads which are the eternal thoughts of God. Creation signifies the act of endowing these monads with free will, with a life of their own. And the development of the human personality is a development of self-consciousness on a basis of preconscious or subconscious levels.

Obviously I. H. Fichte was strongly influenced by the idealist movement. One would hardly expect anything else. But he laid great emphasis on the personal nature of God and on the value and immortality of the human person. And it was in the name of this personalistic idealism that he attacked the Hegelian system in which, he was convinced, finite personality was offered up in sacrifice to the all-devouring Absolute.

CHAPTER XIII

SCHOPENHAUER (1)

Life and writings—Schopenhauer's doctorate dissertation—The world as Idea—The biological function of concepts and the possibility of metaphysics—The world as the manifestation of the Will to live—Metaphysical pessimism—Some critical comments.

1. A PHILOSOPHY'S ability to strike our imaginations by presenting an original and dramatic picture of the universe is obviously not an infallible criterion of its truth. But it certainly adds greatly to its interest. It is not, however, a quality which is conspicuously present in any of the philosophies considered in the last chapter. Herbart, it is true, produced a general system. But if one had to single out the dramatic visions of the world provided by nineteenth-century philosophers, it would hardly occur to anyone to mention Herbart. Hegel, yes; Marx, yes; Nietzsche, yes; but not, I think, Herbart. And still less the sober logician and mathematician Bolzano. In 1819, however, when Herbart was professor at Königsberg and Hegel had recently moved from Heidelberg to Berlin, there appeared the main work of Arthur Schopenhauer, which, though it excited little notice at the time, expressed an interpretation of the world and of human life that was both striking in itself and opposed in certain important respects to the interpretations offered by the great idealists. There are indeed certain family likenesses between the system of Schopenhauer and those of the idealists. But its author, who never minced words, professed an utter contempt for Fichte, Schelling and Hegel, especially the last named, and regarded himself as their great opponent and the purveyor of the real truth to mankind.

Arthur Schopenhauer was born at Danzig on February 22nd, 1788. His father, a wealthy merchant, hoped that his son would follow in his footsteps, and he allowed the boy to spend the years 1803-4 in visiting England, France and other countries on the understanding that at the conclusion of the tour he would take up work in a business house. The young Schopenhauer fulfilled his promise, but he had no relish for a business career and on his father's death in 1803 he obtained his mother's consent to his continuing his studies. In 1809 he entered the University of Göttingen to study medicine, but he changed to philosophy in his second year at the university. As he put it, life is a problem and he had decided to spend his time reflecting on it.

From Göttingen, where he became an admirer of Plato, Schopenhauer went in 1811 to Berlin to listen to the lectures of Fichte and Schleiermacher. The former's obscurity was repugnant to him, while the latter's assertion that nobody could be a real philosopher without being religious elicited the sarcastic comment that nobody who is religious takes to philosophy, as he has no need of it.

Schopenhauer regarded himself as a cosmopolitan, and at no time was he a German nationalist. Having, as he subsequently said, a detestation for all military affairs he prudently left Berlin when Prussia rose against Napoleon and devoted himself in peaceful retirement to the preparation of a dissertation *On the Fourfold Root of the Principle of Sufficient Reason (Ueber die vierfache Wurzel des Satzes vom zureichenden Grunde)* which won for him the doctorate at Jena and was published in 1813. Goethe congratulated the author, and in return Schopenhauer wrote his essay *On Vision and Colours (Ueber das Sehen und die Farben*, 1816) in which he more or less supported Goethe against Newton. But apart from the flattering reception accorded it by the great poet the *Fourfold Root* was practically unnoticed and unsold. The author, however, continued to look on it as an indispensable introduction to his philosophy, and something will be said about it in the next section.

From May 1814 until September 1818 Schopenhauer was living at Dresden. And it was there that he composed his main philosophical work, *The World as Will and Idea (Die Welt als Wille und Vorstellung)*. Having consigned the manuscript to the publishers Schopenhauer left for an art tour of Italy. The work appeared early in 1819, and the author had the consolation of finding that some philosophers, such as Herbart and Beneke, took notice of it. But this consolation was offset by the very small sale of a book which its author believed to contain the secret of the universe.

Encouraged, however, by the fact that his *magnum opus* had not passed entirely unnoticed and eager to expound the truth about the world by word of mouth as well as in writing, Schopenhauer betook himself to Berlin and started lecturing there in 1820. Though he held no university chair, he did not hesitate to choose for his lectures the hour at which Hegel was accustomed to lecture. The enterprise was a complete failure, and Schopenhauer left off lecturing after one semester. His doctrine was scarcely representative of the dominant *Zeitgeist* or spirit of the time. After some wanderings Schopenhauer settled at Frankfurt on the Main in 1833. He read widely in European literature, consulted scientific books and journals, being quick to notice points which would serve as illustrations or empirical confirmation of his philosophical theories, visited the theatre and continued writing. In 1836 he published *On the Will in Nature* (*Ueber den Willen in der Natur*), and in 1839 he won a prize from the Scientific Society of Drontheim in Norway for an essay on freedom. He failed, however, to obtain a similar prize from the Royal Danish Academy of the Sciences for an essay on the foundations of ethics. One of the reasons given for the refusal of the prize was the writer's disrespectful references to leading philosophers. Schopenhauer had a great admiration for Kant, but he had the habit of referring to thinkers such as Fichte, Schelling and Hegel in terms which were, to put it mildly, unconventional, however amusing his expressions may be to later generations. The two essays were published together in 1841 under the title *The Two Fundamental Problems of Ethics* (*Die beiden Grundprobleme der Ethik*).

In 1844 Schopenhauer published a second edition of *The World as Will and Idea* with fifty supplementary chapters. In the preface to this edition he took the opportunity of making quite clear his views about German university professors of philosophy, just in case his attitude might not have been sufficiently indicated already. In 1851 he published a successful collection of essays entitled *Parerga and Paralipomena*, dealing with a wide variety of topics. Finally, in 1859 he published a third and augmented edition of his *magnum opus*.

After the failure of the Revolution of 1848, a revolution for which Schopenhauer had no sympathy at all, people were more ready to pay attention to a philosophy which emphasized the evil in the world and the vanity of life and preached a turning away from life to aesthetic contemplation and asceticism. And in the last decade of his life Schopenhauer became a famous man. Visitors came to see him from all sides and were entertained by his brilliant conversational powers. And though the German professors had not forgotten his sarcasm and abuse, lectures were delivered on his system in several universities, a sure sign that he had at last arrived. He died in September 1860.

Schopenhauer possessed a great breadth of culture, and he could write extremely well. A man of strong character and will, he was never afraid to express his opinions; and he had a gift of wit. He also possessed a considerable fund of practical sense and business acumen. But he was egoistic, vain, quarrelsome and, on occasion, even boorish; and he can hardly be said to have been remarkable for gifts of the heart. His relations with women were not exactly what one expects from a man who discoursed with eloquence on ethical, ascetical and mystical matters; and his literary executors suppressed some of his remarks about the female sex. Further, his theoretical sensitivity to the sufferings of humanity was not accompanied by any very practical efforts to alleviate it. But, as he sagely remarked, it is no more necessary for a philosopher to be a saint than for a saint to be a philosopher. And while as a man he can scarcely be considered as one of the most lovable of philosophers, his outstanding gifts as a writer are, I think, unquestionable.

2. In his doctorate dissertation Schopenhauer writes under the strong influence of Kant. The world of experience is the phenomenal world: it is object for a subject. And as such it is the world of our mental presentations (*Vorstellungen*). But no object is ever presented to us in a state of complete isolation and detachment. That is to say, all our presentations are related to or connected with other presentations in regular ways. And knowledge or science is precisely knowledge of these regular relations. 'Science, that is to say, signifies a *system* of objects known',[1] not a mere aggregate of presentations. And there must be a sufficient reason for this relatedness or correctedness. Thus the general principle which governs our knowledge of objects or phenomena is the principle of sufficient reason.

As a preliminary enunciation of the principle of sufficient reason Schopenhauer chooses 'the Wolffian formulation as the most general: *Nihil est sine ratione cur potius sit quam non sit.* Nothing is without a reason [*Grund*, ground] why it is.'[2] But he goes on to discover four main types or classes of objects and four main types of relatedness or connection. And he draws the conclusion that there are four fundamental forms of the principle of sufficient reason and that the principle in its general enunciation is an abstraction from them. Hence the title of the dissertation, *On the Fourfold Root of the Principle of Sufficient Reason.*

[1] *W*, I, p. 4. References to Schopenhauer's *Works* are given according to volume and page of the edition by J. Frauenstädt (1877).
[2] *W*, I, p. 5.

The first class of objects or presentations is that of our intuitive, empirical and complete[1] presentations. This may not sound very enlightening; but in the language of ordinary realism the objects in question are the physical objects which are causally related in space and time and which form the subject-matter of natural sciences such as physics and chemistry. According to Schopenhauer, this spatial, temporal and causal relatedness is to be ascribed to an activity of the mind which organizes the matter of phenomena, elementary sensations, according to the *a priori* forms of sensibility, namely space and time, and the pure form of causality which is the only category of the understanding. He thus follows Kant, though the Kantian categories of the understanding are reduced to one. And our knowledge of these presentations, of phenomena or, in realist language, of physical objects, is said to be governed by 'the principle of sufficient reason of becoming, *principium rationis sufficientis fiendi*'.[2]

The second class of objects consists of abstract concepts, and the relevant form of relatedness is the judgment. But a judgment does not express knowledge unless it is true. And 'truth is the relation of a judgment to something different from it, which can be called its ground'.[3] The ground or sufficient reason can be of different types. For instance, a judgment can have as its ground another judgment; and when we consider the rules of implication and inference in a formal way, we are in the province of logic.[4] But in any case the judgment, the synthesis of concepts, is governed by 'the principle of sufficient reason of knowing, *principium rationis sufficientis cognoscendi*'.[5]

The third class of objects comprises 'the *a priori* intuitions of the forms of outer and inner sense, space and time'.[6] Space and time are of such a nature that each part is related in a certain way to another. And 'the law according to which the parts of space and time . . . determine one another I call the principle of sufficient reason of being, *principium rationis sufficientis essendi*'.[7] In time, for example, this is the law of irreversible succession; and 'on this connection of the parts of time rests all counting'.[8] Arithmetic, in other words, rests on the law governing the relations between the

---

[1] Complete in the sense that such presentations comprise both the form and the matter of phenomena. In other words, it is not a question here of abstract concepts.
[2] *W*, I, p. 34.   [3] *W*, I, p. 105.
[4] The implication of this is that Hegel's identification of logic with metaphysics, in the sense of the science of the Absolute, is absurd.
[5] *W*, I, p. 105.   [6] *W*, I, p. 130.
[7] *W*, I, p. 131.   [8] *W*, I, p. 133.

parts of time, while geometry rests on the law governing the respective positions of the parts of space. We can say, therefore, that Schopenhauer's third class of objects are mathematical objects, and that the relevant form of the principle of sufficient reason or ground, which governs our knowledge of geometrical and arithmetical relations, is the law, or rather laws, according to which the parts of space and time are respectively related to one another.

The fourth class of objects contains only one member, namely 'the subject of willing considered as object for the knowing subject'.[1] That is to say, the object is the self as source or subject of volition. And the principle governing our knowledge of the relation between this subject and its volitions or acts of will is 'the principle of the ground (or sufficient reason) of acting, *principium rationis sufficientis agendi*; more briefly, the *law of motivation*'.[2] The implication of this is character-determinism. A man acts for motives, and the motives for which he acts have their ground or sufficient reason in his character. We understand the relation between a man's deliberate actions and himself as subject of volition where we see these actions as issuing from the character of the subject. But this subject will be considered later.

Schopenhauer's terminology is based on that of Wolff. But his general position is based on Kant's. The world is phenomenal, object for a subject. And it is the sphere of necessity. True, Schopenhauer recognizes different types of necessity. In the sphere of volition, for example, moral necessity rules, which is to be distinguished both from physical and from logical necessity. But within the sphere of presentations as a whole, the relations between them are governed by certain laws, described as distinct roots of the principle of sufficient reason.

It is to be noted, however, that the principle of sufficient reason applies only within the phenomenal sphere, the sphere of objects for a subject. It does not apply to the noumenon, metaphenomenal reality, whatever this may be. Nor can it be legitimately applied to the phenomenal world considered as a totality. For it governs relations *between* phenomena. Hence no cosmological argument for God's existence can be valid, if it is an argument from the world as a whole to God as cause or as sufficient ground of phenomena. And here again Schopenhauer is in substantial agreement with Kant, though he certainly does not follow

---

[1] *W*, I, p. 140.   [2] *W*, I, p. 145.

Kant in proposing belief in God as a matter of practical or moral faith.

3. The doctorate dissertation which we have just briefly considered appears arid and unexciting in comparison with Schopenhauer's great work *The World as Will and Idea*. Yet Schopenhauer was justified in regarding the former as an introduction to the latter. For his *magnum opus* begins with the statement that 'the world is my idea'.[1] That is to say, the whole visible world or, as Schopenhauer describes it, the sum total of experience is object for a subject: its reality consists in its appearing to or being perceived by a subject. As Berkeley said, the *esse* of sensible things is *percipi*.

The following point should be noticed. The German word translated here by 'idea' is *Vorstellung*. And in the section on Schopenhauer's doctorate dissertation I translated this word by 'presentation', which is preferable to 'idea'. But the title *The World as Will and Idea* has become so familiar that it seems pedantic to insist on a change. At the same time it is important to understand that Schopenhauer distinguishes between intuitive presentations *(intuitive Vorstellungen)* and abstract presentations *(abstrakte Vorstellungen)* or concepts. And when Schopenhauer says that the world is my idea, he is referring to intuitive presentations. He does not mean, for example, that a tree is identical with my abstract concept of a tree. He means that the tree as perceived by me exists only in relation to me as a percipient subject. Its reality is exhausted, so to speak, in its perceptibility. It is simply what I perceive or can perceive it to be.

Schopenhauer's position can be clarified in this way. Abstract concepts are possessed only by man: intuitive presentations are common to man and animals, at least to the higher animals. There is a phenomenal world not only for man but also for animals. For the conditions of its possibility are present also in the latter, these conditions being the *a priori* forms of sensibility, namely space and time, and the category of the understanding, namely causality. In Schopenhauer's view understanding *(Verstand)* is found also in animals. And the *principium rationis sufficientis fiendi* operates, for instance, in a dog, for which there exists a world of causally related things. But animals do not possess reason *(Vernuft)*, the faculty of abstract concepts. A dog perceives things in space and

---

[1] *W*, II, p. 3; *HK*, I, p. 3. In references to *The World as Will and Idea HK* signifies the English translation by R. B. Haldane and J. Kemp.

time, and it can perceive concrete causal relations. But it does not follow that a dog can reflect abstractly about space, time or causality. To put the matter in another way, the statement that the visible world is object for a percipient subject applies as well to a dog as to a man. But it does not follow from this that a dog can know that the statement is true.

It should be added that according to Schopenhauer it was an important discovery of Kant that space and time, as the *a priori* conditions of the visible world, can be intuited in themselves. Hence they can be included in the range of our intuitive presentations which comprise 'the whole visible world, or the whole of experience, together with the conditions of its possibility'.[1] But it does not follow that a dog can intuit space and time in themselves and work out pure mathematics, though there is for it a spatiotemporal world.

Now, if the world is my idea, my body also must be my idea. For it is a visible thing. But we must go further than this. If it is true that the world exists only as object for a subject, it is also true that the percipient subject is correlative with the object. 'For me [Schopenhauer] matter and intelligence are inseparable correlates, existing only for one another, and therefore only relatively . . . the two together constitute *the world as idea*, which is just Kant's *appearance*, and consequently something secondary.'[2] The world as idea or presentation thus comprises both perceiver and perceived. This totality is, as Kant said, empirically real but transcendentally ideal.

For Kant Schopenhauer had a profound respect, and he claimed to be Kant's true successor. But his theory of the phenomenal character of empirical reality was powerfully reinforced by, though not derived from, another factor. Shortly after the publication of his doctorate dissertation in 1813 Schopenhauer met at Weimar an Oriental scholar, F. Mayer, who introduced him to Indian philosophical literature. And he retained an interest in Oriental philosophy up to the end of his life. As an old man he meditated on the text of the Upanishads. It is not surprising, therefore, if he associated his theory of the world as idea or presentation with the Indian doctrine of Maya. Individual subjects and objects are all appearance, Maya.

Now, if the world is phenomenal, the question arises, what is the noumenon? What is the reality which lies behind the veil of Maya?

[1] *W*, II, p. 7; *HK*, I, p. 7.   [2] *W*, III, pp. 19–20; *HK*, II, p. 181.

And Schopenhauer's discussion of the nature of this reality and of its self-manifestation forms the really interesting part of his system. For the theory of the world as idea, though it is in Schopenhauer's opinion an indispensable part of his philosophy, is obviously a development of Kant's position, whereas his theory of the world as will is original[1] and contains the expression of his characteristic interpretation of human life. Before, however, we approach this topic, something must be said about his theory of the practical function of concepts, which possesses an intrinsic interest of its own.

4. As we have seen, besides intuitive presentations man possesses also abstract concepts which are formed by reason and presuppose experience, whether directly or indirectly. But why do we form them? What is their function? Schopenhauer's answer is that their primary function is practical. 'The great utility of concepts consists in the fact that by means of them the original material of knowledge is easier to handle, survey and order.'[2] In comparison with intuitive presentations, with immediate perceptive knowledge, abstract concepts are in a sense poor. For they omit a great deal, the differences, for example, between individual members of a class. But they are required if communication is to be possible and if experimental knowledge is to be retained and handed on. 'The greatest value of rational or abstract knowledge lies in its communicability and in the possibility of retaining it permanently. It is chiefly on this account that it is so inestimably important for practice.'[3] Schopenhauer also mentions the ethical importance of concepts and abstract reasoning. A moral man guides his conduct by principles. And principles require concepts.

But Schopenhauer is not concerned simply with pointing out examples of the practical value of concepts. He is also at pains to show how this practical value is connected with his general theory of cognition. Knowledge is the servant of the will. Or, to omit metaphysics for the present, knowledge is in the first instance the instrument of satisfying physical needs, the servant of the body. In animals needs are less complicated than in man, and they are more easily satisfied. Perception is sufficient, especially as Nature has provided animals with their own means of attack and defence,

---

[1] Schopenhauer liked to regard his philosophy of the Will as a development of Kant's doctrine of the primacy of the practical reason or rational will. But the former's metaphysical voluntarism was really foreign to the latter's mind. It was Schopenhauer's original creation.

[2] *W*, III, p. 89; *HK*, II, p. 258.   [3] *W*, II, p. 66; *HK*, I, p. 72.

such as the claws of the lion and the sting of the wasp. But with the further development of the organism, in particular of the brain, there is a corresponding development of needs and wants. And a higher type of knowledge is required to satisfy them. In man reason appears, which enables him to discover new ways of satisfying his needs, to invent tools, and so on.[1]

Reason, therefore, has a primarily biological function. If one may so speak, Nature intends it as an instrument for satisfying the needs of a more highly complicated and developed organism than that of the animal. But the needs in question are physical needs. Reason is primarily concerned with nourishment and propagation, with the bodily needs of the individual and species. And it follows from this that reason is unfitted for penetrating through the veil of phenomena to the underlying reality, the noumenon. The concept is a practical instrument: it stands for a number of things belonging to the same class and enables us to deal easily and economically with a vast amount of material. But it is not adapted for going beyond phenomena to any underlying essence or thing-in-itself.

In this case, we may well ask, how can metaphysics be possible? Schopenhauer answers that though the intellect is by nature the servant of the will, it is capable in man of developing to such an extent that it can achieve objectivity. That is to say, though man's mind is in the first instance an instrument for satisfying his bodily needs, it can develop a kind of surplus energy which sets it free, at least temporarily, from the service of desire. Man then becomes a disinterested spectator: he can adopt a contemplative attitude, as in aesthetic contemplation and in philosophy.

Clearly, this claim on behalf of the human mind does not by itself dispose of the difficulty which arises out of Schopenhauer's account of the concept. For systematic and communicable philosophy must be expressed in concepts. And if the concept is fitted for dealing only with phenomena, metaphysics appears to be ruled out. But Schopenhauer replies that metaphysical philosophy is possible provided that there is a fundamental intuition on the level of perceptive knowledge, which gives us direct insight into the nature of the reality underlying phenomena, an insight which philosophy endeavours to express in conceptual form. Philosophy, therefore, involves an interplay between intuition and conceptual

---

[1] An obvious line of objection is that there is an element of putting the cart before the horse in all this. It might be claimed, that is to say, that it is precisely because man possesses the power of reasoning that he is able to extend the scope and number of his wants and desires.

reasoning. 'To enrich the concept from intuition is the constant concern of poetry and philosophy.'[1] Concepts do not provide us with new knowledge: intuition is fundamental. But intuition must be raised to the conceptual level if it is to become philosophy.

Schopenhauer is in a rather difficult position. He does not wish to postulate as the basis of philosophy an exceptional intuition which would be something entirely different from perception on the one hand and abstract reasoning on the other. Hence the intuition of which he is speaking must be on the level of perceptive knowledge. But perception is concerned with individual objects, and so with phenomena. For individuality belongs to the phenomenal sphere. He is forced, therefore, to try to show that even on the level of perception there can be an intuitive awareness of the noumenon, an awareness which forms the basis for philosophical mediation.

Leaving the nature of this intuition for consideration in the next section, we can pause to note how in some respects Schopenhauer anticipates certain Bergsonian positions. For Bergson emphasized the practical function of intelligence and the inability of the concept to grasp the reality of life. And he went on to base philosophy on intuition and to depict the philosopher's task as being partly that of endeavouring to mediate this intuition, so far as this is possible, on the conceptual level. Hence for Bergson as for Schopenhauer philosophy involves the interplay of intuition and discursive or conceptual reasoning. I do not mean to imply that Bergson actually took his ideas from Schopenhauer. For I am not aware of any real evidence to show that he did. The notion that if philosopher X holds views which are similar to his predecessor Y, the former must necessarily have borrowed from or been influenced by the latter, is absurd. But the fact remains that though Bergson, when he became aware of the similarity, distinguished between his idea of intuition and that of the German philosopher, there is an obvious analogy between their positions. In other words, the same current or line of thought which found expression in the philosophy of Schopenhauer, when considered under the aspects in question, reappeared in the thought of Bergson. To put the matter in another way, there is some continuity, though there is also difference, between the system of Schopenhauer and the philosophy of Life of which the thought of Bergson is a notable example.

[1] W, III, p. 80; HK, II, p. 248.

5. Kant maintained that the thing-in-itself, the correlative of the phenomenon, is unknowable. Schopenhauer, however, tells us what it is. It is Will. 'Thing-in-itself signifies that which exists independently of our perception, in short that which properly is. For Democritus this was formed matter. It was the same at bottom for Locke. For Kant it was $=X$. For me it is Will.'[1] And this is one single Will. For multiplicity can exist only in the spatio-temporal world, the sphere of phenomena. There cannot be more than one metaphenomenal reality or thing-in-itself. In other words, the inside of the world, so to speak, is one reality, whereas the outside, the appearance of this reality, is the empirical world which consists of finite things.

How does Schopenhauer arrive at the conviction that the thing-in-itself is Will? To find the key to reality I must look within myself. For in inner consciousness or inwardly directed perception lies 'the single narrow door to the truth'.[2] Through this inner consciousness I am aware that the bodily action which is said to follow or result from volition is not something different from volition but one and the same. That is to say, the bodily action is simply the objectified will: it is the will become idea or presentation. Indeed, the whole body is nothing but objectified will, will as a presentation to consciousness. According to Schopenhauer anyone can understand this if he enters into himself. And once he has this fundamental intuition, he has the key to reality. He has only to extend his discovery to the world at large.

This Schopenhauer proceeds to do. He sees the manifestation of the one individual Will in the impulse by which the magnet turns to the north pole, in the phenomena of attraction and repulsion, in gravitation, in animal instinct, in human desire and so on. Wherever he looks, whether in the inorganic or in the organic sphere, he discovers empirical confirmation of his thesis that phenomena constitute the appearance of the one metaphysical Will.

The natural question to ask is this? If the thing-in-itself is manifested in such diverse phenomena as the universal forces of Nature, such as gravity, and human volition, why call it 'Will'? Would not 'Force' or 'Energy' be a more appropriate term, especially as the so-called Will, when considered in itself, is said to be 'without knowledge and merely a blind incessant impulse',[3] 'an endless striving'?[4] For the term 'Will', which implies rationality,

[1] W, VI, p. 96. From Parerga und Paralipomena.
[2] W, III, p. 219; HK, II, p. 406.
[3] W, II, p. 323; HK, I, p. 354.   [4] W, II, p. 195; HK, I, p. 213.

seems to be hardly suitable for describing a blind impulse or striving.

Schopenhauer, however, defends his linguistic usage by maintaining that we ought to take our descriptive term from what is best known to us. We are immediately conscious of our own volition. And it is more appropriate to describe the less well known in terms of the better known than the other way round.

Besides being described as blind impulse, endless striving, eternal becoming and so on, the metaphysical Will is characterized as the Will to live. Indeed, to say 'the Will' and to say 'the Will to live' are for Schopenhauer one and the same thing. As, therefore, empirical reality is the objectification or appearance of the metaphysical Will, it necessarily manifests the Will to live. And Schopenhauer has no difficulty in multiplying examples of this manifestation. We have only to look at Nature's concern for the maintenance of the species. Birds, for instance, build nests for the young which they do not yet know. Insects deposit their eggs where the larva may find nourishment. The whole series of phenomena of animal instinct manifests the omnipresence of the Will to live. If we look at the untiring activity of bees and ants and ask what it all leads to, what is attained by it, we can only answer 'the satisfaction of hunger and the sexual instinct',[1] the means, in other words, of maintaining the species in life. And if we look at man with his industry and trade, with his inventions and technology, we must admit that all this striving serves in the first instance only to sustain and to bring a certain amount of additional comfort to ephemeral individuals in their brief span of existence, and through them to contribute to the maintenance of the species.

All this fits in with what was said in the last section about Schopenhauer's theory of the biological function of reason as existing primarily to satisfy physical needs. We noticed indeed that the human intellect is capable of developing in such a way that it can free itself, at least temporarily, from the slavery of the Will. And we shall see later that Schopenhauer by no means confines the possible range of human activities to eating, drinking and copulation, the means of maintaining the life of the individual and of the species. But the primary function of reason manifests the character of the Will as the Will to live.

6. Now, if the Will is an endless striving, a blind urge or impulse which knows no cessation, it cannot find satisfaction or reach a

---

[1] *W*, III, p. 403; *HK*, III, p. 111.

state of tranquillity. It is always striving and never attaining. And this essential feature of the metaphysical Will is reflected in its self-objectification, above all in human life. Man seeks satisfaction, happiness, but he cannot attain it. What we call happiness or enjoyment is simply a temporary cessation of desire. And desire, as the expression of a need or want, is a form of pain. Happiness, therefore, is 'the deliverance from a pain, from a want';[1] it is 'really and essentially always only *negative* and never positive'.[2] It soon turns to boredom, and the striving after satisfaction reasserts itself. It is boredom which makes beings who love one another so little as men do seek one another's company. And great intellectual powers simply increase the capacity for suffering and deepen the individual's isolation.

Each individual thing, as an objectification of the one Will to live, strives to assert its own existence at the expense of other things. Hence the world is the field of conflict, a conflict which manifests the nature of the Will as at variance with itself, as a tortured Will. And Schopenhauer finds illustrations of this conflict even in the inorganic sphere. But it is naturally to the organic and human spheres that he chiefly turns for empirical confirmation of his thesis. He dwells, for example, on the ways in which animals of one species prey on those of another. And when he comes to man, he really lets himself go. 'The chief source of the most serious evils which afflict man is man himself: *homo homini lupus*. Whoever keeps this last fact clearly in view sees the world as a hell which surpasses that of Dante through the fact that one man must be the devil of another.'[3] War and cruelty are, of course, grist for Schopenhauer's mill. And the man who showed no sympathy with the Revolution of 1848 speaks in the sharpest terms of industrial exploitation, slavery and such like social abuses.

We may note that it is the egoism, rapacity and hardness and cruelty of men which are for Schopenhauer the real justification of the State. So far from being a divine manifestation, the State is simply the creation of enlightened egoism which tries to make the world a little more tolerable than it would otherwise be.

Schopenhauer's pessimism is thus metaphysical in the sense that it is presented as a consequence of the nature of the metaphysical Will. The philosopher is not simply engaged in drawing attention to the empirical fact that there is much evil and suffering in the

[1] *W*, II, p. 376; *HK*, I, pp. 411–12.   [2] *Ibid.*
[3] *W*, III, p. 663; *HK*, III, p. 388.

world. He is also indicating what he believes to be the cause of this empirical fact. The thing-in-itself being what it is, phenomenal reality must be marked with the black features which we actually observe. We can, of course, do something to alleviate suffering. This also is an empirical fact. But it is no good thinking that we can change the fundamental character of the world or of human life. If war, for instance, were abolished and if all men's material needs were met, the result would presumably be, on Schopenhauer's premisses, a condition of intolerable boredom which would be succeeded by the return of conflict. In any case the prevalence of suffering and evil in the world is ultimately due to the nature of the thing-in-itself. And Schopenhauer is not slow to castigate what he regards as the facile optimism of Leibniz and the way in which the German idealists, especially Hegel, slur over the dark side of human existence or, when they admit it, justify it as 'rational'.

7. Needless to say, Schopenhauer thought that his theory of the phenomenal character of empirical reality fitted in well with his theory of the Will. That is to say, he thought that having once accepted Kant's general thesis of the phenomenal character of the world he could then go on, without inconsistency, to reveal the nature of the thing-in-itself. But this is questionable.

Take, for example, Schopenhauer's approach to the Will through inner consciousness. As Herbart remarked, on Schopenhauer's principles the Will, as viewed in inner perception, must be subject to the form of time: it is known in its successive acts. And these are phenomenal. We cannot arrive at the Will as a meta-phenomenal reality. For in so far as we are conscious of it, it is phenomenal. True, we can talk about the metaphysical Will. But in so far as it is thought and spoken about, it must be, it seems, object for a subject, and so phenomenal.

Schopenhauer does indeed admit that we cannot know the metaphysical Will in itself, and that it may have attributes which are unknown by us and indeed incomprehensible to us. But he insists that it is known, even if only partially, in its manifestation or objectification, and that our own volition is for us its most distinct manifestation. In this case, however, the metaphysical Will seems to disintegrate, as it were, into phenomena, as far as our knowledge is concerned. And the conclusion seems to follow that we cannot know the thing-in-itself. To put the matter in another way, Schopenhauer does not wish to base his philosophy on a privileged and exceptional intuition of ultimate reality, but rather on our intuitive perception of our own volition. Yet this intuitive perception seems, on his own premises, to belong to the phenomenal sphere which includes the whole range of the subject-object relationship. In fine, once given the doctrine of *The World as Idea*, the first book of Schopenhauer's *magnum opus*, it is difficult to see how any access to the thing-in-itself is possible. Kant would presumably say that it was impossible.

This line of objection is, I think, justified. But it would, of course, be possible to cut Schopenhauer's philosophy adrift from its Kantian moorings and present it as a kind of hypothesis. The philosopher, let us suppose, was temperamentally inclined to see in a clear light and to emphasize the dark aspects of the world and of human life and history. So far from being secondary features, they seemed to him to constitute the world's most significant and positive aspects. And he considered that analysis of the concepts of happiness and of suffering confirmed this initial vision. On this basis he erected the explanatory hypothesis of the blind and endlessly striving impulse or force which he called the Will. And he could then look round to discover fresh empirical confirmation of his hypothesis in the inorganic, organic and specifically human spheres. Further, the hypothesis enabled him to make some general predictions about human life and history in the future.

It is obviously not my intention to suggest that Schopenhauer would have been willing to surrender his theory of the World as Idea. On the contrary, he laid emphasis on it. Nor is it my intention to suggest that Schopenhauer's picture of the world would be acceptable if it were presented as the lines just indicated above. His analysis of happiness as 'negative', to mention but one point of criticism, seems to me quite untenable. My point is rather that Schopenhauer's philosophy expresses a 'vision' of the world which draws attention to certain aspects of it. And this vision can perhaps be made clearer if his philosophy is expressed in the form of an hypothesis based on an exclusive attention to the aspects in question. To be sure, it is a one-sided vision or picture of the world. But precisely because of its one-sidedness and exaggeration it serves as an effective counter-balance or antithesis to a system such as that of Hegel in which attention is so focused on the triumphant march of Reason through history that the evil and suffering in the world are obscured from view by high-sounding phrases.

CHAPTER XIV

SCHOPENHAUER (2)

Aesthetic contemplation as a temporary escape from the slavery of the Will—The particular fine arts—Virtue and renunciation: the way of salvation—Schopenhauer and metaphysical idealism —The general influence of Schopenhauer—Notes on Eduard von Hartmann's development of Schopenhauer's philosophy.

1. THE root of all evil for Schopenhauer is the slavery of the Will, subservience to the Will to live. But his claim has already been mentioned that the human mind has the capacity for developing beyond the extent required for the satisfaction of physical needs. It can develop, as it were, a surplus of energy over and above the energy required to fulfil its primary biological and practical function. Man is thus able to escape from the futile life of desire and striving, of egoistic self-assertion and conflict.

Schopenhauer describes two ways of escape from the slavery of the Will, the one temporary, an oasis in the desert, the other more lasting. The first is the way of aesthetic contemplation, the way of art; the second is the path of asceticism, the way of salvation. In this section we are concerned with the first, the way of escape through art.

In aesthetic contemplation man becomes the disinterested observer. Needless to say, this does not mean that aesthetic contemplation is uninteresting. If, for example, I regard a beautiful object as an object of desire or as a stimulant to desire, my point of view is not that of aesthetic contemplation: I am an 'interested' spectator. In point of fact I am the servant or instrument of the Will. But it is possible for me to regard the beautiful object neither as itself an object of desire nor as a stimulant to desire but simply and solely for its aesthetic significance. I am then a disinterested, but not an uninterested, spectator. And I am freed, temporarily at least, from the slavery of the Will.

This theory of temporary escape through aesthetic contemplation, whether of natural objects or of works of art, is linked by Schopenhauer with a metaphysical theory of what he calls Platonic Ideas. The Will is said to objectify itself immediately in Ideas which stand to individual natural things as archetypes to copies. They are 'the determinate species or the original unchanging forms and properties of all natural bodies, both inorganic and organic, and also the universal forces which reveal themselves according to natural laws'.[1] There are thus Ideas of natural forces such as gravity, and there are Ideas of species. But there are no Ideas of genuses. For while there are natural species, there are, according to Schopenhauer, no natural genuses.

The Ideas of species must not be confused with the immanent forms of things. The individual members of a species or natural class are said to be 'the empirical correlative of the Idea'.[2] And the Idea is an eternal archetype. It is for this reason, of course, that Schopenhauer identifies his Ideas with the Platonic Forms or Ideas.

How a blind Will or endless striving can reasonably be said to objectify itself immediately in Platonic Ideas, is something which I do not profess to understand. It seems to me that Schopenhauer, sharing the belief of Schelling and Hegel, in spite of his abuse of them, in the metaphysical significance of art and aesthetic intuition, and seeing that aesthetic contemplation offers a temporary escape from the slavery of desire, turns to a philosopher whom he greatly admires, namely Plato, and borrows from him a theory of Ideas which has no clear connection with the description of the Will as a blind, self-tortured impulse or striving. However, it is unnecessary to labour this aspect of the matter. The point is that the artistic genius is capable of apprehending the Ideas and of giving expression to them in works of art. And in aesthetic contemplation the beholder is participating in this apprehension of the Ideas. He thus rises above the temporal and changing and contemplates the eternal and unchanging. His attitude is contemplative, not appetitive. Appetite is stilled during aesthetic experience.

Schopenhauer's exaltation of the role of artistic genius represents a point of affinity with the romantic spirit. He does not, however, speak very clearly about the nature of artistic genius or about the relation between the genius and the ordinary man. Sometimes he seems to imply that genius means not only the ability to apprehend the Ideas but also the ability to express them in works of art. At other times he seems to imply that genius is simply the faculty of intuiting the Ideas, and that the ability to give external expression

---

[1] *W*, II, p. 199; *HK*, I, p. 219.   [2] *W*, III, p. 417; *HK*, III, p. 123.

to them is a matter of technique which can be acquired by training and practice. The first way of speaking fits in best with what is presumably our normal conviction, namely that artistic genius involves the capacity for creative production. If a man lacked this capacity, we would not normally speak of him as an artistic genius or, for the matter of that, as an artist at all. The second way of speaking implies that everyone who is capable of aesthetic appreciation and contemplation participates in genius to some extent. But one might go on to claim with Benedetto Croce that aesthetic intuition involves interior expression, in the sense of imaginative recreation, as distinct from external expression. In this case both the creative artist and the man who contemplates and appreciates the work of art would 'express', though only the first would express externally. However, though it may be possible to bring together the two ways of speaking in some such manner, I think that for Schopenhauer artistic genius really involves both the faculty of intuiting the Ideas and the faculty of giving creative expression to this intuition, though this is aided by technical training. In this case the man who is not capable of producing works of art himself could still share in genius to the extent of intuiting the Ideas in and through their external expression.

The important point, however, in the present context is that in aesthetic contemplation a man transcends the original subjection of knowledge to the Will, to desire. He becomes the 'pure will-less subject of knowledge, who no longer traces relations in accordance with the principle of sufficient reason, but rests and is lost in fixed contemplation of the object presented to him, apart from its connection with any other object'.[1] If the object of contemplation is simply significant form, the Idea as concretely presented to perception, we are concerned with the beautiful. If, however, a man perceives the object of contemplation as having a hostile relation to his body, as menacing, that is to say, the objectification of the Will in the form of the human body by its power of greatness, he is contemplating the sublime. That is, he is contemplating the sublime provided that, while recognizing the menacing character of the object, he persists in objective contemplation and does not allow himself to be overwhelmed by the self-regarding emotion of fear. For instance, a man in a small boat at sea during a terrible storm is contemplating the sublime if he fixes his attention on the

[1] *W*, II, pp. 209–10; *HK*, I, p. 230.

grandeur of the scene and the power of the elements.[1] But whether a man is contemplating the beautiful or the sublime, he is temporarily freed from the servitude of the Will. His mind enjoys a rest, as it were, from being an instrument for the satisfaction of desire and adopts a purely objective and disinterested point of view.

2. Both Schelling and Hegel arranged the particular fine arts in ascending series. And Schopenhauer too engages in this pastime. His standard of classification and arrangement is the series of grades of the Will's objectification. For example, architecture is said to express some low-grade Ideas such as gravity, cohesion, rigidity and hardness, the universal qualities of stone. Moreover, in expressing the tension between gravity and rigidity architecture expresses indirectly the conflict of the Will. Artistic hydraulics exhibits the Ideas of fluid matter in, for instance, fountains and artificial waterfalls, while artistic horticulture or landscape-gardening exhibits the Ideas of the higher grades of vegetative life. Historical painting and sculpture express the Idea of man, though sculpture is concerned principally with beauty and grace while painting is chiefly concerned with the expression of character and passion. Poetry is capable of representing Ideas of all grades. For its immediate material is concepts, though the poet tries by his use of epithets to bring down the abstract concept to the level of perception and thus to stimulate the imagination and enable the reader or hearer to apprehend the Idea in the perceptible object.[2] But though poetry is capable of representing all grades of Ideas, its chief object is the representation of man as expressing himself through a series of actions and through the accompanying thoughts and emotions.

At the time there was controversy among writers on aesthetics about the range of the concept of fine art. But it would hardly be profitable to enter into a discussion about the propriety or impropriety of describing artistic hydraulics and landscape-gardening as fine arts. Nor need we discuss an arrangement of the arts which depends on correlating them with a questionable metaphysical system. Instead we can notice the two following points.

[1] Following Kant, Schopenhauer distinguishes between the dynamical and the mathematically sublime. The man in the boat is contemplating an example of the first type. The mathematically sublime is the statically immense, a great range of mountains, for instance.

[2] For instance, Homer does not simply talk about the sea or the dawn but brings the ideas nearer to the level of perception by the use of epithets such as 'wine-dark' and 'rosy-fingered'.

First, as one would expect, the supreme poetical art is for
Schopenhauer tragedy. For in tragedy we witness the real
character of human life transmuted into art and expressed in
dramatic form, 'the unspeakable pain, the wail of humanity, the
triumph of evil, the mocking mastery of chance and the irretrievable
fall of the just and innocent'.[1]

Secondly, the highest of all arts is not tragedy but music. For
music does not exhibit an Idea or Ideas, the immediate objectification of the Will: it exhibits the Will itself, the inner nature of the
thing-in-itself.[2] In listening to music, therefore, a man receives a
direct revelation, though not in conceptual form, of the reality
which underlies phenomena. And he intuits this reality, revealed
in the form of art, in an objective and disinterested manner, not as
one caught in the grip of the Will's tyranny. Further, if it were
possible to express accurately in concepts all that music expresses
without concepts, we should have the true philosophy.

3. Aesthetic contemplation affords no more than a temporary
or transient escape from the slavery of the Will. But Schopenhauer
offers a lasting release through renunciation of the Will to live.
Indeed, moral progress must take this form if morality is possible
at all. For the Will to live, manifesting itself in egoism, self-
assertion, hatred and conflict, is for Schopenhauer the source of
evil. 'There really resides in the heart of each of us a wild beast
which only waits the opportunity to rage and rave in order to
injure others, and which, if they do not prevent it, would like to
destroy them.'[3] This wild beast, this radical evil, is the direct
expression of the Will to live. Hence morality, if it is possible, must
involve denial of the Will. And as man is an objectification of the
Will, denial will mean self-denial, asceticism and mortification.

Schopenhauer does indeed say that in his philosophy the world
possesses a moral significance. But what he means by this at first
sight astonishing statement is this. Existence, life, is itself a crime:
it is our original sin. And it is inevitably expiated by suffering and
death. Hence we can say that justice reigns and, adapting Hegel's
famous statement, that 'the world itself is the world's court of
judgment'.[4] In this sense, therefore, the world possesses a moral
significance. 'If we could lay all the misery of the world in one

[1] *W*, II, p. 298; *HK*, I, p. 326.
[2] It is for this reason that Schopenhauer condemns imitative music, mentioning
Haydn's *Seasons* as an example.
[3] *W*, VI, p. 230. From *Parerga und Paralipomena*.
[4] *W*, II, p. 415; *HK*, I, p. 454.

scale of the balance and all the guilt of the world in the other, the needle would certainly point to the centre.'[1] Schopenhauer speaks as though it were the Will itself which is guilty and the Will itself which pays the penalty. For it objectifies itself and suffers in its objectification. And this way of speaking may seem to be extravagant. For the sufferings of men must be phenomenal on Schopenhauer's premisses: they can hardly affect the thing-in-itself. Passing over this point, however, we can draw from the statement that existence or life is itself a crime the conclusion that morality, if it is possible, must take the form of denial of the Will to live, of a turning away from life.

Given these premisses, it may well appear to follow that the highest moral act will be suicide. But Schopenhauer argues that suicide expresses a surrender to the Will rather than a denial of it. For the man who commits suicide does so to escape certain evils. And if he could escape from them without killing himself, he would do so. Hence suicide is, paradoxically, the expression of a concealed will to live. Consequently, denial and renunciation must take some form other than suicide.

But is morality possible within the framework of Schopenhauer's philosophy? The individual human being is an objectification of the one individual Will, and his actions are determined. Schopenhauer draws a distinction between the intelligible and empirical characters. The metaphysical Will objectifies itself in the individual will, and this individual will, when considered in itself and anteriorly to its acts, is the intelligible or noumenal character. The individual will as manifested through its successive acts is the empirical character. Now, consciousness has for its object the particular acts of the will. And these appear successively. A man thus comes to know his character only gradually and imperfectly: in principle he is in the same position as an outsider. He does not foresee his future acts of will but is conscious only of acts already posited. He therefore seems to himself to be free. And this feeling of freedom is quite natural. Yet the empirical act is really the unfolding of the intelligible or noumenal character. The former is the consequence of the latter and determined by it. As Spinoza said, the feeling or persuasion of freedom is really the effect of ignorance of the determining causes of one's actions.

At first sight, therefore, there would seem to be little point in indicating how people ought to act if they wish to escape from the

[1] *W*, II, p. 416; *HK*, I, p. 454.

slavery of desire and restless striving. For their actions are determined by their character. And these characters are objectifications of the Will, which is the Will to live and manifests itself precisely in desire and restless striving.

Schopenhauer argues, however, that character-determinism does not exclude changes in conduct. Let us suppose, for example, that I am accustomed to act in the way most calculated to bring me financial gain. One day somebody persuades me that treasure in heaven is more valuable and lasting than treasure on earth. And my new conviction leads to a change in conduct. Instead of trying to avail myself of an opportunity to enrich myself at the expense of Tom Jones I leave the opportunity of financial gain to him. My friends, if I have any, may say that my character has changed. But in point of fact I am the same sort of man that I was before. The actions which I now perform are different from my past actions, but my character has not changed. For I act for the same sort of motive, namely personal gain, though I have changed my view about what constitutes the most gainful line of conduct. In other words, my intelligible character determines what sort of motives move me to act; and the motive remains the same whether I am amassing riches on earth or renouncing them for celestial wealth.

Taken by itself, indeed, this example does not help us to understand how a denial of the Will to live can be possible. For it illustrates the permanence of egoism rather than the emergence of radical self-denial. And though it may be useful as indicating a plausible way of reconciling with the theory of character-determinism the empirical facts which appear to show the possibility of changes in character, it does not explain how the Will to live can turn back on itself, in and through its objectification, and deny itself. But we can pass over this point for the moment. It is sufficient to note that the idea of changing one's point of view plays an important role in Schopenhauer's philosophy as it does in that of Spinoza. For Schopenhauer envisages a progressive seeing through, as it were, the veil of Maya, the phenomenal world of individuality and multiplicity. This is possible because of the intellect's capacity to develop beyond the extent required for the fulfilment of its primary practical functions. And the degrees of moral advance correspond with the degrees of penetration of the veil of Maya.

Individuality is phenomenal. The noumenon is one: a plurality of individuals exists only for the phenomenal subject. And a man may, in the first instance, penetrate the illusion of individuality to the extent that he sets others on the same level as himself and does them no injury. We then have the just man, as distinct from the man who is so enmeshed in the veil of Maya that he asserts himself to the exclusion of others.

But it is possible to go further. A man may penetrate the veil of Maya to the extent of seeing that all individuals are really one. For they are all phenomena of the one undivided Will. We then have the ethical level of sympathy. We have goodness or virtue which is characterized by a disinterested love of others. True goodness is not, as Kant thought, a matter of obeying the categorical imperative for the sake of duty alone. True goodness is love, *agape* or *caritas* in distinction from *eros*, which is self-directed. And love is sympathy. 'All true and pure love is sympathy [*Mitleid*], and all love which is not sympathy is selfishness [*Selbstsucht*]. *Eros* is selfishness; *agape* is sympathy.'[1] Schopenhauer combined his enthusiasm for the Hindu philosophy of Maya with a great admiration for the Buddha. And he had perhaps more sympathy with the Buddhist ethic than with more dynamic western concepts of altruism.

We can, however, go further still. For in and through man the Will can attain such a clear knowledge of itself that it turns from itself in horror and denies itself. The human will then ceases to become attached to anything, and the man pursues the path of asceticism and holiness. Schopenhauer proceeds, therefore, to extol voluntary chastity, poverty and self-mortification and holds out the prospect of a complete deliverance at death from the servitude of the Will.

It was remarked above that it is difficult to understand how the Will's denial of itself is possible. And Schopenhauer recognizes the difficulty. That the Will, manifested or objectified in the phenomenon, should deny itself and renounce what the phenomenon expresses, namely the Will to live, is, Schopenhauer frankly admits, a case of self-contradiction. But, contradiction or not, this radical act of self-denial can take place, even though it happens only in exceptional or rare cases. The Will in itself is free. For it is not subject to the principle of sufficient reason. And in the case of total self-denial, total self-renunciation, the essential freedom of the Will, the thing-in-itself, is made manifest in the phenomenon. In other words, Schopenhauer admits an exception to the principle of

[1] *W*, II, p. 444; *HK*, I, p. 485.

determinism. The free metaphysical Will 'by abolishing the nature which lies at the foundation of the phenomenon, while the phenomenon itself continues to exist in time, brings about a contradiction of the phenomenon with itself'.[1] That is to say, the saint does not kill himself; he continues to exist in time. But he totally renounces the reality which lies at the foundation of himself as a phenomenon and can be said to 'abolish it', namely the Will. This is a contradiction, but it is a contradiction which manifests the truth that the Will transcends the principle of sufficient reason.

What, we may ask, is the final end of virtue and holiness? Obviously, the man who denies the Will treats the world as nothing. For it is simply the appearance of the Will, which he denies. And in this sense at least it is true to say that when the Will turns and denies itself, 'our world with all its suns and milky ways is—nothing'.[2] But what happens at death? Does it mean total extinction or not?

'Before us', says Schopenhauer, 'there is indeed only nothingness.'[3] And if, as seems to be the case, there can be no question on his premisses of personal immortality, there is a sense in which this must obviously be true. For if individuality is phenomenal, Maya, then death, the withdrawal, as it were, from the phenomenal world, means the extinction of consciousness. There remains perhaps the possibility of absorption in the one Will. But Schopenhauer seems to imply, though he does not express himself clearly, that for the man who has denied the Will death means total extinction. In life he has reduced existence to a tenuous thread, and at death it is finally destroyed. The man has reached the final goal of the denial of the Will to live.

Schopenhauer does indeed speak of another possibility.[4] As we have already seen, he admits that the thing-in-itself, the ultimate reality, may possibly possess attributes which we do not and cannot know. If so, these may remain when Will has denied itself as Will. Hence there is presumably the possibility of a state being achieved through self-renunciation which does not amount to nothingness. It could hardly be a state of knowledge, for the subject-object relationship is phenomenal. But it might resemble the incommunicable experience to which mystics refer in obscure terms.

[1] *W*, II, p. 339; *HK*, I, p. 371.   [2] *W*, II, p. 487; *HK*, I, p. 532.
[3] *W*, II, p. 486; *HK*, I, p. 531.
[4] Cp. *W*, II, p. 485 and III, pp. 221–2; *HK*, I, p. 530 and II, p. 408.

But though it is open to anyone to press this admission if he wishes, I should not myself care to do so. Partly, I suppose, Schopenhauer feels bound to make the admission in view of his own statement that we know the ultimate reality in its self-manifestation as Will and not in itself, apart from phenomena. Partly he may feel that the possibility cannot be excluded that the experiences of the mystics are not adequately explicable in terms of his philosophy of the Will. But it would be going too far, were one to represent Schopenhauer as suggesting that either theism or pantheism may be true. Theism he stigmatizes as childish and unable to satisfy the mature mind. Pantheism he judges to be even more absurd and, in addition, to be incompatible with any moral convictions. To identify a world filled with suffering and evil and cruelty with the Godhead or to interpret it as a theophany in a literal sense is utter nonsense, worthy only of a Hegel. Moreover, it leads to a justification of all that happens, a justification which is incompatible with the demands of morality.

In any case, even if the ultimate reality possesses attributes other than those which justify its description as a blind Will, philosophy can know nothing about them. As far as philosophy is concerned, the thing-in-itself is Will. And the denial of the Will thus means for the philosopher the denial of reality, of all that there is, at least of all that he can know that there is. Hence philosophy at any rate must be content with the conclusion: 'no Will; no idea, no world'.[1] If the Will turns on itself and 'abolishes' itself, nothing is left.

4. The reader may perhaps be surprised that the philosophy of Schopenhauer has been considered under the general heading of the reaction to metaphysical idealism. And there is, of course, ground for such surprise. For in spite of Schopenhauer's constant abuse of Fichte, Schelling and Hegel his system undoubtedly belongs in some important respects to the movement of German speculative idealism. Will is indeed substituted for Fichte's Ego and Hegel's *Logos* or Idea, but the distinction between phenomenon and noumenon and the theory of the subjective and phenomenal character of space, time and causality are based on Kant. And it is not unreasonable to describe Schopenhauer's system as transcendental voluntaristic idealism. It is idealism in the sense that the world is said to be our idea or presentation. It is voluntaristic in the sense that the concept of Will rather than that of Reason or

[1] *W*, II, p. 486; *HK*, I, p. 531.

Thought is made the key to reality. And it is transcendental in the sense that the one individual Will is an absolute Will which manifests itself in the multiple phenomena of experience.

But though Schopenhauer's philosophy, when regarded from this point of view, appears as a member of the class of post-Kantian speculative systems which include those of Fichte, Schelling and Hegel, there are also considerable differences between it and the other three philosophies. For example, in the system of Hegel the ultimate reality is Reason, the self-thinking thought which actualizes itself as concrete spirit. The real is the rational and the rational the real. With Schopenhauer, however, reality is not so much rational as irrational: the world is the manifestation of a blind impulse or energy. There are, of course, certain similarities between the cosmic Reason of Hegel and the Schopenhauerian Will. For instance, for Hegel Reason has itself as an end, in the sense that it is thought which comes to think itself, and Schopenhauer's Will also has itself as an end, in the sense that it wills for the sake of willing. But there is a great difference between the idea of the universe as the life of self-unfolding Reason and the idea of the universe as the expression of a blind irrational impulse to existence or life. There are indeed elements of 'irrationalism' in German idealism itself. Schelling's theory of an irrational will in the Deity is a case in point. But with Schopenhauer the irrational character of existence becomes something to be emphasized; it is the cardinal truth rather than a partial truth, to be overcome in a higher synthesis.

This metaphysical irrationalism in Schopenhauer's philosophy may be obscured by his theory of art which sets before us the possibility of transmuting the horrors of existence in the serene world of aesthetic contemplation. But it has important consequences. For one thing there is the substitution of a meta-physically-grounded pessimism for the metaphysically-grounded optimism of absolute idealism. For another thing the deductive character of metaphysical idealism, which is natural enough if reality is regarded as the self-unfolding of Thought or Reason, gives way to a much more empirical approach. To be sure, the comprehensive and metaphysical character of Schopenhauer's philosophy, together with its strongly-marked romantic elements, gives it a family-likeness to the other great post-Kantian systems. At the same time it lends itself very easily to interpretation as a very wide hypothesis based on generalization from empirical data.

And though we naturally and rightly regard it as part of the general movement of post-Kantian speculative metaphysics, it also looks forward to the inductive metaphysics which followed the collapse of absolute idealism.

Further, when we look back on Schopenhauer's system from a much later point in history, we can see in it a transition-stage between the idealist movement and the later philosophies of Life. Obviously, from one point of view the system is simply itself and not a 'transition-stage'. But this does not exclude the point of view which relates the system to the general movement of thought and sees it as a bridge between rationalist idealism and the philosophy of Life in Germany and France. It may be objected, of course, that Schopenhauer emphasizes a no-saying attitude to life. Life is something to be denied rather than affirmed. But Schopenhauer's theory of renunciation and denial is reached only by means of a philosophy which first emphasizes the idea of the Will to live and interprets the world in the light of this idea. Both instinct and reason are described by Schopenhauer as biological instruments or tools, even if he subsequently goes on to speak of the detachment of the human intellect from this practical orientation. Hence he provides the material, as it were, for the substitution of the idea of Life as the central idea in philosophy for that of Thought. Schopenhauer's pessimism no longer appears in the later philosophies of Life; but this does not alter the fact that he brings the idea of Life into the centre of the picture. True, the idea of Life is present in, for example, the philosophies of Fichte and Hegel. But with Schopenhauer the term 'Life' receives a primarily biological significance, and reason (which is also, of course, a form of life) is interpreted as an instrument of Life in a biological sense.

5. After the death of Hegel and after the failure of the Revolution of 1848 the climate of opinion was more prepared for a favourable reconsideration of Schopenhauer's anti-rationalist and pessimistic system, and it became more widely known and won some adherents. Among these was Julius Frauenstädt (1813–79) who was converted from Hegelianism to the philosophy of Schopenhauer in the course of protracted conversations with the philosopher at Frankfurt. He modified somewhat the position of his master, maintaining that space, time and causality are not mere subjective forms and that individuality and multiplicity are not mere appearance. But he defended the theory that the ultimate reality is Will and published an edition of Schopenhauer's writings.

Schopenhauer's writings helped to stimulate in Germany an interest in Oriental thought and religion. Among the philosophers who were influenced by him in this direction we can mention Paul Deussen (1845–1919), founder of the *Schopenhauer-Gesellschaft* (Schopenhauer Society) and a friend of Nietzsche. Deussen occupied a chair in the university of Kiel. In addition to a general history of philosophy he published several works on Indian thought and contributed to bringing about the recognition of Oriental philosophy as an integral part of the history of philosophy in general.

Outside philosophical circles Schopenhauer's influence was considerable. And special mention can be made of his influence on Richard Wagner. The theory that music is the highest of the arts was naturally congenial to Wagner, and he thought of himself as the living embodiment of the Schopenhauerian concept of genius.[1] One cannot, of course, reduce Wagner's outlook on life to Schopenhauer's philosophy. Many of the composer's ideas were formed before he made the acquaintance of this philosophy, and in the course of time he modified and changed his ideas. But when he had been introduced to Schopenhauer's writings in 1854, he sent the philosopher an appreciative letter. And it is said that *Tristan and Isolde* in particular reflects Schopenhauer's influence. One can also mention the writer Thomas Mann as one who owed a debt to Schopenhauer.

Within philosophical circles Schopenhauer's influence was felt more in the form of a stimulus in this or that direction than in the creation of anything which could be called a school. In Germany his writings exercised a powerful influence on Nietzsche in his youth, though he afterwards repudiated Schopenhauer's no-saying attitude to Life. One can also mention the names of Wilhelm Wundt and Hans Vaihinger as philosophers who derived some stimulus from Schopenhauer, though neither man was a disciple of the great pessimist. As for France, it has been already remarked that we must avoid the not uncommon mistake of assuming that similarity of ideas necessarily reveals derivation or borrowing. The development of the philosophy of Life in France explains itself, without the need of involving the name of Schopenhauer. But this does not, of course, exclude a stimulative influence, direct or indirect, by the German philosopher on certain French thinkers.

6. There is at any rate one philosopher of some note whose most

---

[1] Nietzsche, during the halcyon days of their friendship, gave Wagner every encouragement to think this.

obvious affinity is with Schopenhauer and who derived a great deal from him, namely Eduard von Hartmann (1842–1906), a retired artillery officer who gave himself to study and writing. Von Hartmann, who also acknowledged debts to Leibniz and Schelling, endeavoured to develop the philosophy of Schopenhauer in such a way as to lessen the gulf between it and Hegelianism. And he claimed to have worked out his own system on an empirical and scientific basis. His best known work is *The Philosophy of the Unconscious* (*Die Philosophie des Unbewussten*, 1869).

The ultimate reality, according to von Hartmann, is indeed unconscious, but it cannot be, as Schopenhauer thought, simply a blind Will. For the matter of that, even Schopenhauer could not avoid speaking as though the Will had an end in view. Hence we must recognize that the one unconscious principle has two correlative and irreducible attributes, Will and Idea. Or we can express the matter by saying that the one unconscious principle has two co-ordinate functions. As Will it is responsible for the *that*, the existence, of the world: as Idea it is responsible for the *what*, the nature, of the world.

In this way von Hartmann claims to effect a synthesis between Schopenhauer and Hegel. The former's Will could never produce a teleological world-process, and the latter's Idea could never objectify itself in an existent world. The ultimate reality must thus be Will and Idea in one. But it does not follow that the ultimate reality must be conscious. On the contrary, we must turn to Schelling and import the notion of an unconscious Idea behind Nature. The world has more than one aspect. Will manifests itself, as Schopenhauer taught, in pain, suffering and evil. But the unconscious Idea, as Schelling maintained in his philosophy of Nature, manifests itself in finality, teleology, intelligible development and an advance towards consciousness.

Not content with reconciling Schopenhauer, Hegel and Schelling, von Hartmann is also concerned with synthesizing Schopenhauerian pessimism and Leibnizian optimism. The manifestation of the unconscious Absolute as Will gives grounds for pessimism, while its manifestation as Idea gives grounds for optimism. But the unconscious Absolute is one. Hence pessimism and optimism must be reconciled. And this demands a modification of Schopenhauer's analysis of pleasure and enjoyment as 'negative'. The pleasures, for example, of aesthetic contemplation and of intellectual activity are certainly positive.

Now, inasmuch as von Hartmann maintains that the end or *telos* of the cosmic process is the liberation of the Idea from the servitude of the Will through the development of consciousness, we might expect that optimism would have the last word. But though von Hartmann does indeed emphasize the way in which the development of intellect renders possible the higher pleasures, in particular those of aesthetic contemplation, he at the same time insists that the capacity for suffering grows in proportion to intellectual development. For this reason primitive peoples and the uneducated classes are happier than civilized peoples and the more cultured classes.

To think, therefore, that progress in civilization and in intellectual development brings with it an increase in happiness is an illusion. The pagans thought that happiness was attainable in this world. And this was an illusion. The Christians recognized it as such and looked for happiness in heaven. But this too was an illusion. Yet those who recognize it as such tend to fall into a third illusion, namely that of thinking that a terrestrial Paradise can be attained through unending progress. They fail to see two truths. First, increasing refinement and mental development increase the capacity for suffering. Secondly, progress in material civilization and well-being is accompanied by a forgetfulness of spiritual values and by the decadence of genius.

These illusions are ultimately the work of the unconscious principle which shows its cunning by inducing the human race in this way to perpetuate itself. But von Hartmann looks forward to a time when the human race in general will have so developed its consciousness of the real state of affairs that a cosmic suicide will take place. Schopenhauer was wrong in suggesting that an individual can attain annihilation by self-denial and asceticism. What is needed is the greatest possible development of consciousness, so that in the end humanity may understand the folly of volition, commit suicide and, with its own destruction, bring the world-process to an end. For by that time the volition of the unconscious Absolute, which is responsible for the existence of the world, will, von Hartmann hopes, have passed into or been objectified in humanity. Hence suicide on humanity's part will bring the world to an end.

Most people would describe this astonishing theory as pessimism. Not so von Hartmann. The cosmic suicide requires as its condition the greatest possible evolution of consciousness and the triumph of intellect over volition. But this is precisely the end aimed at by the Absolute as Idea, as unconscious Spirit. One can say, therefore, that the world will be redeemed by the cosmic suicide and its own disappearance. And a world which achieves redemption is the best possible world.

There are only two comments which I wish to make on von Hartmann's philosophy. First, if a man writes as much as von Hartmann did, he can hardly avoid making some true and apposite statements, be their setting what it may. Secondly, if the human race destroys itself, which is now a physical possibility, it is much more likely to be due to its folly than to its wisdom or, in von Hartmann's language, to the triumph of Will rather than to that of Idea.

CHAPTER XV

THE TRANSFORMATION OF IDEALISM (1)

Introductory remarks—Feuerbach and the transformation of theology into anthropology—Ruge's criticism of the Hegelian attitude to history—Stirner's philosophy of the ego.

1. WHEN considering the influence of Hegel we noted that after the philosopher's death there emerged a right and a left wing. And something was said about the differences between them in regard to the interpretation of the idea of God in the philosophy of Hegel and about the system's relation to Christianity. We can now turn to consider some of the more radical representatives of the left wing who were concerned not so much with interpreting Hegel as with using some of his ideas to transform metaphysical idealism into something quite different.

These thinkers are commonly known as the Young Hegelians. This term ought indeed to signify the younger generation of those who stood under the influence of Hegel, whether they belonged to the right or to the left wing or to the centre. But it has come to be reserved in practice for the radical members of the left wing, such as Feuerbach. From one point of view they might well be called anti-Hegelians. For they represent a line of thought which culminated in dialectical materialism, whereas a cardinal tenet of Hegel is that the Absolute must be defined as Spirit. From another point of view, however, the name 'anti-Hegelian' would be a misnomer. For they were concerned to set Hegel on his feet, and even if they transformed his philosophy, they made use, as already mentioned, of some of his own ideas. In other words, they represent a left-wing development of Hegelianism, a development which was also a transformation. We find both continuity and discontinuity.

2. Ludwig Feuerbach (1804–72) studied Protestant theology at Heidelberg and then went to Berlin where he attended Hegel's lectures and gave himself to the study of philosophy. In 1828 he became an unsalaried lecturer (*Privatdozent*) at the university of Erlangen. But finding no prospect of advancement in the academic career he retired into a life of private study and writing. At the time of his death he was living near Nuremberg.

If one were to look only at the titles of Feuerbach's writings, one would naturally conclude that he was first and foremost a theologian, or at any rate that he had strong theological interests. True, his earlier works are obviously concerned with philosophy. For example, in 1833 he published a history of modern philosophy from Francis Bacon to Spinoza; in 1837 an exposition and criticism of Leibniz's system; in 1838 a work on Bayle; and in 1839 an essay devoted to criticism of Hegel's philosophy. But then come his important works, such as *The Essence of Christianity* (*Das Wesen des Christentums*, 1841), *The Essence of Religion* (*Das Wesen der Religion*, 1845) and *Lectures on the Essence of Religion* (*Vorlesungen über das Wesen der Religion*, 1851). And these titles, together with such others as *On Philosophy and Christianity* (*Ueber Philosophie und Christentum*, 1839) and *The Essence of Faith in Luther's sense* (*Das Wesen des Glaubens im Sinne Luthers*, 1844), clearly suggest that the author's mind is preoccupied with theological problems.

In a certain sense this impression is quite correct. Feuerbach himself asserted that the main theme of his writings was religion and theology. But he did not mean by this statement that he believed in the objective existence of a God outside human thought. He meant that he was principally concerned with clarifying the real significance and function of religion in the light of human life and thought as a whole. Religion was not for him an unimportant phenomenon, an unfortunate piece of superstition of which we can say that it would have been better if it had never existed and that its effect has been simply that of retarding man's development. On the contrary, the religious consciousness was for Feuerbach an integral stage in the development of human consciousness in general. At the same time he regarded the idea of God as a projection of man's ideal for himself and religion as a temporal, even if essential, stage in the development of human consciousness. He can be said, therefore, to have substituted anthropology for theology.

Feuerbach reaches this position, the substitution of anthropology for theology, through a radical criticism of the Hegelian system. But the criticism is in a sense internal. For it is presupposed that Hegelianism is the highest expression of philosophy up to date. Hegel was 'Fichte mediated through Schelling',[1] and 'the Hegelian philosophy is the culminating point of speculative systematic

[1] *W*, II, p. 180. References to Feuerbach's writings are given according to volume and page of the second edition of his *Works* by Friedrich Jodl (Stuttgart, 1959–60).

philosophy'.[1] But though in the system of Hegel idealism, and indeed metaphysics in general, has attained its most complete expression, the system is not tenable. What is required is to set Hegel on his feet. In particular we have to find our way back from the conceptual abstractions of absolute idealism to concrete reality. Speculative philosophy has tried to make a transition 'from the abstract to the concrete, from the ideal to the real'.[2] But this was a mistake. The passage or transition from the ideal to the real has a part to play only in practical or moral philosophy, where it is a question of realizing ideals through action. When it is a matter of theoretical knowledge, we must start with the real, with Being.

Hegel, of course, starts with Being. But the point is that for Feuerbach Being in this context is Nature, not Idea or Thought.[3] 'Being is subject and thought is predicate.'[4] The fundamental reality is spatio-temporal Nature; consciousness and thought are secondary, derived. True, the existence of Nature can be known only by a conscious subject. But the being which distinguishes itself from Nature knows that it is not the ground of Nature. On the contrary, man knows Nature by distinguishing himself from his ground, sensible reality. 'Nature is thus the ground of man.'[5]

We can say indeed with Schleiermacher that the feeling of dependence is the ground of religion. But 'that on which man depends and feels himself to be dependent is originally nothing else but Nature'.[6] Thus the primary object of religion, if we view religion historically and not simply in the form of Christian theism, is Nature. Natural religion ranges from the deification of objects such as trees and fountains up to the idea of the Deity conceived as the physical cause of natural things. But the foundation of natural religion in all its phases is man's feeling of dependence on external sensible reality. 'The divine essence which manifests itself in Nature is nothing else but Nature which reveals and manifests itself to man and imposes itself on him as a divine being.'[7]

Man can objectify Nature only by distinguishing himself from it. And he can return upon himself and contemplate his own essence. What is this essence? 'Reason, will, heart. To a perfect man there belong the power of thought, the power of willing, the

---

[1] *W*, II, p. 175.   [2] *W*, II, p. 231.
[3] Feuerbach, like Schelling, assumes that Hegel deduces existent Nature from the logical Idea. If this is not assumed, the criticism loses its point.
[4] *W*, II, p. 239.   [5] *W*, II, p. 240.
[6] *W*, VII, p. 434.   [7] *W*, VII, p. 438.

power of the heart.'[1] Reason, will and love in unity constitute the essence of man. Further, if we think any of these three perfections in itself, we think of it as unlimited. We do not conceive, for example, the power of thought as being in itself limited to this or that object. And if we think the three perfections as infinite, we have the idea of God as infinite knowledge, infinite will and infinite love. Monotheism, at least when God is endowed with moral attributes, is thus the result of man's projection of his own essence raised to infinity. 'The divine essence is nothing else but the essence of man; or, better, it is the essence of man when freed from the limitations of the individual, that is to say, actual corporeal man, objectified and venerated as an independent Being distinct from man himself.'[2]

In *The Essence of Christianity* Feuerbach concentrates on the idea of God as a projection of human self-consciousness, whereas in *The Essence of Religion*, in which religion is considered historically, he lays emphasis on the feeling of dependence on Nature as the ground of religion. But he also brings the two points of view together. Man, conscious of his dependence on external reality, begins by venerating the forces of Nature and particular natural phenomena. But he does not rise to the concept of personal gods or of God without self-projection. In polytheism the qualities which differentiate man from man are deified in the form of a multiplicity of anthropomorphic deities, each with his or her peculiar characteristics. In monotheism it is that which unifies men, namely the essence of man as such, which is projected into a transcendent sphere and deified. And a powerful factor in making the transition to some form of monotheism is the consciousness that Nature not only serves man's physical needs but can also be made to serve the purpose which man freely sets before himself. For in this way he comes to think of Nature as existing for him, and so as a unity which embodies a purpose and is the product of an intelligent Creator. But in thinking the Creator man projects his own essence. And if we strip from the idea of God all that is due to this projection, we are left simply with Nature. Hence, though religion is ultimately grounded on man's feeling of dependence on Nature, the most important factor in the formation of the concept of an infinite personal Deity is man's projection of his own essence.

Now, this self-projection expresses man's alienation from himself. 'Religion is the separation of man from himself: he sets God over against himself as an opposed being. God is not what man is, and man is not what God is. God is the infinite Being, man the finite; God is perfect, man is imperfect; God is eternal, man is temporal; God is almighty, man is powerless; God is holy, man is sinful. God and man are extremes: God is the absolutely positive, the essence of all realities, while man is the negative, the essence of all nothingness.'[1] Thus by projecting his essence into a transcendent sphere and objectifying it as God man reduces himself to a pitiful, miserable sinful creature.

In this case, of course, religion is something to be overcome. But it does not follow that religion has not played an essential role in human life. On the contrary, man's objectification of his own essence in the idea of God forms an integral stage in the explicit development of his self-awareness. For he has first to objectify his essence before he can become aware of it as *his* essence. And in the highest or most perfect form of religion, namely Christianity, this objectification reaches the point at which it calls for its own overcoming. Man is a social being, and the power of love belongs to his essence. He is an 'I' in relation to a 'Thou'. And in the Christian religion awareness of this fact finds a projected expression in the doctrine of the Trinity. Further, in the doctrine of the Incarnation, 'the Christian religion has united the word *Man* with the word *God* in the one name *God-Man*, thus making humanity an attribute of the supreme Being'.[2] What remains is to reverse this relation by making Deity an attribute of man. 'The new philosophy has, in accordance with the truth, made this attribute (humanity) the substance; it has made the predicate the subject. The new philosophy is . . . the *truth* of Christianity.'[3]

This last statement recalls to mind Hegel's view of the relation between the absolute religion and the absolute philosophy. But it is certainly not Feuerbach's intention to suggest that 'the new philosophy' can coexist with Christianity in the same mind. On the contrary, the new philosophy abandons the name of Christianity precisely because it gives the rational truth-value of the Christian religion and, in so doing, transforms it from theology into anthropology. Philosophy's elucidation of Christianity is no longer Christianity. Once a man understands that 'God' is a name for his own idealized essence projected into a transcendent sphere, he overcomes the self-alienation involved in religion. And the way then lies open to the objectification of this essence in man's own

[1] *W*, VI, p. 41.   [2] *W*, II, p. 244.   [3] *Ibid.*

activity and social life. Man recovers faith in himself and in his own powers and future.

The abandonment of theology involves the abandonment of historic Hegelianism. For 'the Hegelian philosophy is the last place of refuge, the last rational prop of theology'.[1] And 'he who does not give up the Hegelian philosophy does not give up theology. For the Hegelian doctrine that Nature, reality, is posited by the Idea is simply the *rational* expression of the theological doctrine that Nature has been created by God. . . .'[2] Yet for the overcoming of theology we have to make use of the Hegelian concept of self-alienation. Hegel spoke of the return of absolute Spirit to itself from its self-alienation in Nature. For this concept we must substitute that of man's return to himself. And this means 'the transformation of theology into anthropology, and its dissolution therein'.[3] Yet philosophical anthropology is itself religion. For it gives the truth of religion in the highest form that religion has attained. 'What yesterday was still religion is not religion today, and what is accounted atheism today is accounted religion tomorrow.'[4]

With the substitution of anthropology for theology man becomes his own highest object, an end to himself. But this does not mean egoism. For man is by essence a social being: he is not simply *Mensch* but *Mit-Mensch*. And the supreme principle of philosophy is 'the unity between man and man',[5] a unity which should find expression in love. 'Love is the universal law of intelligence and nature—it is nothing else but the realization of the unity of the species on the plane of feeling.'[6]

Feuerbach is obviously alive to the fact that Hegel emphasized man's social nature. But he insists that Hegel had an erroneous idea of the ground of unity in the species. In absolute idealism men are thought to be united in proportion as they become one with the life of universal spirit, interpreted as self-thinking Thought. It is thus on the level of pure thought that human unity is primarily achieved. But here again Hegel needs to be set squarely on his feet. The special nature of man is grounded on the biological level, 'on the *reality* of the *difference* between I and Thou',[7] that is, on sexual differentiation. The relation between man and woman manifests unity-in-difference and difference-in-unity. This distinction between male and female is not indeed simply a biological distinction. For it determines distinct ways of feeling and thinking and thus affects the whole personality. Nor is it, of course, the only way in which man's social nature is manifested. But Feuerbach wishes to emphasize the fact that man's nature as *Mit-Mensch* is grounded on the fundamental reality, which is sensible reality, not pure thought. In other words, sexual differentiation shows that the individual human being is incomplete. The fact that the 'I' calls for the 'Thou' as its complement is shown in its primary and basic form in the fact that the male needs the female and the female the male.

One might expect that with this insistence on man's special nature, on the unity of the species and on love, Feuerbach would go on to develop the theme of a supranational society or to propose some form of international federation. But in point of fact he is sufficiently Hegelian to represent the State as the living unity of men and the objective expression of the consciousness of this unity. 'In the State the powers of man divide and develop only to constitute an infinite being through this division and through their reunion; many human beings, many powers are one power. The State is the essence of all realities, the State is the providence of man. . . . The true State is the unlimited, infinite, true, complete, divine Man . . . the absolute Man.'[1]

From this it follows that 'politics must become our religion',[2] though, paradoxically, atheism is a condition of this religion. Religion in the traditional sense, says Feuerbach, tends to dissolve rather than to unite the State. And the State can be for us an Absolute only if we substitute man for God, anthropology for theology. 'Man is the fundamental essence of the State. And the State is the actualized, developed and explicit totality of human nature.'[3] Justice cannot be done to this truth if we continue to project human nature into a transcendent sphere in the form of the concept of God.

The State which Feuerbach has in mind is the democratic republic. Protestantism, he remarks, put the monarch in the place of the Pope. 'The Reformation destroyed *religious* Catholicism, but in its place the modern era set *political* Catholicism'.[4] The so-called modern era has been up to now a Protestant Middle Ages. And it is only through the dissolution of the Protestant religion that we can develop the true democratic republic as the living unity of men and the concrete expression of man's essence.

If regarded from a purely theoretical standpoint, Feuerbach's

[1] *W*, II, p. 220.   [2] *W*, II, p. 219.   [3] *W*, II, p. 244.   [4] *W*, II, p. 221.

philosophy is certainly not outstanding. For example, his attempt to dispose of theism by an account of the genesis of the idea of God is superficial. But from the historical point of view his philosophy possesses real significance. In general, it forms part of a movement away from a theological interpretation of the world to an interpretation in which man himself, considered as a social being, occupies the centre of the stage. Feuerbach's substitution of anthropology for theology is an explicit acknowledgement of this. And to a certain extent he is justified in regarding Hegelianism as a half-way house in the process of this transformation. In particular, the philosophy of Feuerbach is a stage in the movement which culminated in the dialectical materialism and the economic theory of history of Marx and Engels. True, Feuerbach's thought moves within the framework of the idea of the State as the supreme expression of social unity and of the concept of political rather than of economic man. But his transformation of idealism into materialism and his insistence on overcoming man's self-alienation as manifested in religion prepared the ground for the thought of Marx and Engels. Marx may have criticized Feuerbach severely, but he certainly owed him a debt.

3. In view of Feuerbach's preoccupation with the subject of religion the shift of emphasis in the Hegelian left wing from logical, metaphysical and religious problems to problems of a social and political nature is perhaps better illustrated by Arnold Ruge (1802–80). Ruge's first two works, written when he was more or less an orthodox Hegelian, were on aesthetics. But his interest came to centre on political and historical problems. In 1838 he founded the *Hallische Jahrbücher für deutsche Wissenschaft und Kunst*, having among his collaborators David Strauss, Feuerbach and Bruno Bauer (1809–82). In 1841 the review was renamed *Deutsche Jahrbücher für Wissenschaft und Kunst*, and at this time Marx began to collaborate with it. Early in 1843, however, the periodical, which had become more and more radical in tone and had aroused the hostile attention of the Prussian government, was suppressed; and Ruge moved to Paris where he founded the *Deutsch-französische Jahrbücher*. But a break between Ruge and Marx and the dispersal of other contributors brought the life of the new review to a speedy close. Ruge went to Zürich. In 1847 he returned to Germany, but after the failure of the Revolution of 1848 he crossed over into England. In his last years he became a supporter of the new German empire. He died at Brighton.

Ruge shared Hegel's belief that history is a progressive advance towards the realization of freedom, and that freedom is attained in the State, the creation of the rational General Will. He was thus prepared to give full marks to Hegel for having utilized Rousseau's concept of the *volonté generale* and for having grounded the State on the universal will which realizes itself in and through the wills of individuals. At the same time he criticized Hegel for having given an interpretation of history which was closed to the future, in the sense that it left no room for novelty. In the Hegelian system, according to Ruge, historical events and institutions were portrayed as examples or illustrations of a dialectical scheme which worked itself out with logical necessity. Hegel failed to understand the uniqueness and non-repeatable character of historical events, institutions and epochs. And his deduction of the Prussian monarchical constitution was a sign of the closed character of his thought, that is, of its lack of openness to the future, to progress, to novelty.

The basic trouble with Hegel, in Ruge's view, was that he derived the scheme of history from the system. We ought not to presuppose a rational scheme and then derive the pattern of history from it. If we do this, we inevitably end by justifying the actual state of affairs. Our task is rather that of *making* history rational, of bringing, for example, new institutions into being which will be more rational than those already in existence. In other words, in place of Hegel's predominantly speculative and theoretical attitude to history and to social and political life we need to substitute a practical and revolutionary attitude.

This does not mean that we have to abandon the idea of a teleological movement in history. But it does mean that the philosopher should endeavour to discern the movement and demands of the spirit of the time (*der Zeitgeist*) and that he should criticize existing institutions in the light of these demands. Hegel's career fell in the period after the French Revolution, but he had little understanding of the real movement of the *Zeitgeist*. He did not see, for instance, that the realization of freedom of which he talked so much could not be achieved without radical changes in the institutions which he canonized.

We can see in Ruge's attitude an attempt to combine belief in a teleological movement in history with a practical and revolutionary attitude. And his criticism of Hegel was congenial to Marx. The great idealist was primarily concerned with understanding history, with seeing the rational in the real. Ruge and Marx were concerned with making history, with understanding the world in order to change it. But Ruge refused to follow Marx in the path of communism. In his opinion Marx's idea of man was very one-sided, and he opposed to it what he called an integral humanism. It is not only man's material and economic needs which require to be satisfied but also his spiritual needs. However, the break between the two men was by no means due simply to ideological differences.

4. A counterblast to the general movement of thought in left-wing Hegelianism came from the somewhat eccentric philosopher Max Stirner (1806–56) whose real name was Johann Kaspar Schmidt. After attending the lectures of Schleiermacher and Hegel at Berlin Stirner taught in a school for a few years and then gave himself to private study. His best known work is *The Individual and His Property (Der Einzige und sein Eigentum,* 1845).

At the beginning of this work Stirner quotes Feuerbach's statement that man is man's supreme being and Bruno Bauer's assertion that man has just been discovered. And he invites his readers to take a more careful look at this supreme being and new discovery. What do they find? What he himself finds is the ego, not the absolute ego of Fichte's philosophy but the concrete individual self, the man of flesh and blood. And the individual ego is a unique reality which seeks from the start to preserve itself and so to assert itself. For it has to preserve itself in the face of other beings which threaten, actually or potentially, its existence as an ego. In other words, the ego's concern is with itself.

It is precisely this unique individual ego which most philosophers pass over and forget. In Hegelianism the individual self was belittled in favour of absolute Thought or Spirit. Paradoxically, man was supposed to realize his true self or essence in proportion as he became a moment in the life of the universal Spirit. An abstraction was substituted for concrete reality. And Feuerbach's philosophy is tarred with the same brush. To be sure, Feuerbach is right in claiming that man should overcome the self-alienation involved in the religious attitude and rediscover himself. For in Judaism and Christianity freedom, the very essence of man, was projected outside the human being in the concept of God, and man was enslaved. He was told to deny himself and obey. But though Feuerbach is justified in his polemics against religious self-alienation and against the abstractions of Hegelianism, he fails to understand the significance of the unique individual and offers us instead the abstraction of Humanity or of absolute Man and the fulfilment of selfhood in and through the State. Similarly, even if in humanistic socialism Humanity is substituted for the Christian God and the Hegelian Absolute, the individual is still sacrificed on the altar of an abstraction. In fine, the left-wing Hegelians can be subjected to the same sort of criticism which they level against Hegel himself.

In place of such abstractions as Absolute Spirit, Humanity and the universal essence of man Stirner enthrones the unique and free individual. In his view freedom is realized through owning. And, as this unique individual, I own all that I can appropriate. This does not mean, of course, that I have in fact to make everything my property. But there is no reason why I should not do so, other than my inability to do it or my own free decision not to do it. I proceed out of and return into the 'creative nothing', and while I exist my concern is with myself alone. My endeavour should be that of expressing my unique individuality without allowing myself to be enslaved or hampered by any alleged higher power such as God or the State or by any abstraction such as Humanity or the universal Moral Law. Subservience to such fictitious entities weakens my sense of my own uniqueness.

Stirner's philosophy of egoism possesses a certain interest and significance in so far as it represents the protest of the concrete human person against the worship of the collectivity or of an abstraction. Moreover some may wish to see in it some spiritual affinity with existentialism. And there is at least some ground for this. It can hardly be said that emphasis on the theme of property is a characteristic of existentialism, but the theme of the unique free individual certainly is.[1] Stirner's philosophy has been mentioned here, however, not for any anticipation of later thought but rather as a phase in the movement of revolt against metaphysical idealism. One can say perhaps that it represents an expression of the nominalistic reaction which over-emphasis on the universal always tends to evoke. It is, of course, an exaggeration. A healthy insistence on the uniqueness of the individual self is coupled with a fantastic philosophy of egoism. But the protest against an exaggeration very often takes the form of an exaggeration in the opposite direction.

Apart, however, from the fact that Stirner was far from being a

[1] Stirner's obscure remarks about 'creative nothing' recall to mind certain aspects of Heidegger's thought.

great philosopher, his thought was out of harmony with the *Zeitgeist*, and it is not surprising if Marx saw in it the expression of the alienated isolated individual in a doomed bourgeois society. Marx and Engels may have incorporated in their philosophy the very features which Stirner so disliked, substituting the economic class for Hegel's national State, the class war for the dialectic of States, and Humanity for absolute Spirit. But the fact remains that their philosophy was, for good or ill, to possess a great historical importance, whereas Max Stirner is remembered only as an eccentric thinker whose philosophy has little significance except when it is seen as a moment in the perennially recurrent protest of the free individual against the voraciously devouring universal.

CHAPTER XVI

THE TRANSFORMATION OF IDEALISM (2)

Introductory remarks—The lives and writings of Marx and Engels and the development of their thought—Materialism—Dialectical materialism—The materialist conception of history—Comments on the thought of Marx and Engels.

1. CONFRONTED with the thought of Marx and Engels the historian of philosophy finds himself in a rather difficult situation. On the one hand the contemporary influence and importance of their philosophy is so obvious that the not uncommon practice of according it little more than a passing mention in connection with the development of left-wing Hegelianism scarcely seems to be justified. Indeed, it might seem more appropriate to treat it as one of the great modern visions of human life and history. On the other hand it would be a mistake to allow oneself to be so hypnotized by the indubitable importance of Communism in the modern world as to tear its basic ideology from its historical setting in nineteenth-century thought. Marxism is indeed a living philosophy in the sense that it inspired and gave impetus and coherence to a force which, for good or ill, exercises a vast influence in the modern world. It is accepted, doubtless with varying degrees of conviction, by a great many people today. At the same time it is arguable that its continued life as a more or less unified system is primarily due to its association with an extra-philosophical factor, a powerful social-political movement, the contemporary importance of which nobody would deny. It is true, of course, that the connection is not accidental. That is to say, Communism did not adopt a system of ideas which lay outside the process of its own birth and development. But the point is that it is the Communist Party which has saved Marxism from undergoing the fate of other nineteenth-century philosophies by turning it into a faith. And the historian of nineteenth-century philosophy is justified in dwelling primarily on the thought of Marx and Engels in its historical setting and in prescinding from its contemporary importance as the basic creed of a Party, however powerful this Party may be.

The present writer has therefore decided to confine his attention to some aspects of the thought of Marx and Engels themselves and to neglect, except for some brief references, the subsequent development of their philosophy as well as its impact on the modern world through the medium of the Communist Party. When it is a question of an inevitably somewhat overcrowded account of philosophy in Germany during the nineteenth century, this restriction does not really stand in need of any defence. But as the importance of Communism in our day may lead the reader to think that a more extended treatment would have been desirable and even that this volume should have culminated in the philosophy of Marx, it may be as well to point out that to depict Marxism as the apex and point of confluence of nineteenth-century German philosophical thought would be to give a false historical picture under the determining influence of the political situation in the world today.

2. Karl Marx (1818–83) was of Jewish descent. His father, a liberal Jew, became a Protestant in 1816, and Marx himself was baptized in 1824. But his father's religious convictions were by no means profound, and he was brought up in the traditions of Kantian rationalism and political liberalism. After his school education at Trier he studied at the universities of Bonn and Berlin. At Berlin he associated with the Young Hegelians, the members of the so-called *Doktorklub*, especially with Bruno Bauer. But he soon became dissatisfied with the purely theoretical attitude of left-wing Hegelianism, and this dissatisfaction was intensified when in 1842 he began to collaborate in editing at Cologne the newly-founded *Rheinische Zeitung*, of which he soon became the chief editor. For his work brought him into closer contact with concrete political, social and economic problems, and he became convinced that theory must issue in practical activity, in action, if it is to be effective. This may indeed seem to be obvious, even a tautology. But the point is that Marx was already turning away from the Hegelian notion that it is the philosopher's business simply to understand the world and that we can trust, as it were, to the working out of the Idea or of Reason. Criticism of traditional ideas and existing institutions is not sufficient to change them unless it issues in political and social action. In fact, if religion signifies man's alienation from himself, so also in its own way does German philosophy. For it divorces man from reality, making him a mere spectator of the process in which he is involved.

At the same time reflection on the actual situation led Marx to

THE TRANSFORMATION OF IDEALISM (2)

adopt a critical attitude towards the Hegelian theory of the State. And it was apparently in this period, between 1841 and 1843, that he wrote a criticism of Hegel's concept of the State under the title *Kritik des Hegelschen Staatsrechts*. According to Hegel objective spirit reaches its highest expression in the State, the family and civil society being moments or phases in the dialectical development of the idea of the State. The State, as the full expression of the Idea in the form of objective Spirit, is for Hegel the 'subject', while the family and civil society are 'predicates'. But this is to put things the wrong way round. The family and civil society, not the State, are the 'subject': they form the basic realities in human society. Hegel's State is an abstract universal, a governmental and bureaucratic institution which stands apart from and over against the life of the people. In fact there is a contradiction between public and private concerns. Transposing on to the political plane Feuerbach's idea of religion as an expression of man's self-alienation, Marx argues that in the State as conceived by Hegel man alienates his true nature. For man's true life is conceived as existing in the State whereas in point of fact the State stands over against individual human beings and their interests. And this contradiction or gulf between public and private concerns will last until man becomes socialized man and the political State, exalted by Hegel, gives way to a true democracy in which the social organism is no longer something external to man and his real interests.

Marx also attacks Hegel's idea of insistence on private property as the basis of civil society. But he has not yet arrived at an explicit communistic theory. He appeals rather for the abolition of the monarchy and the development of social democracy. The idea, however, of a classless economic society is implicit in his criticism of Hegel's political State and in his notion of true democracy. Further, his concern with man as such and his internationalism are also implicit in his criticism of Hegel.

Early in 1843 the life of the *Rheinische Zeitung* was brought to a close by the political authorities, and Marx went to Paris where he collaborated with Ruge in editing the *Deutsch-französische Jahrbücher*. In the first and only number which appeared he published two articles, one a criticism of Hegel's *Philosophy of Right*, the other a review of essays by Bruno Bauer on Judaism. In the first of these articles Marx refers to Feuerbach's analysis of religion as a self-alienation on man's part and asks why it occurs.

Why does man create the illusory world of the supernatural and project into it his own true self? The answer is that religion reflects or expresses the distortion in human society. Man's political, social and economic life is incapable of fulfilling his true self, and he creates the illusory world of religion and seeks his happiness therein, so that religion is man's self-administered opium. Inasmuch as religion prevents man from seeking his happiness where alone it can be found, it must indeed be attacked. But a criticism of religion is of little value if it is divorced from political and social criticism, for it attacks the effect while neglecting the cause. Further, criticism by itself is in any case inadequate. We cannot change society simply by philosophizing about it. Thought must issue in action, that is, in social revolution. For philosophical criticism raises problems which can be solved only in this way. In Marx's language philosophy must be overcome, this overcoming being also the realization (*Verwirklichkung*) of philosophy. It must leave the plane of theory and penetrate to the masses. And when it does so, it is no longer philosophy but takes the form of a social revolution which must be the work of the most oppressed class, namely the proletariat. By abolishing private property consciously and explicitly the proletariat will emancipate itself and, together with itself, the whole of society. For egoism and social injustice are bound up with the institution of private property.

In certain obvious respects Marx's way of thinking is influenced by Hegel's. For example, the idea of alienation and its overcoming is of Hegelian origin. But it is equally obvious that he rejects the notion of history as the self-manifestation or self-expression of the Absolute defined as Spirit. His concept of theory as realizing itself through practice or action reminds us indeed of Hegel's concept of the concrete self-unfolding of the Idea. But the fundamental reality is for him, as for Feuerbach, Nature rather than the Idea or *Logos*. And in his political and economic manuscripts of 1844 Marx emphasizes the difference between his own position and that of Hegel.

True, Marx retains a profound admiration for Hegel. He praises him for having recognized the dialectical character of all process and for having seen that man develops or realizes himself through his own activity, through self-alienation and its overcoming. At the same time Marx sharply criticizes Hegel for his idealist concept of man as self-consciousness and for having conceived human activity as being primarily the spiritual activity of thought. Hegel did indeed look on man as expressing himself outwardly in the objective order and then returning to himself on a higher plane. But his idealism involved the tendency to do away with the objective order by interpreting it simply in relation to consciousness. Hence the process of self-alienation and its overcoming was for him a process in and for thought rather than in objective reality.

Whether Marx does justice to Hegel may be open to question. But in any case he opposes to the primacy of the Idea the primacy of sensible reality. And he maintains that the fundamental form of human work is not thought but manual labour in which man alienates himself in the objective product of his labour, a product which, in society as at present constituted, does not belong to the producer. This alienation cannot be overcome by a process of thought in which the idea of private property is regarded as a moment in the dialectical movement to a higher idea. It can be overcome only through a social revolution which abolishes private property and effects the transition to communism. The dialectical movement is not a movement of thought about reality: it is the movement of reality itself, the historical process. And the negation of the negation (the abolition of private property) involves the positive occurrence of a new historical situation in which man's self-alienation is overcome in actual fact and not simply for thought.

This insistence on the unity of thought and action and on the overcoming of man's self-alienation through social revolution and the transition to communism, an insistence which shows itself in the articles of 1843 and the manuscripts of 1844, can be regarded, in part at least, as the result of a marriage between left-wing Hegelianism and the socialist movement with which Marx came into contact at Paris. Dissatisfied with the predominantly critical and theoretical attitude of the Young Hegelians, Marx found at Paris a much more dynamic attitude. For besides studying the classical English economists, such as Adam Smith and Ricardo, he made the personal acquaintance of German socialists in exile and of French socialists such as Proudhon and Louis Blanc, as well as of revolutionaries such as the Russian Bakunin. And even if he had already shown an inclination to emphasize the need for action, this personal contact with the socialist movement had a profound influence upon his mind. At the same time he came to the conclusion that though the socialists were more in touch with reality than were the German philosophers, they failed to make an adequate appraisal of the situation and its demands. They needed an intellectual instrument to give unity of vision, purpose and method. And though Marx spoke of the overcoming of philosophy and did not regard his own theory of history as a philosophical system, it is clear not only that this is in fact what it became but also that it owed much to a transformation of Hegelianism.

The most important personal contact, however, which Marx made at Paris was his meeting with Engels who arrived in the city from England in 1844. The two men had indeed met one another a couple of years before, but the period of their friendship and collaboration dates from 1844.

Friedrich Engels (1820–95) was the son of a rich industrialist, and he took up a position in his father's firm at an early age. While doing his military service at Berlin in 1841 he associated with the circle of Bruno Bauer and adopted an Hegelian position. The writings of Feuerbach, however, turned his mind away from idealism to materialism. In 1842 he went to Manchester to work for his father's firm and interested himself in the ideas of the early English socialists. It was at Manchester that he wrote his study of the working classes in England (*Die Lage der arbeitenden Klassen in England*) which was published in Germany in 1845. He also composed for the *Deutsch-französische Jahrbücher* his *Outlines of a Critique of National Economy* (*Umrisse einer Kritik der National-ökonomie*).

An immediate result of the meeting between Marx and Engels in Paris was their collaboration in writing *The Holy Family* (*Die heilige Family*, 1845) directed against the idealism of Bruno Bauer and his associates who appeared to think that 'criticism' was a transcendent being which had found its embodiment in the 'Holy Family', namely the members of Bauer's circle. In opposition to the idealist emphasis on thought and consciousness Marx and Engels maintained that the forms of the State, law, religion and morality were determined by the stages of the class-war.

At the beginning of 1845 Marx was expelled from France and went to Brussels where he composed eleven theses against Feuerbach, ending with the famous statement that whereas philosophers have only tried to understand the world in different ways, the real need is to change it. When he had been joined by Engels the two men collaborated in writing *The German Ideology* (*Die deutsche Ideologie*) which remained unpublished until 1932. The work is a criticism of contemporary German philosophy as represented by Feuerbach, Bauer and Stirner and of the German socialists, and it is important for its outline of the materialist conception of history. The fundamental historical reality is social man in his activity in Nature. This material or sensible activity is man's basic life, and it is life which determines consciousness, not, as the idealists imagine, the other way round. In other words, the fundamental factor in history is the process of material or economic production. And the formation of social classes, the warfare between classes and, indirectly, the forms of political life, of law and of ethics are all determined by the varying successive modes of production. Further, the whole historical process is moving dialectically towards the proletarian revolution and the coming of communism, not the self-knowledge of absolute Spirit or any such philosophical illusion.

In 1847 Marx published in French his *Poverty of Philosophy* (*Misère de la philosophie*), a reply to Proudhon's *Philosophy of Poverty* (*Philosophie de la misère*). In it he attacks the notion of fixed categories, eternal truths and natural laws which in his view is characteristic of bourgeois economics. For example, after accepting the description of property as theft Proudhon goes on to envisage a socialist system which will strip property of this character. And this shows that he regards the institution of private property as an eternal or natural value and as a fixed economic category. But there are no such values and categories. Nor is there any philosophy which can be worked out *a priori* and then applied to the understanding of history and society. There can be only a critical knowledge based on the analysis of concrete historical situations. In Marx's view the dialectic is not a law of thought which is expressed in reality: it is immanent in the actual process of reality and is reflected in thought when the mind correctly analyses concrete situations.

Faithful, however, to his idea of the unity of thought and action, Marx was by no means content to criticize the shortcomings of German ideologists such as Bauer and Feuerbach and of socialists such as Proudhon. He joined the Communist League and in 1847 was commissioned, together with Engels, to draw up a summary statement of its principles and aims. This was the famous *Communist Manifesto* or *Manifesto of the Communist Party* which appeared in London early in 1848, shortly before the beginning of the series of revolutions and insurrections which took place in Europe during that year. When the active phase of the revolutionary movement started in Germany, Marx and Engels returned to their native land. But after the failure of the revolution Marx, who had been brought to trial and acquitted, retired to Paris, only to be expelled from France for the second time in 1849. He went to London where he remained for the rest of his life, receiving financial aid from his friend Engels.

In 1859 Marx published at Berlin his *Contribution to a Critique of Political Economy (Zur Kritik der politischen Oekonomie)* which is important, as is also the *Manifesto*, for its statement of the materialist conception of history. And, again uniting action with theory, he founded in 1864 the International Working Men's Association, commonly known as the First International. Its life, however, was beset with difficulties. For example, Marx and his friends considered that it was necessary for authority to be centralized in the hands of the committee if the proletariat was to be led successfully to victory, whereas others, such as Bakunin the anarchist, refused to accept a dictatorship of the central committee. Besides, Marx soon found himself at loggerheads with the French and German socialist groups. After the congress at The Hague in 1872 the central committee was transferred to New York at the instance of Marx. And the First International did not long survive.

The first volume of Marx's famous work *Capital (Das Kapital)* appeared at Hamburg in 1867. But the author did not continue the publication. He died in March 1883, and the second and third volumes were published posthumously by Engels in 1885 and 1894 respectively. Further manuscripts were published in several parts by K. Kautsky in 1905–10. In the work Marx maintains that the bourgeois or capitalist system necessarily involves a class antagonism. For the value of a community is crystallized labour, as it were. That is to say, its value represents the labour put into it. Yet the capitalist appropriates to himself part of this value, paying the worker a wage which is less than the value of the commodity produced. He thus defrauds or exploits the worker. And this exploitation cannot be overcome except by the abolition of capitalism. Marx refers, of course, to contemporary abuses in the economic system, such as the practice of keeping wages as low as possible. But exploitation should not be understood only in this sense. For if the so-called labour theory of value is once accepted, it necessarily follows that the capitalist system involves exploitation or defrauding of the worker. And the payment of high wages would not alter this fact.

In 1878 Engels published as a book, commonly known as *Anti-Dühring*, some articles which he had written against the then influential German socialist Eugen Dühring. One chapter was written by Marx. Engels also occupied himself with composing his *Dialectics of Nature* (*Dialektik der Natur*). But he was too taken up with bringing out the second and third volumes of Marx's *Capital* and with efforts to resuscitate the International to be able to finish the work. And it was not published until 1925, when it appeared at Moscow. Engels lacked his friend's philosophical training, but he had wide interests, and it was he rather than Marx who applied dialectical materialism to the philosophy of Nature. The results were not perhaps such as to enhance Engels' reputation as a philosopher among those who do not accept his writings as part of a creed.

Of Engels' other publications mention should be made of his work on *The Origin of the Family, Private Property and the State* (*Der Ursprung der Familie, des Privateigentums und des Staats*, 1884) in which he tries to derive the origin of class divisions and of the State from the institution of private property. In 1888 a series of articles by Engels were published together as a book under the title *Ludwig Feuerbach and the End of the Classical German Philosophy* (*Ludwig Feuerbach und der Ausgang der klassischen deutschen Philosophie*). Engels died of cancer in August 1895.

3. Whether or not Hegel meant that the Concept (*der Begriff*) or logical Idea is a subsistent reality which externalizes or alienates itself in Nature, is a disputable question. But both Marx and Engels understood him in this sense, namely as holding that the *Logos* is the primary reality which expresses itself in its opposite, namely unconscious Nature, and then returns to itself as Spirit, thus actualizing, as it were, its own essence or definition. Thus in his preface to the second German edition of *Capital* Marx states that 'for Hegel the thought-process, which he goes so far as to transform into an independent Subject under the name "Idea", is the demiurge of the real, the real being simply its external appearance'.[1] And in his book on Feuerbach Engels asserts that 'with Hegel the dialectic is the self-development of the Concept. The absolute Concept is not only present from eternity—who knows where?—but it is also the real living soul of the whole existent world. . . . It alienates itself in the sense that it transforms itself into Nature where, without consciousness of itself and

[1] *Das Kapital*, I, p. xvii (Hamburg, 1922); *Capital*, II, p. 873 (London, Everyman).

disguised as natural necessity, it goes through a new process of development and finally comes again to self-consciousness in man'.[1]

As against this metaphysical idealism Marx and Engels accepted Feuerbach's thesis that the primary reality is Nature. Thus Engels speaks of the liberating effect of Feuerbach's *Essence of Christianity*, which restored materialism to its throne. 'Nature exists independently of all philosophy; it is the basis on which we human beings, ourselves products of Nature, have grown. Apart from Nature and human beings nothing exists; and the higher beings which our religious fantasy created are only the fantastic reflection of our own essence . . . the enthusiasm was general; we were all for the moment followers of Feuerbach. One can see in the *Holy Family* how enthusiastically Marx welcomed the new conception, and how much he was influenced by it, in spite of all critical reservations'.[2]

In this passage Engels speaks of the re-enthronement of materialism. And both Marx and Engels were, of course, materialists. But this obviously does not mean that they denied the reality of mind or that they identified the processes of thought in a crude manner with material processes. What materialism meant for them was in the first place the denial that there is any Mind or Idea which is prior to Nature and expresses itself in Nature. It was certainly not equivalent to denying that human beings have minds. In his *Dialectics of Nature* Engels speaks of the law of the transformation of quantity into quality, and *vice versa*, as the law by which changes in Nature take place.[3] A transformation of this kind occurs when a series of quantitative changes is succeeded by an abrupt qualitative change. Thus when matter has reached a certain pattern of complicated organization mind emerges as a new qualitative factor.

To be sure, the question of the power of the mind is left somewhat obscure by Marx and Engels. In the preface to his *Critique of Political Economy* Marx makes the famous statement that 'it is not the consciousness of human beings which determines their

[1] *Ludwig Feuerbach*, p. 44 (Stuttgart, 1888); *Ludwig Feuerbach*, edited by C. P. Dutt with an introduction by L. Rudas, p. 53 (London, no date).
[2] *Ludwig Feuerbach*, pp. 12–13 (p. 28). When a translated work is referred to more than once, on all occasions but the first I give the pagination of the translation in brackets, without repeating the title.
[3] It is true that in the *Science of Logic* Hegel passes from the category of quality to that of quantity, but when dealing with measure he speaks of nodal points at which a series of quantitative variations is succeeded by an abrupt qualitative change, a leap. This is succeeded in turn by further quantitative variations until a new nodal point is reached.

being, but it is, on the contrary, their social being which determines their consciousness.'[1] And Engels remarks that 'we conceived the concepts in our heads once more from a materialist point of view as copies of real things, instead of conceiving real things as copies of this or that stage of the absolute Concept'.[2] And such passages tend to suggest that human thought is no more than a copy or reflection of material economic conditions or of the processes of Nature. In other words, they tend to suggest the passive character of the human mind. But we have already seen that in his theses against Feuerbach Marx asserts that whereas philosophers have only tried to understand the world, it is man's business to change it. Hence it is not really surprising if in the first volume of *Capital* we find him comparing the human worker with the spider and the bee and remarking that even the worst builder can be distinguished from the best bee by the fact that the former conceives the product of his work before he constructs it whereas the latter does not. In the human worker there is the will which has an end in view and which externalizes itself.[3] Indeed, if Marx and Engels wish to maintain, as they do, the need for revolutionary activity, for correctly analysing the situation and acting accordingly, they obviously cannot maintain at the same time that the mind is no more than a kind of pool on the surface of which natural processes and economic conditions are passively mirrored. When they are engaged in setting Hegel on his feet, that is, in substituting materialism for idealism, they tend to stress the copy-idea of human concepts and thought-processes. But when they are speaking of the need for social revolution and for its preparation, they clearly have to attribute to the human mind and will an active role. Their utterances may not be always perfectly consistent, but their materialism is basically an assertion of the priority of matter, not a denial of the reality of mind.

4. Although, however, Marx and Engels regarded their materialism as a counterblast to Hegel's idealism, they certainly did not look on themselves as being simply opponents of Hegel. For they recognized their indebtedness to him for the idea of the dialectical process of reality, that is, a process by way of negation followed by a negation of the negation, which is also an affirmation of a higher stage. Another way of putting the same thing is to say

---

[1] *Zur Kritik der politischen Oekonomie*, p. xi (Stuttgart, 1897); *Marx-Engels: Selected Works*, 1, p. 363 (London, 1958).
[2] *Ludwig Feuerbach*, p. 45 (p. 54).
[3] *Das Kapital*, 1, p. 140 (1, pp. 169–70).

that process or development takes the form of the contradiction of an existing situation or state of affairs, followed by the contradiction of the contradiction, this contradiction being an overcoming of the first. It is not so much a question of thesis, antithesis and synthesis, as of negation and its negation, though the second negation can be regarded as in some sense a 'synthesis', inasmuch as it is a transition to a higher stage in the dialectical process.

This idea of development as a dialectical process is essential to the thought of Marx and Engels. Obviously, a man can accept the thesis of the priority of matter to mind and some form of what is now called emergent evolution without thereby being a Marxist. The materialism of Marx and Engels is dialectical materialism, to use the descriptive term which is now in general use, even if Marx himself did not employ it.

Marx and Engels were indeed at pains to distinguish between their conception of the dialectic and that of Hegel. In their view Hegel, having seen that thought moves dialectically, hypostatized this process as the process of absolute Thought, the self-development of the Idea. Thus the movement of the dialectic in the world and in human history was regarded by Hegel as the reflection or phenomenal expression of the movement of Thought. For Marx and Engels, however, the dialectical movement is found first of all in reality, that is to say, in Nature and history. The dialectical movement of human thought is simply a reflection of the dialectical process of reality. And this reversal of the relation between thought and reality was for them an essential part of the business of setting Hegel on his feet. At the same time Marx and Engels made no secret of the fact that the idea of the dialectic was derived from Hegel. Hence they regarded their materialism as being essentially a post-Hegelian materialism, and not as a mere return to an earlier type of materialist theory.

Now, though Marx affirms with Feuerbach the priority of matter to mind, he is not really interested in Nature as such, considered apart from man. Sometimes indeed he seems to imply that Nature does not exist except for man. But this must not be taken as meaning that Nature possesses no ontological reality except as object of consciousness. It would be absurd to interpret Marx as an idealist. What he means is that Nature first exists for man when man differentiates himself from it, though at the same time he recognizes a relation between himself and Nature. An animal is a natural product, and we see it as related to Nature. But the animal is not conscious of these relations as such: they do not exist 'for it'. Hence Nature cannot be said to exist 'for the animal'. With the emergence of consciousness, however, and the subject-object relation Nature begins to exist for man. And this is essential for what we may call the becoming of man. To be man, man must objectify himself. And he cannot do so, except by distinguishing himself from Nature.

But man is orientated towards Nature in the sense that he has needs which can be satisfied only through objects other than himself. And Nature is orientated towards man in the sense that it is the means of satisfying these needs. Further, man's satisfaction of his needs involves activity or work on his part. And in a sense the spontaneous satisfaction of a basic physical need by appropriating a ready-made object, so to speak, is work. But it is not specifically human work or activity, not at least if it is considered simply as a physical act. A man may, for example, stoop down and drink from a stream to quench his thirst. But so do many animals. Work becomes specifically human when man consciously transforms a natural object to satisfy his needs, and when he employs means or instruments to do so. In other words, the fundamental form of human work and man's fundamental relation to Nature is his productive activity, his conscious production of the means of satisfying his needs. Man is basically economic man, though this is not to say that he cannot be anything but economic man.

Man cannot, however, objectify himself and become man unless he is also object for another. In other words, man is a social being: a relation to his fellows is essential to his being as man. And the basic form of society is the family. We can say, therefore, that the fundamental reality to which Marx directs his attention is productive man as standing in a twofold relation, to Nature and to other human beings. Or, inasmuch as the term 'productive man' already implies a relation to Nature, we can say that the fundamental reality considered by Marx is productive man in society.

For Marx, therefore, man is basically not a contemplative but an active being, this activity being primarily the material one of production. And the relations between man and Nature are not static but changing relations. He uses means of production to satisfy his needs, and therefore fresh needs present themselves, leading to a further development in the means of production. Further, corresponding to each stage in the development of means of production for the satisfaction of man's needs there are social relations between men. And the dynamic interaction between the means or forces of production and the social relations between men constitute the basis of history. Speaking of man's basic physical needs Marx asserts that 'the first historical fact is the production of the means which enable man to satisfy these needs'.[1] But, as we have seen, this leads to the appearance of fresh needs, to a development in the means of production and to new sets of social relations. Hence the so-called first historical fact contains in itself, as it were in germ, the whole history of man. And this history is for Marx the 'locus', so to speak, of the dialectic. But an account of the dialectic of history according to Marx is best reserved for the next section. It is sufficient to note here that his theory of history is materialist in the sense that the basic factor in history is for him man's economic activity, his activity of production to satisfy his physical needs.

Attention has already been drawn to the fact that Engels extended the dialectic to Nature itself, thus developing what may be called a philosophy of Nature. And there has been some dispute about whether this extension was compatible with the attitude of Marx. Of course, if one assumes that for Marx Nature exists for us only as the field for transformation by human work and that the dialectical movement is confined to history, which presupposes a dynamic relation between man and his natural environment, the extension of the dialectic to Nature in itself would constitute not only a novelty but also a change in the Marxist conception of the dialectic. There might perhaps be a dialectical movement in the development of man's scientific knowledge, but this movement could hardly be attributed to Nature in itself, considered apart from man. It would not be merely a case of Marx having concentrated on human history to the practical exclusion of a philosophy of Nature. It would be a case of an exclusion in principle. But it must be remembered that in Marxism the dialectical movement of history is not the expression of the interior movement of absolute Thought: it is the movement of reality itself. It can be reproduced in the human mind, but in the first instance it is the movement of objective reality. Unless, therefore, we choose to press certain of Marx's utterances to the extent of turning him into an idealist, it does not seem to me that his position excludes in

---

[1] *Deutsche Ideologie, W*, III, p. 28; *The German Ideology*, p. 16 (Parts I and III, translated by W. Lough and C. P. Magill, London, 1942). In references *W* signifies the edition of the *Works* of Marx and Engels published by Dietz Verlag, Berlin, 1957 f.

principle the notion of a dialectic of Nature. Moreover, Marx was well aware that his friend was working at a dialectic of Nature, and he appears to have approved or at any rate not to have shown disapproval. So even if it is arguable that Engels was unfaithful to the thought of Marx and that he was laying the foundation of a mechanistic version of dialectical materialism, in which the movement of history would be regarded as simply a continuation of the necessary movement of autodynamic matter, I should not care to commit myself to the assertion that the extension of the dialectic to Nature in itself was excluded by Marx. Given some of his statements, it may be that he ought to have excluded it. But it does not appear that he did so in point of fact.

However this may be, in what he calls his 'recapitulation of mathematics and the natural sciences'[1] Engels was struck by the fact that in Nature nothing is fixed and static but that all is in movement, change, development. And, as he tells us himself, he was particularly impressed by three factors; first, the discovery of the cell, through the multiplication and differentiation of which plant and animal bodies have developed; secondly, the law of the transformation of energy; and, thirdly, Darwin's statement of the theory of evolution. Reflecting on Nature as revealed by contemporary science Engels came to the conclusion that 'in Nature the same dialectical laws of movement assert themselves in the confusion of innumerable changes which govern the apparent contingency of events in history'.[2]

In his *Dialectics of Nature*[3] Engels summarizes these laws as those of the transformation of quantity into quality, of the mutual penetration of opposites and of the negation of the negation. Some often-quoted examples of this last law, the negation of the negation, are to be found in *Anti-Dühring*. Engels speaks, for instance, of the barley-seed which is said to be negated when it sprouts and the plant begins to grow. The plant then produces a multiplicity of seeds and is itself negated. Thus as 'result of this negation of the negation we have again the original barley-seed, though not as such but tenfold, twentyfold or thirtyfold'.[4] Similarly, the larva or caterpillar negates the egg out of which it comes, is transformed in the course of time into a butterfly and is then itself negated in its death.

---

[1] *Anti-Dühring*, p. xv (Stuttgart, 1919); *Anti-Dühring*, p. 17 (London, 1959, 2nd edition).   [2] *Ibid.*
[3] *Dialektik der Natur*, p. 53 (Berlin, 1952); *Dialectics of Nature*, p. 83 (London, 1954).   [4] *Anti-Dühring*, p. 138 (p. 187).

Whether logical terms such as 'negation' and 'contradiction' are appropriate in this context is, to put it mildly, disputable. But we need not labour this point. Instead we can note that Engels draws an important conclusion in regard to human thought and knowledge from the nature of the twofold field of application of the dialectic, namely Nature and human history.[1] In his view it was Hegel's great discovery that the world is a complex not of finished things but of processes. And it is true both of Nature and of human history that each is a process or complex of processes. From this it follows that human knowledge, as a mirror of this twofold reality, is itself a process which does not and cannot reach a fixed and absolute system of truth. Hegel saw that 'truth lay in the process of knowing itself, in the long historical development of science which rises from lower to ever higher levels of knowledge without ever arriving, through the discovery of a so-called absolute truth, to the point where it can proceed no further, where nothing remains but to lay one's hands on one's lap and wonder at the absolute truth which has been attained'.[2] There is not and cannot be an absolute system of philosophy which only needs to be learned and accepted. Indeed, inasmuch as absolute truth is precisely what philosophers have had in view, we can say that with Hegel philosophy comes to an end. Instead we have a dialectically-advancing progressive scientific knowledge of reality which is always open to further change and development.

Like Marx, therefore, Engels attacks the notion of 'eternal truths'. He finds himself compelled to admit that there are truths which nobody can doubt without being considered mad; for example, that 'two and two make four, that the three angles of a triangle are equal to two right angles, that Paris lies in France, that a man who eats nothing dies of hunger and so on'.[3] But such truths, says Engels, are trivialities or commonplaces. And nobody would dignify them with the solemn title of 'eternal truths' unless he wished to draw from their existence the conclusion that in the field of human history there is an eternal moral law, an eternal essence of justice, and so on. But it is precisely this sort of conclusion which is erroneous. Just as hypotheses in physics and biology are subject to revision and even to revolutionary change, so is morality.

---

[1] Strictly speaking, there are for Engels three fields of application. 'Dialectics is nothing else but the science of the general laws of movement and development in Nature, human society and thought'; *Anti-Dühring*, p. 144 (p. 193).
[2] *Ludwig Feuerbach*, p. 4 (p. 21).   [3] *Anti-Dühring*, p. 81 (p. 122).

Marx and Engels, therefore, did not present their interpretation of reality as being the absolute and final system of philosophy. True, they regarded it as science rather than as speculative philosophy. And this means, of course, that they regarded it as supplanting all previous interpretations, whether idealist or materialist. At the same time science was not for them something which could ever attain a fixed and final form. If reality is a dialectical process, so is human thought, in so far, that is to say, as it reflects reality and does not take refuge in an illusory world of eternal truths and fixed essences.

Taken by itself, this denial of eternal truths, stable positions and final solutions suggests that a detached attitude towards their philosophy would be the appropriate one for Marx and Engels to maintain. But they did not look on it as being simply a theoretical exercise in interpreting the world and history. And it was precisely the detached, theoretical attitude which they decried in Hegel. But the implications of their view of dialectical materialism as a practical instrument or weapon is a topic which must be left aside for the moment.

5. As we have seen, the Marxist theory of history is materialist in the sense that the fundamental situation is depicted as a relation between man, considered as a material being, and Nature: it is man producing by his physical activity the means of satisfying his basic needs. But we must add that historical materialism does not mean only this. It means in addition that man's productive activity determines, directly or indirectly, his political life, his law, his morality, his religion, his art, his philosophy. In the present context materialism does not involve, as has been already remarked, denying the reality of mind or consciousness. Nor does it involve denying all value to the cultural activities which depend on mind. But it maintains that the cultural superstructure in general depends on and is in some sense determined by the economic substructure.

In the economic substructure Marx distinguishes two elements, the material forces of production and the productive relations, the second element depending upon the first. 'In the social production of their life human beings enter into determinate necessary relations which are independent of their will, productive relations [*Produktionsverhältnisse*] which correspond with a determinate stage in the development of their material forces of production [*Produktivkräfte*]. The totality of these productive relations forms the economic structure of society'.[1] In this passage the economic structure of a society is indeed identified with the totality of its productive relations. But inasmuch as these relations are said to correspond with a certain level of development of the productive forces of the society in question, and inasmuch as the emergence of conflicts between the productive forces and the productive relations in a given society is an essential feature in Marx's picture of human history, it is obvious that we must distinguish two main elements in the economic structure of society, a structure which is also described by Marx as a mode of production (*Produktionsweise*).

The term 'material forces of production' (or 'material productive powers') obviously covers all the material things which are used by man as artificial instruments in his productive activity, that is, in the satisfaction of his physical needs, from primitive flint instruments up to the most complicated modern machinery. It also includes natural forces in so far as they are used by man in the process of production. And the term can apparently also cover all such objects as are required for productive activity, even if they do not enter into it directly.[2]

Now, if the term is applied exclusively to things distinct from man himself, man is obviously presupposed. Marx tends to speak of the forces of production as doing this or that, but he is not so stupid as to suppose that these forces develop themselves without any human agency. 'The first condition of all human history is naturally the existence of living human individuals.'[3] And in the *Communist Manifesto* he speaks of the bourgeoisie as revolutionizing the instruments of production and thereby the productive relations. However, in the *German Ideology* he remarks that the production of life, whether of one's own life by work or of that of another through procreation, always involves a social relation, in the sense of the collaboration of several individuals. And after observing that it follows from this that a given mode of production is always linked to a given mode of collaboration, he asserts that this mode of collaboration is itself a 'productive force'.[4] He means, of course, that the social relation between men in the process of production can itself react on men's needs and on the productive forces. But if the mode of collaboration in the labour-process can be reckoned as a productive force, there seems to be no reason why,

---

[1] *Zur Kritik der politischen Oekonomie*, p. x (I, p. 363).
[2] Cf. *Das Kapital*, I, p. 143 (I, pp. 172–3).
[3] *Deutsche Ideologie*, W, III, p. 20 (p. 7).
[4] *Ibid.*, p. 30 (p. 18).

for example, the proletariat should not be accounted a productive force, even if the term is generally used by Marx for instruments or means of production rather than for man himself.[1] In any case it is notoriously difficult to pin him down to a precise and universal use of such terms.

The term 'productive relations' means above all property-relations. Indeed, in the *Critique of Political Economy* we are told that 'property relations' (*Eigentumsverhältnisse*) is simply a juristic expression for 'productive relations'.[2] However, in general the term 'productive relations' refers to the social relations between men as involved in the labour-process. As we have seen, these relations are said to depend on the stage of development of the productive forces. And the two together constitute the economic substructure.

This economic substructure is said to condition the super-structure. 'The mode of production of material life conditions the social, political and mental (*geistigen*) life-process in general. It is not the consciousness of human beings which determines their being, but it is, on the contrary, their social being which determines their consciousness.'[3] Obviously, the statement that the economic substructure 'conditions' (*bedingt*) the superstructure is ambiguous. The statement is not at all startling if it is taken in a very weak sense. It becomes interesting only in proportion as the meaning of the term 'conditions' approaches 'determines'. And it has indeed frequently been taken in this strong sense. Thus it has been maintained, for example, that the celestial hierarchy (from God down to the choirs of angels and the company of the saints) of mediaeval theology was simply an ideological reflection of the mediaeval feudal structure which was itself determined by economic factors. Again, the rise of the bourgeoisie and the arrival of the capitalist mode of production were reflected in the transition from Catholicism to Protestantism. According to Engels the Calvinist doctrine of predestination reflected the supposed economic fact that in commercial competition success or failure does not depend on personal merits but on incomprehensible and uncontrollable economic powers. Yet it was also Engels who protested that the doctrine of Marx and himself had been misunderstood. They had never meant that man's ideas are simply a pale reflection of

[1] In *The Poverty of Philosophy* Marx says explicitly that the revolutionary proletariat is the greatest of all productive forces. See below, p. 328.
[2] *Zur Kritik der politischen Oekonomie*, p. x (I, p. 363).
[3] *Ibid.*, p. xi (I, p. 363).

economic conditions in the sense that the relation of dependence is exclusively unilateral. Ideas (that is to say, men inspired by ideas) can react on the substructure which has conditioned them. The fact of the matter is, I think, that in their reversal of the idealist conception of history Marx and Engels not unnaturally emphasized the determining influence of the economic substructure. But, having once stated their vision of the world in terms which suggested that for them the world of consciousness and ideas was simply determined by the mode of economic production, they found themselves compelled to qualify this simple outlook. Political and legal structures are more directly determined by the economic substructure than are ideological superstructures such as religion and philosophy. And human ideas, though conditioned by economic conditions, can react on these conditions. In fact they had to allow for such reaction if they wished to allow for revolutionary activity.

To turn now to a more dynamic aspect of history. According to Marx 'at a certain stage in their development a society's forces of production come into conflict [literally 'contradiction', *Widerspruch*] with the existing productive relations'.[1] That is to say, when in a given social epoch the forces of production have developed to such a point that the existing productive relations, especially property-relations, have become a fetter on the further development of the forces of production, there is a contradiction within the economic structure of society, and a revolution takes place, a qualitative change to a new economic structure, a new social epoch. And this change in the substructure is accompanied by changes in the superstructure. Man's political, juristic, religious, artistic and philosophical consciousness undergoes a revolution which depends on and is subsidiary to the revolution in the economic sphere.

A revolution of this kind, the change to a new social epoch, does not take place, Marx insists, until the forces of production have developed to the fullest extent that is compatible with the existing productive relations and the material conditions for the existence of the new form of society are already present within the old. For this is the state of affairs which comprises a contradiction, namely that between the forces of production and the existing social relations. The qualitative change in the economic structure of society or mode of production does not occur until a contra-

[1] *Zur Kritik der politischen Oekonomie*, p. xi (I, p. 363).

diction has matured, as it were, within the old society through a series of quantitative changes. Now, if the theory is expressed simply in this way, it gives the impression of being simply a technological and mechanical theory. That is to say, it seems as though social revolution, the transition from one social epoch to another, took place inevitably and mechanically, and as though man's consciousness of the need for a change and his revolutionary activity constituted mere epiphenomena which exercised no real influence on the cause of events. But though this interpretation would fit in with the general doctrine that it is the material conditions of life which determine consciousness and not the other way round, it could scarcely fit in with Marx's insistence on the unity of theory and practice and on the need for the active preparation of the proletariat's revolutionary overthrow of the capitalist economy. Hence, although Marx sometimes tends to speak as though the material forces of production were the real revolutionary agent, we have to introduce the idea of the class war and of human agency.

Marx and Engels envisage at the dawn of history a state of primitive communism in which the land was possessed and tilled by the tribe in common and in which there was no class-division. Once, however, private property had been introduced, a division of society into economic classes soon followed. Marx is aware, of course, that social distinctions in civilized society form a more or less complicated pattern. But his general tendency is to simplify the situation by representing the fundamental distinction as being that between the oppressors and the oppressed, the exploiters and the exploited. In all forms of society, therefore, which presuppose the institution of private property, there is an antagonism between classes, an antagonism now latent, now open. And 'the history of all society hitherto is the history of class struggle'.[1] The State becomes the organ or instrument of the dominant class. So does the law. And the dominant class also tries to impose its own moral conceptions. In the Marxist dialectic of history, therefore, the concept of the class replaces Hegel's concept of the national State, and the class war replaces national wars.[2]

This class war or class struggle becomes particularly significant

---

[1] *Manifest der kommunistischen Partei*, *W*, IV, p. 462; *Communist Manifesto*, p. 125 (edit. H. J. Laski, London, 1948). Obviously, this refers to all known history after the passing of primitive communism.

[2] That is to say, the class war is looked on as more fundamental, and national wars are interpreted in economic terms.

at the period when in a given social epoch the forces of production have developed to such a point that the existing social relations, especially property-relations, are turned into a drag and a fetter. For the hitherto dominant class (individual defections apart) endeavours to maintain the existing productive relations, while it is in the interest of a rising class to overthrow these relations. And when the contradiction between the forces of production and the productive relations has been perceived by the rising class whose interest it is to overthrow the existing and antiquated social order, revolution takes place. Then the new dominant class in its own turn uses the State and the law as its instruments. This process inevitably continues until private property has been abolished and, with it, the division of society into mutually antagonistic classes.

In the preface to his *Contribution to the Critique of Political Economy* Marx observes that we can distinguish in broad outline four progressive social epochs which together form the prehistory (*die Vorgeschichte*) of mankind. The first of these, the asiatic, called by Engels the *gens* organization, is that of primitive communism. As we have seen, this was marked by communal ownership of land, associated labour and absence of private property. But with the institution of private property, associated by Engels with the change from matriarchy to patriarchy and with improvements in methods of production, the accumulation of private wealth was rendered possible. It was possible, for example, for a man to produce more than he required for his own needs. Hence there arose a division between rich and poor, and a new form of economic organization was required. If we ask what was the new productive force which was responsible for the transition, special mention is made of iron, though the subject is not developed. In any case the growth of private property and wealth made it necessary for the prospective rich to have labour at their disposal. But as under primitive communism there was no free labour available, slaves had to be obtained through captives in war.

We thus pass to the antique or ancient period, characterized by slavery and by the class antagonism between freemen and slaves. On this economic structure, represented, for instance, by Greece and Rome, there arose corresponding legal and political institutions and the splendid ideological superstructure of the classical world.

Although Marx and Engels mention various historical factors which contributed to the transition from the antique to the feudal epoch, which reached its culminating phase in the Middle Ages, no convincing explanation is offered of the productive force or forces which were responsible for the transition. However, it took place, and the feudal economy was reflected in the political and legal institutions of the time, as well as, though more indirectly, in mediaeval religion and philosophy.

During the mediaeval period a middle class or bourgoisie gradually developed. But its wealth-amassing propensities were hampered by factors such as feudal restrictions and guild regulations, as also by the lack of free labour for hire. With the discovery of America, however, and the opening-up of markets in different parts of the world, a powerful impetus was given to commerce, navigation and industry. New sources of wealth became available, and at the close of the Middle Ages land-enclosure by the nobility and other factors contributed to the formation of a class of dispossessed people ready to be hired and exploited. The time was ripe for a change, and the guild-system was overthrown by the new middle class in favour of the early phase of capitalist society. Finally, steam and machinery revolutionized industry; the world market was opened up; means of communication underwent a remarkable development; and the bourgeoisie pushed into the background the classes which had lingered from the Middle Ages.

In feudal society, as Marx is aware, the pattern of organization was too complicated to permit of its being reduced to one simple class antagonism, as between barons and serfs. But in capitalist society, to which he naturally devotes most of his attention, we can see, Marx argues, a growing simplification. For there has been a tendency for capital to become concentrated in ever fewer hands, in great combines of a more or less international or cosmopolitan character. At the same time many of the small capitalists have sunk into the ranks of the proletariat[1] which has also tended to take on an international character. Hence we are faced by two prominent classes, the exploiters and the exploited. The term 'exploitation' suggests, of course, the imposition of long hours of work for starvation wages. But though Marx does indeed inveigh against the abuses of the earlier phases of the industrial revolution, the primary meaning of the term is for him technical, not emotive. As we have seen, according to the doctrine expounded in *Capital* the whole value of a commodity is, as it were, crystallized labour;

[1] This is what Marx says in the *Communist Manifesto* which dates, it should be remembered, from the beginning of 1848.

it is due to the labour expended in its production. Hence the wage-system is necessarily exploitation, irrespective of the amount of the wages paid. For in every case the capitalist filches from the worker. The fact that a given capitalist is a humane man who does his best to improve wages and conditions of work makes no difference to the basic situation which is a necessary antagonism between the two classes.

Now, the bourgeoisie has developed the forces of production to a hitherto unknown and undreamed-of extent. But at the same time it has developed them to the point at which they can no longer co-exist with the existing productive relations. According to Marx, this fact is shown, for example, by the periodic recurrence of economic crises. Hence the time is approaching for the overthrow of the capitalist system. And the task of revolutionary activity, particularly of the Communist Party, is to turn the proletariat from a class in itself, to use Hegelian language, into a class for itself, a class conscious of itself and of its mission. The proletariat will then be able to sweep away the capitalist system, seize the organ of the State and use it to establish the dictatorship of the proletariat which will prepare the way for communist society. In this society the political State will wither away. For the State is an instrument for the maintenance of its own position by a dominant class in face of another class or other classes. And under communism class divisions and the class war will disappear.

In view of the fact that the bourgeoisie itself develops the forces of production we may be inclined to ask, what is the new productive force which emerges and which is fettered by the capitalist mode of production? But Marx is ready with his answer. And in the *Poverty of Philosophy* he tells us that the greatest of all productive forces is 'the revolutionary class itself'.[1] This is the productive force which enters into conflict with the existing economic system and overthrows it by revolution.

Human history is thus a dialectical progress from primitive communism to developed communism. And from one point of view at least the intermediary stages are necessary. For it is through them that the forces of production have been developed and that productive relations have been correspondingly changed in such a manner that developed communism is rendered not only possible but also the inevitable result. But the Marxist theory of history is

---

[1] *W*, IV, p. 181; *The Poverty of Philosophy*, edited by C. P. Dutt and V. Chatto-padhyaya, p. 146 (London, no date); p. 174 (London, 1956).

also an instrument or weapon, not merely a spectator's analysis of historical situations. It is the instrument by which the proletariat, through its vanguard the Communist Party, becomes conscious of itself and of the historical task which it has to perform. The theory is also, however, a philosophy of man. Marx assumes the Hegelian thesis that to realize himself man must objectify himself. And the primary form of self-objectification is in labour, production. The product is, as it were, man-in-his-otherness. But in all societies based on private property this self-objectification takes the form of self-alienation or self-estrangement. For the worker's product is treated as something alien to himself. In capitalist society it belongs to the capitalist, not to the worker. Further, this economic self-alienation is reflected in a social self-alienation. For membership of a class does not represent the whole man. Whichever class he belongs to, there is, so to speak, something of himself in the other class. Thus class antagonism expresses a profound division, a self-estrangement, in the nature of man. Religion also represents, as Feuerbach said, human self-alienation. But, as we have seen, self-alienation in the religious consciousness is for Marx a reflection of a profounder self-alienation in the social-economic sphere. And this cannot be overcome except through the abolition of private property and the establishment of communism. If self-alienation on the economic and social level is overcome, its religious expression will disappear. And at last the whole man, the non-divided man, will exist. Human ethics will take the place of class ethics, and a genuine humanism will reign.

It follows from this that the overthrow of the capitalist system by the proletariat is not merely a case of the replacement of one dominant class by another. It is indeed this, but it is also much more. The dictatorship of the proletariat is a temporary phase which prepares the way for the classless communist society from which self-alienation will be absent. In other words, by its revolutionary act the international proletariat saves not simply itself but all mankind. It has a messianic mission.

6. There is no great difficulty in giving a certain plausibility to the materialist theory of history. For example, if I wish to illustrate the conditioning by the economic structure of political and legal forms and of the ideological superstructure, there is a large variety of facts to which I can appeal. I can point to the connection between the then existing economic and class structure and the ferocious penalties which were once inflicted in England for theft, or to the

connection between the economic interests of plantation-owners in the southern States of America and the absence of strong moral feeling against slavery. I can draw attention to the connections between the economic life of a hunting tribe and its ideas of life after death or between class divisions and the lines of the hymn 'The rich man in his castle, the poor man at his gate, God made them high and lowly and ordered their estate'. I can refer to the evident influence of Greek political structures on Plato's picture of the ideal State or, for the matter of that, to the influence of existing conditions in the world of industry on the thought of Marx and Engels.

But though the Marxist theory of the relation between the economic substructure and the superstructure can be rendered plausible, this plausibility depends in large part on one's selecting certain data, slurring over others and circumventing awkward questions. For example, to maintain the theory I have to slur over the fact that Christianity became the dominant religion in the late Roman empire and was then accepted by the peoples who built up the feudal society of the Middle Ages. And I have to avoid awkward questions about the relation between the development of the forces of production and the origins of Islam. If such questions are pressed, I refer to factors which lie outside my original explanation of the ideological superstructure, while at the same time I continue to assert the truth of this explanation. And I blithely admit that the superstructure can itself exercise an influence on the substructure and that changes can take place in the former independently of changes in the latter, while at the same time I refuse to admit that these concessions are inconsistent with my original position. Why, indeed, should I admit this? For I have spoken of the relation between the substructure and the superstructure as a 'conditioning' of the latter by the former. And I can understand this term in a weak or in a strong sense according to the demands of the particular situation which I am considering.

We have seen that for Marx and Engels the dialectic is not something imposed on the world from without, the expression of absolute Thought or Reason. The dialectic as thought is the reflection of the inner movement of reality, of its immanent laws of development. And in this case the movement is presumably necessary and inevitable. This does not mean, of course, that human thought has no part to play. For there is continuity between Nature, human society and the world of ideas. We have already quoted Engels' statement that 'dialectic is nothing else but the science of the general laws of movement and development in Nature, human society and thought'.[1] But the total process would then be the necessary working-out of immanent laws. And in this case there does not seem to be much room for revolutionary activity. Or, rather, revolutionary activity would be a phase of an inevitable process.

From one point of view this mechanical view of the dialectic seems to be required by the conviction of Marx and Engels that the coming of communism is inevitable. But if the dialectic as operating in human history is, as Engels at any rate suggests, continuous with the dialectic as operating in Nature, that is, if it is ultimately a question of the self-development of auto-dynamic matter, it is difficult to see why the process should ever stop or reach a stage where contradictions and antagonisms disappear. Indeed, there is a passage in the *Dialectics of Nature* where Engels remarks that matter goes through an eternal cycle and that with an 'iron necessity' it will exterminate its highest product, namely the thinking mind, and produce it again somewhere else at another time.[2]

But this idea hardly fits in with the apocalyptic aspect of Marxism, which requires the vision of history as moving towards a goal, a terrestrial Paradise. The two ways of looking at the matter are perhaps compatible up to a point. That is to say, it is possible to look on each cycle as leading up to a peak point, as it were. But the more one emphasizes the teleological aspect of history, its movement from primitive communism, the age of innocence, through the Fall, as represented by the introduction of private property and the consequent emergence of selfishness, exploitation and class antagonism, up to the recovery of communism at a higher level and the overcoming of man's self-alienation, so much the more does one tend to reintroduce surreptitiously the notion of the working out of a plan, the realization of an Idea.

In other words, there is a fundamental ambiguity in Marxism. If some aspects are stressed, we have a mechanistic interpretation of the historical process. If other aspects are stressed, the system seems to demand the reintroduction of what Marx and Engels called idealism. Nor is this surprising. For in part Marxism is a transformation of idealism, and elements of this particular source

---

[1] *Anti-Dühring*, p. 144 (p. 193).   [2] *Dialektik der Natur*, p. 28 (p. 54).

linger on. The alliance between dialectic and materialism is not altogether an easy one. For, as Marx and Engels were well aware, dialectics originally referred to a movement of thought. And though they located the movement of the dialectic primarily in the object of thought and only secondarily and by way of reflection in human thinking, this transposition inevitably tends to suggest that the historical process is the self-development of an Idea. The alternative is to interpret the process as a purely mechanical one.[1] This is a matter of some importance. Left to itself, so to speak, Marxism tends to divide into divergent lines of thought. It is possible to emphasize the ideas of necessity, inevitability, determinism, and it is possible to emphasize the ideas of deliberate revolutionary activity and of free action. It is possible to emphasize the materialist element, and it is possible to emphasize the dialectical element. It is also possible, of course, to attempt to hold together all these different aspects, in spite of the ambiguities to which this attempt gives rise. But it is significant that even in the Soviet Union different lines of interpretation and development have manifested themselves. If the emergence of these different lines of thought has been held in check, this has been due to the constraining force of the Party Line, to an extra-philosophical factor and not to any intrinsic consistency and lack of ambiguity in the thought of Marx and Engels themselves.

From one point of view criticism of the type suggested in the foregoing paragraphs[2] is beside the point. That is to say, if we choose to regard Marxism as an interesting 'vision' of the world, detailed criticism necessarily seems pedantic and tiresome. Philosophers who provide striking visions of the world are inclined to take one aspect of reality and to use it as a key to unlock all doors. And detailed criticism, it may be said, is out of place. For it is the very exaggeration involved in the vision which enables us to see the world in a new light. When we have done so, we can forget about the exaggeration: the vision has accomplished its purpose. Thus the philosophy of Marx and Engels enables us to see the importance and far-reaching influence of man's economic life, of the so-called substructure. And it is largely because of the exaggerations involved that it can have this effect, breaking the rigidity of other pictures or interpretations of the world. Once we

[1] It is probably Engels, with his extension of the dialectic to Nature, who provides most ground for a mechanical interpretation.
[2] The lines of criticism suggested are not, of course, in any way new. They are familiar enough to 'bourgeois' philosophers, that is to say, to objective observers.

have seen what Marx and Engels are drawing attention to, we can forget Marxism as expounded in their writings: the essence of their vision passes into the common outlook. It is pedantic to worry about such detailed questions as the precise relation between freedom and necessity, the precise meaning of 'condition', the exact extent to which morality and values are thought to be relative, and so on.

This attitude is indeed understandable. But the Marxist theory of history is not simply a striking nineteenth-century vision of the world which has made its contribution to human thought and then relapsed into the historical background. It is a living and influential system which professes to be a scientific analysis of historical development, an analysis which permits prediction, and it is at the same time the creed or faith of groups whose importance in the modern world nobody would deny. It is therefore appropriate to point out that the transformation of this philosophy into the dogmatic creed of a powerful Party has arrested the natural development of the different lines of thought to which its diverse aspects might otherwise be expected to have given rise.

The Communist theoretician would perhaps reply that it is not a question of the philosophy of Marx and Engels having been adopted by a Party and transformed into a weapon or instrument. For it was this from the beginning. And it is precisely this fact which distinguishes it from all previous philosophies. Marx always thought of his philosophy as a means of transforming the world and not simply as an interpretation of it. But though this is doubtless true, the question then arises whether Marxism falls under its own concept of ideologies as relative to a passing economic structure or whether it transcends this status and represents absolute truth. If Marxism is relative to the situation in which the proletariat is opposed to the bourgeoisie, it should pass away when this antagonism has been overcome. If, however, it represents absolute truth, how is this claim to be reconciled with what Marx and Engels have to say about eternal truths, natural laws and so on?

And yet all criticism based on the internal ambiguities of the philosophy of Marx and Engels seems in a certain sense to be futile. It may have an effect on those, if any, who are attracted to Marxism simply because they think that it is 'scientific'. But it is not likely to have much effect on those who are primarily attracted by the ideal of human society which Marxism represents. What is needed is the delineation of another ideal, based on a more adequate view of man and his vocation and on a more adequate view of the nature of reality.

The philosophy of Marx and Engels has, of course, undergone some development. Attention has been paid, for example, to the theory of knowledge. And certain modern Thomists seem to think that among contemporary philosophical traditions Marxism, as represented by the philosophers of the Soviet Union, offers them a common basis of discussion because of its insistence on realism in epistemology and ontology. This is a theme which goes beyond the scope of this book. But one may remark that even if realism in the sense intended is common to Thomism and to Marxism, Thomism is for the Marxist an 'idealist' system. For it maintains the priority of Mind or Spirit to matter. And it was precisely this doctrine which Marx and Engels were concerned to deny when they affirmed the truth of materialism.

CHAPTER XVII

KIERKEGAARD

Introductory remarks—Life and writings—The individual and the crowd—The dialectic of the stages and truth as subjectivity —The idea of existence—The concept of dread—The influence of Kierkegaard.

1. IN the chapters on the development of Schelling's thought mention was made of the distinction which he came to draw between negative and positive philosophy. The former moves in the realm of ideas: it is a deduction of concepts or essences. The latter is concerned with the *that* of things, with existence. Positive philosophy cannot simply dispense with negative philosophy. At the same time negative philosophy by itself by-passes actual existence. And its chief modern representative is Hegel.

Among Schelling's hearers at Berlin, when he expounded this distinction, was the Dane, Søren Kierkegaard. For the way in which the German thinker developed his own idea of positive philosophy Kierkegaard had little sympathy. But he was in full agreement with Schelling's attack on Hegel. Not that Kierkegaard was lacking in admiration for Hegel or in appreciation of the magnitude of his achievement. On the contrary, he regarded Hegel as the greatest of all speculative philosophers and as a thinker who had achieved a stupendous intellectual *tour de force*. But this, in Kierkegaard's opinion, was precisely the trouble with Hegelianism, namely that it was a gigantic *tour de force* and nothing more. Hegel sought to capture all reality in the conceptual net of his dialectic, while existence slipped through the meshes.

Existence, as will be explained presently, was for Kierkegaard a category relating to the free individual. In his use of the term, to exist means realizing oneself through free choice between alternatives, through self-commitment. To exist, therefore, means becoming more and more an individual and less and less a mere member of a group. It means, one can say, transcending universality in favour of individuality. Hence Kierkegaard has scant sympathy with what he took to be Hegel's view, that a man realizes his true self or essence in proportion as he transcends his particularity and becomes a spectator of all time and existence as a moment in the life of universal thought. Hegelianism, in Kierkegaard's opinion, had no place for the existing individual: it could only universalize him in a fantastic manner. And what could not be universalized it dismissed as unimportant, whereas in point of fact it is that which is most important and significant. To merge or sink oneself in the universal, whether this is conceived as the State or as universal Thought, is to reject personal responsibility and authentic existence.

Kierkegaard's emphasis on self-commitment through free choice, a self-commitment whereby the individual resolutely chooses one alternative and rejects another, is an aspect of his general tendency to underline antitheses and distinctions rather than to gloss them over. For example, God is not man, and man is not God. And the gulf between them cannot be bridged by dialectical thinking. It can be bridged only by the leap of faith, by a voluntary act by which man relates himself to God and freely appropriates, as it were, his relation as creature to the Creator, as a finite individual to the transcendent Absolute. Hegel, however, confounds what ought to be distinguished. And his dialectical mediation between the infinite and the finite, between God and man, leaves us in the end with neither God nor man but only with the pale ghost of hypostatized thought, dignified by the name of absolute Spirit.

With this emphasis on the individual, on choice, on self-commitment, Kierkegaard's philosophical thought tends to become a clarification of issues and an appeal to choose, an attempt to get men to see their existential situation and the great alternatives with which they are faced. It is certainly not an attempt to master all reality by thought and to exhibit it as a necessary system of concepts. This idea was quite foreign and repugnant to his mind. In his view speculative systematic philosophy, the greatest example of which was for him absolute idealism, radically misrepresented human existence. The really important problems, that is, the problems which are of real importance for man as the existing individual, are not solved by thought, by adopting the absolute standpoint of the speculative philosopher, but by the act of choice, on the level of existence rather than on that of detached, objective reflection.

As one might expect, Kierkegaard's philosophy is intensely personal. In one sense, of course, every philosopher worthy of the name is a personal thinker. For it is he who does the thinking.

But with Kierkegaard there is a closer connection between his life and his philosophy than in the case of many other philosophers. He does not simply take over traditional problems or the problems most discussed in contemporary philosophical circles and then attempt to solve them in a purely objective and disinterested spirit. His problems arise out of his own life, in the sense that in the first instance they arise for him in the form of alternatives presented for his own personal choice, a choice involving a radical self-commitment. His philosophy is, as it were, a lived philosophy. And one of his objections to Hegelianism is that one cannot live by it. Obviously, Kierkegaard has to universalize. Without universalization there would be only autobiography. At the same time it is abundantly clear that it is the actor who speaks rather than the spectator.

From one point of view this feature of his philosophy constitutes its weakness. That is to say, his thought may appear too subjective, too hostile to objectivity. In fact, some would refuse it the name of philosophy at all. But from another point of view the intensely personal character of Kierkegaard's thought constitutes its strength. For it gives to his writing a degree of seriousness and depth which sets it entirely outside the concept of philosophy as a game or as an academic pastime for those who have the requisite aptitude and inclination.

In view of the fact that Kierkegaard's thought is developed in conscious opposition to Hegelianism or, if preferred, to speculative philosophy as represented by absolute idealism, as well as for chronological reasons, I have included the chapter on his philosophy in this part of the present volume. But if one were to neglect chronology and take effective influence as a standard, one would have to postpone consideration of his thought to a later stage. For though he was one of the most passionate thinkers of his period, he excited very little real interest at the time. A Dane, he was first discovered, so to speak, by the Germans in the first decades of the present century, and he has exercised a profound influence on some phases of the existentialist movement and on modern Protestant theology of the type represented by Karl Barth. Kierkegaard's preoccupation with Hegelianism as the dominant philosophy of his time and cultural milieu constitutes the dating element in his thought. But the ideas which he opposed to Hegelianism have a quite independent significance, and they have exercised a widespread influence in another and later cultural context.

2. Søren Aabye Kierkegaard was born at Copenhagen on May 15th, 1813. He was given an extremely religious upbringing by his father, a man who suffered from melancholia and imagined that the curse of God hung over him and his family.[1] And Kierkegaard was himself affected to some degree by this melancholy, concealed beneath a display of sarcastic wit.

In 1830 Kierkegaard matriculated in the university of Copenhagen and chose the faculty of theology, doubtless in accordance with his father's wishes. But he paid little attention to theological studies and devoted himself instead to philosophy, literature and history. It was at this time that he gained his knowledge of Hegelianism. During this period Kierkegaard was very much the observer of life, cynical and disillusioned, yet devoted to the social life of the university. Estranged from his father and his father's religion, he spoke of the 'stuffy atmosphere' of Christianity and maintained that philosophy and Christianity were incompatible. Religious disbelief was accompanied by laxity in moral standards. And Kierkegaard's general attitude at this time fell under the heading of what he later called the aesthetic stage on life's way.

In the spring of 1836 Kierkegaard appears to have had a temptation to commit suicide, having been overcome by a vision of his inner cynicism. But in June of that year he underwent a kind of moral conversion, in the sense that he adopted moral standards and made an attempt, even if not always successful, to live up to them.[2] This period corresponds to the ethical stage in his later dialectic.

On May 19th, 1838, the year in which his father died, Kierkegaard experienced a religious conversion, accompanied by an 'indescribable joy'. He resumed the practice of his religion and in 1840 he passed his examinations in theology. He became engaged to Regina Olsen, but a year later he broke off the engagement. He evidently thought that he was unsuited for married life, a correct idea one would imagine. But he had also become convinced that he was a man with a mission, and that marriage would interfere with it.

In 1843 Kierkegaard published *Either-Or*, a title which well expresses his attitude to life and his abhorrence of what he took to be Hegel's 'Both-And', *Fear and Trembling* and *Repetition*. These

[1] As a boy, Kierkegaard's father had tended sheep on a Jutland heath. One day, afflicted with hunger, cold and loneliness, he had cursed God. And this incident was indelibly printed on his memory.

[2] I do not mean to imply that Kierkegaard had ever led what would be generally understood by a thoroughly immoral life. It was more a question of a change of interior attitude from a rejection to an acceptance of ethical self-commitment.

works were followed in 1844 by *The Concept of Dread* and *Philosophical Fragments*, in 1845 by *Stages on Life's Way* and in 1846 by the *Concluding Unscientific Postscript* which, though its name may not suggest it, is a large and weighty tome. He also published some 'edifying discourses' in these years. The works of this period appeared under various pseudonyms, though the identity of the author was well enough known at Copenhagen. As far as the Christian faith was concerned, it was presented from the point of view of an observer, by indirect communication as Kierkegaard put it, rather than from the point of view of an apostle intent on direct communication of the truth.

In the spring of 1848 Kierkegaard enjoyed a religious experience which, as he wrote in his *Journal*, changed his nature and impelled him to direct communication. He did not at once abandon the use of pseudonyms, but with *Anti-Climacus* the change to a direct and positive presentation of the standpoint of Christian faith becomes apparent. The year 1848 saw the publication of *Christian Discourses*, and *The Point of View* was also composed at this time, though it was published only after Kierkegaard's death. *The Sickness unto Death* appeared in 1849.

Kierkegaard was meditating a frontal attack on the Danish State Church which, in his opinion, scarcely deserved any more the name of Christian. For as far as its official representatives at least were concerned, it appeared to him to have watered down Christianity to a polite moral humanism with a modicum of religious beliefs calculated not to offend the susceptibilities of the educated. However, to avoid wounding Bishop Mynster, who had been a friend of his father, Kierkegaard did not open fire until 1854, after the prelate's death. A vigorous controversy ensued in the course of which Kierkegaard maintained that what he represented was simply ordinary honesty. The emasculated Christianity of the established Church should recognize and admit that it was not Christianity.

Kierkegaard died on November 4th, 1855. At his funeral there was an unfortunate scene when his nephew interrupted the Dean to protest against the appropriation by the Danish Church of a man who had so vigorously condemned it.

3. There is an obvious sense in which every human being is and remains an individual, distinct from other persons and things. In this sense of individuality even the members of an enraged mob are individuals. At the same time there is a sense in which the

individuality of the members of such a mob is sunk in a common consciousness. The mob is possessed, as it were, by a common emotion, and it is a notorious fact that a mob is capable of performing actions which its members would not perform precisely as individuals.

This is indeed an extreme example. But I mention it to show in a simple way that we can quite easily give a cash value to the idea of man's being more or less of an individual. One might, of course, take less dramatic examples. Suppose that my opinions are dictated predominantly by what 'one thinks', my emotive reactions by what 'one feels', and my actions by the social conventions of my environment. To the extent that this is the case I can be said to think, feel and act as a member of 'the One', as a member of an impersonal collectivity, rather than as this individual. If, however, I become aware of my anonymous status, so to speak, and begin to form my own principles of conduct and to act resolutely in accordance with them, even if this means acting in a way quite opposed to the customary ways of acting of my social environment, there is a sense in which I can be said to have become more of an individual, in spite of the fact that in another sense I am no more and no less an individual than I was before.

If space permitted, these concepts would obviously require careful analysis. But even in this unanalysed state they may serve to facilitate understanding of the following quotation from Kierkegaard. 'A crowd—not this crowd or that, the crowd now living or the crowd long deceased, a crowd of humble people or of superior people, of rich or of poor, etc.—a crowd in its very concept is the untruth, by reason of the fact that it renders the individual completely impenitent and irresponsible, or at least weakens his sense of responsibility by reducing it to a fraction.'[1] Kierkegaard is not, of course, concerned simply with the dangers of allowing oneself to become a member of a crowd in the sense of a mob. His point is that philosophy, with its emphasis on the universal rather than on the particular, has tried to show that man realizes his true essence in proportion as he rises above what is contemptuously regarded as his mere particularity and becomes a moment in the life of the universal. This theory, Kierkegaard argues, is false, whether the universal is considered as the State or as the economic or social class or as Humanity or as absolute Thought. 'I have endeavoured to express the thought that to

[1] *The Point of View*, p. 114 (translated by W. Lowrie, London, 1939).

employ the category "race" to indicate what it is to be a man, and especially as an indication of the highest attainment, is a misunderstanding and mere paganism, because the race, mankind, differs from an animal race not merely by its general superiority as a race, but by the *human* characteristic that every single individual within the race (not merely distinguished individuals but every individual) is more than the race. For to relate oneself to God is a far higher thing than to be related to the race and through the race to God.'[1]

The last sentence of this quotation indicates the general direction of Kierkegaard's thought. The highest self-actualization of the individual is the relating of oneself to God, not as the universal, absolute Thought, but as the absolute Thou. But further explanation of what Kierkegaard means by becoming the individual is best reserved for the context of his theory of the three stages. For the moment it is sufficient to notice that it means the opposite of self-dispersal in 'the One' or self-submerging in the universal, however this may be conceived. The exaltation of the universal, the collectivity, the totality, is for Kierkegaard 'mere paganism'. But he also insists that historic paganism was orientated towards Christianity, whereas the new paganism is a falling away or an apostasy from Christianity.[2]

4. In *The Phenomenology of Spirit* Hegel expounded his masterly dialectic of the stages by which the mind awakens to self-consciousness, to universal consciousness and to the standpoint of absolute Thought. Kierkegaard also expounds a dialectic. But it is radically different from that of Hegel. In the first place it is the process by which spirit is actualized in the form of individuality, the individual existent, not in the form of the all-comprehensive universal. In the second place the transition from one stage to the next is accomplished not by thinking but by choice, by an act of the will, and in this sense by a leap. There is no question of overcoming antitheses by a process of conceptual synthesis: there is a choice between alternatives, and the choice of the higher alternative, the transition to a higher stage of the dialectic, is a willed self-commitment of the whole man.

The first stage or sphere is described as the aesthetic.[3] And it is

[1] *Ibid*, pp. 88–9, in Note.
[2] See, for example, *The Sickness unto Death*, pp. 73–4 (translated by W. Lowrie, Princeton and London, 1941).
[3] This is discussed, for instance, in the first volume of *Either-Or* and in the first part of *Stages on Life's Way*.

characterized by self-dispersal on the level of sense. The aesthetic man is governed by sense, impulse and emotion. But we must not conceive him as being simply and solely the grossly sensual man. The aesthetic stage can also be exemplified, for instance, in the poet who transmutes the world into an imaginative realm and in the romantic. The essential features of the aesthetic consciousness are the absence of fixed universal moral standards and of determinate religious faith and the presence of a desire to enjoy the whole range of emotive and sense experience. True, there can be discrimination. But the principle of discrimination is aesthetic rather than obedience to a universal moral law considered as the dictate of impersonal reason. The aesthetic man strives after infinity, but in the sense of a bad infinity which is nothing else but the absence of all limitations other than those imposed by his own tastes. Open to all emotional and sense experience, sampling the nectar from every flower, he hates all that would limit his field of choice and he never gives definite form to his life. Or, rather, the form of his life is its very formlessness, self-dispersal on the level of sense.

To the aesthetic man his existence seems to be the expression of freedom. Yet he is more than a psycho-physical organism, endowed with emotive and imaginative power and the capacity for sense enjoyment. 'The soulish-bodily synthesis in every man is planned with a view to being spirit, such is the building; but the man prefers to dwell in the cellar, that is, in the determinants of sensuousness.'[1] And the aesthetic consciousness or attitude to life may be accompanied by a vague awareness of this fact, by a vague dissatisfaction with the dispersal of the self in the pursuit of pleasure and sense enjoyment. Further, the more aware a man becomes that he is living in what Kierkegaard calls the cellar of the building, the more subject he becomes to 'despair'. For he finds that there is no remedy, no salvation, at the level on which he stands. He is faced, therefore, with two alternatives. Either he must remain in despair on the aesthetic level or he must make the transition to the next level by an act of choice, by self-commitment. Mere thinking will not do the trick for him. It is a question of choice; either-or.

The second stage is the ethical. A man accepts determinate moral standards and obligations, the voice of universal reason, and thus gives form and consistency to his life. If the aesthetic stage is

---

[1] *The Sickness unto Death*, p. 67.

typified by Don Juan, the ethical stage is typified by Socrates. And a simple example of the transition from the aesthetic to the moral consciousness is for Kierkegaard that of the man who renounces the satisfaction of his sexual impulse according to passing attraction and enters into the state of marriage, accepting all its obligations. For marriage is an ethical institution, an expression of the universal law of reason.

Now, the ethical stage has its own heroism. It can produce what Kierkegaard calls the tragic hero. 'The tragic hero renounces himself in order to express the universal.'[1] This is what Socrates did, and Antigone was prepared to give her life in defence of the unwritten natural law. At the same time the ethical consciousness as such does not understand sin. The ethical man may take account of human weakness, of course; but he thinks that it can be overcome by strength of will, enlightened by clear ideas. In so far as he exemplifies the attitude characteristic of the ethical consciousness as such he believes in man's moral self-sufficiency. Yet in point of fact a man can come to realize his own inability to fulfil the moral law as it should be fulfilled and to acquire perfect virtue. He can come to an awareness of his lack of self-sufficiency and of his sin and guilt. He has then arrived at the point at which he is faced with the choice or rejection of the standpoint of faith. Just as 'despair' forms, as it were, the antithesis to the aesthetic consciousness, an antithesis which is overcome or resolved by ethical self-commitment, so consciousness of sin forms the antithesis to the ethical stage, and this antithesis is overcome only by the act of faith, by relating oneself to God.

To affirm one's relationship to God, the personal and transcendent Absolute, is to affirm oneself as spirit. 'By relating itself to its own self and by willing to be itself, the self is grounded transparently in the Power which constituted it. And this formula . . . is the definition of faith.'[2] Every man is, as it were, a mixture of the finite and the infinite. Considered precisely as finite, he is separated from God, alienated from him. Considered as infinite, man is not indeed God, but he is a movement towards God, the movement of the spirit. And the man who appropriates and affirms his relationship to God in faith becomes what he really is, the individual before God.

To emphasize the difference between the second and third

[1] *Fear and Trembling*, p. 109 (translated by R. Payne, London, 1939).
[2] *The Sickness unto Death*, p. 216.

stages Kierkegaard uses as a symbol Abraham's willingness to sacrifice his son Isaac at God's command. The tragic hero, such as Socrates, sacrifices himself for the universal moral law; but Abraham, as Kierkegaard puts it, does nothing for the universal. 'So we stand in the presence of the paradox. Either the Individual as the Individual can stand in an absolute relation to the Absolute, and then ethics is not supreme, or Abraham is lost: he is neither a tragic hero nor an aesthetic hero.'[1] Needless to say, Kierkegaard does not intend to enunciate the general proposition that religion involves the negation of morality. What he means is that the man of faith is directly related to a personal God whose demands are absolute and cannot be measured simply by the standards of the human reason. At the back of Kierkegaard's mind there is doubtless the memory of his behaviour towards Regina Olsen. Marriage is an ethical institution, the expression of the universal. And if ethics, the universal, is supreme, Kierkegaard's conduct was inexcusable. He was justified only if he had a personal mission from God whose absolute demands are addressed to the individual. Obviously, I do not intend to suggest that Kierkegaard is universalizing his own experience in the sense of assuming that everyone has the same specific experience. He universalizes it in the sense that he reflects on its general significance.

As Kierkegaard's dialectic is one of discontinuity, in the sense that the transition from one stage to another is made by choice, by self-commitment, and not through a continuous process of conceptual mediation, he not unnaturally plays down the role of reason and emphasizes that of will when he is treating of religious faith. In his view faith is a leap. That is to say, it is an adventure, a risk, a self-commitment to an objective uncertainty. God is the transcendent Absolute, the absolute Thou; he is not an object the existence of which can be proved. True, God reveals himself to the human conscience in the sense that man can become aware of his sin and alienation and his need of God. But man's response is a venture, an act of faith in a Being who lies beyond the reach of speculative philosophy. And this act of faith is not something which can be performed once and for all. It has to be constantly repeated. It is true that God has revealed himself in Christ, the God-Man. But Christ is the Paradox, to the Jews a stumbling-block and to the Greeks foolishness. Faith is always a venture, a leap.

Looked at from one point of view Kierkegaard's account of the

---

[1] *Fear and Trembling*, p. 171.

standpoint of faith is a vigorous protest against the way in which
speculative philosophy, represented principally by Hegelianism,
blurs the distinction between God and man and rationalizes the
Christian dogmas, turning them into philosophically-demonstrated
conclusions. In the Hegelian system 'the qualitative distinction
between God and man is pantheistically abolished'.[1] The system
does indeed hold out the attractive prospect of 'an illusory land,
which to a mortal eye might appear to yield a certainty higher
than that of faith'.[2] But the mirage is destructive of faith, and its
claim to represent Christianity is bogus. 'The entirely unsocratic
tract of modern philosophy is that it wants to make itself and us
believe that it is Christianity.'[3] In other words, Kierkegaard
refuses to admit that in this life there can be a higher standpoint
than that of faith. The vaunted transformation of faith into
speculative knowledge is an illusion.

But though in such passages it is Hegelianism which Kierkegaard
has principally in mind, there is no adequate ground for saying
that he would have had much sympathy with the idea of proving
God's existence by metaphysical argument provided that an
unequivocally theistic idea of God were maintained. In his view
the fact that man is held eternally accountable for belief or disbelief shows that belief is not a matter of accepting the conclusion
of a demonstrative argument but rather a matter of will. Catholic
theologians would obviously wish to make some distinctions here.
But Kierkegaard was not a Catholic theologian. And the point is
that he deliberately emphasized the nature of faith as a leap. It
was not simply a case of opposition to Hegelian rationalism.

This comes out clearly in his famous interpretation of truth as
subjectivity. '*An objective uncertainty held fast in an appropriation-
process of the most passionate inwardness is the truth*, the highest
truth attainable for an *existing* individual.'[4] Kierkegaard is not
denying that there is any such thing as objective, impersonal truth.
But mathematical truths, for example, do not concern the 'existing
individual' as such. That is to say, they are irrelevant to a man's
life of total self-commitment. He accepts them. He cannot do
otherwise. But he does not stake his whole being on them. That on
which I stake my whole being is not something which I cannot

---

[1] *The Sickness unto Death*, p. 192.
[2] *Concluding Unscientific Postscript*, p. 213 (translated by D. F. Swenson,
Princeton and London, 1941).
[3] *The Sickness unto Death*, p. 151.
[4] *Concluding Unscientific Postscript*, p. 182.

deny without logical contradiction or something which is so obviously true that I cannot deny it without palpable absurdity. It is something which I can doubt but which is so important to me that if I accept it, I do so with a passionate self-commitment. It is in a sense *my* truth. 'The truth is precisely the venture which chooses an objective uncertainty with the passion of the infinite. I contemplate the order of nature in the hope of finding God, and I see omnipotence and wisdom; but I also see much else that disturbs my mind and excites anxiety. The sum of all this is an objective uncertainty. But it is for this very reason that the inwardness becomes as intense as it is, for it embraces this objective uncertainty with the entire passion of the infinite.'[1]

Obviously, truth as so described is precisely what Kierkegaard means by faith. The definition of truth as subjectivity and the definition of faith are the same. 'Without risk there is no faith. Faith is precisely the contradiction between the infinite passion of the individual's inwardness and the objective uncertainty.'[2] Kierkegaard does indeed assert more than once that the eternal truth is not in itself a paradox. But it becomes paradoxical in relation to us. One can indeed see some evidence in Nature of God's work, but at the same time one can see much which points in the opposite direction. There is, and remains, 'objective uncertainty', whether we look at Nature or at the Gospels. For the idea of the God-Man is itself paradoxical for the finite reason. Faith grasps the objectively uncertain and affirms it; but it has to maintain itself, as it were, over a fathomless sea. Religious truth exists only in the 'passionate' appropriation of the objectively uncertain.[3]

In point of fact Kierkegaard does not say that there are no rational motives at all for making the act of faith and that it is a purely arbitrary act of capricious choice. But he certainly takes delight in minimizing the rational motives for religious belief and in emphasizing the subjectivity of truth and the nature of faith as a leap. Hence he inevitably gives the impression that faith is for him an arbitrary act of the will. And Catholic theologians at least criticize him on this score. But if we prescind from the theological analysis of faith and concentrate on the psychological aspect of the matter, there is no difficulty in recognizing, whether one is Catholic or Protestant, that there are certainly some who understand very well from their own experience what Kierkegaard is

---

[1] *Concluding Unscientific Postscript*, p. 182.   [2] *Ibid.*
[3] We have to remember that for Kierkegaard faith is a self-commitment to the absolute and transcendent Thou, the personal God, rather than to propositions.

driving at when he describes faith as a venture or risk. And, in general, Kierkegaard's phenomenological analysis of the three distinct attitudes or levels of consciousness which he describes possess a value and a stimulative power which is not destroyed by his characteristic exaggerations.

5. In the passage quoted above which gives Kierkegaard's unconventional definition of truth mention is made of the 'existing individual'. It has already been explained that the term 'existence', as used by Kierkegaard, is a specifically human category which cannot be applied, for example, to a stone. But something more must be said about it here.

To illustrate his use of the concept of existence Kierkegaard employs the following analogy. A man sits in a cart and holds the reins, but the horse goes along its accustomed path without any active control by the driver, who may be asleep. Another man actively guides and directs his horse. In one sense both men can be said to be drivers. But in another sense it is only the second man who can be said to be driving. In an analogous manner the man who drifts with the crowd, who merges himself in the anonymous 'One', can be said to exist in one sense of the term, though in another sense he cannot be said to exist. For he is not the 'existing individual' who strives resolutely towards an end which cannot be realized once and for all at a given moment and is thus in a constant state of becoming, making himself, as it were, by his repeated acts of choice. Again, the man who contents himself with the role of spectator of the world and of life and transmutes everything into a dialectic of abstract concepts exists indeed in one sense but not in another. For he wishes to understand everything and commits himself to nothing. The 'existing individual', however, is the actor rather than the spectator. He commits himself and so gives form and direction to his life. He ex-ists towards an end for which he actively strives by choosing this and rejecting that. In other words, the term 'existence' has with Kierkegaard more or less the same sense as the term 'authentic existence' as used by some modern existentialist philosophers.

If understood simply in this way, the term 'existence' is neutral, in the sense that it can be applied within any of the three stages of the dialectic. Indeed, Kierkegaard says explicitly that 'there are three spheres of existence: the aesthetic, the ethical, the religious'.[1] A man can 'exist' within the aesthetic sphere if he deliberately,

---

[1] *Concluding Unscientific Postscript*, p. 448.

resolutely and consistently acts as the aesthetic man, excluding alternatives. In this sense Don Juan typifies the existing individual within the aesthetic sphere. Similarly, the man who sacrifices his own inclinations to the universal moral law and constantly strives after the fulfilment of a moral ideal which beckons him ever forward is an existing individual within the ethical sphere. 'An existing individual is himself in process of becoming. . . . In existence the watchword is always *forward*.'[1]

But though the term 'existence' has indeed this wide field of application, it tends to take on a specifically religious connotation. Nor is this in any way surprising. For man's highest form of self-realization as spirit is for Kierkegaard his self-relating to the personal Absolute. 'Existence is a synthesis of the infinite and the finite, and the existing individual is both infinite and finite.'[2] But to say that the existing individual is infinite is not to identify him with God. It is to say that his becoming is a constant striving towards God. 'Existence itself, the act of existing, is a striving . . . (and) the striving is infinite.'[3] 'Existence is the child that is born of the infinite and the finite, the eternal and the temporal, and is therefore a constant striving.'[4] One can say, therefore, that existence comprises two moments: separation or finiteness and a constant striving, in this context towards God. The striving must be constant, a constant becoming, because the self-relating to God in faith cannot be accomplished once and for all: it has to take the form of a constantly repeated self-commitment.

It can hardly be claimed that Kierkegaard's definition or descriptions of existence are always crystal clear. At the same time the general notion is intelligible enough. And it is clear that for him the existing individual *par excellence* is the individual before God, the man who sustains the standpoint of faith.

6. In the writings of the existentialists the concept of dread[5] is conspicuous. But the term is used by different writers in different ways. With Kierkegaard it has a religious setting. And in *The Concept of Dread* it has a close association with the idea of sin. However, one can, I think, broaden the range of application and say that dread is a state which precedes a qualitative leap from one stage in life's way to another.

---

[1] *Concluding Unscientific Postscript*, p. 368.
[2] *Ibid.*, p. 350.   [3] *Ibid.*, p. 84.   [4] *Ibid.*, p. 85.
[5] The Germans speak of *Angst*, the French of *angoisse*. Some English writers have employed 'anguish' or even 'anxiety'. I have retained 'dread'. In any case 'fear' should be avoided, for a reason explained in the text.

Dread is defined by Kierkegaard as a '*sympathetic antipathy and an antipathetic sympathy*'.[1] Take the case of the small boy who feels an attraction for adventure, 'a thirst for the prodigious, the mysterious'.[2] The child is attracted by the unknown, yet at the same time is repelled by it, as a menace to his security. Attraction and repulsion, sympathy and antipathy, are interwoven. The child is in a state of dread, but not of fear. For fear is concerned with something quite definite, real or imagined, a snake under the bed, a wasp threatening to sting, whereas dread is concerned with the as yet unknown and indefinite. And it is precisely the unknown, the mysterious, which both attracts and repels the child.

Kierkegaard applies this idea to sin. In the state of innocence, he says, spirit is in a dreaming state, in a state of immediacy. It does not yet know sin. Yet it can have a vague attraction, not for sin as something definite, but for the use of freedom and so for the possibility of sin. 'Dread is the possibility of freedom.'[3] Kierkegaard uses Adam as an illustration. When Adam, in the state of innocence, was told not to eat the fruit of the tree of the knowledge of good and evil under pain of death, he could not know what was meant either by evil or by death. For the knowledge could be obtained only by disobeying the prohibition. But the prohibition awoke in Adam 'the possibility of freedom . . . the alarming possibility of *being able*'.[4] And he was attracted and repelled by it at the same time.

But there is also, Kierkegaard says, a dread in relation to the good. Let us suppose, for example, a man sunk in sin. He may be aware of the possibility of emerging from this state, and he may be attracted by it. But at the same time he may be repelled by the prospect, inasmuch as he loves his state of sin. He is then possessed by dread of the good. And this is really a dread of freedom, if, that is to say, we suppose that the man is in the enslaving grip of sin. Freedom is for him the object of a sympathetic antipathy and an antipathetic sympathy. And this dread is itself the possibility of freedom.

The notion of dread may perhaps become clearer if we can apply it in this way. A man, let us suppose, has become conscious of sin and of his utter lack of self-sufficiency. And he is faced with the possibility of the leap of faith,[5] which, as we have seen, means self-commitment to an objective uncertainty, a leap into the unknown. He is rather like the man on the edge of the precipice

---

[1] *The Concept of Dread*, p. 38 (translated by W. Lowrie, Princeton and London, 1944).   [2] *Ibid.*   [3] *Ibid*, p. 139..   [4] *Ibid.*, p. 40.
[5] 'The opposite of sin is not virtue but faith'; *The Sickness unto Death*, p. 132.

who is aware of the possibility of throwing himself over and who feels attraction and repulsion at the same time. True, the leap of faith means salvation, not destruction. 'The dread of possibility holds him as its prey, until it can deliver him saved into the hands of faith. In no other place does he find repose. . . .'[1] This seems to imply that dread is overcome by the leap. But in so far at least as the maintenance of the standpoint of faith involves a repeated self-commitment to an objective uncertainty, it would appear that dread recurs as the emotive tonality of the repeated leap.

7. Kierkegaard was first and foremost a religious thinker. And though for his actual contemporaries he was pretty well a voice crying in the wilderness, his idea of the Christian religion has exercised a powerful influence on important currents of modern Protestant theology. Mention has already been made of the name of Karl Barth, whose hostility to 'natural theology' is very much in tune with Kierkegaard's attitude towards any invasion by metaphysics into the sphere of faith. It may be said, of course, and with justice, that in the type of theology represented by Karl Barth it is a case not so much of following Kierkegaard as of making a renewed contact with the original well-spring of Protestant thought and spirituality. But inasmuch as some of Kierkegaard's ideas were distinctively Lutheran, this was just one of the effects which his writings could and did exercise.

At the same time his writings are obviously capable of exercising an influence in other directions. On the one hand he had some very hard things to say about Protestantism, and we can discern a movement in his thought not only away from emasculated Protestantism but also from Protestantism as such. It is not my purpose to argue that if he had lived longer, he would have become a Catholic. Whether he would or not is a question which we cannot possibly answer. Hence it is unprofitable to discuss it. But in point of fact his writings have had the effect of turning some people's minds towards Catholicism which, as he remarked, has always maintained the ideal at any rate of what he called No. 1 Christianity. On the other hand one can envisage the possibility of his writings contributing to turn people away from Christianity altogether. One can imagine a man saying, 'Yes, I see the point. Kierkegaard is quite right. I am not really a Christian. And, what is more, I do not wish to be. No leaps for me, no passionate embracing of objective uncertainties.'

---

[1] *The Concept of Dread*, p. 141.

It is not so surprising, therefore, if in the development of the modern existentialist movement we find certain Kierkegaardian themes divorced from their original religious setting and employed in an atheistic system. This is notably the case in the philosophy of M. Sartre. With Karl Jaspers indeed, who of all the philosophers commonly classified as existentialists[1] stands nearest to Kierkegaard, the religious setting of the concept of existence is to a large extent retained.[2] But the philosophy of M. Sartre reminds us that the concepts of authentic existence, of free self-commitment and of dread are capable of displacement from this setting.

These remarks are certainly not meant to imply that the origins of modern existentialism can be attributed simply to the posthumous influence of Kierkegaard. This would be a gross misstatement. But Kierkegaardian themes recur in existentialism, though the historical context has changed. And writers on the existentialist movement are perfectly justified in seeing in the Danish thinker its spiritual ancestor, though not, of course, its sufficient cause. At the same time Kierkegaard has exercised a stimulative influence on many people who would not call themselves existentialists or, for the matter of that, professional philosophers or theologians of any kind. As was remarked in the first section of this chapter, his philosophical thought tends to become both an attempt to get men to see their existential situation and the alternatives with which they are faced and an appeal to choose, to commit themselves, to become 'existing individuals'. It is also, of course, a protest in the name of the free individual or person against submergence in the collectivity. Kierkegaard indeed exaggerates. And the exaggeration becomes more evident when the concept of existence is deprived of the religious significance which he gave it. But exaggeration so often serves to draw attention to what is after all worth saying.

---

[1] Some of these, it is true, have repudiated the label. But we cannot discuss this matter here. In any case, 'existentialism', unless it is confined to the philosophy of M. Sartre, is a portmanteau term.

[2] Jaspers is a professional philosopher and a university professor, whereas it is difficult to imagine the eccentric and passionate Danish thinker as the occupant of any chair. But the life and thought of Kierkegaard (as of Nietzsche) has been for Jaspers a subject of prolonged meditation.

PART III

LATER CURRENTS OF THOUGHT

CHAPTER XVIII

NON-DIALECTICAL MATERIALISM

Introductory remarks—The first phase of the materialist movement—Lange's criticism of materialism—Haeckel's monism —Ostwald's energeticism—Empirio-criticism considered as an attempt to overcome the opposition between materialism and idealism.

1. THE collapse of absolute idealism was soon followed by the rise of a materialistic philosophy which did not stem, as did dialectical materialism, from left-wing Hegelianism but professed to be based on and to follow from serious reflection on the empirical sciences. Science has, of course, no intrinsic connection with philosophical materialism, even if the philosophies of Nature expounded by Schelling and Hegel did little to foster the conviction that the natural complement of science is metaphysical idealism. Further, the leading German philosophers, apart from Marx, have certainly not been materialists. Hence I do not propose to devote much space to the nineteenth-century materialist movement in Germany. But it is as well to understand that there was such a movement. And though it did not represent any profound philosophical thought, it was none the less influential. Indeed, it was precisely because of its lack of profundity and its appeal to the prestige of science that a book such as Büchner's *Force and Matter* enjoyed a wide vogue and passed through a great number of editions.

2. Among the German materialists prominent in the middle of the nineteenth century were Karl Vogt (1817–95), Heinrich Czolbe (1819–73), Jakob Moleschott (1822–93) and Ludwig Büchner (1824–99). Vogt, a zoologist and professor at Giessen for a time, is memorable for his statement that the brain secretes thought as the liver secretes bile. His general outlook is indicated by the title of his polemical work against the physiologist Rudolf Wagner, *Blind Faith and Science* (*Kohlerglaube und Wissenschaft*,

1854, literally *Faith of a Charcoal-burner and Science*). Rudolf Wagner had openly professed belief in divine creation, and Vogt attacked him in the name of science. Czolbe, author of a *New Exposition of Sensualism* (*Neue Darstellung des Sensualismus*, 1855) and of attacks on Kant, Hegel and Lotze, derived consciousness from sensation, which he interpreted in a manner reminiscent of Democritus. At the same time he admitted the presence in Nature of organic forms which are not susceptible of a purely mechanistic explanation.

Moleschott was a physiologist and doctor who had to abandon his chair at Utrecht in consequence of the opposition aroused by his materialistic theories. Subsequently he became a professor in Italy where he exercised a considerable influence on minds inclined to positivism and materialism. In particular he influenced Cesare Lombroso (1836–1909), the famous professor of criminal anthropology at Turin, who translated into Italian Moleschott's *The Cycle of Life* (*Der Kreislauf des Lebens*, 1852). In Moleschott's view the whole history of the universe can be explained in terms of an original matter, of which force or energy is an intrinsic and essential attribute. There is no matter without force, and no force without matter. Life is simply a state of matter itself. Feuerbach prepared the way for the destruction of all anthropomorphic, teleological interpretations of the world, and it is the task of modern science to continue and complete this work. There is no good reason for making a dichotomy between the natural sciences on the one hand and the study of man and his history on the other. Science can use the same principles of explanation in both cases.

The best known product of the earlier phase of German materialism is probably Büchner's *Force and Matter* (*Kraft und Stoff*, 1855), which became a kind of popular textbook of materialism and was translated into a number of foreign languages. The author condemned out of hand all philosophy which could not be understood by the ordinary educated reader. And for this very reason the book enjoyed considerable popularity. As its title indicates, force and matter are taken as sufficient principles of explanation. The spiritual soul, for example, is thrown overboard.

3. In 1866 Friedrich Albert Lange (1828–75) published his famous *History of Materialism* (*Geschichte des Materialismus*) in which he subjected the materialist philosophy to well-founded criticism from the point of view of a Neo-Kantian. If it is considered simply as a methodological principle in natural science,

materialism is to be affirmed. That is to say, the physicist, for
example, should proceed as though there were only material
things. Kant himself was of this opinion. The natural scientist is
not concerned with spiritual reality. But though materialism is
acceptable as a methodological principle in the field of natural
science, it is no longer acceptable when it has been transformed
into a metaphysics or general philosophy. In this form it becomes
uncritical and naïve. For example, in empirical psychology it is
quite right and proper to carry as far as possible the physiological
explanation of psychical processes. But it is a sure sign of an
uncritical and naïve outlook if it is supposed that consciousness
itself is susceptible of a purely materialist interpretation. For it is
only through consciousness that we know anything at all about
bodies, nerves and so on. And the very attempt to develop a
materialist reduction of consciousness reveals its irreducible
character.

Further, the materialists betray their uncritical mentality when
they treat matter, force, atoms and so forth as though they were
things-in-themselves. In point of fact they are concepts formed by
the mind or spirit in its effort to understand the world. We have
indeed to make use of such concepts, but it is naïve to assume that
their utility shows that they can properly be made the basis for a
dogmatist materialist metaphysics. And this is what philosophical
materialism really is.

4. Lange's criticism dealt a telling blow at materialism, all the
more so because he did not confine himself to polemics but was at
pains to show what was, in his opinion, the valid element in the
materialist attitude. But, as one might expect, his criticism did not
prevent a recrudescence of materialism, a second wave which
appealed for support to the Darwinian theory of evolution as a
proved factor which showed that the origin and development of
man was simply a phase of cosmic evolution in general, that man's
higher activities could be adequately explained in terms of this
evolution, and that at no point was it necessary to introduce the
notion of creative activity by a supramundane Being. The fact
that there is no necessary connection between the scientific
hypothesis of biological evolution and philosophical materialism
was indeed clear to some minds at the time. But there were many
people who either welcomed or attacked the hypothesis, as the
case might be, because they thought that materialism was the
natural conclusion to draw from it.

The characteristic popular expression of this second phase of the materialist movement in Germany was Haeckel's *The Riddle of the Universe* (*Die Welträtsel*, 1899). Ernst Haeckel (1834–1919) was for many years professor of zoology at Jena, and a number of his works treated simply of the results of his scientific research. Others, however, were devoted to expounding a monistic philosophy based on the hypothesis of evolution. Between 1859, the year which saw the publication of Darwin's *The Origin of Species by Means of Natural Selection*, and 1871, when Darwin's *The Descent of Man* appeared, Haeckel published several works on topics connected with evolution and made it clear that in his opinion Darwin had at last set the evolutionary hypothesis on a really scientific basis. On this basis Haeckel proceeded to develop a general monism and to offer it as a valid substitute for religion in the traditional sense. Thus in 1892 he published a lecture, with additional notes, bearing the title *Monism as Link between Religion and Science* (*Der Monismus als Band zwischen Religion und Wissenschaft*). And similar attempts to find in his monism a fulfilment of man's need for religion can be seen in *The Riddle of the Universe* and in *God-Nature, Studies in Monistic Religion* (*Gott-Natur, Studien über monistische Religion*, 1914).

Reflection on the world has given rise, Haeckel asserts, to a number of riddles or problems. Some of these have been solved, while others are insoluble and are no real problems at all. 'The monistic philosophy is ultimately prepared to recognize only one comprehensive riddle of the universe, the problem of substance.'[1] If this is understood to mean the problem of the nature of some mysterious thing-in-itself behind phenomena, Haeckel is prepared to grant that we are perhaps as unable to solve it as were 'Anaximander and Empedocles 2400 years ago'.[2] But inasmuch as we do not even know that there is such a thing-in-itself, discussion of its nature is fruitless. What has been made clear is 'the comprehensive law of substance',[3] the law of the conservation of force and matter. Matter and force or energy are the two attributes of substance, and the law of their conservation, when interpreted as the universal law of evolution, justifies us in conceiving the universe as a unity in which natural laws are eternally and universally valid. We thus arrive at a monistic interpretation of the universe which is based on the proofs of its unity and of the causal relation between

[1] *Die Welträtsel*, p. 10 (Leipzig, 1908 edition).
[2] *Ibid.*, p. 239. [3] *Ibid.*

all phenomena. Further, this monism destroys the three principal dogmas of dualistic metaphysics, namely 'God, freedom and immortality'.[1]

Kant's theory of two worlds, the physical, material world and the moral, immaterial world, is thus excluded by the monistic philosophy. But it does not follow that there is no place in monism for an ethics, provided that it is grounded on the social instincts of man and not on some imagined categorical imperative. Monism acknowledges as its highest moral ideal the achievement of a harmony between egoism and altruism, self-love and love of the neighbour. 'Before all others it is the great English philosopher Herbert Spencer whom we have to thank for finding in the theory of evolution a basis for this monistic ethics.'[2]

Haeckel protests that materialism is an entirely inappropriate epithet to apply to his monistic philosophy. For while it does indeed reject the idea of immaterial spirit, it equally rejects the idea of a dead, spiritless matter. 'In every atom both are inseparably combined.'[3] But to say that in every atom spirit and matter (*Geist und Materie*) are combined is really to say that in every atom force and 'stuff' (*Kraft und Stoff*) are combined. And though Haeckel asserts that his philosophy might just as well be labelled spiritualism as materialism, it is evidently what most people would describe as materialism, an evolutionary version of it, it is true, but none the less materialism. His account of the nature of consciousness and reason makes this quite clear, whatever he may say to the contrary.

If the term 'materialism' is objectionable to Haeckel, so also is the term 'atheism'. The monistic philosophy is pantheistic, not atheistic: God is completely immanent and one with the universe. 'Whether we describe this impersonal "Almighty" as "God-Nature" (*Theophysis*) or as "All-God" (*Pantheos*) is ultimately a matter of indifference.'[4] It does not seem to have occurred to Haeckel that if pantheism consists in calling the universe 'God' and if religion consists in cultivating science, ethics and aesthetics as directed respectively towards the ideals of truth, goodness and beauty, pantheism is distinguishable from atheism only by the possible presence of a certain emotive attitude towards the universe in

---

[1] *Die Welträtsel*, pp. 140, 217 and 240.
[2] *Ibid.*, p. 218. If Haeckel were still alive, he would doubtless express appreciation of the ethical ideas of Professor Julian Huxley.
[3] *Der Monismus*, p. 27 (Stuttgart, 1905 edition).
[4] *Gott-Natur*, p. 38 (Leipzig, 1914).

those who call themselves pantheists which is not present in those who call themselves atheists. Haeckel does indeed make the suggestion that 'as the ultimate cause of all things "God" is the hypothetical "original ground of substance"'.[1] But this concept is presumably the same as that of the ghostly impersonal thing-in-itself which, as we have seen, Haeckel elsewhere dismisses from consideration. Hence his pantheism cannot amount to much more than calling the universe 'God' and entertaining a certain emotive attitude towards it.

5. In 1906 a German Monist Society (Monistenbund) was founded at Munich under the patronage of Haeckel,[2] and in 1912 *The Monist Century* (*Das monistische Jahrhundert*) was published by Ostwald, the then president of the Monist Society.

Wilhelm Ostwald (1853–1932) was a famous chemist, professor of chemistry first at Riga and afterwards at Leipzig, a recipient of the Nobel Prize (1909) and founder of the *Annalen der Naturphilosophie* (1901–21), in the last issue of which there appeared the German text of Ludwig Wittgenstein's *Tractatus logico-philosophicus*. In 1906 he resigned from his chair at Leipzig, and in subsequent years he published a considerable number of writings on philosophical topics.

In 1895 Ostwald published a book on *The Overcoming of Scientific Materialism* (*Die Ueberwindung des wissenschaftlichen Materialismus*). But the so-called overcoming of materialism meant for him the substitution of the concept of energy for that of matter. The fundamental element of reality is energy which in a process of transformations takes a variety of distinct forms. The different properties of matter are different forms of energy; and psychic energy, which can be either unconscious or conscious, constitutes another distinct level or form. The different forms or levels are irreducible, in the sense that one distinct form cannot be identified with another. At the same time they arise through transformation of the one ultimate reality, namely energy. Hence 'energeticism' is a monistic theory. It hardly fits in perhaps with Ostwald's own canons of scientific method, which exclude anything approaching metaphysical hypotheses. But when he turned to the philosophy of Nature he was in any case going beyond the limits of empirical science.

6. It is only in its crudest form that materialism involves the

---

[1] *Ibid.*
[2] The Society's guiding idea was that of science as providing a way of life.

assertion that all processes are material. But a philosophy could not be classified as materialist unless it at any rate maintained the priority of matter and that processes which cannot be properly described as material are emergents from matter or epiphenomenal to material processes. Similarly, though idealism does not involve the assertion that all things are ideas in any ordinary sense, a philosophy could not be properly described as a system of metaphysical idealism unless it at any rate held that Thought or Reason or Spirit is prior and that the material world is its expression or externalization. In any case the dispute between materialism and idealism presupposes a *prima facie* distinction between matter and spirit or thought. An attempt is then made to overcome the opposition by subordinating one term of the distinction to the other. One way, therefore, of excluding the dispute between materialism and idealism is to reduce reality to phenomena which cannot properly be described either as material or as spiritual.

We find such an attempt in the phenomenalism of Mach and Avenarius, which is commonly known as empirio-criticism. This is not to say that the two philosophers in question were simply concerned with overcoming the opposition between materialism and idealism. Mach, for instance, was largely concerned with the nature of physical science. At the same time they regarded their phenomenalism as eliminating the dualisms which give rise to metaphysical essays in unification. And it is from this point of view that their theory is considered here.

Richard Avenarius (1843–96), professor of physics at Zürich and author of a *Critique of Pure Experience* (*Kritik der reinen Erfahrung,* 1888–90) and *The Human Concept of the World* (*Der menschliche Weltbegriff,* 1891), sought to reveal the essential nature of pure experience, that is, of experience stripped of all added interpretation. And he found the immediate data or elements of experience in sensations. These depend on changes in the central nervous system which are conditioned by the environment acting either as an external stimulus or by way of the process of nutrition. Further, the more the brain develops, the more is it excited by constant elements in the environment. Thus the impression of a familiar world is produced, a world in which one can feel secure. And increase in these feelings of familiarity and security is accompanied by a decrease in the impression of the world as enigmatic, problematic and mysterious. In fine, the unanswerable problems of metaphysics tend to be eliminated. And the theory of pure experience, with its reduction of both the outer and the inner worlds to sensations, excludes those dichotomies between the physical and the psychical, thing and thought, object and subject, which have formed the basis for such rival metaphysical theories as materialism and idealism.

A similar theory was produced, though by way of a rather different approach, by Ernst Mach (1838–1916) who was for many years a professor in the university of Vienna and published, in addition to works concerned with physical science, *Contributions to the Analysis of Sensations (Beiträge zur Analyse der Empfindungen*, 1886), and *Knowledge and Error (Erkenntnis und Irrtum*, 1905). Experience is reducible to sensations which are neither purely physical nor purely psychical but rather neutral. Mach thus tries to get behind the distinctions which philosophers have used as a basis for the construction of metaphysical theories. But he is more concerned with purifying physical science from metaphysical elements than with developing a general philosophy.[1] Arising out of our biological needs, science aims at control of Nature by enabling us to predict. For this purpose we have to practise an economy of thought, uniting phenomena by means of the fewest and simplest concepts possible. But though these concepts are indispensable instruments for rendering scientific prediction possible, they do not give us insight into causes or essences or substances in a metaphysical sense.

In *Materialism and Empirio-Criticism* (1909) Lenin maintained that the phenomenalism of Mach and Avenarius leads inevitably to idealism and thence to religious belief. For if things are reduced to sensations or sense-data, they must be mind-dependent. And as they can hardly be dependent simply on the individual human mind, they must be referred to a divine mind.

Historically, the phenomenalism of Mach and Avenarius formed part of the line of thought which issued in the neopositivism of the Vienna Circle in the twenties of the present century. It can hardly be said to have led to a revival of idealism, and much less of theism. It does not follow, however, that Lenin's point of view has nothing to be said for it. For example, as Avenarius had no intention of denying that there were things in some sense before there were human beings, he maintained that sensations could

---

[1] Mach rejects the concept of the ego as a spiritual substance standing over against Nature and interprets the self as a complex of phenomena which are continuous with Nature. But he does not work out this theory in any thorough-going manner, and he admits that the ego is the bond which unites experience.

exist before minds, as possible sensations. But unless the reduction of things to sensations is interpreted as equivalent to the statement, with which not even the most resolute realist would quarrel, that physical objects are in principle capable of being sensed if there is any sentient subject at hand, it becomes difficult to avoid some such conclusion as that drawn by Lenin. One can, of course, try to do so by speaking of *sensibilia* rather than of sensations. But in this case one either reinstates physical objects over against the mind or becomes involved in the same difficulty as before. Besides, it is absurd, in the opinion of the present writer, to reduce the self to a complex or succession of *sensibilia*. For the presence of the self as irreducible to *sensibilia* is a condition of the possibility of attempting such a reduction. Hence one would be left with the self on the one hand and *sensibilia* on the other, in other words with a dualism of the very type which empirio-criticism was concerned to overcome.[1] Mach's attempt to purify physical science from metaphysics is one thing: phenomenalism as a philosophical theory is quite another.

[1] The neopositivist attempted to transform phenomenalism from an ontological into a linguistic theory by saying that the statement that physical objects are sense-data means that a sentence in which a physical object is mentioned can be translated into a sentence or sentences in which only sense-data are mentioned, in such a way that if the original sentence is true (or false) the translation will be true (or false) and *vice versa*. But I do not think that this attempt proved to be successful.

CHAPTER XIX

THE NEO-KANTIAN MOVEMENT

Introductory remarks—The Marburg School—The School of Baden—The pragmatist tendency—E. Cassirer; concluding observations—Some notes on Dilthey.

1. IN 1865 Otto Liebmann (1840–1912), in his *Kant und die Epigonen*, raised the cry of 'Back to Kant!' This demand for a return to Kant was indeed perfectly understandable in the circumstances. On the one hand idealist metaphysics had produced a crop of systems which, when the first flush of enthusiasm had passed away, seemed to many to be incapable of providing anything which could properly be called knowledge and thus to justify Kant's attitude towards metaphysics. On the other hand materialism, while speaking in the name of science, proceeded to serve up its own highly questionable form of metaphysics and was blind to the limitations placed by Kant to the use which could legitimately be made of scientific concepts. In other words, both the idealists and the materialists justified by their fruits the limitations which Kant had set to man's theoretical knowledge. Was it not desirable, therefore, to turn back to the great thinker of modern times who by a careful critique of human knowledge had succeeded in avoiding the extravagances of metaphysics without falling into the dogmatism of the materialists? It was not a question of following Kant slavishly, but rather of accepting his general position or attitude and working on the lines which he had followed.

The Neo-Kantian movement became a powerful force in German philosophy. It became in fact the academic philosophy or 'School Philosophy' (*Schulphilosophie*), as the Germans say, and by the turn of the century most of the university chairs of philosophy were occupied by people who were in some degree at least representatives of the movement. But Neo-Kantianism assumed pretty well as many shapes as it had representatives. And we cannot possibly mention them all here. Some general indications of the principal lines of thought will have to suffice.

2. A distinction is drawn within the Neo-Kantian movement

between the Schools of Marburg and Baden. The Marburg School can be said to have concentrated principally on logical, epistemological and methodological themes. And it is associated above all with the names of Hermann Cohen (1842–1918) and Paul Natorp (1854–1924).

Cohen, who was nominated professor of philosophy in the university of Marburg in 1876, concerned himself with both the exegesis and the development of Kant's thought. In a wide sense his principal theme is the unity of the cultural consciousness and its evolution, and whether he is writing on logic, ethics, aesthetics or religion[1] it is noticeable that he is constantly referring to the historical development of the ideas which he is treating and to their cultural significance at different stages of their development. This aspect of his thought makes it less formalistic and abstract than Kant's, though the wealth of historical reflections does not facilitate an immediate grasp of Cohen's personal point of view.

In the first volume of his *System of Philosophy* (*System der Philosophie*, 1902–12) Cohen abandons Kant's doctrine of sensibility, the transcendental aesthetic, and devotes himself entirely to the logic of pure thought or pure knowledge (*die reine Erkenntnis*), especially of the pure or *a priori* knowledge which lies at the basis of mathematical physics. True, logic possesses a wider field of application. But 'the fact that logic must have a relation which extends beyond the field of mathematical natural science to the field of the mental sciences (*Geisteswissenschaften*) in no way affects the fundamental relation of logic to knowledge in mathematical natural science'.[2] Indeed, 'the establishment of the relation between metaphysics and mathematical natural science is Kant's decisive act'.[3]

In the second volume, devoted to the ethics of the pure will (*Ethik des reinen Willens*), Cohen remarks that 'ethics, as the doctrine of man, becomes the centre of philosophy'.[4] But the concept of man is complex and comprises the two principal aspects of man, namely as an individual and as a member of society. Thus the deduction of the adequate concept of man moves

[1] In his *System of Philosophy* the idea of God is discussed in the second volume. Cf. also *The Concept of Religion in the System of Philosophy* (*Der Begriff der Religion im System der Philosophie*, Giessen, 1915). The idea of God is depicted as the unifying ideal of truth and perfection.

[2] *System der Philosophie*, I, p. 15 (Berlin, 1922, 3rd edition). The term *Geisteswissenschaften* will be discussed later.

[3] *Ibid.*, p. 9. Cohen is obviously referring to metaphysics in the sense in which Kant accepted metaphysics.

[4] *System der Philosophie*, II, p. 1 (Berlin 1921, 3rd edition).

through several phases or moments until the two aspects are seen as interpenetrating one another. In his discussion of this matter Cohen observes that philosophy has come to look on the State as the embodiment of man's ethical consciousness. But the empirical or actual State is only too evidently the State 'of the ruling classes'.[1] And the power-State (*der Machtstaat*) can become the State which embodies the principles of right and justice (*der Rechtsstaat*) only when it ceases to serve particular class-interests. In other words, Cohen looks forward to a democratic socialist society which will be the true expression of the ethical will of man considered both as a free individual person and as essentially orientated towards social life and the attainment of a common ideal end.

As the whole system of philosophy is conceived 'from the point of view of the unity of the cultural consciousness'[2] and as this consciousness is certainly not completely characterized by science and morals, Cohen devotes the third volume to aesthetics. As Kant saw, a treatment of aesthetics forms an intrinsic part of systematic philosophy.

Natorp, who also occupied a chair at Marburg, was strongly influenced by Cohen. In his *Philosophical Foundations of the Exact Sciences* (*Die philosophischen Grundlagen der exakten Wissenschaften*, 1910) he tries to show that the logical development of mathematics does not require any recourse to intuitions of space and time. His philosophy of mathematics is thus considerably more 'modern' than Kant's. As for ethics, Natorp shared Cohen's general outlook, and on the basis of the idea that the moral law demands of the individual that he should subordinate his activity to the elevation of humanity he developed a theory of social pedagogy. It can also be mentioned that in a well-known work, *Plato's Theory of Ideas* (*Platons Ideenlehre*, 1903), Natorp attempted to establish an affinity between Plato and Kant.

Both Cohen and Natorp endeavoured to overcome the dichotomy between thought and being which seemed to be implied by the Kantian theory of the thing-in-itself. Thus according to Natorp 'both, namely thought and being, exist and have meaning only in their constant mutual relations to one another'.[3] Being is not something static, set over against the activity of thought; it exists only in a process of becoming which is intrinsically related to this activity. And thought is a process which progressively determines

---

[1] *Ibid.*, p. 620.   [2] *System der Philosophie*, III, p. 4 (Berlin, 1922).
[3] *Philosophie*, p. 13 (Göttingen, 1921, 3rd edition).

its object, being. But though Cohen and Natorp sought to unite thought and being as related poles of one process, it would not have been possible for them to eliminate effectively the thing-in-itself without deserting the Kantian standpoint and making the transition to metaphysical idealism.

3. While the Marburg School emphasized inquiry into the logical foundations of the natural sciences, the School of Baden emphasized the philosophy of values and reflection on the cultural sciences. Thus for Wilhelm Windelband[1] (1848–1915) the philosopher is concerned with inquiry into the principles and presuppositions of value-judgments and with the relation between the judging subject or consciousness and the value or norm or ideal in the light of which the judgment is made.

Given this account of philosophy, it is obvious that ethical and aesthetic judgments provide material for philosophical reflection. The moral judgment, for example, is clearly axiological in character rather than descriptive. It expresses what ought to be rather than what is the case in the world. But Windelband includes also logical judgments. For just as ethics is concerned with moral values, so is logic concerned with a value, namely truth. It is not everything which is thought that is true. The true is that which ought to be thought. Thus all logical thought is guided by a value, a norm. The ultimate axioms of logic cannot be proved; but we must accept them if we value truth. And we must accept truth as an objective norm or value unless we are prepared to reject all logical thinking.

Logic, ethics and aesthetics, therefore, presuppose the values of truth, goodness and beauty. And this fact compels us to postulate a transcendental norm-setting or value-positing consciousness which lies, as it were, behind empirical consciousness. Further, inasmuch as in their logical, ethical and aesthetic judgments all individuals appeal implicitly to universal absolute values, this transcendental consciousness forms the living bond between individuals.

Absolute values, however, require a metaphysical anchoring (*eine metaphysische Veränkerung*). That is to say, recognition and affirmation of objective values leads us to postulate a metaphysical foundation in a supersensible reality which we call God. And there thus arises the values of the holy. 'We do not understand by the

---

[1] Windelband, the well-known historian of philosophy, occupied chairs successively at Zürich, Freiburg and Strasbourg. In 1903 he was nominated professor of philosophy at Heidelberg. He was the first major figure of the so-called Baden School.

holy a particular class of universally valid values, such as the classes constituted by the true, the good and the beautiful, but rather all these values themselves in so far as they stand in relation to a supersensible reality.'[1]

Windelband's philosophy of values was developed by Heinrich Rickert (1863–1936), his successor in the chair of philosophy at Heidelberg. Rickert insists that there is a realm of values which possess reality but cannot properly be said to exist.[2] They possess reality in the sense that the subject recognizes and does not create them. But they are not existing things among other existing things. In value-judgments, however, the subject brings together the realm of values and the sensible world, giving valuational significance to things and events. And though values themselves cannot be properly said to exist, we are not entitled to deny the possibility of their being grounded in an eternal divine reality which transcends our theoretical knowledge.

In accordance with his general outlook Rickert emphasizes the place of the idea of value in history. Windelband had maintained[3] that natural science is concerned with things in their universal aspects, as exemplifying types, and with events as repeatable, that is, as exemplifying universal laws, whereas history is concerned with the singular, the unique. The natural sciences are 'nomothetic' or law-positing, whereas history (that is, the science of history) is 'idiographic'.[4] Rickert agrees that the historian is concerned with the singular and unique, but insists that he is interested in persons and events only with reference to values. In other words, the ideal of historiography is a science of culture which depicts historical development in the light of the values recognized by different societies and cultures.

As far as one particular aspect of his thought is concerned, Hugo Münsterberg (1863–1916), who was a friend of Rickert, can be associated with the Baden School of Neo-Kantianism. In his *Philosophy of Values (Philosophie der Werte*, 1908), he expounded

---

[1] *Einleitung in die Philosophie*, p. 390 (Tübingen, 1914).
[2] In his *System of Philosophy (System der Philosophie*, 1921) Rickert attempts to classify values in six groups or spheres; the values of logic (truth values), aesthetics (values of beauty), mysticism (values of impersonal sanctity or holiness), ethics (moral values), erotics (values of happiness) and religion (values of personal sanctity).
[3] In his *History and Natural Science (Geschichte und Naturwissenschaft*, 1894).
[4] A science is not 'idiographic' by reason simply of the fact that it treats of human beings. Empirical psychology, for instance, treats of human beings, but it is none the less a 'nonothetic' science. In Scholastic language, the distinction is formal rather than material.

the idea of giving meaning to the world in terms of a system of values. But as professor of experimental psychology at Harvard he gave his attention mainly to the field of psychology, where he had been strongly influenced by Wundt.

4. We have seen that Windelband regarded the existence of a supersensible divine reality as a postulate of the recognition of absolute values. At the same time he was concerned to argue that the term 'postulate', as used in this context, means much more than 'useful fiction'. There were, however, some Neo-Kantians who interpreted Kant's postulate-theory in a definitely pragmatist sense.

Thus Friedrich Albert Lange (1828–75), who has already been mentioned as a critic of materialism, interpreted metaphysical theories and religious doctrines as belonging to a sphere between knowledge and poetry. If such theories and doctrines are presented as expressing knowledge of reality, they are open to all the objections raised by Kant and other critics. For we cannot have theoretical knowledge of metaphenomenal reality. But if they are interpreted as symbols of a reality which transcends knowledge and if at the same time their value for life is emphasized, they become immune from objections which have point only if cognitive value is claimed for metaphysics and theology.

The useful-fiction version of the theory of postulates was developed in a more systematic way by Hans Vaihinger (1852–1933), author of the celebrated work *The Philosophy of As-If* (*Die Philosophie des Als-Ob*, 1911). With him metaphysical theories and religious doctrines become only particular instances of the application of a general pragmatist view of truth. Only sensations and feelings are real: otherwise the whole of human knowledge consists of 'fictions'. The principles of logic, for example, are fictions which have proved their real utility in experience. And to say that they are undeniably true is to say that they have been found indispensably useful. Hence the question to ask in regard, say, to a religious doctrine is whether it is useful or valuable to act as though it were true rather than whether it is true. Indeed, the question whether the doctrine is 'really' true or not hardly arises, not simply because we have no means of knowing whether it is true or not but rather because the concept of truth is given a pragmatist interpretation.[1]

---

[1] To do Vaihinger justice, it must be added that he endeavours to sort out the different ways in which the concepts of 'as-if' and 'fiction' operate. He does not simply throw the principles of logic, scientific hypotheses and religious doctrines indiscriminately into the same basket.

This pragmatist fictionalism evidently goes a long way beyond the position of Kant. Indeed, it really deprives the Kantian theory of postulates of its significance, inasmuch as it does away with the sharp contrast established by Kant between theoretical knowledge on the one hand and the postulates of the moral law on the other. But though I have included Vaihinger among the Neo-Kantians, he was strongly influenced by the vitalism and fiction-theory of Nietzsche on whom he published a well-known work, *Nietzsche as Philosopher* (*Nietzsche als Philosoph*, 1902).

5. As we have seen, Neo-Kantianism was by no means a homogeneous system of thought. On the one hand we have a philosopher such as Alois Riehl (1844–1924), professor at Berlin, who not only rejected decisively all metaphysics but also maintained that value-theory must be excluded from philosophy in the proper sense.[1] On the other hand we have a philosopher such as Windelband who developed the theory of absolute values in such a way as practically to reintroduce metaphysics, even if he still spoke about 'postulates'.

Such differences naturally become all the more marked in proportion as the field of application of the term 'Neo-Kantian' is extended. For instance, the term has sometimes been applied to Johannes Volkelt (1848–1930), professor of philosophy at Leipzig. But as Volkelt maintained that the human spirit can enjoy an intuitive certitude of its unity with the Absolute, that the Absolute is infinite spirit, and that creation can be conceived as analogous to aesthetic production, the propriety of calling him a Neo-Kantian is obviously questionable. And in point of fact Volkelt was strongly influenced by other German philosophers besides Kant.

It will have been noticed that most of the philosophers mentioned lived into the twentieth century. And the Neo-Kantian movement has indeed had one or two eminent representatives in comparatively recent times. Notable among these is Ernst Cassirer (1874–1945) who occupied chairs successively at Berlin, Hamburg, Göteborg and Yale in the United States. The influence of the Marburg School contributed to directing his attention to problems of knowledge. And the fruit of his studies was his three-volume work on *The Problem of Knowledge in the Philosophy and*

---

[1] According to Riehl, a philosophy which deserves to be called scientific must confine itself to the critique of knowledge as realized in the natural sciences. He did not, of course, deny the importance of values in human life; but he insisted that recognition of them is not, properly speaking, a cognitive act and falls outside the scope of scientific philosophy.

Science of the Modern Era (*Das Erkenntnisproblem in der Philosophie und Wissenschaft der neueren Zeit*, 1906–20). This was followed in 1910 by a work on the concepts of substance and function (*Substanzbegriff und Funktionsbegriff*). Cassirer was struck by the progressive mathematization of physics, and he concluded that in modern physics sensible reality is transformed into and reconstructed as a world of symbols. Further reflection on the function of symbolism led him to develop a large-scale *Philosophy of Symbolic Forms* (*Philosophie der symbolischen Formen*, 1923–9) in which he maintained that it is the use of symbols which distinguishes man from the animals. It is by means of language that man creates a new world, the world of culture. And Cassirer used the idea of symbolism to unlock many doors. For example, he tried to explain the unity of the human person as a functional unity which unites man's different symbolic activities. He devoted special attention to the function of symbolism in the form of myth, and he studied such activities as art and historiography in the light of the idea of symbolic transformation.

But though Neo-Kantianism lasted on into the present century, it can scarcely be called a twentieth-century philosophy. The emergence of new movements and lines of thought has pushed it into the background. It is not so much that the subjects with which it dealt are dead. It is rather that they are treated in different settings or frameworks of thought. Inquiry into the logic of the sciences and the philosophy of values are cases in point. Further, epistemology or theory of knowledge no longer enjoys the central position which Kant and his disciples attributed to it.

This is not to say, of course, that the influence of Kant is exhausted. Far from it. But it is not felt, at any rate on a significant scale, in the continuance of any movement which could appropriately be called Neo-Kantian. Further, Kant's influence is sometimes exercised in a direction which is thoroughly un-Kantian. For example, while positivists believe that Kant was substantially right in excluding metaphysics from the field of knowledge, there is a current of thought in modern Thomism which has interpreted and developed Kant's transcendental method for the very un-Kantian purpose of establishing a systematic metaphysics.

6. This is a convenient place at which to make a few remarks about Wilhelm Dilthey (1833–1911), who occupied chairs successively at Basel, Kiel, Breslau and finally Berlin, where he succeeded Lotze as professor of philosophy. True, though Dilthey entertained

a profound admiration for Kant he cannot properly be described as a Neo-Kantian. He did indeed endeavour to develop a critique of historical reason (*Kritik der historischen Vernunft*) and a corresponding theory of categories. And this activity can be regarded from one point of view as an extension of Kant's critical work to what the Germans call the *Geisteswissenschaften*. At the same time he insisted that the categories of the historical reason, that is, of reason engaged in understanding and interpreting history, are not *a priori* categories which are then applied to some raw materials to constitute history. They arise out of the living penetration by the human spirit of its own objective manifestation in history. And in general, especially from 1883 onwards, Dilthey drew a sharp distinction between the abstractness of Kant's thought and his own concrete approach. However, the fact that we have already had occasion in this chapter to refer to the distinction between the natural sciences and the *Geisteswissenschaften* provides, I think, sufficient reason for mentioning Dilthey here.

The fact that the term 'mental sciences' is a misleading translation of *Geisteswissenschaften* can easily be seen by considering the examples given by Dilthey. Alongside the natural sciences, he says, there has grown up a group of other sciences which together can be called the *Geisteswissenschaften* or *Kulturwissenschaften*. Such are 'history, national economy, the sciences of law and of the State, the science of religion, the study of literature and poetry, of art and music, of philosophical world-views, and systems, finally psychology'.[1] The term 'mental sciences' tends to suggest only psychology. But in a similar list of examples Dilthey does not even mention psychology.[2] The French are accustomed to speak of 'the moral sciences'. But in English this term suggests primarily ethics. Hence I propose to speak of 'the cultural sciences'. It is true that this term would not normally suggest national economy. But it is sufficient to say that the term is being used to cover what Dilthey calls *Kulturwissenschaften* or *Geisteswissenschaften*.

It is clear that we cannot distinguish between the cultural sciences on the one hand and the natural sciences on the other by the simple expedient of saying that the former are concerned with man whereas the latter are not. For physiology is a natural

---

[1] *Gesammelte Schiften*, VII, p. 79. This collection of Dilthey's *Works* will be referred to hereafter as *GS*.

[2] *GS*, VII, p. 70.

science; yet it treats of man. And the same can be said of experimental psychology. Nor can we say simply that the natural sciences are concerned with the physical and sensible, including the physical aspects of man, whereas the cultural sciences are concerned with the psychical, the interior, with that which does not enter into the sensible world. For it is evident that in the study of art, for instance, we are concerned with sensible objects such as pictures rather than with the psychical states of the artists. True, works of art are studied as objectifications of the human spirit. But they are none the less sensible objectifications. Hence we must find some other way of distinguishing between the two groups of sciences.

Man stands in a living felt unity with Nature, and his primary experience of his physical milieu are personal lived experiences (*Erlebnisse*), not objects of reflection from which man detaches himself. To construct the world of natural science, however, man has to prescind from the aspect of his impressions of his physical milieu under which they are his personal lived experiences; he has to put himself out of the picture as far as he can[1] and develop an abstract conception of Nature in terms of relations of space, time, mass and motion. Nature has to become for him the central reality, a law-ordered physical system, which is considered, as it were, from without.

When, however, we turn to the world of history and culture, the objectifications of the human spirit, the situation is different. It is a question of penetration from within. And the individual's personal lived relations with his own social milieu become of fundamental importance. For example, I cannot understand the social and political life of ancient Greece as an objectification of the human spirit if I exclude my own lived experiences of social relations. For these form the basis of my understanding of the social life of any other epoch. True, a certain unity in the historical and social life of humanity is a necessary condition of the possibility of my own *Erlebnisse* providing a key to the understanding of history. But the 'original cell of the historical world,'[2] as Dilthey calls it, is precisely the individual's *Erlebnis*, his lived experience of interaction with his own social milieu.

But though what Dilthey calls *Erlebnisse* are a necessary condition for the development of the cultural sciences, they do not

---

[1] In the science of physiology man regards himself from an impersonal and external point of view as a physical object, as part of Nature.

[2] *GS*, VII, p. 161.

by themselves constitute a science of any kind. Understanding
(*Verstehen*) is also necessary. And what we have to understand in
history and the other cultural sciences is not the human spirit in
its interiority, so to speak, but the external objectification of this
spirit, its objective expression, as in art, law, the State and so on.
We are concerned in other words with the understanding of
objective spirit.[1] And to understand a phase of objective spirit
means relating its phenomena to an inner structure which finds
expression in these phenomena. For example, the understanding of
Roman law involves penetrating beneath the external apparatus,
so to speak, to the spiritual structure which find expression in the
laws. It means penetrating what can be called the spirit of Roman
law, just as understanding Baroque architecture would involve
penetrating the spirit, the structure of purposes and ideals, which
found expression in this style. We can say, therefore, that 'the
cultural sciences rest on the relation of lived experience, expression
and understanding'.[2] Expression is required because the underlying spiritual structure is grasped only in and through its external
expression. Understanding is a movement from the outside to the
inside. And in the process of understanding a spiritual object rises
before our vision, whereas in the natural sciences a physical object
is constructed (though not in the Kantian sense) in the process of
scientific knowledge.

We have seen that a man's personal experience of his own social
milieu is a necessary condition of his being able to live over again
the experience of men in the past. *Erleben* is a condition of the
possibility of *Nacherleben*. And the former renders the latter
possible because of the continuity and fundamental unity of the
developing historical-cultural reality which Dilthey describes as
Life (*Leben*). Cultures are, of course, spatially and temporally
distinct. But if we conceive the reciprocal relations between
persons, under the conditions set by the external world, as a
structural and developing unity which persists throughout spatial
and temporal differentiations, we have the concept of Life. And
in studying this Life the historical reason employs certain categories.
As has already been remarked, these categories are not *a priori*

[1] Dilthey was influenced by Hegel's concept of 'objective spirit'. But his own
use of the term is obviously somewhat different from that of Hegel who classified
art and religion under the heading of 'absolute spirit'. Hegel's use of the term is
connected, of course, with his idealist metaphysics, for which Dilthey had no use.
Further, Dilthey rejected what he regarded as Hegel's *a priori* methods of interpreting history and human culture.
[2] *Auf dem Verhältnis von Erlebnis, Ausdruck und Verstehen*; GS, VII, p. 131.

forms or concepts applied to some raw material: 'they lie in the nature of Life itself'[1] and are conceptualized abstractly in the process of understanding. We cannot determine the exact number of such categories or turn them into a tidy abstract logical scheme for mechanical application. But among them we can name 'meaning, value, purpose, development, ideal'.[2]

These categories should not be understood in a metaphysical sense. It is not a question, for example, of defining the end or meaning of history in the sense of an end which the process of historical development is predestined to attain. It is a question rather of understanding the meaning which Life has for a particular society and the operative ideals which find expression in that society's political and legal institutions, in its art, religion and so on. 'The category of meaning signifies the relations of parts of Life to the whole.'[3] But 'our conception of the meaning of Life is always changing. Each life-plan expresses an idea of the meaning of Life. And the purpose which we set for the future conditions our account of the meaning of the past.'[4] If we say that the task for the future is to achieve this or that, our judgment conditions our understanding of the meaning of the past. And, of course, the other way round as well.

It can hardly be denied that Dilthey's thought contains a prominent element of historical relativism. For example, all world-views or *Weltanschauungen* are partial views of the world, relative to distinct cultural phases. And a study of such world-views or metaphysical systems would exhibit their relativity. At the same time Dilthey does not maintain that there is no universally valid truth at all. And he regards the study of Life, of history as a whole, as a constant approximation to an objective and complete self-knowledge by man. Man is fundamentally an historical being, and he comes to know himself in history. This self-knowledge is never actually complete, but the knowledge which man attains through a study of history is no more purely subjective than is the knowledge attained through the natural sciences. How far Dilthey actually succeeds in overcoming pure historicism is doubtless open to discussion. But he certainly does not intend to assert an extreme relativism which would necessarily invalidate his conception of world-history.

At a time when the natural sciences appear to be threatening to engulf the whole field of knowledge, the question whether and how

[1] *GS*, VII, p. 232.   [2] *Ibid.*   [3] *GS*, VII, p. 233.   [4] *Ibid.*

one could distinguish between the natural and the cultural sciences naturally becomes an issue of importance. And Dilthey's account of the matter was one of the most signal contributions to the discussion. What one thinks of its value seems to depend very largely on one's view of the historian's function. If, for example, one thinks that Dilthey's idea of getting behind the external expression to an inward spiritual structure (the 'spirit' of Roman law, of Baroque art and architecture, and so on) smacks of the transcendental metaphysics which Dilthey himself professed to reject, and if at the same time one disapproves of such transcendental metaphysics, one will hardly be disposed to accept Dilthey's account of the differences between the two groups of sciences. If, however, one thinks that an understanding of man's cultural life does in fact demand this passage from the external phenomena to the operative ideals, purposes and values which are expressed in them, one can hardly deny the relevance of the concepts of *Erleben* and *Nacherleben*. For historical understanding would then necessarily involve a penetration of the past from within, a reliving, so far as this is possible, of past experience, of past attitudes, valuations and ideals. And this would be at any rate one distinguishing characteristic of the historical and cultural sciences. For the physicist can scarcely be said to attempt to relive the experience of an atom or to penetrate behind the relations of infra-atomic particles to a spiritual structure expressed in them. To introduce such notions into mathematical physics would mean its ruin. Conversely, to fail to introduce them into the theory of the cultural sciences is to forget that 'he who explores history is the same who makes history'.[1]

[1] *GS*, VII, p. 278.

CHAPTER XX

THE REVIVAL OF METAPHYSICS

Remarks on inductive metaphysics—Fechner's inductive metaphysics—The teleological idealism of Lotze—Wundt and the relation between science and philosophy—The vitalism of Driesch —Eucken's activism—Appropriation of the past: Trendelenburg and Greek thought; the revival of Thomism.

1. In spite of their own excursions into metaphysics both the materialists and the Neo-Kantians were opposed to the idea of metaphysics as a source of positive knowledge about reality, the former appealing to scientific thinking in justification of their attitude, the latter to Kant's theory of the limitations of man's theoretical knowledge. But there was also a group of philosophers who came to philosophy from some branch or other of empirical science and who were convinced that the scientific view of the world demands completion through metaphysical reflection. They did not believe that a valid system of metaphysics could be worked out *a priori* or without regard to our scientific knowledge. And they tended to look on metaphysical theories as hypothetical and as enjoying a higher or lower degree of probability. Hence in their case we can speak of inductive metaphysics.

Inductive metaphysics has, of course, had its notable representatives, above all perhaps Henri Bergson. But there are probably few people who would be prepared to claim that the German inductive metaphysicians of the second half of the nineteenth century were of the same stature as the great idealists. And one of the weak points of inductive metaphysics in general is that it tends to leave unexamined and unestablished the basic principles on which it rests. However, it is as well to realize that we cannot simply divide the German philosophers into two classes, those who constructed metaphysics in an *a priori* manner and those who rejected metaphysics in the name of science or in that of the limitations of the human mind. For there were also those who attempted to achieve a synthesis between science and metaphysics, not by trying to harmonize science with an already-made philosophical system but rather by trying to show that reflection on the world as known through the particular sciences reasonably leads to metaphysical theories.

2. Among the representatives of inductive metaphysics, we can mention Gustav Theodor Fechner (1801–87), for many years professor of physics at Leipzig and celebrated as one of the founders of experimental psychology. Continuing the studies of E. H. Weber (1795–1878) on the relation between sensation and stimulus, Fechner gave expression in his *Elements of Psychophysics* (*Elemente des Psychophysik*, 1860) to the 'law' which states that the intensity of the sensation varies in proportion to the logarithm of the intensity of the stimulus. Fechner also devoted himself to the psychological study of aesthetics, publishing his *Propaedeutics to Aesthetics* (*Vorschule der Aesthetik*) in 1876.

These studies in exact science did not, however, lead Fechner to materialist conclusions.[1] In psychology he was a parallelist. That is to say, he thought that psychical and physical phenomena correspond in a manner analogous to the relation between a text and its translation or between two translations of a text, as he explained in his *Zend-Avesta* (1851) and in his *Elements of Psychophysics*. In fact, the psychical and the physical were for him two aspects of one reality. And in accordance with this view he postulated the presence of a psychical life even in plants, though of a lower type than in animals.[2] Moreover, he extended this parallelism to the planets and stars and indeed to all material things, justifying this panpsychism by a principle of analogy which states that when objects agree in possessing certain qualities or traits, one is entitled to assume hypothetically that they agree also in other qualities, provided that one's hypotheses do not contradict established scientific facts.

This is hardly a very safe rule of procedure, but, to do Fechner justice, it should be added that he demanded some positive ground for metaphysical theories, as distinct from a mere absence of contradiction of scientific facts. At the same time he also made use of a principle which is not calculated to commend his metaphysics in the eyes of anti-metaphysicians or, for the matter of that, of many metaphysicians themselves. I refer to the principle

[1] As a youth Fechner went through an atheistic phase, but a book by Oken, one of Schelling's disciples, convinced him that materialism and atheism were by no means entailed by an acceptance of exact science.

[2] In 1848 Fechner published *Nanna, or the Soul-Life of Plants* (*Nanna, oder das Seelenleben der Pflanzen*).

which states that an hypothesis which has some positive ground and does not contradict any established fact is to be the more readily embraced the more it renders man happy.[1]

In the spirit of this principle Fechner contrasted what he called the day-view with the night-view, to the detriment of the latter.[2] The night-view, attributed not only to the materialists but also to the Kantians, is the view of Nature as dumb and dead and as affording no real clue to its teleological significance. The day-view is the vision of Nature as a living harmonious unity, animated by a soul. The soul of the universe is God, and the universe considered as a physical system is the divine externality. Fechner thus uses his principle of analogy to extend psychophysical parallelism not only from human beings to other classes of particular things but also from all particular things to the universe as a whole. He employs it also as a basis for belief in personal immortality. Our perceptions persist in memory and enter once again into consciousness. So, we may suppose, our souls persist in the divine memory but without simple absorption in the Deity.

Panpsychism is indeed a very ancient theory, and it is one which tends to recur. It is far from being Fechner's private invention. However, it is difficult to avoid the impression that when Fechner leaves the purely scientific sphere and embarks on philosophy he becomes a kind of poet of the universe. But it is interesting to observe the pragmatist element in his thought. We have seen that in his view, other things being equal, the theory which makes for happiness is to be preferred to the theory which does not. But Fechner does not make it a matter simply of individual preference. Another of his principles states that the probability of a belief increases in proportion to the length of its survival, especially if acceptance of it increases together with the development of human culture. And it is not surprising that William James derived inspiration from Fechner.

3. A much more impressive figure as a philosopher is Rudolf Hermann Lotze (1817–81) who studied medicine and philosophy at Leipzig, where he also listened to Fechner's lectures on physics. In 1844 he was nominated professor of philosophy at Göttingen and in 1881, shortly before his death, he accepted a chair of philosophy at Berlin. Besides works on physiology, medicine and

---

[1] Happiness for Fechner does not mean simply sense-pleasure. It includes joy in the beautiful, the good and the true and in the religious feeling of union with God.

[2] Cf. *Die Tagesansicht gegenüber der Nachtansicht*, 1879.

psychology he published a considerable number of philosophical writings.[1] In 1841 there appeared a *Metaphysics*, in 1843 a *Logic*, in 1856–64 a large three-volume work entitled *Microcosm* (*Mikrokosmus*) on philosophical anthropology, in 1868 a history of aesthetics in Germany and in 1874–9 a *System of Philosophy* (*System der Philosophie*). After Lotze's death a series of volumes were published which were based on lecture-notes taken by his students. These covered in outline the fields of psychology, ethics, philosophy of religion, philosophy of Nature, logic, metaphysics, aesthetics and the history of post-Kantian philosophy in Germany. A three-volume collection of his minor writings (*Kleine Schriften*) appeared in 1885–91.

According to Lotze himself it was his inclination to poetry and art which originally turned his mind to philosophy. Hence it can be somewhat misleading to say that he came to philosophy from science. At the same time he had a scientific training at the university of Leipzig, where he enrolled in the faculty of medicine, and it is characteristic of his systematic philosophical thinking that he presupposed and took seriously what he called the mechanical interpretation of Nature.

For example, while recognizing, of course, the evident fact that there are differences in behaviour between living and non-living things, Lotze refused to allow that the biologist must postulate some special vital principle which is responsible for the maintenance and operation of the organism. For science, which seeks everywhere to discover connections which can be formulated in terms of general laws, 'the realm of life is not divided from that of inorganic Nature by a higher force peculiar to itself, setting itself up as something alien above other modes of action . . . but simply by the peculiar kind of connection into which its manifold constituents are woven. . . .'[2] That is to say, the characteristic behaviour of the organism can be explained in terms of the combination of material elements in certain ways. And it is the biologist's business to push this type of explanation as far as he can and not to have recourse to the expedient of invoking special vital principles. 'The connection of vital phenomena demands throughout a mechanical treatment which explains life not by a peculiar principle of operation but by

---

[1] Some of his medico-psychological publications, such as his *Medical Psychology or Physiology of the Soul* (*Medizinische Psychologie oder Physiologie der Seele*, 1852) are of importance for his philosophy.
[2] *Mikrokosmus*, Bk. i, ch. 3, sect. i (in 5th German edition, Leipzig, 1896–1909, i, p. 58).

a characteristic application of the general principles of physical process.'¹

This mechanical interpretation of Nature, which is necessary for the development of science, should be extended as far as possible. And this is as true of psychology as of biology. At the same time we are certainly not entitled to rule out *a priori* the possibility of finding facts of experience which limit the applicability of the mechanical view. And we do find such facts. For example, the unity of consciousness, which manifests itself in the simple act of comparing two presentations and judging them to be like or unlike, at once sets a limit to the possibility of describing man's psychical life in terms of causal relations between distinct psychical events. It is not a question of inferring the existence of a soul as a kind of unalterable psychical atom. It is 'the fact of the unity of consciousness which is *eo ipso* at the same time the fact of the existence of a substance',² namely the soul. In other words, to affirm the existence of the soul is neither to postulate a logical condition of the unity of consciousness nor to infer from this unity an occult entity. For recognition of the unity of consciousness is at the same time recognition of the existence of the soul, though the proper way of describing the soul is obviously a matter for further reflection.

Thus there are certain empirical facts which set a limit to the field of application of the mechanical interpretation of Nature. And it is no good suggesting that further scientific advance can abolish these facts or show that they are not facts. This is quite evident in the case of the unity of consciousness. For any further scientific advances in empirical and physiological psychology depend on and presuppose the unity of consciousness. And as for Lotze reflection on the unity of consciousness shows that psychical states must be referred to an immaterial reality as their subject, the point at which the limitation of the mechanical interpretation of man's psychical life becomes decisively evident is also the point at which the need for a metaphysical psychology becomes clear.

It is not, however, Lotze's intention to construct a two-storey system, as it were, in which the mechanical interpretation of material Nature would form the lower storey and a superimposed metaphysics of spiritual reality the higher. For he argues that even as regards Nature itself the mechanical interpretation gives but a

¹ *System der Philosophie*, II, p. 447 (Leipzig, 1912; Bk. 2, ch. 8, sect. 229).
² *Ibid.*, p. 481 (sect. 243).

one-sided picture, valid indeed for scientific purposes but inadequate from a metaphysical point of view.

The mechanical interpretation of Nature presupposes the existence of distinct things which are in causal relations of interaction and each of which is relatively permanent, that is, in relation to its own changing states. But interaction between A and B is possible, according to Lotze, only if they are members of an organic unity. And permanence in relation to changing states can best be interpreted on an analogy with the permanent subject of change which is best known to us, namely the human soul as revealed in the unity of consciousness. We are thus led not only to the concept of Nature as an organic unity but also to the idea of things as in some sense psychical or spiritual entities. Further, the ground of this unity must be conceived on an analogy with the highest thing known to us, namely the human spirit. Hence the world of finite spirits is to be conceived as the self-expression of infinite Spirit or God. All things are immanent in God, and what the scientist sees as mechanical causality is simply the expression of the divine activity. God does not create a world and then sit back, as it were, while the world obeys the laws he has given it. The so-called laws are the divine action itself, the mode of God's operation.

From a rather hard-headed starting-point in the mechanical conception of Nature Lotze thus goes on to expound a metaphysical theory which recalls the monadology of Leibniz and which entails the conclusion that space is phenomenal. But though Lotze did indeed derive stimulus from Leibniz and Herbart, he also drew inspiration, as he himself says, from the ethical idealism of Fichte. He was not a disciple of Fichte, and he disapproved of the *a priori* method of the post-Kantian idealists, especially of Hegel. At the same time Fichte's conception of the ultimate principle expressing itself in finite subjects with a view to a moral end exercised a powerful attraction on Lotze's mind. And it is to the philosophy of values that he turns for the key to the meaning of creation. Sense experience tells us nothing about the final cause of the world. But that the world cannot be without end or purpose is a moral conviction. And we must conceive God as expressing himself in the world for the realization of value, of a moral ideal which is being constantly fulfilled in and through the divine activity. As for our knowledge of what this end or aim is, we can come to some knowledge of it only by an analysis of the notion of the Good, of the highest value. A phenomenological analysis of values is thus an integral part of philosophy. Indeed, our belief in God's existence ultimately rests on our moral experience and appreciation of value.[1] God is for Lotze a personal Being. The notion of impersonal spirit he dismisses as contrary to reason. As for the view of Fichte and other philosophers that personality is necessarily finite and limited and so cannot be predicated of the infinite, Lotze replies that it is only infinite spirit which can be personal in the fullest sense of the word: finitude involves a limitation of personality. At the same time all things are immanent in God, and, as we have seen, mechanical causality is simply the divine action. In this sense God is the Absolute. But he is not the Absolute in the sense that finite spirits can be considered modifications of the divine substance. For each exists 'for itself' and is a centre of activity. From a metaphysical point of view, says Lotze, pantheism could be accepted as a possible view of the world only if it renounced all inclination to conceive the infinite as anything else but Spirit. For the spatial world is phenomenal and cannot be identified with God under the name of Substance. From a religious point of view 'we do not share the inclination which commonly governs the pantheistic imagination to suppress all that is finite in favour of the infinite. . . .'[2]

Lotze's teleological idealism has obvious affinities with the post-Kantian idealist movement. And his vision of the world as an organic unity which is the expression of infinite Spirit's realization of ideal value may be said to have given fresh life to idealist thought. But he did not believe that we can deduce a metaphysical system, descriptive of existent reality, from ultimate principles of thought or self-evident truths. For the so-called eternal truths of logic are hypothetical in character, in the sense that they state conditions of possibility. Hence they cannot be used as premises for an *a priori* deduction of existent reality. Nor can human beings achieve an absolute point of view and describe the whole process of reality in the light of a final end which they already know. Man's metaphysical interpretation of the universe must be based on

---

[1] When discussing the traditional proofs of God's existence, Lotze remarks that the immediate moral conviction that that which is greatest, most beautiful and most worthy has reality lies at the foundation of the ontological argument, just as it is the factor which carries the teleological argument far beyond any conclusions which could be logically derived from its assumptions. *Mikrokosmus*, Bk. IX, ch. 4, sect. 2 (5th German edition, III, p. 561).

[2] *Mikrokosmus*, Bk. IX, ch. 4, sect. 3 (5th German edition, III, p. 569).

experience. And, as we have seen, Lotze attributes a profound significance to the experience of value. For it is this experience which lies at the root of the conviction that the world cannot be simply a mechanical system without purpose or ethical value but must be conceived as progressively realizing a spiritual end. This is not to say that the metaphysician, once armed with this conviction, is entitled to indulge in flights of the imagination uncontrolled by logical thinking about the nature of reality. But in the philosopher's systematic interpretation of the universe there will inevitably be much that is hypothetical.

The influence of Lotze was considerable. For instance, in the field of psychology it was felt by Carl Stumpf (1848–1936) and Franz Brentano, of whom something will be said in the last chapter. But it was perhaps in the field of the philosophy of values that his influence was most felt. Among a number of English thinkers who derived stimulus from Lotze we may mention in particular James Ward (1843–1925). In America the idealist Josiah Royce (1855–1916) was influenced by Lotze's personalistic idealism.

4. Among the German philosophers of the second half of the nineteenth century who came from science to philosophy mention must be made of Wilhelm Wundt (1832–1920). After studying medicine Wundt gave himself to physiological and psychological research, and in 1863–4 he published a series of *Lectures on the Human and Animal Soul* (*Vorlesungen über die Menschen- und Tierseele*). After nine years as an 'extraordinary' professor of physiology at Heidelberg he was nominated to the chair of inductive philosophy at Zürich in 1874. In the following year he moved to Leipzig where he occupied the chair of philosophy until 1918. And it was at Leipzig that he founded the first laboratory of experimental psychology. The first edition of his *Outlines of Physiological Psychology* (*Grundzüge der physiologischen Psychologie*) was published in 1874. In the philosophical field he published a two-volume *Logic* in 1880–3,[1] an *Ethics* in 1886, a *System of Philosophy* in 1889,[2] and a *Metaphysics* in 1907. But he did not abandon his psychological studies, and in 1904 he published a two-volume *Psychology of Peoples* (*Völkerpsychologie*) of which a new and greatly enlarged edition appeared in 1911–20.

When Wundt speaks about experimental psychology and the experimental method he is generally referring to introspective

---

[1] An enlarged edition in 3 vols. appeared in 1919–21.
[2] A two-volume edition appeared in 1919.

psychology and the introspective method. Or, more accurately, he regards introspection as the appropriate method of investigation for individual, as distinct from social, psychology. Introspection reveals, as its immediate data, a connection of psychical events or processes, not a substantial soul, nor a set of relatively permanent objects. For no one of the events revealed by introspection remains precisely the same from one moment to another. At the same time there is a unity of connection. And just as the natural scientist tries to establish the causal laws which operate in the physical sphere, so should the introspective psychologist endeavour to ascertain the fundamental laws of relation and development which give content to the idea of psychical causality. In interpreting man's psychical life Wundt lays emphasis on volitional rather than on cognitive elements. The latter are not denied, of course, but the volitional element is taken as fundamental and as providing the key for the interpretation of man's psychical life as a whole.

When we turn from the psychical life as manifested in introspection to human societies, we find common and relatively permanent products such as language, myth and custom. And the social psychologist is called on to investigate the psychical energies which are responsible for these common products and which together form the spirit or soul of a people. This spirit exists only in and through individuals, but it is not reducible to them when taken separately. In other words, through the relations of individuals in a society there arises a reality, the spirit of a people, which expresses itself in common spiritual products. And social psychology studies the development of these realities. It also studies the evolution of the concept of humanity and of the general spirit of man which manifests itself, for example, in the rise of universal instead of purely national religions, in the development of science, in the growth of the idea of common human rights, and so on. Wundt thus allots to social psychology a far-reaching programme. For its task is to study from a psychological point of view the development of human society and culture in all its principal manifestations.

Philosophy, according to Wundt, presupposes natural science and psychology. It builds upon them and incorporates them into a synthesis. At the same time philosophy goes beyond the sciences. Yet there can be no reasonable objection to this procedure on the ground that it is contrary to the scientific spirit. For in the particular sciences themselves explanatory hypotheses are constructed which go beyond the empirical data. At the level of knowledge of the understanding (*Verstandeserkenntnis*), the level at which sciences such as physics and psychology arise, presentations are synthesized with the aid of logical method and techniques. At the level of rational knowledge (*Vernunfterkenntnis*) philosophy, especially metaphysics, tries to construct a systematic synthesis of the results of the previous level. At all levels of cognition the mind aims at absence of contradiction in a progressive synthesis of presentations, which form the fundamental point of departure for human knowledge.

In his general metaphysical picture of reality Wundt conceives the world as the totality of individual agents or active centres which are to be regarded as volitional unities of different grades. These volitional unities form a developing series which tends towards the emergence of a total spirit (*Gesamtgeist*). In more concrete terms, there is a movement towards the complete spiritual unification of man or humanity, and individual human beings are called on to act in accordance with the values which contribute to this end. Metaphysics and ethics are thus closely connected, and both receive a natural completion in religious idealism. For the concept of a cosmic process directed towards an ideal leads to a religious view of the world.

5. We have seen that though Lotze went on to develop a metaphysical theory about the spiritual nature of reality, he would not allow that the biologist has any warrant for setting aside the mechanical interpretation of Nature which is proper to the empirical sciences and postulating a special vital principle to explain the behaviour of the organism. When, however, we turn to Hans Driesch (1867–1941) we find this onetime pupil of Haeckel being led by his biological and zoological researches to a theory of dynamic vitalism and to the conviction that finality is an essential category in biology. He became convinced that in the organic body there is an autonomous active principle which directs the vital processes and which cannot be accounted for by a purely mechanistic theory of life.

To this principle Driesch gave the name of *entelechy*, making use of an Aristotelian term. But he was careful to refrain from describing the entelechy or vital principle as psychical. For this term, he considered, is inappropriate in view both of its human associations and of its ambiguity.

Having formed the concept of entelechies Driesch proceeded to blossom out as a philosopher. In 1907–8 he gave the Gifford Lectures at Aberdeen, and in 1909 he published his two-volume *Philosophy of the Organic (Philosophie des Organischen)*. In 1911 he obtained a chair of philosophy at Heidelberg, and subsequently he was professor first at Cologne and later at Leipzig. In his general philosophy[1] the concept of the organism was extrapolated to apply to the world as a whole, and his metaphysics culminated in the idea of a supreme entelechy, God. The picture was that of a cosmic entelechy, the teleological activity of which is directed towards the realization of the highest possible level of knowledge. But the question of theism or pantheism was left in suspense.

Through his attack on mechanistic biology Driesch exercised a considerable influence. But of those who agreed with him that a mechanistic interpretation was inadequate and that the organism manifests finality by no means all were prepared to accept the theory of entelechies. To mention two Englishmen who, like Driesch, came to philosophy from science and in due course delivered series of Gifford Lectures, Lloyd Morgan (1852–1936) rejected Driesch's neo-vitalism, while J. A. Thomson (1861–1933) tried to steer a middle path between what he regarded as the metaphysical Scylla of the entelechy theory and the Charybdis of mechanistic materialism.

6. The philosophers whom we have been considering in this chapter had a scientific training and either turned from the study of some particular science or sciences to philosophical speculation or combined the two activities. We can now consider briefly a thinker, Rudolf Eucken (1846–1926), who certainly did not come to philosophy from science but who was already interested as a school-boy[2] in philosophical and religious problems and who devoted himself to the study of philosophy at the universities of Göttingen and Berlin. In 1871 he was appointed professor of philosophy at Basel, and in 1874 he accepted the chair of philosophy at Jena.

Eucken had little sympathy with the view of philosophy as a purely theoretical interpretation of the world. Philosophy was for him, as for the Stoics, a wisdom for life. Further, it was for him an expression of life. In his opinion the interpretation of philosophical systems as so many life-views (*Lebensanschauungen*) contained a

---

[1] In epistemology Driesch was influenced by Kant, but he departed from Kantian doctrine by attributing an objective character to the categories, such as to render possible a metaphysics of reality.

[2] At school Eucken came under the influence of a certain Wilhelm Reuter who was a disciple of the philosopher Krause.

profound truth, namely that philosophy is rooted in life and continuous with it. At the same time he wished to overcome the fragmentation of philosophy, its falling apart into purely personal reactions to life and ideals for life. And he concluded that if philosophy, as the expression of life, is to possess a more than subjective and purely personal significance, it must be the expression of a universal life which rescues man from his mere particularity.

This universal life is identified by Eucken with what he calls Spiritual Life (*das Geistesleben*). From the purely naturalistic point of view psychical life 'forms a mere means and instrument for the preservation of beings in the hard fight for existence'.[1] Spiritual Life, however, is an active reality which produces a new spiritual world. 'There thus arise whole fields such as science and art, law and morals, and they develop their own contents, their own motive forces, their own laws.'[2] Provided that he breaks with the naturalistic and egoistic point of view man can rise to a participation in this Spiritual Life. He then becomes 'more than a mere point; a universal Life becomes for him his own life'.[3]

Spiritual Life, therefore, is an active reality which operates in and through man. And it can be regarded as the movement of reality towards the full actualization of Spirit. It is, as it were, reality organizing itself from within into a spiritual unity. And as it is through participation in this Life that man achieves real personality, the Life which is the foundation of human personality can be regarded as being itself personal. It is in fact God. 'The concept of God receives here the meaning of an absolute Spiritual Life,'[4] 'the Spiritual Life which attains to complete independence and at the same time to the embracing in itself of all reality.'[5]

Philosophy is or should be the expression of this Life. 'The synthesis of the manifold which philosophy undertakes must not be imposed on reality from without but should proceed out of reality itself and contribute to its development.'[6] That is to say, philosophy should be the conceptual expression of the unifying activity of the Spiritual Life, and it should at the same time contribute to the development of this Life by enabling men to understand their relation to it.

[1] *Einführung in eine Philosophie des Geisteslebens*, p. 9 (Leipzig, 1908).
[2] *Ibid.*, p. 8.
[3] *Grundlinien einer neuen Lebensanschauung*, p. 117 (Leipzig, 1907).
[4] *Der Wahrheitsgehalt der Religion*, p. 138 (Leipzig, 1905, 2nd edition).
[5] *Ibid.*, p. 150.
[6] *Einführung in eine Philosophie des Geisteslebens*, p. 10.

The concept of *das Geistesleben* naturally recalls to mind the philosophy of Hegel. And from this point of view Eucken's thought can be described as neo-idealism. But whereas Hegel emphasized the conceptual solution of problems, Eucken is inclined to say that the important problems of life are solved by action. A man attains to truth in so far as he overcomes the pull of his non-spiritual nature and participates actively in the one Spiritual Life. Hence Eucken described his philosophy as 'activism'.[1] As for the affinities between his own philosophy and pragmatism, Eucken was inclined to interpret pragmatism as involving the reduction of truth to an instrument in the service of 'mere man's' egoistic search for satisfaction and thus as favouring the very fragmentation of philosophy which he wished to overcome. In his view truth is that towards which Spiritual Life actively strives.

In his own day Eucken had a considerable reputation. But what he offers is obviously one more world-view, one more *Lebensanschauung*, rather than an effective overcoming of the conflict of systems. And his philosophy is one in which the element of precise statement and explanation is by no means always conspicuous. It is all very well, for example, to talk about problems being solved by action. But when it is a question of theoretical problems, the concept of solution through action requires much more careful analysis than is given it by Eucken.

7. Hegel, as we have seen, gave a powerful impetus to the study of the history of philosophy. But for him the history of philosophy was absolute idealism in the making or, to express the matter metaphysically, absolute Spirit's progressive understanding of itself. And the historian of philosophy who is thoroughly imbued with Hegelian principles sees in the development of philosophical thought a constant dialectical advance, later systems presupposing and subsuming in themselves earlier phases of thought. It is understandable, however, that there should be other philosophers who look back to past phases of thought as valuable sources of insights which have been later forgotten or overlooked rather than taken up and elevated in succeeding systems.

As an example of the philosophers who have emphasized the objective study of the past with a view to rethinking and re-appropriating its perennially valuable elements we can mention Adolf Trendelenburg (1802-72) who occupied the chair of philosophy at Berlin for many years and exercised a considerable

[1] *Einführung in eine Philosophie des Geisteslebens*, p. 155.

influence on the development of historical studies. He applied himself especially to the study of Aristotle, though his historical writings dealt also with Spinoza, Kant, Hegel and Herbart. A vigorous opponent both of Hegel and Herbart, he contributed to the decline of the former's prestige in the middle of the century. And he directed men's attention to the perennially valuable sources of European philosophy in Greek thought, though he was convinced that the insights of Greek philosophy needed to be rethought and appropriated in the light of the modern scientific conception of the world.

Trendelenburg's own philosophy, described by him as the 'organic world-view' (*organische Weltanschauung*) was developed in his two-volume *Logical Inquiries* (*Logische Untersuchungen*, 1840). It owed much to Aristotle, and, as in Aristotelianism, the idea of finality was fundamental. At the same time Trendelenburg endeavoured to reconcile Aristotle and Kant by depicting space, time and the categories as forms both of being and of thought. He also attempted to give a moral foundation to the ideas of right and law in his works on *the Moral Idea of Right* (*Die sittliche Idee des Rechts*, 1849) and *Natural Right on the Foundation of Ethics* (*Naturrecht auf dem Grunde der Ethik*, 1860).

Aristotelian studies were also pursued by Gustav Teichmüller (1832–88) who came under Trendelenburg's influence at Berlin. But Teichmüller subsequently developed a philosophy inspired by Leibniz and Lotze, especially by the former.

Among Trendelenburg's pupils was Otto Willmann (1839–1920) whose mind moved from the thought of Aristotle through criticism of both idealism and materialism to Thomist philosophy. And some allusion can be made here to the reappropriation of mediaeval philosophy, in particular of the thought of St. Thomas Aquinas. It is indeed rather difficult to treat this subject simply within the context of German philosophy in the nineteenth century. For the rise of Thomism was a phenomenon within the intellectual life of the Catholic Church in general, and it can hardly be claimed that the German contribution was the most important. At the same time the subject cannot be simply passed over in silence.

In the seventeenth, eighteenth and early part of the nineteenth centuries philosophy in ecclesiastical seminaries and teaching institutions generally tended to take the form of an uninspired Scholastic Aristotelianism amalgamated with ideas taken from other currents of thought, notably Cartesianism and, later, the philosophy of Wolff. And it lacked the intrinsic vigour which was required to make its presence felt in the intellectual world at large. Further, in the first half of the nineteenth century there were a number of Catholic thinkers in France, Italy and Germany whose ideas, developed either in dialogue with or under the influence of contemporary thought, seemed to the ecclesiastical authorities to compromise, whether directly or indirectly, the integrity of the Catholic faith. Thus in Germany Georg Hermes (1775–1831), professor of theology first at Münster and then at Bonn, was judged by the Church to have adopted far too much from the philosophers whom he tried to oppose, such as Kant and Fichte, and to have thrown Catholic dogma into the melting-pot of philosophical speculation. Again, in his enthusiasm for the revivification of theology Anton Günther (1783–1863) attempted to make use of the Hegelian dialectic to explain and prove the doctrine of the Trinity,[1] while Jakob Froschhammer (1821–93), a priest and a professor of philosophy at Munich, was judged to have subordinated supernatural faith and revelation to idealist philosophy.[2]

In the course of the nineteenth century, however, a number of Catholic thinkers raised the call for a reappropriation of mediaeval thought, and especially of the theological-philosophical synthesis developed in the thirteenth century by St. Thomas Aquinas. As far as Germany was concerned, the revival of interest in Scholasticism in general and Thomism in particular owed much to the writings of men such as Joseph Kleutgen (1811–83), Albert Stöckl (1832–95) and Konstantin Gutberlet (1837–1928). Most of Gutberlet's works appeared after the publication in 1879 of Pope Leo XIII's encyclical letter *Aeterni Patris* in which the Pope asserted the permanent value of Thomism and urged Catholic philosophers to draw their inspiration from it while at the same time developing it to meet modern needs. But Stöckl's *Textbook of Philosophy* (*Lehrbuch der Philosophie*) had appeared in 1868, and the first editions of Kleutgen's *The Theology of Early Times Defended* (*Die Theologie der Vorzeit verteidigt*) and *The Philosophy of Early Times Defended* (*Die Philosophie der Vorzeit verteidigt*) had appeared respectively in 1853–60 and 1860–3. Hence it is not quite accurate to say that Leo XIII inaugurated the revival of

---

[1] Accused by the Church of rationalism, Günther submitted to her judgment.

[2] Froschhammer, who refused to submit to ecclesiastical authority when his views were censured, was later one of the opponents of the dogma of papal infallibility.

Thomism. What he did was to give a powerful impetus to an already existing movement.

The revival of Thomism naturally demanded a real knowledge and understanding not only of the thought of Aquinas in particular but also of mediaeval philosophy in general. And it is natural that the first phase of the revival should have been succeeded by specialist studies in the sphere, such as we associate with the names of Clemens Baeumker (1853–1924) and Martin Grabmann (1875–1949) in Germany, of Maurice De Wulf (1867–1947) in Belgium, and of Pierre Mandonnet (1858–1936) and Étienne Gilson (b. 1884) in France.

At the same time, if Thomism was to be presented as a living system of thought and not as possessing a purely historical interest, it had to be shown, first that it was not entangled with antiquated physics and discarded scientific hypotheses, and secondly that it was capable of development and of throwing light on philosophical problems as they present themselves to the modern mind. In the fulfilment of the first task much was accomplished by the work of Cardinal Mercier (1851–1926) and his collaborators and successors at the university of Louvain.[1] In regard to the fulfilment of the second task we can mention the names of Joseph Geyser (1869–1948) in Germany and of Jacques Maritain (b. 1882) in France.

Having established itself as, so to speak, a respectable system of thought, Thomism had then to show that it was capable of assimilating the valuable elements in other philosophies without self-destruction. But this is a theme which belongs to the history of Thomist thought in the present century.

---

[1] Mercier was not concerned simply with showing that Thomism did not conflict with the sciences. He envisaged the development of Thomism in close connection with the positive and purely objective study of the sciences. An eminent representative of the fulfilment of Mercier's project is the Louvain psychologist Albert Michotte (b. 1881).

CHAPTER XXI

NIETZSCHE (1)

*Life and writings—The phases of Nietzsche's thought as 'masks'
—Nietzsche's early writings and the critique of contemporary
culture—The critique of morals—Atheism and its consequences.*

1. As we have already strayed into the twentieth century, it may
seem inappropriate to reserve to this stage of the volume two
chapters on a philosopher who died physically in 1900 and, as far
as writing was concerned, some ten years previously. But though
this procedure is questionable from the chronological point of view,
one can also argue in favour of closing a volume on nineteenth-
century German philosophy with a thinker who died in 1900 but
whose influence was not fully felt until the present century.
Whatever one may think about Nietzsche's ideas, one cannot
question his vast reputation and the power of his ideas to act like
a potent wine in the minds of a good many people. And this is
something which can hardly be said about the materialists, Neo-
Kantians and the inductive metaphysicians whom we have been
considering in the foregoing chapters.

Friedrich Wilhelm Nietzsche was born on October 15th, 1844,
at Röcken in Prussian Saxony. His father, a Lutheran pastor, died
in 1849, and the boy was brought up at Naumburg in the feminine
and pious society of his mother, his sister, a grandmother and two
aunts. From 1854 to 1858 he studied at the local *Gymnasium*, and
from 1858 to 1864 he was a pupil at the celebrated boarding-school
at Pforta. His admiration for the Greek genius was awakened during
his schooldays, his favourite classical authors being Plato and
Aeschylus. He also tried his hand at poetry and music.

In October 1864 Nietzsche went to the university of Bonn in
company with his school friend Paul Deussen, the future orientalist
and philosopher. But in the autumn of the following year he
moved to Leipzig to continue his philological studies under
Ritschl. He formed an intimate friendship with Erwin Rohde, then
a fellow student, later a university professor and author of *Psyche*.
By this time Nietzsche had abandoned Christianity, and when at
Leipzig he made the acquaintance of Schopenhauer's main work

one of the features which attracted him was, as he himself said, the author's atheism.

Nietzsche had published some papers in the *Rheinisches Museum*, and when the university of Basel asked Ritschl whether their author was a suitable person to occupy the chair of philosophy at Basel, Ritschl had no hesitation in giving an unqualified testimonial on behalf of his favourite pupil. The result was that Nietzsche found himself appointed a university professor before he had even taken the doctorate.[1] And in May 1869 he delivered his inaugural lecture on *Homer and Classical Philology*. On the outbreak of the Franco-Prussian war Nietzsche joined the ambulance corps of the German army; but illness forced him to abandon this work, and after an insufficient period of convalescence he resumed his professional duties at Basel.

Nietzsche's great consolation at Basel lay in his visits to Richard Wagner's villa on the lake of Lucerne. He had already been seized with admiration for Wagner's music while he was still a student at Leipzig, and his friendship with the composer had a possibly unfortunate effect on his writing. In *The Birth of Tragedy from the Spirit of Music* (*Die Geburt der Tragödie aus dem Geiste der Musik*) which appeared in 1872, he first drew a contrast between Greek culture before and after Socrates, to the disadvantage of the latter, and then argued that contemporary German culture bore a strong resemblance to Greek culture after Socrates and that it could be saved only if it were permeated with the spirit of Wagner. Not unnaturally, the work met with an enthusiastic reception from Wagner, but the philologists reacted somewhat differently to Nietzsche's views about the origins of Greek tragedy. Wilamowitz-Moellendorff in particular, then a young man, launched a devastating attack against the book. And not even Rohde's loyal defence of his friend could save Nietzsche from losing credit in the world of classical scholarship. Not that this matters much to us today. For it is Nietzsche as philosopher, moralist and psychologist who interests us, not as professor of philology at Basel.

In the period 1873-6 Nietzsche published four essays with the common title *Untimely Meditations* or *Considerations* (*Unzeitgemässe Betrachtungen*) which is rendered as *Thoughts out of Season* in the English translation of his works. In the first he vehemently attacked the unfortunate David Strauss as a representative of German culture-philistinism, while in the second he attacked the

[1] The university of Leipzig thereupon conferred the degree without examination.

idolization of historical learning as a substitute for a living culture. The third essay was devoted to extolling Schopenhauer as an educator, to the disadvantage of the university professors of philosophy, while the fourth depicted Wagner as originating a rebirth of the Greek genius.

By 1876, the date of publication of the fourth essay, entitled *Richard Wagner in Bayreuth*, Nietzsche and Wagner had already begun to drift apart.[1] And his break with the composer represented the end of the first phase or period in Nietzsche's development. If in the first period he decries Socrates, the rationalist, in the second he tends to exalt him. In the first period culture, and indeed human life in general, is depicted as finding its justification in the production of the genius, the creative artist, poet and musician: in the second Nietzsche prefers science to poetry, questions all accepted beliefs and pretty well plays the part of a rationalistic philosopher of the French Enlightenment.

Characteristic of this second period is *Human, All-too-Human* (*Menschliches, Allzumenschliches*) which was originally published in three parts, 1878–9. In a sense the work is positivistic in outlook. Nietzsche attacks metaphysics in an indirect manner, trying to show that the features of human experience and knowledge which had been supposed to necessitate metaphysical explanations or to justify a metaphysical superstructure are capable of explanation on materialistic lines. For instance, the moral distinction between good and bad had its origin in the experience of some actions as beneficial to society and of others as detrimental to it, though in the course of time the utilitarian origin of the distinction was lost sight of. Again, conscience originates in a belief in authority: it is the voice not of God but of parents and educators.

A combination of bad health and dissatisfaction, amounting to disgust, with his professional duties led Nietzsche to resign from his chair at Basel in the spring of 1879. And for the next ten years he led a wandering life, seeking health in various places in Switzerland and Italy, with occasional visits to Germany.

In 1881 Nietzsche published *The Dawn of Day* (*Morgenröte*) in which, as he declared, he opened his campaign against the morality of self-renunciation. And this was followed in 1882[2] by *Joyful*

---

[1] Nietzsche thought, no doubt rightly, that Wagner regarded him as a tool to promote the cause of Wagnerism. But he also came to feel that the real Wagner was not all that he had imagined him to be. The publication of *Parsifal* was for Nietzsche the last straw.

[2] The fifth part of *Joyful Wisdom* was not added until 1887.

Wisdom (*Die fröhliche Wissenschaft*) in which we find the idea of Christianity as hostile to life. The report that God is dead, as Nietzsche puts it, opens up vast horizons to free spirits. Neither book was successful. Nietzsche sent a copy of *The Dawn of Day* to Rohde, but his former friend did not even acknowledge it. And the indifference with which his writings were met in Germany was not calculated to increase Nietzsche's fondness for his fellow countrymen.

In 1881 the idea of the eternal recurrence came to Nietzsche while he was at Sils-Maria in the Engadine. In infinite time there are periodic cycles in which all that has been is repeated over again. This somewhat depressing idea was scarcely new, but it came to Nietzsche with the force of an inspiration. And he conceived the plan of presenting the ideas which were fermenting in his mind through the lips of the Persian sage Zarathustra. The result was his most famous work, *Thus Spake Zarathustra* (*Also sprach Zarathustra*). The first two parts were published separately in 1883. The third, in which the doctrine of the eternal recurrence was proclaimed, appeared at the beginning of 1884, and the fourth part was published early in 1885.

Zarathustra, with its ideas of Superman and the transvaluation of values, expresses the third phase of Nietzsche's thought. But its poetic and prophetical style gives it the appearance of being the work of a visionary.[1] Calmer expositions of Nietzsche's ideas are to be found in *Beyond Good and Evil* (*Jenseits von Gut und Böse*, 1886) and *A Genealogy of Morals* (*Zur Genealogie der Moral*, 1887), which, together with *Zarathustra*, are probably Nietzsche's most important writings. *Beyond Good and Evil* elicited an appreciative letter from Hippolyte Taine, and after the publication of *A Genealogy of Morals*, Nietzsche received a similar letter from Georg Brandes, the Danish critic, who later delivered a course of lectures on Nietzsche's ideas at Copenhagen.

Beyond Good and Evil had as its subtitle *Prelude to a Philosophy of the Future*. Nietzsche planned a systematic exposition of his philosophy, for which he made copious notes. His idea of the appropriate title underwent several changes. At first it was to be *The Will to Power, a New Interpretation of Nature* or *The Will to Power, an Essay towards a New Interpretation of the Universe*. In

---

[1] Rudolf Carnap remarks that when Nietzsche wished to take to metaphysics, he very properly had recourse to poetry. Carnap thus looks on *Zarathustra* as empirical confirmation of his own neopositivist interpretation of the nature of metaphysics.

other words, just as Schopenhauer had based a philosophy on the concept of the will to life, so would Nietzsche base a philosophy on the idea of the will to power. Later the emphasis changed, and the proposed title was *The Will to Power, an Essay towards the Trans-valuation of all Values (Der Wille zur Macht: Versuch einer Umwerthung aller Werthe)*. But in point of fact the projected *magnum opus* was never completed, though *The Antichrist (Der Antichrist)* was meant to be the first part of it. Nietzsche's notes for the work which he planned have been published posthumously.

Nietzsche turned aside from his projected work to write a ferocious attack on Wagner, *The Case of Wagner (Der Fall Wagner*, 1888), and followed it up with *Nietzsche contra Wagner*. This second essay was published only after Nietzsche's breakdown, as were also other writings of 1888, *The Twilight of the Idols (Die Götzen-dämmerung)*, *The Antichrist* and *Ecce Homo*, a kind of auto-biography. The works of this year show evident signs of extreme tension and mental instability, and *Ecce Homo* in particular, with its exalted spirit of self-assertion, gives a marked impression of psychical disturbance. At the end of the year definite signs of madness began to show themselves, and in January 1889 Nietzsche was taken from Turin, where he then was, to a clinic at Basel. He never really recovered, but after treatment at Basel and then at Jena he was able to go to his mother's home at Naumburg.[1] After her death he lived with his sister at Weimar. By that time he had become a famous man, though he was hardly in a position to appreciate the fact. He died on August 25th, 1900.

2. In the foregoing section reference has been made to periods or phases in the development of Nietzsche's thought. The philosopher himself, as he looked back, described these phases as so many masks. For example, he asserted that the attitude of a free spirit, that is, of a critical, rationalistic and sceptical observer of life, which he adopted in his second period, was an 'eccentric pose', a second nature, as it were, which was assumed as a means whereby he might win through to his first or true nature. It had to be discarded as the snake sloughs its old skin. Further, Nietzsche was accustomed to speak of particular doctrines or theories as though they were artifices of self-preservation or self-administered tonics. For instance, the theory of the eternal recurrence was a test of

---

[1] Nietzsche was indeed dogged by bad health and insomnia. And loneliness and neglect preyed on his mind. But it seems probable, in spite of his sister's attempts to deny it, that as a university student he contracted a syphilitic infection and that the disease, after running an atypical course, finally affected the brain.

strength, of Nietzsche's power to say 'yes' to life instead of the Schopenhauerian 'no'. Could he face the thought that his whole life, every moment of it, every suffering, every agony, every humiliation, would be repeated countless times throughout endless time? Could he face this thought and embrace it not only with stoical resignation but also with joy? If so, it was a sign of inner strength, of the triumph in Nietzsche himself of the yea-saying attitude of life.

Obviously, Nietzsche did not say to himself one fine day: 'I shall now pose for a time as a positivist and a coolly critical and scientific observer, because I think that it would be good for my mental health.' It is rather that he seriously attempted to play such a part until, having grown out of it, he recognized it in retrospect as a self-administered tonic and as a mask under which the real direction of his thought could develop unseen. But what was the real direction of his thought? In view of what Nietzsche says about winning through to his true nature, one is inclined, of course, to assume that the doctrine of his later works and of the posthumously-published notes for *The Will to Power* represents his real thought. Yet if we press the theory of masks, we must apply it also, I think, to his third period. As already mentioned, he spoke of the theory of the eternal recurrence as a trial of strength; and this theory belongs to his third period. Further, it was in the third period that Nietzsche explicitly stated his relativistic and pragmatist view of truth. His general theory of truth was indeed social rather than personal, in the sense that those theories were said to be true which are biologically useful for a given species or for a certain kind of man. Thus the theory of Superman would be a myth which possessed truth in so far as it enabled the higher type of man to develop his potentialities. But if we press the idea of masks, we must take such a statement as 'the criterion of truth lies in the intensification of the feeling of power'[1] in a personal sense and apply it to the thought of Nietzsche's third period no less than to that of the first and second periods.

In this case, of course, there remains no 'real thought' of Nietzsche which is statable in terms of definite philosophical theories. For the whole of his expressed thought becomes an

[1] *W*, III, p. 919 (xv, p. 49). Unless otherwise stated, references are given according to volume and page of the three-volume (incomplete) edition of Nietzsche's *Works* by K. Schlechta (Munich, 1954–6). The references in brackets are always to the English translation of Nietzsche's *Works* edited by Dr. Oscar Levy (see Bibliography). The critical German edition of Nietzsche's writings is still unfinished.

instrument whereby Nietzsche as an existing individual, to use Kierkegaard's phrase, seeks to realize his own possibilities. His ideas represent a medium through which we have to try to discern the significance of an existence. We then have the sort of interpretation of Nietzsche's life and work of which Karl Jaspers has given us a fine example.[1]

The present writer has no intention of questioning the value of the existential interpretation of Nietzsche's life and thought. But in a book such as this the reader has a right to expect a summary account of what Nietzsche said, of his public face or appearance, so to speak. After all, when a philosopher commits ideas to paper and publishes them, they take on, as it were, a life of their own and exercise a greater or lesser influence, as the case may be. It is true that his philosophy lacks the impressiveness of systems such as those of Spinoza and Hegel, a fact of which Nietzsche was well aware. And if one wishes to find in it German 'profundity', one has to look beneath the surface. But though Nietzsche himself drew attention to the personal aspects of his thinking and to the need for probing beneath the surface, the fact remains that he held certain convictions very strongly and that he came to think of himself as a prophet, as a reforming force, and of his ideas as 'dynamite'. Even if on his own view of truth his theories necessarily assume the character of myth, these myths were intimately associated with value-judgments which Nietzsche asserted with passion. And it is perhaps these value-judgments more than anything else which have been the source of his great influence.

3. We have already referred to Nietzsche's discovery, when he was a student at Leipzig, of Schopenhauer's *World as Will and Idea*. But though Nietzsche received a powerful stimulus from the great pessimist, he was at no time a disciple of Schopenhauer. In *The Birth of Tragedy*, for example, he does indeed follow Schopenhauer to the extent of postulating what he calls a 'Primordial Unity' which manifests itself in the world and in human life. And, like Schopenhauer, he depicts life as terrible and tragic and speaks of its transmutation through art, the work of the creative genius. At the same time even in his early works, when the inspiration derived from Schopenhauer's philosophy is evident, the general direction of Nietzsche's thought is towards the affirmation of life rather than towards its negation. And when in 1888 he looked back on *The*

[1] In his *Nietzsche: Einführung in das Verständnis seines Philosophierens* (Berlin 1936). For Jaspers Nietzsche and Kierkegaard represent two 'exceptions', two embodiments of different possibilities of human existence.

Birth of Tragedy and asserted that it expressed an attitude to life which was the antithesis of Schopenhauer's, the assertion was not without foundation.

The Greeks, according to Nietzsche in *The Birth of Tragedy*, knew very well that life is terrible, inexplicable, dangerous. But though they were alive to the real character of the world and of human life, they did not surrender to pessimism by turning their backs on life. What they did was to transmute the world and human life through the medium of art. And they were then able to say 'yes' to the world as an aesthetic phenomenon. There were, however, two ways of doing this, corresponding respectively to the Dionysian and Apollonian attitudes or mentalities.

Dionysus is for Nietzsche the symbol of the stream of life itself, breaking down all barriers and ignoring all restraints. In the Dionysian or Bacchic rites we can see the intoxicated votaries becoming, as it were, one with life. The barriers set up by the principle of individuation tend to break down; the veil of Maya is turned aside; and men and women are plunged into the stream of life, manifesting the Primordial Unity. Apollo, however, is the symbol of light, of measure, of restraint. He represents the principle of individuation. And the Apollonian attitude is expressed in the shining dream-world of the Olympic deities.

But we can, of course, get away from metaphysical theories about the Primordial Unity and Schopenhauer's talk about the principle of individuation, and express the matter in a psychological form. Beneath the moderation so often ascribed to the Greeks, beneath their devotion to art and beauty and form, Nietzsche sees the dark, turgid and formless torrent of instinct and impulse and passion which tends to sweep away everything in its path.

Now, if we assume that life is in itself an object of horror and terror and that pessimism, in the sense of the no-saying attitude to life, can be avoided only by the aesthetic transmutation of reality, there are two ways of doing this. One is to draw an aesthetic veil over reality, creating an ideal world of form and beauty. This is the Apollonian way. And it found expression in the Olympic mythology, in the epic and in the plastic arts. The other possibility is that of triumphantly affirming and embracing existence in all its darkness and horror. This is the Dionysian attitude, and its typical art forms are tragedy and music. Tragedy does indeed transmute existence into an aesthetic phenomenon, but it does not draw a veil over existence as it is. Rather does it exhibit existence in aesthetic form and affirm it.

In *The Birth of Tragedy*, as its title indicates, Nietzsche is concerned immediately with the origins and development of Greek tragedy. But we cannot discuss the matter here. Nor does it matter for our present purposes how far Nietzsche's account of the origins of tragedy is acceptable from the point of view of classical scholarship. The important point is that the supreme achievement of Greek culture, before it was spoiled by the spirit of Socratic nationalism, lay for Nietzsche in a fusion of Dionysian and Apollonian elements.[1] And in this fusion he saw the foundation for a cultural standard. True culture is a unity of the forces of life, the Dionysian element, with the love of form and beauty which is characteristic of the Apollonian attitude.

If existence is justified as an aesthetic phenomenon, the fine flower of humanity will be constituted by those who transmute existence into such a phenomenon and enable men to see existence in this way and affirm it. In other words, the creative genius will be the highest cultural product. Indeed, in the period which we are considering Nietzsche speaks as though the production of genius were the aim and end of culture, its justification. He makes this quite clear in, for instance, his essay on *The Greek State* (*Der griechische Staat*, 1871). Here and elsewhere he insists that the toil and labour of the majority in the struggle of life are justified by forming the substructure on which the genius, whether in art, music or philosophy, can arise. For the genius is the organ whereby existence is, as it were, redeemed.

On the basis of these ideas Nietzsche proceeds to give a highly critical evaluation of contemporary German culture. He contrasts, for example, historical knowledge about past cultures with culture itself, described as 'unity of artistic style in all the expressions of the life of a people'.[2] But his critique of the German culture of his time need not detain us here. Instead we can note two or three general ideas which also look forward to Nietzsche's later thought.

Nietzsche varies the question whether life should dominate knowledge or knowledge life. 'Which of the two is the higher and decisive power? Nobody will doubt that life is the higher and dominating power. . . .'[3] This means that the nineteenth-century culture, characterized by the domination of knowledge and

---

[1] According to Nietzsche, the tragedies of Aeschylus were the supreme artistic expression of this fusion.
[2] *W*, I, p. 140 (I, p. 8).   [3] *W*, I, p. 282 (II, p. 96).

science, is exposed to the revenge, as it were, of the vital forces, the explosion of which will produce a new barbarism. Beneath the surface of modern life Nietzsche sees vital forces which are 'wild, primitive and completely merciless. One looks at them with a fearful expectancy as though at the cauldron in a witch's kitchen . . . for a century we have been ready for world-shaking convulsions.'[1] In nineteenth-century society we can see both a complacency in the condition which man has already reached and a widespread tendency, fostered by the national State and manifested in the movements towards democracy and socialism, to promote a uniform mediocrity, hostile to genius. But there is no reason to suppose that the development of man's potentialities has reached its term. And the emergence of the latent destructive forces will pave the way for the rise of higher specimens of humanity in the form of outstanding individuals.

Obviously, this view involves a supra-historical outlook, as Nietzsche puts it. It involves, that is to say, a rejection of the Hegelian canonization of the actual in the name of a necessary self-manifestation of the *Logos* or Idea, and a vision of values which transcend the historical situation. The human being is plastic; he is capable of transcending himself, of realizing fresh possibilities; and he needs a vision, a goal, a sense of direction. Empirical science cannot provide this vision. And though Nietzsche does not say much about Christianity in his early writings, it is clear that he does not look to the Christian religion as the source of the requisite vision.[2] There remains philosophy, not indeed as represented by learned university professors, but in the guise of the lonely thinker who has a clear vision of the possibilities of man's self-transcendence and who is not afraid to be 'dangerous'. Once it has been decided how far things are alterable, philosophy should set itself 'with ruthless courage to the task of *improving that aspect of the world which has been recognized as susceptible to being changed*'.[3] When in later years Nietzsche looks back on these early essays, he

---

[1] *W*, I, p. 313 (II, p. 137).
[2] In *Schopenhauer as Educator* Nietzsche remarks that 'Christianity is certainly one of the purest manifestations of that impulse towards culture and, precisely, towards the ever renewed production of the saint'; *W*, I, p. 332 (II, p. 161). But he goes on to argue that Christianity has been used to turn the mill-wheels of the State and that it has become hopelessly degenerate. It is clear that he regards the Christian religion as a spent force. Looking back later on *The Birth of Tragedy* he sees in its silence about Christianity a hostile silence. For the book in question recognized only aesthetic values, which, Nietzsche maintains, Christianity denies.
[3] *W*, I, p. 379 (I, p. 120).

sees in this ideal of the philosopher as judge of life and creator of values Zarathustra or himself. It comes to the same thing.

4. A criticism of the ethical attitude in so far as this involves the assertion of a universal moral law and of absolute moral values is implicit in Nietzsche's early writings. We have seen that according to his own statement only aesthetic values were recognized in *The Birth of Tragedy*. And in his essay on David Strauss Nietzsche refers to Strauss's contention that the sum and substance of morality consists in looking on all other human beings as having the same needs, claims and rights as oneself and then asks where this imperative comes from. Strauss seems to take it for granted that the imperative has its basis in the Darwinian theory of evolution. But evolution provides no such basis. The class *Man* comprises a multitude of different types, and it is absurd to claim that we are required to behave as though individual differences and distinctions were non-existent or unimportant. And we have seen that Nietzsche lays stress on outstanding individuals rather than on the race or species.

However, it is in *Human, All-too-Human* that Nietzsche begins to treat of morality in some detail. The work is indeed composed of aphorisms; it is not a systematic treatise. But if we compare the remarks relating to morality, a more or less coherent theory emerges.

It is the first sign that the animal has become man when its notions are no longer directed simply to the satisfaction of the moment but to what is recognized as useful in an enduring manner.[1] But we can hardly talk about morality until utility is understood in the sense of usefulness for the existence, survival and welfare of the community. For 'morality is primarily a means of preserving the community in general and warding off destruction from it'.[2] Compulsion has first to be employed to make the individual conform his conduct to the interests of society. But compulsion is succeeded by the force of custom, and in time the authoritative voice of the community takes the form of what we call conscience. Obedience can become a second nature, as it were, and be associated with pleasure. At the same time moral epithets come to be extended from actions to the intentions of the agents. And the concepts of virtue and of the virtuous man arise. In other words, morality is interiorized through a process of progressive refinement.

[1] *W*, I, p. 502 (VII/1, p. 92).   [2] *W*, I, p. 900 (VII/2, p. 221).

So far Nietzsche speaks like a utilitarian. And his concept of morality bears some resemblance to what Bergson calls closed morality. But once we look at the historical development of morality we see a 'twofold early history of good and evil'.[1] And it is the development of this idea of two moral outlooks which is really characteristic of Nietzsche. But the idea is best discussed in relation to his later writings.

In *Beyond Good and Evil* Nietzsche says that he has discovered two primary types of morality, 'master-morality and slave-morality'.[2] In all higher civilizations they are mixed, and elements of both can be found even in the same man. But it is important to distinguish them. In the master-morality or aristocratic morality 'good' and 'bad' are equivalent to 'noble' and 'despicable', and the epithets are applied to men rather than to actions. In the slave-morality the standard is that which is useful or beneficial to the society of the weak and powerless. Qualities such as sympathy, kindness and humility are extolled as virtues, and the strong and independent individuals are regarded as dangerous, and therefore as 'evil'. By the standards of the slave-morality the 'good' man of the master-morality tends to be accounted as 'evil'. Slave-morality is thus herd-morality. Its moral valuations are expressions of the needs of a herd.

This point of view is expounded more systematically in *The Genealogy of Morals* where Nietzsche makes use of the concept of resentment. The higher type of man creates his own values out of the abundance of his life and strength. The meek and powerless, however, fear the strong and powerful, and they attempt to curb and tame them by asserting as absolute the values of the herd. 'The revolt of the slaves in morals begins with resentment becoming creative and giving birth to values.'[3] This resentment is not, of course, openly acknowledged by the herd, and it can work by devious and indirect paths. But the psychologist of the moral life can detect and bring to light its presence and complex modes of operation.

What we see, therefore, in the history of morals is the conflict of two moral attitudes or outlooks. From the point of view of the higher man there can in a sense be coexistence. That is to say, there could be coexistence if the herd, incapable of anything higher, was content to keep its values to itself. But, of course, it is not content

---

[1] *W*, I, p. 483 (VII/1, p. 64). [2] *W*, II, p. 730 (V, p. 227).
[3] *W*, II, p. 782 (XIII, p. 34).

to do this. It endeavours to impose its own values universally. And according to Nietzsche it succeeded in doing this, at least in the West, in Christianity. He does not indeed deny all value to Christian morality. He admits, for instance, that it has contributed to the refinement of man. At the same time he sees in it an expression of the resentment which is characteristic of the herd-instinct or slave-morality. And the same resentment is attributed to the democratic and socialist movements which Nietzsche interprets as derivatives of Christianity.

Nietzsche maintains, therefore, that the concept of a uniform, universal and absolute moral system is to be rejected. For it is the fruit of resentment and represents inferior life, descending life, degeneracy, whereas the aristocratic morality represents the movement of ascending life.[1] And in place of the concept of one universal and absolute moral system (or indeed of different sets of values, relative to different societies, if each set is regarded as binding all the members of the society) we must put the concept of a gradation of rank among different types of morality. The herd is welcome to its own set of values, provided that it is deprived of the power of imposing them on the higher type of man who is called upon to create his own values which will enable man to transcend his present condition.

When, therefore, Nietzsche speaks of standing beyond good and evil, what he has in mind is rising above the so-called herd-morality which in his opinion reduces everyone to a common level, favours mediocrity and prevents the development of a higher type of man. He does not mean to imply that all respect for values should be abandoned and all self-restraint thrown overboard. The man who rejects the binding force of what is customarily called morality may be himself so weak and degenerate that he destroys himself morally. It is only the higher type of man who can safely go beyond good and evil in the sense which these terms bear in the morality of resentment. And he does so in order to create values which will be at once an expression of ascending life and a means of enabling man to transcend himself in the direction of Superman, a higher level of human existence.

When it comes to describing the content of the new values, Nietzsche does not indeed afford us very much light. Some of the virtues on which he insists look suspiciously like old virtues,

---

[1] The general philosophy of life which these judgments require as a background will be considered later.

though he maintains that they are 'transvalued', that is, made different by reason of the different motives, attitudes and valuations which they express. However, one can say in general that what Nietzsche looks for is the highest possible integration of all aspects of human nature. He accuses Christianity of depreciating the body, impulse, instinct, passion, the free and untrammelled exercise of the mind, aesthetic values, and so on. But he obviously does not call for the disintegration of the human personality into a bundle of warring impulses and unbridled passions. It is a question of integration as an expression of strength, not of extirpation or mortification out of a motive of fear which is based on a consciousness of weakness. Needless to say, Nietzsche gives a very one-sided account of the Christian doctrine of man and of values. But it is essential for him to insist on this one-sided view. Otherwise he would find it difficult to assert that he had anything new to offer, unless it were the type of ideal for man which some of the Nazis liked to attribute to him.

5. In *Joyful Wisdom* Nietzsche remarks that 'the greatest event of recent times—that 'God is dead', that belief in the Christian God has become unworthy of belief—already begins to cast its first shadows over Europe. . . . At last the horizon lies free before us, even granted that it is not bright; at least the sea, *our* sea, lies open before us. Perhaps there has never been so open a sea.'[1] In other words, decay of belief in God opens the way for man's creative energies to develop fully; the Christian God, with his commands and prohibitions, no longer stands in the path; and man's eyes are no longer turned towards an unreal supernatural realm, towards the other world rather than towards this world.

This point of view obviously implies that the concept of God is hostile to life. And this is precisely Nietzsche's contention, which he expresses with increasing vehemence as time goes on. 'The concept *God*', he says in *The Twilight of the Idols*, 'was up to now the greatest *objection* against existence.'[2] And in *The Antichrist* we read that 'with God war is declared on life, Nature and the will to live! God is the formula for every calumny against this world and for every lie concerning a beyond!'[3] But it is unnecessary to multiply quotations. Nietzsche is willing to admit that religion in some of its phases has expressed the will to life, or rather to power; but his general attitude is that belief in God, especially in the God

[1] *W*, II, pp. 205–6 (x, pp. 275–6).   [2] *W*, II, p. 978 (XVI, p. 43).
[3] *W*, II, p. 1178 (XVI, p. 146). Nietzsche is speaking specifically of the Christian concept of God.

of the Christian religion, is hostile to life, and that when it expresses the will to power, the will in question is that of the lower types of man.

Given this attitude, it is understandable that Nietzsche tends to make the choice between theism, especially Christian theism, and atheism a matter of taste or instinct. He recognizes that there have been great men who were believers, but he maintains that nowadays at least, when the existence of God is no longer taken for granted, strength, intellectual freedom, independence and concern for the future of man demand atheism. Belief is a sign of weakness, cowardice, decadence, a no-saying attitude to life. True, Nietzsche attempts a sketch of the origins of the idea of God. And he cheerfully commits the genetic fallacy, maintaining that when it has been shown how the idea of God could have originated, any disproof of God's existence becomes superfluous. He also occasionally alludes to theoretical objections against belief in God. But, generally speaking, the illusory character of this belief is assumed. And the decisive motive for its rejection is that man (or Nietzsche himself) may take the place of God as legislator and creator of values. Considered as a purely theoretical attack, Nietzsche's condemnation of theism in general and of Christianity in particular is worth very little. But it is not an aspect of the matter to which he attaches much importance. As far as theology is concerned, there is no need to bother about such fables. Nietzsche's hatred of Christianity proceeds principally from his view of its supposed effect on man, whom it renders weak, submissive, resigned, humble or tortured in conscience and unable to develop himself freely. It either prevents the growth of superior individuals or ruins them, as in the case of Pascal.[1]

It is indeed noticeable that in his attack on Christianity Nietzsche often speaks of the seductiveness and fascination of Christian beliefs and ideals. And it is clear that he himself felt the attraction and that he rejected it partly in order to prove to himself that 'apart from the fact that I am a *decadent*, I am also the opposite of such a being'.[2] His rejection of God proved to himself his inner strength, his ability to live without God. But from the

---

[1] Nietzsche does occasionally say something in favour of Christian values. But his admissions are by no means always calculated to afford consolation to Christians. For instance, while admitting that Christianity has developed the sense of truth and the ideal of love, he insists that the sense of truth ultimately turns against the Christian interpretation of reality and the ideal of love against the Christian idea of God.

[2] *W*, II, p. 1072 (XVII, p. 12).

purely philosophical point of view the conclusions which he draws from atheism are more important than the psychological factors bearing on his rejection of the Christian God.

Some people have imagined, Nietzsche maintains, that there is no necessary connection between belief in the Christian God and acceptance of Christian moral standards and values. That is to say, they have thought that the latter can be maintained more or less intact when the former has been discarded. We have thus witnessed the growth of secularized forms of Christianity, such as democracy and socialism, which have tried to maintain a considerable part of the Christian moral system without its theological foundations. But such attempts are, in Nietzsche's opinion, vain. The 'death of God' will inevitably be followed, sooner or later, by the rejection of absolute values and of the idea of an objective and universal moral law.

The European man, however, has been brought up to recognize certain moral values which have been associated with Christian belief and, Nietzsche maintains, in a certain sense depend on it. If, therefore, European man loses his faith in these values, he loses his faith in all values. For he knows only 'morality', the morality which was canonized, as it were, by Christianity and given a theological foundation. And disbelief in all values, issuing in the sense of the purposelessness of the world of becoming, is one of the main elements in nihilism. 'Morality was the greatest *antidote* (*Gegenmittel*) against practical and theoretical *nihilism*.'[1] For it ascribed an absolute value to man and 'prevented man from despising himself as man, from turning against life and from despairing of the possibility of knowledge; it was a *means of preservation*'.[2] True, the man who was preserved in this way by the Christian morality was the lower type of man. But the point is that the Christian morality succeeded in imposing itself generally, whether directly or in the form of its derivatives. Hence the breakdown of belief in the Christian moral values exposes man to the danger of nihilism, not because there are no other possible values, but because most men, in the West at least, know no others.

Nihilism can take more than one form. There is, for instance, passive nihilism, a pessimistic acquiescence in the absence of values and in the purposelessness of existence. But there is also active nihilism which seeks to destroy that in which it no longer believes. And Nietzsche prophesies the advent of an active nihilism,

[1] *W*, III, p. 852 (IX, p. 9).   [2] *Ibid*.

showing itself in world-shaking ideological wars. 'There will be wars such as there have never been on earth before. Only from my time on will there be on earth *politics on the grand scale.*'[1]

The advent of nihilism is in Nietzsche's opinion inevitable. And it will mean the final overthrow of the decadent Christian civilization of Europe. At the same time it will clear the way for a new dawn, for the transvaluation of values, for the emergence of a higher type of man. For this reason 'this most gruesome of all guests',[2] who stands at the door, is to be welcomed.

[1] *W*, II, p. 1153 (XVII, p. 132).   [2] *W*, III, p. 881 (IX, p. 5).

CHAPTER XXII

NIETZSCHE (2)

The hypothesis of the Will to Power—The Will to Power as manifested in knowledge; Nietzsche's view of truth—The Will to Power in Nature and man—Superman and the order of rank— The theory of the eternal recurrence—Comments on Nietzsche's philosophy.

1. *'This world'*, Nietzsche asserts, *'is the Will to Power—and nothing else!* And you yourselves too are this Will to Power—and nothing else!'[1] These words are an adaptation of Schopenhauer's statements at the close of his *magnum opus*; and the way in which Nietzsche is accustomed to speak of 'the Will to Power' naturally gives the impression that he has transformed Schopenhauer's Will to Existence or Will to Live into the Will to Power. But though the impression is, of course, correct in a sense, we must not understand Nietzsche as meaning that the world is an appearance of a metaphysical unity which transcends the world. For he is never tired of attacking the distinction between this world, identified with merely phenomenal reality, and a transcendent reality which is 'really real'. The world is not an illusion. Nor does the Will to Power exist in a state of transcendence. The world, the universe, is a unity, a process of becoming; and it is the Will to Power in the sense that this Will is its intelligible character. Everywhere, in everything, we can see the Will to Power expressing itself. And though one can perhaps say that for Nietzsche the Will to Power is the inner reality of the universe, it exists only in its manifestations. Nietzsche's theory of the Will to Power is thus an interpretation of the universe, a way of looking at it and describing it, rather than a metaphysical doctrine about a reality which lies *behind* the visible world and transcends it.

Nietzsche had, of course, Schopenhauer at the back of his mind. But he did not jump straight from his reading of *The World as Will and Idea* to a general theory of the universe. Rather did he discern manifestations of the Will to Power in human psychical processes and then extend this idea to organic life in general. In *Beyond Good and Evil* he remarks that logical method compels us to inquire

[1] *W*, III, p. 917 (XV, p. 432).

whether we can find one principle of explanation, one fundamental form of causal activity, through which we can unify vital phenomena. And he finds this principle in the Will to Power. 'A living thing seeks above all to *discharge* its force—life itself is Will to Power: self-preservation is only one of the indirect and most common *consequences* thereof.'[1] Nietzsche then proceeds to extend this principle of explanation to the world as a whole. 'Granted that we succeed in explaining our whole instinctive life as the development and ramification of *one* fundamental form of will—namely the Will to Power, as *my* thesis says; granted that one could refer all organic functions to this Will to Power, . . . one would have thereby acquired the right to define unequivocally *all* active force as *Will to Power*. The world as seen from within, the world as defined and characterized according to its "intelligible character", would be precisely "Will to Power" and nothing else.'[2]

Thus Nietzsche's theory of the Will to Power is not so much an *a priori* metaphysical thesis as a sweeping empirical hypothesis. If, he says, we believe in the causality of the will, a belief which is really belief in causality itself, 'we *must* make the attempt to posit hypothetically the causality of the will as the only form of causality'.[3] In Nietzsche's intention at least the theory was an explanatory hypothesis, and in his projected *magnum opus* he planned to apply it to different classes of phenomena, showing how they could be unified in terms of this hypothesis. The notes which he made for this work indicate the lines of his thought, and in the next two sections I propose to give some examples of his reflections.

2. 'Knowledge', Nietzsche insists, 'works as an instrument of power. It is therefore obvious that it grows with every increase of power. . . .'[4] The desire of knowledge, the will to know, depends on the will to power, that is, on a given kind of being's impulse to master a certain field of reality and to enlist it in its service. The aim of knowledge is not to know, in the sense of grasping absolute truth for its own sake, but to master. We desire to schematize, to impose order and form on the multiplicity of impressions and sensations to the extent required by our practical needs. Reality is Becoming: it is we who turn it into Being, imposing stable patterns on the flux of Becoming. And this activity is an expression of the Will to Power. Science can thus be defined or described as the

---

[1] *W*, II, p. 578 (v, p. 20).   [2] *W*, II, p. 601 (v, p. 52).
[3] *Ibid.*   [4] *W*, III, p. 751 (xv, p. 11).

'transformation of Nature into concepts for the purpose of governing Nature'.[1]

Knowledge is, of course, a process of interpretation. But this process is grounded on vital needs and expresses the will to master the otherwise unintelligible flux of Becoming. And it is a question of reading an interpretation into reality rather than of reading it, so to speak, off or in reality. For instance, the concept of the ego or self as a permanent substance is an interpretation imposed upon the flux of Becoming: it is our creation for practical purposes. To be sure, the idea that 'we' interpret psychical states as similar and attribute them to a permanent subject involves Nietzsche in obvious and, in the opinion of the present writer, insoluble difficulties. His general contention is, however, that we cannot legitimately argue from the utility of an interpretation to its objectivity. For a useful fiction, an interpretation which was devoid of objectivity in the sense in which believers in absolute truth would understand objectivity, might be required and thereby justified by our needs.

But there is, according to Nietzsche, no absolute truth. The concept of absolute truth is an invention of philosophers who are dissatisfied with the world of Becoming and seek an abiding world of Being. '*Truth is that sort of error* without which a particular type of living being could not live. The value for *life* is ultimately decisive.'[2]

Some 'fictions', of course, prove to be so useful, and indeed practically necessary, to the human race that they tend to become unquestioned assumptions; for example, 'that there are enduring things, that there are equal things, that there are things, substances, bodies. . . .'[3] It was necessary for life that the concept of a thing or of substance should be imposed on the constant flux of phenomena. 'The beings which did not see correctly had an advantage over those who saw everything "in flux".'[4] Similarly, the law of causality has become so assimilated by human belief that '*not* to believe in it would mean the ruin of our species'.[5] And the same can be said of the laws of logic.

The fictions which have shown themselves to be less useful than other fictions, or even positively harmful, are reputed as 'errors'. But those which have proved their utility to the species and have attained the rank of unquestioned 'truths' become embedded, as

---

[1] *W*, III, p. 440 (xv, p. 105).   [2] *W*, III, p. 844 (xv, p. 20).
[3] *W*, II, p. 116 (x, p. 153).   [4] *W*, II, p. 119 (x, p. 157).
[5] *W*, III, p. 443 (xv, pp. 21–2).

it were, in language. And here lies a danger. For we may be misled by language and imagine that our way of speaking about the world necessarily mirrors reality. 'We are still being constantly led astray by words and concepts into thinking things are simpler than they are, as separate from one another, indivisible and existing each on its own. A philosophical mythology lies hidden in *language*, and it breaks out again at every moment, however careful one may be.'[1]

All 'truths' are 'fictions'; all such fictions are interpretations; and all interpretations are perspectives. Even every instinct has its perspective, its point of view, which it endeavours to impose on other instincts. And the categories of reason are also logical fictions and perspectives, not necessary truths, nor *a priori* forms. But the perspectival view of truth admits, of course, of differences. Some perspectives, as we have seen, have proved to be practically necessary for the welfare of the race. But there are others which are by no means necessary. And here the influence of valuations becomes especially evident. For example, the philosopher who interprets the world as the appearance of an Absolute which transcends change and is alone 'really real' expounds a perspective based on a negative evaluation of the world of becoming. And this in turn shows what sort of a man he is.

The obvious comment on Nietzsche's general view of truth is that it presupposes the possibility of occupying an absolute standpoint from which the relativity of all truth or its fictional character can be asserted, and that this presupposition is at variance with the relativist interpretation of truth. Further, this comment by no means loses its point if Nietzsche is willing to say that his own view of the world, and even of truth, is perspectival and 'fictional'.[2] A few moments' reflection is sufficient to show this. Still, it is interesting to find Nietzsche anticipating John Dewey in applying a pragmatist or instrumentalist view of truth to such strongholds of the absolute truth theory as logic. For him, even the fundamental principles of logic are simply expressions of the Will to Power, instruments to enable man to dominate the flux of Becoming.

3. If Nietzsche is prepared to apply his view of truth to alleged eternal truths, he must obviously apply it *a fortiori* to scientific

---

[1] *W*, I, pp. 878–9 (VII/2, p. 192).
[2] No doubt, Nietzsche would admit this in principle, while insisting that his interpretation of the world was the expression of a higher form of the Will to Power. But what is the standard of higher and lower?

hypotheses. The atomic theory, for example, is fictional in character; that is to say, it is a schema imposed on phenomena by the scientist with a view to mastery.[1] We cannot indeed help speaking as though there was a distinction between the seat of force or energy and the force itself. But this should not blind us to the fact that the atom, considered as an entity, a seat of force, is a symbol invented by the scientist, a mental projection.

However, if we presuppose the fictional character of the atomic theory, we can go on to say that every atom is a quantum of energy or, better, of the Will to Power. It seeks to discharge its energy, to radiate its force or power. And so-called physical laws represent relations of power between two or more forces. We need to unify, and we need mathematical formulas for grasping, classifying, mastering. But this is no proof either that things obey laws in the sense of rules or that there are substantial things which exercise force or power. There are simply 'dynamic quanta in a relation of tension to all other dynamic quanta'.[2]

To turn to the organic world. 'A plurality of forces, united by a common nutritive process, we call *Life*.'[3] And life might be defined as 'a lasting form of processes of assertions of force, in which the various combatants on their side grow unequally'.[4] In other words, the organism is an intricate complexity of systems which strive after an increase in the feeling of power. And being itself an expression of the Will to Power, it looks for obstacles, for something to overcome. For example, appropriation and assimilation are interpreted by Nietzsche as manifestations of the Will to Power. And the same can be said of all organic functions.

When treating of biological evolution Nietzsche attacks Darwinism. He points out, for instance, that during most of the time taken up in the formation of a certain organ or quality, the inchoate organ is of no use to its possessor and cannot aid it in its struggle with external circumstances and foes. 'The influence of "external circumstances" is absurdly *overrated* by Darwin. The essential factor in the vital process is precisely the tremendous power to shape and create forms from within, a power which *uses* and *exploits* the environment.'[5] Again, the assumption that natural selection works in favour of the progress of the species and of its better-constituted and individually stronger specimens is

---

[1] Mastery is not to be understood, of course, in a vulgarly utilitarian sense. Knowledge itself is mastery, an expression of the Will to Power.
[2] *W*, III, p. 778 (xv, p. 120).   [3] *W*, III, p. 874 (xv, p. 123).
[4] *W*, III, p. 458 (xv, p. 124).   [5] *W*, III, p. 889 (xv, p. 127).

unwarranted. It is precisely the better specimens which perish and the mediocre which survive. For the exceptions, the best specimens, are weak in comparison with the majority. Taken individually, the members of the majority may be inferior, but when grouped together under the influence of fear and the gregarious instincts they are powerful.

Hence if we based our moral values on the facts of evolution, we should have to conclude that 'the mediocre are more valuable than the exceptional specimens, and that the *decadent* are more valuable than the mediocre'.[1] For higher values we have to look to superior individuals who in their isolation are stimulated to set before themselves lofty aims.

In the field of human psychology Nietzsche finds ample opportunity for diagnosing the manifestations of the Will to Power. For example, he dismisses as quite unfounded the psychological theory presupposed by hedonism, namely the theory that pursuit of pleasure and avoidance of pain are the fundamental motives of human conduct. In Nietzsche's view pleasure and pain are concomitant phenomena in the striving after an increase of power. Pleasure can be described as the feeling of increased power, while pain results from a felt hindrance to the Will to Power. At the same time pain often provides a stimulus to this Will. For every triumph presupposes an obstacle, a hindrance, which is overcome. It is thus absurd to look on pain as an unmixed evil. Man is constantly in need of it as a stimulus to fresh effort and, for the matter of that, as a stimulus to obtaining new forms of pleasure as accompanying results of the triumphs to which pain urges him on.

Though we cannot enter in detail into Nietzsche's psychological analyses, it is worth noting the role played in these analyses by the concept of sublimation. For example, in his view self-mortification and asceticism can be sublimated forms of a primitive cruelty which is itself an expression of the Will to Power. And he raises the question, what instincts are sublimated in, say, the aesthetic view of the world? Everywhere Nietzsche sees the operation, often devious and hidden, of the Will to Power.

4. According to Nietzsche, rank is determined by power. 'It is quanta of power, and nothing else, which determine and distinguish rank.'[2] And one might well draw the conclusion that if the mediocre

[1] *W*, III, pp. 748–9 (xv, p. 159).
[2] *W*, x, p. 105 (xv, p. 295). The first reference here is not to the Schlechta edition but to the *Taschen-Ausgabe* published by A. Kroner of Stuttgart, the date of the volume in question being 1921.

majority possesses greater power than individuals who are not mediocre, it also possesses greater value. But this, of course, is by no means Nietzsche's view. He understands power in the sense of an intrinsic quality of the individual. And he tells us, 'I distinguish between a type which represents ascending life and a type which represents decadence, decomposition, weakness'.[1] And even if the mediocre majority, united together, happens to be powerful, it does not, for Nietzsche, represent ascending life.

Yet the mediocre are necessary. For 'a high culture can exist only on a broad basis, on a strongly and soundly consolidated mediocrity'.[2] In fact, from this point of view Nietzsche welcomes the spread of democracy and socialism. For they help to create the requisite basis of mediocrity. In a famous passage in the first part of *Zarathustra* Nietzsche launches an attack against the national State, 'the coldest of all cold monsters'[3] and the new idol which sets itself up as an object of worship and endeavours to reduce all to a common state of mediocrity. But though he condemns the national State from this point of view, namely as preventing the development of outstanding individuals, he none the less insists that the mediocre masses are a necessary means to an end, the emergence of a higher type of man. It is not the mission of the new higher caste or type to lead the masses as a shepherd leads his flock. Rather is it the mission of the masses to form the foundation on which the new so-called lords of the earth can lead their own life and make possible the emergence of still higher types of man. But before this can happen there will come the new barbarians, as Nietzsche calls them, who will break the actual dominion of the masses and thus render possible the free development of out-standing individuals.

As a spur and goal to the potentially higher man Nietzsche offers the myth of Superman (*der Uebermensch*). 'Not "humanity" but *Superman* is the goal.'[4] 'Man is something which must be surpassed; man is a bridge and not a goal.'[5] But this must not be taken to mean that man will evolve into Superman by an inevitable process. Superman is a myth, a goal for the will. 'Superman is the meaning of the earth. Let your will say: Superman *is to be* the meaning of the earth.'[6] Nietzsche does indeed assert that 'man is a rope stretched between animal and Superman—a rope over an abyss'.[7]

[1] *W*, III, p. 829 (xv, p. 296).   [2] *W*, III, p. 709 (xv, pp. 302-3).
[3] *W*, II, p. 313 (IV, p. 54).   [4] *W*, III, p. 440 (xv, p. 387).
[5] *W*, II, p. 445 (IV, p. 241).   [6] *W*, II, p. 280 (IV, p. 7).
[7] *W*, II, p. 281 (IV, p. 9).

But it is not a question of man evolving into Superman by a process of natural selection. For the matter of that, the rope might fall into the abyss. Superman cannot come unless superior individuals have the courage to transvalue all values, to break the old table of values, especially the Christian tables, and create new values out of their superabundant life and power. The new values will give direction and a goal to the higher man, and Superman is, as it were, their personification.

If he were taxed with his failure to give a clear description of Superman, Nietzsche might reply that as Superman does not yet exist he can hardly be expected to supply a clear description. At the same time, if the idea of Superman is to act as a spur, stimulus and goal, it must possess some content. And we can say perhaps that it is the concept of the highest possible development and integration of intellectual power, strength of character and will, independence, passion, taste and physique. Nietzsche alludes in one place to 'the Roman Caesar with Christ's soul'.[1] Superman would be Goethe and Napoleon in one, Nietzsche hints, or the Epicurean god appearing on earth. He would be a highly-cultured man, we may say, skilful in all bodily accomplishments, tolerant out of strength, regarding nothing as forbidden unless it is weakness either under the form of 'virtue' or under that of 'vice', the man who has become fully free and independent and affirms life and the universe. In fine, Superman is all that ailing, lonely, tormented, neglected Herr Professor Dr. Friedrich Nietzsche would like to be.

5. The reader of *Zarathustra* may easily and not unnaturally assume that the idea of Superman, if taken in conjunction with that of the transvaluation of values, is the main idea of the book. And he may be inclined to conclude that Nietzsche hopes at least for a constant development of man's potentialities. But Zarathustra is not only the prophet of Superman but also the teacher of the doctrine of the eternal recurrence. Further, in *Ecce Homo* Nietzsche informs us that the fundamental idea of *Zarathustra* is that of the eternal recurrence as 'the highest formula of the yea-saying (attitude to life) which can ever be attained'.[2] He also tells us that this 'fundamental thought'[3] of the work was first presented in the last aphorism but one of *Joyful Wisdom*. If, therefore, the doctrine of the eternal recurrence is the fundamental thought of *Zarathustra*,

---

[1] *W*, III, p. 422 (xv, p. 380).   [2] *W*, II, p. 1128 (xvII, p. 96).
[3] *Ibid.*

it can hardly be dismissed as a strange excrescence in Nietzsche's philosophy.

To be sure, Nietzsche found the idea of the eternal recurrence somewhat dismaying and oppressive. But, as was remarked earlier, he used the idea as a test of his strength, of his ability to say 'yes' to life as it is. Thus in the relevant aphorism of *Joyful Wisdom* he imagines a spirit appearing to him and telling him that his life, even in all its smallest details, will recur again innumerable times; and he raises the question whether he would be prostrated by this thought and curse the speaker or whether he would welcome the message in a spirit of affirmation of life, inasmuch as the eternal recurrence sets the seal of eternity on the world of Becoming. Similarly, in *Beyond Good and Evil* Nietzsche speaks of the world-approving man who wishes to have the play all over again a countless number of times and who cries *encore* not only to the play but also to the players. And he sets this idea against the 'half-Christian, half-German narrowness and simplicity'[1] with which pessimism was presented in Schopenhauer's philosophy. Again, in the third part of *Zarathustra* Nietzsche speaks of feeling disgust at the thought that even the most inferior man will return and that he himself is to 'come again eternally to this self same life, in its greatest and smallest (events)'.[2] And he proceeds to welcome this return. 'Oh, how should I not be ardent for eternity and for the marriage-ring of rings—the ring of the return?'[3] Similarly, in the notes for his *magnum opus* he speaks several times of the theory of the eternal recurrence as a great disciplinary thought, at once oppressive and liberating.

At the same time the theory is presented as an empirical hypothesis, and not merely as a disciplinary thought or test of inner strength. Thus we read that 'the principle of conservation of energy demands the *eternal* recurrence'.[4] If the world can be looked at as a determinate quantum of force or energy and as a determinate number of centres of force, it follows that the world-process will take the form of successive combinations of these centres, the number of these combinations being in principle determinable, that is, finite. And 'in an infinite time every possible combination would have been realized at some point; further, it would be realized an infinite number of times. And as between each combination and its next recurrence all other possible combinations

[1] *W*, II, p. 617 (v, p. 74).   [2] *W*, II, p. 467 (IV, p. 270).
[3] *W*, II, p. 474 (IV, p. 280).   [4] *W* III, p. 861 (XV, p. 427).

would have to occur, and as each of these combinations conditions the whole sequence of combinations in the same series, a cycle of absolutely identical series would be proved.'[1]

One main reason why Nietzsche lays stress on the theory of the eternal recurrence is that it seems to him to fill a gap in his philosophy. It confers on the flux of Becoming the semblance of Being, and it does so without introducing any Being which transcends the universe. Further, while the theory avoids the introduction of a transcendent Deity, it also avoids pantheism, the surreptitious reintroduction of the concept of God under the name of the universe. According to Nietzsche, if we say that the universe never repeats itself but is constantly creating new forms, this statement betrays a hankering after the idea of God. For the universe itself is assimilated to the concept of a creative Deity. And this assimilation is excluded by the theory of the eternal recurrence. The theory also excludes, of course, the idea of personal immortality in a 'beyond', though at the same time it provides a substitute for this idea, even if the notion of living one's life over again in all its details a countless number of times is unlikely to exercise a more than limited appeal. In other words, the theory of the eternal recurrence expresses Nietzsche's resolute will to this-worldliness, to *Diesseitigkeit*. The universe is shut in, as it were, on itself. Its significance is purely immanent. And the truly strong man, the truly Dionysian man, will affirm this universe with steadfastness, courage and even joy, shunning the escapism which is a manifestation of weakness.

It is sometimes said that the theory of the eternal recurrence and the theory of Superman are incompatible. But it can hardly be claimed, I think, that they are logically incompatible. For the theory of recurrent cycles does not exclude the recurrence of the will to Superman or, for the matter of that, of Superman himself. It is, of course, true that the theory of the eternal recurrence rules out the concept of Superman as the final end of a non-repeatable creative process. But Nietzsche does not admit this concept. On the contrary, he excludes it as being equivalent to a surreptitious reintroduction of a theological manner of interpreting the universe.

6. There have been disciples of Nietzsche who endeavoured to make his thought into a system which they then accepted as a kind of gospel and tried to propagate. But, generally speaking, his

[1] *W*, III, p. 704 (xv, p. 430).

influence has taken the form of stimulating thought in this or that direction. And this stimulative influence has been widespread. But it certainly has not been uniform in character. Nietzsche has meant different things to different people. In the field of morals and values, for example, his importance for some people has lain primarily in his development of a naturalistic criticism of morality, while others would emphasize rather his work in the phenomenology of values. Others again, of a less academically philosophical turn of mind, have stressed his idea of the transvaluation of values. In the field of social and cultural philosophy some have portrayed him as attacking democracy and democratic socialism in favour of something like Nazism, while others have represented him as a great European, or as a great cosmopolitan, a man who was above any nationalistic outlook. To some he has been primarily the man who diagnosed the decadence and imminent collapse of western civilization, while others have seen in him and his philosophy the embodiment of the very nihilism for which he professed to supply a remedy. In the field of religion he has appeared to some as a radical atheist, intent on exposing the baneful influence of religious belief, while others have seen in the very vehemence of his attack on Christianity evidence of his fundamental concern with the problem of God. Some have regarded him first and foremost from the literary point of view, as a man who developed the potentialities of the German language; others, such as Thomas Mann, have been influenced by his distinction between the Dionysian and Apollonian outlooks or attitudes; others again have emphasized his psychological analyses.

Obviously, Nietzsche's method of writing is partly responsible for the possibility of diverse interpretations. Many of his books consist of aphorisms. And we know that in some cases he jotted down thoughts which came to him on his solitary walks and later strung them together to form a book. The results are what might be expected. For instance, reflection on the tameness of bourgeois life and on the heroism and self-sacrifice occasioned by war might produce an aphorism or passage in praise of war and warriors, while on another occasion reflection on the way in which war leads to the waste and destruction of the best elements of a nation, and often for no appreciable gain to anyone except a few selfish individuals, might produce, and indeed did produce, a condemnation of war as stupid and suicidal for both victors and vanquished. It is then possible for the commentator to depict Nietzsche either as a lover of war or as almost a pacifist. A judicious selection of texts is all that is required.

The situation is complicated, of course, by the relation between the philosophizing of Nietzsche and his personal life and struggles. Thus while it is possible to confine one's attention to the written word, it is also possible to develop a psychological interpretation of his thought. And, as already noted, there is the possibility of giving an existentialist interpretation of the significance of the whole complex of his life and thought.

That Nietzsche was in some respects an acute and far-seeing thinker is hardly open to question. Take, for example, his excursions into psychology. It is not necessary to regard all his analyses as acceptable before one is prepared to admit that he divined, as it were, a number of important ideas which have become common coin in modern psychology. We have only to recall his notion of concealed operative ideals and motives or his concept of sublimation. As for his use of the concept of the Will to Power as a key to human psychology, an idea which found its classical expression in the psychological theory of Alfred Adler, we can say indeed that it was exaggerated and that the more widely the concept is applied the more indefinite does its content become.[1] At the same time Nietzsche's experimentation with the use of the concept as a key to man's psychical life helped to focus attention on the operation of a powerful drive, even if it is not the only one. Again, as we look back in the light of the events of the twentieth century on Nietzsche's anticipation of the coming of the 'new barbarism' and of world-wars we can hardly fail to recognize that he had a deeper insight into the situation than those of his contemporaries who showed a complacent optimistic belief in the inevitability of progress.

But though Nietzsche was clear-sighted in some respects, he was myopic in others. For instance, he certainly failed to give sufficient attention to the question whether his distinctions between ascending and descending life and between higher and lower types of men did not tacitly presuppose the very objectivity of values which he rejected. It would be open to him, of course, to make it a matter of taste and aesthetic preference, as he sometimes said that it was. But then a similar question can be raised about aesthetic values, unless perhaps the distinction between higher and lower is to become simply a matter of subjective feeling and no claim is

---

[1] Obviously, similar remarks can be made about Freud's concept of *libido*.

made that one's own feelings should be accepted as a norm by anyone else. Again, as has already been hinted, Nietzsche failed to give the requisite prolonged consideration to the question how the subject can impose an intelligible structure on the flux of Becoming when the subject is itself resolved into the flux and exists as a subject only as part of the structure which it is said to impose.

As for Nietzsche's attitude to Christianity, his increasingly shrill attack on it is accompanied by an increasing inability to do justice to his foe. And it is arguable that the vehemence of his attack was partly an expression of an inner tension and uncertainty which he endeavoured to stifle.[1] As he himself put it, he had the blood of theologians in his veins. But if we abstract from the shrillness and one-sidedness of his attack on Christianity in particular, we can say that this attack forms part of his general campaign against all beliefs and philosophies, such as metaphysical idealism, which ascribe to the world and to human existence and history a meaning or purpose or goal other than the meaning freely imposed by man himself.[2] The rejection of the idea that the world has been created by God for a purpose or that it is the self-manifestation of the absolute Idea or Spirit sets man free to give to life the meaning which he wills to give it. And it has no other meaning.

The idea of God, whether theistically or pantheistically conceived, thus gives way to the concept of man as the being who confers intelligibility on the world and creates values. But are we to say that in the long run it is the world itself which has, so to speak, the last word, and that man, the moral legislator and conferer of meaning, is absorbed as an insignificant speck in the meaningless cycles of history? If so, man's effort to confer meaning and value on his life appear as a defiant 'No', a rejection

[1] To claim that a professed atheist was 'really' a believer simply because he attacked theism persistently and vehemently would be extravagant and paradoxical. But Nietzsche, who as a boy was profoundly religious, was never indifferent to the problems of Being and of the meaning or purpose of existence. Further, his dialogue, as it were, with Christ, culminating in the final words of *Ecce Homo*, '*Dionysus* versus *the Crucified*', shows clearly enough that 'the Antichrist' had to do violence to himself, even if he thought of it as a case of transcending his own inclinations to weakness. In spite of his rejection of God he was very far from being what would generally be thought of as an 'irreligious man'.

[2] Nietzsche insists indeed that his main objection against Christianity is against the system of morals and values. At the same time he joins Christianity with German idealism, which he regards as a derivative of Christianity or as a masked form of it, in his attack on the view that the world has a given meaning or goal.

of the meaningless universe, rather than as a yea-saying attitude.[1] Or are we to say that the interpretation of the world as without a given meaning or goal and as a series of endless cycles is a fiction which expresses man's Will to Power? If so, the question whether the world has or has not a given meaning or goal remains open.

A final remark. Professional philosophers who read Nietzsche may be interested principally in his critique of morality or in his phenomenological analyses or in his psychological theories. But it is probably true to say that the attention of the general reader is usually concentrated on the remedies which he offers for the overcoming of what he calls nihilism, the spiritual crisis of modern man. It is the idea of the transvaluation of values, the concept of the order of rank and the myth of Superman which strike their attention. It is arguable, however, that what is really significant in what one may call the non-academic Nietzsche is not his proposed antidotes to nihilism but rather his existence and thought considered precisely as a dramatic expression of a lived spiritual crisis from which there is no issue in terms of his own philosophy.

[1] Unless indeed we understand by a yea-saying attitude an acceptance of the fact of differences between the strong and the weak, as opposed to an attempt to set all on the same level. But in this case a yea-saying attitude should also involve acceptance of the fact that the majority sets limits to the activities of the independent rebels.

CHAPTER XXIII

RETROSPECT AND PROSPECT

Some questions arising out of nineteenth-century German philosophy—The positivist answer—The philosophy of existence —The rise of phenomenology; Brentano, Meinong, Husserl, the widespread use of phenomenological analysis—Return to ontology; N. Hartmann—The metaphysics of Being; Heidegger, the Thomists—Concluding reflections.

1. KANT endeavoured to overcome what he regarded as the scandal of conflicting metaphysical systems and to set philosophy on a secure basis. And at the beginning of the period covered in this volume we find Fichte insisting that philosophy is the fundamental science which grounds all other sciences. But when Fichte declared that philosophy was the fundamental science, he was referring, of course, to the *Wissenschaftslehre*, that is, to his own philosophy. And his system simply forms one member of the series of highly personal, though interesting and often fascinating, interpretations of reality which span the nineteenth century like a series of mountain peaks. Other examples are the speculative theism of Schelling, the absolute idealism of Hegel, Schopenhauer's philosophy of the world as presentation and will, Kierkegaard's vision of human history and Nietzsche's philosophy of the Will to Power. And it would need a bold man to maintain that the series provides empirical confirmation of the validity of Fichte's claim on behalf of the scientific character of philosophy.

It is indeed arguable that the differences between philosophies, even when these differences are very considerable, do not prove that philosophy has no cognitive value. For it may be that each philosophy expresses a truth, an apprehension of a real aspect of reality or of human life and history, and that these truths are mutually complementary. That is to say, the element of conflict does not arise from any incompatibility between the fundamental ideas which lie at the bases of the different systems, but rather from the fact that each philosopher exaggerates one aspect of the world or of human life and history, thus turning a part into the whole. For example, Marx undoubtedly draws attention to real aspects of man and of human history; and there is no fundamental incompatibility between these aspects and, say, the religious aspects of human existence which are emphasized by Schelling. The incompatibility arises when Marx turns one idea which expresses a partial aspect of man and his history into a key-idea to unlock all doors.

One trouble, however, with this way of looking at things is that it involves whittling down philosophical systems to what amount practically to truisms, and that this process deprives the systems of most of their interest. It can be argued, for example, that Marx's philosophy is of interest precisely because of the element of exaggeration which sets the whole of human history in a certain perspective. If Marxism is whittled down to indubitable truths such as that without man's economic life there could be no philosophy or art or science, it loses a great deal of its interest and all of its provocative character. Similarly, if Nietzsche's philosophy is whittled down to the statement that the will to power or drive to power is one of the influential factors in human life, it becomes compatible with the reduced version of Marxism, but only at the cost of being itself reduced to a fairly obvious proposition.

A possible way of countering this line of argument is to say that the exaggerations in a philosophical system serve a useful purpose. For it is precisely the element of striking and arresting exaggeration which serves to draw attention in a forcible way to the basic truth which is contained in the system. And once we have digested this truth, we can forget about the exaggeration. It is not so much a question of whittling down the system as of using it as a source of insight and then forgetting the instrument by which we attained this insight, unless indeed we need to refer to it again as a means of recovering the insight in question.

But though this is in itself a not unreasonable line of thought, it is of very little use for supporting Fichte's contention that philosophy is the science of sciences. For suppose that we reduce the philosophies of Schopenhauer, Marx and Nietzsche respectively to such statements as that there is a great deal of evil and suffering in the world, that we have to produce food and consume it before we can develop the sciences, and that the will to power can operate in devious and concealed forms. We then have three propositions of which the first two are for most people obviously true while the third, which is rather more interesting, is a psychological proposition. None of them would normally be called a specifically philosophical proposition. The philosophical propositions of

Schopenhauer, Marx and Nietzsche would thus become instruments for drawing attention to propositions of some other type. And this is obviously not at all the sort of thing which Fichte had in mind when he claimed that philosophy was the basic science.

It may be objected that I have been concentrating simply on the outstanding original systems, on the mountain peaks, and neglecting the foothills, the general movements such as Neo-Kantianism. It may be suggested, that is to say, that while it is true that if we are looking for highly personal imaginative interpretations of the universe or of human life we must turn to the famous philosophers, it is also true that in those general movements in which the particular tends to be merged in the universal we can find more plebeian scientific work in philosophy, patient co-operative efforts at tackling separate problems.

But is it true? In Neo-Kantianism, for example, there are, of course, family-likenesses which justify our describing it as a definite movement, distinct from other movements. But once we start to inspect it at close hand we see not only somewhat different general tendencies within the movement as a whole but also a multitude of individual philosophies. Again, in the movement of inductive metaphysics this philosopher uses one idea as a key-idea for interpreting the world while that philosopher uses another. Wundt uses his voluntaristic interpretation of human psychology as a basis for a general philosophy, while Driesch uses his theory of entelechies, derived from reflection on biological processes. True, a sense of proportion and the requirements of mental economy suggest that in many cases individual systems are best forgotten or allowed to sink into the background of a general movement. But this does not alter the fact that the closer we look at the philosophy of the nineteenth century, the more do the massive groupings tend to break up into individual philosophies. Indeed, it is not altogether an exaggeration to say that as the century wears on each professor of philosophy seems to think it necessary to produce his own system.

Obviously, there can be different opinions within the framework of a common conviction about the nature and function of philosophy. Thus the Neo-Kantians were more or less agreed about what philosophy is incompetent to achieve. But though conflicting views about the nature and function of philosophy are not necessarily coextensive with different philosophical views or even systems, there were obviously in nineteenth-century German thought some very different concepts about what philosophy ought to be. For instance, when Fichte said that philosophy ought to be a science, he meant that it should be derived systematically from one fundamental principle. The inductive metaphysicians, however, had a different idea of philosophy. And when we turn to Nietzsche, we find him rejecting the concept of absolute truth and emphasizing the valuational foundations of different kinds of philosophy, the value-judgments themselves depending on the types of men who make them.[1]

Needless to say, the fact that two philosophers differ does not of itself prove that neither is right. And even if they are both wrong, some other philosopher may be right. At the same time the conflicting systems of the nineteenth century, and still more perhaps the conflicting views about the nature and competence of philosophy, show that Kant's attempt to settle once and for all the true nature and function of philosophy was from the historical point of view a failure. And the old questions present themselves to the mind with renewed force. Can philosophy be a science? If so, how? What sort of knowledge can we legitimately expect from it? Has philosophy been superseded by the growth and development of the particular sciences? Or has it still a field of its own? If so, what is it? And what is the appropriate method for investigating this field?

It is not indeed surprising that Kant's judgment about the nature and limits of scientific philosophy should have failed to win universal acceptance. For it was closely related to his own system. In other words, it was a philosophical judgment, just as the pronouncements of Fichte, Hegel, Marx, Nietzsche, Eucken and others were philosophical judgments. In fact, provided that one is not making a statement either about the current conventional use of terms or about the various uses of the word 'philosophy' in history, any pronouncement that one may make about the 'true' nature and function of philosophy is a philosophical statement, one which is made from within philosophy and commits one to or expresses a particular philosophical position.

[1] This view naturally brings to mind Fichte's statement that the kind of philosophy which a man chooses depends on the kind of man that he is. But even if we prescind from the fact that Fichte did not intend this statement to be understood in a sense which would exclude the concept of philosophy as a science and see in it an anticipation of the tendency to subordinate the concept of truth to the concept of human life or existence, in tracing the concrete development of this tendency we find it splitting up into different conceptions of man and of human life and existence. One has only to mention the names of Kierkegaard and Nietzsche, for example.

It is obviously not the intention of the present writer to suggest that no definite philosophical position should be adopted or that it is improper to make philosophical judgments about the nature and function of philosophy. Nor is it his intention to suggest that no good reasons can be adduced in favour of accepting one judgment rather than another. At the same time he does not wish to make an abrupt transition at this moment from the role of historian to the role of one who speaks in the name of a definite philosophical system. He prefers instead to take a brief glance at some of the general lines of answer which have been offered in German thought during the first part of the twentieth century to the type of question mentioned above. This procedure will serve to provide some sort of bridge between past and present.

2. One possible line of answer to questions about the scope of philosophy is to maintain that the particular sciences are the only source of knowledge about the world and that philosophy has no field of its own in the sense that its function is to investigate a special level or type of being. It is indeed perfectly understandable that at one time men sought to acquire knowledge about the world through philosophical speculation. But in the course of their development the various sciences have taken over one part after another of the field of exploration which was once attributed to philosophy. There has thus been a gradual substitution of scientific knowledge for philosophical speculation. And it is no wonder if philosophers who think that they can increase our knowledge of reality by other means than the employment of the scientific method of hypothesis, deduction and verification only succeed in producing conflicting systems which may possess some aesthetic value or emotive significance but which can no longer be seriously considered as possessing cognitive value. If philosophy is to be scientific and not a form of poetry masquerading as science, its function must be purely analytic in character. For example, it may be able to clarify some of the fundamental concepts employed in the sciences and to inquire into scientific methodology, but it cannot go beyond the sciences by adding to or supplementing our scientific knowledge of the world.

This general positivist attitude, the conviction that the empirical sciences are the only reliable source of knowledge about the world, is obviously widespread. In the nineteenth century it attained its classical expression in the philosophy of Auguste Comte, and we have seen that it also found expression, though on a less impressive scale, in the materialist and positivist current of thought in Germany. But we also noted how some of the German philosophers who represented this current of thought went well beyond the particular sciences by developing a general view of reality. Haeckel's monism was a case in point. And it was just this tendency of philosophy to develop into a *Weltanschauung* or world-view which the positivism of the twentieth century was concerned to exclude.

An obvious objection to the reduction of philosophy to the position of a handmaid of science is that there are questions and problems which are not raised by any particular science, which demand answers and which have been traditionally and properly regarded as belonging to the field of philosophical inquiry. The positivist is convinced, of course, that questions about ultimate reality or the Absolute, about the origin of finite existents, and so on have not in fact been answered by the metaphysical philosophers, such as Schelling for instance. But even if one agreed that the questions had not in fact been definitely answered, or even that we were not in a position to answer them, one might still wish to say that the raising and discussion of such questions has a great value. For it helps to show the limits of scientific knowledge and reminds us of the mysteries of finite existence. Hence an effective exclusion of metaphysical philosophy requires the establishment of two complementary theses. It must be shown that metaphysical problems are unanswerable in principle and not merely in the sense that we are not in a position to answer them here and now. And it must further be shown that problems which are unanswerable in principle are pseudo-problems in the sense that they are not real questions at all but verbal expressions which lack any clear meaning.

This is precisely what the neopositivists of the Vienna Circle and their associates set out to show in the twenties of the present century by developing a criterion of meaning, the so-called principle of verifiability, which would effectively exclude metaphysical problems and statements from the class of meaningful problems and statements. Apart from the purely formal propositions of logic and pure mathematics, meaningful propositions were interpreted as empirical hypotheses, the meaning of which was coincident with the thinkable, though not necessarily practically realizable, mode of verification in sense-experience. And as, for instance, we can conceive no empirical verification in sense-experience of the statement of Parmenides that all things are really one changeless being, this statement could not be accepted as meaningful.[1] As stated in this form, however, the neopositivist criterion of meaning was unable to stand up to criticism, whether from outside or inside the neopositivist movement, and it either came to be interpreted as a purely methodological principle for the purpose of delimiting the range of what could properly be called scientific hypotheses or was so whittled down and explained away that it became quite ineffective for excluding speculative philosophy.

The fact of the matter is, I think, that neopositivism as a philosophy was an attempt to provide a theoretical justification of positivism as a mentality or attitude. And the neopositivist criterion of meaning was heavily loaded with the implicit philosophical presuppositions of this attitude. Further, its effectiveness as a weapon against metaphysical philosophy depended on these presuppositions not being made explicit. For once they have been made explicit, neopositivism stands revealed as one more questionable philosophy. This obviously does not entail the disappearance of positivism as a mentality or attitude. But the whole episode of the rise and criticism (partly autocriticism) of neopositivism had the great advantage of dragging concealed presuppositions into the light of day. It was a question of the positivist mentality, which had become widespread in the nineteenth century, becoming reflectively conscious of itself and seeing its own presuppositions. True, this self-consciousness was attained within the philosophical field and left untouched great areas of the positivist mentality or attitude. But this simply helps to illustrate the need of philosophy, one of the functions of which is precisely to render explicit and subject to critical examination the concealed implicit presuppositions of non-reflective philosophical attitudes.[2]

3. According to the neopositivists, philosophy can become scientific, but only at the cost of becoming purely analytic and relinquishing any claim to increase our factual knowledge of

---

[1] That is to say, the statement might be expressive and evocative of emotive attitudes, thus possessing 'emotive' significance; but according to strict neopositivist principles it would be meaningless in the sense that it would be incapable of being either true or false.

[2] A bibliography of neopositivism is provided in *Logical Positivism* (an anthology), edited by A. J. Ayer, Glencoe, Ill., and London, 1959. Some writings illustrating the discussion of the principle of verifiability, together with a selected bibliography, can be found in *A Modern Introduction to Philosophy* edited by P. Edwards and A. Pap, pp. 543–621, Glencoe, Ill. 1957. Cf. also *Contemporary Philosophy*, by F. C. Copleston, pp. 26–60, London, 1956, for a critical discussion of neopositivism.

reality. Another possible way of describing the function and nature of philosophy is to say that it has a field of its own, inasmuch as it is concerned with Being, and at the same time to deny that it is or can be a science, whether a universal science or a special science alongside the particular empirical sciences. In one sense philosophy is what it always has been, namely concerned with Being (*das Sein*) as distinct from *die Seienden*. But it was a mistake to suppose that there can be a science of Being. For Being is unobjectifiable; it cannot be turned into an object of scientific investigation. The primary function of philosophy is to awaken man to an awareness of Being as transcending beings and grounding them. But as there can be no science of Being, no metaphysical system can possess universal validity. The different systems are so many personal decipherings of unobjectifiable Being. This does not mean, however, that they are valueless. For any great metaphysical system can serve to push open, as it were, the door which positivism would keep shut. Thus to speak of the scandal of conflicting systems betrays a misconception of the true nature of philosophy. For the objection is valid only if philosophy, to be justified at all, should be a science. And this is not the case. True, by claiming that philosophy is a science, the metaphysicians of the past have themselves provided the ground for talk about the scandal of different and incompatible systems. But once this claim is relinquished and we understand the true function of metaphysics as being that of awakening man to an awareness of the enveloping Being in which he and all other finite existents are grounded, the ground for scandal disappears. For that there should be different personal decipherings of transcendent Being is only what one ought to expect. The important thing is to see them for what they are and not to take the extravagant claims of their authors at their face value.

This point of view represents one aspect of the philosophy of Professor Karl Jaspers (b. 1883). But he combines acceptance of the Kantian contention that speculative metaphysics cannot provide us with theoretical knowledge with a theory of 'existence' which shows the influence of Kierkegaard. The human being can be objectified and studied scientifically by, say, the physiologist and the psychologist. The individual is then exhibited as classifiable in this or that way. But when looked at from the point of view of the free agent himself, from within the life of free choice, the individual is seen as this unique existent, the being who freely transcends what he already is and creates himself, as it were, through the exercise of his freedom. Indeed, from this point of view man is always in the making, his own making: *Existenz* is always possible existence, *mögliche Existenz*. Of man regarded under this aspect there can be no scientific study. But philosophy can draw attention to or illuminate 'existence' in such a way as to enable the existing individual to understand what is meant in terms of his own experience. It can also draw attention to the movement by which, especially in certain situations, the individual becomes aware both of his finitude and of the enveloping presence of Being as the Transcendent in which he and all other beings are grounded. But as transcendent Being can be neither objectified nor reduced to the conclusion of a demonstration or proof, the man who becomes aware of it as the unobjectifiable complement and ground of finite beings is free either to affirm it with Kierkegaard, through what Jaspers calls 'philosophical faith', or to reject it with Nietzsche.

We cannot enter into further descriptions of the philosophy of Karl Jaspers,[1] as it has been mentioned less for its own sake than as one of the ways of depicting the nature and functions of philosophy which have been exemplified in German thought during the first half of the twentieth century. It should be noted, however, that Jaspers, like Kant before him, endeavours to place belief in human freedom and in God beyond the reach of scientific criticism. Indeed, we can see an evident recurrence of Kantian themes. For example, Jaspers' distinction between man as seen from the external scientific point of view and man as seen from the internal point of view of 'existence' corresponds in some way to the Kantian distinction between the phenomenal and noumenal levels. At the same time there are also evident differences between Kant and Jaspers. For instance, Kant's emphasis on the moral law, on which practical faith in God is grounded, disappears, and the Kierkegaardian concept of the existing individual comes to the fore. Besides, Jaspers' 'philosophical faith', which is a more academic version of Kierkegaard's leap of faith, is directed towards God as Being, not, as with Kant, to the idea of God as an instrument for synthesizing virtue and happiness.

An obvious objection to Jaspers' way of setting metaphysics beyond the reach of scientific criticism is that in speaking at all about freedom and, still more, about Being he is inevitably objectifying what according to him cannot be objectified. If Being is really unobjectifiable, it cannot be mentioned. We can only remain silent. But one might, of course, employ Wittgenstein's distinction and say that for Jaspers philosophy tries to 'show' what cannot be 'said'. Indeed, Jaspers' emphasis on the 'illuminating' function of philosophy points in precisely this direction.

4. For the neopositivists, philosophy can be scientific, but by the very fact of becoming scientific it is not a science in the sense of having a field peculiar to itself. For Jaspers philosophy has in a sense a field of its own,[1] but it is not a science and moves on a different plane from those of the sciences. The phenomenologists, however, have tried both to assign to philosophy a field or fields and to vindicate its scientific character.

(i) In a few notes on the rise of phenomenology there is no need to go back beyond Franz Brentano (1838–1917). After studying with Trendelenburg Brentano became a Catholic priest. In 1872 he was appointed to a chair at Würzburg, and in 1874 at Vienna. But in 1873 he had abandoned the Church, and his status as a married ex-priest did not make his life as a university professor in the Austrian capital an easy one. In 1895 he retired from teaching and took up residence at Florence, moving to Switzerland on the outbreak of the First World War.

In 1874 Brentano published a book bearing the title *Psychology from the Empirical Standpoint* (*Psychologie vom empirischen Standpunkt*).[2] Empirical psychology, he insists, is not a science of the soul, a term which has metaphysical implications, but of psychical phenomena. Further, when Brentano talks about empirical psychology, it is descriptive rather than genetic psychology which he has in mind. And descriptive psychology is for him an inquiry into psychical acts or acts of consciousness as concerned with 'inexistent' objects, that is, with objects as contained within the acts themselves. All consciousness is consciousness *of*. To think is to think of something, and to desire is to desire something. Thus every act of consciousness is 'intentional': it 'intends' an object. And

---

[1] The term 'philosophy of existence' suggests that *Existenz* constitutes this field. But Jaspers insists more on Being, the illumination of 'existence' being the path to the awareness of Being. Being, however, is not a field for scientific investigation by philosophy, though the philosopher may be able to reawaken or keep alive the awareness of Being.

[2] Among other writings we can mention *On the Origin of Moral Knowledge* (*Vom Ursprung der sittlichen Erkenntnis*, 1889), *On the Future of Philosophy* (*Ueber die Zukunft der Philosophie*, 1893) and *The Four Phases of Philosophy* (*Die vier Phasen der Philosophie*, 1895).

we can consider the object precisely as intended and as inexistent, without raising questions about its extramental nature and status.

This theory of the intentionality of consciousness, which goes back to Aristotelian-Scholastic thought, is not in itself a subjectivist theory. The descriptive psychologist, as Brentano interprets his function, does not say that the objects of consciousness have no existence apart from consciousness. But he considers them only as inexistent, for the good reason that he is concerned with psychical acts or acts of consciousness and not with ontological questions about extramental reality.

Now, it is clear that in considering consciousness one can concentrate either on the inexistent objects of consciousness or on the intentional reference as such. And Brentano tends to concentrate on the second aspect of consciousness, distinguishing three main types of intentional reference. First there is simple presentation, in which there is no question of truth or falsity. Secondly there is judgment which involves recognition (*Anerkennen*) or rejection (*Verwerfen*), in other words affirmation or denial. Thirdly there are the movements of the will and of feelings (*Gemütsbewegungen*), where the fundamental attitudes or structures of consciousness are love and hate or, as Brentano also says, of pleasure and displeasure.

We may add that just as Brentano believed that there are logical judgments which are evidently true, so did he believe that there are moral sentiments which are evidently correct or right. That is to say, there are goods, objects of moral approval or pleasure, which are evidently and always preferable. But from the point of view of the rise of phenomenology the important feature of Brentano's thought is the doctrine of the intentionality of consciousness.

(ii) Brentano's reflections exercised an influence on a number of philosophers who are sometimes grouped together as the Austrian School, such as Anton Marty (1847–1914), a professor at Prague, Oskar Kraus (1872–1942), a pupil of Marty and himself a professor at Prague, and Carl Stumpf (1848–1936), who was a noted psychologist and had Edmund Husserl among his pupils.

Special mention, however, must be made of Alexius Meinong (1853–1920) who studied under Brentano at Vienna and subsequently became professor of philosophy at Graz. In his theory of objects (*Gegenstandstheorie*) Meinong distinguished different types of objects. In ordinary life we generally understand by the term 'objects' particular existing things such as trees, stones, tables, and so on. But if we consider 'objects' as objects of consciousness, we can easily see that there are other types as well. For example, there are ideal objects, such as values and numbers, which can be said to possess reality though they do not exist in the sense in which trees and cows exist. Again, there are imaginary objects such as a golden mountain or the king of France. There is no existing golden mountain and there has been no king of France for many years. But if we can talk about golden mountains, we must be talking about something. For to talk about nothing is not to talk. There is an object present to consciousness, even if there is no corresponding extramentally existent thing.

Bertrand Russell's theory of descriptions was designed to circumvent Meinong's line of argument and to depopulate, as it were, the world of objects which are in some sense real but do not exist. However, this is irrelevant to our present purpose. The main point is that Meinong's theory helped to concentrate attention on objects considered precisely as objects of consciousness, as, to use Brentano's term, inexistent.

(iii) The effective founder of the phenomenological movement was, however, neither Brentano nor Meinong but Edmund Husserl (1859–1938). After having taken his doctorate in mathematics Husserl attended Brentano's lectures at Vienna (1884–6) and it was Brentano's influence which led him to devote himself to philosophy. He became professor of philosophy at Göttingen and subsequently at Freiburg-im-Breisgau where Martin Heidegger was one of his pupils.

In 1891 Husserl published a *Philosophy of Arithmetic* (*Philosophie der Arithmetik*) in which he showed a certain tendency to psychologism, that is, to grounding logic on psychology. For example, the concept of multiplicity, which is essential for the concept of number, is grounded on the psychical act of binding together diverse contents of consciousness in one representation. This view was subjected to criticism by the celebrated mathematician and logician Gottlob Frege (1848–1925) and in his *Logical Investigations* (*Logische Untersuchungen*, 1900–1) Husserl maintained clearly that logic is not reducible to psychology.[1] Logic is concerned with the sphere of meaning, that is, with what is meant (*gemeint*) or intended, not with the succession of real psychical acts. In other words, we must distinguish between consciousness

[1] In his rejection of psychologism Husserl was probably influenced not only by Frege but also by Bolzano (see pp. 256–9).

as a complex of psychical facts, events or experiences (*Erlebnisse*) and the objects of consciousness which are meant or intended. The latter 'appear' to or for consciousness: in this sense they are phenomena. The former, however, do not appear: they are lived through (*erlebt*) or experienced. Obviously, this does not mean that psychical acts cannot themselves be reduced to phenomena by reflection; but then, considered precisely as appearing to consciousness, they are no longer real psychical acts.

This involves a distinction between meanings and things, a distinction which is of considerable importance. For failure to make this distinction was one of the main reasons why the empiricists found it necessary to deny the existence of universal concepts or ideas. Things, including real psychical acts, are all individual or particular, whereas meanings can be universal. And as such they are 'essences'.

In the work which in its English translation bears the title *Ideas: General Introduction to Pure Phenomenology* (*Ideen zu einer reinen Phänomenologie und phänomenologischen Philosophie*, 1913) Husserl calls the act of consciousness *noesis* and its correlative object, which is meant or intended, *noema*. Further, he speaks of the intuition of essences (*Wesensschau*). In pure mathematics, for example, there is an intuition of essences which gives rise to propositions which are not empirical generalizations but belong to a different type, that of *a priori* propositions. And phenomenology in general is the descriptive analysis of essences or ideal structures. There could thus be, for example, a phenomenology of values. But there could also be a phenomenological analysis of the fundamental structures of consciousness, provided, of course, that these structures are 'reduced' to essences or *eidē*.

A point insisted on by Husserl is the suspension of judgment (the so-called *epoche*) in regard to the ontological or existential status or reference of the objects of consciousness. By means of this suspension existence is said to be 'bracketed'. Suppose, for example, that I wished to develop a phenomenological analysis of the aesthetic experience of beauty. I suspend all judgment about the subjectivity or objectivity of beauty in an ontological sense and direct my attention simply to the essential structure of aesthetic experience as 'appearing' to consciousness.

The reason why Husserl insists on this suspension of judgment can be seen by considering the implications of the title of one of his writings, *Philosophy as Strict Science* (*Philosophie als strenge*

Wissenschaft, 1910–11). Like Descartes before him, Husserl wished to put philosophy on a firm basis. And in his opinion this meant going behind all presuppositions to that which one cannot doubt or question. Now, in ordinary life we make all sorts of existential assumptions, about, for instance, the existence of physical objects independently of consciousness. We must therefore prescind from or bracket this 'natural attitude' (*natürliche Einstellung*). It is not a question of saying that the natural attitude is wrong and its assumptions unjustified. It is a question of methodologically prescinding from such assumptions and going behind them to consciousness itself which it is impossible either to doubt or to prescind from. Further, we cannot, for example, profitably discuss the ontological status of values until we are quite clear what we are talking about, what value 'means'. And this is revealed by phenomenological analysis. Hence phenomenology is fundamental philosophy: it must precede and ground any ontological philosophy, any metaphysics.

As already hinted, Husserl's employment of the *epoche* bears a resemblance to Descartes' use of methodological doubt. And in point of fact Husserl saw in Descartes' philosophy a certain measure of anticipation of phenomenology. At the same time he insisted that the existence of a self in the sense of a spiritual substance or, as Descartes put it, a 'thinking thing' (*res cogitans*) must itself be bracketed. True, the ego cannot be simply eliminated. But the subject which is required as correlative to the object of consciousness is simply the pure or transcendental ego, the pure subject as such, not a spiritual substance or soul. The existence of such a substance is something about which we must suspend judgment, so far as pure phenomenology is concerned.

The methodological use of the *epoche* does not by itself commit Husserl to idealism. To say that the existence of consciousness is the only undeniable or indubitable existence is not necessarily to say that consciousness is the only existent. But in point of fact Husserl proceeds to make the transition to idealism by trying to deduce consciousness from the transcendental ego and by making the reality of the world relative to consciousness. Nothing can be conceived except as an object of consciousness. Hence the object must be constituted by consciousness.[1]

Already discernible in *Ideas*, this idealistic orientation of

---

[1] Constituting an object can mean making it an object *for* consciousness. And this does not necessarily mean idealism. Or it can be taken to refer to a creative

Husserl's thought became more marked in *Formal and Transcendental Logic* (*Formale und transzendentale Logik*, 1929) where logic and ontology tend to coincide, and in *Cartesian Meditations* (*Méditations cartésiennes*, 1931). It is understandable that this transition to idealism did not favour the acceptance by other phenomenologists of Husserl's original insistence on the *epoche*. Martin Heidegger, for example, decisively rejected the demand for the *epoche* and attempted to use the phenomenological method in the development of a non-idealistic philosophy of Being.

(iv) Phenomenological analysis is capable of fruitful application in a variety of fields. Alexander Pfänder (1870–1941) applied it in the field of psychology, Oskar Becker (b. 1889), a disciple of Husserl, in the philosophy of mathematics, Adolf Reinach (1883–1917) in the philosophy of law, Max Scheler (1874–1928) in the field of values, while others have applied it in the fields of aesthetics and the religious consciousness. But the use of the method does not necessarily mean that the user can be called a 'disciple' of Husserl. Scheler, for example, was an eminent philosopher in his own right. And phenomenological analysis has been practised by thinkers whose general philosophical position is markedly different from Husserl's. One has only to mention the French existentialists Jean-Paul Sartre (b. 1905) and Maurice Merleau-Ponty (b. 1908) or indeed the contemporary Thomists.

It is not unreasonable to argue that this widespread use of phenomenological analysis not only constitutes an eloquent testimony to its value but also shows that it is a unifying factor. At the same time it is also arguable that the fact that Husserl's demand for the *epoche* has generally been disregarded or rejected and that phenomenology has been used within the frameworks of different philosophies rather than as a foundation for a philosophy to put an end to conflicting systems shows that it has not fulfilled Husserl's original hopes. Besides, the nature of what is called phenomenological analysis can itself be called in question. For example, though the relations between continental phenomenology and the conceptual or 'linguistic' analysis practised in England is one of the main themes which permit a fruitful dialogue between groups of philosophers who in other respects may find it difficult to understand one another, one of the principal issues in such a dialogue is precisely the nature of what is called phenomenological activity by which things are given the only reality they possess, namely as related to consciousness, as consciousness-dependent. It is the transition to this second meaning which involves idealism.

analysis. Is it legitimate to speak of a phenomenological analysis of 'essences'? If so, in what precise sense? Is phenomenological analysis a specifically philosophical activity? Or does it fall apart into psychology on the one hand and so-called linguistic analysis on the other? We cannot discuss such questions here. But the fact that they can be raised suggests that Husserl was as over-optimistic as Descartes, Kant and Fichte before him in thinking that he had at last overcome the fragmentation of philosophy.

5. We have seen that at the turn of the century Neo-Kantianism was the dominant academic philosophy or *Schulphilosophie* in the German universities. And one obviously associates with this tradition a concern with the forms of thought and of the judgment rather than with objective categories of things. Yet it was a pupil of Cohen and Natorp at Marburg, namely Nicolai Hartmann (1882–1950), who expressed in his philosophy what we may call a return to things and developed an impressive realist ontology. And though it would be out of place to dwell here at any length on the ideas of a philosopher who belonged so definitely to the twentieth century, some general indication of his line of thought will serve to illustrate an important view of the nature and function of philosophy.

In his *Principles of a Metaphysics of Knowledge* (*Grundzüge einer Metaphysik der Erkenntnis*, 1921) Nicolai Hartmann passed from Neo-Kantianism to a realist theory of knowledge, and in subsequent publications he developed an ontology which took the form of an analysis of the categories of different modes or levels of being. Thus in his *Ethics* (*Ethik*, 1926) he devoted himself to a phenomenological study of values, which possess ideal being, while in *The Problem of Spiritual Being* (*Das Problem des geistigen Seins*, 1933) he considered the life of the human spirit both in its personal form and in its objectification. *A Contribution to the Foundation of Ontology* (*Zur Grundlegung der Ontologie*, 1935), *Possibility and Actuality* (*Möglichkeit und Wirklichkeit*, 1938), *The Construction of the Real World. Outline of the General Doctrine of Categories* (*Der Aufbau der realen Welt. Grundriss der allgemeinen Kategorienlehre*, 1940) and *New Ways in Ontology* (*Neue Wege der Ontologie*, 1941) represent general ontology, while in *Philosophy of Nature* (*Philosophie der Natur*, 1950) special attention is paid to the categories of the inorganic and organic levels.[1]

---

[1] We can also mention the posthumously-published works, *Teleological Thought* (*Teleologisches Denken*, 1951) and *Aesthetics* (*Aesthetik*, 1953), a study of beauty and aesthetic values.

In general, therefore, Hartmann's thought moves from a study of the universal structural principles or categories of being, such as unity and multiplicity, persistence and becoming or change, to regional ontologies, that is, to the analysis of the specific categories of inorganic being, organic being and so on. And to this extent he distinguishes between being-there (*Dasein*) and being-thus-or-thus (*Sosein*). But his ontology takes throughout the form of a phenomenological analysis of the categories exemplified in the beings given in experience. The idea of subsistent being, in the sense of the infinite act of existence, *ipsum esse subsistens*, is entirely foreign to his thought. And any metaphysics of transcendent being, in the sense in which God is transcendent, is excluded. Indeed, metaphysics for Hartmann deals with insoluble problems, whereas ontology in his sense is perfectly capable of attaining definite results.

Hartmann's ontology, therefore, is an overcoming of Neo-Kantianism inasmuch as it involves a study of the objective categories of real being. It is an overcoming of positivism inasmuch as it assigns to philosophy a definite field of its own, namely the different levels or types of being considered precisely as such. And though Hartmann employs the method of phenomenological analysis, he is not involved in that restriction to a subjective sphere to which an observance of Husserl's *epoche* would have condemned him. At the same time his ontology is a doctrine of categories, not a metaphysics of Being (*das Sein*) as grounding beings (*die Seienden*). In his view scientific philosophy has no place for an inquiry into Being which goes beyond a study of beings as beings. There is indeed the ideal being of values which are recognized in varying degrees by the human mind. But though these values possess ideal reality, they do not, as such, exist. And existent beings are those which form the world.

6. (i) The recall of philosophy to the thought of Being (*das Sein*) is principally represented in contemporary German thought by that enigmatic thinker, Martin Heidegger (b. 1889). According to Heidegger the whole of western philosophy has forgotten Being and immersed itself in the study of beings.[1] And the idea of Being has meant either an empty and indeterminate concept, obtained by thinking away all the determinate characteristics of beings, or the supreme being in the hierarchy of beings, namely God. Being as the Being of beings, as that which is veiled by beings and as that

[1] Obviously, Nicolai Hartmann is included in this judgment.

which grounds the duality of subject and object that is presupposed by the study of beings, is passed over and forgotten: it remains hidden, veiled. Heidegger asks, therefore, what is the meaning of Being? For him this is not a grammatical question. It is to ask for an unveiling of the Being of beings.

The very fact that man can ask this question shows, for Heidegger, that he has a pre-reflective sense of Being. And in the first part of Being and Time (Sein und Zeit, 1927) Heidegger sets out to give a phenomenological-ontological analysis of man as the being who is able to raise the question and who is thus open to Being. What he calls fundamental ontology thus becomes an existential analysis of man as 'existence' (Dasein). But though Heidegger's aim is in this way to bring Being to show itself, as it were, he never really gets further than man. And inasmuch as man's finitude and temporality are brought clearly to light, the work not unnaturally tends to give the impression, even if incorrect, that Being is for the author essentially finite and temporal. The second part of Being and Time has never been published.

In Heidegger's later writings we hear a great deal about man's openness to Being and of the need for keeping it alive, but it can hardly be said that he has succeeded in unveiling Being. Nor indeed would he claim to have done so. In fact, though Heidegger proclaims that the world in general and philosophers in particular have forgotten Being, he seems unable to explain clearly what they have forgotten or why this forgetfulness should be as disastrous as he says it is.

(ii) Heidegger's pronouncements about Being, as distinct from his existential analysis of man, are so oracular that they cannot be said to amount to a science of Being. The idea of metaphysics as a science of Being is most clearly maintained by the modern Thomists, especially by those who employ what they call the transcendental method. Inspired by Kant and, more particularly (inasmuch as Kant is concerned only with the transcendental deduction of the forms of thought) by German idealists such as Fichte, the transcendental method contains two main phases. To establish metaphysics as a science it is necessary to work backwards, as it were, to a foundation which cannot itself be called in question; and this is the reductive phase or moment.[1] The other

[1] Some see the proper starting-point in an analysis of the judgment as an act of absolute affirmation. So, for example, J. B. Lotz in Das Urteil und das Sein. Eine Grundlegung der Metaphysik (Pullach bei München, 1957) and Metaphysica operationis humanae methodo transcendentali explicata (Rome, 1958). Others go

phase consists in the systematic deduction of metaphysics from the ultimate starting-point.

In effect the transcendental method is used by the philosophers in question to establish Thomist metaphysics on a secure foundation and deduce it systematically, not to produce a new system of metaphysics as far as content is concerned, still less to discover startling new truths about the world. Hence to the outsider at least it seems to be a question of putting the same old wine into a new bottle. At the same time it is obvious that the question of scientific method inevitably tends to loom large and to grow in importance in proportion as emphasis is placed, as with the Thomists under discussion, on the task of converting man's unreflective and implicit apprehension of Being into systematically-grounded explicit knowledge.

7. This admittedly sketchy outline of some currents in thought in German philosophy during the first half of the twentieth century does not afford much ground for saying that the divergencies of systems and tendencies has been at last overcome. At the same time it suggests that in order to justify its claim to be more than a mere handmaid of the sciences philosophy must be metaphysical. If we assume that the aspects of the world under which it is considered by the particular sciences are the only aspects under which it can properly be considered, philosophy, if it is to continue to exist at all, must concern itself either with the logic and methodology of the sciences or with the analysis of ordinary language. For it obviously cannot compete with the sciences on their own ground. To have a field of its own other than analysis of the language of the sciences or of ordinary language, it must consider beings simply as beings. But if it confines itself, as with Nicolai Hartmann, to an inquiry into the categories of the different levels of finite being as revealed in experience, the crucial question of the being or existence of beings is simply passed over. And unless this question is ruled out as meaningless, there can be no justification for this neglect. If, however, the question is once admitted as a genuine philosophical question, the problem of the Absolute comes once more into the foreground. And in the long run Schelling will be shown to be justified in claiming that no more important philosophical problem can be conceived than that of the relation of finite existence to the unconditioned Absolute.

behind the judgment to the *question*, what is the ultimate foundation of all knowledge and judgment? So E. Coreth in *Metaphysik. Eine methodisch-systematische Grundlegung* (Innsbruck, Vienna and Munich, 1961).

This reference to Schelling is not equivalent to a demand for a return to German idealism. What I have in mind is this. Man is spirit-in-the-world. He is in the world not only as locally present in it but also as, by nature, involved in it. He finds himself in the world as dependent on other things for his life, for the satisfaction of his needs, for the material of his knowledge, for his activity. At the same time, by the very fact that he conceives himself as a being in the world he stands out from the world: he is not, as it were, totally immersed in the world-process. He is an historical being, but in the sense that he can objectify history he is a supra-historical being. It is not, of course, possible to make a complete separation between these two aspects of man. He is a being in the world, a 'worldly' being, as standing out from the world; and he stands out from the world as a being in the world. Considered as spirit, as standing out from the world, he is able, and indeed impelled, to raise metaphysical problems, to seek a unity behind or underlying the subject-object situation. Considered as a being involved in the world, he is naturally inclined to regard these problems as empty and profitless. In the development of philosophical thought these divergent attitudes or tendencies recur, assuming different historical, and historically explicable, forms. Thus German idealism was one historically-conditioned form assumed by the metaphysical tendency or drive. Inductive metaphysics was another. And we can see the same fundamental tendency reasserting itself in different ways in the philosophies of Jaspers and Heidegger.

On the plane of philosophy each tendency or attitude seeks to justify itself theoretically. But the dialectic continues. I do not mean to imply that there is no means of discriminating between the proffered justifications. For example, inasmuch as man can objectify himself and treat himself as an object of scientific investigation, he is inclined to regard talk about his standing out from the world or as having a spiritual aspect as so much nonsense. Yet the mere fact that it is he who objectifies himself shows, as Fichte well saw, that he cannot be completely objectified, and that a phenomenalistic reduction of the self is uncritical and naïve. And once reflective thought understands this, metaphysics begins to reassert itself. Yet the pull of the 'worldly' aspect of man also reasserts itself, and insights once gained are lost sight of, only to be regained once more.

Obviously, reference to two tendencies or attitudes based on the dual nature of man would be a gross over-simplification if it were taken to be a sufficient key to the history of philosophy. For in explaining the actual development of philosophy very many factors have to be taken into account. Yet even if there is no simple repetition in history, it is only to be expected that persistent tendencies should constantly tend to recur in varying historical shapes. For, as Dilthey remarked, he who understands history also made history. The dialectic of philosophy reflects the complex nature of man.

The conclusion may appear to be pessimistic, namely that there is no very good reason to suppose that we shall ever reach universal and lasting agreement even about the scope of philosophy. But if fundamental disagreements spring from the very nature of man himself, we can hardly expect anything else but a dialectical movement, a recurrence of certain fundamental tendencies and attitudes in different historical shapes. This is what we have had hitherto, in spite of well-intentioned efforts to bring the process to a close. And it can hardly be called undue pessimism if one expects the continuation of the process in the future.

APPENDIX

A SHORT BIBLIOGRAPHY

General Works

Abbagnano, N. *Storia della filosofia:* II, *parte seconda.* Turin, 1950.
Adamson, R. *The Development of Modern Philosophy, with other Lectures and Essays.* Edinburgh, 1908 (2nd edition).
Alexander, A. B. D. *A Short History of Philosophy.* Glasgow, 1922 (3rd edition).
Bosanquet, B. *A History of Aesthetic.* London, 1892.
Bréhier, E. *Histoire de la philosophie:* II, *deuxième partie.* Paris, 1944.
   (Bréhier's work is one of the best histories of philosophy, and it contains brief, but useful, bibliographies.)
   Histoire de la philosophie allemande. Paris, 1933 (2nd edition).
Castell, A. *An Introduction to Modern Philosophy in Six Problems.* New York, 1943.
Catlin, G. *A History of the Political Philosophers.* London, 1950.
Collins, J. *A History of Modern European Philosophy.* Milwaukee, 1954.
   (This work by a Thomist can be highly recommended. It contains useful bibliographies.)
   God in Modern Philosophy. London, 1960. (In the relevant period this work contains treatments of Hegel, Feuerbach, Marx and Kierkegaard.)
De Ruggiero, G. *Storia della filosofia:* IV, *la filosofia moderna. L'età del romanticismo.* Bari, 1943.
   Hegel. Bari, 1948.
Deussen, P. *Allgemeine Geschichte der Philosophie:* II, 3, *Neuere Philosophie von Descartes bis Schopenhauer.* Leipzig, 1922 (3rd edition).
Devaux, P. *De Thalès à Bergson. Introduction historique à la philosophie.* Liège, 1948.
Erdmann, J. E. *A History of Philosophy:* II, *Modern Philosophy,* translated by W. S. Hough. London, 1889, and subsequent editions.
Falckenberg, R. *Geschichte der neuern Philosophie.* Berlin, 1921 (8th edition).
Fischer, K. *Geschichte der neuern Philosophie.* 10 vols. Heidelberg, 1897–1904. (This work includes separate volumes on Fichte, Schelling, Hegel and Schopenhauer, as listed under these names.)
Fischl, J. *Geschichte der Philosophie,* 5 vols. III, *Aufklärung und deutscher Idealismus.* IV, *Positivismus und Materialismus.* Vienna, 1950.
Fuller, B. A. G. *A History of Philosophy.* New York, 1945 (revised edition).

Hegel, G. W. F. *Lectures on the History of Philosophy*, translated by E. S. Haldane and F. H. Simson. Vol. III. London, 1895. (Hegel's history of philosophy forms part of his system.)

Heimsoeth, H. *Metaphysik der Neuzeit*. Munich, 1929.

Hirschberger, J. *The History of Philosophy*, translated by A. Fuerst, 2 vols. Milwaukee, 1959. (The second volume treats of modern philosophy.)

Höffding, H. *A History of Philosophy* (modern), translated by B. E. Meyer, 2 vols. London, 1900 (American reprint, 1924). *A Brief History of Modern Philosophy*, translated by C. F. Sanders, London, 1912.

Jones, W. T. *A History of Western Philosophy: II, The Modern Mind*. New York, 1952.

Klimke, F., S.J. and Colomer, E., S.J. *Historia de la filosofía*. Barcelona, 1961 (3rd edition).

Marías, J. *Historia de la filosofía*. Madrid, 1941.

Meyer, H. *Geschichte der abendländischen Weltanschauung: IV, Von der Renaissance zum deutschen Idealismus: V, Die Weltanschauung der Gegenwart*. Würzburg, 1950.

Oesterreich, T. K. *Die deutsche Philosophie des XIX Jahrhunderts*. Berlin, 1923 (reproduction, 1953). (This is the fourth volume of the new revised edition of Ueberweg's *Grundriss der Geschichte der Philosophie*. It contains extensive bibliographies and is useful as a work of reference.)

Randall, H., Jr. *The Making of the Modern Mind*. Boston, 1940 (revised edition).

Rogers, A. K. *A Student's History of Philosophy*. New York, 1954 (3rd edition reprinted). (A straightforward textbook.)

Russell, Bertrand. *History of Western Philosophy and its connection with Political and Social Circumstances from the Earliest Times to the Present Day*. London, 1946, and reprints. *Wisdom of the West. An Historical Survey of Western Philosophy in its Social and Political Setting*. London, 1959. (For German philosophy in the nineteenth century the last-named work is to be preferred to the first.)

Sabine, G. H. *A History of Political Theory*. London, 1941. (A valuable study of the subject.)

Schilling, K. *Geschichte der Philosophie: II, Die Neuzeit*. Munich, 1953. (Contains useful bibliographies.)

Souilhé, J. *La philosophie chrétienne de Descartes à nos jours*. 2 vols. Paris, 1934.

Thilly, F. *A History of Philosophy*, revised by L. Wood. New York, 1951.

Thonnard, F. J. *Précis d'histoire de la philosophie.* Paris, 1941 (revised edition).

Turner, W. *History of Philosophy.* Boston and London, 1903.

Vorländer, K. *Geschichte der Philosophie: II, Philosophie der Neuzeit.* Leipzig, 1919 (5th edition).

Webb, C. C. J. *A History of Philosophy.* (Home University Library.) London, 1915 and reprints.

Windelband, W. *A History of Philosophy, with especial reference to the Formation and Development of its Problems and Conceptions,* translated by J. A. Tufts. New York and London, 1952 (reprint of 1901 edition). (This notable work treats the history of philosophy according to the development of problems.)
Lehrbuch der Geschichte der Philosophie, edited by H. Heimsoeth with a concluding chapter, *Die Philosophie im 20 Jahrhundert mit einer Uebersicht über den Stand der philosophie-geschichtlichen Forschung.* Tübingen, 1935.

Wright, W. K. *A History of Modern Philosophy.* New York, 1941.

Chapter I: General Works Relating to the German Idealist Movement

Benz, R. *Die deutsche Romantik,* Leipzig, 1937.

Cassirer, E. *Das Erkenntnisproblem in der Philosophie und Wissenschaft der neueren Zeit: III, Die nachkantischen Systeme.* Berlin, 1920.

Delbos, V. *De Kant aux Postkantiens.* Paris, 1940.

Flügel, O. *Die Religionsphilosophie des absoluten Idealismus: Fichte, Schelling, Hegel, Schopenhauer.* Langensalza, 1905.

Gardeil, H.-D. *Les étages de la philosophie idéaliste.* Paris, 1935.

Groos, H. *Der deutsche Idealismus und das Christentum.* Munich, 1927.

Hartmann, N. *Die Philosophie des deutschen Idealismus.* Berlin, 1960. 2nd edition (originally 2 vols., 1923–9).

Haym, R. *Die romantische Schule.* Berlin, 1928 (5th edition).

Hirsch, E. *Die idealistische Philosophie und das Christentum.* Gütersloh, 1926.

Kircher, E. *Philosophie der Romantik.* Jena, 1906.

Kroner, R. *Von Kant bis Hegel.* 2 vols. Tübingen, 1921–4. (This work and that of N. Hartmann are classical treatments of the subject, from different points of view.)

Lutgert, W. *Die Religion des deutschen Idealismus und ihr Ende.* Gütersloh, 1923.

Maréchal, J., S.J. *Le point de départ de la métaphysique.* Cahier IV: *Le système idéaliste chez Kant et les postkantiens.* Paris, 1947.

Michelet, C. L. *Geschichte der letzten Systeme der Philosophie in Deutschland von Kant bis Hegel.* 2 vols. Berlin, 1837–8.
Entwicklungsgeschichte der neuesten deutschen Philosophie. Berlin, 1843.

Chapters II–IV: Fichte

Texts

Sämmtliche Werke, edited by I. H. Fichte. 8 vols. Berlin, 1845–6.
Nachgelassene Werke, edited by I. H. Fichte. 3 vols. Bonn, 1834–5.
Werke, edited by F. Medicus. 6 vols. Leipzig, 1908–12. (This edition does not contain all Fichte's works.)
Fichtes Briefwechsel, edited by H. Schulz. 2 vols. Leipzig, 1925.
Die Schriften zu J. G. Fichte's Atheismus-streit, edited by H. Lindau. Munich, 1912.
Fichte und Forberg. Die philosophischen Scriften zum Atheismus-streit, edited by F. Medicus. Leipzig, 1910.
The Science of Knowledge, translated by A. E. Kroeger. Philadelphia, 1868; London, 1889.
New Exposition of the Science of Knowledge, translated by A. E. Kroeger. St. Louis, 1869.
The Science of Rights, translated by A. E. Kroeger. Philadelphia, 1869; London, 1889.
The Science of Ethics, translated by A. E. Kroeger. London, 1907.
Fichte's Popular Works, translated, with a memoir of Fichte, by W. Smith. 2 vols. London, 1889 (4th edition).
Addresses to the German Nation, translated by R. F. Jones and G. H. Turnbull. Chicago, 1922.
J. G. Fichtes Leben und literarischer Briefwechsel, by I. H. Fichte. Leipzig, 1862 (2nd edition).

Studies

Adamson, R. *Fichte.* Edinburgh and London, 1881.
Bergmann, E. *Fichte der Erzieher.* Leipzig, 1928 (2nd edition).
Engelbrecht, H. C. *J. G. Fichte: A Study of His Political Writings with special Reference to His Nationalism.* New York, 1933.
Fischer, K. *Fichtes Leben, Werke und Lehre.* Heidelberg, 1914 (4th edition).
Gogarten, F. *Fichte als religiöser Denker.* Jena, 1914.
Gueroult, M. *L'évolution et la structure de la doctrine de la science chez Fichte.* 2 vols. Paris, 1930.
Heimsoeth, H. *Fichte.* Munich, 1923.
Hirsch, E. *Fichtes Religionsphilosophie.* Göttingen, 1914.
    Christentum und Geschichte in Fichtes Philosophie. Göttingen, 1920.

Léon, X. *La philosophie de Fichte*. Paris, 1902.
    Fichte et son temps. 2 vols. (in 3). Paris, 1922–7.
Pareyson, L. *Fichte*. Turin, 1950.
Rickert, H. *Fichtes Atheismusstreit und die kantische Philosophie*.
    Berlin, 1899.
Ritzel, W. *Fichtes Religionsphilosophie*. Stuttgart, 1956.
Stine, R. W. *The Doctrine of God in the Philosophy of Fichte*.
    Philadelphia, 1945 (dissertation).
Thompson, A. B. *The Unity of Fichte's Doctrine of Knowledge*.
    Boston, 1896.
Turnbull, G. H. *The Educational Theory of Fichte*. London, 1926.
Wallner, F. *Fichte als politischer Denker*. Halle, 1926.
Wundt, M. *Fichte*. Stuttgart, 1937 (2nd edition).

Chapters V–VII: Schelling

Texts

Sämmtliche Werke, edited by K. F. A. Schelling. *Erste Abteilung*,
    10 vols., 1856–61; *Zweite Abteilung*, 4 vols. 1856–8. Stuttgart
    and Augsburg.
Werke, edited by M. Schröter. 6 vols. Munich, 1927–8; 2 supplementary
    vols. Munich, 1943–56.
Of Human Freedom, translated by J. Gutman. Chicago, 1936.
The Ages of the World, translated by F. Bolman, Jr. New York, 1942.
*The Philosophy of Art: An Oration on the Relation between the Plastic
    Arts and Nature*, translated by A. Johnson. London, 1845.
Essais, translated by S. Jankélévitch. Paris, 1946.
Introduction à la philosophie de la mythologie, translated by S.
    Jankélévitch. Paris, 1945.

Studies

Bausola, A. *Saggi sulla filosofia di Schelling*. Milan, 1960.
Benz, E. *Schelling, Werden und Wirkung seines Denkens*. Zürich and
    Stuttgart, 1955.
Bréhier, E. *Schelling*. Paris, 1912.
Dekker, G. *Die Rückwendung zum Mythos. Schellings letzte Wandlung*.
    Munich and Berlin, 1930.
Drago del Boca, S. *La filosofia di Schelling*. Florence, 1943.
Fischer, K. *Schellings Leben, Werke und Lehre*. Heidelberg, 1902 (3rd
    edition).
Fuhrmans, H. *Schellings letzte Philosophie. Die negative und positive
    Philosophie im Einsatz des Spätidealismus*. Berlin,
    1940.
    Schellings Philosophie der Weltalter. Düsseldorf, 1954.

Gibelin, J. *L'ésthetique de Schelling d'après la philosophie de l'art.* Paris, 1934.
Gray-Smith, R. *God in the Philosophy of Schelling.* Philadelphia, 1933 (dissertation).
Hirsch, E. D., Jr. *Wordsworth and Schelling.* London, 1960.
Jankélévitch, V. *L'odysée de la conscience dans la dernière philosophie de Schelling.* Paris, 1933.
Jaspers, K. *Schelling: Grösse und Verhängnis.* Munich, 1955.
Knittermeyer, H. *Schelling und die romantische Schule.* Munich, 1929.
Koehler, E. *Schellings Wendung zum Theismus.* Leipzig, 1932 (dissertation).
Massolo, A. *Il primo Schelling.* Florence, 1953.
Mazzei, V. *Il pensiero etico-politico di Friedrich Schelling.* Rome, 1938.
Noack, L. *Schelling und die Philosophie der Romantik.* Berlin, 1859.
Schulz, W. *Die Vollendung des deutschen Idealismus in der Spätphilosophie Schellings.* Stuttgart and Cologne, 1955.
Watson, J. *Schelling's Transcendental Idealism.* Chicago, 1892 (2nd edition).
For a further bibliography see: *Friedrich Wilhelm Joseph von Schelling. Eine Bibliographie,* by G. Schneeberger. Bern, 1954.

Chapter VIII: Schleiermacher

Texts

Werke, Berlin, 1835–64. (Section I, theology, 13 vols.; Section II, sermons, 10 vols.; Section III, philosophy, 9 vols.)
Werke (selections), edited by O. Braun. 4 vols. Leipzig, 1910–13.
Addresses on Religion, translated by J. Oman. London, 1894.
The Theology of Schleiermacher, a Condensed Presentation of His Chief Work 'The Christian Faith', by G. Cross. Chicago, 1911.

Studies

Baxmann, R. *Schleiermacher, sein Leben und Wirken.* Elberfeld, 1868.
Brandt, R. B. *The Philosophy of Schleiermacher.* New York, 1941.
Dilthey, W. *Leben Schleiermachers.* Berlin, 1920 (2nd edition).
Fluckinger, F. *Philosophie und Theologie bei Schleiermacher.* Zürich, 1947.
Keppstein, T. *Schleiermachers Weltbild und Lebensanschauung.* Munich, 1921.
Neglia, F. *La filosofia della religione di Schleiermacher.* Turin, 1952.
Neumann, J. *Schleiermacher.* Berlin, 1936.
Reble, A. *Schleiermachers Kulturphilosophie.* Erfurt, 1935.
Schultz, L. W. *Das Verhältnis von Ich und Wirklichkeit in der religiösen Antropologie Schleiermachers.* Göttingen, 1935.
Schutz, W. *Schleiermacher und der Protestantismus.* Hamburg, 1957.

Visconti, L. *La dottrina educativa di F. D. Schleiermacher.* Florence, 1920.

Wendland, I. *Die religiöse Entwicklung Schleiermachers.* Tübingen, 1915.

Chapters IX–XI: Hegel

Texts

Werke, Jubiläumsausgabe, edited by H. G. Glockner. 26 vols. Stuttgart, 1927–39. The first 20 vols., containing Hegel's writings, are a reprint of the 1832–87 edition (19 vols.). Vols. 21–2 contain Glockner's *Hegel* and Vols. 23–6 his *Hegel-Lexikon.*

Sämmtliche Werke, kritische Ausgabe, edited by G. Lasson and J. Hoffmeister. This critical edition, originally published at Leipzig (F. Meiner), was begun by G. Lasson (1862–1932) in 1905. On Lasson's death it was continued by J. Hoffmeister, and from 1949 it was published at Hamburg (F. Meiner). It was planned to contain 24 (later 26 and then 27) vols. Some of the vols. went through several editions. For example, a third edition of Vol. 2 (*Die Phänomenologie des Geistes*) appeared in 1929 and a third edition of Vol. 6 (*Grundlinien der Philosophie des Rechts*) in 1930. The total work remains unfinished.

Sämmtliche Werke, neue kritische Ausgabe, edited by J. Hoffmeister. This edition, planned to contain 32 vols., is published at Hamburg (F. Meiner) and is designed both to complete and to supersede the Lasson-Hoffmeister edition, now known as the *Erste kritische Ausgabe.* The situation is somewhat complicated as some of the volumes of the Lasson-Hoffmeister edition are being taken over by the new critical edition. For instance, the first part of Hoffmeister's edition of Hegel's *Vorlesungen über die Geschichte der Philosophie*, which was published in 1940 as Vol. 15a in the *Kritische Ausgabe*, becomes Vol. 20 in the *Neue kritische Ausgabe.* Again, the first volume of Hoffmeister's edition of letters written by and to Hegel (1952) bore the title *Kritische Ausgabe* and mention was made of Lasson as the original editor, whereas the second volume (1953) bore the title *Neue kritische Ausgabe* and no mention was made of Lasson. (The *Briefe von und an Hegel* form Vols. 27–30 in the new critical edition.)

Hegels theologische Jugendschriften, edited by H. Nohl. Tübingen, 1907.

Dokumente zu Hegels Entwicklung, edited by J. Hoffmeister. Stuttgart, 1936.

G. W. F. Hegel: Early Theological Writings, translated by T. M. Knox with an introduction by R. Kroner. Chicago, 1948.

The Phenomenology of Mind, translated by J. Baillie. London, 1931 (2nd edition).

Encyclopaedia of Philosophy, translated and annotated by G. E. Mueller New York, 1959.

Science of Logic, translated by W. H. Johnston and L. G. Struthers. 2 vols. London, 1929. (This is the so-called 'Greater Logic' of Hegel.)

The Logic of Hegel, translated from the Encyclopaedia of the Philosophical Sciences, translated by W. Wallace. Oxford, 1892 (2nd edition). (This is the so-called 'Lesser Logic'.)

Hegel's Philosophy of Mind, translated from the Encyclopaedia of the Philosophical Sciences, translated by W. Wallace. Oxford, 1894.

The Philosophy of Right, translated and annotated by T. M. Knox. Oxford, 1942.

Philosophy of History, translated by J. Sibree. London, 1861.

The Philosophy of Fine Art, translated by F. P. B. Osmaston. 4 vols. London, 1920.

Lectures on the Philosophy of Religion, together with a Work on the Proofs of the Existence of God, translated by E. B. Speirs and J. B. Sanderson. 3 vols. London, 1895 (reprint 1962).

Lectures on the History of Philosophy, translated by E. S. Haldane and F. H. Simpson. 3 vols. London, 1892–6.

Studies

Adams, G. P. *The Mystical Element in Hegel's Early Theological Writings*. Berkeley, 1910.

Aspelin, G. *Hegels Tübinger Fragment*. Lund, 1933.

Asveld, P. *La pensée religieuse du jeune Hegel. Liberté et aliénation.* Louvain, 1953.

Baillie, J. *The Origin and Significance of Hegel's Logic*. London, 1901.

Balbino, G. *Der Grundirrtum Hegels*. Graz, 1914.

Brie, S. *Der Volksgeist bei Hegel und die historische Rechtsschule.* Berlin, 1909.

Bullinger, A. *Hegelsche Logik und gegenwärtig herrschender anti-hegelische Unverstand.* Munich, 1901.

Bülow, F. *Die Entwicklung der Hegelschen Sozialphilosophie.* Leipzig, 1920.

Caird, E. *Hegel.* London and Edinburgh, 1883. (This is still an excellent introduction to Hegel.)

Cairns, H. *Legal Philosophy from Plato to Hegel.* Baltimore, 1949.

Coreth, E., S.J. *Das dialektische Sein in Hegels Logik.* Vienna, 1952.

Cresson, A. *Hegel, sa vie, son œuvre.* Paris, 1949.

Croce, B. *What is Living and What is Dead in the Philosophy of Hegel*, translated by D. Ainslie. London, 1915.

Cunningham, G. W. *Thought and Reality in Hegel's System.* New York, 1910.

De Ruggiero, G. *Hegel.* Bari, 1948.
Dilthey, W. *Die Jugendgeschichte Hegels.* Berlin, 1905. (Contained in Dilthey's *Gesammelte Schriften,* IV; Berlin, 1921.)
Dulckeit, G. *Die Idee Gottes im Geiste der Philosophie Hegels.* Munich, 1947.
Emge, C. A. *Hegels Logik und die Gegenwart.* Karlsruhe, 1927.
Findlay, J. N. *Hegel. A Re-Examination.* London, 1958. (A sympathetic and systematic account of Hegel's philosophy, in which the metaphysical aspect is minimized.)
Fischer, K. *Hegels Leben, Werke und Lehre.* 2 vols. Heidelberg, 1911 (2nd edition).
Foster, M. B. *The Political Philosophies of Plato and Hegel.* Oxford, 1935.
Glockner, H. *Hegel.* 2 vols. Stuttgart. (Vols. 21 and 22 in Glockner's edition of Hegel's *Works* mentioned above.)
Grégoire, F. *Aux sources de la pensée de Marx: Hegel, Feuerbach.* Louvain, 1947.
Études hégéliennes. Louvain, 1958.
Häring, T. *Hegel, sein Wollen und sein Werk.* 2 vols. Leipzig, 1929–38.
Haym, R. *Hegel und seine Zeit.* Leipzig, 1927 (2nd edition).
Heimann, B. *System und Methode in Hegels Philosophie.* Leipzig, 1927.
Hoffmeister, J. *Hölderlin und Hegel.* Tübingen, 1931.
Goethe und der deutsche Idealismus. Eine Einführung zu Hegels Realphilosophie. Leipzig, 1932.
Die Problematik des Völkerbundes bei Kant und Hegel. Tübingen, 1934.
Hyppolite, J. *Genèse et structure de la Phénomenologie de l'Esprit de Hegel.* Paris, 1946. (A very valuable commentary.)
Introduction à la philosophie de l'histoire de Hegel. Paris, 1948.
Logique et existence: Essai sur la logique de Hegel. Paris, 1953.
Iljin, I. *Die Philosophie Hegels als kontemplative Gotteslehre.* Bern, 1946.
Kojève, A. *Introduction à la lecture de Hegel.* Paris, 1947 (2nd edition). (The author gives an atheistic interpretation of Hegel.)
Lakebrink, B. *Hegels dialektische Ontologie und die thomistiche Analektik.* Cologne, 1955.
Lasson, G. *Was heisst Hegelianismus?* Berlin, 1916.
Einführung in Hegels Religionsphilosophie. Leipzig, 1930. (This book constitutes an introduction to Vol. 12 of Lasson's critical edition of Hegel's *Works,* mentioned above. There are similar introductions by Lasson; for example, *Hegel als Geschichtsphilosoph,* Leipzig, 1920.)

Litt, T. *Hegel. Versuch einer kritischen Erneuerung.* Heidelberg, 1953.
Lukács, G. *Der junge Hegel. Ueber die Beziehungen von Dialektik und Oekonomie.* Berlin, 1954 (2nd edition). (The author writes from the Marxist point of view.)
Maggiore, G. *Hegel.* Milan, 1924.
Maier, J. *On Hegel's Critique of Kant.* New York, 1939.
Marcuse, M. *Reason and Revolution: Hegel and the Rise of Social Theory.* New York, 1954 (2nd edition).
McTaggart, J. McT. E. *Commentary on Hegel's Logic.* Cambridge, 1910.
        Studies in the Hegelian Dialectic. Cambridge, 1922 (2nd edition).
        Studies in Hegelian Cosmology. Cambridge, 1918 (2nd edition).
Moog, W. *Hegel und die Hegelsche Schule.* Munich, 1930.
Mure, G. R. G. *An Introduction to Hegel.* Oxford, 1940. (Stresses Hegel's relation to Aristotle.)
        A Study of Hegel's Logic. Oxford, 1950.
Negri, A. *La presenza di Hegel.* Florence, 1961.
Niel, H., S.J. *De la médiation dans la philosophie de Hegel.* Paris, 1945. (A study of Hegel's philosophy in the light of the pervading concept of mediation.)
Nink, C., S.J. *Kommentar zu den grundlegenden Abschnitten von Hegels Phänomenologie des Geistes.* Regensburg, 1931.
Ogiermann, H. A., S.J. *Hegels Gottesbeweise.* Rome, 1948.
Olgiati, F. *Il panlogismo hegeliano.* Milan, 1946.
Pelloux, L. *La logica di Hegel.* Milan, 1938.
Peperzak, A. T. B. *Le jeune Hegel et la vision morale du monde.* The Hague, 1960.
Pringle-Pattison, A. S. (=A. Seth). *Hegelianism and Personality.* London, 1893 (2nd edition).
Reyburn, H. A. *The Ethical Theory of Hegel: A Study of the Philosophy of Right.* Oxford, 1921.
Roques, P. *Hegel, sa vie et ses œuvres.* Paris, 1912.
Rosenkranz, K. *G. W. F. Hegels Leben.* Berlin, 1844.
        Erläuterungen zu Hegels Enzyklopädie der Philosophie. Berlin, 1870.
Rosenzweig, F. *Hegel und der Staat.* 2 vols. Oldenburg, 1920.
Schmidt, E. *Hegels Lehre von Gott.* Gütersloh, 1952.
Schneider, R. *Schellings und Hegels schwäbische Geistesahnen.* Würzburg, 1938.
Schwarz, J. *Die anthropologische Metaphysik des jungen Hegel.* Hildesheim, 1931.
        Hegels philosophische Entwicklung. Frankfurt a. M., 1938.
Specht, E. K. *Der Analogiebegriff bei Kant and Hegel.* Cologne, 1952.

Stace, W. T. *The Philosophy of Hegel*. London, 1924 (new edition, New York, 1955). (A systematic and clear account.)

Steinbüchel, T. *Das Grundproblem der Hegelschen Philosophie*. Vol. 1. Bonn, 1933. (The author, a Catholic priest, died before the completion of the work.)

Stirling, J. H. *The Secret of Hegel*. London, 1865.

Teyssedre, B. *L'ésthetique de Hegel*. Paris, 1958.

Vanni Rovighi, S. *La concezione hegeliana della Storia*. Milan, 1942.

Wacher, H. *Das Verhältnis des jungen Hegel zu Kant*. Berlin, 1932.

Wahl, J. *Le malheur de la conscience dans la philosophie de Hegel*. Paris, 1951 (2nd edition). (A valuable study.)

Wallace, W. *Prolegomena to the Study of Hegel's Philosophy and especially of his Logic*. Oxford, 1894 (2nd edition).

Weil, E. *Hegel et l'état*. Paris, 1950.

Chapters XIII–XIV: Schopenhauer

Texts

Werke, edited by J. Frauenstädt. 6 vols. Leipzig, 1873–4 (and subsequent editions). New edition by A. Hübscher, Leipzig, 1937–41.

Sämmtliche Werke, edited by P. Deussen and A. Hübscher. 16 vols. Munich, 1911–42.

On the Fourfold Root of the Principle of Sufficient Reason, and On the Will in Nature, translated by K. Hillebrand. London, 1907 (revised edition).

The World as Will and Idea, translated by R. B. Haldane and J. Kemp. 3 vols. London, 1906 (5th edition).

The Basis of Morality, translated by A. B. Bullock. London, 1903.

Selected Essays, translated by E. B. Bax. London, 1891.

Studies

Beer, M. *Schopenhauer*. London, 1914.

Caldwell, W. *Schopenhauer's System in Its Philosophical Significance*. Edinburgh, 1896.

Copleston, F. C., S.J. *Arthur Schopenhauer, Philosopher of Pessimism*. London, 1946.

Costa, A. *Il pensiero religioso di Arturo Schopenhauer*. Rome, 1935.

Covotti, A. *La vita a il pensiero di A. Schopenhauer*. Turin, 1909.

Cresson, A. *Schopenhauer*. Paris, 1946.

Faggin, A. *Schopenhauer, il mistico senza Dio*. Florence, 1951.

Fauconnet, A. *L'ésthetique de Schopenhauer*. Paris, 1913.

Frauenstädt, J. *Schopenhauer-Lexikon*. 2 vols. Leipzig, 1871.

Grisebach, E. *Schopenhauer*. Berlin, 1897.

Hasse, H. *Schopenhauers Erkenntnislehre*. Leipzig, 1913.

Hübscher, A. *Arthur Schopenhauer. Ein Lebensbild.* Wiesbaden, 1949 (2nd edition).

Knox, I. *Aesthetic Theories of Kant, Hegel and Schopenhauer.* New York, 1936.

McGill, V. J. *Schopenhauer, Pessimist and Pagan.* New York, 1931.

Méry, M. *Essai sur la causalité phénoménale selon Schopenhauer.* Paris, 1948.

Neugebauer, P. *Schopenhauer in England, mit besonderer Berüktsichtigung seines Einflusses auf die englische Literatur.* Berlin, 1931.

Padovani, U. A. *Arturo Schopenhauer: L'ambiente, la vita, le opere.* Milan, 1934.

Robot, T. *La philosophie de Schopenhauer.* Paris, 1874.

Ruyssen, T. *Schopenhauer.* Paris, 1911.

Sartorelli, F. *Il pessimismo di Arturo Schopenhauer, con particolare riferimento alla dottrina del diritto e dello Stato.* Milan, 1951.

Schneider, W. *Schopenhauer.* Vienna, 1937.

Seillière, E. *Schopenhauer*, Paris. 1912.

Simmel, G. *Schopenhauer und Nietzsche.* Leipzig, 1907.

Siwek, P., S.J. *The Philosophy of Evil* (Ch. X). New York, 1951.

Volkelt, J. *Arthur Schopenhauer, seine Persönlichkeit, seine Lehre, seine Glaube.* Stuttgart, 1907 (3rd edition).

Wallace, W. *Schopenhauer.* London, 1891.

Whittaker, T. *Schopenhauer.* London, 1909.

Zimmern, H. *Schopenhauer: His Life and Philosophy.* London, 1932 (revised edition). (A short introduction.)

Zint, H. *Schopenhauer als Erlebnis.* Munich and Basel, 1954.

Chapter XV: Feuerbach

Texts

Sämmtliche Werke, edited by L. Feuerbach (the philosopher himself). 10 vols. Leipzig, 1846–66.

Sämmtliche Werke, edited by W. Bolin and F. Jodl. 10 vols. Stuttgart, 1903–11.

The Essence of Christianity, translated by G. Eliot. New York, 1957. (London, 1881, 2nd edition, with translator's name given as M. Evans.)

Studies

Arvon, H. *Ludwig Feuerbach ou la transformation du sacré.* Paris, 1957.

Bolin, W. *Ludwig Feuerbach, sein Wirken und seine Zeitgenossen.* Stuttgart, 1891.

Chamberlin, W. B. *Heaven Wasn't His Destination: The Philosophy of Ludwig Feuerbach.* London, 1941.

Engels, F. *Ludwig Feuerbach and the Outcome of Classical German Philosophy*. (Contained in *Karl Marx, Selected Works*, edited by C. P. Dutt. See under Marx and Engels.)

Grégoire, F. *Aux Sources de la pensée de Marx, Hegel, Feuerbach*. Louvain, 1947.

Grün, K. *Ludwig Feuerbach in seinem Briefwechsel und Nachlass*. 2 vols. Leipzig, 1874.

Jodl, F. *Ludwig Feuerbach*. Stuttgart, 1904.

Lévy, A. *La philosophie de Feuerbach et son influence sur la littérature allemande*. Paris, 1904.

Lombardi, F. *Ludwig Feuerbach*. Florence, 1935.

Löwith, K. *Von Hegel bis Nietzsche*. Zurich, 1941.

Nüdling, G. *Ludwig Feuerbachs Religionsphilosophie*. Paderborn, 1936.

Rawidowicz, S. *Ludwig Feuerbachs Philosophie*. Berlin, 1931.

Schilling, W. *Feuerbach und die Religion*. Munich, 1957.

Secco, L. *L'etica nella filosofia di Feuerbach*. Padua, 1936.

Chapter XVI: Marx and Engels

Texts

Marx-Engels, Historisch-kritische Gesamtausgabe: Werke, Schriften, Briefe, edited by D. Ryazanov (from 1931 by V. Adoratsky). Moscow and Berlin. This critical edition, planned to contain some 42 vols., was undertaken by the Marx-Engels Institute in Moscow. It remains, however, sadly incomplete. Between 1926 and 1935 there appeared 7 vols. of the writings of Marx and Engels, with a special volume to commemorate the fortieth anniversary of Engels' death. And between 1929 and 1931 there appeared 4 vols. of correspondence between Marx and Engels.

Karl Marx–Friedrich Engels, Werke. 5 vols. Berlin, 1957-9. This edition, based on the one mentioned above, covers the writings of Marx and Engels up to November 1848. It is published by the Dietz Verlag. And a large number of the works of Marx and Engels have been reissued in this publisher's Library of Marxism-Leninism (*Bücherei des Marximus-Leninismus*).

Gesammelte Schriften von Karl Marx und Friedrich Engels, 1852–1862, edited by D. Ryazanov. 2 vols. Stuttgart, 1920 (2nd edition). (Four volumes were contemplated.)

Aus dem literarischen Nachlass von Karl Marx, Friedrich Engels und Friedrich Lassalle, 1841–1850, edited by F. Mehring. 4 vols. Berlin and Stuttgart, 1923 (4th edition).

Karl Marx. Die Frühschriften, edited by S. Landshut. Stuttgart, 1953.

Der Briefwechsel zwischen F. Engels und K. Marx, edited by A. Bebel and E. Bernstein. 4 vols. Stuttgart, 1913.

A number of the writings of Marx and Engels have been translated into English for the Foreign Languages Publishing House in Moscow and have been published in London (Lawrence and Wishart). For example: Marx's *The Poverty of Philosophy* (1956), Engels' *Anti-Dühring* (1959, 2nd edition) and *Dialectics of Nature* (1954), and *The Holy Family* (1957) by Marx and Engels.

Of older translations one can mention the following. Marx: *A Contribution to the Critique of Political Economy* (New York, 1904); *Selected Essays*, translated by H. J. Stenning (London and New York, 1926); *The Poverty of Philosophy* (New York, 1936). Engels: *The Origin of the Family, Private Property and the State* (Chicago, 1902); *Ludwig Feuerbach* (New York, 1934); *Herr Dühring's Revolution in Science*, i.e. *Anti-Dühring* (London, 1935). Marx and Engels: *The German Ideology* (London, 1938).

There are several English translations of *Capital*. For example: *Capital*, revised and amplified according to the 4th German edition by E. Untermann (New York, 1906), and the two-volume edition of *Capital* in the Everyman Library (London), introduced by G. D. H. Cole and translated from the 4th German edition by E. and C. Paul.

Of the English editions of *The Communist Manifesto* we can mention that by H. J. Laski: *Communist Manifesto: Socialist Landmark*, with an introduction (London, 1948).

Other Writings

Marx-Engels. Selected Correspondence. London, 1934.

Karl Marx. Selected Works, edited by C. P. Dutt. 2 vols. London and New York, 1936, and subsequent editions.

Karl Marx. Selected Writings in Sociology and Social Philosophy, edited by T. Bottomore and M. Rubel. London, 1956.

Three Essays by Karl Marx, translated by R. Stone. New York, 1947.

Karl Marx and Friedrich Engels. Basic Writings on Politics and Philosophy, edited by L. S. Feuer. New York, 1959.

Studies

Acton, H. B. *The Illusion of the Epoch, Marxism-Leninism as a Philosophical Creed.* London, 1955. (An excellent criticism.)

Adams, H. P. *Karl Marx in His Earlier Writings.* London, 1940.

Adler, M. *Marx als Denker.* Berlin, 1908.
      Engels als Denker. Berlin, 1921.

Aron, R., and Others. *De Marx au Marxisme.* Paris, 1948.

Aron, H. *Le marxisme.* Paris, 1955.

Baas, E. *L'humanisme marxiste.* Paris, 1947.

Barbu, Z. *Le développement de la pensée dialectique.* (By a Marxist.) Paris, 1947.

Bartoli, H. *La doctrine économique et sociale de Karl Marx*. Paris, 1950.
Beer, M. *Life and Teaching of Karl Marx*, translated by T. C. Partington and H. J. Stenning. London, 1934 (reprint).
Bekker, K. *Marx's philosophische Entwicklung, sein Verhältnis zu Hegel*. Zürich, 1940.
Berdiaeff, N. *Christianity and Class War*. London, 1934.
    The Origin of Russian Communism. London, 1937.
Berlin, I. *Karl Marx*. London, 1939 and subsequent editions. (A useful small biographical study.)
Bober, M. *Karl Marx's Interpretation of History*. Cambridge (U.S.A.), 1927.
Bohm-Bawerk, E. von. *Karl Marx and The Close of His System*. London, 1898.
Boudin, L. B. *Theoretical System of Karl Marx in the Light of Recent Criticism*. Chicago, 1907.
Bouquet, A. C. *Karl Marx and His Doctrine*. London and New York, 1950. (A small work published by the S.P.C.K.)
Calvez, J.-V. *La pensée de Karl Marx*. Paris, 1956. (An outstanding study of Marx's thought.)
Carr, H. *Karl Marx. A Study in Fanaticism*. London, 1934.
Cornu, A. *Karl Marx, sa vie et son œuvre*. Paris, 1934.
    The Origins of Marxian Thought. Springfield (Illinois), 1957.
Cottier, G. M.-M. *L'athéisme du jeune Marx: ses origines hégéliennes*. Paris, 1959.
Croce, B. *Historical Materialism and the Economics of Karl Marx*, translated by C. M. Meredith. Chicago, 1914.
Desroches, H. C. *Signification du marxisme*. Paris, 1949.
Drahn, E. *Friedrich Engels*. Vienna and Berlin, 1920.
Gentile, G. *La filosofia di Marx*. Milan, 1955 (new edition).
Gignoux, C. J. *Karl Marx*. Paris, 1950.
Grégoire, F. *Aux sources de la pensée de Marx: Hegel, Feuerbach*. Louvain, 1947.
Haubtmann, P. *Marx et Proudhon: leurs rapports personels, 1844–47*. Paris, 1947.
Hook, S. *Towards the Understanding of Karl Marx*. New York, 1933.
    From Hegel to Marx. New York, 1936.
    Marx and the Marxists. Princeton, 1955.
Hyppolite, J. *Études sur Marx et Hegel*. Paris, 1955.
Joseph, H. W. B. *Marx's Theory of Value*. London, 1923.
Kamenka. E. *The Ethical Foundations of Marxism*. London, 1962.
Kautsky, K. *Die historische Leistung von Karl Marx*. Berlin, 1908.
Laski, H. J. *Karl Marx*. London, 1922.
Lefebvre, H. *Le matérialisme dialectique*. Paris, 1949 (3rd edition).
    Le marxisme. Paris, 1958. (By a Marxist author.)

Leff, G. *The Tyranny of Concepts: A Critique of Marxism*. London, 1961.

Lenin, V. I. *The Teachings of Karl Marx*. New York, 1930.
Marx, Engels, Marxism. London, 1936.

Liebknecht, W. *Karl Marx, Biographical Memoirs*. Chicago, 1901.

Loria, A. *Karl Marx*. New York, 1920.

Löwith, K. *Von Hegel bis Nietzsche*. Zürich, 1947.

Lunau, H. *Karl Marx und die Wirklichkeit*. Brussels, 1937.

Marcuse, H. *Reason and Revolution*. London, 1941.

Mandolfo, R. *Il materialismo storico in Friedrich Engels*. Genoa, 1912.

Mascolo, D. *Le communisme*. Paris, 1953. (By a Marxist.)

Mayer, G. *Friedrich Engels*. 2 vols. The Hague, 1934 (2nd edition).

Mehring, F. *Karl Marx: the Story of His Life*, translated by E. Fitzgerald. London, 1936. (The standard biography.)

Meyer, A. G. *Marxism. The Unity of Theory and Practice. A Critical Essay*. Cambridge (U.S.A.) and Oxford, 1954.

Nicolaievsky, N. *Karl Marx*. Philadelphia, 1936.

Olgiati, F. *Carlo Marx*. Milan, 1953 (6th edition).

Pischel, G. *Marx giovane*. Milan, 1948.

Plenge, J. *Marx und Hegel*. Tübingen, 1911.

Robinson, J. *An Essay in Marxian Economics*. London, 1942.

Rubel, M. *Karl Marx. Essai de biographie intellectuelle*. Paris, 1957.

Ryazanov, D. *Karl Marx and Friedrich Engels*. New York, 1927.
Karl Marx, Man, Thinker and Revolutionist. London, 1927.

Schlesinger, R. *Marx: His Time and Ours*. London, 1950.

Schwarzschild, L. *Karl Marx*. Paris, 1950.

Seeger, R. *Friedrich Engels*. Halle, 1935.

Somerhausen, L. *L'humanisme agissant de Karl Marx*. Paris, 1946.

Spargo, J. *Karl Marx. His Life and Work*. New York, 1910.

Tönnies, F. *Marx. Leben und Lehre*. Jena, 1921.

Touilleux, P. *Introduction aux systèmes de Marx et Hegel*. Tournai, 1960.

Tucker, R. C. *Philosophy and Myth in Karl Marx*. Cambridge, 1961.

Turner, J. K. *Karl Marx*. New York, 1941.

Vancourt, R. *Marxisme et pensée chrétienne*. Paris, 1948.

Van Overbergh, C. *Karl Marx, sa vie et son œuvre. Bilan du marxisme*. Brussels, 1948 (2nd edition).

Vorländer, K. *Kant und Marx*. Tübingen, 1911.
Marx Engels und Lassalle als Philosophen. Stuttgart, 1920.

Wetter, G. A. *Dialectical Materialism* (based on 4th German edition). London, 1959. (This outstanding work is devoted mainly to the development of Marxism-Leninism in the Soviet Union. But the author treats first of Marx and Engels.)

Chapter XVII: Kierkegaard

Texts

Samlede Vaerker, edited by A. B. Drachmann, J. L. Herberg and H. O. Lange. 14 vols. Copenhagen, 1901–6. A critical Danish edition of Kierkegaard's *Complete Works* is being edited by N. Thulstrup. Copenhagen, 1951 ff. A German translation of this edition is being published concurrently at Cologne and Olten. (There are, of course, previous German editions of Kierkegaard's writings.)

Papirer (Journals), edited by P. A. Heiberg, V. Kuhr and E. Torsting. 20 vols. (11 vols. in 20 parts). Copenhagen, 1909–48.

Breve (Letters), edited by N. Thulstrup. 2 vols. Copenhagen, 1954.

There is a Danish *Anthology* of Kierkegaard's writings, *S. Kierkegaard's Vaerker i Udvalg*, edited by F. J. Billeskov-Jansen. 4 vols. Copenhagen, 1950 (2nd edition).

English translations, mainly by D. F. Swenson and W. Lowrie, of Kierkegaard's more important writings are published by the Oxford University Press and the Princeton University Press. Exclusive of the Journals (mentioned separately below) there are 12 vols. up to date, 1936–53. Further references to individual volumes are made in the footnotes to the chapter on Kierkegaard in this book.

Johannes Climacus, translated by T. H. Croxall. London, 1958.

Works of Love, translated by H. and E. Hong. London, 1962.

Journals (selections), translated by A. Dru. London and New York, 1938 (also obtainable in Fontana Paperbacks).

A Kierkegaard Anthology, edited by R. Bretall. London and Princeton, 1946.

Diario, with introduction and notes by C. Fabro (3 vols., Brescia, 1949–52), is a useful Italian edition of selections from Kierkegaard's *Journals* by an author who has also published an *Antologia Kierkegaardiana*, Turin, 1952.

Studies

Bense, M. *Hegel und Kierkegaard*. Cologne and Krefeld, 1948.

Bohlin, T. *Sören Kierkegaard, l'homme et l'œuvre*, translated by P. H. Tisseau. Bazoges-en-Pareds, 1941.

Brandes, G. *Sören Kierkegaard*. Copenhagen, 1879.

Cantoni, R. *La coscienza inquieta: S. Kierkegaard*. Milan, 1949.

Castelli, E. (editor). Various Authors. *Kierkegaard e Nietzsche*. Rome, 1953.

Chestov, L. *Kierkegaard et la philosophie existentielle*, translated from the Russian by T. Rageot and B. de Schoezer. Paris, 1948.

Collins, J. *The Mind of Kierkegaard*. Chicago, 1953.

Croxall, T. H. *Kierkegaard Commentary*. London, 1956.

Diem, H. *Die Existenzdialektik von S. Kierkegaard*. Zürich, 1950.

Fabro, C. *Tra Kierkegaard e Marx*. Florence, 1952.

Fabro, C., and Others. *Studi Kierkegaardiani*. Brescia, 1957.

Friedmann, K. *Kierkegaard, the Analysis of His Psychological Personality*. London, 1947.

Geismar, E. *Sören Kierkegaard. Seine Lebensentwicklung und seine Wirksamkeit als Schriftsteller*. Göttingen, 1927.
   Lectures on the Religious Thought of Sören Kierkegaard. Minneapolis, 1937.

Haecker, T. *Sören Kierkegaard*, translated by A. Dru. London and New York, 1937.

Hirsch, E. *Kierkegaardstudien*. 2 vols. Gütersloh, 1930–3.

Höffding, H. *Sören Kierkegaard als Philosoph*. Stuttgart, 1896.

Hohlenberg, J. *Kierkegaard*. Basel, 1949.

Jolivet, R. *Introduction to Kierkegaard*, translated by W. H. Barber. New York, 1951.

Lombardi, F. *Sören Kierkegaard*. Florence, 1936.

Lowrie, W. *Kierkegaard*. London, 1938. (A very full bibliographical treatment.)
   Short Life of Kierkegaard. London and Princeton, 1942.

Martin, H. V. *Kierkegaard the Melancholy Dane*. New York, 1950.

Masi, G. *La determinazione de la possibilità dell' esistenza in Kierkegaard*. Bologna, 1949.

Mesnard, P. *Le vrai visage de Kierkegaard*. Paris, 1948.
   Kierkegaard, sa vie, son œuvre, avec un exposé de sa philosophie. Paris, 1954.

Patrick, D. *Pascal and Kierkegaard*. 2 vols. London, 1947.

Roos, H., S.J. *Kierkegaard et le catholicisme*, translated from the Danish by A. Renard, O.S.B. Louvain, 1955.

Schremf, C. *Kierkegaard*. 2 vols. Stockholm, 1935.

Sieber, F. *Der Begriff der Mitteilung bei Sören Kierkegaard*. Würzburg, 1939.

Thomte, R. *Kierkegaard's Philosophy of Religion*. London and Princeton, 1948.

Wahl, J. *Études kierkegaardiennes*. Paris, 1948 (2nd edition).

Chapters XXI–XXII: Nietzsche

Texts

A complete critical edition of Nietzsche's writings and correspondence, *Nietzsches Werke und Briefe, historisch-kritische Ausgabe*, was begun at Munich in 1933 under the auspices of the Nietzsche-Archiv. Five volumes of the *Werke* (comprising the *juvenilia*) appeared between 1933 and 1940, and four volumes of the *Briefe* between 1938 and 1942. But the enterprise does not seem to be making much progress.

Gesammelte Werke, Grossoktav Ausgabe. 19 vols. Leipzig, 1901–13. In 1926 R. Oehler's *Nietzsche-Register* was added as a 20th vol.

Gesammelte Werke, Musarionausgabe. 23 vols. Munich, 1920–9.

Werke, edited by K. Schlechta. 3 vols. Munich, 1954–6. (Obviously incomplete, but a handy edition of Nietzsche's main writings, with lengthy selections from the *Nachlass.*)

There are other German editions of Nietzsche's *Works*, such as the *Taschenausgabe* published at Leipzig.

Gesammelte Briefe. 5 vols. Berlin and Leipzig, 1901–9. A volume of correspondence with Overbeck was added in 1916. And some volumes, such as the correspondence with Rohde, have been published separately.

The Complete Works of Friedrich Nietzsche, translated under the general editorship of O. Levy. 18 vols. London, 1909–13. (This edition is not complete in the sense of containing the *juvenilia* and the whole *Nachlass*. Nor are the translations above criticism. But it is the only edition of comparable scope in the English language.)

Some of Nietzsche's writings are published in *The Modern Library Giant*, New York. And there is the *Portable Nietzsche*, translated by W. A. Kaufmann. New York, 1954.

Selected Letters of Friedrich Nietzsche, edited by O. Levy. London. 1921.

The Nietzsche-Wagner Correspondence, edited by E. Förster-Nietzsche. London, 1922.

Friedrich Nietzsche. Unpublished Letters. Translated and edited by K. F. Leidecker. New York, 1959.

Studies

Andler, C. *Nietzsche: sa vie et sa pensée.* 6 vols. Paris, 1920–31.

Banfi, A. *Nietzsche.* Milan, 1934.

Bataille, G. *Sur Nietzsche. Volonté de puissance.* Paris, 1945.

Bäumler, A. *Nietzsche der Philosoph und Politiker.* Berlin, 1931.

Benz, E. *Nietzsches Ideen zur Geschichte des Christentums.* Stuttgart, 1938.

Bertram, E. *Nietzsche. Versuch einer Mythologie.* Berlin, 1920 (3rd edition).

Bianquis, G. *Nietzsche en France.* Paris, 1929.

Bindschedler, M. *Nietzsche und die poetische Lüge.* Basel, 1954.

Brandes, G. *Friedrich Nietzsche.* London, 1914.

Brinton, C. *Nietzsche.* Cambridge (U.S.A.) and London, 1941.

Brock, W. *Nietzsches Idee der Kultur.* Bonn, 1930.

Chatterton Hill, G. *The Philosophy of Nietzsche.* London, 1912.

Copleston, F. C., S.J. *Friedrich Nietzsche, Philosopher of Culture.* London, 1942.

Cresson, A. *Nietzsche, sa vie, son œuvre, sa philosophie.* Paris, 1943.

Deussen, P. *Erinnerungen an Friedrich Nietzsche.* Leipzig, 1901.

Dolson, G. N. *The Philosophy of Friedrich Nietzsche.* New York, 1901.

Drews, A. *Nietzsches Philosophie.* Heidelberg, 1904.

Förster-Nietzsche, E. *Das Leben Friedrich Nietzsches.* 2 vols. in 3. Leipzig, 1895–1904.

    Der junge Nietzsche. Leipzig, 1912.

    Der einsame Nietzsche. Leipzig, 1913. (These books by Nietzsche's sister have to be used with care, as she had several axes to grind.)

Gawronsky, D. *Friedrich Nietzsche und das Dritte Reich.* Bern, 1935.

Goetz, K. A. *Nietzsche als Ausnahme. Zur Zerstörung des Willens zur Macht.* Freiburg, 1949.

Giusso, L. *Nietzsche.* Milan, 1943.

Halévy, D. *Life of Nietzsche.* London, 1911.

Heidegger, M. *Nietzsche.* 2 vols. Pfulligen, 1961.

Jaspers, K. *Nietzsche: Einführung in das Verständnis seines Philosophierens.* Berlin, 1936. (The two last-mentioned books are profound studies in which, as one might expect, the respective philosophical positions of the writers govern the interpretations of Nietzsche.)

Joël, K. *Nietzsche und die Romantik.* Jena, 1905.

Kaufmann, W. A. *Nietzsche: Philosopher, Psychologist, Antichrist.* Princeton, 1950.

Klages, L. *Die psychologischen Errungenschaften Nietzsches.* Leipzig, 1930 (2nd edition).

Knight, A. H. J. *Some Aspects of the Life and Work of Nietzsche, and particularly of His Connection with Greek Literature and Thought.* Cambridge, 1933.

Lannoy, J. C. *Nietzsche ou l'histoire d'un égocentricisme athée.* Paris, 1952. (Contains a useful bibliography, pp. 365–92.)

Lavrin, J. *Nietzsche. An Approach.* London, 1948.

Lea, F. A. *The Tragic Philosopher. A Study of Friedrich Nietzsche.* London, 1957. (A sympathetic study by a believing Christian.)

Lefebvre, H. *Nietzsche.* Paris, 1939.

Lombardi, R. *Federico Nietzsche.* Rome, 1945.

Lotz, J. B., S.J. *Zwischen Seligkeit und Verdamnis. Ein Beitrag zu dem Thema: Nietzsche und das Christentum.* Frankfurt a. M., 1953.

Löwith, K. *Von Hegel bis Nietzsche.* Zürich, 1941.

    Nietzsches Philosophie der ewigen Wiederkehr des Gleichen. Stuttgart, 1956.

Ludovici, A. M. *Nietzsche, His Life and Works*. London, 1910.
    Nietzsche and Art. London, 1912.
Mencken, H. L. *The Philosophy of Friedrich Nietzsche*. London, 1909.
Mess, F. *Nietzsche als Gesetzgeber*. Leipzig, 1931.
Miéville, H. L. *Nietzsche et la volonté de puissance*. Lausanne, 1934.
Mittasch, A. *Friedrich Nietzsche als Naturphilosoph*. Stuttgart, 1952.
Molina, E. *Nietzsche, dionisiaco y asceta*. Santiago (Chile), 1944.
Morgan, G. A., Jr. *What Nietzsche Means*. Cambridge (U.S.A), 1941.
    (An excellent study.)
Mügge, M. A. *Friedrich Nietzsche: His Life and Work*. London, 1909.
Oehler, R. *Nietzsches philosophisches Werden*. Munich, 1926.
Orestano, F. *Le idee fondamentali di Friedrich Nietzsche nel loro
    progressivo svolgimento*. Palermo, 1903.
Paci, E. *Federico Nietzsche*. Milan, 1940.
Podach, E. H. *The Madness of Nietzsche*. London, 1936.
Reininger, F. *Friedrich Nietzsches Kampf um den Sinn des Lebens*.
    Vienna, 1922.
Reyburn, H. A., with the collaboration of H. B. Hinderks and
    J. G. Taylor. *Nietzsche: The Story of a Human philosopher*.
    London, 1948. (A good psychological study of Nietzsche.)
Richter, R. *Friedrich Nietzsche*. Leipzig, 1903.
Riehl, A. *Friedrich Nietzsche, der Künstler und der Denker*. Stuttgart,
    1920 (6th edition).
Römer, H. *Nietzsche*. 2 vols. Leipzig, 1921.
Siegmund, G. *Nietzsche, der 'Atheist' und 'Antichrist'*. Paderborn,
    1946 (4th edition).
Simmel, G. *Schopenhauer und Nietzsche*. Leipzig, 1907.
Steinbüchel, T. *Friedrich Nietzsche*. Stuttgart, 1946.
Thibon, G. *Nietzsche ou le déclin de l'esprit*. Lyons, 1948.
Vaihinger, H. *Nietzsche als Philosoph*. Berlin, 1905 (3rd edition).
Wolff, P. *Nietzsche und das christliche Ethos*. Regensburg, 1940.
Wright, W. H. *What Nietzsche Taught*. New York, 1915. (Mainly
    excerpts.)

INDEX

(The principal references are in heavy type. Asterisked numbers refer to bibliographical information. References in ordinary type to a continuous series of pages, e.g. 195–8, do not necessarily indicate continuous treatment. References to two persons together are usually under the person criticized or influenced. Footnote abbreviations given in italics, e.g. *B*, are referred to the pages explaining them.)

316; Marxism 307, 316, 320, 324 ff, 331; *also* 250 f, 284 f, 346 *and below*

contradiction, principle of *see* non-contradiction

contradictions, reconciliation of: Fichte 47, 57; Hegel 166, 176, 184 f, 192; Herbart 251

contraries: Hegel 177

Copenhagen 338 f, 393

Copernican revolution 3

Coreth, E. 439*

corporations: Hegel 212 n, 214

corporativism: Hegel 214

correspondence theory of knowledge 106

creation: Fichte 9, 80, 92; Hegel 9, 196, 235, 239; Schelling 9, 128 f, 132, 135 f, 143; *also* 258 ff, 298, 353 f, 367, 419

purpose of 135, 260, 379

creative nothing: Stirner 302

creative human powers: Nietzsche 392, 396, 398, 403; *also* 15 f, 279

creaturehood acknowledged: Kierkegaard 336, 341

crime and the criminal: Hegel 205, 213

critical philosophy of Kant: Fichte 3-6, 7 f, 15, 32 f, 39-42, 44, 52, 56 ff, 60, 64, 78 f; Hegel 5, 10, 167, 189 f; Schelling 101, 123, 137; *also* 248 ff, 257

German idealism and 10, 21, 23-6

See also Kant

criticism: Schelling 94, 100-3

Croce, Benedetto (1866-1952) 241, 247, 279

cruelty: Nietzsche 412; Schopenhauer 274, 286

cult, worship: Hegel 237, 240

cultural sciences *see Geisteswissenschaften*

culture, cultures: Fichte 74; Hegel 30, 202, 216, 220; Nietzsche 391 f, 398, 399 n, 413 f; *also* 16, 321, 362 f, 368, 370 f, 382

German culture 74, 391, 398

history and 365, 370 f, 398

'cunning of reason': Hegel 222, 223 n; *also* 291

curiosity: Fichte 68

custom 382, 400

cycles of history *see* eternal recurrence

Czolbe, Heinrich (1819-73) 352 f

Danzig 261

darkness and light: Baader 146; Schelling 131

Darwin, Charles (1809-82), Darwinism: Nietzsche 400, 411 f; *also* 319, 354 f

Dasein: Fichte 86, 88, 93; N. Hartmann 437; Heidegger 438

See also existence

Daub, Karl (1765-1836) 245

dawn, new: Nietzsche 406

day-view and night-view: Fechner 376

death: Kierkegaard 349; Schopenhauer 281, 284 f

decadence: Nietzsche 404, 406, 412 f, 417

deduction: Fichte 48, 50 f, 119, *see also* transcendental D. *below*, *and* consciousness, D. of; Hegel 48, 168, 178, 199, 201, 203, 259, 301; Kant 11, 438; Schelling 22, 116, 127 f, 135 f, 139, 335; *also* 259 f, 287, 362, 439

consciousness, D. of *see* consciousness, D. of

Nature, D. of: Hegel 168 f, 197; Schelling 109-14

transcendental D: Fichte 57, 78, 438; *also* 115, 438 f

definition: Bolzano 257

deification: Feuerbach 295

deism: Fichte 76

demiurge 313

democracy: Cohen 363; Feuerbach 299; Fichte 72; Hegel 214 f; Marx 307; Nietzsche 399, 402, 405, 413, 417

Democritus (B.C. 460-370) 252, 272, 353

demythologization: Fichte 88; Hegel 225, 241; *also* 12

dependence, feeling of: Feuerbach 295 f; Schleiermacher 152 f, 155, 157 f, 295

Descartes, René (1596-1650) 6, 434

descriptions, theory of 432

desire: Fichte 50, 55 f, 61; Hegel 183; Schopenhauer 270, 274,

476 INDEX

Hölderlin, Friedrich (1770–1843)
16, 94, 159 and n, 164
holiness: Nietzsche 399n, Schopenhauer 284f; Windelband 364f
Holy family, The, of Marx and Engels 310, 314
Holy Spirit, The: Hegel 187; *also* 245
Homer 280n.2
horticulture 280
HS 242n
human activity, primary: Hegel 308f; Marx 308f, 317
See also work, human
human beings *see* ego, human
humanism: Marx 329; Ruge 302
humanity 363, 382
an abstraction: Kierkegaard 340; Stirner 303f
Hume, David (1711–76) and self-knowledge 43
humility: Nietzsche 401, 404
Husserl, Edmund (1859–1938) 259, 431, 432–5
hydraulics 280
hypothesis: Fechner 375f; *also* 381f, 411

Idea, the: Fichte 86, 89 (called Concept); E. von Hartmann 290; Hegel 172, 194f, 230f, 243, 290, 306f, 313, 316, 399 *and see* Nature and I. *below*; Marxism 313–16, 331f; *also* 17, 129
Absolute as *see s.v.* — meaning in Hegel 172—Nature and I. 198, 200, 226, 298 — unconscious I. 290
idea: absolute Idea: Hegel 137, 191, 194f; Schelling 135, 137; *also* 259, 315, 419
divine idea *see* ideas, divine
eternal Idea: Hegel 170, 172f; Schelling 126ff
human idea *see* concept
Kantian regulative idea 107
logical Idea: Hegel (*also called* Concept, *Logos,* Notion) 172f, 191, 195–9, 202, 226, 235, 239, 242, 259, 313
Platonic Idea: Schopenhauer 277–80
plurality of ideas: Schelling *see*

ideas, divine
in one Idea 126
Ideal, the: Hegel 230
ideal or aim: Schelling 116, 118; *also* 295, 418
ideal (historical category): Dilthey 372f
ideal and real (phenomenal and noumenal): Feuerbach 295; Hegel 162, 167, 170, 174, 179, 189f, 198, 200; Kant 123, 189f, 268, 429; Nietzsche 407, 409; Schelling 105–9, 113, 115f, 118–27, 129, 134, 170; Schleiermacher 150f; Schopenhauer 266ff, 270f, 275, 281ff, 286; *also* 147, 249, 260, 363f, 429, 432
identity of: Schelling 123ff, 170
idealism: Part I (*see* Contents pp. v–vi). Feuerbach 295, 300; Fichte 38ff, 51, 83, 86, 100, 152; Husserl 434f; Lotze 380f; Marxism 308–11, 315, 331; *also* 9, 125, 260f, 288, 358f, 386f
absolute idealism: Feuerbach 295, 298; Hegel 90f, 240f, 243f, 386; Kant and 10, 21, 23–6; Kierkegaard 336f; *also* 2, 10, 19, 24f, 259f, 287f, 352
Christianity and 245
ethical I: Fichte 34, 51, 91, 93
German I. *see* Contents, pp. v–vi. Nietzsche 419n.2; Schelling 113f, 143; Schopenhauer 275, 286; *also* 1ff, 5f, 8ff, 242f, 287, 440, 445*
anthropomorphism in 24ff, 86; and philosophy of man 26–31; and religion 10–13, 19, 149; romanticism and 13–21; subjectivism 113
'magical' I. 15
metaphysical I: after Kant 3, 5–10, 12, 14, 20f, 24, 26, 190; Fichte 40, 43f, 46n, 56, 58; Schelling 22, 138, 144, 148; Schopenhauer 286f; *also* 257, 293, 303, 314, 352, 358f, 419
pure I. = metaphysical I. (q.v.)
subjective I: after Kant 8; Fichte 84, 90f; Schelling 104
teleological I: Lotze 380

transcendental I: Fichte 15, 21,
74, 78ff, 103; Hegel 168, 170;
Schelling 95, 103, **114–19**, 121,
123, 125, 144, 147, 168, 170;
Schopenhauer 286f
ideas: association of—Herbart 253;
divine ideas—Schelling 121f,
124, 126f; Platonic Ideas see
s.v.
identity
absolute or pure I: Schelling 121,
123, 132, 189
Absolute as identity: Hegel 168f,
172, 174, 179, 189; Schelling
107, 118, 121, **123ff**, 126, 134,
143n, 144f, 168f, 189; Schleiermacher 151, 153ff, 157; also
145
I. in difference: Hegel 172, 174f,
177, 179, 183, 185ff, 193, 200,
213, 216, 226f and see Absolute
as I. above
principle of: Fichte 49f; Hegel
168; Schelling 130, 168
system or theory of: Schelling see
Absolute as I. above
idiographic science 365
image: Fichte 52, 83, 85, 87; Schelling 122, 127f
imagination: Fichte 15, 52–5, 57,
100; Hegel 203, 235, 239, 241;
Kant 52; Schelling 122; Schopenhauer 280; also 14, 257
immanence of God or the Absolute:
Hegel 185, 238; Schelling 130
immanence of knowledge: Schelling
115, 121
immediacy: Hegel 194, 210, 230;
Kierkegaard 349
immortality of the soul: affirmed
246, 257, 259f, 376; denied 247,
285, 356, 416
impartiality: Hegel 219
imperative, categorical see categorical I.
implication: Schleiermacher 154;
Schopenhauer 265
causality and 9, 199
impotence of Nature: Hegel 199
impulse: Fichte 54ff, 61ff, 77, 87;
Hegel 164, 203, 208; Herbart
253, 254n; Schelling 116, 131;
Schleiermacher 155f; Schopenhauer 273, 276, 278, 287;

Nietzsche 397, 403; also 256,
342f
imputability: Hegel 207
Incarnation, the: Feuerbach 297;
Hegel 187, 235, 240; Kierkegaard 344, 346
'inclination and interest': Fichte
39f
inclination and morality: Hegel 208
independence see freedom
Indian philosophy: Schopenhauer
268; also x, 289
indifference or identity of ideal and
real: Schelling 121, 123
and see identity
indifference, liberty of see freedom
of I.
individual: person see person,
human; thing see particular
individuality: of persons see personality; of things see particularity
individuals in society: Fichte 68ff,
81f; Hegel 187, 210, 212–15;
Nietzsche 400–3; Schleiermacher 150, 156; also 362f,
370f, 382
individuation, principle of 397
inductive philosophy 381
Industrial Revolution, the 327
industry: Marx 327, 330
inference 265
infinite: Fichte 21, 44, 71, 87; Hegel
18ff, 22f, 165; Kierkegaard
342, 346; Schleiermacher 152f,
155, 157; also 143n, 257*, 437
Absolute I. see s.v. — bad I. 342
— consciousness in 24f, 79 —
God infinite see s.v.
infinite and finite **11f**, 17–20, 22ff,
260, 429 and: Fichte 47, 83f,
88f, 92f; Hegel 11, 160, 164–9,
174f, 179, 197f, 227f, 235–8,
260; N. Hartmann 437, 439;
Kierkegaard 343, 348; Schelling 11, 99, 101ff, 108, 121,
123f, 125, 127, 129f, 439;
Schleiermacher 154, 157
inheritance, law of 245
injustice, social: Marx 308
innocence, state of: Kierkegaard 349
inorganic being: N. Hartmann 437
insight: Hegel 178; Schopenhauer
270; also 422

pacifism: Nietzsche 418
paganism: Schelling 140f; also 291, 341
pain: Nietzsche 412; also 274, 290
painting: 122, 233f, 280
panpsychism: Fechner 375f
panentheism: Fichte 84
Pan-Slavists 147
pantheism: Fichte 92f; Haeckel 356f; Hegelianism 237, 247, 345; Lotze 380; Nietzsche 416, 419; Schelling 130, 134, 143, 145; Schleiermacher 157; Schopenhauer 286; also 12, 145
paradise on earth 291, 331
Paradoxes of the infinite, Bolzano's 257
parallelism, psychophysical: Fechner 375f
Paris 300, 307, 309f, 312
Parmenides (c. 540–470 B.C.) 242, 252
Parsifal, Nietzsche and 392n
participation: Hegel 180, 186, 212, 238; Schelling 121
particular, individual, things: Hegel 199; Schelling 121; Schopenhauer 278, 284f
particularity: Hegel 195, 202, 211f, 236f; Schelling 127; Schopenhauer 285
Pascal, Blaise (1623–62) 404
Paul, St, Apostle 130, 238
passion: Hegel 164, 222; Nietzsche 397, 403, 414; Schopenhauer 280; also 77
Pavlov, M. G. (1773–1840) 147
peace, perpetual 218
peace, personal 101
pedagogy 256
perception; Hegel 182; Schopenhauer 269–72, 279f; also 259
perfection, absolute: Hegel 185
permanence: Lotze 379; also 382, 437
Persian religion 237
person, human: Fichte 69ff, 81, 83; Hegel 183, 203f, 213, 215f, 224; Kierkegaard 335f, 339ff, 344f, 351; Schelling 101, 131, 137; Schleiermacher 155ff; Stirner 302ff; also 146, 260, 368, 428f, 436

person and society *see* individuals in society
See also ego, human
personality, individuality, of persons: Feuerbach 298f; Fichte 81, 83, 92, 380; Hegel 215; Kierkegaard 339ff; Lotze 380; Schelling 30, 131f; Schleiermacher 155ff; also 14ff, 17f, 29f, 260, 385
sex and P. 298f
pessimism: E. von Hartmann 290f; Nietzsche 397, 405, 415; Schopenhauer 274f, 276, 287f, 415
Pestalozzi, Johann Heinrich (1746–1827) 249, 255
Peter, St, Apostle 133
Pfänder, Alexander (1870–1941) 435
Pforta 32, 390
phenomena, appearances: Hegel 182f; Herbart 251f; Schelling 106, 124, 128f; Schopenhauer 264f, 268, 270–3; also 86, 189, 359 and n, 371, 373, 433
See also ideal and real
phenomenal and noumenal *see* ideal and real
phenomenalism: Herbart 256; Mach, Avenarius 358ff
re self 360, 440
phenomenology 430–6, 437 and Hegel 180; Heidegger 438; Husserl 432–4; Nietzsche 420
consciousness, P. of *see s.v.*
Phenomenology of spirit, Hegel's The 96, 161f, 169, 180–8, 202, 227, 341
philology, classical 391
philosophy: Fichte 21, 31, 37–40, 48, 88, 100, 421–4, 424n; Hegel 10f, 21, 160, 170–80, 195, 202 and below; Herbart 250f, 252, 255; Kierkegaard 336ff, 340, 344f; Marxism 306, 308, 320f, 324, 327, 332f; Nietzsche 398ff, 419; Schelling 95, 100f, 105ff, 122f, 135–8, 139, 168, 439 and below; Schopenhauer 270f, 281, 286; also 7, 9, 146, 364, 367, 421–8, 439ff
absolute P: Hegel 240f, 244, 297
aesthetic P. *see* art, P. of
art, P. of *see s.v.*

religion, philosophy of: Hegel 161, 228 ff, **234-9**; idealists 10-13, 17; Schelling 17, 25, 99, 122, 138, 141 f, 144, 147, 259; *also* 155, 249*, 259, 377

religious consciousness, experience: Hegel 11, 181, 185-8, 229, 234-7, 239 f; Schelling 25, 99, 138, 140 f, 144, 148; Schleiermacher 149 f, **151-5**, 157; *also* 6, 13, 24, 246, 249, 294, 329, 339, 435
language of : Hegel 196, 198, 239 ff

religious doctrines: Lange 366

religious experience *see* religious consciousness *above*

renunciation *see* mortification

representation: Bolzano 259; Engels 315 (on concept); Fichte 52, 57; Schelling 100, 105 f, 108 f, 112 ff
See also Vorstellung

reproduction of species 111, 270, 273, 291

republic, democratic: Feuerbach 299

Republic, Plato's 215 f

repulsion and attraction 111, 272

research, scholarly: Fichte 68

resentment: Nietzsche 401 f

responsibility: Kierkegaard 336, 340

resurrection: Hegel 233

retribution: Herbart 254

return to God: Baader 146; Schelling 129, 135, 138 f

Reuter, Wilhelm 384 n

revelation: Fichte 33, 77 f; Hegel 163, 240 f; Schelling 118, 122 f, 130, 137, **138-42**, 144, 148; Schleiermacher 155; *also* 281, 388

Revolution of 1848 263, 274, 288, 311 f

revolution, social: Marxism 308 f, 311, 315, 324 ff, 328

revolutionary spirit and activity 301 f, 308, 315, 323 n, 324 f, 328, 331 f

reward for moral action: Schopenhauer 283

Rheinische Zeitung 306 f

Ricardo, David (1772-1823) 309

Rickert, Heinrich (1863-1936) **365**

Riehl, Alois (1844-1924) 367

Riga 357

right, concept of : Fichte 60, 70; Hegel 60, 161*, 204, 209, 224; *also* 387

right, rule of : Fichte 70

rights, moral: Fichte 51, 59 f, **69 ff**, 72 f, 119; Hegel 60; Schelling 117; *also* 248

Ritschl 391

Röcken 390

Rötscher, Heinrich Theodor (1803-71) 245

Rohde, Erwin (1845-98) 390 f, 393

romantic art: Hegel 233

romantic movement **13-21**, 35, 95, 150, 152, 278, 287

Rome, ancient 203, 221, 223, 238, 326

Rosenkranz, Johann K. F. (1805-79) 246

Rousseau, Jean-Jacques (1712-78): Fichte 32, 71; Hegel 159, 213 general will 28, 71, 213, 301

Royce, Josiah (1855-1916) 381

Ruge, Arnold (1802-80) **300 ff**

Russell, Bertrand (*b.* 1872) 432

Russia 147

S 218 n.3

sacrifice 238

salvation: Kierkegaard 342, 350; *also* 237, 277

sanctions 205, 254, 283

sanctity *see* holiness

Sartre, Jean-Paul (*b.* 1905) 79, 134, 351, 435

satisfaction: Eucken 386; Fichte 62 f, 87; Schopenhauer 273 f
See also pleasure

Scheler, Max (1874-1928) 435

Schelling, Friedrich Wilhelm (1775-1854) **94-148** (*see* Contents, pp. v-vi): Boehme *see* s.v.; Fichte 36, 94-100, 102 ff, 114 ff, 121; Hegel 94-8, 144, 160, 168 ff, 243; Kierkegaard 335; Schopenhauer 261, 263, 286; Spinoza 94, 143; *also* frequently 5-30, 145 f, 149, 290, 422, 439 f, 447 f*

Schlegel, August Wilhelm (1767-1845): Fichte and 35; Schelling 95 f

war: Baader 146; Hegel **217f**;
Marx 325; Nietzsche 406,
417f; Schopenhauer 274f; *also*
117, 256
Ward, James (1843–1925) 381
Warsaw 33
*Way to the blessed life or the doctrine
of religion,* Fichte's 36, 86, 88
weak, morality of the: Nietzsche
401, 404, 414
Weber, E. H. (1795–1878) 375
Weimar 268, 394
Weisse, Christian Hermann (1801–
60) **259f**
welfare: Hegel 207f, 212
Weltanschauung see world-view
Weltgeist: Hegel 219 *and see* world-
spirit
Wilamowitz-Moellendorff, U. von
(1848–1931) 391
will: Feuerbach 295f; Fichte 65,
67–70, 83f, 91; Hegel 28, 185ff,
203–9, 212f, 216, 301; Herbart
254; Nietzsche 414 *and see* will
to power *below*; Schelling 116,
131–7, 141; Schopenhauer 269f,
272–5, 277–85, 287–9; *also* 295,
315, 431
acts of will: Schopenhauer 282f
— blind W. *see* unconscious W.
below — finite W. *see* human W.
below — free W. *see s.v.* —
General W: Fichte 70f, 74;
Hegel 186f, 213, 216, 301;
Ruge 301; morality and 28, 70f
— good W: Fichte 65; Hegel
209 — human W: Fichte 68ff;
Hegel 206; Schopenhauer 282,
284 — individual W. *see* human
W. *above* — infinite W: Fichte
68, 83f, 91; Hegel 206 — intellect and W. *see s.v.* — irrational
W. *see* unconscious W. *below* —
will to live: Nietzsche 403, 407;
Schopenhauer 273, 281–5,
288f, 394 — metaphysical W:
Schopenhauer 272–5, 282, 285
— moral W: Cohen 363;
Fichte 69, 84; Hegel 206 —
objectification of *see s.v.* — particular W: Hegel 28, 205f, 208,
212f; and will of the State 71,
212f — Will to Power: Nietzsche
393f, 403f, **407f**, 410 and n,

411f, 418, 420, 422 — rational
W: Hegel 185f, 203f, 208, 212,
301; Ruge 301; Schelling 131f,
135, 137; Schopenhauer 269n
— reason and W: Kierkegaard
344; Schopenhauer **269f**;
Wundt 382 — self-determining W: Schelling 116 —
slavery of W: E. von Hartmann
291; Schopenhauer 277–81,
283f — subjective W: Hegel
206f — unconscious, blind,
W: Schelling 131f, 134, 141;
Schopenhauer 278, 287 — universal W: Hegel 205f, 208,
212f
Willman, Otto (1839–1920) 387
Windelband, Wilhelm (1848–1915)
364f, 366f
wisdom: Hegel 203; *also* 142, 147n,
384
Wissenschaft der Logik, Hegel's 161
Wissenschaftslehre, Fichte's 33f and
see *Basis of the entire theory of
science*
Wittenberg 32
Wittgenstein, Ludwig (1889–1951)
430
Wolff, Christian (1659–1754) 19, 32,
264, 266, 388
Word, the divine: Fichte 88; Hegel
187; Schelling 127
work, human: Marx 309, 317, 329
and see labour
working classes: Marxism 310, 312,
329
world, the: Fichte 80, 89, 91;
Nietzsche 407f, 410, 415f, 419,
423, 425; Schelling 100, 127,
135; *also* 150, 302, 355
eternal world: Oken 145 — God and
see Nature and God — history,
world- *see s.v.* — World as Idea:
E. von Hartmann 290ff, Schopenhauer 264, 266, 268, 275f, 288
and see World as Will and Idea
— world-order, moral: Fichte
28f, 34, 68, 80–3, 91; Schelling:
117ff, 119 — world-organization *see* community, universal
— phenomenal W. *see* world as
Idea — purpose of W: E. von
Hartmann 291; Lotze 379, 381
and see finality of Nature —

A
HISTORY OF PHILOSOPHY

VOLUME VIII
BENTHAM TO RUSSELL

BY

FREDERICK COPLESTON, S.J.

CONTENTS

iii

PART II

THE IDEALIST MOVEMENT IN GREAT BRITAIN

PART III

IDEALISM IN AMERICA

CONTENTS

PART IV

THE PRAGMATIST MOVEMENT

PART V

THE REVOLT AGAINST IDEALISM

PREFACE

IN the preface to Volume VII of this *History of Philosophy* I said that I hoped to devote a further volume, the eighth, to some aspects of French and British thought in the nineteenth century. This hope has been only partially fulfilled. For the present volume contains no treatment of French philosophy but is devoted exclusively to some aspects of British and American thought. It covers rather familiar ground. But in a general history of Western philosophy this ground obviously ought to be covered.

As I have strayed over well into the twentieth century, some explanation may be needed of the fact that the philosophy of Bertrand Russell, who is happily still with us, has been accorded relatively extensive treatment, whereas the thought of Ludwig Wittgenstein, who died in 1951, has been relegated to the epilogue, apart from a few allusions in the chapter on Russell. After all, it may be pointed out, Russell was himself influenced to a certain extent by Wittgenstein, both in regard to the interpretation of the logical status of the propositions of logic and pure mathematics and in regard to logical atomism.

The explanation is simple enough. Russell's thought fits naturally into the context of the revolt against idealism; and though he has obviously exercised a powerful influence on the rise and development of the analytic movement in twentieth-century British thought, in some important respects he has maintained a traditional view of the function of philosophy. His lack of sympathy with Wittgenstein's later ideas and with certain aspects of recent 'Oxford philosophy' is notorious. Further, though he has emphasized the limitations of empiricism as a theory of knowledge, in some respects he can be regarded as prolonging the empiricist tradition into the twentieth century, even if he has enriched it with new techniques of logical analysis. Wittgenstein, however, frankly proposed a revolutionary concept of the nature, function and scope of philosophy. Certainly, there is a very considerable difference between the ideas of language expounded in the *Tractatus* and those expounded in *Philosophical Investigations*; but in both cases the concept of philosophy is far from being a traditional one. And as limitations of space excluded the possibility of according extensive treatment to the concentration on language which is associated with the name of Wittgenstein, I decided to confine my discussion of the subject to some brief remarks in an epilogue. This fact should not, however, be interpreted as implying a judgment of value in regard to the philosophy either of Russell or of Wittgenstein. I mean, the fact that I have devoted three chapters to Russell does not signify that in my opinion his thought is simply a hangover from the nineteenth century. Nor does the fact that I have relegated Wittgenstein to the epilogue, apart from some allusions in the chapters on Russell, mean that I fail to appreciate his originality and importance. Rather is it a matter of not being able to give equally extensive treatment to the ideas of both these philosophers.

A word of explanation may also be appropriate in regard to my treatment of Cardinal Newman. It will be obvious to any attentive reader that in distinguishing the currents of thought in the nineteenth century I have used traditional labels, 'empiricism', 'idealism' and so on, none of which can properly be applied to Newman. But to omit him altogether, because of the difficulty of classifying him, would have been absurd, especially when I have mentioned a considerable number of much less distinguished thinkers. I decided, therefore, to make a few remarks about some of his philosophical ideas in an appendix. I am well aware, of course, that this will not satisfy Newman enthusiasts; but a writer cannot undertake to satisfy everybody.

Volumes VII and VIII having been devoted respectively to German and British-American philosophy in the nineteenth century, the natural procedure would be to devote a further volume, the ninth, to aspects of French and other European philosophy during the same period. But I am inclined to postpone the writing of this volume and to turn my attention instead to the subject to which I referred in the preface to Volume VII, that is, to what may be called the philosophy of the history of philosophy or general reflection on the development of philosophical thought and on its implications. For I should like to undertake this task while there is a reasonable possibility of fulfilling it.

ACKNOWLEDGMENTS

THE author has pleasure in expressing his gratitude to the Right Hon. the Earl Russell, O.M., for his generous permission to quote from his writings, and to the following publishers and holders of copyright for permission to quote from the works indicated below.

The Clarendon Press: *Collected Essays, Ethical Studies, Principles of Logic, Appearance and Reality, Essays on Truth and Reality,* by F. H. Bradley; *The Idea of God in the Light of Recent Philosophy* by A. S. Pringle-Pattison; *The Nature of Truth* by H. H. Joachim; *Statement and Inference* by J. Cook Wilson; and *Essays in Ancient and Modern Philosophy* by H. W. B. Joseph.

The Oxford University Press: *The Problems of Philosophy* and *Religion and Science* by Bertrand Russell; and *A Common Faith* by John Dewey.

Macmillan and Co., Ltd. (London): *Logic, Essentials of Logic, The Philosophical Theory of the State, The Principle of Individuality and Value, The Value and Destiny of the Individual* by Bernard Bosanquet; *Humanism, Formal Logic* and *Axioms as Postulates* (contained in *Personal Idealism,* edited by H. Sturt) by F. C. S. Schiller; and *Space, Time and Deity* by S. Alexander.

The Cambridge University Press: *The Nature of Existence* by J. M. E. McTaggart.

W. Blackwood and Sons, Ltd: *Hegelianism and Personality* by A. S. Pringle-Pattison.

A. and C. Black, Ltd.: *Naturalism and Agnosticism* by James Ward.

Miss S. C. Campbell: *The Realm of Ends* by James Ward.

The Belknap Press of the Harvard University Press: *Collected Papers of Charles Sanders Peirce*; Vols. I and II, copyright 1931, 1932, 1959, 1960; Vols. III and IV, copyright 1933, 1961; Vols. V and VI, copyright 1934, 1935, 1962, 1963 by the President and Fellows of Harvard College.

G. Bell and Sons, Ltd.: *The Influence of Darwin on Philosophy* by John Dewey.

Constable and Co., Ltd.: *Experience and Nature* by John Dewey.

Yale University Press: *A Common Faith* by John Dewey; *The*

ix

Meaning of God in Human Experience and *Human Nature and Its Remaking* by W. E. Hocking. Acknowledgment is also due to Professor W. E. Hocking.

The University of Chicago Press: *Theory of Valuation* by John Dewey. (*International Encyclopaedia of Unified Science*, Vol. 2, no. 4, copyright 1939.)

The Philosophical Library Inc. (N.Y.): *Problems of Men* (copyright 1946) by John Dewey and *The Development of American Pragmatism* by John Dewey (contained in *Twentieth Century Philosophy*, edited by Dagobert D. Runes, copyright 1943).

Holt, Rinehart and Winston Inc. (N.Y.) and the John Dewey Foundation: *Human Nature and Conduct*, *Logic: The Theory of Inquiry* and *The Public and Its Problems* by John Dewey.

Putnam's and Coward-McCann (N.Y.): *Quest For Certainty* (copyright 1929, renewed 1957) by John Dewey.

The Macmillan Co. Inc. (N.Y.): *Democracy and Education* (copyright 1916) by John Dewey; *The New Realism: Cooperative Studies in Philosophy* (copyright 1912) by E. B. Holt and Others; *Process and Reality* (copyright 1929 and 1949) by A. N. Whitehead.

Professor G. Ryle, Editor of *Mind: The Nature of Judgment* (*Mind*, 1899) by G. E. Moore.

Mrs. G. E. Moore: *Principia Ethica* by G. E. Moore.

Routledge and Kegan Paul, Ltd.: *Philosophical Studies* by G. E. Moore; and *What I Believe* by Bertrand Russell.

George Allen and Unwin, Ltd.: *The Metaphysical Theory of the State* by L. T. Hobhouse; *Philosophical Papers and Some Main Problems of Philosophy* by G. E. Moore; *The Principles of Mathematics, Introduction to Mathematical Philosophy, Philosophical Essays, The Analysis of Mind, Our Knowledge of the External World, Principles of Social Reconstruction, Mysticism and Logic, An Outline of Philosophy, The Scientific Outlook, Power, An Inquiry into Meaning and Truth, A History of Western Philosophy, Human Knowledge: Its Scope and Limits, Logic and Knowledge, My Philosophical Development, Unpopular Essays* and *Authority and the Individual* by Bertrand Russell; *Contemporary British Philosophy*, First Series (1924) and Second Series (1925), edited by J. H. Muirhead.

W. W. Norton and Co., Inc. (N.Y.): *The Principles of Mathematics* by Bertrand Russell.

Simon and Schuster Inc. (N.Y.): *A History of Western Philosophy* (c. 1945), *Human Knowledge: Its Scope and Limits* (c. 1948),

ACKNOWLEDGMENTS xi

Authority and the Individual (*c.* 1949), *Unpopular Essays* (*c.* 1950) and *My Philosophical Development* (*c.* 1959), by Bertrand Russell.

Macdonald and Co., Ltd. (London) and Doubleday and Co. Inc. (N.Y.): *Wisdom of the West* by Bertrand Russell (copyright Rathbone Books Ltd., London 1959).

The Library of Living Philosophers Inc., formerly published by The Tudor Publishing Co., N.Y., and now published by The Open Court Publishing Co., La Salle, Illinois: *The Philosophy of John Dewey* (1939 and 1951) and *The Philosophy of Bertrand Russell* (1946), both edited by Paul Arthur Schilpp.

ACKNOWLEDGMENTS

PART I

BRITISH EMPIRICISM

CHAPTER I

THE UTILITARIAN MOVEMENT (1)

Introductory remarks—The life and writings of Bentham—The principles of Benthamism, followed by some critical comments—The life and writings of James Mill—Altruism and the associationist psychology; Mill's polemic against Mackintosh—James Mill on the mind—Remarks on Benthamite economics.

1. THE philosophy of David Hume, which represented the culmination of classical British empiricism, called forth a lively reaction on the part of Thomas Reid and his successors.[1] Indeed, as far as the Universities were concerned, in the first decades of the nineteenth century the so-called Scottish School was the one living and vigorous movement of thought. Moreover, though in the meantime it had received some serious blows and had lost its first vigour, its place in the Universities was eventually taken by idealism rather than by empiricism.

It would, however, be a great mistake to suppose that empiricism was reduced to a moribund condition by Reid's attack on Hume, and that it remained in this position until it was given a fresh lease of life by J. S. Mill. Philosophy is not confined to the Universities. Hume himself never occupied an academic chair, though, admittedly, this was not due to lack of effort on his part. And empiricism continued its life, despite attack by Reid and his followers, though its leading representatives were not university professors or lecturers.

The first phase of nineteenth-century empiricism, which is known as the utilitarian movement, may be said to have originated with Bentham. But though we naturally tend to think of him as a philosopher of the early part of the nineteenth century, inasmuch as it was then that his influence made itself felt, he was born in 1748, twenty-eight years before the death of Hume. And some of his works were published in the last three decades of the eighteenth

[1] See Vol. V of this *History*, pp. 364–94.

century. It is no matter of surprise, therefore, if we find that there is a conspicuous element of continuity between the empiricism of the eighteenth century and that of the nineteenth. For example, the method of reductive analysis, the reduction, that is to say, of the whole to its parts, of the complex to its primitive or simple elements, which had been practised by Hume, was continued by Bentham. This involved, as can be seen in the philosophy of James Mill, a phenomenalistic analysis of the self. And in the reconstruction of mental life out of its supposed simple elements use was made of the associationist psychology which had been developed in the eighteenth century by, for instance, David Hartley,[1] not to speak of Hume's employment of the principles of association of ideas. Again, in the first chapter of his *Fragment on Government* Bentham gave explicit expression to his indebtedness to Hume for the light which had fallen on his mind when he saw in the *Treatise of Human Nature* how Hume had demolished the fiction of a social contract or compact and had shown how all virtue is founded on utility. To be sure, Bentham was also influenced by the thought of the French Enlightenment, particularly by that of Helvétius.[2] But this does not alter the fact that in regard to both method and theory there was a notable element of continuity between the empiricist movements of the eighteenth and nineteenth centuries in Great Britain.

But once the element of continuity has been noted, attention must be drawn to the considerable difference in emphasis. As traditionally represented at any rate, classical British empiricism had been predominantly concerned with the nature, scope and limits of human knowledge, whereas the utilitarian movement was essentially practical in outlook, orientated towards legal, penal and political reform. It is true that emphasis on the role of the theory of knowledge in classical empiricism can be overdone. Hume, for example, was concerned with the development of a science of human nature. And it can be argued, and has indeed been argued, that he was primarily a moral philosopher.[3] But Hume's aim was chiefly to understand the moral life and the moral judgment, whereas Bentham was mainly concerned with providing the criterion for judging commonly received moral ideas and legal and political institutions with a view to their reformation. Perhaps we can apply Marx's famous assertion and

[1] See Vol. V of this *History*, pp. 191–3.
[2] See Vol. VI of this *History*, pp. 35–8.
[3] Cf. Vol. V of this *History*, pp. 260–3, 318–19 and 342–3.

say that Hume was primarily concerned with understanding the world, whereas Bentham was primarily concerned with changing it.

Of the two men Hume was, indeed, by far the greater philosopher. But Bentham had the gift of seizing on certain ideas which were not his own inventions, developing them and welding them into a weapon or instrument of social reform. Benthamism in a narrow sense, and utilitarianism in general, expressed the attitude of liberal and radical elements in the middle class to the weight of tradition and to the vested interests of what is now often called the Establishment. The excesses connected with the French Revolution produced in England a strong reaction which found notable expression in the reflections of Edmund Burke (1729–97), with their emphasis on social stability and tradition. But after the Napoleonic Wars at any rate the movement of radical reform was more easily able to make its influence felt. And in this movement utilitarianism possesses an undeniable historical importance. Considered as a moral philosophy, it is over-simplified and skates lightly over awkward and difficult questions. But its over-simplified character, together with an at least *prima facie* clarity, obviously facilitated its use as an instrument in the endeavour to secure practical reforms in the social and political fields.

During the nineteenth century social philosophy in Great Britain passed through several successive phases. First, there was the philosophical radicalism which is associated with the name of Bentham and which had been already expressed by him in the closing decades of the eighteenth century. Secondly, there was Benthamism as modified, added to and developed by J. S. Mill. And thirdly, there was the idealist political philosophy which arose in the last part of the nineteenth century. The term 'utilitarianism' covers the first two phases, but not, of course, the third. Utilitarianism was individualistic in outlook, even though it aimed at the welfare of society, whereas in idealist political theory the idea of the State as an organic totality came to the fore under the influence of both Greek and German thought.

This and the following chapters will be devoted to an account of the development of utilitarianism from Bentham to J. S. Mill inclusively. The latter's theories in the fields of logic, epistemology and ontology will be discussed separately in a subsequent chapter.

2. Jeremy Bentham was born on February 15th, 1748. A

precocious child, he was learning Latin grammar at the age of four. Educated at Westminster School and the University of Oxford, neither of which institutions captivated his heart, he was destined by his father for a career at the Bar. But he preferred the life of reflection to that of a practising lawyer. And in the law, the penal code and the political institutions of his time he found plenty to think about. To put the matter in simple terms, he asked questions on these lines. What is the purpose of this law or of this institution? Is this purpose desirable? If so, does the law or institution really conduce to its fulfilment? In fine, how is the law or institution to be judged from the point of view of utility?

In its application to legislation and to political institutions the measure of utility was for Bentham the degree of conduciveness to the greater happiness of the greatest possible number of human beings or members of society. Bentham himself remarks that the principle of utility, as so interpreted, occurred to him when he was reading the *Essay on Government* (1768) by Joseph Priestley (1733–1804) who stated roundly that the happiness of the majority of the members of any State was the standard by which all the affairs of the State should be judged. But Hutcheson, when treating of ethics, had previously asserted that that action is best which conduces to the greatest happiness of the greatest number.[1] Again, in the preface to his famous treatise on crimes and punishments (*Dei delitti e delle pene*, 1764), Cesare Beccaria (1738–94) had spoken of the greatest happiness divided among the greatest possible number. There were utilitarian elements in the philosophy of Hume, who declared, for example, that 'public utility is the sole origin of justice'.[2] And Helvétius, who, as already noted, strongly influenced Bentham, was a pioneer in utilitarian moral theory and in its application to the reform of society. In other words, Bentham did not invent the principle of utility: what he did was to expound and apply it explicitly and universally as the basic principle of both morals and legislation.

Bentham was at first principally interested in legal and penal reform. Radical changes in the British constitution did not enter into his original schemes. And at no time was he an enthusiast for democracy as such. That is to say, he had no more belief in the sacred right of the people to rule than he had in the theory of

[1] See Vol. V of this *History*, p. 182.
[2] *An Enquiry concerning the Principles of Morals*, 3, 1, 145.

natural rights in general, which he considered to be nonsense. But whereas he seems to have thought at first that rulers and legislators were really seeking the common good, however muddled and mistaken they might be about the right means for attaining this end, in the course of time he became convinced that the ruling class was dominated by self-interest. Indifference and opposition to his plans for legal, penal and economic reform doubtless helped him to come to this conclusion. Hence he came to advocate political reform as a prerequisite for other changes. And eventually he proposed the abolition of the monarchy and the House of Lords, the disestablishment of the Church of England, and the introduction of universal suffrage and annual parliaments. His political radicalism was facilitated by the fact that he had no veneration for tradition as such. He was far from sharing Burke's view of the British constitution; and his attitude had much more affinity with that of the French *philosophes*,[1] with their impatience with tradition and their belief that everything would be for the best if only reason could reign. But his appeal throughout was to the principle of utility, not to any belief that democracy possesses some peculiarly sacred character of its own.

Nor was Bentham primarily moved by humanitarian considerations. In the movement of social reform in Great Britain throughout the nineteenth century, humanitarianism, sometimes based on Christian beliefs and sometimes without any explicit reference to Christianity, undoubtedly played a very important role. But though, for example, in his campaign against the outrageously severe penal code of his time and against the disgraceful state of the prisons, Bentham often demanded changes which humanitarian sentiment would in fact suggest, he was primarily roused to indignation by what he considered, doubtless rightly, to be the irrationality of the penal system, its incapacity to achieve its purposes and to serve the common good. To say this is not, of course, to say that he was what would normally be called inhumane. It is to say that he was not primarily moved by compassion for the victims of the penal system, but rather by the 'inutility' of the system. He was a man of the reason or understanding rather than of the heart or of feeling.

In 1776 Bentham published anonymously his *Fragment on Government* in which he attacked the famous lawyer Sir William

---

[1] Allusion to the influence of Helvétius's writings on Bentham's mind has already been made. We may add that he corresponded with d'Alembert.

Blackstone (1723–80) for his use of the fiction of a social compact or contract. The work had no immediate success, but in 1781 it brought Bentham the friendship of Lord Shelburne, afterwards Marquis of Lansdowne, who was Prime Minister from July 1782 to February 1783. And through Shelburne the philosopher met several other important people. He also formed a friendship with Étienne Dumont, tutor to Shelburne's son, who was to prove of invaluable help in publishing a number of his papers. Bentham not infrequently left manuscripts unfinished and went on to some other topic. And many of his writings were published through the agency of friends and disciples. Sometimes they first appeared in French. For example, a chapter of his *Manual of Political Economy*, written in 1793, appeared in the *Bibliothèque britannique* in 1798; and Dumont made use of the work in his *Théorie des peines et des récompenses* (1811). Bentham's work was published in English for the first time in John Bowring's edition of his *Works* (1838–43).

Bentham's *Defence of Usury* appeared in 1787 and his important *Introduction to the Principles of Morals and Legislation* in 1789.[1] The *Introduction* was intended as a preparation and scheme for a number of further treatises. Thus Bentham's *Essay on Political Tactics* corresponded to one section in this scheme. But though a part of this essay was sent to the Abbé Morellet in 1789, the work was first published by Dumont in 1816,[2] together with *Anarchical Fallacies* which had been written in about 1791.

In 1791 Bentham published his scheme for a model prison, the so-called *Panopticon*. And he approached the French National Assembly with a view to the establishment of such an institution under its auspices, offering his gratuitous services as supervisor. But though Bentham was one of the foreigners on whom the Assembly conferred the title of citizen in the following year, his offer was not taken up.[3] Similar efforts to induce the British government to implement the scheme for a model prison promised at first to be successful. But they eventually failed, partly, so Bentham at any rate liked to believe, through the machinations of King George III. However, in 1813 Parliament voted the philosopher a large sum of money in compensation for his expenditure on the Panopticon scheme.

[1] This work had been printed in 1788.
[2] A partial English text appeared in 1791.
[3] Obviously, the prisoners whom Bentham had in mind were not at all of the type of those who later became victims of the Jacobin Terror. He turned to the new French Assembly in the hope that now at last the reign of unclouded reason was beginning, that philosophy was coming into its own.

In 1802 Dumont published a work entitled *Traités de législation de M. Jérémie Bentham*. This consisted partly of papers written by Bentham himself, some of which had been originally composed in French, and partly of a digest by Dumont of the philosopher's ideas. And the work contributed greatly to the rise of Bentham's fame. At first this was more evident abroad than in England. But in the course of time the philosopher's star began to rise even in his own country. From 1808 James Mill became his disciple and a propagator of his doctrines. And Bentham became what might be called the background leader or inspirer of a group of radicals devoted to the principles of Benthamism.

In 1812 James Mill published an *Introductory View of the Rationale of Evidence*, a version of some of Bentham's papers. A French version of the papers was published by Dumont in 1823 under the title *Traité des preuves judiciaires*; and an English translation of this work appeared in 1825. A five-volume edition of Bentham's papers on jurisprudence which was much fuller than James Mill's was published by J. S. Mill in 1827 under the title *Rationale of Judicial Evidence*.

Bentham also gave his attention both to questions of constitutional reform and to the subject of the codification of the law. Characteristically, he was impatient of what he regarded as the chaotic condition of English law. His *Catechism of Parliamentary Reform* appeared in 1817, though it had been written in 1809. The year 1817 also saw the publication of *Papers upon Codification and Public Instruction*. In 1819 Bentham published a paper entitled *Radical Reform Bill, with Explanations*, and in 1823 *Leading Principles of a Constitutional Code*. The first volume of his *Constitutional Code*, together with the first chapter of the second volume, appeared in 1830. The whole work, edited by R. Doane, was published posthumously in 1841.

It is not possible to list all Bentham's publications here. But we can mention two or three further titles. *Chrestomathia*, a series of papers on education, appeared in 1816, while in the following year James Mill published his edition of Bentham's *Table of the Springs of Action*[1] which is concerned with the analysis of pains and pleasures as springs of action. The philosopher's *Deontology or Science of Morality* was published posthumously by Bowring in 1834 in two volumes, the second volume being compiled from notes. Reference has already been made to Bowring's edition of

[1] The work had been written at a considerably earlier period.

Bentham's *Works*.[1] A complete and critical edition of the philosopher's writings is yet to come.

Bentham died on June 6th, 1832, leaving directions that his body should be dissected for the benefit of science. It is preserved at University College, London. This College was founded in 1828, largely as a result of pressure from a group of which Bentham himself was a member. It was designed to extend the benefits of higher education to those for whom the two existing universities did not cater. Further, there were to be no religious tests, as there still were at Oxford and Cambridge.

3. Benthamism rested on a basis of psychological hedonism, the theory that every human being seeks by nature to attain pleasure and avoid pain. This was not, of course, a novel doctrine. It had been propounded in the ancient world, notably by Epicurus, while in the eighteenth century it was defended by, for example, Helvétius in France and Hartley and Tucker in England.[2] But though Bentham was not the inventor of the theory, he gave a memorable statement of it. 'Nature has placed mankind under the governance of two sovereign masters, *pain* and *pleasure*. . . . They govern us in all we do, in all we say, in all we think: every effort we can make to throw off our subjection will serve but to demonstrate and confirm it. In words a man may pretend to abjure their empire, but in reality he will remain subject to it all the while.'[3]

Further, Bentham is at pains to make clear what he means by pleasure and pain. He has no intention of restricting the range of meaning of these terms by arbitrary or 'metaphysical' definitions. He means by them what they mean in common estimation, in common language, no more and no less. 'In this matter we want no refinement, no metaphysics. It is not necessary to consult Plato, nor Aristotle. *Pain* and *pleasure* are what everybody feels to be such.'[4] The term 'pleasure' covers, for example, the pleasures of eating and drinking; but it also covers those of

[1] In the *Works* Bowring included a number of fragments, some of which are of philosophical interest. Thus in the fragment entitled *Ontology* Bentham distinguishes between real entities and fictitious entities. The latter, which are not to be compared with fabulous entities, the products of the free play of the imagination, are creations of the exigencies of language. For example, we require to be able to speak of relations, using the noun 'relation'. But though things can be related, there are no separate entities called 'relations'. If such entities are postulated through the influence of language, they are 'fictitious'.

[2] For Tucker see Vol. V of this *History*, pp. 193–4.

[3] *An Introduction to the Principles of Morals and Legislation*, ch. 1, sect. 1. This work will be referred to in future as *Introduction*.

[4] *Theory of Legislation*, translated from the French of Étienne Dumont by R. Hildreth, p. 3 (London, 1896).

reading an interesting book, listening to music or performing a kind action.

But Bentham is not concerned simply with stating what he takes to be a psychological truth, namely that all men are moved to action by the attraction of pleasure and the repulsion of pain. He is concerned with establishing an objective criterion of morality, of the moral character of human actions. Thus after the sentence quoted above, in which Bentham says that Nature has placed mankind under the government of pain and pleasure, he adds that 'it is for them alone to point out what we ought to do, as well as to determine what we shall do. On the one hand the standard of right and wrong, on the other the chain of causes and effects, are fastened to their throne.'[1] If, therefore, we assume that pleasure, happiness and good are synonymous terms and that pain, unhappiness and evil are also synonymous, the question immediately arises whether it makes any sense to say that we ought to pursue what is good and avoid what is evil, if, as a matter of psychological fact, we always do pursue the one and endeavour to avoid the other.

To be able to answer this question affirmatively, we have to make two assumptions. First, when it is said that man seeks pleasure, it is meant that he seeks his greater pleasure or the greatest possible amount of it. Secondly, man does not necessarily perform those actions which will as a matter of fact conduce to this end.[2] If we make these assumptions and pass over the difficulties inherent in any hedonistic ethics, we can then say that right actions are those which tend to increase the sum total of pleasure while wrong actions are those which tend to diminish it, and that we ought to do what is right and not do what is wrong.[3]

We thus arrive at the principle of utility, also called the greatest happiness principle. This 'states the greatest happiness of all those whose interest is in question, as being the right and proper, and only right and proper and universally desirable, end of human

---

[1] *Introduction*, ch. 1, sect. 1.

[2] For example, under the attraction of an immediate pleasure a man might neglect the fact that the course of action which causes this pleasure leads to a sum total of pain which outweighs the pleasure.

[3] Strictly speaking, an action which tends to add to the sum total of pleasure is for Bentham a 'right' action, in the sense of an action which we ought to perform, or at any rate not an action which we are obliged not to perform, that is, a 'wrong' action. It may not always be the case that an addition to the sum of pleasure cannot exist otherwise than through my action here and now. Hence I may not be obliged to act, though, if I do, the action will certainly not be wrong.

action'.[1] The parties whose interest is in question may, of course, differ. If we are thinking of the individual agent as such, it is his greatest happiness which is referred to. If we are thinking of the community, it is the greater happiness of the greatest possible number of the members of the community which is being referred to. If we are thinking of all sentient beings, then we must also consider the greater pleasure of animals. Bentham is chiefly concerned with the greater happiness of the human community, with the common good or welfare in the sense of the common good of any given human political society. But in all cases the principle is the same, namely that the greatest happiness of the party in question is the only desirable end of human action.

If we mean by proof deduction from some more ultimate principle or principles, the principle of utility cannot be proved. For there is no more ultimate ethical principle. At the same time Bentham tries to show that any other theory of morals involves in the long run an at least tacit appeal to the principle of utility. Whatever may be the reasons for which people act or think that they act, if we once raise the question why we *ought* to perform a certain action, we shall ultimately have to answer in terms of the principle of utility. The alternative moral theories which Bentham has in mind are principally intuitionist theories or theories which appeal to a moral sense. In his opinion such theories, taken by themselves, are incapable of answering the question why we ought to perform this action and not that. If the upholders of such theories once try to answer the question, they will ultimately have to argue that the action which ought to be performed is one which conduces to the greater happiness or pleasure of whatever party it is whose interest is in question. In other words, it is utilitarianism alone which can provide an objective criterion of right and wrong.[2] And to show that this is the case, is to give the only proof of the principle of utility which is required.

In passing we can note that though hedonism represented only one element in Locke's ethical theory,[3] he explicitly stated that

---

[1] *Introduction*, ch. 1, sect. 1, note 1.
[2] Bentham insists that the rightness or wrongness of actions depends on an objective criterion and not simply on the motive with which they are performed. 'Motive' and 'intention' are often confused, though they ought, Bentham maintains, to be carefully distinguished. If 'motive' is understood as a tendency to action when a pleasure, or the cause of a pleasure, is contemplated as the consequent of one's action, it makes no sense to speak of a bad motive. But in any case the criterion of right and wrong is primarily an objective criterion, not a subjective one.
[3] See Vol. V of this *History*, pp. 123-7.

'things then are good or evil only in reference to pleasure or pain. That we call good which is apt to cause or increase pleasure or diminish pain in us. . . . And on the contrary we name that evil which is apt to increase any pain or diminish any pleasure in us. . . .'[1] The property which is here called 'good' by Locke is described by Bentham as 'utility'. For 'utility is any property in any object, whereby it tends to produce benefit, advantage, pleasure, good or happiness, or . . . to prevent the happening of mischief, pain, evil or unhappiness to the party whose interest is considered.'[2]

Now, if actions are right in so far as they tend to increase the sum total of pleasure or diminish the sum total of pain of the party whose interest is in question, as Bentham puts it, the moral agent, when deciding whether a given action is right or wrong, will have to estimate the amount of pleasure and the amount of pain to which the action seems likely to give rise, and to weigh the one against the other. And Bentham provides a hedonistic or 'felicific' calculus for this purpose.[3] Let us suppose that I wish to estimate the value of a pleasure (or pain) for myself. I have to take into account four factors or dimensions of value: intensity, duration, certainty or uncertainty, propinquity or remoteness. For example, one pleasure might be very intense but of short duration, while another might be less intense but so much more lasting that it would be quantitatively greater than the first. Further, when considering actions which tend to produce pleasure or pain, I have to bear in mind two other factors, fecundity and purity. If of two types of action, each of which tends to produce pleasurable sensations, the one type tends to be followed by further pleasurable sensations while the other type does not or only in a lesser degree, the first is said to be more fecund or fruitful than the second. As for purity, this signifies freedom from being followed by sensations of the opposite kind. For instance, the cultivation of an appreciation of music opens up a range of enduring pleasure which does not yield those diminishing returns that result from the action of taking certain habit-forming drugs.

So far Bentham's calculus follows the same lines as that of Epicurus. But Bentham is chiefly concerned, in the application of his ethical theory, with the common good. And he adds that when a number of persons or community is the party whose interest is in question, we have to take into account a seventh factor in

[1] *Essay*, Bk. 2, ch. 20, sect. 2.   [2] *Introduction*, ch. 1, sect. 3.
[3] *Ibid.*, ch. 4.

addition to the six just mentioned. This seventh factor is extent, that is, the number of persons who are affected by the pleasure or pain in question.

It has sometimes been said that Bentham's calculus is useless but that one could quite well discard it while retaining his general moral theory. But it seems to the present writer that some distinctions are required. If one chose to look on this theory as no more than an analysis of the meaning of certain ethical terms, it would doubtless be possible to maintain that the analysis is correct and at the same time to disregard the hedonistic calculus. But if one looks on Bentham's moral theory as he himself looked on it, that is, not simply as an analysis but also as a guide for action, the case is somewhat different. We could indeed maintain, and rightly, that no exact mathematical calculation of pains and pleasures can be made. It is fairly obvious, for example, that in many cases a man cannot make a precise mathematical calculation of the respective quantities of pleasure which would probably result from alternative courses of action. And if it is the community whose interest is in question, how are we going to calculate the probable sum total of pleasure when it is a notorious fact that in many cases what is pleasurable to one is not pleasurable to another? At the same time, if we admit, as Bentham admitted, only quantitative differences between pleasures, and if we regard hedonistic ethics as providing a practical rule for conduct, some sort of calculation will be required, even if it cannot be precise. And in point of fact people do make such rough calculations on occasion. Thus a man may very well ask himself whether it is really worth while pursuing a certain course of pleasurable action which will probably involve certain painful consequences. And if he does seriously consider this question, he is making use of one of the rules of Bentham's calculus. What relation this sort of reasoning bears to morality is another question. And it is irrelevant in the present context. For the hypothesis is that Bentham's general moral doctrine is accepted.

Now, the sphere of human action is obviously very much wider than legislation and acts of government. And in some cases it is the individual agent as such whose interest is in question. Hence I can have duties to myself. But if the sphere of morality is coterminous with the sphere of human action, legislation and acts of government fall within the moral sphere. Hence the principle of utility must apply to them. But here the party whose interest is in question is the community. Although, therefore, as Bentham says, there are many actions which are as a matter of fact useful to the community but the regulation of which by law would not be in the public interest, legislation ought to serve this interest. It ought to be directed to the common welfare or happiness. Hence an act of legislation or of government is said to conform with or be dictated by the principle of utility when 'the tendency which it has to augment the happiness of the community is greater than any which it has to diminish it'.[1]

The community, however, is 'a fictitious *body*, composed of the individual persons who are considered as constituting as it were its members'.[2] And the interest of the community is 'the sum of the interests of the several members who compose it'.[3] To say, therefore, that legislation and government should be directed to the common good is to say that they should be directed to the greater happiness of the greatest possible number of individuals who are members of the society in question.

Obviously, if we assume that the common interest is simply the sum total of the private interests of the individual members of the community, we might draw the conclusion that the common good is inevitably promoted if every individual seeks and increases his own personal happiness. But there is no guarantee that individuals will seek their own happiness in a rational or enlightened manner, and in such a way that they do not diminish the happiness of other individuals, thus diminishing the sum total of happiness in the community. And in point of fact it is clear that clashes of interest do occur. Hence a harmonization of interests is required with a view to the attainment of the common good. And this is the function of government and legislation.[4]

It is sometimes said that any such harmonization of interests presupposes the possibility of working altruistically for the common good, and that Bentham thus makes an abrupt and unwarranted transition from the egoistic or selfish pleasure-seeker to the public-spirited altruist. But some distinctions are required. In the first place Bentham does not assume that all men are by

---

[1] *Introduction*, ch. 1, sect. 7.
[2] *Ibid.*, ch. 1, sect. 4. For Bentham's use of the word 'fictitious' see Note 1 on p. 15.
[3] *Ibid.*
[4] Bentham and his followers were indeed convinced that in the sphere of the economic market the removal of legal restrictions and the introduction of free trade and competition would, in the long run at any rate, inevitably make for the greater happiness of the community. But further reference to Benthamite economics will be made in the last section of this chapter.

nature necessarily egoistic or selfish in the sense in which these terms would generally be understood. For he recognizes social affections as well as their contrary. Thus in his table of pleasures he includes among the so-called simple pleasures those of benevolence, which are described as 'the pleasures resulting from the view of any pleasures supposed to be possessed by the beings who may be the objects of benevolence; to wit the sensitive beings we are acquainted with'.[1] In the second place, though Benthamism doubtless assumes that the man who takes pleasure in witnessing the pleasure of another does so originally because it is pleasurable to himself, it invokes the principles of the associationist psychology to explain how a man can come to seek the good of others without any advertence to his own.[2]

At the same time there is obviously no guarantee that those whose task it is to harmonize private interests will be notably endowed with benevolence, or that they will in fact have learned to seek the common good in a disinterested spirit. Indeed, it did not take Bentham long to come to the conclusion that rulers are very far from constituting exceptions to the general run of men, who, left to themselves, pursue their own interests, even if many of them are perfectly capable of being pleased by the pleasure of others. And it was this conclusion which was largely responsible for his adoption of democratic ideas. A despot or absolute monarch generally seeks his own interest, and so does a ruling aristocracy. The only way, therefore, of securing that the greater happiness of the greatest possible number is taken as the criterion in government and legislation is to place government, so far as this is practicable, in the hands of all. Hence Bentham's proposals for abolishing the monarchy[3] and the House of Lords and for introducing universal suffrage and annual parliaments. As the common interest is simply the sum total of private interests, everyone has a stake, so to speak, in the common good. And education can help the individual to understand that in acting for the common good he is also acting for his own good.

To avoid misunderstanding, it must be added that the harmonization of interests by law which Bentham demanded was primarily a removal of hindrances to the increase of the happiness of the greatest possible number of citizens rather than what would

---

[1] *Introduction*, ch. 5, sect. 10. 'Sensitive beings' includes animals.
[2] This theme will be treated in connection with James Mill.
[3] In Bentham's time the British monarch was able to exercise considerably more effective influence in political life than is possible today.

generally be thought of as positive interference with the freedom of the individual. This is one reason why he gave so much attention to the subject of penology, the infliction of penal sanctions for diminishing the general happiness or good by infringing laws which are or at any rate ought to be passed with a view to preventing actions which are incompatible with the happiness of the members of society in general. In Bentham's opinion the primary purpose of punishment is to deter, not to reform. Reformation of offenders is only a subsidiary purpose.

Bentham's remarks on concrete issues are often sensible enough. His general attitude to penal sanctions is a case in point. As already remarked, the primary purpose of punishment is to deter. But punishment involves the infliction of pain, of a diminution of pleasure in some way or other. And as all pain is evil, it follows that 'all punishment in itself is evil'.[1] And the conclusion to be drawn is that the legislator ought not to attach to the infringement of the law a penal sanction which exceeds what is strictly required to obtain the desired effect. True, it might be argued that if the primary aim of punishment is to deter, the most ferocious penalties will be the most efficacious. But if punishment is in itself an evil, even though in the concrete circumstances of human life in society a necessary evil, the relevant question is, what is the least amount of punishment which will have a deterrent effect? Besides, the legislator has to take into account public opinion, though this is indeed a variable factor. For the more people come to consider a given penal sanction to be grossly excessive or inappropriate, the more they tend to withhold their co-operation in the execution of the law.[2] And in this case the supposedly deterrent effect of the punishment is diminished. Again, it has a bad educative effect and is not for the public good if some heavy penalty, such as the death penalty, is inflicted for a variety of offences which differ very much in gravity, that is, in the amount of harm which they do to others or to the community at large. As for the subsidiary aim of punishment, namely to contribute to the reformation of offenders, how can this aim be fulfilled when the prisons are notoriously hotbeds of vice?

[1] *Introduction*, ch. 13, sect. 2.
[2] It was certainly not unknown at the time for juries to refuse to convict even when they were well aware that the accused was guilty. Further, the death sentence, when passed for what would now be considered comparatively minor offences and even on children, was frequently commuted. In other words, there was a growing discrepancy between the actual state of the law and educated opinion as to what it should be.

It is possible, of course, to hold a different view about the primary purpose of punishment. But it would require a considerable degree of eccentricity for a man of today to disagree with Bentham's conclusion that the penal system of his time stood in need of reform. And even if we do hold a `somewhat different view about the function of punishment, we can none the less recognize that his arguments in favour of reform are, generally speaking, intelligible and persuasive.

But when we turn from such discussions about the need for reform to Bentham's general philosophy, the situation is somewhat different. For example, J. S. Mill objected that Bentham's idea of human nature betrayed a narrowness of vision. And inasmuch as Bentham tends to reduce man to a system of attractions and repulsions in response to pleasures and pains, together with an ability to make a quasi-mathematical computation of the pluses of pleasures and the minuses of pains, many would find themselves in full agreement with Mill on this point.

At the same time J. S. Mill awards high marks to Bentham for employing a scientific method in morals and politics. This consists above all in 'the method of detail; of treating wholes by separating them into their parts, abstractions by resolving them into things —classes and generalities by distinguishing them into the individuals of which they are made up; and breaking every question into pieces before attempting to solve it'.[1] In other words, Mill commends Bentham for his thoroughgoing use of reductive analysis and for this reason regards him as a reformer in philosophy.

In regard to the question of fact Mill is, of course, quite right. We have seen, for example, how Bentham applied a kind of quantitative analysis in ethics. And he applied it because he thought that it was the only proper scientific method. It was the only method which would enable us to give clear meanings to terms such as 'right' and 'wrong'. Again, for Bentham terms such as 'community' and 'common interest' were abstractions which stood in need of analysis if they were to be given a cash-value. To imagine that they signified peculiar entities over and above the elements into which they could be analysed was to be misled by language into postulating fictitious entities.

But though there can obviously be no valid *a priori* objection to experimenting with the method of reductive analysis, it is also clear that Bentham skates lightly over difficulties and treats that

---

[1] *Dissertations and Discussions*, I, pp. 339–40 (2nd edition, 1867).

which is complicated as though it were simple. For example, it is admittedly difficult to give a clear explanation of what the common good is, if it is not reducible to the private goods of the individual members of the community. But it is also difficult to suppose that a true statement about the common good is always reducible to true statements about the private goods of individuals. We cannot legitimately take it for granted that such a reduction or translation is possible. Its possibility ought to be established by providing actual examples. As the Scholastics say, *ab esse ad posse valet illatio*. But Bentham tends to take the possibility for granted and to conclude without more ado that those who think otherwise have fallen victims to what Wittgenstein was later to call the bewitchment of language. In other words, even if Bentham was right in his application of reductive analysis, he did not pay anything like sufficient attention to what can be said on the other side. Indeed, Mill draws attention to 'Bentham's contempt of all other schools of thinkers'.[1]

According to Mill, Bentham 'was not a great philosopher, but he was a great reformer in philosophy'.[2] And if we are devotees of reductive analysis, we shall probably agree with this statement. Otherwise we may be inclined to omit the last two words. Bentham's habit of over-simplifying and of skating over difficulties, together with that peculiar narrowness of moral vision to which Mill aptly alludes, disqualifies him from being called a great philosopher. But his place in the movement of social reform is assured. His premisses are often questionable but he is certainly skilled in drawing from them conclusions which are frequently sensible and enlightened. And, as has already been remarked, the over-simplified nature of his moral philosophy facilitated its use as a practical instrument or weapon.

4. James Mill, Bentham's leading disciple, was born on April 6th, 1773, in Forfarshire. His father was a village shoemaker. After schooling at the Montrose Academy Mill entered the University of Edinburgh in 1790, where he attended the lectures of Dugald Stewart.[3] In 1798 he was licensed to preach; but he never received a call from any Presbyterian parish, and in 1802 he went to London with the hope of earning a living by writing and editorship. In 1805 he married. At the end of the following year he began work on his history of British India which appeared in three

---

[1] *Ibid.*, 1, p. 353. [2] *Ibid.*, 1, p. 339.
[3] See Vol. V of this *History*, pp. 375–83.

volumes in 1817. In 1819 this brought him a post in the East India Company, and subsequent advancement, with increases in salary, set him free at last from financial worries.

In 1808 Mill met Bentham and became a fervent disciple. By this time the would-be Presbyterian minister had become an agnostic. For some years he wrote for the *Edinburgh Review*, but he was too much of a radical to win the real confidence of the editors. In 1816–23 he wrote for the *Supplement* to the *Encyclopaedia Britannica* series of political articles which set forth the views of the utilitarian circle.[1] In 1821 he published his *Elements of Political Economy* and in 1829 his *Analysis of the Phenomena of the Human Mind*. Between these two dates he contributed for a time to the *Westminster Review*, which was founded in 1824 as an organ of the radicals.

James Mill died on June 23rd, 1836, a champion of Benthamism to the last. He was not perhaps a particularly attractive figure. A man of vigorous though somewhat narrow intellect, he was extremely reserved and apparently devoid of any poetic sensibility, while for passionate emotions and for sentiment he had little use. His son remarks that though James Mill upheld an Epicurean ethical theory (Bentham's hedonism), he was personally a Stoic and combined Stoic qualities with a Cynic's disregard for pleasure. But he was certainly an extremely hard-working and conscientious man, devoted to propagating the views which he believed to be true.

With James Mill, as with Bentham, we find a combination of *laissez-faire* economics with a reiterated demand for political reform. As every man naturally seeks his own interest, it is not surprising that the executive does so. The executive, therefore, must be controlled by the legislature. But the House of Commons is itself the organ of the interests of a comparatively small number of families. And its interest cannot be made identical with that of the community in general unless the suffrage is extended and elections are frequent.[2] Like other Benthamites, Mill also had a

[1] This circle comprised, among others, the economists David Ricardo and J. R. McCulloch, T. R. Malthus, the famous writer on population, and John Austin, who applied utilitarian principles to jurisprudence in his work *The Province of Jurisprudence Determined* (1832).

[2] Mill was indeed quite right in thinking that the House of Commons of his time was effectively representative of only a small part of the population. He seems, however, to have thought that a legislature which represented the prosperous middle classes would represent the interests of the country as a whole. At the same time he saw no logical stopping-point in the process of extending the suffrage, though he assumed, rather surprisingly, that the lower classes would be governed by the wisdom of the middle class.

somewhat simple faith in the power of education to make man see that their 'real' interests are bound up with the common interest. Hence political reform and extended education should go hand in hand.

5. James Mill undertook to show, with the aid of the associationist psychology, how altruistic conduct on the part of the pleasure-seeking individual is possible. He was indeed convinced that 'we never feel any pains or pleasures but our own. The fact, indeed, is, that our very idea of the pains or pleasures of another man is only the idea of our own pains, or our own pleasures, associated with the idea of another man.'[1] But these remarks contain also the key to understanding the possibility of altruistic conduct. For an inseparable association can be set up, say between the idea of my own pleasure and the idea of that of the other members of the community to which I belong, an association such that its result is analogous to a chemical product which is something more than the mere sum of its elements. And even if I originally sought the good of the community only as a means to my own, I can then seek the former without any advertence to the latter.

Given this point of view, it may seem strange that in his *Fragment on Mackintosh*, which was published in 1835 after having been held up for a time, Mill indulges in a vehement attack on Sir James Mackintosh (1765–1832), who in 1829 had written on ethics for the *Encyclopaedia Britannica*. For Mackintosh not only accepted the principle of utility but also made use of the associationist psychology in explaining the development of the morality which takes the general happiness as its end. But the reason for the attack is clear enough. If Mackintosh had expounded an ethical theory quite different from that of the Benthamites, the Kantian ethics for example, Mill would presumably not have been so indignant. As it was, Mackintosh's crime in Mill's eyes was to have adulterated the pure milk of Benthamism by adding to it the moral sense theory, derived from Hutcheson and to a certain extent from the Scottish School, a theory which Bentham had decisively rejected.

Although Mackintosh accepted utility as the criterion for

---

[1] *Analysis of the Phenomena of the Human Mind*, II, p. 217 (1869, edited by J. S. Mill). Commenting on his father's statement, J. S. Mill draws attention to its ambiguity. To say that if I take pleasure in another man's pleasure, the pleasure which I feel is my own and not the other man's, is one thing. And it is obviously true. To imply that if I seek another man's pleasure I do so as a means to my own, is something different.

distinguishing between right and wrong actions, he also insisted on the peculiar character of the moral sentiments which are experienced in contemplating such actions and, in particular, the qualities of the agents as manifested in such actions. If we group together these sentiments as forming the moral sense, we can say that it is akin to the sense of beauty. True, a virtuous man's moral qualities are indeed useful in that they contribute to the common good or happiness. But one can perfectly well approve and admire them without any more reference to utility than when we appreciate a beautiful painting.[1]

In discussing Mackintosh's view James Mill urged that if there were a moral sense, it would be a peculiar kind of faculty, and that we ought logically to admit the possibility of its overriding the judgment of utility. True, Mackintosh believed that in point of fact the moral sentiments and the judgment of utility are always in harmony. But in this case the moral sense is a superfluous postulate. If, however, it is a distinct faculty which, in principle at least, is capable of overriding the judgment of utility, it should be described as an immoral rather than a moral sense. For the judgment of utility is the moral judgment.

Many people would probably feel that, apart from the question whether the term 'moral sense' is appropriate or inappropriate, we certainly can experience the kind of sentiments described by Mackintosh. So what is all the fuss about? A general answer is that both Bentham and Mill looked on the theory of the moral sense as a cloudy and in some respects dangerous doctrine which had been superseded by utilitarianism, so that any attempt to reintroduce it constituted a retrograde step. In particular, Mill doubtless believed that Mackintosh's theory implied that there is a superior point of view to that of utilitarianism, a point of view, that is to say, which rises above such a mundane consideration as that of utility. And any such claim was anathema to Mill.

The long and the short of it is that James Mill was determined to maintain a rigid Benthamism.[2] Any attempt, such as that made by Mackintosh, to reconcile utilitarianism with intuitionist ethics simply aroused his indignation. As will be seen later, however, his son had no such devotion to the letter of the Benthamite gospel.

---

[1] Similarly, the sentiments which we feel in contemplating the undesirable qualities of a bad man need not involve any reference to their lack of utility.

[2] This determination also shows itself in Mill's attack on Mackintosh for making the morality of actions depend on motive, when Bentham had shown that it does not.

6. Obviously, the use made by James Mill of the associationist psychology in explaining the possibility of altruistic conduct on the part of the individual who by nature seeks his own pleasure presupposes a general employment of the method of reductive analysis which was characteristic of classical empiricism, especially in the thought of Hume, and which was systematically practised by Bentham. Thus in his *Analysis of the Phenomena of the Human Mind* Mill tries to reduce man's mental life to its basic elements. In general he follows Hume in distinguishing between impressions and ideas, the latter being copies or images of the former. But Mill actually speaks of sensations, not of impressions. Hence we can also say that he follows Condillac[1] in depicting the development of mental phenomena as a process of the transformation of sensations. It must be added, however, that Mill groups together sensations and ideas under the term 'feelings'. 'We have two classes of feelings; one, that which exists when the object of sense is present; another, that which exists after the object of sense has ceased to be present. The one class of feelings I call sensations; the other class of feelings I call *ideas*.'[2]

After reducing the mind to its basic elements Mill is then faced with the task of reconstructing mental phenomena with the aid of the principles of the association of ideas. Hume, he remarks, recognized three principles of association, namely contiguity in time and place, causation and resemblance. But causation, in Mill's view, can be identified with contiguity in time, that is, with the order of regular succession. 'Causation is only a name for the order established between an antecedent and consequent; that is, the established or constant antecedence of the one, and consequence of the other.'[3]

Mill's work covers such topics as naming, classification, abstraction, memory, belief, ratiocination, pleasurable and painful sensations, the will and intentions. And at the end the author remarks that the work, which constitutes the theoretical part of the doctrine of the mind, should be followed by a practical part comprising logic, considered as practical rules for the mind in its search for truth, ethics and the study of education as directed to training the individual to contribute actively to the greatest possible good or happiness for himself and for his fellow men.

We cannot follow Mill in his reconstruction of mental

---

[1] See Vol. VI of this *History*, pp. 28–35.   [2] *Analysis*, I, p. 52.
[3] *Ibid.*, I, p. 110.

phenomena. But it is worth while drawing attention to the way in which he deals with reflection, which was described by Locke as the notice which the mind takes of its own operations. The mind is identified with the stream of consciousness. And consciousness means having sensations and ideas. As, therefore, 'reflection is nothing but consciousness',[1] to reflect on an idea is the same thing as to have it. There is no room for any additional factor.

Commenting on his father's theory J. S. Mill remarks that 'to reflect on any of our feelings or mental acts is more properly identified with *attending* to the feeling than (as stated in the text) with merely having it'.[2] And this seems to be true. But James Mill is so obstinately determined to explain the whole mental life in terms of the association of primitive elements reached by reductive analysis that he has to explain away those factors in consciousness to which it is difficult to apply such treatment. In other words, empiricism can manifest its own form of dogmatism.

7. To turn briefly to Benthamite economics. As far as the economic market was concerned, Bentham believed that in a freely competitive market a harmony of interest is inevitably attained, at least in the long run. Such State action as he demanded consisted in the removal of restrictions, such as the abolition of the tariffs which protected the English market in grain and which Bentham thought of as serving the sectional interest of the land-owners.

Behind this *laissez-faire* theory lay the influence of the French physiocrats, to whom allusion has already been made, though elements were also derived, of course, from English writers, particularly from Adam Smith.[3] But it was obviously not simply a question of deriving ideas from previous writers. For the *laissez-faire* economics can be said to have reflected the needs and aspirations of the expanding industrial and capitalist system of the time. In other words, it reflected the interests, real or supposed, of that middle class which James Mill considered to be the wisest element in the community.

The theory found its classical expression in the writings of David Ricardo (1772–1823), especially in his *Principles of Political Economy*, which was published in 1817. Bentham is reported to have said that James Mill was his spiritual child, and that Ricardo was the spiritual child of James Mill. But though it was largely

[1] *Analysis*, II, p. 177.   [2] *Ibid.*, II, p. 179, note 34.
[3] See Vol. V of this *History*, pp. 354–5.

as a result of Mill's encouragement that Ricardo published his *Principles* when he did, in economic theory Mill was more dependent on Ricardo than the other way round. In any case it was Ricardo's work which became the classical statement of Benthamite economics.

In the view of his disciple J. R. McCulloch (1789–1864) Ricardo's great service was to state the fundamental theorem of the science of value. This was to the effect that in a free market the value of commodities is determined by the amount of labour required for their production. In other words, value is crystallized labour.

Now, if this theory were true, it would appear to follow that the money obtained from the sale of commodities belongs rightfully to those whose labour produced the commodities in question. That is to say, the conclusion drawn by Marx[1] from the labour theory of value appears to be amply justified, unless perhaps we wish to argue that the capitalist is to be included among the labourers. But Ricardo and the other economists of the *laissez-faire* School were far from using the labour theory of value as a means of showing that capitalism by its very nature involves exploitation of the workers. For one thing they were conscious that the capitalist contributes to production by the investment of capital in machinery and so on. For another thing they were interested in arguing that in a competitive market, free from all restrictions, prices tend naturally to represent the real values of commodities.

This line of argument seems to involve the at least implicit assumption that a free market is governed by some sort of natural economic law which ultimately ensures a harmonization of interests and operates for the common good, provided that nobody attempts to interfere with its functioning. But this optimistic view represents only one aspect of Benthamite economics. According to T. R. Malthus (1766–1834), population always increases when living becomes easier, unless, of course, its rate of increase is restricted in some way. Thus population tends to outrun the means of subsistence. And it follows that wages tend to remain constant, at a subsistence level that is to say. Hence there is a law of wages which can hardly be said to operate in favour of the greater happiness of the greatest possible number.

If the Benthamites had made in the economic sphere a thoroughgoing application of the principle of utility, they would have had to demand in this sphere a harmonization of interests through legislation similar to the harmonization of interests through legislation which they demanded in the political sphere. Indeed, in his essay on government for the *Encyclopaedia Britannica* James Mill declared that the general happiness is promoted by assuring to every man the greatest possible amount of the fruit of his own labour, and that the government should prevent the powerful robbing the weak. But their belief in certain economic laws restricted the Benthamites' view both of the possibility and of the desirability of State action in the economic sphere.

And yet they themselves made breaches in the wall set up round the economic sphere by the belief in natural economic laws. For one thing Malthus argued that while wages tend to remain constant, rents tend to increase with the increasing fertility of the land. And these rents represent profit for the landlords though they contribute nothing to production. In other words, the landlords are parasites on society. And it was the conviction of the Benthamites that their power should be broken. For another thing, while those who were strongly influenced by Malthus's reflections on population may have thought that the only way of increasing profits and wages would be by restricting the growth of population, and that this would be impracticable, the very admission of the possibility in principle of interfering with the distribution of wealth in one way should have encouraged the exploration of other ways of attaining this end. And in point of fact J. S. Mill came to envisage legislative control, in a limited form at least, of the distribution of wealth.

In other words, if the Benthamite economists began by separating the economic sphere, in which a *laissez-faire* policy should reign, from the political sphere, in which a harmonization of interests through legislation was demanded, in J. S. Mill's development of utilitarianism the gap between the economic and political spheres tended to close. As will be seen presently, J. S. Mill introduced into the utilitarian philosophy elements which were incompatible with strict Benthamism. But it seems to the present writer at any rate that in proposing some State interference in the economic sphere with a view to the general happiness, Mill was simply applying the principle of utility in a way in which it might well have been applied from the start, had it not been for the belief in the autonomy of the economic sphere, governed by its own iron laws.

CHAPTER II

THE UTILITARIAN MOVEMENT (2)

Life and writings of J. S. Mill—Mill's development of the utilitarian ethics—Mill on civil liberty and government—Psychological freedom.

1. JOHN STUART MILL was born in London on May 20th, 1806. A fascinating account of the extraordinary education to which he was subjected by his father is to be found in his *Autobiography*. Having apparently started to learn Greek at the age of three, by the time he was about twelve years old he was sufficiently acquainted with Greek and Latin literature, history and mathematics to enter on what he calls more advanced studies, including logic. In 1819 he was taken through a complete course of political economy, during which he read Adam Smith and Ricardo. As for religion, 'I was brought up from the first without any religious belief, in the ordinary acceptation of the term',[1] though his father encouraged him to learn what religious beliefs mankind had in point of fact held.

In 1820 J. S. Mill was invited to stay in the South of France with Sir Samuel Bentham, brother of the philosopher. And during his time abroad he not only studied the French language and literature but also followed courses at Montpellier on chemistry, zoology, logic and higher mathematics, besides making the acquaintance of some economists and liberal thinkers. Returning to England in 1821 Mill started to read Condillac, studied Roman law with John Austin (1790–1859), and gave further attention to the philosophy of Bentham. He also extended his philosophical reading to the writings of thinkers such as Helvétius, Locke, Hume, Reid and Dugald Stewart. Through personal contact with men such as John Austin and his younger brother Charles, Mill was initiated into the utilitarian circle. Indeed, in the winter of 1822–3 he founded a little Utilitarian Circle of his own, which lasted for about three and a half years.

---

[1] *Autobiography*, p. 38 (2nd edition, 1873). Though James Mill was an agnostic rather than a dogmatic atheist, he refused to admit that the world could possibly have been created by a God who combined infinite power with infinite wisdom and goodness. Moreover, he thought that this belief had a detrimental effect upon morality.

In 1823 Mill obtained, through his father's influence, a clerkship in the East India Company. And after successive promotions he became head of the office in 1856 with a substantial salary. Neither father nor son ever held an academic chair.

Mill's first printed writings consisted of some letters published in 1822, in which he defended Ricardo and James Mill against attack. After the foundation of the *Westminster Review* in 1824 he became a frequent contributor. And in 1825 he undertook the editing of Bentham's *Rationale of Evidence* in five volumes, a labour which, so he tells us, occupied about all his leisure time for almost a year.

It is hardly surprising that prolonged overwork, culminating in the editing of Bentham's manuscripts, resulted in 1826 in what is popularly called a nervous breakdown. But this mental crisis had a considerable importance through its effect on Mill's outlook. In his period of dejection the utilitarian philosophy, in which he had been indoctrinated by his father, lost its charms for him. He did not indeed abandon it. But he came to two conclusions. First, happiness is not attained by seeking it directly. One finds it by striving after some goal or ideal other than one's own happiness or pleasure. Secondly, analytic thought needs to be complemented by a cultivation of the feelings, an aspect of human nature which Bentham had mistrusted. This meant in part that Mill began to find some meaning in poetry and art.[1] More important, he found himself able to appreciate Coleridge and his disciples, who were generally regarded as the antithesis to the Benthamites. In the course of time he even came to see some merit in Carlyle, a feat which his father was never able to achieve. True, the effect of Mill's crisis should not be exaggerated. He remained a utilitarian, and, though modifying Benthamism in important ways, he never went over to the opposite camp. As he himself puts it, he did not share in the sharp reaction of the nineteenth century against the eighteenth, a reaction represented in Great Britain by the names of Coleridge and Carlyle. At the same time he became conscious of the narrowness of Bentham's view of human nature, and he formed the conviction that the emphasis laid by the French *philosophes* and by Bentham on the analytic reason needed to be supplemented, though not supplanted, by an understanding of the importance of other aspects of man and his activity.

In 1829–30 Mill became acquainted with the doctrines of the

[1] Mill started to read Wordsworth in 1828.

followers of Saint-Simon.[1] While he disagreed with them on many issues, their criticism of the *laissez-faire* economics appeared to him to express important truths. Further, 'their aim seemed to me desirable and rational, however their means might be inefficacious'.[2] In a real sense Mill always remained an individualist at heart, a staunch upholder of individual liberty. But he was quite prepared to modify individualism in the interest of the common welfare.

In 1830–1 Mill wrote five *Essays on Some Unsettled Questions of Political Economy*, though they were not published until 1844.[3] In 1843 he published his famous *System of Logic*, on which he had been working for some years. For part of the work he found stimulus in W. Whewell's *History of the Inductive Sciences* (1837) and in Sir John Herschel's *Discourse on the Study of Natural Philosophy* (1830), while in the final rewriting of the work he found further help in Whewell's *Philosophy of the Inductive Sciences* (1840) and the earlier volumes of Auguste Comte's *Cours de philosophie positive*.[4] His correspondence with the celebrated French positivist, whom he never actually met, began in 1841. But in the course of time this epistolary friendship waned and then ceased. Mill continued to respect Comte, but he found himself entirely out of sympathy with the positivist's later ideas for the spiritual organization of humanity.

In 1848 Mill published his *Principles of Political Economy*.[5] In 1851 he married Harriet Taylor, with whom he had been on terms of intimate friendship from 1830 and whose first husband died in 1849. In 1859, the year following that of his wife's death, Mill published his essay *On Liberty*, in 1861 his *Considerations on Representative Government*, and in 1863 *Utilitarianism*.[6] *An Examination of Sir William Hamilton's Philosophy* and the small volume on *Auguste Comte and Positivism* appeared in 1865.

From 1865 until 1868 Mill was a Member of Parliament for Westminster. He spoke in favour of the Reform Bill of 1867, and he denounced the policy of the British government in Ireland. Of his pamphlet *England and Ireland* (1868) he remarks that it 'was

[1] Comte Claude Henri de Rouvroy de Saint-Simon (1760–1825) was a French socialist, whose ideas gave rise to a group or School.
[2] *Autobiography*, p. 167. Mill is referring to the aim or ideal of organizing labour and capital for the general good of the community.
[3] The fifth essay was partially rewritten in 1833.
[4] Auguste Comte (1798–1857) published the first volume of this work in 1830.
[5] Subsequent editions appeared in 1849 and 1852.
[6] This short work had previously appeared in instalments in *Fraser's Magazine*.

not popular, except in Ireland, as I did not expect it to be.'[1] Mill also advocated proportional representation and the suffrage for women.

Mill died at Avignon on May 8th, 1873. His *Dissertations and Discussions* appeared in four volumes between 1859 and 1875, while his *Essays in Religion* were published in 1874. Further reference to the last-named work, in which Mill discusses sympathetically the hypothesis of a finite God, that is, God limited in power, will be made in the next chapter.

2. In *Utilitarianism* Mill gives an often-quoted definition or description of the basic principle of utilitarian ethics which is quite in accord with Benthamism. 'The creed which accepts as the foundation of morals, Utility, or the Greatest Happiness Principle, holds that actions are right in proportion as they tend to promote happiness, wrong as they tend to produce the reverse of happiness. By happiness is intended pleasure, and the absence of pain; by unhappiness, pain, and the privation of pleasure.'[2]

True, Mill is anxious to show that utilitarianism is not a philosophy either of egoism or of expediency. It is not a philosophy of egoism because happiness, in the moral context, 'is not the agent's own greatest happiness, but the greatest amount of happiness altogether'.[3] As for expediency, the expedient as opposed to the right generally means that which serves the interests of the individual as such, without regard to the common good, 'as when a minister sacrifices the interests of his country to keep himself in place'.[4] Such conduct is clearly incompatible with the greatest happiness principle. At the same time, though Mill is anxious to show that utilitarianism does not deserve the accusations to which Bentham's doctrine seemed to some people to lay it open, he provides plenty of evidence that his thought moves within a Benthamite framework. This can be seen easily enough if one considers his discussion of the sense in which the principle

[1] *Autobiography*, p. 294.
[2] *Utilitarianism*, pp. 9–10 (2nd edition, 1864).
[3] *Ibid.*, p. 16.
[4] *Ibid.*, p. 32. Mill recognizes that the expedient may mean that which is expedient or useful for securing some temporary advantage when the securing of this advantage involves violation of a rule 'whose observance is expedient in a much higher degree' (*ibid.*). And it is clear that not only the individual but also the community, as represented by public authority, might succumb to the temptation to seek its immediate temporary advantage in this way. But Mill argues that the expedient in this sense is not really 'useful' at all. It is harmful. Hence there can be no question of choice of the expedient being justified by the principle of utility.

of utility is susceptible of proof.[1] Mill's first point is that happiness is universally recognized to be a good. 'Each person's happiness is a good to that person, and the general happiness, therefore, a good to the aggregate of all persons.'[2] This remark implies an acceptance of Bentham's analysis of such terms as 'community' and 'common interest'. Mill then goes on to argue that happiness is not merely *a* good but *the* good: it is the one ultimate end which all desire and seek. True, it can be objected that some people seek virtue or money or fame for its own sake, and that such things cannot properly be described as happiness. But the fact that such things can be sought for their own sakes is explicable in terms of the association of ideas. Take virtue, for example. 'There was no original desire of it, or motive to it, save its conduciveness to pleasure; and especially to protection from pain.'[3] But that which is originally sought as a means to pleasure can, by association with the idea of pleasure, come to be sought for its own sake. And it is then sought not as a means to pleasure or happiness but as a constituent part of it. Evidently, this line of argument, with its appeal to the associationist psychology, is in line with Benthamism.

Nobody, of course, disputes the facts that Mill began with the Benthamism in which he had been indoctrinated by his father, and that he never formally rejected it, and that he always retained elements of it. The significant aspect of Mill's brand of utilitarianism, however, is not to be found in the ideas which he took over from Bentham and James Mill. It is to be found in the ideas which Mill himself added, and which strained the original Benthamite framework to such an extent that it ought to have been radically refashioned or even abandoned.

Foremost among the ideas which Mill introduced was that of intrinsic qualitative differences between pleasures. He does indeed admit that 'utilitarian writers in general have placed the superiority of mental over bodily pleasures chiefly in the greater permanency, safety, uncostliness, etc., of the former—that is, in their circumstantial advantages rather than in their intrinsic

---

[1] Mill agrees with Bentham that the principle of utility cannot be proved by deduction from any more ultimate principle or principles. For the point at issue is the ultimate end of human action. And 'questions of ultimate ends do not admit of proof, in the ordinary acceptation of the term' (*Utilitarianism*, p. 52). It can, however, be shown that all men seek happiness, and only happiness, as the end of action. And this is sufficient proof of the statement that happiness is the one ultimate end of action.

[2] *Utilitarianism*, p. 53.   [3] *Ibid.*, pp. 56–7.

nature'.[1] But he goes on to argue that the utilitarians in question might have adopted another point of view 'with entire consistency. It is quite compatible with the principle of utility to recognize the fact, that some *kinds* of pleasure are more desirable and more valuable than others. It would be absurd that while, in estimating all other things, quality is considered as well as quantity, the estimation of pleasures should be supposed to depend on quantity alone.'[2]

Mill may be quite right in claiming that it is absurd that in discriminating between pleasures no account should be taken of qualitative differences. But the suggestion that the recognition of intrinsic qualitative differences is compatible with Benthamism is quite unjustified. And the reason is clear. If we wish to discriminate between different pleasures without introducing any standard or criterion other than pleasure itself, the principle of discrimination can only be quantitative, whatever Mill may say to the contrary. In this sense Bentham adopted the only possible consistent attitude. If, however, we are determined to recognize intrinsic qualitative differences between pleasures, we have to find some standard other than pleasure itself. This may not be immediately evident. But if we reflect, we can see that when we say that one kind of pleasure is qualitatively superior to another, we really mean that one kind of pleasure-producing activity is qualitatively superior to or intrinsically more valuable than another. And if we try to explain what this means, we shall probably find ourselves referring to some ideal of man, to some idea of what the human being ought to be. For example, it makes little sense to say that the pleasure of constructive activity is qualitatively superior to that of destructive activity except with reference to the context of man in society. Or, to put the matter more simply, it makes little sense to say that the pleasure of listening to Beethoven is qualitatively superior to the pleasure of smoking opium, unless we take into account considerations other than that of pleasure itself. If we decline to do this, the only relevant question is, which is the greater pleasure, quantity being measured not simply by intensity but also according to the other criteria of the Benthamite calculus.

In point of fact Mill does introduce a standard other than pleasure itself. On occasion at least he appeals to the nature of man, even if he does not clearly understand the significance of

---

[1] *Utilitarianism*, p. 11.   [2] *Ibid.*, pp. 11–12.

what he is doing. 'It is better to be a human being dissatisfied than a pig satisfied; better to be Socrates dissatisfied than a fool satisfied.'[1] After all, when Mill is engaged in discussing explicitly Bentham's strong and weak points, one of the main features of Bentham's thought to which he draws attention is its inadequate conception of human nature. 'Man is conceived by Bentham as a being susceptible of pleasures and pains, and governed in all his conduct partly by the different modifications of self-interest, and the passions commonly classed as selfish, partly by sympathies, or occasionally antipathies, towards other beings. And here Bentham's conception of human nature stops. . . . Man is never recognized by him as a being capable of pursuing spiritual perfection as an end; of desiring, for its own sake, the conformity of his own character to his standard of excellence, without hope of good or fear of evil from other source than his own inward consciousness.'[2]

It is very far from being the intention of the present writer to find fault with Mill for introducing the idea of human nature as a standard for determining qualitative differences between pleasure-producing activities. The point is rather that he does not appear to understand the extent to which he is subjecting the original Benthamite framework of his thought to acute stresses and strains. There is no need to consult Aristotle, said Bentham. But to come closer to Aristotle is precisely what Mill is doing. In his essay *On Liberty* he remarks that 'I regard utility as the ultimate appeal on all ethical questions; but it must be utility in the largest sense, grounded on the permanent interests of man as a progressive being.'[3] Mill does not hesitate to refer to man's 'higher faculties',[4] to which higher or superior pleasures are correlative. And in the essay *On Liberty* he quotes with approval the statement of Wilhelm von Humboldt that 'the end of man is the highest and most harmonious development of his powers to a complete and consistent whole.'[5] True, Mill does not produce a clear and full account of what he means by human nature. He lays stress, indeed, on the perfecting and improving of human nature, and he emphasizes the idea of individuality. Thus he says, for example, that 'individuality is the same thing with development', and that 'it is only the cultivation of individuality which

[1] *Dissertations and Discussions*, I, pp. 358-9.   [2] *Ibid.*
[3] *On Liberty*, p. 9 (edited by R. B. McCallum, Oxford, 1946).
[4] *Utilitarianism*, pp. 13 and 16.
[5] *On Liberty*, p. 50.

produces, or can produce, well-developed human beings'.[1] But he makes it clear that individual self-development does not mean for him a surrender to any impulses which the individual is inclined to follow, but rather the individual fulfilment of the ideal of harmonious integration of all one's powers. It is not a question of sheer eccentricity, but of unity in diversity. Hence there must be a standard of excellence; and this is not fully worked out. The relevant point in the present context, however, is not Mill's failure to elaborate a theory of human nature. Rather is it the fact that he grafts on to Benthamism a moral theory which has little or nothing to do with the balancing of pleasures and pains according to the hedonistic calculus of Bentham, and that he does not see the necessity of subjecting his original starting-point to a thorough criticism and revision. As we have seen, he does indeed criticize Bentham's narrowness of moral vision. But at other times he tends to slur over the differences between them, especially, of course, when it is a question of uniting against what they would consider reactionary forces.

The reference to Aristotle in the last paragraph is not so far-fetched as may at first sight appear. As Bentham was primarily interested in questions of practical reform, he not unnaturally emphasized the consequences of actions. The moral character of actions is to be estimated according to the consequences which they tend to have. This view is, of course, essential to utilitarianism, in some form or other at least. And Mill often speaks in the same way. But he also sees, as Aristotle saw, that the exercise of human activities cannot properly be described as a means to an end, happiness, when the end is taken to be something purely external to these activities. For the exercise of the activities can itself constitute a part of happiness. The enjoyment of good health, for example, and the appreciative hearing of good music are, or can be, constituent elements in happiness, and not simply means to some abstract external end. 'Happiness is not an abstract idea, but a concrete whole.'[2] This is a thoroughly Aristotelian notion.

Now, in the first two paragraphs of this section we saw that according to Mill actions are right in proportion as they tend to promote happiness, wrong in so far as they tend to produce the reverse of happiness. We also noted Mill's explanation that in this ethical context happiness does not mean the individual agent's

----

[1] *On Liberty*, p. 56.   [2] *Utilitarianism*, p. 56.

own greater happiness, but the greatest amount of happiness altogether. And if we ask why the general happiness is desirable, Mill answers that 'no reason can be given why the general happiness is desirable, except that each person, so far as he believes it to be attainable, desires his own happiness'.[1] It is therefore incumbent on him to make clear the relation between the agent's own happiness and the general happiness.

One line of argument employed by Mill represents orthodox Benthamism. 'Each person's happiness is a good to that person, and the general happiness, therefore, a good to the aggregate of all persons.'[2] If the general happiness is related to my happiness as a whole to a part, in desiring the general happiness I am desiring my own. And by the force of association of ideas I can come to desire the general happiness without adverting to my own. It can thus be explained not only how altruism is possible but also how egoism is possible. For it is no more necessary that all should attain to an altruistic point of view than it is necessary that all those who desire money as a means to an end should become misers, seeking money for its own sake.

This may sound reasonable. But reflection discloses a difficulty. If the general happiness is, as Bentham maintained, nothing but the sum total resulting from an addition of the happinesses of individuals, there is no reason why I should be unable to seek my own happiness without seeking the general happiness. And if I ask why I ought to seek the latter, it is no use replying that I seek the former. For this reply to have any relevance, it must be assumed that the general happiness is not simply the result of an addition sum, the aggregate which results from a juxtaposition of individual happinesses, but rather an organic whole of such a kind that he who promotes his own happiness necessarily promotes the general happiness. For he actualizes a constituent part of an organic whole. But it can hardly be shown that this is the case unless emphasis is placed on the social nature of man. For one can then argue that the individual does not attain his own real happiness except as a social being, a member of society, and that his happiness is a constituent element in an organic whole.

This seems indeed to be the sort of idea towards which Mill is working. He remarks, for example, that the firm foundation of the utilitarian morality is to be found in 'the social feelings of mankind'.[3] These social feelings can be described as the 'desire to be in

[1] *Ibid.*, p. 53.   [2] *Ibid.*   [3] *Ibid.*, p. 46.

unity with our fellow creatures, which is already a powerful principle in human nature, and happily one of those which tend to become stronger, even without express inculcation, from the influences of advancing civilization. The social state is at once so natural, so necessary, and so habitual to man, that, except in some unusual circumstances, or by an effort of voluntary abstraction, he never conceives himself otherwise than as a member of a body.'[1] True, Mill emphasizes the fact that the social feelings grow through the influence of education and of advancing civilization, and that the more they grow the more does the common good or general happiness appear as desirable, as an object to be sought. At the same time he also emphasizes the fact that social feeling has its root in human nature itself, and that 'to those who have it, it possesses all the characters of a natural feeling. It does not present itself to their minds as a superstition of education, or a law despotically imposed by the power of society, but as an attitude which it would not be well for them to be without. This conviction is the ultimate sanction of the greatest happiness morality.'[2]

Once again, therefore, we receive the impression that Mill is working away from Benthamism to an ethics based on a more adequate view of the human person. At the same time the new theory is not developed in such a way as to make clear its relations to and differences from the framework of thought with which Mill started and which he never actually abandoned.

Though, however, the difficulty of passing from the man who seeks his own personal happiness to the man who seeks the common good is diminished in proportion as emphasis is laid on the nature of man as a social being, there remains an objection which can be brought against the utilitarian theory of obligation, whether utilitarianism is understood in its original Benthamite form or as developed by Mill.[3] For anyone at least who accepts Hume's famous assertion that an 'ought' cannot be derived from an 'is', an ought-statement from a purely factual or empirical statement, is likely to object that this is precisely what the utilitarians try to do. That is to say, they first assert that as a matter of empirical fact man seeks happiness, and they then

---

[1] *Utilitarianism*, p. 46.   [2] *Ibid.*, p. 50.
[3] This line of objection is not confined, of course, to utilitarianism. It can be brought against any form of teleological ethics which interprets the moral imperative as what Kant would call an assertoric hypothetical imperative. (See Vol. VI of this *History*, pp. 321–3.)

conclude that he ought to perform those actions which are required to increase happiness and that he ought not to perform those actions which diminish happiness or increase pain or unhappiness.

One possible way of dealing with this objection is, of course, to challenge its validity. But if it is once admitted that an ought-statement cannot be derived from a purely factual statement, then, to defend utilitarianism, we have to deny the applicability of the objection in this case. Obviously, we cannot deny that the utilitarians start with a factual statement, namely that all men seek happiness. But it might be argued that this factual statement is not the only statement which functions as a premiss. For example, it might be maintained that a judgment of value about the end, namely happiness, is tacitly understood. That is to say, the utilitarians are not simply stating that as a matter of empirical fact all men pursue happiness as the ultimate end of action. They are also stating implicitly that happiness is the only end worthy of being an ultimate end. Or it might be maintained that together with the factual statement that all men seek for happiness as the ultimate end of action, the utilitarians tacitly include the premisses that to act in the way which effectively increases happiness is the only rational way of acting (given the fact that all seek this end), and that to act in a rational manner is worthy of commendation. Indeed, it is fairly clear that Bentham does assume that, as all seek pleasure, to act in the way which will effectively increase pleasure is to act rationally, and that to act rationally is commendable. And it is also clear that Mill assumes that to act in such a way as to develop a harmonious integration of the powers of human nature or of the human person is commendable.

It is not the purpose of these remarks to suggest that in the opinion of the present writer utilitarianism either in its original Benthamite form or in the somewhat incoherent shape that it assumes with J. S. Mill, is the correct moral philosophy. The point is that though in word the utilitarians derive ought-statements from a purely factual, empirical statement, it is perfectly reasonable to argue that they tacitly presuppose other premisses which are not purely factual statements. Hence, even if it is admitted that an ought-statement cannot be derived from a purely factual statement, the admission is not by itself necessarily fatal to utilitarian moral theory.

As for the general merits and demerits of utilitarian moral theory, this is too broad a question for discussion here. But we can

make two points. First, when we are asked why we think that one
action is right and another action wrong, we frequently refer to
consequences. And this suggests that a teleological ethics finds
support in the way in which we ordinarily think and speak about
moral questions. Secondly, the fact that a man of the calibre of
J. S. Mill found himself driven to transcend the narrow hedonism
of Bentham and to interpret happiness in the light of the idea of
the development of the human personality suggests that we cannot
understand man's moral life except in terms of a philosophical
anthropology. Hedonism certainly tends to recur in the history of
ethical theory. But reflection on it prompts the mind to seek for a
more adequate theory of human nature than that which is
immediately suggested by the statement that all men pursue
pleasure. This fact is well illustrated by Mill's development of
Benthamism.

3. Mill's idea of the self-development of the individual plays a
central role in his reflections on civil or social liberty. As he
follows Hume and Bentham in rejecting the theory of 'abstract
right, as a thing independent of utility',[1] he cannot indeed appeal
to a natural right on the part of the individual to develop himself
freely. But he insists that the principle of utility demands that
every man should be free to develop his powers according to his
own will and judgment, provided that he does not do so in a way
which interferes with the exercise of a similar freedom by others.
It is not in the common interest that all should be moulded or
expected to conform to the same pattern. On the contrary, society
is enriched in proportion as individuals develop themselves freely.
'The free development of individuality is one of the principal
ingredients of human happiness, and quite the chief ingredient of
individual and social progress.'[2] Hence the need for liberty.

When he is thinking of the value of free self-development on
the part of the individual, Mill not unnaturally pushes the idea of
liberty to the fullest extent which is consistent with the existence
and maintenance of social harmony. 'The liberty of the individual
must be thus far limited; he must not make himself a nuisance to
other people.'[3] Provided that he refrains from interfering with
other people's liberty and from actively inciting others to crime,
the individual's freedom should be unrestricted. 'The only part of

---

[1] *On Liberty*, p. 9. All page references to this essay and to that *On Representative
Government* are to the edition of the two essays in one volume by R. B. McCallum
(Oxford, 1946).
[2] *Ibid.*, p. 50.   [3] *Ibid.*, p. 49.

the conduct of anyone, for which he is amenable to society, is that which concerns others. In the part which merely concerns himself, his independence is, of right, absolute. Over himself, over his own body and mind, the individual is sovereign.'[1]

In the passage just cited the phrase 'of right' suggests, at first sight at least, that Mill has forgotten for the moment that the theory of natural rights does not form part of his intellectual baggage. It would not indeed be matter for astonishment if after inheriting the rejection of this theory from Bentham and his father Mill then tended to reintroduce the theory. But presumably he would comment that what he rejects is the theory of 'abstract' rights which are not based on the principle of utility and which are supposed to be valid irrespective of the historical and social context. 'Liberty, as a principle, has no application to any state of things anterior to the time when mankind have become capable of being improved by free and equal discussion.'[2] In a society of barbarians despotism would be legitimate, 'provided that the end be their improvement, and the means justified by actually effecting that end'.[3] But when civilization has developed up to a certain point, the principle of utility demands that the individual should enjoy full liberty, except the liberty to do harm to others. And if we presuppose a society of this sort, we can reasonably talk about a 'right' to liberty, a right grounded on the principle of utility.

Mill's general thesis is, therefoıe, that in a civilized community the only legitimate ground for the exercise of coercion in regard to the individual is 'to prevent harm to others. His own good, either physical or moral, is not a sufficient warrant.'[4] But where does the boundary lie between what does harm to others and what does not, between purely self-regarding conduct and conduct which concerns others? We have noted that Mill quotes with approval Wilhelm von Humboldt's statement that the end of man is 'the highest and most harmonious development of his powers to a complete and consistent whole'.[5] And Mill is, of course, convinced that the common happiness is increased if individuals do develop themselves in this way. Might it not be argued, therefore, that harm is done to others, to the community, if the individual acts in such a way as to prevent the harmonious integration of his powers and becomes a warped personality?

This difficulty is, of course, seen and discussed by Mill himself.

[1] *Ibid.*, p. 9.   [2] *Ibid.*   [3] *Ibid.*   [4] *Ibid.*, p. 8.   [5] *Ibid.*, p. 50.

And he suggests various ways of dealing with it. In general, however, his answer is on these lines. The common good demands that as much liberty as possible should be conceded to the individual. Hence injury to others should be interpreted as narrowly as possible. The majority is by no means infallible in its judgments about what would be beneficial to an individual. Hence it should not attempt to impose its own ideas about what is good and bad on all. The community should not interfere with private liberty except when 'there is a definite damage, or a definite risk of damage, either to an individual or to the public'.[1]

Obviously, this does not constitute a complete answer to the objection from the purely theoretical point of view. For questions can still be asked about what constitutes 'definite damage' or 'a definite risk of damage'.[2] At the same time Mill's general principle is, by and large, that which tends to be followed in our Western democracies. And most of us would doubtless agree that restrictions on private liberty should be kept to the minimum demanded by respect for the rights of others and for the common interest. But it is idle to suppose that any philosopher can provide us with a formula which will settle all disputes about the limits of this minimum.

Mill's insistence on the value of private liberty and on the principle of individuality or originality, the principle, that is to say, of individual self-development, naturally affects his ideas on government and its functions. It affects his concept of the most desirable form of government, and it also leads him to see how democracy can be threatened by a danger to which Bentham and James Mill had not really paid attention. We can consider these two points successively.

Though Mill is well aware of the absurdity of supposing that the form of constitution which one considers to be, abstractly speaking, the best is necessarily the best in the practical sense of being suited to all people and to all stages of civilization, he none the less insists that 'to inquire into the best form of government in the abstract (as it is called) is not a chimerical, but a highly practical

---

[1] *On Liberty*, p. 73.
[2] Mill makes a distinction between violating specific duties to society and causing perceptible hurt to assignable individuals on the one hand and merely 'constructive injury' on the other (cf. *On Liberty*, p. 73). But though most people would make a clear distinction between, say, driving a car to the danger of the public when the driver is drunk and getting drunk in the privacy of one's own home, there are bound to be many cases in which the application of general categories is a matter for dispute.

employment of scientific intellect'.[1] For political institutions do not simply grow while men sleep. They are what they are through the agency of the human will. And when a political institution has become obsolete and no longer corresponds to the needs and legitimate demands of a society, it is only through the agency of the human will that it can be changed or developed or supplanted by another institution. But this demands thought about what is desirable and practicable, about the ideally best form of government. For, 'the ideally best form of government, it is scarcely necessary to say, does not mean one which is practicable or eligible in all states of civilization, but the one which, in the circumstances in which it is practicable and eligible, is attended with the greatest amount of beneficial consequences, immediate and prospective.'[2]

If we presuppose that a stage of civilization has been reached in which democracy is practicable, the ideally best form of government is, for Mill, that in which sovereignty is vested in the community as a whole, in which each citizen has a voice in the exercise of sovereignty, and in which each citizen is sometimes called on to take an actual part in government, whether local or national, in some capacity or other. For one thing, the individual is more secure from being harmed by others in proportion as he is able to protect himself. And he can do this best in a democracy. For another thing, a democratic constitution encourages an active type of character, gifted with initiative and vigour. And it is more valuable to promote an active than a passive type of character. Obviously, this consideration weighs heavily with Mill. In his opinion a democratic constitution is the most likely to encourage that individual self-development on which he lays so much emphasis. Further, it promotes the growth in the individual of a public spirit, of concern with the common good, whereas under a benevolent despotism individuals are likely to concentrate simply on their private interests, leaving care for the common good to a government in which they have no voice or share.

It is clear that Mill is not primarily concerned with an external harmonization of interests among atomic human individuals, each of which is supposed to be seeking simply his own pleasure. For if this were the chief concern of government, one might conclude that benevolent despotism is the ideal form of government and that democracy is preferable only because despots are, in practice,

[1] *On Representative Government*, p. 115.   [2] *Ibid.*, p. 141.

generally as self-seeking as anyone else. It was partly this idea that drove Bentham to adopt a radically democratiç point of view. Mill, however, while by no means blind to the need for harmonizing interests, is concerned above all with the superior educative effect of democracy. True, it presupposes a certain level of education. At the same time it encourages, more than any other form of government, private liberty and free self-development on the part of the individual.

Ideally, direct democracy would be the best form of government, at least in the sense of a democracy in which all citizens would have the opportunity of sharing in government in some capacity. 'But since all cannot, in a community exceeding a single small town, participate personally in any but some very minor portions of the public business, it follows that the ideal type of a perfect government must be representative.'[1]

Mill is not, however, so naïve as to suppose that a democratic constitution automatically ensures a due respect for individual liberty. When democracy means in effect the rule, by representation, of a numerical majority, there is no guarantee that the majority will not oppress the minority. For example, legislation might be made to serve the interest of a racial or religious majority or that of a particular economic class[2] rather than the interests of the whole community. In fine, what Bentham called 'sinister interests' can operate in a democracy as elsewhere.

As a safeguard against this danger Mill insists that minorities must be effectively represented. And to secure this he advocates a system of proportional representation, referring to Thomas Hare's *Treatise on the Election of Representatives* (1859) and to Professor Henry Fawcett's pamphlet *Mr. Hare's Reform Bill Simplified and Explained* (1860). But constitutional devices such as universal suffrage and proportional representation will not be sufficient without a process of education which inculcates a genuine respect for individual liberty and for the rights of all citizens, whatever may be their race, religion or position in society.

Given Mill's insistence on the value of individual self-development and initiative, it is not surprising that he disapproves of any tendency on the part of the State to usurp the functions of

---

[1] *On Representative Government*, p. 151.
[2] Mill envisages the possibility of a majority of unskilled workers obtaining legislation to protect what it conceives to be its own interest, to the detriment of the interests of skilled workers and of other classes. Cf. *On Representative Government*, p. 183.

voluntary institutions and to hand them over to the control of a State bureaucracy. 'The disease which afflicts bureaucratic governments, and which they usually die of, is routine. . . . A bureaucracy always tends to become a pedantocracy.'[1] The tendency for all the more able members of the community to be absorbed into the ranks of State functionaries 'is fatal, sooner or later, to the mental activity and progressiveness of the body itself.'[2]

This does not mean, however, that Mill condemns all legislation and State control other than that required to maintain peace and order in the community. It seems true to say that he is drawn in two directions. On the one hand the principle of individual liberty inclines him to disapprove of any legislation or State control of conduct which goes beyond what is required for preventing or deterring the individual from injuring others, whether assignable individuals or the community at large. On the other hand the principle of utility, the greatest happiness principle, might well be used to justify a very considerable amount of legislation and State control with a view to the common good or happiness. But, as we have seen, the principle of individuality is itself grounded on the principle of utility. And the idea of preventing the individual from injuring others can be interpreted in such a way as to justify a good deal of State 'interference' with the individual's conduct.

Education is a case in point. We have seen that according to Mill the community has no right to coerce the individual simply for his own good. But this applies, as Mill explains, only to adults, not to children. For the latter must be protected not only from being harmed by others but also from harming themselves. Hence Mill does not hesitate to say, 'is it not almost a self-evident axiom, that the State should require and compel the education, up to a certain standard, of every human being who is born its citizen?'[3] He is not suggesting that parents should be compelled to send their children to State schools. For 'a general State education is a mere contrivance for moulding people to be exactly like one another':[4] it might easily become an attempt to establish 'a despotism over the mind'.[5] But if parents do not provide in some way for the education of their children, they are failing in their duty and are harming both individuals, namely the children, and

[1] *Ibid.*, p. 179.   [2] *Ibid.*, p. 102.
[3] *On Liberty*, p. 94.   [4] *Ibid.*, p. 95.   [5] *Ibid.*

the community.[1] Hence the State should prevent them from injuring others in this way. And if the parents are genuinely unable to pay for their children's education, the State should come to their aid.

On occasion Mill's interpretation of the principle of preventing the individual from injuring others is astonishingly broad. Thus in the essay *On Liberty* he remarks that in a country in which the population is or threatens to become so great that wages are reduced through superabundant labour, with the consequence that parents are unable to support their children, a law to forbid marriages unless the parties could show that they had the means of supporting a family would not exceed the legitimate power of the State. True, the expediency of such a law is open to dispute. But the law would not constitute a violation of liberty. For its aim would be to prevent the parties concerned from injuring others, namely the prospective offspring. And if anyone objected to the law simply on the ground that it would violate the liberty of parties who wished to marry, he would give evidence of a misplaced notion of liberty.

In point of fact Mill came to modify his view that no man should be compelled to act or to refrain from acting in a certain way simply for his own good. Take the case of proposed legislation to reduce the hours of labour. Mill came to the conclusion that such legislation would be perfectly legitimate, and also desirable, if it were in the real interest of the workmen. To pretend that it violates the worker's freedom to work for as many hours as he likes is absurd. It is indeed obviously true that he would choose to work for an excessive length of time, if the alternative were to starve. But it by no means follows that he would not choose to work for shorter hours, provided that the reduction were universally enforced by law. And in enacting such a law the legislator would be acting for the good of the worker and in accordance with his real desire.

Given his belief in the value of voluntary associations and of initiative uncontrolled by the State, together with his rooted mistrust of bureaucracy, Mill would hardly take kindly to the idea of the so-called Welfare State. At the same time in his later years he came to envisage a degree of State-control of the distribution of wealth which he at any rate was prepared to describe as

[1] Mill insists, for example, that some education is a prerequisite for exercise of the suffrage, and so for democracy.

socialist in character. And the development of his thought on social legislation has often been depicted, though not necessarily with disapproval of course, as constituting an implicit desertion of his original principles. But though it is perfectly reasonable to see in his thought a shift of emphasis from the idea of private liberty to that of the demands of the common good, it seems to the present writer that the charge of inconsistency or of making a *volte-face* can easily be overdone. After all, Mill did not mean by liberty merely freedom from external control. He emphasized liberty as freedom to develop oneself as a human being in the full sense, a freedom which is demanded by the common good. Hence it is reasonable to conclude that it is the business of the community, that it makes for the common good or general happiness, to remove obstacles to such self-development on the part of the individual. But the removal of obstacles may very well entail a considerable amount of social legislation.

What is true, of course, is that Mill departs very far from Benthamism. And this departure from Benthamism can also be seen in the sphere of economics. For example, when Mill condemned laws against trade unions and associations formed to raise wage-levels, the condemnation may have been based primarily on his belief that free rein should be given to private enterprises in general and to voluntary economic experiments in particular. But it implied that, within the limits set by other factors, something can be done to raise wages by human effort. In other words, there is no iron law of wages which renders nugatory all attempts to raise them.

To conclude this section. Bentham, with what we may call his quantitative point of view, naturally emphasized the individual unit. Each is to count, so to speak, as one and not as more than one. And this idea naturally led him in the direction of democratic convictions. Mill shared these convictions; but he came to lay the emphasis on quality, on the development of the individual personality, a value which is best assured in a democratically constituted society. And this shift in emphasis, involving a change from the concept of the pleasure-seeking and pain-avoiding unit to the concept of the personality seeking the harmonious and integrated active development of all his powers, is perhaps the most salient characteristic of Mill's development of utilitarianism from the philosophical point of view. From the practical point of view, that of the reformer, the feature of Mill's thought which usually strikes the observer is the way in which he discerns the growing movement towards social legislation and approves it in so far as he feels that he can reconcile it with his profound belief in the value of individual liberty. But the two points of view go together, as has already been remarked. For Mill's qualified approval of social legislation is motivated very largely by his conviction that such legislation is required to create the conditions for, by the removal of hindrances to, the fuller self-development of the individual. To the extent that he envisages the removal by the State of obstacles or hindrances to the leading by all of a full human life, Mill approximates to the point of view expounded by the British idealists in the latter part of the nineteenth century. But veneration for the State as such, the kind of veneration which had been shown by Hegel, is entirely absent from his outlook. In a very real sense he remains an individualist to the last. What exists is the individual, though the individual character and personality cannot be fully developed apart from social relations.

4. The topics of civil liberty and government are obviously connected. Freedom of the will or liberty in a psychological sense is discussed by Mill in his *A System of Logic*, under the general heading of the logic of the mental sciences, and in his *An Examination of Sir William Hamilton's Philosophy*. But as interest in the problem of freedom of the will is generally prompted by its bearing on ethics and on questions, whether moral or legal, about responsibility, it seems permissible to take the problem out of the general logical setting in which Mill actually discusses it and to consider it here.

Mill assumes that according to libertarians, upholders, that is to say, of the doctrine of freedom of the will, 'our volitions are not, properly speaking, the effects of causes, or at least have no causes which they uniformly and implicitly obey'.[1] And as he himself believes that all volitions or acts of the will are caused, he embraces, to this extent at least, what he calls the doctrine of philosophical necessity. By causation he understands 'invariable, certain and unconditional sequence',[2] a uniformity of order or sequence which permits predictability. And it is this empiricist idea of causation which he applies to human volitions and actions.

The causes which are relevant in this context are motives and

---

[1] *A System of Logic*, II, p. 421 (10th edition, 1879). All further page-references to this work will be to this edition, denoted by the title *Logic*.

[2] *Logic*, II, p. 423.

character. Hence the doctrine of philosophical necessity means that, 'given the motives which are present to an individual's mind, and given likewise the character and disposition of the individual, the manner in which he will act might be unerringly inferred'.[1] It is scarcely necessary to say that Mill is referring to predictability in principle. The less knowledge we have of a man's character and of the motives which present themselves to his mind with varying degrees of force, the less able are we to predict his actions in practice.

One obvious objection to this theory is that it presupposes either that a man's character is fixed from the start or that it is formed only by factors which lie outside his control. In point of fact, however, Mill is quite prepared to admit that 'our character is formed by us as well as for us'.[2] At the same time he adds, and indeed must add if he is to preserve consistency with his premiss about causality, that the will to shape our character is formed for us. For example, experience of painful consequences of the character which he already possesses, or some other strong feeling, such as admiration, which has been aroused in him, may cause a man to desire to change his character.

It is true that when we yield, for example, to a stray temptation, we tend to think of ourselves as capable of having acted differently. But, according to Mill, this does not mean that we are actually aware or conscious that we could have acted in a different manner, all other things being equal. We are not conscious of liberty of indifference in this sense. What we are conscious of is that we could have acted differently if we had preferred to do so, that is, if the desire not to act in the way in which we did act or to act in a different manner had been stronger than the desire which, as a matter of fact, operated in us and caused our choice.

We can say, therefore, if we like, that Mill embraces a theory of character-determinism. But though he speaks, as we have seen, about the doctrine of philosophical necessity, he does not relish the use of such terms as 'necessity' and 'determinism'. He argues instead that the predictability in principle of human actions is perfectly compatible with all that the upholders of freedom of the will can reasonably maintain. Some religious metaphysicians, for instance, have found no difficulty in claiming both that God foresees all human actions and that man acts freely. And if God's foreknowledge is compatible with human liberty, so is any other

[1] *Ibid.*, II, p. 422.   [2] *Ibid.*, II, p. 426.

foreknowledge. Hence an admission of predictability in principle does not prevent us from saying that man acts freely. It is rather a question of analysing what is meant by freedom. If it is taken to mean that when I am faced with alternative courses of action, I could make a different choice from the one which I actually make, even though all factors, including character, desires and motives, are assumed to be the same, it cannot be allowed that man is free. For freedom in this sense would be incompatible with predictability in principle: it would follow that human actions are uncaused and random events. But if by saying that man is free we mean simply that he could act differently from the way in which he does act if his character and motives were otherwise than they are, and that he himself has a hand in shaping his character, it is then quite legitimate to say that man is free. Indeed, those who assert human freedom can mean no more than this unless they are prepared to say that human actions are chance, inexplicable events.

Mill is naturally convinced that his analysis of human freedom is not at odds with the utilitarian ethics. For he does not deny that character is malleable or that moral education is possible. All that follows from the causal activity of motives, in conjunction with character, is that moral education must be directed to the cultivation of the right desires and aversions, that is, to the cultivation of those desires and aversions which are demanded by the principle of utility. 'The object of moral education is to educate the will: but the will can only be educated through the desires and aversions.'[1] As for penal sanctions and punishment in general, the statement that all human actions are in principle predictable does not entail the conclusion that all punishment is unjust. Let us assume that punishment has two ends, 'the benefit of the offender himself and the protection of others'.[2] Appropriate punishment can serve to strengthen the offender's aversion to wrong-doing and his desire to obey the law. As for protection of others, punishment, provided that unnecessary suffering is not inflicted, needs no defence other than that provided by common sense. Whatever position we may adopt on the subject of free will, murderers can no more be allowed to commit their crimes with impunity than a mad dog can be allowed to roam the streets.

[1] *An Examination of Sir William Hamilton's Philosophy*, p. 505 (2nd edition, 1865). This work will be referred to in future page-references as *Examination*.
[2] *Ibid.* p. 511

In maintaining that all human actions are predictable in principle, Mill can draw, of course, on some empirical evidence. For it is an undoubted fact that the better we know a man the more confident we feel that in a given set of circumstances he would act in one way rather than in another. And if he does not act as we expected, we may conclude either that his character was stronger than we suspected or that there was a hidden flaw in his character, as the case may be. Similarly, if we find that our friends are surprised that we have resisted, say, a temptation to use a given opportunity of making money by some shady means, we may very well comment that they ought to have known us better. But though plenty of examples can be found in ordinary speech which seem to imply that a perfect knowledge of a man's character would enable the possessor of the knowledge to predict the man's actions, examples can also be found which suggest a belief to the contrary. After all, there are occasions on which we resent the suggestion that all our utterances and actions can be predicted, as though we were automata, incapable of any originality. Ultimately, however, Mill asserts the predictability in principle of all human actions more as the alternative to admitting uncaused events than as an empirical generalization.

If we assume that Mill is right in saying that we have to choose between these two alternatives, and if we are not prepared to describe human volitions and actions as chance or random events which happen without being caused, the question then arises whether the admission that all human volitions and actions are predictable in principle is or is not compatible with describing some actions as free. In one sense at any rate it is certainly compatible. For some of our actions are performed deliberately, with a conscious purpose, while others are not, reflex acts for instance. And if we wish to use the word 'free' simply to describe actions of the first kind, as distinct from the second kind, the question of predictability is irrelevant. For even if actions of both types are predictable in principle, the difference between them remains. And the word 'free' is being used simply to mark this difference. If, however, we wish to maintain that to say that an action is performed freely necessarily implies that the agent could act otherwise without being a different sort of person, unerring predictability in virtue of a knowledge of the person's character is ruled out. And if we have already accepted the validity of Mill's thesis that we have to choose between asserting predictability in principle and asserting that free actions are random events, we shall find it difficult to claim at the same time that an agent is morally responsible for his free actions.

If, however, we wish to maintain that Mill is not justified in forcing us to choose between admitting that all human actions are predictable in principle in virtue of the agent's character and admitting that free actions are random or chance events, we have to find an acceptable alternative. And this is not easy to do. It is hardly sufficient to say that the action is indeed caused but that it is caused by the agent's will, and that no other cause is required save a final cause, namely a purpose or motive. For Mill would immediately ask, what is the cause of the volition? Or is it an uncaused event? As for the motive, what causes this motive rather than another to be the stronger, actually prevailing motive? Must it not be the agent's character, the fact that he is the sort of man that he is?

It may be said that Mill himself gets into difficulties. For example, he admits that the individual can play a part in shaping his own character. And it is indeed essential for him to admit this, if any sense is to be given to his idea of civil liberty as required for self-development. But on Mill's own premises every effort that a man makes with a view to self-improvement must be caused. And in the long run what can be meant by the statement that a man plays an active part in shaping his own character except that the causes of his character are not simply external, educational and environmental, but also internal, physiological and psychological? But this hardly squares with what the ordinary person understands by the claim that man is free, and that he is not simply a product of his environment, but can freely play an active part in shaping his character. Hence Mill should either embrace and assert determinism, which he tries to avoid, or make it clear that he is using terms such as 'free' and 'freedom' in some peculiar sense of his own, in what Bentham would call a 'metaphysical' sense.

But the fact that difficulties can be raised in regard to Mill's position does not necessarily get other people out of their difficulties. And it might very well be argued that we cannot escape these difficulties if we once allow ourselves to share Mill's analytic approach, speaking about the agent, his character and his motives as though they were distinct entities which interact on one another. We ought instead to find another way of talking, based on a conception of the human person and his acting which cannot be expressed in Mill's terms. Bergson made an attempt to develop, or at least to indicate, such a language. And others have followed suit. We cannot talk about God in the language of, say, physics. For the concept of God is not a concept of physical science. Nor can we talk about freedom in the language used by Mill. If we try to do so, we shall find freedom being translated into something else.

The aim of the foregoing remarks is not to solve the problem of freedom, but simply to indicate some lines of reflection which arise out of Mill's discussions of the matter. For the matter of that, there is a great deal more that could be said in connection with Mill's approach and line of thought. But it would be inappropriate to devote more space to the subject in a book which is not intended to be a treatise on human liberty, whether in the civil or in the psychological sense of the term.

CHAPTER III

J. S. MILL: LOGIC AND EMPIRICISM

Introductory remarks—Names and propositions, real and verbal—The nature of mathematics—Syllogistic reasoning—Induction and the principle of the uniformity of Nature—The law of causation—Experimental inquiry and deduction—Method in the Moral Sciences—Matter as a permanent possibility of sensations—The analysis of mind and the spectre of solipsism—Mill on religion and natural theology.

1. In the eighteenth century the study of logic had been comparatively neglected. And in the introduction to his *System of Logic* Mill pays a tribute to Richard Whateley (1787–1863), Archbishop of Dublin, as 'a writer who has done more than any other person to restore this study to the rank from which it had fallen in the estimation of the cultivated class in our own country.'[1] But it does not follow, of course, that Mill is in full agreement with Whateley's idea of the nature and scope of logic. Logic was defined by Whateley as the science and art of reasoning.[2] But this definition, Mill contends, is in any case too narrow to cover all logical operations. More important, Whateley regarded syllogistic deduction as the standard and type of all scientific inference, and he refused to admit that the logic of induction could be given a scientific form analogous to the theory of the syllogism. He did not mean, he explained, that no rules for inductive investigation could be laid down. But in his opinion such rules must always remain comparatively vague and could not be synthesized in a properly scientific theory of inductive logic. Mill, however, sets out with the aim of showing that the opposite is true. He is careful to remark that he does not despise the syllogism. And in his *System of Logic* he deals with syllogistic inference. But he lays emphasis on the nature of logic as 'the science which treats of the operations of the human mind in the pursuit of truth'.[3] That is to say, he lays emphasis on the function of logic in generalizing and

[1] *Logic*, 1, p. 2 (1, *Introduction*, 2). Whateley's *Elements of Logic* appeared in 1826.
[2] Whateley regarded the description of logic as the art of reasoning as inadequate. Logic is also the science of reasoning. As far as this emendation is concerned, Mill agrees with him.
[3] *Logic*, 1, p. 4 (1, *Introduction*, 4).

synthesizing the rules for estimating evidence and advancing from known to unknown truths rather than on its function as providing rules for formal consistency in reasoning. Hence what is primarily required for the development of logic is precisely the fulfilment of the task which according to Whateley could not be fulfilled, or at least not with any degree of scientific exactitude, namely to generalize 'the modes of investigating truth and estimating evidence, by which so many important and recondite laws of nature have, in the various sciences, been aggregated to the stock of human knowledge'.[1]

But Mill is not interested simply in developing a systematic theory of inductive logic as employed in natural science. He is also concerned with working out a logic of what he calls the moral sciences, which include psychology and sociology. True, he actually considered this topic before he found himself able to complete a satisfactory account of inductive logic as given in the third book of the *System of Logic*. But this does not prevent Mill from presenting the sixth book, which deals with the logic of the moral sciences, as an application to them of the experimental method of the physical sciences. He thus makes his own the programme envisaged by David Hume, namely that of employing the experimental method in the development of a science of human nature.[2]

If it is asked whether Mill's point of view is that of an empiricist, the answer obviously depends to a great extent on the meaning which is given to this term. As Mill himself uses the term, he is not, or at any rate does not wish to be, an empiricist. Thus in the *System of Logic* he speaks of 'bad generalization *a posteriori* or empiricism properly so called',[3] as when causation is inferred from casual conjunction. Again, Mill refers to induction by simple enumeration as 'this rude and slovenly mode of generalization',[4] a mode of generalization which was demanded by Francis Bacon and which confuses merely empirical laws with causal laws. A simple example is offered by the way in which many people generalize from the people of their own country to the peoples of other countries, 'as if human beings felt, judged and acted everywhere in the same manner'.[5] Again, in Mill's work on Comte we are told that 'direct induction [is] usually no better than

---

[1] *Ibid.*, I, p. vii (in the Preface to the first edition).
[2] See Vol. V of this *History*, pp. 260–2.   [3] *Logic*, II, p. 368 (II, 5, 5, 5).
[4] *Ibid.*, II, p. 363 (II, 5, 5, 4).
[5] *Ibid.*, II, p. 368 (II, 5, 5, 4).

empiricism',[1] 'empiricism' being obviously employed in a deprecia-
tory sense. And similar remarks occur elsewhere.

But though Mill certainly rejects empiricism in the sense in
which he understands the term, in the sense, that is to say, of bad
and slovenly generalization, of a procedure which bears little
relation to scientific method or methods, he equally certainly takes
his stand with Locke in holding that the material of all our
knowledge is provided by experience. And if this is what is meant
by empiricism, Mill is indubitably an empiricist. True, he admits
intuition as a source of knowledge. Indeed, 'the truths known by
intuition are the original premises from which all others are
inferred'.[2] But by intuition Mill means consciousness, immediate
awareness of our sensations and feelings. If by intuition is meant
'the direct knowledge we are supposed to have of things external
to our minds',[3] he is not prepared to admit that there is any
such thing. Indeed, the *System of Logic* 'supplies what was
much wanted, a text-book of the opposite doctrine—that which
derives all knowledge from experience, and all moral and
intellectual qualities principally from the direction given to the
associations'.[4]

Mill's rejection of what he calls the German or *a priori* view of
human knowledge, which is to be found in the philosophy of
Coleridge and to a certain extent in that of Whewell, is complicated by the fact that he regards it as having undesirable
consequences in moral and political theory, or even as being
invoked to support undesirable social attitudes and convictions.
'The notion that truths external to the mind may be known by
intuition or consciousness, independently of observation and
experience, is, I am persuaded, in these times the great intellectual
support of false doctrines and bad institutions. . . . There never
was such an instrument devised for consecrating all deep-seated
prejudices.'[5] Hence when the *System of Logic* endeavours to
explain mathematical knowledge, the stronghold of the intuitionists, without recourse to the idea of intuitive or *a priori*
knowledge, it is performing a valuable social service as well as
attempting to settle a purely theoretical problem.

It may be objected that these remarks are really quite inadequate for settling the question whether or not Mill is to be

---

[1] *Auguste Comte and Positivism*, p. 121 (2nd edition, 1866).
[2] *Logic*, I, p. 5 (I, *Introduction*, 4).   [3] *Ibid.*, I, footnote (I, *Introduction*, 4).
[4] *Autobiography*, p. 225.
[5] *Ibid.*, pp. 225–6.

described as an empiricist. On the one hand, if empiricism is equated with bad and slovenly generalization, it is indeed obvious that neither Mill nor any other serious thinker would wish to be called an empiricist. For the term becomes one of abuse or at least of depreciation. On the other hand, a conviction that the material of our knowledge is furnished by experience is not by itself sufficient warrant for calling a philosopher an empiricist. Hence to observe that Mill attacks empiricism in a certain sense of the term while at the same time he maintains that all our knowledge is grounded in experience, does not do more than narrow down the question to a certain extent. It does not answer it. We are not told, for instance, whether Mill admits metaphysical principles which, though we come to know them as a basis of experience and not *a priori*, nevertheless go beyond any actual experience, in the sense that they apply to all possible experience.

This line of objection is perfectly reasonable. But it is difficult to give a simple answer to the question raised. On the one hand Mill certainly takes up an empiricist position when he explicitly asserts that we cannot attain absolute truth and that all generalizations are revisable in principle. On the other hand, when he is differentiating between properly scientific induction and slovenly generalization, he tends to speak in such a way as to imply that hitherto unknown truths can be inferred with certainty from known truths and, consequently, that Nature possesses a stable structure, as it were, which could be expressed in statements which would be true of all possible experience. In view of Mill's general position in the history of British philosophy and in view of the influence exercised by his thought it is perfectly natural that we should emphasize the first aspect of his thought and call him an empiricist. But it is as well to remember that he sometimes adopts positions which imply a different point of view. In any case the different strands in his thought can be seen only by considering what he says on particular topics.

2. Logic, Mill maintains, is concerned with inferences from truths previously known, not, of course, in the sense that the logician increases our knowledge of the world by actually making substantial inferences, but in the sense that he provides the tests or criteria for determining the value of inference or proof, and consequently of belief in so far as it professes to be grounded on proof. But inference is 'an operation which usually takes place by means of words, and in complicated cases can take place in no

other way'.[1] Hence it is proper to begin a systematic study of
logic by a consideration of language.

We might perhaps expect that Mill would turn immediately to
propositions. For it is propositions which are inferred. But as he
regards the proposition as always affirming or denying a predicate
of a subject, one name, as he puts it, of another name, he actually
begins by discussing names and the process of naming.

It is unnecessary to mention here all the distinctions which Mill
draws between different types of names. But the following points
can be noted. According to Mill, whenever a name given to objects
has in the proper sense a meaning, its meaning consists in what it
connotes, not in what it denotes. All concrete general names are
of this kind. For example, the word 'man' can denote or refer to
an indefinite number of individual things which together are said
to form a class; but its meaning resides in what it connotes, namely
the attributes which are predicated when the word 'man' is applied
to certain beings. It follows, therefore, that proper names, such as
John, which can be applied to more than one individual but which
have no connotation, possess, strictly speaking, no meaning. It
does not follow, however, that the word 'God' has no meaning.
For this term is not, according to Mill, a proper name. To be sure,
as used by the monotheist the term is applicable to only one
being. But this is because, as so used, it connotes a certain union
of attributes which in fact limits its range of application. It is thus
a connotative term, not a proper name like John or Mary.

Mill does indeed distinguish between words which name things
or attributes and words which enter into the naming-process. For
instance, in 'the wife of Socrates' the word 'of' is not itself a
name.[2] But Mill has been criticized by later logicians for passing
over words such as 'or' and 'if', which can certainly not be
described as parts of names.

Turning to propositions, we find, as already indicated, that
Mill's over-emphasis on names and naming leads him to regard all
propositions as affirming or denying one name or another. The
words which are commonly, though not necessarily, used to
signify affirmative or negative predication are 'is' or 'is not', 'are'
or 'are not'. Thus Mill takes the subject-copula-predicate form of
proposition as the standard, though not invariable, form. And he

---

[1] *Logic*, 1, p. 17 (1, 1, 1, 1).
[2] The phrase 'the wife of Socrates' would be for Mill a name, but not a proper
name. For it is a connotative name, whereas proper names, such as John, are not
connotative but solely denotative.

warns his readers about the ambiguity of the term 'is'. For example, if we fail to distinguish between the existential use of the verb 'to be' and its use as a copula, we may be led into such absurdities as supposing that unicorns must possess some form of existence because we can say that the unicorn is an animal with one horn, or even because we can say that it is an imaginary beast.

In the course of his discussion of the import or meaning of propositions Mill distinguishes between real and verbal propositions. In a real proposition we affirm or deny of a subject an attribute which is not already connoted by its name, or a fact which is not already comprised in the signification of the name of the subject. In other words, a real proposition conveys new factual information, true or false as the case may be, information which is new in the sense that it cannot be obtained simply by analysis of the meaning of the subject term. As proper names are not connotative terms and, strictly speaking, possess no 'meaning', every proposition, such as 'John is married', which has as its subject a proper name, must necessarily belong to this class. Verbal propositions, however, are concerned simply with the meanings of names: the predicate can be obtained by analysis of the connotation or meaning of the subject term. For example, in 'man is a corporeal being' the predicate already forms part of the connotation or meaning of the term 'man'. For we would not call anything a man unless it were a corporeal being. Hence the proposition says something about the meaning of a name, about its usage: it does not convey factual information in the sense that 'John is married' or 'the mean distance of the moon from the earth is 238,860 miles' conveys factual information.

The most important class of verbal propositions are definitions, a definition being 'a proposition declaratory of the meaning of a word: namely, either the meaning which it bears in common acceptance or that which the speaker or writer, for the particular purposes of his discourse, intends to annex to it'.[1] Mill thus does not exclude the use of words in new ways for specific purposes. But he insists on the need for examining ordinary usage very carefully before we undertake to reform language. For an examination of the different shades of meaning which a word has in common usage, or changes in its use, may bring to light distinctions and

---

[1] *Logic*, I, p. 151 (I, I, 8, I). As proper names do not possess meaning, they cannot be defined.

other relevant factors which it is important that the would-be reformer of language should bear in mind.

Obviously, when Mill says that definitions are verbal propositions, he does not intend to imply that they are by nature purely arbitrary or that inquiries into matters of fact are never relevant to the framing of definitions. It would be absurd, for example, to define man with complete disregard for the attributes which those beings whom we call men possess in common. Mill's point is that though the connotation of the term 'man' is grounded in experience of men, and though inquiries into matters of fact can render this connotation less vague and more distinct, what the definition as such does is simply to make this connotation or meaning explicit, either wholly or in part, that is, by means of selected differentiating attributes. True, we may be inclined to suppose that the definition is not purely verbal. But the inclination can be easily explained if we bear in mind the ambiguity of the copula. A general connotative term such as 'man' denotes an indefinite number of things and connotes certain attributes which they have in common. When, therefore, it is said that 'man is . . .', we may be inclined to suppose that the definition asserts that there are men. In this case, however, we tacitly presuppose the presence of two propositions, corresponding to two possible uses of the verb 'to be'; on the one hand the definition, which simply makes explicit the meaning of the term 'man', and on the other hand an existential proposition which asserts that there are beings which possess the attributes mentioned in the definition. If we omit the existential proposition which we have surreptitiously introduced, we can see that the definition is purely verbal, concerned simply with the meaning of a name.

Let us return for a moment to real propositions and consider a general proposition such as 'All men are mortal.'[1] Looked at from one point of view, as a portion of speculative truth, as Mill puts it, this means that the attributes of man are always accompanied by the attribute of being mortal. And under analysis this means that certain phenomena are regularly associated with other phenomena. But we can also look at the proposition under the aspect of a memorandum for practical use. And it then means that 'the attributes of man are *evidence of*, are a *mark* of, mortality'.[2] In other words, it tells us what to expect. According to Mill these

[1] This is, for Mill, a real proposition, and not an 'essential' or purely verbal proposition.

[2] *Logic*, I, p. 13 (I, I, 6, 5).

different meanings are ultimately equivalent. But in scientific inference it is the practical aspect of meaning, its predictive aspect, which is of special importance.

We have, therefore, a distinction between verbal propositions in which the predicate is either identical with or a part of the meaning of the subject term, and real propositions, in which the predicate is not contained in the connotation of the subject. And Mill remarks that 'this distinction corresponds to that which is drawn by Kant and other metaphysicians between what they term analytic and synthetic judgments; the former being those which can be evolved from the meaning of the terms used'.[1] We may add that Mill's distinction also corresponds more or less to Hume's distinction between propositions which state relations between ideas and propositions which state matters of fact.

If we mean by truth correspondence between a proposition and the extra-linguistic fact to which it refers,[2] it obviously follows that no purely verbal proposition can be properly described as true. A definition can be adequate or inadequate; it can correspond or not correspond with linguistic usage. But by itself it makes no statement about matters of extra-linguistic fact. The question arises, however, whether for Mill there are real propositions which are necessarily true. Does he agree with Hume that no real proposition can be necessarily true? Or, to use Kantian terminology, does he recognize the existence of synthetic *a priori* propositions?

It is a notorious fact that Mill tends to speak in different ways, his way of speaking being influenced by his reaction to the type of theory which he happens to be discussing. Hence it is difficult to say what *the* view of Mill is. However, he is undoubtedly opposed to the view that there is any *a priori* knowledge of reality. And this opposition naturally inclines him to reject synthetic *a priori* propositions. Mill is not indeed prepared to say that when the negation of a given proposition appears to us as unbelievable, the proposition must be merely verbal. For there are doubtless some real propositions which reflect a uniformity or regularity of experience such that the negations of these propositions seem to us unbelievable. And for all practical purposes we are justified in treating them as though they were necessarily true. Indeed, we

---

[1] *Ibid.*, 1, p. 129, footnote (1, 1, 6, 4, footnote). Mill tends to use the term 'metaphysics' in the sense of theory of knowledge.
[2] It is not denied, of course, that there can be true propositions which state matters of linguistic fact, propositions about the English language, for example.

can hardly do otherwise, because *ex hypothesi* we have had no experience which has led us to question their universal applicability. But a real proposition can be necessarily true in the psychological sense that we find its opposite unbelievable, without being necessarily true in the logical sense that it must be true of all possible experience, of all unobserved or unexperienced phenomena.

This seems to be more or less Mill's characteristic position. But to appreciate the complexity of the situation it is advisable to consider what he has to say about mathematical propositions, the great stronghold of intuitionists and upholders of *a priori* knowledge.

3. It is scarcely necessary to say that Mill recognizes that mathematics possesses some peculiar characteristics. He remarks, for example, that 'the propositions of geometry are independent of the succession of events'.[1] Again, the truths of mathematics 'have no connection with laws of causation. . . . That when two straight lines intersect each other the opposite angles are equal, is true of all such lines and angles, by whatever cause produced.'[2] Again, mathematical reasoning 'does not suffer us to let in, at any of the joints in the reasoning, an assumption which we have not faced in the shape of an axiom, postulate or definition. This is a merit which it has in common with formal Logic.'[3]

When, however, we start inquiring into Mill's general theory of mathematics, complications arise. Dugald Stewart maintained that mathematical propositions do not express matters of fact but only connections between suppositions or assumptions and certain consequences. He further maintained that the first principles of geometry are Euclid's definitions, not the postulates and axioms. And as he regarded the definitions as arbitrary, he made it difficult to explain how pure mathematics can be applied. That mathematics can fit reality, so to speak, and be successfully applied in physics becomes for him a matter of pure coincidence. Mill, however, was not satisfied with this position. He wished to say that mathematical propositions are true. Hence he could not admit that Euclid's theorems are deducible from definitions. For Mill held, as we have seen, that definitions are neither true nor false. He had to maintain, therefore, that Euclid's theorems are deduced from postulates, which can be true or false. And he

[1] *Logic*, I, p. 373 (I, 3, 5, 1).   [2] *Ibid.*, II, p. 147 (II, 3, 24, 2).
[3] *Examination*, p. 526.

argued that any Euclidean definition is only partly a definition. For it also involves a postulate. In other words, any Euclidean definition can be analysed into two propositions, of which one is a postulate or assumption in regard to a matter of fact while the other is a genuine definition. Thus the definition of a circle can be analysed into the following two propositions: 'a figure may exist, having all the points in the line which bounds it equally distant from a single point within it', (and) 'any figure possessing this property is called a circle'.[1] The first proposition is a postulate; and it is such postulates, not the pure definitions, which form the premisses for the deduction of Euclid's theorems. The gap which Stewart created between pure and applied mathematics is thus closed. For the propositions of geometry, for instance, are not derived from arbitrary definitions but from postulates or assumptions concerning matters of fact.

We can say, therefore, that in geometry 'our reasonings are grounded on the matters of fact postulated in definitions, and not on the definitions themselves'.[2] And 'this conclusion', Mills remarks, 'is one which I have in common with Dr. Whewell'.[3] But though Mill may find himself in agreement with Whewell when it is a question of attacking Stewart's idea that the theorems of Euclidean geometry are deduced from definitions, agreement immediately ceases when it is a question of our knowledge of the first principles of mathematics. According to Whewell these first principles are self-evident, underived from experience and known intuitively. They constitute examples of *a priori* knowledge. And this is a position which Mill is unwilling to accept. He maintains instead that in mathematics 'these original premisses, from which the remaining truths of the science are deduced, are, notwithstanding all appearances to the contrary, results of observations and experiences, founded, in short, on the evidence of the senses'.[4] We have never come across a case which would refute a mathematical axiom; and the operation of the laws of association is quite sufficient to explain our belief in the necessity of such axioms.

In the general class of 'original premisses' Mill makes a distinction between axioms and the postulates involved in definitions. Axioms are exactly true. 'That things which are equal to the same thing are equal to one another, is as true of the lines and figures in

[1] *Logic*, I, p. 165 (I, I, 8, 5).   [2] *Ibid.*, I, p. 171 (I, I, 8, 6).   [3] *Ibid.*
[4] *Ibid.*, II, pp. 148–9 (II, 3, 24, 4).

nature, as it would be of the imaginary ones assumed in the definitions.'[1] But the postulates or assumptions involved in the definitions of Euclidean geometry 'are so far from being necessary, that they are not even true; they purposely depart, more or less widely, from the truth'.[2] For example, it is not true that a line as defined by the geometer can exist. But it does not follow that the geometer intuits some peculiar mathematical entity. When he defines the line as having length but not breadth, he is deciding, for his own purposes, to ignore the element of breadth, to abstract from it, and to consider only length. Hence both axioms and postulates are derived from experience.

Obviously, when Mill describes the first principles of mathematics as generalizations from experience, he is not suggesting that our knowledge of all mathematical propositions is in fact the result of inductive generalization. What he is saying in effect is that the ultimate premisses of mathematical demonstration are empirical hypotheses. He therefore finds himself in agreement with Dugald Stewart as against Whewell. As we have seen, he disagrees with Stewart's derivation of Euclidean geometry from pure definitions; but this disagreement is played down when it is a question of noting their substantial agreement about the nature of mathematics. 'The opinion of Dugald Stewart respecting the foundations of geometry is, I conceive, substantially correct; that it is built on hypotheses.'[3] All that Whewell can show, when arguing against this opinion, is that the hypotheses are not arbitrary. But 'those who say that the premisses of geometry are hypotheses, are not bound to maintain them to be hypotheses which have no relation whatever to fact'.[4]

Having said this, Mill then proceeds to get himself into an impossible position. An hypothesis, he remarks, is usually taken to be a postulate or assumption which is not known to be true but is surmised to be true, because, if it were true, it would account for certain facts. But the hypotheses of which he is speaking are not at all of this kind. For, as we have seen, the postulates involved in the definitions of Euclidean geometry are known *not* to be literally true. Further, as much as is true in the hypotheses under discussion 'is not hypothetical, but certain'.[5] The hypotheses, therefore, appear to fall into two parts, one part being known not to be literally true, the other part being certain. And it is thus

[1] *Logic*, I, p. 265 (I, 2, 5, 3).   [2] *Ibid.*, I, p. 262 (I, 2, 5, 1).
[3] *Ibid.*, I, p. 261 (I, 2, 5, 1).   [4] *Ibid.*, I, p. 263 (I, 2, 5, 2).
[5] *Ibid.*, I, p. 261, note (I, 2, 5, 1, note).

rather difficult to see what justification there is for speaking of 'hypotheses' at all. Nor is the situation improved when Mill says that to call the conclusions of geometry necessary truths is really to say that they follow correctly from suppositions which 'are not even true'.[1] What he means, of course, is that the necessity of the conclusions consists in the fact that they follow necessarily from the premisses. But if we were to take literally the suggestion that necessary truths are necessary because they follow from untrue assumptions, we should have to say that Mill was talking nonsense. However, it would be unfair to understand him in this way.

In his *Autobiography* Mill makes it clear that the interpretation of mathematics which he regards as his own is the explanation of so-called necessary truths in terms of 'experience and association'.[2] Hence it would be going too far if one suggested that after the publication of the *System of Logic* Mill later produced a new interpretation of mathematics. It may even be going too far if one suggests that he consciously entertained second thoughts about the interpretation, or interpretations, given in the *Logic*. But it can hardly be denied that he made remarks which implied a different conception of mathematics. For example, in his *Examination of Sir William Hamilton's Philosophy* Mill informs his readers that the laws of number underlie the laws of extension, that these two sets of laws underlie the laws of force, and that the laws of force 'underlie all the other laws of the material universe'.[3] Similarly, in the Address which he wrote in 1866 for the University of St. Andrews Mill implies that mathematics gives us the key to Nature, and that it is not so much that the first principles of mathematics are formed by inductive generalization from observation of phenomena which might be otherwise than they are as that phenomena are what they are because of certain mathematical laws. Obviously, this would not necessarily affect the thesis that we come to know mathematical truths on a basis of experience and not *a priori*. But it would certainly affect the thesis that the necessity of mathematics is purely hypothetical.

Perhaps the situation can be summed up in this way. According to Mill, for the development of the science of number or arithmetic no more is required than two fundamental axioms, namely 'things which are equal to the same thing are equal to one another' and

---

[1] *Ibid.*, I, p. 262 (I, 2, 5, I).   [2] *Autobiography*, p. 226.
[3] *Examination*, p. 533.

'equals added to equals make equal sums', 'together with the definitions of the various numbers'.[1] These axioms can hardly be described as empirical hypotheses, unless one resolutely confuses the psychological question of the way in which we come to recognize them with the question of their logical status. And though Mill speaks of them as inductive truths, he also speaks of their 'infallible truth'[2] being recognized 'from the dawn of speculation'.[3] It would thus be quite possible to regard such axioms as necessarily true by virtue of the meanings of the verbal symbols used, and to develop a formalist interpretation of mathematics. But Mill was not prepared to admit that the fundamental axioms of mathematics are verbal propositions. Hence, if he was determined, as he was, to undermine the stronghold of the intuitionists, he had to interpret them as inductive generalizations, as empirical hypotheses. And the necessity of mathematical propositions had to be interpreted simply as a necessity of logical connection between premisses and the conclusions derived from them. At the same time Mill was acutely conscious of the success of applied mathematics in increasing our knowledge of the world; and he came to make remarks which remind us of Galileo, not to mention Plato. He thought, no doubt, that talk about laws of number lying at the basis of the phenomenal world was quite consistent with his interpretation of the basic principles of mathematics. But though it was consistent with the psychological statement that our knowledge of mathematical truths actually presupposes experience of things, it was hardly consistent with the logical statement that mathematical axioms are empirical hypotheses. And we have seen how Mill got himself into a difficult position when he tried to explain in what sense they are hypotheses.

In fine, we can say one of two things. Either we can say that Mill held an empiricist view of mathematics, but that he made assertions which were inconsistent with this view. And this is the traditional way of depicting the situation. Or we can say with certain writers[4] that though Mill seems to have thought that he was expounding one unified interpretation of mathematics, in actual fact we can discern several alternative interpretations in his writings, interpretations between which he continued to hesitate, in practice if not in theory.

[1] *Logic*, II, p. 150 (II, 3, 24, 5).   [2] *Ibid.*, II, p. 149 (II, 3, 24, 4).   [3] *Ibid.*
[4] Notably R. P. Anschutz in *The Philosophy of J. S. Mill*, ch. 9.

4. Most of the propositions which we believe, Mill remarks, are believed not because of any immediate evidence for their truth but because they are derived from other propositions, the truth of which we have already assumed, whether justifiably or not. In short, most of the propositions which we believe are inferred from other propositions. But inference can be of two main kinds. On the one hand we can infer propositions from others which are equally or more general. On the other hand we can infer propositions from others which are less general than the propositions inferred from them. In the first case we have what is commonly called deductive inference or ratiocination, while in the second case we have inductive inference.

Now, according to Mill there is 'real' inference only when a new truth is inferred, that is, a truth which is not already contained in the premisses. And in this case only induction can be accounted real inference, inasmuch as 'the conclusion or induction embraces more than is contained in the premisses'.[1] When the conclusion is precontained in the premisses inference makes no real advance in knowledge. And this is true of syllogistic inference. For 'it is universally allowed that a syllogism is vicious if there be anything more in the conclusion than was assumed in the premisses. But this is, in fact, to say that nothing ever was, or can be, proved by syllogism, which was not known, or assumed to be known, before.'[2]

If this were all that Mill had to say on the matter, it would be natural to conclude that for him there are two distinct types of logic. On the one hand there is deductive inference, in which from more general propositions we infer less general propositions. And as the inference is invalid unless the conclusion is precontained in the premisses, no new truth can be discovered in this way. Syllogistic reasoning can ensure logical consistency in thought. For example, if someone speaks in such a way as to show that he is really asserting both that all X's are Y and that a particular X is not Y, we can employ the forms of syllogistic reasoning to make clear to him the logical inconsistency of his thought. But no new truth is, or can be, discovered in this way. For to say that all X's are Y is to say that every X is Y. On the other hand we have inductive inference, the inference employed in physical science, whereby the mind moves from what is known to a truth which is unknown before the process of inference establishes it. In short,

---

[1] *Logic*, I, p. 187 (I, 2, 1, 3).   [2] *Ibid.*, I, p. 209 (I, 2, 3, 1).

on the one hand we have a logic of consistency, on the other hand a logic of discovery.

In reality, however, the situation is much more complicated than this preliminary account suggests. Consider one of the arguments mentioned by Mill: 'All men are mortal; the Duke of Wellington is a man: therefore the Duke of Wellington is mortal.' It is indeed obvious that to concede the major and minor premisses and deny the conclusion would involve one in logical inconsistency. But Mill sometimes speaks as though to assume the truth of the major premiss is to assume the truth of the conclusion in such a way that to know the truth of the major is already to know the truth of the conclusion. And this seems to be questionable on either of the interpretations of the major premiss which he puts forward.

We have already seen that according to Mill the proposition 'all men are mortal', when it is considered as what he calls a portion of speculative truth, means that 'the attributes of man are always accompanied by the attribute mortality'.[1] Mill here fixes his attention on the connotation of the word 'man'. And if the proposition 'all men are mortal' is interpreted in terms of the connotation of the word 'man', it is natural to say that the proposition concerns universals, not particulars. Further, if we were to interpret 'always' as meaning 'necessarily', there would be no cogent ground for saying that the man who asserts that the attributes which make up the connotation of the word 'man' are always accompanied by the attribute of mortality, must already know that the Duke of Wellington is mortal. True, the assertion in question can be said to imply that if there is a being which can properly be described as the Duke of Wellington and which also possesses the attributes that make up the connotation of the word 'man', this being also possesses the attribute of mortality. But the fact remains that the assertion does not necessarily presuppose any knowledge whatsoever of the Duke of Wellington.

It may be objected that Mill does not interpret 'always' as 'necessarily'. If he did, this would make 'all men are mortal' an essential or verbal proposition. For mortality would then be one of the attributes which make up the connotation of the word 'man'. In point of fact Mill regards 'all men are mortal' as a real proposition. Hence 'always' does not mean 'necessarily' but 'so far as all observation goes'. Moreover, though Mill may some-

[1] *Logic*, I, p. 130 (I, I, 6, 5).

times speak in a way which implies or suggests a realistic theory of universals, it is a notorious fact that in the course of his discussion of the syllogism he supports a nominalist theory. In other words, 'all men' must be understood in terms of denotation. It means 'all particular men'. And if we *know* that *all* particular men are mortal, we know that any particular man is mortal.

The premisses of this argument are correct. That is to say, Mill does regard 'all men are mortal' as a real and not as a verbal proposition, and he does take up a nominalist position in his discussion of the syllogism. But the conclusion of the argument does not follow from the premisses. For according to Mill's nominalist theory 'all men are mortal' is a record of experience of particular facts, that is, of facts such as that Socrates and Julius Caesar both died. And if the Duke of Wellington is a living man, his death is obviously not included among these particular facts. Hence it cannot be reasonably claimed that to know that all men are mortal presupposes or includes knowledge of the mortality of the Duke of Wellington. The conclusion that the Duke of Wellington is mortal is not precontained in the proposition 'all men are mortal'. And it seems to follow that inference from 'all men are mortal' to 'the Duke of Wellington is mortal' is invalid.

In order to make the inference valid we have to say that 'all men are mortal' is not simply a record of past experience of people dying but also an inductive inference which goes beyond the empirical evidence and serves as a prediction, telling us what to expect. Having observed in the past that the attributes which make up the connotation of the term 'man' have in fact been accompanied by mortality, we infer that the same is to be expected in the future. In other words, 'all men are mortal' becomes not so much a premiss from which the mortality of living and future men is deduced as a formula for making future inferences, that is, from the possession of certain other attributes to the attribute of mortality. And this is precisely what Mill says. 'General propositions are merely registers of such inferences already made, and short formulae for making more. The major premiss of a syllogism, consequently, is a formula of this description: and the conclusion is not an inference drawn *from* the formula, but an inference drawn *according* to the formula.'[1] And the rules of syllogistic

---

[1] *Ibid.*, I, p. 221 (I, 2, 3, 4). The notion of a formula 'according to which' was suggested to Mill by Dugald Stewart's doctrine that the axioms of geometry are principles according to which, not from which, we reason.

inferences are rules for the correct interpretation of the formula. As such, they are useful. And Mill can enter 'a protest, as strong as that of Archbishop Whateley himself, against the doctrine that the syllogistic art is useless for the purposes of reasoning'.[1]

But if the major premiss is not a proposition *from* which the conclusion is derived but a formula *according to which* the conclusion is drawn, it follows that it is particular observed facts which constitute the real logical antecedent. In other words 'all inference is from particulars to particulars'.[2] A multitude of particular factual connections between being a man and being mortal have been observed.in the past. As we cannot carry them all in our heads, we record them in a compendious memorandum. But the record is not simply an historical note. It runs beyond the empirical evidence observed in the past and predicts the future, serving as a guide to or formula for making inferences. And though we need not cast our reasoning according to the formula in syllogistic form, we can do so. The rules of syllogistic inference are a set of rules or precautions for ensuring correctness and consistency in our interpretation of the formula, correctness being measured by our purpose in establishing the formula, namely to simplify the making of future inferences in accordance with our past inferences. Syllogistic reasoning then becomes the latter half in the total process, as Mill puts it, of travelling from premisses to conclusions, that is, from particulars to particulars. In other words, the gap between deductive and inductive inference is diminished.

But there is more to come. Mill admits that there are cases in which syllogistic reasoning constitutes the whole process of reasoning from premisses to conclusion. These cases occur, for example, in theology and in law, when the major premiss is derived from the appropriate authority, and not by inductive inference from particular cases. Thus a lawyer may receive his major premiss, in the form of a general law, from the legislator and then argue that it applies or does not apply in some particular case or set of circumstances. But Mill adds that the lawyer's process of reasoning is then 'not a process of inference, but a process of interpretation'.[3]

We have already seen, however, that when syllogistic inference constitutes the second half of a total process of reasoning from

[1] *Logic*, I, p. 225 (I, 2, 3, 5).   [2] *Ibid.*, I, p. 221 (I, 2, 3, 4).
[3] *Ibid.*, I, p. 223 (I, 2, 3, 4).

premisses to conclusion, it is in effect a process of interpreting a formula, namely the major premiss. And in this case the sharp distinction between two kinds of logic collapses. Syllogistic reasoning is simply a process of interpretation. It can stand on its own, so to speak, as may happen when a theologiaᵩ takes his major premiss from the authority of the Scripture or the Church. Or it can form one phase in a total process of inference from particulars to particulars. But in neither case is it, taken in itself, an example of inference. And the rules of the syllogism are rules for the correct interpretation of a general proposition, not rules of inference, in the proper sense of the term at least.

5. In view of the fact that Mill represents syllogistic reasoning as a process of interpreting a general proposition which is itself the result of induction, it is not surprising that he defines inductive inference as 'the operation of discovering and proving general propositions'.[1] At first sight the definition may indeed appear somewhat strange. For, as we have seen, all inference is said to be from particulars to particulars. However, 'generals are but collections of particulars definite in kind but indefinite in number'.[2]

This amounts to saying that to prove a general proposition is to prove that something is true of a whole class of particulars. Hence induction can be defined as 'that operation of the mind by which we infer that what we know to be true in a particular case or cases will be true in all cases which resemble the former in certain assignable respects'.[3] Obviously, Mill is not thinking of so-called perfect induction, in which the general proposition simply records what has already been observed to be true in regard to every single member of a class. For induction in this sense does not represent any advance in knowledge.[4] He is thinking of inference which goes beyond the actual data of experience and argues, for example, from the known truth that some X's are Y to the conclusion that anything at any time which possesses the attributes in virtue of which X's are considered as members of a class will also be found to possess the attribute Y.

The basic presupposition implied by this process of going

---

[1] *Ibid.*, I, p. 328 (I, 3, I, 2). [2] *Ibid.*

[3] *Ibid.*, I, p. 333 (I, 3, 2, I). The use of the word 'will' should not be taken to mean that inductive inference is exclusively a process of inferring the future from the past. The general proposition refers also, of course, to unobserved contemporary members of a class, and indeed to unobserved past members.

[4] If, for instance, I first discover that each Apostle is a Jew and then say, 'all the Apostles are Jews', this general proposition does not represent any real advance in knowledge.

beyond the actual empirical data to the enunciation of a general proposition is, according to Mill, the principle of the uniformity of Nature, that all phenomena take place according to general laws. 'The proposition that the course of Nature is uniform, is the fundamental principle, or general axiom, of Induction.'[1] And he goes on to say that if inductive inference from particulars to particulars were to be put in syllogistic form by supplying a major premiss, this same principle would constitute the ultimate major premiss.

Now, if the principle of the uniformity of Nature is described as a fundamental principle or axiom or postulate of induction, this may tend to suggest that the principle is explicitly conceived and postulated before any particular scientific inference is made. But this is not at all Mill's point of view. He means rather that the uniformity of Nature is the necessary condition for the validity of scientific inference, and that in embarking on any particular inference we tacitly presuppose it, even though we are not consciously aware of the fact. When, therefore, he says that if an inductive inference were to be cast into syllogistic form, the principle of the uniformity of Nature would be found to constitute the ultimate major premiss, he means that the principle is the 'suppressed' premiss of induction. And, following his general doctrine of syllogistic reasoning, he means that it is a tacit formula or axiom *in accordance with which* inferences are made, not a proposition *from* which the conclusion of the inference is deduced. True, mention of the syllogism is rather confusing. For, as we have seen, Mill regards syllogistic reasoning as the interpretation of a formula; and this suggests deliberate interpretation of a consciously conceived and enunciated formula. But though the principle of the uniformity of Nature would obviously have to be explicitly enunciated if we were actually to cast inference into syllogistic form by supplying the suppressed major premiss, it by no means follows that all scientific inference involves conscious awareness of the principle or axiom in accordance with which it operates.

Mill has no intention, therefore, of suggesting that the principle of the uniformity of Nature is a self-evident truth which is known antecedently to the discovery of particular regularities or uniformities. On the contrary, 'this great generalization is itself founded on prior generalizations.'[2] And so far from being the first

---

[1] *Logic*, I, p. 355 (I, 3, 3, I). [2] *Ibid*.

induction to be made, it is one of the last. This may indeed appear at first sight to be incompatible with Mill's view that the uniformity of Nature is the basic presupposition of scientific inference. But his position seems to be more or less as follows. Scientific inference would not be valid unless there was uniformity in Nature. Hence when we turn to the investigation of Nature and embark on scientific inference, we tacitly presuppose that there is uniformity in Nature, even though we are unaware of the fact. The explicit idea of the uniformity of Nature arises through the discovery of particular uniformities. And the more we discover such uniformities, the more we tend to prove the validity of the idea, and thus of the implicit presupposition of all inference.

Now, if the principle of the uniformity of Nature is taken to mean that the course of Nature is always uniform in the sense that the future will always repeat or resemble the past, the principle, as a universal proposition, is patently untrue. As Mill observes, the weather does not follow a uniform course in this sense, nor does anyone expect it to do so. But what is called the uniformity of Nature 'is itself a complex fact, compounded of all the separate uniformities which exist in respect to single phenomena',[1] these separate uniformities being commonly called laws of Nature. Presumably, therefore, to say that scientific inference presupposes the uniformity of Nature is simply to say that the scientific investigation of Nature tacitly presupposes that there are uniformities in Nature. In other words, the condition of the validity of scientific inference is that there should be uniformities in the context or sphere with which the inference is concerned. And the progressive discovery of particular uniformities constitutes the progressive validation of scientific inference.

It is often said that Mill attempts to 'justify' scientific inference from the unknown to the known. And so he does in a sense. But in what sense? He tells us indeed that 'the real proof that what is true of John, Peter, etc. is true of all mankind, can only be, that a different supposition would be inconsistent with the uniformity which we know to exist in the course of Nature'.[2] But we do not know in advance that the course of Nature is uniform. We may assume it, and if the assumption is partly a rule for making inferences, consistency demands that we should follow it. But consistency alone can hardly constitute a proof of the assumption. If at any rate we concentrate our attention on the empiricist

[1] *Ibid.*, I, p. 364 (I, 3, 4, 1).   [2] *Ibid.*, I, p. 357 (I, 3, 3, 1).

aspects of Mill's thought, on his denial of *a priori* knowledge and on his view that all inference is from particulars to particulars, generals being but collections of particulars, it seems that the only possible justification of inductive generalization is partial verification coupled with absence of falsification. We cannot observe all possible instances of a law or asserted uniformity. But if the law is verified in those cases where we do test it empirically and if we know of no case in which it is falsified, this appears to be the only sort of justification of the inductive leap from the known to the unknown, from the observed to the unobserved, from 'some' to 'all', which can be provided. And if the uniformity of Nature is simply the complex of particular uniformities, it follows that the uniformity of Nature in a general sense tends to be proved, in the only sense in which it can ever be proved, in proportion as particular inductive generalizations are found, through partial verification and absence of falsification, to be successful predictions of phenomena.

6. In common parlance, as Mill puts it, the various uniformities in Nature are called the laws of Nature. But in stricter scientific language the laws of Nature are the uniformities in Nature when reduced to their simplest expression. They are 'the fewest and simplest assumptions, which being granted, the whole existing order of Nature would result',[1] or 'the fewest general propositions from which all the uniformities which exist in the universe might be deductively inferred'.[2] The task of the scientific study of Nature is to ascertain what these laws are and what subordinate uniformities can be inferred from them, while the task of inductive logic is to determine the principles and rules governing the arguments by which such knowledge is established.

We can note in passing how Mill shifts his position under the influence of the actual nature of science. When speaking as an empiricist, he tells us that all inference is from particulars to particulars, and that general propositions, reached by inductive generalization, are formulas for making inferences but not propositions *from* which conclusions are deduced. Now he tells us that the scientific study of Nature involves deducing less general from more general laws. Obviously, it remains true that particulars as such cannot be deduced from any general proposition. The general proposition tells us what to expect, and we then have to examine empirically whether the prediction is confirmed or

---

[1] *Logic*, I, p. 366 (I, 3, 4, I).   [2] *Ibid.*

falsified. At the same time there seems to be a change of emphasis. When discussing the syllogism, Mill gives a nominalist account of the process of inference. When he turns to induction he tends to adopt a more realist position. He tends to assume that Nature possesses a stable structure which can be represented in the edifice of science.

Some laws or uniformities, such as the propositions of geometry, are unrelated to temporal succession. Others, such as the propositions of arithmetic, apply both to synchronous or coexisting and to successive phenomena. Others again are related only to temporal succession. And the most important of these is the law of causation. 'The truth that every fact which has a beginning has a cause, is coextensive with human experience.'[1] Indeed, recognition of the law of causation is 'the main pillar of inductive science'.[2] That is to say, inductive science establishes causal laws, and it presupposes that every event happens in accordance with such a law. Hence in developing a theory of induction it is essential to define the idea of causality as clearly as possible.

Mill disclaims any intention of concerning himself with ultimate causes in a metaphysical sense.[3] Moreover, as he intends to determine the idea of causality only in so far as it can be obtained from experience, he does not propose to introduce the notion of any mysterious necessary bond between cause and effect. Such a notion is not required for a theory of inductive science. There is no need to go beyond 'the familiar truth, that invariability of succession is found by observation to obtain between every fact in nature and some other fact which has preceded it'.[4]

At the same time it is misleading to assert that Mill reduces the causal relation to invariable sequence. For this might be taken to imply that in his view the cause of a given phenomenon can be identified with any other phenomenon which is found by experience always to precede it. Rather does he identify the cause of a given phenomenon with the totality of antecedents, positive and negative, which are required for the occurrence of the phenomenon and which are sufficient for its occurrence. 'Invariable sequence, therefore, is not synonymous with causation, unless the sequence, besides being invariable, is unconditional.'[5] And the cause of a phenomenon is, properly speaking, 'the antecedent, or the

---

[1] *Ibid.*, I, p. 376 (I, 3, 5, 1).   [2] *Ibid.*, I, p. 377 (I, 3, 5, 2).
[3] Adopting a distinction made by Reid, Mill says that he is concerned only with 'physical' causes, and not with 'efficient' causes.
[4] *Logic*, I, p. 377 (I, 3, 5, 2).   [5] *Ibid.*, I, p. 392 (I, 3, 5, 6).

concurrence of antecedents, on which it is invariably and *un-conditionally* consequent'.[1]

Now, Mill says of the law of causation that 'on the universality of this truth depends the possibility of reducing the inductive process to rules'.[2] And he certainly assumes in practice that every phenomenon has a cause in the sense explained above. All the phenomena of Nature are the 'unconditional' consequences of previous collocations of causes.[3] And any mind which knew all the causal agents existing at a given moment, together with their positions and the laws of their operations, 'could predict the whole subsequent history of the universe, at least unless some new volition of a power capable of controlling the universe should supervene'.[4]

But how do we know that the law of causation is a universal truth? Mill is certainly not prepared to say that it is a self-evident *a priori* proposition, nor that it is deducible from any such proposition. Hence he must hold that it is a product of inductive inference. But what sort of inductive inference? In ascertaining particular causal laws the method recommended by Mill is that of elimination, as will be seen in the next section. But the method, or rather methods, of experimental inquiry by the process of elimination presuppose the truth of the law of causation. Hence it can hardly be itself established by this process. And this means that we have to fall back on induction by simple enumeration. That is to say, we find in ordinary experience that every event has a cause. And when we come to the scientific study of Nature, we already believe in and expect to find causal connections.

It can hardly be denied, I think, that Mill is in rather a difficult position. On the one hand he wishes to say that the law of causation is a universal and certain truth which validates scientific inference. And he maintains that induction by simple enumeration becomes more and more certain in proportion as the sphere of observation is widened. Hence 'the most universal class of truths, the law of causation for instance, and the principles of number and of geometry, are duly and satisfactorily proved by that method alone, nor are they susceptible of any other proof'.[5] The law of causation 'stands at the head of all observed uniformities, in point of universality, and therefore (if the preceding observations are

---

[1] *Logic*, I, p. 392 (I, 3, 5, 6).   [2] *Ibid.*, I, p. 378 (I, 3, 5, 2).
[3] Mill recognizes in the universe 'permanent causes', natural agents which precede all human experience and of whose origin we are ignorant.
[4] *Logic*, I, p. 400 (I, 3, 5, 8).   [5] *Ibid.*, II, p. 102 (II, 3, 21, 3).

correct) in point of certainty'.[1] Again, 'the law of cause and effect, being thus certain, is capable of imparting its certainty to all other inductive propositions which can be deduced from it'.[2] On the other hand Mill maintains that induction by simple enumeration is fallible. True, the certainty of the law of causation is 'for all practical purposes complete'.[3] At the same time 'the uniformity in the succession of events, otherwise called the law of causation, must be received not as a law of the universe, but of that portion of it only which is within the range of our means of sure observation, with a reasonable degree of extension to adjust cases. To extend it further is to make a supposition without evidence, and to which, in the absence of any ground of experience for estimating its degree of probability, it would be idle to attempt to assign any.'[4]

The upshot seems to be more or less this. In ordinary experience we find that events have causes. And experience, together with the operation of the laws of the association of ideas, can explain our undoubting assurance in the universal validity of the law of causation. And the law can thus fulfil, in regard to scientific inference, the function which Mill assigns to the major premiss in a syllogism. That is to say, it is at once a record of past experience and a prediction of what we are to expect. It is a rule or formula for scientific induction. Moreover, scientific inference always confirms the law of causation and never falsifies it. If we in fact arrive at a wrong conclusion and assert that A is the cause of C when it is not, we eventually find that something else, say B, is the cause of C, not that C is uncaused. Hence for all practical purposes the law of causation is certain, and we can safely rely on it. But from the purely theoretical point of view we are not entitled to say that it infallibly holds good in regions of the universe which lie outside all human experience.

If it is objected that Mill clearly wishes to attribute to the law of causation an absolute certainty which enables it to constitute the absolutely sure foundation of scientific inference, the objection can be conceded. 'That every fact which begins to exist has a cause . . . may be taken for certain. The whole of the present facts are the infallible result of all past facts, and more immediately of all facts which existed at the moment previous. Here, then, is a great sequence, which we know to be uniform. If the whole prior

[1] *Ibid.*, II, p. 103 (II, 3, 21, 3).   [2] *Ibid.*, II, p. 104 (II, 3, 21, 3).
[3] *Ibid.*, II, p. 106 (II, 3, 21, 4).   [4] *Ibid.*, II, p. 108 (II, 3, 21, 4).

state of the entire universe could again recur, it would again be followed by the present state.'[1] But though Mill may believe in the universality and infallibility of the law of causation, the point is that on his premisses he has no adequate justification for his belief. And, as we have seen, he finds himself compelled to recognize this fact.

7. Mill is very far from thinking that empiricism, in the sense of mere observation, can do much to advance scientific knowledge. Nor does he think that experimentalism, in the sense of the making of controlled experiments, constitutes the whole of scientific method. He is conscious that the function of hypotheses is 'one which must be reckoned absolutely indispensable in science. . . . Without such assumptions, science could never have attained its present state; they are necessary steps in the progress to something more certain; and nearly everything which is now theory was once hypothesis.'[2] Nor, of course, does he pass over the role of deduction. 'To the Deductive Method, thus characterized in its three constituent parts, Induction, Ratiocination and Verification, the human mind is indebted for its most conspicuous triumphs in the investigation of Nature.'[3] As attention is generally concentrated on Mill's methods of experimental inquiry, of which a brief account will shortly be given, it is as well to recognize from the outset that the experimentalism which he contrasts with mere empiricism does not involve a total blindness to the actual nature of scientific method.

A distinction is made by Mill between purely descriptive and explanatory hypotheses. Take the bare assertion that the orbits of the planets are ellipses. This merely describes the movements of the planets without offering any causal explanation. And if the hypothesis is verified, this is the only proof of its truth which is required. 'In all these cases, verification is proof; if the supposition accords with the phenomena there needs no other evidence of it.'[4] But in the case of explanatory hypotheses the situation is different. Let us suppose that from hypothesis X we deduce that if the hypothesis is true, phenomena a, b and c should occur in certain given circumstances. And let us suppose that the prediction is verified. The verification does not prove the truth of X; for the same consequences might also be deducible from hypotheses Y and Z. We are then faced with three possible causes. And in order to

---

[1] *Logic*, I, p. 437 (I, 3, 7, I).
[2] *Ibid.*, II, pp. 16–17 (II, 3, 14, 5).
[3] *Ibid.*, I, p. 538 (I, 3, 11, 3).
[4] *Ibid.*, II, p. 15 (II, 3, 14, 4).

discover the true one we have to eliminate two. When this has been done, what was originally an hypothesis becomes a law of Nature. The implied view of physical science is clearly realistic. Mill speaks as though we already know that Nature is uniform, in the sense that 'the whole of the present facts are the infallible result of all past facts'.[1] But when we contemplate Nature, we are not immediately presented with particular uniformities. And no amount of mere observation will enable us to resolve general uniformity into particular uniformities. For 'the order of Nature, as perceived at a first glance, presents at every instant a chaos followed by another chaos'.[2] In other words, when we look for the cause of a given event, we are faced with a plurality of *prima facie* causes or of possible causes; and observation alone will not enable us to determine the true cause. Nor for the matter of that will purely mental analysis or reasoning. Reasoning is indeed indispensable. For in science we have to form hypotheses and deduce their consequences. But an hypothesis cannot be turned into a law of Nature unless alternative possibilities are eliminated. And this requires methods of experimental inquiry. Obviously, all this presupposes the existence of an objective uniformity of Nature, and so of real causal laws waiting to be discovered. Given the empiricist aspects of Mill's thought, we cannot indeed prove the general uniformity of Nature except *a posteriori* and progressively, in proportion as we discover factual causal connections. But this does not alter the fact that Mill is clearly convinced that there are such connections to be discovered. And this is doubtless why he tends to speak, as we have seen, as though the general uniformity of Nature can be known in advance of the scientific discovery of particular causal laws.

Mill gives four methods of experimental inquiry. The first two methods are respectively those of agreement and disagreement. The canon or regulating principle of the method of agreement states that 'if two or more instances of the phenomenon under investigation have only one circumstance in common, the circumstance in which alone all the instances agree is the cause (or effect) of the given phenomenon'.[3] The canon of the method of disagreement states that if we consider a case in which the phenomenon under investigation occurs and a case in which it does not occur, and if we find that the two cases have all circumstances in common save one, which is present only in the former case, this one

---

[1] *Ibid.*, I, p. 437 (I, 3, 7, I).   [2] *Ibid.*   [3] *Ibid.*, I, p. 451 (I, 3, 8, I).

circumstance is the effect or the cause, or an indispensable part of the cause, of the phenomenon in question. Both methods are obviously methods of elimination, the first resting on the axiom that whatever can be eliminated is not connected by any causal law with the occurrence of the phenomenon under investigation, the second on the axiom that whatever cannot be eliminated is so connected. And Mill combines the two methods in the joint method of agreement and disagreement.[1]

The canon of the third experimental method, the method of residues, is stated as follows. 'Subduct from any phenomenon such part as is known by previous inductions to be the effect of certain antecedents, and the residue of the phenomenon is the effect of the remaining antecedents.'[2] The fourth method, that of concomitant variations, is especially used in cases where artificial experiment is not practicable. Its canon declares that whatever phenomenon varies whenever another phenomenon varies in a given manner is either a cause of this phenomenon or its effect or connected with it through some causal fact. For example, if we find that variations in the moon's position are always followed by corresponding variations in the tides, we are entitled to conclude that the moon is the cause, total or partial, which determines the tides, even though we are obviously not able to remove the moon and see what happens in its absence.

Now, Mill does indeed speak as though his four methods of experimental inquiry, which he regards as 'the only possible modes of experimental inquiry',[3] were methods of discovery. And it has been sometimes objected that they are in reality only ways of checking the validity of scientific hypotheses which have been worked out by other means. But in justice to Mill it must be added that he insists more on the status of the methods as methods of proof than on their function as possible methods of discovery. 'If discoveries are ever made by observation and experiment without Deduction, the four methods are methods of discovery: but even if they were not methods of discovery, it would not be the less true that they are the sole methods of Proof; and in that character even the results of deduction are amenable to them.'[4]

Mill recognizes, of course, that experimentation has a limited field of application. In astronomy we cannot perform the experiments which we can perform in chemistry. And the same is more

---

[1] *Logic*, I, p. 458 (I, 3, 8, 4).　　[2] *Ibid.*, I, p. 460 (I, 3, 8, 5).
[3] *Ibid.*, I, p. 470 (I, 3, 8, 7).　　[4] *Ibid.*, I, p. 502 (I, 3, 9, 6).

or less true of psychology and sociology. Hence the method of these sciences, 'in order to accomplish anything worthy of attainment, must be to a great extent, if not principally deductive'.[1] But his general principle is that 'observation without experiment (supposing no aid from deduction) can ascertain sequences and coexistences, but cannot prove causation'.[2] And the four methods mentioned above are the methods of proof, the methods of turning an hypothesis into an assured causal law. Mill is therefore not prepared to accept the view, which he attributes to Whewell, that in the absence of empirical falsification we should be content to let an hypothesis stand until a simpler hypothesis, equally consistent with the empirical facts, presents itself. In his opinion absence of falsification is by no means the only proof of physical laws which is required. And for this reason he insists on the use of the methods of experimental inquiry, whenever this is practicable.

Does Mill succeed in justifying inductive inference from the observed to the unobserved, from the known to the unknown? If we concentrate attention on his explicit assertion that all inference is from particulars to particulars, and if we take it that particulars are all entirely separate entities (that is, if we concentrate attention on the nominalist elements in Mill's thought), a negative answer must be given. Mill might, of course, have tried to work out a theory of probability. But in the absence of such a theory he would perhaps have done best to say that science is justified by its success and requires no further theoretical justification. At the same time we can say that he does provide such a justification. But he provides it only by assuming that throughout Nature there is a structure of real uniformities which are something more than purely factual sequences. In other words, he justifies scientific inference by assuming a realist position and forgetting the implications of nominalism.

8. Hume's programme of extending the reign of science from the study of the non-human material world to man himself, by creating a science of human nature, had found a partial fulfilment in Mill's empiricist predecessors. The associationist psychologists aimed at setting psychology, the study of man's mental life, on a scientific basis. And Bentham thought of himself as developing a science of man's moral life and of man in society. As we have seen, J. S. Mill considered that Bentham's idea of human nature was narrow and short-sighted. And he was well aware that the science

[1] *Ibid.*, I, p. 443 (I, 3, 7, 3).   [2] *Ibid.*, I, p. 446 (I, 3, 7, 4).

of human nature had not made an advance comparable to that made by the physical sciences. Hence for the would-be creator of a logic of the 'moral sciences' it could not be simply a question of stating in abstract and explicit form a method or methods of proof which had already been employed to obtain impressive concrete results. His work must be necessarily in large measure tentative, a pointing out of a path to be followed in the future rather than a reflection on a road already traversed. But in any case it was natural that Mill should lay emphasis on the need for developing a logic of the moral sciences. I do not intend to imply that he was influenced exclusively by his British predecessors. For French social philosophy was also a stimulative factor. But, given the general movement of thought, it was natural that a man who wished to work out a logic of inductive inference and who was at the same time deeply interested in social thought and reform, should include man in society in the field of his reflections about scientific method.

The sixth book of the *System of Logic* is entitled 'On the Logic of the Moral Sciences'. By the moral sciences Mill means those branches of study which deal with man, provided that they are neither strictly normative in character nor classifiable as parts of physical science. The first condition excludes practical ethics or 'morality', that is, ethics in so far as it is expressed in the imperative mood. 'The imperative mood is the characteristic of art, as distinguished from science.'[1] The second condition excludes consideration of states of mind in so far as they are considered as caused immediately by bodily states. Study of the laws governing the relations between states of mind belongs to psychology as a moral science; but study of the laws governing sensations regarded as proximately dependent on physical conditions belongs to physiology, which is a natural science. Provided that we bear in mind these qualifications, we can say that the moral sciences include psychology, ethology or the science of the formation of character,[2] sociology and history, though the science of history is really part of general sociology, the science of man in society.

What is needed, in Mill's opinion, is to rescue the moral sciences from 'empiricism'. That is to say, purely empirical descriptive laws must be turned into explanatory or causal laws or deduced from such laws. We may, for example, have observed that in all

---

[1] *Logic*, II, p. 546 (II, 6, 12, 1).
[2] The study of the formation of national character had been suggested, for example, by Montesquieu.

known cases human beings behave in a certain way in certain circumstances. We then state in a generalized form that human beings behave in this way. But mere observation of a certain number of instances does not really provide us with any reliable assurance that the empirical law holds universally. Such assurance can be provided only by ascertaining the cause or causes which determine human behaviour under given conditions. And it is only by ascertaining such causal connections that a genuine science of human nature can be developed. It does not follow, of course, that we can always ascertain exact laws in practice. But this at least is the ideal. Thus once more, in the distinction between empiricism and science we see evidence of Mill's firm belief in the existence of objective causal connections waiting to be discovered.

The subject-matter of psychology as a moral science is 'the uniformities of succession, the laws, whether ultimate or derivative, according to which one mental state succeeds another; is caused by, or at least is caused to follow, another'.[1] These laws are those of the association of ideas, which have been ascertained, and in Mill's opinion could only be ascertained, by the methods of experimental inquiry. Hence psychology is 'altogether, or principally, a science of observation and experiment'.[2]

When, however, in ethology we turn to the formation of character, especially national character, there is little room for experiment. But mere observation is not sufficient to establish ethology as a science. Hence its method must be 'altogether deductive'.[3] That is to say, it must presuppose psychology, and its principles must be deduced from the general laws of psychology, while the already accepted empirical laws relating to the formation of character, individual or national, must be shown to be derivable from, and hence to function as verifications of, these principles. Moreover, once the principles of ethology have been firmly established, the way will lie open for the development of a corresponding art, namely that of practical education, which will be able to make use of the principles with a view to producing desirable effects or preventing undesirable effects.

Social science, the science of man in society, studies 'the actions of collective masses of mankind, and the various phenomena which constitute social life'.[4] It includes, of course, the study of politics. In social science or sociology, as in ethology, the making

---

[1] *Logic*, II, p. 439 (II, 6, 4, 3).
[3] *Ibid.*
[2] *Ibid.*, II, p. 458 (II, 6, 5, 5).
[4] *Ibid.*, II, p. 464 (II, 6, 6, 1).

of artificial experiments is impracticable, while mere observation is not sufficient to create a science. At the same time the deductive method as practised in geometry does not provide an appropriate model. Bentham, indeed, endeavoured to deduce a social-political theory from one principle, namely that men always seek their own interests. But in point of fact it is not always true that men are always governed in their actions by selfish interests. Nor, for that matter, is it universally true that they are governed by altruistic motives. In general, social phenomena are too complex and are the results of too many diverse factors for it to be possible to deduce them from one principle. If he is seeking a model of method, the sociologist should look not to geometry but to physical science. For the physical scientist allows for a variety of causes contributing to the production of an effect, and so for a variety of laws.

Mill emphasizes the utility in social science of what he calls the inverse deductive or historical method. In employing this method the sociologist does not deduce conclusions *a priori* from laws and then verify them by observation. He first obtains the conclusions, as approximate empirical generalizations, from experience and then connects them 'with the principles of human nature by *a priori* reasonings, which reasonings are thus a real Verification'.[1] This idea was borrowed, as Mill frankly acknowledges, from Auguste Comte. 'This was an idea entirely new to me when I found it in Comte: and but for him I might not soon (if ever) have arrived at it.'[2]

But while he emphasizes the utility of the inverse deductive method Mill is not prepared to allow that it is the only method suitable for employment in sociology. For we can also make use of the direct deductive method, provided that we recognize its limitations. For example, if we know that X is a law of human nature, we can deduce that human beings will tend to act in a certain manner. But we cannot know and positively predict that they will act in this way in concrete fact. For we cannot know in advance, or at any rate only rarely, all the other causal agents at work, which may counteract the operation of the cause which we have in mind or combine with it to produce an effect rather different from that which would be produced if there were no other causal agents. However, the direct deductive method

---

[1] *Logic*, II, p. 490 (II, 6, 9, 1). That is to say, the empirical generalizations are verified by ascertaining whether they follow from known general principles relating to human nature.

[2] *Autobiography*, p. 211.

undoubtedly has its own use in predicting tendencies to action.
And this is of value for practical politics. Further, it is especially
fitted for use in a science such as political economy which 'considers mankind as occupied solely in acquiring and consuming
wealth'.[1] Obviously, this is not all that mankind does. But the
point is that the more simplified a view of man we take, the more
scope can we attribute to the direct deductive method. Conversely, the more complex the situation considered, the more we
have to turn to the inverse deductive method.

In sociology Mill follows Comte in making a distinction between
social statics and dynamics. The former is concerned with ascertaining and verifying uniformities of coexistence in society. That
is to say, it investigates the mutual actions and reactions of con-
temporaneous social phenomena, abstracting, as far as possible,
from the continuous process of change which is always, if gradually,
modifying the whole complex of phenomena. Social dynamics,
however, studies society considered as being in a constant state of
movement or change, and it tries to explain the historical
sequences of social conditions. But though we can ascertain some
general laws of historical change or progress, we cannot predict
the rate of progress. For one thing, we cannot predict the appearance of those exceptional individuals who exercise a marked
influence on the course of history.

In this connection Mill refers to Macaulay's essay on Dryden
and criticizes the view, there expressed, of the comparative
inoperativeness of great historical individuals. We cannot legitimately assume, for example, that without Socrates, Plato and
Aristotle European philosophy would have developed as it did, or
even that it would have developed at all. Nor can we justifiably
assume that if Newton had not lived his natural philosophy would
have been worked out practically just as soon by someone else.
It is a complete mistake to suppose that the truth that all human
volitions and actions are caused, entails the conclusion that out-
standingly gifted individuals cannot exercise an exceptional
influence.

Obviously, Mill's conception of social science as involving the
explanation of human behaviour in terms of causal laws presupposes the predictability in principle of all human volitions and
actions. This subject has already been touched on in connection
with Mill's ethical theory. But he insists that this predictability is

[1] *Logic*, II, p. 496 (II, 6, 9, 3).

not to be confused with 'fatalism', when fatalism is understood as meaning that the human will is of no account in determining the cause of events. For the human will is itself a cause, and a powerful one.[1] Further, in sociology we have to steer a middle course between thinking that no definite causal laws can be ascertained and imagining that it is possible to predict the course of history. Social laws are hypothetical, and statistically-based generalizations by their very nature admit of exceptions.

Mill does indeed express his belief that with the progress of civilization collective agencies tend to predominate more and more, and that in proportion as this happens prediction becomes easier. But he is thinking, for example, of the difference between a society in which much depends on the caprices of an individual, the absolute monarch, and a society in which the people at large expresses its will through universal suffrage. In other words, empirical generalizations have a greater predictive power when we are dealing with men in the mass than when we are dealing with the individual agent.[2] True, one of the main aims of social science is to connect these empirical generalizations with the laws of human nature. But the situation is too complex for it to be possible to predict infallibly the course of history, even if, in Mill's opinions, changes in human society have made it easier to approximate to a science of history or of social dynamics.

9. Mill's whole conception of the sciences, whether physical or moral, obviously presupposes the existence of the external world. And we can now turn to his discussion of the grounds of our belief in such a world, a discussion which is carried on for the most part within the framework of his criticism of Sir William Hamilton's philosophy.

Hamilton maintained that in perception we have an immediate knowledge of the ego and the non-ego, of the self and of something existing which is external to the self. Mill, however, while readily admitting that we have, as Hume claimed, a natural belief in the existence of an external world, endeavours to show how this belief can be psychologically explained without its being necessary

[1] Mill can, of course, evade fatalism, if fatalism is understood as omitting the human will from the chain of operative causes. At the same time if, given the antecedent conditions, a human volition cannot be otherwise than it is, it is difficult to see how he can evade fatalism if this is understood as synonymous with rejection of liberty of indifference.,

[2] For instance, statistically-based generalizations may enable us to predict the approximate number of people in a given county who will post letters incorrectly addressed. But the statistician is not in a position to say which individual citizens will be guilty of this oversight.

to suppose that it expresses an original datum of consciousness. He makes two postulates. The first is that the mind is capable of expectation, while the second is the validity of the associationist psychology. On the basis of these two postulates he argues that there are associations 'which, supposing no intuition of an external world to have existed in consciousness, would inevitably generate the belief in a permanent external world, and would cause it to be regarded as an intuition'.[1]

Let us suppose that I have certain visual and tactual sensations which produce in my mind an association of ideas. For example, when sitting at the table in my study, I have those visual sensations which I call seeing the table and the tactual sensations which I call touching or feeling the table. And an association is set up such that when I have a visual sensation of this kind, a tactual sensation is present as a possibility. Conversely, when I have only a tactual sensation, as when the room is completely dark, a visual sensation is there as a possibility. Further, when I leave the room and later re-enter it, I have similar sensations. Hence an association is formed in my mind of such a kind that when I am out of the room, I am firmly persuaded that, if I were at any moment to re-enter it, I should or could have similar sensations. Further, as these possible sensations form a group, and as moreover the group is found to enter into various causal relations, I inevitably think of the permanent possibilities of sensations as an abiding physical object. Actual sensations are transient and fugitive. But the possibilities of sensation, associated as a group, remain. Hence we come to distinguish between sensations and physical objects. But the ground of our belief in these external objects is the existence of different mutually associated clusters or groups of possible sensations, these groups being permanent in comparison with actual sensations.[2]

A further point. We find that the permanent possibilities of sensation which we think of as physical objects 'belong as much to other human or sentient beings as to ourselves',[3] though they certainly do not experience the same actual sensations as we do. And this puts the final seal to our belief in a common external world.

---

[1] *Examination*, p. 192.
[2] Obviously, in the illustration which has just been given of someone sitting at a table, a belief in the existence of an external world is already present. But it can serve to show the general line of Mill's psychological reconstruction of the belief.
[3] *Examination*, p. 196.

Now, Mill's theory, as so far outlined, might possibly be taken as being simply a psychological account of the genesis of a belief. That is to say, it might be understood as being free from any ontological commitment, as not involving any statement about the ontological nature of physical objects. In point of fact, however, Mill proceeds to define matter as 'a Permanent Possibility of Sensation',[1] bodies being groups of simultaneous possibilities of sensation. To be sure, he remarks that it is a question of defining matter rather than of denying its existence. But he makes it clear that he, like 'all Berkeleians',[2] believes in matter only in the sense of this definition, a definition which, he claims, includes the whole meaning which ordinary people attach to the term, whatever some philosophers and theologians may have done. Hence Mill clearly commits himself to an ontological statement.

The definition of matter as a permanent possibility of sensation is, however, ambiguous. For it easily suggests the idea of a permanent ground of possible sensations, a ground which is itself unknowable. And if this were what Mill intended to imply, a rift would inevitably be introduced between the world of science and the underlying physical reality. Scientific truths would relate to phenomena, not to things-in-themselves. But though he remarks elsewhere that 'all matter apart from the feelings of sentient beings has but an hypothetical and unsubstantial existence: it is a mere assumption to account for our sensations',[3] he makes it clear that he does not intend to assert the validity of this hypothesis.

Of course, if we interpret Mill on the lines on which Berkeley is often interpreted, namely as saying simply that material things are simply what we perceive and can perceive them to be, and that there is no unknowable substratum as postulated by Locke, the nature of science, as depicted by Mill, does not appear to be affected. But though it is doubtless part of what Mill means, as is shown by his conviction that in defining matter as he does he is on the side of the common man, the fact remains that he speaks of material things as 'sensations'. Thus he says, for example, that 'the brain, just as much as the mental functions, is, like matter

---

[1] *Examination*, p. 198.
[2] *Ibid.* Needless to say, Mill does not accept the theological conclusions which Berkeley drew from his theory of material things as 'ideas'. But he regards his own analysis of what it means to say that there are material things which continue to exist even when unperceived, as being substantially the same as that given by the good bishop.
[3] *Three Essays on Religion*, p. 86 (1904 edition).

itself, merely a set of human sensations either actual or inferred as possible—namely, those which the anatomist has when he opens the skull. . . .'[1] And from this it appears to follow that physical science inquires into the relations between sensations, principally, of course, possible sensations, but still sensations. Indeed, Mill himself speaks of causal relations or constant sequences as being found to exist between sets of possible sensations.

It is understandable that later empiricists have endeavoured to avoid this conclusion by forbearing from saying that material things *are* sensations or sense-data. Instead they have contented themselves with claiming that a sentence in which a physical or material object is mentioned can in principle be translated into other sentences in which only sense-data are mentioned, the relation between the original sentence and the translation being such that if the former is true (or false), the latter is true (or false), and conversely. The question whether this claim has been made good need not detain us here.[2] The point is that, as far as Mill himself is concerned, he speaks in such a way that the subject-matter of physical science is human sensations.

This, however, is a very difficult position to maintain. Let us suppose that sensations are to be understood as subjective states. This would make great difficulties in regard to Mill's account of the genesis of our belief in an external world, as outlined above. For instance, Mill says that we 'find' that there are possibilities of sensation which are common to other people as well as to ourselves. But other people will be for me simply permanent possibilities of sensation. And if the word 'sensation' is understood in terms of a subjective state, it seems to follow that other people, and indeed everything else, are reduced to my subjective states. As for science, this would become a study of the relations between my sensations. But is it credible that if an anatomist looks at a human brain, the object of his examination is simply a set of his own subjective states, actual and possible? In short, the logical result of defining physical objects in terms of sensations, when sensation is understood as a subjective state, is solipsism. And nobody really believes that solipsism is true.

It may be objected that Mill never intended to say that science

[1] *Ibid.*, p. 85.
[2] It is widely recognized that the only sufficient proof of the possibility of such a translation would be to perform it, and that no adequate translation has in fact been made.

is simply concerned with subjective states in any ordinary sense of the term. And the objection is obviously valid. It is perfectly clear that Mill had no intention of maintaining that the whole physical world consisted of his, Mill's, sensations in a subjective sense. But then we must either reify sensations, turning them into public physical objects, or we must assume that to say that a physical object is a permanent possibility of sensations is to say that a physical object is that which is capable of causing sensations in a sentient subject. The first alternative would be a very peculiar thesis, while the second would tend to reintroduce the concept of things-in-themselves and the rift between the world of science and physical reality to which allusion has already been made.

The fact of the matter is that after showing, to his own satisfaction at least, how our belief in the external world can be explained genetically in terms of the association of ideas, Mill slides into ontological assertions without really considering their implications in regard to the nature of physical science. And it seems clear to the present writer at any rate that Mill's empiricist analysis of the physical object is not really compatible with the realist conception of science which underlies his doctrine about causal laws.

10. Mill was obviously predisposed by the empiricist tradition to give an analogous analysis of the concept of the mind. 'We have no conception of Mind itself, as distinguished from its conscious manifestations. We neither know nor can imagine it, except as represented by the succession of manifold feelings which metaphysicians call by the name of States or Modifications of Mind.'[1] It is quite true, of course, that we tend to speak of the mind as something permanent in comparison with changing mental states. But if there were no special factor in the situation to be considered, we could perfectly well define the mind as a permanent possibility of mental states.

In point of fact, however, the phenomenalistic analysis of the mind presents special difficulties. For 'if we speak of the Mind as a series of feelings, we are obliged to complete the statement by calling it a series of feelings which is aware of itself as past and

---

[1] *Examination*, p. 205. According to Mill's use of the term, metaphysics is 'that portion of mental philosophy which attempts to determine what part of the furniture of the mind belongs to it originally, and what part is constructed out of materials furnished to it from without'. *Logic*, I, p. 7 (I, *Introduction*, 4). For the use of the term 'feeling' see reference on p. 21 to James Mill's use of the word.

future'.[1] And how can the series be aware of itself as a series? We have no reason to suppose that the material thing enjoys self-consciousness. But the mind certainly does.

But though he draws attention to this difficulty and admits that language suggests the irreducibility of the mind to the series of mental phenomena, Mill is unwilling to sacrifice phenomenalism. Hence he is compelled to hold that the series of feelings, as he puts it, can be aware of itself as a series, even though he is admittedly unable to explain how this is possible. 'I think, by far the wisest thing we can do, is to accept the inexplicable fact, without any theory of how it takes place; and when we are obliged to speak of it in terms which assume a theory, to use them with a reservation as to their meaning.'[2]

In connection with the analysis of the concept of mind Mill raises the question of solipsism. According to Reid, he remarks, I have no evidence at all of the existence of other selves if I am but a series of feelings or a thread of consciousness. My so-called awareness of other selves is simply an awareness of my own private feelings. But this line of argument, Mill contends, is 'one of Reid's most palpable mistakes'.[3] For one thing, even if I believe that my own mind is a series of feelings, there is nothing to prevent my conceiving other minds as similar series of feelings. For another thing, I have inferential evidence of the existence of minds other than my own, as the following line of reflection shows.

Modifications in the permanent possibility of sensations which I call my body evoke in me actual sensations and mental states which form part of the series which I call my mind. But I am aware of the existence of other permanent possibilities of sensations which are not related to my mental life in this way. And at the same time I am aware of actions and other external signs in these permanent possibilities of sensation or bodies, which I am warranted in interpreting as signs or expressions of inner mental states analogous to my own.

The view that we know the existence of other minds by inference from overt bodily behaviour is common enough. The trouble is, however, that Mill has already analysed bodies in terms of sensations. Obviously, he never intended to say or to imply that another person's body is simply and solely a group of *my* sensations, actual and possible. But he has at any rate to meet the objection that I am aware of another person's body only through

---

[1] *Examination*, p. 212.   [2] *Ibid.*, p. 213.   [3] *Ibid.*, p. 207.

my sensations, and that if the body is defined in terms of sensations, he must admit either that these sensations are mine or that sensations can exist on their own or that a body is a ground of possible sensations. In the first case solipsism is the logical conclusion. In the second case we are presènted with a very peculiar thesis. In the third case, as has already been noted, the phenomenalistic analysis of the material thing collapses. And as, on Mill's own explicit admission, there is a special difficulty in the phenomenalistic analysis of mind, this is *a fortiori* subject to doubt.

Solipsism has proved the haunting spectre of phenomenalism. It is not that phenomenalists have actually embraced solipsism. For they have done nothing of the kind. The difficulty has been rather that of stating phenomenalism in such a way that it leads neither to a solipsistic conclusion on the one hand nor to an implicit abandonment of phenomenalism on the other. Perhaps the most successful attempt to state the phenomenalist position has been the modern linguistic version, to which reference was made in the previous section. But this can easily appear as an evasion of critical problems. At the same time, if we once start looking for hidden substrates, we shall find ourselves in other difficulties. And one can sympathize with the down-to-earth common-sense approach of some recent devotees of the cult of ordinary language. The trouble is, however, that once we have brought things back to ordinary language, the familiar philosophical problems tend to start up all over again.

11. Mill, as was mentioned in the sketch of his life, was brought up by his father without any religious beliefs. But he did not share James Mill's marked hostility to religion as inherently detrimental to morality. Hence he was more open to considering evidence for the existence of God. Of the ontological argument in its Cartesian form he remarks that it 'is not likely to satisfy anyone in the present day'.[1] And as he regarded the causal relation as being essentially a relation between phenomena, it is not surprising that he argues with Hume and Kant that 'the First Cause argument is in itself of no value for the establishment of Theism'.[2] But he is prepared to give serious consideration to the argument from design in Nature, as this is 'an argument of a really scientific character, which does not shrink from scientific tests, but claims

[1] *Three Essays on Religion*, p. 70. This work will be referred to as *Three Essays*.
[2] *Ibid.*, p. 67.

to be judged by the established canons of Induction. The design argument is wholly grounded on experience.'[1] Whether any argument to a metaphenomenal reality can properly be called a 'scientific' argument is open to question. But Mill's main point is that even if the argument from design in Nature concludes with affirming the existence of a divine being which in itself transcends the reach of scientific inquiry, it bases itself on empirical facts in a manner which is easily understood and makes an inference, the validity of which is open to reasonable discussion.

Paley's form of the argument will not do. It is true that if we found a watch on a desert island, we should indeed infer that it had been left there by a human being. But we should do so simply because we already know by experience that watches are made and carried by human beings. We do not, however, have previous experience of natural objects being made by God. We argue by analogy. That is to say, we argue from resemblances between phenomena which we already know to be products of human design and other phenomena which we then attribute to the productive work of a supramundane intelligence.

It must be added, however, that the argument from design in Nature rests on a special resemblance, namely the working together of various factors to one common end. For instance, the argument infers the operation of a supramundane intelligence from the arrangement and structure of the various parts of the visual apparatus which together produce sight. We cannot indeed exclude all other explanations of such phenomena. Hence the argument cannot lead to a conclusion which possesses more than some degree of probability. But the argument is none the less a reasonable inductive inference.[2] 'I think it must be allowed that, in the present state of our knowledge, the adaptations in Nature afford a large balance of probability in favour of creation by intelligence.'[3]

In Mill's opinion, however, we cannot accept the existence of God as a probable truth and at the same time affirm the divine omnipotence. For design implies the adaptation of means to an end, and the need to employ means reveals a limitation of power. 'Every indication of Design in the Kosmos is so much evidence against the omnipotence of the designer.'[4]

---

[1] *Ibid.*, p. 72.
[2] Mill does not think that an account of the matter simply in terms of the survival of the fittest is at all conclusive.
[3] *Three Essays*, p. 75. [4] *Ibid.*

This does not seem to me a very telling argument. For though the argument from design, taken by itself, concludes simply with assertion of the existence of a designer, not a creator, this does not show that the designer is not the creator. And it is difficult to see how the mere fact of using means to an end is any argument against omnipotence. But Mill's chief interest lies elsewhere, namely in arguing that there is an evident incompatibility between asserting at the same time that God is omnipotent and infinitely good. And this is a much more impressive line of argument.

Mill's point is that if God is omnipotent, he can prevent evil, and that if he does not do so, he cannot be infinitely good. It is no use saying with Dean Mansel that the term 'good' is predicated of God analogically and not in the same sense in which it is used of human beings. For this is really equivalent to saying that God is not good in any sense which we can give to the term. In fine, if we wish to maintain that God is good, we must also say that his power is limited or finite.

Mill is prepared to admit the reasonableness of believing that God desires the happiness of man. For this is suggested by the fact that pleasure seems to result from the normal functioning of the human organism and pain from some interference with this functioning. At the same time we can hardly suppose that God created the universe for the sole purpose of making men happy. Appearances suggest that if there is an intelligent creator, he has other motives besides the happiness of mankind, or of sentient beings in general, and that these other motives, whatever they may be, are of greater importance to him.

In other words, natural theology does not carry us very far. It is not indeed unreasonable, at least in the present state of the evidence, to believe in an intelligent divine being of limited power. But the proper attitude to adopt is what Mill calls a rational scepticism, which is more than sheer agnosticism but less than firm assent.

This might be all very well if those who are really interested in the question of the existence of God were concerned simply and solely with finding an explanatory hypothesis. But it is quite evident that they are not. For a religious person belief in the existence of God is not quite like belief that the architect of St. Paul's Cathedral was Sir Christopher Wren. And Mill sees this to the limited extent of raising the question of the pragmatic value or utility of religion. While recognizing that much evil has been done in the name of religion and that some religious beliefs can be detrimental to human conduct, he is not prepared to subscribe to his father's view that religion is 'the greatest enemy of morality'.[1] For religion, like poetry, can supply man with ideals beyond those which we actually find realized in human life. 'The value, therefore, of religion to the individual, both in the past and present, as a source of personal satisfaction and of elevated feelings, is not to be disputed.'[2] And in Christianity we find a conception of ideal goodness embodied in the figure of Christ.

To be sure, some people look on any suggestion that the pragmatic value of religion provides a reason for believing in God as an immoral suggestion, a betrayal of our duty to pay attention simply to the weight of the empirical evidence. But though this point of view is understandable, Mill does at any rate see that the function of religion in human history is something more than the solving of an intellectual puzzle in terms of an inductive hypothesis.

At the same time Mill raises the question whether the moral uplift of the higher religions cannot be preserved without belief in a supernatural Being. And as far as the provision of an ideal object of emotion and desire is concerned, he suggests that the 'need is fulfilled by the Religion of Humanity in as eminent a degree, and in as high a sense, as by the supernatural religions even in their best manifestations, and far more so than in any of the others'.[3] True, some religions have the advantage of holding out the prospect of immortality. But as the conditions of this life improve and men grow happier and more capable of deriving happiness from unselfish action, human beings, Mill thinks, 'will care less and less for this flattering expectation'.[4] However, if we include in the religion of humanity that belief in the existence of a God of limited power which natural theology justifies as a probable truth, it superadds to other inducements for working for the welfare of our fellow men the conviction that 'we may be co-operating with the unseen Being to whom we owe all that is enjoyable in life'.[5] Hence even if the religion of humanity is destined to be the religion of the future, this does not necessarily exclude belief in God.

Mill is thus in agreement with Auguste Comte that the so-called

---

[1] *Autobiography*, p. 40.   [2] *Three Essays*, p. 48.   [3] *Ibid.*, p. 50.
[4] *Ibid.*, p. 54. Mill maintains that while science does not provide any cogent evidence against immortality, there is no positive evidence in favour of it.
[5] *Ibid.*, p. 108.

religion of humanity is the religion of the future, though he has no sympathy with Comte's fantastic proposals for the organization of this religion. At the same time he does not rule out belief in a finite God with whom man can co-operate. And though his idea of religion is clearly not such as to satisfy Kierkegaard or indeed anyone who understands religion as involving absolute self-commitment to the personal Absolute, he does not think, like some empiricists before him, that religion can be disposed of either by a psychological account of the way in which religious belief could have arisen or by drawing attention to the evils which have been done in the name of religion. Though his empiricist premisses actually determine his evaluation of the force of the arguments for God's existence, he endeavours to keep an open mind. And though he regarded the evidence as amounting 'only to one of the lower degrees of probability',[1] when the *Three Essays on Religion* were published posthumously in 1874 some surprise was felt in positivist circles at the extent to which Mill made concessions to theism. He had travelled at any rate a modest distance beyond the point at which his father had stopped.

[1] *Three Essays*, p. 102.

CHAPTER IV

EMPIRICISTS, AGNOSTICS, POSITIVISTS

Alexander Bain and the associationist psychology—Bain on utilitarianism—Henry Sidgwick's combination of utilitarianism and intuitionism—Charles Darwin and the philosophy of evolution—T. H. Huxley; evolution, ethics and agnosticism—Scientific materialism and agnosticism; John Tyndall and Leslie Stephen—G. J. Romanes and religion—Positivism; the Comtist groups, G. H. Lewes, W. K. Clifford, K. Pearson—B. Kidd; concluding remarks.

1. THE associationist psychology was further developed by Alexander Bain (1818-1903), who occupied the chair of logic in the University of Aberdeen from 1860 until 1880. He was of some help to J. S. Mill in the preparation of his *System of Logic*,[1] and prepared some of the psychological notes for Mill's edition of his father's *Analysis of the Phenomena of the Human Mind*. But though he is sometimes described as a disciple of Mill, Mill himself remarks that the younger man did not really stand in need of any predecessor except the common precursors of them both.

Bain was primarily interested in developing empirical psychology as a separate science, rather than in employing the principle of the association of ideas to solve specifically philosophical problems. Further, he was particularly concerned with correlating psychical processes with their physiological bases, and in this respect he continued the interests of Hartley rather than of the two Mills.[2] While, however, his thought remained within the general framework of the associationist psychology,[3] the titles of his chief works, *The Senses and the Intellect* (1855) and *The Emotions and the Will* (1859), show that he extended his field of study from sensation and intellectual activity to the emotive and volitional aspects of human nature.[4] And this shift of emphasis

---

[1] See J. S. Mill's *Autobiography*, p. 245, note.

[2] Though certainly not blind to the relevance of physiological investigations, J. S. Mill, like his father, was chiefly interested in the psychology of consciousness and in its philosophical relevance.

[3] Bain introduced, however, a good many modifications into the associationist psychology as received from his predecessors.

[4] Mind is thus described from the start. 'It has Feeling, in which term I include what is commonly called Sensation and Emotion. It can Act according to Feeling. It can Think.' *The Senses and the Intellect*, p. 1 (1st edition).

enabled him to surmount, to some extent at least, the tendency of associationist psychologists to depict man's mental life as the result of a purely mechanical process.

Bain's emphasis on human activity shows itself, for example, in his account of the genesis of our belief in an external, material world. If we were simply subjects of purely passive sensations, of sensations or impressions, that is to say, considered apart from any activity or putting forth of energy on our part, our waking state of consciousness would resemble the dream-state. In point of fact, however, 'in us sensation is never wholly passive, and in general is much the reverse. Moreover, the tendency to movement exists before the stimulus of sensation; and movement gives a new character to our whole percipient existence'.[1] Impressions received from without arouse movement, activity, the display of energy or force; and 'it is in this exercise of force that we must look for the peculiar feeling of externality of objects'.[2] For instance, in the case of touch, the sense which is the first to make us clearly aware of an external world, 'it is hard contact that suggests externality; and the reason is that in this contact we put forth force of our own'.[3] Reacting to a sensation of touch by muscular exertion, we have a sense of resistance, 'a feeling which is the principal foundation of our notion of externality'.[4] In fine, 'the sense of the external is the consciousness of particular energies and activities of our own';[5] and our external world, the external world as it is presented to our minds, can be described as 'the sum total of all the occasions for putting forth active energy, or for conceiving this as possible to be put forth'.[6] Bain thus defines the external world, as it exists for our consciousness,[7] in terms of possible active responses to sensations rather than, as Mill defined it, of possible sensations.

It is not surprising, therefore, that Bain emphasizes the intimate connection between belief in general and action. 'Belief has no meaning, except in reference to our actions.'[8] Whenever a man, or an animal for the matter of that, performs an action as a means to an end, the action is sustained by a primitive belief or credulity which can be described 'as expectation of some contingent future about to follow on an action'.[9] It is this primitive credulity which leads a sentient being to repeat its successful experiment,

---

[1] *The Senses and the Intellect*, p. 371.   [2] *Ibid.*   [3] *Ibid.*, p. 372.
[4] *Ibid.*   [5] *Ibid.*, p. 371.   [6] *Ibid.*, p. 372.
[7] According to Bain, we cannot even discuss the existence of a material world entirely apart from consciousness.
[8] *The Emotions and the Will*, p. 524 (2nd edition).   [9] *Ibid.*, p. 525.

say of running to a brook to quench its thirst. It does not follow, however, that the force of belief rises gradually from zero to a state of full development in proportion to the length and uniformity of experience. For there is a primitive impulse or tendency to belief, which is derived from the natural activity of the organic system, and the strength of which is proportionate to the strength of the 'will'. 'The creature that wills strongly believes strongly at the origin of its career.'[1] What experience does is to determine the particular forms taken by a primitive impulse which it does not itself generate. And the factor which is of most importance in establishing sound belief is absence of contradiction or factual invariability of sequence, between, that is, expectation and its fulfilment.

If we assume, therefore, our instinctive responses in action to pleasure and pain, we can say that experience, with the inferences which follow on it, is the cardinal factor in stabilizing beliefs. But it is certainly not the only factor which is influential in shaping particular beliefs. For though feeling and emotion do not alter the objective facts, they may, and often do, affect our way of seeing and interpreting the facts. Evidence and feeling: 'the nature of the subject, and the character of the individual mind, determine which is to predominate; but in this life of ours, neither is the exclusive master'.[2]

If one wished to draw general conclusions about Bain's philosophical position, one could draw different conclusions from different groups of statements. On the one hand the emphasis which he lays on the physiological correlates of psychical processes might suggest a materialistic position. On the other hand a position of subjective idealism is suggested when he speaks, for example, of 'the supposed perception of an external and independent material world'[3] and adds that 'what is here said to be perceived is a convenient fiction, which by the very nature of the case transcends all possible experience'.[4] In point of fact, however, Bain tries to steer clear of metaphysics and to devote himself to empirical and genetic psychology, even if some of his statements have philosophical implications.

Bain's psychological investigations were continued by James Sully (1842–1923), who occupied the chair of philosophy at University College, London, from 1892 until 1903. In his *Outlines of Psychology* (1884) and in his two-volume work *The Human*

---

[1] *Ibid.*, p. 538.　　[2] *Ibid.*, p. 548.
[3] *Ibid.*, p. 585.　　[4] *Ibid.*

Mind (1892) he followed Bain in emphasizing the physiological correlates of psychical processes and in employing the principle of the association of ideas. Further, he extended his reflections into the field of the theory of education and applied himself to child-psychology in his *Studies of Childhood* (1895).

Already in Bain's lifetime, however, the associationist psychology was subjected to attack by James Ward and others. It is doubtless true that the emphasis laid by Bain on the emotive and volitional aspects of man gave to his thought a rather more modern tone than one finds in his predecessors. But it can also be argued that his introduction of fresh ideas into the old psychology helped to prepare the way for the lines of thought which supplanted it. Obviously, association continued to be recognized as a factor in mental life. But it could no longer be taken as a key to unlock all doors to the understanding of psychical processes, and the old atomistic associationist psychology had had its day.

2. In the ethical field Bain introduced into utilitarianism important modifications or supplementary considerations. These modifications doubtless impaired the simple unity of the utilitarian ethics. But Bain considered them necessary if an adequate account was to be given of the moral consciousness as it actually exists, that is, as Bain saw it in himself and in the members of the society or culture to which he belonged.

Utilitarianism, Bain remarks, has this great advantage over the moral sense theory, that it provides an external standard of morality, substituting 'a regard to consequences for a mere unreasoning sentiment, or feeling'.[1] It is also opposed to the theory that all human actions are the result of selfish impulses, a theory which is committed to misinterpreting affection and sympathy, 'the main foundations of disinterestedness'.[2] To be sure, these impulses belong to the self. But it does not follow that they can properly be described as 'selfish' impulses. In point of fact selfishness has never been the sole foundation of men's ideas of what is right. And it certainly is not the present sole foundation of men's moral convictions. This is recognized by the utilitarians, who connect the notion of utility with that of the common good.

At the same time utilitarianism cannot constitute the whole truth about morality. For one thing, we must find room for a distinction between 'utility made compulsory and what is left

[1] *The Emotions and the Will*, p. 272.
[2] *Ibid.*, p. 258. Bain also notes that we can have disinterested antipathies and aversions.

free'.[1] After all, there are many actions which are useful to the community but which are not regarded as obligatory. For another thing, it is clear that the moral rules which prevail in most communities are grounded partly on sentiment, and not only on the idea of utility. Hence, even though the principle of utility is an essential feature of ethics, we must add sentiment and also tradition, 'which is the continuing influence of some former Utility or Sentiment'.[2] That is to say, we must add them if we wish to give a comprehensive account of existing moral practices.

Bain is not concerned, therefore, with working out an *a priori* theory of ethics. He is concerned with exhibiting the empirical foundations of morality as it exists. He approaches morality very much from the point of view of a psychologist. And if we bear this approach in mind, we can understand his genetic treatment of conscience and the feeling of obligation. In contrast to the view of Dugald Stewart that conscience is 'a primitive and independent faculty of the mind, which would be developed in us although we never had any experience of external authority',[3] Bain holds that 'conscience is an imitation within us of the government without us'.[4] In other words, conscience is an interior reflection of the voices of parents, educators and external authority in general. And the sense of obligation and duty arises out of the association established in the infant mind between the performance of actions forbidden by external authority and the sanctions imposed by this authority.

Now, if we interpret J. S. Mill as offering utilitarianism as an adequate description of the existing moral consciousness, Bain is doubtless right in saying that for an adequate description other factors have to be taken into account besides the principle of utility. But if we interpret Mill as recommending a particular system of ethics and as preferring this system to the moral sense theory on the ground that the principle of utility provides a criterion of moral conduct which is lacking in any pure moral sense theory, it is arguable that Bain is really more of a positivist than Mill. For though, as we have seen, he recognizes the advantage which utilitarianism possesses in having an external standard, he tends to emphasize the relativity of moral convictions. If someone asks, what is the moral standard? the proper answer would be that it is 'the enactments of the existing society, as

[1] *Ibid.*, p. 274.   [2] *Ibid.*, p. 277.
[3] *Ibid.*, p. 283.   [4] *Ibid.*

derived from some one clothed in his day with a moral legislative authority'.[1] Instead of treating morality as if it were one indivisible whole, we ought to consider particular codes and moral rules separately. And then we shall see that behind the phenomena of conscience and obligation there lies authority. Bain allows for the influence of outstanding individuals; but the assent of the community at large, whatever it may be, is required to complete the legislative process. And once it is completed, the external authority is present which shapes conscience and the sense of duty in the individual.

Bain would have done well to reflect on his own admission that outstanding individuals are capable of moulding afresh the moral outlook of a society. That is to say, he might well have asked himself whether this admission was really consistent with an ethics of social pressure. Some have concluded that there is a field of objective values into which different degrees of insight are possible, while Bergson thought it necessary to make a distinction between what he called 'closed' and 'open' morality. But the problem does not seem to have troubled Bain, even though the data for the raising of the problem were present in his account of morality.

3. A much more radical change in the utilitarian ethics was made by Henry Sidgwick (1838–1900), Fellow of Trinity College, Cambridge, who was elected to the chair of moral philosophy in that university in 1883. His reputation rests principally on *The Methods of Ethics* (1874). Other writings include his *Outlines of the History of Ethics for English Readers* (1886) and his posthumously published *Lectures on the Ethics of Green, Spencer and Martineau* (1902).

In Sidgwick's account of the development of his ethical views, which was printed in the sixth edition (1901) of *The Methods of Ethics*, he remarked that 'my first adhesion to a definite Ethical system was to the Utilitarianism of Mill'.[2] But he soon came to see a discrepancy between psychological hedonism, the thesis that every man seeks his own pleasure, and ethical hedonism, the thesis that every man ought to seek the general happiness. If psychological hedonism is taken to mean that as a matter of fact every man seeks exclusively his own pleasure, the thesis is questionable, or, rather, false. But in any case a purely psychological thesis

---

[1] *The Emotions and the Will*, p. 281.
[2] *The Methods of Ethics*, p. XV (6th edition.)

cannot establish an ethical thesis. As Hume maintained, we cannot deduce an 'ought' from an 'is', an ought-statement from a purely factual descriptive statement. James Mill may have tried to show how it is psychologically possible for a person who by nature pursues his own pleasure or happiness to act altruistically. But even if his account of the matter were valid from a psychological point of view, this would not show that we *ought* to act altruistically. If, therefore, ethical or universalistic hedonism is to have a philosophical basis, we must look elsewhere for it than in psychology.

Sidgwick came to the conclusion that this philosophical basis could be found only in the intuition of some fundamental moral principle or principles. He was thus drawn away from the utilitarianism of Bentham and J. S. Mill to intuitionism. But further reflection convinced him that the principles which were implicit in the morality of common sense, as distinct from philosophical theories about morality, were either utilitarian in character or at any rate compatible with utilitarianism. 'I was then a Utilitarian again, but on an Intuitional basis.'[1]

In Sidgwick's view, therefore, there are certain moral principles which are self-evidently true. Thus it is evident that one should prefer a future greater good to a present lesser one.[2] This is the principle of prudence. It is also self-evident that as rational beings we ought to treat others in the way in which we think that we ought to be treated, unless there is some difference 'which can be stated as a reasonable ground for difference of treatment'.[3] This is the principle of justice. It is also self-evident both that from the point of view of the Universe the good of any one individual is of no more importance than the good of any other individual, and that as a rational being I ought to aim at the general good, so far as it is attainable by my efforts. From these two propositions we can deduce the principle of benevolence, namely that 'each one is morally bound to regard the good of any other individual as much as his own, except in so far as he judges it to be less, when impartially viewed, or less certainly knowable or attainable by him'.[4]

[1] *Ibid.*, p. XX.
[2] This does not mean that we ought to prefer a future uncertain good to a lesser but certain present one. As self-evident, the principle simply states that priority in time, considered simply by itself, is not a reasonable ground for preferring one good to another. Cf. *The Methods of Ethics*, p. 381.
[3] *The Methods of Ethics*, p. 380. The difference might be one of circumstances or between the persons considered. We would not necessarily think it right to treat a child in the way that we consider we ought to be treated.
[4] *Ibid.*, p. 382.

The principle of prudence or of 'rational egoism', as mentioned above, implies that a man ought to seek his own good. And Sidgwick is in fact convinced, with Butler, that this is a manifest obligation. The principle of rational benevolence, however, states that we ought to seek for the good of others, under certain conditions at any rate. If therefore we combine them, we have the command to seek the good of all, including one's own, or to seek one's own good as a constituent part of the general good. For the general good is made up of individual goods. Now, the general good can be equated with universal happiness, provided that we do not understand by happiness simply the pleasures of sense, and provided that we do not intend to imply that happiness is always best attained by aiming at it directly. Hence 'I am finally led to the conclusion that the Intuitional method rigorously applied yields as its final result the doctrine of pure Universalistic Hedonism—which it is convenient to denote by the single word, Utilitarianism'.[1]

If we look at Sidgwick's moral philosophy in the light of the utilitarian tradition, we naturally tend to focus our attention on his rejection of the claims of genetic psychology to provide an adequate basis for our moral convictions, especially of the consciousness of obligation, and on his use of the idea of intuitively perceived moral axioms, a use which was encouraged by his reading of Samuel Clarke and other writers.[2] He can be described as an intuitionist utilitarian or as an utilitarian intuitionist, if such descriptions do not involve a contradiction in terms. Sidgwick, indeed, maintained that there is no real incompatibility between utilitarianism and intuitionism. At the same time he was too honest a thinker to assert that he had given a definitive solution to the problem of reconciling the claims of interest and duty, of prudence or rational egoism and of benevolence, a benevolence capable of expressing itself not only in altruistic conduct but also in complete self-sacrifice in the service of others or in the pursuit of some ideal end.

If, however, we look at Sidgwick's moral philosophy in relation to what was to come later instead of in relation to what went before, we shall probably lay more stress on his method. He laid emphasis on the need for examining what he called the morality of common sense; and he attempted to discover the principles

---

[1] *The Methods of Ethics*, pp. 406–7.
[2] For Samuel Clarke see Vol. V of this *History*, pp. 160–1.

which are implicit in the ordinary moral consciousness, to state
them precisely and to determine their mutual relations. His
method was analytic. He selected a problem, considered it from
various angles, proposed a solution and raised objections and
counter-objections. He may have tended to lose himself in details
and to suspend final judgment because he was unable to see his
way clearly through all difficulties. To say this, however, is in a
sense to commend his thoroughness and careful honesty. And
though his appeal to self-evident truths may not appear very
convincing, his devotion to the analysis and clarification of the
ordinary moral consciousness puts one in mind of the later
analytic movement in British philosophy.

4. The associationist psychology, the phenomenalism of J. S.
Mill and the utilitarian ethics, all had their roots in the eighteenth
century. Soon after the middle of the nineteenth century, however, a new idea began to colour the empiricist current of thought.
This was the idea of evolution. We cannot indeed fix on a certain
date and say that after this date empiricism became a philosophy
of evolution. Herbert Spencer, the great philosopher of evolution
in nineteenth-century England, had started publishing his *System
of Philosophy* before J. S. Mill published his work on Hamilton,
and Bain, who died in the same year as Spencer, continued the
tradition represented by the two Mills. Moreover, it is less a
question of the empiricist movement as a whole coming under the
domination of the idea of evolution than of the idea becoming
prominent in certain representatives of the movement. We can,
however, say that in the second half of the century the theory of
evolution invaded and occupied not only the relevant parts of the
scientific field but also a considerable part of the field of empiricist
philosophy.

The idea of biological evolution was not, of course, an invention
of the middle of the nineteenth century. As a purely speculative
idea it had appeared even in ancient Greece. In the eighteenth
century the way had been prepared for it by Georges-Louis de
Buffon (1707–88), while Jean-Baptiste Pierre Lamarck (1744–
1829) had proposed his theories that in response to new needs
brought about by changes in the environment changes take place
in the organic structure of animals, some organs falling into disuse
and others being evolved and developed, and that acquired habits
are transmitted by heredity. Moreover, when the idea of evolution
was first publicized in Britain, the publicist was a philosopher,

Spencer, rather than a scientist. At the same time this does not affect the importance of Darwin's writings in setting the theory of evolution on its feet and in giving an enormously powerful impetus to its propagation.

Charles Robert Darwin (1809–82) was a naturalist, not a philosopher. During his famous voyage on the 'Beagle' (1831–6), observation of variations between differently situated animals of the same species and reflection on the differences between living and fossilized animals led him to question the theory of the fixity of species. In 1838 study of Malthus's *Essay on the Principle of Population* helped to lead him to the conclusions that in the struggle for existence favourable variations tend to be preserved and unfavourable variations to be destroyed, and that the result of this process is the formation of new species, acquired characteristics being transmitted by heredity.

Similar conclusions were reached independently by another naturalist, Alfred Russel Wallace (1823–1913), who, like Darwin, was influenced by a reading of Malthus in arriving at the idea of the survival of the fittest in the struggle for existence. And on July 1st, 1858, a joint communication by Wallace and Darwin was presented at a meeting of the Linnean Society in London. Wallace's contribution was a paper *On the Tendency of Varieties to Depart Indefinitely from the Original Type*, while Darwin contributed an abridgment of his own ideas.

Darwin's famous work on the *Origin of Species by Means of Natural Selection, or The Preservation of Favoured Races in the Struggle for Life* was published in November 1859, all copies being sold out on the day of publication. This was followed in 1868 by *The Variation of Animals and Plants under Domestication*. And the year 1871 saw the publication of *The Descent of Man, and Selection in Relation to Sex*. Darwin published a number of further works, but he is chiefly known for *The Origin of Species* and *The Descent of Man*.

Being a naturalist, Darwin was sparing of philosophical speculation and devoted himself primarily to working out a theory of evolution based on the available empirical evidence. He did indeed interpret morality as evolving out of the purposiveness of animal instinct and as developing through changes in social standards which confer survival value on societies. And he was obviously well aware of the flutter in theological dovecotes which was caused by his theory of evolution, particularly in its application to man. In 1870 he wrote that while he could not look on the universe as the product of blind chance, he could see no evidence of design, still less of beneficent design, when he came to consider the details of natural history. And though he was originally a Christian, he arrived in the course of time at an agnostic suspension of judgment. He tended, however, to avoid personal involvement in theological controversy.

Unless perhaps we happen to live in one of the few surviving pockets of fundamentalism, it is difficult for us now to appreciate the ferment which was caused in the last century by the hypothesis of organic evolution, particularly in its application to man. For one thing, the idea of evolution is now common coin and is taken for granted by very many people who would be quite unable either to mention or to weigh the evidence adduced in its favour. For another thing, the hypothesis is no longer an occasion for bitter theological controversy. Even those who question the sufficiency of the evidence to prove the evolution of the human body from some other species commonly recognize that the first chapters of *Genesis* were not intended to solve scientific problems, and that the matter is one which has to be settled according to the available empirical evidence. Again, if we except the Marxists, who are in any case committed to materialism, reflective unbelievers do not generally maintain that the hypothesis of organic evolution, taken by itself, disproves Christian theism or is incompatible with religious belief. After all, the presence of evil and suffering in the world, which constitutes one of the main objections to Christian theism, remains an indubitable fact whether the hypothesis is accepted or rejected. Further, we have seen philosophers such as Bergson developing a spiritualistic philosophy within the framework of the general idea of creative evolution, and, more recently, a scientist such as Teilhard de Chardin making an enthusiastic use of the same idea in the service of a religious world-view. Hence the controversies of the last century naturally seem to many people to have accumulated a great deal of dust and cobwebs in the interval.

We have to remember, however, that in the middle of the last century the idea of the evolution of species, especially as applied to man himself, was for the general educated public a complete novelty. Moreover, the impression was commonly given, not only by exponents of the idea but also by some of its critics, that the Darwinian theory rendered superfluous or, rather, positively excluded any teleological interpretation of the cosmic process. For example, T. H. Huxley wrote as follows. 'That which struck the present writer most forcibly on his first perusal of the *Origin of Species* was the conviction that Teleology, as commonly understood, had received its deathblow at Mr. Darwin's hands.'[1] Those species survive which are the best fitted for the struggle for existence; but the variations which make them the best fitted are fortuitous.

Our concern here is with the impact of the theory of evolution on philosophy rather than with the theological controversies to which it gave rise. Herbert Spencer, the foremost philosopher of evolution in the nineteenth century, merits a chapter to himself. Meanwhile we can consider briefly two or three writers who contributed to publicizing the idea of evolution and to developing some philosophical theories based on or connected with this idea. It is to be noted, however, that they were scientists who made excursions into philosophy, rather than professional philosophers. Generally speaking, the academic or university philosophers held aloof from the topic and maintained a reserved attitude. As for Spencer, he never occupied an academic post.

5. The name which immediately suggests itself in this context is that of Thomas Henry Huxley (1825-95). As a naval surgeon aboard the 'Rattlesnake' Huxley had opportunity for studying the marine life of the tropical seas, and as a result of his researches he was elected a Fellow of the Royal Society in 1851. In 1854 he was appointed lecturer in natural history at the School of Mines. In the course of time he became more and more involved in public life, serving on some ten royal commissions and taking an active part in educational organization. From 1883 to 1885 he was president of the Royal Society.

In Huxley's opinion Darwin had placed the theory of evolution on a sound footing by following a method in accordance with the rules of procedure laid down by J. S. Mill. 'He has endeavoured to determine great facts inductively, by observation and experiment; he has then reasoned from the data thus furnished; and lastly, he has tested the validity of his ratiocination by comparing his deductions with the observed facts of Nature.'[2] It is true that the

---

[1] *Lectures and Essays* (The People's Library edition), pp. 178-9. Huxley was commenting on an essay by a certain Professor Kolliker of Würzburg who had interpreted Darwin as a teleologist and had criticized him on this score.

[2] *Lay Sermons, Addresses and Reviews*, p. 294 (6th edition). The quotation is taken from an 1860 article on *The Origin of Species*.

origin of species by natural selection has not been proved with certainty. The theory remains an hypothesis which enjoys only a high degree of probability. But it is 'the only extant hypothesis which is worth anything in a scientific point of view'.[1] And it is a marked improvement on Lamarck's theory.[2]

But though Huxley accepted the view that organic evolution proceeds by natural selection or the survival of the fittest in the struggle for existence, he made a sharp distinction between the evolutionary process and man's moral life. Those who expound an ethics of evolution, according to which man's moral life is a continuation of the evolutionary process, are probably right in maintaining that what we call the moral sentiments have evolved like other natural phenomena. But they forget that the immoral sentiments are also the result of evolution. 'The thief and the murderer follow nature just as much as the philanthropist.'[3]

In fine, morality involves going against the evolutionary process. In the struggle for existence the strongest and most self-assertive tend to trample down the weaker, whereas 'social progress means a checking of the cosmic process at every step and the substitution for it of another, which may be called the ethical process'.[4] Originally, human society was probably just as much a product of organic necessity as the societies of bees and ants. But in the case of man social progress involves strengthening the bonds of mutual sympathy, consideration and benevolence, and self-imposed restrictions on anti-social tendencies. True, in so far as this process renders a society more fitted for survival in relation to Nature or to other societies, it is in harmony with the cosmic progress. But in so far as law and moral rules restrict the struggle for existence between members of a given society, the ethical process is plainly at variance with the cosmic process. For it aims at producing quite different qualities. Hence we can say that 'the ethical progress of society depends, not on imitating the cosmic process, still less in running away from it, but in combating it'.[5]

[1] *Ibid.*, p. 295.
[2] In regard to Lamarck's theory that environmental changes produce new needs in animals, that new needs produce new desires, and that new desires result in organic modifications which are transmitted by heredity, Huxley remarks that it does not seem to have occurred to Lamarck to inquire 'whether there is any reason to believe that there are any limits to the amount of modifications producible, or to ask how long an animal is likely to endeavour to gratify an impossible desire;' *Lectures and Essays*, p. 124. The quotation is taken from an 1850 essay on 'The Darwinian Hypothesis'.
[3] *Evolution and Ethics and Other Essays*, p. 80. The discourse on *Evolution and Ethics* was originally given at Oxford as the second Romanes lecture.
[4] *Ibid.*, p. 81.   [5] *Ibid.*, p. 83.

There is thus a marked difference between the views of T. H. Huxley and his grandson, Sir Julian Huxley, on the relation between evolution and ethics. I do not mean to imply, of course, that Sir Julian Huxley rejects the moral qualities and ideals which his grandfather considered desirable. The point is that whereas Sir Julian Huxley emphasizes the element of continuity between the general movement of evolution and moral progress, T. H. Huxley emphasized the element of discontinuity, maintaining that 'the cosmic process has no sort of relation to moral ends'.[1] T. H. Huxley might, of course, have called for a new type of ethics, involving a Nietzschean exaltation of Nature's strong men, which could have been interpreted as a continuation of what he called the cosmic process. But he did not aim at any such transvaluation of values. Rather did he accept the values of sympathy, benevolence, consideration for others, and so on; and in the cosmic process he found no respect for such values.

Though, however, man's moral life formed for Huxley a world of its own within the world of Nature, it does not follow that he looked on man as possessing a spiritual soul which cannot be accounted for in terms of evolution. He maintained that 'consciousness is a function of the brain'.[2] That is to say, consciousness is an epiphenomenon which arises when matter has developed a special form of organization. And this theory, together with his defence of determinism, led to his being described as a materialist.

Huxley, however, stoutly denied the applicability to himself of this description. One reason which he gave for this denial is perhaps not very impressive, because it involved a very narrow interpretation of materialism. Materialism, according to Huxley, maintains that there is nothing in the universe but matter and force, whereas the theory of the epiphenomenal nature of consciousness neither denies the reality of consciousness nor identifies it with the physical processes on which it depends.[3] But Huxley went on to remark, with a rather charming unexpectedness, that 'the arguments used by Descartes and Berkeley to show that our certain knowledge does not extend beyond our states of consciousness, appear to me to be as impregnable now as they did when I first became acquainted with them some half-century ago. . . . Our one certainty is the existence of the mental world, and that of

---

[1] *Evolution and Ethics, and Other Essays*, p. 83.　　　　[2] *Ibid.*, p. 135.
[3] The Marxist, for example, does not deny the reality of mind. Nor does he identify psychical with physical processes. But he looks on himself none the less as a materialist. And so he is in a metaphysical sense.

Kraft und Stoff falls into the rank of, at best, a highly probable hypothesis.'[1] Further, if material things are resolved into centres of force, one might just as well speak of immaterialism as of materialism.

It is not perhaps very easy to understand how the doctrine that we can never really know anything with certainty but our states of consciousness can be harmonized with the doctrine that consciousness is a function of the brain. But the first doctrine enables Huxley to say that 'if I were forced to choose between Materialism and Idealism, I should elect for the latter'.[2]

It must be added, however, that Huxley has no intention of letting himself be forced to choose between materialism and idealism. And the same applies to the issue between atheism and theism. Huxley proclaims himself an agnostic, and in his work on David Hume he expresses agreement with the Scottish philosopher's suspension of judgment about metaphysical problems. We have our scientific knowledge, and 'the man of science has learned to believe in justification, not by faith, but by verification'.[3] In regard to that which lies beyond the scope of verification we must remain agnostic, suspending judgment.

As one might expect in the case of a naturalist who makes excursions into philosophy, Huxley's philosophical theories are not well worked out. Nor is their mutual consistency clearly exhibited, to put it mildly. At the same time they manifest the not uncommon English attitude which shows itself in a dislike of extremes and a reluctance to submit to the imposition of restrictive labels. Huxley was quite prepared to defend evolution against attack, as he did in his famous encounter with Bishop Samuel Wilberforce in 1860. And he was prepared to criticize orthodox theology. But though he clearly did not believe in the Christian doctrine of God, he refused to commit himself either to atheism or to materialism. Behind the veil of phenomena lies the unknowable. And in regard to the unknowable agnosticism is, by definition, the appropriate attitude.

6. (i) The label 'materialist', repudiated by Huxley, was accepted by John Tyndall (1820–93), who in 1853 was appointed professor of natural philosophy in the Royal Institution, where he

---

[1] *Evolution and Ethics, and Other Essays*, p. 130. *Kraft und Stoff* is the title of a well-known book by the German materialist, Ludwig Büchner. See Vol. VII of this *History*, pp. 352–3.
[2] *Ibid.*, p. 133.
[3] *Lay Sermons, Addresses and Reviews*, p. 18.

was a colleague of Faraday.[1] Tyndall was chiefly concerned with inorganic physics, particularly with the subject of radiant heat; and he was much less inclined than Huxley to make prolonged excursions into the field of philosophy. But he did not hesitate to profess openly what he called 'scientific materialism'.

The scientific materialism accepted by Tyndall was not, however, the same thing as the materialism which was rejected by Huxley. For it meant in large part the hypothesis that every state of consciousness is correlated with a physical process in the brain. Thus in his address to the British Association in 1868 on the *Scope and Limit of Scientific Materialism* Tyndall explained that 'in affirming that the growth of the body is mechanical, and that thought, as exercised by us, has its correlative in the physics of the brain, I think that the position of the "Materialist" is stated, as far as that position is a tenable one'.[2] In other words, the materialist asserts that two sets of phenomena, mental processes and physical processes in the brain, are associated, though he is 'in absolute ignorance'[3] of the real bond of union between them. Indeed, in his so-called Belfast Address, delivered before the British Association in 1874, Tyndall asserted roundly that 'man the *object* is separated by an impassible gulf from man the *subject*. There is no motor energy in the human intellect to carry it, without logical rupture, from the one to the other.'[4]

Tyndall did indeed understand scientific materialism as involving 'a provisional assent'[5] to the hypothesis that the mind and all its phenomena 'were once latent in a fiery cloud'[6] and that they are 'a result of the play between organism and environment through cosmic ranges of time'.[7] But the conclusion which he drew from the theory of evolution was that matter could not properly be looked on as mere 'brute' matter. It had to be regarded as potentially containing within itself life and mental phenomena. In other words, scientific materialism demanded a revision of the concept of matter as something essentially dead and opposed to biological and mental life.

Beyond the phenomena of matter and force, which form the object of scientific inquiry, 'the real mystery of the universe lies

[1] On Faraday's death in 1867 Tyndall succeeded him as Superintendent of the Institution.
[2] *Fragments of Science for Unscientific People*, pp. 121–2 (2nd edition).
[3] *Ibid.*, p. 122.
[4] *Lectures and Essays*, p. 40 (Rationalist Press Association edition, 1903).
[5] *Fragments of Science*, p. 166.
[6] *Ibid.*, p. 163.   [7] *Lectures and Essays*, p. 40.

unsolved, and, as far as we are concerned, is incapable of solution'.[1] But this acknowledgment of mystery in the universe was not intended by Tyndall as a support for belief in God as conceived by Christians. In his *Apology for the Belfast Address* (1874), he spoke of the idea of creative activity by 'a Being standing outside the nebula'[2] not only as based on no empirical evidence but also as 'opposed to the very spirit of science'.[3] Further, when answering a Catholic critic he remarked, in the same *Apology*, that he would not disavow the charge of atheism, as far as any concept of the Supreme Being was concerned which his critics would be likely to accept.

Tyndall's scientific materialism was not confined, therefore, to a methodological point of view presupposed by scientific inquiry. He was not simply saying, for example, that the scientific psychologist should pursue his inquiries into the relation between mind and body on the assumption that we shall find a correlation between any given mental phenomenon and a physical process. He was saying that as far as knowledge is concerned, science is omnicompetent. Problems which cannot be answered by science are unanswerable in principle. Religion, for example, is immune from disproof as long as it is regarded simply as a subjective experience.[4] But if it is regarded as claiming to extend our knowledge, its claim is bogus. In a general sense of the term, therefore, Tyndall was a positivist. By admitting a sphere for agnosticism, mysteries or enigmas, that is to say, which cannot be solved, he stopped short of the position to be adopted later by the neopositivists or logical positivists. But this does not alter the fact that scientific materialism involved for him a positivist view of the omnicompetence of science in the field of knowledge.

(ii) The view that agnosticism is the only attitude which is really in harmony with the genuinely scientific spirit was also maintained by Sir Leslie Stephen (1832–1904), author of a two-volume *History of English Thought in the Eighteenth Century* (1876) and of a three-volume work on *The English Utilitarians* (1900). At first a clergyman, he came successively under the influence of J. S. Mill, Darwin and Spencer, and in 1875 he finally abandoned his clerical status.

In a discussion of the nature of materialism Stephen maintains

---

[1] *Fragments of Science*, p. 93.   [2] *Lectures and Essays*, p. 47.   [3] *Ibid.*
[4] 'No atheistic reasoning can, I hold,'dislodge religion from the human heart. Logic cannot deprive us of life, and religion is life to the religious. As an experience of consciousness it is beyond the assaults of logic', *ibid.*, p. 45.

that it 'represents the point of view of the physical inquirer. A man is a materialist for the time being so long as he has only to do with that which may be touched, handled, seen or otherwise perceived through the senses'.[1] In other words, scientific inquiry demands a methodical materialism. It does not demand acceptance of the doctrine that matter is the ultimate reality.

It by no means follows, however, that we are entitled to assert spiritualism, the doctrine that mind is the ultimate reality. The truth of the matter is that 'we cannot get behind the curtain, which is reality'.[2] If we try to do so, we are at once plunged into 'the transcendental region of antinomies and cobwebs of the brain'.[3] The unknowable which lies beyond 'reality' is 'a mere blank':[4] it is not itself converted into a reality by being spelt with a capital letter. 'The ancient secret is a secret still; man knows nothing of the Infinite and Absolute.'[5]

One would have thought that if the phenomenal world is once equated with 'reality', there is no good reason for supposing that there is any unknowable beyond it. What is the reason for supposing that there *is* a secret which always remains a secret? Conversely, if there is good reason for supposing that there is an unknowable Absolute, there is no good reason for equating the phenomenal world with reality. But Stephen's agnosticism represents less a carefully thought out position than a general attitude. Science alone provides us with definite knowledge. Science knows nothing of any meta-empirical Absolute. But we feel that even if all scientific problems were answered, the universe would still be mysterious, enigmatic. The enigma, however, is insoluble.

Needless to say, scientific materialism and agnosticism were by no means regarded as entailing the rejection of moral values. Tyndall insisted that moral values are independent of religious creeds, and that scientific materialism must not be understood as involving or implying a belittlement of man's highest ideals. As for Sir Leslie Stephen, in his work *The Science of Ethics* (1882) he tried to continue and develop Spencer's attempt to ground morals on evolution. Abstractly considered, the function of morality is to further the health and vitality of the social organism. Historically considered, moral principles undergo a process of natural selection, and those which are most effective in furthering the good

[1] *An Agnostic's Apology and Other Essays*, p. 52 (Rationalist Press Association edition, 1904). The quotation is taken from an 1886 essay. *What is Materialism?*
[2] *Ibid.*, p. 66. [3] *Ibid.*, p. 57. [4] *Ibid.* [5] *Ibid.*, p. 20.

of the social organism prevail over the less effective. That is to say, they are approved by the society in question. Thus even morality is brought under the law of the survival of the fittest. Obviously, Stephen's point of view was different from that of T. H. Huxley.

7. Agnosticism was not, of course, the only attitude adopted by those who embraced the theory of evolution. Henry Drummond (1851–97), for example, a writer whose books once enjoyed great popularity, tried to bring together science and religion, Darwinism and Christianity, in terms of the operation of one law of continuing evolution. More interesting, however, is the case of George John Romanes (1848–94), biologist and author of a number of works on evolution, who passed from early religious belief to agnosticism and from agnosticism by way of pantheism back in the direction of Christian theism.

The agnostic phase in Romanes's thought found expression in *A Candid Examination of Theism*, which he published in 1878 under the pseudonym of *Physicus*. There is, he maintained, no real evidence for the existence of God, though it may possibly be true, for all we know, that there would be no universe unless there were a God. Some years later, however, in a lecture entitled *Mind, Motion and Monism* (1885), Romanes proposed a form of pantheism, while his adoption of a more sympathetic attitude towards Christian theism was represented by *Thoughts on Religion* (1895), edited by Charles Gore, later Bishop of Oxford. This work comprises some articles which Romanes wrote for the *Nineteenth Century* but did not publish, together with notes for a second *Candid Examination of Theism* which was to have been signed *Metaphysicus*.

In the articles on the influence of science on religion, which form part of *Thoughts on Religion*, Romanes argues that this influence has been destructive in the sense that it has progressively revealed the invalidity of appeals to direct intervention in Nature or to alleged evidence of special cases of design. At the same time science necessarily presupposes the idea of Nature as a system, as exemplifying universal order; and theism provides a reasonable explanation of this universal order. If, however, we wish to speak of the postulated creator of universal order as a divine Mind, we must remember that none of the qualities which characterize the minds with which we are acquainted can be properly attributed to God. Hence 'the word

Mind, as applied to the supposed agency, stands for a blank'.[1] In this sense, therefore, the argument for theism leads to agnosticism. In his notes for the proposed second version of his *Candid Examination of Theism* Romanes adopts a somewhat different point of view by arguing that the advance of science, 'far from having weakened religion, has immeasurably strengthened it. For it has proved the uniformity of natural causation'.[2] But the question whether one is to look on the universal causal order as a continuing expression of the divine will or simply as a natural fact, is not one which can be settled by the human understanding alone. Science provides an empirical basis, as it were, for a religious vision of the world, but the transition to this vision requires an act of faith. True, 'no one is entitled to deny the possibility of what may be termed an organ of spiritual discernment',[3] manifested in the religious consciousness; and 'reason itself tells me it is not unreasonable to expect that the heart and will should be required to join with reason in seeking God'.[4] The way to become a Christian is to act as one, 'and if Christianity be true, the verification will come, not indeed immediately through any course of speculative reason, but immediately by spiritual intuition'.[5] At the same time faith, definite self-commitment to a religious view of the world, demands 'a severe effort of the will',[6] an effort which Romanes himself is not prepared to make.

It is thus a mistake to say that Romanes came to commit himself definitely to a theistic position. In a sense he not only begins but also ends with agnosticism. At the same time there is a considerable difference between the initial and the terminal agnosticism. For whereas in one period of his life Romanes was evidently convinced that his scientific conscience demanded of him an agnostic position, in later years he came to insist that the religious view of the world may be justified, though it would be justified by something of the nature of spiritual intuition. The agnostic has no right to rule out this possibility or to say that the venture of faith is a fool's venture. For the experiment of faith may well have its own peculiar mode of verification, about which science cannot pronounce judgment. In other words, Romanes was neither satisfied with agnosticism nor fully prepared to reject it. He developed a sympathy with religious belief which Tyndall did not share. But he did not feel able to commit himself to it by

[1] *Thoughts on Religion*, p. 87.   [2] *Ibid.*, p. 124.   [3] *Ibid.*, p. 140.
[4] *Ibid.*, p. 132.   [5] *Ibid.*, p. 168.   [6] *Ibid.*, p. 131.

that effort of the will which he considered necessary before the internal validation of the religious consciousness could manifest itself.

8. (i) As we have seen, J. S: Mill admired Auguste Comte and was prepared to talk in a general way about the religion of humanity. But he had no use for Comte's proposals for organizing a cult for the new religion or for his dreams of a spiritual and intellectual domination to be exercised by the positivist philosophers. Again, Spencer, who also derived stimulus from Comte, adopted a critical attitude towards some of the Frenchman's theories,[1] while T. H. Huxley described the philosophy of Comte as Catholicism minus Christianity. For real disciples of Comte we have to turn to Richard Congreve (1818–99), Fellow of Wadham College, Oxford, who translated Comte's positivist catechism into English and to his circle. This included John Henry Bridges (1832–1906), Frederic Harrison (1831–1923) and Edward Spencer Beesley (1831–1915).

The London Positivist Society was founded in 1867, and in 1870 it opened a positivist temple in Chapel Street. But after some years a split occurred in the ranks of the Comtists, and those who accepted the leadership of Pierre Laffitte (1823–1903), friend and successor of Comte as high priest of positivism, formed the London Positivist Committee which opened a centre of its own in 1881. Bridges was the first president of the new Committee (1878–80), and he was succeeded by Harrison. The original group was led by Congreve. In 1916 the two groups were reunited.[2]

(ii) The independent thinkers are obviously of more interest than those who were primarily engaged in spreading the pure word of Comtism. One of these independent thinkers was George Henry Lewes (1817–78), author of the once popular but long superseded two-volume *Biographical History of Philosophy* (1845–6). In his earlier years Lewes was an enthusiastic follower of Comte, and in 1853 he published *Comte's Philosophy of the Positive Sciences*. But though he remained a positivist in the sense of holding that philosophy consists in the widest generalizations from the results of the particular sciences and should abstain from any treatment of the meta-empirical, he moved away from Comte and came more under the influence of Spencer. In 1874–9 he published five volumes of *Problems of Life and Mind*.

[1] In 1864 Spencer wrote his *Reasons for Dissenting from the Philosophy of Comte*.
[2] In 1893 the London Positivist Committee founded *The Positivist Review*. But the periodical ceased publication in 1925, after having been called *Humanity* during the last two years of its life.

Lewes made a distinction between the phenomenon which is understandable simply in terms of its constituent factors and the phenomenon which emerges from its constituent factors as something new, a novelty. The former he called a 'resultant', the latter an 'emergent'. The idea of this distinction was not Lewes's invention, but he appears to have coined the term 'emergent', which was later to play a conspicuous role in the philosophy of evolution.

(iii) A more interesting figure was William Kingdon Clifford (1845–79), who from 1871 was professor of applied mathematics in University College, London. An eminent mathematician, he was also extremely interested in philosophical topics. And he was a fervent preacher of the religion of humanity.

Clifford's best known philosophical idea is probably that of 'mind-stuff', which he proposed as a means of solving the problem of the relation between the psychical and the physical and of avoiding the necessity of postulating the emergence of mind from a completely heterogeneous matter. Like other defenders of the ancient theory of panpsychism, Clifford did not mean to imply that all matter enjoys consciousness. His thesis was that the relation between the psychical and the physical is comparable to that between a read sentence and the same sentence as written or printed. There is a complete correspondence, and every atom, for example, has a psychical aspect. Emergence is not indeed excluded. For consciousness arises when a certain organization of mind-stuff has developed. But any leap from the physical to the psychical, which might seem to imply the causal activity of a creative agent, is avoided.[1]

In the field of ethics Clifford emphasized the idea of the tribal self. The individual has indeed his egoistic impulses and desires. But the concept of the human atom, the completely solitary and self-contained individual, is an abstraction. In actual fact every individual is by nature, in virtue of the tribal self, a member of the social organism, the tribe. And moral progress consists in subordinating the egoistic impulses to the interests or good of the tribe, to that which, in Darwinian language, makes the tribe most fit for survival. Conscience is the voice of the tribal self; and the

[1] As Clifford presupposed something like the phenomenalism of Hume, he had to maintain that impressions or sensations, composed of mind-stuff, can exist antecedently to consciousness. When consciousness arises, they become, or can become, its objects; but to be objects of consciousness is not essential for their existence.

ethical ideal is to become a public-spirited and efficient citizen. In other words, morality as described by Clifford corresponds pretty well to what Bergson was later to call 'closed morality'. On the subject of religion Clifford was something of a fanatic. Not only did he speak of the clergy as enemies of humanity, and of Christianity as a plague, but he also attacked all belief in God. He was thus more akin to some of the writers of the French Enlightenment than to the nineteenth-century English agnostics, who were generally polite in what they said about religion and its official representatives. And he has been compared not inaptly with Nietzsche. At the same time he proclaimed a substitute religion, that of humanity, though he looked to the progress of science to establish the kingdom of man rather than to any organization on the lines proposed by Comte. Clifford did indeed speak of the 'cosmic emotion' which man can feel for the universe; but it was not his intention to replace theism by pantheism. He was concerned rather with substituting man for God, as he thought that belief in God was inimical to human progress and morality.

(iv) Clifford's successor in his chair of applied mathematics was Karl Pearson (1857–1936), who was later (1911–33) Galton professor of eugenics in the University of London.[1] In Pearson's writings we find a clear exposition of the positivist spirit. He was not indeed the man to look with a kindly eye on Comte's ideas about religious cult, but he was a firm believer in the omni-competence of science. And his attitude towards metaphysics and theology was very similar to that advanced later by the neopositivists.

According to Pearson, the function of science is 'the classification of facts, the recognition of their sequence and relative significance',[2] while the scientific frame of mind is the habit of forming impersonal judgments upon the facts, judgments, that is to say, which are unbiased by personal feeling and by the idiosyncrasies of the individual temperament. This is not, however, a frame of mind which is characteristic of the metaphysician. Metaphysics, in fact, is poetry which masquerades as something else. 'The poet is a valued member of the community, for he is known to be a poet. . . . The metaphysician is a poet, often a very great one, but unfortunately he is not known to be a poet, because he strives to

---

[1] Sir Francis Galton (1822–1911), a cousin of Darwin, was the founder of the science of eugenics and envisaged the deliberate application in human society of the principle of selection which works automatically in Nature.
[2] *The Grammar of Science*, p. 6 (2nd edition, revised and enlarged, 1900).

clothe his poetry in the language of reason, and hence it follows that he is liable to be a dangerous member of the community.'[1] Rudolf Carnap was to expound exactly the same point of view. What, then, are the facts which form the basis for scientific judgment? Ultimately they are simply sense-impressions or sensations. These are stored up in the brain, which acts as a kind of telephone exchange; and we project groups of impressions outside ourselves and speak of these as external objects. 'As such we call it [a group thus projected] a *phenomenon*, and in practical life term it *real*.'[2] What lies behind sense-impressions, we do not and cannot know. The claims of philosophers to have penetrated to things-in-themselves are completely bogus. Indeed, we cannot with propriety even raise the question what causes sense-impressions. For the causal relation is simply a relation of regular sequence between phenomena. Pearson therefore prefers the term 'sensations' to 'sense-impressions', as the latter term naturally suggests the causal activity of an unknown agent.

Obviously, Pearson does not intend to say that science consists simply of noting sensations or sense-impressions. Concepts are derived from sensations; and deductive inference is an essential feature of scientific method. But science is grounded in sensations and it also terminates in them, in the sense that we test the conclusions of an inference by the process of verification. As a body of propositions science is a mental construction, but it rests at either end, so to speak, on sense-impressions.

The statement that science is a mental construction is to be taken literally. On the level of pre-scientific thought the permanent physical object is, as we have seen, a mental construct. And on the level of scientific thought both laws and scientific entities are both mental constructs. The descriptive laws of science[3] are general formulas constructed for economy of thought, and 'the logic man finds in the universe is but the reflection of his own reasoning faculty'.[4] As for postulated entities such as atoms, the term 'atom' denotes neither an observed object nor a thing-in-itself. 'No physicist ever saw or felt an individual atom. Atom and molecule are intellectual conceptions by aid of which physicists

---

[1] *The Grammar of Science*, p. 17.
[2] *Ibid.*, p. 64.
[3] Science, Pearson insists, is purely descriptive, and not explanatory. Scientific laws 'simply *describe*, they never explain the routine of our perceptions, the sense-impressions we project into an "outside world" ', *ibid.*, p. 99.
[4] *Ibid.*, p. 91. No argument from 'design' to the existence of God, therefore, could ever be valid.

classify phenomena, and formulate the relationships between their sequences.'[1] In other words, it is not sufficient to write off metaphysics as a possible source of knowledge about things-in-themselves. Science itself needs to be purified of its superstitions and of the tendency to think that its useful concepts refer to hidden entities or forces.

The beneficent social effects of science are strongly emphasized by Pearson. In addition to the technical application of scientific knowledge and its use in special departments such as that of eugenics, there is the general educative effect of scientific method. 'Modern science, as training the mind to an exact and impartial analysis of facts, is an education specially fitted to promote sound citizenship.'[2] Indeed, Pearson goes so far as to quote with approval a remark by Clifford to the effect that scientific thought is human progress itself, and not simply an accompaniment to or condition of such progress.

On the basis, therefore, of a phenomenalism which stood in the tradition of Hume and J. S. Mill Pearson developed a theory of science akin to that of Ernst Mach.[3] In fact, Mach dedicated to Pearson his *Beiträge zur Analyse der Empfindungen*. Common to both men is the idea of science as enabling us to predict and as practising, for this purpose, a policy of economy of thought by linking phenomena in terms of the fewest and simplest concepts possible. And both men interpret unobserved scientific entities as mental constructions. Further, as both Pearson and Mach resolve phenomena ultimately into sensations, we seem to arrive at the odd conclusion that though science is purely descriptive, there is really no world to be described, apart from the contents of consciousness. Thus empiricism, which began by stressing the experimental foundations of all knowledge, ends, through its phenomenalistic analysis of experience, in having no world left, outside the sphere of sensations. To put the matter in another way, empiricism started with the demand for respect for facts and then went on to resolve facts into sensations.

9. Generally speaking, the thinkers mentioned in this chapter can be said to have given expression to a vivid recognition of the part played by scientific method in the enormous increase in man's knowledge of the world. And it is understandable that this recognition was accompanied by the conviction that scientific

---

[1] *Ibid.*, p. 95.
[3] See Vol. VII of this *History*, p. 359.

[2] *Ibid.*, p. 9.

method was the only means of acquiring anything that could properly be called knowledge. Science, they thought, continually extends the frontiers of human knowledge; and if there is anything which lies beyond the reach of science, it is unknowable. Metaphysics and theology claim to make true statements about the metaphenomenal; but their claims are bogus.

In other words, the growth of a genuinely scientific outlook is necessarily accompanied by a growth of agnosticism. Religious belief belongs to the childhood of the human race, not to a truly adult mentality. We cannot indeed prove that there is no reality beyond the phenomena, the relations between which are studied by the scientist. Science is concerned with description, not with ultimate explanations. And there may be, for all we know, such an explanation. Indeed, the more phenomena are reduced to sensations or sense-impressions, the more difficult it is to avoid the concept of a metaphenomenal reality. But in any case a reality of this kind could not be known. And the adult mind simply accepts this fact and embraces agnosticism.

With Romanes, it is true, agnosticism came to mean something much more than a mere formal acknowledgment of the impossibility of proving the non-existence of God. But with the more positivist-minded thinkers religion, as far as the adult man was concerned, was deprived of intellectual content. That is to say, it would not comprise belief in the truth of propositions about God. In so far as religion could be retained by the adult mind, it would be reduced to an emotive element. But the emotive attitude would be directed either to the cosmos, as the object of cosmic emotion or feeling, or to humanity, as in the so-called religion of humanity. In fine, the emotive element in religion would be detached from the concept of God and re-directed elsewhere, traditional religion being something that should be left behind in the onward march of scientific knowledge.

We can say, therefore, that a large number of thinkers considered in this chapter were forerunners of the so-called scientific humanists of today, who look on religious belief as lacking any rational support and tend to emphasize the alleged detrimental effect of religion on human progress and morality. Obviously, if one is convinced that man is essentially related to God as his last end, one will question the propriety of the use of the term 'humanism' for any atheistic philosophy of man. But if one regards the movement of evolution in human society as simply an advance in the scientific knowledge and control by man both of his environment and of himself, one can hardly keep any room for religion in so far as it directs man's attention to the transcendent. Scientism is necessarily opposed to traditional religion.

A rather different point of view was advanced by Benjamin Kidd (1858–1916), author of the once popular works *Social Evolution* (1894), *The Principles of Western Civilization* (1902), and *The Science of Power* (1918). In his opinion natural selection in human society tends to favour the growth of man's emotional and affective rather than of his intellectual qualities. And as religion is grounded on the emotive aspects of human nature, it is not surprising if we find that religious peoples tend to prevail over communities in the struggle for existence. For religion encourages, in a way that science can never do, altruism and devotion to the interests of the community. In its ethical aspects especially religion is the most potent of social forces. And the highest expression of the religious consciousness is Christianity, on which Western civilization is built.

In other words, Kidd belittled the reason as a constructive force in social evolution and laid the emphasis on feeling. And as he deprived religion of its intellectual content and interpreted it as the most powerful expression of the emotive aspect of man's nature, he depicted it as an essential factor in human progress. Hostile criticism of religion by the destructive reason was thus for him an attack on progress.

Kidd's recognition of the influence of religion in human history was obviously quite justified. But the emphasis which he placed on the emotive aspects of religion laid him open to the retort that religious beliefs belong to the class of emotively-sustained myths which have as a matter of fact exercised a great influence but the need of which should be outgrown by the adult mentality. Kidd would answer, of course, that such a retort presupposes that progress is secured by the exercise of the critical reason, whereas in his view progress is secured by the development of the emotional and affective aspects of man, not by the development of a reason which is destructive rather than constructive. It seems, however, to be obvious that though the emotive aspects of man are essential to his nature, reason should retain control. And if religion has no rational warrant at all, it is necessarily suspect. Further, though the influence exercised by religions on human societies is an undoubted fact, it by no means necessarily follows that this influence has been invariably beneficial. We need rational principles of discrimination.

There is, however, one main belief which is common to both Kidd and those whom he attacked, namely the belief that in the struggle for existence the principle of natural selection works automatically for progress.[1] And it is precisely this dogma of progress which has been called in question in the course of the twentieth century. In view of the cataclysmic events of this century we can hardly retain a serene confidence in the beneficent effects of collective emotion. But, equally, we find it difficult to suppose that the advance of science, taken by itself, is synonymous with social progress. There is the all-important question of the purposes to be realized by scientific knowledge. And consideration of this question takes us outside the sphere of descriptive science. Obviously, we should all agree that science should be used in the service of man. But the question arises, how are we to interpret man? And our answer to this question will involve metaphysics, either explicit or implicit. The attempt to by-pass or exclude metaphysics will often be found to involve a concealed metaphysical assumption, an unavowed theory of being. In other words, the idea that scientific advance pushes metaphysics out of the picture is mistaken. Metaphysics simply reappears in the form of concealed assumptions.

[1] As we have seen, T. H. Huxley was an exception, inasmuch as he believed that moral progress runs counter to the process of evolution in Nature.

CHAPTER V

THE PHILOSOPHY OF HERBERT SPENCER

Life and writings—The nature of philosophy and its basic concepts and principles—The general law of evolution: the alternation of evolution and dissolution—Sociology and politics —Relative and absolute ethics—The Unknowable in religion and science—Final comments.

1. In 1858, the year preceding that of the publication of Darwin's *The Origin of Species*, Herbert Spencer mapped out a plan for a system which was to be based on the law of evolution or, as he expressed it, the law of progress. He is one of the few British thinkers who have deliberately attempted the construction of a comprehensive philosophical system. He is also one of the few British philosophers who have acquired a world-wide reputation during their lifetime. Seizing on an idea which was already in the air and to which Darwin gave an empirical basis in a restricted field, Spencer turned it into the key-idea of a synoptic vision of the world and of human life and conduct, an optimistic vision which appeared to justify nineteenth-century belief in human progress and which made of Spencer one of the major prophets of an era.

Though, however, Spencer remains one of the great figures of the Victorian age, he now gives the impression of being one of the most dated of philosophers. Unlike Mill, whose writings well repay study, whether one agrees or not with the views expressed. Spencer is little read nowadays. It is not merely that the idea of evolution has become common coin and no longer arouses much excitement. It is rather that after the brutal challenges of the twentieth century we find it difficult to see how the scientific hypothesis of evolution, taken by itself, can provide any adequate basis for that optimistic faith in human progress which was, generally speaking, a characteristic feature of Spencer's thought. On the one hand positivism has changed its character and fights shy of explicit and comprehensive world-visions. On the other hand those philosophers who believe that the trend of evolution is in some real sense beneficent to man generally appeal to metaphysical theories which were foreign to the mind of Spencer. Moreover, while Mill not only dealt with many problems which are still examined by British philosophers but also treated them in a way which is still considered relevant, Spencer is notable for his large-scale exploration of one leading idea rather than for any detailed analyses. However, though Spencer's thought is so closely wedded to the Victorian era that it can scarcely be described as a living influence today, the fact remains that he was one of the leading representative members of the nineteenth century. Hence he cannot be passed over in silence.

Herbert Spencer was born at Derby on April 27th, 1820. Whereas Mill began Greek at the age of three, Spencer admits that at the age of thirteen he knew nothing worth mentioning of either Latin or Greek. By the age of sixteen, however, he had at any rate acquired some knowledge of mathematics; and after a few months as a schoolmaster at Derby he became a civil engineer employed by the Birmingham and Gloucester Railway. When the line was completed in 1841, Spencer was discharged. 'Got the sack—very glad', as he noted in his diary. But though in 1843 he moved to London to take up a literary career, he returned for a short while to the service of the railways and also tried his hand at inventions.

In 1848 Spencer became sub-editor of the *Economist*, and he entered into relations of friendship with G. H. Lewes, Huxley, Tyndall and George Eliot. With Lewes in particular he discussed the theory of evolution; and among the articles which he wrote anonymously for Lewes's *Leader* there was one on 'The Development Hypothesis', in which the idea of evolution was expounded on Lamarckian lines. In 1851 he published *Social Statics* and in 1855, at his own expense, *The Principles of Psychology*. At this time the state of his health was causing him serious concern, and he made several excursions to France, where he met Auguste Comte. He was able, however, to publish a collection of his essays in 1857.

At the beginning of 1858 Spencer drew up a scheme for *A System of Synthetic Philosophy*; and the prospectus, distributed in 1860, envisaged ten volumes. *First Principles* appeared in one volume in 1862, and *The Principles of Biology* in two volumes in 1864–7. *The Principles of Psychology*, originally published in one volume in 1855, appeared in two volumes in 1870–2, while the three volumes of *The Principles of Sociology* were published in 1876–96. *The Data of Ethics* (1879) was subsequently included with two other parts to form the first volume of *The Principles of Ethics* (1892), while the second volume of this work (1893) utilized

Justice (1891). Spencer also published new editions of several volumes of the *System*. For example, the sixth edition of *First Principles* appeared in 1900, while a revised and enlarged edition of *The Principles of Biology* was published in 1898–9. Spencer's *System of Synthetic Philosophy* constituted a remarkable achievement, carried through in spite of bad health and, at first at any rate, of serious financial difficulties. Intellectually, he was a self-made man; and the composition of his great work involved writing on a number of subjects which he had never really studied. He had to collect his data from various sources, and he then interpreted them in the light of the idea of evolution. As for the history of philosophy, he knew little about it, except from secondary sources. He did indeed make more than one attempt to read Kant's first *Critique*; but when he came to the doctrine of the subjectivity of space and time, he laid the book aside. He had little appreciation or understanding of points of view other than his own. However, if he had not practised what we might call a rigid economy of thought, it is unlikely he would ever have completed his self-imposed task.

Of Spencer's other publications we can mention *Education* (1861), a small but very successful book, *The Man Versus the State* (1884), a vigorous polemic against what the author regarded as the threatening slavery, and the posthumous *Autobiography* (1904). In 1885 Spencer published in America *The Nature and Reality of Religion*, comprising a controversy between himself and the positivist Frederic Harrison. But the work was suppressed, as Harrison protested against the re-publication of his articles without permission, especially as an introduction in support of Spencer's position by a Professor Yeomans had been included in the volume.

With the exception of membership of the Athenaeum Club (1868) Spencer consistently refused all honours. When invited to stand for the chair of mental philosophy and logic at University College, London, he refused; and he also declined membership of the Royal Society. He seems to have felt that when he had really had need of such offers they had not been made, and that when they were made, he no longer had need of them, his reputation being already established. As for honours offered by the government, his opposition to social distinctions of this kind militated against acceptance, quite apart from his annoyance at the lateness of the offers.

Spencer died on December 8th, 1903. At the time of his death he was extremely unpopular in his own country, mainly because of his opposition to the Boer War (1899–1902), which he regarded as an expression of the militaristic spirit that he so much hated.[1] Abroad, however, there was considerable criticism of English indifference to the passing of one of the country's outstanding figures. And in Italy the Chamber adjourned on receiving the news of Spencer's death.

2. Spencer's general account of the relation between philosophy and science bears a marked resemblance to that given by the classical positivists such as Auguste Comte. Both science and philosophy treat of phenomena, of, that is to say, the finite, conditioned and classifiable. True, in Spencer's opinion phenomena are manifestations to consciousness of infinite, unconditioned Being. But as knowledge involves relating and classification, whereas infinite, unconditional Being is by its very nature unique and unclassifiable, to say that such Being transcends the sphere of phenomena is to say that it transcends the sphere of the knowable.[2] Hence it cannot be investigated by the philosopher any more than by the scientist. Metaphenomenal or 'ultimate' causes lie outside the reach of both philosophy and science.

If, therefore, we are to distinguish between philosophy and science, we cannot do so simply in terms of the objects of which they treat. For both are concerned with phenomena. We have to introduce the idea of degrees of generalization. 'Science' is the name of the family of particular sciences. And though every science, as distinct from the unco-ordinated knowledge of particular facts, involves generalization, even the widest of such generalizations are partial in comparison with those universal truths of philosophy which serve to unify the sciences. 'The truths of Philosophy thus bear the same relation to the highest scientific truths, that each of these bears to lower scientific truths. . . . Knowledge of the lowest kind is un-unified knowledge; Science is *partially-unified* knowledge; Philosophy is *completely-unified* knowledge.'[3]

The universal truths or widest generalizations of philosophy can be considered in themselves, as 'products of exploration'.[4] And we are then concerned with general philosophy. Or the universal truths can be considered according to their active role as 'instruments of exploration'.[5] That is to say, they can be considered as

---

[1] Spencer's attitude to the Boer War prompted an attack on him by *The Times*.
[2] We shall return later to Spencer's doctrine of the 'unknowable'.
[3] *First Principles*, p. 119 (6th edition).   [4] *Ibid.*, p. 120.   [5] *Ibid.*

truths in the light of which we investigate different specific areas of phenomena, such as the data of ethics and sociology. And we are then concerned with special philosophy. Spencer's *First Principles* is devoted to general philosophy, while subsequent volumes of the *System* deal with the parts of special philosophy. Taken by itself, Spencer's account of the relation between science and philosophy in terms of degrees of unification tends to suggest that in his view the basic concepts of philosophy are derived by generalization from the particular sciences. But this is not the case. For he insists that there are fundamental concepts and assumptions which are involved in all thinking. Let us suppose that a philosopher decides to take one particular datum as the point of departure for his reflections, and that he imagines that by acting in this way he is making no assumptions. In actual fact the choice of one particular datum implies that there are other data which the philosopher might have chosen. And this involves the concept of existence other than the existence actually asserted. Again, no particular thing can be known except as like some other things, as classifiable in virtue of a common attribute, and as different from or unlike other things. In fine, the choice of one particular datum involves a number of 'unacknowledged postulates',[1] which together provide the outlines of a general philosophical theory. 'The developed intelligence is framed upon certain organized and consolidated conceptions of which it cannot divest itself; and which it can no more stir without using than the body can stir without help of its limbs.'[2]

It can hardly be claimed that Spencer makes his position crystal clear. For he speaks of 'tacit assumptions',[3] 'unavowed data',[4] 'unacknowledged postulates',[5] 'certain organized and consolidated conceptions',[6] and 'fundamental intuitions',[7] as though the meanings of these phrases stood in no need of further elucidation and as though they all meant the same thing. It is indeed clear that he does not intend to assert a Kantian theory of the *a priori*. The fundamental concepts and assumptions have an experimental basis. And sometimes Spencer speaks as though it were a question of the individual experience or consciousness. He says, for example, that 'we cannot avoid accepting as true the verdict of consciousness that some manifestations are like one another and some are unlike one another'.[8] The situation is

[1] *Ibid.*, p. 123.   [2] *Ibid.*   [3] *Ibid.*, p. 122.   [4] *Ibid.*, p. 123.
[5] *Ibid.*   [6] *Ibid.*   [7] *Ibid.*   [8] *Ibid.*, p. 125.

complicated, however, by the fact that Spencer accepts the idea of a relative *a priori*, that is, of concepts and assumptions which are, from the genetic point of view, the product of the accumulated experience of the race[1] but which are *a priori* in relation to a given individual mind, in the sense that they came to it with the force of 'intuitions'. The basic assumptions of the process of thought have to be taken provisionally as unquestionable. They can be justified or validated only by their results, that is, by showing the agreement or congruity between the experience which the assumptions logically lead us to expect and the experiences which we actually have. Indeed, 'the complete establishment of the congruity becomes the same thing as the complete unification of knowledge in which Philosophy reaches its goal'.[2] Thus general philosophy makes explicit the basic concepts and assumptions, while special philosophy shows their agreement with the actual phenomena in distinct fields or areas of experience.

Now, according to Spencer 'knowing is classifying, or grasping the like and separating the unlike'.[3] And as likeness and unlikeness are relations, we can say that all thinking is relational, that '*relation* is the universal form of thought'.[4] We can distinguish, however, between two kinds of relations, those of sequence and those of co-existence.[5] And each gives rise to an abstract idea. 'The abstract of all sequences is Time. The abstract of all co-existences is Space.'[6] Time and Space are not indeed original forms of consciousness in an absolute sense. But as the generation of these ideas takes place through an organization of experiences which proceeds throughout the entire evolution of mind or intelligence, they can have a relatively *a priori* character, as far as a given individual mind is concerned.

Our concept of Space is fundamentally that of co-existent positions which offer no resistance. And it is derived by abstraction from the concept of Matter, which in its simplest form is that of co-existent positions which offer resistance. In turn, the concept of Matter is derived from an experience of force. For 'forces, standing in certain co-relations, form the whole content of our

---

[1] Some of these may have their remoter origin in animal experience.
[2] *First Principles*, p. 125. [3] *Ibid.*, p. 127. [4] *Ibid.*, p. 145.
[5] In Spencer's opinion the idea of co-existence is derived from that of sequence, inasmuch as we find that the terms of certain relations of sequence can be presented with equal facility in reverse order. Co-existence cannot be an original datum of a consciousness which consists in serial states.
[6] *First Principles*, p. 146.

idea of Matter'.[1] Similarly, though the developed concepts of Motion involves the ideas of Space, Time and Matter, the rudimentary consciousness of Motion is simply that of 'serial impressions of force'.[2]

Spencer argues, therefore, that psychological analysis of the concepts of Time, Space, Matter and Motion shows that they are all based on experiences of Force. And the conclusion is that 'we come down, then, finally to Force, as the ultimate of ultimates'.[3] The principle of the indestructibility of matter is really that of the indestructibility of force. Similarly, all proofs of the principle of the continuity of motion 'involve the postulate that the quantity of Energy is constant',[4] energy being the force possessed by matter in motion. And in the end we arrive at the principle of the persistence of Force, 'which, as being the basis of science, cannot be established by science',[5] but transcends demonstration, a principle which has as its corollary that of the uniformity of law, the persistence of relations between forces.

It may be objected that such principles as that of the indestructibility of matter belong to science rather than to philosophy. But Spencer answers that they are 'truths which unify concrete phenomena belonging to all divisions of Nature, and so must be components of that all-embracing conception of things which Philosophy seeks'.[6] Further, though the word 'force' ordinarily signifies 'the consciousness of muscular tension',[7] the feeling of effort which we have when we set something in motion or resist a pressure is a symbol of Absolute Force. And when we speak of the persistence of Force, 'we really mean the persistence of some Cause which transcends our knowledge and conception'.[8] How we can intelligibly predicate persistence of an unknowable reality is not perhaps immediately evident. But if the assertion of the persistence of Force really means what Spencer says that it means, it clearly becomes a philosophical principle, even apart from the fact that its character as a universal truth would in any case qualify it for inclusion among the truths of philosophy according to Spencer's account of the relation between philosophy and science.

3. Though, however, such general principles as the indestructibility of matter, the continuity of motion and the persistence of force are components of the synthesis which philosophy seeks to

[1] *Ibid.*, p. 149. [2] *Ibid.*, p. 151. [3] *Ibid.*
[4] *Ibid.*, p. 167. [5] *Ibid.*, p. 175. [6] *Ibid.*, p. 249.
[7] *Ibid.*, p. 175. [8] *Ibid.*, p. 176.

achieve, they do not, even when taken together, constitute this synthesis. For we require a formula or law which specifies the course of the transformations undergone by matter and motion, and which thus serves to unify all the processes of change which are examined in the several particular sciences. That is to say, if we assume that there is no such thing as absolute rest or permanence but that every object is constantly undergoing change, whether by receiving or losing motion or by changes in the relations between its parts, we need to ascertain the general law of the continuous redistribution of matter and motion.

Spencer finds what he is looking for in what he calls indiscriminately a 'formula', 'law' or 'definition' of evolution. 'Evolution is an integration of matter and concomitant dissipation of motion; during which the matter passes from a relatively indefinite, incoherent homogeneity to a relatively definite, coherent heterogeneity; and during which the retained motion undergoes a parallel transformation.'[1] This law can be established deductively, by deduction from the persistence of force. It can also be established or confirmed inductively. For whether we contemplate the development of solar systems out of the nebular mass, or that of more highly organized and complex living bodies out of more primitive organisms, or that of man's psychological life, or the growth of language, or the evolution of social organization, we find everywhere a movement from relative indefiniteness to relative definiteness, from incoherence to coherence, together with a movement of progressive differentiation, the movement from relative homogeneity to relative heterogeneity. For example in the evolution of the living body we see a progressive structural and functional differentiation.

But this is only one side of the picture. For the integration of matter is accompanied by a dissipation of motion. And the process of evolution tends towards a state of equilibrium, of a balance of forces, which is succeeded by dissolution or disintegration. For example, the human body dissipates and loses its energies, dies and disintegrates; any given society loses its vigour and decays; and the heat of the sun is gradually dissipated.

Spencer is careful to avoid claiming that we can legitimately extrapolate what is true of a relatively closed system to the totality of things, the universe as a whole. We cannot, for example,

---

[1] *First Principles*, p. 367. In a note Spencer remarks that the word 'relatively', omitted in the original text, needs to be inserted in two places as above.

argue with certainty from the running-down, so to speak, of our solar system to the running-down of the universe. And it is possible, for all we know, that when life has been extinguished on our planet through the dissipation of the sun's heat, it will be in process of development in some other part of the universe. In fine, we are not entitled to argue that what happens to a part *must* happen to the whole.

'At the same time, if there is an alternation of evolution and dissolution in the totality of things, we must 'entertain the conception of Evolutions that have filled an immeasurable past and Evolutions that will fill an immeasurable future'.[1] And if this represents Spencer's personal opinion, we can say that he gives an up-to-date version of certain early Greek cosmologies, with their ideas of a cyclic process. In any case there is a rhythm of evolution and dissolution in the parts, even if we are not in a position to make dogmatic assertions about the whole. And though at first Spencer spoke about the law of evolution as the law of progress, his belief in alternations of evolution and dissolution evidently set limits to his optimism.

4. Spencer's ideal of a complete philosophical synthesis demands the inclusion of a systematic treatment of the inorganic world in the light of the idea of evolution. And he remarks that if this topic had been treated in the *System of Philosophy*, it 'would have occupied two volumes, one dealing with Astrogeny and the other with Geogeny'.[2] In point of fact, however, Spencer confines himself, in special philosophy, to biology, psychology, sociology and ethics. He alludes, of course, to astronomical, physical and chemical topics, but the *System* contains no systematic treatment of evolution in the inorganic sphere.

As limitations of space exclude a recapitulation of all the parts of Spencer's system, I propose to pass over biology and psychology and to make some remarks in this section about his sociological and political ideas, devoting the following section to the subject of ethics.

The sociologist is concerned with the growth, structures, functions and products of human societies.[3] The possibility of a science of sociology follows from the fact that we can find regular sequences among social phenomena, which permit prediction; and

[1] *Ibid.*, p. 506.　　　　[2] *The Principles of Sociology*, I, p. 3.
[3] The study of what Spencer calls super-organic evolution, which presupposes organic or biological evolution, would include, if understood in the widest sense, the study of, for example, the societies of bees and ants.

it is not excluded by the fact that social laws are statistical and predictions in this field approximate. 'Only a moiety of science is exact science.'[1] It is the possibility of generalization which is required, not quantitative exactitude. As for the utility of sociology, Spencer claims in a somewhat vague way that if we can discern an order in the structural and functional changes through which societies pass, 'knowledge of that order can scarcely fail to affect our judgments as to what is progressive and what retrograde—what is desirable, what is practicable, what is Utopian'.[2]

When we consider the struggle for existence in the general process of evolution, we find obvious analogies between the inorganic, organic and super-organic (social) spheres. The behaviour of an inanimate object depends on the relations between its own forces and the external forces to which it is exposed. Similarly, the behaviour of an organic body is the product of the combined influences of its intrinsic nature and of its environment, both inorganic and organic. Again, every human society 'displays phenomena that are ascribable to the character of its units and to the conditions under which they exist'.[3]

It is indeed true that the two sets of factors, intrinsic and extrinsic, do not remain static. For example, man's powers, physical, emotional and intellectual, have developed in the course of history, while evolving society has produced remarkable changes in its organic and inorganic environment. Again, the products of evolving society, its institutions and cultural creations, bring fresh influences into being. Further, the more human societies develop, so much the more do they react on one another, so that the super-organic environment occupies a position of even greater importance. But in spite of the growing complexity of the situation an analogous interplay of forces, intrinsic and extrinsic, is discernible in all three spheres.

Though, however, there is continuity between the inorganic, organic and super-organic spheres, there is also discontinuity. If there is similarity, there is also dissimilarity. Consider, for example, the idea of a society as an organism. As in the case of an organic body in the proper sense, the growth of society is accompanied by a progressive differentiation of structures, which results in a progressive differentiation of functions. But this point of similarity between the organic body and human society is also

---

[1] *The Study of Sociology*, p. 44 (26th thousand, 1907).   [2] *Ibid.*, p. 70.
[3] *The Principles of Sociology*, I, pp. 9–10.

a point of dissimilarity between them both and the inorganic body. For according to Spencer the actions of the different parts of an inorganic thing cannot properly be regarded as functions. Further, there is an important difference between the process of differentiation in an organic body and that in the social organism. For in the latter we do not find that kind of differentiation which in the former results in one part alone becoming the organ of intelligence and in some parts becoming sense-organs while others do not. In the organic body 'consciousness is concentrated in a small part of the aggregate', whereas in the social organism 'it is diffused throughout the aggregate: all the units possess the capacity for happiness and misery, if not in equal degrees, still in degrees that approximate'.[1]

An enthusiast for the interpretation of political society as an organism might, of course, try to find detailed analogies between differentiation of functions in the organic body and in society. But this might easily lead him into speaking, for example, as though the government were analogous to the brain and as though the other parts of society should leave all thinking to the government and simply obey its decisions. And this is precisely the sort of conclusion which Spencer wishes to avoid. Hence he insists on the relative independence of the individual members of a political society and denies the contention that society is an organism in the sense that it is more than the sum of its members and possesses an end which is different from the ends of the members. 'As, then, there is no social sensorium, it results that the welfare of the aggregate, considered apart from that of the members, is not an end to be sought. The society exists for the benefit of its members; not its members for the benefit of society.'[2] In other words, we can say that the arms and the legs exist for the good of the whole body. But in the case of society we have to say that the whole exists for the parts. Spencer's conclusion at any rate is clear. And even if his arguments are sometimes obscure and perplexing, it is also clear that in his opinion the analogy of an organism, as applied to a political society, is not only misleading but also dangerous.

The situation is in fact this. Spencer's determination to use the idea of evolution throughout all fields of phenomena leads him to speak of political society, the State, as a super-organism. But as he is a resolute champion of individual liberty against the claims

[1] *Ibid.*, I, p. 479.   [2] *Ibid.*

and encroachment of the State, he tries to deprive this analogy of
its sting by pointing out essential differences between the organic
body and the body political. And he does this by maintaining that
while political development is a process of integration, in the
sense that social groups become larger and individual wills are
merged together, it is also a movement from homogeneity to
heterogeneity, so that differentiation tends to increase. For
example, with the advance of civilization towards the modern
industrialized State the class-divisions of relatively more primitive
societies tend, so Spencer believes, to become less rigid and even
to break down. And this is a sign of progress.

Spencer's point depends in part on his thesis that 'the state of
homogeneity is an unstable state; and where there is already
some heterogeneity, the tendency is towards greater heterogeneity'.[1] Given this idea of the movement of evolution, it
obviously follows that a society in which differentiation is
relatively greater is more evolved than one in which there is
relatively less differentiation. At the same time it is clear that
Spencer's point of view also depends on a judgment of value,
namely that a society in which individual liberty is highly
developed is intrinsically more admirable and praiseworthy than
a society in which there is less individual liberty. True, Spencer
believes that a society which embodies the principle of individual
liberty possesses a greater survival-value than societies which do
not embody the principle. And this can be understood as a purely
factual judgment. But it seems obvious to me at any rate that
Spencer considers the first type of society to be more deserving of
survival because of its greater intrinsic value.

If we pass over Spencer's account of primitive societies and
their development, we can say that he concentrates most of his
attention on the transition from the militaristic or militant type
of society to the industrial type. The militant society is basically
'one in which the army is the nation mobilized while the nation is
the quiescent army, and which, therefore, acquires a structure
common to army and nation'.[2] There can indeed be development
within this kind of society. For example, the military leader
becomes the civil or political head, as in the case of the Roman
emperor; and in the course of time the army becomes a specialized
professional branch of the community instead of being coextensive with the adult male population. But in the militant

---

[1] *The Principles of Sociology*, II, p. 288.   [2] *Ibid.*, I, p. 577.

society in general integration and cohesion are dominant features. The primary aim is the preservation of the society, while the preservation of individual members is a matter for concern only as a means to the attainment of the primary aim. Again, in this kind of society there is constant regulation of conduct, and 'the individuality of each member has to be so subordinated in life, liberty, and property, that he is largely, or completely *owned* by the State'.[1] Further, as the militant type of society aims at self-sufficiency, political autonomy tends to be accompanied by economic autonomy.[2] The Germany of National Socialism would doubtless have represented for Spencer a good example of a revival of the militant type of society in the modern industrial era.

Spencer does not deny that the militant type of society had an essential role to play in the process of evolution considered as a struggle for existence in which the fittest survive. But he maintains that though inter-social conflict was necessary for the formation and growth of societies, the development of civilization renders war increasingly unnecessary. The militant type of society thus becomes an anachronism, and a transition is required to what Spencer calls the industrial type of society. This does not mean that the struggle for existence ceases. But it changes its form, becoming 'the industrial struggle for existence',[3] in which that society is best fitted to survive which produces 'the largest number of the best individuals—individuals best adapted for life in the industrial state'.[4] In this way Spencer tries to avoid the accusation that when he has arrived at the concept of the industrial type of society, he abandons the ideas of the struggle for existence and of the survival of the fittest.

It would be a great mistake to suppose that by the industrial type of society Spencer means simply a society in which the citizens are occupied, exclusively or predominantly, in the economic life of production and distribution. For an industrial society in this narrow sense would be compatible with a thoroughgoing regulation of labour by the State. And it is precisely this element of compulsion which Spencer is concerned to exclude. On the economic level, he is referring to a society dominated by the principle of *laissez-faire*. Hence in his view socialist and communist

[1] *Ibid.*, II, p. 607.
[2] The militant type of society also tends to manifest itself in characteristic forms of law and judicial procedure.
[3] *The Principles of Sociology*, II, p. 610.   [4] *Ibid.*

States would be very far from exemplifying the essence of the industrial type of society. The function of the State is to maintain individual freedom and rights, and to adjudicate, when necessary, between conflicting claims. It is not the business of the State to interfere positively with the lives and conduct of the citizens, except when interference is required for the maintenance of internal peace.

In other words, in the ideal type of industrial society, as Spencer interprets the term, emphasis is shifted from the totality, the society as a whole, to its members considered as individuals. 'Under the industrial *régime* the citizen's individuality, instead of being sacrificed by the society, has to be defended by the society. Defence of his individuality becomes the society's essential duty.'[1] That is to say, the cardinal function of the State becomes that of equitably adjusting conflicting claims between individual citizens and preventing the infringement of one man's liberty by another.

Spencer's belief in the universal applicability of the law of evolution obviously committed him to maintaining that the movement of evolution tends to the development of the industrial type of State, which he regarded, rather over-optimistically, as an essentially peaceful society. But the tendencies to interference and regulation by the State which were showing themselves in the last decades of his life led him to express his fear of what he called 'the coming slavery'[2] and to attack violently any tendency on the part of the State or of one of its organs to regard itself as omnicompetent. 'The great political superstition of the past was the divine right of kings. The great political superstition of the present is the divine right of parliaments.'[3] Again, 'the function of Liberalism in the past was that of putting a limit to the powers of kings. The function of true Liberalism in the future will be that of putting a limit to the powers of Parliaments.'[4]

Obviously, in this resolute attack on 'the coming slavery' Spencer could not appeal simply to the automatic working-out of any law of evolution. His words are clearly inspired by a passionate conviction in the value of individual liberty and initiative, a conviction which reflected the character and temperament of a man who had never at any period of his life been inclined to bow before constituted authority simply because it was authority. And it is a notorious fact that Spencer carried his attack on what

[1] *The Principles of Sociology*, II, p. 607.
[2] This is the title of one of his essays.
[3] *The Man Versus the State*, p. 78 (19th thousand, 1910).   [4] *Ibid.*, p. 107.

he regarded as encroachments by the State on private liberty to the extent of condemning factory legislation, sanitary inspection by government officials, State management of the Post Office, poor relief by the State and State education. Needless to say, he did not condemn reform as such or charitable relief work or the running of hospitals and schools. But his insistence was always on voluntary organization of such projects, as opposed to State action, management and control. In short, his ideal was that of a society in which, as he put it, the individual would be everything and the State nothing, in contrast with the militant type of society in which the State is everything and the individual nothing.

Spencer's equation of the industrial type of society with peace-loving and anti-militaristic society is likely to strike us as odd, unless we make the equation true by definition. And his extreme defence of the policy of *laissez-faire* is likely to appear to us as eccentric, or at least as a hangover from a bygone outlook. He does not seem to have understood, as Mill came to understand, at least in part, and as was understood more fully by an idealist such as T. H. Green, that social legislation and so-called interference by the State may very well be required to safeguard the legitimate claims of every individual citizen to lead a decent human life.

At the same time Spencer's hostility to social legislation which nowadays is taken for granted by the vast majority of citizens in Great Britain should not blind us to the fact that he, like Mill, saw the dangers of bureaucracy and of any exaltation of the power and functions of the State which tends to stifle individual liberty and originality. To the present writer at any rate it seems that concern with the common good leads to an approval of State action to a degree far beyond what Spencer was prepared to endorse. But it should never be forgotten that the common good is not something entirely different from the good of the individual. And Spencer was doubtless quite right in thinking that it is for the good both of individuals and of society in general that citizens should be able to develop themselves freely and show initiative. We may well think that it is the business of the State to create and maintain the conditions in which individuals can develop themselves, and that this demands, for example, that the State should provide for all the means of education according to the individual's capacity for profiting by it. But once we accept the principle that the State should concern itself with positively creating and maintaining the conditions which will make it possible for every individual to lead a decent human life in accordance with his or her capacities, we expose ourselves to the danger of subsequently forgetting that the common good is not an abstract entity to which the concrete interests of individuals have to be ruthlessly sacrificed. And Spencer's attitude, in spite of its eccentric exaggerations, can serve to remind us that the State exists for man and not man for the State. Further, the State is but one form of social organization: it is not the only legitimate form of society. And Spencer certainly understood this fact.

As has already been indicated, Spencer's political views were partly the expression of factual judgments, connected with his interpretation of the general movement of evolution, and partly an expression of judgments of value. For example, his assertion that what he calls the industrial type of society possesses a greater survival value than other types was partly equivalent to a prediction that it would in fact survive, in virtue of the trend of evolution. But it was also partly a judgment that the industrial type of society deserved to survive, because of its intrinsic value. Indeed, it is clear enough that with Spencer a positive evaluation of personal liberty was the really determining factor in his view of modern society. It is also clear that if a man is resolved that, as far as depends on him, the type of society which respects individual freedom and initiative *will* survive, this resolution is based primarily on a judgment of value rather than on any theory about the automatic working-out of a law of evolution.

5. Spencer regarded his ethical doctrine as the crown of his system. In the preface to *The Data of Ethics* he remarks that his first essay, on *The Proper Sphere of Government* (1842), vaguely indicated certain general principles of right and wrong in political conduct. And he adds that 'from that time onwards my ultimate purpose, lying behind all proximate purposes, has been that of finding for the principles of right and wrong in conduct at large, a scientific basis'.[1] Belief in supernatural authority as a basis for ethics has waned. It thus becomes all the more imperative to give morality a scientific foundation, independent of religious beliefs. And for Spencer this means establishing ethics on the theory of evolution.

Conduct in general, including that of animals, consists of acts

---

[1] *The Data of Ethics*, p. V (1907 edition). This preface is reprinted in the first volume of *The Principles of Ethics*, the reference being to p. VII (1892 edition).

adjusted to ends.[1] And the higher we proceed in the scale of evolution, the clearer evidence do we find of purposeful actions directed to the good either of the individual or of the species. But we also find that teleological activity of this kind forms part of the struggle for existence between different individuals of the same species and between different species. That is to say, one creature tries to preserve itself at the expense of another, and one species maintains itself by preying on another.

This type of purposeful conduct, in which the weaker goes to the wall, is for Spencer imperfectly evolved conduct. In perfectly evolved conduct, ethical conduct in the proper sense, antagonisms between rival groups and between individual members of one group will have been replaced by co-operation and mutual aid. Perfectly evolved conduct, however, can be achieved only in proportion as militant societies give place to permanently peaceful societies. In other words it cannot be achieved in a stable manner except in the perfectly evolved society, in which alone can the clash between egoism and altruism be overcome and transcended.

This distinction between imperfectly and perfectly evolved conduct provides the basis for a distinction between relative and absolute ethics. Absolute ethics is 'an ideal code of conduct formulating the behaviour of the completely adapted man in the completely evolved society',[2] while relative ethics is concerned with the conduct which is the nearest approximation to this ideal in the circumstances in which we find ourselves, that is, in more or less imperfectly evolved societies. According to Spencer, it is simply not true that in any set of circumstances which call for purposeful action on our part we are always faced with a choice between an action which is absolutely right and one which is absolutely wrong. For example, it may happen that circumstances are such that, however I act, I shall cause some pain to another person. And an action which causes pain to another cannot be absolutely right. In such circumstances, therefore, I have to try to estimate which possible course of action is relatively right, that is, which possible course of action will probably cause the greatest amount of good and the least amount of evil. I cannot expect to make an infallible judgment. I can only act as seems to me best, after devoting to the matter the amount of reflection which appears to be demanded by the relative importance of the issue.

[1] Purposeless actions are excluded from 'conduct'.
[2] *The Data of Ethics*, p. 238.

I can indeed bear in mind the ideal code of conduct of absolute ethics; but I cannot legitimately assume that this standard will serve as a premiss from which I can infallibly deduce what action would be relatively best in the circumstances in which I find myself.

Spencer accepts the utilitarian ethics in the sense that he takes happiness to be the ultimate end of life and measures the rightness or wrongness of actions by their relation to this end. In his opinion the 'gradual rise of a utilitarian ethic has, indeed, been inevitable'.[1] True, there was from the start a nascent utilitarianism, in the sense that some actions were always felt to be beneficial and other injurious to man and society. But in past societies ethical codes were associated with authority of some sort or another, or with the idea of divine authority and divinely imposed sanctions, whereas in the course of time ethics has gradually become independent of non-ethical beliefs, and there has been growing up a moral outlook based simply on the ascertainable natural consequences of actions. In other words, the trend of evolution in the moral sphere has been towards the development of utilitarianism. It must be added, however, that utilitarianism must be understood in such a way that room is found for the distinction between relative and absolute ethics. Indeed, the very idea of evolution suggests progress towards an ideal limit. And in this progress advance in virtue cannot be separated from social advance. 'The co-existence of a perfect man and an imperfect society is impossible.'[2]

As Spencer regards utilitarianism as the scientifically-based ethics, it is understandable that he wishes to show that it is not simply one among many mutually exclusive systems, but that it can find room for the truths contained in other systems. Thus he maintains, for example, that utilitarianism, when rightly understood, finds room for the point of view which insists on the concepts of right, wrong and obligation rather than on the attainment of happiness. Bentham may have thought that happiness is to be aimed at directly, by applying the hedonistic calculus. But he was wrong. He would indeed have been right if the attainment of happiness did not depend on the fulfilment of conditions. But in this case any action would be moral if it produced pleasure. And this notion is incompatible with the moral consciousness. In point of fact the attainment of happiness depends on the fulfilment of

---

[1] *The Principles of Ethics*, I, p. 318.   [2] *The Data of Ethics*, p. 241.

certain conditions, that is, on the observance of certain moral precepts or rules.[1] And it is at the fulfilment of these conditions that we ought to aim directly. Bentham thought that everyone knows what happiness is, and that it is more intelligible than, say, the principles of justice. But this view is the reverse of the truth. The principles of justice are easily intelligible, whereas it is far from easy to say what happiness is. Spencer advocates, therefore, what he calls a 'rational' utilitarianism, one which 'takes for its immediate object of pursuit conformity to certain principles which, in the nature of things, causally determine welfare'.[2]

Again, the theory that moral rules can be inductively established by observing the natural consequences of actions does not entail the conclusion that there is no truth at all in the theory of moral intuitionism. For there are indeed what can be called moral intuitions, though they are not something mysterious and inexplicable but 'the slowly organized results of experiences received by the race'.[3] What was originally an induction from experience can come in later generations to have for the individual the force of an intuition. The individual may see or feel instinctively that a certain course of action is right or wrong, though this instinctive reaction is the result of the accumulated experience of the race.

Similarly, utilitarianism can perfectly well recognize truth in the contention that the perfection of our nature is the object for which we should seek. For the trend of evolution is towards the emergence of the highest form of life. And though happiness is the supreme end, it is 'the concomitant of that highest life which every theory of moral guidance has distinctly or vaguely in view'.[4] As for the theory that virtue is the end of human conduct, this is simply one way of expressing the doctrine that our direct aim should be that of fulfilling the conditions for the attainment of the highest form of life to which the process of evolution tends. If it were attained, happiness would result.

Needless to say, Spencer could not reasonably claim to ground his ethical theory on the theory of evolution without admitting a continuity between evolution in the biological sphere and that in the moral sphere. And he maintains, for example, that 'human justice must be a further development of sub-human justice'.[5]

---

[1] Obviously, the idea of moral precepts must be understood in such a way as to admit the distinction between principles of conduct in an imperfectly evolved society and the ideal principles which would obtain in a perfectly evolved society.
[2] *The Data of Ethics*, p. 140.　　　[3] *Ibid.*, p. 148.　　　[4] *Ibid.*
[5] *Justice* (*The Principles of Ethics*, Part IV), p. 17.

At the same time, in a preface, subsequently withdrawn, to the fifth and sixth parts of *The Principles of Ethics* he admits that the doctrine of evolution has not furnished guidance to the hoped-for extent. He seems, however, never to have understood clearly that the process of evolution, considered as an historical fact, could not by itself establish the value-judgments which he brought to bear upon its interpretation. For example, even if we grant that evolution is moving towards the emergence of a certain type of human life in society and that this type is therefore shown to be the most fitted for survival, it does not necessarily follow that it is morally the most admirable type. As T. H. Huxley saw, factual fitness for survival in the struggle for existence and moral excellence are not necessarily the same thing.

Of course, if we assume that evolution is a teleological process directed towards the progressive establishment of a moral order, the situation is somewhat different. But though an assumption of this kind may have been implicit in Spencer's outlook, he did not profess to make any such metaphysical assumptions.

6. The explicit metaphysical element in Spencer's thought is, somewhat paradoxically, his philosophy of the Unknowable. This topic is introduced in the context of a discussion about the alleged conflict between religion and science. 'Of all antagonisms of belief the oldest, the widest, the most profound, and the most important is that between Religion and Science.'[1] Of course, if religion is understood simply as a subjective experience, the question of a conflict between it and science hardly arises. But if we bear in mind religious beliefs, the case is different. In regard to particular events supernatural explanations have been superseded by scientific or natural explanations. And religion has had to confine itself more or less to offering an explanation of the existence of the universe as a totality.[2] But the arguments are unacceptable to anyone who possesses a scientific outlook. In this sense, therefore, there is a conflict between the religious and scientific mentalities. And it can be resolved, according to Spencer, only through a philosophy of the Unknowable.

If we start from the side of religious belief, we can see that both pantheism and theism are untenable. By pantheism Spencer

---

[1] *First Principles*, p. 9.
[2] It may occur to the reader that religion and the offering of explanations are not precisely the same thing. But in ordinary language 'religion' is generally understood as involving an element or elements of belief. And Spencer obviously understands the term in this way.

understands the theory of a universe which develops itself from potential to actual existence. And he contends that this idea is inconceivable. We do not really know what it means. Hence the question of its truth or falsity hardly arises. As for theism, understood as the doctrine that the world was created by an external agent, this too is untenable. Apart from the fact that the creation of space is inconceivable, because its non-existence cannot be conceived, the idea of a self-existent Creator is as inconceivable as that of a self-existent universe. The very idea of self-existence is inconceivable. 'It is not a question of probability, or credibility, but of conceivability.'[1]

It is true, Spencer concedes, that if we inquire into the ultimate cause or causes of the effects produced on our senses, we are led inevitably to the hypothesis of a First Cause. And we shall find ourselves driven to describe it as both infinite and absolute. But Mansel[2] has shown that though the idea of a finite and dependent First Cause involves manifest contradictions, the idea of a First Cause which is infinite and absolute is no more free from contradictions, even if they are not so immediately evident. We are unable, therefore, to say anything intelligible about the nature of the First Cause. And we are left in the end with nothing more than the idea of an inscrutable Power.

If, however, we start from the side of science, we are again brought face to face with the Unknowable. For science cannot solve the mystery of the universe. For one thing, it cannot show that the universe is self-existent, for the idea of self-existence is, as we have seen, inconceivable or unintelligible. For another thing, the ultimate ideas of science itself 'are all representative of realities that cannot be comprehended'.[3] For example, we cannot understand what force is 'in itself'. And in the end 'ultimate religious ideas and ultimate scientific ideas alike turn out to be merely symbols of the actual, not cognitions of it'.[4]

This point of view is supported by an analysis of human thought. All thinking, as we have seen, is relational. And that which is not classifiable by being related to other things through relations of similarity and dissimilarity is not a possible object of knowledge. Hence we cannot know the unconditioned and

---

[1] First Principles, p. 29.
[2] Henry L. Mansel (1820–71), who became Dean of St. Paul's, developed Sir William Hamilton's doctrine about the unknowable unconditioned and gave the Bampton lectures on The Limits of Religious Thought (1858) from which Spencer quotes (First Principles, pp. 33–6) in support of his own agnosticism.
[3] First Principles, p. 55.   [4] Ibid., p. 57.

absolute. And this applies not only to the Absolute of religion but also to ultimate scientific ideas if considered as representing meta-phenomenal entities or things-in-themselves. At the same time to assert that all knowledge is 'relative' is to assert implicitly that there exists a non-relative reality. 'Unless a real Non-relative or Absolute be postulated, the Relative itself becomes absolute, and so brings the argument to a contradiction.'[1] In fact, we cannot eliminate from our consciousness the idea of an Absolute behind appearances.

Thus whether we approach the matter through a critical examination of religious beliefs or through reflection on our ultimate scientific ideas or through an analysis of the nature of thought and knowledge, we arrive in the end at the concept of an unknowable reality. And a permanent state of peace between religion and science will be achieved 'when science becomes fully convinced that its explanations are proximate and relative, while Religion becomes fully convinced that the mystery it contemplates is ultimate and absolute'.[2]

Now, the doctrine of the Unknowable forms the first part of *First Principles* and thus comes at the beginning of Spencer's system of philosophy as formally arranged. And this fact may incline the unwary reader to attribute to the doctrine a funda-mental importance. When, however, he discovers that the inscrutable Absolute or Power of religion is practically equiparated with Force, considered in itself, he may be led to conclude that the doctrine is not much more, if anything, than a sop politely offered to the religious-minded by a man who was not himself a believer in God and who was buried, or rather cremated, without any religious ceremony. It is thus easy to understand how some writers have dismissed the first part of *First Principles* as an unhappy excrescence. Spencer deals with the Unknowable at considerable length. But the total result is not impressive from the metaphysical point of view, as the arguments are not well thought out, while the scientist is likely to demur at the notion that his basic ideas pass all understanding.

The fact remains, however, that Spencer recognizes a certain mystery in the universe. His arguments for the existence of the Unknowable are indeed somewhat confused. Sometimes he gives the impression of accepting a Humian phenomenalism and of arguing that the modifications produced on our senses must be

---

[1] *First Principles*, pp. 82–3.   [2] *Ibid.*, p. 92.

caused by something which transcends our knowledge. At other times he seems to have at the back of the mind a more or less Kantian line of thought, derived from Hamilton and Mansel. External things are phenomena in the sense that they can be known only in so far as they conform to the nature of human thought. Things-in-themselves or noumena cannot be known; but as the idea of the noumenon is correlative to that of the phenomenon, we cannot avoid postulating it.[1] Spencer also relies, however, on what he calls an all-important fact, namely that besides 'definite' consciousness 'there is also an *indefinite* consciousness which cannot be formulated'.[2] For example, we cannot have a definite consciousness of the finite without a concomitant indefinite consciousness of the infinite. And this line of argument leads to the assertion of the infinite Absolute as a positive reality of which we have a vague or indefinite consciousness. We cannot know *what* the Absolute is. But even though we deny each successive definite interpretation or picture of the Absolute which presents itself, 'there ever remains behind an element which passes into new shapes'.[3]

This line of argument appears to be intended seriously. And though it might be more convenient to turn Spencer into a complete positivist by dismissing the doctrine of the Unknowable as a patronizing concession to religious people, there does not seem to be any adequate justification for this summary dismissal. When Frederic Harrison, the positivist, exhorted Spencer to transform the philosophy of the Unknowable into the Comtist religion of humanity, Spencer turned a deaf ear. It is easy to poke fun at him for using a capital letter for the Unknowable, as though, as it has been said, he expected one to take off one's hat to it. But he seems to have been genuinely convinced that the world of science is the manifestation of a reality which transcends human knowledge. The doctrine of the Unknowable is unlikely to satisfy many religious people. But this is another question. As far as Spencer himself is concerned, he appears to have sincerely believed that the vague consciousness of an Absolute or Unconditioned is an uneliminable feature of human thought, and that it is, as it were, the heart of religion, the permanent element which survives the succession of different creeds and different metaphysical systems.

7. Needless to say, Spencer's philosophy contains a good deal

---

[1] Spencer actually employs the Kantian terms.   [2] *First Principles*, p. 74.
[3] *Ibid.*, p. 80.

of metaphysics. Indeed, it is difficult to think of any philosophy which does not. Is not phenomenalism a form of metaphysics? And when Spencer says, for example, that 'by reality we mean *persistence* in consciousness',[1] it is arguable that this is a metaphysical assertion. We might, of course, try to interpret it as being simply a definition or as a declaration about the ordinary use of words. But when we are told that 'persistence is our ultimate test of the real whether as existing under its unknown form or under the form known to us',[2] it is reasonable to classify this as a metaphysical assertion.

Obviously, Spencer cannot be described as a metaphysician if we mean by this a philosopher who undertakes to disclose the nature of ultimate reality. For in his view it cannot be disclosed. And though he is a metaphysician, to the extent of asserting the existence of the Unknowable, he then devotes himself to constructing a unified overall interpretation of the knowable, that is, of phenomena. But if we like to call this general interpretation 'descriptive metaphysics', we are, of course, free to do so.

In developing this interpretation Spencer adheres to the empiricist tradition. It is true that he is anxious to reconcile conflicting points of view. But when he is concerned with showing that his own philosophy can recognize truth in non-empiricist theories, his method of procedure is to give an empiricist explanation of the data on which the theories are based. As has already been mentioned, he is quite prepared to admit that there are what can be called moral intuitions. For an individual may very well feel a quasi-instinctive approval or disapproval of certain types of action and may 'see', as though intuitively and without any process of reasoning, that such actions are right or wrong. But in Spencer's opinion moral intuitions in this sense are 'the results of accumulated experiences of Utility, gradually organized and inherited'.[3] Whether there are such things as inherited experiences of utility, is open to question. But in any case it is abundantly clear that Spencer's way of showing that there is truth in moral intuitionism is to give an empiricist explanation of the empirical data to which this theory appeals.

Similarly, Spencer is prepared to admit that there is something which can be called an intuition of space, in the sense that as far as the individual is concerned it is practically a form independent

[1] *First Principles*, p. 143.   [2] *Ibid.*, pp. 143-4.
[3] *The Data of Ethics*, p. 106.

of experience. But it by no means follows that Spencer is trying
to incorporate into his own philosophy the Kantian doctrine of the
a priori. What he does is to argue that this theory is based on a
real fact, but that this fact can be explained in terms of the
'organized and consolidated experiences of all antecedent individuals who bequeathed to him [a given subsequent individual]
their slowly-developed nervous organizations'.[1]

Though, however, we are not entitled to conclude from Spencer's
concern with reconciling conflicting points of view that he throws
empiricism overboard, he is, we can say, an empiricist with a
difference. For he does not simply tackle individual problems
separately, as many empiricists are apt to do. In his autobiography he speaks of his architectonic instinct, his love for
system-building. And in point of fact his philosophy was designed
as a system: it did not simply become a system in the sense that
different lines of investigation and reflection happened to converge towards the formation of an overall picture. Spencer's
general principle of interpretation, the so-called law of evolution,
was conceived at an early stage and then used as an instrument
for the unification of the sciences.

It can hardly be claimed that Spencer's architectonic instinct,
his propensity for synthesis, was accompanied by an outstanding
gift for careful analysis or for the exact statement of his meaning.
But his weak health and the obstacles which he had to face in the
fulfilment of his self-imposed mission did not in any case leave
him the time or the energy for much more than he was able in
fact to achieve. And though most readers probably find his writings extremely dull, his ambitions and pertinacious attempt to
unify our knowlege of the world and of man, as well as our moral
consciousness and social life, in the light of one all-pervading idea
demands the tribute of our admiration. He has relapsed, as it
were, into the Victorian era; and, as has already been remarked,
in regard to living influence there is no comparison between
Spencer and J. S. Mill. But though Spencer's philosophy may be
covered with dust it deserves something better than the contemptuous attitude adopted by Nietzsche, who regarded it as a
typical expression of the tame and limited mentality of the
English middle class.

[1] *Ibid.*

PART II

THE IDEALIST MOVEMENT IN GREAT BRITAIN

CHAPTER VI
THE BEGINNINGS OF THE MOVEMENT

Introductory historical remarks—Literary pioneers; Coleridge and Carlyle—Ferrier and the subject-object relation—John Grote's attack on phenomenalism and hedonism—The revival of interest in Greek philosophy and the rise of interest in Hegel; B. Jowett and J. H. Stirling.

1. IN the second half of the nineteenth century idealism became the dominant philosophical movement in the British universities. It was not, of course, a question of subjective idealism. If this was anywhere to be found, it was a logical consequence of the phenomenalism associated with the names of Hume in the eighteenth century and J. S. Mill in the nineteenth century. For the empiricists who embraced phenomenalism tended to reduce both physical objects and minds to impressions or sensations, and then to reconstruct them with the aid of the principle of the association of ideas. They implied that, basically, we know only phenomena, in the sense of impressions, and that, if there are metaphenomenal realities, we cannot know them. The nineteenth-century idealists, however, were convinced that things-in-themselves, being expressions of the one spiritual reality which manifests itself in and through the human mind, are essentially intelligible, knowable. Subject and object are correlative because they are both rooted in one ultimate spiritual principle. It was thus a question of objective rather than subjective idealism.[1]

Nineteenth-century British idealism thus represented a revival of explicit metaphysics.[2] That which is the manifestation of Spirit can in principle be known by the human spirit. And the whole

[1] The foregoing remarks constitute a generalization which is open to criticism on a number of counts. But in such introductory observations one has to prescind from the differences between the various idealist systems.

[2] Empiricism, it is true, had its own implicit metaphysics. And the empiricists not infrequently used the term 'metaphysics' in regard to some of their tenets. But in so far as metaphysics involves an attempt to disclose the nature of ultimate reality, idealism can legitimately be said to represent a revival of metaphysics.

world is the manifestation of Spirit. Science is simply one level of knowledge, one aspect of the complete knowledge to which the mind tends, even if it cannot fully actualize its ideal. Metaphysical philosophy endeavours to complete the synthesis.

The idealist metaphysics was thus a spiritualist metaphysics, in the sense that for it ultimate reality was in some sense spiritual. And it follows that idealism was sharply opposed to materialism. In so far indeed as the phenomenalists tried to go beyond the dispute between materialism and spiritualism by reducing both minds and physical objects to phenomena which cannot properly be described either as spiritual or as material, we cannot legitimately call them materialists. But these phenomena were evidently something very different from the one spiritual reality of the idealists. And in any case we have seen that on the more positivistic side of the empiricist movement there appeared an at least methodological materialism, the so-called scientific materialism, a line of thought for which the idealists had no sympathy.

With its emphasis on the spiritual character of ultimate reality and on the relation between the finite spirit and infinite Spirit idealism stood for a religious outlook as against materialistic positivism and the tendency of empiricism in general to by-pass religious problems or to leave room, at best, for a somewhat vague agnosticism. Indeed, a good deal of the popularity of idealism was due to the conviction that it stood firmly on the side of religion. To be sure, with Bradley, the greatest of the British idealists, the concept of God passed into that of the Absolute, and religion was depicted as a level of consciousness which is surpassed in metaphysical philosophy, while McTaggart, the Cambridge idealist, was an atheist. But with the earlier idealists the religious motive was much in evidence, and idealism seemed to be the natural home of those who were concerned with preserving a religious outlook in face of the threatening incursions of agnostics, positivists and materialists.[1] Further, after Bradley and Bosanquet idealism turned from absolute to personal idealism and was once again favourable to Christian theism, though by that time the impetus of the movement was already spent.

It would, however, be a mistake to conclude that British

[1] In Catholic countries idealism, with its tendency to subordinate theology to speculative philosophy, was commonly regarded as a disintegrating influence, so far as the Christian religion was concerned. In England the situation was somewhat different. A good many of the British idealists were themselves religious men, who found in their philosophy both an expression of and a support for their religious view of the world and of human life.

idealism in the nineteenth century represented simply a retreat from the practical concerns of Bentham and Mill into the metaphysics of the Absolute. For it had a part to play in the development of social philosophy. Generally speaking, the ethical theory of the idealists emphasized the idea of self-realization, of the perfecting of the human personality as an organic whole, an idea which had more in common with Aristotelianism than with Benthamism. And they looked on the function of the State as that of creating the conditions under which individuals could develop their potentialities as persons. As the idealists tended to interpret the creation of such conditions as a removal of hindrances, they could, of course, agree with the utilitarians that the State should interfere as little as possible with the liberty of the individual. They had no wish to replace freedom by servitude. But as they interpreted freedom as freedom to actualize the potentialities of the human personality, and as the removal of hindrances to freedom in this sense involved in their opinion a good deal of social legislation, they were prepared to advocate a measure of State-activity which went beyond anything contemplated by the more enthusiastic adherents of the policy of *laissez faire*. We can say, therefore, that in the latter part of the nineteenth century idealist social and political theory was more in tune with the perceived needs of the time than the position defended by Herbert Spencer. Benthamism or philosophical radicalism doubtless performed a useful task in the first part of the century. But the revised liberalism expounded by the idealists later in the century was by no means 'reactionary'. It looked forward rather than backward.

The foregoing remarks may appear to suggest that nineteenth-century idealism in Great Britain was simply a native reaction to empiricism and positivism and to *laissez faire* economic and political theory. In point of fact, however, German thought, especially that of Kant and Hegel successively, exercised an important influence on the development of British idealism. Some writers, notably J. H. Muirhead,[1] have maintained that the British idealists of the nineteenth century were the inheritors of a Platonic tradition which had manifested itself in the thought of the Cambridge Platonists in the seventeenth century and in the philosophy of Berkeley in the eighteenth century. But though it is useful to draw attention to the fact that British philosophy has not been exclusively empiricist in character, it would be difficult

[1] In *The Platonic Tradition in Anglo-Saxon Philosophy* (1931).

to show that nineteenth-century idealism can legitimately be considered as an organic development of a native Platonic tradition. The influence of German thought, particularly of Kant and Hegel,[1] cannot be dismissed as a purely accidental factor. It is indeed true that no British idealist of note can be described as being in the ordinary sense a disciple of either Kant or Hegel. Bradley, for example, was an original thinker. But it by no means follows that the stimulative influence of German thought was a negligible factor in the development of British idealism.

A limited knowledge of Kant was provided for English readers even during the philosopher's lifetime. In 1795 a disciple of Kant, F. A. Nitzsch, gave some lectures on the critical philosophy at London, and in the following year he published a small work on the subject. In 1797 J. Richardson published his translation of *Principles of Critical Philosophy* by J. J. Beck, and in 1798 A. F. M. Willich published *Elements of Critical Philosophy*. Richardson's translation of Kant's *Metaphysic of Morals* appeared in 1799; but the first translation of the *Critique of Pure Reason*, by F. Haywood, did not appear until 1838. And the serious studies of Kant, such as E. Caird's great work, *A Critical Account of the Philosophy of Kant* (1877), did not appear until a considerably later date. Meanwhile the influence of the German philosopher, together with a host of other influences, was felt by the poet Coleridge, whose ideas will be discussed presently, and in a more obvious way by Sir William Hamilton, though the element of Kantianism in Hamilton's thought was most conspicuous in his doctrine about the limits of human knowledge and in his consequent agnosticism in regard to the nature of ultimate reality.

Among the British idealists proper, Kant's influence may be said to have been felt particularly by T. H. Green and E. Caird. But it was mixed with the influence of Hegel. More accurately, Kant was seen as looking forward to Hegel or was read, as it has been put, through Hegelian spectacles. Indeed, in J. H. Stirling's *The Secret of Hegel* (1865) the view was explicitly defended that the philosophy of Kant, if properly understood and evaluated, leads straight to Hegelianism. Hence, though we can say with truth that the influence of Hegel is more obvious in the absolute

[1] Fichte and Schelling exercised little influence, though the former had some stimulative effect on Carlyle, and the latter on Coleridge. There is one obvious reason for this. The classical German idealist movement was already over when the British began; and it was regarded as having culminated in Hegel, considered as the true successor of Kant.

idealism of Bradley and Bosanquet than in the philosophy of Green, there is no question of suggesting that we can divide up the British idealists into Kantians and Hegelians. Some pioneers apart, the influence of Hegel was felt from the beginning of the movement. And it is thus not altogether unreasonable to describe British idealism, as is often done, as a Neo-Hegelian movement, provided at least that it is understood that it was a question of receiving stimulus from Hegel rather than of following him in the relation of pupil to master.

In its earlier phases the British idealist movement was characterized by a marked concentration on the subject-object relationship. In this sense idealism can be said to have had an epistemological foundation, inasmuch as the subject-object relationship is basic in knowledge. The metaphysics of the Absolute was not indeed absent. For subject and object were regarded as grounded in and manifesting one ultimate spiritual reality. But the point of departure affected the metaphysics in an important way. For the emphasis placed in the first instance on the finite subject militated against any temptation to interpret the Absolute in such a manner as to entail the conclusion that the finite is no more than its 'unreal' appearance. In other words, the earlier idealists tended to interpret the Absolute in a more or less theistic, or at any rate in a panentheistic, sense, the monistic aspect of metaphysical idealism remaining in the background. And this, of course, made it easier to represent idealism as an intellectual support for traditional religion.

Gradually, however, the idea of the all-comprehensive organic totality came more and more into the foreground. Thus with Bradley the self was depicted as a mere 'appearance' of the Absolute, as something which is not fully real when regarded in its *prima facie* independence. And this explicit metaphysics of the Absolute was understandably accompanied by a greater emphasis on the State in the field of social philosophy. While Herbert Spencer on the one hand was engaged in asserting an opposition between the interests of the free individual and those of the State, the idealists were engaged in representing man as achieving true freedom through his participation in the life of the totality.

In other words, we can see in the idealist movement up to Bradley and Bosanquet the increasing influence of Hegelianism. As has already been indicated, the influence of Kant was never unmixed. For the critical philosophy was seen as looking forward to metaphysical idealism. But if we make allowances for this fact and also for the fact that there were very considerable differences between Bradley's theory of the Absolute and that of Hegel, we can say that the change from emphasis on the subject-object relationship to emphasis on the idea of the organic totality represented a growing predominance of the stimulative influence of Hegelianism over that of the critical philosophy of Kant.

In the final phase of the idealist movement emphasis on the finite self became once again prominent, though it was a question this time of the active self, the human person, rather than of the epistemological subject. And this personal idealism was accompanied by a reapproximation to theism, except in the notable case of McTaggart, who depicted the Absolute as the system of finite selves. But though this phase of personal idealism is of some interest, inasmuch as it represents the finite self's resistance to being swallowed up in some impersonal Absolute, it belongs to a period when idealism in Britain was giving way to a new current of thought, associated with the names of G. E. Moore, Bertrand Russell, and, subsequently, Ludwig Wittgenstein.

2. As far as the general educated public was concerned, the influence of German thought first made itself felt in Great Britain through the writings of poets and literary figures such as Coleridge and Carlyle.

(i) Samuel Taylor Coleridge (1772–1834) seems to have made his first acquaintance with philosophy through the writings of Neo-Platonists, when he was a schoolboy at Christ's Hospital. This early attraction for the mystical philosophy of Plotinus was succeeded, however, by a Voltairean phase, during which he was for a short time a sceptic in regard to religion. Then at Cambridge Coleridge developed a perhaps somewhat surprising enthusiasm for David Hartley and his associationist psychology.[1] Indeed, Coleridge claimed to be more consistent than Hartley had been. For whereas Hartley, while maintaining that psychical processes depend on and are correlated with vibrations in the brain, had not asserted the corporeality of thought, Coleridge wrote to Southey in 1794 that he believed thought to be corporeal, that is, motion. At the same time Coleridge combined his enthusiasm for Hartley with religious faith.[2] And he came to think that the scientific

---

[1] That is to say, it is from one point of view somewhat surprising to find that the romantic poet was ever an enthusiast for Hartley of all people. But the associationist psychology was then regarded as 'advanced', and this doubtless helped to commend it to the intellectually alive undergraduate.

[2] For the matter of that, Hartley himself had been a religious believer.

understanding is inadequate as a key to reality, and to speak of
the role of intuition and the importance of moral experience. Later
on he was to declare that Hartley's system, in so far as it differs
from that of Aristotle, is untenable.[1]

Coleridge's distinction between the scientific understanding
and the higher reason or, as the Germans would put it, between
Verstand and *Vernunft* was one expression of his revolt against
the spirit of the eighteenth-century Enlightenment. He did not,
of course, mean to imply that the scientific and critical understanding should be rejected in the name of a higher and intuitive
reason. His point was rather that the former is not an omnicompetent instrument in the interpretation of reality, but that it
needs to be supplemented and balanced by the latter, namely the
intuitive reason. It can hardly be claimed that Coleridge made his
distinction between understanding and reason crystal clear. But
the general line of his thought is sufficiently plain. In *Aids to
Reflection* (1825) he describes the understanding as the faculty
which judges according to sense. Its appropriate sphere is the
sensible world, and it reflects and generalizes on the basis of
sense-experience. Reason, however, is the vehicle of ideas which
are presupposed by all experience, and in this sense it predetermines and governs experience. It also perceives truths which are
incapable of verification in sense-experience, and it intuitively
apprehends spiritual realities. Further, Coleridge identifies it with
the practical reason, which comprises the will and the moral aspect
of the human personality. J. S. Mill is thus perfectly justified in
saying in his famous essay on Coleridge that the poet dissents
from the 'Lockian' view that all knowledge consists of generalizations from experience, and that he claims for the reason, as
distinct from the understanding, the power to perceive by direct
intuition realities and truths which transcend the reach of the
senses.[2]

In his development of this distinction Coleridge received
stimulus from the writings of Kant, which he began to study
shortly after his visit to Germany in 1798–9.[3] But he tends to
speak as though Kant not only limited the scope of the understanding to knowledge of phenomenal reality but also envisaged

[1] See Coleridge's *Biographia Literaria*, ch. 6.
[2] See Mill's *Dissertations and Discussions*, I, p. 405.
[3] 'The writings of the illustrious sage of Koenigsberg, the founder of the
Critical Philosophy, more than any other works, at once invigorated and dis-
ciplined my understanding', *Biographia Literaria*, p. 76 (Everyman's Library
edition).

an intuitive apprehension of spiritual realities by means of the reason, whereas in point of fact in attributing this power to the reason, identified moreover with the practical reason, Coleridge obviously parts company with the German philosopher. He is on firmer ground when he claims an affinity with Jacobi[1] in maintaining that the relation between reason and spiritual realities is analogous to that between the eye and material objects.

Nobody, however, would wish to maintain that Coleridge was a Kantian. It was a question of stimulus, not of discipleship. And though he recognized his debt to German thinkers, especially to Kant, it is clear that he regarded his own philosophy as being fundamentally Platonic in inspiration. In *Aids to Reflection* he asserted that every man is born either a Platonist or an Aristotelian. Aristotle, the great master of understanding, was unduly earthbound. He 'began with the sensual, and never received that which was above the senses, but by necessity, but as the only remaining hypothesis. . . .'[2] That is to say, Aristotle postulated spiritual reality only as a last resort, when forced to do so by the need of explaining physical phenomena. Plato, however, sought the supersensible reality which is revealed to us through reason and our moral will. As for Kant, Coleridge sometimes describes him as belonging spiritually to the ranks of the Aristotelians, while at other times he emphasizes the metaphysical aspects of Kant's thought and finds in him an approach to Platonism. In other words, Coleridge welcomes Kant's restriction of the reach of understanding to phenomenal reality and then tends to interpret his doctrine of reason in the light of Platonism, which is itself interpreted in the light of the philosophy of Plotinus.

These remarks should not be understood as implying any contempt for Nature on Coleridge's part. On the contrary, he disliked Fichte's 'boastful and hyperstoic hostility to Nature, as lifeless, godless, and altogether unholy'.[3] And he expressed a warm sympathy with Schelling's philosophy of Nature, as also with his system of transcendental idealism, in which 'I first found a genial coincidence with much that I had toiled out for myself, and a powerful assistance in what I had yet to do'.[4] Coleridge is indeed at pains to reject the charge of plagiarism, and he maintains that both he and Schelling have drunk at the same springs, the writings of Kant, the philosophy of Giordano Bruno and the

[1] See Vol. VI of this *History*, pp. 146–8.
[2] *Philosophical Lectures*, edited by K. Coburn, p. 186.
[3] *Biographia Literaria*, p. 78.   [4] *Ibid.*, p. 79.

speculations of Jakob Boehme. However, the influence of Schelling seems to be sufficiently evident in the line of thought which we can now briefly outline.

'All knowledge rests on the coincidence of an object with a subject.'[1] But though subject and object are united in the act of knowledge, we can ask which has the priority. Are we to start with the object and try to add to it the subject? Or are we to start with the subject and try to find a passage to the object? In other words, are we to take Nature as prior and try to add to it thought or mind, or are we to take thought as prior and try to deduce Nature? Coleridge answers that we can do neither the one nor the other. The ultimate principle is to be sought in the identity of subject and object.

Where is this identity to be found? 'Only in the self-consciousness of a spirit is there the required identity of object and of representation.'[2] But if the spirit is originally the identity of subject and object, it must in some sense dissolve this identity in order to become conscious of itself as object. Self-consciousness, therefore, cannot arise except through an act of will, and 'freedom must be assumed as a *ground* of philosophy, and can never be deduced from it'.[3] The spirit becomes a subject knowing itself as object only through 'the act of constructing itself objectively to itself'.[4]

This sounds as though Coleridge begins by asking the sort of question which Schelling asks, then supplies Schelling's answer, namely that we must postulate an original identity of subject and object, and finally switches to Fichte's idea of the ego as constituting itself as subject and object by an original act. But Coleridge has no intention of stopping short with the ego as his ultimate principle, especially if we mean by this the finite ego. Indeed, he ridicules the 'egoism' of Fichte.[5] Instead, he insists that to arrive at the absolute identity of subject and object, of the ideal and the real, as the ultimate principle not only of human knowledge but also of all existence we must 'elevate our conception to the absolute self, the great eternal *I am*'.[6] Coleridge criticizes Descartes's *Cogito, ergo sum* and refers to Kant's distinction between the empirical and the transcendental ego. But he then tends to speak as though the transcendental ego were the absolute

---

[1] *Biographia Literaria*, p. 136.   [2] *Ibid.*, p. 145.   [3] *Ibid.*
[4] *Ibid.*, p. 144.
[5] Fichte did not, of course, make the finite ego or self his ultimate principle. And Coleridge tends to caricature his thought.   [6] *Biographia Literaria*, p. 144.

I am that I am of *Exodus*[1] and the God in whom the finite self is called to lose and find itself at the same time.

All this is obviously cloudy and imprecise. But it is at any rate clear that Coleridge opposes a spiritualistic interpretation of the human self to materialism and phenomenalism. And it is clearly this interpretation of the self which in his view provides the basis for the claim that reason can apprehend supersensible reality. Indeed, in his essay on faith Coleridge describes faith as fidelity to our own being in so far as our being is not and cannot become an object of sense-experience. Our moral vocation demands the subordination of appetite and will to reason; and it is reason which apprehends God as the identity of will and reason, as the ground of our existence, and as the infinite expression of the ideal which we are seeking as moral beings. In other words, Coleridge's outlook was essentially religious, and he tried to bring together philosophy and religion. He may have tended, as Mill notes, to turn Christian mysteries into philosophical truths. But an important element in the mission of idealism, as conceived by its more religious adherents, was precisely that of giving a metaphysical basis to a Christian tradition which seemed to be signally lacking in any philosophical backbone.

In the field of social and political theory Coleridge was conservative in the sense that he was opposed to the iconoclasm of the radicals and desired the preservation and actualization of the values inherent in traditional institutions. At one time he was indeed attracted, like Wordsworth and Southey, by the ideas which inspired the French Revolution. But he came to abandon the radicalism of his youth, though his subsequent conservatism arose not from any hatred of change as such but from a belief that the institutions created by the national spirit in the course of its history embodied real values which men should endeavour to realize. As Mill put it, Bentham demanded 'the extinction of the institutions and creeds which had hitherto existed', whereas Coleridge demanded 'that they be made a reality'.[2]

(ii) Thomas Carlyle (1795–1881) belonged to a later generation than that of Coleridge; but he was considerably less systematic in the presentation of his philosophical ideas, and there are doubtless very many people today who find the turbulent prose of *Sartor Resartus* quite unreadable. However, he was one of the channels

---

[1] *Exodus*, 3, 14.
[2] *Dissertations and Discussions*, I, p. 436.

through which German thought and literature were brought to the attention of the British public.

Carlyle's first reaction to German philosophy was not exactly favourable, and he made fun both of Kant's obscurity and of the pretensions of Coleridge. But in his hatred of materialism, hedonism and utilitarianism he came to see in Kant the brilliant foe of the Enlightenment and of its derivative movements. Thus in his essay on the *State of German Literature* (1827) he praised Kant for starting from within and proceeding outwards instead of pursuing the Lockian path of starting with sense-experience and trying to build a philosophy on this basis. The Kantian, according to Carlyle, sees that fundamental truths are apprehended by intuition in man's inmost nature. In other words, Carlyle ranges himself with Coleridge in using Kant's restriction of the power and scope of the understanding as a foundation for asserting the power of reason to apprehend intuitively basic truths and spiritual realities.

Characteristic of Carlyle was his vivid sense of the mystery of the world and of its nature as an appearance of, or veil before, supersensible reality. In the *State of German Literature* he asserted that the ultimate aim of philosophy is to interpret phenomena or appearances, to proceed from the symbol to the reality symbolized. And this point of view found expression in *Sartor Resartus*,[1] under the label of the philosophy of clothes. It can be applied to man, the microcosm. 'To the eye of vulgar Logic what is man? An omnivorous Biped that wears Breeches. To the eye of Pure Reason what is he? A Soul, a Spirit, and divine Apparition. . . . Deep-hidden is he under that strange Garment.'[2] And the analogy is applicable also to the macrocosm, the world in general. For the world is, as Goethe divined, *'the living visible Garment of God'*.[3]

In the *State of German Literature* Carlyle explicitly connects his philosophy of symbolism with Fichte, who is regarded as having interpreted the visible universe as the symbol and sensible manifestation of an all-pervading divine Idea, the apprehension of which is the condition of all genuine virtue and freedom. And there is indeed no great difficulty in understanding Carlyle's predilection for Fichte. For seeing, as he does, human life and

---

[1] As no publisher would accept this work, it first appeared in instalments in *Fraser's Magazine*, 1833-4. An American edition of the book appeared in 1836, and an English edition in 1838.
[2] *Sartor Resartus*, I, 10, p. 57 (Scott Library edition). The 'Garment' is, of course, the body.
[3] *Ibid.*, I, 8, p. 48.

history as a constant struggle between light and darkness, God
and the devil, a struggle in which every man is called to play a
part and to make an all-important choice, he naturally feels an
attraction for Fichte's moral earnestness and for his view of
Nature as being simply the field in which man works out his moral
vocation, the field of obstacles, so to speak, which man has to
overcome in the process of attaining his ideal end.

This outlook helps to explain Carlyle's concern with the hero,
as manifested in his 1840 lectures *On Heroes, Hero-Worship and
the Heroic in History*. Over against materialism and what he calls
profit-and-loss philosophy he sets the ideas of heroism, moral
vocation and personal loyalty. Indeed, he is prepared to assert
that 'the life-breath of all society [is] but an effluence of Hero-
worship, submissive admiration for the truly great. Society is
founded on Hero-worship.'[1] Again, 'Universal History, the history
of what man has accomplished in the world, is at bottom the
History of the Great Men who have worked here'.[2]

In his insistence on the role of history's 'great men' Carlyle
resembles Hegel[3] and anticipates Nietzsche in some aspects,
though hero-worship in the political field is an idea which we are
likely to regard with mixed feelings nowadays. However, it is
clear that what especially attracted Carlyle in his heroes was their
earnestness and self-devotion and their freedom from a morality
based on the hedonistic calculus. For example, while aware of
Rousseau's shortcomings and faults of character, which made him
'a sadly *contracted* Hero',[4] Carlyle insists that this unlikely
candidate for the title possessed 'the first and chief characteristic
of a Hero: he is heartily *in earnest*. In earnest, if ever man was; as
none of these French Philosophes were.'[5]

3. In spite of the fact that both men delivered lectures it would
be idle to look either to Coleridge or Carlyle for a systematic
development of idealism. For a pioneer in this field we have to
turn rather to James Frederick Ferrier (1808–64), who occupied
the chair of moral philosophy in the University of St. Andrews
from 1845 until the year of his death, and who made a great point
of systematic procedure in philosophy.

In 1838–9 Ferrier contributed a series of articles to *Blackwood's*

[1] *On Heroes*, lecture I, p. 193 (London, Chapman and Hall).
[2] *Ibid.*, p. 185.
[3] Hegel, however, regarded his 'word-historical individuals' as instruments of
the World-Spirit.
[4] *On Heroes*, lecture V, p. 323.   [5] *Ibid.*

Magazine, which was published with the title *Introduction to the Philosophy of Consciousness.* In 1854 he published his main work, *The Institutes of Metaphysics,* which is remarkable for the way in which the author develops his doctrine in a series of propositions, each of which, with the exception of the first fundamental proposition, is supposed to follow with logical rigour from its predecessor. In 1856 he published *Scottish Philosophy,* while his *Lectures on Greek Philosophy and Other Philosophical Remains* appeared posthumously in 1866.

Ferrier claimed that his philosophy was Scottish to the core. But this does not mean that he regarded himself as an adherent of the Scottish philosophy of common sense. On the contrary, he vigorously attacked Reid and his followers. In the first place a philosopher should not appeal to a multitude of undemonstrated principles, but should employ the deductive method which is essential to metaphysics and not an optional expository device. In the second place the Scottish philosophers of common sense tended to confuse metaphysics with psychology, trying to solve philosophical problems by psychological reflections, instead of by rigorous logical reasoning.[1] As for Sir William Hamilton, his agnosticism about the Absolute was quite misplaced.

When Ferrier said that his philosophy was Scottish to the core, he meant that he had not borrowed it from the Germans. Though his system was not uncommonly regarded as Hegelian, he claimed that he had never been able to understand Hegel.[2] Indeed, he expressed a doubt whether the German philosopher had been able to understand himself. In any case Hegel starts with Being, whereas his own system took knowledge as its point of departure.[3]

Ferrier's first move is to look for the absolute starting-point of metaphysics in a proposition which states the one invariable and essential feature in all knowledge, and which cannot be denied without contradiction. This is that 'along with whatever any intelligence knows, it must, as the ground or condition of its knowledge, have some cognizance of itself'.[4] The object of know-

---

[1] According to Ferrier, if we wish to find the solution to a metaphysical problem, we might well inquire what the psychologists have said about the matter and then assert the exact opposite.

[2] This did not prevent Ferrier from writing articles on Schelling and Hegel for the *Imperial Dictionary of Universal Biography.*

[3] We can hardly exclude all influence of German thought on Ferrier's mind. But he was doubtless right in claiming that his system was his own creation, and not the result of borrowing.

[4] *Institutes of Metaphysics,* I, prop. 1, p. 79 (Works, I, 3rd edition). This work will henceforth be referred to simply as *Institutes.*

ledge is a variable factor. But I cannot know anything without knowing that I know. To deny this is to talk nonsense. To assert it is to admit that there is no knowledge without self-consciousness, without some awareness of the self.

It follows from this, Ferrier argues, that nothing can be known except in relation to a subject, a self. In other words, the object of knowledge is essentially object-for-a-subject. And Ferrier draws the conclusion that nothing is thinkable except in relation to a subject. From this it follows that the material universe is unthinkable as existing without any relation to subject.

The critic might be inclined to comment that Ferrier is really saying no more than that I cannot think of the universe without thinking of it, or know it without knowing it. If anything more is being said, if, in particular, a transition is being made from an epistemological point to the assertion of an ontological relation, a solipsistic conclusion seems to follow, namely that the existence of the material world is unthinkable except as dependent on myself as subject.

Ferrier, however, wishes to maintain two propositions. First, we cannot think of the universe as 'dissociated from *every* me. You cannot perform the abstraction.'[1] Secondly, each of us can dissociate the universe from himself in particular. And from these two propositions it follows that though 'each of us can unyoke the universe (so to speak) from himself, he can do this only by yoking it on, in thought, to some other self'.[2] This is an essential move for Ferrier to make, because he wishes to argue that the universe is unthinkable except as existing in synthesis with the divine mind.

The first section of the *Institutes of Metaphysics* thus purports to show that the absolute element in knowledge is the synthesis of subject and object. But Ferrier does not proceed at once to his final conclusion. Instead, he devotes the second section to 'agnoiology', the theory of 'ignorance'. We can be said to be in a state of nescience in regard to the contradictions of necessarily true propositions. But this is obviously no sign of imperfection in our minds. As for ignorance, we cannot properly be said to be ignorant except of what is in principle knowable. Hence we cannot be ignorant of, for example, matter 'in itself' (without relation to a subject). For this is unthinkable and unknowable. Further, if we

---

[1] *Ibid.*, 1, prop. 13, observation 3, p. 312.
[2] *Ibid.*, observation 2, p. 311.

assume that we are ignorant of the Absolute, it follows that the Absolute is knowable. Hence Hamilton's agnosticism is untenable. But what is the Absolute or, as Ferrier expresses it, Absolute Existence? It cannot be either matter *per se* or mind *per se*. For neither is thinkable. It must be, therefore, the synthesis of subject and object. There is, however, only one such synthesis which is necessary. For though the existence of a universe is not conceivable except as object-for-a-subject, we have already seen that the universe can be unyoked or dissociated from any given finite subject. Hence 'there is one, but only one, Absolute Existence which is strictly *necessary*; and that existence is a supreme, and infinite, and everlasting Mind in synthesis with all things'.[1]

By way of comment it is not inappropriate to draw attention to the rather obvious fact, that the statement 'there can be no subject without an object and no object without a subject' is analytically true, if the terms 'subject' and 'object' are understood in their epistemological senses. It is also true that no material thing can be conceived except as object-for-a-subject, if we mean by this that no material thing can be conceived except by constituting it ('intentionally', as the phenomenologists would say) as an object. But this does not seem to amount to much more than saying that a thing cannot be thought of unless it is thought of. And from this it does not follow that a thing cannot exist unless it is thought of. Ferrier could retort, of course, that we cannot intelligibly speak of a thing as existing independently of being conceived. For by the mere fact that we speak of it, we conceive it. If I try to think of material thing X as existing outside the subject-object relationship, my effort is defeated by the very fact that I am thinking of X. In this case, however, the thing seems to be irrevocably yoked, as Ferrier puts it, to me as subject. And how can I possibly unyoke it? If I try to unyoke it from myself and yoke it to some other subject, whether finite or infinite, does not this other subject, on Ferrier's premises, become object-for-a-subject, the subject in question being myself?

It is not my intention to suggest that in point of fact the material universe could exist independently of God. The point is rather that the conclusion that it cannot so exist does not really follow from Ferrier's epistemological premises. The conclusion which does seem to follow is solipsism. And Ferrier escapes from

---

[1] *Institutes*, III, prop. 11, p. 522. It will be noted that for Ferrier the Absolute is not God alone but the synthesis of God and the world, of the infinite subject and its object in relation to one another.

this conclusion only by an appeal to common sense and to our knowledge of historical facts. That is to say, as I cannot seriously suppose that the material universe is simply object for me as subject, I must postulate an eternal, infinite subject, God. But on Ferrier's premisses it appears to follow that God Himself, as thought by me, must be object-for-a-subject, the subject being myself.

4. Among Ferrier's contemporaries John Grote (1813-66), brother of the historian, deserves mention. Professor of moral philosophy at Cambridge from 1855 until 1866, he published the first part of *Exploratio philosophica* in 1865. The second part appeared posthumously in 1900. His *Examination of Utilitarian Philosophy* (1870) and *A Treatise on the Moral Ideals* (1876) were also published after his death. It is true that nowadays Grote is even less known than Ferrier; but his criticism of phenomenalism and of hedonistic utilitarianism is not without value.

Grote's critique of phenomenalism can be illustrated in this way. One of the main features of positivistic phenomenalism is that it first reduces the object of knowledge to a series of phenomena and then proceeds to apply a similar reductive analysis to the subject, the ego or self. In effect, therefore, the subject is reduced to its own object. Or, if preferred, subject and object are both reduced to phenomena which are assumed to be the basic reality, the ultimate entities out of which selves and physical objects can be reconstructed by thought. But this reduction of the self or subject can be shown to be untenable. In the first place talk about phenomena is not intelligible except in relation to consciousness. For that which appears, appears to a subject, within the ambit, so to speak, of consciousness. We cannot go behind consciousness; and analysis of it shows that it essentially involves the subject-object relationship. In primitive consciousness subject and object are virtually or confusedly present; and they are progressively distinguished in the development of consciousness until there arises an explicit awareness of a world of objects on the one hand and of a self or subject on the other, this awareness of the self being developed especially by the experience of effort. As, therefore, the subject is present from the start as one of the essential poles even in primitive consciousness, it cannot be legitimately reduced to the object, to phenomena. At the same time reflection on the essential structure of consciousness shows that we are not presented with a self-enclosed ego from which we have to find a bridge, as in the philosophy of Descartes, to the non-ego.

In the second place it is important to notice the way in which the phenomenalists overlook the active role of the subject in the construction of an articulated universe. The subject or self is characterized by teleological activity; it has ends. And in pursuit of its ends it constructs unities among phenomena, not in the sense that it imposes *a priori* forms on a mass of unrelated, chaotic data,[1] but rather in the sense that it builds up its world in an experimental way by a process of auto-correction. On this count too, therefore, namely the active role of the self in the construction of the world of objects, it is clear that it cannot be reduced to a series of phenomena, its own immediate objects.[2]

In the sphere of moral philosophy Grote was strongly opposed to both egoistic hedonism and utilitarianism. He did not object to them for taking into account man's sensibility and his search for happiness. On the contrary, Grote himself admitted the science of happiness, 'eudaemonics' as he called it, as a part of ethics. What he objected to was an exclusive concentration on the search for pleasure and a consequent neglect of other aspects of the human personality, especially man's capacity for conceiving and pursuing ideals which transcend the search for pleasure and may demand self-sacrifice. Hence to 'eudaemonics' he added 'aretaics', the science of virtue. And he insisted that the moral task is to achieve the union of the lower and higher elements of man's nature in the service of moral ideals. For our actions become moral when they pass from the sphere of the merely spontaneous, as in following the impulse to pleasure, into the sphere of the deliberate and voluntary, impulse supplying the dynamic element and intellectually-conceived principles and ideals the regulative element?

Obviously, Grote's attack on utilitarianism as neglecting the higher aspects of man through an exclusive concentration on the search for pleasure was more applicable to Benthamite hedonism than to J. S. Mill's revised version of utilitarianism. But in any case it was a question not so much of suggesting that a utilitarian philosopher could not have moral ideals as of maintaining that the utilitarian ethics could not provide an adequate theoretical frame-

[1] According to Grote, in its construction of an articulated world the self discovers or recognizes categories in Nature, which are the expression of the divine mind.
[2] In Grote's view, things-in-themselves are known intuitively, even if not distinctly, through knowledge by acquaintance, as contrasted with knowledge about.

work for such ideals. Grote's main point was that this could be provided only by a radical revision of the concept of man which Bentham inherited from writers such as Helvétius. Hedonism, in Grote's opinion, could not account for the consciousness of obligation. For this arises when man, conceiving moral ideals, feels the need of subordinating his lower to his higher nature.

5. We can reasonably see a connection between the idealists' perception of the inadequacy of the Benthamite view of human nature and the revival of interest in Greek philosophy which occurred in the universities, especially at Oxford, in the course of the nineteenth century. We have already seen that Coleridge regarded his philosophy as being fundamentally Platonic in inspiration and character. But the renewal of Platonic studies at Oxford can be associated in particular with the name of Benjamin Jowett (1817–93), who became a Fellow of Balliol College in 1838 and occupied the chair of Greek from 1855 to 1893. The defects in his famous translation of Plato's *Dialogues* are irrelevant here. The point is that in the course of his long teaching career he contributed powerfully to a revival of interest in Greek thought. And it is not without significance that T. H. Green and E. Caird, both prominent in the idealist movement, were at one time his pupils. Interest in Plato and Aristotle naturally tended to turn their minds away from hedonism and utilitarianism towards an ethics of self-perfection, based on a theory of human nature within a metaphysical framework.

The revival of interest in Greek thought was accompanied by a growing appreciation of German idealist philosophy. Jowett himself was interested in the latter, particularly in the thought of Hegel;[1] and he helped to stimulate the study of German idealism at Oxford. The first large-scale attempt, however, to elucidate what Ferrier had considered to be the scarcely intelligible profundities of Hegel was made by the Scotsman, James Hutchison Stirling (1820–1909), in his two-volume work *The Secret of Hegel*, which appeared in 1865.[2]

Stirling developed an enthusiasm for Hegel during a visit to Germany, especially during a stay at Heidelberg in 1856; and the result was *The Secret of Hegel*. In spite of the comment that if the

[1] While he explicitly acknowledged the stimulus which he had received from Hegel, Jowett gradually moved further away from rather than nearer to Hegelianism.

[2] A one-volume edition appeared in 1898. Stirling never held an academic post; but he gave the Gifford Lectures at Edinburgh in 1899–90. These were published in 1890 with the title *Philosophy and Theology*.

author knew the secret of Hegel, he kept it successfully to himself, the book marked the beginning of the serious study of Hegelianism in Great Britain. In Stirling's view Hume's philosophy was the culmination of the Enlightenment, while Kant,[1] who took over what was valuable in Hume's thought and used it in the development of a new line of reflection, fulfilled and at the same time overcame and transcended the Enlightenment. While, however, Kant laid the foundations of idealism, it was Hegel who built and completed the edifice. And to understand the secret of Hegel is to understand how he made explicit the doctrine of the concrete universal, which was implicit in the critical philosophy of Kant.

It is noteworthy that Stirling regarded Hegel not only as standing to modern philosophy in the relation in which Aristotle stood to preceding Greek thought but also as the great intellectual champion of the Christian religion. He doubtless attributed to Hegel too high a degree of theological orthodoxy; but his attitude serves to illustrate the religious interest which characterized the idealist movement before Bradley. According to Stirling, Hegel was concerned with proving, among other things, the immortality of the soul. And though there is little evidence that Hegel felt much interest in this matter, Stirling's interpretation can be seen as representing the emphasis placed by the earlier idealists on the finite spiritual self, an emphasis which harmonized with their tendency to retain a more or less theistic outlook.

[1] Stirling published a *Text-Book to Kant* in 1881.

CHAPTER VII

THE DEVELOPMENT OF IDEALISM

T. H. Green's attitude to British empiricism and to German thought—Green's doctrine of the eternal subject, with some critical comments—The ethical and political theory of Green— E. Caird and the unity underlying the distinction between subject and object—J. Caird and the philosophy of religion— W. Wallace and D. G. Ritchie.

1. PHILOSOPHERS are not infrequently more convincing when they are engaged in criticizing the views of other philosophers than when they are expounding their own doctrines. And this perhaps somewhat cynical remark seems to be applicable to Thomas Hill Green (1836–82), Fellow of Balliol College, Oxford, and Whyte professor of moral philosophy in that university from 1878 to the year of his death. In his *Introductions to Hume's Treatise of Human Nature*,[1] which he published in 1874 for the Green and Grose edition of Hume, he made an impressive broadside attack on British empiricism. But his own idealist system is no less open to criticism than the views against which he raised objections.

From Locke onwards, according to Green, empiricists have assumed that it is the philosopher's business to reduce our knowledge to its primitive elements, to the original data, and then to reconstruct the world of ordinary experience out of these atomic data. Apart, however, from the fact that no satisfactory explanation has ever been offered of the way in which the mind can go behind the subject-object relationship and discover the primitive data out of which both minds and physical objects are supposed to be constructed, the empiricist programme lands us in an impasse. On the one hand, to construct the world of minds and physical objects the mind has to relate the primitive atomic data, discrete phenomena. In other words, it has to exercise activity. On the other hand, the mind's activity is inexplicable on empiricist principles. For it is itself reduced to a series of phenomena. And how can it construct itself? Further, though empiricism professes to account for human knowledge, it does not in fact do anything of the kind. For the world of ordinary experience is interpreted

---

[1] This work will be referred to as *Introductions*.

as a mental construction out of discrete impressions; and we have no way of knowing that the construction represents objective reality at all. In other words, a consistent empiricism leads inevitably to scepticism.

Hume himself, as Green sees him, was an outstanding thinker who discarded compromise and carried the principles of empiricism to their logical conclusion. 'Adopting the premisses and method of Locke, he cleared them of all illogical adaptations to popular belief, and experimented with them on the basis of professed knowledge. . . . As the result of the experiment, the method, which began with professing to explain knowledge, showed knowledge to be impossible.'[1] 'Hume himself was perfectly cognizant of this result, but his successors in England and Scotland would seem so far to have been unable to look it in the face.'[2]

Some philosophers after Hume, and here Green is evidently referring to the Scottish philosophers of common sense, have thrust their heads back into the thicket of uncriticized belief. Others have gone on developing Hume's theory of the association of ideas, apparently oblivious of the fact that Hume himself had shown the insufficiency of the principle of association to account for anything more than natural or quasi-instinctive belief.[3] In other words, Hume represented both the culmination and the bankruptcy of empiricism. And the torch of inquiry 'was transferred to a more vigorous line in Germany'.[4]

Kant, that is to say, was the spiritual successor of Hume. 'Thus the *Treatise of Human Nature* and the *Critique of Pure Reason*, taken together, form the real bridge between the old world of philosophy and the new. They are the essential "Propaedeutik" without which no one is a qualified student of modern philosophy.'[5] It does not follow, however, that we can remain in the philosophy of Kant. For Kant looks forward to Hegel or at any rate to something resembling Hegelianism. Green agrees with Stirling that Hegel developed the philosophy of Kant in the right direction; but he is not prepared to say that Hegel's system as it stands is satisfactory. It is all very well for the Sundays of speculation, as Green puts it; but it is more difficult to accept on the weekdays of ordinary thought. There is need for reconciling the judgments of

---

[1] *Introductions*, 1, 2–3. Green and Grose edition of Hume's *Treatises*, 1, p. 2.
[2] *Ibid.*, 3.
[3] Green is clearly thinking of philosophers such as the two Mill's.
[4] *Introductions*, 1, 3. Green and Grose, 1, pp. 2–3.
[5] *Ibid.* Green and Grose, 1, p. 3.

speculative philosophy with our ordinary judgments about matters of fact and with the sciences. Hegelianism, however, if taken as it stands, cannot perform this task of synthesizing different tendencies and points of view in contemporary thought. The work has to be done over again.

In point of fact the name of Hegel does not loom large in the writings of Green. The name of Kant is far more prominent. But Green maintained that by reading Hume in the light of Leibniz and Leibniz in the light of Hume, Kant was able to free himself from their respective presuppositions. And we can justifiably say that though Green derived a great deal of stimulus from Kant, he read him in the light of his conviction that the critical philosophy needed some such development, though not precisely the same, as that which it actually received at the hands of the German metaphysical idealists, and of Hegel in particular.

2. In the introduction to his *Prolegomena to Ethics*, which was published posthumously in 1883, Green refers to the temptation to treat ethics as though it were a branch of natural science. This temptation is indeed understandable. For growth in historical knowledge and the development of theories of evolution suggest the possibility of giving a purely naturalistic and genetic explanation of the phenomena of the moral life. But what becomes then of ethics considered as a normative science? The answer is that the philosopher who 'has the courage of his principles, having reduced the speculative part of them [our ethical systems] to a natural science, must abolish the practical or preceptive part altogether'.[1] The fact, however, that the reduction of ethics to a branch of natural science involves the abolition of ethics as a normative science should make us reconsider the presuppositions or conditions of moral knowledge and activity. Is man merely a child of Nature? Or is there in him a spiritual principle which makes knowledge possible, whether it be knowledge of Nature or moral knowledge?

Green thus finds it necessary to start his inquiry into morals with a metaphysics of knowledge. And he argues in the first place that even if we were to decide in favour of the materialists all those questions about particular facts which have formed the subject of debate between them and the spiritualists, the possibility of our explaining the facts at all still remain to be accounted for. 'We shall still be logically bound to admit that in a man who

---

[1] *Prolegomena to Ethics*, p. 9 (first edition). This work will be referred to henceforth as *Prolegomena*.

can know a Nature—for whom there is a "cosmos of experience" —there is a principle which is not natural and which cannot without a ϑοτερον πρότερον be explained as we explain the facts of nature.'[1]

According to Green, to say that a thing is real is to say that it is a member in a system of relations, the order of Nature. But awareness or knowledge of a series of related events cannot itself be a series of events. Nor can it be a natural development out of such a series. In other words, the mind as an active synthesizing principle is irreducible to the factors which it synthesizes. True, the empirical ego belongs to the order of Nature. But my awareness of myself as an empirical ego manifests the activity of a principle which transcends that order. In fine, 'an understanding—for that term seems as fit as any other to denote the principle of consciousness in question—irreducible to anything else, "makes nature" for us, in the sense of enabling us to conceive that there is such a thing'.[2]

We have just seen that for Green a thing is real in virtue of its membership in a system of related phenomena. At the same time he holds that 'related appearances are impossible apart from the action of an intelligence'.[3] Nature is thus made by the synthesizing activity of a mind. It is obvious, however, that we cannot seriously suppose that Nature, as the system of related phenomena, is simply the product of the synthesizing activity of any given finite mind. Though, therefore, it can be said that each finite mind constitutes Nature in so far as it conceives the system of relations, we must also assume that there is a single spiritual principle, an eternal consciousness, which ultimately constitutes or produces Nature.

From this it follows that we must conceive the finite mind as participating in the life of an eternal consciousness or intelligence which 'partially and gradually reproduces itself in us, communicating piece-meal, but in inseparable correlation, understanding and the facts understood, experience and the experienced world'.[4] This amounts to saying that God gradually reproduces his own knowledge in the finite mind. And, if this is the case, what are we to say about the empirical facts relating to the origin and

---

[1] *Prolegomena*, p. 14. The phrase 'cosmos of experience' is taken from G. H. Lewes, one of Green's targets of attack.
[2] *Ibid.*, p. 22. Clearly, Kant's transcendental ego is given an ontological status.
[3] *Ibid.*, p. 28.
[4] *Ibid.*, p. 38.

growth of knowledge? For these hardly suggest that our knowledge is imposed by God. Green's answer is that God reproduces his own knowledge in the finite mind by making use, so to speak, of the sentient life of the human organism and of its response to stimuli. There are thus two aspects to human consciousness. There is the empirical aspect, under which our consciousness appears to consist 'in successive modifications of the animal organism'.[1] And there is the metaphysical aspect, under which this organism is seen as gradually becoming 'the vehicle of an eternally complete consciousness'.[2]

Green thus shares with the earlier idealists the tendency to choose an epistemological point of departure, the subject-object relationship. Under the influence of Kant, however, he depicts the subject as actively synthesizing the manifold of phenomena, as constituting the order of Nature by relating appearances or phenomena. This process of synthesis is a gradual process which develops through the history of the human race towards an ideal term. And we can thus conceive the total process as an activity of one spiritual principle which lives and acts in and through finite minds. In other words, Kant's idea of the synthesizing activity of the mind leads us to the Hegelian concept of infinite Spirit.

At the same time Green's religious interests militate against any reduction of infinite Spirit to the lives of finite spirits considered simply collectively. It is true that he wishes to avoid what he regards as one of the main defects of traditional theism, namely the representation of God as a Being over against the world and the finite spirit. Hence he depicts the spiritual life of man as a participation in the divine life. But he also wishes to avoid using the word 'God' simply as a label either for the spiritual life of man considered universally, as something which develops in the course of the evolution of human culture, or for the ideal of complete knowledge, an ideal which does not yet exist but towards which human knowledge progressively approximates. He does indeed speak of the human spirit as 'identical' with God; but he adds, 'in the sense that He *is* all which the human spirit is capable of becoming'.[3] God is the infinite eternal subject; and His complete knowledge is reproduced progressively in the finite subject in dependence, from the empirical point of view, on the modifications of the human organism.

[1] *Ibid.*, pp. 72–3.   [2] *Ibid.*, p. 72.   [3] *Ibid.*, p. 198.

If we ask why God acts in this way, Green implies that no answer can be given. 'The old question, why God made the world, has never been answered, nor will be. We know not why the world should be; we only know that there it is. In like manner we know not why the eternal subject of that world should reproduce itself, through certain processes of the world, as the spirit of mankind, or as the particular self of this or that man in whom the spirit of mankind operates. We can only say that, upon the best analysis we can make of our experience, it seems that so it does.'[1]

In Green's retention of the idea of an eternal subject which 'reproduces itself' in finite subjects and therefore cannot be simply identified with them it is not unreasonable to see the operation of a religious interest, a concern with the idea of a God in whom we live and move and have our being. But this is certainly not the explicit or formal reason for postulating an eternal subject. For it is explicitly postulated as the ultimate synthesizing agent in constituting the system of Nature. And in making this postulate Green seems to lay himself open to the same sort of objection that we brought against Ferrier. For if it is once assumed, at least for the sake of argument, that the order of Nature is constituted by the synthesizing or relating activity of intelligence, it is obvious that I cannot attribute this order to an eternal intelligence or subject unless I have myself first conceived, and so constituted, it. And it then becomes difficult to see how, in Ferrier's terminology, I can unyoke the conceived system of relations from the synthesizing activity of my own mind and yoke it on to any other subject, eternal or otherwise.

It may be objected that this line of criticism, though possibly valid in the case of Ferrier, is irrelevant in that of Green. For Green sees the individual finite subject as participating in a general spiritual life, the spiritual life of humanity, which progressively synthesizes phenomena in its advance towards the ideal goal of complete knowledge, a knowledge which would be itself the constituted order of Nature. Hence there is no question of unyoking my synthesis from myself and yoking it to any other spirit. My synthesizing activity is simply a moment in that of the human race as a whole or of the one spiritual principle which lives in and through the multiplicity of finite subjects.

In this case, however, what becomes of Green's eternal subject? If we wish to represent, say, the advancing scientific knowledge

[1] *Prolegomena*, pp. 103–4.

of mankind as a life in which all scientists participate and which moves towards an ideal goal, there is, of course, no question of 'unyoking' and 'yoking'. But a concept of this sort does not by itself call for the introduction of any eternal subject which reproduces its complete knowledge in a piecemeal manner in finite minds.

Further, how precisely, in Green's philosophy, are we to conceive the relation of Nature to the eternal subject or intelligence? Let us assume that the constitutive activity of intelligence consists in relating or synthesizing. Now if God can properly be said to create Nature, it seems to follow that Nature is reducible to a system of relations without terms. And this is a somewhat perplexing notion. If, however, the eternal subject only introduces relations, so to speak, between phenomena, we seem to be presented with a picture similar to that painted by Plato in the *Timaeus*, in the sense, that is to say, that the eternal subject or intelligence would bring order out of disorder rather than create the whole of Nature out of nothing. In any case, though it may be possible to conceive a divine intelligence as creating the world by thinking it, terms such as 'eternal subject' and 'eternal consciousness' necessarily suggest a correlative eternal object. And this would mean an absolutization of the subject-object relationship, similar to that of Ferrier.

Objections of this sort may appear to be niggling and to indicate an inability to appreciate Green's general vision of an eternal consciousness in the life of which we all participate. But the objections serve at any rate the useful purpose of drawing attention to the fact that Green's often acute criticism of other philosophers is combined with that rather vague and woolly speculation which has done so much to bring metaphysical idealism into disrepute.[1]

3. In his moral theory Green stands in the tradition of Plato and Aristotle, in the sense that for him the concept of good is primary, not that of obligation. In particular, his idea of the good for man as consisting in the full actualization of the potentialities of the human person in an harmonious and unified state of being recalls the ethics of Aristotle. Green does indeed speak of 'self-satisfaction' as the end of moral conduct, but he makes it clear

[1] Obviously, metaphysical idealists are by no means the only philosophers whose criticism of their opponents has been more telling than their own positive contributions to philosophy. Indeed, the frequency with which this situation occurs raises general problems about philosophy. But they cannot be discussed here.

that self-satisfaction signifies for him self-realization rather than pleasure. We must distinguish between 'the quest for self-satisfaction which all moral activity is rightly held to be, and the quest for pleasure which morally *good* activity is not'.[1] This does not mean that pleasure is excluded from the good for man. But the harmonious and integrated actualization of the human person's potentialities cannot be identified with the search for pleasure. For the moral agent is a spiritual subject, not simply a sensitive organism. And in any case pleasure is a concomitant of the actualization of one's powers rather than this actualization itself.

Now it is certain that it is only through action that a man can realize himself, in the sense of actualizing his potentialities and developing his personality towards the ideal state of harmonious integration of his powers. And it is also obvious that every human act, in the proper sense of the term, is motivated. It is performed in view of some immediate end or goal. But it is arguable that a man's motives are determined by his existing character, in conjunction with other circumstances, and that character is itself the result of empirical causes. In this case are not a man's actions determined in such a way that what he will be depends on what he is, what he is depending in turn on circumstances other than his free choice? True, circumstances vary; but the ways in which men react to varying circumstances seem to be determined. And if all a man's acts are determined, is there any room for an ethical theory which sets up a certain ideal of human personality as that which we ought to strive to realize through our actions?

Green is quite prepared to concede to the determinists a good deal of the ground on which they base their case. But at the same time he tries to take the sting out of these concessions. 'The propositions, current among "determinists", that a man's action is the joint result of his character and circumstances, is true enough in a certain sense, and, in that sense, is quite compatible with an assertion of human freedom.'[2] In Green's view, it is not a necessary condition for the proper use of the word 'freedom' that a man should be able to do or to become anything whatsoever. To justify our describing a man's actions as free, it is sufficient that they should be his own, in the sense that he is truly the author of them. And if a man's action follows from his character, if, that is to say, he responds to a situation which calls for action in a certain way because he is a certain sort of man, the action is his own; he, and nobody else, is the responsible author of it.

In defending this interpretation of freedom Green lays emphasis on self-consciousness. In the history of any man there is a succession of natural empirical factors of one kind or another, natural impulses for example, which the determinist regards as exercising a decisive influence on the man's conduct. Green argues, however, that such factors become morally relevant only when they are assumed, as it were, by the self-conscious subject, that is, when they are taken up into the unity of self-consciousness and turned into motives. They then become internal principles of action; and, as such, they are principles of free action.

This theory, which is in some respects reminiscent of Schelling's theory of freedom, is perhaps hardly crystal clear. But it is clear at least that Green wishes to admit all the empirical data to which the determinist can reasonably appeal,[1] and at the same time to maintain that this admission is compatible with an assertion of human freedom. Perhaps we can say that the question which he asks is this. Given all the empirical facts about human conduct, have we still a use for words such as 'freedom' and 'free' in the sphere of morals? Green's answer is affirmative. The acts of a self-conscious subject, considered precisely as such, can properly be said to be free acts. Actions which are the result of physical compulsion, for example, do not proceed from the self-conscious subject as such. They are not really his own actions; he cannot be considered the true author of them. And we need to be able to distinguish between actions of this type and those which are the expression of the man himself, considered not merely as a physical agent but also as a self-conscious subject or, as some would say, a rational agent.

Mention of the fact that for Green self-realization is the end of moral conduct may suggest that his ethical theory is individualistic. But though he does indeed lay emphasis on the individual's realization of himself, he is at one with Plato and Aristotle in regarding the human person as essentially social in character. In other words, the self which has to be realized is not an atomic self, the potentialities of which can be fully actualized and harmonized without any reference to social relations. On the contrary, it is only in society that we can fully actualize our

---

[1] Obviously, if Green had lived at a later date, he would have had to cope with theories of the infra-conscious springs of human action.

potentialities and really live as human persons. And this means in effect that the particular moral vocation of each individual has to be interpreted within a social context. Hence Green can use a phrase which Bradley was afterwards to render famous, by remarking that 'each has primarily to fulfil the duties of his station'.[1]

Given this outlook, it is understandable that Green lays emphasis, again with Plato and Aristotle but also, of course, with Hegel, on the status and function of political society, the State, which is 'for its members the society of societies'.[2] It will be noted that this somewhat grandiloquent phrase itself indicates a recognition of the fact that there are other societies, such as the family, which are presupposed by the State. But Hegel himself recognized this fact, of course. And it is clear that among societies Green attributes a pre-eminent importance to the State.

Precisely for this reason, however, it is important to understand that Green is not recanting, either explicitly or implicitly, his ethical theory of self-realization. He continues to maintain his view that 'our ultimate standard of worth is an ideal of *personal* worth. All other values are relative to value for, of, or in a person.'[3] This ideal, however, can be fully realized only in and through a society of persons. Society is thus a moral necessity. And this applies to that larger form of social organization which we call political society or the State as well as to the family. But it by no means follows that the State is an end itself. On the contrary, its function is to create and maintain the conditions for the good life, that is, the conditions in which human beings can best develop themselves and live as persons, each recognizing the others as ends, not merely as means. In this sense the State is an instrument rather than an end in itself. It is indeed an error to say that a nation or a political society is *merely* an aggregate of individuals. For use of the word 'merely' shows that the speaker overlooks the fact that the individual's moral capacities are actualized only in concrete social relations. It implies that individuals could possess their moral and spiritual qualities and fulfil their moral vocation quite apart from membership of society. At the same time the premiss that the nation or the State is not 'merely' a collection of individuals does not entail the conclusion that it is a kind of self-subsistent entity over and above the individuals who compose it.

---

[1] *Prolegomena*, p. 192.
[2] *Lectures on the Principles of Political Obligation*, p. 146 (1901 edition). This work will be referred to as *Political Obligation*.
[3] *Prolegomena*, p. 193.

'The life of the nation has no real existence except as the life of the individuals composing the nation.'[1]

Green is therefore quite prepared to admit that in a certain sense there are natural rights which are presupposed by the State. For if we consider what powers must be secured for the individual with a view to the attainment of his moral end, we find that the individual has certain claims which should be recognized by society. It is true that rights in the full sense of the term do not exist until they have been accorded social recognition. Indeed, the term 'right', in its full sense, has little or no meaning apart from society.[2] At the same time, if by saying that there are natural rights which are antecedent to political society we mean that a man, simply because he is a man, has certain claims which ought to be recognized by the State as rights, it is then perfectly true to say that 'the State presupposes rights, and rights of individuals. It is a form which society takes in order to maintain them.'[3]

It is sufficiently obvious from what has been said that in Green's view we cannot obtain a philosophical understanding of the function of the State simply by conducting an historical investigation into the ways in which actual political societies have in fact arisen. We have to consider the nature of man and his moral vocation. Similarly, to have a criterion for judging laws we have to understand the moral end of man, to which all rights are relative. 'A law is not good because it enforces "natural rights", but because it contributes to the realization of a certain end. We only discover what rights are natural by considering what powers must be secured to a man in order to the attainment of this end. These powers a perfect law will secure to their full extent.'[4]

From this close association of political society with the attainment of man's moral end it follows that 'morality and political subjection have a common source, "*political* subjection" being distinguished from that of a slave, as a subjection which secures

---

[1] *Ibid.*, p. 193. Hegel could, of course, say the same. For the universal, in his view, exists only in and through particulars. At the same time, in speaking of the State, Green does not employ the exalted epithets used by the German philosopher.

[2] Society in this context does not necessarily mean the State. The members of a family, for example, enjoy rights. The point is that 'right' is, so to speak, a social term.

[3] *Political Obligation*, p. 144. The State, of course, presupposes the family, a form of society in which the claims of individuals are already recognized. The State maintains these rights.

[4] *Ibid.*, p. 41.

rights to a subject. That common source is the rational recognition by certain human beings—it may be merely by children of the same parent—of a common well-being which is their well-being, and which they conceive as their well-being, whether at any moment any one of them is inclined to it or no, . . .'[1] Obviously, any given individual may be disinclined to pursue what promotes this common well-being or good. Hence there is need for moral rules or precepts and, in the political sphere, for laws. Moral obligation and political obligation are thus closely linked by Green. The real basis of an obligation to obey the law of the State is neither fear nor mere expediency but man's moral obligation to avoid those actions which are incompatible with the attainment of his moral end and to perform those actions which are required for its attainment.

It follows that there can be no right to disobey or rebel against the State as such. That is to say, 'so far as the laws anywhere or at any time in force fulfil the idea of a State, there can be no right to disobey them'.[2] But, as Hegel admitted, the actual State by no means always measures up to the idea or ideal of the State; and a given law may be incompatible with the real interest or good of society as a whole. Hence civil disobedience in the name of the common good or well-being can be justifiable. Obviously, men have to take into account the fact that it is in the public interest that laws should be obeyed. And the claim of this public interest will usually favour working for the repeal of the objectionable law rather than downright disobedience to it. Further, men ought to consider whether disobedience to an objectionable law might result in some worse evil, such as anarchy. But the moral foundation of political obligation does not entail the conclusion that civil disobedience is never justified. Green sets rather narrow limits to the scope of civil disobedience by saying that to justify our practising it we ought to be able 'to point to some public interest, generally recognized as such'.[3] But from what he subsequently says it does not seem that the proviso 'generally recognized as such' is intended to exclude entirely the possibility of a right to civil disobedience in the name of an ideal higher than that shared by the community in general. The reference is rather to an appeal to a generally recognized public interest against a law which is promulgated not for the public good but in the private interest of a special group or class.

[1] *Political Obligation*, p. 125.   [2] *Ibid.*, p. 147.   [3] *Ibid.*, p. 149.

Given Green's view that the State exists to promote the common good by creating and maintaining the conditions in which all its citizens can develop their potentialities as persons, it is understandable that he has no sympathy with attacks on social legislation as violating individual liberty, when liberty signifies the power to do as one likes without regard to others. Some people, he remarks, say that their rights are being violated if they are forbidden, for example, to build houses without any regard to sanitary requirements or to send their children out to work without having received any education. In point of fact, however, no rights are being violated. For a man's rights depend on social recognition in view of the welfare of society as a whole. And when society comes to see, as it has not seen before, that the common good requires a new law, such as a law enforcing elementary education, it withdraws recognition of what may formerly have been accounted a right.

Clearly, in certain circumstances the appeal from a less to a more adequate conception of the common good and its requirements might take the form of insisting on a greater measure of individual liberty. For human beings cannot develop themselves as persons unless they have scope for the exercise of such liberty. But Green is actually concerned with opposing *laissez-faire* dogmas. He does not advocate curtailment of individual liberty by the State for the sake of such curtailment. Indeed, he looks on the social legislation of which he approves as a removal of obstacles to liberty, that is, the liberty of all citizens to develop their potentialities as human beings. For example, a law determining the minimum age at which children can be sent to work removes an obstacle to their receiving education. It is true that the law curtails the liberty of parents and prospective employers to do what they like without regard to the common good. But Green will not allow any appeal from the common good to liberty in this sense. Private, sectional and class interests, however hard they may mask themselves under an appeal to private liberty, cannot be allowed to stand in the way of the creation by the State of conditions in which all its citizens have the opportunity to develop themselves as human beings and to live truly human lives.

With Green, therefore, we have a conspicuous example of the revision of liberalism in accordance with the felt need for an increase in social legislation. He tries to interpret, we can say, the operative ideal of a movement which was developing during the closing decades of the nineteenth century. His formulation of a theory may be open to some criticism. But it was certainly preferable not only to *laissez-faire* dogmatism but also to attempts to retain this dogmatism in principle while making concessions which were incompatible with it.

In conclusion it is worth remarking that Green is not blind to the fact that fulfilment of our moral vocation by performing the duties of our 'station' in society may seem to be a rather narrow and inadequate ideal. For 'there may be reason to hold that there are capacities of the human spirit not realizable in persons under the conditions of any society that we know, or can positively conceive, or that may be capable of existing on the earth'.[1] Hence, unless we judge that the problem presented by unfulfilled capacities is insoluble, we may believe that the personal life which is lived on earth in conditions which thwart its full development is continued in a society in which man can attain his full perfection. 'Or we may content ourselves with saying that the personal self-conscious being, which comes from God, is for ever continued in God.'[2] Green speaks in a rather non-committal fashion. But his personal attitude seems to be much more akin to that of Kant, who postulated continued life after death as an unceasing progress in perfection, than to that of Hegel, who does not appear to have been interested in the question of personal immortality, whether he believed in it or not.

4. The idea of a unity underlying the distinction between subject and object becomes prominent in the thought of Edward Caird (1835–1908), Fellow of Merton College, Oxford (1864–6), professor of moral philosophy in the University of Glasgow (1866–93) and Master of Balliol College, Oxford (1893–1907). His celebrated work, *A Critical Account of the Philosophy of Kant*, appeared in 1877, a revised edition in two volumes being published in 1889 under the title *The Critical Philosophy of Kant*. In 1883 Caird published a small work on Hegel,[3] which is still considered one of the best introductions to the study of this philosopher. Of Caird's other writings we may mention *The Social Philosophy and Religion of Comte* (1885), *Essays on Literature and Philosophy* (two volumes, 1892), *The Evolution of Religion* (two volumes, 1893) and *The Evolution of Theology in the Greek Philosophers* (two volumes,

---

[1] *Prolegomena*, p. 195.   [2] *Ibid.*
[3] *Hegel*, published in Blackwood's Philosophical Classics series.

1904). The two last named works are the published versions of sets of Gifford Lectures.

Though Caird wrote on both Kant and Hegel, and though he used metaphysical idealism as an instrument in interpreting human experience and as a weapon for attacking materialism and agnosticism, he was not, and did not pretend to be, a disciple of Hegel or of any other German philosopher. Indeed, he considered that any attempt to import a philosophical system into a foreign country was misplaced.[1] It is idle to suppose that what satisfied a past generation in Germany will satisfy a later generation in Great Britain. For intellectual needs change with changing circumstances.

In the modern world, Caird maintains, we have seen the reflective mind questioning man's spontaneous certainties and breaking asunder factors which were formerly combined. For example, there is the divergence between the Cartesian point of departure, the self-conscious ego, and that of the empiricists, the object as given in experience. And the gulf between the two traditions has grown so wide that we are told that we must either reduce the physical to the psychical or the psychical to the physical. In other words, we are told that we must choose between idealism and materialism, as their conflicting claims cannot be reconciled. Again, there is the gulf which has developed between the religious consciousness and faith on the one hand and the scientific outlook on the other, a gulf which implies that we must choose between religion and science, as the two cannot be combined.

When oppositions and conflicts of this kind have once arisen in man's cultural life, we cannot simply return to the undivided but naïve consciousness of an earlier period. Nor is it sufficient to appeal with the Scottish School to the principles of common sense. For it is precisely these principles which have been called in question, as by Humian scepticism. Hence the reflective mind is forced to look for a synthesis in which opposed points of view can be reconciled at a higher level than that of the naïve consciousness.

Kant made an important contribution to the fulfilment of this task. But its significance has, in Caird's opinion, been misunderstood, the misunderstanding being due primarily to Kant himself.

---

[1] On this subject see Caird's Preface to *Essays in Philosophical Criticism*, edited by A. Seth and R. B. Haldane (1883).

For instead of interpreting the distinction between appearance and reality as referring simply to different stages in the growth of knowledge, the German philosopher represented it as a distinction between phenomena and unknowable things-in-themselves. And it is precisely this notion of the unknowable thing-in-itself which has to be expelled from philosophy, as indeed Kant's successors have done. When we have got rid of this notion, we can see that the real significance of the critical philosophy lies in its insight into the fact that objectivity exists only for a self-conscious subject. In other words, Kant's real service was to show that the fundamental relationship is that between subject and object, which together form a unity-in-difference. Once we grasp this truth, we are freed from the temptation to reduce subject to object or object to subject. For this temptation has its origin in an unsatisfactory dualism which is overcome by the theory of an original synthesis. The distinction between subject and object emerges within the unity of consciousness, a unity which is fundamental.

According to Caird, science itself bears witness in its own way to this unity-in-difference. True, it concentrates on the object. At the same time it aims at the discovery of universal laws and at correlating these laws; and it thus tacitly presupposes the existence of an intelligible system which cannot be simply heterogeneous or alien to the thought which understands it. In other words, science bears witness to the correlativity of thought and its object.

Though, however, one of the tasks allotted to the philosopher by Caird is that of showing how science points to the basic principle of the synthesis of subject and object as a unity-in-difference, he himself gives his attention chiefly to the religious consciousness. And in this sphere he finds himself driven to go behind subject and object to an underlying unity and ground. Subject and object are distinct. Indeed, 'all our life moves between these two terms which are essentially distinct from, and even opposed to, each other'.[1] Yet they are at the same time related to each other in such a way that neither can be conceived without the other.[2] And 'we are forced to seek the secret of their being in a higher principle, of whose unity they in their action and reaction are the manifestations, which they presuppose as their beginning and to which they point as their end'.[3]

---

[1] *The Evolution of Religion*, I, p. 65.
[2] This is obviously true in regard to the *terms* 'subject' and 'object'.
[3] *The Evolution of Religion*, I, p. 67.

This enveloping unity, which is described in Platonic phrases as being 'at once the source of being to all things that are, and of knowing to all beings that know',[1] is the presupposition of all consciousness. And it is what we call God. It does not follow, Caird insists, that all men possess an explicit awareness of God as the ultimate unity of being and knowing, of objectivity and subjectivity. An explicit awareness is in the nature of the case the product of a long process of development. And we can see in the history of religion the main stages of this development.[2]

The first stage, that of 'objective religion', is dominated by awareness of the object, not indeed as the object in the abstract technical sense of the term, but in the form of the external things by which man finds himself surrounded. At this stage man cannot form an idea of anything 'which he cannot body forth as an existence in space and time'.[3] We can assume that he has some dim awareness of a unity comprehending both himself and other things; but he cannot form an idea of the divine except by objectifying it in the gods.

The second stage in the development of religion is that of 'subjective religion'. Here man returns from absorption in Nature to consciousness of himself. And God is conceived as a spiritual being standing apart from both Nature and man, and as revealing Himself above all in the inner voice of conscience.

In the third stage, that of 'absolute religion', the self-conscious subject and its object, Nature, are seen as distinct yet essentially related, and at the same time as grounded in an ultimate unity. And God is conceived 'as the Being who is at once the source, the sustaining power, and the end of our spiritual lives'.[4] This does not mean, however, that the idea of God is completely indeterminate, so that we are forced to embrace the agnosticism of Herbert Spencer. For God manifests Himself in both subject and object; and the more we understand the spiritual life of humanity on the one hand and the world of Nature on the other, so much the more do we learn about God who is 'the ultimate unity of our life and of the life of the world'.[5]

Insofar as Caird goes behind the distinction between subject and object to an ultimate unity, we can say that he does not

---

[1] *Ibid.*, I, p. 68.
[2] Caird's three stages correspond more or less to Hegel's stages; natural religion, the religion of spiritual individuality and absolute religion.
[3] *The Evolution of Religion*, I, p. 189.
[4] *Ibid.*, I, p. 195.   [5] *Ibid.*, I, p. 140.

absolutize the subject-object relationship in the way that Ferrier does. At the same time his epistemological approach, namely by way of their relationship, seems to create a difficulty. For he explicitly recognizes that 'strictly speaking, there is but one object and one subject for each of us'.[1] That is to say, for me the subject-object relationship is, strictly, that between myself as subject and my world as object. And the object must include other people. Even if, therefore, it is granted that I have from the beginning a dim awareness of an underlying unity, it seems to follow that this unity is the unity of myself as subject and of my object, other persons being part of 'my object'. And it is difficult to see how it can then be shown that there are other subjects, and that there is one and only one common underlying unity. Common sense may suggest that these conclusions are correct. But it is a question not of common sense but rather of seeing how the conclusions can be established, once we have adopted Caird's approach. Taken by itself, the idea of an underlying unity may well be of value.[2] But arrival at the conclusion at which Caird wishes to arrive is not facilitated by his point of departure. And it is certainly arguable that Hegel showed wisdom in starting with the concept of Being rather than with that of the subject-object relationship.

5. It has been said of John Caird (1820–98), brother of Edward, that he preached Hegelianism from the pulpit. A Presbyterian theologian and preacher, he was appointed professor of divinity in the University of Glasgow in 1862, becoming Principal of the University in 1873. In 1880 he published *An Introduction to the Philosophy of Religion*, and in 1888 a volume on Spinoza in Blackwood's Philosophical Classics. Some other writings, including his Gifford Lectures on *The Fundamental Ideas of Christianity* (1899), appeared posthumously.

In arguing against materialism John Caird maintains not only that it is unable to explain the life of the organism and of consciousness,[3] but also that the materialists, though undertaking to reduce the mind to a function of matter, tacitly and inevitably

---

[1] *Evolution of Religion*, 1, p. 65.

[2] This idea appears, for example, though in a rather different setting, in the philosophy of Karl Jaspers, under the form of The Comprehensive.

[3] In the organism, John Caird argues, we find immanent teleology which shows itself in the way that an internal spontaneity or energy differentiates members and functions and at the same time reintegrates them into a common unity, realizing the immanent end of the whole organism. As for the life of reflective consciousness, the idea of mechanical causality loses all relevance in this sphere.

presuppose from the outset that the mind is something different from matter. After all, it is the mind itself which has to perform the reduction. In an analogous manner he argues that the agnostic who says that God is unknowable betrays by his very statement the fact that he has an implicit awareness of God. 'Even in maintaining that the human mind is incapable of absolute knowledge the sceptic presupposes in his own mind an ideal of absolute knowledge in comparison with which human knowledge is pronounced defective. The very denial of an absolute intelligence in us could have no meaning but for a tacit appeal to its presence. An implicit knowledge of God in this sense is proved by the very attempt to deny it.'[1]

As expressed in this particular quotation, Caird's theory is obscure. But it can be elucidated in this way. Caird is applying to knowledge in particular Hegel's thesis that we cannot be aware of finitude without being implicitly aware of infinity. Experience teaches us that our minds are finite and imperfect. But we could not be aware of this except in the light of an implicit idea of complete or absolute knowledge, a knowledge which would be in effect the unity of thought and being. It is this implicit or virtual idea of absolute knowledge which constitutes a vaguely-conceived standard in comparison with which our limitations become clear to us. Further, this idea draws the mind as an ideal goal. It thus operates in us as a reality. And it is in fact an absolute intelligence, in the light of which we participate.

Obviously, it is essential for Caird to maintain the view expressed in the last two sentences. For if he said simply that we strive after complete or absolute knowledge as an ideal goal, we should probably conclude that absolute knowledge does not yet exist, whereas Caird wishes to arrive at the conclusion that in affirming the limitations of our knowledge we are implicitly affirming a living reality. Hence he has to argue that in asserting the limitations of my intelligence I am implicitly asserting the existence of an absolute intelligence which operates in me and in whose life I participate. He thus utilizes the Hegelian principle that the finite cannot be understood except as a moment in the life of the infinite. Whether the employment of these Hegelian principles can really serve the purpose for which Caird employed them, namely to support Christian theism, is open to dispute. But he at any rate is convinced that they can.

[1] *An Introduction to the Philosophy of Religion*, p. 112.

John Caird also argues, in the same way as his brother, that the interrelation of subject and object reveals an ultimate unity underlying the distinction. As for the traditional proofs of God's existence, they are exposed to the customary objections, if they are taken as claiming to be strictly logical arguments. If, however, they are interpreted more as phenomenological analyses of ways 'by which the human spirit rises to the knowledge of God, and finds therein the fulfilment of its own highest nature, these proofs possess great value'.[1] It is not quite clear perhaps where this great value is supposed to lie. Caird can hardly mean that logically invalid arguments possess great value if they exhibit ways in which the human mind has as a matter of fact reached a conclusion by faulty reasoning. So presumably he means that the traditional arguments possess value as illustrating ways in which the human mind can become explicitly conscious of an awareness which they already possess in an implicit and obscure manner. This point of view would allow him to say both that the arguments beg the question by presupposing the conclusion from the start and that this does not really matter, inasmuch as they are really ways of making the implicit explicit.[2]

Like Hegel, John Caird insists on the need for advancing from the level of ordinary religious thought to a speculative idea of religion, in which 'contradictions' are overcome. For example, the opposed and equally one-sided positions of pantheism and deism are both overcome in a truly philosophical conception of the relation between the finite and the infinite, a conception which is characteristic of Christianity when rightly understood. As for specifically Christian doctrines, such as that of the Incarnation, Caird's treatment of them is more orthodox than Hegel's. He is, however, too convinced of the value of the Hegelian philosophy as an ally in the fight against materialism and agnosticism to consider seriously whether, as McTaggart was later to put it, the ally may not turn out in the long run to be an enemy in disguise, inasmuch as the use of Hegelianism in the interpretation of Christianity tends, by the very nature of the Hegelian system, to involve the subordination of the content of the Christian faith

---

[1] *An Introduction to the Philosophy of Religion*, p. 125.

[2] In more recent times, it has sometimes been said that the traditional proofs of God's existence, while logically invalid, possess value as 'pointers' to God. But unless we know what is meant by saying this, it is difficult to discuss the thesis. We need to be told something more than that the traditional proofs are 'pointers to God' or, as by Caird, that they possess great value as phenomenological analyses. This is the point that I have been trying to make.

to speculative philosophy and, indeed, a tie-up with a particular system.

In point of fact, however, John Caird does not adopt the Hegelian system lock, stock and barrel. What he does is rather to adopt from it those general lines of thought which seem to him to possess intrinsic validity and to be of service in supporting a religious outlook in the face of contemporary materialist and positivist tendencies. He thus provides a good example of the religious interest which characterized a large part of the idealist movement in Great Britain.

6. Among those who contributed to spreading a knowledge of Hegelianism in Great Britain William Wallace (1844–97), Green's successor as Whyte professor of moral philosophy at Oxford, deserves a mention. In 1874 he published a translation, furnished with prolegomena or introductory material, of Hegel's *Logic* as contained in the *Encyclopaedia of the Philosophical Sciences*.[1] He later published a revised and enlarged edition in two volumes, the translation appearing in 1892 and the greatly augmented *Prolegomena*[2] in 1894. Wallace also published in 1894 a translation, with five introductory chapters, of Hegel's *Philosophy of Mind*, again from the *Encyclopaedia*. In addition he wrote the volume on Kant (1882) for Blackwood's Philosophical Classics series and a *Life of Schopenhauer* (1890). His *Lectures and Essays on Natural Theology and Ethics*, which appeared posthumously in 1898, show clearly the affinity between his thought and John Caird's speculative interpretation of religion in general and of Christianity in particular.

Though we must refrain from multiplying brief references to philosophers who stood within the ambit of the idealist movement, there is a special reason for mentioning David George Ritchie (1853–1903), who was converted to idealism by Green at Oxford and who in 1894 became professor of logic and metaphysics in the University of St. Andrews. For while the idealists in general were unsympathetic to systems of philosophy based on Darwinism, Ritchie undertook to show that the Hegelian philosophy was perfectly capable of assimilating the Darwinian theory of evolution.[3] After all, he argued, does not Darwin's theory of the survival of the fittest harmonize very well with Hegel's doctrine that the real is the rational and the rational the real, and that the

---

[1] This is, of course, the so-called shorter or lesser *Logic*, of Hegel.
[2] *Prolegomena to the Study of Hegel, and especially of his Logic.*
[3] Cf. for example, *Darwin and Hegel, with Other Philosophical Studies* (1893).

rational, representing a value, triumphs over the irrational? And does not the disappearance of the weaker and less fitted for survival correspond with the overcoming of the negative factor in the Hegelian dialectic?

It is true, Ritchie admitted, that the Darwinians were so concerned with the origin of species that they failed to understand the significance of the movement of evolution as a whole. We must recognize the facts that in human society the struggle for existence takes forms which cannot be properly described in biological categories, and that social progress depends on co-operation. But it is precisely at this point that Hegelianism can shed a light which is shed neither by the biological theory of evolution taken purely by itself nor by the empiricist and positivist systems of philosophy which are professedly based on this theory.

Though, however, Ritchie made a valiant attempt to reconcile Darwinism and Hegelianism, the construction of 'idealist' philosophies of evolution, in the sense of philosophies which endeavoured to show that the total movement of evolution is towards an ideal term or goal, was actually to take place outside rather than inside the Neo-Hegelian current of thought.

CHAPTER VIII

ABSOLUTE IDEALISM: BRADLEY

Introductory remarks—The Presuppositions of Critical History
—*Morality and its self-transcending in religion*—*The relevance
of logic to metaphysics*—*The basic presupposition of meta-
physics*—*Appearance: the thing and its qualities, relations and
their terms, space and time, the self*—*Reality: the nature of the
Absolute*—*Degrees of truth and reality*—*Error and evil*—*The
Absolute, God and religion*—*Some critical discussion of
Bradley's metaphysics.*

1. IT was in the philosophy of Francis Herbert Bradley (1846–
1924) that emphasis on the subject-object relationship was
decisively supplanted by the idea of the supra-relational One, the
all-embracing Absolute. Of Bradley's life there is little which
needs to be said. In 1870 he was elected a Fellow of Merton
College, Oxford, and he retained this post until his death. He did
not lecture. And the quantity of his literary output, though
substantial, was not exceptional. But as a thinker he is of considerable interest, especially perhaps for the way in which he
combines a radical criticism of the categories of human thought,
when considered as instruments for apprehending ultimate reality,
with a firm faith in the existence of an Absolute in which all contradictions and antinomies are overcome.

In 1874 Bradley published an essay on *The Presuppositions of
Critical History*, to which reference will be made in the next
section. *Ethical Studies* appeared in 1876, *The Principles of Logic*
in 1883,[1] *Appearance and Reality* in 1893,[2] and *Essays on Truth
and Reality* in 1914. Other essays and articles were collected
and published posthumously in two volumes in 1935 under the
title *Collected Essays*.[3] A small book of *Aphorisms* appeared in
1930.

Bradley's enemies were those of the idealists in general, namely
empiricists, positivists and materialists, though in his case we have
to add the pragmatists. As a polemical writer he did not always
represent his opponents' views in a manner which they considered

[1] The second edition appeared in two volumes in 1922.
[2] A second edition, with an added Appendix, appeared in 1897.
[3] *The Presuppositions of Critical History* is reprinted in the first volume.

fair; but he could be devastating, and on occasion none too polite.
His own philosophy has often been described as Neo-Hegelian.
But though he was undoubtedly influenced by Hegelianism, the
description is not altogether appropriate. It is true that both
Hegel and Bradley were concerned with the totality, the Absolute.
But the two men held markedly different views about the capacity
of the human reason to grasp the Absolute. Hegel was a rationalist,
in the sense, that is to say, that he regarded reason (*Vernunft*), as
distinct from understanding (*Verstand*), as capable of penetrating
the inner life of the Absolute. He endeavoured to lay bare the
essential structure of the self-developing universe, the totality of
Being; and he showed an overwhelming confidence in the power of
dialectical thought to reveal the nature of the Absolute both in
itself and in its concrete manifestations in Nature and Spirit.
Bradley's dialectic, however, largely took the form of a systematic
self-criticism by discursive thought, a criticism which, in his
opinion at least, made clear the incapacity of human thought to
attain any adequate grasp of ultimate reality, of what is really
real. The world of discursive thought was for him the world of
appearance; and metaphysical reflection showed that it was
precisely this, by revealing the antinomies and contradictions
engendered by such thought. Bradley was indeed convinced that
the reality which is distorted by discursive thought is in itself free
from all contradictions, a seamless whole, an all-comprehensive
and perfectly harmonious act of experience. The point is, however,
that he did not pretend to be able to show dialectically precisely
how antinomies are overcome and contradictions solved in the
Absolute. To be sure, he did in fact say a good deal about the
Absolute. And in view of his thesis that ultimate reality transcends
human thought, it is arguable that in doing so he showed a certain
inconsistency. But the point which is relevant here is that Bradley
gave expression not so much to Hegelian rationalism as to a
peculiar combination of scepticism and fideism; of scepticism
through his depreciation of human thought as an instrument of
grasping reality as it really is, and of fideism by his explicit
assertion that belief in a One which satisfies all the demands of
ideal intelligibility rests on an initial act of faith that is presupposed by all genuinely metaphysical philosophy.

In reaching this characteristic position Bradley was influenced
to a certain extent by Herbart's view that contradictions do not
belong to reality itself but emerge only through our inadequate

ways of conceiving reality.[1] This is not to suggest that Bradley was an Herbartian. He was a monist, whereas the German philosopher was a pluralist. But the late Professor A. E. Taylor relates that when he was at Merton College, he was recommended by Bradley to study Herbart as a wholesome correction to undue absorption in Hegelian ways of thinking.[2] And an understanding of Herbart's influence on Bradley helps to correct any over-emphasis on Hegelian elements in the latter's philosophy.

Bradley's philosophy, however, cannot be adequately described in terms of influence exercised by other thinkers. It was in fact an original creation, in spite of the stimulus derived from such different German philosophers as Hegel and Herbart. In some respects, for instance in the way in which the concept of 'God' is represented as transcended in that of the suprapersonal Absolute, Bradley's thought shows clear signs of the influence of German absolute idealism. And the way in which the tendency of earlier British idealists to absolutize the subject-object relationship gives way before the idea of the totality, the One, can be said to represent the triumph of the absolute idealism which is associated above all with the name of Hegel. But British absolute idealism, especially in the case of Bradley, was a native version of the movement. It may not be as impressive as the Hegelian system; but this is no good reason for depicting it as no more than a minor replica of Hegelianism.

2. In his essay on *The Presuppositions of Critical History* Bradley writes that the critical mind must provisionally suspect the reality of everything before it. At the same time 'critical history must have a presupposition, and this presupposition is the uniformity of law'.[3] That is to say, 'critical history assumes that its world is one',[4] this unity being that of the universality of law and of 'what loosely may be termed causal connection'.[5] History does not start by proving this unity; it presupposes it as the condition of its own possibility, though developed history confirms the truth of the presupposition.

There is no mention here of the Absolute. Indeed, the world of causal connections is relegated by Bradley in his metaphysics to the sphere of appearance. But in the light of the later development of his thought we can see in the idea of the unity of the world of

---

[1] See Vol. VII of this *History*, p. 251.
[2] See *Contemporary British Philosophy, Second Series*, p. 271, edited by J. H. Muirhead (1925).
[3] *Collected Essays*, I, p. 24.   [4] *Ibid.*, I, p. 20.   [5] *Ibid.*, I, p. 21.

history as a presupposition of historiography a hint of the idea of a total organic unity as the presupposition of metaphysics. And this suggestion seems to be supported by Bradley's assertion in a note that 'the universe seems to be one system; it is an organism (it would appear) and more. It bears the character of the self, the personality to which it is relative, and without which it is as good as nothing. Hence any portion of the universe by itself cannot be a consistent system; for it refers to the whole, and has the whole present in it. Potentially the whole (since embodying that which is actually the whole), in trying to fix itself on itself, it succeeds only in laying stress on its character of relativity; it is carried beyond and contradicts itself'.[1] To be sure, this is not precisely a statement of the doctrine of the Absolute as we find it in *Appearance and Reality*, where the Absolute is certainly not depicted as a self. At the same time the passage serves to show how Bradley's mind was dominated by the idea of the universe as an organic whole.

3. Bradley's *Ethical Studies* is not a metaphysical work. Indeed, on reading the first essay one may receive the impression that the writer's line of thought has more affinity with the modern analytic movement than with what would naturally be expected from a metaphysical idealist. For Bradley concerns himself with examining what the ordinary man understands by responsibility and imputability, and he then shows how two theories of human action are incompatible with the conditions of moral responsibility which are implicitly presupposed by 'the vulgar'.

On the one hand, the ordinary man implicitly assumes that he cannot legitimately be held morally responsible for an action unless he is the same man who performed the action. And if this assumption is taken to be correct, it excludes that form of determination which is based on the associationist psychology and to all intents and purposes does away with any permanent self-identity. 'Without personal identity responsibility is sheer nonsense; and to the psychology of our Determinists personal identity (with identity in general) is a word without a vestige of meaning.'[2] On the other hand, the ordinary man assumes that he cannot legitimately be held morally responsible for an action unless he is truly the author of it, unless it proceeds from him as effect from

---

[1] *Collected Essays*, I, pp. 69–70.
[2] *Ethical Studies*, p. 36 (2nd edition). It is in this context that Bradley makes his famous comment: 'Mr Bain collects that the mind is a collection. Has he ever thought who collects Mr Bain?' (p. 39, note 1).

cause. And this assumption rules out any theory of indeterminism which implies that human free actions are uncaused and does away with the relation between a man's action and his self or character. For the agent as described by this sort of theory is 'a person who is *not* responsible, who (if he is anything) is idiotic'.[1]

Bradley is, of course, the last man to suggest that we should take the beliefs of the ordinary man as a final court of appeal. But for the moment he is concerned not with expounding a metaphysical theory of the self but with arguing that both determinism and indeterminism, when understood in the senses mentioned above, are incompatible with the presuppositions of the moral consciousness. And the positive conclusion to be drawn is that the moral consciousness of the ordinary man implies a close relation between actions for which one can legitimately be held responsible and one's self in the sense of character.

Though, however, *Ethical Studies* is not a metaphysical work, either in the sense that Bradley sets out to derive ethical conclusions from metaphysical premises or in the sense that he explicitly introduces his metaphysical system,[2] it certainly has a metaphysical bearing or significance. For the upshot of the work is that morality gives rise to contradictions which cannot be resolved on the purely ethical level, and that it points beyond itself. True, in this work morality is depicted as leading on to religion. But elsewhere religion is depicted as leading on to the philosophy of the Absolute.

For Bradley the end of morality, of moral action, is self-realization. And it follows that the good for man cannot be identified with 'the feeling of self-realizedness',[3] or indeed with any feeling. Hedonism therefore, which looks on the feeling of pleasure as the good for man, is ruled out. In Bradley's view, as in that of Plato, the hedonist should logically assert that any action is moral which produces greater pleasure in the agent. For consistent hedonism admits only of a quantitative standard of discrimination. Once we introduce, with J. S. Mill, a qualitative distinction between pleasures, we require a standard other than the feeling of pleasure and have thus in effect abandoned hedonism. The truth of the matter is that Mill's utilitarianism expresses a groping after the ethical idea of self-realization, and that it is hindered

[1] *Ibid.*, p. 12.
[2] The book includes indeed some metaphysical excursions; but Bradley does not explicitly introduce his metaphysics of the Absolute.
[3] *Ethical Studies*, p. 125.

from arriving fully at this idea by its illogical attempt to retain hedonism at the same time. 'May we suggest, in conclusion, that of all our utilitarians there is perhaps not one who has not still a great deal to learn from Aristotle's *Ethics?*'[1]

In making pleasure the sole good hedonism is a hopelessly one-sided theory. Another one-sided theory is the Kantian ethics of duty for duty's sake. But here the trouble is the formalism of the theory. We are told to realize the good will, 'but as to that which the good will is, it [the ethics of duty for duty's sake] tells us nothing, and leaves us with an idle abstraction'.[2] Bradley safeguards himself from the charge of caricaturing the Kantian ethics by saying that he does not intend to give an exegesis of Kant's moral theory. At the same time he states his belief that the Kantian ethical system 'has been annihilated by Hegel's criticism'.[3] And Hegel's main criticism was precisely that the Kantian ethics was involved in an empty formalism.

Bradley does not disagree, any more than Hegel did, with the view that the end of morality is the realization of a good will. His point is that content must be given to this idea. And to do this we must understand that the good will is the universal will, the will of a social organism. For this means that one's duties are specified by one's membership of the social organism, and that 'to be moral, I must will my station and its duties'.[4]

At first sight this Hegelian point of view, with its reminiscences of Rousseau, may seem to be at variance with Bradley's doctrine that the end of morality is self-realization. But all depends, of course, on how the term 'self' is understood. For Bradley, as for Hegel, the universal will, which is a concrete universal existing in and through its particulars, represents the individual's 'true' self. Apart from his social relations, his membership of a social organism, the individual man is an abstraction. 'And individual man is what he is because of and by virtue of community.'[5] Hence to identify one's private will with the universal will is to realize one's true self.

What does this mean in less abstract terms? The universal will is obviously the will of a society. And as the family, the basic society, is at the same time preserved and taken up in political society, the State, the emphasis is placed by Bradley, as by Hegel, on the latter. To realize oneself morally, therefore, is to

---

[1] *Ethical Studies*, pp. 125–6.   [2] *Ibid.*, p. 159.   [3] *Ibid.*, p. 148, note 1.
[4] *Ibid.*, p. 180.   [5] *Ibid.*, p. 166.

act in accordance with social morality, that is, with 'the morality already existing ready to hand in laws, institutions, social usages, moral opinions and feelings'.[1]

This view obviously gives content to the moral law, to the command of reason to realize the good will. But, equally obviously, morality becomes relative to this or that human society. Bradley does indeed try to maintain a distinction between lower and higher moral codes. It is true that the essence of man is realized, however imperfectly, at any and every stage of moral evolution. But 'from the point of view of a higher stage, we can see that lower stages failed to realize the truth completely enough, and also, mixed and one with their realization, did present features contrary to the true nature of man as we now see it'.[2] At the same time Bradley's view that one's duties are specified by one's station, by one's place and function in the social organism, leads him to assert that morality not only is but ought to be relative. That is to say, it is not simply a question of noting the empirical fact that moral convictions have differed in certain respects in different societies. Bradley maintains in addition that moral codes would be of no use unless they were relative to given societies. In fine, 'the morality of every stage is justified for that stage; and the demand for a code of right in itself, apart from any stage, is seen to be the asking for an impossibility'.[3]

It scarcely needs saying that the very idea of a moral code involves the idea of a relation to possible conduct, and that a code which has no relation at all to a man's historical and social situation would be useless to him. But it does not necessarily follow that I must identify morality with the existing moral standards and outlook of the society to which I happen to belong. Indeed if, as Bradley admits, a member of an existing society can see the defects in the moral code of a past society, there does not seem to be any adequate reason why an enlightened member of the past society should not have seen these defects for himself and have rejected social conformism in the name of higher moral standards and ideals. This is, after all, precisely what has happened in history.

In point of fact, however, Bradley does not reduce morality simply to social morality. For in his view it is a duty to realize the ideal self; and the content of this ideal self is not exclusively social. For example, 'it is a moral duty for the artist or the

---

[1] *Ibid.*, pp. 199–200.   [2] *Ibid.*, p. 192.   [3] *Ibid.*

inquirer to lead the life of one, and a moral offence when he fails to do so'.[1] True, the activities of an artist or of a scientist can, and generally do, benefit society. But 'their social bearing is indirect, and does not lie in their very essence'.[2] This idea is doubtless in tune with Hegel's attribution of art to the sphere of absolute spirit, rather than that of objective spirit, where morality belongs. But the point is that Bradley's assertion that 'man is not man at all unless social, but man is not much above the beasts unless more than social'[3] might well have led him to revise such statements as that 'there is nothing better than my station and its duties, nor anything higher or more truly beautiful'.[4] If morality is self-realization, and if the self cannot be adequately described in purely social categories, morality can hardly be identified with conformity to the standards of the society to which one belongs.

Yet in a sense all this is simply grist to Bradley's mill. For, as has already been mentioned, he wishes to show that morality gives rise to antinomies or contradictions which cannot be overcome on the purely ethical level. For example, and this is the principal contradiction, the moral law demands the perfect identification of the individual will with the ideally good and universal will, though at the same time morality cannot exist except in the form of an overcoming of the lower self, a striving which presupposes that the individual will is not identified with the ideally good will. In other words, morality is essentially an endless process; but by its very nature it demands that the process should no longer exist but should be supplanted by moral perfection.

Obviously, if we deny either that overcoming of the lower or bad self is an essential feature of the moral life or that the moral law demands the cessation of this overcoming, the antinomy disappears. If, however, we admit both theses, the conclusion to be drawn is that morality seeks its own extinction. That is to say, it seeks to transcend itself. 'Morality is an endless process and therefore a self-contradiction; and, being such, it does not remain standing in itself, but feels the impulse to transcend its existing reality.'[5] If the moral law demands the attainment of an ideal which cannot be attained as long as there is a bad self to be overcome, and if the existence in some degree of a bad self is a necessary presupposition of morality, the moral law, we must conclude,

---

[1] *Ethical Studies*, p. 223.   [2] *Ibid.*   [3] *Ibid.*
[4] *Ibid.*, p. 201.   [5] *Ibid.*, p. 313.

demands the attainment of an ideal or end which can be attained only in a supra-ethical sphere.

As far as *Ethical Studies* is concerned, this sphere is that of religion. The moral ideal is 'not realized in the objective world of the State';[1] but it can be realized for the religious consciousness. It is true that 'for religion the world is alienated from God, and the self is sunk in sin'.[2] At the same time for the religious consciousness the two poles, God and the self, the infinite and the finite, are united in faith. For religious faith the sinner is reconciled with God and justified, and he is united with other selves in the community of the faithful. Thus in the sphere of religion man reaches the term of his striving and he fulfils the demand of morality that he should realize himself as 'an infinite whole',[3] a demand which can be only imperfectly fulfilled on the ethical level through membership in political society.

Morality, therefore, consists in the realization of the true self. The true self, however, is 'infinite'. This means that morality demands the realization of the self as a member of an infinite whole. But the demand cannot be fully met on the level of the ethics of my station and its duties. Ultimately, indeed, it can be met only by the transformation of the self in the Absolute. And in this sense Bradley's account of morality is pregnant with metaphysics, the metaphysics of the Absolute. But in *Ethical Studies* he is content to take the matter as far as the self-transcending of morality in religion. The self-transcending of religion is left to the explicit metaphysics of *Appearance and Reality*.

4. Turning to Bradley's logical studies, we must note in the first place his concern with separating logic from psychology. Needless to say, he does not question the legitimacy of inquiries into the origin of ideas and into the association between ideas, inquiries which had occupied so prominent a place in empiricist philosophy from Locke to J. S. Mill. But he insists that they belong to the province of psychology, and that if we confuse logical and psychological inquiries, we shall find ourselves giving psychological answers to logical questions, as the empiricists were inclined to do. 'In England at all events we have lived too long in the psychological attitude.'[4]

Bradley starts his logical studies with an examination of the judgment, considered not as a combination of ideas, which have

---

[1] *Ibid.*, p. 316.   [2] *Ibid.*, p. 322.   [3] *Ibid.*, p. 74.
[4] *The Principles of Logic*, I, p. 2 (2nd edition).

to be previously treated, but as an act of judging that something is or is not the case. It is true, of course, that we can distinguish various elements within the judgment. But the logician is concerned not with the psychological origin of ideas or concepts nor with the influence of mental associations but with the symbolic function, the reference, which concepts acquire in the judgment. 'For logical purposes ideas are symbols, and they are nothing but symbols.'[1] Terms acquire a definite meaning or reference in the proposition; and the proposition says something which is either true or false. The logician should concern himself with these aspects of the matter, leaving psychological questions to the psychologist.

Bradley's anti-psychologizing attitude in logic has won him a good mark from modern logicians including those whose general philosophical outlook is more or less empiricist. But the connection between his logic and his metaphysics is generally regarded much less benevolently. On this point, however, we have to be careful. On the one hand Bradley does not identify logic with metaphysics. And he regards his inquiries into the forms, quantity and modality of judgments and into the characteristics and types of inference as pertaining to logic, not to metaphysics. On the other hand in the preface to the first edition of *The Principles of Logic* he implicitly admits that 'I am not sure where logic begins or ends'.[2] And some of his logical theories have an obvious connection with his metaphysics, a connection which I wish to illustrate briefly by one or two examples.

As every judgment is either true or false, we are naturally inclined to assume that it asserts or denies a fact, its truth or falsity depending on its correspondence or lack of correspondence with some factual state of affairs. But while a singular judgment such as 'I have a toothache' or 'This leaf is green' seems at first sight to mirror a particular fact, reflection shows that the universal judgment is the result of inference and that it is hypothetical in character. For example, if I say that all mammals are warm-blooded, I infer from a limited number of instances a universal conclusion; and what I am actually asserting is that if at any time there is something which possesses the other attributes of being a mammal, it also possesses that of warm-bloodedness.[3] The judgment is thus hypothetical; and a gap is introduced between ideal

---

[1] *The Principles of Logic*, I, pp. 2–3.   [2] *Ibid.*, I, p. ix.
[3] It is presupposed that the judgment is not what Bradley calls a 'collective' judgment, a mere summation of observed cases, but a genuine abstract universal judgment.

content and actual fact. For the judgment is asserted as being true even if at any given time there are no actually existing mammals.

According to Bradley, however, it is a mistake to assume that though the universal judgment is hypothetical, the singular affirmative judgment enjoys the privilege of being tied to a particular fact or experience, which it mirrors. If I say that I have a toothache, I am referring, of course, to a particular pain of my own; but the judgment which I enunciate could perfectly well be enunciated by someone else, who would obviously be referring to a different toothache, his own and not mine. True, we can try to pin down the reference of singular judgments by the use of words, such as 'this', 'that', 'here' and 'now'. But though this device serves very well for practical purposes, it is not possible to eliminate every element of generality from the meaning of these particularizing expressions.[1] If someone holds an apple in his hand and says 'This apple is unripe', I am obviously perfectly well aware what apple is being referred to. But the judgment 'This apple is unripe' is not tied to this particular apple: it could be uttered by someone else, or indeed by the same man, with reference to some other apple. The singular affirmative judgment, therefore, does not enjoy any special privilege of being a mirror of existent fact.

The conclusion which Bradley wishes to draw is that if the judgment is regarded as a synthesis or union of ideas, every judgment is general, and that a gap is thus introduced between ideal content and reality. 'Ideas are universal, and, no matter what it is that we try to say and dimly mean, what we really express and succeed in asserting is nothing individual.'[2] If, therefore, an abstract universal judgment is hypothetical and so divorced to some extent from actual reality, it is no use thinking that in the singular judgment we can find an unequivocal reference to a particular fact. All judgments are tarred with the same brush.

In point of fact, however, 'judgment is not the synthesis of ideas, but the reference of ideal content to reality'.[3] And it is Bradley's contention that the latent and ultimate subject of any judgment is reality as a whole, reality, we may say, with a capital letter. 'Not only (this is our doctrine) does all judgment affirm of Reality, but in every judgment we have the assertion that

[1] Hegel had already drawn attention to this point. See Vol. VII of this *History*, p. 182.
[2] *The Principles of Logic*, I, p. 49.   [3] *Ibid.*, I, p. 56.

"Reality is such that S is P".[1] If, for example, I assert that this leaf is green, I am asserting that reality as a whole, the universe, is such that this leaf is green. There is no such thing as an isolated particular fact. So-called particular facts are what they are only because reality as a whole is what it is.

This point of view has an evident bearing on the relative adequacy of different types of judgment. For if reality as a whole is the latent ultimate subject of every judgment, it follows that the more particular a judgment is, the less adequate is it as a description of its ultimate subject. Further, an analytic judgment, in the sense of one which analyses a particular given sense-experience, distorts reality by arbitrarily selecting elements from a complex whole and treating them as though they constituted a self-sufficient particular fact, whereas there are no such facts. The only self-sufficient fact is reality as a whole.

Bradley thus turns his back on the empiricist belief that the more we analyse, the closer we approach to truth.[2] It has been assumed that 'analysis is no alteration, and that, whenever we distinguish, we have to do with divisible existence'.[3] This assumption, however, is a 'cardinal principle of error and delusion'.[4] In reality truth, as Hegel saw, is the whole.

This may suggest that we shall come nearer to an apprehension of reality if we turn away from the immediate judgments of sense to the general hypotheses of the sciences. But though in this sphere there is less fragmentation, there is also a much higher degree of abstraction and of mental construction. If reality consists of what is presented to the senses, the abstractions of the sciences seem to be further removed from reality than the immediate judgments of sense. And if reality does not consist of the wealth of sensuous phenomena, can we really suppose that it consists of logical constructions and scientific abstractions? 'It may come from a failure in my metaphysics, or from a weakness of the flesh which continues to blind me, but the notion that existence could be the same as understanding strikes as cold and ghost-like as the dreariest materialism. That the glory of this world in the end is appearance leaves the world more glorious, if we feel it is a show of some fuller splendour; but the sensuous

[1] *The Principles of Logic*, II, p. 623 (terminal essays, 2).
[2] As Bradley turned his back on Hume, so have modern logical atomists turned their back on Bradley. Thus for Bertrand Russell analysis is the path to truth, to a knowledge of reality, rather than a distortion or mutilation of reality. In actual fact, however, we need both analysis and synthesis.
[3] *The Principles of Logic*, I, p. 95.   [4] *Ibid.*

curtain is a deception and a cheat, if it hides some colourless movement of atoms, some spectral woof of impalpable abstractions, or unearthly ballet of bloodless categories.'[1]

This oft-quoted passage is directed not only against the reduction of reality to scientific generalizations which form a web through whose meshes there slips the whole wealth of sensible particulars, but also against the Hegelian idea that logical categories reveal to us the essence of reality and that the movement of dialectical logic represents the movement of reality.[2] And Bradley's general point of view is that the process of judgment and inference, or, better, the process of discursive thought, is unable to grasp and represent reality. To be sure, for the purposes of practical life and of the sciences discursive thought is a perfectly adequate instrument. This is shown by its success. But it does not necessarily follow that it is a fit instrument for grasping ultimate reality as it is in itself.

When Bradley was writing *The Principles of Logic*, he tried to avoid metaphysics as much as he felt possible. In the second edition, published twenty-nine years after the publication of *Appearance and Reality*, there is naturally more reference to metaphysics, together with modifications or corrections of some of the logical views advanced in the first edition. In other words, Bradley's explicit metaphysics reacted on his logic. In any case, however, it is quite clear that his logical theories have from the start a metaphysical relevance, even if the main conclusion is perhaps a negative one, namely that discursive thought cannot comprehend reality. At the same time, as Bradley remarks in his additional notes, if reality is the whole, the totality, it must somehow include thought within itself.

5. In his introduction to *Appearance and Reality* Bradley remarks that 'we may agree, perhaps, to understand by metaphysics an attempt to know reality as against mere appearance, or the study of first principles or ultimate truths, or again the effort to comprehend the universe, not simply piecemeal or by fragments, but somehow as a whole'.[3] Most of us would probably accept his contention that a dogmatic and *a priori* assertion of the impossibility of metaphysics should be ruled out of court. And it is obviously reasonable to say that if we are going to make the

[1] *Ibid.*, II, p. 591.
[2] In Bradley's developed metaphysics movement, becoming, belongs to the sphere of appearance.
[3] *Appearance and Reality*, p. 1 (2nd edition, 1897).

attempt to understand reality as a whole, it should be made 'as thoroughly as our nature permits'.[1] But in view of what has been said in the last section about the shortcomings of discursive thought it may seem odd that Bradley is prepared to make the attempt at all. He insists, however, that it is natural for the reflective mind to desire to comprehend reality, and that even if comprehension in the full sense turns out to be unattainable, a limited knowledge of the Absolute is none the less possible.

Now, if we describe metaphysics from the start as an attempt to know reality as contrasted with appearance, we presuppose that this distinction is meaningful and valid. And if we say that metaphysics is an attempt to understand reality as a whole, we assume, at least by way of hypothesis, that reality is a whole, that there is in the same sense a One. But Bradley is perfectly prepared to admit that metaphysics rests on an initial presupposition. 'Philosophy demands, and in the end it rests on, what may fairly be termed faith. It has, we may say, to presuppose its conclusion in order to prove it.'[2]

What precisely is the content of this assumption or presupposition or initial act of faith? In the appendix which he added to the second edition of *Appearance and Reality* Bradley tells us that 'the actual starting-point and basis of this work is an assumption about truth and reality. I have assumed that the object of metaphysics is to find a general view which will satisfy the intellect, and I have assumed that whatever succeeds in doing this is real and true, and that whatever fails is neither. This is a doctrine which, so far as I can see, can neither be proved nor questioned.'[3]

The natural way of interpreting this passage, if it is taken simply by itself, seems to be this. The scientist assumes that there are uniformities to be discovered within his field of investigation. Otherwise he would never look for them. And he has to assume that the generalizations which satisfy his intellect are true. Further investigations may lead him to modify or change his conclusions. But he cannot proceed at all without making some presupposition. Similarly, we are free to pursue metaphysics or to leave it alone; but if we pursue it at all, we inevitably assume that a 'general view' of reality is possible, and therefore that reality as a whole is intelligible in principle. We further inevitably assume that we can recognize the truth when we find it. We assume, that

---

[1] *Appearance and Reality*, p. 4.   [2] *Essays on Truth and Reality*, p. 15.
[3] *Appearance and Reality*, pp. 553-4.

is to say, that the general view which satisfies the intellect is true and valid. For our only way of discriminating between rival general views is by choosing the one which most adequately satisfies the demands of the intellect. Considered in itself this point of view is reasonable enough. But difficulties arise when we bear in mind Bradley's doctrine about the shortcomings of discursive thought. And it is perhaps not surprising to find expression being given to a somewhat different view. Thus in a supplementary note to the sixth chapter of his *Essays on Truth and Reality* Bradley maintains that the One which is sought in metaphysics is not reached simply by a process of inference but is given in a basic feeling-experience. 'The subject, the object, and their relation, are experienced as elements or aspects in a One which is there from the start.'[1] That is to say, on the pre-reflective level there is an experience 'in which there is no distinction between my awareness and that of which it is aware. There is an immediate feeling, a knowing and being in one, with which knowledge begins.'[2] Indeed, 'at no stage of mental development is the mere correlation of subject and object actually given'.[3] Even when distinctions and relations emerge in consciousness, there is always the background of 'a felt totality'.[4]

This point of view is possibly compatible with that previously mentioned, though one would not normally describe a basic immediate experience as an 'assumption'. In any case Bradley's thesis that there is such an experience enables him to give some content to the idea of the Absolute, in spite of the shortcomings of discursive thought. Metaphysics is really an attempt to think the One which is given in the alleged primitive feeling-experience. In a sense this attempt is foredoomed to failure. For thought is inevitably relational. But inasmuch as thought can recognize the 'contradictions' which emerge when reality is conceived as a Many, as a multiplicity of related things, it can see that the world of common sense and of science is appearance. And if we ask, 'Appearance of what?', reference to the basic experience of a felt totality enables us to have some inkling at any rate of what the Absolute, ultimate reality, must be. We cannot attain a clear vision of it. To do so, we should have to be the comprehensive unified experience which constitutes the Absolute. We should have to get outside our own skins, so to speak. But we can have a

---

[1] *Essays on Truth and Reality*, p. 200.   [2] *Ibid.*, p. 159.
[3] *Ibid.*, p. 200.   [4] *Ibid.*

limited knowledge of the Absolute by conceiving it on an analogy with the basic sentient experience which underlies the emergence of distinctions between subject and object and between different objects. In this sense the experience in question can be regarded as an obscure, virtual knowledge of reality which is the 'presupposition' of metaphysics and which the metaphysician tries to recapture at a higher level.

In other words, Bradley admits the truth of the objection that metaphysics presupposes its own conclusion, but he regards it not as an objection but rather as a clarification of the nature of metaphysics. In view, however, of the importance of the theme it is regrettable that he does not develop his thesis more at length. As it is, he speaks in a variety of ways, employing terms such as presupposition, assumption, faith and immediate experience. And though these different ways of speaking may be compatible, we are left in some doubt about his precise meaning. However, we are probably justified in laying emphasis on Bradley's thesis that there is an immediate experience of 'a many felt in one',[1] and that this experience gives us an inkling of the nature of the Absolute.

6. By the nature of the case there is not much that can be said by way of positive description either about the alleged prereflective experience of a felt totality or about the infinite act of experience which constitutes the Absolute. And it is hardly surprising if Bradley concentrates his attention on showing that our ordinary ways of conceiving reality give rise to contradictions and cannot yield a 'general view' capable of satisfying the intellect. But it is not possible to enter here into all the details of his dialectic. We must confine ourselves to indicating some of the phases of his line of thought.

(i) We are accustomed to group the world's contents into things and their qualities, in Scholastic language into substances and accidents, or, as Bradley puts it, into the substantive and adjectival. But though this way of regarding reality is embedded in language and undoubtedly has a practical utility, it gives rise, Bradley maintains, to insoluble puzzles.

Consider, for example, a lump of sugar which is said to have the qualities of whiteness, hardness and sweetness. If we say that the sugar is white, we obviously do not mean that it is identical with the quality of whiteness. For if this were what we meant, we could

---

[1] *Essays on Truth and Reality*, p. 174. Bradley argued against James Ward that there is in fact such an experience.

not then say that the lump of sugar is hard, unless indeed we were prepared to identify whiteness and hardness. It is natural, therefore, to conceive the sugar as a centre of unity, a substance which possesses different qualities.

If, however, we try to explain what this centre of unity is in itself, we are entirely at a loss. And in our perplexity we are driven to say that the sugar is not an entity which possesses qualities, a substance in which accidents inhere, but simply the qualities themselves as related to one another. Yet what does it mean to say, for example, that the quality of whiteness is related to the quality of sweetness? If, on the one hand, being related to sweetness is identical with being white, to say that whiteness is related to sweetness is to say no more than that whiteness is whiteness. If, on the other hand, being related to sweetness is something different from being white, to say that whiteness is related to sweetness is to predicate of it something different from itself, that is, something which it is not.[1]

Obviously, Bradley is not suggesting that we should cease to speak about things and their qualities. His contention is that once we try to explain the theory implied by this admittedly useful language, we find the thing dissolving into its qualities, while at the same time we are unable to give any satisfactory explanation of the way in which the qualities form the thing. In brief, no coherent account can be given either of the substance-accident theory or of phenomenalism.

(ii) Now let us rule out the substance-accident theory and confine our attention to qualities and relations. In the first place we can say that qualities without relations are unintelligible. For one thing, we cannot think of a quality without conceiving it as possessing a distinct character and so as different from other qualities. And this difference is itself a relation.

In the second place, however, qualities taken together with their relations are equally unintelligible. On the one hand qualities cannot be wholly reduced to their relations. For relations require terms. The qualities must support their relations; and in this sense qualities can be said to make their relations. On the other hand a relation makes a difference to what is related. Hence we can also say that qualities are made by their relations. A quality must be 'at once condition and result'.[1] But no satisfactory account of this paradoxical situation can be given.

---

[1] *Appearance and Reality*, p. 31.

Approaching the matter from the side of relations we can say at once that without qualities they are unintelligible. For relations must relate terms. But we are also driven to say that relations are unintelligible even when they are taken together with their terms, namely qualities. For a relation must be either nothing or something. If it is nothing, it cannot do any relating. But if it is something, it must be related to each of its terms by another relation. And we are then involved in an endless series of relations.

A Scholastic reader of this ingenious piece of dialectic would probably be inclined to remark that a relation is not an 'entity' of the same logical category as its terms, and that it makes no sense to say that it requires to be related to its terms by other relations. But Bradley does not, of course, intend to say that it is sensible to talk about relations being related to their terms. His point is that they must either be so related or be nothing at all, and that both theses are unacceptable.[1] And his conclusion is that 'a relational way of thought—any one that moves by the machinery of terms and relations—must give appearance, and not truth. It is a makeshift, a device, a mere practical compromise, most necessary, but in the end most indefensible.'[2]

To say roundly that thinking which employs the categories of terms and relations does not give us truth, seems to be an exaggeration even on Bradley's premises. For, as will be seen later, he expounds a theory of degrees of truth, a theory which does not admit any simple distinction between truth and error. It is clear, however, that what he means is that relational thinking cannot give us Truth with a capital letter. That is to say, it cannot disclose the nature of reality as contrasted with appearance. For if the concept of relations and their terms gives rise to insoluble puzzles, it cannot be an instrument for attaining the 'general view' which will satisfy the intellect.

Bradley's position can be clarified in this way. It has sometimes been said that he denied external relations and accepted only internal relations. But this statement can be misleading. It is true that in Bradley's view all relations make a difference to their terms. In this sense they are internal. At the same time they cannot be simply identified with the terms which they relate. And in this sense there not only can but also must be external relations,

---

[1] Obviously, if we wish to avoid Bradley's conclusion, we must refuse to be compelled to choose between these bald theses. For example, we can distinguish two possible meanings of the statement 'a relation is nothing'.

[2] *Appearance and Reality*, p. 33.

though there cannot indeed be a relation which exists entirely on its own, and to which it is purely accidental whether it happens to connect terms or not. Hence Bradley can say: 'External relations, if they are to be absolute, I in short cannot understand except as the supposed necessary alternative when internal relations are denied. But the whole "Either-Or", between external and internal relations, to me seems unsound.'[1]

At the same time it is precisely the rejection of 'Either-Or' and the assertion of 'Both-And' which gives rise to Bradley's critique of relational thought. Relations cannot be external in an absolute sense. But neither can they be wholly internal, completely merged with their terms. And it is the difficulty in combining these two points of view which leads Bradley to conclude that relational thought is concerned with the sphere of appearance, and that ultimate reality, the Absolute, must be supra-relational.

(iii) Bradley remarks that anyone who has understood the chapter in *Appearance and Reality* on relation and quality 'will have seen that our experience, where relational, is not true; and he will have condemned, almost without a hearing, the great mass of phenomena'.[2] We need not, therefore, say much about his critique of space, time, motion and causality. It is sufficient to illustrate his line of thought by reference to his critique of space and time.

On the one hand space cannot be simply a relation. For any space must consist of parts which are themselves spaces. And if space were merely a relation, we should thus be compelled to make the absurd statement that space is nothing but the relation which connects spaces. On the other hand, however, space inevitably dissolves into relations and cannot be anything else. For space is infinitely differentiated internally, consisting of parts which themselves consist of parts, and so on indefinitely. And these differentiations are clearly relations. Yet when we look for the terms, we cannot find them. Hence the concept of space, as giving rise to a contradiction, must be relegated to the sphere of appearance.

A similar critique is applied to the concept of time. On the one hand time must be a relation, namely that between 'before' and 'after'. On the other hand it cannot be a relation. If it is a relation between units which have no duration, 'then the whole time has no duration, and is not time at all'.[3] If, however, time is a relation

[1] *Essays on Truth and Reality*, p. 238.
[2] *Appearance and Reality*, p. 34.   [3] *Ibid.*, p. 37.

between units which themselves possess duration, the alleged units cannot be really units but dissolve into relations. And there are no terms. It may be said that time consists of 'now's'. But as the concept of time involves the ideas of before and after, diversity is inevitably introduced into the 'now'; and the game starts once more.

(iv) Some people, Bradley remarks, are quite prepared to see the external spatio-temporal world relegated to the sphere of appearance, but will assure us that the self at least is real. For his own part, however, he is convinced that the idea of the self, no less than the ideas of space and time, gives rise to insoluble puzzles. Obviously, the self exists in some sense. But once we start to ask questions about the nature of the self, we soon see how little value is to be attached to people's spontaneous conviction that they know perfectly well what the term means.

On the one hand a phenomenalistic analysis of the self cannot be adequate. If we try to equate a man's self with the present contents of his experience, our thesis is quite incompatible with our ordinary use of the word 'self'. For we obviously think and speak of the self as having a past and a future, and so as enduring beyond the present moment. If, however, we try to find a relatively enduring self by distinguishing between the relatively constant average mass of a man's psychical states and those states which are clearly transitory, we shall find that it is impossible to say where the essential self ends and the accidental self begins. We are faced with 'a riddle without an answer'.[1]

On the other hand, if we abandon phenomenalism and locate the self in a permanent unit or monad, we are again faced with insoluble difficulties. If all the changing states of consciousness are to be attributed to this unit, in what sense can it be called a unit? And how is personal identity to be defined? If, however, the unit or monad is depicted as underlying all these changing states, 'it is a mere mockery to call it the self of a man'.[2] It would be absurd to identify a man's self with a kind of metaphysical point.

Bradley's conclusion is that 'the self is no doubt the highest form of experience which we have, but, for all that, is not a true form'.[3] The earlier idealists may have thought that the subject-object relationship was a firm rock on which to build a philosophy of reality, but in Bradley's opinion the subject, no less than the object, must be relegated to the sphere of appearance.

[1] *Appearance and Reality*, p. 80.   [2] *Ibid.*, p. 87.   [3] *Ibid.*, p. 119.

7. Reality for Bradley is one. The splintering of reality into finite things connected by relations belongs to the sphere of appearance. But to say of something that it is appearance is not to deny that it exists. 'What appears, for that sole reason, most indubitably *is*; and there is no possibility of conjuring its being away from it.'[1] Further, inasmuch as they exist, appearances must be comprised within reality; they are real appearances. Indeed, 'reality, set on one side and apart from all appearance, would assuredly be nothing'.[2] In other words, the Absolute is the totality of its appearances: it is not an additional entity lying behind them.

At the same time appearances cannot exist in the Absolute precisely as appearances. That is to say, they cannot exist in the Absolute in such a way as to give rise to contradictions or antinomies. For the whole which we seek in metaphysics must be one which completely satisfies the intellect. In the Absolute, therefore, appearances must be transformed and harmonized in such a way that no contradictions remain.

What must the Absolute, or reality, be, for such a transformation of appearances to be possible? Bradley answers that it must be an infinite act of experience, and moreover, sentient experience. 'Being and reality are, in brief, one thing with sentience; they can neither be opposed to, nor even in the end distinguished from it.'[3] Again, 'the Absolute is one system, and its contents are nothing but sentient experience. It will hence be a single and all-inclusive experience, which embraces every partial diversity in concord.'[4]

Use of the term 'sentient experience' should not, of course, be taken to imply that according to Bradley the Absolute can be identified with the visible universe as animated by some kind of world-soul. The Absolute is spirit. 'We may fairly close this work then by insisting that Reality is spiritual. . . . Outside of spirit there is not, and there cannot be, any reality, and, the more that anything is spiritual, so much the more is it veritably real.'[5]

We may very well ask, however, what Bradley means by saying that reality is spiritual, and how this statement is compatible with describing reality as sentient experience. And to answer these questions we must recall his theory of an immediate basic feeling-experience or sentient experience in which the distinction between

---

[1] *Ibid.*, p. 132.   [2] *Ibid.*   [3] *Ibid.*, p. 146.
[4] *Ibid.*, pp. 146–7.   [5] *Ibid.*, p. 552.

subject and object, with the consequent sundering of ideal content from that of which it is predicated, has not yet emerged. On the level of human reflection and thought this basic unity, a felt totality, breaks up and externality is introduced. The world of the manifold appears as external to the subject. But we can conceive as a possibility an experience in which the immediacy of feeling, of primitive sentient experience, is recovered, as it were, at a higher level, a level at which the externality of related terms such as subject and object ceases utterly. The Absolute is such an experience in the highest degree. In other words, the Absolute is not sentient experience in the sense of being below thought and infra-relational: it is above thought and supra-relational, including thought as transformed in such a way that the externality of thought to being is overcome.

When, therefore, the Absolute is described as sentient experience, this term is really being used analogically. 'Feeling, as we have seen, supplies us with a positive idea of non-relational unity. The idea is imperfect, but is sufficient to serve as a positive basis',[1] as a positive basis, that is to say, for conceiving ultimate reality. And reality or the Absolute can properly be described as spiritual inasmuch as spirit is definable as 'a unity of the manifold in which the externality of the manifold has utterly ceased'.[2] In the human mind we find a unification of the manifold; but the externality of the manifold has by no means utterly ceased. The human mind is thus only imperfectly spiritual. 'Pure spirit is not realized except in the Absolute.'[3]

It is important to understand that when Bradley describes the Absolute as spiritual, he does not mean to imply that it is a spirit, a self. Inasmuch as the Absolute *is* its appearances, as transformed, it must include within itself all the elements, so to speak, of selfhood. 'Every element of the universe, sensation, feeling, thought and will, must be included within one comprehensive sentience.'[4] But it would be extremely misleading to apply to the infinite universe a term such as 'self', which connotes finitude, limitation. The Absolute is supra-personal, not infra-personal; but it is not a person, and it should not be described as a personal being.

In other words, the Absolute is not a sentient life below consciousness. But consciousness involves externality; and though it

[1] *Appearance and Reality*, p. 530.   [2] *Ibid.*, p. 498.
[3] *Ibid.*, p. 499   [4] *Ibid.*, p. 159.

must be comprised within the Absolute, it must be comprised within it as transformed in such a way that it is no longer what it appears to us to be. Hence we cannot properly speak of the Absolute as conscious. All that we can say is that it includes and at the same time transcends consciousness.

As for personal immortality, Bradley admits that it is just possible. But he considers that a future life 'must be taken as decidedly improbable'.[1] And he evidently does not believe in it, though his main concern is with arguing that a belief in personal immortality is required neither for morality nor for religion. True, the finite self, as an appearance of the Absolute, must be included within it. But it is included only as somehow transformed. And it is clear that the transformation required is for Bradley of such a kind that an assertion of the personal immortality of the finite self would be quite inappropriate.

8. The Absolute, therefore, is all its appearances, every one of them; but 'it is not all equally, but one appearance is more real than another'.[2] That is to say, some appearances or phenomena are less far removed than others from all-inclusiveness and self-consistency. Hence the former require less alteration than the latter in order to fit into the harmonious, all-inclusive and self-consistent system which constitutes reality. 'And this is what we mean by degrees of truth and reality.'[3]

The criteria of truth are coherence and comprehensiveness. 'Truth is an ideal expression of the Universe, at once coherent and comprehensive. It must not conflict with itself, and there must be no suggestion which fails to fall inside it. Perfect truth in short must realize the idea of a systematic whole.'[4] Thought sunders, as Bradley puts it, the *what* from the *that*. We try to reconstitute the unity of ideal content and being by proceeding beyond singular judgments of perception to ever more comprehensive descriptions of the universe. Our goal is thus a complete apprehension of the universe in which every partial truth would be seen as internally, systematically and harmoniously related to every other partial truth in a self-coherent whole.

This goal is, however, unattainable. We cannot combine comprehensiveness with an understanding of all particular facts. For the wider and more comprehensive our relational scheme becomes, the more abstract it becomes: the meshes of the net become wider,

---

[1] *Ibid.*, p. 506.   [2] *Ibid.*, p. 487.   [3] *Ibid.*, p. 365.
[4] *Essays on Truth and Reality*, p. 223.

and particular facts fall through. Further, our relational thinking, as we have already seen, is not in any case fitted to grasp reality as it is, as one fully coherent and comprehensive whole. 'There is no possible relational scheme which in my view in the end will be truth. . . . I had long ago made it clear (so I thought) that for me no truth in the end was quite true. . . .'[1]

Now, if we take it that for Bradley the standard in reference to which we have to measure degrees of truth is the ideal truth which perpetually eludes our grasp, we seem to be left without any standard or criterion which can be of practical use. But Bradley's line of thought seems to be this. 'The criterion of truth, I should say, as of everything else, is in the end the satisfaction of a want of our nature.'[2] We do not know in advance what satisfies the intellect. But by using our intellect in the attempt to understand the world we discover that what satisfies us is coherence and comprehensiveness, as far as we are able to find them. This, then, is what we are aiming at, the ideal goal of perfect coherence and comprehensiveness. But to be able to distinguish between different degrees of truth it is not necessary to have attained this goal. For reflection on the degrees of satisfaction and dissatisfaction which we experience in our actual attempt to understand the world will enable us to make corresponding distinctions between degrees of truth.

9. If the Absolute is its appearances, it must in some sense be or contain error and evil. And though Bradley disclaims the ability to explain precisely how they are transformed in the Absolute, he at any rate feels that it is incumbent on him to show that they are not positively incompatible with his theory of ultimate reality.

The line which Bradley takes in regard to error follows from his theory of degrees of truth. If undiluted truth, so to speak, is identified with the complete truth, every partial truth must be infected with some degree of error. In other words, any sharp distinction between truth and error disappears. An erroneous judgment does not constitute a peculiar kind of judgment. All human judgments are appearance; and all are transformed in the Absolute, though some need a more radical transformation than others. The transformation of what we call erroneous judgments, therefore, does not demand special treatment. It is all a question of degree.

[1] *Essays on Truth and Reality*, p. 239.　　[2] *Ibid.*, p. 219.

As for evil in the sense of pain and suffering, Bradley suggests that it does not exist, as such, in the infinite act of experience which constitutes the Absolute. The possibility of this can be verified to some extent within the field of our own experience, by the way in which a small pain can be swallowed up, as it were, or neutralized by an intense pleasure. This suggestion is hardly a source of much consolation to the finite sufferer; but Bradley is understandably unwilling to envisage the Absolute as undergoing pain. In treating of moral evil Bradley makes use of the interpretation to which reference has already been made. Moral evil is in a sense a condition of morality, inasmuch as the moral life consists in an overcoming of the lower self. But morality tends, as we have seen, to transcend itself. And in the Absolute it no longer exists as morality. Absolute experience transcends the moral order, and moral evil has no meaning in this context.

10. Can Bradley's Absolute be properly described as God? Bradley's answer is plain enough: 'for me the Absolute is not God'.[1] Obviously, if we meant by God simply ultimate reality, without any further specification, the Absolute would be God. But Bradley is thinking of the concept of God as a personal being; and he will not allow that personality can be predicated of the Absolute. True, to speak of the Absolute as impersonal would be misleading. For this would suggest that the Absolute is infra-personal. In point of fact personality must be contained within reality, so that the Absolute cannot be less than personal. But, as so contained, personality is transformed to such an extent that we cannot speak of the Absolute as personal 'if the term "personal" is to bear anything like its ordinary sense'.[2] Reality 'is not personal, because it is personal and more. It is, in a word, suprapersonal.'[3]

Some theistic philosophers would obviously comment that they predicate personality of God in an analogical sense and not, as Bradley seems to suppose, in a univocal sense. As predicated of God, the term 'personal' does not imply finitude or limitation. This, however, is precisely the line of argument to which Bradley objects. In his view theistic philosophers begin by wishing to satisfy the demands of the religious consciousness.[4] That is to say, they desire to reach the conclusion that God is personal, a being

---

[1] *Ibid.*, p. 335.
[2] *Appearance and Reality*, p. 531. [3] *Ibid.*
[4] When speaking of the religious consciousness, it is primarily Christianity which Bradley has in mind. It can hardly be claimed that in all forms of religion the divine, or ultimate reality, is conceived as personal.

to whom man can pray and who can hear man's prayers. But they then pursue a line of argument which progressively eliminates from the concept of personality all that gives it concrete content or meaning for us. And the proper conclusion of this line of argument is that God is not personal but super-personal, above personality. The conclusion, however, which these philosophers actually assert is the one which they wish to arrive at, not the one which follows from the line of argument which they actually employ. It is not that they are deliberately dishonest. It is rather that they take a word which has a definite range of meaning when applied to human beings, evacuate it of its content and then imagine that it can be meaningfully applied to God. In point of fact, if we once admit that terms such as 'personal' cannot be applied to God in the sense which they ordinarily bear in our language, we create a chasm between personality and God. 'Nor will you bridge the chasm by the sliding extension of a word. You will only make a fog, where you can cry out that you are on both sides at once. And towards increasing this fog I decline to contribute.'[1]

The question, however, is not simply whether God should be called personal or super-personal. It must be remembered that Bradley's Absolute *is* its appearances. It is the universe as transformed. If therefore we understand by God a being who transcends the world in such a way that he cannot be identified with it, it is obvious that God and the Absolute cannot be equated. We *could* call the Absolute 'God'. But Bradley's contention is that the term already has in ordinary speech a meaning which is different from that of the term 'Absolute'. Hence confusion results if the two are identified. And in the interest of clarity, and of intellectual honesty, it is preferable to say that the Absolute is not 'God'.

This point of view affects what Bradley has to say of religion. If we assume that for the religious consciousness God is a being distinct from the external world and the finite self, we can only conclude that this consciousness is involved in a self-contradiction. On the one hand it looks on God as the one true reality. And in this case God must be infinite. On the other hand it conceives God as distinct from the multiplicity of creatures and so as one being, even if the greatest, among many. And in this case God must be limited, finite. If, therefore, when we speak of religion, we are thinking of its concept of ultimate reality, we are compelled to

---

[1] *Appearance and Reality*, p. 533.

conclude that it belongs to the sphere of appearance, and that, just as morality passes into religion, so does religion pass into the metaphysics of the Absolute. 'If you identify the Absolute with God, that is not the God of religion. . . . Short of the Absolute God cannot rest, and having reached that goal, he is lost and religion with him.'[1]

There is, however, another point of view to which Bradley gives expression. The essence of religion he maintains is not knowledge. Nor is it feeling. 'Religion is rather the attempt to express the complete reality of goodness through every aspect of our being. And, so far as this goes, it is at once something more, and something higher, than philosophy.'[2] The precise meaning of this definition of religion may not be immediately evident; but it is at any rate clear that there is no question of religion, as so defined, passing into metaphysics. Religion may still be appearance; but so is philosophy. And 'the completion of each is not to be found except in the Absolute'.[3] It is obvious from what has been said that Bradley by no means has the desire of some of the earlier British idealists to use metaphysics to support the Christian religion. But it is equally obvious that he does not share Hegel's sublime confidence in the power of speculative philosophy.

In conclusion we can mention Bradley's passing suggestion of the need for a new religion and religious creed. He obviously does not think that metaphysics can justify Christianity, as Hegel thought that it could. Indeed, Bradley would doubtless think it misleading to apply the name of Christianity to 'absolute religion' as interpreted by Hegel. At the same time it might be possible to have 'a religious belief founded otherwise than on metaphysics, and a metaphysics able in some sense to justify that creed. . . . Though this fulfilment is a thing which I cannot myself expect to see, and though the obstacles in the way are certainly great, on the other hand I cannot regard it as impossible.'[4]

11. In the preface to *Appearance and Reality* Bradley quotes from his note-book the celebrated aphorism, 'metaphysics is the finding of bad reasons for what we believe upon instinct, but to find these reasons is no less an instinct'.[5] This remark is clearly not intended as a flat denial of the view expressed in the same preface that 'the metaphysician cannot perhaps be too much in earnest

---

[1] *Ibid.*, p. 447. [2] *Ibid.*, p. 453. [3] *Ibid.*, p. 454.
[4] *Essays on Truth and Reality*, pp. 446-7.
[5] *Appearance and Reality*, p. XIV.

with metaphysics',[1] provided at any rate that he recognizes the limitations of metaphysics and does not exaggerate its importance. Bradley himself takes seriously his own contention that 'the chief need of English philosophy is, I think, a sceptical study of first principles . . . an attempt to become aware of and to doubt all preconceptions'.[2] This element of scepticism, 'the result of labour and education',[3] is represented by the dialectic of appearance, the critique of our ordinary ways of thought. At the same time the element of belief 'upon instinct' is represented by Bradley's explicit statement, to which reference has already been made, that metaphysics rests on a basic presupposition or assumption or initial act of faith,[4] and by the whole doctrine of the Absolute as a completely self-coherent and comprehensive totality.

This element of belief 'upon instinct' occupies a prominent position in the development of Bradley's metaphysics. Consider, for example, the theory of the transformation of appearances in the Absolute. The theory is not, of course, eschatological in character. That is to say, Bradley is not suggesting that at some future apocalyptic date the phenomena which give rise to contradictions or antinomies will undergo a transformation. He maintains that they exist here and now in the Absolute otherwise than they appear to us to exist. The completely harmonious and all-inclusive experience which constitutes the Absolute is a present reality, not simply something which will come into being in the future. But Bradley does not profess to be able to tell us precisely in what this transformation consists. What he does is to argue from possibility to actuality. We can show, for instance, that the transformation of error is not impossible. And if it is not impossible, it is possible. And if it is possible, it is an actual reality. 'For what is *possible*, and what a general principle compels us to say *must be*, that certainly *is*.'[5]

The same holds good of the transformation of pain. 'That which is both possible and necessary we are bound to think real.'[6] Similarly, of the transformation of moral evil Bradley remarks that 'if possible, then, as before, it is indubitably real'.[7] Again, 'the "this" and "mine" are now absorbed as elements within our Absolute. For their resolution must be, and it may be, and so certainly is *is*.'[8] And as a final example we can mention the

---

[1] *Appearance and Reality*, p. XIV.   [2] *Ibid.*, p. XII.   [3] *Ibid.*
[4] As we have seen, this is also described by Bradley as a dim virtual knowledge.
[5] *Appearance and Reality*, p. 196.
[6] *Ibid.*, p. 201.   [7] *Ibid.*, p. 203.   [8] *Ibid.*, p. 240.

transformation of finite centres of consciousness, which 'evidently is real, because on our principle it is necessary, and because again we have no reason to doubt that it is possible'.[1]

An obvious objection to this line of argument is that we can hardly be said to know that the required transformation is possible, unless we are able to show how it can take place. How, for example, can we legitimately claim to know that finite centres of consciousness can exist as elements within one infinite absolute experience without any disharmony or 'contradiction', unless we are able to show how they can so exist? It is really not enough to say that nobody can prove the impossibility of our thesis. After all, there is very considerable difficulty, *prima facie* at least, in seeing how finite centres of consciousness can be said to exist as elements within one unified and harmonious experience. And the burden of proof lies on the shoulders of those who claim that it is possible rather than of those who say that it is not possible.

It may be said in reply that as Bradley believes both that reality is one infinite self-coherent and all-inclusive experience and that appearances are real, and not simply illusory, appearances, he must also believe that the required transformation of appearances is not only possible but also actual. This is quite true. The point is, however, that Bradley is forced to draw this conclusion only because of an initial assumption or presupposition or hypothesis about reality. The assumption is not proved by the dialectic of appearance. True, the elimination of substance, of the substantial, is skilfully used to suggest that all finite things are adjectival to one reality. But Bradley's criticism of substance is itself open to criticism. And in any case the fact, if it is a fact, that our ordinary ways of conceiving reality give rise to contradictions and antinomies does not of itself prove that reality is a self-coherent whole. For reality might be precisely what the dialectic reveals it as being, namely incoherent. If we go on to assert that reality, as contrasted with appearance, is a self-coherent totality, this is because we have already decided that reality *must* be of this nature. References to a primitive sentient experience of a 'felt totality' will not help us much. The idea of such an experience may indeed serve as an analogue for conceiving the Absolute, if we have already decided that there must be an Absolute. But it can hardly be said to prove that it is necessary to postulate the Absolute, as Bradley conceives it.

[1] *Ibid.*, p. 227.

It is true that Bradley's line of thought can be presented in a plausible way. If we are going to try to understand reality at all, we must assume that reality is intelligible. Hence we must take it that the real is that which satisfies the demands of the intellect. An account of reality which is riddled with self-contradictions does not satisfy the intellect. We must therefore conclude that in reality, as contrasted with appearance, all contradictions are overcome. And in the end this means that we must accept the doctrine of a completely harmonious and all-inclusive totality, the Absolute.

Though, however, it is reasonable to claim that no account of reality which is riddled with contradictions can be accepted as true, it obviously does not follow that we have to accept Bradley's contention that all our ordinary and scientific ways of conceiving reality are in fact riddled with contradictions. True, concepts such as those of space, time and the self have for centuries provided philosophers with problems or puzzles. But we would probably not be inclined to acquiesce in the conclusion that the problems are insoluble on the ground that the concepts are inherently self-contradictory, unless we already believed that reality is different from what it appears to be.

Further, when Bradley makes statements about the Absolute, they are apt to cause no less difficulty than, say, the concept of an enduring self. For example, we are told that 'the Absolute has no history of its own, though it contains histories without number. . . . The Absolute has no seasons, but all at once it bears its leaves, fruit and blossoms.'[1] Now if Bradley's Absolute were transcendent, we could understand the statement that it has no history of its own. But, in his view, the appearances of the Absolute are internal to it: it is nothing apart from them. Hence history, change, development are internal to it. Yet at the same time it 'has no seasons'. The thesis is, of course, that change is 'transformed' in the Absolute. But if it is so transformed that it is no longer what we call change, it is difficult to see how the Absolute can be said to contain histories without number. And if change is not so transformed as to be no longer change, it is difficult to see how the Absolute can be said to have no history. For, to repeat, it *is* its appearances.

The obvious answer to this line of criticism is that it is illegitimate to expect perfect self-coherence from metaphysics. For,

[1] *Appearance and Reality*, pp. 499–500.

given Bradley's interpretation of the shortcomings of human thought, it follows necessarily that any concept of the Absolute which we are capable of forming belongs itself to the sphere of appearance. Indeed, the whole of metaphysics is appearance. Nor does Bradley hesitate to admit this. As we have seen, he declares that philosophy, no less than religion, reaches its completion in the Absolute. That is to say, philosophy is an appearance which, as transformed, is included in the infinite experience which constitutes the Absolute but which transcends our grasp. It is no matter for surprise, therefore, if metaphysical statements themselves fail to attain an ideal standard of self-coherence.

This is true enough. But it simply adds point to the contention that in the long run Bradley's assertion of the Absolute rests on an initial act of faith. In the long run it is the '*must* be' which is decisive. For Bradley's sceptical mind all constructions of human thought, including the metaphysics of the Absolute, must be relegated to the sphere of appearance. He allows indeed for degrees of truth. And he is convinced that the metaphysics of the Absolute in truer than, say, a concept of reality as consisting of many separate things linked by relations. But this does not alter the fact that speculative philosophy is appearance, and not identical with absolute experience. As has been already noted, Bradley does not share Hegel's confident 'rationalism'. Hence we can say that his scepticism extends even to metaphysics, as is indeed suggested by the aphorism quoted at the beginning of this section. This scepticism is combined, however, with a firm belief that reality in itself, transcending our powers of comprehension, is a comprehensive, completely harmonious totality, an all-embracing perfectly self-coherent eternal experience.

It is not altogether surprising if contemporary British philosophers, when writing on Bradley, have tended to concentrate on the puzzles which he raises in regard to our ordinary ways of thought and to pass over his doctrine of the Absolute in a rather cursory manner. One reason for this is that the logical puzzles raised by Bradley can often be treated on their own, without reference to any act of faith in the One, and that they are in principle capable of being definitely solved. For example, in order to decide whether it is true to say that space cannot be and at the same time must be a relation or set of relations, it is not necessary to discuss the transformation of space in the Absolute. What we need in the first place is to clarify the meaning or meanings of 'space'. Again, if we take Bradley's thesis that the concept of relation is self-contradictory, as on the one hand all relations make a difference to their terms and so must be internal to them, while on the other hand they must in some sense fall between and connect their terms and so be external to them, we have a problem which we can hope to solve, provided that we are prepared for the requisite clarificatory analysis. We can understand what is meant by Bradley's thesis and what questions have to be answered in order to decide whether or not it is true.

At the same time we obviously miss what one might call the essential Bradley, if we use *Appearance and Reality* simply as a quarry for detached logical puzzles. For the philosopher is clearly a man who is possessed by the idea of the Absolute, of a completely self-consistent and all-inclusive whole. And it is easy to understand how his philosophy has been able to arouse the interest of Indian thinkers who have not abandoned the native traditions of Hindu speculation, and of some Western philosophers who have an initial sympathy with this line of speculation. For there is at any rate some affinity between Bradley's theory of speculation and the Indian doctrine of Maya, the phenomenal world which veils the one true reality. Obviously, both Bradley and the Indian philosophers in question are faced with the same difficulty, namely that every concept which we can form of ultimate reality must itself belong to the sphere of appearance. But their initial 'visions' are similar, and it is a vision which can exercise a powerful attraction on some minds. Perhaps what we need is a serious inquiry into the bases of this vision or initial inspiration, an inquiry which is not dominated by the *a priori* assumption that what Bradley speaks of as a presupposition or act of faith must be devoid of objective value. It is an inquiry which possesses considerable importance in regard to the foundations of speculative metaphysics.

CHAPTER IX

ABSOLUTE IDEALISM: BOSANQUET

Life and writings—Logic; judgment and reality—The meta-physics of individuality—Bosanquet's philosophy of the State—Hobhouse's criticism of Bosanquet—R. B. Haldane; Hegelianism and relativity—H. H. Joachim and the coherence theory of truth.

1. BRADLEY was a recluse. The other leading absolute idealist in Great Britain, Bernard Bosanquet (1848–1923), was not. After studying at Balliol College, Oxford, where he came under the influence of T. H. Green and R. L. Nettleship, he was elected a Fellow of University College, Oxford, in 1871. But in 1881 he took up residence in London with a view to devoting himself not only to writing but also to lecturing for the adult education movement, which was just beginning, and to social work. From 1903 until 1908 he occupied the chair of moral philosophy in the University of St. Andrews.

Bosanquet was a prolific writer. In 1883 his essay on *Logic as the Science of Knowledge* appeared in *Essays in Philosophical Criticism*, edited by A. Seth and R. B. Haldane. *Knowledge and Reality* was published in 1885 and the two-volume *Logic or the Morphology of Knowledge* in 1888.[1] There followed in quick succession *Essays and Addresses* (1889), *A History of Aesthetic* (1892, 2nd edition 1904), *The Civilization of Christendom and Other Studies* (1893), *Companion to Plato's Republic* (1895), *Essentials of Logic* (1895), and *The Psychology of the Moral Self* (1897). In 1899 Bosanquet published what is probably his best known work, *The Philosophical Theory of the State*.[2] Two sets of Gifford lectures, *The Principle of Individuality and Value* and *The Value and Destiny of the Individual*, appeared respectively in 1912 and 1913. Among other publications we may mention *The Distinction between Mind and Its Objects* (1913), *Three Lectures on Aesthetic* (1915), *Social and International Ideals* (1917), *Some Suggestions in Ethics* (1918), *Implication and Linear Inference* (1920), *What Religion Is* (1920), *The Meeting of Extremes in Contemporary Philosophy* (1921) and *Three chapters on the Nature of Mind* (1923).

[1] A second edition appeared in 1911.
[2] A fourth edition appeared in 1923, the year of Bosanquet's death.

In spite of this extensive literary activity Bosanquet has tended to pass into oblivion and, in comparison with Bradley, is rarely mentioned nowadays, except perhaps in connection with a certain brand of political theory.[1] One reason is probably that Bosanquet is a duller and less paradoxical thinker than Bradley. A more important factor, however, seems to be the belief that, political and aesthetic theory apart, he has little to offer that is not to be found in the writings of his more famous contemporary. Indeed, in 1920 Bosanquet himself wrote to an Italian philosopher that from the publication of *Ethical Studies* in 1876 he had recognized Bradley as his master. But this modest remark hardly does justice to the facts. For example, Bosanquet strongly criticized Bradley's work *The Principles of Logic* on the ground that it created a gulf between thought and reality. And Bradley recognized his indebtedness to Bosanquet's ideas in connection with the material added to the second edition of *The Principles of Logic*. As for *Appearance and Reality*, Bosanquet was deeply influenced by it; but, though he was, like Bradley, a monist, he developed his own metaphysics which in some respects stood closer to Hegelianism. He was convinced of the truth of Hegel's principle that the rational is the real and the real the rational, and he did not share Bradley's marked sceptical tendencies.

2. In a certain sense, Bosanquet maintains, it is true to say that the world is for every individual *his* world, the course of his consciousness, built up out of his perceptions. 'The real world for every individual is emphatically *his* world; an extension and determination of his present perception, which perception is to him not indeed reality as such, but his point of contact with reality as such.'[2] That is to say, we must distinguish between the course of consciousness considered as a series of psychical phenomena and consciousness considered as 'intentional', as presenting a system of interrelated objects.[3] 'Consciousness is consciousness of a world only in so far as it *presents* a system, a whole of objects, acting on one another, and therefore independent of the presence or absence of the consciousness which presents them.'[4] We must also allow for a distinction between my objective world and the creations of

---

[1] Bosanquet's history of aesthetic theory remains, however, a valuable contribution to the subject.

[2] *Logic*, I, p. 3.

[3] Bosanquet is concerned with phenomenology rather than with psychology. The individual's world is not built up out of his perceptions considered as psychological entities, but rather out of his perceptions considered as presenting objects.

[4] *Essentials of Logic*, p. 15.

my imagination. Hence we can say that 'the whole world, for each of us, *is* our course of consciousness, in so far as this is regarded as a system of objects which we are obliged to think'.[1] Reflection on this factor of constraint shows us that the worlds of different individuals are constructed by definite processes common to intelligence as such. In a sense each of us begins with his or her private world. But the more the constructive process of building up a systematic world of objects is developed, so much the more do these several worlds correspond with one another and tend to merge into a common world.

This process of constructing a world is the same as knowledge, in the sense of coming to know. Thus knowledge is the mental construction of reality, the medium in which the world exists for us as a system of interrelated objects. And logic is the analysis of this constructive process. 'The work of intellectually constituting that totality which we call the real world is the work of knowledge. The work of analyzing the process of this constitution or determination is the work of logic, which might be described as the self-consciousness of knowledge, or the reflection of knowledge upon itself.'[2]

Now, knowledge exists in the judgment. And it follows, therefore, if logic is the self-consciousness of knowledge, that the study of the judgment is fundamental in logic. True, we can say that the proposition, the expression of the judgment, has 'parts'. And the enunciation of a proposition is a temporal process. But the judgment in itself is an identity-in-difference: it is 'not a relation between ideas, nor a transition from one idea to another, nor does it contain a third idea which indicates a particular kind of connection between two other ideal contents'.[3]

The ultimate subject of the judgment is reality as a whole, and 'the essence of Judgment is the reference of an ideal content to Reality'.[4] Hence every judgment could be introduced by some such phrase as 'Reality is such that . . .' or 'The real world is characterized by. . . .'[5]

As for inference, we can indeed make a *prima facie* distinction between judgment and inference by saying that the former is the immediate and the latter the mediate reference of an ideal content to reality. But on closer examination the distinction tends to

---

[1] *Ibid.*, pp. 14–15.   [2] *Logic*, I, p. 3.
[3] *Ibid.*, I, pp. 83–4. By 'a third idea' Bosanquet means the copula considered as a distinct element in the judgment.
[4] *Ibid.*, II, p. 1.   [5] *Ibid.*, I, p. 78.

break down. For, properly speaking, no judgment can be said to express knowledge unless it possesses the characteristics of necessity and 'precision', precision depending on the mediating conditions being made explicit. And in this case no absolute distinction between judgment and inference is possible. Instead we have the ideal of one ultimate judgment which would predicate the whole of reality, as an ideal content, of itself. This ultimate judgment would not, of course, be simple. For it would include within itself all partial truths as organically interrelated, as coherent. It would be the all-inclusive identity-in-difference in the form of knowledge. 'The whole is the truth.'[1] And particular truths are true in so far as they cohere with other truths in this whole.

Obviously, Bosanquet is in agreement with Bradley on many points: on the fundamental importance of the judgment in logic, on reality as the ultimate subject of every judgment, and on truth in the full sense as being the complete system of truth. But in spite of the many points of agreement there are important differences of attitude. Thus for Bosanquet reality or the universe is 'not only of such a nature that it can be known by intelligence, but further of such a nature that it can be known and handled by *our* intelligence'.[2] True, Bosanquet carefully refrains from claiming that the finite mind can fully comprehend reality. At the same time he is anxious to avoid what he regards as Bradley's marked tendency to drive a wedge between human thought on the one hand and reality on the other. Every finite mind approaches reality from a particular point of view and builds up its own conception of reality. But though there are degrees of truth, and so of error, no judgment is entirely out of touch with reality; and intelligence as such forces us to conceive the universe in certain ways, so that, despite private points of view, a common objective world is presented in consciousness. Further, human thought as a whole approximates more and more to a comprehension of reality, even though the ideal ultimate judgment is a goal which transcends the capacity of any given finite mind.[3]

3. With Bosanquet, as with Bradley, there is evidently a close connection between logic and metaphysics. For both hold that the

---

[1] *The Principle of Individuality and Value*, p. 43.
[2] *Essentials of Logic*, p. 166.
[3] To a certain extent Bradley would be prepared to speak in much the same way. But it is true that he so emphasizes the deficiencies of human thought that Bosanquet is justified in seeing in Bradley's philosophy the creation of a gap between thought and reality.

ultimate subject of every judgment is reality as a whole. But it would be a mistake to think that because Bosanquet describes logic as the self-consciousness of knowledge, he intends to imply that logic can provide us with factual knowledge about the world. He does not maintain this any more than Bradley does. Logic is the morphology of knowledge: it does not provide us with the content of knowledge.

Indeed, it is a mistake to look to philosophy at all for a knowledge of hitherto unknown facts. 'Philosophy can tell you no new facts, and can make no discoveries. All that it can tell you is the significant connection of what you already know. And if you know little or nothing, philosophy has little or nothing to tell you.'[1] In other words, we acquire factual knowledge by ordinary experience and by the study of physics, chemistry, and so on. Philosophy neither deduces nor adds to this knowledge. What it does is to exhibit a pattern of connections between already known facts.

Obviously, the sciences do not present us with unrelated atomic facts; they exhibit relations, connections, bringing facts under what we call laws. Hence, if philosophy has any such function to perform, to exhibit the 'significant connection' of what we already know must mean showing how the facts which are known otherwise than through philosophy are members of an overall system in which each member contributes to the total unity in virtue of the very characteristics which distinguish it from other members. In other words, the philosopher is not primarily concerned with class-concepts formed by abstraction from differentiating characteristics but rather with the concrete universal, which is an identity-in-difference, the universal existing in and through its particulars.

The concrete universal is called by Bosanquet, following Hegel, the 'individual'. And it is clear that in the fullest sense of the term there can be only one individual, namely the Absolute. For this universal of universals is the all-embracing system which alone can fully satisfy the criteria proposed by Bosanquet, that is, non-contradiction and wholeness. These criteria are said to be really one. For it is only in the complete whole or totality that there is complete absence of contradiction.

Though, however, individuality belongs in a pre-eminent sense to the Absolute, it is also attributed to human beings, even if in a secondary sense. And when examining this use of the term

[1] *Essentials of Logic*, p. 166.

Bosanquet insists that individuality should not be understood in a predominantly negative fashion, as though it consisted chiefly in not being someone else. After all, in the case of the supreme individual, the Absolute, there is no other individual from which it can be distinguished. Rather should individuality be conceived positively, as consisting 'in the richness and completeness of a self'.[1] And it is in social morality, art, religion and philosophy that 'the finite mind begins to experience something of what individuality must ultimately mean'.[2] In social morality, for example, the human person transcends what Bosanquet calls the repellent self-consciousness, for the private will is united with other wills without being annulled in the process. Again, in religion the human being transcends the level of the narrow and poverty-stricken self and feels that he attains a higher level of richness and completeness in union with the divine. At the same time morality is subsumed within religion.

Reflection on the development of the individual self can thus give us some idea of how various levels of experience can be comprehended and transformed in the one unified and all-inclusive experience which constitutes the Absolute. And here Bosanquet has recourse to the analogy of Dante's mind as expressed in the *Divine Comedy*. The external world and the world of selves are both present in the poet's mind and find expression in the poem. The human selves are indeed presented as thinking and acting beings, as real selves existing in an external sphere. At the same time all these selves live only through their participation in the thoughts, emotions and acts which make up the poet's mind as expressed in the poem.

This analogy should not be interpreted as meaning that for Bosanquet the Absolute is a mind behind the universe, a mind which composes a divine poem. The Absolute is the totality. Hence it cannot be a mind. For mind is a perfection which depends on physical preconditions and constitutes a certain level of reality. Nor can the Absolute be simply equated with the God of the religious consciousness, who is a being distinct from the world and who does not contain evil. 'The whole, considered as a perfection in which the antagonism of good and evil is unnoted, is not what religion means by God, and must rather be taken as the Absolute.'[3] Here Bosanquet is at one with Bradley.

---

[1] *The Principle of Individuality and Value*, p. 69.   [2] *Ibid.*, p. 80.
[3] *The Value and Destiny of the Individual*, p. 251.

Though, however, the Absolute cannot be a mind or a self, reflection on self-consciousness, the chief characteristic of mind, can furnish us with clues for deciphering the nature of reality. For example, the self attains satisfaction and richness of experience only by passing out of itself: it must die, as it were, to live. And this suggests that a perfect experience embodies the character of the self to this extent at least, that it passes out of itself to regain itself. In other words, Bosanquet, unlike Bradley, is attempting to offer some explanation of the existence of finite experience. 'Not of course that the infinite being can lose and regain its perfection, but that the burden of the finite is inherently a part or rather an instrument of the self-completion of the infinite. The view is familiar. I can only plead that it loses all point if it is not taken in bitter earnest.'[1] One objection against this Hegelian idea of a self-developing Absolute is that it seems to introduce temporal succession into the infinite being. But unless we are prepared to say that the concept of the Absolute is for us a vacuous concept, we cannot help ascribing to the Absolute a content which, from our point of view, is developed in time.

It may be objected that Bosanquet has done nothing to show that there is an Absolute. He simply assumes its existence and tells us what it must be. His reply, however, is that at all levels of experience and thought there is a movement from the contradictory and partial to the non-contradictory and complete, and that the movement can find no end save in the concept of the Absolute. 'I am aware of no point at which an arrest in the process can be justified.'[2] The idea of the Absolute, the totality, is in fact the motive-force, the final end, of all thought and reflection.

Now, individuality is the criterion of value, a concept on which much more emphasis is laid by Bosanquet than by Bradley. And as individuality is to be found in its complete form only in the Absolute, the Absolute must be the ultimate standard of value, as well as of truth and reality. It follows from this that we cannot attribute an ultimate or absolute value to the finite self. And as Bosanquet conceives self-perfection as involving an overcoming of self-enclosedness and a conscious entry into membership of a greater whole, we would hardly expect him to regard personal immortality as the destiny of the finite self. He claims indeed that the best in the finite self is preserved, in a transformed state, in the Absolute. But he also admits that that which persists of myself

---

[1] *The Principle of Individuality and Value*, pp. 243–4.   [2] *Ibid.*, pp. 267–8.

would not appear to my present consciousness to be a continuation of 'myself'. This, however, is not for Bosanquet any cause for regret. The self, as we know it, is a mixture, as it were, of the finite and the infinite; and it is only in shedding the restricting vesture of finite limited selfhood that it achieves its destiny.

As has already been noted, Bosanquet is much less concerned than Bradley with illustrating the defectiveness of human thought as an instrument for grasping reality, and much more concerned with understanding the universe as a whole and with determining degrees of perfection or value. Yet in the long run both maintain that the universe is something very different from what it appears to be. Bosanquet rather plays down this aspect of the matter. And for this reason his thought may appear less exciting than that of Bradley. But both men represent the universe as an infinite experience, as something, that is to say, which it certainly does not appear to be at first sight. Though, however, there is a fundamental affinity, Bosanquet is notable as making explicit the value-judgment which is basic in idealist monism, namely that the supreme value and the ultimate criterion of all value is the totality, the all-inclusive concrete universal in which all 'contradictions' are overcome.

4. Given Bosanquet's absolute idealism, one would not expect him to favour the type of political theory which regards the State as a device for enabling individuals (in the ordinary sense of the term) to pursue their private ends in peace and security. All such theories are condemned as superficial, as theories 'of the first look'. 'It is the first look of the man in the street or of the traveller, struggling at a railway station, to whom the compact self-containedness and self-direction of the swarming human beings before him seems an obvious fact, while the social logic and spiritual history which lie behind the scene fail to impress themselves on his perceptive imagination.'[1]

These theories assume that every man is a self-enclosed unit which undergoes the impact of other such units. And government tends to appear as the impact of others when systematized, regularized and reduced to a minimum. In other words, it appears as something alien to the individual, bearing upon him from without, and so as an evil, though admittedly a necessary evil.

A quite different point of view is represented by Rousseau's theory of the General Will. Here we have the idea of an 'identity

[1] *The Philosophical Theory of the State*, p. 80 (1st edition).

between my particular will and the will of all my associates in the body politic which makes it possible to say that in all social co-operation, and in submitting even to forcible restraint, when imposed by society in the true common interest, I am obeying only myself, and am actually attaining my freedom'.[1] Yet in the process of expressing his enthusiasm for direct democracy and his hostility to representative government Rousseau really enthrones the Will of All in the place of the General Will, which becomes a nonentity.

We must therefore go beyond Rousseau and give a real content to the idea of the General Will, without reducing it in effect to the Will of All. And this means identifying it with the State when considered not merely as a governmental structure but rather as 'a working conception of life . . . the conception by the guidance of which every living member of the commonwealth is enabled to perform his function, as Plato has taught us'.[2] If the State or political society is understood in this way, we can see that the relation of the individual mind and will to the mind of society and the General Will is comparable to the relation between the individual physical object and Nature as a whole. In both cases the self-enclosed individual is an abstraction. The individual man's real will, therefore, by which he wills his own nature as a rational being, is identical with the General Will. And in this identification 'we find the only true account of political obligation'.[3] In obeying the State the individual obeys his real will. And when he is constrained by the State to act in a certain manner, he is constrained to act in accordance with his real will, and so to act freely.

In other words, the alleged antithesis between the individual and the State is for Bosanquet a false antithesis. And it follows that the alleged problem of justifying interference by the State with private liberty is not a genuine problem. But this is not to say that no genuine problem can arise in regard to some particular concrete issue. For the ultimate end of the State, as of its members, is a moral end, the attainment of the best life, the life which most develops man's potentialities or capacities as a human being. Hence we can always ask, in regard to a proposed law for example, 'how far and in what way the use of force and the like by the State is a hindrance to the end for which the States exists',[4] and which is at the same time the end of each of its members. An appeal simply to private liberty against so-called State interference

[1] *Ibid.*, p. 107.
[2] *Ibid.*, p. 151.
[3] *Ibid.*, p. 154.
[4] *Ibid.*, p. 183.

in general betrays a misunderstanding of the nature of the State and of its relations to its members. But it by no means follows that any and every use of compulsion contributes to the end for which the State exists.

Bosanquet's point of view can be clarified in this way. As the end of the State is a moral end, it cannot be attained unless the citizens act morally, which includes intention as well as external action. Morality in this full sense, however, cannot be enforced by law. Individuals can be compelled, for instance, to refrain from certain actions; but they cannot be compelled to refrain from them for high moral motives. It is indeed clearly conducive to the common good that people should refrain from murder, even if their motive is simply the avoidance of punishment. It remains true, however, that the employment of force, so far as it is the determining cause of an action, reduces the resultant actions to a lower level than they would occupy if they were the result of reason and free choice. Hence the employment of force and compulsion should be restricted as far as possible, not because it is thought to represent an interference by society with self-enclosed individuals (for this is a false antithesis), but because it interferes with the attainment of the end for which the State exists.

In other words, Bosanquet shares the view of T. H. Green that the primary function of legislation is to remove hindrances to the development of the good life. How far, for example, social legislation should extend is not a question which can be answered *a priori*. As far as general principles go, we can only say that to justify compulsion we ought to be able to show that 'a definite tendency to growth, or a definite reserve of capacity, . . . is frustrated by a known impediment, the removal of which is a small matter compared to the capacities to be set free'.[1] On this principle we can justify, for instance, compulsory education as the removal of a hindrance to the fuller and wider development of human capacities. Obviously, the legislation itself is positive. But the object of the law is primarily that of removing hindrances to the attainment of the end for which political society exists, an end which is 'really' willed by every member as a rational being.

If we assume that the moral end is the fullest possible development of man's capacities, and that it is attained or at any rate approached only in the context of society, it seems only natural to look beyond the national State to the ideal of a universal society,

---

[1] *The Philosophical Theory of the State*, p. 192.

humanity in general. And Bosanquet does at least admit that the idea of humanity must have a place 'in any tolerably complete philosophical thinking'.[1] At the same time he claims that the ethical idea of humanity does not form an adequate basis for an effective community. For we cannot presuppose in mankind at large a sufficient unity of experience, such as exists in a national State, for the exercise of a General Will. Further, Bosanquet condemns proposals for a World-State with plans for substituting a universal language for national languages, a substitution which, in his opinion, would destroy literature and poetry and reduce intellectual life to a level of mediocrity. Like Hegel, therefore, Bosanquet is unable to transcend the idea of the national State, animated by a common spirit which expresses itself in objective institutions and submits these institutions to a critical evaluation in the light of experience and present needs.

Again, like Hegel, Bosanquet is prepared to admit that no actual State is immune from criticism. It is possible in principle for the State to act 'in contravention of its main duty to sustain the conditions of as much good life as possible'.[2] But though this admission would appear to most people to be obviously justified, it creates a special difficulty for anyone who holds with Bosanquet that the State is in some sense identical with the General Will. For by definition the General Will wills only what is right. Hence Bosanquet tends to make a distinction between the State as such and its agents. The latter may act immorally, but the former, the State as such, cannot be saddled with responsibility for the misdeeds of its agents 'except under circumstances which are barely conceivable'.[3]

It can hardly be claimed that this is a logically satisfactory position. If the State as such means the General Will, and if the General Will always wills what is right, it seems to follow that there are no conceivable circumstances in which the State as such could be said to act immorally. And in the long run we are left with a tautology, namely that a will which always wills what is right, always wills what is right. Indeed, Bosanquet himself seems to feel this, for he suggests that on a strict definition of State action we ought to say that the State does not really will an immoral action which we would ordinarily attribute to 'the State'. At the same time he understandably feels bound to admit that there may be circumstances in which we can legitimately speak of

---

[1] *Ibid.*, p. 328.   [2] *Ibid.*, p. 327.   [3] *Ibid.*, p. 322.

the State acting immorally. But by speaking of 'barely conceivable' circumstances he inevitably gives the impression that for practical purposes the State is immune from criticism. For those who maintain that statements about action by the State are always reducible in principle to statements about individuals, there is obviously no difficulty in speaking about the State as acting immorally. But if we assume that we can make meaningful statements about 'the State as such' which are not reducible in principle to a set of statements about assignable individuals, the question certainly arises whether we can legitimately apply the criteria of personal morality when judging the actions of this somewhat mysterious entity.

5. It is understandable that when some British writers undertook to show that ultimate responsibility for the First World War rested fairly and squarely on the shoulders of German philosophers such as Hegel, Bosanquet's political philosophy came in for its share of criticism. For example, in *The Metaphysical Theory of the State* (1918) by L. T. Hobhouse,[1] the author, though principally concerned with Hegel, devoted a good deal of criticism to Bosanquet, in whom he rightly saw the British political philosopher who stood nearest to Hegel.

Hobhouse sums up what he calls the metaphysical theory of the State in the three following propositions. 'The individual attains his true self and freedom in conformity to his real will'; 'this real will is the general will'; and 'the general will is embodied in the State'.[2] The State is thus identified to all intents and purposes with the entire social fabric, with society in general; and it is regarded as the guardian and expression of morality, as the highest moral entity. But if the State is identified with society, the result is the absorption of the individual by the State. And why should the national State be regarded as the highest product of social development? If we assume for the sake of argument that there is such a thing as the General Will and that it is the real or true will of man,[3] it should find a much more adequate expression in a universal world-society than in the national State. True, a world-society is not yet in existence. But the creation of such a

---

[1] Leonard Trelawny Hobhouse (1864–1929), professor of sociology in the University of London from 1907 until the year of his death, was a philosopher of wide interests and the author of a number of books on philosophical and sociological topics. The work mentioned in the text represents a course of lectures given at the London School of Economics in 1917.

[2] *The Metaphysical Theory of the State*, pp. 117–18.

[3] As a matter of fact, Hobhouse denies all three propositions mentioned above.

society should be held up as an ideal towards which we ought to strive effectively, whereas in point of fact Bosanquet, following Hegel, shows an unwarranted prejudice in favour of the national State. In this sense idealist political theory is unduly conservative. Further, if the State is regarded as the guardian and expression of morality and as the highest moral entity, the logical consequence is a disastrous moral conformism. In any case, if the State is really, as Bosanquet supposes it to be, a moral entity of a higher order than the individual moral agent, it is very odd that these sublime moral entities, namely different States, have not succeeded in regularizing their mutual relations according to moral standards.[1] In brief, 'to confuse the State with society and political with moral obligation is the central fallacy of the metaphysical theory of the State'.[2]

Having summed up the metaphysical theory of the State in a number of theses, Hobhouse then finds himself driven to admit that Bosanquet sometimes speaks in ways which do not easily fit into this abstract scheme. But his way of coping with this difficulty is to argue that Bosanquet is guilty of inconsistency. He notes, for example, that in the introduction to the second edition of *The Philosophical Theory of the State* Bosanquet refers to a social co-operation which does not belong strictly either to the State or to private individuals simply as such. And he finds this inconsistent with the thesis that every man's true self finds its adequate embodiment in the State. Again, Hobhouse notes that in *Social and International Ideals* Bosanquet speaks of the State as an organ of the community, which has the function of maintaining the external conditions required for the development of the best life. And he finds this way of speaking inconsistent with the thesis that the State is identical with the whole social fabric. Hobhouse's conclusion, therefore, is that if such passages represent what Bosanquet really thinks about the State, he ought to undertake 'the reconstruction of his entire theory'.[3]

By and large, of course, Hobhouse is quite justified in finding in Bosanquet the so-called metaphysical theory of the State.[4] True,

---

[1] According to Bosanquet, 'moral relations presuppose an organized life; but such a life is only within the State, not in relations between the States and other communities'. *The Philosophical Theory of the State*, p. 325.

[2] *The Metaphysical Theory of the State*, p. 77.   [3] *Ibid.*, p. 121, note 1.

[4] If one sums up a trend of thought common to several philosophers in a number of theses, it is not surprising if the resultant scheme is not fully applicable to all of them, or perhaps to any of them. And one can then find examples of 'inconsistency'. Still, the inconsistency may be with the main operative ideas of a given philosopher's thought.

it is an exaggeration to say that according to Bosanquet a man's true self finds its adequate embodiment in the State, if we mean by this that man's potentialities are completely actualized in what would normally be regarded as his life as a citizen. Like Hegel, Bosanquet considers art, for instance, separately from the State, even if it presupposes society. At the same time it is undoubtedly true that he maintains an organic theory of the State, according to which statements about the State 'as such' are irreducible in principle to statements about assignable individuals. It is also true that Bosanquet ascribes to the national State a pre-eminent role as the embodiment of the General Will, and that he is comparatively insensitive to the ideal of a wider human society. As for the confusion of political with moral obligation, which Hobhouse mentions as a cardinal feature of the metaphysical theory of the State and to which he strongly objects, it seems to the present writer that a distinction must be made.

If we hold a teleological interpretation of morality, in which obligation is regarded as falling on us in regard to those actions which are required for the attainment of a certain end (for example, the actualization and harmonious integration of one's potentialities as a human being), and if at the same time we regard life in organized society as one of the normally requisite means for attaining this end, we can hardly avoid looking on political obligation as one of the expressions of moral obligation. But it by no means follows that we are committed to confusing moral with political obligation, if by this is meant reducing the former to the latter. This confusion can arise only if the State is regarded as being itself the basis and interpreter of the moral law. If we do look on the State in this way, a disastrous conformism is, as Hobhouse notes, the result. But though Bosanquet's theory of the General Will as finding its adequate embodiment in the State undoubtedly favours this exalted view of the latter's moral function, we have seen that he allows, even if with reluctance, for moral criticism of any actual State. Hobhouse's comment, however, is that Bosanquet is here guilty of inconsistency, and that if he really wishes to allow for moral criticism of the State, he should revise his theory of the General Will. The comment seems to the present writer to be just.

6. We have noted that Bosanquet stood closer than Bradley to Hegel. But if we are looking for a British philosopher who openly shared Stirling's enthusiastic veneration for Hegel as the

great master of speculative thought, we must turn rather to Richard Burdon Haldane (1856–1928), the distinguished statesman who in 1911 was created Viscount Haldane of Cloan. In his two-volume work *The Pathway to Reality* (1903–4) Haldane declared that Hegel was the greatest master of speculative method since Aristotle, and that he himself was not only prepared but also desirous to be called an Hegelian.[1] Indeed, his undisguised admiration for German thought and culture led to a rather shameful attack on him at the beginning of the First World War.[2]

Haldane made an attempt to show that the theory of relativity is not only compatible with Hegelianism but also demanded by it. In *The Pathway to Reality* he proposed a philosophical theory of relativity; and when Einstein published his papers on the subject, Haldane regarded them as providing confirmation of his own theory, which he developed in *The Reign of Relativity* (1921). In brief, reality as a whole is one, but knowledge of this unity is approached from various points of view, such as those of the physicist, the biologist and the philosopher. And each point of view, together with the categories which it employs, represents a partial and relative view of the truth and should not be absolutized. This idea not only fits in with but is also demanded by a philosophical outlook for which reality is ultimately Spirit and for which truth is the whole system of truth, reality's complete self-reflection or self-knowledge, a goal which is approached through dialectical stages.

It can hardly be claimed that this general philosophical theory of relativity was, in itself, a novelty. And in any case it was rather late in the day for an attempt to infuse fresh life into Hegelianism by emphasizing the relativistic aspects of the system and by invoking the name of Einstein as a patron. However, it is worth mentioning Haldane as one of those prominent figures in British public life who have had a lasting interest in philosophical problems.

7. We have already had occasion to mention the coherence theory of truth, namely that any particular truth is true in virtue

[1] In the biographical note which prefaces his contribution to the first volume of *Contemporary British Philosophy*, edited by J. H. Muirhead, Haldane remarks that he was influenced more by Hegel's method than by his detailed theory of the Absolute. But he adds that in his opinion Hegel came nearer to the ultimately true view than anyone since the ancient Greeks.

[2] Though he had become Lord Chancellor in 1912, after having done excellent work as Secretary of State for War, Haldane was omitted from the reconstituted ministry of 1915, not indeed because his colleagues had any doubt of his patriotism but rather as a measure of expediency in view of popular prejudice.

of its place in a total system of truth. This theory was discussed and defended in *The Nature of Truth* (1906) by Harold Henry Joachim (1868–1938), who occupied the Wykeham chair of logic at Oxford from 1919 until 1935. And it is not altogether super-fluous to say something about the book, because the author showed his awareness of the difficulties to which the theory gives rise and did not attempt to slur them over.

Joachim approaches the coherence theory of truth by way of a critical examination of other theories. Consider, for example, the correspondence theory, according to which a factual statement is true if it corresponds with extra-linguistic reality. If somebody asks us to tell him what the reality is with which, say, a true scientific statement corresponds, our reply will necessarily be expressed in a judgment or set of judgments. When therefore we say that the scientific statement is true because it corresponds with reality, what we are really saying is that a certain judgment is true because it coheres systematically with other judgments. Hence the correspondence of truth is seen to pass into the coherence theory.

Or take the doctrine that truth is a quality of certain entities called 'propositions', a quality which is simply perceived im-mediately or intuitively. According to Joachim the claim of an immediate experience to be an experience of truth can be recog-nized only in so far as the intuition is shown to be the outcome of rational mediation, that is, in so far as the truth in question is seen to cohere with other truths. A proposition considered as an independent entity which possesses the quality of truth or of falsity, is a mere abstraction. Hence once more we are driven on to the interpretation of truth as coherence.

Joachim is thus convinced that the coherence theory of truth is superior to all rival theories. 'That the truth itself is one, and whole, and complete, and that all thinking and all experience moves within its recognition and subject to its manifest authority; this I have never doubted.'[1] Similarly, Joachim does not doubt that different judgments and partial systems of judgments are 'more or less true, i.e. as approximating more or less closely to the one standard'.[2] But once we begin to make the coherence theory explicit, really to think out its meaning and implications, difficul-ties arise which cannot be ignored.

In the first place coherence does not mean simply formal

---

[1] *The Nature of Truth*, p. 178.   [2] *Ibid.*, pp. 178–9.

consistency. It refers in the long run to one all-inclusive significant whole in which form and matter, knowledge and its object, are inseparably united. In other words, truth as coherence means absolute experience. And an adequate theory of truth as coherence would have to provide an intelligible account of absolute experience, the all-inclusive totality, and to show how the various levels of incomplete experience form constitutive moments in it. But it is impossible in principle that these demands should be met by any philosophical theory. For every such theory is the result of finite and partial experience and can be at best only a partial manifestation of the truth.

In the second place truth, as it is attained in human knowledge, involves two factors, thought and its object. And it is precisely this fact which gives rise to the correspondence theory of truth. An adequate theory of truth as coherence must therefore be able to explain how we are to conceive that self-diremption of the totality, absolute experience, which brings about the relative independence of subject and object, of ideal content and external reality, within human knowledge. But no such explanation, Joachim admits, has ever been given.

In the third place, as all human knowledge involves thought about an Other (that is, an other than itself), every theory of the nature of truth, including the coherence theory, must be a theory about truth as its Other, as something about which we think and pronounce judgment. And this is equivalent to saying that 'the coherence theory of truth *on its own admission* can never rise above the level of knowledge which at the best attains to the "truth" of correspondence'.[1]

With admirable candour Joachim is quite ready to speak of the 'shipwreck' of his endeavours to state an adequate theory of truth. In other words, he cannot meet the difficulties to which the coherence theory gives rise. At the same time he is still convinced that this theory carries us further than rival theories into the problem of truth, and that it can maintain itself against objections which are fatal to them, even if it itself gives rise to questions which cannot be answered. It is, however, clear enough that the ultimate reason why Joachim sticks to the coherence theory, in spite of the difficulties to which it admittedly gives rise, is a metaphysical reason, a belief about the nature of reality. Indeed, he explicitly says that he does not believe that 'the Metaphysician is

[1] *Ibid.*, p. 175.

entitled to acquiesce in logical theories, when their success demands that he should accept within the sphere of Logic assumptions which his own metaphysical theory condemns'.[1] In other words, absolute idealism in metaphysics demands the coherence theory of truth in logic. And in spite of the difficulties to which this theory gives rise we are justified in accepting it, if other theories of truth inevitably pass into the coherence theory when we try to state them precisely.

In judging whether other theories of truth do in fact pass into the coherence theory we have to bear in mind Joachim's own observation that coherence in this context does not mean simply formal consistency. An admission that two mutually incompatible propositions cannot both be true at the same time is not equivalent to embracing the coherence theory of truth. As Joachim presents the theory, when he is discussing the difficulties to which it gives rise, it is clearly a metaphysical theory, part and parcel of absolute idealism. Hence it is a question of whether all other theories of truth can be seen ultimately either to suffer complete collapse under critical examination or to imply the validity of absolute idealism. And nobody who is not already an absolute idealist is likely to admit that this is the case. It is not indeed the intention of the present writer to suggest that coherence has nothing to do with truth. In point of fact we often use coherence as a test, coherence with already established truths. And it is arguable that this implies a metaphysical belief about the nature of reality. But it does not necessarily follow that this is an implicit belief in absolute idealism. In any case, as Joachim himself frankly recognizes, if a true proposition is true only in so far as it is included as a moment in an absolute experience which transcends our grasp, it is very difficult to see how we can ever know that any proposition is true. And yet we are sure that we can have some knowledge. Perhaps an essential preliminary to any attempt to formulate 'the' theory of truth is a careful examination of the ways in which terms such as 'true' and 'truth' are used in ordinary discourse.

---

[1] *The Nature of Truth*, p. 179.

CHAPTER X

THE TURN TOWARDS PERSONAL IDEALISM

Pringle-Pattison and the value of the human person—The pluralistic idealism of McTaggart—The pluralistic spiritualism of J. Ward—General comments.

1. THE attitude adopted by Bradley and Bosanquet to finite personality not unnaturally led to a reaction even within the idealist movement. One of the chief representatives of this reaction was Andrew Seth Pringle-Pattison (1856–1931).[1] In his first work, *The Development from Kant to Hegel* (1882), he described the transition from the critical philosophy of Kant to the metaphysical idealism of Hegel as an inevitable movement. And he always maintained that the mind cannot rest in a system which involves the doctrine of unknowable things-in-themselves. But in 1887 he published *Hegelianism and Personality* in which, somewhat to the surprise of his readers, he submitted absolute idealism to outspoken criticism.

At first sight, Pringle-Pattison admits, Hegelianism appears to magnify man. For, obscure though Hegel's utterances may be, his philosophy certainly suggests that God or the Absolute is identical with the whole historical process, considered as developing dialectically towards self-knowledge in and through the human mind. 'The philosopher's knowledge of God is God's knowledge of himself.'[2] The ground is thus prepared for the Left-wing Hegelian transformation of theology into anthropology.

Reflection, however, shows that in Hegelianism the individual person is of little account. For human beings become 'the foci in which the impersonal life of thought momentarily concentrates itself, in order to take stock of its own contents. These foci appear only to disappear in the perpetual process of this realization.'[3] The human person, in other words, is simply a means whereby impersonal Thought comes to a knowledge of itself. And from the

---

[1] Originally called Andrew Seth, he adopted the name Pringle-Pattison in 1898 in fulfilment of a condition for succeeding to an estate. He successively occupied chairs of philosophy at Cardiff (1883–7), St. Andrews (1887–91) and Edinburgh (1891–1919).

[2] *Hegelianism and Personality*, p. 196 (2nd edition).

[3] *Ibid.*, p. 199.

point of view of anyone who attaches a real value to personality
it is clear that 'Hegel's determination to have one process and one
subject was the original fountain of error'.[1] The radical mistake
both of Hegelianism itself and of its British derivatives is 'the
identification of the human and the divine self-consciousness or,
to put it more broadly, the unification of consciousness in a single
self'.[2] This unification is ultimately destructive of the reality of
both God and man.

Pringle-Pattison insists, therefore, on two points. First, we
should recognize a real self-consciousness in God, even though we
have to avoid ascribing to it the features of finite self-consciousness
considered precisely as finite. Secondly, we must assert the value
and relative independence of the human person. For each person
has a centre of its own, a will, which is 'impervious' to any other
person, 'a centre which I maintain even in my dealings with God
Himself'.[3] 'The two positions—the divine personality and human
dignity and immortality—are two complementary sides of the
same view of existence.'[4]

This sounds like an abandonment of absolute idealism in favour
of theism. But in his later writings Pringle-Pattison reaffirms
absolute idealism or, more accurately, attempts to revise it in
such a way that it permits more value being attached to finite
personality than in the philosophies of Bradley and Bosanquet.
The result is an unsatisfactory amalgam of absolute idealism and
theism.

In the first place we cannot prove, by the sort of arguments
employed by the earlier British idealists, that the world of Nature
can exist only as object for a subject. Ferrier's line of argument,
for example, is quite unsound. It is indeed obviously true that we
cannot conceive material things without conceiving them; but
'this method of approach cannot possibly prove that they do not
exist out of that relation'.[5] As for Green's argument that relations
cannot exist except through the synthesizing activity of a universal
consciousness, this presupposes a defunct psychology, according
to which experience begins with unrelated sensations. In point of

---

[1] *Hegelianism and Personality*, p. 203.
[2] *Ibid.*, p. 226. Strictly speaking, neither Bradley nor Bosanquet regarded the
Absolute as a 'self'. But they did, of course, merge all finite experiences in the
unity of a single absolute experience.
[3] *Ibid.*, p. 217.
[4] *Ibid.*, p. 238.
[5] *The Idea of God in the Light of Recent Philosophy* (1917), p. 192. This work
will be referred to as *The Idea of God*.

fact relations are just as much given realities as the things related.

It does not follow, however, that, as the 'lower naturalism' maintains, Nature exists apart from a total system which embodies value. On the contrary, we can see in Nature a continuity of process combined with the emergence of qualitatively distinct levels. Man appears as 'the organ through which the universe beholds and enjoys itself'.[1] And among the emergent qualities which characterize the universe we must recognize not only the so-called secondary qualities but also 'the aspects of beauty and sublimity which we recognize in nature and those finer insights which we owe to the poet and the artist'.[2] Moral values too must be taken as qualifying the universe. And the whole process of Nature, with the emergence of qualitatively different levels, is to be looked on as a progressive manifestation of the Absolute or God.

According to Pringle-Pattison, the idea of God as existing 'before' the world and as creating it out of nothing is philosophically untenable. 'The idea of creation tends to pass into that of manifestation';[3] and the infinite and the finite stand to one another in a relation of mutual implication. As for man, 'he exists as an organ of the universe or of the Absolute, the one Being',[4] which should be conceived in terms of its highest manifestation and so as one spiritual life or absolute experience.

Whatever *Hegelianism and Personality* may have seemed to imply, there is thus no radical rejection of absolute idealism in Pringle-Pattison's later work. On the contrary, there is a large measure of agreement with Bosanquet. At the same time Pringle-Pattison is not prepared to accept Bosanquet's view of the destiny of the human individual. In his view differentiation constitutes the very essence of absolute life, and 'every individual is a unique nature . . . an expression or focalization of the universe which is nowhere else repeated'.[5] The higher we ascend in the scale of life, the clearer becomes the uniqueness of the individual. And if value increases in proportion to unique individuality, we cannot suppose that distinct selves achieve their destiny by being merged without distinction in the One. Each must be preserved in its uniqueness.

Pringle-Pattison is thus not prepared to say with Bradley that

[1] *Ibid.*, p. 211.   [2] *Ibid.*, p. 212.   [3] *Ibid.*, p. 308.
[4] *Ibid.*, p. 259.   [5] *Ibid.*, p. 267.

the temporal world is appearance. And as he retains the doctrine of the Absolute, he seems to be committed to saying that the Absolute is subject to temporal succession. But he also wishes to maintain that there is a real sense in which the Absolute or God transcends time. Hence he has recourse to the analogies of the drama and the symphony. Where, for example, a symphony is played, the notes succeed one another; yet in a real sense the whole is there from the beginning, giving meaning to and unifying the successive units. 'Somewhat in this fashion we may perhaps conceive that the time-process is retained in the Absolute and yet transcended.'[1]

If such analogies were pressed, the natural conclusion would be that the Absolute is simply the Idea, or perhaps more properly the Value, of the entire cosmic and historical process. But Pringle-Pattison clearly wishes to maintain that God is an absolute personal experience, which could hardly be described as simply the meaning and value of the world. In other words, he tries to combine absolute idealism with elements of theism. And the ambiguous result suggests that he would have done better either to retain the Absolute and identify it with the historical process considered as moving towards the emergence of new values or to make a clear break with absolute idealism and embrace theism. However, it is at any rate clear that within the general framework of absolute idealism he tried to preserve and assert the value of the finite personality.

2. We can now turn to a Cambridge philosopher, John McTaggart Ellis McTaggart (1866–1925), for whom the problem of the relation between finite selves and the Absolute did not and could not arise, inasmuch for him there was no Absolute apart from the society or system of selves. In his philosophy the Absolute as understood by Bradley and Bosanquet simply disappeared from the scene.

McTaggart was elected a Fellow of Trinity College, Cambridge, in 1891. In his view Hegel had penetrated further than any other philosopher into the nature of reality. And he devoted himself to a prolonged study of Hegelianism, which bore fruit in *Studies in the Hegelian Dialectic* (1896; second edition, 1922), *Studies in the Hegelian Cosmology* (1901; second edition, 1918), and *A Commentary on Hegel's Logic* (1910). But McTaggart was by no means only a student of and commentator on Hegel: he was an

[1] *The Idea of God*, p. 363.

original thinker. This fact shows itself indeed in the commentaries but much more in the two volumes of *The Nature of Existence*,[1] which together contain his system of philosophy.

In the first part of his sytem McTaggart is concerned with determining the characteristics which belong to all that exists or, as he puts it, to existence as a whole.[2] More accurately, he is concerned with determining the characteristics which the existent *must* have. Hence the method to be employed will be that of *a priori* deduction. McTaggart is thus very far from being what is often described as an inductive metaphysician.

Even in the first part of the system, however, McTaggart admits two empirical premisses, namely that something exists and that what exists is differentiation. The truth of the first premiss is known by immediate experience. For everyone is aware that he at any rate exists. And he cannot deny this without implicitly affirming it. As for the second premiss, 'it would indeed be possible to reach this result *a priori*. For I shall argue later that it is certain *a priori* that no substance can be simple.'[3] But an appeal to perception 'seems more likely to command assent'.[4] What McTaggart really wishes to show is that existence as a whole is differentiated, that there is a plurality of substances. And this is shown by the very fact of perception. If, for example, perception is interpreted as a relation, there must be more than one term.

We can take it, therefore, that something exists. This cannot be existence itself.[5] For if we say that what exists is existence, we are left with an absolute blank. That which exists must possess some quality besides existence. And the compound quality, composed of all the qualities of a thing, can be called its nature. But we cannot resolve a thing without residue into its qualities. 'At the head of the series there will be something existent which has qualities without being itself a quality. The ordinary name for

[1] The first volume appeared in 1921. The second, edited by Professor C. D. Broad, was published posthumously in 1927. A summary of the system is presented by McTaggart himself in his contribution to the first volume of *Contemporary British Philosophy*, edited by J. H. Muirhead.

[2] Existence is said to be an indefinable quality which is such that everything which exists is real, though not everything which is real is necessarily existent. In other words, reality or being is for McTaggart a wider concept than that of existence.

[3] *The Nature of Existence*, 45. The work is divided into sections numbered successively from the beginning of the first to the end of the second volume. And references are given here according to these numbered sections.

[4] *Ibid.*

[5] Obviously, McTaggart, interpreting existence as an indefinable quality, could not accept the Thomist thesis that ultimate reality is precisely *ipsum esse subsistens*.

this, and I think the best name, is substance.'[1] It may be objected
that substance apart from its qualities is an inconceivable nothing;
but it does not follow that substance is 'not anything in conjunction with its qualities'.[2]

If therefore there is anything existing, and we know from
experience that there is, there must be at least one substance. But
we have already accepted the empirical premiss of pluralism, of the
differentiation of existence as a whole. It follows therefore that there
must be relations.[3] For if there is a plurality of substances, they
must be similar and dissimilar, similar in being substances, dissimilar
in being distinct.[4] And similarity and dissimilarity are relations.

Now, according to McTaggart every relation generates a
derivative quality in each of its terms, namely the quality of
being a term in this relationship. Further, a derivative relationship is generated between every relation and each of its terms. We
therefore get infinite series. But 'these infinite series are not
vicious, because it is not necessary to complete them to determine
the meaning of the earlier terms'.[5] Hence Bradley's argument to
show that qualities and relations cannot be truly real loses its force.

Substances, we have seen, must be dissimilar in some way. But
there are similarities which permit their arrangement in collections
and collections of collections. A collection is called a 'group', and
the substances which compose it are its 'members'.[6] Taken by
itself, this is a straightforward idea. But there are several points
to notice. First, a group is for McTaggart a substance. Thus the
group of all French citizens is a substance which possesses qualities
of its own, such as being a nation. Secondly, as no substance is
ever absolutely simple, a compound substance cannot have simple
substances as its members. Thirdly, we cannot assume without
more ado that two groups are necessarily two substances. If the
contents are the same, the groups are one substance. For example,
the counties of England and the parishes of England form two
groups but only one substance.

---

[1] *The Nature of Existence*, 65.   [2] *Ibid.*, 68.
[3] The term 'relation' is for McTaggart indefinable, though we can clarify the
difference in meaning between words such as 'relation' and 'quality'. For instance,
qualities are not said to exist 'between' terms, whereas relations are.
[4] According to McTaggart, following Leibniz, if two substances had precisely
the same nature, they would be indistinguishable, and therefore one and the same
substance.
[5] *The Nature of Existence*, 88.
[6] We must distinguish between members and parts. 'If we take the group of
all the counties in Great Britain, neither England nor Whitechapel are members
of the group, but they are parts, of which the group is the whole.' *Ibid.*, 123.

Now, there must be one compound substance which contains all existent content and of which every other substance is a part. 'This substance is to be called the Universe.'[1] It is an organic unity in which 'all that exists, both substances and characteristics, are bound together in one system of extrinsic determination'.[2] At the same time there seems to be a major objection against admitting this idea of an all-inclusive substance. On the one hand McTaggart takes it that a sufficient description of any substance must be possible in principle. On the other hand no sufficient description of the universe seems to be possible. For a sufficient description would have, it appears, to indicate the parts and also their relations to one another and to the whole. But how can this be possible if no substance is simple and is consequently infinitely divisible?[3]

The details of McTaggart's solution of this difficulty are too complicated for discussion here. His general principle, as stated in his summary of his system, is that to avoid a contradiction between the thesis that a sufficient description of any substance is possible and the thesis that no substance is simple 'there must be some description of any substance, A, which implies sufficient descriptions of the members of all its sets of parts which are sequent to some given sets of parts'.[4] Taken by itself, this statement does not indeed convey very much. But McTaggart's line of thought is this. A sufficient description of a substance is possible in principle, if certain conditions are fulfilled. Consider the all-inclusive substance, the universe. This consists of one or more primary wholes, which in turn consist of primary parts. These parts can be differentiated by, for example, distinct qualities. And a sufficient description of the universe is possible in principle, provided that descriptions of the primary parts *imply* sufficient descriptions of the secondary parts, the series of which is indefinitely prolonged. For this implication to be a reality, however, the secondary parts must be related to one another by what McTaggart calls the relation of determining correspondence. For example, let us suppose that A and B are primary parts of a given

[1] *Ibid.*, 135.
[2] *Ibid.*, 137. If, for instance, a substance X possesses qualities a, b and c, an alteration in one quality produces an alteration in the nature (composed of the qualities) and so in the substance which is manifested in the nature. The qualities are then said to stand to one another in a relation of extrinsic determination.
[3] As no substance is absolutely simple, the difficulty occurs in regard to every substance.
[4] *Contemporary British Philosophy*, First Series, p. 256.

substance, and that A and B are sufficiently described in terms of the qualities of x and y respectively. The relation of determining correspondence demands that a secondary part of A should be sufficiently describable in terms of y and that a secondary part of B should be sufficiently describable in terms of x. Given such interlocking determining correspondences throughout the whole hierarchy of consequent sets of parts, sufficient descriptions of the primary parts will imply sufficient descriptions of the secondary parts. And a sufficient description of the substance is thus possible in principle, notwithstanding the fact that it is indefinitely divisible.

As McTaggart maintains that a sufficient description of every substance must be possible, it follows that the relation of determining correspondence must hold between the parts of a substance. And if we look on determining correspondence as a label for types of causal relations, we can then say that McTaggart attempts to prove *a priori* the necessity of a certain pattern of causal relations within the universe. That is to say, if, as he assumes, the universe is an intelligible organic unity, there must exist in the hierarchy of its parts a certain pattern of determining correspondence.

Now, we have referred, for instance, to the counties of England, and we have been speaking of the universe. But though in the first part of the system some empirical illustrations are given to facilitate understanding, the conclusions reached are intended to be purely abstract. For example, though it is argued *a priori* that, if anything exists, there must be an all-inclusive substance which we can call the universe, it is a mistake to suppose that this term necessarily refers to the whole complex of entities which we are ordinarily accustomed to think of as the universe. The first part of the system established simply that there must be a universe. It does not tell us which, if any, empirical entities are members of the all-inclusive group which is called the universe. It is only in the second part of the system that McTaggart applies the conclusions of the first part, asking, for instance, whether the characteristics of substance which have been determined *a priori* can belong to those kinds of things which at first sight appear to be substances, or, rather, whether the characteristics which are encountered in or suggested by experience really belong to the existent.

In this field of inquiry, however, McTaggart insists, we cannot obtain absolute certainty. We may indeed be able to show that certain characteristics presented in or suggested by experience cannot belong to the existent, and that they must therefore be assigned to the sphere of appearance. But we cannot show with absolute certainty that characteristics suggested by experience *must* belong to the existent. For there might be characteristics never experienced or imagined by us which would equally well or better satisfy the *a priori* requirements of the first part of the system. However, if it can be shown that characteristics suggested by experience do in fact satisfy these *a priori* demands, and that no others which we know of or can imagine will do so, we have reasonable, though not absolute, certainty. In other words, McTaggart ascribes absolute certainty only to the results of *a priori* demonstration.

'The universe appears, *prima facie*, to contain substances of two very different kinds—Matter and Spirit.'[1] But McTaggart refuses to admit the reality of matter, mainly on the ground that nothing which has the quality of being material can have between its parts that relation of determining correspondence which must exist between the secondary parts of a substance. Let us suppose, for the sake of argument, that a given material thing has two primary parts, one of which can be sufficiently described as blue, while the other can be sufficiently described as red. According to the requirements of the principle of determining correspondence there would have to be a secondary part of the primary part described as blue which would correspond with the primary part described as red. That is to say, this secondary part would be red. But this is not logically possible. For a primary part could not be sufficiently described as blue, if one of its secondary parts were red. And analogous conclusions can be drawn if we consider qualities such as size and shape. Hence matter cannot belong to the existent: it cannot qualify the universe.[2]

We are left therefore with spirit. There is indeed no demonstrative proof that nothing exists save spirit. For there might possibly be a form of substance, which we had never experienced or imagined, which would satisfy the requirements for being a substance and yet not be spiritual. But we have no positive ground for claiming that there is such a substance. Hence it is reasonable to conclude that all substance is spiritual.

[1] *The Nature of Existence*, 352.
[2] According to McTaggart, it is no good saying that the existence of matter can be proved inferentially from sense-data. For what we call sense-data might be caused by spiritual causes. And if we claim that sense-data are themselves material substances, we shall have to meet the arguments which show, in general, that substance cannot be material.

As for the nature of spirit, 'I propose to define the quality of spirituality by saying that it is the quality of having content, all of which is the content of one or more selves'.[1] Thus selves are spiritual, and so are parts of selves and groups of selves, though in deference to common usage the term 'a spirit' can be reserved for a self.[2]

If spirit, therefore, is the only form of substance, the universe or Absolute will be the all-inclusive society or system of selves, selves being its primary parts. The secondary parts, of all grades, are perceptions, which form the contents of selves. In this case there must be relations of determining correspondence between these parts. True, this demands the fulfilment of certain conditions; that 'a self can perceive another self, and a part of another self',[3] that a perception is part of a percipient self, and that a perception of a part of a whole can be part of a perception of this whole. But the fulfilment of these conditions cannot be shown to be impossible; and there are reasons for thinking that they are in fact fulfilled. So we can take it that the Absolute is the system or society of selves.

Are selves immortal? The answer to this question depends on the point of view which we adopt. On the one hand McTaggart denies the reality of time, on the ground that an assertion of the reality of the temporal series of past, present and future compels us to attribute to any given event mutually incompatible determinations.[4] Hence if we adopt this point of view, we should describe selves as timeless or eternal rather than as immortal, a term which implies unending temporal duration. On the other hand time certainly belongs to the sphere of appearance. And the self will appear to persist through all future time. 'In consequence of this, I think we may properly say that the self is immortal',[5] though immortality must then be understood as including pre-existence, before, that is, its union with the body.

Professor C. D. Broad has remarked[6] that he does not suppose that McTaggart made a single disciple, though he exercised a considerable influence on his pupils by his logical subtlety, his intellectual honesty and his striving after clarity. It is not indeed

---

[1] *The Nature of Existence*, 381.
[2] For McTaggart the self is indefinable and is known by acquaintance.
[3] *The Nature of Existence*, 408.
[4] Cf. *The Nature of Existence*, 332, and McTaggart's article on *The Unreality of Time* in *Mind*, 1908.
[5] *The Nature of Existence*, 503.
[6] In *British Philosophy in the Mid-Century*, edited by C. A. Mace, p. 45.

surprising if McTaggart failed to make disciples. For, apart from the fact that he does not explain, any more than Bradley did, how the sphere of appearance arises in the first place, his system provides a much clearer example than the philosophies of either Bradley or Bosanquet of the account of metaphysics which has sometimes been given by anti-metaphysicians, namely as an alleged science which professes to deduce the nature of reality in a purely *a priori* manner. For having worked out in the first part of his system what characteristics the existent must possess, McTaggart blithely proceeds in the second part to reject the reality of matter and time on the ground that they do not fulfil the requirements established in the first part. And though his conclusions certainly make his philosophy more interesting and exciting, their strangeness is apt to make most readers conclude without more ado that there must be something wrong with his arguments. Most people at any rate find it difficult to believe that reality consists of a system of selves, the contents of which are perceptions. 'Ingenious but unconvincing', is likely to be their verdict about McTaggart's arguments.

It may be objected that this is a very philistinian point of view. If McTaggart's arguments are good ones, the strangeness of his conclusions does not alter the fact. And this is true enough. But it is also a fact that few philosophers have been convinced by the arguments adduced to show that reality must be what McTaggart says it is.

3. McTaggart combined the doctrine that existing reality consists of spiritual selves with atheism.[1] But the personal idealists generally adopted some form of theism. We can take as an example James Ward (1843–1925), naturalist, psychologist and philosopher, who studied for a while in Germany, where he came under the influence of Lotze, and eventually occupied the chair of logic and mental philosophy at Cambridge (1897–1925).

In 1886 Ward contributed to the *Encyclopaedia Britannica* a famous article on psychology, which later provided the basis for his *Psychological Principles* (1918), a work which clearly shows the influence of German philosophers such as Lotze, Wundt and Brentano. Ward was strongly opposed to the associationist psychology. In his view the content of consciousness consists of

---

[1] McTaggart admitted the bare possibility of there being within the society of selves a self which from the standpoint of experience might appear to exercise some controlling, though not creative, function. But he added that we have no reason to suppose that there is in fact such a self. And even if there were, it would not be equivalent to God as customarily represented in theistic thought.

'presentations'; but these form a continuum. They are not discrete isolated events or impressions, into which the presentational continuum can be broken up. Obviously, a new presentation introduces fresh material; but it does not constitute simply an additional item in a series, for it modifies or partially changes the pre-existing field of consciousness. Further, every presentation is a presentation for a subject, being an experience of the subject. The idea of the 'soul' is not for Ward a concept of psychology; but we cannot dispense with the idea of the subject. For consciousness involves selective attention to this or that feature or aspect of the presentational continuum; and this is an activity of the subject under the influence of feelings of pleasure and pain. It is, however, a mistake to regard the subject of consciousness as merely a spectator, a purely cognitive subject. For the conative aspect of experience is fundamental, and the selective activity in question is teleological in character, the active subject selecting and attending to presentational data in view of an end or purpose.[1]

In the first series of his Gifford Lectures, published in 1899 as *Naturalism and Agnosticism*, Ward attacked what he called the naturalistic view of the world. We must distinguish between natural science on the one hand and philosophical naturalism on the other. For example, mechanics which deals simply 'with the quantitative aspects of physical phenomena'[2] should not be confused with the mechanical theory of Nature, 'which aspires to resolve the actual world into an actual mechanism'.[3] The philosopher who accepts this theory believes that the formulas and laws of mechanics are not simply abstract and selective devices for dealing with an environment under certain aspects, devices which possess a limited validity, but that they reveal to us the nature of concrete reality in an adequate manner. And in this belief he is mistaken. Spencer, for instance, attempts to deduce the movement of evolution from mechanical principles and is blind to the fact that in the process of evolution different levels emerge which require their own appropriate categories and concepts.[4]

Dualism, however, as a possible alternative to naturalism, is untenable. It is true that the fundamental structure of experience is the subject-object relationship. But this distinction is not

[1] In the opinion of the present writer this approach to psychology was much superior to that of the associationists.
[2] *Naturalism and Agnosticism*, I, p. viii.   [3] *Ibid.*
[4] Ward is not always careful to observe his own distinction between natural science and philosophical naturalism. And he tends to speak as though the science of mechanics does not treat of 'the actual'.

equivalent to a dualism between mind and matter. For even when the object is what we call a material thing, the fact that it is comprised together with the subject within the unity of the subject-object relationship shows that it cannot be entirely heterogeneous to the subject. No ultimate dualism between mind and matter can stand up to criticism.

Having rejected, therefore, materialism, in the form of the mechanical theory of Nature, and dualism, Ward has recourse to what he calls spiritualistic monism. This term does not, however, express a belief that there is only one substance or being. Ward's view is that all entities are in some sense spiritual. That is to say, they all possess a psychical aspect. His theory is thus pluralistic; and in his second set of Gifford Lectures, which appeared in 1911 under the title *The Realm of Ends or Pluralism and Theism* he speaks of pluralistic spiritualism rather than of spiritualistic monism, though, if the latter term is properly understood, both names have the same meaning.

To some readers it may appear extraordinary that a Cambridge professor of comparatively recent date should embrace a theory of panpsychism. But Ward does not intend to imply, any more than Leibniz did,[1] that every entity or monad enjoys what we call consciousness. The idea is rather that there is no such thing as 'brute' matter, but that every centre of activity possesses some degree, often a very low degree, of 'mentality'. Moreover, Ward claims that pluralistic spiritualism is not a doctrine which has been deduced *a priori* but is based on experience.[2] 'The world is taken simply as we find it, as a plurality of active individuals unified only in and through their mutual interactions. These interactions again are interpreted throughout on the analogy of social transactions, as a mutuum commercium; that is to say, as based on cognition and conation.'[3]

---

[1] Ward's pluralism resembles the monadology of Leibniz, except that Ward's monads are not 'windowless' but act on one another.

[2] According to Ward, the only *a priori* statements which are beyond challenge are 'purely formal statements' (*The Realm of Ends*, p. 227), those of logic and mathematics. These do not give factual information about the world. If, however, a philosopher professes to deduce the nature of reality from a table of categories and these are found to apply to the world, it will also be found that they were taken from experience in the first place.

[3] *The Realm of Ends*, p. 225. Obviously, the less fantastic panpsychism is made to appear, the more does it lie open to the comment that no new information is being given, but that it consists simply in interpreting the empirically observable behaviour of things according to certain selected analogies. The question whether it is true or not then appears as a question whether a certain description is appropriate, not whether certain behaviour takes place or not.

Now, Ward admits that it is possible to stop at this idea of a plurality of finite active centres of experience. For Kant has exposed the fallacies in the alleged demonstrative proofs of God's existence. At the same time theism supplies a unity which is missing in pluralism without God. Further, the concepts of creation and conservation throw light on the existence of the Many, though creation should be understood in terms of ground and consequent rather than of cause and effect. 'God is the ground of the world's being, its *ratio essendi*.'[1] In addition, Ward argues in a pragmatist-like way that acceptance of the idea of God has the benefit of increasing the pluralist's confidence in the significance of finite existence and in the eventual realization of the ideal of the kingdom of ends. Without God as both transcendent and immanently active in the universe, 'the world may well for ever remain that *rerum concordia discors*, which at present we find it'.[2]

4. We can safely venture the generalization that one of the basic factors in personal idealism is a judgment of value, namely that personality represents the highest value within the field of our experience. This statement may indeed appear inapplicable to the philosophy of McTaggart, who professes to demonstrate by *a priori* reasoning what characteristics must belong to the existent and then inquires which of the kinds of things that are *prima facie* substances actually possess these characteristics. But it does not necessarily follow, of course, that a judgment of value does not constitute an effective implicit factor even in his philosophy. In any case it is clear that Pringle-Pattison's revision of absolute idealism was prompted by a conviction of the ultimate value of personality, and that James Ward's pluralistic spiritualism was connected with a similar conviction.

Obviously, personal idealism does not consist simply of this judgment of value. It involves also the conviction that personality should be taken as the key to the nature of reality, and a sustained attempt to interpret reality in the light of this conviction. This means that personal idealism tends to pluralism rather than to monism. In the philosophies of McTaggart and Ward a pluralistic conception of the universe is clearly dominant. With Pringle-Pattison it is held in check by his retention of the idea of the Absolute as a single all-inclusive experience. At the same time the value which he attaches to finite personality drives him to

---

[1] *The Realm of Ends*, p. 234.   [2] *Ibid.*, p. 421.

endeavour to interpret the doctrine of the One in such a way as not to involve the submerging or obliteration of the Many in the One.

The natural result in metaphysics of the turning from monism to pluralism in the light of a conviction of the value of personality is the assertion of some form of theism. In the exceptional case of McTaggart the Absolute is indeed interpreted as the society or system of finite spiritual selves. And with Pringle-Pattison the change to unequivocal theism is checked by the influence which the tradition of absolute idealism still exercises on his mind. But the inner dynamic, so to speak, of personal idealism is towards the interpretation of ultimate reality as being itself personal in character and of such a kind as to allow for the dependent reality of finite persons. According to the absolute idealists, as we have seen, the concept of God must be transformed into the concept of the Absolute. In personal idealism the concept of the Absolute tends to be re-transformed into the concept of God. True, McTaggart looks on his idea of the society or system of spiritual selves as the proper interpretation of the Hegelian Absolute. But with James Ward we find a clear transition to theism. And it is no matter for surprise that he explicitly asserts his affinity with Kant rather than with Hegel.

How far we extend the application of the term 'personal idealism' is, within limits, a matter of choice. Consider, for example, William Ritchie Sorley (1855–1935), who occupied the chair of moral philosophy at Cambridge from 1900 until 1932. He was mainly concerned with problems connected with the nature of values and the judgment of value, and it may be preferable to label him a philosopher of value. But he also inquired into the sort of general philosophical theory which we must embrace when we take values seriously into account as factors in reality. Thus he insisted that persons are 'the bearers of value',[1] and that metaphysics culminates in the idea of God, conceived not only as creator but also as 'the essence and source of all values, and as willing that these values should be shared by the free minds who owe their being to him'.[2] And the total result of his reflections is such that he can reasonably be labelled as a personal idealist.

We cannot, however, be expected to outline the ideas of all those British philosophers who can reasonably be described as personal idealists. Instead we can draw attention to the differences in

---

[1] *Contemporary British Philosophy*, Second Series, p. 254. [2] *Ibid.*, p. 265.

attitude towards the sciences between the absolute idealists and the personal idealists. Bradley does not, of course, deny the validity of science at its own level. But inasmuch as he relegates all discursive thought to the sphere of appearance, he is involved in holding that the sciences are incapable of revealing to us the nature of reality as distinct from appearance. True we find much the same attitude in McTaggart, for whom the spatio-temporal world is appearance. And even James Ward, in his polemic against naturalism and the mechanical theory of the world, plays down the ability of science to disclose to us the nature of reality and emphasizes the man-made character of abstract scientific concepts, which have to be judged by their utility rather than by any claim to absolute truth. At the same time he is convinced that the concrete sciences, such as biology and psychology, suggest and confirm his pluralistic philosophy. And, in general, the personal idealists are concerned not so much with sitting in judgment on science and relegating it to the sphere of appearance as with challenging the claim of materialist and mechanist philosophies to be the logical outcome of the sciences. The general tendency at any rate of personal idealism is to appeal to the fact that different sciences require different categories to cope with different levels of experience or aspects of reality, and to regard metaphysics as a legitimate and indeed necessary enlargement of the field of interpretation rather than as the unique path to a knowledge of reality from which the empirical sciences, confined to the sphere of appearance, are necessarily debarred. This observation may not apply to McTaggart. But he is really *sui generis*. The general attitude of the personal idealists is to argue that experience and an empirical approach to philosophy support pluralism rather than the type of monism characteristic of absolute idealism, and that if we bear in mind the different types of science,[1] we can see that metaphysical philosophy is not a counterblast to science but a natural crown to that interpretation of reality in which the sciences have their own parts to play.

A final point. If we except the system of McTaggart, personal idealism was calculated by its very nature to appeal to religiously minded philosophers, to the sort of philosophers who would be considered suitable persons to receive invitations to give series of Gifford Lectures. And what the personal idealists wrote was

---

[1] When Ward writes as though science does not provide us with knowledge of the concretely real, he is thinking primarily of mechanics which he regards as a branch of mathematics. As already noted, he was himself a psychologist.

generally religiously edifying. Their style of philosophy was obviously much less destructive of Christian faith than the absolute idealism of Bradley.[1] But though the various philosophies which can reasonably be regarded as representative of personal idealism are edifying enough from the moral and religious points of view, they tend to give the impression, at least in their more metaphysical aspects, of being a series of personal statements of belief which owe less to rigorous argument than to a selective emphasis on certain aspects of reality.[2] And it is understandable that during the lifetime of Ward and Sorley other Cambridge philosophers were suggesting that instead of rushing to produce large-scale interpretations of reality we should do better to make our questions as clear and precise as possible and treat them one by one. However, though this sounds a very reasonable and practical suggestion, the trouble is that philosophical problems are apt to interlock. And the idea of breaking up philosophy into clearly defined questions which can be answered separately has not in practice proved to be as fruitful as some people hoped. Still, it is undeniable that the idealist systems appear, in the present climate of British philosophy, to belong to a past phase of thought. This makes them indeed apt material for the historian. But it also means that the historian cannot help wondering whether there is really much justification for devoting space to minor systems which do not strike the imagination in the way that the system of Hegel makes an impression. There is, however, this to be said, that personal idealism represents the recurrent protest of the finite personality to absorption in a One, however it is conceived. It is easy to say that personality is 'appearance'; but no monistic system has ever explained how the sphere of appearance arises in the first place.

[1] I do not mean to imply that Bradley can properly be described as an irreligious thinker. At the same time the concept of 'God' belongs for him to the sphere of appearance, and it would be absurd to claim him as a Christian thinker. He was not.

[2] McTaggart certainly professed to reach his conclusion by rigorous argument. But then his conclusions were not particularly edifying from the religious point of view, unless one is prepared to maintain that the existence or non-existence of God is a matter of indifference to religion.

PART III

IDEALISM IN AMERICA

CHAPTER XI

INTRODUCTORY

The beginnings of philosophy in America; S. Johnson and J. Edwards—The Enlightenment in America; B. Franklin and T. Jefferson—The influence of the Scottish philosophy—R. W. Emerson and Transcendentalism—W. T. Harris and his programme for speculative philosophy.

1. THE remote origins of philosophical reflection in America can be traced back to the Puritans of New England. Obviously, the primary aim of the Puritans was to organize their lives according to the religious and moral principles in which they believed. They were idealistic in the non-philosophical sense of the term. They were also Calvinists who allowed no dissent from what they regarded as the principles of orthodoxy. At the same time we can find among them an element of philosophical reflection, stimulated mainly by the thought of Petrus Ramus or Pierre de la Ramée (1515–72) and by the *Encyclopaedia* of Johann Heinrich Alsted (1588–1638). Petrus Ramus, the celebrated French humanist and logician, became a Calvinist in 1561, expounded a congregationalist theory of the Church, and eventually perished in the massacre of St. Bartholomew's Eve. He thus had special qualifications for being regarded as an intellectual patron by the Congregationalists of New England. Alsted, a follower of Melanchthon and also a disciple of Petrus Ramus, published an encyclopaedia of the arts and sciences in 1630. This work, which had a Platonic colouring, contained a section devoted to what Alsted called *archeologia*, the system of the principles of knowledge and being. And it became a popular textbook in New England.

The religious affiliations of the first phase of American philosophical thought are shown by the fact that the earliest philosophers were clerics. Samuel Johnson (1696–1772) is an example. At first a Congregationalist minister, he entered the Anglican Church in 1772 and subsequently received Anglican orders. In

1754 he was appointed first president of King's College, New York, which is now Columbia University.

In his autobiography Johnson remarks that when he was studying at Yale the standard of education was low. Indeed, it showed a decline in comparison with the standards of the original settlers who had been brought up in England. True, the names of Descartes, Boyle, Locke and Newton were not unknown, and the introduction of the writings of Locke and Newton were gradually opening up fresh lines of thought. But there was a strong tendency to equate secular learning with some of the works of Ramus and Alsted and to regard the new philosophical currents as a danger to the purity of religious faith. In other words, a 'scholasticism' which had served a useful purpose in the past was being used to check the spread of new ideas.

Johnson himself came under the influence of Berkeley. He made the acquaintance of the philosopher during the latter's sojourn on Rhode Island (1729–31) and it was to Berkeley that he dedicated his *Elementa Philosophica*, which appeared in 1752.[1]

But though deeply impressed by Berkeley's immaterialism, Johnson was not prepared to accept his view that space and time are particular relations between particular ideas, and that infinite space and time are simply abstract ideas. He wished to retain the Newton-Clarke theory of absolute and infinite space and time, on the ground that they are entailed by admission of the existence of a plurality of finite spirits. For example, unless there were absolute space, all finite spirits would coincide with one another. Further, Johnson tried to fit Berkeley's theory of ideas into a Platonic mould, by maintaining that all ideas are ectypes of archetypes existing in the divine mind. In other words, while welcoming Berkeley's immaterialism Johnson endeavoured to adapt it to the Platonic tradition already present in American thought.

A better-known representative of eighteenth-century American thought is Jonathan Edwards (1703–58), a noted Congregationalist theologian. Educated at Yale, in 1717 he made the acquaintance of Locke's *Essay* and in 1730 of Hutcheson's *Inquiry into the Original of Our Ideas of Beauty and Virtue*. Though primarily a Calvinist theologian who for most of his life occupied pastoral posts, he attempted to achieve a synthesis between the Calvinist theology and the new philosophy. Or, to put the matter in another

[1] Johnson's philosophical correspondence with Berkeley can be found in the second volume of the critical edition of the bishop's *Works* edited by Professor T. E. Jessop.

way, he used ideas taken from contemporary philosophy in interpreting the Calvinist theology. In 1757 he became president of the college at Princeton, New Jersey, which is now Princeton University; but he died of smallpox in the following year.

Edwards sees the universe as existing only within the divine mind or spirit. Space, necessary, infinite and eternal, is in fact an attribute of God. Further, it is only spirits which are, properly speaking, substances. There are no quasi-independent material substances which exercise real causal activity. To be sure, Nature exists as appearance; and from the point of view of the scientist, who is concerned with phenomena or appearances, there is uniformity in Nature, a constant order. The scientist as such can speak quite legitimately of natural laws. But from a profounder and philosophical point of view we can admit only one real causal activity, that of God. Not only is the divine conservation of finite things a constantly repeated creation, but it is also true that the uniformity of Nature is, from the philosophical standpoint, an arbitrary constitution, as Edwards puts it, of the divine will. There is really no such thing in Nature as a necessary relation or as efficient causality; all connections depend ultimately as the arbitrary *fiat* of God.

The fact that Edwards rejects, with Berkeley, the existence of material substance but admits the existence of spiritual substances must not, however, be taken to mean that in his view human volition constitutes an exception to the general truth that God is the only real cause. From one point of view, of course, we can say that he gives an empiricist analysis of relations, in particular of the causal relation. But this analysis is combined with the Calvinist idea of the divine omnipotence or causality to produce metaphysical idealism in which God appears as the sole genuine cause. In his work on the *Freedom of the Will* Edwards explicitly rejects the idea of the self-determining human will. In his view it is absurd, and also an expression of Arminianism, to maintain that the human will can choose against the prevailing motive or inclination.[1] Choice is always determined by the prevailing motive, and this in turn is determined by what appears to be the greatest good. Theologically speaking, a man's choice is predetermined by his Creator. But it is a mistake to suppose that this relieves man

[1] Obviously if by prevailing inclination or strongest motive we mean the motive which actually 'prevails', it *would* be absurd to claim that we can resist it. But then the statement that we always follow it becomes tautological.

of all moral responsibility. For a moral judgment about an action depends simply on the nature of the action, not on its cause. A bad action remains a bad action, whatever its cause.

An interesting feature of Edwards' thought is his theory of a sense of God or direct awareness of the divine excellence. In general, he was in sympathy with the revivalist 'Great Awakening' of 1740–1. And he considered that the religious affections, on which he wrote a treatise, manifest an apprehension of the divine excellence which is to be attributed to the heart rather than to the head. At the same time he tried to distinguish between the sense of God and the highly emotive states which are characteristic of revivalist meetings. In doing this he developed a theory of the sense of God in which it is reasonable to see the influence of Hutcheson's aesthetic and moral ideas.

According to Edwards, just as a sense of the sweetness of honey precedes and lies at the basis of our theoretical judgment that honey is sweet, so does a sentiment or sense of, say, the divine holiness lie at the basis of the judgment that God is holy. In general, just as a sense of the beauty of an object or of the moral excellence of a person is presupposed by judgments which give expression to this sense or feeling, so is a sense of the divine excellence presupposed by our 'cerebral' judgments about God. Perhaps the term 'just as' is open to criticism. For the sense of God is for Edwards a consent of our being to the divine being and is of supernatural origin. But the point is that man can be aware of God through a form of experience analogous to sense-experience and to the pleasure which we feel in beholding a beautiful object or an expression of moral excellence.

Perhaps we can see in this theory the influence of Lockian empiricism. I do not mean to imply, of course, that Locke himself based belief in God on feeling and intuition. In regard to this matter his approach was rationalistic; and his mistrust of 'enthusiasm' is notorious. But his general insistence on the primacy of sense-experience may well have been one of the factors which influenced Edwards' mind, though the influence of Hutcheson's idea of the sense of moral beauty or excellence is certainly more obvious.

Edwards did not live long enough to carry out his project of writing a complete theology, developed systematically according to a new method. But he was extremely influential as a theologian; and his attempt to bring together Calvinist theology, idealism,

Lockian empiricism and the world-view of Newton constituted the first major expression of American thought.

2. In Europe the eighteenth century was the age of the Enlightenment. And America too had what is customarily called its Enlightenment. In the field of philosophy it does not indeed bear comparison with its counterparts in England and France. But it is none the less of importance in the history of American life.

The first characteristic which we can notice is the attempt to separate the Puritan moral virtues from their theological setting, an attempt which is well exemplified by the reflections of Benjamin Franklin (1706–90). An admirer of William Wollaston, the English deist, he was certainly not the man to walk in the footsteps of Samuel Johnson or Jonathan Edwards. Revelation, as he declared, had for him no weight. And he was convinced that morals should be given a utilitarian in place of a theological basis. Some types of action are beneficial to man and society, while other types of action are detrimental. The former can be regarded as commanded, the latter as forbidden. Virtues such as temperance and diligence are justified by their utility. Their opposites are blameworthy because they are prejudicial to the interests of society and of personal success.

Famous as he is, Franklin can hardly be described as a profound philosopher, in spite of the fact that he was one of the founders of the American Philosophical Society. And it is a simple matter to caricature his ethical outlook. To be sure, Franklin exalted truthfulness, sincerity and integrity, virtues highly esteemed by the Puritans, as essential for human well-being. But once these virtues are extolled because, on balance, people who are truthful and sincere are more likely to be successful in life than the untruthful and insincere, a certain banal pragmatism takes the place of the religious idealism of the Puritan mind at its best. It is no longer a case of man becoming the image of God, as it was with the more Platonic-minded Puritan theologians. Rather is it a case of 'early to bed and early to rise makes a man healthy and wealthy and wise'. A sensible maxim perhaps, but not particularly uplifting.

However, even if Franklin's reflections tended to assume a somewhat banal character, they represented the same movement to set ethics on its own feet and to separate it from theology which we find in more sophisticated forms in eighteenth-century

European philosophy. And the retention of Puritan virtues in a secularized dress was of considerable historical importance in the development of the American outlook.

Another important feature of the Enlightenment in America was the secularization of the idea of society. Calvinism was opposed from the start to control of the Church by the State. And though the general tendency of the Calvinists was to secure, when possible, widespread control over society, in principle at any rate they recognized a distinction between the body of true believers and political society. Moreover, Calvinism in New England took the form of Congregationalism. And though in practice the clergy, once appointed, exercised great power, the congregations were in theory simply voluntary unions of likeminded believers. When stripped, therefore, of its theological and religious associations, this idea of society lent itself to exploitation in the interest of democratic republicanism. And Locke's theory of the social contract or compact was at hand to serve as an instrument.

The process of secularizing the theory of religious society associated with the Congregationalists of New England was, however, only one factor in a complex situation. Another factor was the growth in the New World of pioneer societies which were not primarily associated, if at all, with particular religious bodies and movements. The new frontier societies[1] had to adapt the ideas of law and social organization which they carried with them to the situations in which they found themselves. And their main desire was clearly that of securing, as far as possible, such conditions of order as would prevent anarchy and enable individuals to pursue their several ends in comparative peace. Needless to say, the members of the pioneer societies were not much concerned with political philosophy, or with philosophy of any sort. At the same time they represented a growing society which tacitly implied a Lockian theory of a free union of human beings organizing themselves and submitting themselves to law with a view to preserving a social fabric and order which would permit the peaceful, though competitive, exercise of individual initiative. Further, the growth of these societies, with emphasis on temporal success, favoured the spread of the idea of toleration, which was scarcely a strong point of the Calvinist theologians and ministers.

The idea of political society as a voluntary union of human

[1] Benjamin Franklin, it may be noted, emphasized the virtues and values which proved to be of advantage in the frontier societies.

beings for the purpose of establishing social order as a framework for the peaceful exercise of private initiative was understandably associated with the idea of natural rights which are presupposed by organized society and should be protected by it. The theory of natural rights, sponsored by Locke and by other English and French writers, found expression in *The Rights of Man*[1] by Thomas Paine (1737–1809), a deist who insisted on the sovereignty of reason and on the equal rights of all men. It also found a powerful exponent in Thomas Jefferson (1743–1826) who, as is well known, drafted the Declaration of Independence of 1776. This famous document asserts that it is self-evidently true that all men are created equal, that they are endowed by their Creator with certain inalienable rights, and that among these are the right to life, liberty and the pursuit of happiness. The Declaration further asserts that governments are instituted to secure these rights, and that they derive their powers from the consent of the governed.

It is scarcely necessary to remark that the Declaration of Independence was a national act, not an exercise in political philosophy. And, quite apart from the fact that a good deal of it consists of animadversions on the British monarch and government, the philosophy behind its opening sentences was not fully developed in eighteenth-century America. Thus Jefferson himself simply assumed that the statement that all men are endowed by their Creator with certain inalienable rights is a matter of common sense. That is to say, common reason sees that it must be true, without any need of proof, though, once its truth has been recognized, moral and social conclusions can be drawn from it. At the same time the philosophical portion of the Declaration admirably illustrates the spirit and fruit of the American Enlightenment. And there is, of course, no doubt about its historical importance.

3. Men such as Franklin and Jefferson were obviously not professional philosophers. But in the course of the nineteenth century academic philosophy underwent a very considerable development in the United States. And among the influences contributing to this development was the thought of Thomas Reid and his successors in the Scottish School. In religious quarters the Scottish philosophical tradition was regarded with favour as being at the same time realist in character and a much needed antidote

---

[1] Part I, 1791; Part II, 1792. Paine was also the author of the *Age of Reason*, the two parts of which appeared respectively in 1794 and 1796.

to materialism and positivism. It thus became popular with those Protestant divines who were conscious of the lack of an adequate rational basis for the Christian faith.

One of the principal representatives of this tradition was James McCosh (1811–94), himself a Scottish Presbyterian, who occupied for sixteen years the chair of logic and metaphysics at Queen's College, Belfast, and then in 1868 accepted the presidency of Princeton and made the university a stronghold of the Scottish philosophy. Besides writing a number of other philosophical works, such as *An Examination of John Stuart Mill's Philosophy* (1866) and *Realistic Philosophy* (1887), he published a well-known study, *The Scottish Philosophy*, in 1875.

Among the effects of the popularization in America of the Scottish tradition was the widespread habit of dividing philosophy into mental and moral, the former, namely the science of the human mind or psychology, being looked on as providing the basis for the latter, namely ethics. This division is reflected in the titles of the much-used textbooks published by Noah Porter (1811–92), who in 1847 was nominated to the chair of moral philosophy and metaphysics at Yale, where he was also president for some years. For instance, in 1868 he published *The Human Intellect*, in 1871 *The Elements of Intellectual Science*, an abridgement of the first-named book, and in 1885 *The Elements of Moral Science*. Porter was not, however, simply an adherent of the Scottish School. He had made a serious study not only of British empiricists such as J. S. Mill and Bain but also of Kantian and post-Kantian German thought. And he attempted to effect a synthesis of the Scottish philosophy and German idealism. Thus he maintained that the world is to be regarded as a thought rather than as a thing, and that the existence of the Absolute is a necessary condition of the possibility of human thought and knowledge.

An attempt at combining themes from empiricism, the Scottish philosophy of common sense and German idealism had been made by the French philosopher, Victor Cousin (1792–1867). As rector of the *École normale*, rector of the University of Paris and finally minister of public instruction, Cousin had been in a position to impose his ideas as a kind of philosophical orthodoxy in the centre of French academic life. But an eclectic philosophy, formed from such heterogeneous elements, was obviously open to serious criticism on the ground of incoherence. However, the relevant point here is that his thought exercised a certain influence in America, especially in encouraging a combination of ideas inspired by the Scottish tradition with a transcendentalism inspired by German idealism.

As an example we can mention Caleb Sprague Henry (1804–84), a professor at the University of New York. To all intents and purposes Cousin had based metaphysics on psychology. Psychological observation, properly employed, reveals in man the presence of a spontaneous reason which acts as a bridge between consciousness and being and enables us to pass beyond the limits of subjective idealism, by apprehending, for example, finite substances as objectively existent. Philosophy, as the work of reflective reason, makes explicit and develops the objective truths apprehended immediately by spontaneous reason. This distinction between spontaneous and reflective reason was accepted by Henry who, as a devout Anglican, proceeded to use it in a theological setting and drew the conclusions that religious or spiritual experience precedes and grounds religious knowledge.[1] By religious or spiritual experience, however, he meant primarily the moral consciousness of good and obligation, a consciousness which manifests the power of God to raise man to a new life. Further, with Henry material civilization becomes the fruit of the 'understanding', whereas Christianity, considered historically as the redemptive work of God, aiming at the creation of an ideal society, is the response to the demands of 'reason' or spirit.

4. At the same time that the Scottish philosophy was penetrating into university circles, the famous American writer Ralph Waldo Emerson (1803–82) was preaching his gospel of transcendentalism. In 1829 he became a Unitarian minister. But the man who found inspiration in Coleridge and Carlyle, who laid emphasis on moral self-development and tended to divest religion of its historical associations, who was more concerned with giving expression to his personal vision of the world than with transmitting a traditional message, was not really suited for the ministry. And in 1832 he abandoned it and gave himself to the task of developing and expounding a new idealist philosophy which, he was confident, was capable of renewing the world in a

---

[1] In using the distinction in this way Henry was not simply following Cousin. For Cousin insisted that the existence of God is known by inductive reasoning from the existence of finite substances, though he tried to combine this thesis with an idea of God inspired by German metaphysical idealism, an idea which led to accusations of pantheism by clerical critics. Henry was interested chiefly in the redemptive power of Christianity in history, and while accepting Cousin's idea of reason, he transposed it into the setting of Christian theology.

way in which not only materialism but also traditional religion was incapable of renewing it.

In 1836 Emerson published anonymously a little work entitled *Nature*, which contained the essence of his message. His celebrated *Address*, delivered in 1838 in the divinity school of Harvard, aroused considerable opposition among those who considered it unorthodox. In 1841 and 1844 he published two series of *Essays*, while his *Poems* appeared in 1846. In 1849 he published *Representative Men*, a series of lectures which he had given in 1845-6 on selected famous men from Plato to Napoleon and Goethe. In later years he became a national institution, the Sage of Concord, a fate which sometimes overtakes those who are at first regarded as purveyors of dangerous new ideas.

In a lecture delivered in 1842 in the Masonic Temple at Boston Emerson declares that what are called the 'new views' are really very old thoughts cast into a mould suited to the contemporary world. 'What is popularly called Transcendentalism among us is Idealism; Idealism as it appears in 1842.'[1] The materialist takes his stand on sense-experience and on what he calls facts, whereas 'the idealist takes his departure from his consciousness, and reckons the world an appearance'.[2] Materialism and idealism thus appear to be sharply opposed. Yet once we begin to ask the materialist what the basic facts really are, his solid world tends to break up. And with phenomenalism all is ultimately reduced to the data of consciousness. Hence under criticism materialism tends to pass into idealism, for which 'mind is the only reality . . . [and] Nature, literature, history are only subjective phenomena'.[3]

It does not follow, however, that the external world is simply the creation of the individual mind. Rather is it the product of the one universal spirit or consciousness, 'that Unity, that Over-Soul, within which every man's particular being is contained and made one with all other'.[4] This Over-Soul or eternal One or God is the sole ultimate reality, and Nature is its projection. 'The world proceeds from the same spirit as the body of man. It is a remoter and inferior projection of God, a projection of God in the unconscious. But it differs from a body in one important respect. It is not, like that, now subjected to the human will. Its serene order is inviolable by us. It is, therefore, to us, the present expositor of the divine mind.'[5]

[1] *Complete Works*, II, p. 279 (London, 1866). References are given according to volume and page of this edition. [2] *Ibid.*, II, p. 280.
[3] *Ibid.*, II, pp. 280-1. [4] *Ibid.*, I, p. 112. [5] *Ibid.*, II, p. 167.

If we ask how Emerson knows all this, it is no good expecting any systematically developed proofs. He does indeed insist that the human reason presupposes and seeks an ultimate unity. But he also insists that 'we know truth when we see it, let sceptic and scoffer say what they choose'.[1] When foolish people hear what they do not wish to hear, they ask how one knows that what one says is true. But 'we know truth when we see it, from opinion, as we know when we are awake that we are awake'.[2] The announcements of the soul, as Emerson puts it, are 'an influx of the divine mind into our mind':[3] they are a revelation, accompanied by the emotion of the sublime.

We might expect that from this doctrine of the unity of the human soul with the Over-Soul or divine spirit Emerson would draw the conclusion that the individual as such is of little importance, and that moral or spiritual progress consists in submerging one's personality in the One. But this is not at all his point of view. The Over-Soul incarnates itself, as Emerson expresses it, in a particular way in each individual. Hence 'each man has his own vocation. The talent is the call.'[4] And the conclusion is drawn: 'Insist on yourself, never imitate'.[5] Conformism is a vice: self-reliance is a cardinal virtue. 'Whoso would be a man must be a nonconformist.'[6] Emerson provides indeed a theoretical reason for this exaltation of self-reliance. The divine spirit is self-existent, and its embodiments are good in proportion as they share in this attribute. At the same time it is not unreasonable to see in Emerson's moral doctrine the expression of the spirit of a young, vigorous, developing and competitive society.

In Emerson's opinion this self-reliance, if universally practised, would bring about a regeneration of society. The State exists to educate the wise man, the man of character; and 'with the appearance of the wise man, the State expires. The appearance of character makes the State unnecessary.'[7] What is meant is doubtless that if individual character were fully developed, the State as an organ of force would be unnecessary, and that in its place there would be a society based on moral right and love.

It scarcely needs saying that Emerson, like Carlyle, was a seer rather than a systematic philosopher. Indeed, he went so far as to say that 'a foolish consistency is the hobgoblin of little minds, adored by little statesmen and philosophers and divines. With

[1] *Works*, I, p. 117.   [2] *Ibid.*   [3] *Ibid.*   [4] *Ibid.*, I, p. 59.
[5] *Ibid.*, I, p. 35.   [6] *Ibid.*, I, p. 20.   [7] *Ibid.*, I, p. 244.

consistency a great soul has simply nothing to do.'[1] True his principal point is that a man should preserve his intellectual integrity and not be afraid to say what he really thinks today simply because it contradicts what he said yesterday. But he remarks, for example, that if in metaphysics we deny personality to God, this should not prevent us from thinking and speaking in a different way 'when the devout motions of the soul come'.[2] And though we can understand what Emerson means, a systematic philosopher who held this point of view would be more likely to follow Hegel in drawing an explicit distinction between the language of speculative philosophy and that of religious consciousness than to content himself with dismissing consistency as a hobgoblin of little minds. In other words, Emerson's philosophy was impressionistic and what is sometimes called 'intuitive'. It conveyed a personal vision of reality, but it was not presented in the customary dress of impersonal argument and precise statement. Some, of course, may consider this to be a point in its favour, but the fact remains that if we are looking for a systematic development of idealism in American thought, we have to look elsewhere.

Emerson was the chief figure in the Transcendentalist Club which was founded at Boston in 1836. Another member, highly esteemed by Emerson, was Amos Bronson Alcott (1799–1888), a deeply spiritual man who, in addition to his attempts to introduce new methods into education, founded a utopian community in Massachusetts, though it did not last long. Given to vague and oracular utterances, he was later pushed by the St. Louis Hegelians into trying to clarify and define his idealism. Among others associated in some way with New England Transcendentalism we may mention Henry David Thoreau (1817–62) and Orestes Augustus Brownson (1803–76). Thoreau, a famous literary figure, was attracted to Emerson when the latter delivered his Phi Beta Kappa Society address on 'The American Scholar' at Harvard in 1857. As for Brownson, his spiritual pilgrimage led him by various stages from Presbyterianism to Catholicism.

5. In 1867 there appeared at St. Louis, Missouri, the first number of *The Journal of Speculative Philosophy*, edited by William Torrey Harris (1835–1909). Harris and his associates contributed powerfully to spreading in America a knowledge of German idealism, and the group are known as the St. Louis

[1] *Ibid.*, I, p. 24.   [2] *Ibid.*

Hegelians. Harris was also one of the founders of the Kant-Club (1874). The group had some relations with the Transcendentalists of New England; and Harris helped to start the Concord Summer School of Philosophy in 1880, with which Alcott collaborated. In 1889 he was appointed United States Commissioner of Education by President Harrison.

In the first number of *The Journal of Speculative Philosophy* Harris spoke of the need for a speculative philosophy which would fulfil three main tasks. In the first place it should provide a philosophy of religion suitable for a time when traditional dogmas and ecclesiastical authority were losing their hold on men's minds. In the second place it should develop a social philosophy in accordance with the new demands of the national consciousness, which was turning away from sheer individualism. In the third place it should work out the deeper implications of the new ideas in the sciences, in which field, Harris maintained, the day of simple empiricism was definitely over. As speculative philosophy meant for Harris the tradition which started with Plato and attained its fullest expression in the system of Hegel, he was calling in effect for a development of idealism under the inspiration of post-Kantian German philosophy but in accordance with American needs.

There were various attempts to fulfil this sort of programme, ranging from the personal idealism of Howison and Bowne to the absolute idealism of Josiah Royce. And as both Howison and Bowne were born before Royce, they should perhaps be treated first. I propose, however, to devote the next chapter to Royce and in the following chapter to discuss briefly the personal idealists and some other philosophers who belonged to the idealist tradition, mentioning the names of some thinkers who were junior to Royce.

It may be as well, however, to point out at once that it is difficult to make any very sharp division between personal and absolute idealism in American thought. In a real sense Royce too was a personalist idealist. In other words, the form which absolute idealism took with Bradley, involving the relegation of personality to the sphere of appearances as contrasted with that of reality, was not congenial to the American mind. And, in general, it was felt that the proper fulfilment of Harris's programme required that human personality should not be sacrificed on the altar of the One, though there were, of course, differences in emphasis, some thinkers placing the emphasis on the Many, others more on the

One. Hence a distinction between personal and absolute idealism is legitimate, provided that we allow for the qualification which has just been made.

We may also remark that the term 'personal idealism' is somewhat ambiguous in the context of American thought. It was used, for example, by William James of his own philosophy. But though the use of the term was doubtless justified, James is best discussed under the heading of pragmatism.

CHAPTER XII

THE PHILOSOPHY OF ROYCE

*Remarks on Royce's writings previous to his Gifford Lectures
—The meaning of Being and the meaning of ideas—Three
inadequate theories of Being—The fourth conception of Being—
The finite self and the Absolute; moral freedom—The social
aspect of morality—Immortality—Infinite series and the idea
of a self-representative system—Some critical comments.*

1. JOSIAH ROYCE (1855–1916) entered the University of California
at the age of sixteen and received his baccalaureate in 1875. A
paper which he wrote on the theology of the *Prometheus Bound* of
Aeschylus won him a grant of money that enabled him to spend
two years in Germany, where he read German philosophers such
as Schelling and Schopenhauer, and studied under Lotze at
Göttingen. After taking his doctorate in 1878 at Johns Hopkins
University he taught for a few years in the University of California and then went to Harvard as a lecturer in philosophy. In
1885 he was nominated as assistant professor, and in 1892
professor. In 1914 he accepted the Alford chair of philosophy at
Harvard.

In 1885 Royce published *The Religious Aspect of Philosophy*.
In it he argues that the impossibility of proving the universal and
absolute validity of the moral ideal embraced by any given
individual tends to produce moral scepticism and pessimism.
Reflection, however, shows that the very search for a universal
and absolute ideal reveals in the seeker a moral will which wills the
harmonization of all particular ideals and values. And there then
arises in the mind of the individual the consciousness that he
ought so to live that his life and the lives of other men may form
a unity, converging towards a common ideal goal or end. With this
idea Royce associates an exaltation of the social order, in particular of the State.[1]

Turning to the problem of God, Royce rejects the traditional
proofs of God's existence and develops an argument for the
Absolute from the recognition of error. We are accustomed to

[1] The exaltation of the State, which is even described as 'divine', reappears in
Royce's essay, *California: A Study of American Character* (1886).

think that error arises when our thought fails to conform with its intended object. But we obviously cannot place ourselves in the position of an external spectator, outside the subject-object relationship, capable of seeing whether thought conforms with its object or not. And reflection on this fact may lead to scepticism. Yet it is clear that we are capable of recognizing error. We can not only make erroneous judgments but also know that we have made them. And further reflection shows that truth and falsity have meaning only in relation to a complete system of truth, which must be present to absolute thought. In other words, Royce accepts a coherence theory of truth and passes from it to the assertion of absolute thought. As he was later to express it, an individual's opinions are true or false in relation to a wider insight. And his argument is that we cannot stop until we arrive at the idea of an all-inclusive divine insight which embraces in a comprehensive unity our thinking and its objects and is the ultimate measure of truth and falsity.

In *The Religious Aspect of Philosophy*, therefore, the Absolute is described as thought. 'All reality must be present to the unity of the Infinite Thought.'[1] But Royce does not understand this term in a sense which would exclude descriptions of the Absolute in terms of will or of experience. And in *The Conception of God* (1897) he argues that there is an absolute experience which is related to ours as an organic whole is related to its constituent elements. Though, therefore, Royce frequently uses the term 'God', it is obvious that the divine being is for him the One, the totality.[2] At the same time God or the Absolute is conceived as self-conscious. And the natural conclusion to draw is that finite selves are thoughts of God in his own act of self-knowledge. It is thus perfectly understandable that Royce drew upon himself the criticism of the personal idealists.[3] In point of fact, however, he had no wish to submerge the Many in the One in such a way as to reduce finite self-consciousness to an inexplicable illusion. Hence he had to develop a theory of the relation between the One and the Many which would neither reduce the Many to illusory appearance nor make the term 'One' altogether inappropriate. And this was

---

[1] *The Religious Aspect of Philosophy*, p. 433.
[2] In *The Spirit of Modern Philosophy* (1892), Royce speaks of the one infinite Self of which all finite selves are moments or organic parts.
[3] The sub-title of *The Conception of God* is *A Philosophical Discussion Concerning the Nature of the Divine Idea as a Demonstrable Reality*. Howison, the personal idealist, was one of the participants in the original discussion of 1895.

one of the main themes of Royce's Gifford Lectures, to which we shall turn in the next section.

Royce's idea of God as the absolute and all-inclusive experience naturally compels him, like Bradley, to devote attention to the problem of evil. In *Studies in Good and Evil* (1898) he rejects any attempt to evade the issue by saying that suffering and moral evil are illusions. On the contrary, they are real. We cannot avoid the conclusion, therefore, that God suffers when we suffer. And we must suppose that suffering is necessary for the perfecting of the divine life. As for moral evil, this too is required for the perfection of the universe. For the good will presupposes the evil as something to be overcome. True, from the point of view of the Absolute the world, the object of infinite thought, is a perfect unity in which evil is already overcome and subordinated to the good. But it is none the less a constituent element in the whole.

If God is a name for the universe, and if suffering and evil are real, we must obviously locate them in God. If, however, there is an absolute point of view from which evil is eternally overcome and subordinated to the good, God can hardly be simply a name for the universe. In other words, the problem of the relation between God and the world becomes acute. But Royce's ideas on this subject are best discussed in connection with his main presentation of his philosophy.

2. The two volumes of *The World and the Individual*, representing series of Gifford Lectures, appeared respectively in 1900 and 1901. In them Royce sets out to determine the nature of Being. If it is asserted that God is, or that the world is, or that the finite self is, we can always ask for the meaning of 'is'. This term, which Royce calls 'the existential predicate',[1] is often assumed to be simple and indefinable. But in philosophy the simple and ultimate is as much a subject for reflection as the complex and derived. Royce is not, however, concerned with the verb 'to be' simply in the sense of exist. He is also concerned with determining 'the special sorts of Reality that we attribute to God, to the World, and to the Human Individual'.[2] In traditional language he is concerned with essence as well as with existence, in his own language with the *what* as well as with the *that*. For if we assert

[1] *The World and the Individual*, I, p. 12 (1920 edition). This work will be referred to simply as *The World*.
[2] *Ibid.*, I, p. 12.

that X is or exists, we assert that there is an X, something possessing a certain nature.

In point of fact the problem of determining the meaning of what Royce calls the existential or ontological predicate immediately becomes for him the problem of determining the nature of reality. And the question arises, how are we to tackle this problem? It might perhaps appear that the best way to approach it would be to look at reality as presented in experience and try to understand it. But, Royce insists, we can understand reality only by means of ideas. And it thus becomes all-important to understand what an idea is and how it stands to reality. 'I am one of those who hold that when you ask the question: What is an Idea? and: How can Ideas stand in any true relation to Reality? you attack the world-knot in the way that promises most for the untying of its meshes.'[1]

After his initial announcement that he is going to deal with the problem of Being, Royce's shift of attention to the nature of ideas and their relation to reality is likely to appear both disappointing and exasperating to his readers. But his method of procedure is easily explicable. We have seen that in *The Religious Aspect of Philosophy* Royce described God as absolute thought. And his approach to the problem of Being by way of a theory of ideas is suggested by the metaphysical position which he has already adopted, namely the primacy of thought. Thus when he asserts 'the primacy of the World as Idea over the World as Fact',[2] he is speaking in terms of the idealist tradition as he sees it, the tradition according to which the world is the self-realization of the absolute Idea.

In the first place Royce draws a distinction between the external and internal meanings of an idea. Let us suppose that I have an idea of Mount Everest. It is natural to think of this idea as referring to and representing an external reality, namely the actual mountain. And this representative function is what Royce understands by the external meaning of an idea. But now let us suppose that I am an artist, and that I have in my mind an idea of the picture which I wish to paint. This idea can be described as 'the partial fulfilment of a purpose'.[3] And this aspect of an idea is what Royce calls its internal meaning.

Common sense would doubtless be prepared to admit that the idea in the mind of an artist can reasonably be described as the

[1] *Ibid.*, I, pp. 16–17.　　[2] *Ibid.*, I, p. 19.　　[3] *Ibid.*, I, p. 25.

partial fulfilment of a purpose.[1] And to this extent it recognizes
the existence of internal meaning. But, left to itself, common
sense would probably regard the representative function of the
idea as primary, even though it is a question of representing what
does not yet exist, namely the projected work of art. And if we
consider an idea such as that of the number of the inhabitants of
London, common sense would certainly emphasize its representative character and ask whether or not it corresponds with external
reality.

Royce, however, maintains that it is the internal meaning of an
idea which is primary, and that in the long run external meaning
turns out to be only 'an aspect of the completely developed
internal meaning'.[2] Suppose, for example, that I wish to ascertain
the number of people, or of families, resident in a certain area.
Obviously, I have a purpose in wishing to ascertain these facts.
Perhaps I am in charge of a housing scheme and wish to ascertain
the number of individuals and of families in order to be able to
estimate the number of houses or flats required for the already
resident population in a district which is to be reconstructed. It
is clearly important that my idea of the population should be
accurate. External meaning is thus of importance. At the same
time I try to obtain an accurate idea with a view to the fulfilment
of a purpose. And the idea can be regarded as a partial or incomplete fulfilment of this purpose. In this sense the internal meaning
of the idea is primary. According to Royce, its external meaning,
taken simply by itself, is an abstraction, an abstraction, that is to
say, from its context, namely the fulfilment of a purpose. When it
is replaced in its context, the internal meaning is seen to take
precedence.

What, it may be asked, is the connection between this theory of
the meaning of ideas and the solution of the problem of reality?
The answer is obviously that Royce intends to represent the
world as the embodiment of an absolute system of ideas which are,
in themselves, the incomplete fulfilment of a purpose. 'We propose
to answer the question: What is to be? by the assertion that: To

---

[1] It is certainly not the intention of the present writer to suggest that the artist
or poet necessarily first forms a clear idea of the work to be done and then gives
concrete embodiment to this idea. If, for example, the poet had a clear idea of
the poem, the poem would already have been composed. And all that remained
would be to write down a poem already existing in the poet's mind. At the same
time the poet would not start working without some sort of conceived purpose,
some sort of 'idea' which could reasonably be regarded as the beginning of a total
action.
[2] *The World*, I, p. 36.

be means simply to express, to embody the complete internal meaning of a certain absolute system of ideas—a system, moreover, which is genuinely implied in the true internal meaning or purpose of every finite idea, however fragmentary.'[1] Royce admits that this theory is not novel. For example, it is essentially the same as the line of thought which 'led Hegel to call the world the embodied Idea'.[2] But though the theory is not novel, 'I believe it to be of fundamental and of inexhaustible importance'.[3]

In other words, Royce first interprets the function of human ideas in the light of an already existing idealist conviction about the primacy of thought. And he then uses this interpretation as the basis for an explicit metaphysics. At the same time he works dialectically towards the establishment of his own view of the meaning of 'to be' by examining in turn different types of philosophy with a view to exhibiting their inadequacy. And though we cannot enter into the details of this discussion, it is appropriate to indicate its general lines.

3. The first type of philosophy discussed by Royce is what he calls realism. By this he understands the doctrine that 'the mere knowledge of any Being by any one who is not himself the Being known, "makes no difference whatever" to that known Being'.[4] In other words, if all knowledge were to disappear from the world, the only difference that this would make to the world would be that the particular fact of knowledge would no longer exist. Truth and falsity consist in the correspondence or non-correspondence of ideas with things: and nothing exists simply in virtue of the fact that it is known. Hence we cannot tell by inspecting the relations between ideas whether the objects referred to exist or not. Hence the *what* is sundered from the *that*. And this, Royce remarks, is why the realist has to deny the validity of the ontological argument for God's existence.

Royce's criticism of 'realism' is not always very clear. But his general line of thought is as follows. By realism in this context he evidently means an extreme nominalistic empiricism, according to which the world consists of a plurality of entities that are mutually independent. The disappearance of one would not affect the existence of the rest. Any relations which are superadded to these entities must, therefore, be themselves independent entities. And in this case, Royce argues, the terms of the relations cannot really

[1] *Ibid.*, I, p. 36.   [2] *Ibid.*, I, p. 32.
[3] *Ibid.*   [4] *Ibid.*, I, p. 93.

be related. If we start with entities which are sundered from one another, they remain sundered. Royce then argues that ideas must themselves be entities, and that on realist premises an unbridgeable gulf yawns between them and the objects to which they are thought to refer. In other words, if ideas are entities which are completely independent of other entities, we can never know whether they correspond with objects external to themselves, nor indeed whether there are such objects at all. Hence we can never know whether realism, as an idea or set of ideas, is true or false. And in this sense realism, as a theory of reality, is self-defeating: it undermines its own foundations.[1]

From realism Royce proceeds to a consideration of what he calls 'mysticism'. As the core of realism consists in defining as 'real' any being which is essentially independent of any idea which refers to it from without, the realist, Royce claims, is committed to dualism. For he must postulate the existence of at least one idea and one object which is external to it. Mysticism, however, rejects dualism and asserts the existence of a One in which the distinctions between subject and object, idea and the reality to which it refers, vanish.

Mysticism, as understood in this sense, is as self-defeating as realism. For if there is only one simple and indivisible Being, the finite subject and its ideas must be accounted illusory. And in this case the Absolute cannot be known. For it could be known only by ideas. In fact any assertion that there is a One must be illusory. It is true that our fragmentary ideas need completion in a unified system, and that the whole is the truth. But if a philosopher stresses unity to such an extent that ideas have to be accounted illusion, he cannot at the same time consistently maintain that there is a One or Absolute. For it is plain that the Absolute has meaning for us only in so far as it is conceived by means of ideas.

If therefore we wish to maintain that knowledge of reality is possible at all, we cannot take the path of mysticism. We must allow for plurality. At the same time we cannot return to realism as described above. Hence realism must be modified in such a way that it is no longer self-defeating. And one way of attempting such a modification is to take the path of what Royce calls 'critical rationalism'.

The critical rationalist undertakes to 'define Being in terms of

[1] The argument might perhaps be summed up in this way. If things are completely independent of ideas, ideas are completely independent of things. And in this case truth, considered as a relation between idea and things, is unattainable.

validity, to conceive that whoever says, of any object, *It is*, means
only that a certain idea . . . *is valid*, has truth, defines an experience that, at least as a mathematical ideal, and perhaps as an
empirical event, is determinately *possible*'.[1] Suppose that I assert
that there are human beings on the planet Mars. According to the
critical rationalist, I am asserting that in the progress of possible
experience a certain idea would be validated or verified. Royce
gives as examples of critical rationalism Kant's theory of possible
experience and J. S. Mill's definition of matter as a permanent
possibility of sensations. We might add logical positivism, provided that we substitute for 'idea' 'empirical proposition'.

In Royce's view critical rationalism has this advantage over
realism that by defining Being in terms of possible experience, the
validation of an idea (better, the verification of a proposition),
it avoids the objections which arise from realism's complete
sundering of ideas from the reality to which they are assumed to
refer. At the same time critical rationalism has this great draw-
back that it is incapable of answering the question, '*what is a valid
or a determinately possible experience at the moment when it is
supposed to be only possible?* What is a valid truth at the moment
when nobody verifies its validity?'[2] If I assert that there are men
on Mars, this statement doubtless implies, in a definable sense of
this term, that the presence of men on Mars is an object of possible
experience. But if the statement happens to be true, their existence
is not simply possible existence. Hence we can hardly define
Being simply in terms of the possible validation or verification of
an idea. And though critical rationalism does not make knowledge
of reality impossible, as is done by both realism and mysticism,
it is unable to provide an adequate account of reality. Hence we
must turn to another and more adequate philosophical theory,
which will subsume in itself the truths contained in the three
theories already mentioned but which will at the same time be
immune from the objections which can be brought against them.

4. It has already been indicated that by 'realism' Royce understands nominalism rather than realism as this term is used in the
context of the controversy about universals. And if we bear this
fact in mind, we shall not be so startled by his assertion that for
the realist the only ultimate form of being is the individual. For
the nominalist slogan was that only individuals exist. At the same
time we must also bear in mind the fact that Hegel, who was no

[1] *The World*, I, pp. 226–7. [2] *Ibid.*, I, p. 260.

nominalist, used the term 'individual' to mean the concrete universal, and that in the Hegelian philosophy the ultimate form of being is the individual in this sense of the term, the Absolute being the supreme individual, the all-inclusive concrete universal. Hence when Royce asserts that the truth contained in realism is that the only ultimate form of being is the individual, it would be misleading to say simply that he is accepting the nominalist slogan. For he re-interprets the term 'individual' under the inspiration of the idealist tradition. According to his use of the term 'an individual being is a Life of Experience fulfilling Ideas, in an absolutely final form. . . . The essence of the Real is to be Individual, or permit no other of its own kind, and this character it possesses only as the unique fulfilment of purpose.'[1]

Now we have seen that an idea is the incomplete or partial fulfilment of a purpose, the expression of will. And the complete embodiment of the will is the world in its entirety. Hence any idea ultimately 'means'[2] the totality. And it follows that in the totality, the world as a whole, I can recognize myself. To this extent therefore we can find truth in 'mysticism' and agree with the oriental mystic who 'says of the self and the World: *That art Thou*'.[3]

It is evident, however, that as embodied in any particular phase of consciousness the will expresses itself in attention only to a part of the world or to certain facts in the world. The rest relapses into a vague background at the margin of consciousness. It becomes in fact the object of possible experience. In other words, it is necessary to introduce a concept from critical rationalism.

So far we have been thinking of the point of view of the individual finite subject. But though there is an obvious sense in which the world is 'my world' and nobody else's, it is also obvious that if I regard the world as being simply and solely the embodiment of my will, I am committed to solipsism. It is also clear that if I postulate the existence of other lives of experience besides my own but regard each life as completely self-enclosed, I fall back into the thesis of realism, namely that reality consists of completely separate and mutually independent entities. Hence to avoid solipsism without returning to the realist thesis which we

[1] *The World*, I, p. 348. For example, 'my world' is the embodiment of my will, the fulfilment of my purpose, the expression of my interests. And it is thus unique. But, as is explained in the following paragraphs, we cannot remain simply with the concept of 'my world'.
[2] We must remember that for Royce 'internal meaning' is primary.
[3] *The World*, I, p. 355.

have already rejected we must introduce a new dimension or plane, that of intersubjectivity.

It is commonly said, Royce remarks, that we come to know the existence of other persons by analogical reasoning. That is to say, observing certain patterns of external behaviour we attribute to them wills like our own. But if this means that we first have a clear knowledge of ourselves and then infer the existence of other persons, 'it is nearer the truth to say that we first learn about ourselves from and through our fellows, than that we learn about our fellows by using the analogy of ourselves'.[1] We have indeed ever-present evidence of the existence of others. For they are the source of new ideas. They answer our questions; they tell us things; they express opinions other than our own; and so on. Yet it is precisely through social intercourse or at least in the consciousness of the presence of others, that we form our own ideas and become aware of what we really will and aim at. As Royce puts it, our fellows 'help us to find out what our true meaning is'.[2]

If, however, Royce rejects the view that we first possess a clear consciousness of ourselves and then infer the existence of other persons, still less does he intend to imply that we first have a clear and definite idea of other persons and then infer that we too are persons. He says, indeed, that 'a vague belief in the existence of our fellows seems to antedate, to a considerable extent, the definite formation of any consciousness of ourselves'.[3] But his thesis is that the clear awareness of ourselves and of other persons arises out of a kind of primitive social consciousness, so that it is a question of differentiation rather than of inference. Empirical self-consciousness depends constantly upon a series of contrast-effects. 'The Ego is always known as in contrast to the Alter.'[4] Both emerge from the original social consciousness.

As experience develops, the individual comes more and more to regard the inner lives of others as something private, removed from his direct observation. At the same time he becomes progressively conscious of external objects as instruments of purposes which are common to himself and others as well as of his and their particular purposes or interests. There thus arises the consciousness of a triad, 'my fellow and Myself, with Nature between us'.[5]

[1] *Ibid.*, II, pp. 170-1.   [2] *Ibid.*, II, p. 172.   [3] *Ibid.*, II, p. 170.
[4] *Ibid.*, II, p. 264. Royce expresses his general agreement with the theory of the origins of self-consciousness given in the second volume of *Mental Development in the Child and the Race* (1896), by James Mark Baldwin (1861-1934), of Princeton University.
[5] *The World*, II, p. 177.

The world of Nature is known by us only in part, a great deal
remaining for us the realm of possible experience. But we have
already noted the difficulty encountered by critical rationalism in
explaining the ontological status of objects of possible experience;
and in any case science makes it impossible for us to believe that
Nature is simply and solely the embodiment of human will and
purpose. The hypothesis of evolution, for example, leads us to
conceive finite minds as products. In this case, however, the
question arises, how can we save the idealist definition of Being
in terms of the internal meaning of ideas considered as the partial
fulfilment of a purpose?

Royce's answer to this question is easy to foresee. The world is
ultimately the expression of an absolute system of ideas which is
itself the partial fulfilment of the divine will. God, expressing
himself in the world, is the ultimate Individual. Or, to put the
matter in another way, the ultimate Individual is the life of
absolute experience. Each finite self is a unique expression of the
divine purpose; and each embodies or expresses itself in its world.
But 'my world' and 'your world' are unique facets of 'the world',
the embodiment of the infinite divine will and purpose. And what
is for us simply the object of possible experience is for God the
object of actual creative experience. 'The whole world of truth
and being must exist only as present, in all its variety, its wealth,
its relationships, its entire constitution, to the unity of a single
consciousness, which includes both our own and all finite conscious meanings in one final eternally present insight.'[1] Royce is
thus able to preserve his theory of Being, namely that 'whatever
is, is consciously known as the fulfilment of some idea, and is so
known either by ourselves at this moment, or by a consciousness
inclusive of our own'.[2]

5. We have seen that for Royce the individual is a *life* of
experience. And if we are looking for the nature of the self in a
meta-empirical sense,[3] we have to conceive it in ethical terms, not
in terms of a soul-substance. For it is through the possession of a
unique ideal, a unique vocation, a unique life-task which is what
my past has 'meant' and which my future is to fulfil that '*I am
defined and created a Self*'.[4] Perhaps, therefore, we can say,

---

[1] *The World*, I, p. 397.   [2] *Ibid.*, I, p. 396.
[3] That is to say, if we are looking for a metaphysical concept of the self rather
than for an empirical account of, say, the origins and development of self-
consciousness.
[4] *The World*, II, p. 276.

speaking in a manner that puts us in mind of existentialism, that for Royce the finite individual continually creates himself as this unique self by realizing a unique ideal, by fulfilling a certain unique vocation.[1]

It is in terms of this idea of the self that Royce attempts to meet the objection that absolute idealism deprives the finite self of reality, value and freedom. He has, of course, no intention of denying any of the empirical data relating to the dependence of the psychical on the physical or to the influence on the self of social environment, education and such like factors. But he insists that each finite self has its own unique way of acknowledging and responding by its deeds to this dependence,[2] while from the metaphysical point of view the life of each finite self is a unique contribution to the fulfilment of the general purpose of God. Royce has indeed to admit that when I will, God wills in me, and that my act is part of the divine life. But this admission, he maintains, is quite compatible with the statement that the finite self can act freely. For by the very fact that I am a *unique* expression of the divine will, the will from which my acts proceed is *my* will. 'Your individuality in your act *is* your freedom.'[3] That is to say, my way of expressing the divine will is myself; and if my acts proceed from myself, they are free acts. There is indeed a sense in which it is true to say that the divine Spirit compels us, but 'in the sense that it compels you to be an individual, and to be free'.[4]

Now, Royce maintains that every finite will seeks the Absolute, so much so that 'to seek anything but the Absolute itself is, indeed, even for the most perverse Self, simply impossible'.[5] In other words, every finite self tends by its very nature, whether it is aware of the fact or not, to unite its will ever more closely with the divine will. Obligation bears on us in relation to conduct which would bring us nearer to this end. And a moral rule is a rule which, if followed, would bring us nearer to the end than if we acted in a manner contrary to the rule. It is thus clear enough that in Royce's ethics the concept of the good is paramount, and that obligation bears on us in relation to the means necessary to attain this good, namely the conscious union of our will with the divine will. But it is not so clear how any room can be left for rebellion against the divine will or against a known dictate of the moral

---

[1] Needless to say, for the atheist existentialist, such as Sartre, the idea of a God-given vocation is devoid of validity.
[2] Here again one is put in mind of modern existentialism.
[3] *The World*, I, p. 469.   [4] *Ibid.*, II, p. 293.   [5] *Ibid.*, II, p. 347.

law. For if we all inevitably seek the Absolute, it appears to follow that if a person acts in a manner which will not as a matter of fact bring him nearer to the final end which he is always seeking, he does so simply out of ignorance, out of defective knowledge. Hence the question arises, 'can a finite self, knowing the Ought, in any sense freely choose to rebel or to obey?'[1]

Royce answers in the first place that though a man who has clear knowledge of what he ought to do will act in accordance with this knowledge, he can voluntarily concentrate his attention elsewhere, so that here and now he no longer has clear knowledge of what he ought to do. 'To sin is *consciously to forget*, through a narrowing of the field of attention, an Ought that one already recognizes.'[2]

Given Royce's premisses, this answer is hardly adequate. We can, of course, easily give a cash-value to his idea of a shift of attention. Suppose, for example, that I am sincerely convinced that it would be wrong for me to act in a certain way which I regard as productive of sensual pleasure. The more I concentrate my attention on the pleásurable aspects of this way of acting, so much the more does my conviction of its wrongness tend to retreat to the margin of consciousness and become ineffective. We all know that this sort of situation occurs frequently enough. And the ordinary comment would be that the agent should be careful not to concentrate his attention on the pleasurable aspects of a way of acting which he sincerely believes to be wrong. If he concentrates his attention in this manner, he is ultimately responsible for what happens. But though this point of view is clearly reasonable, the question immediately arises, how can the agent be properly held responsible for choosing to concentrate his attention in a certain direction if he is in his entirety an expression of the divine will? Have we simply not pushed the difficulty a stage further back?

Royce rather tends to evade the issue by turning to the subject of the overcoming of evil in the totality. But his general line of answer seems to be that as a man's direction of his attention proceeds from his will, the man is himself responsible for it and thus for the outcome. The fact that the man's will is itself the expression of the divine will does not alter the situation. In the circumstances it does not appear that Royce can very well say anything else. For though he certainly wishes to maintain human

---

[1] *The World*, II, p. 351.   [2] *Ibid.*, II, p. 359.

freedom and responsibility in a real sense, his determination to maintain at the same time the doctrine of the all-comprehensive Absolute inevitably influences his account of freedom. Moral freedom becomes 'simply this freedom to hold by attention, or to forget by inattention, an Ought already present to one's finite consciousness'.[1] If it is asked whether the holding or forgetting is not itself determined by the Absolute, Royce can only answer that it proceeds from a man's own will, and that to act in accordance with one's will *is* to act freely, even if one's finite will is a particular embodiment of the divine will.

6. As Royce lays great emphasis, in a manner which reminds us of Fichte, on the uniqueness of the task which each finite self is called to perform, he can hardly be expected to devote much time to developing a theory of universal moral rules.[2] And it is perhaps not an exaggeration to say that the fundamental precept is for him, as for Emerson, 'Be an individual! That is, find and fulfil your unique task.' At the same time it would be quite wrong to depict him as belittling the idea of the community. On the contrary, his ethical theory can be regarded as a contribution to the demand made by Harris in his programme for speculative philosophy, that a social theory should be developed which would fulfil the needs of a national consciousness that was moving away from sheer individualism. For Royce all finite selves are mutually related precisely because they are unique expressions of one infinite will. And all individual vocations or life-tasks are elements in a common task, the fulfilment of the divine purpose. Hence Royce preaches loyalty to the ideal community, the Great Community as he calls it.[3]

In *The Problem of Christianity* (1913) Royce defines loyalty as 'the willing and thoroughgoing devotion of a self to a cause, when the cause is something which unites many selves in one, and which is therefore the interest of a community'.[4] And he sees in the Church, the community of the faithful, especially as represented in the Pauline Epistles, the embodiment of the spirit of loyalty, of

[1] *Ibid.*, II, p. 360.
[2] 'By the Ought you mean, at any temporal instant, a rule that, if followed, would guide you so to express, at that instant, your will, that you should be thereby made nearer to union with the divine, nearer to a consciousness of the oneness of your will and the Absolute Will, than you would if you acted counter to this Ought', *The World*, II, pp. 347-8. Here the emphasis is placed on 'the instant', not on the universal.
[3] In 1908 Royce published *The Philosophy of Loyalty* and in 1916 *The Hope of the Great Community*.
[4] *The Problem of Christianity*, I, p. 68.

devotion to a common ideal and of loyalty to the ideal community which should be loved as a person. It does not follow, however, that Royce intended to identify what he calls the Great Community with an historic Church, any more than with an historic State. The Great Community is more like Kant's kingdom of ends; it is the ideal human community. Yet though it is an ideal to be sought after rather than an actual historic society existing here and now, it none the less lies at the basis of the moral order, precisely because it is the goal or *telos* of moral action. It is true that the individual alone can work out his moral vocation; it cannot be done for him. But because of the very nature of the self genuine individuality can be realized only through loyalty to the Great Community, to an ideal cause which unites all men together.

Largely under the influence of C. S. Peirce, Royce came to emphasize the role of interpretation in human knowledge and life; and he applied this idea in his ethical theory. For example, the individual cannot realize himself and attain true selfhood or personality without a life-goal or life-plan, in relation to which concepts such as right and wrong, higher self and lower self, become concretely meaningful. But a man comes to apprehend his life-plan or ideal goal only through a process of interpreting himself to himself. Further, this self-interpretation is achieved only in a social context, through interaction with other people. Others inevitably help me to interpret myself to myself; and I help others to interpret themselves to themselves. In a sense this process tends to division rather than to union, inasmuch as each individual becomes thereby more aware of himself as possessing a unique life-task. But if we bear in mind the social structure of the self, we are led to form the idea of an unlimited community of interpretation, of humanity, that is to say, as engaged throughout time in the common task of interpreting both the physical world and its own purposes, ideals and values. All growth in scientific knowledge and moral insight involves a process of interpretation.

The supreme object of loyalty as a moral category is, Royce came to think, this ideal community of interpretation. But towards the close of his life he stressed the importance of limited communities both for moral development and for the achievement of social reform. If we consider, for instance, two individuals who are disputing about, say, the possession of some property, we can see that this potentially dangerous situation is transformed by the intervention of a third party, the judge. A tryadic relation is substituted for the potentially dangerous dyadic relation; and a small-scale community of interpretation is set up. Thus Royce tries to exhibit the mediating or interpretative and morally educative functions of such institutions as the judicial system, always in the light of the idea of interpretation. He applies this idea even to the institution of insurance and develops, as a safeguard against war, a scheme of insurance on an international scale.[1] Some of his commentators may have seen in such ideas a peculiarly American fusion of idealism with a rather down-to-earth practicality. But it does not follow, of course, that such a fusion is a bad thing. In any case Royce evidently felt that if substantive proposals were to be put forward in ethical theory, something more was required than exhorting men to be loyal to the ideal community of interpretation.

7. From what has been said hitherto it is clear that Royce attaches to the unique personality a value which could not be attributed to it in the philosophy of Bradley. It is not surprising, therefore, that he is far more interested than Bradley in the question of immortality, and that he maintains that the self is preserved in the Absolute.

In discussing this subject Royce dwells, among other aspects of the matter, on the Kantian theme that the moral task of the individual can have no temporal end. 'A consciously last moral task is a contradiction in terms. . . . The service of the eternal is an essentially endless service. There can be no last moral deed.'[2] Obviously, this line of argument could not by itself prove immortality. It is true that if we recognize a moral law at all, we have to regard it as bearing upon us as long as we live. But it does not follow from this premiss alone that the self survives bodily death and is able to continue fulfilling a moral vocation. But for Royce as a metaphysician the universe is of such a kind that the finite self, as a unique expression of the Absolute and as representing an irreplaceable value, must be supposed to continue in existence. The ethical self is always something in the making; and as the divine purpose must be fulfilled, we are justified in believing that after the death of the body the self attains genuine individuality in a higher form. But 'I know not in the least, I pretend not to guess, by what processes the individuality of our human life is further expressed. I wait until this mortal shall put

[1] Cf. *War and Insurance* (1914), and *The Hope of the Great Community* (1916).
[2] *The World*, I, pp. 444–5

on—Individuality.'[1] Evidently, in Royce's assertion of immortality what really counts is his general metaphysical vision of reality, coupled with his evaluation of personality.

8. At the end of the first volume of Royce's Gifford Lectures there is a Supplementary Essay in which he takes issue with Bradley on the subject of an infinite multitude. Bradley, it will be remembered, maintains that relational thought involves us in infinite series. If, for example, qualities A and B are related by relation R, we must choose between saying that R is reducible without residue to A and B or that it is not so reducible. In the first case we shall be compelled to conclude that A and B are not related at all. In the second case we shall have to postulate further relations to relate both A and B with R, and so on without end. We are then committed to postulating an actually infinite multitude. But this concept is self-contradictory. Hence we must conclude that relational thought is quite incapable of giving a coherent account of how the Many proceed from and are unified in the One, and that the world as presented in such thought belongs to the sphere of appearance as contrasted with that of reality. Royce, however, undertakes to show that the One can express itself in infinite series which are 'well-ordered' and involve no contradiction, and that thought is thus capable of giving a coherent account of the relation between the One and the Many. It is perhaps disputable whether Bradley's difficulties are really met by first ascribing to him the thesis that an actually infinite multitude is 'a self-contradictory conception'[2] and then arguing that an endless series in mathematics does not involve a contradiction. But though Royce develops his own conception of the relation between the One and the Many in the context of a controversy with Bradley, what he is really interested in is, of course, the explanation of his own ideas.

Royce's attention was directed by C. S. Peirce to the logic of mathematics;[3] and the Supplementary Essay shows the fruit of Royce's reflections on this subject. In an endless mathematical series, such as that of the whole numbers, the endlessness of the series is due to a recurrent operation of thought, a recurrent operation of thought being describable as 'one that, *if once finally expressed*, would involve, in the region where it had received

---

[1] *The Conception of Immortality*, p. 80.
[2] *The World*, I, p. 475.
[3] Royce's interest in mathematical logic found expression in *The Relation of the Principles of Logic to the Foundation of Geometry* (1905).

expression, an infinite variety of serially arranged facts, corresponding to the purpose in question'.[1] In general, if we assume a
purpose of such a kind that if we try to express it by means of a
succession of acts, the ideal data which begin to express it demand
as part of their own 'meaning' additional data which are themselves further expressions of the original meaning and at the same
time demand still further expressions, we have an endless series
produced by a recurrent operation of thought.

A series of this kind can properly be regarded as a totality. To
be sure, it is not a totality in the sense that we can count to the
end and complete the series. For it is *ex hypothesi* infinite or endless. But if we take, for example, the series of whole numbers, 'the
mathematician can view them all as *given* by means of their
universal definition, and their consequent clear distinction from
all other objects of thought'.[2] In other words, there is no intrinsic
repugnance between the idea of a totality and that of an infinite
series. And we can conceive the One as expressing itself in an
infinite series or, rather, a plurality of co-ordinate infinite series,
the plurality of lives of experience. This gives us, of course, a
dynamic rather than a static concept of the One. And this is
essential to Royce's metaphysics, with its emphasis on divine will
and purpose and on the 'internal meaning' of ideas.

An infinite series of this kind is described by Royce as a self-
representative system. And he finds examples in 'all continuous
and discrete mathematical systems of any infinite type'.[3] But a
simple illustration given by Royce himself will serve better to
clarify what he means by a self-representative system. Suppose
that we decide that on some portion of England a map is to be
constructed which will represent the country down to the smallest
detail, including every contour and marking, whether natural or
artificial. As the map itself will be an artificial feature of England,
another map will have to be constructed within the first map and
representing it too, if, that is to say, our original purpose is to be
carried out. And so on without end. True, this endless representation of England would not be physically possible. But we can
conceive an endless series of maps within maps, a series which,
though it cannot be completed in time, can be regarded as already
given in our original purpose or 'meaning'. The observer who
understood the situation and looked at the series of maps, would
not see any last map. But he would know why there could be no

[1] *The World*, I, p. 507.   [2] *Ibid.*, I, p. 515.   [3] *Ibid.*, I, p. 513.

last map. Hence he would see no contradiction or irrationality in the endlessness of the series. And the series would constitute a self-representative system.

If we apply this idea in metaphysics, the universe appears as an infinite series, an endless whole, which expresses a single purpose or plan. There are, of course, subordinate and co-ordinate series, in particular the series which constitute the lives of finite selves. But they are all comprised within one unified infinite series which has no last member but which is 'given' as a totality in the internal meaning of the divine idea or absolute system of ideas. The One, according to Royce, must express itself in the endless series which constitutes its life of creative experience. In other words, it must express itself in the Many. And as the endless series is the progressive expression or fulfilment of a single purpose, the whole of reality is one self-representative system.

9. It is clear that Royce, with his emphasis on personality, has no intention of abandoning theism altogether and of using the term 'the Absolute' simply as a name for the world considered as an open totality, a series which has no assignable last member. The world is for him the embodiment of the internal meaning of a system of ideas which are themselves the partial fulfilment of a purpose. And the Absolute is a self; it is personal rather than impersonal; it is an eternal and infinite consciousness. Hence it can reasonably be described as God. And Royce depicts the infinite series which constitutes the temporal universe as present all at once, *tota simul*, to the divine consciousness. Indeed, he is quite prepared to commend St. Thomas Aquinas for his account of the divine knowledge; and he himself uses the analogy of our awareness of a symphony as a whole, an awareness which is obviously quite compatible with the knowledge that this part precedes that. So, according to Royce, God is aware of temporal succession, though the whole temporal series is none the less present to the eternal consciousness.

At the same time Royce rejects the dualistic sundering of the world from God which he regards as characteristic of theism, and he blames Aquinas for conceiving 'the temporal existence of the created world as sundered from the eternal life which belongs to God'.[1] The Many exist within the unity of the divine life. 'Simple unity is a mere impossibility. God cannot be One except by being Many. Nor can we various Selves be Many, unless in Him we are One.'[2]

---

[1] *The World*, II, p. 143.   [2] *Ibid.*, II, p. 331.

In other words, Royce tries to re-interpret theism in the light of absolute idealism. He tries to preserve the idea of a personal God while combining it with the idea of the all-comprehensive Absolute represented as the Universal of universals.[1] And this is not an easy position to maintain. In fact its ambiguity is well illustrated by Royce's use of the term 'individual'. If we speak of God as the supreme or ultimate Individual, we naturally tend to think of him as a personal being and of the world as the 'external' expression of his creative will. But for Royce the term 'individual' means, as we have seen, a life of experience. And according to this meaning of the term God becomes the life of absolute and infinite experience, in which all finite things are immanent. Whereas the interpretation of the existence of finite things as the expression of purposeful will suggests creation in a theistic sense, the description of God as absolute experience suggests a rather different relation. No doubt Royce tries to bring the two concepts together through the conception of creative experience; but there seems to be in his philosophy a somewhat unstable marriage between theism and absolute idealism.

It is, of course, notoriously difficult to express the relation between the finite and the infinite without tending either to a monism in which the Many are relegated to the sphere of appearance or are submerged in the One or to a dualism which renders the use of the term 'infinite' quite inappropriate. And it is certainly not possible to avoid both positions without a clear theory of the analogy of being. But Royce's statements on the subject of being are somewhat perplexing.

On the one hand we are told that being is the expression or embodiment of the internal meaning of an idea, and so of purpose or will. But though the subordination of being to thought may be characteristic of metaphysical idealism, the question obviously arises whether thought itself is not a form of being. And the same question can be asked in regard to will. On the other hand we are told that the ultimately real, and so presumably the ultimate form of being, is the individual. And as God is the Individual of individuals, it appears to follow that he must be the supreme and absolute being. Yet we are also told to regard 'individuality, and consequently Being, as above all an expression of Will'.[2] To regard individuality as an expression of will is not so difficult, if,

---

[1] The term 'universal' is used here, needless to say, in the sense of the concrete universal.

[2] *The World*, I, p. 588.

that is to say, we interpret individuality as a life of expression. But to regard being as an expression of will is not so easy. For the question again arises, is will not being? Of course, it would be possible to restrict the use of the term 'being' to material being. But then we could hardly regard individuality, in Royce's sense of the term, as being.

In spite, however, of the ambiguity and lack of precision in his writing, Royce's philosophy impresses by its sincerity. It is evidently the expression of a deeply held faith, a faith in the reality of God, in the value of the human personality and in the unity of mankind in and through God, a unity which can be adequately realized only through individual contributions to a common moral task. Royce was indeed something of a preacher. But the philosophy which he preached certainly meant for him a great deal more than an intellectual exercise or game.

It should be added that in the opinion of some commentators[1] Royce came to abandon his theory of the Absolute Will and to substitute for it the idea of an unlimited community of interpretation, an unlimited community, that is to say, of finite individuals. And from the purely ethical point of view such a change would be understandable. For it would dispose of the objection, of which Royce himself was aware, that it is difficult, if indeed possible at all, to reconcile the theory of the Absolute Will with the view of human beings as genuine moral agents. At the same time the substitution of a community of finite individuals for the Absolute would be a pretty radical change. And it is by no means easy to see how such a community could take over, as it were, the cosmological function of the Absolute. Even if, therefore, the idea of the Absolute retreats into the background in Royce's latest writings, one hesitates to accept the view that he positively rejected the idea, unless, of course, one is driven to do so by strong empirical evidence. There is indeed some evidence. In his last years Royce himself referred to a change in his idealism. Hence we cannot say that the claim that he substituted the unlimited community of interpretation for his earlier concept of the Absolute is unfounded. Royce does not seem, however, to have been explicit as one could wish about the precise nature and extent of the change to which he refers.

[1] Cf., the Appendix to *The Moral Philosophy of Josiah Royce* by Peter Fuss (Cambridge, Mass., 1965).

CHAPTER XIII

PERSONAL IDEALISM AND OTHER TENDENCIES

Howison's criticism of Royce in favour of his own ethical pluralism—The evolutionary idealism of Le Conte—The personal idealism of Bowne—The objective idealism of Creighton—Sylvester Morris and dynamic idealism—Notes on the prolongation of idealism into the twentieth century—An attempt at transcending the opposition between idealism and realism.

1. GEORGE HOLMES HOWISON (1834–1916), a member of the Philosophical Society of St. Louis and of W. T. Harris's Kant-Club, was at first a professor of mathematics. But in 1872 he accepted the chair of logic and philosophy in the Massachusetts Institute of Technology at Boston, a post which he occupied until 1878 when he went to Germany for two years. In Germany he came under the influence of the right-wing Hegelian Ludwig Michelet (1801–93), and, like Michelet himself, he interpreted Hegel's absolute Idea or cosmic Reason as a personal being, God. In 1884 Howison became a professor in the University of California. His work *The Limits of Evolution and Other Essays*, appeared in 1901.

It has already been mentioned that Howison participated in the discussion which formed the basis for *The Conception of God* (1897), a work to which reference was made in the chapter on Royce. In his introduction to the book Howison draws attention to the existence of a certain measure of basic agreement among the participants in the discussion, particularly in regard to the personality of God and about the close relation between the concepts of God, freedom and immortality. But though he recognizes certain family likenesses between different types of idealism, this does not prevent him from developing a sharp criticism of Royce's philosophy.

In the first place, if being is defined in terms of its relation to the internal meaning of an idea, how, Howison asks, are we to decide whether the idea in question is my idea or that of an infinite all-inclusive self? The factor which leads Royce and those who share his general outlook to reject solipsism in favour of absolute idealism is an instinctive response to the demands of common sense rather than any logical and compelling argument. In the second place, though Royce certainly intends to preserve individual freedom and responsibility, he can do so only at the cost of consistency. For absolute idealism logically involves the merging of finite selves in the Absolute.

Howison's own philosophy has been described as ethical pluralism. Existence takes the form of spirits and of the contents and order of their experience, the spatio-temporal world owing its being to the co-existence of spirits. Each spirit is a free and active efficient cause, having the origin of its activity within itself. At the same time each spirit is a member of a community of spirits, the City of God, the members being united in terms of final causality, that is, by their attraction to a common ideal, the full realization of the City of God. The human consciousness is not simply self-enclosed, but, when developed, it sees itself as a member of what Howison describes as Conscience or Complete Reason. And the movement towards a common ideal or end is what is called evolution.

This may sound remarkably like Royce's view, except perhaps for Howison's insistence that the spring of the activity of each spirit is to be sought within itself. But Howison tries to avoid what he regards as the logical and disastrous consequences of Royce's philosophy by emphasizing final causality. God is represented as the personified ideal of every spirit. By this Howison does not mean that God has no existence except as a human ideal. He means that the mode of divine action on the human spirit is that of final causality, rather than that of efficient causality. God draws the finite self as an ideal; but the self's response to God is its own activity rather than the action of God or the Absolute. In other words, God acts by illuminating the reason and attracting the will to the ideal of the unity of free spirits in himself rather than by determining the human will through efficient causality or the exercise of power.

2. Another participant in the discussion referred to above was Joseph Le Conte (1823–1901), professor in the University of California. Trained as a geologist, Le Conte interested himself in the philosophical aspects of the theory of evolution and expounded what can be described as evolutionary idealism.[1] As the ultimate source of evolution he saw a divine Energy which expresses itself

---

[1] Le Conte's writings include *Religion and Science* (1874), and *Evolution: Its Nature, Its Evidence and Its Relation to Religious Thought* (1888).

immediately in the physical and chemical forces of Nature. But the efflux of this divine Energy becomes progressively individuated concomitantly with the advancing organization of matter. Le Conte's philosophy is thus pluralistic. For he maintains that in the process of evolution we find the emergence of successively higher forms of self-active individuals, until we reach the highest form of individual being yet attained, namely the human being. In man the efflux or spark of the divine life is able to recognize and to enter into conscious communion with its ultimate source. In fact we can look forward to a progressive elevation of man to the level of 'regenerated' man, enjoying a higher degree of spiritual and moral development.

Howison's approach to philosophy tended to be through the critical philosophy of Kant, when rethought in the light of metaphysical idealism. Le Conte's approach was rather by way of an attempt to show how the theory of evolution liberates science from all materialistic implications and points the way to a religious and ethical idealism. He exercised some influence on the mind of Royce.

3. Besides Howison, whose philosophy has been labelled as ethical idealism, one of the most influential representatives of personal idealism in America was Borden Parker Bowne (1847–1910). As a student at New York Bowne wrote a criticism of Spencer. During subsequent studies in Germany he came under the influence of Lotze, especially in regard to the latter's theory of the self.[1] In 1876 Bowne became Professor of Philosophy in the University of Boston. His writings include *Studies in Theism* (1879), *Metaphysics* (1882), *Philosophy of Theism* (1887), *Principles of Ethics* (1892), *The Theory of Thought and Knowledge* (1897), *The Immanence of God* (1905), and *Personalism* (1908). These titles show clearly enough the religious orientation of his thought.

Bowne at first described his philosophy as transcendental empiricism, in view of the conspicuous role played in his thought by a doctrine of categories inspired by Kant. These are not simply empirically derived, fortuitous results of adaptation to environment in the process of evolution. At the same time they are the expression of the nature of the self and of its self-experience. And this shows that the self is an active unity and not a mere logical

[1] See Vol. VII of this *History*, p. 378. For Lotze, to recognize the fact of the unity of consciousness is *eo ipso* to recognize the existence of the soul. He thus tries to avoid phenomenalism on the one hand and postulating an occult soul-substance on the other. For Bowne, the self is an immediate datum of consciousness, not a hidden entity which has to be inferred from the existence of faculties and their acts.

postulate, as Kant thought. Indeed, the self or person, characterized by intelligence and will, is the only real efficient cause. For efficient causality is essentially volitional. In Nature we find indeed uniformities, but no causality in the proper sense. This idea of Nature forms the basis for a philosophy of God. Science describes how things happen. And it can be said to explain events, if we mean by this that it exhibits them as examples or cases of empirically discovered generalizations which are called 'laws'. 'But in the causal sense science explains nothing. Here the alternative is supernatural explanation or none.'[1] True, in science itself the idea of God is no more required than in shoemaking. For science is simply classificatory and descriptive. But once we turn to metaphysics, we see the order of Nature as the effect of the constant activity of a supreme rational will. In other words, as far as its causation is concerned, any event in Nature is as supernatural as a miracle would be. 'For in both alike God would be equally implicated.'[2]

We can now take a broad view of reality. If, as Bowne believes, to be real is to act, and if activity in the full sense can be attributed only to persons, it follows that it is only persons who are, so to speak, fully real. We thus have the picture of a system of persons standing to one another in various active relations through the instrumentality of the external world. And this system of persons must, according to Bowne, be the creation of a supreme Person, God. On the one hand a being which was less than personal could not be the sufficient cause of finite persons. On the other hand, if we can apply the category of causality to a world in which the infra-personal exercises no real efficient causality, this can only be because the world is the creation of a personal being who is immanently active in it. Ultimate reality thus appears as personal in character, as a system of persons with a supreme Person at their head.

Personalism, as Bowne came to call his philosophy, is 'the only metaphysics that does not dissolve away into self-cancelling abstractions'.[3] Auguste Comte, according to Bowne, was justified not only in confining science to the study of uniformities of co-existence and sequence among phenomena and in excluding from it all properly causal inquiry but also in rejecting metaphysics in so far as this is a study of abstract ideas and categories which are supposed to provide causal explanations. But personalism is

[1] *The Immanence of God*, p. 19.   [2] *Ibid.*, p. 18.   [3] *Ibid.*, p. 32.

immune from the objections which can be raised against meta-physics as Comte understood the term. For it does not seek the causal explanations which, on Comte's own showing, science cannot provide, in abstract categories. It sees in these categories simply the abstract forms of self-conscious life, and the ultimate causal explanation is found in a supreme rational will. True, personalist metaphysics may seem to involve a return to what Comte regarded as the first stage of human thought, namely the theological stage, in which explanations were sought in divine wills or in a divine will. But in personalism this stage is raised to a higher level, inasmuch as capricious wills are replaced by an infinite rational will.[1]

4. Objective idealism, as it is commonly called, had as its principal representative James Edwin Creighton (1861–1924), who in 1892 succeeded J. G. Schurman[2] as head of the Sage School at Cornell University. In 1920 he became the first president of the American Philosophical Association. His principal articles were collected and published posthumously in 1925 with the title *Studies in Speculative Philosophy*.[3]

Creighton distinguishes two types of idealism. The first, which he calls mentalism, is simply the antithesis of materialism. While the materialist interprets the psychical as a function of the physical, the mentalist reduces material things to psychical phenomena, to states of consciousness or to ideas. And as the material world cannot without absurdity be reduced to any given finite individual's states of consciousness, the mentalist is in-evitably driven to postulate an absolute mind. The clearest example of this type of idealism is the philosophy of Berkeley. But there are variants, such as panpsychism.

The other main type of idealism is objective or speculative idealism, which does not attempt to reduce the physical to the psychical but regards Nature, the self and other selves as three distinct but co-ordinate and complementary moments or factors

---

[1] Obviously, what really needs to be shown is that metaphysical explanation is required at all. That empirical science cannot provide it is clear enough.

[2] Jack Gould Schurman (1854–1942), who became President of Cornell University in 1892, the same year in which he founded *The Philosophical Review*, believed that American culture was destined to prove the great mediator between East and West, and that idealism was peculiarly suited both to America and to the fulfilment of this task. Just as Kant mediated between rationalism and empiricism, so can speculative idealism mediate between the sciences and the arts. It has a synthesizing function in cultural life.

[3] Though not a prolific writer, Creighton's influence as a teacher was con-siderable. And he and his colleagues at Cornell were responsible for the philo-sophical education of a good many future American professors.

within experience. In other words, experience presents us with the ego, other selves and Nature as distinct and irreducible factors which are at the same time comprised within the unity of experience. And objective idealism attempts to work out the implications of this basic structure of experience.

For example, though Nature is irreducible to mind, the two are mutually related. Nature, therefore, cannot be simply heterogeneous to mind; it must be intelligible. And this means that though philosophy cannot do the work of the empirical sciences it is not committed merely to accepting the scientific account of Nature, without adding anything. Science puts Nature in the centre of the picture: philosophy exhibits it as a co-ordinate of experience, in its relation to spirit. This does not mean that the philosopher is competent to contradict, or even to call in question scientific discoveries. It means that it is his business to show the significance of the world as represented by the sciences in reference to the totality of experience. In other words, there is room for a philosophy of Nature.

Again, objective idealism is careful to avoid placing the ego in the centre of the picture by taking it as an ultimate point of departure and then trying to prove, for example, the existence of other selves. The objective idealist, while recognizing the distinction between individuals, recognizes also that there are no isolated individual selves apart from society. And he will study, for instance, the significance of morality, political institutions and religion as activities or products, as the case may be, of a society of selves within the human environment, namely Nature.

In conformity with these ideas, which have an obvious affinity with Hegelianism, the Cornell School of idealism emphasized the social aspect of thought. Instead of being divided up into as many systems as there are philosophers, philosophy should be, like science, a work of co-operation. For it is the reflection of spirit, existing in and through a society of selves, rather than of the individual thinker considered precisely as such.

5. Objective idealism, represented chiefly by Creighton, was associated with Cornell University. Another form of idealism, so-called dynamic idealism, was associated with the University of Michigan, where it was expounded by George Sylvester Morris (1840–89).[1] After having studied at Dartmouth College and the

---

[1] Another representative of this form of idealism at Michigan was the author of *Dynamic Idealism* (1898), Alfred Henry Lloyd.

Union Theological Seminary at New York, Morris passed some years in Germany, where he came under the influence of Trendelenburg[1] at Berlin. In 1870 he began to teach modern languages and literature at Michigan, and from 1878 he also lectured on ethics and the history of philosophy at Johns Hopkins University. Subsequently he became dean of the philosophical faculty at Michigan. His writings include *British Thought and Thinkers* (1880), *Philosophy and Christianity* (1883), and *Hegel's Philosophy of the State and of History: An Exposition* (1887). He also translated into English Ueberweg's *History of Philosophy* (1871-3), in the second volume of which he inserted an article on Trendelenburg.

Under the influence of Trendelenburg Morris placed in the forefront of his philosophy the Aristotelian idea of movement, that is, of the actualization of a potentiality, of the active expression of an entelechy. Life is obviously movement, energy; but thought too is a spontaneous activity, akin to other forms of natural energy. And it follows from this that the history of thought is not properly described as a dialectical development of abstract ideas or categories. Rather is it the expression of the activity of the spirit or mind. And philosophy is the science[2] of the mind as an active entelechy. That is to say, it is the science of experience in act or of lived experience.

To say that philosophy is the science of the activity of the spirit or mind, of experience in act, is not, however, to say that it has no connection with being. For the analysis of experience shows that subject and object, knowledge and being, are correlative terms. That which exists or has being is that which is known or knowable. It is that which falls within the potential field of active experience. And this is why we have to reject the Kantian Theory of the unknowable thing-in-itself, together with the phenomenalism which produces this theory.[3]

In his later years Morris moved closer to Hegel, whom he regarded as an 'objective empiricist', concerned with the integration of human experience by the reason. His most famous pupil was John Dewey, though Dewey came to abandon idealism for the instrumentalism associated with his name.

6. Idealism in America obviously owed much to the influence of

---

[1] See Vol. VII of this *History*, pp. 386-7.
[2] For Morris philosophy is as much a science as other sciences.
[3] That is to say, if we regard the object of knowledge as phenomena, in the sense of appearances of what does not itself appear, we are led inevitably to postulate unknowable things-in-themselves.

European thought. But equally obviously, it proved congenial to many minds and received a native stamp, which is shown above all perhaps in the emphasis so often placed on personality. It is not surprising, therefore, that American idealism was by no means simply a nineteenth-century phenomenon, due to the discovery of German thought and to influence from British idealism. It has shown a vigorous life in the present century.

Among the representatives of personal idealism in the first half of the twentieth century we can mention the names of Ralph Tyler Flewelling (1871–), for many years a Professor of Philosophy in the University of South California and founder of *The Personalist* in 1920,[1] Albert Cornelius Knudson (1873–1953)[2] and Edgar Sheffield Brightman (1884–1953), Bowne Professor of Philosophy in the University of Boston.[3] The titles of their publications provide abundant evidence of the continuation of that religious orientation of personalism which we have already had occasion to notice. But apart from the fact that it is so often religiously minded people who are attracted in the first instance to personal idealism, there is, as has been mentioned above, an intrinsic reason for the religious orientation of this line of thought. The basic tenet of personalism has been stated as the principle that reality has no meaning except in relation to persons; that the real is only in, of or for persons. In other words, reality consists of persons and their creations. It follows, therefore, that unless the personal idealist equates ultimate reality with the system of finite selves, as McTaggart did, he must be a theist. There is room, of course, for somewhat different conceptions of God. Brightman, for example, maintained that God is finite.[4] But a concern not only with philosophical theism but also with religion as a form of experience is a universal feature of American personal idealism.

This is not to say, however, that the personal idealists have been

[1] Among Flewelling's publications are *Personalism and The Problems of Philosophy* (1915), *The Reason in Faith* (1924), *Creative Personality* (1925) and *Personalism in Theology* (1943).
[2] Knudson is the author of *The Philosophy of Personalism* (1927), *The Doctrine of God* (1930), and *The Validity of Religious Experience* (1937).
[3] Brightman published among other writings, *Religious Values* (1925), *A Philosophy of Ideals* (1928), *The Problem of God* (1930), *Is God a Person?* (1932), *Moral Laws* (1933), *Personality and Religion* (1934), *A Philosophy of Religion* (1940), and *The Spiritual Life* (1942).
[4] Brightman argues, for instance, that the 'waste' involved in the process of evolution suggests the idea of a finite God who meets with opposition. Again, the divine reason sets limits to the divine will and power. Further, there is in God a 'given' element which he progressively masters. But where this 'given' element comes from is left obscure.

concerned only with the defence of a religious outlook. For they have also devoted their attention to the subject of values, connecting them closely with the idea of the self-realization or development of personality. And this in turn has reacted on the theory of education, emphasis being laid on moral development and the cultivation of personal values. Finally, in political theory this type of idealism, with its insistence on freedom and on respect for the person as such, has been sharply opposed to totalitarianism and a strong advocate of democracy.

Evolutionary idealism has been represented in the first half of the present century by John Elof Boodin (1869–1950).[1] The main idea of this type of idealism is familiar enough, namely that in the evolutionary process we can see the emergence of successively higher levels of development through the creative activity of an immanent principle, the nature of which should be interpreted in the light of its higher rather than of its lower products.[2] In other words, evolutionary idealism substitutes for a purely mechanistic conception of evolution, based on laws relating to the redistribution of energy, a teleological conception according to which mechanical processes take place within a general creative movement tending towards an ideal goal.[3] Thus Boodin distinguishes between different interacting levels or fields in the evolutionary process or processes, in each of which there are interacting individual systems of energy. These levels or fields range from the primary physico-chemical level up to the ethical-social level. And the all-inclusive field is the divine creative spirit, 'the spiritual field in which everything lives and moves and has its being'.[4]

Evolutionary idealism does not indeed deny the value of human personality. For Boodin the human spirit participates in the divine creativity by the realization of values. At the same time, inasmuch as the evolutionary idealist fixes his attention chiefly on

[1] Author of *Time and Reality* (1904), *Truth and Reality* (1911), *A Realistic Universe* (1916), *Cosmic Evolution* (1925), *God and Creation* (2 volumes, 1934), and *Religion of Tomorrow* (1943).

[2] In distinguishing between 'lower' and 'higher' judgments of value obviously play an important part.

[3] It would, however, be a mistake to suppose that all philosophers who believe in creative evolution have postulated a fixed, preconceived goal or *telos* of the evolutionary process. Indeed, unless the creative agent is conceived in a recognizably theistic manner, such a postulate is inappropriate.

[4] *God and Creation*, II, p. 34. According to Boodin, God, as conceived according to his intrinsic essence, is eternal; but from another point of view, namely when he is considered as the creative activity comprising the whole history of the cosmos, he is temporal.

the total cosmic process rather than on the finite self,[1] he is more inclined than the personal idealist to a pantheistic conception of God. And this tendency is verified in the case of Boodin.

Absolute idealism has been continued in the present century by the well-known philosopher William Ernest Hocking (b. 1873), a pupil of Royce and William James at Harvard and later Alford Professor of Philosophy in that University.[2] At the level of common sense, Hocking argues, physical objects and other minds appear as entities which are purely external to myself. And it is at this level that the question arises how we come to know that there are other minds or other selves. But reflection shows us that there is an underlying social consciousness which is as real as self-consciousness. In fact they are interdependent. After all, the very attempt to prove that there are other minds presupposes an awareness of them. And further reflection, Hocking maintains, together with intuitive insight, reveals to us the presence of the enveloping divine reality which renders human consciousness possible. That is to say, our participation in social consciousness involves an implicit awareness of God and is in some sense an experience of the divine, of absolute mind. Hence the ontological argument can be stated in this way: 'I have an idea of God, therefore I have an experience of God'.[3]

We have noted that Hocking was a pupil of Royce. And like his former professor he insists that God is personal, a self. For 'there is nothing higher than selfhood and nothing more profound'.[4] At the same time he insists that we cannot abandon the concept of the Absolute. And this means that we must conceive God as in some sense including within himself the world of finite selves and the world of Nature. Indeed, just as the human self, taken apart from its life of experience, is empty, so is the concept of God an empty concept if he is considered apart from his life of absolute experience. 'The domain of religion in fact is a divine self, a Spirit which is as Subject to all finite things, persons and arts as Object,

---

[1] The personal idealist is not, of course, committed to denying the hypothesis of evolution. But he takes the idea of personality as his point of departure and as the fixed point, as one might put it, in his reflections, whereas the evolutionary idealist emphasizes the aspect of the person as a product of a general creative activity immanent in the whole cosmos.

[2] Hocking's writings include *The Meaning of God in Human Experience* (1912), *Human Nature and Its Remaking* (1918), *Man and the State* (1926), *The Self, Its Body and Freedom* (1928), *Lasting Elements of Individualism* (1937), *Thoughts on Life and Death* (1937), *Living Religions and a World Faith* (1940), *Science and the Idea of God* (1944) and *Experiment in Education* (1954).

[3] *The Meaning of God in Human Experience*, p. 314.

[4] *Types of Philosophy*, p. 441.

and presumably to much else that these categories do not include.'[1] The world is thus necessary to God, though at the same time we can conceive it as created. For Nature is in fact an expression of the divine mind, as well as the means by which finite selves communicate with one another and pursue common ideals. In addition to the scientific view of Nature, which treats Nature as a self-contained whole, we need the concept of it as a divine communication to the finite self. As for the divine essence in itself, it transcends the grasp of discursive thought, though mystical experience yields a valid insight.

With Hocking, therefore, as with Royce, we find a form of personalistic absolute idealism. He tries to find a middle position between a theism which would reduce God to the level of being a self among selves, a person among persons, and an absolute idealism which would leave no room for the concept of God as personal. And this desire to find a middle position is shown in Hocking's treatment of religion. On the one hand he dislikes the tendency, shown by some philosophers, to offer as the alleged essence of religion a concept which abstracts from all historical religion. On the other hand he rejects the notion of one particular historical faith becoming the world-faith by displacing all others. And though he attributes to Christianity a unique contribution to the recognition of the ultimate personal structure of reality, he looks to a process of dialogue between the great historical religions to produce, by a convergent movement, the world-faith of the future.

We have already had occasion more than once to note the concern of American idealists with religious problems. It is hardly an exaggeration to say that with some of the personal idealists, such as Bowne, philosophy was practically used as an apologetic in defence of the Christian religion. In the case of personalistic absolute idealism,[2] however, as with Hocking, it is more a question of developing a religious view of the world and of suggesting a religious vision for the future than of defending a particular historical religion. And this is clearly more in line with W. T. Harris's programme for speculative philosophy. For Harris assumed that traditional doctrines and ecclesiastical organization were in process of losing their grip on men's minds, that a new

[1] *Human Nature and Its Remaking*, p. 329.
[2] The line of thought of Royce and Hocking is sometimes described as absolutistic personalism in distinction from the pluralistic personalism of Bowne and other 'personal idealists'.

religious outlook was needed, and that it was part of the business of speculative philosophy or metaphysical idealism to meet this need. At the same time idealism does not necessarily involve either the defence of an already existing religion or positive preparation for a new one. It is, of course, natural to expect of the metaphysical idealist some interest in religion or at least an explicit recognition of its importance in human life. For he aims, in general, at a synthesis of human experience, and in particular, at doing justice to those forms of experience which the materialist and positivist tend either to belittle or to exclude from the scope of philosophy. But it would be a mistake to think that idealism is necessarily so connected either with Christian faith or with the mystical outlook of a philosopher such as Hocking that it is inseparable from profoundly held religious convictions. A preoccupation with religious problems was not a characteristic of the objective idealism of Creighton; nor is it a characteristic of the thought of Brand Blanshard (b. 1892), Sterling Professor of Philosophy at Yale, the twentieth-century American idealist who is best known in Great Britain.[1]

In his notable two-volume work, *The Nature of Thought* (1939–40), Blanshard devotes himself to critical analyses of interpretations of thought and knowledge which he considers false or inadequate and to a defence of reason conceived primarily as the discovery of necessary connections. He rejects the restriction of necessity to purely formal propositions and its reduction to convention, and he represents the movement of thought as being towards the logical ideal of an all-inclusive system of interdependent truths. In other words, he maintains a version of the coherence theory of truth. Similarly, in *Reason and Analysis* (1962) Blanshard devotes himself on the negative side to a sustained criticism of the analytic philosophy of the last forty years, including logical positivism, logical atomism and the so-called linguistic movement, and on the positive side to an exposition and defence of the function of reason as he conceives it. True, he has given two series of Gifford Lectures. But in *Reason and Goodness* (1961), which represents the first series, the emphasis is laid on vindicating the function of reason in ethics, as against, for example, the emotive theory of ethics, certainly not on edification, either moral or religious.[2]

[1] Blanshard studied at Oxford, and he is regarded as carrying on the tradition of Oxford idealism.
[2] The second volume has not appeared at the time of writing.

These remarks are not intended either as commendation or as criticism of Blanshard's freedom from the preoccupation with religious problems and from the tone of uplift which have been conspicuous features of many of the publications of American idealists. The point is rather that the example of Blanshard shows that idealism is able to make out a good case for itself and to deal shrewd blows at its enemies without exhibiting the features which in the eyes of some of its critics rule it out of court from the start, as though by its very nature it served extra-philosophical interests. After all, Hegel himself deprecated any confusion between philosophy and uplift and rejected appeals to mystical insights.

7. In Marxist terminology idealism is commonly opposed to materialism, as involving respectively the assertion of the ultimate priority of mind or spirit to matter and the assertion of the ultimate priority of matter to mind or spirit. And if idealism is understood in this way, no synthesis of the opposites is possible. For the essential dispute is not about the reality of either mind or matter. It is about the question of ultimate priority. And both cannot be ultimately prior at the same time.

Generally, however, idealism is contrasted with realism. It is by no means always clear how these terms are being understood. And in any case their meanings can vary with different contexts. But an attempt has been made by an American philosopher, Wilbur Marshall Urban (b. 1873),[1] to show that idealism and realism are ultimately based on certain judgments of value about the conditions of genuine knowledge, and that these judgments can be dialectically harmonized. He does not mean, of course, that opposed philosophical systems can be conflated. He means that the basic judgments on which idealist and realist philosophies ultimately rest can be so interpreted that it is possible to transcend the opposition between idealism and realism.

The realist, Urban maintains, believes that there cannot be genuine knowledge unless things are in some sense independent of mind. In other words, he asserts the priority of being to knowledge. The idealist, however, believes that there can be no genuine knowledge unless things are in some sense dependent on mind. For their intelligibility is bound up with this dependence. At first sight, therefore, realism and idealism are incompatible, the first

[1] Urban is the author of, among other writings, *Valuation: Its Nature and Laws* (1909), *The Intelligible World: Metaphysics and Value* (1929), *Language and Reality* (1939) and *Beyond Realism and Idealism* (1949). In the present context the relevant work is the last-named one.

asserting the priority of being to thought and knowledge, the second asserting the priority of thought to being. But if we consider the basic judgments of value, we can see the possibility of overcoming the opposition between them. For example, the realist claim that knowledge cannot be described as genuine knowledge of reality unless things are in some sense independent of mind can be satisfied provided that we are willing to admit that things are not dependent simply on the human mind, while the idealist claim that knowledge cannot be described as genuine knowledge of reality unless things are in some sense mind-dependent can be satisfied if it is assumed that the reality on which on all finite things ultimately depend is spirit or mind.

It seems to the present writer that there is a great deal of truth in this point of view. Absolute idealism, by rejecting the claim of subjective idealism that the human mind can know only its own states of consciousness, goes a long way towards meeting the realist's claim that genuine knowledge of reality is not possible unless the object of knowledge is in some real sense independent of the subject. And a realism that is prepared to describe ultimate reality as spirit or mind goes a long way towards meeting the idealist claim that nothing is intelligible unless it is either spirit or the self-expression of spirit. At the same time the dialectical harmonization of opposed views, which Urban has in mind, seems to demand certain stipulations. We have to stipulate, for example, that the idealist should cease talking like Royce, who uses the word 'being' for the expression of will and purpose, for the embodiment of the internal meaning of an idea, and should recognize that will is itself a form of being. In fact, to reach agreement with the realist he must, it appears, recognize the priority of existence; *prius est esse quam esse tale*. If, however, he admits this, he has to all intents and purposes been converted to realism. We also have to stipulate, of course, that realism should not be understood as equivalent to materialism. But then many realists would insist that realism in no way entails materialism.

The ideal of transcending the traditional oppositions in philosophy is understandable, and doubtless laudable. But there is this point to consider. If we interpret realism in terms of basic judgments of value about the conditions of genuine knowledge, we have implicitly adopted a certain approach to philosophy. We are approaching philosophy by way of the theme of knowledge, by way of the subject-object relationship. And many philosophers who are customarily labelled realists doubtless do this. We speak, for example, of realist theories of knowledge. But some realists would claim that they take as their point of departure being, particularly in the sense of existence, and that their approach is recognizably different from that of the idealist, and that it is the different approaches to philosophy which determine the different views of knowledge.

PART IV

THE PRAGMATIST MOVEMENT

CHAPTER XIV
THE PHILOSOPHY OF C. S. PEIRCE

The life of Peirce—The objectivity of truth—Rejection of the method of universal doubt—Logic, ideas and the pragmatist analysis of meaning—Pragmatism and realism—The pragmatist analysis of meaning and positivism—Ethics, pure and practical—Peirce's metaphysics and world-view—Some comments on Peirce's thought.

1. ALTHOUGH it is possible to find pragmatist ideas in the writings of some other thinkers,[1] the originator of the pragmatist movement in America was to all intents and purposes Charles Sanders Peirce (1839–1914). To be sure, the term 'pragmatism' is associated chiefly with the name of William James. For James's style as lecturer and writer and his obvious concern with general problems of interest to reflective minds quickly brought him before the public eye and kept him there, whereas during his lifetime Peirce was little known or appreciated as a philosopher. But both James and Dewey recognized their indebtedness to Peirce. And after his death Peirce's reputation has steadily increased, even if, by the nature of his thought, he remains very much a philosopher's philosopher.

Peirce was the son of a Harvard mathematician and astronomer, Benjamin Peirce (1809–80), and his own formal education culminated in the chemistry degree which he received at Harvard in 1863. From 1861 until 1891 he was on the staff of the United States Coast and Geodetic Survey, though from 1869 he was also associated for some years with the Harvard Observatory. And the one book which he published, *Photometric Researches* (1878), embodied the results of a series of astronomical observations which he had made.

In the academic years of 1864–5 and 1869–70 Peirce lectured at

---

[1] See, for example, *Chauncey Wright and the Foundations of Pragmatism* by E. H. Madden (Seattle, 1963).

Harvard on the early history of modern science, and in 1870–1 on logic.[1] From 1879 until 1884 he was a lecturer on logic at Johns Hopkins University; but for various reasons his appointment was not renewed.[2] And he never again held any regular academic post, in spite of William James's efforts on his behalf.

In 1887 Peirce settled with his second wife in Pennsylvania and tried to make ends meet by writing reviews and articles for dictionaries. He wrote indeed a great deal, but apart from a few articles his work remained unpublished until the posthumous publication of his *Collected Papers*, six volumes appearing in 1931–5 and two further volumes in 1958.

Peirce did not approve of the way in which William James was developing the theory of pragmatism, and in 1905 he changed the name of his own theory from pragmatism to pragmaticism, remarking that the term was ugly enough to render it secure from kidnappers. At the same time he appreciated the friendship of James, who did what he could to put remunerative work in the way of the neglected and poverty-stricken philosopher. Peirce died of cancer in 1914.

2. It is probably correct to say that in the minds of most people for whom the word 'pragmatism' has any definite meaning, it is associated primarily with a certain view of the nature of truth, namely with the doctrine that a theory is to be accounted true in so far as it 'works', in so far, for example, as it is socially useful or fruitful. It is therefore just as well to understand from the outset that the essence of Peirce's pragmatism or pragmaticism lies in a theory of meaning rather than in a theory of truth. This theory of meaning will be examined presently. Meanwhile we can consider briefly what Peirce has to say about truth. And it will be seen that whether or not the identification of truth with 'what works' represents the real view of William James, it certainly does not represent that of Peirce.

Peirce distinguishes different kinds of truth. There is, for example, what he calls transcendental truth, which belongs to

---

[1] In 1868 Peirce published some articles in *The Journal of Speculative Philosophy* on certain alleged faculties of the human mind, such as that of recognizing intuitively, without the need of any previous knowledge, the premisses which constitute the absolute points of departure for reasoning.

[2] The fact that in 1883 Peirce divorced his first wife and subsequently remarried probably contributed to the termination of his appointment at Johns Hopkins. But there appear to have been other factors too, such as the offence which he sometimes gave by intemperate expressions of moral indignation and his lack of conformity on some points with the requirements of academic life.

things as things.[1] And if we say that science is looking for truth in this sense, we mean that it is inquiring into the real characters of things, the characters which they have whether we know that they have them or not. But here we are concerned with what Peirce calls complex truth, which is the truth of propositions. This again can be subdivided. There is, for example, ethical truth or veracity, which lies in the conformity of a proposition with the speaker's or writer's belief. And there is logical truth, the conformity of a proposition with reality in a sense which must now be defined.

'When we speak of truth and falsity, we refer to the possibility of the proposition being refuted.'[2] That is to say, if we could legitimately deduce from a proposition a conclusion which would conflict with an immediate perceptual judgment, the proposition would be false. In other words, a proposition would be false if experience would refute it. If experience would not refute a proposition, the proposition is true.

This may suggest that for Peirce truth and verification are the same thing. But reflection will show that he is perfectly justified in rejecting this identification. For he is saying, not that a proposition is true if it is empirically verified, but that it is true if it would not be empirically falsified, supposing that such a testing were possible. In point of fact it may not be possible. But we can still say that a proposition is false if, to put it crudely, it *would* conflict with reality as revealed in experience if a confrontation were possible, and that otherwise it is true. Peirce can therefore say without inconsistency that 'every proposition is either *true* or *false*'.[3]

Now, there are some propositions which could not conceivably be refuted. Such, for example, are the propositions of pure mathematics. Hence on the interpretation of truth mentioned above the truth of a proposition in pure mathematics lies in 'the impossibility of ever finding a case in which it fails'.[4] Peirce sometimes writes in a rather disconcerting way about mathematics. He says, for instance, that the pure mathematician deals exclusively with hypotheses which are the products of his own imagination, and that no proposition becomes a statement of pure mathematics 'until it is devoid of all definite meaning'.[5] But

---

[1] Peirce refers in this context to the Scholastic maxim that every being is one, true and good.
[2] 5.569. References are given in the customary way to volume and numbered paragraph of the *Collected Papers of Charles Sanders Peirce*.
[3] 2.327.   [4] 5.567.   [5] *Ibid.*

'meaning' has to be understood here in the sense of reference. A proposition of pure mathematics does not say anything about actual things:[1] the pure mathematician, as Peirce puts it, does not care whether or not there are real things corresponding to his signs. And this absence of 'meaning' is, of course, the reason why the propositions of pure mathematics cannot possibly be refuted and so are necessarily true.

There are other propositions, however, of which we do not know with absolute certainty whether they are true or false. These are what Leibniz calls truths of fact, in distinctions from truths of reason. And they include, for example, scientific hypotheses and metaphysical theories about reality. In the case of a proposition which cannot possibly be refuted we know that it is true.[2] But a scientific hypothesis can *be* true without our knowing that it is. And in point of fact we cannot know with certainty that it is true. For while empirical refutation shows that an hypothesis is false, what we call verification does not prove that an hypothesis is true, though it certainly provides a ground for accepting it provisionally. If from hypothesis x it is legitimately deduced that in certain circumstances event y should occur, and if in these circumstances y does not occur, we can conclude that x is false. But the occurrence of y does not prove with certainty that x is true. For it may be the case, for example, that the conclusion that in the same set of circumstances event y should occur, can be deduced from hypothesis z, which on other grounds is preferable to x. Scientific hypotheses can enjoy varying degrees of probability, but they are all subject to possible revision. In fact all formulations of what passes for human knowledge are uncertain, fallible.[3]

It should not be necessary to add that Peirce's principle of fallibilism does not entail a denial of objective truth. Scientific inquiry is inspired by a disinterested search for objective truth. Nobody would ask a theoretical question unless he believed that there was such a thing as truth. And 'truth consists in a conformity of something *independent of his thinking it to be so*, or of

---

[1] The question whether it concerns a realm of possibility, as contrasted with actuality, is a question for the metaphysician.
[2] Peirce remarks that an entirely meaningless proposition is to be classed with true propositions, because it cannot be refuted. But he adds the saving provision, 'if it be called a proposition at all' (2.327).
[3] When asked whether his principle of fallibilism, as it is called, the assertion that all assertions are uncertain, is itself fallible or infallible, uncertain or certain, Peirce answers that he does not intend to claim that his assertion is absolutely certain. This may be logical, but it involves a certain weakening of his position.

any man's opinion on that subject'.[1] But if we combine the idea
of the disinterested search for objective truth, known as such,
with the principle of fallibilism, according to which dogmatism is
the enemy of the pursuit of truth, we must conceive absolute and
final truth as the ideal goal of inquiry. This ideal stands eternally
above our struggles to attain it, and we can only approximate
to it.

Truth, therefore, can be defined from different points of view.
From one point of view truth can be taken to mean 'the Universe
of all Truth'.[2] 'All propositions refer to one and the same determinately singular subject . . . namely, to The Truth, which is the
universe of all universes, and is assumed on all hands to be real.'[3]
From an epistemological point of view, however, truth can be
defined as 'that concordance of an abstract statement with the
ideal limit towards which endless investigation would tend to
bring scientific belief'.[4]

If such passages recall to our minds the idealist notion of truth
as the whole, the total system of truth, rather than anything
which would normally be associated with the term 'pragmatism',
there is nothing to be surprised at in this. For Peirce openly
acknowledged points of similarity between his own philosophy and
that of Hegel.

3. In regard to the pursuit of truth Peirce rejects the Cartesian
thesis that we should begin by doubting everything until we can
find an indubitable and presuppositionless point of departure. In
the first place we cannot doubt simply at will. Real or genuine
doubt arises when some experience, external or internal,
clashes or appears to clash with one of our beliefs. And when this
occurs, we undertake further inquiry with a view to overcoming
the state of doubt, either by re-establishing our former belief on a
firmer basis or by substituting for it a better-grounded belief.
Doubt is thus a stimulus to inquiry, and in this sense it has a
positive value. But to doubt the truth of a proposition, we must
have a reason for doubting the truth of *this* proposition or of a
proposition on which it depends. Any attempt to apply the method
of universal doubt simply leads to pretended or fictitious doubt.
And this is not genuine doubt at all.

Peirce is obviously thinking in the first place of scientific
inquiry. But he applies his ideas in a quite general way. We all
start with certain beliefs, with what Hume called natural beliefs.

And the philosopher will indeed try to make explicit our un-criticized natural beliefs and subject them to critical scrutiny. But even he cannot doubt them at will: he requires a reason for doubting the truth of this or that particular belief. And if he has or thinks that he has such a reason, he will also find that his very doubt presupposes some other belief or beliefs. In other words, we cannot have, nor do we need, an absolutely presuppositionless point of departure. Cartesian universal doubt is not genuine doubt at all. 'For genuine doubt does not talk of beginning with doubting.'[1] The follower of Descartes would presumably reply that he is primarily concerned with 'methodic' rather than with 'real' or 'genuine' doubt. But Peirce's point is that methodic doubt, in so far as it is distinguishable from genuine doubt, is not really doubt at all. Either we have a reason for doubting or we do not. In the first case the doubt is genuine. In the second case we have only pretended or fictitious doubt.

If we bear in mind this point of view, we can understand Peirce's claim that 'the scientific spirit requires a man to be at all times ready to dump his whole cartload of beliefs, the moment experience is against them'.[2] He is obviously speaking of theoretical beliefs, which are characterized above all by expectation. If a man holds belief x, he believes, for example, that in certain circumstances event y should occur. And if it does not occur, he will, of course, doubt the truth of the belief. Antecedently to a clash between experience and belief, anyone who possesses the scientific spirit will be prepared to abandon any belief about the world if such a clash should occur. For, as we have already seen, he regards all such beliefs as subject to possible revision. But it by no means follows from this that he will begin or should begin with universal doubt.

4. Pragmatism, as Peirce conceives it, is 'not a *Weltanschauung* but is a method of reflection having for its purpose to render ideas clear'.[3] It belongs, therefore, to methodology, to what Peirce calls 'methodeutic'. And as he emphasizes the logical foundations and connections of pragmatism, it is appropriate to say something first about his account of logic.

Peirce divides logic into three main parts, the first of which is speculative grammar. This is concerned with the formal conditions of the meaningfulness of signs. A sign, called by Peirce a 'representamen', stands for an object to someone in whom it arouses a

[1] 6.498.   [2] 1.55.   [3] 5.13, note.

more developed sign, the 'interpretant'. A sign stands, of course, for an object in respect of certain 'characters', and this respect is called the 'ground'. But we can say that the relation of significance or the semiotic function of signs is for Peirce a triadic relation between representamen, object and interpretant.[1]

The second main division of logic, critical logic, is concerned with the formal conditions of the truth of symbols. Under this heading Peirce treats of the syllogism or argument, which can be divided into deductive, inductive and 'abductive' argument. Inductive argument, which is statistical in character, assumes that what is true of a number of members of a class is true of all members of the class. And it is in connection with induction that Peirce considers the theory of probability. Abductive argument is predictive in character. That is to say, it formulates an hypothesis from observed facts and deduces what should be the case if the hypothesis is true. And we can then test the prediction. When looked at from one point of view, Royce tells us, pragmatism can be described as the logic of abduction. The force of this remark will become clear presently.

The third main division of logic, speculative rhetoric, deals with what Peirce calls the formal conditions of the force of symbols or 'the general conditions of the reference of Symbols and other Signs to the Interpretants which they aim to determine'.[2] In communication a sign arouses another sign, the interpretant, in an interpreter. Peirce insists that the interpreter is not necessarily a human being. And as he wishes to avoid psychology as much as possible, he lays emphasis on the interpretant rather than on the interpreter. In any case it simplifies matters if we think of a sign arousing a sign in a person. We can then see that speculative rhetoric will be concerned in large measure with the theory of meaning. For meaning is 'the intended interpretant of a symbol'.[3] Whether we are speaking of a term, a proposition or an argument, its meaning is the entire intended interpretant. And as pragmatism is for Peirce a method or rule for determining meaning, it obviously belongs to or is closely connected with speculative rhetoric, which is also called 'methodeutic'.

More precisely, pragmatism is a method or rule for making ideas clear, for determining the meaning of ideas. But there are

---

[1] Under the general heading of speculative grammar Peirce also considers terms, propositions and the fundamental principles of logic, those of identity, non-contradiction and excluded middle.
[2] 2.93.   [3] 5.175.

different types of ideas.[1] First, there is the idea of a percept or sense-datum considered in itself, without relation to anything else. Such would be the idea of blueness or of redness. In Peirce's terminology this is the idea of a 'firstness'. Secondly, there is the idea of acting which involves two objects, namely the agent and the patient or that which is acted upon. This is the idea of a 'secondness'.[2] Thirdly, there is the idea of a sign relation, of a sign signifying to an interpreter that a certain property belongs to a certain object or, rather, to a certain kind of object. This is an idea of a 'thirdness'. And such ideas, which can be thought of as universal ideas, are called by Peirce intellectual concepts or conceptions.[3] In practice pragmatism is a method or rule for determining their meaning.

Peirce formulates the principle of pragmatism in several ways. One of the best known is as follows. *'In order to ascertain the meaning of an intellectual conception one should consider what practical consequences might conceivably result by necessity from the truth of that conception; and the sum of these consequences will constitute the entire meaning of the conception.'*[4] For example, suppose that someone tells me that a certain kind of object is hard, and suppose that I do not know what the word 'hard' means. It can be explained to me that to say that an object is hard means, among other things, that if one exerts moderate pressure on it, it does not give in the way that butter does; that if someone sits on it, he does not sink through; and so on. And the sum total of 'practical consequences' which necessarily follow if it is true to say that an object is hard, gives the entire meaning of the concept. If I do not believe this, I have only to exclude all such 'practical consequences' from the meaning of the term. I shall then see that it becomes impossible to distinguish between the meanings of 'hard' and 'soft'.

Now, if we understand Peirce as saying that the meaning of an intellectual concept is reducible to the ideas of certain sense-data,

---

[1] Strictly speaking, the theory of ideas belongs to epistemology. But Peirce insists that it is grounded on the logic of relations. And he emphasizes the relevance of the theory to pragmatism.

[2] As in human experience acting involves an act of the will, Peirce tends to speak of this type of idea as the idea of a volition. In any case he insists that an idea of a 'secondness' cannot be simply reduced to ideas of 'firstness'. If, for example, we try to reduce the idea of the wind moving the blind to simpler ideas of sense-data, taken separately, the whole idea of acting disappears.

[3] In theory at least Peirce distinguishes between 'idea' and 'concept', a universal idea being subjectively apprehended in an intellectual concept.

[4] 5.9.

we shall have to conclude that he is contradicting his assertion that intellectual concepts are not reducible to ideas of 'firstness'. And if we understand him as saying that the meaning of an intellectual concept is reducible to the ideas of certain actions, we shall have to conclude that he is contradicting his assertion that such concepts are not reducible to ideas of 'secondness'. But he is saying neither the one nor the other. His view is that the meaning of an intellectual concept can be explicated in terms of the ideas of necessary relations between ideas of secondness and ideas of firstness, between, that is to say, ideas of volition or action and ideas of perception. As he explains, when he talks about 'consequences', he is referring to the relation (*consequentia*) between a consequent and an antecedent, not simply about the consequent (*consequens*).

From this analysis it obviously follows that the meaning of an intellectual concept has a relation to conduct. For the conditional propositions in which the meaning is explicated are concerned with conduct. But, equally obviously, Peirce is not suggesting that in order to understand or to explain the meaning of an intellectual concept we have actually to do something, to perform certain actions mentioned in the explication of the meaning. I can explain to an interpreter the meaning of 'hard' by causing to arise in his mind the idea that if he were to perform a certain action in regard to the object which is described as hard, he *would* have a certain experience. It is not required that he should actually perform the action before he can understand what 'hard' means. It is not even necessary that the action should be practicable, provided that it is conceivable. In other words, the meaning of an intellectual concept is explicable in terms of conditional propositions; but, for the meaning to be understood, it is not necessary that the conditions should be actually fulfilled. It is only necessary that they should be conceived.

It is to be noted that this theory of meaning does not contradict Peirce's view, which has been mentioned above, that we must distinguish between truth and verification. If, for example, I say that a given object has weight, and if I explain that this means that in the absence of an opposing force it will fall, the fulfilment of the conditional proposition is said to verify my statement. But to verify means to show that a proposition is true, that is, that it is true antecedently to any verification, true independently of any action performed by me or by anyone else.

5. Although it involves touching on ontology, it is convenient at this point to draw attention to Peirce's conviction that the pragmatist theory of meaning demands the rejection of nominalism and the acceptance of realism. An intellectual concept is a universal concept; and its meaning is explicated in conditional propositions. These conditional propositions are in principle verifiable. And the possibility of verification shows that some at least of the propositions which explicate the meaning of intellectual concepts express something in reality which is so independently of its being expressed in a judgment. For example, a statement such as 'iron is hard' is a prediction: if x, then y. And regularly successful or verified prediction shows that there must be something real now, of a general nature, which accounts for a future actuality. This something real now is for Peirce a real possibility. He compares it to the essence or common nature in the philosophy of Duns Scotus;[1] but for him it has a relational structure, expressed in the conditional proposition which explicates the meaning of a universal concept. Hence he calls it a 'law'. Universal concepts, therefore, have an objective foundation or counterpart in reality, namely 'laws'.

We have been speaking of ideas of thirdness. But Peirce's realism can also be seen in his account of ideas of firstness. The idea of white, for example, has its objective counterpart in reality, namely, not simply white things but whiteness, an essence. Whiteness as such does not indeed exist as an actuality. Only white things exist in this way. But for Peirce whiteness is a real possibility. From the epistemological point of view it is the real possibility of an idea, an idea of a firstness.[2]

In general, human knowledge and science demand as a necessary condition the existence of a realm of real possibilities, 'essences', of a general nature. Hence we cannot accept the nominalist thesis that generality belongs only to words in their function as standing for a plurality of individual entities.[3]

6. When we read the formulation of the pragmatist principle

[1] Peirce's realism was not derived from Scotus, but it was to a great extent developed through reflection on and a transformation of the doctrine of the mediaeval Franciscan, or of what Peirce believed to be his doctrine. Indeed, on occasion Peirce even called himself a 'Scotistic realist'. On this subject see *Charles Peirce and Scholastic Realism: A Study of Peirce's Relation to John Duns Scotus*, by John F. Boler (Seattle, 1963).

[2] The 'essence' of whiteness is embodied in an idea through the power of attention, which is said to 'abstract' it.

[3] What Peirce calls 'realism' is not what everyone would understand by the term. But we are concerned here with his use of the word.

which is quoted in the fourth section of this chapter,[1] we are naturally put in mind of the neopositivist criterion of meaning. But in order to be able to discuss the relation between Peirce's theory of meaning and positivism, we have first to make some distinctions with a view to clarifying the issue.

In the first place, when Peirce himself talks about positivism, he is speaking, needless to say, of classical positivism as represented, for example, by Auguste Comte and Karl Pearson. And while he allows that positivism in this sense has been of service to science, he also explicitly attacks some features which he finds in it or at any rate attributes to it. For instance, he attributes to Comte the view that a genuine hypothesis must be practically verifiable by direct observation; and he proceeds to reject this view, on the ground that for an hypothesis to be meaningful it is required only that we should be able to *conceive* its practical consequences, not that it should be practically verifiable. Again, Peirce refuses to allow that nothing except what is directly observable should be postulated in an hypothesis. For in an hypothesis we infer the future, a 'will be' or 'would be', and a 'would be' is certainly not directly observable.[2] Further, it is a mistake to regard hypotheses as being simply fictional devices for stimulating observation. An hypothesis can have, for example, an initial probability, as being the result of legitimate inference. In general, therefore, Peirce regards the positivists as too preoccupied with the process of practical verification and as being far too quick to say that this or that is inconceivable.

We cannot, however, infer without more ado from Peirce's criticism of Comte and Pearson that his theory of meaning has nothing in common with neopositivism (or logical positivism as it is generally called in England). For though the neopositivists were originally given to identifying the meaning of an empirical hypothesis with its mode of verification, they did not intend to imply that its meaning can be identified with the actual process of verification. They identified the meaning with the *idea* of the mode of verification, considered, in Peirce's terminology, as the practical consequences of the hypothesis. Further, they did not insist that an hypothesis should be directly verifiable, in order to

---

[1] P. 311.

[2] Obviously, when a prediction is fulfilled, the result may be directly observable. But Peirce's point is that a scientific hypothesis states what *would* be the case *if* a condition were fulfilled, and that a 'would be' is not, *as such*, directly observable.

be meaningful. It is not the intention of the present writer to express agreement with the neopositivist criterion of meaning. In point of fact he does not agree with it. But this is irrelevant. The relevant point is that the theory of meaning expounded by the neopositivists escapes at any rate some of the criticisms which Peirce levelled, whether fairly or unfairly, against positivism as he knew it.

It must also be emphasized that the question is not whether Peirce was or was not a positivist. For it is perfectly clear that he was not. As will be seen presently, he sketched a metaphysics which under some aspects at least bore a resemblance to Hegelian absolute idealism. The question is rather whether the neopositivists are justified in looking on Peirce as a predecessor, not only in the sense that his 'pragmaticist' analysis of meaning has a clear affinity to their own but also in the sense that genuine consistency with his theory of meaning would have ruled out the sort of metaphysics which he in fact developed. In other words, once given his theory of meaning, ought Peirce to have been a positivist? That is to say, ought he to have anticipated neopositivism to a much great extent than was in fact the case?

In his well-known paper on *How to make our ideas clear* Peirce asserts that 'the essence of belief is the establishment of a habit; and different beliefs are distinguished by the different modes of action to which they give rise'.[1] If there is no difference at all between the lines of conduct or action to which two *prima facie* different beliefs give rise, they are not two beliefs but one.

It is easy to think of a simple example. If one man says that he believes that there are other persons besides himself while another man says that he believes the opposite, and if we find them acting in precisely the same way by talking with others, questioning them, listening to them, writing them letters and so on, we naturally conclude that, whatever he may say, the second man really has exactly the same belief as the first man, namely that there are other persons besides himself.

Peirce applies this idea to the alleged difference in belief between Catholics and Protestants in regard to the Eucharist,[2] maintaining that as there is no difference in action or conduct

---

[1] 5.398.
[2] The term 'Protestant' in this context is ambiguous. For there is no one belief about the Eucharist which can be called *the* Protestant belief. But Peirce obviously has in mind those who deny the real presence of Christ in the Sacrament, and, more particularly, those who deny a change which justifies the statement that the consecrated bread and wine *are* the Body and Blood of Christ.

between the two parties, there cannot be any real difference in belief. At first sight at any rate this thesis appears to be in flat contradiction with the facts. For example, practising Catholics genuflect before the Blessed Sacrament, pray before the Tabernacle in which the Blessed Sacrament is reserved, and so on, while the Protestants whom Peirce has in mind do not, for the very good reason that they do not believe in the 'real presence'. But closer inspection of what Peirce says on the subject shows that he is really arguing that Catholics and Protestants have the same expectations in regard to the sensible effects of the Sacrament. For, irrespective of their theological beliefs, both parties expect, for example, that consumption of the consecrated bread will have the same physical effects as consumption of unconsecrated bread. And this is, of course, quite true. The Catholic who believes in transubstantiation does not deny that after the consecration the 'species' of bread will have the same sensible effects as unconsecrated bread.

The relevance of Peirce's argument to the subject of his relation to positivism may not be immediately apparent. But in point of fact his line of argument is extremely relevant. For he explicitly says that he wishes to point out 'how impossible it is that we should have an idea in our minds which relates to anything but conceived sensible effects of things. Our idea of anything *is* our idea of its sensible effects; and if we fancy that we have any other we deceive ourselves, and mistake a mere sensation accompanying the thought for a part of the thought itself.'[1] In the immediate context this means that to agree that an object has all the sensible effects of bread and to claim at the same time that it is really the Body of Christ is to indulge in 'senseless jargon'.[2] In a wider context it seems to follow clearly from Peirce's thesis that all metaphysical talk about spiritual realities which cannot be construed as talk about 'sensible effects' is nonsense, or that it has no more than emotive significance.

Needless to say, we are not concerned here with theological controversy between Catholics and Protestants. The point of referring to the passage in which Peirce mentions the matter is simply that in it he explicitly states that our idea of anything *is* the idea of its sensible effects. If such a statement does not give good ground for the contention that certain aspects of Peirce's thought constitute an anticipation of neopositivism, it is difficult to think of statements which would do so. But this does not alter the fact that there are other aspects of his thought which differentiate it sharply enough from positivism. Nor, as far as I know, has anyone attempted to deny the fact.

7. Turning to ethics, we can note that it is described by Peirce in various ways, as, for example, the science of right and wrong, the science of ideals, the philosophy of aims. But he also tells us that 'we are too apt to define ethics to ourselves as the science of right and wrong'.[1] To be sure, ethics is concerned with right and wrong; but the fundamental question is, 'What am I to aim at, what am I after?'[2] In other words, the fundamental problem of ethics is that of determining the end of ethical conduct, conduct meaning here deliberate or self-controlled action. The concept of the good is thus basic in Peirce's ethics.

For Peirce, therefore, ethics consists of two main divisions. Pure ethics inquires into the nature of the ideal, the *summum bonum* or ultimate aim of conduct. 'Life can have but one end. It is Ethics which defines that end.'[3] Practical ethics is concerned with the conformity of action to the ideal, to the end. The former, pure ethics, can be called a pre-normative science, while practical ethics is strictly normative in character. Both are required. On the one hand a system of practical ethics gives us a programme for future deliberate or controlled conduct. But all deliberate conduct has an aim; it is for the sake of an end. And as the ultimate end or aim is determined in pure ethics, this is presupposed by practical ethics. On the other hand pragmatism requires that the concept of the end should be explicated in terms of conceived practical consequences, in conditional propositions relating to deliberate or controlled conduct. It does not follow, however, that in ethics a pragmatist will be an advocate of action for the sake of action. For, as we have seen, deliberate or rational action, and it is with this that ethics is concerned, is directed to the realization of an end, an ideal.

'Pure ethics,' Peirce tells us, 'has been, and always must be, a theatre of discussion, for the reason that its study consists in the gradual development of a distinct recognition of a satisfactory aim.'[4] This satisfactory aim or end of conduct must be an infinite end, that is, one which can be pursued indefinitely. And this is to be found in what we may call the rationalization of the universe. For the rational or reasonable is the only end which is fully

---

[1] 2.198.   [2] *Ibid.*   [3] *Ibid.*   [4] 4.243.

satisfactory in itself. And this means in effect that the *summum bonum* or supreme good is really the evolutionary process itself considered as the progressive rationalization of reality, as the process whereby that which exists comes more and more to embody rationality. The ultimate end is thus a cosmic end. But 'in its higher stages evolution takes place more and more largely through self-control'.[1] And this is where specifically human action comes in. It is self-control which makes possible 'an ought-to-be of conduct'.[2]

Peirce thus has the vision of the cosmic process as moving towards the realization of reason or rationality, and of man as co-operating in the process. Further, as the ultimate end is a general end, a cosmic aim, so to speak, it follows that it must be a social end, common to all men. Conscience, created and modified by experience, is in a sense pre-ethical: it belongs to what Peirce calls a community-consciousness, existing at a level of the soul at which there are hardly distinct individuals. And in point of fact a great part of one's moral vocation is settled by one's place and function in the community to which one belongs. But our vision should rise above the limited social organism to 'a conceived identification of one's interests with those of an unlimited community'.[3] And universal love is the all-important moral ideal.

Inasmuch as Peirce's pragmatism is primarily a theory of meaning and a method of making our concepts clear, it is primarily a matter of logic. But it has, of course, an application in ethics. For ethical concepts are to be interpreted in terms of conceived modes of conduct, though, as we have seen, reflection or deliberate or controlled conduct leads inevitably to reflection on the end of conduct. If we interpret ethical concepts and propositions in terms of good and bad consequences, we cannot avoid asking the question, what is the good? In other words, pragmatism is not a doctrine simply of practice, of action for action's sake. Theory and practice, Peirce insists, go together. For the matter of that, pragmatism in its application to science is not a doctrine of action for action's sake. We have already noted how Peirce rejected what he regarded as the positivist worship of actual verification. True, the pragmatist analysis of scientific hypotheses can be said to look forward to conduct or action; but in itself the analysis is a theoretical inquiry. Similarly, ethics looks forward to moral conduct; it is a normative science. But it is none the less a science, a

[1] 5.433.   [2] 4.540.   [3] 2.654.

theoretical inquiry, though it would, of course, be barren if no conduct resulted.

Sometimes Peirce speaks as though ethics were fundamental and logic an application of it. For thinking or reasoning is itself a form of conduct, and it is 'impossible to be thoroughly and rationally logical except upon an ethical basis'.[1] Indeed, logic, as concerned with what we ought to think, 'must be an application of the doctrine of what we deliberately choose to do, which is ethics'.[2] At the same time Peirce does not really mean that logic can be derived from ethics, any more than ethics can be derived from logic. They are for him distinct normative sciences. But inasmuch as pragmatism teaches that 'what we think is to be interpreted in terms of what we are prepared to do',[3] there must be connections between logic and ethics.

One connection worth noting is this. We have seen that according to Peirce absolute certainty concerning the truth of an hypothesis cannot be attained at any given moment by any given individual. At the same time there can be an 'infinite' or unending approximation to it through the unlimited or continuing community of observers, by means of repeated verification which raises probability towards the ideal limit of certainty. So in the moral sphere the experiment of conduct, so to speak, tends to increase, through the unlimited community of mankind, clear recognition of the nature of the supreme end of life and of its 'meaning', its implications in regard to concrete action. And we can envisage, at any rate as an ideal limit, universal agreement.

Indeed, Peirce does not hesitate to say that 'in regard to morals we can see ground for hope that debate will ultimately cause one party or other to modify their sentiments up to complete accord'.[4] This obviously presupposes that the basis of morality is objective, that the supreme good or ultimate end is something to be discovered and about which agreement is possible in principle. And this point of view obviously differentiates Peirce's ethics from the emotive theory, especially in its older and cruder form, which is associated with the early phase of modern neopositivism. So does his idea of analyzing moral propositions on lines analogous to his analysis of scientific propositions,[5] not to speak of his general

[1] 2.198.   [2] 5.35.   [3] *Ibid.*   [4] 2.151.
[5] The upholder of the emotive theory of ethics would claim that this analysis fails to do justice to the peculiar character of moral utterances. But to say this is, of course, to recognize the difference between Peirce's theory of ethics and the emotive theory.

vision of evolution as moving towards the embodiment of reason in the unlimited community, a vision which has much more affinity with absolute idealism than with positivism.

8. Sometimes Peirce speaks of metaphysics in a thoroughly positivist manner. For example, in a paper on pragmatism he states that pragmatism will serve to show that 'almost every proposition of ontological metaphysics is either meaningless gibberish—one word being defined by other words, and they by still others, without any real conception ever being reached—or else is downright absurd'.[1] When this rubbish has been swept away, philosophy will be reduced to problems capable of investigation by the observational methods of the genuine sciences. Pragmatism is thus 'a species of prope-positivism'.[2]

At the same time Peirce goes on to say that pragmatism does not simply jeer at metaphysics but 'extracts from it a precious essence, which will serve to give life and light to cosmology and physics'.[3] In any case he has no intention of rejecting metaphysics, provided that he himself is practising it. And while it is only right to mention the fact that Peirce sometimes derides metaphysics, this does not alter the fact that he has his own brand of it.

Peirce gives a number of different definitions or descriptions of metaphysics, when, that is to say, the term 'metaphysics' is not being used as a term of abuse. We are told, for example, that 'metaphysics consists in the results of the absolute acceptance of logical principles not merely as regulatively valid, but as truths of being'.[4] It is in accordance with this view that Peirce connects the fundamental ontological categories with the logical categories of firstness, secondness and thirdness. And he asserts that as metaphysics results from the acceptance of logical principles as principles of being, the universe must be regarded as having a unifying explanation. At other times Peirce emphasizes the observational basis of metaphysics. 'Metaphysics, even bad metaphysics, really rests on observations, whether consciously or not.'[5] And it is in accordance with this view that Peirce derives the fundamental ontological categories from phenomenology or 'phaneroscopy', by inquiring into the irreducible formal elements in any and every

¹ 5.423.   ² Ibid.
³ Ibid. Elsewhere (6.3) Peirce says that the chief cause of the backwardness of metaphysics is that it has been so often in the hands of theologians, who have an axe to grind.
⁴ 1.487.   ⁵ 6.2

experience. We are also told that 'metaphysics is the science of Reality',[1] reality including for Peirce not only the actually existent but also the sphere of real possibility.

To a certain extent at least these various ways of describing metaphysics can be harmonized. For example, to say that metaphysics is the science of reality is not incompatible with saying that it is based on experience or observation. It may even be possible to harmonize the view that metaphysics rests on observations with the view that it results from the acceptance of logical principles, providing at any rate that we do not interpret this second view as meaning that metaphysics can be deduced from logic without any recourse to experience. At the same time it does not seem to be possible to construct from Peirce's various utterances an absolutely consistent and unambiguous account of metaphysics. For one thing, he does not appear to have made up his mind definitely about the precise relation between ontology and logic. For present purposes, therefore, we had better confine ourselves to indicating briefly some of Peirce's metaphysical ideas. We cannot undertake here to create that consistent system which the philosopher himself did not achieve.

We can start with Peirce's three fundamental categories. The first, that of 'firstness', is 'the idea of that which is such as it is regardless of anything else'.[2] And Peirce calls it the category of quality, in the sense of 'suchness'. From the phenomenological point of view we can conceive a feeling, as of sadness, or a sensed quality, as of blueness, without reference to subject or object but simply as a unique something, 'a purely monadic state of feeling'.[3] To convert the psychological concept into a metaphysical one, Peirce tells us, we have to think of a monad as 'a pure nature, or quality, in itself without parts or features, and without embodiment'.[4] But the term 'monad', with its Leibnizian associations, can be misleading. For Peirce goes on to say that the meanings of the names of the so-called secondary qualities are as good examples of monads as can be given. It is understandable therefore that he speaks of the category of firstness as that of quality. In any case firstness is a pervasive feature of the universe, representing the element of uniqueness, freshness and originality which is everywhere present, in every phenomenon, every fact, every event. To obtain some idea of what is meant, Peirce suggests that we should imagine to ourselves the universe as it appeared to Adam when

[1] 5.21.   [2] 5.66.   [3] 1.303.   [4] Ibid.

he looked on it for the first time, and before he had drawn distinctions and become reflectively aware of his own experience.

The second fundamental category, that of 'secondness', is dyadic, corresponding to the idea of secondness in logic. That is to say, secondness is 'the conception of being relative to, the conception of reaction with, something else'.[1] From one point of view secondness can be called 'fact', while from another point of view it is existence or actuality. For 'existence is that mode of being which lies in opposition to another'.[2] And this category too pervades the universe. Facts are facts, as we say; and this is why we sometimes speak of 'brute' facts. Actuality or existence involves everywhere effort and resistance. It is in this sense dyadic.

The third fundamental category, that of 'thirdness', is said to be the category of mediation, its logical prototype being the mediating function of a sign between object and interpretant. Ontologically, thirdness mediates between firstness, in the sense of quality, and secondness, in the sense of fact or of action and reaction. It thus introduces continuity and regularity, and it takes the form of laws of various types or grades. For instance, there can be laws of quality, determining 'systems of qualities, of which Sir Isaac Newton's law of colour-mixture, with Dr. Thomas Young's supplement thereto, is the most perfect known example'.[3] There can also be laws of fact. Thus if a spark falls into a barrel of gunpowder (treated as a first), it causes an explosion (treated as a second); and it does so according to an intelligible law, which thus has a mediating function.[4] Then again there are laws of regularity which enable us to predict that future facts of secondness will always take on a certain determinate character or quality. In its various forms, however, the category of thirdness, like those of firstness and secondness, pervades the universe; and we can say that everything stands in some relation to every other thing.[5]

Now, quality can be said, in Mill's language, to be a permanent possibility of sensation. It is, however, a real possibility, independent of subjective experience. And we can thus say that the first quality gives us the first mode of being, namely real possibility, though the concept of possibility is admittedly wider than that of quality. Similarly, the second category, being from one point of

---

[1] 6.32.   [2] 4.457.   [3] 1.482.
[4] According to Peirce laws of fact can be divided into logically necessary and logically contingent laws, while logically contingent laws can be subdivided into metaphysically necessary and metaphysically contingent laws (1.483).
[5] Cf. 4.319.

view that of actuality or existence, gives us the second mode of being, namely actuality as distinct from possibility. Again, by involving the concept of law the third category gives us the third mode of being, which Peirce calls 'destiny', as governing future facts. But it must be understood that in Peirce's use of the term the concept of 'destiny' is wider than the concept of law, if we mean by law the idea of it which is associated with determinism. For to be free from determining law is as much 'destiny' as to be subject to it.

We have, therefore, three fundamental ontological categories and three corresponding metaphysical modes of being. Peirce also distinguishes three modes or categories of existence or actuality. The first is what he calls 'chance', a term used 'to express with accuracy the characteristics of freedom or spontaneity'.[1] The second mode of existence is law, laws being of various types but all being the result of evolution. The third mode of existence is habit, or, rather, the tendency to habit-making. The word 'habit', however, must be understood in a wide sense. For, according to Peirce, all things possess a tendency to take habits,[2] whether they are human beings, animals, plants or chemical substances. And the laws which state uniformities or regularities are the results of long periods of such habit-taking.

We can now briefly consider the actual world or universe in the light of these modes or categories of actuality or existence.[3] 'Three elements are active in the world: first, chance; second, law; and third, habit-taking.'[4] We are invited to think of the universe as being originally in a state of pure indetermination, a state in which there were no distinct things, no habits, no laws, a state in which absolute chance reigned. From one point of view this absolute indetermination was 'nullity',[5] the negation of all determination, while from another point of view, considered, that is to say, as the real possibility of all determination, it was 'being'.[6] At the same time chance is spontaneity, freedom, creativity. It thus annuls itself as unlimited possibility or potentiality by taking the form of possibilities of this or that sort, that is to say, of some definite qualities or suchnesses, falling under the ontological category of firstness. And as the universe evolves and

[1] 6.201.   [2] Cf. 1.409.
[3] The actual world, it will be remembered, is for Peirce part of the wider sphere of real possibility. It consists of actualized possibilities and of possibilities in the process of actualization.
[4] 1.409.   [5] 1.447.   [6] Ibid.

'monads' act and react in 'secondnesses', habits are formed and there are produced those regularities or laws which fall into the category of thirdness. The ideal limit of the process is the complete reign of law, the opposite of the reign of absolute chance. The first stage is evidently, in a real sense, an abstraction. For if chance is spontaneity and creativity, we can hardly speak, as Peirce explicitly recognizes, of an assignable time or period during which there was absolutely no determination. Similarly, the complete reign of law, in which all chance or spontaneity is absent, is also in a sense an abstraction, an ideal limit. For according to Peirce's principle of 'tychism',[1] chance is always present in the universe. Hence we can say that the universe is a process of creative and continuous determination, moving from the ideal limit of absolute indetermination to the ideal limit of absolute determination, or, better, from the ideal limit of bare possibility to the ideal limit of the complete actualization of possibility. Another way of putting the matter is to say that evolution is a process of advance from absolute chance considered as 'a chaos of unpersonalized feeling'[2] to the reign of pure reason embodied in a perfectly rational system. We have already seen, in connection with his ethical doctrine, how Peirce regards the universe as moving towards an ever fuller embodiment of rationality.

It does not follow from Peirce's doctrine of absolute chance as the primitive state of the universe that chance is the sole explanation of evolution. On the contrary, 'evolution is nothing more nor less than the working out of a definite end',[3] a final cause. And this idea enables Peirce to adopt and adapt the old idea of the cosmic significance of love, an idea which goes back at any rate to the Greek philosopher Empedocles. A final end works by attraction, and the response is love. To the idea of 'tychism', therefore, we have to add that of 'agapism' as a cosmological category. And to these two we must add a third, namely 'synechism', which is 'the doctrine that all that exists is continuous'.[4]

Synechism, we may note, rules out any ultimate dualism between matter and mind. Indeed, 'what we call matter is not completely dead, but is merely mind hidebound with habits'[5] which make it act with a specially high degree of mechanical regularity. And Peirce remarks that 'tychism' must give rise to a 'Schelling-fashioned idealism which holds matter to be mere

---

[1] 'Tychism' or 'chance-ism', coined by Peirce from the Greek word *tyche*.
[2] 6.33.   [3] 1.204.   [4] 1.172.   [5] 6.158.

specialized and partially deadened mind'.[1] So convinced is he of this, that he does not hesitate to say that 'the one intelligible theory of the universe is that of objective idealism, that matter is effete mind, inveterate habits becoming physical laws'.[2]

Now, if it is asked whether Peirce believed in God, the answer is affirmative. But if it is asked what part is played in his philosophy by the concept of God, the answer is more complex. His general principle is that philosophy and religion should not be mixed up. Not that this prevents him from writing about God. But when he talks about 'musement' as an activity of the mind which leads directly to God, he is not thinking of what would normally be called a systematic metaphysical argument. If, for example, I contemplate the starry heavens, as Kant did, and allow instinct and the heart to speak, I cannot help believing in God. Appeal to one's own 'instinct' is more effective than any argument.[3] Peirce does indeed make it clear that in his opinion contemplation of the 'three universes' of tychism, agapism and synechism 'gives birth to the hypothesis and ultimately to the belief that they, or at any rate two of the three, have a Creator independent of them'.[4] But he calls this the 'neglected argument', also the 'humble argument', and he brings it under the heading of 'musement'. The direction of Peirce's thought is, however, perfectly plain. A theory of evolution which enthroned mechanical law above the principle of creative growth or development would be hostile to religion; but 'a genuine evolutionary philosophy . . . is so far from being antagonistic to the idea of a personal creator that it is really inseparable from that idea'.[5] While, therefore, in his systematic metaphysics Peirce concentrates on the doctrine of categories, his general world-view is certainly theistic.

9. From the point of view of the history of pragmatism Peirce's chief contribution is, of course, his analysis of meaning, his rule for making concepts clear. And if this is considered in a general way, it has an obvious value. For it can serve as a useful goad or stimulus, making us give concrete content to our concepts, instead of letting words do duty for clear ideas. In other words, it stimulates

[1] 6.102. Tychism is mentioned because Peirce connects mind with firstness, and so, rather surprisingly, with chance, while matter is connected with secondness, and with agapism, and evolution with thirdness, synechism (6.32).
[2] 6.25.
[3] Peirce believed that God's existence is from one point of view evident enough. 'Where would such an idea, say as that of God, come from if not from direct experience?' (6.493).
[4] 6.483.   [5] 6.157.

to conceptual analysis. It seems to me pretty obvious, for example, that if there were no assignable difference between what Peirce calls the 'practical consequences' or 'practical effects' of the words 'hard' and 'soft', there would in fact be no difference in meaning. True, as a general criterion of meaning Peirce's principle of pragmaticism lies open to the same sort of objections which have been brought against the neopositivist criterion of meaning. There is great difficulty in interpreting all factual statements as predictions or sets of predictions. But this does not alter the fact that the principle of pragmaticism brings out aspects of the semantic situation which have to be taken into account in developing a theory of meaning. In other words, Peirce made a valuable contribution to logic. And if he allowed what he saw clearly to obscure other aspects of the situation, there is nothing exceptional in this.

We have seen, however, that when applying the principle of pragmaticism in a particular context Peirce states roundly that our idea of anything *is* our idea of its sensible effects. If this statement is taken seriously in its universal form, it appears to undermine Peirce's own metaphysical world-view. He does indeed make an attempt to apply his principle to the concept of God without dissolving the concept.[1] And he suggests[2] that if the pragmaticist is asked what he means by 'God', he can reply that just as long acquaintance with the works of Aristotle makes us familiar with the philosopher's mind, so does study of the physico-psychical universe give us an acquaintance with what may be called in some analogous sense the divine 'mind'. But if his statement elsewhere about 'sensible effects' is taken seriously, it seems to follow either that we have no clear concept of God or that the idea of God is simply the idea of his sensible effects. And in point of fact Peirce himself suggests in one place[3] that the question whether there really is such a being as God is the question whether physical science is something objective or simply a fictional construction of the scientists' minds.

It may be objected that the last sentence involves taking a remark out of its general context, and that in any case too much emphasis has been placed on the statement that our idea of anything is the idea of its sensible effects. After all, when he made the statement Peirce was talking about the sensible effects of bread. Further, he gives various formulations of the principle of pragmatism, and in view of the way in which he often uses the principle

[1] 6.489–490.   [2] 6.502.   [3] 6.503.

we ought not to over-emphasize a statement made in a particular context. This is doubtless true. But Peirce made the statement in question. And the point which we are trying to make here is that he did not construct a system in which all the elements of his thought were harmonized and rendered consistent. Peirce approached philosophy through mathematics and science, and his theory of meaning was doubtless largely suggested by reflection on scientific statements considered as fallible hypotheses, as verifiable or falsifiable predictions. But his interests were wide and his mind was original and fertile; and he developed a metaphysical world-view in which pragmatism was not forgotten but which demanded reconsideration of the nature and scope of the pragmatist principle. To claim that it is impossible to synthesize Peirce's logic and his metaphysics would be to claim too much, at least if synthesis is understood as permitting revision and modification of the elements to be synthesized. But two things at any rate are clear; first that Peirce did not himself work out such a synthesis, and, secondly, that no synthesis is possible if the pragmatic principle is understood in such a way that it leads straight to neopositivism.

To say, however, that Peirce did not achieve a fully coherent synthesis of the various elements in his thought is not to deny that he was in a real sense a systematic thinker. Indeed, from one point of view it is hardly an exaggeration to claim that he was possessed by a passion for system. We have only to think, for example, of the way in which he used the ideas of firstness, secondness and thirdness, employing them to link together logic, epistemology, ontology and cosmology. It is undeniable that out of his various papers there arise the general outlines of an imposing system.

We have said that Peirce approached philosophy by way of mathematics and science. And we would naturally expect his metaphysics to be a prolongation or extension of his reflections on the scientific view of the world. So it is to some extent. At the same time the general results have a marked affinity with metaphysical idealism. But Peirce was well aware of this; and he considered that if one constructs a world-view based on the scientific conception of the world, one is inevitably pushed in the direction of metaphysical idealism, an idealism which is able to accommodate the 'Scholastic realism' on which Peirce always insisted. In other words, he did not start with idealist premises.

He started with realism and was determined to maintain it. But he recognized that though his approach was different from that of the idealists, his conclusions had a recognizable resemblance to theirs. We find much the same situation in the case of Whitehead in the present century.

We have already noted Peirce's commendation of Schelling's view of matter, and his explicit statement that objective idealism is the one intelligible theory of the universe. Here we can note his partial affinity with Hegel. Sometimes indeed Peirce speaks against Hegel, maintaining, for example, that he was too inclined to forget that there is a world of action and reaction, and that Hegel deprived 'firstness' and 'secondness' of all actuality. But when speaking of his own doctrine of categories, logical and metaphysical, Peirce notes the 'Hegelian sound'[1] of what he has to say and remarks that his statements are indeed akin to those of Hegel. 'I sometimes agree with the great idealist and sometimes diverge from his footsteps.'[2] While prepared to say on occasion that he entirely rejects the system of Hegel, Peirce is also prepared to say on occasion that he has resuscitated Hegelianism in a new form, and even to claim that, so far as a philosophical concept can be identified with the idea of God, God is the absolute Idea of Hegel, the Idea which manifests itself in the world and tends towards its complete self-revelation in the ideal limit or term of the evolutionary process.[3] It is not altogether surprising, therefore, if Peirce speaks of Hegel as 'in some respects the greatest philosopher that ever lived',[4] even if he also criticizes Hegel for a lamentable deficiency in 'critical severity and sense of fact'.[5]

We have mentioned the name of Whitehead. There does not seem to be any evidence that Whitehead was influenced by Peirce, or even that he had studied Peirce's writings. But this renders the resemblance between their thought all the more notable. It is, of course, a limited resemblance, but it is none the less real. For example, Whitehead's doctrine of eternal objects and actual entities was anticipated to some extent by Peirce's distinction between 'generals' and facts. Again, Whitehead's doctrine of novelty in the universe, in the cosmic process, recalls Peirce's doctrine of spontaneity and originality. Further, it is perhaps not

---

[1] 1.453.   [2] *Ibid.*
[3] One can compare Peirce's different ways of alluding to Hegelianism with the different ways in which he speaks of metaphysics. Needless to say, the different statements must in both cases he interpreted in the light of their immediate contexts.
[4] 1.524.   [5] *Ibid.*

altogether fanciful to see in Peirce's thought an anticipation of Whitehead's famous distinction between the primordial and consequent natures of God. For Peirce tells us that God as Creator is the 'Absolute First',[1] while as terminus of the universe, as God completely revealed, he is the 'Absolute Second'.[2] Perhaps one is put in mind more of Hegel than of Whitehead; but then the philosophy of Whitehead himself, anti-idealist though it was by original intention, bears some resemblance in its final form to absolute idealism.

To return finally to Peirce in himself. He was an original philosopher and powerful thinker. Indeed, the claim that he is the greatest of all purely American philosophers is by no means unreasonable. He had a strong tendency to careful analysis and was far from being one of those philosophers whose chief concern appears to be that of providing uplift and edification. At the same time he had a speculative mind which sought for a general or overall interpretation of reality. And this combination is, we may well think, precisely what is required. At the same time the example of Peirce is a living illustration of the difficulty of effecting such a combination. For we find in his thought unresolved ambiguities. For instance, Peirce is a resolute realist. Reality is independent of human experience and thought. Indeed, the real is to be defined precisely in terms of this independence. And it is this account of the real which permits Peirce to attribute independent reality to the world of possibles and to depict God as the only absolute reality. At the same time his pragmatism or pragmaticism seems to demand what Royce called the 'critical rationalist' interpretation of reality, namely in terms of conceivable human experience. That which gives rise to actual experience is actually real. That which is conceived as giving rise to possible experience is potentially actual, a real possibility. On this interpretation of reality we could not claim that God is an actually existing being without claiming that he is the object of actual experience. Alternatively, we would have to analyze the concept of God in such a way as to reduce it to the idea of those effects which we do experience. So we are back once more with the latent tension in Peirce's philosophy as a whole between his metaphysics and a logical analysis of the meaning of concepts which appears to point in quite a different direction from that of his speculative metaphysics.

[1] 1.362.
[2] *Ibid*. The 'third' would be every state of the universe at an assignable point of time, mediating between God as First and God as Second.

CHAPTER XV

THE PRAGMATISM OF JAMES AND SCHILLER

The life and writings of William James—James's conception of radical empiricism and pure experience—Pragmatism as theory of meaning and as theory of truth—The relations between radical empiricism, pragmatism and humanism in the philosophy of James—Pragmatism and belief in God—Pragmatism in America and England—The humanism of C. F. S. Schiller.

1. WILLIAM JAMES (1842–1910) was born at New York and received his school education partly in America and partly abroad, acquiring in the process a fluency in the French and German languages. In 1864 he entered the Harvard Medical School, receiving the degree of doctor of medicine in 1869. After a period of bad health and mental depression he became an instructor in anatomy and physiology at Harvard. But he was also interested in psychology, and in 1875 he began giving courses in the subject. In 1890 he published his *Principles of Psychology* in two volumes.

Apart from an early attempt to become a painter, James's higher education was thus mainly scientific and medical. But like his father, Henry James, senior,[1] he was a man of deep religious feeling, and he found himself involved in a mental conflict between the scientific view of the world, interpreted as a mechanistic view which excluded human freedom, and a religious view which would include belief not only in God but also in the freedom of man. As far as the legitimacy of belief in freedom was concerned, James found help in the writing of the French philosopher Charles Renouvier (1815–1903). And it was largely the desire to overcome the opposition between the outlook to which science seemed to him to point and the outlook suggested by his religious and humanistic inclinations which drove James to philosophy. In 1879 he started to lecture on the subject at Harvard, and in the following year he became an assistant professor of philosophy. In 1885 he was nominated professor of philosophy.

In 1897 James published *The Will to Believe and Other Essays in Popular Philosophy.*[2] His famous *Varieties of Religious*

---

[1] Henry James, junior, the novelist, was a younger brother of William.
[2] The copyright date is 1896, but the volume appeared in 1897.

Experience,[1] appeared in 1902. This was followed by *Pragmatism* in 1907, *A Pluralistic Universe*[2] in 1909 and, in the same year, *The Meaning of Truth*. James's posthumously published writings include *Some Problems of Philosophy* (1911), *Memories and Studies* (1911), *Essays in Radical Empiricism* (1912), and *Collected Essays and Reviews* (1920). His *Letters*, edited by his son, Henry James, appeared in 1926.

2. In the preface to *The Will to Believe* James describes his philosophical attitude as that of radical empiricism. He explains that by empiricism he understands a position which is 'contented to regard its most assured conclusions concerning matters of fact as hypotheses liable to modification in the course of future experience'.[3] As for the word 'radical', this indicates that the doctrine of monism itself is treated as an hypothesis. At first hearing this sounds very odd. But in this context James understands by monism the view that the multiplicity of things forms an intelligible unity. He does not mean by monism the theory that the world is one single entity or one single fact. On the contrary, he excludes this theory in favour of pluralism. What he is saying is that radical empiricism postulates a unity which is not immediately given, but that this postulate, which stimulates us to discover unifying connections, is treated as itself an hypothesis which has to be verified, and not as an unquestionable dogma.[4]

In *Some Problems of Philosophy*, in the context of a discussion of types of metaphysics, empiricism is contrasted with rationalism. 'Rationalists are the men of principles, empiricists the men of facts.'[5] The rationalist philosopher, as James sees him, moves from the whole to its parts, from the universal to the particular, and he endeavours to deduce facts from principles. Further, he tends to claim final truth on behalf of his system of deduced conclusions. The empiricist, however, starts with particular facts; he moves from parts to wholes; and he prefers, if he can, to explain principles as inductions from facts. Further, the claim to final truth is foreign to his mind.

Obviously, there is nothing new here. Familiar lines of contrast between rationalism and empiricism are presented by James in a more or less popular manner. But in the preface to *The Meaning*

---

[1] This work represents Gifford Lectures given at Edinburgh in 1901–2.
[2] This work represents the Hibbert Lectures given at Oxford in 1908–9.
[3] *The Will to Believe*, p. vii (1903 edition).
[4] We shall mention presently another sense of the word 'monism'.
[5] *Some Problems of Philosophy*, p. 35.

of Truth we can find a more clearly defined account of radical empiricism. It is there said to consist 'first of a postulate, next of a statement of fact, and finally of a generalized conclusion'.[1] The postulate is that only those matters which are definable in terms drawn from experience should be considered debatable by philosophers. Hence if there is any being which transcends all possible experience, it also transcends philosophical discussion. The statement of fact is that relations, conjunctive and disjunctive, are as much objects of experience as the things related. And the generalized conclusion from this statement of fact is that the knowable universe possesses a continuous structure, in the sense that it does not consist simply of entities which can be related only through categories imposed from without.

James is insistent on the reality of relations. 'Radical empiricism takes conjunctive relations at their face value, holding them to be as real as the terms united by them.'[2] And among conjunctive relations is the causal relation. Hence what James calls radical empiricism differs from the empiricism of Hume, according to whom 'the mind never perceives any real connection among distinctive existences'.[3] It is also opposed to Bradley's theory of relations. "Mr. Bradley's understanding shows the most extraordinary power of perceiving separations and the most extraordinary impotence in comprehending conjunctions.'[4]

The meaning of the word 'experience' is notoriously imprecise. But according to James ordinary experience, in which we are aware of distinct things of various kinds and of relations of different types, grows out of pure experience, described as 'the immediate flux of life which furnishes the material to our later reflection with its conceptual categories'.[5] True, only new-born infants and people in a state of semi-coma can be said to enjoy in its purity a state of pure experience, which is 'but another name for feeling or sensation'.[6] But pure experience, the immediacy of feeling or sensation, is the embryo out of which articulated experience develops; and elements or portions of it remain even in our ordinary experience.

From this doctrine of pure experience we can draw two conclusions. First, in this basic flux of experience the distinctions of reflective thought, such as those between consciousness and

---

[1] *The Meaning of Truth*, p. xii.   [2] *Essays in Radical Empiricism*, p. 107.
[3] *Treatise of Human Nature*, Appendix, p. 636 (Selby-Bigge edition).
[4] *Essays in Radical Empiricism*, p. 117.
[5] *Ibid.*, p. 93.   [6] *Ibid.*, p. 94.

content, subject and object, mind and matter, have not yet emerged in the forms in which we make them. In this sense pure experience is 'monistic'. And James can speak of it as the 'one primal stuff or material in the world, a stuff of which everything is composed'.[1] This is the doctrine of 'neutral monism', which James associates with radical empiricism. Pure experience cannot be called, for example, either physical or psychical: it logically precedes the distinction and is thus 'neutral'.

Secondly, however, the fact that radical empiricism is pluralistic rather than monistic in the ontological sense and asserts the reality of many things and of the relations between them, means that pure experience must be regarded as containing in itself potentially the distinctions of developed experience. It is shot through, as James expresses the matter, not only with nouns and adjectives but also with prepositions and conjunctions. The causal relation, for example, is present in the flux of sensation, inasmuch as all sensation is teleological in character.

Now, if pure monism is understood in a purely psychological sense, as simply stating, that is to say, that the primitive and basic form of experience is a state of 'feeling' in which distinctions, such as that between subject and object, are not as yet present, it is doubtless compatible with a realistic pluralism. But if it is understood in an ontological sense, as meaning that the flux of undifferentiated experience is the ontological 'stuff' out of which all emerges, it is difficult to see how it does not lead straight to some form of monistic idealism. However, James assumes that the doctrine of pure experience, which is obviously psychological in origin, is compatible with the pluralistic view of the universe that he associates with radical empiricism.

In so far as radical empiricism involves pluralism and belief in the reality of relations, it can be said to be a world-view. But if it is understood simply in terms of the three elements mentioned above, namely a postulate, a statement of fact, and a generalized conclusion, it is an embryonic rather than a full-grown world-view. The problem of God, for example, is left untouched. James does indeed maintain that there are specifically religious experiences which suggest the existence of a superhuman consciousness that is limited and not all-inclusive in a sense which would conflict with pluralism. And he remarks that if empiricism were to become 'associated with religion, as hitherto, through some strange

[1] *Ibid.*

misunderstanding, it has been associated with irreligion, I believe that a new era of religion as well as of philosophy will be ready to begin'.[1] But James's theism will be more conveniently treated after we have outlined the basic tenets of pragmatism and the relation between pragmatism and radical empiricism.

3. In origin and primarily pragmatism is, James tells us, 'a method only'.[2] For it is in the first place 'a method of settling metaphysical disputes that might otherwise be interminable'.[3] That is to say, if A proposes theory x while B proposes theory y, the pragmatist will examine the practical consequences of each theory. And if he can find no difference between the respective practical consequences of the two theories, he will conclude that they are to all intents and purposes one and the same theory, the difference being purely verbal. In this case further dispute between A and B will be seen to be pointless.

What we have here is obviously a method for determining the meanings of concepts and theories. In an address delivered in 1881 James remarked that if two apparently different definitions of something turn out to have identical consequences, they are really one and the same definition.[4] And this is the theory of meaning which finds expression in *Pragmatism*. 'To attain perfect clearness in our thoughts of an object, we need only consider what conceivable effects of a practical kind the object may involve—what sensations we are to expect from it, and what reactions we must prepare. Our conception of these effects, whether immediate or remote, is then for us the whole of our conception of the object, so far as that conception has positive significance at all.'[5]

As so described, the pragmatism of James evidently follows the main lines of the pragmatist method as conceived by Peirce. James was, indeed, influenced by some other thinkers as well, such as the scientists Louis Agassiz and Wilhelm Ostwald; but he made no secret of his indebtedness to Peirce. He refers to him in a footnote relating to the address of 1881.[6] He again admits his debt to Peirce in a public lecture given in 1898.[7] And after the passage quoted in the last paragraph he adds that 'this is the principle of Peirce, the principle of pragmatism',[8] and remarks that Peirce's doctrine remained unnoticed until he, James, brought it forward in the lecture of 1898 and applied it to religion.

[1] *A Pluralistic Universe*, p. 314.   [2] *Pragmatism*, p. 51.
[3] *Ibid.*, p. 45.   [4] *The Will to Believe*, p. 124.
[5] *Pragmatism*, p. 47.   [6] *The Will to Believe*, p. 124, note 1.
[7] *Collected Essays and Reviews*, p. 410.   [8] *Pragmatism*, p. 47.

There are, it is true, certain differences between the positions of Peirce and James. For example, when Peirce spoke about the practical consequences of a concept he emphasized the general idea of a habit of action, the idea of the general manner in which the concept could conceivably modify purposive action. James, however, tends to emphasize particular practical effects. As we have seen in the passage which is quoted above from *Pragmatism*, he there emphasizes particular sensations and reactions. Hence Peirce accused him of having been led away from the universal to the particular under the influence of an ultra-sensationalistic psychology, of being, as Dewey put it, more of a nominalist. In Peirce's terminology, James is concerned with antecedents and consequents more than with consequences, a consequence being the conceived relation between an antecedent and a consequent.

At the same time, if James's pragmatism were simply a method for making concepts clear, for determining their meanings, we could say that he adopts Peirce's principle, even if he gives it, as Dewey expresses it, a 'nominalistic' twist. In point of fact, however, pragmatism is not for James simply a method of determining the meanings of concepts. It is also a theory of truth. Indeed, James explicitly states that 'the pivotal part of my book named *Pragmatism* is its account of the relation called "truth" which may obtain between our idea (opinion, belief, statement, or what not) and its object'.[1] And it was largely James's development of pragmatism into a theory of truth which led Peirce to re-name his own theory 'pragmaticism'.

It is important to understand that James's theory of truth does not presuppose a denial of the correspondence theory. Truth is for him a property of certain of our beliefs, not of things. 'Realities are not *true*, they *are*; and beliefs are true *of* them.'[2] In modern language, logical truth and falsity are predicated of propositions, not of things or of facts. Strictly speaking at any rate, it is the proposition enunciating a fact which is true, not the fact itself. Julius Caesar's existence at a certain period of history cannot properly be called true; but the statement that he existed is true, while the statement that he did not exist is false. At the same time the statement that Julius Caesar existed is not true in virtue of the meanings of the symbols or words employed in the statement. Hence we can say that it is true in virtue of a relation of correspondence with reality or fact.

[1] *The Meaning of Truth*, p. v. [2] *Ibid.*, p. 196.

In James's opinion, however, to say that a true belief (he also speaks of true ideas) is one which corresponds or agrees with reality raises rather than solves a problem. For what precisely is meant by correspondence in this context? Copying? An image of a sensible object might be called a copy of the object. But it is not so easy to see how a true idea of, say, justice can reasonably be described as a copy. James's analysis of 'correspondence' is on these lines. Truth is a relation between one part of experience and another. The *terminus a quo* of the relation is an idea, which belongs to the subjective aspect of experience, while the *terminus ad quem* is an objective reality. What, then, is the relation between the terms? Here we have to employ the pragmatist interpretation of an idea as a plan or rule of action. If our following out this plan leads us to the *terminus ad quem*, the idea is true. More accurately, 'such mediating events *make* the idea true'.[1] In other words, the truth of an idea is the process of its verification or validation. If, for example, I am lost in a wood and then come upon a path which I think of as possibly or probably leading to an inhabited house where I can obtain directions or help, my idea is a plan of action. And if my following out this plan verifies or validates the idea, this process of verification constitutes the truth of the idea: it is the 'correspondence' to which the correspondence theory of truth really refers.

Now, it is noticeable that on the same page on which James tells us that an idea 'becomes true, is made true by events',[2] he also tells us that 'true ideas are those that we can assimilate, validate, corroborate and verify'. In other words, he cannot help admitting that there are truths which can or could be verified, but which have not yet been verified. Indeed, he is prepared to state that unverified truths 'form the overwhelmingly large number of the truths we live by',[3] and that truth lives 'for the most part on a credit system'.[4]

If, however, truths are *made* true by verification or validation, it follows that unverified truths are potentially true, truths *in posse*. And this enables James to deal a blow at the philosophical rationalists or intellectualists who exalt static, timeless truths which are true prior to any verification. 'Intellectualist truth is only pragmatist truth *in posse*.'[5] And the total fabric of truth

[1] *The Meaning of Truth*, p. 202.   [2] *Pragmatism*, p. 201.
[3] *Ibid.*, p. 206.   [4] *Ibid.*, p. 207.   [5] *The Meaning of Truth*, p. 205.

would collapse if it did not rest on some actually verified truths, that is, on some actual truths, just as a financial system would collapse if it possessed no solid basis in cash. In discussing James's theory of truth it is obviously important not to caricature it. James was inclined to write in a popular style and to use some rather down-to-earth phrases which gave rise to misunderstanding. For example, his expression of the view that an idea or belief is true if it 'works' was apt to suggest the conclusion that even a falsehood could be called 'true' if it were useful or expedient to believe it. But when James speaks about a theory 'working', he means that it 'must mediate between all previous truths and certain new experiences. It must derange common sense and previous belief as little as possible, and it must lead to some sensible terminus or other that can be verified exactly. To "work" means both these things.'[1]

Misunderstanding was also caused by the way in which James spoke of satisfaction as a basic element in truth. For his way of speaking suggested that in his view a belief could be accounted true if it caused a subjective feeling of satisfaction, and that he was thus opening the door to every kind of wishful thinking. But this was not at any rate his intention. 'Truth in science is what gives us the maximum possible sum of satisfaction, taste included, but consistency both with previous truth and with novel fact is always the most imperious claimant.'[2] The successful 'working' of an hypothesis, in the sense explained above, involves the satisfaction of an interest. But the hypothesis is not accepted simply because one wishes it to be true. If, however, there is no evidence which compels us to choose one rather than the other of two hypotheses which purport to explain the same set of phenomena, it is a matter of scientific 'taste' to choose the more economical or the more elegant hypothesis.

It is indeed true that in his famous essay on *The Will to Believe* James explicitly declares that 'our passional nature not only lawfully may, but must, decide our option between propositions, whenever it is a genuine option that cannot by its nature be decided on intellectual grounds'.[3] But he makes it clear that by a genuine option he means one 'of the forced, living, and momentous kind'.[4] That is to say, when it is a question of a living and important issue, one which influences conduct, when we cannot avoid

---

[1] *Pragmatism*, pp. 216–17.   [2] *Ibid*., p. 217.
[3] *The Will to Believe*, p. 11.   [4] *Ibid*., p. 3.

choosing one of two beliefs, and when the issue cannot be decided on intellectual grounds, we are entitled to choose on 'passional' grounds, to exercise the will to believe, provided that we recognize our option for what it is. It is then a question of the right to believe in certain circumstances. And whether one agrees with James's thesis or not, one should not represent him as claiming that we are entitled to believe any proposition which affords us consolation or satisfaction, even if the balance of evidence goes to show that the proposition is false.[1] It is true, for instance, that according to James we are entitled, other things being equal, to embrace a view of reality which satisfies the moral side of our nature better than another view. And it is by no means everyone who would agree with him. But this is no reason for disregarding the qualification 'other things being equal', where 'other things' include, of course, already known truths and the conclusions deducible from them.

Though, however, we should be careful not to caricature the pragmatist theory of truth, it by no means follows that it is immune from serious criticism. One obvious line of criticism, attributed by James to the 'rationalists', is that in so far as it identifies truth with verification the pragmatist theory confuses the truth of a proposition with the process of showing that it is true. This was one of Peirce's objections to turning pragmatism from a method of determining meaning into a theory of truth.

James's reply is to challenge his critic, the rationalist as he calls him, to explain 'what the *word* true *means*, as applied to a statement, without invoking the *concept of the statement's workings*'.[2] In James's opinion the rationalist cannot explain what he means by correspondence with reality without referring to the practical consequences of the proposition in question, to what would verify or validate it, if it were true. The rationalist thus implicitly commits himself to the pragmatist theory of truth, though he proposes to attack it in the name of a different theory.

In a discussion of this topic confusion is only too apt to arise. Suppose that I say that the statement that Julius Caesar crossed the Rubicon is true in virtue of its correspondence with reality, with historical fact. And suppose that I am asked to explain what

---

[1] One might, however, object against James's thesis that if a question is in principle unanswerable on intellectual grounds, it cannot, on the pragmatist analysis of meaning, be a meaningful question, and that in this case the issue of belief or unbelief does not arise.

[2] *The Meaning of Truth*, p. 221.

I mean by this relation of correspondence with reality. I can hardly do so without mentioning the state of affairs or, rather, the action or series of actions which are referred to in the statement. And it is perfectly true that the occurrence of this series of actions at an assignable date in history is ultimately what validates or 'verifies' the statement. In this sense I cannot explain what I mean by correspondence without referring to what would validate or verify the statement. At the same time the term 'verification' would normally be understood to refer to the measures which we might conceivably take to show that a statement is true, when we already know what the statement means. That is to say, verification would normally be understood as referring to conceivable means of showing that the state of affairs which must obtain or must have obtained if the statement is true actually does or did obtain. And if verification is understood in this sense, it seems perfectly correct to say with the 'rationalist' that it is a case of *showing* a statement to be true rather than of *making* it true.

We might, however, first define 'true' in such a way that it would follow logically that only an actually verified statement is true. A statement which could be verified but has not yet been verified would then be potentially true, a truth *in posse*. But it is evident that James does not regard the pragmatist theory of truth as being simply and solely the result of arbitrary definition. Hence it is not unreasonable to claim that the theory is acceptable or unacceptable according as it is reduced or not reduced to a thesis which, once understood, appears obvious. That is to say, if it is reduced to the thesis that an empirical statement is true or false according as the state of affairs asserted or denied is (was or will be) the case or not, the theory is acceptable, though what is stated is 'trivial'. If, however, the theory identifies the truth of a statement with the process which would show that the state of affairs asserted or denied is the case or not, it is very difficult to see how it does not stand wide open to the objections of the 'rationalists'.

It is not suggested that these remarks constitute an adequate answer to James's question about the nature of correspondence. From the point of view of a professional logician to say, for example, that a proposition is a copy or picture of reality simply will not do. Even apart from the fact that it will not fit the propositions of pure mathematics and formal logic,[1] it is far too

---

[1] For James such propositions are truths *in posse*, which are made (actually) true by successful application, by their 'working'. But this implies that they are empirical hypotheses, a view which is not favoured by most modern logicians.

imprecise a description of the relation between a true empirical proposition and the state of affairs asserted or denied. And it is to James's credit that he saw this. But it is worth noting that he also seems to have felt that his theory of truth ran the risk of being reduced to a triviality. For he says that one can expect the theory to be first attacked, then to be admitted as true but obvious and insignificant, and finally to be regarded as 'so important that its adversaries claim that they themselves discovered it'.[1] If, however, the theory contains something more than what is 'obvious', it is this something more which we may well be inclined to consider the questionable element in James's pragmatism.

4. How does pragmatism stand to radical empiricism? According to James, there is no logical connection between them. Radical empiricism 'stands on its own feet. One may entirely reject it and still be a pragmatist.'[2] And yet he also tells us that 'the establishment of the pragmatist theory of truth is a step of first rate importance in making radical empiricism prevail'.[3]

Up to a certain point James is doubtless justified in saying that radical empiricism and pragmatism are independent of one another. For instance, it is perfectly possible to hold that relations are as real as their terms and that the world has a continuous structure without accepting the pragmatist conceptions of meaning and truth. At the same time the postulate of radical empiricism is, as we have seen, that only those matters should be considered as subjects of philosophical debate which are definable in terms derived from experience. And the pragmatist is said to hold of the truth-relation that 'everything in it is experienceable. ... The "workableness" which ideas must have, in order to be true, means particular workings, physical or intellectual, actual or possible, which they may set up from next to next inside of concrete experience.'[4] In other words, pragmatism will regard as possessing a claim to truth only those ideas which can be interpreted in terms of experienceable 'workings'. And acceptance of this view would obviously tend to make radical empiricism prevail, if by radical empiricism we mean the above-mentioned postulate.

We can put the matter in this way. Pragmatism, James remarks, has 'no doctrines save its method'.[5] Radical empiricism, however, which James develops into a metaphysics or world-view, has its

[1] *Pragmatism*, p. 198.   [2] *Ibid.*, p. ix.
[3] *The Meaning of Truth*, p. xii.   [4] *Ibid.*, p. xiv.
[5] *Pragmatism*, p. 54.

doctrines. These doctrines, considered in themselves, can be held on other grounds than those provided by radical empiricism. This is true, for example, of belief in God. But in James's view the use of the pragmatist theory of truth or method of determining truth and falsity would contribute greatly to making the doctrines of radical empiricism prevail. He may have been over-optimistic in thinking this; but it is what he thought.

Now, James also makes use of the word 'humanism' to describe his philosophy. In a narrower sense of the term he uses it to refer to the pragmatist theory of truth when considered as emphasizing the 'human' element in belief and knowledge. For example, 'humanism says that satisfactoriness is what distinguishes the true from the false'.[1] It sees that truth is reached 'by ever substituting more satisfactory for less satisfactory opinions'.[2] We have already noted that James tries to avoid pure subjectivism by insisting that a belief cannot be accounted satisfactory and so true, if it is incompatible with previously verified beliefs or if the available evidence tells against it. But in his view no belief can be final, in the sense of being incapable of revision. And this is precisely what the 'humanist' sees. He sees, for example, that our categories of thought have been developed in the course of experience, and that even if we cannot help employing them, they might conceivably change in the future course of evolution.

To borrow a Nietzschean phrase, the humanist understands that our beliefs are human, all-too-human. And it is in this sense that we should understand James's definition of humanism as the doctrine that '*though one part of our experience may lean upon another part to make it what it is in any one of several aspects in which it may be considered, experience as a whole is self-containing and leans on nothing*'.[3] What he means is that while there are standards which grow up *within* experience, there is no absolute standard of truth *outside* all experience, to which all our truths must conform. The humanist regards truth as relative to changing experience, and so as relative to man; and he regards absolute truth as 'that ideal vanishing-point towards which we imagine that all our temporary truths will some day converge'.[4] And, to do him justice, James is prepared to apply this outlook to humanism itself.[5]

---

[1] *Essays in Radical Empiricism*, p. 253. [2] *Ibid.*, p. 255.
[3] *The Meaning of Truth*, p. 124. [4] *Ibid.*, p. 85.
[5] See, for example, *The Meaning of Truth*, p. 90.

The term 'humanism', however, is also used by James in a wider sense. Thus he tells us that the issue between pragmatism and rationalism, and so between humanism and rationalism, is not simply a logical or epistemological issue: '*it concerns the structure of the universe itself*'.[1] The pragmatist sees the universe as unfinished, changing, growing and plastic. The rationalist, however, maintains that there is one 'really real' universe, which is complete and changeless. James is thinking partly of 'Vivekanda's mystical One'.[2] But he is also thinking, of course, of Bradley's monism, according to which change is not fully real and degrees of truth are measured in relation to a unique absolute experience which transcends our apprehension.[3]

Now, James himself remarks that the definition of humanism which is quoted above in the last paragraph but one seems at first sight to exclude theism and pantheism. But he insists that this is not really the case. 'I myself read humanism theistically and pluralistically.'[4] Humanism thus becomes a pluralistic and theistic metaphysics or world-view, coinciding with developed radical empiricism. But James's theism can be considered separately in the next section.

5. When discussing the application of pragmatism as a method to substantial philosophical problems, James remarks that Berkeley's criticism of the idea of material substance was thoroughly pragmatist in character. For Berkeley gives the 'cash-value',[5] as James puts it, of the term 'material substance' in ideas or sensations. Similarly, when examining the concept of the soul Hume and his successors 'redescend into the stream of experience with it, and cash it into so much small-change value in the way of "ideas" and their peculiar connections with each other'.[6]

James himself applies the pragmatist method to a problem of intimate personal concern, namely to the issue between theism and materialism. In the first place we can consider theism and materialism retrospectively, as James puts it. That is to say, we can suppose that the theist and the materialist see the world itself and its history in the same way, and that the theist then adds the hypothesis of a God who set the world going, while the materialist

---

[1] *Pragmatism*, p. 259.   [2] *Ibid.*, p. 262.
[3] James relates rival theories of the universe to different types of temperament.
[4] *The Meaning of Truth*, p. 125.
[5] James's talk about cash-value is apt to create an unfortunate impression. But he is referring, of course, to analyzing ideas on beliefs in terms of their 'practical consequences'.
[6] *Pragmatism*, p. 92.

excludes this hypothesis as unnecessary and invokes 'matter' instead. How are we to choose between these two positions? On pragmatist principles at any rate we cannot choose. For 'if no future detail of experience or conduct is to be deduced from our hypothesis, the debate between materialism and theism becomes quite idle and insignificant'.[1]

When, however, theism and materialism are considered 'prospectively', in relation to what they promise, to the expectations which they respectively lead us to entertain, the situation is quite different. For materialism leads us to expect a state of the universe in which human ideals, human achievements, consciousness and the products of thought will be as if they had never been,[2] whereas theism 'guarantees an ideal order that shall be permanently preserved'.[3] Somehow or other God will not allow the moral order to suffer shipwreck and destruction.

Looked at from this point of view, therefore, theism and materialism are very different. And on pragmatist principles we are entitled, other things being equal, to embrace that belief which corresponds best with the demands of our moral nature. But James does not mean to imply that there is no evidence at all in favour of theism, other than a desire that it should be true. 'I myself believe that the evidence for God lies primarily in inner personal experiences.'[4] In *A Pluralistic Universe* he resumes what he has already maintained in *The Varieties of Religious Experience* by arguing that 'the believer is continuous, to his own consciousness at any rate, with a wider self from which saving experiences flow in'.[5] Again, 'the drift of all the evidence we have seems to me to sweep us very strongly towards the belief in some form of superhuman life with which we may, unknown to ourselves, be co-conscious'.[6] At the same time the evil and suffering in the world suggest the conclusion that this superhuman consciousness is finite, in the sense that God is limited 'either in power, or in knowledge, or in both at once'.[7]

This idea of a finite God is used by James in his substitution of 'meliorism' for optimism on the one hand and pessimism on the other. According to the meliorist the world is not necessarily becoming better, nor is it necessarily becoming worse: it *can*

---

[1] *Ibid.*, p. 99.
[2] James quotes a well-known passage from A. J. Balfour's *The Foundations of Belief* (p. 30).
[3] *Pragmatism*, p. 106.   [4] *Ibid.*, p. 109.
[5] *A Pluralistic Universe*, p. 307.   [6] *Ibid.*   [7] *Ibid.*, p. 311.

344 THE PRAGMATIST MOVEMENT

become better, if, that is to say, man freely co-operates with the
finite God in making it better.[1] In other words, the future is not
inevitably determined, either for better or for worse, not even by
God. There is room in the universe for novelty, and human effort
has a positive contribution to make in the establishment of a
moral order.

James thus used pragmatism to support a religious world-view.
But we have seen that when stating the pragmatist theory of
meaning he declared that our whole conception of an object is
reducible to our ideas of the 'conceivable effects of a practical kind
the object may involve',[2] explicitly mentioning the sensations we
may expect and the reactions we should prepare. And we may well
doubt whether this is a promising foundation for a theistic world-
view. But as was noted in the section on his life, the reconciliation
of a scientific with a religious outlook constituted for him a
personal problem. And taking a theory of truth which was built
on to a theory of meaning that originated in an analysis of
empirical hypotheses, he used it to support the only world-view
which really satisfied him. In the process, of course, he extended
the concept of experience far beyond sense-experience. Thus he
maintained that religious empiricism is much more truly
'empirical' than irreligious empiricism, inasmuch as the former
takes seriously the varieties of religious experience whereas the
latter does not. In a sense his problem was the same as that of
Kant, to reconcile the scientific outlook with man's moral and
religious consciousness. His instrument of unification or harmonization was pragmatism. The result was presented as the development of radical empiricism. And the attitude adopted was
described as humanism.

6. The pragmatist movement was above all an American
phenomenon. True, one can find manifestations of the pragmatist
attitude even in German philosophy. In the seventh volume of this
History mention was made of the emphasis laid by F. A. Lange[3]
on the value for life of metaphysical theories and religious
doctrines at the expense of their cognitive value, and the way in
which Hans Vaihinger[4] developed what we may call a pragmatist
view of truth which had obvious affinities with Nietzsche's fiction-
theory.[5] Attention was also drawn to the influence exercised on

---

[1] James applied the pragmatist method to the issue between the theories of
free will and determinism, as also to that between pluralism and monism.
[2] *Pragmatism*, p. 47.   [3] Vol. VII, p. 366.
[4] *Ibid.*, pp. 366–7.   [5] *Ibid.*, pp. 408–10.

THE PRAGMATISM OF JAMES AND SCHILLER 345

William James by G. T. Fechner,[1] especially through his distinction between the 'day' and 'night' views of the universe and his claim that, other things being equal, we are entitled to give preference to the view which most contributes to human happiness and cultural development. As for French thought, mention was made in the first section of this chapter of the help derived by James from the writings of Charles Renouvier. And Renouvier, it may be noted, maintained that belief and even certitude are not exclusively intellectual affairs, but that affirmation involves also feeling and will. Though, however, we can certainly find affinities with pragmatism not only in German but also in French thought,[2] the pragmatist movement remains primarily associated with the names of three American philosophers, Peirce, James and Dewey.

This does not mean that England was without its pragmatist movement. But English pragmatism was neither so influential nor so impressive as its American counterpart. It would not be possible to give a reasonable account of American philosophy without including pragmatism. Peirce was an outstanding thinker on any count and nobody would question the influence exercised by James and Dewey on intellectual life in the United States. They brought philosophy to the fore, so to speak, to public notice; and Dewey especially applied it in the educational and social fields. But no great sin of omission would be committed if in an account of the development of modern British philosophy no mention were made of pragmatism, even though it caused a temporary flutter in the philosophical dovecotes. However, in an account of nineteenth-century British thought in which allusion has been made to a considerable number of minor philosophers some mention of pragmatism seems to be desirable.

In 1898 the Oxford Philosophical Society was founded, and an outcome of its discussions was the publication in 1902 of *Personal Idealism*, edited by Henry Sturt. In his preface to this collection of essays by eight members of the Society Sturt explained that the contributors were concerned with developing the theme of personality and with defending personality against naturalism on the one hand and absolute idealism on the other. The naturalist

[1] Vol. VII, pp. 375–6. James refers frequently to Fechner in his writings.
[2] It is worth mentioning that Maurice Blondel once used the term *pragmatism* for his philosophy of action. But when he became acquainted with American pragmatism, he dropped the term, as he did not agree with the interpretation given to it by William James.

maintains that the human person is a transitory product of physical processes, while the absolute idealist holds that personality is an unreal appearance of the Absolute.[1] In fine, 'Naturalism and Absolutism, antagonistic as they seem to be, combine in assuring us that personality is an illusion'.[2] Oxford idealism, Sturt went on to say, had always been opposed to naturalism; and to this extent absolute and personal idealism maintained a common front. But for this very reason the personal idealists felt that absolute idealism was a more insidious adversary than naturalism. The absolute idealists adopted the impracticable course of trying to criticize human experience from the point of view of absolute experience. And it failed to give any adequate recognition to the volitional aspect of human nature. Absolute idealism, in brief, was insufficiently empirical. And Sturt suggested 'empirical idealism' as an appropriate name for personal idealism. For personal life is what is closest to us and best known by us.

Needless to say, personal idealism and pragmatism are not interchangeable terms. Of the eight contributors to *Personal Idealism* some became well known outside the sphere of philosophy. R. R. Marett, the anthropologist, is an example. Others, such as G. F. Stout, were philosophers but not pragmatists. The volume contained, however, an essay by F. C. S. Schiller, who was the principal champion of pragmatism in England. And the point which we have been trying to make is that British pragmatism had a background of what we may call 'humanism'. It was to a considerable extent a protest on behalf of the human person not only against naturalism but also against the absolute idealism which was then the dominant factor in Oxford philosophy. It thus had more affinity with the pragmatism of William James than with the pragmatism of Peirce, which was essentially a method or rule for determining the meaning of concepts.

Ferdinand Canning Scott Schiller (1864–1937), came of German ancestry, though he was educated in England. In 1893 he became an instructor at Cornell University in America. In 1897 he was elected to a Tutorial Fellowship at Corpus Christi College, Oxford; and he remained a Fellow of the College until his death, though in 1929 he accepted a chair of philosophy in the University of Southern California at Los Angeles. In 1891 he published anony-

[1] Strictly speaking, Bradley did not hold that personality is an 'unreal appearance' of the Absolute. It is a real appearance; but, being appearance, it cannot be fully real.
[2] *Personal Idealism*, p. vi.

mously *Riddles of the Sphinx*,[1] and this was followed in 1902 by his essay, *Axioms as Postulates*, in *Personal Idealism*, the volume referred to above. *Humanism: Philosophical Essays* appeared in 1903, *Studies in Humanism* in 1907, *Plato or Protagoras?* in 1908, *Formal Logic* in 1912, *Problems of Belief* and *Tantalus, or The Future of Man* in 1924, *Eugenics and Politics* in 1926, *Logic for Use* in 1929 and *Must Philosophers Disagree? and Other Essays in Popular Philosophy* in 1934. Schiller also contributed a paper entitled *Why Humanism?* to the first series of *Contemporary British Philosophy* (1924), edited by J. H. Muirhead, and wrote the article on pragmatism for the fourteenth edition of the *Encyclopaedia Britannica* (1929).

7. As the titles of his writings suggest, Schiller's thought centres round man. In his essay *Plato or Protagoras?* he explicitly places himself on the side of Protagoras and makes his own the famous dictum that man is the measure of all things. *In Riddles of the Sphinx*, where he had attacked the absolute idealist theory of the One in the name of pluralistic personalism, he had declared that all our thinking must be anthropomorphic. But he did not at first use the term 'pragmatism' to describe his humanistic outlook. And in the preface to the first edition of *Humanism*, written after he had come under the influence of American pragmatism, especially that of William James, Schiller remarks that 'I was surprised to find that I had all along been a pragmatist myself without knowing it, and that little but the name was lacking to my own advocacy of an essentially cognate position in 1892'.[2] But though Schiller makes frequent use of the term 'pragmatism', once he has taken it over from William James, he insists that humanism is the basic concept. Humanism, which holds that man, and not the Absolute, is the measure of all experience and the maker of the sciences, is the fundamental and permanent attitude of thought of James and himself. Pragmatism 'is in reality only the application of Humanism to the theory of knowledge'.[3] The general need is to re-humanize the universe.

Re-humanization of the universe, humanism in other words, demands in the first place a humanization of logic. This demand is in part a protest against the arid subtleties and mental gymnastics

[1] A second edition, with the author's name, appeared in 1894 and a new edition in 1910.
[2] *Humanism*, p. xiii (2nd edition, 1912). Schiller's reference is to an essay, *Reality and Idealism*, which he published in 1892. It is reprinted in *Humanism*, pp. 110–27.
[3] *Ibid.*, p. xxv.

of formal logicians who treat logic as a game to be played for its own sake, a protest which, Schiller notes, was expressed by Albert Sidgwick, himself a logician, whose first work bore the title *Fallacies: A View of Logic from the Practical Side* (1883). But Schiller's demand for a humanization of logic is much more than a protest against the aridities and hair-splitting of some logicians. For it rests on the conviction that logic does not represent a realm of absolute and timeless truth which is unaffected by human interest and purposes. In Schiller's view the idea of absolute truth is an *'ignis fatuus'*,[1] in formal logic as well as in empirical science. The fundamental principles or axioms of logic are not *a priori* necessary truths; they are postulates, demands on experience,[2] which have shown themselves to possess a wider and more lasting value for the fulfilment of human purposes than is possessed by other postulates. And to bring out this aspect of the principles or axioms of logic is one of the tasks involved in the humanization of this science.

But we can go considerably further than this. The pragmatist believes that the validity of any logical procedure is shown by its successful working. But it works only in concrete contexts. And it is therefore idle to suppose that complete abstraction from all subject-matter introduces us into a realm of changeless, absolute truth. Indeed, Schiller goes so far as to say that formal logic *'is in the strictest and completest sense meaningless'*.[3] If someone says, 'it is too light' and we do not know the context, his statement is for us meaningless. For we do not know whether he is referring to the weight of an object, to the colour of something or to the quality of a lecture or a book. Similarly, we cannot abstract completely from the use of logic, from its application, *'without incurring thereby a total loss, not only of truth but also of meaning'*.[4]

If, therefore, logical principles are postulates made in the light of human desires and purposes, and if their validity depends on their success in fulfilling these desires and purposes, it follows that we cannot divorce logic from psychology. 'Logical value must be found in psychological fact *or nowhere*. . . . Logical possibilities (or even "necessities") are nothing until they have somehow become psychologically actual and active.'[5] So much for all attempts to de-psychologize logic and to set it on its own feet.

---

[1] *Contemporary British Philosophy*, First Series, p. 401.
[2] See *Axioms as Postulates* in *Personal Idealism*, p. 64.
[3] *Formal Logic*, p. 382.   [4] *Ibid.*, p. ix.
[5] *Axioms as Postulates* in *Personal Idealism*, p. 124.

What has been said of logical truth, namely that it is relative to human desires and aims, can be said of truth in general. Truths are in fact valuations. That is to say, to assert that a proposition is true is to say that it possesses practical value by fulfilling a certain purpose. 'Truth is the useful, efficient, workable, to which our practical experience tends to restrict our truth-valuations.'[1] Conversely, the false is the useless, what does not work. This is *the great Pragmatist principle of selection*.[2]

Schiller sees, of course, that ' "working" is clearly a vague generic term, and it is legitimate to ask what precisely is covered by it'.[3] But he finds this a difficult question to answer. It is comparatively easy to explain what is meant by the working of a scientific hypothesis. But it is not at all so easy to explain, for example, what forms of 'working' are to be accounted relevant to assessing the truth of an ethical theory. We have to admit that 'men take up different attitudes towards different workings because they themselves are temperamentally different'.[4] In other words, no clear and precise general answer can be given to the question.

As one would expect, Schiller is anxious to show that a distinction can be made on pragmatist principles between 'all truths are useful' and 'everything useful is true'. One of his arguments is that 'useful' means useful for a particular purpose, which is determined by the general context of a statement. For example, if I were threatened with torture if I did not say that the earth is flat, it would certainly be useful for me to say this. But the utility of my statement would not make it true. For statements about the shape of the earth pertain to empirical science; and it is certainly not useful for the advancement of science to assert that the earth is flat.

Another way of dealing with the matter is to insist on social recognition. But Schiller is alive to the fact that to recognize a truth is to recognize it as true. And on his principles to recognize it as true is to recognize it as useful. Hence social recognition cannot make a proposition useful, and so true. It is accorded to propositions which have already shown their utility. 'The use-criterion selects the individual truth-valuations, and constitutes thereby the objective truth which obtains social recognition.'[5]

Schiller tends to fall back on a biological interpretation of truth

---

[1] *Humanism*, p. 59.   [2] *Ibid.*, p. 58.
[3] *Contemporary British Philosophy*, First Series, p. 405.
[4] *Ibid.*, p. 406.   [5] *Humanism*, p. 59.

and to stress the idea of survival-value.[1] There is a process of natural selection among truths. Truths of inferior value are eliminated, while truths of superior value survive. And the belief which proves to have most survival-value shows itself to be the most useful, and so the most true. But what is survival-value? It can be described as 'a sort of working, which, while wholly devoid of any rational appeal, yet exercises a far-reaching influence on our beliefs, and is capable of determining this adoption and the elimination of their contraries'.[2] So we are back once more with the admittedly imprecise and vague idea of 'working'.

As we have seen, Schiller maintains that from 'all truths are useful' it does not follow that 'any proposition which is useful is true'. This is perfectly correct, of course. But then one might quite well hold that all truths are 'useful' in some sense or other without holding that their utility constitutes their truth. If one *does* hold that truth is constituted by utility, one can hardly deny at the same time that every useful proposition is true in so far as it is useful. And if the doctrine of non-convertibility is to be maintained successfully one has to show that true propositions possess some property or properties which useful falsehoods do not. Human beings are organisms, but not all organisms are human beings. And this is so because human beings possess properties which are not possessed by all organisms. What are the properties which are peculiar to true propositions over and above a utility which can also be possessed by a proposition which is false? This is a question to which Schiller never really faces up. Mention has been made of Sturt's opinion that absolute idealism did not give sufficient recognition to the volitional side of human nature. One of the troubles with Schiller is that he accords it too much recognition.

Schiller was much less inclined than James to indulge in metaphysical speculation. He did indeed maintain that humanism, an anthropocentric outlook, demands that we should look on the world as 'wholly plastic',[3] as indefinitely modifiable, as what we can make of it. But though he allows that humanists or pragmatists will regard the efforts of metaphysicians with tolerance and will concede aesthetic value to their systems, at the same time 'metaphysics seem doomed to remain *personal guesses* at ultimate reality, and to remain inferior in objective value to the

[1] See especially *Logic in Use*, also *Problems of Belief*, chapters XI–XII.
[2] *Contemporary British Philosophy*, First Series, p. 406.
[3] *Axioms as Postulates* in *Personal Idealism*, p. 61.

sciences, which are essentially "common" *methods* for dealing with phenomena'.[1] Here again we see the difficulty encountered by Schiller in explaining precisely what 'working' can mean outside the sphere of scientific hypotheses. So he attributes aesthetic value rather than truth-value to metaphysical theories. This is obviously because he regards scientific hypotheses as empirically verifiable whereas metaphysical systems are not. And we are back again with the question whether verification, a species of 'working', does not show an hypothesis to be true (or tend to show it) rather than constitute its truth.

Schiller's main contribution to pragmatism lay in his treatment of logic, which was more professional and detailed than that of William James. But his overall interpretation of logic cannot be said to have demonstrated its 'survival-value'.

---

[1] *Contemporary British Philosophy*, First Series, p. 409.

CHAPTER XVI

THE EXPERIMENTALISM OF JOHN DEWEY

Life and writings—Naturalistic empiricism: thought, experience and knowledge—The function of philosophy—Instrumentalism: logic and truth—Moral theory—Some implications in social and educational theory—Religion in a naturalistic philosophy —Some critical comments on Dewey's philosophy.

1. JOHN DEWEY (1859–1952) was born at Burlington, Vermont. After studying at the University of Vermont he became a high school teacher. But his interest in philosophy led him to submit to W. T. Harris an essay on the metaphysical assumptions of materialism with a view to publication in *The Journal of Speculative Philosophy*,[1] and the encouragement which he received resulted in his entering Johns Hopkins University in 1882. At the university Dewey attended courses on logic by C. S. Peirce, but the chief influence on his mind was exercised by G. S. Morris, the idealist, with whom Dewey entered into relations of personal friendship.

From 1884 until 1888 Dewey lectured at the University of Michigan, first as an instructor in philosophy and later as an assistant professor, after which he spent a year as professor at the University of Minnesota. In 1889 he returned to Michigan as head of the department of philosophy, and he occupied this post until 1894 when he went to Chicago. During this period Dewey occupied himself with logical, psychological and ethical questions, and his mind moved away from the idealism which he had learned from Morris.[2] In 1887 he published *Psychology*, in 1891 *Outlines of a Critical Theory of Ethics*, and in 1894 *The Study of Ethics: A Syllabus*.

From 1894 until 1904 Dewey was head of the department of philosophy in the University of Chicago, where he founded his Laboratory School[3] in 1896. The publications of this period include *My Pedagogic Creed* (1897), *The School and Society* (1900), *Studies in Logical Theory* (1903) and *Logical Conditions of a Scientific Treatment of Morality* (1903).

---

[1] The article was published in the issue of April, 1882.
[2] In this connection Dewey notes the influence exercised on his mind by William James's *Principles of Psychology*.
[3] An experimental school, commonly known as The Dewey School.

In 1904 Dewey went as professor of philosophy to Columbia University, becoming professor emeritus in 1929.[1] In 1908 he published *Ethics*,[2] in 1910 *How We Think* and *The Influence of Darwin and Other Essays in Contemporary Thought*, in 1915 *Schools of Tomorrow*, in 1916 *Democracy and Education* and *Essays in Experimental Logic*, in 1920 *Reconstruction in Philosophy*, in 1922 *Human Nature and Conduct*, in 1925 *Experience and Nature*, and in 1929 *The Quest for Certainty*. As for later publications *Art as Experience* and *A Common Faith* appeared in 1934, *Experience and Education* and *Logic: The Theory of Inquiry* in 1938, *Theory of Valuation* in 1939, *Education Today* in 1940, *Problems of Men* in 1946 and *Knowing and The Known* in 1949.

Outside the United States at least Dewey is probably best known for his instrumentalism, his version of pragmatism. But he was certainly not the man to concern himself simply with general theories about thought and truth. As the foregoing partial list of his publications indicates, he was deeply interested in problems of value and of human conduct, of society and of education. In the last-named field especially he exercised a great influence in America. Obviously, his ideas did not win universal acceptance. But they could not be ignored. And, in general, we can say that William James and John Dewey were the two thinkers who did most to bring philosophy to the attention of the educated public in the United States.

2. Dewey often describes his philosophy as empirical naturalism or naturalistic empiricism. And the meaning of these descriptions can perhaps best be illustrated by saying something about his account of the nature and function of thought. We can begin by considering the bearing in this context of the term 'naturalism'.

In the first place thought is not for Dewey an ultimate, an absolute, a process which creates objective reality in a metaphysical sense. Nor is it something in man which represents a non-natural element, in the sense that it sets man above or over against Nature. It is in the long run a highly developed form of the active relation between a living organism and its environment. To be sure, in spite of a tendency to use behaviourist language Dewey is well aware that the intellectual life of man has its own peculiar characteristics. The point is, however, that he refuses to start, for instance, from the distinction between subject and object as from

[1] During this period Dewey made several journeys abroad, to Europe, the Far East, Mexico and, in 1928, to Russia.
[2] Written in collaboration with J. H. Tufts.

an absolute and ultimate point of departure, but sees man's intellectual life as presupposing and developing out of antecedent relations, and thus as falling wholly within the sphere of Nature. Thought is one among other natural processes or activities.

All things react in some way to their environment. But they obviously do not all react in the same way. In a given set of circumstances an inanimate thing, for example, can be said simply to react or not to react. A situation does not pose any problem which the thing can recognize as a problem and to which it can react in a selective manner. When, however, we turn to the sphere of life, we find selective responses. As living organisms become more complex, their environment becomes more ambivalent. That is to say, it becomes more uncertain what responses or actions are called for in the interests of living, what actions will best fit into a series which will sustain the continuity of life. And 'in the degree that responses take place to the doubtful *as* the doubtful, they acquire *mental* quality'.[1] Further, when such responses possess a directed tendency to change the precarious into the secure and the problematic into the resolved, 'they are *intellectual* as well as mental'.[2]

We can say therefore that for Dewey thought is a highly developed form of the relation between stimulus and response on the purely biological level. True, in its interaction with its environment the human organism, like any other organism, acts primarily according to established habits. But situations arise which reflection recognizes as problematic situations, and thus as calling for inquiry or thought, the immediate response being thus in a sense interrupted. But in another sense the response is not interrupted. For the aim of thought, stimulated by a problematic situation, is to transform or reconstruct the set of antecedent conditions which gave rise to the problem or difficulty. In other words, it aims at a change in the environment. 'There is no inquiry that does not involve the making of *some* change in environing conditions.'[3] That is to say, the conclusion at which the process of inquiry arrives is a projected action or set of actions, a plan of possible action which will transform the problematic situation. Thought is thus instrumental and has a practical function. It is not, however, quite accurate to say that it subserves activity. For it is itself a form of activity. And it can be seen as part of a total process of activity whereby man seeks to resolve problematic

---

[1] *The Quest for Certainty*, p. 225.   [2] *Ibid*.   [3] *Logic*, I, p. 42.

situations by effecting changes in his environment, by changing an 'indeterminate' situation, one in which the elements clash or do not harmonize and so give rise to a problem for reflection, into a 'determinate' situation, a unified whole. In this sense, therefore, thought does not interrupt the process of response; for it is itself part of the total response. But the process of inquiry presupposes recognition of a problematic situation *as* problematic. It can thus be said to interrupt the response, if we mean by response one that is instinctive or follows simply in accordance with some established habit.

A man can, of course, react to a problematic situation in an unintelligent manner. To take a simple example, he may lose his temper and smash a tool or instrument which is not functioning properly. But this sort of reaction is clearly unhelpful. To solve his problem the man has to inquire into what is wrong with the instrument and consider how to put things right. And the conclusion at which he arrives is a plan of possible action calculated to transform the problematic situation.

This is an example taken from the level of common sense. But Dewey will not allow that there is any impassable gulf or rigid distinction between the level of common sense and that of, say, science. Scientific inquiry may involve prolonged operations which are not overt actions in the ordinary sense but operations with symbols. Yet the total process of hypothesis, deduction and controlled experiment simply reproduces in a much more sophisticated and complex form the process of inquiry which is stimulated by some practical problem in everyday life. Even the complicated operations with symbols aim at transforming the problematic situation which gave rise to the hypothesis. Thus thought is always practical in some way, whether it takes place at the level of common sense or at the level of scientific theory. In both cases it is a way of dealing with a problematic situation.

It is to be noted that when Dewey speaks of effecting a change in the environment, the last-mentioned term should not be understood as referring exclusively to man's physical environment, the world of physical Nature. 'The environment in which human beings live, act and inquire, is not simply physical. It is cultural as well.'[1] And a clash of values, for example, in a given society gives rise to a problematic situation, the resolution of which would effect a change in the cultural environment.

[1] *Ibid.*, p. 42.

This account of thought and its basic function corresponds with the fact that 'man who lives in a world of hazards is compelled to seek for security'.[1] And it is, of course, obvious that when man is faced with threatening and perilous situations, recognized as such, it is action which is called for, not simply thought. At the same time Dewey is, needless to say, well aware that inquiry and thought do not necessarily lead to action in the ordinary sense. For example, a scientist's inquiry may terminate in an idea or set of ideas, that is, in a scientific theory or hypothesis. Dewey's account of thought does indeed entail the view that 'ideas are anticipatory plans and designs which take effect in concrete reconstruction of antecedent conditions of existence'.[2] A scientific hypothesis is predictive, and it thus looks forward, so to speak, to verification. But the scientist may not be in a position to verify it here or now. Or he may not choose to do so. His inquiry then terminates in a set of ideas; and he does not possess warranted knowledge. But this does not alter the fact that the ideas are predictive, that they are plans for possible action.

Analogously, if a man is stimulated to inquiry or reflection by a morally problematic situation, the moral judgment which he finally makes is a plan or directive for possible action. When a man commits himself to a moral principle, he expresses his preparedness to act in certain ways in certain circumstances. But though his thought is thus directed to action, action does not necessarily follow. The judgment which he makes is a direction for possible action.

Now, there is a real sense in which each problematic situation is unique and unrepeatable. And when Dewey is thinking of this aspect of the matter, he tends to depreciate general theories. But it is obvious that the scientist works with general concepts and theories; and Dewey's recognition of the fact is shown in his insistence that a theory's connection with action is 'with *possible* ways of operation rather than with those found to be *actually* and immediately required'.[3] At the same time the tension between a tendency to depreciate general concepts and theories, in view of the fact that inquiry is stimulated by particular problematic situations and aims at transforming them, and a recognition of the fact that scientific thought operates with general ideas and constructs general theories, general solutions, shows itself in what

[1] *The Quest for Certainty*, p. 3.   [2] *Ibid.*, p. 166.
[3] *Logic*, p. 49.

Dewey has to say about the nature of philosophy. But this matter can be left to the next section.

We have seen that Dewey's account of thought is 'naturalistic' in the sense that it depicts thought as developing out of the relation between an organism and its environment. 'Intellectual operations are foreshadowed in behaviour of the biological kind, and the latter prepares the way for the former.'[1] Naturalism does not deny differences, of course, but it is committed to accounting for these differences without invoking any non-natural source or agent. In other words, thought must be represented as a product of evolution.

Further, Dewey's account of thought can be described as 'empiricist' in the sense that thought is depicted as starting from experiences and as leading back to experiences. The process of inquiry is set in motion when the subject encounters a problematic situation in its environment, and it terminates, whether actually or ideally, in some change in the environment, or indeed in man himself. At the same time Dewey asserts that the object of knowledge is made or constructed by thought. And as this statement seems at first sight to represent an idealist rather than an empiricist position, it stands in need of some explanation.

Experience in general is said to be a transaction, a process of doing and undergoing, an active relation between an organism and its environment. And according to Dewey primary or immediate experience is non-cognitive in character. It contains 'no division between act and material, subject and object, but contains them both in an unanalyzed totality'.[2] What is experienced is not objectified by a subject as a sign possessing significance or meaning. Distinctions such as that between subject and object arise only for reflection. And a thing assumes, or, rather, is clothed with significance only as the result of a process of inquiry or thought. A fountain pen, for example, takes on significance for me in terms of its function or functions. And it does so as the result of a process of inquiry or thought. Inasmuch, therefore, as Dewey reserves the term 'object of knowledge' for the term of this process, he can say that thought makes or constructs the object of knowledge.

On the one hand Dewey is at pains to point out that his account of the activity of knowing does not entail the conclusion that

---

[1] *Ibid.*, p. 43.
[2] *Experience and Nature*, p. 8 (Dover Publications edition 1958).

things do not exist antecedently to being experienced or to being thought about.[1] On the other hand by identifying the object of knowledge with the term of inquiry he is committed to saying that it is in some sense the product of thought. For the term of inquiry is the determinate situation which replaces an indeterminate or problematic situation. Dewey argues, however, that 'knowledge is not a distortion or perversion which confers upon *its* subject-matter traits which *do* not belong to it, but is an act which confers upon non-cognitive material traits which *did* not belong to it'.[2] The resolution of a problematic situation or the process of clothing with determinate significance is no more a distortion or perversion than is the act of the architect who confers upon stone and wood qualities and relations which they did not formerly possess.

If it is asked why Dewey adopts this odd theory of knowledge, which identifies the object of knowledge with the term of the process of inquiry, one reason is that he wishes to get rid of what he calls 'the spectator theory of knowledge'.[3] According to this theory we have on the one hand the knower and on the other the object of knowledge, which is entirely unaffected by the process of knowing. We are then faced with the problem of finding a bridge between the process of knowing which takes place wholly within the spectator-subject and the object which is indifferent to being known. If, however, we understand that the object of knowledge as such comes into being through the process of knowing, this difficulty does not arise.

The statement that the object of knowledge comes into being through the process of knowing might, considered by itself, be a tautology. For it is tautological to say that nothing is constituted an object of knowledge except by being known. But Dewey obviously does not intend the statement to be a tautology: he intends to say something more. And what he intends is to depict the process of knowing as a highly developed form of the active relation between an organism and its environment, a relation whereby a change is effected in the environment. In other words, he is concerned with giving a naturalistic account of knowledge and with excluding any concept of it as a mysterious phenomenon which is entirely *sui generis*. He is also concerned with uniting theory and practice. Hence knowledge is represented as being

[1] Dewey remarks, for example, that 'I should think it fairly obvious that we experience most things *as* temporally prior to our experiencing of them', *The Influence of Darwin*, p. 240.
[2] *Experience and Nature*, p. 381.   [3] *The Quest for Certainty*, p. 23.

itself a doing or making rather than, as in the so-called spectator theory, a 'seeing'.

3. Dewey's account of thought and knowledge is obviously relevant to his concept of philosophy and to his judgments about other philosophers. For example, he is sharply opposed to the idea of philosophy as being concerned with a sphere of unchanging, timeless being and truth. We can indeed explain the genesis of this idea. 'The *world* is precarious and perilous.'[1] That is to say, the hazards to which men are exposed are objective situations. And when they are recognized as hazards, they become problematic situations which man seeks to resolve. But his means for doing so are limited. Further, in his search for security, and so for certainty, man becomes aware that the empirical world, which is a changing world, cannot provide him with absolute security and certainty. And we find Greek philosophers such as Plato making a sharp distinction between the changing, empirical world and the sphere of immutable being and truth. Theory thus becomes divorced from practice.[2] True, philosophy remains an activity. For thought is always an activity. But with Aristotle, for example, purely theoretical activity, the life of contemplation, is exalted above the practical life, the life of action in a changing world. And it becomes necessary to recall thought to its true function of being directed to resolving indeterminate or problematic situations by effecting changes in the environment and in man himself. Thought and practice have to be once more joined together.

This union of thought and practice is seen most strikingly in the rise of modern science. In the early stages of history man either tried to control the mysterious and threatening forces of Nature by magic or personified them and sought to appease them, though he also practised simple acts such as that of agriculture. Later, as we have seen, there arose that divorce between theory and practice which was effected by philosophy, the idea of man as spectator being substituted for that of man as actor. But with the rise of modern science a new attitude to change shows itself. For the scientist sees that it is only by correlating phenomena that we can understand the process of change and, within limits, control it, bringing about the changes which we desire and preventing

---

[1] *Experience and Nature*, p. 42.
[2] Dewey is, of course, aware of the practical aspects of the thought of Plato and Aristotle. But he is opposed to the whole idea of a sphere of immutable Being and Truth, and the dichotomy between the sphere of Being and the sphere of Becoming is the aspect of Plato's philosophy which he emphasizes.

those which we regard as undesirable. Thought is thus no longer directed to a celestial sphere of unchanging being and truth; it is redirected to the experienced environment, though on a surer basis than it was in the early stages of humanity. And with the constant growth and progress of the sciences the whole attitude of man towards thought and knowledge has been altered. And this new attitude or vision of the function of thought and knowledge needs to be reflected in our concept of philosophy.

Now, the particular sciences are not themselves philosophy. But science has been commonly conceived as presenting us with the picture of a world which is indifferent to moral values, as eliminating from Nature all qualities and values. And 'thus is created the standing problem of modern philosophy: the relation of science to the things we prize and love and which have authority in the direction of conduct'.[1] This problem, which occupied the mind of, for example, Immanuel Kant, became 'the philosophic version of the popular conflict of science and religion'.[2] And philosophers of the spiritualistic and idealistic traditions, from the time of Kant, or rather from that of Descartes, onwards have tried to solve the problem by saying that the world of science can safely be presented as the sphere of matter and mechanism, stripped of qualities and values, because 'matter and mechanism have their foundation in immaterial mind'.[3] In other words, philosophers have tried to reconcile the scientific view of the world, as they conceived it, with an assertion of the reality of values by developing their several versions of the same sort of dichotomy or dualism which was characteristic of Platonism.

Obviously, Dewey will have nothing to do with this way of solving the problem. For in his view it amounts simply to a resuscitation of an outmoded metaphysics. But though he rejects the notion that there are immutable values, transcending the changing world, he has not the slightest intention of belittling, much less of denying, values. Hence he is committed by his naturalism to maintaining that they are in some sense comprised within Nature, and that advance in scientific knowledge constitutes no threat whatever to the reality of value. 'Why should we not proceed to employ our gains in science to improve our judgments about values, and to regulate our actions so as to make values more secure and more widely shared in existence?'[4] It is not

---

[1] *The Quest for Certainty*, p. 103.   [2] *Ibid.*, p. 41.
[3] *Ibid.*, p. 42.   [4] *Ibid.*

the business of the philosopher to prove in general that there are values. For beliefs about values and value-judgments are inevitable characteristics of man; and any genuine philosophy of experience is aware of this fact. 'What is inevitable needs no proof for its existence.'[1] But man's affections, desires, purposes and devices need direction; and this is possible only through knowledge. Here philosophy can give guidance. The philosopher can examine the accepted values and ideals of a given society in the light of their consequences, and he can at the same time attempt to resolve the conflicts between values and ideals which arise within a society by pointing the way to new possibilities, thus transforming indeterminate or problematic situations in the cultural environment into determinate situations.

The function of philosophy is thus both critical and constructive or, rather, reconstructive. And it is critical with a view to reconstruction. Hence we can say that philosophy is essentially practical. And inasmuch as there is no question of the philosopher competing with the scientist on his own ground, Dewey naturally lays emphasis on moral and social philosophy and on the philosophy of education. True, the philosopher is by no means confined to these topics. As Dewey maintains in *Studies in Logical Theory*, a philosophy of experience includes within its area of inquiry all modes of human experience, including the scientific as well as the moral, religious and aesthetic, and also the social-cultural world in its organized form. And it should investigate the interrelations between these different fields. But if we are thinking of the resolution of specific problematic situations, the philosopher is obviously not in a better position than the scientist to solve scientific problems. From this point of view, therefore, it is natural that Dewey should have come to say that 'the task of future philosophy is to clarify men's ideas as to the social and moral strifes of their own day. Its aim is to become so far as is humanly possible an organ for dealing with these conflicts.'[2]

Now, if the philosopher is conceived as being called upon to throw light on specific problematic situations, it is understandable that general notions and theories should be depreciated. We can understand, for example, Dewey's assertion that whereas philosophical discussion in the past has been carried on 'in terms of *the* state, *the* individual',[3] what is really required is light upon 'this

---

[1] *Ibid.*, p. 299.   [2] *Reconstruction in Philosophy*, p. 26.
[3] *Ibid.*, p. 188.

or that group of individuals, this or that concrete human being, this or that special institution or social arrangement'.[1] In other words, when he is concerned with emphasizing the practical function of philosophy, Dewey tends to depreciate general concepts and theories as divorced from concrete life and experience and as associated with a view of philosophy as a purely contemplative activity. His attitude is an expression of his protest against the divorce of theory from practice.

The reader will doubtless object that it is no more the business of the philosopher as such to solve, for instance, specific political problems than it is to solve specific scientific problems. But Dewey does not really intend to say that it is the philosopher's business to do this. What he claims is that 'the true impact of philosophical reconstruction'[2] is to be found in the development of *methods* for reconstructing specific problematic situations. In other words, Dewey is concerned with the 'transfer of experimental method from the technical field of physical experience to the wider field of human life'.[3] And this transfer obviously requires a general theory of experimental method, while the use of the method 'implies direction by ideas and knowledge'.[4] True, Dewey has not the slightest intention of encouraging the development of a method which is supposed to possess an *a priori*, absolute and universal validity. He insists that what is needed is an intelligent examination of the actual consequences of inherited and traditional customs and institutions with a view to intelligent examination of the ways in which their customs and institutions should be modified in order to produce the consequences which we consider desirable. But this does not alter the fact that a great part of his reflection is devoted to developing a general logic of experience and a general theory of experimental method.

It would thus be a gross caricature of Dewey's actual practice if one were to represent him as despising all general concepts and all general theories, still more if we were to represent him as actually doing without such concepts and theories. Without them one could not be a philosopher at all. It is true that in his contribution to a volume of essays entitled *Creative Intelligence* (1917) Dewey roundly asserts that because 'reality' is a denotative term, designating indifferently everything that happens, no general theory of reality 'is possible or needed',[5] a conclusion which does

---

[1] *Reconstruction in Philosophy*, p. 188.   [2] *Ibid.*, p. 193.
[3] *The Quest for Certainty*, p. 273.   [4] *Ibid.*
[5] *Creative Intelligence*, p. 55.

not appear to follow from the premises. But in *Experience and Nature* (1925) he can fairly be said to have himself developed such a theory, though admittedly not a theory of any reality transcending Nature. Similarly, though in *Reconstruction in Philosophy* he rules out talk about 'the State', this does not prevent him from developing a theory of the State. Again, when he asserts that any philosophy which is not isolated from modern life must grapple with 'the problem of restoring integration and co-operation between man's beliefs about the world in which he lives and his beliefs about the values and purposes that should direct his conduct',[1] he is indicating a problem which cannot possibly be discussed without general ideas. It is not indeed a question of maintaining that Dewey is perpetually contradicting himself. For example, one might rule out talk about 'the State', meaning by this an eternal essence, and yet make generalizations based on reflection about actual States. Rather is it a question of maintaining that Dewey's insistence on practice, as the termination of inquiry in the reconstruction of a specific problematic situation, leads him at times to speak in a way which does not square with his actual practice.

4. We have noted the stress which Dewey lays on inquiry, inquiry being defined as 'the controlled or directed transformation of an indeterminate situation into one that is so determinate in its constituent distinctions and relations as to convert the elements of the original situation into a unified whole'.[2] He calls, therefore, for a new logic of inquiry. If the Aristotelian logic is considered purely historically, in relation to Greek culture, 'it deserves the admiration it has received'.[3] For it is an admirable analysis of 'discourse in isolation from the operations in which discourse takes effect'.[4] At the same time the attempt to preserve the Aristotelian logic when the advance of science has undermined the ontological background of essences and species on which it rested is 'the main source of existing confusion in logical theory'.[5] Moreover, if this logic is retained when its ontological presuppositions have been repudiated, it inevitably becomes purely formal and quite inadequate as a logic of inquiry. True, Aristotle's logic remains a model in the sense that it combined in a unified scheme both the

---

[1] *The Quest for Certainty*, p. 255.
[2] *Logic*, pp. 104–5. Bertrand Russell objects that this definition would apply to the activity of a drill sergeant in transforming a collection of new recruits into a regiment, though this activity could hardly be described as a process of inquiry. Cf. *The Philosophy of John Dewey*, edited by P. A. Schilpp, p. 143.
[3] *Ibid.*, p. 94.   [4] *Ibid.*   [5] *Ibid.*

common sense and the science of his day. But his day is not our day. And what we need is a unified theory of inquiry which will make available for use in other fields 'the authentic pattern of experimental and operational inquiry in science'.[1] This is not to demand that all other fields of inquiry should be reduced to physical science. It is rather that the logic of inquiry has hitherto found its chief exemplification in physical science, and that it needs to be abstracted, so to speak, and turned into a general logic of inquiry which can be employed in all 'inquiries concerned with deliberate reconstruction of experience'.[2] We are thus reminded of Hume's demand that the experimental method of inquiry which had proved so fruitful in physical science or natural philosophy should be applied in the fields of aesthetics, ethics and politics. But Dewey, unlike Hume, develops an elaborate account of this logic of inquiry.

It would be impracticable to summarize this account here. But certain features can be mentioned. In general, logic is regarded, of course, as instrumental, that is, as a means of rendering intelligent, instead of blind, the action involved in reconstructing a problematic or indeterminate situation. Intelligent action presupposes a process of thought or inquiry, and this requires symbolization and propositional formulation. Propositions in general are the necessary logical instruments for reaching a final judgment which has existential import; and the final judgment is reached through a series of intermediate judgments. Hence judgment can be described as 'a continuous process of resolving an indeterminate, unsettled situation into a determinately unified one, through operations which transform subject-matter originally given'.[3] The whole process of judgment and ratiocination can thus be considered as a phase of intelligent actions, and at the same time as instrumental to actual reconstruction of a situation. Universal propositions, for instance, are formulations of possible ways of acting or operating.[4] They are all of the 'if/then' type.

If logical thought is instrumental, its validity is shown by its success. Hence the standard of validity is 'precisely the degree in which the thinking actually disposes of the difficulty [the problematic situation] and allows us to proceed with more direct modes of experiencing that are forthwith possessed of more assured and deepened value'.[5] In accordance with this view Dewey rejects the

---

[1] *Logic*, p. 98. [2] *Reconstruction in Philosophy*, p. 138.
[3] *Logic*, p. 283. [4] *Ibid.*, p. 264.
[5] *Studies in Logical Theory*, p. 3. Dewey often depicts the term of inquiry as an enrichment and deepening of experience.

idea of the basic principles of logic as being *a priori* truths which are fixed antecedently to all inquiry and represents them as generated in the process of inquiry itself. They represent conditions which have been found, during the continued process of inquiry, to be involved in or demanded by its success. Just as causal laws are functional in character, so are the so-called first principles of logic. Their validity is measured by their success. Instrumentalism in logic thus has a connection with Dewey's naturalism. The basic logical principles are not eternal truths, transcending the changing empirical world and to be apprehended instinctively; they are generated in the actual process of man's active relation with his environment.

In an essay on the development of American pragmatism Dewey defines instrumentalism as 'an attempt to constitute a precise logical theory of concepts, of judgments and inferences in their various forms, by considering primarily how thought functions in the experimental determinations of future consequences'.[1] But there is also an instrumentalist theory of truth. And some brief remarks must be made about this topic.

In a footnote in his *Logic* Dewey remarks that 'the best definition of *truth* from the logical standpoint which is known to me is that of Peirce',[2] namely that the true is that opinion which is fated to be ultimately accepted by all investigators. He also quotes with approval Peirce's statement that truth is the concordance of an abstract statement with the ideal limit towards which endless inquiry would tend to bring scientific belief. Elsewhere, however, Dewey insists that if it is asked what truth is here and now, so to speak, without reference to an ideal limit of all inquiry, the answer is that a statement or an hypothesis is true or false in so far as it leads us to or away from the end which we have in view. In other words, 'the hypothesis that works is the *true* one'.[3] In Dewey's opinion this view of truth follows as a matter of course from the pragmatist concept of meaning.

Dewey is careful to point out that if it is said that truth is utility or the useful, this statement is not intended to identify truth with 'some purely personal end, some profit upon which a particular individual has set his heart'.[4] The idea of utility in this context must be interpreted in relation to the process of

---

[1] *Twentieth Century Philosophy*, edited by D. D. Runes, pp. 463-4 (New York, 1943).
[2] *Logic*, p. 345, note 6.
[3] *Reconstruction in Philosophy*, p. 156.   [4] *Ibid.*, p. 157.

transforming a problematic situation. And a problematic situation is something public and objective. A scientific problem, for example, is not a private neurotic worry but an objective difficulty which is resolved by appropriate objective methods. For this reason Dewey avoids speaking with James of truth as the satisfactory or that which satisfies. For this way of speaking suggests a private emotive satisfaction. And if the term 'the satisfactory' is employed, we must understand that the satisfaction in question is that of the demands of a public problematic situation, not the satisfaction of the emotive needs of any individual. For the matter of that, the solution of a scientific problem might occasion great unhappiness to the human race. Yet in so far as it worked or manifested its utility by transforming an objective problematic situation, it would be true and 'satisfactory'.

Though, however, he insists that instrumentalism does not deny the objectivity of truth by making it relative to the individual's whims, wishes and emotive needs, Dewey is, of course, well aware that his theory is opposed to that of eternal, unchanging truths. Indeed, he obviously intends this opposition. He regards the theory of eternal, unchanging truths as implying a certain metaphysics or view of reality, namely the distinction between the phenomenal sphere of becoming and the sphere of perfect and unchanging being, which is apprehended in the form of eternal truths. This metaphysics is, of course, at variance with Dewey's naturalism. Hence the so-called timeless truths have to be represented by him as being simply instruments for application in knowing the one world of becoming, instruments which constantly show their value in use. In other words, their significance is functional rather than ontological. No truth is absolutely sacrosanct, but some truths possess in practice a constant functional value.

This theory that there are no sacrosanct eternal truths, but that all statements which we believe to be true are revisible in principle or from the purely logical point of view, obviously has important implications in the fields of morals and politics. 'To generalize the recognition that the true means the verified and nothing else places upon men the responsibility for surrendering political and moral dogmas, and subjecting to the test of consequences their most cherished prejudices.'[1] In Dewey's opinion this is one of the main reasons why the instrumentalist theory of truth raises fear and hostility in many minds.

[1] *Reconstruction in Philosophy*, p. 160.

5. Passing over for the present any criticism of the instrumentalist theory of truth, we can turn to ethics which Dewey regards as concerned with intelligent conduct in view of an end, with consciously directed conduct. A moral agent is one who proposes to himself an end to be achieved by action.[1] But Dewey insists that activity, consciously directed to an end which is thought worth while by the agent, presupposes habits as acquired dispositions to respond in certain ways to certain classes of stimuli. 'The act must come before the thought, and a habit before an ability to evoke the thought at will.'[2] As Dewey puts it, it is only the man who already has certain habits of posture and who is capable of standing erect that can form for himself the idea of an erect stance as an end to be consciously pursued. Our ideas, like our sensations, depend on experience. 'And the experience upon which they both depend is the operation of habits—originally of instincts.'[3] Our purposes and aims in action come to us through the medium of habits.

Dewey's insistence on the relevance to ethics of the psychology of habit is partly due to his conviction that habits, as demands for certain kinds of action, 'constitute the self',[4] and that 'character is the interpenetration of habits'.[5] For if such interpenetration, in the sense of an harmonious and unified integration, is something to be achieved rather than an original datum, it obviously follows that moral theory must take habits into account, in so far as it is concerned with the development of human nature.

But Dewey's emphasis on the psychology of habit is also due to his determination to include ethics in his general naturalistic interpretation of experience. Naturalism cannot accommodate such ideas as those of eternal norms, subsistent absolute values or a supernatural moral legislator. The whole moral life, while admittedly involving the appearance of fresh elements, must be represented as a development of the interaction of the human organism with its environment. Hence a study of biological and social psychology is indispensable for the moral philosopher who is concerned with the moral life as it actually exists.

It has already been noted that for Dewey environment does not mean simply the physical, non-human environment. Indeed, from the moral point of view man's relations with his social environment are of primary importance. For it is a mistake to think that

[1] Cf., for example, *Outlines of a Critical Theory of Ethics*, p. 3.
[2] *Human Nature and Conduct*, p. 30.   [3] *Ibid.*, p. 32.
[4] *Ibid.*, p. 25.   [5] *Ibid.*, p. 38.

morality *ought* to be social: 'morals *are* social'.[1] This is simply an empirical fact. It is true that to a considerable extent customs, which are widespread uniformities of habit, exist because individuals are faced by similar situations to which they react in similar ways. 'But to a larger extent customs persist because individuals form their personal habits under conditions set by prior customs. An individual usually acquires the morality as he inherits the speech of his social group.'[2] This may indeed be more obvious in the case of earlier forms of society. For in modern society, at least of the Western democratic type, the individual is offered a wide range of custom-patterns. But in any case, customs, as demands for certain ways of acting and as forming certain outlooks, constitute moral standards. And we can say that 'for practical purposes morals mean customs, folk-ways, established collective habits'.[3]

At the same time customs, as widespread uniformities of habit, tend to perpetuate themselves even when they no longer answer the needs of man in his relations with his environment. They tend to become matter of mechanical routine, a drag on human growth and development. And to say this is to imply that there is in man another factor, besides habit, which is relevant to morals. This factor is impulse. Indeed, habits, as acquired dispositions to act in certain ways, are secondary to unacquired or unlearned impulses.

This distinction, however, gives rise to a difficulty. On the one hand impulse represents the sphere of spontaneity and thus the possibility of reorganizing habits in accordance with the demands of new situations. On the other hand man's impulses are for the most part not definitely organized and adapted in the way in which animal instincts are organized and adapted. Hence they acquire the significance and definiteness which are required for human conduct only through being canalized into habits. Thus 'the direction of native activity depends upon acquired habits, and yet acquired habits can be modified only by redirection of impulses'.[4] How, then, can man be capable of changing his habits and customs to meet fresh situations and the new demands of a changing environment? How can he change himself?

This question can be answered only by introducing the idea of intelligence. When changing conditions in the environment render a habit useless or detrimental or when a conflict of habits occurs,

[1] *Human Nature and Conduct*, p. 319.   [2] *Ibid.*, p. 58.
[3] *Ibid.*, p. 75.   [4] *Ibid.*, p. 126.

impulse is liberated from the control of habit and seeks redirection. Left to itself, so to speak, it simply bursts the chains of habit asunder in a wild upsurge. In social life this means that if a society's customs have become outmoded or harmful, and if the situation is left to itself, revolution inevitably occurs, unless perhaps the society simply becomes lifeless and fossilized. The alternative is obviously the intelligent redirection of impulse into new customs and the intelligent creation of fresh institutions. In fine, a 'breach in the crust of the cake of custom releases impulses; but it is the work of intelligence to find the ways of using them'.[1]

In some sense, therefore, intelligence, when seeking to transform or reconstruct a problematic moral situation, has to deliberate about ends and means. But for Dewey there are no fixed ends which the mind can apprehend as something given from the start and perennially valid. Nor will he allow that an end is a value which lies beyond the activity which seeks to attain it. 'Ends are foreseen consequences which arise in the cause of activity and which are employed to give activity added meaning and to direct its further course.'[2] When we are dissatisfied with existing conditions, we can, of course, picture to ourselves a set of conditions which, if actualized, would afford satisfaction. But Dewey insists that an imaginary picture of this kind becomes a genuine aim or end-in-view only when it is worked out in terms of the concrete, possible process of actualizing it, that is, in terms of 'means'. We have to study the ways in which results similar to those which we desire are actually brought about by causal activity. And when we survey the proposed line of action, the distinction between means and ends arises within the series of contemplated acts.

It is obviously possible for intelligence to operate with existing moral standards. But we are considering problematic situations which demand something more than manipulating the current moral ideas and standards of a society. And in such situations it is the task of intelligence to grasp and actualize possibilities of growth, of the reconstruction of experience. Indeed, 'growth itself is the only moral "end"'.[3] Again, 'growing, or the continuous reconstruction of experience, is the only end'.[4]

A natural question to ask is, growth in what direction? Reconstruction for what purpose? But if such questions concern a final end other than growth itself, reconstruction itself, they can have

---

[1] *Ibid.*, p. 170.   [2] *Ibid.*, p. 225.
[3] *Reconstruction in Philosophy*, p. 177.   [4] *Ibid.*, p. 184.

no meaning in terms of Dewey's philosophy. He does indeed admit that happiness or the satisfaction of the forces of human nature is the moral end. But as happiness turns out to be living, while 'life means growth',[1] we seem to be back at the same point. The growth which is the moral end is one which makes possible further growth. In other words, growth itself is the end.

We must remember, however, that for Dewey no genuine end is separable from the means, from the process of its actualization. And he tells us that 'good consists in the meaning that is experienced to belong to an activity when conflict and entanglement of various incompatible impulses and habits terminate in a unified orderly release in action'.[2] So we can say perhaps that for Dewey the moral end is growth in the sense of the dynamic development of harmoniously integrated human nature, provided that we do not envisage a fixed and determinate state of perfection as the final end. There is for Dewey no final end save growth itself. The attainment of a definite and limited end-in-view opens up new vistas, new tasks, fresh possibilities of action. And it is in grasping and realizing these opportunities and possibilities that moral growth consists.

Dewey tries, therefore, to get rid of the concept of a realm of values distinct from the world of fact. Values are not something given; they are constituted by the act of evaluating, by the value-judgment. This is not a judgment that something is 'satisfying'. For to say this is simply to make a statement of fact, like the statement that something is sweet or white. To make a value-judgment is to say that something is 'satisfactory' in the sense that it fulfils specifiable conditions.[3] For example, does a certain activity create conditions for further growth or does it prevent them? If I say that it does, I declare the activity to be valuable or a value.

It may be objected that to say that something fulfils certain specifiable conditions is no less a statement of fact than to say that an object is satisfying, in the sense that I myself or many people or all men find it satisfying. But Dewey is aware that to ask whether something is a value is to ask whether it is 'something to be prized and cherished, to be enjoyed',[4] and that to say that it is a value is to say that it is something to be desired and enjoyed.[5]

---

[1] Democracy and Education, p. 61.   [2] Human Nature and Conduct, p. 210.
[3] Cf. The Quest for Certainty, p. 260.   [4] Ibid., p. 260.
[5] 'A judgment about what is to be desired and enjoyed is therefore a claim on future action; it possesses de jure and not merely de facto quality', Ibid., p. 263.

Hence the following definition. 'Judgments about values are judgments about the conditions and the results of experienced objects; judgments about that which should regulate the formation of our desires, affections and enjoyments.'[1]

The emphasis, however, is placed by Dewey on the judgment of value as the term of a process of inquiry, stimulated by a problematic situation. For this enables him to say that his theory of values does not do away with their objectivity. Something is a value if it is adapted 'to the needs and demands imposed by the situation',[2] that is to say, if it meets the demands of an objective problematic situation, in regard to its transformation or reconstruction. A judgment of value, like a scientific hypothesis, is predictive, and it is thus empirically or experimentally verifiable. 'Appraisals of courses of action as better and worse, more or less serviceable, are as experimentally justified as are non-valuative propositions about impersonal subject matter.'[3] The transfer of the experimental method from physics to ethics would mean, of course, that all judgments and beliefs about values would have to be regarded as hypotheses. But to interpret them in this way is to transfer them from the realm of the subjective into that of the objective, of the verifiable. And as much care should be devoted to their framing as is devoted to the framing of scientific hypotheses.

6. Dewey's insistence on growth obviously implies that personality is something to be achieved, something in the making. But the human person is not, of course, an isolated atom. It is not simply a question of the individual being under an obligation to consider his social environment: he *is* a social being, whether he likes it or not. And all his actions 'bear the stamp of his community as assuredly as does the language he speaks'.[4] This is true even of those courses of activity of which society in general disapproves. It is a man's relations with his fellow-men which provide him both with the opportunities for action and with the instruments for taking advantage of such opportunities. And this is verified in the case of the burglar or the dealer in the white slave traffic no less than in that of the philanthropist.

At the same time the social environment, with its institutions, has to be organized and modified in the manner best suited for promoting the fullest possible development in desirable ways of

[1] *Ibid.*, p. 265.   [2] *Theory of Valuation*, p. 17.
[3] *Ibid.*, p. 22.   [4] *Human Nature and Conduct*, p. 317.

the capacities of individuals. And at first sight we are faced with a vicious circle. On the one hand the individual is conditioned by the existing social environment in regard to his habits of action and his aims. On the other hand, if the social environment is to be changed or modified, this can be accomplished only by individuals, even though by individuals working together and sharing common aims. How, then, is it possible for the individual, who is inevitably conditioned by his social environment, to devote himself to changing that environment in a deliberate and active manner?

Dewey's answer is what one would expect, namely that when a problematic situation arises, such as a clash between man's developing needs on the one hand and existing social institutions on the other, impulse stimulates thought and inquiry directed to transforming or reconstructing the social environment. As in morals, the task-in-hand is always in the forefront of Dewey's mind. The function of political philosophy is to criticize existing institutions in the light of man's development and changing needs and to discern and point out practical possibilities for the future to meet the needs of the present. In other words, Dewey looks on political philosophy as an instrument for concrete action. This means that it is not the business of the political philosopher to construct Utopias. Nor should he allow himself to succumb to the temptation of delineating 'the State', the essential concept of a state, which is supposed to be perennially valid. For to do this is in effect to canonize, even though unconsciously, an existing state of affairs, probably one that has already been challenged and subjected to criticism. In any case inquiry is hindered rather than helped by solutions which purport to cover all situations. If, for example, we are concerned with determining the value of the institution of private property in a given society at a certain period, it is no help to be told either that private property is a sacred, inviolable and perennial right or that it is always theft.

Obviously, the process of criticizing existing social institutions and of pointing the way to fresh concrete possibilities requires some standard to which men can refer. And for Dewey the test for all such institutions, whether political, juridical or industrial, is 'the contributions they make to the all-around growth of every member of society'.[1] It is for this reason that he favours democracy, namely as founded on 'faith in the capacities of human nature, faith in human intelligence and in the power of pooled and

[1] *Reconstruction in Philosophy*, p. 186.

co-operative experience'.[1] Yet 'the prime condition of a democratically organized public is a kind of knowledge and insight which
does not yet exist',[2] though we can indicate some of the conditions which have to be fulfilled if it is to exist. Democracy as we
know it is thus the settling for the free use of the experimental
method in social inquiry and thought, which is required for the
solution of concrete social, political and industrial problems.

We have seen that for Dewey the moral end is growth, and that
the degree to which they facilitate growth provides a test for
assessing the value of social and political institutions. The idea
of growth is also the key to his educational theory. Indeed, 'the
educative process is all one with the moral process'.[3] And education is 'getting from the present the degree and kind of growth
there is in it'.[4] It follows that as the potentiality for growth or
development does not cease with the close of adolescence, education should not be regarded as a preparation for life. It is itself a
process of living.[5] In fact, 'the educational process has no end
beyond itself; it is its own end'.[6] True, formal schooling comes to
an end; but the educative influence of society, social relations and
social institutions affects adults as well as the young. And if we
take, as we should, a broad view of education, we can see the
importance of effecting those social and political reforms which
are judged most likely to foster the capacity for growth and to
evoke those responses which facilitate further development.
Morals, education and politics are closely interconnected.

Given this general view of education, Dewey naturally stresses
the need of making the school as far as possible a real community,
to reproduce social life in a simplified form and thus to promote
the development of the child's capacity to participate in the life
of society in general. Further, he emphasizes, as one would expect,
the need for training children in intelligent inquiry. Struck by the
contrast between the lack of interest shown by many children in
their school instruction and their lively interest in those activities
outside the school in which they are able to share personally and
actively, he concludes that scholastic methods should be so
changed as to allow the children to participate actively as much

---

[1] *Problems of Men*, p. 59.
[2] *The Public and Its Problems*, p. 166. It is in this work that Dewey's most
detailed discussion of the State is to be found.
[3] *Reconstruction in Philosophy*, p. 183.
[4] *Ibid.*, pp. 184–5.
[5] This point of view is expanded in, for example, *My Pedagogic Creed*.
[6] *Democracy and Education*, p. 59.

as possible in concrete processes of inquiry leading from problematic situations to the overt behaviour or actions needed to transform the situation. But we cannot enter into further details of Dewey's ideas about education in the ordinary sense. His main conviction is that education should not be simply instruction in various subjects but rather a coherent unified effort to foster the development of citizens capable of promoting the further growth of society by employing intelligence fruitfully in a social context.

7. For many years Dewey was comparatively reticent about religion. In *Human Nature and Conduct* (1922), he spoke of religion as 'a sense of the whole',[1] and remarked that 'the religious experience is a reality in so far as in the midst of effort to foresee and regulate future objects we are sustained and expanded in feebleness and failure by the sense of an enveloping whole'.[2] And in *The Quest for Certainty* (1929) we find him maintaining that Nature, including humanity, when it is considered as the source of ideals and possibilities of achievement and as the abode of all attained goods, is capable of evoking a religious attitude which can be described as a sense of the possibilities of existence and as devotion to the cause of their actualization.[3] But these were more or less incidental remarks, and it was not until 1934 that Dewey really tackled the subject of religion in *A Common Faith*, which was the published version of a series of Terry Foundation Lectures delivered at Yale University.

Although, however, Dewey had previously written little about religion, he made it clear that he himself rejected all definite creeds and religious practices. And it was indeed obvious that his empirical naturalism had no room for belief in or worship of a supernatural divine being. At the same time Dewey had also made it clear that he attached some value to what he called a religious attitude. And in *A Common Faith* we find him distinguishing between the noun 'religion' and the adjective 'religious'. The noun he rejects, in the sense of rejecting definite religious creeds, institutions and practices. The adjective he accepts, in the sense that he affirms the value of religion as a quality of experience.

It must be understood, however, that Dewey is not speaking of any specifically religious and mystical experience, such as might be used to support belief in a supernatural Deity. The quality which he has in mind is one which can belong to an experience

---

[1] *Human Nature and Conduct*, p. 331.   [2] *Ibid.*, p. 264.
[3] Cf. *The Quest for Certainty*, pp. 288–91.

that would not ordinarily be described as religious. For example, the experience or feeling of being at one with the universe, with Nature as a whole, possesses this quality. And in *A Common Faith* Dewey associates the quality of being 'religious' with faith in 'the unification of the self through allegiance to inclusive ideal ends, which imagination presents to us and to which the human will responds as worthy of controlling our desires and choices'.[1]

As for the word 'God', Dewey is prepared to retain it, provided that it is used to signify not an existent supernatural being but rather the unity of the ideal possibilities which man can actualize through intelligence and action. 'We are in the presence neither of ideals completely embodied in existence nor yet of ideals that are mere rootless ideals, fantasies, utopias. For there are forces in nature and society that generate and support the ideals. They are further unified by the action that gives them coherence and solidity. It is this *active* relation between ideal and actual to which I would give the name "God".'[2]

A naturalistic philosophy, in other words, can find no room for God as conceived in the Jewish, Christian and Mohammedan religions. But a philosophy of experience must find room for religion in some sense of the term. Hence the quality of being 'religious' must be detached, as it were, from specifically religious experiences, in the sense of experience which purports to have for its object a supernatural being, and reattached to other forms of experience. As Dewey notes in *A Common Faith* the adjective 'religious' can apply to attitudes which can be adopted towards any object or any ideal. It can apply to aesthetic, scientific or moral experience or to experience of friendship and love. In this sense religion can pervade the whole of life. But Dewey himself emphasizes the religious character of the experience of the unification of the self. As 'the self is always directed toward something beyond itself',[3] its ideal unification depends upon a harmonizing of the self with the universe, with Nature as a totality. And here Dewey stresses, as we have seen, the movement towards the realization of ideal possibilities. One might perhaps expect him to recognize an active divine principle operating in and through Nature for the realization and conservation of values. But even if much of what he says points in the direction of some such idea, his naturalism effectively prevents him from taking such a step.

[1] *A Common Faith*, p. 33.   [2] *Ibid.*, pp. 50–1.   [3] *Ibid.*, p. 19.

8. Obviously, Dewey's philosophy is not a metaphysics if by this term we mean a study or doctrine of meta-empirical reality. But though, as has already been noted, he denies, in one place at least, that any general theory of reality is needed or even possible, it is clear enough that he develops a world-view. And world-views are generally classed under the heading of metaphysics. It would be ingenuous to say that Dewey simply takes the world as he finds it. For the plain fact is that he interprets it. For the matter of that, in spite of all that he has to say against general theories, he does not really prohibit all attempts to determine the generic traits, as he puts it, of existence of all kinds. What he does is to insist that 'the generic insight into existence which alone can define metaphysics in any empirically intelligible sense is itself an added fact of interaction, and is therefore subject to the same requirement of intelligence as any other natural occurrence: namely, inquiry into the bearings, leadings and consequences of what it discovers. The universe is no infinite self-representative series, if only because the addition within it of a representation makes it a different universe.'[1] So far as metaphysics in the sense of ontology is admitted,[2] its findings become working hypotheses, as much subject to revision as are the hypotheses of physical science. Presumably Dewey's own world-view is such a working hypothesis.

It is arguable that this world-view shows traces of its author's Hegelian past, in the sense at any rate that Nature is substituted for Hegel's Spirit and that Dewey tends to interpret the philosophical systems of the past in relation to the cultures which gave birth to them. This second point helps to explain the fact that when Dewey is treating of past systems, he bothers very little, if at all, about the arguments advanced on their behalf by their authors and dwells instead on the inability of these systems to deal with the problematic situations arising out of contemporary culture. This attitude is, of course, in accordance with his instrumentalist view of truth. But the result is that the attentive and critical reader of his books receives the impression that the naturalistic view of the world is assumed, not proved. And in the opinion of the present writer this impression is justified. Dewey simply assumes, for example, that the day of theological and metaphysical explanations is past, and that such explanations

---

[1] *Experience and Nature*, pp. 414–15. The reference to an infinite self-representative series is to the doctrine of Royce.
[2] Dewey himself deals, for example, with the category of causality.

were bogus. And the observation that such explanations do not serve as instruments to solve, say, contemporary social problems is insufficient to show the validity of the assumption.

The reply may be made that if Dewey's philosophy of experience, his general world-view, succeeds in giving a coherent and unified account of experiences as a whole, no further justification is required for excluding superfluous hypotheses which go beyond the limits of naturalism. But it is open to question whether Dewey's philosophy as a whole is really coherent. Consider, for example, his denial of absolute values and fixed ends. He asserts, as we have seen, the objectivity of values; but he regards them as relative to the problematic situations which give rise to the processes of inquiry that terminate in value-judgments. Yet it certainly appears that Dewey himself speaks of 'growth' as though it were an absolute value and an end in itself, an end fixed by the nature of man and ultimately by the nature of reality. Again, Dewey is careful to explain that he has no intention of denying the existence of a world antecedently to human experience; and he asserts that we experience many things *as* antecedently prior to our experiencing them. At the same time there is a strong tendency to interpret 'experience' in terms of the reconstruction of situations, a reconstruction which makes the world different from what it would have been without human operational thinking. And this points to a theory of creative experience which tends to turn the antecedently given into a kind of mysterious thing-in-itself.

Obviously, the presence of inconsistencies in Dewey's thought does not disprove naturalism. But it does at any rate render an assumption of a naturalistic point of view more open to criticism than it would have been if Dewey had succeeded in giving a perfectly unified and coherent world-view or interpretation of experience. It is clearly not sufficient to answer that on Dewey's own premises his world-view is a working hypothesis which must be judged by its 'consequences' and not by the comparative absence of antecedent arguments in its favour. For the 'working' of a world-view is shown precisely in its ability to give us a coherent and unified conceptual mastery over the data.

If we turn to Dewey's logical theory, we again encounter difficulties of some moment. For instance, though he recognizes, of course, that there are basic logical principles which have constantly shown themselves to be objectively useful instruments in coping with problematic situations, he insists that from a purely logical point of view no principle is sacrosanct; all are revisible in principle. At the same time Dewey evidently assumes that intelligence cannot rest satisfied with a problematic situation, with an unresolved conflict or 'contradiction'. As in the philosophy of Hegel, the mind is forced on towards an overcoming of such contradictions.[1] And this seems to imply an absolute demand of the intellect, a demand which it is difficult to reconcile with the view that no logical principles are absolute.

Again, there seems to be some ambiguity in the use of the word 'consequences'. A scientific hypothesis is interpreted as predictive, and it is verified if the predicted consequences, which constitute the meaning of the hypothesis, are realized. Whether verification brings subjective satisfaction to people or not, is irrelevant. In this context Dewey is careful to avoid the objection, to which James exposes himself, that the 'satisfying' character of a proposition is the test of its truth. But when we come to the social and political spheres, we can see a tendency to slide into the interpretation of 'consequences' as desirable consequences. Dewey would probably reply that what he is talking about is 'intended' consequences. The solution to a social or political problematic situation 'intends', has as its meaning, certain consequences. And, as in the case of scientific hypotheses, verification validates the proposed solution. Whether people like the solution or not is beside the point. In both cases, in that of the social or political solution or plan as in that of the scientific hypothesis, the test of truth or validity is objective. Yet it seems fairly obvious that in practice Dewey discriminates between political plans and solutions and theories in terms of their contribution to 'growth', their promotion of an end which he considers desirable. One might, of course, apply the same criterion in an analogous sense to scientific hypotheses. For example, an hypothesis which tends to arrest further scientific inquiry and advance cannot be accepted as true. But then the test of truth is no longer simply the verification of the consequences which are said to form the meaning of the hypothesis, though it may indeed tend to coincide with Peirce's conception of truth as the ideal limit to which all inquiry converges.

The strength of Dewey's philosophy doubtless lies in the fact

[1] There is, of course, a big difference between the attitudes of Hegel and Dewey. For Dewey is concerned with the active transformation of a situation, and not simply with the dialectical overcoming of a contradiction. But both men assume that contradiction *is* something to be overcome.

that its author always has his eye on empirical reality, or concrete situations and on the power of human intelligence and will to deal with these situations and to create possibilities of further development. Dewey brings philosophy down to earth and tries to show its relevance to concrete problems, moral, social and educational. And this helps to explain his great influence. He is a rather dull writer. And he is not a conspicuously precise and clear writer. His success in bringing his ideas to the attention of so many of his fellow-countrymen is not due to his literary gifts: it must be attributed in great part to the practical relevance of his ideas. Besides, his general world-view is undoubtedly capable of appealing to those who look on theological and metaphysical tenets as outmoded, and perhaps also as attempts to preserve vested interests, and who at the same time seek a forward-looking philosophy which does not appeal in any way to supernatural realities but in some sense justifies a faith in indefinite human progress.

For these reasons the activity of finding inconsistencies and ambiguities in Dewey's thought may appear to some minds a poor sort of game to play, a futile sniping at a philosophy which, by and large, is firmly rooted in the soil of experience. To others, however, it may well appear that practical relevance is bought, so to speak, at the expense of a thorough explicitation, examination and justification of the foundations of the philosophy. It may also appear that in the long run Dewey's philosophy rests on a judgment of value, the value of action. One can, of course, base a philosophy on a judgment or on judgments of value. But it is desirable that in this case the judgments should be brought into the open. Otherwise one may think, for example, that the instrumentalist theory of truth is simply the result of a dispassionate analysis.

PART V

THE REVOLT AGAINST IDEALISM

CHAPTER XVII
REALISM IN BRITAIN AND AMERICA

An introductory remark—Some Oxford realists—Brief notes on an ethical discussion at Oxford—American neo-realism—Critical realism in America—The world-view of Samuel Alexander—A reference to A. N. Whitehead.

1. WHEN we think of the revolt against idealism in Great Britain, the names which immediately come to mind are those of two Cambridge men, G. E. Moore and Bertrand Russell. Moore, however, is universally acknowledged to be one of the chief inspirers of the analytic movement, as it is commonly called, which has enjoyed a spectacular success in the first half of the twentieth century. And Russell, besides being another of the principal pioneers of this movement, is by far the most widely known British philosopher of this century. The present writer, therefore, has decided to postpone the brief treatment of them which is all that the scope of this volume allows and to treat first of a number of comparatively minor figures, even if this means neglecting the demands of chronological order.

2. Mention has already been made of the way in which idealism came to occupy a dominating position in the British universities, especially at Oxford, during the second half of the nineteenth century. But even at Oxford the triumph of idealism was not complete. For example, Thomas Case (1844–1925), who occupied the chair of metaphysics from 1899 until 1910 and was President of Corpus Christi College from 1904 until 1924, published *Realism in Morals* in 1877 and *Physical Realism* in 1888. It is indeed true that in itself Case's realism was opposed to subjective idealism and to phenomenalism rather than to objective or to absolute idealism. For it consisted basically in the thesis that there is a real and knowable world of things existing independently of sense-data.[1]

---

[1] It must be noted, however, that though for Case independent physical things are knowable, their existence and nature is known mediately, being inferred from sense-data, which are caused modifications of the nervous system.

At the same time, while in the war against materialism Case was on the side of the idealists, he regarded himself as continuing or restoring the realism of Francis Bacon and of scientists such as Newton and as an opponent of the then fashionable idealist movement.[1]

A more notable opponent of idealism was John Cook Wilson (1849–1915), who occupied the chair of logic at Oxford from 1889 until the year of his death. He published very little, his main influence being exercised as a teacher. But a two-volume collection of lectures on logic, essays and letters, together with a memoir by the editor, A. S. L. Farquharson, appeared posthumously in 1926 with the title *Statement and Inference*.

As an undergraduate Cook Wilson had been influenced by T. H. Green, and later he went to Göttingen to hear Lotze. But he gradually became a sharp critic of idealism. He did not, however, oppose to it a rival world-view. His strength lay partly in attack and partly in the way in which he selected particular problems and tried to follow them through with meticulous care and thoroughness. In this sense his thought was analytic. Further, he had an Aristotelian respect for the distinctions expressed in or implied by ordinary language. And he was convinced that logicians would do well to pay both attention and defence to the natural logic of common linguistic usage.

One of Cook Wilson's grievances against the logic of Bradley and Bosanquet is their doctrine of judgment. In his view they assume that there is one mental act, namely judging, which finds expression in every statement. And to make this assumption is to confuse mental activities, such as knowing, opining and believing, which ought to be distinguished. Further, it is a serious mistake to suppose that there is an activity called judging which is distinct from inference. 'There is no such thing.'[2] If logicians paid more attention to the ways in which we ordinarily use such terms as 'judge', they would see that to judge that something is the case is to infer it. In logic we can get along quite well with statement and inference, without introducing a fictitious separate activity, namely judging.

A statement, therefore, can express various activities. But of these knowing is fundamental. For we cannot understand what is

---

[1] It is significant that Case was the author of the article on Aristotle in the eleventh edition of the *Encyclopædia Britannica*.
[2] *Statement and Inference*, I, p. 87.

meant by, for example, having an opinion or wondering whether something is true except by way of a contrast with knowledge. It by no means follows, however, that knowledge can be analyzed and defined. We can indeed ask how we come to know or what we know, but the question, What is knowledge itself? is absurd. For to demand an answer is to presuppose that we can estimate its truth, and it is thus presupposed that we are already aware what knowledge is. Knowledge can be exemplified but not explained or defined. Nor does it stand in need of any further justification than pointing to examples of it.

We can indeed exclude false accounts of knowledge. These take two main forms. On the one hand there is the attempt to reduce the object to the act of apprehension by interpreting knowledge as a making, a construction of the object. On the other hand there is the tendency to describe the act of apprehension in terms of the object, by maintaining that what we know is a 'copy' or representation of the object. This thesis makes knowledge impossible. For if what we know immediately is always a copy or idea, we can never compare it with the original, to see whether it tallies or not.

Refutations of false accounts of knowledge presuppose, however, that we are already well aware of what knowledge is. And we are aware of it by actually knowing something. Hence to ask what is knowledge? as though we were ignorant, is just as much an improper question as Bradley's query, how is a relation related to its term? A relation is simply not the sort of thing which can be intelligibly said to be related. And knowledge is an indefinable and *sui generis* relation between a subject and an object. We can say what it is not, that it neither makes the object nor terminates in a copy of the object; but we cannot define what it is.

Cook Wilson's realism obviously assumes that we perceive physical objects which exist independently of the act of perception. In other words, he denies the thesis that *esse est percipi*, to be is to be perceived.[1] At the same time he finds it necessary to qualify his realism. Thus when dealing with the so-called secondary qualities he takes the example of heat and maintains that what we perceive is our own sensation of heat, while that which exists in the physical object is simply a power to cause or produce this sensation in a subject. This power 'is not perceived but inferred

[1] According to G. E. Moore, *esse est percipi* is the basic tenet of idealism. But he understands the thesis in a wide sense.

by a scientific theory'.[1] When, however, he is dealing with the so-called primary qualities, Cook Wilson maintains that we feel, for example, the extension of an actual body and not simply our tactual and muscular sensations. In other words, in his discussion of the relation of qualities to physical things he occupies a position close to that of Locke.

Indeed, we can say that Cook Wilson's realism involves the contention that the world which we know is simply the world as conceived by the classical Newtonian scientists. Thus he rejects the idea of non-Euclidean space or spaces. In his view mathematicians actually employ only the Euclidean concept of space, 'none other of course being possible for thought, while they imagine themselves to be talking of another kind of space'.[2]

The general outlook of Cook Wilson was shared by H. A. Prichard (1871–1947), who occupied the chair of moral philosophy at Oxford. In the first place 'it is simply *impossible* to think that any reality depends upon our knowledge of it, or upon any knowledge of it. If there is to be knowledge, there must first *be* something to be known.'[3] Obviously, the activities of Sherlock Holmes, as related by Conan Doyle, depend upon the mind in a sense in which stones and stars do not. But I could not claim to 'know' what Sherlock Holmes did unless there was first something to be known. In the second place 'knowledge is *sui generis*, and, as such, cannot be explained'.[4] For any alleged explanation necessarily presupposes that we are aware what knowledge is. In the third place secondary qualities cannot exist independently of a percipient subject, and consequently they 'cannot be qualities of things, since the qualities of a thing must exist independently of the perception of a thing'.[5]

In view of the last-mentioned point it is not surprising to find Prichard maintaining, in his posthumously published collection of essays *Knowledge and Perception* (1950), that we never actually see physical objects but only coloured and spatially related extensions, which we 'mistake' for physical bodies. If we ask how it comes about that we judge these sense-data to be physical

---

[1] *Statement and Inference*, II, p. 777. Cook Wilson prefers the example of heat to that of colour. For people who are innocent of theory are accustomed to speak of themselves as 'feeling hot', whereas nobody speaks of 'feeling coloured'. To see the relation between colour and the subject, a greater degree of reflection is required.
[2] *Ibid.*, II, p. 567.
[3] *Kant's Theory of Knowledge* (1909), p. 118.
[4] *Ibid.*, p. 124.　　　　　　　　　　[5] *Ibid.*, p. 86.

objects, Prichard replies that it is not a case of judging at all.[1] We are naturally under the impression that what we see are physical bodies existing independently of perception. And it is only in the course of subsequent reflection that we come to infer or judge that this is not the case.

If, therefore, we start with the position of common sense or naïve realism, we must say that both Cook Wilson and Prichard modified this position, making concessions to the other side. Further concessions were made by H. W. B. Joseph (1867-1943), Fellow of New College, Oxford, and an influential teacher. Thus in a paper on Berkeley and Kant which he read to the British Academy Joseph remarks that common sense realism is badly shaken by reflection, and he suggests that though the things outside us are certainly not private in the sense in which my pain is private, they may be bound up 'with the being of knowing and perceiving minds'.[2] Joseph also suggests that reflection on the philosophies of Berkeley and Kant points to the conclusion that the conditions of our knowledge of objects may depend 'upon a reality or intelligence which shows itself in nature to itself in minds'.[3]

The last remark is clearly a concession to metaphysical idealism rather than to any form of subjective idealism. But this simply illustrates the difficulty in maintaining that in our knowledge of physical objects knowing is a relation of compresence between a subject and an object which is entirely heterogeneous to mind. As for the discussion of sense-data, a discussion which received a powerful impetus at Oxford from Professor H. H. Price's *Perception*,[4] this illustrates the difficulty in maintaining successfully a position of naïve realism. That is to say, problems arise for reflection which suggest that the position has to be modified. One way of coping with this situation is to dismiss the problems as pseudo-problems. But this was not an expedient adopted by the older Oxford philosophers whom we have been considering.

3. H. A. Prichard, who was mentioned in the last section, is probably best known for his famous essay in *Mind* (1912) on the

---

[1] According to Prichard, we could judge or infer that the direct objects of perception are physical bodies which are entirely independent of the perceiving subject, if we could be said to 'know' the former. But perception, for Prichard, is never knowledge.

[2] *Essays in Ancient and Modern Philosophy*, p. 231.   [3] *Ibid.*

[4] This book, published in 1932, shows the influence of Cambridge thinkers, such as Moore and Russell, whereas Cook Wilson had shown little respect for Cambridge thought.

question, 'Does Moral Philosophy rest on a Mistake?'[1] Moral philosophy is conceived by Prichard as being largely concerned with trying to find arguments to prove that what seem to be our duties really are our duties. And his own thesis is that in point of fact we simply see or intuit our duties, so that the whole attempt to prove that they are duties is mistaken. True, there can be argument in some sense. But what is called argument is simply an attempt to get people to look more closely at actions in order that they may see for themselves the characteristic of being obligatory. There are, of course, situations which give rise to what we are accustomed to call a conflict of duties. But in the case of an apparent conflict of this kind it is a mistake to try to resolve it by arguing, as so many philosophers have done, that one of the alternative actions will produce a greater good of some sort, this good being external to and a consequence of the action. The question at issue is, which action has the greater degree of obligatoriness? And the question cannot be answered in any other way than by looking closely at the actions until we *see* which is the greater obligation. This is, after all, what we are accustomed to do in practice.

This ethical intuitionism obviously implies that the concepts of right and obligation are paramount in ethics and take precedence over the concept of good. In other words, teleological ethical systems, such as the Aristotelian and the Utilitarian, rest on a fundamental mistake. And in the period after the First World War a discussion took place at Oxford on the themes raised by Prichard. It was conducted more or less independently of, though not without some reference to, the views of G. E. Moore. But we can say that it expressed a strong reaction against the type of position represented by the Cambridge philosopher. For though Moore had maintained in *Principia Ethica* (1903) that goodness is an indefinable quality,[2] he made it quite clear that in his opinion a moral obligation is an obligation to perform that action which will produce the greater amount of goodness.

In 1922 Prichard devoted his inaugural lecture as professor of moral philosophy at Oxford to the theme 'Duty and Interest', developing therein his point of view. In 1928 E. F. Carritt published *The Theory of Morals* in which he maintained that the idea of a *summum bonum*, a supreme good, is the *ignis fatuus* of moral

---

[1] Reprinted in *Moral Obligation: Essays and Lectures* (1949).
[2] This does not mean that we cannot say what things possess this quality or have intrinsic value. Moore was convinced that we can.

philosophy, and that any attempt to prove that certain actions are duties because they are means to the realization of some end considered as good is foredoomed to failure. The famous Aristotelian scholar, Sir W. D. Ross, then Provost of Oriel College, Oxford, contributed to the discussion by his book on *The Right and The Good* (1930). And this was followed in 1931 by Joseph's *Some Problems in Ethics*, in which the author characteristically tried to combine admission of the thesis that obligation is not derived from the goodness of the consequences of an action with the thesis that obligation is none the less not independent of any relation to goodness.

In other words, Joseph attempted to compromise between Prichard's view and the Aristotelian tradition. And in his little work *Rule and End in Morals* (1932), which was intended as a summing-up of the Oxford discussions, Professor J. H. Muirhead of the University of Birmingham drew attention to signs of a return, welcomed by himself, towards an Aristotelian-idealist view of ethics. But in 1936 there appeared *Language, Truth and Logic*, the celebrated logical positivist manifesto by A. J. Ayer, in which a statement such as 'actions of type X are wrong' was interpreted, not as the expression of any intuition, but as an utterance expressing an emotive attitude towards actions of type X and as also calculated to arouse a similar emotive attitude in others. And though the emotive theory of ethics certainly cannot be said to have won the universal assent of British moral philosophers, it stimulated a new phase of discussion in ethical theory, a phase which lies outside the scope of this volume.[1] Hence when Sir David Ross published *The Foundations of Ethics* in 1939, his intuitionism seemed to some at any rate to belong to a past phase of thought. However, on looking back we can see how the discussion by Prichard, Ross, Joseph and others of concepts such as those of the right and the good represented an analytic approach to moral philosophy which was different from the idealist tendency to treat ethics as a subordinate theme dependent on a metaphysical world-view. Yet we can also see how in the subsequent phase of ethical discussion philosophers have at length been led to doubt whether ethics can profitably be confined in a watertight compartment as a study of the language of morals.[2]

4. To turn now to realism in the United States of America. In

[1] See, for example, *Ethics Since 1900* by M. Warnock (London, 1960).
[2] Professor Stuart Hampshire's *Thought and Action* (London, 1959) is an example of this tendency.

March 1901 William Pepperell Montague (1873–1953) published in *The Philosophical Review* an article entitled 'Professor Royce's Refutation of Realism'. And in October of the same year Ralph Barton Perry (1876–1957) published in *The Monist* a paper on 'Professor Royce's Refutation of Realism and Pluralism'. Both articles, therefore, were answers to Royce's attack on realism as destructive of the possibility of knowledge. And in 1910 the two writers, together with E. B. Holt (1873–1946), W. T. Marvin (1872–1944), W. B. Pitkin (1878–1953), and E. G. Spaulding (1873–1940), published in the *Journal of Philosophy* 'The Program and First Platform of Six Realists'.[1] This was followed by the publication in 1912 of a volume of essays by these authors under the title, *The New Realism: Co-operative Studies in Philosophy*.

As was stated in the 1910 programme and as the sub-title of *The New Realism* indicates, this group of philosophers aimed at making philosophy a genuine co-operative pursuit, at least among those thinkers who were prepared to accept the basic tenets of realism. They insisted on a scrupulous care of language as the instrument of all philosophy, on analysis considered as 'the careful, systematic and exhaustive examination of any topic of discourse',[2] on separating vague complex problems into definite questions which should be dealt with separately, and on a close association with the special sciences. By this approach to philosophy the new realist hoped, therefore, to overcome the subjectivism, looseness of thought and language, and disregard of science which in their opinion had tended to bring philosophy into disrepute. In other words, a reform of philosophy in general was to go hand in hand with the development of a realist line of thought.

The new realists were at any rate agreed on the truth of a basic tenet, namely that, as Pitkin expressed it, 'things known are not products of the knowing relation nor essentially dependent for their existence or behaviour upon that relation'.[3] This tenet corresponds with our natural spontaneous belief, and it is demanded by the sciences. Hence the burden of proof rests fairly and squarely on the shoulders of those who deny it. But the disproofs offered by the idealists are fallacious. For instance, they slide from a truism, that it is only when objects are known that we

---

[1] This programme was reprinted as an Appendix in *The New Realism*.

[2] *The New Realism*, p. 24. As far as care for language and breaking up vague and complex problems into manageable and quite definite questions were concerned, the new realists' idea of proper philosophical procedure was similar to that of G. E. Moore in England.

[3] *Ibid.*, p. 477.

know that they exist, or from the tautology 'no object without a subject', to a substantial but unproven conclusion, namely that we know that objects exist only as objects, that is, only when they are known, as terms of the knowing relation.

This obviously implies that knowledge is an external relation. As Spaulding puts it, knowledge is 'eliminable',[1] in the sense that a thing can exist when it is not known and that, when not known, it can be precisely what it is when it is known, with the obvious difference that it is then not the term of the external relation of knowing. There must thus be at least one kind of external relation. And we can say in general that the new realists accepted the theory of relations as external to their terms. This view obviously favoured pluralism rather than monism in metaphysics. And it also pointed to the impossibility of deducing the world-system *a priori*.

The ordinary man's spontaneous reaction to the basic tenet of realism would undoubtedly be one of unqualified acceptance. For he is obviously accustomed to think of physical objects as existing quite independently of the knowing relation and as being entirely unaffected by this relation in their natures or characteristics. But reflection shows us that some account has to be taken of illusions, hallucinations and such like phenomena. Are they to be described as objects of knowledge? If so, can they reasonably be said to be real independently of the subject? And what of apparently converging railway-lines, sticks which appear bent when half immersed in water, and so on? Can we say that such percepts exist independently of perception? Must we not at any rate modify realism in such a way as to be able to assert that some objects of consciousness exist independently while others do not?

Holt's way of dealing with the matter is to make a distinction between being and reality. Realism does not commit us to holding that all perceived things are real. 'While all perceived things are things, *not* all perceived things are *real* things.'[2] It does not follow, however, that 'unreal' objects of perception or of thought are to be described as 'subjective' in character. On the contrary, the unreal has being and 'subsists of its own right in the all-inclusive universe of being'.[3] In fine, 'the universe is not all real; but the universe all is'.[4]

[1] *The New Realism*, p. 478.   [2] *Ibid.*, p. 358.
[3] *Ibid.*, p. 366. The unreal object must be distinguished from the unthinkable, such as a round square.
[4] *Ibid.*, p. 360.

Obviously, some explanation of this use of terms is required. And in the first place what does Holt mean by reality? The answer, 'as to what reality is, I take no great interest',[1] is not very promising. But Holt goes on to say that, if challenged, he would 'hazard the guess that perhaps reality is some very comprehensive system of terms in relation. . . . This would make reality closely related to what logic knows as "existence" '.[2] This suggests that an hallucinatory object, for example, is unreal in the sense that it cannot be fitted, without contradiction, into the most universal system of related terms. But Holt remarks that 'I shall not call an hallucinatory object necessarily "unreal" '.[3] The point on which he insists, however, is that unreality does not exclude objectivity. If, for instance, I assume certain geometrical premises at will and deduce a consistent system, the system is 'objective', even if it is described as 'unreal'. And to say that the unreal is objective, not subjective, is what Holt means by saying that it has being.

As for converging railway lines, sticks which appear bent in water and so on, Holt maintains that a physical object has innumerable projective properties, with which there correspond different specific responses in the nervous systems of different percipient organisms. Hence if we abstract from the particular purpose or purposes which lead us to select one appearance as a thing's 'real' appearance, we can say that all its appearances are on the same footing. They are all objective, and they subsist as projective properties. We are thus offered the picture of 'a general universe of being in which all things physical, mental, and logical, propositions and terms, existent and non-existent, false and true, good and evil, real and unreal *subsist*'.[4]

As Montague was afterwards to point out when discussing the differences between himself and some of his colleagues in the neo-realist group, there are considerable objections to putting all these things on the same footing. In the first place, the relations between objects of perception can be asymmetrical. For instance, on the assumption that the stick partly immersed in water is straight, we can easily explain why it appears bent. But if we assume that it is bent, we cannot explain why it appears straight in the circumstances in which it does appear to be straight. And this difficulty is certainly not overcome by saying that the stick is bent when it is partly immersed in water, while it is straight

---

[1] *Ibid.*, p. 366.
[2] *Ibid.*,
[3] *Ibid.*, p. 367.
[4] *Ibid.*, p. 372.

when it is out of the water. Again, some objects can produce effects only indirectly by means of the subject which conceives them, while other objects can also produce effects directly. For example, a dragon, as object of thought, might conceivably stimulate a man to make a voyage of exploration; but it could not produce the effects which can be produced by a lion. And we need to be able to make clear distinctions between the ontological statuses of these different classes of objects.

The new realists also concerned themselves with discussing the nature of consciousness. Holt and Perry, partly under the influence of William James, accepted the doctrine of neutral monism, according to which there is no ultimate substantial difference between mind and matter. And they tried to eliminate consciousness as a peculiar entity by explaining awareness of an object as a specific response by an organism. Montague interpreted this as meaning that the response consists of a motion of particles. And he asked how this theory, which he described as behaviourism, could possibly explain, for example, our awareness of past events. He himself identified the specific response which constitutes consciousness with 'the relation of self-transcending implication, which the brain-states sustain to their extra-organic causes'.[1] But it is not at all clear how brain-states can exercise any such self-transcending function. Nor does it help very much to be told that the possibility of the cortical states transcending themselves and providing awareness of objects is 'a matter for psychology rather than epistemology'.[2]

However, it is at any rate clear that the new realists were intent on maintaining that, as Montague put it, 'cognition is a peculiar type of relation which may subsist between a living being and any entity . . . [that it] belongs to the same world as that of its objects . . . [and that] there is nothing transcendental or supernatural about it'.[3] They also rejected all forms of representationalism. In perception and knowledge the subject is related directly to the object, not indirectly by means of an image or some sort of mental copy which constitutes the immediate term of the relation.

5. This rejection by the neo-realists of all representationalism seemed to some other philosophers to be naïve and uncritical. It was this rejection which led to physical and hallucinatory objects

---

[1] *The New Realism*, p. 482.　　[2] *Ways of Knowing* (1925), p. 396.
[3] *The New Realism*, p. 475.

being placed on the same footing. And it made it impossible to explain, for instance, our perception of a distant star when the star has ceased to exist. Thus there soon arose a movement of critical realism, formed by philosophers who agreed with the neo-realists in rejecting idealism but who found themselves unable to accept their thoroughgoing rejection of representationalism.

Like neo-realism, critical realism found expression in a joint-volume, *Essays in Critical Realism: A Co-operative Study of the Problems of Knowledge*, which appeared in 1920. The contributors were D. Drake (1898–1933), A. O. Lovejoy (1873–1962), J. B. Pratt (1875–1944), A. K. Rogers (1868–1936), G. Santayana (1863–1952), R. W. Sellars (b. 1880), and C. A. Strong (1862–1940).

The strength of critical realism lay in attack. For example, in *The Revolt against Dualism* (1930), Lovejoy argued that while neo-realists originally appealed to common sense in their rejection of representationalism, they then proceeded to give an account of objects which was incompatible with the common sense point of view. For to maintain with Holt that all the appearances of a thing are on the same footing as its objective projective properties is to commit oneself to saying that railway lines are both parallel and convergent, and that the surface of, say, a penny is both circular and elliptical.

In expounding their own doctrine, however, the critical realists encountered considerable difficulties. We can say that they were agreed in maintaining that what we directly perceive is some character-complex or immediate datum which functions as a sign of or guide to an independently existing thing. But they were not in full agreement about the nature of the immediate datum. Some were prepared to speak about such data as mental states.[1] And in this case they would presumably be in the mind. Others, such as Santayana, believed that the immediate data of consciousness are essences, and ruled out any question as to their whereabouts on the ground that they exist only as exemplified. In any case, if representationalism is once admitted, it seems to follow that the existence of physical objects is inferred. And there then arises the problem of justifying this inference. What reason have I for supposing that what I actually perceive represents something

---

[1] In an essay on the development of American realism Montague attributes to the critical realists in general the doctrine that we know directly only 'mental states or ideas'. Cf. *Twentieth Century Philosophy* (1943). edited by D. D. Runes, p. 441.

other than itself? Further, if we never perceive physical objects directly, how can we discriminate between the representative values of different sense-data?

The critical realists tried to answer the first question by maintaining that from the very start and by their very nature the immediate data of perception point to physical objects beyond themselves. But they differed in their accounts of this external reference. Santayana, for instance, appealed to animal faith, to the force of instinctive belief in the external reference of our percepts, a belief which we share with the animals, while Sellars relied on psychology to explain how our awareness of externality develops and grows in definiteness.

As for the question, how can we discriminate between the representative values of sense-data if we never perceive physical objects directly? one may be tempted to answer, 'In the way that we actually do discriminate, namely by verification'. And this may be an excellent answer from the practical point of view. After all, travellers in the desert, interpreting a mirage as a prediction that they will find water ahead of them, find by bitter experience that the prediction is not verified. At the same time a theoretical difficulty still remains for the representationalist to solve. For on his premises the process of verification terminates in sensory experience or the having of sense-data and is not a magic wand which, when waved, gives us direct access to what lies beyond sense-data. True, if what we are seeking is the sensory experience of a slaking of thirst, having this experience is all that is required from the practical point of view. But from the point of view of the theory of knowledge the representationalist seems to remain immersed in the world of 'representation'.

The fact of the matter is, of course, that on the level of common sense and practical life we can get along perfectly well. And in ordinary language we have developed distinctions which are quite sufficient to cope for all practical purposes with sticks partially immersed in water, converging railway lines, pink rats, and so on. But once we start to reflect on the epistemological problems to which such phenomena appear to give rise, there is the temptation to embrace some overall solution, either by saying that all the objects of awareness are objective and on the same footing or by saying that they are all subjective mental states or sense-data which are somehow neither subjective nor objective. In the first case we have neo-realism, in the second critical realism, provided, of course, that the immediate data are regarded as representative of or in some way related to independent physical objects. Both positions can be regarded as attempts to reform ordinary language. And though this enterprise cannot be ruled out *a priori*, the fact that both positions give rise to serious difficulties may well prompt us, with the late Professor J. L. Austin, to take another look at ordinary language.

The word 'realism' can have different shades of meaning. In this chapter it has as its basic meaning the view that knowledge is not a construction of the object, that knowing is a relation of compresence between a subject and an object, which makes no difference to the object. We have seen, however, that in the realist movement problems arose about the immediate objects of perception and knowledge. At the same time we do not wish to give the quite erroneous impression that the American philosophers who belonged to the two groups which have been mentioned were exclusively concerned with the problems to which attention has been drawn in this and the preceding sections. Among the neo-realists Perry, for example, became well known as a moral philosopher,[1] and also devoted himself to political and social themes. Among the critical realists Santayana developed a general philosophy,[2] while Strong and Drake expounded a panpsychistic ontology, taking introspection as a key to the nature of reality.[3] Sellars defended a naturalistic philosophy,[4] based on the idea of emergent evolution with irreducible levels and comprising a theory of perception as an interpretative operation. Lovejoy exercised a considerable influence by his studies in the history of ideas.[5]

6. A realist theory of knowledge, in the sense already described, obviously does not exclude the construction of a metaphysical system or world-view. All that is excluded is a metaphysics based on the theory that knowledge is a construction of the object or on

---

[1] He published his *General Theory of Value* in 1926.

[2] Santayana's *Realms of Being* comprises four volumes: *The Realm of Essence* (1927), *The Realm of Matter* (1930), *The Realm of Truth* (1938), and *The Realm of Spirit* (1940).

[3] According to Strong, introspection is the one case in which we are directly aware of 'stuff' as distinct from structure. But neither Strong nor Drake meant to imply that stones, for instance, are conscious. Their panpsychism was linked with the idea of emergent evolution. Even those things which we call 'material' possess a potential energy which at a certain level of evolution manifests itself in consciousness.

[4] As in *The Philosophy of Physical Realism* (1932).

[5] Lovejoy published, for instance, *The Great Chain of Being* in 1936 and *Essays in the History of Ideas* in 1948.

the theory that creative thought or experience is the basic, primary reality. And in point of fact there have been a considerable number of world-views in modern philosophy, which presupposed a realist theory of knowledge. To mention them all is, however, out of the question. And I propose to confine myself to making some remarks about the world-view of Samuel Alexander.

Samuel Alexander (1859–1938) was born in Sydney, Australia, but went to Oxford in 1877, where he came under the influence of Green and Bradley. This influence, however, was supplanted by that of the idea of evolution, as well as by an interest in empirical psychology, which was scarcely a characteristic of Oxford at the time.[1] Later on Alexander received stimulus from the realism of Moore and Russell and came to approach, though he did not altogether accept, the position of American neo-realism. But he regarded the theory of knowledge as preparatory to metaphysical synthesis. And it may well be true that his impulse to metaphysical construction, though not the actual content of his system, was due in some measure to the early influence of idealism on his mind.

In 1882 Alexander was elected a Fellow of Lincoln College, Oxford. And the influence of evolutionary thought can be seen in the book which he published in 1889, *Moral Order and Progress: An Analysis of Ethical Conceptions*. As the title of the book indicates, Alexander considered ethics to be concerned with the analysis of moral concepts, such as good and evil, right and wrong. But he also regarded it as a normative science. In his interpretation of the moral life and of moral concepts he carried on the line of thought represented by Herbert Spencer and Sir Leslie Stephen. Thus in his view the struggle for survival in the biological sphere takes the form in the ethical sphere of a struggle between rival moral ideals. And the law of natural selection, as applying in the moral field, means that that set of moral ideals tends to prevail which most conduces to the production of a state of equilibrium or harmony between the various elements and forces in the individual, between the individual and society, and between man and his environment. There is thus an ultimate and overall ideal of harmony which in Alexander's view includes within itself the ideals upheld by other ethical systems, such as happiness and self-realization. At the same time the conditions of life, physical and

[1] Bradley was interested in psychology. But it is notorious that for many years psychology was frowned on at Oxford and regarded as not qualifying for recognition as a science.

social, are constantly changing, with the result that the concrete meaning of equilibrium or harmony assumes fresh forms. Hence, even though there is in a real sense an ultimate end of moral progress, it cannot be actually attained in a fixed and unalterable shape, and ethics cannot be expressed in the form of a set of static principles which are incapable of modification or change.

To turn to Alexander's realism.[1] His basic idea of knowledge is that it is simply a relation of compresence or togetherness between some object and a conscious being. The object, in the sense of the thing known, is what it is whether it is known or not. Further, Alexander rejects all forms of representationalism. We can, of course, direct our attention explicitly to our mental acts or states. But they do not serve as copies or signs of external things which are known only indirectly. Rather do we 'enjoy' our mental acts while knowing directly objects which are other than the acts by which we know them. Nor are sense-data intermediate objects between consciousness and physical things, they are perspectives of things. Even a so-called illusion is a perspective of the real world, though it is referred by the mind to a context to which it does not belong.[2] Further, in knowing the past by memory we really do know the past. That is to say, pastness is a direct object of experience.

In 1893 Alexander was appointed professor of philosophy in the University of Manchester. In the years 1916–18 he delivered the Gifford Lectures at Glasgow, and the published version appeared in 1920 under the title *Space, Time and Deity*. In this work we are told that metaphysics is concerned with the world as a whole, thus carrying comprehensiveness to its furthest limits. In Aristotelian language we can say that it is the science of being and its essential attributes, investigating 'the ultimate nature of existence if it has any, and those pervasive characters of things, or categories'.[3] But though metaphysics has a wider subject-matter than any special science, its method is empirical, in the sense that, like the sciences, it uses 'hypotheses by which to bring its data into verifiable connection'.[4] At the same time the pervasive and essential attributes of things can be described as non-empirical or

---

[1] The best known of Alexander's articles illustrating his realist theory of knowledge is 'The Basis of Realism', which appeared in the *Proceedings of the British Academy* for 1914.

[2] In other words, the mind does not create the materials of an illusion but derives them from sensible experience. But it can be said to constitute the illusion *as* an illusion by an erroneous judgment in regard to context.

[3] *Space, Time and Deity*, I, p. 2.   [4] *Ibid.*, I, p. 4.

a priori provided that we understand that the distinction between the empirical and the non-empirical lies within the experienced and is not equivalent to a distinction between experience and what transcends all experience. Bearing this in mind, we can define metaphysics as 'the experiential or empirical study of the non-empirical or *a priori*, and of such questions as arise out of the relation of the empirical to the *a priori*'.[1]

According to Alexander, ultimate reality, the basic matrix of all things, is space-time. Precisely how he arrived at this notion, it is difficult to say. He mentions, for example, the idea of a world in space and time formulated by H. Minkowski in 1908. And he refers to Lorentz and Einstein. Further, he speaks with approval of Bergson's concept of real time, though with disapproval of the French philosopher's subordination of space to time. In any case Alexander's notion of space-time as the ultimate reality is obviously opposed to Bradley's relegation of space and time to the sphere of appearance and to McTaggart's theory of the unreality of time. Alexander is concerned with constructing a naturalistic metaphysics or world-view; and he begins with what is for him both the ultimate and, when considered purely in itself, the primitive phase of the evolutionary process.

The naïve way of conceiving space and time is as receptacles or containers. And a natural corrective to this crude image is to depict them as relations between individual entities, relations respectively of co-existence and succession. But this view clearly implies that individual entities are logically prior to space and time, whereas the hypothesis embraced by Alexander is that space and time constitute 'the stuff or matrix (or matrices) out of which things or events are made, the medium in which they are precipitated and crystallized'.[2] If we consider either space or time by itself, its elements or parts are indistinguishable. But 'each point of space is determined and distinguished by an instant in time, and each instant of time by its position in space'.[3] In other words, space and time together constitute one reality, 'an infinite continuum of pure events or point-instants'.[4] And empirical things are groupings or complexes of such events.

Alexander proceeds to discuss the pervasive categories or fundamental properties of space-time, such as identity, diversity and existence, universal and particular, relation, causality and so

[1] *Space, Time and Deity*, I, p. 4.   [2] *Ibid.*, I, p. 38.
[3] *Ibid.*, I, p. 60.   [4] *Ibid.*, I, p. 66.

on. The stage is thus set for an examination of the emergence of qualities and of levels of empirical reality, from matter up to conscious mental activity. We cannot discuss all these themes here. But it is worth drawing attention to Alexander's doctrine of 'tertiary qualities'.

The tertiary qualities are values, such as truth and goodness. They are called 'tertiary' to distinguish them from the primary and secondary qualities of traditional philosophy. But as applied to values the term 'qualities' should really be placed in inverted commas, to indicate that 'these values are not qualities of reality in the same sense as colour, or form, or life'.[1] To speak of them as objective qualities of reality can be misleading. For instance, reality is not, properly speaking, either true or false: it is simply reality. Truth and falsity are properly predicated of propositions as believed, that is, in relation to the mind which believes them, not of things, nor even of propositions when considered simply as mental facts. Similarly, a thing is good, according to Alexander, only in relation to a purpose, as when we speak of a good tool. Again, though a red rose is red whether anyone perceives it or not, it is beautiful only in relation to the mind which appreciates its 'coherence'. But it by no means follows that we are entitled to speak of the tertiary qualities or values as purely subjective or as unreal. They emerge as real features of the universe, though only in relation to minds or conscious subjects. They are, in fine, 'subject-object determinations',[2] which 'imply the amalgamation of the object with the human appreciation of it'.[3]

The relation between subject and object is not, however, invariable. In the case of truth, for example, appreciation by the subject is determined by the object. For in knowledge reality is discovered, not made. But in the case of goodness the quality of being good is determined primarily by the subject, that is, by purpose, by the will. There is, however, a common factor which must be noted, namely that the appreciation of values in general arises in a social context, out of the community of minds. For instance, it is in relation to the judgment of others that I become aware that a proposition is false; and in my judgments about truth or falsity I represent what we can call the collective mind. 'It is social intercourse, therefore, which makes us aware that there is a reality compounded of ourselves and the object, and that in

[1] *Ibid.*, II, p. 237.   [2] *Ibid.*, II, p. 238.
[3] *Ibid.*

that relation the object has a character which it would not have except for that relation.'[1]

This doctrine of the emergence of tertiary qualities enables Alexander to insist that evolution is not indifferent to values. 'Darwinism is sometimes thought to be indifferent to value. It is in fact the history of how values come into existence in the world of life.'[2] We thus have the general picture of a process of evolution in which different levels of finite being emerge, each level possessing its own characteristic empirical quality. 'The highest of these empirical qualities known to us is mind or consciousness.'[3] And at this level the tertiary qualities or values emerge as real features of the universe, though this reality involves a relation to the subject, the human mind.

Now, Alexander's work is entitled *Space, Time and Deity*. Hence the question arises, how does Deity fit into this scheme or worldview? The philosopher's answer is that 'Deity is the next higher empirical quality to the highest we know'.[4] We obviously cannot say what this quality is. But we know that it is not any quality with which we are already acquainted. For that it should be any such quality is ruled out by definition.

Does it follow from this that God exists only in the future, so to speak, being identifiable with the next level of finite being to emerge in the process of evolution? To this question Alexander gives a negative answer. As an actually existent being, God is the universe, the whole space-time continuum. 'God is the whole world as possessing the quality of deity. . . . As an actual existent, God is the infinite world with its nisus towards deity, or, to adapt a phrase of Leibniz, as big or in travail with deity.'[5]

Alexander was of Jewish origin and it is not unreasonable to see in his view of God a dynamic version of Spinoza's pantheism, adapted to the theory of evolution. But there is an obvious difficulty in maintaining both that God is the whole world as possessing the quality of Deity and that this quality is a future emergent. Alexander is aware of this, of course. And he concludes that 'God as an actual existent is always becoming deity but never attains it. He is the ideal God in embryo.'[6] As for religion, it can be described as 'the sentiment in us that we are drawn towards Him [God], and caught in the movement of the world to a higher level of existence'.[7]

[1] *Space, Time and Deity*, II, p. 240.   [2] *Ibid.*, II, p. 309.   [3] *Ibid.*, II, p. 345.
[4] *Ibid.*   [5] *Ibid.*, II, p. 353.   [6] *Ibid.*, II, p. 365.
[7] *Ibid.*, II, p. 429.

Given his premisses, Alexander's position is understandable. On the one hand, if Deity is the quality of a future level of being, and if God were identifiable with the actual bearer of this quality, he would be finite. On the other hand, the religious consciousness, Alexander assumes, demands a God who is not only existent but also infinite. Hence God must be identified with the infinite universe as striving after the quality of Deity. But to say this is really to do no more than to apply a label, 'God', to the evolving universe, the space-time continuum. To be sure, there is some similarity between Alexander's view and that of Hegel. At the same time Hegel's Absolute is defined as Spirit, whereas Alexander's is defined as Space-Time. And this renders the label 'God' even more inappropriate. What is appropriate is the description of religion as a 'sentiment'. For in a naturalistic philosophy this is precisely what religion becomes, namely some kind of cosmic emotion.

7. Owing to the development and spread of a current of thought which has been accompanied by a marked distrust of all comprehensive world-views, little attention has been paid to Alexander's philosophy.[1] In any case, in the field of speculative philosophy his star has been completely eclipsed by that of Alfred North Whitehead (1861–1947), the greatest English metaphysical philosopher since Bradley. True, it can hardly be claimed that the influence of Whitehead as a speculative philosopher on recent British philosophy has been extensive or profound. Given the prevailing climate of philosophical thought, one would hardly expect it to have been. Whitehead's influence has in fact been greater in America, where he worked from 1924 until his death, than in his native land. In the last few years, however, interest in his thought has shown itself in a considerable number of books and articles published in Great Britain.[2] And his name has become increasingly known in Europe. In other words, Whitehead is recognized as a major thinker, whereas Alexander tends to be forgotten.

From one point of view, Whitehead's philosophy certainly qualifies for inclusion in this chapter. True, he himself drew attention to the affinity between the results of his philosophizing and absolute idealism. Thus in his preface to *Process and Reality* he notes that 'though throughout the main body of the work I am

---

[1] In Mr. G. J. Warnock's excellent little book, *English Philosophy Since 1900*, Alexander is passed over in silence.
[2] The increase not only in tolerance of but also in sympathy with 'descriptive metaphysics' has, of course, contributed to this revival of interest in Whitehead.

in sharp disagreement with Bradley, the final outcome is after all not so greatly different'.[1] At the same time Whitehead, who came from mathematics to the philosophy of science and Nature, and thence to metaphysics, intended to return to a pre-idealist attitude and point of departure. That is to say, just as some of the pre-Kantian philosophers had philosophized in close association with the science of their time, Whitehead considered that the new physics demanded a fresh effort in speculative philosophy. He did not start from the subject-object relation or from the idea of creative thought, but rather from reflection on the world as presented in modern science. His categories are not simply imposed by the *a priori* constitution of the human mind; they belong to reality, as pervasive features of it, in much the same sense as Aristotle's categories belonged to reality. Again, Whitehead gives a naturalistic interpretation of consciousness, in the sense that it is depicted as a developed, emergent form of the relation of 'prehension' which is found between all actual entities. Hence when he notes the affinity between the results of his speculative philosophy and some features of absolute idealism he also suggests that his type of thought may be 'a transformation of some main doctrines of Absolute Idealism on to a realistic basis'.[2]

But though Whitehead's philosophy, as standing on what he calls a realistic basis, certainly qualifies for consideration in this chapter, it is far too complicated to summarize in a few paragraphs. And after some consideration the present writer has decided not to make the attempt. It is, however, worth noting that Whitehead was convinced of the inevitability of speculative or metaphysical philosophy. That is to say, unless a philosopher deliberately breaks off at a certain point the process of understanding the world and of generalization, he is inevitably led to 'the endeavour to frame a coherent, logical, necessary system of general ideas in terms of which every element of our experience can be interpreted'.[3] Moreover, it is not simply a question of synthesizing the sciences. For the analysis of any particular fact and the determination of the status of any entity require in the long run a view of the general principles and categories which the fact embodies and of the entity's status in the whole universe. Linguistically speaking, every proposition stating a particular fact requires for its complete analysis an exhibition of the general character of the universe as exemplified in this fact. Ontologically

[1] *Process and Reality*, p. vii (1959 edition).   [2] *Ibid.*, p. viii.   [3] *Ibid.*, p. 4.

speaking, 'every definite entity requires a systematic universe to supply its requisite status'.[1] Wherever we start, therefore, we are led to metaphysics, provided that we do not break off the process of understanding on the way. This point of view assumes, of course, that the universe is an organic system. And it is Whitehead's sustained attempt to show that the universe is in fact a unified dynamic process, a plurality-in-unity which is to be interpreted as a creative advance into novelty, that constitutes his philosophical system. As already noted, the total result of his speculation bears some resemblance to absolute idealism. But the world as presented by Whitehead is certainly not the dialectical working-out of an absolute Idea. The total universe, comprising both God and the world, is said to be caught 'in the grip of the ultimate metaphysical ground, the creative advance into novelty'.[2] It is 'creativity',[3] not thought, which is for him the ultimate factor.

[1] *Ibid*, p. 17. [2] *Ibid.*, p. 529.
[3] 'Creativity', as described by Whitehead, is not an actual entity, like God, but 'the universal of universals' (*Process and Reality*, p. 31).

CHAPTER XVIII

G. E. MOORE AND ANALYSIS

Life and writings—Common sense realism—Some remarks on Moore's ethical ideas—Moore on analysis—The sense-datum theory as an illustration of Moore's practice of analysis.

1. IN the last chapter we had occasion to consider briefly some Oxford realists. But when one thinks of the collapse of idealism in England and of the rise of a new dominating current of thought, one's mind naturally turns to the analytic movement which had its origins at Cambridge and which in the course of time established itself firmly at Oxford and in other universities. It is true that in its later phase it has become commonly known as 'Oxford philosophy'; but this does not alter the fact that the three great pioneers of and stimulative influences in the movement, Moore, Russell and Wittgenstein, were all Cambridge men.

George Edward Moore (1873–1958) went up to Cambridge in 1892, where he began by studying classics. He has remarked that he does not think that the world or the sciences would ever have suggested to him philosophical problems. In other words, left to himself he tended to take the world as he found it and as it was presented by the sciences. He appears to have been entirely free from Bradley's dissatisfaction with all our ordinary ways of conceiving the world, and he did not hanker after some superior way of viewing it. Still less was he tortured by the problems which beset Kierkegaard, Jaspers, Camus and such-like thinkers. At the same time Moore became interested in the queer things which philosophers have said about the world and the sciences; for example, that time is unreal or that scientific knowledge is not really knowledge. And he was diverted from classics to philosophy, partly under the influence of his younger contemporary, Bertrand Russell.

In 1898 Moore was awarded a Prize-Fellowship at Trinity College, Cambridge. And in 1903 he published *Principia Ethica*. After an absence from Cambridge he was appointed Lecturer in Moral Science in 1911; and in the following year he published his little work, *Ethics*, in the Home University Library Series. In 1921 he succeeded G. F. Stout as editor of *Mind*; and in 1922 he published *Philosophical Studies*, consisting for the most part of reprinted articles. In 1925 Moore was elected to the Chair of Philosophy at Cambridge on the retirement of James Ward. In 1951 he was awarded the *Order of Merit*; and in 1953 he published *Some Main Problems of Philosophy*. *Philosophical Papers*, a collection of essays prepared for publication by Moore himself, appeared posthumously in 1959, while his *Commonplace Book*, 1919–53, a selection from his notes and jottings, was published in 1962.

2. According to Bertrand Russell, it was Moore who led the rebellion against idealism. And Moore's early realism can be illustrated by reference to an article on the nature of judgment, which he published in *Mind* during the year 1899.

In this article Moore takes as his text Bradley's statement that truth and falsity depend on the relation between ideas and reality, and he refers with approval to Bradley's explanation that the term 'ideas' does not signify mental states but rather universal meanings.[1] Moore then proceeds to substitute 'concept' for 'idea' and 'proposition' for 'judgment', and to maintain that what is asserted in a proposition is a specific relation between concepts. In his view this holds good also of existential judgments. For 'existence is itself a concept'.[2] But Moore rejects the theory that a proposition is true or false in virtue of its correspondence or lack of correspondence with a reality or state of affairs other than itself. On the contrary, the truth of a proposition is an identifiable property of the proposition itself, belonging to it in virtue of the relation obtaining, within the proposition, between the concepts which compose it. 'What kind of relation makes a proposition true, what false, cannot be further defined, but must be immediately recognized.'[3] It is not, however, a relation between the proposition and something outside it.

Now, as Moore says that concepts are 'the only objects of knowledge',[4] and as propositions assert relations between concepts and are true or false simply in virtue of the relation asserted, it looks at first sight as though he were expounding a theory which is the reverse of anything which could reasonably be described as realism. That is to say, it looks as though Moore were creating an unbridgeable gulf between the world of propositions, which is the sphere of truth and falsity, and the world of non-propositional reality or fact.

[1] In other words, Moore approves of Bradley's protest against the psychologizing of logic.
[2] *Mind*, Vol. 8 (1899), p. 180.   [3] *Ibid.*   [4] *Ibid.*, p. 182.

We have to understand, however, that for Moore concepts are not abstractions, mental constructs formed on the basis of the material provided by sense-data, but rather objective realities, as with Meinong. Further, we are invited 'to regard the world as formed of concepts'.[1] That is to say, an existent thing is a complex of concepts, of universals such as whiteness for example, 'standing in a unique relation to the concept of existence'.[2] To say this is not to reduce the world of existing things to mental states. On the contrary, it is to eliminate the opposition between concepts and things. And to say that concepts are the objects of knowledge is to say that we know reality directly. When, therefore, Moore says of concepts that they must *be* something before they can enter into a relation with a cognitive subject and that 'it is indifferent to their nature whether anybody thinks them or not',[3] we can see what he means. He is saying that knowledge makes no difference to the object. It doubtless has its causes and effects; but 'these are to be found only in the subject'.[4] Construction of the object is certainly not one of the effects of knowing.

If a proposition consists of concepts standing in a specific relation to one another, and if concepts are identical with the realities conceived, it obviously follows that a true proposition must be identical with the reality which it is commonly considered as representing and with which it is commonly said to correspond. And in an article on truth,[5] Moore did not hesitate to maintain that the proposition 'I exist' does not differ from the reality 'my existence'.

As Moore was well aware at the time of writing, this theory sounds extremely odd. But what is more serious than its oddity is the difficulty in seeing how it does not eliminate the distinction between true and false propositions. Suppose, for example, that I believe that the earth is flat. If what I believe is a proposition, it seems to follow from the account of propositions explained above, that the earth being flat is a reality. Moore, therefore, came to throw overboard the idea that what we believe is propositions. In fact he came to jettison the idea of propositions at all, at any rate in the sense in which he had formerly postulated them. At the same time he clung to a realist view of knowledge as a unique unanalyzable relation between a cognitive subject and an object, a relation which makes no difference to the nature of the object.

[1] *Mind*, Vol. 8, p. 182.   [2] *Ibid.*, p. 183.   [3] *Ibid.*, p. 179.   [4] *Ibid.*
[5] In Baldwin's *Dictionary of Philosophy and Psychology*.

As for the truth or falsity of beliefs, he came to admit that this must depend in some sense on correspondence or the lack of it, though he felt unable to give any clear account of the nature of this correspondence.

Now, if being the term of the unique and indefinable relation in which knowledge consists makes no difference to the nature of the object, there must be at any rate one external relation. And in point of fact Moore, having ascribed to the idealists the view that no relation is purely external, in the sense that there is no relation which does not affect the natures or essences of the terms, proceeds to reject it. Thus in an article on the concept of the relative[1] he distinguishes between the terms 'relative' and 'related' and asserts that the former term, when predicated of a thing, implies that the relation or relations referred to are essential to the subject of which the term is predicated. But this implies that the relation of something which is a whole to something else is identical with or a part of the whole. And this notion, Moore maintains, is self-contradictory. In other words, a thing is what it is, and it is not definable in terms of its relations to anything else. Hence a thing's nature cannot be constituted by the nature of the system to which it belongs; and idealist monism is thus deprived of one of its main foundations.

Moore's best-known criticism of idealism is, of course, his article entitled *The Refutation of Idealism*.[2] In it he maintains that if modern idealism makes any general assertion at all about the universe, it is that the universe is spiritual. But it is not at all clear what this statement means. And it is thus very difficult to discuss the question whether the universe is or is not spiritual. When we examine the matter, however, we find that there is a large number of different propositions which the idealist has to prove if he is to establish the truth of his general conclusion. And we can inquire into the weight of his arguments. Obviously, the statement that the universe is spiritual in character might still be true even if all the arguments advanced by idealists to prove its truth were fallacious. At the same time to show that the arguments were fallacious would be at any rate to show that the general conclusion was entirely unproved.

According to Moore, every argument used to prove that reality is spiritual has as one of its premisses the proposition *esse est*

<hr>

[1] Article 'Relative' in Baldwin's *Dictionary of Philosophy and Psychology*.
[2] *Mind*, Vol. 12 (1903), reprinted in *Philosophical Studies*.

percipi, to be is to be perceived. And one's natural reaction to this contention is to comment that belief in the truth of *esse est percipi* is characteristic of Berkeley's idealism, and that it should not be attributed to Hegel, for instance, or to Bradley. But Moore understands *percipi* as including 'that other type of mental fact, which is called "thought" ',[1] and as meaning, in general, to be experienced. And on this interpretation of *percipi* Bradley could be counted as subscribing to the thesis *esse est percipi*, inasmuch as everything is for him a constituent element in one all-comprehensive absolute experience.

As Moore understands *esse est percipi* in such a broad sense, it is not surprising that he finds the thesis ambiguous and capable of being interpreted in several ways. However, let us take it that acceptance of the thesis commits one to holding, among other things, that the object of a sensation cannot be distinguished from the sensation itself, or that, insofar as a distinction is made, it is the result of illegitimate abstraction from an organic unity. Moore undertakes to show that this view is false.

In the first place we are all aware, for example, that the sensation of blue differs from that of green. Yet if they are both sensations, they must have something in common. And Moore calls this common element 'consciousness', while the differentiating elements in the two sensations he calls their respective 'objects'. Thus 'blue is one object of sensation and green is another, and consciousness, which both sensations have in common, is different from either'.[2] On the one hand, as consciousness can co-exist with other objects of sensation besides blue, we obviously cannot legitimately claim that blue is the same thing as consciousness alone. On the other hand, we cannot legitimately claim that blue is the same thing as blue together with consciousness. For if we could, the statement that blue exists would have the same meaning as the statement that blue co-exists with consciousness. And this cannot be the case. For if, as has already been admitted, consciousness and blue are distinct elements in the sensation of blue, it makes sense to ask whether blue can exist without consciousness. And it would not make sense if the statement that blue exists and the statement that blue co-exists with consciousness had exactly the same meaning.

It may be objected that by using the term 'object' instead of 'content' this line of argument simply begs the question. In point

[1] *Philosophical Studies*, p. 7.   [2] *Ibid.*, p. 17.

of fact blue is the content, rather than the object, of the sensation of blue. And any distinction which we may make between the elements of content and consciousness or awareness is the result of an operation of abstraction performed on an organic unity. For Moore, however, an appeal to the concept of organic unity is tantamount to an attempt to have things both ways. That is to say, a distinction is allowed and prohibited at the same time. In any case Moore is not prepared to admit that 'content' is a more appropriate term than 'object'. It is legitimate to speak of blue as part of the content of a blue flower. But a sensation of blue is not itself blue: it is awareness or consciousness of blue as an object. And 'this relation is just that which we mean in every case by "knowing"'.[1] To know or be aware of blue is not to have in the mind a representative image of which blue is the content or part of the content; it is to be directly aware of the object 'blue'.

According to Moore, therefore, the awareness which is included in sensation is the same unique relation which basically constitutes every kind of knowledge. And the problem of getting out of the subjective sphere or circle of our sensations, images and ideas is a pseudo-problem. For 'merely to have a sensation is already to be outside that circle. It is to know something which is as truly and really *not* a part of *my* experience, as anything which I can ever know.'[2]

It can be added, with reference to the idealist thesis that reality is spiritual, that according to Moore we possess precisely the same evidence for saying that there are material things as we possess for saying that we have sensations. Hence to doubt the existence of material things entails doubting the existence of our sensations, and of experience in general. To say this is not to say, or even to suggest, that nothing is spiritual. It is to say that if the statement that reality is spiritual entails denying the existence of material things, we have no possible reason for making the statement. For 'the only *reasonable* alternative to the admission that matter exists *as well as* spirit, is absolute scepticism—that, as likely as not, *nothing* exists at all'.[3] And this is not a position which we can consistently propose and maintain.

In his discussion of sensation and perception, a discussion to which we shall have to return presently, Moore can be said to be concerned with phenomenological analysis. But it is obvious that his general attitude is founded on a common sense realism. And

[1] *Ibid.*, p. 25.   [2] *Ibid.*, p. 27.   [3] *Ibid.*, p. 30.

this element in his thought comes out clearly in the famous essay entitled *A Defence of Common Sense*,[1] where he maintains that there are a number of propositions, the truth of which is known with certainty. Thus I know that there is at present a living human body which is my body. I know also that there are other living bodies besides my own. I know too that the earth has existed for many years. Further, I know that there are other people, each of whom knows that there is a living body which is his own body, that there are other living bodies besides his own, and that the earth has existed for many years. Again, I know not only that these people are aware of the truth of these propositions but also that each of them knows that there are other people who are aware of the same truths. Such propositions belong to the common sense view of the world. And it follows, according to Moore, that they are true. There may indeed be differences of opinion about whether a given proposition belongs or not to the common sense view of the world. But if it does, it is true. And if it is known to belong, it is known to be true. And it is known to be true because of the reasons which we actually have for stating that it is true, not for any supposedly better reasons which philosophers may claim to be able to provide. It is no more the philosopher's business to prove the truth of propositions which we already know to be true than it is his business to disprove them.

Moore's defence of common sense has been referred to here simply as an illustration of one aspect of his realism. We shall have to return to the subject in connection with his conception of analysis. Meanwhile we can profitably take a glance at some of his ethical ideas, which, apart from their intrinsic interest, seem to illustrate the fact that his realism is not a 'naturalistic' realism.

3. Some moral philosophers, Moore remarks, have considered adequate the description of ethics as being concerned with what is good and what is bad in human conduct. In point of fact this description is too narrow. For other things besides human conduct can be good, and ethics can be described as 'the general inquiry into what is good'.[2] In any case, before we ask the question 'what is good?', meaning 'what things and which kinds of conduct possess the property of being good?', it seems logically proper to ask and answer the question, 'what is good?', meaning 'how is

[1] *Contemporary British Philosophy*, Second Series, edited by J. H. Muirhead (1925) and reprinted in *Philosophical Papers* (1959).
[2] *Principia Ethica*, p. 2, s.2 (1959 reprint). In reference to this work the letter 's' signifies the section.

good to be defined?', 'what is goodness in itself?' For unless we know the answer to this question, it may be argued, how can we discriminate between good and bad conduct and say what things possess the property of goodness?

Moore insists that when he raises the question, 'how is good to be defined?', he is not looking for a purely verbal definition, the sort of definition which consists simply in substituting other words for the word to be defined. Nor is he concerned with establishing or with justifying the common usage of the word 'good'. 'My business is solely with that object or idea, which I hold, rightly or wrongly, that the word is generally used to stand for. What I want to discover is the nature of that object or idea.'[1] In other words, Moore is concerned with phenomenological rather than with linguistic analysis.

Having raised the question, Moore proceeds to assert that it cannot be answered, not because good is some mysterious, occult and unrecognizable quality but because the idea of good is a simple notion, like that of yellow. Definitions which describe the real nature of an object are only possible when the object is complex. When the object is simple, no such definition is possible. Hence good is indefinable. This does not entail the conclusion that the things which are good are indefinable. All that is being maintained is that the notion of good as such is a simple notion and hence 'incapable of any definition, in the most important sense of that word'.[2]

From this doctrine of good as an indefinable property or quality there follow some important conclusions. Suppose, for example, that someone says that pleasure is the good. Pleasure may be one of the things which possess the property of being good; but if, as is probably the case, the speaker imagines that he is giving a definition of good, what he says cannot possibly be true. If good is an indefinable property, we cannot substitute for it some other property, such as pleasurable. For even if we admitted, for the sake of argument, that all those things which possess the property of being good also possess the property of being pleasurable, pleasure would still not be, and could not be, the same as good. And anyone who imagines that it is or could be the same, is guilty of the 'naturalistic fallacy'.[3]

Now, the fallacy in question is basically 'the failure to distinguish clearly that unique and indefinable quality which we mean

[1] *Ibid.*, p. 6, s.6.   [2] *Ibid.*, p. 9, s.10.   [3] *Ibid.*, p. 10, s.10.

by good'.[1] Anyone who identifies goodness with some other quality or thing, whether it be pleasure or self-perception or virtue or love, saying that this is what 'good' *means*, is guilty of this fallacy. These things may perfectly well possess the quality of goodness in the sense, for example, that what is pleasurable also possesses the quality of being good. But it no more follows that to be pleasurable is the same thing as to be good than it would follow, on the supposition that all primroses are yellow, that to be a primrose and to be yellow are the same thing.

But, it may well be asked, why should this fallacy be described as 'naturalistic'? The only real reason for so describing it would obviously be the belief that goodness is a 'non-natural' quality. Given this belief, it would follow that those who identify goodness with a 'natural' quality are guilty of a naturalistic fallacy. But though in *Principia Ethica* Moore does indeed maintain that goodness is a non-natural quality, he greatly complicates matters by distinguishing between two groups of philosophers who are both said to be guilty of the naturalistic fallacy. The first group consists of those who uphold some form of naturalistic ethics by defining good in terms of 'some one property of things, which exists in time'.[2] Hedonism, which identifies pleasure and goodness, would be an example. The second group consists of those who base ethics on metaphysics and define good in metaphysical terms, in terms of or by reference to a supersensible reality which transcends Nature and does not exist in time. According to Moore, Spinoza is an example, when he tells us that we become perfect in proportion as we are united with Absolute Substance by what he calls the intellectual love of God. Another example is provided by those who say that our final end, the supreme good, is the realization of our 'true' selves, the 'true' self not being anything which exists here and now in Nature. What, then, is meant by saying that good is a 'non-natural' quality, if at the same time those who define good in terms of or with reference to a 'non-natural' reality or quality or experience are said to be guilty of the naturalistic fallacy?

The answer which immediately suggests itself is that there is no incompatibility between asserting that good is an indefinable non-natural quality and denying that it can be defined in terms of some other non-natural quality. Indeed, the assertion entails the denial. But this consideration by itself does not tell us in what

---

[1] *Principia Ethica*, p. 59, s.36.   [2] *Ibid.*, p. 41, s.27.

sense good is a non-natural quality. In *Principia Ethica* Moore makes it clear that he has not the slightest intention of denying that good can be a property of natural objects. 'And yet I have said that "good" itself is not a natural property.'[1] What, then, is meant by saying that good can be, and indeed is, a non-natural property of at least some natural objects?

The answer provided in *Principia Ethica* is extremely odd. A natural property, or at any rate most natural properties, can exist by themselves in time, whereas good cannot. 'Can we imagine "good" as existing *by itself* in time, and not merely as a property of some natural object?'[2] No, we certainly cannot imagine this. But neither can we imagine a natural quality such as being brave existing *by itself* in time. And when Professor C. D. Broad, for example, pointed this out, Moore said that he completely agreed. It is not surprising, therefore, to find him eventually admitting roundly that 'in *Principia* I did not give any tenable explanation of what I meant by saying that "good" was not a natural property'.[3]

In his essay on the conception of intrinsic value in *Philosophical Studies* Moore gave another account of the distinction between natural and non-natural properties. He later admitted that this account was really two accounts; but he maintained that one of them might possibly be true. If one ascribes to a thing a natural intrinsic quality, one is always describing it to some extent. But if one ascribes to a thing a non-natural intrinsic quality, one is not describing the thing at all.

Obviously, if good is a non-natural intrinsic quality, and if to ascribe this quality to an object is not to describe the object in any way at all, the temptation immediately arises to conclude that the term 'good' expresses an evaluative attitude, so to speak, and that to call a thing good is to express this attitude and at the same time a desire that others should share this attitude. But if this conclusion is drawn, the view that goodness is an intrinsic quality of things has to be abandoned. And Moore was not prepared to abandon it. He believed that we can recognize what things possess the quality of being good, though we cannot define the quality. And when he wrote *Principia Ethica*, he was convinced that it is one of the main tasks of moral philosophy to determine values in this sense, namely to determine what things possess the

---

[1] *Ibid.*, p. 41, s.26. [2] *Ibid.*, p. 41, s.26.
[3] In 'A Reply to my Critics' contained in *The Philosophy of G. E. Moore*, edited by P. A. Schilpp, p. 582 (New York, 1952, 2nd edition).

quality of goodness and what things possess it in a higher degree than others.[1]

Obligation was defined by Moore in terms of the production of good. 'Our "duty", therefore, can be defined as that action which will cause more good to exist in the Universe than any possible alternative.'[2] Indeed, in *Principia Ethica* Moore went so far as to say that it is demonstrably certain that the assertion that one is morally bound to perform an action is identical with the assertion that this action will produce the greatest possible amount of good in the Universe. When, however, he came to write *Ethics*, he was no longer prepared to claim that the two statements were identical. And later on he recognized the necessity of distinguishing clearly between the statement that that action is morally obligatory which will produce the greatest amount of good as an effect *subsequent* to the action and the statement that that action is morally obligatory which, by reason of its being performed, by reason of its intrinsic nature, makes the Universe intrinsically better than it would be if some other action were performed. In any case the point to notice is that Moore does not regard his theory of good as an indefinable non-natural property as being in any way incompatible with a teleological view of ethics, which interprets obligation in terms of the production of good, that is, in terms of the production of things or experiences possessing the intrinsic quality of goodness. Nor in fact does there appear to be any incompatibility.

From this theory of obligation it does not follow, however, that in any set of circumstances whatsoever we are morally obliged to perform a certain action. For there might be two or more possible actions which, as far as we can see, would be equally productive of good. We can then describe these actions as right or morally permissible, but not as morally obligatory, even though we were obliged to perform either the one or the other.

Moore certainly assumed and implied that if a man passes a specifically moral judgment or an action, his statement, considered precisely as a moral judgment, is capable of being true or false. Take, for example, the assertion that it was right of Brutus to stab Julius Caesar. If this assertion is intended in a specifically

---

[1] In *Principia Ethica* Moore laid most stress on the values of personal affection and aesthetic enjoyment, that is, the appreciation of the beautiful in art and Nature. And this attitude exercised a considerable influence at the time on what was known as the Bloomsbury Circle.

[2] *Ibid.*, p. 148, s.89.

ethical sense, it is reducible neither to the statement that the speaker has a subjective attitude of approval towards Brutus's action nor to the statement that as a matter of historical fact Brutus stabbed Caesar. And in its irreducible moral character it is either true or false. Hence the dispute between the man who says that Brutus's action was right and the man who says that it was wrong is a dispute about the truth or falsity of a moral proposition.

When, however, he was confronted with the so-called emotive theory of ethics, Moore began to feel doubt about the truth of the position which he had hitherto adopted. As can be seen from his 'A Reply to My Critics', he conceded that Professor C. L. Stevenson might be right in maintaining that the man who says that Brutus's action was right, when the word 'right' is being used in a specifically ethical sense, is not saying anything of which truth or falsity can be predicated, except perhaps that Brutus actually did stab Caesar, a statement which is clearly historical and not ethical. Further, Moore conceded that if one man says that Brutus's action was right while another says that it was wrong, 'I feel some inclination to think that their disagreement *is* merely a disagreement in attitude, like that between the man who says "Let's play poker" and the other who says, "No; let's listen to a record": and I do not know that I am not *as much* inclined to think this as to think that they are making incompatible assertions'.[1] At the same time Moore confessed that he was also inclined to think that his old view was true; and he maintained that in any case Stevenson had not shown that it was false. 'Right', 'wrong', 'ought', may have merely emotive meaning. And in this case the same must be said of 'good' too. 'I am *inclined* to think that this is so, but I am also inclined to think that it is not so; and I do not know which way I am inclined most strongly.'[2]

These hesitations can reasonably be described as typical of Moore. He was, as has often been remarked, a great questioner. He raised a problem, tried to define it precisely and offered a solution. But when he was faced with criticism, he never brushed it aside. When he thought that it was based on misunderstanding of what he had said, he tried to explain his meaning more clearly. When, however, the criticism was substantial and not simply the fruit of misunderstanding, it was his habit to give serious

[1] *The Philosophy of G. E. Moore*, edited by P. A. Schilpp, pp. 546–7.
[2] *Ibid.*, p. 554.

consideration to the critic's remarks and to give due weight to his point of view. Moore never assumed that what he had said must be true and what the other fellow said must be false. And he did not hesitate to give a candid expression to his reflections and perplexities. We have to remember, therefore, that he is thinking aloud, so to speak, and that his hesitations are not necessarily to be taken as a definite retraction of his former views. He is engaged in weighing a new point of view, suggested to him by a critic, and in trying to estimate the amount of truth in it. Further, as we have seen, he is extremely frank about his subjective impressions, letting his readers know, without any attempt at concealment, that he is inclined to accept the new point of view, while at the same time he is inclined to stick to his own former view. Moore never felt that he was irretrievably committed to his own past, that is, to what he had said in the past. And when he became convinced that he had been wrong, he said so plainly.

In regard, however, to the question whether truth and falsity can legitimately be predicated of moral judgments, we are not entitled to say that Moore became *convinced* that his former view had been wrong. In any case the ethical theses which are for ever associated with his name are those of the indefinability of good, considered as a non-natural intrinsic quality, and of the need for avoiding any form of the so-called naturalistic fallacy. Moore's ethical position, especially as developed in *Principia Ethica*, can be said to be realist but not naturalistic; realist in the sense that good is regarded as an objective and recognizable intrinsic quality, not naturalistic in the sense that this quality is described as non-natural. But Moore never succeeded in explaining satisfactorily what was meant by saying, for example, that good is a non-natural quality of natural objects. And it is understandable that the emotive theory of ethics eventually came to the fore in philosophical discussion. After all, this theory can itself claim to be free from the 'naturalistic fallacy' and can use this claim as a weapon for dealing blows at rival theories. At the same time the theory is immune from the accusation of committing what Moore called the naturalistic fallacy only because 'good' is removed altogether from the sphere of objective intrinsic qualities.[1]

[1] It is not, of course, my intention to suggest that Moore's ethics must pass into the emotive theory. What I suggest is simply that it is understandable if to some minds the emotive theory appears more intelligible and tenable. But this theory in its original form was very soon seen to constitute a gross over-simplification of complex issues, And subsequent ethical discussion became much more sophisticated and also, in a real sense, more ecumenical.

4. Mention has already been made of the fact that as an under-graduate at Cambridge Moore was struck by some of the odd things which philosophers have said about the world. McTaggart's denial of the reality of time was a case in point. What, Moore wondered, could McTaggart possibly mean by this? Was he using the term 'unreal' in some peculiar sense which would deprive the statement that time is unreal of its paradoxical character? Or was he seriously suggesting that it is untrue to say that we have our lunch after we have had our breakfast? If so, the statement that time is unreal would be exciting but at the same time preposterous: it could not possibly be true. In any case, how can we profitably discuss the question whether time is real or unreal unless we first know precisely what is being asked? Similarly, according to Bradley reality is spiritual. But it is not at all clear what it means to say that reality is spiritual. Perhaps several different proposi-tions are involved. And before we start discussing whether reality is spiritual or not, we must not only clarify the question but make sure that it is not really several separate questions. For if it is, these questions will have to be treated in turn.

It is important to understand that Moore had no intention whatsoever of suggesting that all philosophical problems are pseudo-problems. He was suggesting that the reason why philo-sophical problems are often so difficult to answer is sometimes that it is not clear in the first place precisely what is being asked. Again, when, as so often happens, disputants find themselves at cross-purposes, the reason may sometimes be that the question under discussion is not really one question but several. Such suggestions have nothing at all to do with any general dogma about the meaninglessness of philosophical problems. They represent an appeal for clarity and accuracy from the start, an appeal prompted by enlightened common sense. They express, of course, the predominantly analytic turn of Moore's mind; but they do not make him a positivist, which he certainly was not.

When, however, we think of Moore's idea of philosophical analysis, we generally think of it in connection with his contention that there are common sense propositions which we all know to be true. If we know them to be true, it is absurd for the philosopher to try to show that they are not true. For he too knows that they are true. Nor is it the business of the philosopher, according to Moore, to attempt to prove, for example, that there are material things outside the mind. For there is no good reason to suppose that the philosopher can provide better reasons than those which we already have for saying that there are material things external to the mind. What, however, the philosopher can do is to analyze propositions, the truth or the falsity of which is established by other than specifically philosophical argument. The philosopher can, of course, try to make explicit the reasons which we already have for accepting some common sense propositions. But this does not turn the reasons into specifically philosophical reasons, in the sense that they have been added, as it were, by the philosopher to our stock of reasons.[1]

The question arises, therefore, what is meant by analyzing a proposition? It obviously cannot signify simply 'giving the meaning'. For if I know that a proposition is true, I must know what it means. Normally at any rate we would not be prepared to say that a man knew, or could know, that a proposition was true, if at the same time he had to admit that he did not know what the proposition meant.[2] And from this we can infer that analysis, as envisaged by Moore, does not consist simply in putting what has been said into other words. For instance, if an Italian asks me what it means to say 'John is the brother of James' and I reply that it means 'Giovanni è il fratello di Giacomo', I have explained to the Italian what the English sentence means, but I can hardly be said to have analyzed a proposition. I have not analyzed anything.

Analysis means for Moore conceptual analysis. He admitted later that he had sometimes spoken as though to give the analysis of a proposition was to give its 'meaning'. But he insisted that what he really had in mind was the analysis of concepts. The use of the word 'means' implies that analysis is concerned with verbal

---

[1] In a well-known essay on 'Moore and Ordinary Language' (*The Philosophy of G. E. Moore*, edited by P. A. Schilpp, Chapter 13), Professor N. Malcolm maintained that Moore's way of proving the denials of common sense propositions to be false was to appeal to ordinary language. Moore himself (*ibid.*, pp. 668–9) admitted that he considered the sort of argument referred to by Malcolm as a good argument, and that he himself had said that this sort of argument amounted to a disproof of the proposition 'there are no material things'. He added, however, that in the case of such a proposition as 'we do not know for certain that there are material things', something more is required if the proposition is to be proved to be false. For in point of fact many more philosophers have held that we do not *know* that there are material things than have held that there are actually no material things.

[2] I say 'normally at any rate', because if a man was convinced that all statements made by a certain authority were necessarily true, he might wish to claim that he knew that any such statement was true, even if he was not at all sure of what it meant.

expression, with defining words, whereas it is really concerned with defining concepts. The *analyzandum*, that which is to be analyzed, is a concept, and the *analyzans*, the analysis, must also be a concept. The expression used for the *analyzans* must be different from the expression used for the *analyzandum*, and it must be different in that it explicitly means or expresses à concept or concepts not explicitly mentioned by the expression used for the *analyzandum*. For instance, to give an example employed by Moore himself, '*x* is a male sibling' would be an analysis of '*x* is a brother'. It is not a question of merely substituting one verbal · expression for another in the sense in which 'fratello' can be substituted for 'brother'. 'Male sibling' is indeed a different verbal expression from 'brother', but at the same time it explicitly mentions a concept which is not explicitly mentioned in '*x* is a brother'.

And yet, of course, as Moore admits, if the analysis is correct, the concepts in the *analyzandum* and the *analyzans*, in the proposition to be analyzed and in its analysis, must be in some sense the same. But in what sense? If they are the same in the sense that no distinction can be made between them except in terms of verbal expression, analysis seems to be concerned simply with the substitution of one verbal expression for another. But Moore has said that this is not the case. He is therefore faced with the task of explaining in what sense the concepts in *analyzandum* and *analyzans* must be the same if the analysis is to be correct, and in what sense they must be distinct if analysis is to be more than the mere substitution of an equivalent verbal expression for a given verbal expression. But Moore does not feel able to give a really clear explanation.

In a general way it is, of course, easy enough to give a cash-value to the idea of philosophical analysis. True, if we are told that '*x* is a male sibling' is an analysis of '*x* is a brother', we may be inclined to wonder what possible philosophical relevance analysis of this kind can possess. But consider the non-philosopher who knows perfectly well how to use causal expressions in concrete contexts. If someone tells him that the banging of the door was caused by a sudden gust of wind through the open window, he knows perfectly well what is meant. He can distinguish between cases of *post hoc* and cases of *propter hoc*, and he can recognize particular causal relations. In a sense, therefore, he is well aware what causality means. But if the non-philosopher were asked to give an abstract analysis of the concept of causality, he would find himself at a loss. Like Socrates's young friends in a similar situation, he would probably mention instances of the causal relation and be unable to do anything more. Yet philosophers from Plato and Aristotle onwards have tried to give abstract analyses of concepts such as causality. And we can call this sort of thing philosophical analysis.

Though, however, this idea of philosophical analysis seems at first sight to be plain sailing, it can be and has been challenged. Thus those who sympathize with the attitude expressed in certain remarks in Wittgenstein's *Philosophical Investigations* would maintain that if one is asked what causality is, the proper answer is precisely to mention examples of the causal relation. It is a mistake to look for one single and profounder 'meaning' of the term. Either we already know what causality is (how the word is used) or we do not. And if we do not, we can be informed by having examples of the causal relation pointed out to us. Similarly, it is a mistake to suppose that because we describe a variety of things as beautiful, there must necessarily be one single 'real' meaning, one genuine analysis of a unitary concept, which the philosopher can, as it were, dig out. We can, of course, say that we are looking for a definition. But one can be found in the dictionary. And if this is not what we are looking for, then what we really need is to be reminded of the ways in which the word in question is actually used in human language. We shall then know what is 'means'. And this is the only 'analysis' which is really required.

It is not the intention of the present writer to defend this more 'linguistic' idea of analysis. His sympathies lie rather with the older idea of philosophical analysis, provided, of course, that we avoid the fallacy of 'one word, one meaning'. At the same time the notion of conceptual analysis is not at all so clear as it may seem to be at first sight. Difficulties arise which require to be considered and, if possible, met. But we cannot find any adequate answers to such difficulties in Moore's account of analysis.

This is not, however, surprising. For the fact of the matter is that Moore devoted himself for the most part to the *practice* of philosophical analysis. That is to say, he concerned himself with the analysis of particular propositions rather than with analyzing the concept of analysis. And when he was challenged to give an abstract account of his method and its aims, he felt able to remove some misunderstandings but unable to answer all questions to his own satisfaction. With his characteristic honesty, he did not hesitate to say so openly.

Obviously, therefore, to obtain some concrete idea of what Moore understood by analysis we have to look primarily at his actual practice. But before we turn to a line of analysis which occupied a great deal of his attention, there are two points which must be emphasized. In the first place Moore never said, and never intended to say, that philosophy and analysis are the same thing, and that the philosopher can do nothing more than analyze propositions or concepts. And when this view was attributed to him, he explicitly rejected it. The bent of his mind was indeed predominantly analytic; but he never laid down any dogma about the limits of philosophy. Other people may have done so, but not Moore. In the second place he never suggested that all concepts are analyzable. We have already seen, for example, that according to him the concept of good is simple and unanalyzable. And the same can be said of the concept of knowing.

5. In his well-known paper *Proof of an External World*, which he read to the British Academy in 1939,[1] Moore maintained that it is a good argument for, and indeed sufficient proof of, the existence of physical objects external to the mind if we can indicate one or more such objects. And he proceeded to claim that he could prove that two hands exist by the simple expedient of holding up his two hands, making a gesture with the right hand while saying 'here is one hand' and then making a gesture with the left hand while saying 'and here is the other'.

This may sound extremely naïve. But, as someone has said, Moore always had the courage to appear naïve. The trouble is, however, that while we may all come to believe that there is an external world by becoming aware of external objects, the only person who can possibly need a proof of the existence of an external world is the person who professes to doubt it. And if he professes to doubt, his doubt covers the existence of any extra-mental physical object. Hence he is not likely to be impressed when Moore, or anyone else, exhibits two hands. He will simply say that he doubts whether what he sees, when he is shown two hands, are really external physical objects.

And yet, of course, Moore's position is not really as naïve as it appears to be at first sight. For the determined sceptic is not going to be convinced by any proof. And what Moore is saying to the sceptic is more or less this: 'The only evidence which I can offer you is the evidence which we already have. And this is sufficient evidence. But you are looking for evidence or proof which we have not got, and which in my opinion we can never have. For I see no reason to believe that the philosopher can offer better evidence than the evidence we have. What you are really demanding is something which can never be provided, namely proof that the existence of an external world is a necessary truth. But it is not a necessary truth. Hence it is futile to look for the sort of evidence or proof which you insist on demanding.' This is clearly a reasonable point of view.

Now, as we have already indicated, while thinking that it is not the philosopher's job to try to prove by some special means of his own the truth of such a proposition as 'there are material things' or 'there are extra-mental physical objects', Moore believes that analysis of such propositions does form part of the philosopher's job. For while the truth of a proposition may be certain, its correct analysis may not be at all certain. But the correct analysis of such general propositions such as those just mentioned 'depends on the question how propositions of another and simpler type are to be analyzed'.[1] And an example of a simpler proposition would be 'I am perceiving a human hand'.

This proposition, however, is itself a deduction from two simpler propositions which can be expressed as 'I am perceiving *this*' and '*this* is a human hand'. But what is '*this*'? In Moore's opinion it is a sense-datum. That is to say, what I directly apprehend when I perceive a human hand is a sense-datum. And a sense-datum, even if we assume it to be somehow part of a human hand, cannot be identified with the hand. For the hand is in any case much more than what I actually see at a given moment. Hence a correct analysis of 'I perceive a human hand' involves one in specifying the nature of a sense-datum and its relation to the relevant physical object.

In a paper entitled *The Nature and Reality of Objects of Perception* which he read to the Aristotelian Society in 1905 Moore maintained that if we look at a red book and a blue book standing side by side on a shelf, what we really see are red and blue patches of colour of certain sizes and shapes, 'having to one another the spatial relation which we express by saying they are side by side'.[2] Such objects of direct perception he called 'sense-contents'. In the

---

[1] *Philosophical Papers*, p. 53.   [2] *Philosophical Studies*, p. 68.

lectures which he gave in the winter of 1910–11[1] Moore used the term 'sense-data'. True, in a paper entitled *The Status of Sense-Data*, which he read to the Aristotelian Society during the session 1913–14, Moore admitted that the term 'sense-datum' is ambiguous. For it suggests that the objects to which this term is applied can exist only when they are given, a view to which Moore did not wish to commit himself. Hence he proposed as 'more convenient'[2] the use of the term 'sensible'. But to all intents and purposes 'sense-data' is Moore's name for the immediate objects of direct perception. And in *A Defence of Common Sense* we find him saying that 'there is no doubt at all that there are sense-data, in the sense in which I am now using the term,'[3] that is, in a sense which makes it true to say that what we directly perceive when we look at a hand or at an envelope is a sense-datum but which leaves open the question whether this sense-datum is or is not part of the physical object which in ordinary language we are said to be seeing.

Now, Moore was careful to distinguish between sensations and sense-data. When, for example, I see a colour, the *seeing* the colour is the sensation and *what* is seen, the object, is the sense-datum. It therefore makes sense, at any rate at first sight, to ask whether sense-data can exist when they are unperceived. It would hardly make sense to ask whether a 'seeing' can exist when no sentient subject is seeing. But it does make sense to ask whether a colour exists when it is not perceived. If, of course, sense-data were described as existing 'in the mind', it would hardly make sense to ask whether they can exist unperceived. But Moore was unwilling to describe sense-data in this way, namely as being 'in the mind'.

But if sense-data are not 'in the mind', *where* are they? Provided that sense-data exist, and do not exist in the mind, the question arises whether or not they exist when they are not objects of perception. Do they then exist in a public physical space? One difficulty in saying this is the following. When two men look at a white envelope, we commonly say that they are seeing the same object. But according to the sense-datum theory there must be two sense-data. Further, the shape and spatial relations of one man's sense-datum do not seem to be precisely the same as those of the other man's sense-datum. If, therefore, we take it that the

---

[1] These lectures form the text of *Some Main Problems of Philosophy*, which will be referred to in notes as *Main Problems*.
[2] *Philosophical Studies*, p. 171.
[3] *Philosophical Papers*, p. 54.

shape and size and spatial relations of a physical object existing in public space are the same for all, must we not say that the one man's sense-datum exists in one private space and the other man's sense-datum in another private space?

Further, what is the relation between a sense-datum and the relevant physical object? For example, if I look at a coin from such an angle of vision that its surface appears to me as elliptical, is my sense-datum a part of the coin as a physical object, the surface of which we take to be roughly circular? Ordinary language suggests that it is. For I should normally be said to be seeing the coin. But if I look at the coin at another moment from a different position, or if another man looks at the same coin at the same moment as I do, there are different sense-data. And they differ not merely numerically but also qualitatively or in content. Are all these sense-data parts of the physical object? If they are, this suggests that the surface of a coin can be both elliptical and circular at the same time. If they are not, how are we to describe the relations between the sense-data and the physical object? Indeed, how do we know that there is a physical object for the sense-data to be related to?

These are the sort of problems with which Moore grappled on and off throughout his life. But he did not succeed in solving them to his own satisfaction. For example, we have already seen that in his attack on idealism Moore denied the truth of 'to be is to be perceived'; and his natural inclination was to claim that sense-data can exist even when they are unperceived. But though this point of view may appear reasonable when it is a question of a visual sense-datum such as a colour, it by no means appears reasonable if a toothache, for instance, is admitted into the category of sense-data, nor perhaps if sweet and bitter are taken as examples of sense-data rather than colour, size and shape. And in 'A Reply to My Critics' we find Moore saying that while he had once certainly suggested that sense-data such as blue and bitter could exist unperceived, 'I am inclined to think that it is as impossible that anything which has the sensible quality "blue", and more generally, *anything whatever which is directly appre-hended*, any *sense-datum*, that is, should exist unperceived, as it is that a headache should exist unfelt'.[1]

In this case, of course, as Moore notes, it follows that no sense-datum can possibly be identical with or part of the surface of a

[1] *The Philosophy of G. E. Moore*, edited by P. A. Schilpp, p. 658.

physical object. And to say this is to say that no physical surface can be directly perceived. The question, therefore, of how we know that there are physical objects distinct from sense-data becomes acute. Needless to say, Moore is well aware of the fact. But he is certainly not prepared to jettison his conviction that we do know the truth of the propositions which he regards as propositions of common sense. He is not prepared to throw overboard what, in *A Defence of Common Sense*, he called 'the Common Sense view of the world'.[1] And in a lecture entitled *Four Forms of Scepticism*, which Moore delivered on various occasions in the United States during the period 1940-4, we find a characteristic denial of Russell's contention that 'I do not know for certain that this is a pencil or that you are conscious'.[2] I call the denial 'characteristic' for this reason. Moore remarks that Russell's contention seems to rest on four distinct assumptions; that one does not know these things (that this is a pencil or that you are conscious) immediately; that they do not follow logically from anything which one does know immediately; that, in this case, one's knowledge of or belief in the propositions in question must be based on an analogical or inductive argument; and that no such argument can yield certain knowledge. Moore then proceeds to say that he agrees that the first three assumptions are true. At the same time 'of no one even of these three do I feel *as* certain as that I do know for certain that this is a pencil. Nay more: I do not think it is *rational* to be as certain of any one of these four propositions, as of the proposition that I do know that this is a pencil.'[3]

It is, of course, open to anyone to say that in his opinion the sense-datum theory as expounded by Moore leads logically to scepticism or at any rate to agnosticism in regard to the physical world as distinct from sense-data. But it is certainly not correct to speak of Moore as a sceptic. He was no such thing. He started, as we have seen, with the assumption that we know with certainty that there are external physical objects or material things; but he was doubtful of the correct analysis of such a proposition. And though his analysis may have led him into a position which was difficult to reconcile with his initial conviction, he did not abandon this conviction.

It has not been possible here to follow Moore through all his struggles with the theory of sense-data and its implications. The fulfilment of such a task would require a whole book. The theme

[1] *Philosophical Papers*, p. 45.   [2] *Ibid.*, p. 226.   [3] *Ibid.*

has been discussed in brief primarily in order to illustrate Moore's practice of analysis. But what sort of analysis is it? In a sense, of course, it is concerned with language. For Moore is out to analyze propositions, such as 'I see a human hand' or 'I see a penny'. But to describe his analysis as being concerned 'simply with words', as though it were a case of choosing between two sets of linguistic conventions, would be grossly misleading. Part at any rate of what he does can best be described, I think, as phenomenological analysis. For example, he raises the question, what exactly is it that happens when, as would ordinarily be said, we see a material object? He then explains that he is in no way concerned with the physical processes 'which occur in the eye and the optic nerves and the brain'.[1] What he is concerned with is 'the mental occurrence—the act of consciousness—which occurs (as is supposed) as a consequence of or accompaniment—of these bodily processes'.[2] Sense-data are introduced as objects of this act of consciousness. Or, rather, they are 'discovered', as Moore believes, as its immediate objects. And the process by which they are discovered is phenomenological analysis. But sense-data are not, of course, confined to visual sense-data. Hence we can say that Moore is concerned with the phenomenological analysis of sense-perception in general.

It is not my intention to suggest that this is all that Moore is concerned with, even within the restricted context of the sense-datum theory. For if we assume that sense-data can properly be said to exist, the question of their relation to physical objects can be described as an ontological question. Further, Moore concerns himself with epistemological questions; how do we know this or that? But part at any rate of his activity can better be described as phenomenological analysis than as linguistic analysis. And though the stock of the sense-datum theory has slumped greatly in recent years,[3] the judgment of Dr. Rudolf Metz was not entirely unreasonable, that in comparison with Moore's meticulous phenomenological analysis of perception 'all earlier studies of the problem seem to be coarse and rudimentary'.[4]

[1] *Main Problems*, p. 29.   [2] *Ibid.*
[3] We have only to think, for example, of the late J. L. Austin's attack on the theory.
[4] *A Hundred Years of British Philosophy*, p. 547 (London, 1938).

CHAPTER XIX

BERTRAND RUSSELL (1)

Introductory remarks—Life and writings up to the publication of Principia Mathematica; *Russell's idealist phase and his reaction against it, the theory of types, the theory of descriptions, the reduction of mathematics to logic—Ockham's razor and reductive analysis as applied to physical objects and to minds— Logical atomism and the influence of Wittgenstein—Neutral monism—The problem of solipsism.*

1. WE have already had occasion to remark that of all present-day British philosophers Bertrand Russell is by far the best known to the world at large. This is partly due to the fact that he has published a very considerable number of books and essays on moral, social and political topics which are salted with amusing and provocative remarks and are written at a level which can be understood by a public that is scarcely capable of appreciating his more technical contributions to philosophical thought. And it is largely this class of publications which has made of Russell a prophet of liberal humanism, a hero of those who regard themselves as rationalists, free from the shackles of religious and metaphysical dogma and yet at the same time devoted to the cause of human freedom, as against totalitarianism, and of social and political progress according to rational principles. We can also mention, as a contributing cause to Russell's fame, his active self-commitment at various periods of his life to a particular side, sometimes an unpopular side, in issues of general concern and importance. He has always had the courage of his convictions. And the combination of aristocrat, philosopher, Voltairean essayist and ardent campaigner has naturally made an impact on the imagination of the public.

It scarcely needs to be said that the fame of a philosopher during his lifetime is not an infallible indication of the value of his thought, especially if his general reputation is largely due to his more ephemeral writings. In any case the varied character of Russell's writing creates a special difficulty in estimating his status as a philosopher. On the one hand he is justly renowned for his work in the field of mathematical logic. But he himself regards this subject as belonging to mathematics rather than to philosophy. On the other hand it is not fair to Russell to estimate his status as a thinker in terms of his popular writings on concrete moral issues or on social and political topics. For though in view of the traditional and common view of the word 'philosophy' he recognizes that he has to resign himself to having his moral writings labelled as philosophical works, he has said that the only ethical topic which he regards as belonging properly to philosophy is the analysis of the ethical proposition as such. Concrete judgments of value should, strictly speaking, be excluded from philosophy. And if such judgments express, as Russell believes that they do, basic emotive attitudes, he is doubtless entitled to express his own emotive attitudes with a vehemence which would be out of place in discussing problems which, in princir˙ɔ at leas*, can be solved by logical argument.

If we exclude from philosophy mathematical logic on the one hand and concrete moral, valuational and political judgments on the other, we are left with what can perhaps be called Russell's general philosophy, consisting, for example, of discussions of epistemological and metaphysical questions. This general philosophy has passed through a series of phases and mutations, and it represents a strange mixture of acute analysis and of blindness to important relevant factors. But it is unified by his analytic method or methods. And the changes are hardly so great as to justify a literal interpretation of Professor C. D. Broad's humorous remark that, 'as we all know, Mr. Russell produces a different system of philosophy every few years.'[1] In any case Russell's general philosophy represents an interesting development of British empiricism in the light of later ways of thought, to which he himself made an important contribution.

In the following pages we shall be concerned mainly, though not exclusively, with Russell's idea and practice of analysis. But a thorough treatment, even of this limited theme, will not be possible. Nor indeed could it legitimately be expected in a general history of western philosophy.

2. (i) Bertrand Arthur William Russell was born in 1872. His parents, Lord and Lady Amberley, died when he was a small child,[2] and he was brought up in the house of his grandfather,

[1] In *Contemporary British Philosophy*, First Series, edited by J. H. Muirhead, p.79.
[2] In 1937 Russell published, together with Patricia Russell, *The Amberley Papers* in two volumes, containing the letters and diaries of his parents.

Lord John Russell, afterwards Earl Russell.[1] At the age of eighteen he went up to Cambridge, where he at first concentrated on mathematics. But in his fourth year at the university he turned to philosophy, and McTaggart and Stout taught him to regard British empiricism as crude and to look instead to the Hegelian tradition. Indeed, Russell tells us of the admiration which he felt for Bradley. And from 1894, the year in which he went down from Cambridge, until 1898 he continued to think that metaphysics was capable of proving beliefs about the universe which 'religious' feeling led him to think important.[2]

For a short while in 1894 Russell acted as an honorary attaché at the British Embassy in Paris. In 1895 he devoted himself to the study of economics and German social democracy at Berlin. The outcome was the publication of *German Social Democracy* in 1896. Most of his early essays were indeed on mathematical and logical topics, but it is worth noting that his first book was concerned with social theory.

Russell tells us that at this period he was influenced by both Kant and Hegel but sided with the latter when the two were in conflict.[3] He has described as 'unadulterated Hegel'[4] a paper on the relations of number and quantity which he published in *Mind* in 1896. And of *An Essay on the Foundations of Geometry* (1897), an elaboration of his Fellowship dissertation for Trinity College, Cambridge, he has said that the theory of geometry which he presented was 'mainly Kantian',[5] though it was afterwards swept away by Einstein's theory of relativity.

In the course of the year 1898 Russell reacted strongly against idealism. For one thing, a reading of Hegel's *Logic* convinced him that what the author had to say on the subject of mathematics was nonsense. For another thing, while lecturing on Leibniz at Cambridge in place of McTaggart, who was abroad, he came to the conclusion that the arguments advanced by Bradley against the reality of relations were fallacious. But Russell has laid most emphasis on the influence of his friend G. E. Moore. Together with Moore he adhered to the belief that, whatever Bradley or

[1] Bertrand Russell succeeded to the earldom in 1931.
[2] Russell abandoned belief in God at the age of eighteen. But he continued to believe for some years that metaphysics could provide a theoretical justification of emotive attitudes of awe and reverence towards the universe.
[3] Whether Russell ever had a profound knowledge of Hegel's general system is, of course, another question.
[4] *My Philosophical Development*, p. 40.
[5] *Ibid.*

McTaggart might say to the contrary, all that common sense takes to be real is real. Indeed, in the period in question Russell carried realism considerably further than he was later to do. It was not simply a question of embracing pluralism and the theory of external relations, nor even of believing in the reality of secondary qualities. Russell also believed that points of space and instants of time are existent entities, and that there is a timeless world of Platonic ideas or essences, including numbers. He thus had, as he has put it, a very full or luxuriant universe.

The lectures on Leibniz, to which reference has been made above, resulted in the publication in 1900 of Russell's notable work *A Critical Exposition of the Philosophy of Leibniz*. In it he maintained that Leibniz's metaphysics was in part a reflection of his logical studies and in part a popular or exoteric doctrine expounded with a view to edification and at variance with the philosopher's real convictions.[1] From then on Russell remained convinced that the substance-attribute metaphysics is a reflection of the subject-predicate mode of expression.

(ii) Considerable importance is attached by Russell to his becoming acquainted at an international congress at Paris in 1900 with the work of Giuseppe Peano (1858–1932), the Italian mathematician. For many years, in fact since he began to study geometry, Russell had been perplexed by the problem of the foundations of mathematics. At this time he did not know the work of Frege, who had already attempted to reduce arithmetic to logic. But the writings of Peano provided him with the stimulus for tackling his problem afresh. And the immediate result of his reflections was *The Principles of Mathematics*, which appeared in 1903.

But there were weeds in the mathematical garden. Russell finished the first draft of *The Principles of Mathematics* at the end of 1900, and early in 1901 he came upon what seemed to him to be an antinomy or paradox in the logic of classes. As he defined number in terms of the logic of classes, a cardinal number being 'the class of all classes similar to the given class',[2] the antinomy evidently affected mathematics. And Russell had either to solve it or to admit an insoluble antinomy within the mathematical field.

The antinomy can be illustrated in this way. The class of pigs is

[1] For some brief comments on Russell's view of Leibniz see Vol. IV of this *History*, pp. 270–2.
[2] *The Principles of Mathematics*, p. 115 (2nd edition, 1937). Two classes are said to be 'similar' when they 'have the same number' (*ibid.*, p. 113).

evidently not itself a pig. That is to say, it is not a member of itself. But consider the notion of the class of all classes which are not members of themselves. Let us call this class X and ask whether X is a member of itself or not. On the one hand, it seems that it cannot be a member of itself. For if we assume that it is, it follows logically that X has the defining property of its members. And this defining property is that any class of which it is a property is not a member of itself. Hence X cannot be a member of itself. On the other hand, it seems that X must be a member of itself. For if we begin by assuming that it is not a member of itself, it follows logically that it is not a member of those classes which are not members of themselves. And to say this is to say that X is a member of itself. Hence whether we begin by assuming that X is a member of itself or that it is not a member of itself, we seem in either case to be involved in self-contradiction.

Russell communicated this antinomy or paradox to Frege, who replied that arithmetic was tottering. But after some struggles Russell hit upon what seemed to him to be a solution. This was the doctrine or theory of types, a preliminary version of which was presented in *Appendix B* in *The Principles of Mathematics*. Every propositional function, Russell maintained, 'has in addition to its range of truth, a range of significance.'[1] For example, in the propositional function 'X is mortal', we can obviously substitute for the variable X a range of values such that the resultant propositions are true. Thus 'Socrates is mortal' is true. But there are also values which, if substituted for X, would make the resultant propositions neither true nor false but meaningless. For instance, 'the class of men is mortal' is meaningless. For the class of men is not a thing or object of which either mortality or immortality can be meaningfully predicated. From 'if X is a man, X is mortal' we can infer 'if Socrates is a man, Socrates is mortal'; but we cannot infer that the class of men is mortal. For the class of men neither is nor could be a man. In other words, the class of men cannot be a member of itself: in fact it is really nonsense to speak of its either being or not being a member of itself. For the very idea of a class being a member of itself is nonsensical. To take an example given by Russell,[2] a club is a class of individuals. And it can be a member of a class of another type, such as an association of clubs, which would be a class of classes. But neither the class nor the class of classes could possibly be a member of itself.

[1] *Ibid.*, p. 523.   [2] *Ibid.*, p. 524.

And if the distinctions between types are observed, the antinomy or paradox in the logic of classes does not arise.

To deal with further difficulties Russell produced a 'branching' or ramified theory of types. But we cannot discuss it here. Instead we can draw attention to the following point. Having made it clear that a class of things is not itself a thing, Russell goes on in *Principia Mathematica* to what he has called 'the abolition of classes'.[1] That is to say, he interprets classes as 'merely symbolic or linguistic conveniences'[2] as incomplete symbols. And it is not surprising to find him later on adopting a sympathetic attitude towards a linguistic interpretation of the theory of types and saying, for example, that 'difference of type means difference of syntactical function'.[3] Having once implied that differences between types are differences between types of entities, Russell came to recognize that the differences lie between different types of symbols, which 'acquire their type-status through the syntactical rules to which they are subject'.[4] In any case it is safe to say that one of the general effects of Russell's theory of types was to encourage belief in the relevance to philosophy of 'linguistic analysis'.

The theory of types has, of course, a variety of possible applications. Thus in his introduction to Ludwig Wittgenstein's *Tractatus Logico-Philosophicus* Russell, writing in 1922, suggested that Wittgenstein's difficulty about not being able to say anything within a given language about the structure of this language could be met by the idea of a hierarchy of languages. Thus even if one were unable to say anything within language *A* about its structure, one might be able to do so within language *B*, when they belong to different types, *A* being a first-order language, so to speak, and *B* a second-order language. If Wittgenstein were to reply that his theory of the inexpressible in language applies to the totality of languages,[5] the retort could be made that there is not, and cannot

---

[1] *The Principles of Mathematics*, p. x (Introduction to 2nd edition).
[2] *Principia Mathematica*, I, p. 72.
[3] *The Philosophy of Bertrand Russell*, edited by P. A. Schilpp, p. 692. As Russell notes in the introduction to the second edition of *The Principles of Mathematics*, he had been convinced by F. P. Ramsey's *The Foundations of Mathematics* (1931), that there are two classes of paradoxes. Some are purely logical or mathematical and can be cleared up by the simple (original) theory of types. Others are linguistic or semantic, such as the paradox arising out of the statement 'I am lying'. These can be cleared up by linguistic considerations.   [4] *Ibid*.
[5] It seems to the present writer that in the *Tractatus* Wittgenstein so defines the essence of the proposition that it follows logically that any proposition *about* propositions is a pseudo-proposition, devoid of 'sense' (*Sinn*). In this case to avoid the conclusion one has to reject the definition.

be, such a thing as a totality of languages.[1] The hierarchy is without limit.

What Russell has to say in developing the theory of types also has its application in metaphysics. For example, if we once accept the definition of the world as the class of all finite entities, we are debarred from speaking of it as being itself a contingent entity or being, even if we regard contingency as belonging necessarily to every finite being. For to speak in this way would be to make a class a member of itself. It does not follow, however, that the world must be described as a 'necessary entity'. For if the world is to be defined as the class of entities, it cannot itself be an entity, whether contingent or necessary.

(iii) It has already been mentioned, by way of anticipation, that in *Principia Mathematica* Russell maintains that the symbols for classes are incomplete symbols. 'Their *uses* are defined, but they themselves are not assumed to mean anything at all.'[2] That is to say, the symbols for classes undoubtedly possess a definable use or function in sentences, but, taken by themselves, they do not denote entities. Rather are they ways of referring to other entities. In this respect the symbols for classes are 'like those of descriptions'.[3] And something must now be said about Russell's theory of descriptions, which he developed between the writing of *The Principles of Mathematics* and the publication of *Principia Mathematica*.[4]

Let us consider the sentence 'the golden mountain is very high'. The phrase 'the golden mountain' functions as the grammatical subject of the sentence. And it may appear that as we can say something about the golden mountain, namely that it is very high, the phrase must denote an entity of some sort. True, it does not denote any existing entity. For though it is not logically impossible for there to be a golden mountain, we have no evidence that there is one. Yet even if we say 'the golden mountain does not exist', we seem to be saying something intelligible *about* it, namely that it does not exist. And in this case it appears to follow that 'the golden mountain' must denote an entity, not indeed an actually existing entity, but none the less a reality of some sort.

---

[1] That is, there can no more be a totality of languages than there can be a class of all classes. The latter notion was for Russell self-contradictory. A class of *all* classes would be additional to *all* classes. It would also be a member of itself which is ruled out by the theory of types.

[2] *Principia Mathematica*, I, p. 71.   [3] *Ibid.*

[4] The theory found a preliminary expression in Russell's article *On Denoting* in *Mind* for 1905.

This line of reasoning can be applied, of course, to the grammatical subjects in sentences such as 'the king of France is bald' (uttered or written when there is no king of France) or 'Sherlock Holmes wore a deerstalker's cap'. We thus get the sort of over-populated, or at any rate very well populated, universe in which Russell originally believed in the first flush of his realist reaction against the way in which idealists such as Bradley and McTaggart described as unreal several factors in the universe which common sense spontaneously regards as real. It is understandable, therefore, that Russell devoted himself to the study of Meinong, who also accepted a luxuriant universe in which room was found for entities which do not actually exist but which are none the less realities in some sense. At the same time it was precisely his study of Meinong which raised serious doubts in Russell's mind about the validity of the principle that phrases such as 'the golden mountain', which can function as grammatical subjects in sentences, denote entities of some sort. Indeed, when taken by themselves, have such phrases as 'the golden mountain', 'the king of France' and so on any 'meaning'? It was one of the functions of the theory of descriptions to show that they have not.

According to this theory such phrases are not 'names', denoting entities, but 'descriptions'. In his *Introduction to Mathematical Philosophy* (1919) Russell distinguishes between two sorts of descriptions, indefinite and definite.[1] Phrases such as 'the golden mountain' and 'the king of France' are definite descriptions; and we can confine our attention here to this class. The theory of descriptions purports to show that they are incomplete symbols, and though they can function as grammatical subjects in sentences, these sentences can be restated according to their logical form in such a way that it becomes clear that the phrases in question are not the real logical subjects in the sentences in which they occur as grammatical subjects. When this has become clear, the temptation to think that they must denote entities should vanish. For it is then understood that, taken by themselves, the phrases in question have no denoting function. The phrase 'the golden mountain', for example, does not denote anything at all.

Let us take the sentence 'the golden mountain does not exist'. If this is translated as 'the propositional function "X is golden and a mountain" is false for all values of X', the meaning of the

---

[1] 'An indefinite description is a phrase of the form "a so-and-so" and a definite description is a phrase of the form "the so-and-so" (in the singular)', *Introduction to Mathematical Philosophy*, p. 167.

original sentence is revealed in such a way that the phrase 'the golden mountain' disappears and, with it, the temptation to postulate a subsisting non-actual entity. For we are no longer involved in the awkward situation which arises in view of the fact that the statement 'the golden mountain does not exist' can prompt the question *'what* does not exist?', implying that the golden mountain must have some sort of reality if we can say of it significantly that it does not exist.

This is all very well, it may be said, but it is extremely odd to claim, in regard to descriptions in general, that they have no meaning when they are taken by themselves. It seems indeed to be true that 'the golden mountain' does not mean anything, provided that by meaning one understands denoting an entity. But what about a phrase such as 'the author of *Waverley*'? According to Russell, it is a description, not a proper name. But is it not evident that it means Scott?

If 'the author of *Waverley*' meant Scott, Russell replies, 'Scott is the author of *Waverley*' would be a tautology, declaring that Scott is Scott. But it is evidently not a tautology. If, however, 'the author of *Waverley*' meant anything else but Scott, 'Scott is the author of *Waverley*' would be false, which it is not. The only thing to say is, therefore, 'the author of *Waverley*' means nothing. That is to say, taken in isolation it does not denote anyone. And the statement 'Scott is the author of *Waverley*' can be restated in such a way that the phrase 'the author of *Waverley*' is eliminated. For example, 'for all values of X, "X wrote *Waverley*" is equivalent to "X is Scott" '.[1]

It seems indeed that we can very well say 'the author of *Waverley* is Scotch', and that in this case we are predicating an attribute, namely being Scotch, of an entity, namely the author of *Waverley*. Russell, however, maintained that 'the author of *Waverley* is Scotch' implies and is defined by three distinct propositions; 'at least one person wrote *Waverley*', 'at most one person wrote *Waverley*', and 'whosoever wrote *Waverley* was Scotch'.[2] And this can be stated formally as 'there is a term c such that "X wrote *Waverley*" is equivalent, for all values of X, to "X is c", and "c is Scotch" '.

Needless to say, Russell has no doubt that the author of *Waverley* was Scotch, in the sense that Sir Walter Scott wrote

[1] *My Philosophical Development*, p. 84.
[2] *Introduction to Mathematical Philosophy*, p. 177.

Waverley and was a Scotsman. The point is, however, that if the descriptive term 'the author of *Waverley*' is not a proper name and does not denote anyone, the same can be said of such a descriptive term as 'the king of France'. 'The author of *Waverley* was Scotch' can be restated in such a way that the translation is a true proposition but does not contain the descriptive phrase 'the author of *Waverley*', and 'the king of France is bald' can be restated in such a way that the translation does not contain the descriptive phrase 'the king of France' but is a false, though significant proposition. It is thus in no way necessary to postulate any non-actual entity denoted by 'the king of France'.

It is understandable that Russell's theory of descriptions has been subjected to criticism. For example, G. E. Moore has objected[1] that if in 1700 an Englishman had made the statement 'the king of France is wise', it would certainly have been correct to say that 'the king of France' denoted an entity, namely Louis XIV. In this case, therefore, 'the king of France' would not have been an incomplete symbol. But in other circumstances it might be. There can be sentences in which 'the king of France' does not denote anyone; but, equally, there can be sentences in which it does denote someone.

It seems to the present writer that in his criticism of Russell's theory of descriptions Moore is appealing to ordinary linguistic usage. This is, of course, the strength of his criticism. Russell himself, however, is concerned not so much with mapping-out ordinary language as with constructing a theory which will deprive of its linguistic basis the notion that it is necessary to postulate non-existent but real entities such as 'the golden mountain', 'the king of France' (when there is no king of France), and so on. It is perfectly legitimate criticism, it seems to me, to object that the theory involves an interpretation of such phrases which is too narrow to square with actual linguistic usage.[2] But in the present context it is more important to draw attention to Russell's aim, to what he thinks that he is accomplishing by means of his theory.

It would obviously be a great mistake to suppose that Russell imagines that translation of 'the golden mountain is very high' into a sentence in which the descriptive phrase 'the golden

---

[1] *The Philosophy of Bertrand Russell*, edited by P. A. Schilpp, ch. 5.
[2] Some analytic philosophers might wish to say that Russell was trying to 'reform' language, to create an ideal language. But he did not intend, of course, to prohibit people from saying what they are accustomed to say.

mountain' does not occur proves that there is no golden mountain. Whether there is or is not a golden mountain in the world is an empirical question; and Russell is perfectly well aware of the fact. Indeed, if the translation to which reference has just been made proved that there is in fact no golden mountain, then the fact that 'the author of *The Principles of Mathematics* is English' can be restated in such a way that the descriptive phrase 'the author of *The Principles of Mathematics*' disappears would prove that there is no Bertrand Russell.

It would also be a mistake to suppose that according to Russell the ordinary man, the non-philosopher, is misled into thinking that there must be some sort of non-existing but real object corresponding to the phrase 'the golden mountain' because we can say 'the golden mountain does not exist'. Russell is not attributing any mistakes of this kind to the ordinary man. His point is that for philosophers, who reflect on the implications or apparent implications of linguistic expressions, descriptive phrases such as 'the golden mountain' may occasion, and in Russell's opinion have occasioned, the temptation to postulate entities with a queer status between actual existence and non-entity. And the function of the theory of descriptions is to remove this temptation by showing that descriptive phrases are incomplete symbols which, according to Russell, mean nothing, that is, do not denote any entity. The paradoxical aspect of the theory of descriptions is that, because of its generality, it applies equally both to phrases such as 'the golden mountain' or 'the king of France' and to phrases such as 'the author of *The Principles of Mathematics*', not to speak of the other class of phrases such as 'the round square'. But its function is to contribute to clearing away the fictitious entities with which certain philosophers, not the man in the street, have over-populated the universe. It thus serves the purpose of Ockham's razor and can be brought under the general heading of reductive analysis, a theme to which we shall have to return.

A final point. We have noted that when a phrase such as 'the golden mountain' or 'the author of *Waverley*' occurs as the grammatical subject of a sentence, Russell maintains that it is not the logical subject. The same line of reasoning can, of course, be applied to grammatical objects. In 'I saw nobody on the road' the grammatical object is 'nobody'. But 'nobody' is not a special kind of 'somebody'. And the sentence can be restated in such a way (for example, 'it is not the case that I saw any person on the road') that the word 'nobody' disappears. In general, therefore, Russell's contention is that the grammatical form of a sentence is by no means the same as its logical form, and that philosophers can be seriously misled if they do not understand this fact. But though Russell may have generalized this idea, it is historically inaccurate to suggest that he was the first man to make this discovery.[1] For example, in the twelfth century St. Anselm pointed out that to say that God created the world out of nothing is not to say that the world was created out of nothing as some kind of pre-existing material. It is to say that God did not create the world out of anything, that is, out of any pre-existing material.

(iv) The three volumes of *Principia Mathematica*, which were the fruit of the joint work of Russell and A. N. Whitehead, appeared in 1910–13. The point which aroused most interest was the attempt to show that pure mathematics is reducible to logic, in the sense that it can be shown to follow from purely logical premisses and employs only concepts which are capable of being defined in logical terms.[2] In practice, of course, we cannot simply take a complicated mathematical formula at random and express it without more ado in purely logical terms. But in principle the whole of pure mathematics is ultimately derivable from logical premisses, mathematics being, as Russell has put it, the manhood of logic.

As Russell believed that in *Principia Mathematica* he had demonstrated the truth of his thesis, he also believed that he had provided a decisive refutation of Kantian theories of mathematics. For example, if geometry is derivable from purely logical premisses, to postulate an *a priori* intuition of space is entirely superfluous.

Russell and Whitehead had, needless to say, their predecessors. George Boole (1815–64)[3] had attempted to 'algebraicize' logic and had developed a calculus of classes. But he regarded logic as subordinate to mathematics, whereas William Stanley Jevons (1835–82)[4] was convinced that logic is the fundamental science. John Venn

---

[1] This is understood nowadays. But in the past statements have sometimes been made which said or implied that Russell was the discoverer of this distinction between grammatical and logical form.

[2] Russell has expressed his disappointment that comparatively little attention was paid to the mathematical techniques developed in the course of the work.

[3] Author of *The Mathematical Analysis of Logic* (1847), and *An Investigation of the Laws of Thought* (1854).

[4] Author of *Pure Logic* (1864) and other logical studies. Whereas Boole was a professor of mathematics, Jevons occupied a chair of political economy and did not possess Boole's 'mathematicizing' turn of mind, though he invented a calculating machine to carry out the processes of inference.

(1834-1923),[1] however, while attempting to remedy the defects in Boole's system and to overcome the contemporary chaos in symbolic notation, looked on logic and mathematics as separate branches of symbolic language, neither being subordinate to the other. In America C. S. Peirce modified and developed the logical algebra of Boole and showed how it could accommodate a revised version of the logic of relations formulated by Augustus De Morgan (1806-71). In Germany Friedrich Wilhelm Schröder (1841-1902) gave a classical formulation to Boole's logical algebra as modified by Peirce.

More important, Gottlob Frege (1848-1925) attempted to derive arithmetic from logic in his works *Die Grundlagen der Arithmetik* (1884) and *Grundgesetze der Arithmetik* (1893-1903). As has been mentioned, Russell was not at first aware that he had rediscovered for himself ideas which had already been proposed by Frege. But when he became aware of Frege's work, he drew attention to it,[2] though it was not until a considerably later period that the German mathematician's studies obtained general recognition in England.

In Italy Peano and his collaborators tried to show, in their *Formulaires de mathématiques* (1895-1908), that arithmetic and algebra can be derived from certain logical ideas, such as those of a class and of membership of a class, three primitive mathematical concepts and six primitive propositions. As we have seen, Russell became acquainted with Peano's work in 1900. And he and Whitehead made use of Peano's logical symbolism or notation in the construction of *Principia Mathematica*, which carried further the work of both Peano and Frege.

The present writer is not competent to pass any judgment on the contents of *Principia Mathematica*. It must suffice to say that though the thesis of the reducibility of mathematics to logic has by no means won the consent of all mathematicians,[3] nobody would question the historic importance of the work in the development of mathematical logic. Indeed, it stands out above all other English contributions to the subject.[4] In any case, though Russell

[1] Author of *The Logic of Chance* (1866), *Symbolic Logic* (1881), and *The Principles of Empirical or Inductive Logic* (1889).
[2] *Appendix A* in *The Principles of Mathematics* is devoted to 'the logical and arithmetical doctrines of Frege'.
[3] It was rejected both by the 'Formalists', such as David Hilbert (1862-1943) and by the 'Intuitionists' who followed Luitzen Brouwer (b. 1881).
[4] It is a notorious fact that since the publication of *Principia Mathematica* comparatively little attention has been paid in England to symbolic logic. This is not to say that no good work has subsequently been done in England on logical theory. But, generally speaking, the attention of philosophers has been concentrated rather on 'ordinary language'. It is Polish and American logicians who have been most prominent in the field of symbolic logic.

himself may understandably regret that more attention was not paid to the mathematical techniques evolved in the work, the present writer's principal aim in drawing attention here to *Principia Mathematica* is to illustrate the background to Russell's conception of reductive analysis. For example, to say that mathematics is reducible to logic obviously does not mean that there is no such thing as mathematics. Nor is it tantamount to a denial that there are any differences between logic and mathematics as they actually exist or have actually been developed. Rather does it mean that pure mathematics can in principle be derived from certain fundamental logical concepts and certain primitive indemonstrable propositions, and that, in principle, mathematical propositions could be translated into logical propositions with equivalent truth-values.

Before we pass on to Russell's general idea of reductive analysis, it is worth noting that the reducibility of mathematics to logic does not mean that mathematics is based on laws of thought in the psychological sense of laws governing human thinking. In the earlier years of this century Russell believed that mathematics carries us beyond what is human 'into the region of absolute necessity, to which not only the actual world, but every possible world, must conform'.[1] In this ideal world mathematics forms an eternal edifice of truth; and in the contemplation of its serene beauty man can find refuge from a world full of evil and suffering. Gradually, however, though reluctantly, Russell came to accept Wittgenstein's view that pure mathematics consists of 'tautologies'. This change of mind he has described as 'a gradual retreat from Pythagoras'.[2] One effect of the First World War on Russell's mind was to turn it away from the idea of an eternal realm of abstract truth, where one can take refuge in the contemplation of timeless and non-human beauty, to concentration on the actual concrete world. And this meant, in part at least, a turning away from purely logical studies to the theory of knowledge and to the parts of psychology and linguistics which seemed to be relevant to epistemology.

3. We have seen Russell getting rid of superfluous entities such as 'the golden mountain'. And in the course of writing *Principia Mathematica* he found that the definition of cardinal numbers as

[1] From *The Study of Mathematics*, written in 1902 and first published in the *New Quarterly* in 1907. See *Philosophical Essays*, p. 82, and *Mysticism and Logic*, p. 69.
[2] *My Philosophical Development*, p. 208.

classes of classes, together with the interpretation of class-symbols as incomplete symbols, rendered it unnecessary to regard cardinal numbers as entities of any kind. But there remained, for example, points, instants and particles as factors in the physical world. And these figured in *The Problems of Philosophy* (1912), which can be said to represent Russell's incursion into the general philosophical field, as distinct from the more restricted sphere of logical and mathematical theory. Whitehead, however, woke him from his 'dogmatic slumbers' by inventing a way of constructing points, instants and particles as sets of events, or as logical constructions out of sets of events.[1]

The technique of reductive analysis as illustrated in the case of points, instants and particles was regarded by Russell as an application of the method already employed in *Principia Mathematica*. In this work the task was to find for mathematics a minimum vocabulary in which no symbol would be definable in terms of the others. And the result of the inquiry was the conclusion that the minimum vocabulary for mathematics is the same as that for logic. In this sense mathematics was found to be reducible to logic. If a similar technique, Russell came to think, is applied to the language used to describe the physical world, it will be found that points, instants and particles do not appear in the minimum vocabulary.

Now, talk about finding a minimum vocabulary tends to suggest that the operation in question is purely linguistic, in the sense of being concerned only with words. But in the context of propositions about the physical world finding a minimum vocabulary means for Russell discovering by analysis the uneliminable entities in terms of which inferred entities can be defined. If, for example, we find that the inferred non-empirical entity, or putative entity, X can be defined in terms of a series of empirical entities a, b, c, and d, X is said to be a logical construction out of a, b, c, and d. This reductive analysis as applied to X has indeed a linguistic aspect. For it means that a proposition in which X is mentioned can be translated into a set of propositions in which there is no mention of X but only of a, b, c, and d, the relation between the original proposition and the translation being such that if the former is true (or false) the latter is true (or false) and *vice versa*. But the reductive analysis has at the same time an

---

[1] See *My Philosophical Development*, p. 103 and *The Principles of Mathematics*, p. xi (in the Introduction to the second edition).

ontological aspect. True, if X can be interpreted as a logical construction out of a, b, c, and d, we are not necessarily committed to denying the existence of X as a non-empirical entity distinct from or over and above a, b, c, and d. But it is unnecessary to postulate the existence of such an entity. Hence the principle of parsimony (or economy) or Ockham's razor forbids us to *assert* the existence of X as an inferred non-empirical entity. And the principle itself can be stated in this form: 'whenever possible logical constructions are to be substituted for inferred entities'.[1]

This quotation is taken from a paper on the relation of sense-data to physics, which Russell wrote at the beginning of 1914. In this paper he maintains that physical objects can be defined as functions of sense-data, a sense-datum being a particular object, such as a particular patch of colour, of which a subject is directly aware. Sense-data, therefore, are not to be confused with sensations, that is, with the acts of awareness of which they are the object.[2] Nor are they mental entities, in the sense of being purely within the mind. We must thus admit, to speak paradoxically, sense-data which are not actual data, not objects of actual awareness on the part of a subject. But the paradox can be avoided by calling these unsensed sense-data *sensibilia*, potential sense-data. And the physical objects of common sense and of science are to be interpreted as functions of sense-data and *sensibilia* or, to put the matter in another way, as the classes of their appearances.

There is, however, a major difficulty in admitting *sensibilia* as being on the same level, so to speak, as actual sense-data. For Russell's programme demands that the physical objects of common sense and of science should be interpreted, if possible, as logical constructions out of purely empirical, non-inferred entities. But *sensibilia* are inferred entities. The only relevant non-inferred entities are *actual* sense-data. Hence it is not surprising to find Russell saying, in his paper on the relation of sense-data to physics, that 'a complete application of the method which substitutes constructions for inferences would exhibit matter wholly in terms of sense-data, and even, we may add, of the sense-data of a single person, since the sense-data of others cannot be known without some element of inference'.[3] But he goes on to add that the carrying out of this programme is extremely difficult, and that

[1] *Mysticism and Logic*, p. 155.
[2] It will be noted that Russell and Moore are at one on this matter.
[3] *Mysticism and Logic*, p. 157.

he proposes to allow himself two kinds of inferred entities, the sense-data of other people and *sensibilia*.

In *Our Knowledge of the External World* (1914) Russell depicts the physical objects of common sense and science as logical constructions out of actual sense-data, *sensibilia* or possible sense-data being defined with reference to them. At any rate, 'I think it may be laid down quite generally that, *in so far* as physics or common sense is verifiable, it must be capable of interpretation in terms of actual sense-data alone'.[1] However, in a lecture on the ultimate constituents of matter which he delivered early in 1915, Russell remarks that while the particles of mathematical physics are logical constructions, useful symbolic fictions, 'the actual data in sensation, the immediate objects of sight or touch or hearing, are extra-mental, purely physical, and among the ultimate constituents of matter'.[2] Similarly, 'sense-data are merely those among the ultimate constituents of the physical world, of which we happen to be immediately aware'.[3] Whether the statement that sense-data are 'among' the ultimate constituents of the physical world is equivalent to the admission of *sensibilia* as members of this class, or whether it means simply that sense-data are the only ultimate constituents of which we are directly aware, is not quite clear. In any case, if the world of common sense and of science is to be regarded as a logical construction, or hierarchy of logical constructions, out of the actual sense-data of a single person, it is difficult to see how solipsism can be successfully avoided. However, it was not long before Russell abandoned the doctrine of sense-data as here presented. And his ideas on solipsism will be considered later.

So far we have been concerned only with analysis of the physical objects of common sense and science. But what of the subject or mind which is aware of objects? When Russell rejected monism and embraced pluralism, he made a sharp distinction between the act of awareness and its object. Originally indeed, as he himself tells us, he accepted the view of Brentano that in sensation there are three distinct elements, 'act, content and object'.[4] He then came to think that the distinction between content and object is superfluous; but he continued to believe in the relational character of sensation, that is to say, that in sensation a subject is aware of an object. And this belief found

---

[1] *Our Knowledge of the External World*, pp. 88–9.
[2] *Mysticism and Logic*, p. 128.   [3] *Ibid.*, p. 143.
[4] *My Philosophical Development*, p. 134.

expression in, for example, *The Problems of Philosophy* (1912). In this work Russell admitted, even if tentatively, that the subject can be known by acquaintance. It does not follow, of course, that he accepted the idea of a permanent mental substance. But he held at any rate that we are acquainted with what one might perhaps call the momentary self, the self precisely as apprehending an object in a given act of awareness. In other words, it was a question of the phenomenological analysis of consciousness rather than of metaphysical theory.

When, however, we turn to an essay on the nature of acquaintance, which Russell wrote in 1914, we find him expressing his agreement with Hume that the subject is not acquainted with itself. He does indeed define acquaintance as 'a dual relation between a subject and an object which need not have any community of nature'.[1] But the term 'subject', instead of denoting an entity with which we can be acquainted, becomes a description. In other words, the self or mind becomes a logical construction; and in his 1915 address on the ultimate constituents of matter Russell suggests that 'we might regard the mind as an assemblage of particulars, namely, what would be called "states of mind", which belong together in virtue of some specific common quality. The common quality of all states of mind would be the quality designated by the word "mental".'[2] This suggestion is indeed advanced only in the context of a discussion of the theory, rejected by Russell, that sense-data are 'in the mind'. But it is clear that the subject, considered as a single entity, has become a class of particulars. At the same time these particulars possess a quality which marks them off as mental. In other words, an element of dualism is still retained by Russell. He has not yet adopted the neutral monism, of which something will be said presently.

Needless to say, the theory of logical constructions is not intended to imply that we ought to give up talking about minds on the one hand and the physical objects of common sense and science on the other. To say, for example, that sentences in which a table is mentioned can in principle be translated into sentences in which only sense-data are referred to and the word 'table' does not occur is not equivalent to a denial of the utility of talking about tables. Indeed, within the context of ordinary language and its purposes it is perfectly true to say that there are tables, though

---

[1] *Logic and Knowledge*, p. 127.   [2] *Mysticism and Logic*, pp. 131-2.

from the point of view of the analytic philosopher a table is a logical construction out of sense-data. The language of atomic physics, for instance, does not render ordinary language illegitimate. For the purposes of ordinary life we are perfectly entitled to go on talking about trees and stones; we do not have to talk about atoms instead. And if philosophical analysis leads us to regard the entities of physical science, such as atoms, as logical constructions, this does not render illegitimate the language of physical science. The different levels of language can co-exist and are employed for different purposes, within different contexts. They should not, of course, be confused; but the one level does not exclude the other levels.

It is thus easy to understand the contention that the issue between the sense-datum theory and the common sense view of the world is a purely linguistic matter; that is, that it is simply a question of choosing between two alternative languages. But, as has already been indicated, this contention does not adequately represent Russell's point of view. Obviously, analysis as he practises it takes different forms.[1] Sometimes it is predominantly a logical analysis which has ontological implications only in the sense that it removes the ground for postulating superfluous entities. But in its application to the physical objects of common sense and science it professes to reveal the ultimate constituents of such objects. In other words it professes to increase our understanding not only of language but also of extra-linguistic reality. To be sure, Russell has at times expressed a very sceptical view about the knowledge which is actually attainable in philosophy. But his aim at any rate has been that of attaining impersonal truth. And the primary method of doing so is for him analysis. His point of view is thus opposed to that of Bradley, who thought that analysis, the breaking-up of a whole into its constituent elements, distorts reality and leads us away from the truth which is, as Hegel said, the whole. Later on, especially when treating of the relation of philosophy to the empirical sciences, Russell is ready to emphasize the role of synthesis, of bold and wide philosophical hypotheses about the universe. But at the period of which we have been writing the emphasis is placed on analysis.

[1] So far as the present writer is aware, Russell has never given a systematic account of the methods of analysis practised by himself, comparing them with one another and noting both their common and their differentiating features. On this subject the reader can profitably consult *The Unity of Russell's Philosophy* by Morris Weitz in *The Philosophy of Bertrand Russell*, edited by P. A. Schilpp.

And it would be extremely misleading to describe analysis, as practised by Russell, as being purely 'linguistic'. This point can also be illustrated in the following way. In *The Problems of Philosophy* Russell accepted universals as ultimate conceptual constituents of reality, universals being said 'to *subsist* or *have being*, where "being" is opposed to "existence" as being timeless'.[1] And though he has progressively depopulated the world of universals, he has never entirely rejected his former view. For he has continued to believe not only that a minimum vocabulary for the description of the world requires some universal term or terms but also that this fact shows something about the world itself, even if he has ended by being uncertain about precisely what it shows.

4. In *My Philosophical Development*,[2] Russell tells us that from August 1914 until the end of 1917 he was wholly occupied with matters arising out of his opposition to the war. These matters presumably cover *Principles of Social Reconstruction* and *Justice in War-Time*, both of which appeared in 1916, in addition to a number of articles and addresses relating to the war. However, during the period 1914–19 Russell published an important series of philosophical articles in *The Monist*.[3] In 1918 he published *Mysticism and Logic and Other Essays* and *Roads to Freedom: Socialism, Anarchism and Syndicalism*. His *Introduction to Mathematical Philosophy*, to which reference has already been made, was written in 1918, during his six months imprisonment,[4] and was published in 1919.

Shortly before the First World War Wittgenstein gave Russell some notes on various logical points. And these, together with the conversations which the two men had had during Wittgenstein's first sojourn at Cambridge, 1912–13, affected Russell's thought during the years when he was cut off from contact with his friend and former pupil.[5] In fact he prefaced his 1918 lectures on the philosophy of logical atomism with the remark that they were largely concerned with ideas which he had learned from Wittgenstein.

As for the term 'atomism' in 'logical atomism' Russell says that

[1] *The Problems of Philosophy*, p. 156.   [2] P. 128.
[3] The lectures on logical atomism which Russell delivered in 1918 and which were published in *The Monist*, 1918–19, have been reprinted in *Logic and Knowledge*, edited by R. Marsh (London, 1956).
[4] This was the result of a second prosecution, arising, like the first, out of Russell's outspoken opposition to the First World War.
[5] Wittgenstein, then still an Austrian citizen, joined the Austrian army and was subsequently a prisoner-of-war of the Italians.

he wishes to arrive at the ultimate constituent elements of reality in a manner analogous to that in which in *Principia Mathematica* he worked back from 'result' to the uneliminable logical 'premisses'. But he is looking, of course, for logical and not physical atoms. Hence the use of the term 'logical'. 'The point is that the atom I wish to arrive at is the atom of logical analysis, not the atom of physical analysis.'[1] The atom of physical analysis (or, more accurately, whatever physical science at a given time takes to be ultimate physical constituents of matter) is itself subject to logical analysis. But though in his final lecture on logical atomism Russell makes what he calls an excursus into metaphysics and introduces the idea of logical constructions or, as he puts it, logical fictions, he is mainly concerned with discussing propositions and facts.

We can, of course, understand the meaning of a proposition without knowing whether it is true or false. But a proposition which asserts or denies a fact is either true or false; and it is its relation to a fact which makes it true or false.[2] As we have seen, the grammatical form of a sentence may be different from its logical form. But in a logically perfect language 'the words in a proposition would correspond one by one with the components of the corresponding fact, with the exception of such words as "or", "not", "if", "then", which have a different function'.[3] In such a language therefore there would be an identity of structure between the fact asserted or denied and its symbolic representation, the proposition. Hence if there are atomic facts, there can be atomic propositions.

The simplest imaginable kind of fact, according to Russell, is that which consists in the possession of a quality by a particular, the quality being called a 'monadic relation'. This kind of fact is an atomic fact, though not the only kind. For it is not required, in order that a fact should be atomic, that it should comprise only one term and a monadic relation. There can be a hierarchy of atomic facts; facts which comprise two particulars and a (dyadic) relation, facts which comprise three particulars and a (triadic) relation, and so on. It must be understood, however, that 'particulars',

---

[1] *Logic and Knowledge*, p. 179.
[2] Russell notes that it was Wittgenstein who first drew his attention to the truth that propositions are not names for facts. For to every proposition there 'correspond' at least two propositions, one true, the other false. The false proposition 'corresponds with' the fact in the sense that it is its relation to the fact which makes it false.
[3] *Logic and Knowledge*, p. 197.

defined by Russell as the terms of relations in atomic facts, are to be understood in the sense of what would be for him genuine particulars, such as actual sense-data, not in the sense of logical constructions. 'This is white' would thus be an atomic proposition, provided that 'this' functions as a proper name denoting a sense-datum. So would 'these are white', provided again that 'these' denotes genuine particulars.

Now, an atomic proposition contains a single verb or verbal phrase. But by the use of words such as 'and', 'or' and 'if', we can construct complex or molecular propositions.[1] It would appear to follow, therefore, that there are molecular facts. But Russell shows hesitation on this point. Let us suppose, for example, that 'either today is Sunday or I made a mistake in coming here' is a molecular proposition. Does it make any sense to speak of a disjunctive fact? However, though Russell expresses some doubt about molecular facts, he admits 'general facts'. For instance, if we could enumerate all the atomic facts in the world, the proposition 'these are all the atomic facts there are' would express a general fact. Russell is also prepared to admit negative facts, even if with some hesitation. He suggests, for example, that 'Socrates is not alive' expresses an objective negative fact, an objective feature of the world.

We cannot refer to all the topics mentioned by Russell in his lectures on logical atomism. But there are two points to which attention can profitably be drawn. The first is the doctrine that every genuine particular is completely self-subsistent, in the sense that it is logically independent of every other particular. 'There is no reason why you should not have a universe consisting of one particular and nothing else.'[2] True, it is an empirical fact that there is a multitude of particulars. But it is not logically necessary that this should be the case. Hence it would not be possible, given knowledge of one particular, to deduce from it the whole system of the universe.

The second point is Russell's analysis of existence-propositions. I know, for example, that there are men in Canton; but I cannot mention any individual who lives there. Hence, Russell argues, the proposition 'there are men in Canton' cannot be about actual individuals. 'Existence is essentially a property of a propositional

---

[1] When the truth or falsity of a molecular proposition depends simply on the truth or falsity of its constituent propositions it is said to be a truth-function of these constituents.
[2] *Logic and Knowledge*, p. 202.

function.'[1] If we say 'there are men' or 'men exist', this means that there is at least one value of X for which it is true to say 'X is a man'. At the same time Russell recognizes 'existence-facts', such as that corresponding to 'there are men', as distinct from atomic facts.

It has already been mentioned that according to Russell's own explicit declaration his 1918 lectures on logical atomism were partly concerned with explaining theories suggested to him by Wittgenstein. But at that time, of course, he was acquainted with Wittgenstein's ideas only in a preliminary or immature form. Shortly after the armistice, however, Russell received from Wittgenstein the typescript of the *Tractatus Logico-Philosophicus*. And though he found himself in agreement with some of the ideas expressed in it, there were others which he was unable to accept. For example, at that time Russell accepted Wittgenstein's picture-theory of the proposition,[2] his view that atomic propositions are all logically independent of one another, and his doctrine that the propositions of logic and pure mathematics are 'tautologies' which, in themselves,[3] neither say anything about the actual existing world nor reveal to us another world of subsistent entities and timeless truths. But Russell did not accept, for instance, Wittgenstein's contention that the form which a true proposition has in common with the corresponding fact cannot be 'said' but can only be 'shown'. For Russell, as we have already noted, believed in a hierarchy of languages. Even if in language *a* nothing can be said *about* this language, there is nothing to prevent us employing language *b* to talk about *a*. Again, Wittgenstein's denial that anything can be said about the world as a whole, for example about 'all the things that there are in the world,' was more than Russell could stomach.[4]

Every student of recent British philosophy is aware that Russell has shown a marked lack of sympathy with Wittgenstein's later ideas, as expressed above all in *Philosophical Investigations*. But he admired the *Tractatus*; and in spite of the important points on which he disagreed with its author, his own logical atomism was, as we have seen, influenced by Wittgenstein's ideas. It does not follow, however, that the approaches of the two men

---

[1] *Ibid.*, p. 232.
[2] Later on Russell came to doubt this theory and to believe that, even if it is true in some sense, Wittgenstein exaggerated its importance.
[3] Needless to say, neither Wittgenstein nor Russell questioned the fact that logic and mathematics can be applied.
[4] Russell discusses the impact of Wittgenstein on his thought in ch. X of *My Philosophical Development*.

were precisely the same. Wittgenstein thought of himself as writing simply as a logician. He thought that logical analysis demanded elementary propositions, atomic facts and the simple objects which enter into atomic facts and are named in elementary propositions.[1] But he did not think that it was his business as a logician to give any examples of simple objects, atomic facts or elementary propositions. Nor did he give any. Russell, however, while approaching analysis by way of mathematical logic rather than from the point of view of classical empiricism, very soon became interested in discovering the actual ultimate constituents of the world. And, as we have seen, he did not hesitate to give examples of atomic facts. 'This is white' would be an example, when 'this' denotes an actual sense-datum. Similarly, while in the *Tractatus* Wittgenstein described psychology as a natural science and so as having nothing to do with philosophy, Russell, in his lectures on logical atomism, applied reductive analysis not only to the physical objects of common sense and science but also to the human person. 'A person is a certain series of experiences',[2] the members of the series having a certain relation R between them, so that a person can be defined as the class of all those experiences which are serially related by R.

It is true that while he had previously regarded the goal of analysis as a knowledge of simple particulars, Russell later came to think that while many things can be known to be complex, nothing can be *known* to be simple.[3] But the reason why he came to think this was because in science what was formerly thought to be simple has often turned out to be complex. And the conclusion which he drew was simply that the logical analyst should refrain from any dogmatic assertion that he has arrived at a knowledge of what is simple. In other words, though Russell undoubtedly approached logical atomism with a background of mathematical logic, his attitude was much more empirical than that of Wittgenstein as manifested in the *Tractatus*. And in the application of reductive analysis to physical objects and minds he

[1] In the opinion of the present writer the theory of the world which is found at the beginning of the *Tractatus* has nothing to do with inductive metaphysics. For Wittgenstein, the world exists for us only in so far as it is describable, in so far as we can speak meaningfully about states of affairs in the world. And the theory of atomic facts and simple objects is really an answer to the question, what *must* the world (any world) be like as a necessary condition for meaningful descriptive language? The approach, in other words, is *a priori*. The theory of the world is not an induction from observation of simple objects and atomic facts.
[2] *Logic and Knowledge*, p. 277.
[3] Cf. *My Philosophical Development*, pp. 165–6.

carried on the tradition of British empiricism, a tradition which hardly figured in Wittgenstein's mental furniture.

5. After the First World War Russell found his mind turning to the theory of knowledge and relevant topics, mathematical logic remaining more or less a past interest. This is not to say that his interest in social and political subjects abated. In 1920 he visited Russia, though his impressions were unfavourable, as is clear from *The Practice and Theory of Bolshevism* (1920). A succeeding visit to China bore fruit in *The Problems of China* (1922). Meanwhile he had published in 1921 *The Analysis of Mind*,[1] one of his best known books in the field of philosophy as he understands the term.

When Russell embraced pluralism in 1898, he accepted a dualist position. And, as we have seen, this position was maintained for some time, even if in an attenuated form. Russell was indeed acquainted with William James's theory of neutral monism, according to which the mental and physical are composed of the same material, so to speak, and differ only in arrangement and context.[2] But in his 1914 essay on the nature of acquaintance he first quoted passages from Mach and James and then expressed his disagreement with neutral monism as being incapable of explaining the phenomenon of acquaintance, which involves a relation between subject and object.

In the 1918 lectures on logical atomism, however, the sharpness of Russell's rejection of neutral monism is greatly diminished. In fact he states roundly that 'I feel more and more inclined to think that it may be true'.[3] He is indeed conscious of difficulties in accepting a view which does not distinguish between a particular and experiencing it. At the same time he is no longer sure that the difficulties are insuperable. And it is clear that while he has not yet embraced neutral monism, he would like to be able to do so.

It is thus no matter for surprise if in *The Analysis of Mind* we find Russell announcing his conversion to neutral monism,[4]

---

[1] This was followed by *The Analysis of Matter* in 1927, the same year in which *An Outline of Philosophy* appeared. Needless to say, the intervening period between 1921 and 1927 was punctuated not only by articles but also by books, such as *The Prospects of Industrial Civilization* (1923), *The ABC of Atoms* (1923), *The ABC of Relativity* (1925), and *On Education* (1926).

[2] As Russell notes, this was much the same view as that held by Ernst Mach. See Vol. VII of this *History*, p. 359.

[3] *Logic and Knowledge*, p. 279.

[4] It should hardly be necessary to point out that neutral monism is not the opposite of pluralism. It is 'monistic' in the sense that it admits no ultimate specific difference between the natures of mental and physical particulars or events. In themselves these particulars are neither specifically mental nor specifically physical or material. Hence the term 'neutral'.

which is conceived as providing a harmonization of two conflicting tendencies in contemporary thought. On the one hand many psychologists emphasize more and more the dependence of mental on physical phenomena; and one can see a definite tendency, especially among the behaviourists, to a form of methodological materialism. Obviously psychologists of this kind really consider physics, which has made a much greater advance than psychology, as the basic science. On the other hand there is a tendency among the physicists, particularly with Einstein and other exponents of the theory of relativity, to regard the matter of old-fashioned materialism as a logical fiction, a construction out of events. These two apparently conflicting tendencies can be harmonized in neutral monism, that is, by recognizing that 'physics and psychology are not distinguished by their material'.[1] Both mind and matter are logical constructions out of particulars which are neither mental nor material but neutral.

Obviously, Russell has now to abandon his former sharp distinction between the sense-datum and awareness of it. He mentions Brentano's theory of the intentionality of consciousness,[2] the theory that all consciousness is consciousness 'of' (an object), and Meinong's distinction between act, content and object. And he then remarks that 'the *act* seems unnecessary and fictitious. . . . Empirically, I cannot discover anything corresponding to the supposed act; and theoretically I cannot see that it is indispensable.'[3] Russell also tries to get rid of the distinction between content and object, when the content is supposed to be something in the external physical world. In fine, 'my own belief is that James was right in rejecting consciousness as an entity'.[4] Russell admits, of course, that he formerly maintained that a sense-datum, a patch of colour for example, is something physical, not psychical or mental. But he now holds that 'the patch of colour may be both physical and psychical',[5] and that 'the patch of colour and our sensation in seeing it are identical'.[6]

How, then, are the spheres of physics and psychology to be distinguished? One way of doing so is by distinguishing between different methods of correlating particulars. On the one hand we can correlate or group together all those particulars which common sense would regard as the appearances of a physical thing in

[1] *The Analysis of Mind*, p. 307.
[2] For some brief remarks about Brentano see Vol. VII of this *History*, pp. 430–1.
[3] *The Analysis of Mind*, pp. 17–18.
[4] *Ibid.*, p. 25.   [5] *Ibid.*, p. 143.   [6] *Ibid.*

different places. This leads to the construction of physical objects as sets of such appearances. On the other hand we can correlate or group together all events in a given place, that is, events which common sense would regard as the appearances of different objects as viewed from a given place. This gives us a perspective. And it is correlation according to perspectives which is relevant to psychology. When the place concerned is the human brain, the perspective 'consists of all the perceptions of a certain man at a given time'.[1]

Now, we have spoken of Russell's 'conversion' to neutral monism. It must be added, however, that this conversion was not complete. For example, while accepting the idea that sensation can be described in terms of a neutral material which in itself is neither mental nor material, he adds that in his opinion 'images belong only to the mental world, while those occurrences (if any) which do not form part of any "experience" belong only to the physical world'.[2] Russell does indeed say that he would be 'glad to be convinced that images can be reduced to sensations of a peculiar kind';[3] but this does not alter the fact that in *The Analysis of Mind* he maintains, even if hesitantly, that images are purely mental. Again, when discussing differentiation between physics and psychology in terms of causal laws, Russell is prepared to admit that 'it is by no means certain that the peculiar causal laws which govern mental events are not really physiological';[4] but at the same time he expresses his belief that images are subject to peculiar psychological laws, which he calls 'mnemic' and that the unperceived entities of physics cannot be brought under psychological causal laws. Further, though, as we have seen, Russell expresses agreement with James in rejecting consciousness as an entity, he clearly feels some hesitation on the point, as well he might. Thus he remarks that whatever the term 'consciousness' may mean, consciousness is 'a complex and far from universal characteristic of mental phenomena'.[5] It thus cannot be used to distinguish the psychical from the physical. And we ought to try to exhibit its derivative character. But to say this is not quite the same thing as to deny the existence of consciousness.

In 1924 Russell published a well-known essay on logical atomism, his contribution to the First Series of *Contemporary British Philosophy*, edited by J. H. Muirhead. The ultimate constituents

---

[1] *Ibid.*, p. 105. [2] *Ibid.*, p. 25. [3] *Ibid.*, p. 156.
[4] *Ibid.*, p. 139. [5] *Ibid.*, p. 308.

of the world are there said to be 'events',[1] each of which stands to a certain number of other events in a relation of compresence. The mind is defined as 'a track of sets of compresent events in a region of space-time where there is matter peculiarly liable to form habits'.[2] As this refers especially to the brain, the definition is more or less the same as the provisional definition offered in 1927 in *An Outline of Philosophy*.[3] But though both minds and physical objects are interpreted as logical constructions out of events, the former are constructed out of sensations and images, while the latter are constructions out of sensations and unperceived events.[4] And we have seen that Russell finds difficulty in regarding images as being anything else but purely mental, and unperceived events as anything else but purely physical.

Reviewing the course of his reflections in *My Philosophical Development* (1959) Russell remarks that 'in *The Analysis of Mind* (1921), I explicitly abandoned "sense-data" '.[5] That is to say, he abandoned the relational theory of sensation, according to which sensation is a cognitive act, sense-data being physical objects of psychical awareness. This meant that there was not the same need as before to regard physical and psychical occurrences as fundamentally different; and to this extent he was able to embrace neutral monism. He adds, however, that when dualism has been got rid of at one point, it is very difficult not to re-introduce it at another, and that it is necessary to re-interpret and re-define such terms as 'awareness', 'acquaintance' and 'experience'. An effort in this direction was made in *An Inquiry into Meaning and Truth* (1940);[6] but Russell does not pretend to have solved all his problems. It is thus not quite accurate to say that Russell embraced neutral monism only to reject it. It is rather that he has found himself unable in practice to carry through the requisite programme of re-interpretation, without, however, being prepared to assert that it could not be carried through.

6. Now, if the physical objects of common sense and science are first interpreted as logical constructions out of sense-data, and if sense-data, considered as extra-mental objects of awareness, are

---

[1] In *An Outline of Philosophy* an event is said to be 'something occupying a small finite amount of space-time' (p. 287), and each minimal event is said to be a 'logically self-subsistent entity' (p. 293).
[2] *Contemporary British Philosophy*, First Series, p. 382.
[3] P. 300.
[4] On unperceived events see *The Analysis of Matter*, pp. 215–16.
[5] *My Philosophical Development*, p. 135.
[6] In this work 'acquaintance' is replaced by 'noticing'. Cf. pp. 49f.

then eliminated, it seems to follow that we have no direct knowledge or awareness of any external object. For example, when the occurrence takes place which would ordinarily be called seeing the sun, the direct object of my awareness seems to be an event or events, sensations, which are in some sense 'in me'.[1] And the same must be said about my awareness of other persons. We are then faced with the difficulty that the direct objects of experience or awareness are not the physical objects of common sense and of science, while at the same time it is only what we directly experience that gives us any real reason for believing that there are such objects.

Of the possible ways of dealing with this problem 'the simplest is that of solipsism',[2] which Russell is prepared to admit as a logically possible position. For example, after saying that in his opinion the universe in itself is without unity and continuity he remarks, 'indeed there is little but prejudice and habit to be said for the view that there is a world at all'.[3] Similarly, though as a matter of fact my experience leads me to believe in the existence of other minds, 'as a matter of pure logic, it would be possible for me to have these experiences even if other minds did not exist'.[4] One can, of course, appeal to causal inference. But even at best such inference cannot provide demonstrative certainty and thus cannot show that solipsism is utterly untenable.

Though, however, solipsism may be logically possible, it is hardly credible. If it is taken as involving the dogmatic assertion that 'I alone exist', nobody really believes it. If it is taken to mean simply that there is no valid reason either for asserting or denying anything except one's own experiences, consistency demands that one should doubt whether one has had a past and whether one will have a future. For we have no better reason for believing that we have had experiences in the past than we have for believing in external objects. Both beliefs depend on inference. And if we doubt the second, we should also doubt the first. But 'no solipsist has ever gone as far as this'.[5] In other words, no solipsist is ever consistent.

The alternative to what Russell calls 'solipsism of the moment',[6] the hypothesis that the whole of my knowledge is limited to what I am now noticing at this moment, is the hypothesis that there are

[1] Cf. *The Analysis of Matter*, p. 197, and *The Scientific Outlook* (1931), pp. 74-5.
[2] *My Philosophical Development*, p. 104.   [3] *The Scientific Outlook*, p. 98.
[4] *My Philosophical Development*, p. 195.   [5] *Ibid.*
[6] *Human Knowledge, Its Scope and Limits* (1948), p. 197.

THE REVOLT AGAINST IDEALISM

principles of non-deductive inference which justify our belief in the existence of the external world and of other people. When these two alternatives are clearly presented, nobody, Russell argues, would honestly and sincerely choose solipsism. He is doubtless right. But in this case an examination of the relevant principles of inference becomes a matter of importance.[1]

[1] Obviously, the problem of solipsism presupposes the epistemological theses which give rise to it. And one's natural comment is that these theses might well be re-examined. But this is not the path which Russell chooses.

CHAPTER XX

BERTRAND RUSSELL (2)

The postulates of non-demonstrative inference and the limits of empiricism—Language; the complexity of language and the idea of a hierarchy of languages, meaning and significance, truth and falsity—Language as a guide to the structure of the world.

1. RUSSELL has drawn attention to three books in particular as representing the outcome of his reflections in the years after the First World War on the theory of knowledge and relevant subjects.[1] These are *The Analysis of Mind* (1921), *An Inquiry into Meaning and Truth* (1940), and *Human Knowledge: Its Scope and Limits* (1948). In this section, where we shall be considering Russell's ideas about non-demonstrative inference, we shall be referring mainly to the last-named book.[2]

If we assume with Russell that the physical objects of common sense and of science are logical constructions out of events and that each event is a logically self-sufficient entity, it follows that from one event or group of events we cannot infer with certainty the occurrence of any other event or group of events. Demonstrative inference belongs to logic and pure mathematics, not to the empirical sciences. Indeed, on the face of it it appears that we have no real ground for making any inferences at all in science. At the same time we are all convinced that valid inferences, leading to conclusions which possess varying degrees of probability, can be made both on the level of common sense and in science. To be sure, not all inferences are valid. Many scientific hypotheses have had to be discarded. But this does not alter the fact that no sane man doubts that by and large science has increased and is increasing human knowledge. On this assumption, therefore, the question arises, how can scientific inference be theoretically justified?

Some philosophers would say, and the plain man would probably be inclined to agree with them, that scientific inference stands in need of no other justification than a pragmatic one, namely its success. Scientists can and do make successful predictions.

[1] Cf. *My Philosophical Development*, p. 128.
[2] It will be referred to simply as *Human Knowledge*.

Science works. And the philosopher who looks for a further justification is looking for what cannot be had and is in any case not required.

In Russell's opinion this attitude is equivalent to blocking inquiry from the outset. He is, needless to say, as well aware as anyone else that by and large science delivers the goods. But he is also acutely aware of the fact that purely empiricist premises lead to the conclusion that the factual success of scientific inference is simply fortuitous. Yet nobody really believes that this is the case. Hence we must look for some justification of scientific inference other than its factual success. To attempt to block inquiry at the outset is unworthy of a genuine philosopher. And if inquiry leads us to the conclusion that pure empiricism is an inadequate theory of knowledge, we just have to accept the fact and not shut our eyes to it.

Russell regards his task as that of finding 'the minimum principles required to justify scientific inference'.[1] Such principles or premises[2] must state something about the world. For inference from the observed to the unobserved or from one group of events to another can be justified only 'if the world has certain characteristics which are not logically necessary'.[3] It is not a question of logically necessary principles which are known to possess absolute validity independently of all experience. For scientific inference is non-demonstrative inference. Rather is it a question of reflecting on actual scientific inference and discovering the minimum number of principles, premises or postulates which are required to justify them.

The matter has, however, to be expressed more precisely. There is obviously no question of justifying all inferences and generalizations. For, as we know by experience, some generalizations are false. What we are looking for is the minimum number of principles which will confer an antecedent finite probability on certain inferences and generalizations and not on others. In other words, we have to examine what are universally regarded as genuine instances of scientific inference and generalization and discover the principles which are required in order to justify these types of inference and generalization by conferring on them an antecedent finite probability that is not conferred on the types which

---

[1] *Human Knowledge*, p. 11.
[2] Russell calls them 'postulates'. The reason for this will be discussed presently.
[3] *Human Knowledge*, p. 10.

experience has taught us to reject as inherently fallacious and unscientific.[1]

To cut a long story short, Russell finds five principles or premisses of scientific inference. But he lays no particular emphasis upon the number five. He considers indeed that the principles which he enunciates are sufficient; but he allows for the possibility that the number might be reduced. Further, he does not insist on his actual formulation of the principles.[2] Greater precision might well be possible. It is to be noted, however, that all the principles state probabilities only, not certainties, and that they are conceived as conferring a finite antecedent probability on certain types of inductive inference.

The first principle, described by Russell as the postulate of quasi-permanence, states that, given any event A, it frequently happens that an event very similar to A occurs in a neighbouring place at a neighbouring time. This postulate enables us to operate, for instance, with the common sense concepts of person and thing without introducing the metaphysical notion of substance. For the 'very similar' event can be regarded as part of the history of the series of events which constitutes the person or thing.

The second principle, the postulate of separable causal lines, states that it is often possible to form a series of events such that from one or two members of the series we can infer something about the other members. This principle or postulate is clearly essential for scientific inference. For it is only on the basis of the idea of causal lines that we can infer distant from near events.

The third principle, the postulate of spatio-temporal continuity, which presupposes the second principle and refers to causal lines, denies action at a distance and states that when there is a causal connection between non-contiguous events, there will be found to be intermediate links in the chain.

The fourth principle, 'the structural postulate', states that when a number of structurally similar complex events occur around a centre from which they are not too widely separated, it is generally the case that all are members of causal lines which have their origin in an event of similar structure at the centre. Suppose, for

[1] Russell thus presupposes that what is generally regarded as scientific knowledge really is knowledge. If we start with undiluted scepticism, we shall get nowhere. After all, the problem of justifying scientific inference only arises because we are convinced that there is such a thing but at the same time see no adequate basis for it in pure empiricism.

[2] For Russell's actual formulation of the five principles the reader is referred to *Human Knowledge*, pp. 506 ff.

example, that a number of persons are situated in different parts of a public square where an orator is holding forth or a radio is blaring, and that they have similar auditory experiences. This postulate confers antecedent probability on the inference that their similar experiences are causally related to the sounds made by the orator or radio.[1]

The fifth principle, the postulate of analogy, states that if, when two classes of events, A and B, are observed, there is reason to believe that A causes B, then if, in a given case, A occurs but we cannot observe whether B occurs or not, it is probable that it does occur. Similarly, if the occurrence of B is observed while the occurrence of A cannot be observed, it is probable that A has occurred. According to Russell, an important function of this postulate is to justify belief in other minds.

This doctrine of the principles of non-demonstrative inference is partly intended to solve a problem raised by J. M. Keynes (1883–1946) in his *Treatise on Probability* (1921).[2] But the point to which we wish to draw attention here is the unprovability of the principles. They are not offered as eternal truths which can be intuited *a priori*. Nor are they supposed to be deducible from such truths. At the same time they cannot be proved nor even rendered probable by empirical arguments. For they are the very principles on which the validity of such arguments rests. If we tried to justify them by appealing to scientific inference, we should be involved in a vicious circle. Hence the principles must necessarily be described as 'postulates' of scientific inference.

In view of the fact that these postulates cannot be proved, nor even rendered probable, by empirical argument, Russell explicitly admits the failure of empiricism, in the sense that it is inadequate as a theory of knowledge and is unable to justify the presuppositions on which all inferred empirical knowledge depends for its validity. It has therefore sometimes been said that he approaches a Kantian position. But the similarity is limited to a common recognition of the limitations of pure empiricism. Russell is very far from developing a theory of the *a priori* on the lines of Kant's first *Critique*. Instead he proceeds to give a biological-psychological account of the origins of the postulates of non-demonstrative

---

[1] Obviously, the ordinary man would comment: 'I don't need any postulate to know this'. But it must be remembered that for Russell it is *logically* possible that the similarity of experiences should be causally independent, and that in pure empiricism there is nothing which makes it objectively more probable that the similar experiences have a common causal origin than that they do not.

[2] Cf. *My Philosophical Development*, pp. 200f.

inference. If, for example, an animal has a habit of such a kind that in the presence of an instance of A it behaves in a manner in which, before acquiring the habit, it behaved in the presence of an instance of B, it can be said to have 'inferred' and to 'believe' that every instance of A is usually followed by an instance of B. This is, of course, an anthropomorphic way of speaking. The animal does not consciously make inferences. None the less there is such a thing as animal inference. It is a feature of the process of adaptation to environment, and there is continuity between it and inference in man. That is to say, our 'knowledge' of the principles or postulates of non-demonstrative inference 'exists at first solely in the form of a propensity to inferences of the kind that they justify'.[1] Man, unlike the animal, is capable of reflecting on examples of these inferences, of making the postulates explicit and of using logical technique to improve their foundations. But the relatively *a priori* character[2] of the principles is explicable in terms of a propensity to make inferences in accordance with them, a propensity which is continuous with that manifested in animal inference.

Now, we have seen that Russell set out to discover a theoretical justification of scientific inference. But though he justifies scientific inference in terms of certain postulates, the postulates themselves are then explained through a biological-psychological account of their origin. And this account, which goes back ultimately to the process of adaptation to environment, appears to be quite compatible with the theory of what Nietzsche called biologically useful fictions. In other words, it is arguable that Russell does not in fact fulfil his programme of providing a theoretical justification of non-demonstrative inference, not at least if to justify this inference theoretically means to supply premises which warrant the assertion that it is theoretically valid.

It may appear, therefore, that in the long run we are thrown back on a pragmatic justification, on an appeal to the fact that the postulates work, that 'their verifiable consequences are such as experience will confirm'.[3] Indeed, Russell explicitly says that the

---

[1] *Human Knowledge*, p. 526
[2] The postulates are *a priori* in the sense of being logically antecedent to the inferences made in accordance with them; but they exist first of all in the form of an empirical propensity and are recognized as postulates only through an examination of examples of non-demonstrative inferences. They are not absolutely *a priori* eternal truths.
[3] *Human Knowledge*, p. 527.

postulates 'are justified by the fact that they are implied in inferences which we all accept as valid, and that, although they cannot be proved in any formal sense, the whole system of science and everyday knowledge, out of which they have been distilled, is, within limits, self-confirmatory'.[1] The fact that the postulates or principles lead to results which are in conformity with experience 'does not logically suffice to make the principles even probable'.[2] At the same time the whole system of science, of probable knowledge, which rests on the postulates, is self-confirmatory, self-justifying in a pragmatic sense. Hence Russell can say that while he does not accept the idealist coherence theory of truth, there is, in an important sense, a valid coherence theory of probability.[3]

In this case we may be inclined to ask why Russell does not accept from the start the position of those who claim that scientific inference is sufficiently justified by its results, by the fact that it leads to verifiable predictions. But Russell would presumably answer that to content oneself with this position from the start is equivalent to suppressing a real problem, to shutting one's eyes to it. Consideration of the problem leads to a recognition of the indemonstrable postulates of scientific inference, and thus to a recognition of the limitations and inadequacy of pure empiricism as a theory of knowledge. Recognition of these facts is a real intellectual gain; and it cannot be obtained if the attempt to discover a theoretical justification of non-demonstrative inference is prohibited from the outset.

The comment might be made, of course, that though this attitude is reasonable enough when considered within the framework of Russell's general empiricist analysis of the world, the fact remains that while explicitly recognizing the limitations of pure empiricism as a theory of knowledge he does not really go beyond it. His biological explanation of the origin of a propensity to make inferences in accordance with certain implicit postulates or expectations can be seen as a continuation and development of Hume's doctrine of natural beliefs. But to go beyond empiricism, in the sense of substituting for it a genuinely non-empiricist theory of knowledge, would obviously have demanded a much more radical revision of his opinions than Russell was prepared either to undertake or to recognize as justified.

2. We have noted Russell's statement that after the First World

---

[1] *My Philosophical Development*, p. 204.   [2] *Human Knowledge*, p. 526.
[3] Cf. *My Philosophical Development*, p. 204.

War his thoughts turned to the theory of knowledge and to the relevant parts of psychology and linguistics. It is appropriate, therefore, to say something about the last-mentioned theme, Russell's theory of language. Reference has already been made, however, to the theory of the relation between language and fact as expounded in the 1918 lectures on logical atomism. And we can confine ourselves here mainly to Russell's ideas as set out in *An Inquiry into Meaning and Truth* and as repeated or modified in *Human Knowledge*.[1]

(i) Philosophers, Russell remarks, have been chiefly interested in language as a means of making statements and conveying information. But 'what is the purpose of language to a sergeant-major?'[2] The purpose of commands is obviously to influence the behaviour of others rather than to state facts or convey information. Besides, the sergeant-major's language is also sometimes directed to expressing emotive attitudes. Language, in other words, has a variety of functions.

Though, however, Russell recognizes the complex and flexible character of language, he himself is chiefly interested, like the philosophers to whom he vaguely refers, in descriptive language. This is indeed only to be expected. For Russell regards philosophy as an attempt to understand the world. And his attention is thus naturally centred on language as an instrument in fulfilling this task.[3] This is indeed one reason for his marked lack of sympathy with any tendency to treat language as though it were an autonomous, self-sufficient entity, which can be profitably studied by the philosopher without reference to its relation to non-linguistic fact.[4]

Reference has already been made to Russell's idea of a hierarchy of languages, an idea which is connected with the theory of types. In *An Inquiry into Meaning and Truth* he assumes this idea and maintains that though the hierarchy extends indefinitely upwards, it cannot extend indefinitely downwards. In other words, there

[1] Some discussion of language can also be found in *The Analysis of Mind* and *The Outline of Philosophy*.
[2] *Human Knowledge*, p. 71.
[3] Russell refuses to commit himself to the general statement that there can be no thought without language. But in his opinion complicated, elaborate thought at any rate requires language.
[4] Russell's well-known reference to the type of linguistic analysis which 'is, at best, a slight help to lexicographers, and, at worst, an idle tea-table amusement' (*My Philosophical Development*, p. 217), is obviously polemical and constitutes an exaggeration if considered as a description of 'Oxford philosophy' as a whole; but at the same time it illustrates, by way of contrast, the direction of his own interest, namely in language as an instrument in understanding the world.

must be a basic or lowest-type language. And Russell proceeds to discuss one possible form of such a language, though he does not claim that it is the only possible form.

The basic or primary language suggested by Russell is an object-language, consisting, that is to say, of object-words. A word of this type can be defined in two ways. Logically, it is a word which has meaning in isolation. Hence the class of object-words would not include terms such as 'or'. Psychologically, an object-word is one the use of which can be learned without its being necessary to have previously learned the uses or meanings of other words. That is to say, it is a word the meaning of which can be learned by ostensive definition, as when one says to a child 'pig', while pointing to an example of this kind of animal.

It does not follow, however, that an object-language of this kind would be confined to nouns. For it would admit verbs such as 'run' and 'hit' and adjectives such as 'red' and 'hard'. And, according to Russell, 'theoretically, given sufficient capacity, we could express in the object-language every non-linguistic occurrence',[1] though this would admittedly involve translating complicated sentences into a kind of 'pidgin'.

Now, meaningful statements expressed in this primary language would *be* either true or false. But we should not be able to *say*, within the limits of the primary language, that any statement expressed in it was true or false. For these logical terms would not be available. It would be necessary to use a second-order language for this purpose. Actual language, of course, includes both object-words and logical words. But the artificial isolation of a possible object-language serves to illustrate the idea of a hierarchy of languages and shows how we can cope with any difficulty arising out of the contention that nothing can be said within a given language *about* this language.[2]

(ii) Truth and falsity obviously presuppose meaning. We could not properly say of a meaningless statement that it was either true or false. For there would be nothing to which these terms could apply. But it does not follow that every meaningful utterance is either true or false. 'Right turn!' and 'Are you feeling better?' are meaningful utterances, but we would not say of either that it is true or false. The range of meaning is thus wider than the

---

[1] *An Inquiry into Meaning and Truth*, p. 77. This work will be referred to henceforth as *Inquiry*.

[2] Reference has already been made to the special case of Wittgenstein's contention in the *Tractatus*.

range of logical truth and falsity.[1] And in the *Inquiry* Russell tells us that indicative sentences 'alone are true or false',[2] though subsequently we are told that 'truth and falsehood, in so far as they are public, are attributes of sentences, either in the indicative or in the subjective or conditional'.[3]

Hitherto we have attributed 'meaning' both to object-words and to sentences. But Russell tends, though without uniform consistency, to restrict the term 'meaning' to object-words and to speak of sentences as having 'significance'. And we can say that 'although meanings must be derived from experience, significance need not'.[4] That is to say, we can understand the significance of a sentence which refers to something which we have never experienced, provided that we know the meanings of the words and that the sentence observes the rules of syntax.

Meaning, when attributed to object-words, signifies reference. And it is said to be fundamental. For it is through the meanings of object-words, learned by experience, that 'language is connected with non-linguistic occurrences in the way that makes it capable of expressing empirical truth or falsehood'.[5] But whereas we might expect a purely logical definition of meaning in this sense, Russell introduces psychological considerations based on what he believes to be the way in which a child, for example, comes to acquire the habit of using certain words correctly. Thus we are told that a word is said to mean an object 'if the sensible presence of the object causes the utterance of the word, and the hearing of the word has effects analogous, in certain respects, to the sensible presence of the object'.[6]

This methodological, though not dogmatic, behaviourism can be found also in, for instance, Russell's account of imperatives. An uttered imperative 'expresses' something in the speaker, a desire coupled with an idea of the intended effect, while it 'means' the external effect intended and commanded. And the heard imperative is understood 'when it causes a certain kind of bodily movement, or an impulse towards such a movement'.[7]

Imperative sentences, however, though significant, are not said to be true or false. So let us consider indicative sentences, which are said to indicate fact. Russell also calls them assertions, maintaining that 'an assertion has two sides, subjective and

[1] This follows in any case from Russell's view of object-words as meaningful in isolation. 'Hard' by itself, for example, is neither true nor false.
[2] *Inquiry*, p. 30.   [3] *Human Knowledge*, p. 127.   [4] *Inquiry*, p. 193.
[5] *Ibid.*, p. 29.   [6] *Human Knowledge*, p. 85.   [7] *Ibid.*, p. 86.

objective'.[1] Subjectively, an assertion expresses a state of the person who makes the assertion, a state which can be called a belief.[2] Objectively, the assertion is related to something which makes it true or false. An assertion is false if it intends to indicate a fact but fails to do so, true if it succeeds. But true and false assertions are equally meaningful. Hence the significance of an assertion cannot be equated with actual indication of a fact, but lies rather in what the assertion expresses, namely a certain belief or, more accurately, the object of this belief, what is believed. And a heard assertion is said to be significant, from a psychological point of view, if it can cause belief, disbelief or doubt in the hearer.

Russell's insistence on studying language in the context of human life is doubtless largely responsible for his introducing a number of perhaps somewhat confusing psychological considerations. But the main issue can be simplified in this way. The significance of a sentence is that which is common to a sentence in one language and its translation into another language. For example, 'I am hungry' and 'J'ai faim' have a common element which constitutes the significance of the sentence. This common element is the 'proposition'. We cannot ask, therefore, if a proposition is significant. For it *is* the significance. But in the case of indicative sentences at any rate we can properly ask whether the proposition is true or false. Significance is thus independent of truth.

Now, we have noted Russell's insistence that, given certain conditions, we can understand the significance of an assertion which refers to something which we have not personally experienced. It can now be added that he does not wish to tie down the significance of assertions or statements even to the experienceable. And this naturally leads him to adopt a critical attitude towards the logical positivist criterion of meaning. True, in some respects he regards logical positivism with a benevolent eye, chiefly perhaps because of its interpretation of logic and pure mathematics and its serious concern with empirical science. But though he agrees with the positivists in rejecting the idea of 'ineffable knowledge',[3] he has consistently refused to accept the criterion of

[1] *Inquiry*, p. 171.
[2] Russell uses the term 'belief' in such a wide sense that even animals can be said to have beliefs. Cf. *Inquiry*, p. 171 and *Human Knowledge*, p. 329. But we are here concerned with language, and so with human beings.
[3] 'Ineffable knowledge' is not identical with knowledge of what goes beyond our experience.

meaning, according to which the meaning of a factual proposition is identical with the mode of its verification.

In general, Russell argues, the logical positivist criterion of meaning implies two things. First, what cannot be verified or falsified is meaningless. Secondly, two propositions verified by the same occurrences have the same meaning or significance. 'I reject both.'[1] In regard to the first point, the propositions which are most nearly certain, namely judgments of perception, cannot be verified, 'since it is they that constitute the verification of all other empirical propositions that can be in any degree known. If Schlick were right, we should be committed to an endless regress.'[2] In regard to the second point, the hypothesis that the stars exist continuously and the hypothesis that they exist only when I see them are identical in their testable consequences. But they do not have the same significance. Of course, the principle of verifiability can be modified and interpreted as claiming that a factual statement is meaningful if we can imagine sensible experiences which would verify it, if it were true. But Russell comments that in his opinion this is a sufficient but not a necessary criterion of significance.[3]

(iii) In 1906-9 Russell wrote four essays dealing with the subject of truth, especially in relation to pragmatism, which were reprinted in *Philosophical Essays*. At a later date he took up the subject again, the results of this second phase of reflection being embodied in the *Inquiry*. The topic is also treated in *Human Knowledge*. And in *My Philosophical Development* Russell devotes the fifteenth chapter to a review of the course of his investigations.

A certain looseness in the use of terminology is characteristic of Russell. Thus in different places we are told that truth and falsity are predicated of indicative sentences, of sentences in the indicative or in the subjunctive or conditional, of assertions, of propositions and of beliefs. But it does not follow, of course, that all these ways of speaking are mutually incompatible. The significance of a sentence is a proposition; but propositions, according to Russell, express states of belief. Hence we can say that 'it is in fact primarily beliefs that are true or false; sentences only become so through the fact that they can express beliefs'.[4] In any case the main lines of Russell's theory of truth are clear enough.

In the first place Russell rejects the idealist interpretation of

---

[1] *Human Knowledge*, p. 465.   [2] *Inquiry*, p. 308.
[3] Cf. *Inquiry*, pp. 175 and 309.   [4] *Human Knowledge*, p. 129.

truth as coherence. In an early article he argued that if every particular true judgment, when isolated from the total system of truth, is only partially true, and if what would normally be called false judgments are partially true and have their place in the complete system of truth, it follows that the statement 'Bishop Stubbs was hanged for murder' is not completely false but forms part of the whole truth.[1] But this is incredible. And, in general, the coherence theory simply blurs the distinction between truth and falsehood.

In the second place Russell rejects the pragmatist theory of truth. When he paraphrased William James's statement that the true is only the expedient in our way of thinking as 'a truth is anything which it pays to believe', he was accused of gross misinterpretation. Russell retorted, however, that James's explanation of the real meaning of the statement was even sillier than what he, Russell, had taken the statement to mean. Russell did indeed owe a number of important ideas to James; but he had no sympathy with the American philosopher's account of truth.

In the third place Russell protests against any confusion between truth and knowledge. Obviously, if I can properly be said to know that something is the case, the statement which expresses my knowledge is true. But it by no means follows that a true proposition must be known to be true. Indeed, Russell is prepared to admit the possibility of propositions which are true, though we cannot know them to be true. And if it is objected that this admission is tantamount to an abandonment of pure empiricism, he replies that 'pure empiricism is believed by no one'.[2]

We are left, therefore, with the correspondence theory of truth, according to which 'when a sentence or belief is "true", it is so in virtue of some relation to one or more facts'.[3] These facts are called by Russell 'verifiers'. To know what an assertion or statements means, I must, of course, have some idea of the state of affairs which would make it true. But I need not know that it is true. For the relation between statement and verifier or verifiers is an objective one, independent of my knowledge of it. Indeed, in Russell's opinion I need not be able to mention any particular instance of a verifier in order to know that a statement is meaningful and that it is thus either true or false. And this thesis enables him to maintain that a statement such as 'there are facts which I

[1] Cf. *Philosophical Essays*, p. 156.   [2] *Inquiry*, p. 305.
[3] *My Philosophical Development*, p. 189. Cf. *Human Knowledge*, pp. 164–5.

cannot imagine' is meaningful and either true or false. In Russell's view at any rate I could not mention any particular instance of a fact which cannot be imagined. At the same time I can conceive 'general circumstances'[1] which would verify the belief that there are facts which I cannot imagine. And this is sufficient to render the statement intelligible and capable of being true or false. Whether it *is* true or false, however, depends on a relation which is independent of my knowledge of it. In popular language the statement either corresponds or does not correspond with the facts. And the relation which actually obtains is unaffected by my knowing or not knowing it.

The theory of truth as correspondence with fact does not apply, of course, to the analytic propositions of logic and pure mathematics. For in their case truth 'follows from the form of the sentence'.[2] But in its application to empirical statements or assertions the theory can be said to represent a common sense position. The ordinary man would certainly argue that an empirical factual statement is made true or false by its relation to a fact or facts.[3] Difficulty arises only when we try to give a precise and adequate account of the idea of correspondence in this context. What precisely is meant by it? Russell is conscious of this difficulty. But he tells us that 'every belief which is not merely an impulse to action is in the nature of a picture, combined with a yes-feeling or a no-feeling; in the case of a yes-feeling it is "true" if there is a fact having to the picture the kind of similarity that a prototype has to an image; in the case of a no-feeling it is "true" if there is no such fact. A belief which is not true is called "false". This is a definition of "truth" and "falsehood".'[4]

In the opinion of the present writer the introduction of terms such as 'yes-feeling' and 'no-feeling' into a definition of truth is hardly felicitous. This point apart, however, it is clear that correspondence is conceived by Russell according to the analogy of pictorial representation. But though we may perhaps speak of true and false pictures, that which is strictly speaking true or

---

[1] *Human Knowledge*, p. 169. Some further specification of these 'general circumstances' seems to be required.

[2] *Ibid.*, p. 128.

[3] It is not necessary that the facts should be extra-linguistic. For we can, of course, make statements about *words*, which are made true or false by their relation to linguistic facts. Obviously, this would not apply, for example, to stipulative definitions. But these would in any case be excluded by Russell's custom of predicating truth or falsity of *beliefs*. For a mere declaration that one intends to use a given word in a certain sense cannot be described as a belief.

[4] *Human Knowledge*, p. 170.

false is not the picture but the statement that it does or does not correspond with an object or set of objects. So presumably the relation of correspondence which makes a statement true must be, as in Wittgenstein's *Tractatus*, a structural correspondence between the proposition and the fact or facts which count as its verifier or verifiers. Russell notes, however, that the relation is by no means always simple or of one invariable type.

3. It scarcely needs saying that no amount of inspection of a belief, as Russell puts it, or of an empirical statement will tell us whether it is true or false. To ascertain this we have to consider the factual evidence. But Russell has claimed that in some other sense or senses we can infer something about the world from the properties of language. Moreover, this is not a claim which he has put forward only once or in passing. For example, in *The Principles of Mathematics* he remarked that though grammatical distinctions cannot legitimately be assumed without more ado to indicate genuine philosophical distinctions, 'the study of grammar, in my opinion, is capable of throwing far more light on philosophical questions than is commonly supposed by philosophers'.[1] Again, even in *An Outline of Philosophy*, where he went as far as he could in a behaviourist interpretation of language, he suggested that 'quite important metaphysical conclusions, of a more or less sceptical kind',[2] can be derived from reflection on the relation between language and things. At a later date, in the *Inquiry*, he explicitly associated himself with those philosophers who 'infer properties of the world from properties of language'[3] and asserted his belief that 'partly by means of the study of syntax, we can arrive at considerable knowledge concerning the structure of the world'.[4] Moreover, in *My Philosophical Development* he quotes the paragraph in which this last assertion occurs with the endorsement 'I have nothing to add to what I said there'.[5]

Russell obviously does not mean that we can infer, without more ado, properties of the world from grammatical forms as they exist in ordinary language. If we could do this, we could infer the substance-accident metaphysics from the subject-predicate form of sentence, whereas we have seen that Russell eliminates the concept of substance by reductive analysis.[6] Nor does Russell mean that from the fact that a term can be eliminated, in the sense that sentences in which this term occurs can be translated into

[1] P. 42.   [2] P. 275.   [3] P. 341.   [4] P. 347.   [5] P. 173.
[6] According to Russell, if Aristotle had thought and written in Chinese instead of in Greek, he would have evolved a somewhat different philosophy.

sentences of equivalent truth-value in which the term does not
occur, we can infer that no entity exists corresponding to the term
in question. As has already been noted, the fact that the term 'the
golden mountain' can be eliminated does not prove that there is
no golden mountain. It may show that we need not postulate such
a mountain. But our grounds for thinking that there actually is
no such mountain are empirical, not linguistic, grounds. Similarly,
if 'similarity' can be eliminated, this does not by itself prove that
there is no entity corresponding to 'similarity'. It may show that
we cannot legitimately infer such an entity from language; but to
show that language does not provide any adequate ground for
inferring a subsistent entity 'similarity' is not the same thing as
to prove that there is in fact no such entity. When referring to
sentences in which the word 'similarity' cannot be replaced by
'similar' or some such word, Russell remarks that 'these latter
need not be admitted'.[1] And it seems obvious that he has already
decided, and rightly decided, but on grounds which were not
purely linguistic, that it would be absurd to postulate an entity
named 'similarity'. For this reason he says that if there are
sentences in which 'similarity' cannot be replaced by 'similar',
sentences of this class 'need not be admitted'.

The question can thus be formulated in this way. Can we infer
properties of the world from the indispensable properties of a
logically purified and reformed language? And the answer to this
question seems to depend very largely on the sense which is given
to the term 'infer' in this context. If it is suggested that a logically
purified language can serve as an ultimate premiss from which we
can deduce properties of the world, the validity of this idea
appears to me questionable. For one thing it would have to be
shown that no ontological decisions, made on grounds which
could not reasonably be described as purely linguistic, had
influenced the construction of the logically purified language. In
other words, it would have to be shown that assessment of the
indispensable features of language had not been influenced and
guided by empirically-based convictions about features of extra-
linguistic reality.

If, however, the claim that we can infer properties of the world
from properties of language simply means that if we find that it is
necessary to speak of things in certain ways, there is at least a
strong presumption that there is some reason in things themselves

[1] *Inquiry*, p. 347.

for this necessity, the claim seems to be reasonable. Language has developed through the centuries in response to man's experience and needs. And if we find, for example, that we cannot get along without being able to say of two or more things that they are similar or alike, it is probable that some things are indeed of such a kind that they can be appropriately described as similar or alike, and that the world does not consist simply of entirely heterogeneous and unrelated particulars. But in the long run the question whether there actually are things which can appropriately be described in this way, is a question which has to be decided empirically.

It might perhaps be objected that we cannot talk of 'things' at all without implying similarity. For if there are things, they are necessarily similar in being things or beings. This is doubtless true. And in this sense we can infer from language that similarity is a feature of the world. But this does not alter the fact that it is ultimately through experience, and not from language, that we know that there are things. Reflection on language can doubtless serve to sharpen our awareness of features of extra-linguistic reality and to make us notice what we possibly had not noticed before. But that language can serve as an ultimate premiss for inferring properties of the world seems to be highly questionable.

CHAPTER XXI

BERTRAND RUSSELL (3)

Introductory remarks—Russell's earlier moral philosophy and the influence of Moore—Instinct, mind and spirit—The relation of the judgment of value to desire—Social science and power—Russell's attitude towards religion—The nature of philosophy as conceived by Russell—Some brief critical comments.

1. WE have been concerned so far with the more abstract aspects of Russell's philosophy. But we noted that his first book was on *German Social Democracy* (1896). And concomitantly with or in the intervals between his publications on mathematics, logic, the theory of knowledge, the philosophy of science and so on he has produced a spate of books and articles on ethical, social and political topics. At the 1948 International Philosophical Congress at Amsterdam a Communist professor from Prague took it upon himself to refer to Russell as an example of an ivory-tower philosopher. But whatever one's estimate may be of Russell's ideas in this or that field of inquiry and reflection, this particular judgment was patently absurd. For Russell has not only written on matters of practical concern but also actively campaigned in favour of his ideas. His imprisonment towards the close of the First World War has already been mentioned. During the Second World War he found himself in sympathy with the struggle against the Nazis, and after the war, when the Communists were staging take-overs in a number of countries, he vehemently criticized some of the more unpleasant aspects of Communist policy and conduct. In other words, his utterances were for once in tune with the official attitude in his own country. And in 1949 he received the Order of Merit from King George VI.[1] In more recent years he has not only campaigned for the introduction of a system of world-government but also sponsored the movement for nuclear disarmament. In fact he carried his sponsorship to the extent of taking a personal part in the movement of civil disobedience. And as he refused to pay the imposed fine, this activity earned him a week or so in gaol.[2] Thus

---

[1] I do not mean to imply, of course, that this high honour was not a tribute to Russell's eminence as a philosopher.

[2] The short period was passed in the prison infirmary, it is only fair to add, not in the usual conditions of prison life.

even at a very advanced age Russell has continued to battle on behalf of the welfare of humanity, as he sees it. And the charge of 'ivory-tower philosopher' is obviously singularly inappropriate.

In the following section, however, we shall be concerned with the more theoretical aspects of Russell's ethical and political thought. To the general public he is, of course, best known for his writing on concrete issues. But it would be out of place in a history of philosophy to discuss Russell's opinions about, say, sex[1] or nuclear disarmament, especially as he himself does not regard discussion of such concrete issues as pertaining to philosophy in a strict sense.

2. The first chapter in *Philosophical Essays* (1910) is entitled 'The Elements of Ethics' and represents a conflation of an article on determinism and morals which appeared in the *Hibbert Journal* in 1908 and of two articles on ethics which appeared in 1910 in the February and May issues of the *New Quarterly*. At this period Russell maintained that ethics aims at discovering true propositions about virtuous and vicious conduct, and that it is a science. If we ask why we ought to perform certain actions, we eventually arrive at basic propositions which cannot themselves be proved. But this is not a feature peculiar to ethics, and it does not weaken its claim to be a science.

Now, if we ask for reasons why we ought to perform certain actions and not to perform others, the answer generally refers to consequences. And if we assume that an action is right because it produces good consequences or leads to the attainment of a good, it is clear that some things at any rate must be good in themselves. Not all things can be good. If they were, we could not distinguish between right and wrong actions. And some things may be considered good as means to something else. But we cannot do without the concept of things which are intrinsically good, possessing the property of goodness 'quite independently of our opinion on the subject, or of our wishes or other people's'.[2] True, people often have different opinions about what is good. And it may be difficult to decide between these opinions. But it does not follow from this that there is nothing which *is* good. Indeed, *'good* and *bad* are

---

[1] We may remark in passing that in 1940 Russell's appointment to the College of the City of New York was cancelled because of his views on marriage and sexual conduct. True, he was given a chair at the Barnes Foundation, Philadelphia, but this appointment lasted only until 1943. The New York episode led to a good deal of acrid controversy, on which the present writer does not feel called upon to pass any comment.

[2] *Philosophical Essays*, p. 10.

qualities which belong to objects independently of our opinions, just as much as *round* and *square* do'.[1]

Though goodness is an objective property of certain things, it is indefinable. It cannot therefore be identified with, say, the pleasant. That which gives pleasure may be good. But, if it is, this is because it possesses, over and above pleasantness, the indefinable quality of goodness. 'Good' no more means 'pleasant' than it means 'existent'.

Now if we assume that goodness is an intrinsic, indefinable property of certain things, it can be perceived only immediately. And the judgment in which this perception is expressed will be insusceptible of proof. The question arises, therefore, whether differences between such judgments do not weaken or even entirely undermine the thesis that there can be knowledge of what is good. Russell obviously does not deny that there have been and are different judgments about what things are good and bad. At the same time such differences, in his opinion, are neither so great nor so widespread as to compel us to relinquish the idea of moral knowledge. In fact, genuine differences between the judgments of different people in regard to intrinsic goodness and badness 'are, I believe, very rare indeed'.[2] Where they exist, the only remedy is to take a closer look.

In Russell's view genuine differences of opinion arise not so much in regard to intrinsic goodness and badness as in regard to the rightness and wrongness of actions. For an action is objectively right 'when, of all that are possible, it is the one which will probably have the best results'.[3] And it is obvious that people may come to different conclusions about means, even when they are in agreement about ends. In these circumstances the moral agent will act in accordance with the judgment at which he arrives after the amount of reflection which is appropriate in the given case.

The thesis that goodness is an intrinsic, indefinable property of certain things, together with the subordination of the concepts of right and obligation to the concept of the good, obviously show the influence of Russell's friend, G. E. Moore. And this influence persists, to some extent at least, in *Principles of Social Reconstruction* (1916). Russell is here mainly concerned with social and political themes; and he tells us that he did not write the book in his capacity as a philosopher. But when he says that 'I consider

[1] *Ibid.*, p. 11.   [2] *Ibid.*, p. 53.   [3] *Ibid.*, p. 30.

the best life that which is most built on creative impulses'[1] and explains that what he means by creative impulses are those which aim at bringing into existence good or valuable things such as knowledge, art and goodwill, his point of view is certainly in harmony with that of Moore.

3. At the same time, though there is certainly no explicit recantation in *Principles of Social Reconstruction* of the views which Russell took over from Moore, we can perhaps see in certain aspects of what he says the manifestation of a tendency to make good and bad relative to desire. In any case there is a marked tendency to interpret morality in the light of anthropology, of a certain doctrine about human nature. I do not mean to imply that this is necessarily a bad thing. I mean rather that Russell is moving away from a purely Moorean point of view in ethics.

'All human activity', Russell agrees, 'springs from two sources: impulse and desire.'[2] As he goes on to say that the suppression of impulse by purposes, desires and will means the suppression of vitality, one's natural tendency is to think that he is talking about conscious desire. But the desire which lies at the basis of human activity is presumably in the first instance unconscious desire. And in *The Analysis of Mind* Russell insists, under the influence of psycho-analytic theory, that 'all primitive desire is unconscious'.[3]

The expression of natural impulse is in itself a good thing because men possess 'a central principle of growth, an instinctive urgency leading them in a certain direction, as trees seek the light'.[4] But this approval of natural impulse, which sometimes puts us in mind of Rousseau, stands in need of qualification. If we follow natural impulse alone, we remain in bondage to it, and we cannot control our environment in a constructive manner. It is mind, impersonal objective thought, which exercises a critical function in regard to impulse and instinct and enables us to decide what impulses need to be suppressed or diverted because they conflict with other impulses or because the environment makes it impossible or undesirable to satisfy them. It is also mind which enables us to control our environment to a certain extent in a constructive manner. So while he insists on the principles of 'vitality', Russell does not give a blanket approval to impulse.

We have seen that Russell attributes human activities to two sources, impulse and desire. Later on he attributes it to 'instinct,

[1] *Principles of Social Reconstruction*, p. 5.
[2] *Ibid.*, p. 12.   [3] P. 76.
[4] *Principles of Social Reconstruction*, p. 24.

mind and spirit'.[1] Instinct is the source of vitality, while mind exercises a critical function in regard to instinct. Spirit is the principle of impersonal feelings and enables us to transcend the search for purely personal satisfaction by feeling the same interest in other people's joys and sorrows as in our own, by caring about the happiness of the human race as a whole and by serving ends which are in some sense supra-human, such as truth or beauty or, in the case of religious people, God.

Perhaps we can adopt the suggestion of Professor J. Buchler[2] that for Russell impulse and desire are the basic modes of initial stimulus, while instinct, mind and spirit are the categories under which human activities as we know them can be classified. In any case Russell obviously has in mind a progressive integration of desires and impulses under the control of mind, both in the individual and in society. At the same time he insists on the function of spirit, considered as the capacity for impersonal feeling. For 'if life is to be fully human it must serve some end which seems, in some sense, outside human life'.[3]

4. Even if in *Principles of Social Reconstruction* Russell retained, though with some misgiving, the Moorean idea that we can have intuitive knowledge of intrinsic goodness and badness, he did not retain the idea very long. For example, after having remarked in a popular essay, *What I Believe* (1925), that the good life is one inspired by love and guided by knowledge, he explains that he is not referring to ethical knowledge. For 'I do not think there is, strictly speaking, such a thing as ethical knowledge'.[4] Ethics is distinguished from science by desire rather than by any special form of knowledge. 'Certain ends are desired, and right conduct is what conduces to them.'[5] Similarly, in *An Outline of Philosophy* (1927) Russell explicitly says that he has abandoned Moore's theory of goodness as an indefinable intrinsic quality, and he refers to the influence on his mind in this respect of Santayana's *Winds of Doctrine* (1926). He now holds that good and bad are 'derivative from desire'.[6] Language is, of course, a social pheno-menon, and, generally speaking, we learn to apply the word 'good' to the things desired by the social group to which we belong. But 'primarily, we call something "good" when we desire it, and "bad" when we have an aversion from it'.[7]

[1] *Ibid.*, p. 205.
[2] In *The Philosophy of Bertrand Russell*, edited by P. A. Schilpp, p. 524.
[3] *Principles of Social Reconstruction*, p. 245.   [4] P. 37.   [5] P. 40.
[6] *An Outline of Philosophy*, p. 238.   [7] *Ibid.*, p. 242.

To say nothing more than this, however, would be to give an over-simplified account of Russell's ethical position. In the first place the utilitarian element in his earlier ethical ideas, an element common to him and to Moore, has remained unchanged. That is to say, he has continued to regard as right those actions which produce good consequences and as wrong those actions which produce bad consequences. And in this restricted field knowledge is possible. For example, if two men agree that a certain end X is desirable and so good, they can perfectly well argue about which possible action or series of actions is most likely to attain this end. And in principle they can come to an agreed conclusion representing probable knowledge.[1] But though the context would be ethical, the knowledge attained would not be in any way specifically different from knowledge of the appropriate means for attaining a certain end in a non-ethical context. In other words it would not be a case of a peculiar kind of knowledge called 'ethical' or 'moral'.

When we turn, however, from an examination of the appropriate means for attaining a certain end to value-judgments about ends themselves, the situation is different. We have seen that Russell once maintained that differences of opinion about values are not so great as to make it unreasonable to hold that we can and do have immediate knowledge of intrinsic goodness and badness, ethical intuition in other words. But he abandoned this view and came to the conclusion that a difference of opinion about values is basically 'one of tastes, not one as to any objective truth'.[2] If, for instance, a man tells me that cruelty is a good thing,[3] I can, of course, agree with him in the sense of pointing out the practical consequences of such a judgment. But if he still stands by his judgment, even when he realizes what it 'means', I can give him no theoretical proof that cruelty is wrong. Any 'argument' that I may employ is really a persuasive device designed to change the man's desires. And if it is unsuccessful there is no more to be said. Obviously, if someone professes to deduce a certain value-judgment from other value-judgments and one thinks that the alleged deduction is logically erroneous, one can point this out. And if a man meant by 'X is good' no more than

---

[1] It would not be certain or demonstrative knowledge. But neither is scientific knowledge certain knowledge.

[2] *Religion and Science* (1935), p. 238.

[3] The statement 'I think that cruelty is good' or 'I approve of cruelty' would be an ordinary empirical statement, relating to a psychological fact. 'Cruelty is good', however, is a value-judgment.

that X has certain empirical consequences, we could argue about whether X does or does not tend in practice to produce these effects. For this would be a purely empirical matter. But the man would not be likely to say, even in this case, 'X is good' unless he approved of the consequences; and his approval would express a desire or taste. In the long run, therefore, we ultimately reach a point where theoretical proof and disproof no longer have a role to play.

The matter can be clarified in this way. Russell may have sometimes expressed himself in such a way as to imply that in his opinion judgments of value are a matter of purely personal taste, without involving other people in any way. But this is certainly not his considered opinion. In his view judgments of value are really in the optative mood. To say 'X is good' is to say 'would that everyone desired X', and to say 'y is bad' is to say 'would that everyone felt an aversion from y'.[1] And if this analysis is accepted, it is obvious that 'cruelty is bad', when taken as meaning 'would that everyone had an aversion from cruelty', is no more describable as true or false than 'would that everyone appreciated good claret'. Hence there can be no question of proving that the judgment 'cruelty is bad' is true or false.

Obviously, Russell is perfectly aware that there is a sense in which it is true to say that it does not matter much if a man appreciates good wine or not, whereas it may matter very much whether people approve of cruelty or not. But he would regard these practical considerations as irrelevant to the purely philosophical question of the correct analysis of the value-judgment. If I say 'cruelty is bad', I shall obviously do anything which lies in my power to see that education, for example, is not so conducted as to encourage the belief that cruelty is admirable. But if I accept Russell's analysis of the value-judgment, I must admit that my own evaluation of cruelty is not theoretically provable.

Now, Russell has sometimes been criticized for giving vehement expression to his own moral convictions, as though this were inconsistent with his analysis of the value-judgment. But he can make, and has made, the obvious retort that as in his opinion judgments of value express desires, and as he himself has strong desires, there is no inconsistency in giving them vehement expression. And this reply seems to be quite valid, as far as it goes.

[1] In his *Replies to Criticism* Russell says: 'I do not think that an ethical judgment *merely* expresses a desire; I agree with Kant that it must have an element of universality'. *The Philosophy of Bertrand Russell*, edited by P. A. Schilpp, p. 722.

At the same time, when we remember that he is prepared to condemn certain lines of conduct, such as the treatment of the unfortunate prisoners at Ausschwitz, even if it could be shown that such conduct would ultimately benefit the human race and increase the general happiness, it is very difficult to avoid the impression that he really does think after all that some things are intrinsically bad, whether other people think they are bad or not.

Indeed, Russell himself seems to have a suspicion that this is the case. For after having remarked that he sees no logical inconsistency between his ethical theory and the expression of strong moral preferences, he adds that he is still not quite satisfied. His own theory of ethics does not satisfy him, but then other people's theories he finds even less satisfactory.[1] Hence we can perhaps say that while Russell would like to be able to return to the idea of intrinsic goodness and badness, he is at the same time convinced that a truly empirical and scientific philosophy can neither discover Moore's indefinable property of goodness nor admit self-evident moral principles.

One possible line of objection against Russell's analysis of the value-judgment is that it does not at all represent what ordinary people think that they are saying when they make such judgments. But Russell has never been the man to worry much about what the non-philosopher thinks. Nor has he ever been a devotee of 'ordinary language'. It is understandable, however, if some younger moral philosophers[2] have tried to give an account of the judgment of values, which pays more attention to ordinary language and its implications and yet refrains from re-introducing Moore's indefinable non-natural property.

5. There is at least one part of ethics which Russell regards as belonging to philosophy in a strict sense, namely the analysis of the judgment of value, the doctrine that to exhibit the logical form of such judgments one has to express them in the optative rather than in the indicative mood. But social and political theory is regarded by Russell as lying wholly outside the sphere of philosophy in the proper sense. Hence, though it might be considered odd to say nothing at all about them, no apology is needed for treating them in a very brief and sketchy manner.

In a famous essay which he wrote in 1902 Russell spoke of 'the

[1] Cf. *The Philosophy of Bertrand Russell*, edited by P. A. Schilpp, p. 724.
[2] I am thinking, for example, of Mr. R. M. Hare of Oxford.

tyranny of non-human power',[1] Nature's triumphant indifference to human ideals and values, and he also condemned the worship of naked power, of force, and the creed of militarism. He envisaged man turning his back on unthinking power and creating his own realm of ideal values, even if this realm is doomed in the end to utter extinction. It may therefore be somewhat surprising at first sight to find Russell saying in 1938 that those economists are mistaken who think that self-interest is the fundamental motive in social life, and that the basic concept in social science is that of power.[2] For if the word 'power' were interpreted in the same sense in which Russell condemned power in 1902, it would seem to follow that in 1938 he has either radically altered his opinions or is urging men to turn their backs on social and political life, something which is very far from being his intention.

In point of fact, however, Russell has never altered his dislike of 'naked power' and his condemnation of the love of power for its own sake. When he says that power is the basic concept in social science and that the laws of social dynamics cannot be stated except in terms of it, he is using the term to mean 'the production of intended effects'.[3] And when he says that though the desire of commodities and material comfort certainly operates in human life, the love of power is more fundamental, he means by 'love of power' 'the desire to be able to produce intended effects upon the outer world, whether human or non-human'.[4] Whether the love of power in this sense is a good or a bad thing depends on the nature of the effects which a man or group desires to produce.

The matter can be put in this way. In *Power* Russell assumes that energy is the basic concept in physics. He then looks for a basic concept in social science and finds it in power. And as power, like energy, is constantly passing from one form to another, he assigns to social science the task of discovering the laws of the transformation of power. But though Russell rejects the economic theory of history as unrealistic, that is, as minimizing the role of the fundamental motive-force in social life, he does not attempt to classify all human activities in terms of power. For example, it is possible to pursue knowledge for the sake of power, that is, of control; and this impulse has become increasingly conspicuous in modern science. But it is also possible to pursue knowledge in a

---

[1] *Mysticism and Logic*, p. 49 (also *Philosophical Essays*, p. 62).
[2] Cf. *Power: A New Social Analysis* (1938), p. 10. This work will be referred to simply as *Power*.
[3] *Power*, p. 35.   [4] *Ibid.*, p. 274

contemplative spirit, for love of the object itself. Indeed, 'the lover, the poet and the mystic find a fuller satisfaction than the seeker after power can ever know, since they can rest in the object of their love'.[1]

If power is defined as the production of intended effects and love of power as the desire to produce such effects, it obviously follows that power is not an end in itself but a means to the attainment of ends other than itself. And in Russell's opinion 'the ultimate aim of those who have power (and we all have some) should be to promote social co-operation, not in one group as against another, but in the whole human race'.[2] Democracy is upheld as a safeguard against the arbitrary exercise of power.[3] And the ideal of social co-operation in the whole human race is represented as leading to the concept of a world-government possessing the authority and power to prevent the outbreak of hostility between nations.[4] Science has helped to unify the world on the technological plane. But politics has lagged behind science; and we have not yet achieved an effective world-organization capable of utilizing the benefits conferred by science and at the same time of preventing the evils which science has made possible.

It does not follow, of course, that social organization is for Russell the one worthwhile aim of life. In fact it is itself a means rather than an end, a means to the promotion of the good life. Man has acquisitive and predatory impulses; and it is an essential function of the State to control the expression of these impulses in individuals and groups, just as it would be the function of a world-government to control their expression as manifested by States. But man also has his creative impulses, 'impulses to put something into the world which is not taken away from anybody else'.[5] And it is the function of government and law to facilitate the expression of such impulses rather than to control them. Applied to world-government, this idea implies that different nations should remain free to develop their own cultures and ways of life.

---

[1] *The Scientific Outlook* (1931), p. 275.   [2] *Power*, p. 283.
[3] Russell can be called a socialist, but he has emphasized the dangers of socialism when divorced from effective democracy.
[4] If in recent years Russell has paid more attention to campaigning for nuclear disarmament than for a world-government, this is doubtless because the prospect of achieving effective world-government by agreement seems to be somewhat remote, whereas a suicidal world-war could break out at any time.
[5] *Authority and the Individual* (1949), p. 105. In this work Russell discusses the problem of combining social cohesion with individual liberty in the light of concrete possibilities.

Russell's analysis of social dynamics in terms of the idea of power is doubtless open to criticism on the ground of over-simplification. But the point to notice is that he has consistently subordinated fact to value, in the sense that he has always insisted on the primacy of ethical ends and on the need for organizing human society with a view to facilitating the harmonious development of the human personality. It scarcely needs to be added that Russell does not claim that his judgments about the ethical ends of social and political organization and about what constitutes a good life are exempt from his own analysis of the judgment of value. He would admit that they express personal desires, personal recommendations. And it is for this very reason, of course, that he does not regard them as pertaining to philosophy in a strict sense.

6. Except for noting that Russell abandoned belief in God at an early age, we have not yet said anything about his attitude to religion. To look for a profound philosophy of religion in his writings would be to look in vain. But as he has often referred to the subject, it seems appropriate to give a general indication of his views.

Though, like J. S. Mill before him, Russell evidently thinks that the evil and suffering in the world constitute an unanswerable objection to belief in a God who is described both as infinitely good and as omnipotent, he would not claim that the non-existence of a divine being transcending the world can be proved. Technically speaking, therefore, he is an agnostic. At the same time he does not believe that there is any real evidence for the existence of a God. And it is indeed clear from the whole character of his philosophy that the traditional arguments for God's existence are excluded. On a phenomenalistic analysis of causality no causal inference to a meta-phenomenal being can be valid. And if 'order, unity and continuity are human inventions just as truly as are catalogues and encyclopaedias',[1] we cannot get very far with an argument based on order and finality in the world. As for the arguments adduced by some modern scientists, there is, for example, nothing in evolution to warrant the hypothesis that it manifests a divine purpose. And even if a case can be made out for the thesis that the world had a beginning in time, we are not entitled to infer that it was created. For it might have begun spontaneously. It may seem odd that it should have done so;

[1] *The Scientific Outlook*, p. 101.

'but there is no law of nature to the effect that things which seem odd to us must not happen'.[1]

Though, however, Russell does not think that there is any evidence for the existence of God, he has made it clear that belief in God, taken by itself, would no more arouse his hostility than belief in elves or fairies. It would simply be an example of a comforting but unsupported belief in a hypothetical entity, which does not necessarily make a man a worse citizen than he would otherwise be. Russell's attacks are directed primarily against the Christian religious bodies, which in his view have generally done more harm than good, and against theology only in so far as it has been invoked in support of persecution and religious wars and as a warrant for preventing the taking of means to certain ends which he considers desirable.

At the same time, though Russell often writes in a Voltairean manner, he is not simply a spiritual descendant of *les philosophes*. He attaches value to what we may call religious emotion and a religious attitude of serious concern about life. And in so far as he can be said to have a religion, it is the life of the 'spirit' as sketched in *Principles of Social Reconstruction*. True, this book appeared in 1916, but at a much later date he has remarked that the expression of his own personal religion which seems to him 'least unsatisfactory is the one in *Social Reconstruction*'.[2]

Russell's polemics against Christianity do not concern us here. It is sufficient to point out that though on occasion he pays tribute to, for example, the ideal of love and to the Christian idea of the value of the individual, attack is more prominent than commendation. And while Russell undoubtedly draws attention to some familiar black patches in Christian history, he tends to exaggerate and, sometimes, to sacrifice accuracy to wit and sarcasm. More relevant here, however, is the consideration that he has never tried systematically to dissociate what he regards as valuable in religion from theological belief. If he had, he might possibly have had second thoughts about his position, though it is probably too much to expect that he would ask himself seriously whether God is not in some sense an implicit presupposition of some of the problems which he himself has raised.

7. It is not possible to sum up Russell's view of the nature of philosophy in a concise statement. For he speaks in different ways

---

[1] *The Scientific Outlook*, p. 122.
[2] *The Philosophy of Bertrand Russell*, edited by P. A. Schilpp, p. 726.

at different times.[1] And he has never been a man for gathering together all the threads and showing in detail how they fit together, how they form an intelligible pattern. He has been too intent with getting on with the next matter in hand. At the same time it is not, I think, very difficult to understand how he came to express rather different views about the nature and scope of philosophy. Nor is it very difficult to discover persistent elements in his concept of philosophy.

As far as its basic motive is concerned, philosophy has always been for Russell a pursuit of knowledge, of objective truth. And he has expressed his conviction that one of the main tasks of philosophy is to understand and interpret the world, even to discover, as far as this is possible, the ultimate nature of reality. True, Russell believes that in practice philosophers have often set out to prove preconceived beliefs; and he has referred to Bradley's famous saying that metaphysics is the finding of bad reasons for what one believes by instinct. He is also convinced that in practice some philosophers have employed thought and argument to establish comforting beliefs which have seemed to them to possess pragmatic value. Further, when comparing the aims and ambitions of philosophy with the actual results achieved, he has sometimes spoken as though science were the only means of attaining anything which could properly be called knowledge. But all this does not alter the fact that in regard to what ought to be the attitude, motive and aims of the philosopher Russell has maintained what can reasonably be described as a traditional view. This is apparent in his earlier writings; and it is also apparent in his later attack on 'linguistic' philosophy, that is, on philosophy as concerned exclusively with mapping out so-called ordinary language, on the ground that the philosophers who represent this tendency have abandoned the important task of interpreting the world.[2]

As we have noted, however, the method on which Russell lays the chief emphasis is analysis. In general philosophy this means that the philosopher starts with a body of common knowledge or what is assumed to be knowledge. This constitutes his data. He then reduces this complex body of knowledge, expressed in

[1] Russell is, of course, as free as anybody else to change his mind. But, this fact apart, we have to remember, in regard to utterances which, abstractly considered, are scarcely compatible, that in a given context and for polemical reasons he sometimes exaggerates one particular aspect of a subject.
[2] Cf. *My Philosophical Development*, p. 230.

propositions which are somewhat vague and often logically inter-dependent, to a number of propositions which he tries to make as simple and precise as possible. These are then arranged in deductive chains, depending logically on certain initial propositions which serve as premisses. 'The discovery of these premisses belongs to philosophy; but the work of deducing the body of common knowledge from them belongs to mathematics, if "mathematics" is interpreted in a somewhat liberal sense.'[1] In.other words, philosophy proceeds by logical analysis from the complex and relatively concrete to what is simpler and more abstract. It thus differs from the special sciences, which proceed from the simpler to the more complex, and also from purely deductive mathematics.

The philosopher may find, however, that some of the logically implied premisses of a common body of assumed knowledge are themselves open to doubt. And the degree of probability of any consequence will depend on the degree of probability of the premiss which is most open to doubt. Thus logical analysis does not simply serve the purpose of discovering implied initial propositions or premisses. It also serves the purpose of helping us to estimate the degree of probability attaching to what commonly passes for knowledge, the consequences of the premisses.

Now, there can be little doubt that the method of analysis was suggested to Russell by his work in mathematical logic. And it is thus understandable that he has spoken of logic as the essence of philosophy and has declared that every philosophical problem, when properly analyzed, is found to be either not really a philosophical problem at all or else a logical problem, in the sense of being a problem of logical analysis.[2] This analysis is inspired by the principle of economy or Ockham's razor and leads to logical atomism.

We have noted, however, how Russell was converted to Wittgenstein's theory of the propositions of formal logic and pure mathematics as systems of 'tautologies'. And if we look at the matter from this point of view, it is perfectly understandable that he has emphasized the difference between logic and philosophy. For example, 'logic, I maintain, is not part of philosophy'.[3] But to say that formal logic, as a system of tautologies, falls outside philosophy is not, of course, incompatible with an insistence on

---

[1] *Our Knowledge of the External World*, p. 214. [2] Cf. *Ibid.*, p. 42.
[3] *Human Knowledge*, p. 5.

the importance in philosophy of logical analysis, the reductive analysis which has been characteristic of Russell's thought. True, in proportion as his early work in mathematical logic has receded into the distance, Russell has become less and less inclined to speak of logic as the essence of philosophy. And the more he has come to emphasize the tentative character of philosophical hypotheses, so much the wider has he made the gap between philosophy and logic in the strict sense. Thus there is no question of maintaining that there has been no change in Russell's attitude. After all, having once said that logic is the essence of philosophy, he has declared at a later date that logic is not part of philosophy at all. At the same time we have to remember that when Russell made the first of these statements he meant, in part at any rate, that the method of philosophy is or ought to be the method of logical analysis. And he has never abandoned belief in the value of this method.

Though, however, Russell has retained his belief in the value of the reductive analysis which is a characteristic feature of his thought and has defended this sort of analysis against recent criticism, it is undeniable that his general conception of philosophy underwent a considerable change. We have seen that there was a time when he sharply distinguished between philosophical method on the one hand and scientific method on the other. Later on, however, we find him saying that the philosopher should learn from science 'principles and methods and general conceptions'.[1] In other words, Russell's reflections on the relation between philosophy and science, reflections which were posterior to his work in mathematical logic and to the first conception and employment of reductive analysis, had a considerable influence on his general idea of philosophy. Thus whereas at the time when he was saying that logic is the essence of philosophy, he tended to give the impression that if philosophical problems were properly analyzed and reduced to precise manageable questions they could be solved one by one, he later came to emphasize the need for bold and sweeping provisional hypotheses in philosophy. At the same time he has shown a marked tendency on occasion to question the philosopher's ability to find any real solutions to his problems. Perhaps the following remarks on Russell's ideas about the relation between philosophy and the empirical sciences may serve to make his different utterances more intelligible.

---

[1] *An Outline of Philosophy*, p. 2.

Philosophy, according to Russell, presupposes science, in the sense that it should be built upon a foundation of empirical knowledge.[1] It must therefore in some sense go beyond science. It is obvious that the philosopher is not in a better position than the scientist to solve problems which are recognized as pertaining to science. He must therefore have his own problems to solve, his own work to do. But what is this work?

Russell has said that the most important part of philosophy consists in criticism and clarification of notions which are apt to be regarded as ultimate and to be accepted in an uncritical manner.[2] This programme presumably covers the critical examination and 'justification' of scientific inference to which reference was made in the previous chapter. But it also includes criticism and clarification of supposedly basic concepts such as those of minds and physical objects. And the fulfilment of this task leads with Russell, as we have seen, to the interpretation of minds and physical objects as logical constructions out of events. But we have also seen that Russell does not consider reductive analysis in this context to be simply a linguistic affair, that is, simply a matter of finding an alternative language to that of minds and physical objects. In a real sense analysis is conceived as aiming at a knowledge of the ultimate constituents of the universe. And the entities of physical science, atoms, electrons and so on, are themselves interpreted as logical constructions. Philosophical analysis, therefore, does not go beyond science in the sense of trying to clarify confused concepts which science takes for granted. On the scientific level the concept of the atom is not confused. Or, if it is, it is hardly the philosopher's business to clarify it. Philosophy goes beyond science in the sense that it advances an ontological or metaphysical hypothesis.

It is in no way surprising, therefore, that Russell should have asserted that one of the jobs of philosophy is to suggest bold hypotheses about the universe. But a question at once arises. Are these hypotheses to be regarded exclusively as hypotheses which science is not yet in a position to confirm or refute, though it could in principle do so? Or is the philosopher entitled to propose hypotheses which are in principle unverifiable by science? In other

[1] Cf. for example, *My Philosophical Development*, p. 230, where Russell is criticizing linguistic philosophy, which he regards as trying to effect a divorce of philosophy from science.

[2] *Contemporary British Philosophy*, First Series, p. 379, and *Logic and Knowledge*, p. 341.

words, has philosophy or has it not problems about the universe which are peculiarly its own?

Russell does indeed speak of the problems of philosophy as problems which 'do not, at least at present, belong to any of the special sciences',[1] and which science is thus not yet in a position to solve. Moreover, if the hypotheses of science are provisional,the hypotheses which philosophy advances as solutions to its problems are much more provisional and tentative. In fact, 'science is what you more or less know and philosophy is what you do not know'.[2] True, Russell has admitted that this particular statement was a jocular remark; but he considers that it is a justifiable joke provided that we add that 'philosophical speculation as to what we do not yet know has shown itself a valuable preliminary to exact scientific knowledge'.[3] If philosophical hypotheses are verified, they then become part of science and cease to be philosophical.

This point of view represents what we may call the positivist side of Russell. I do not mean to suggest that he has ever been a 'logical positivist'. For, as we have seen, he has always rejected the logical positivist criterion of meaning. When he says that unverified philosophical hypotheses do not constitute knowledge, he is not saying that they are meaningless. At the same time the statement that 'all *definite* knowledge—so I should contend— belongs to science'[4] can be described as positivist, if we mean by positivism the doctrine that it is only science which provides positive knowledge about the world. It is, however, worth remarking that when Russell makes statements of this nature, he seems to forget that on his theory of the unprovable postulates of scientific inference it is difficult to see how science can be asserted with confidence to provide definite knowledge, though, admittedly, we all believe that it is capable of doing so.

This positivist attitude, however, represents only one aspect of Russell's conception of the problems of philosophy. For he has also depicted the philosopher as considering problems which are not in principle capable of receiving scientific solutions. True, he seems generally to be referring to philosophy in the popular or in the historical sense. But he certainly remarks that 'almost all the questions of most interest to speculative minds are such as science cannot answer'.[5] Further, it is in the business of philosophy to study such questions, for example the problem of the end or ends

[1] *An Outline of Philosophy*, p. 1.   [2] *Logic and Knowledge*, p. 281.
[3] *Unpopular Essays* (1950), p. 39.
[4] *History of Western Philosophy* (1945), p. 10.   [5] *Ibid.*

of life, even if it cannot answer them. Obviously, such problems would be essentially philosophical problems. And even if Russell is sceptical about philosophy's capacity to answer them, he certainly does not regard them as meaningless. On the contrary, 'it is one of the functions of philosophy to keep alive interest in such questions'.[1]

There are indeed some perplexing juxtapositions of conflicting statements in Russell's writings. For example, in the very paragraph in which he says that 'philosophy should make us know the ends of life'[2] he also states that 'philosophy cannot itself determine the ends of life'.[3] Again, having said, as already mentioned, that philosophy should keep alive an interest in such problems as whether the universe has a purpose, and that 'some kind of philosophy is a necessity to all but the more thoughtless',[4] he proceeds to say that 'philosophy is a stage in intellectual development, and is not compatible with mental maturity'.[5]

It is, of course, possible that such apparent inconsistencies can be made to disappear by suitable distinctions in meaning and context. But it is unnecessary to embark here upon detailed exegesis of this sort. It is more to the point to suggest that in Russell's view of philosophy there are two main attitudes. On the one hand he feels strongly that through its impersonal pursuit of truth and its indifference to preconceived beliefs and to what one would like to be true science provides a model for theoretical thinking, and that metaphysical philosophy has a bad record in this respect. He is convinced too that though scientific hypotheses are always provisional and subject to possible revision, science gives us the nearest approach to definite knowledge about the world which we are capable of attaining. Hence such statements as 'whatever can be known, can be known by means of science'.[6] From this point of view the ideal situation would be that philosophy should give way altogether to science. And if in practice it cannot, as there will always be problems which science is not yet in a position to solve, philosophy should become as 'scientific' as possible. That is to say, the philosopher should resist the temptation to use philosophy to prove preconceived or comforting beliefs or to serve as a way of salvation.[7] And concrete judgments of

[1] *Unpopular Essays*, p. 41.   [2] *An Outline of Philosophy*, p. 312.
[3] *Ibid.*   [4] *Unpopular Essays*, p. 41.
[5] *Ibid.*, p. 77.   [6] *History of Western Philosophy*, p. 863.
[7] 'In itself philosophy sets out neither to solve our troubles nor to save our souls', *Wisdom of the West* (1959), p. 6.

value, as well as reflections depending on such judgments, should be excluded from 'scientific' philosophy.

On the other hand not only is Russell well aware that 'philosophy' in the popular and historical senses of the term covers a great deal more than would be admitted by the concept of 'scientific' philosophy, but he also feels that there are significant and important questions which science cannot answer but awareness of which broadens our mental horizons. He refuses to rule out such questions as meaningless. And even if he thinks that 'what science cannot discover, mankind cannot know',[1] he is also convinced that if such problems were to be forgotten 'human life would be impoverished',[2] if only because they show the limitations of scientific knowledge. In other words, a certain sympathy with positivism in a general sense is balanced by a feeling that the world has enigmatic aspects, and that to refuse to recognize them is the expression either of an unwarranted dogmatism or of a narrow-minded philistinism.

The matter can be expressed in this way. On his own confession one of the sources of Russell's original interest in philosophy was the desire to discover whether philosophy could provide any defence for some sort of religious belief.[3] He also looked to philosophy to provide him with certain knowledge. On both counts he was disappointed. He came to the conclusion that philosophy could not provide him either with a rational foundation for religious belief or with certainty in any field. There was, of course, mathematics; but mathematics is not philosophy. Russell thus came to the conclusion that science, however provisional its hypotheses may be and to whatever extent scientific inference may rest on unprovable postulates, is the only source of what can reasonably be called definite knowledge. Hence philosophy in a strict sense cannot be much more than philosophy of science and general theory of knowledge, together with an examination of problems which science is not yet in a position to solve but the raising and discussion of which can have a positive stimulative value for science by supplying the required element of anticipatory vision. At the same time Russell has always been passionately interested in the welfare of humanity, as he sees it. Hence he has never hesitated to go beyond the limits of 'scientific' philosophy and to treat of those subjects which involve explicit judgments of

[1] *Religion and Science*, p. 243.   [2] *Unpopular Essays*, p. 41.
[3] Cf. *My Philosophical Development*, p. 11.

value and which are certainly covered by 'philosophy' in the popular sense of the term. A good many at any rate of the apparent inconsistencies in his thought are explicable in terms of these considerations. Some of the rest may be partly due to his reluctance to go back over his writings and to exclude differences in the use of the same term or, alternatively, to explain on each occasion in what precise sense he is using the term. It is also perhaps a relevant point that while Russell has recommended the piecemeal tackling of philosophical problems by logical analysis, he has always shown himself appreciative of the grandeur and attraction of sweeping hypotheses and theories.

8. In 1950 Russell received the Nobel Prize for Literature. And there is no doubt but that he is an elegant and, if one prescinds from a certain looseness in the use of terminology, clear writer. Obviously, his early work in mathematical logic is not for the general public. But apart from this, he has brought philosophical reflection to a wide circle of readers who would be unlikely to embark on Kant's first *Critique* or Hegel's *Phenomenology of Spirit*. In literary style he thus stands in the tradition of Locke and Hume and J. S. Mill, though his more popular writings remind one more of the French philosophers of the Enlightenment. In fact with the general public Russell has become the patron of rationalism and non-religious humanism.

Among philosophers nobody questions, of course, Russell's influence on modern British philosophy and similar currents of thought elsewhere. There has doubtless been a tendency in some countries, notably Germany, to dismiss him as an 'empiricist' who did some good work in mathematics in his early days. But he has discussed philosophical problems of interest and importance, such as the foundations of scientific inference and the nature of the judgment of value. And though some of the devotees of the cult of ordinary language may have criticized Russell's reductive analysis, in the opinion of the present writer such criticism is quite inadequate if it is framed entirely in linguistic terms. For example, if reductive analysis is taken to imply that in principle 'Russia invaded Finland' could be translated into a number of sentences in which the term 'Russia' would not occur but individuals only would be mentioned,[1] the relation between the original sentence and the translation being such that if the former is true (or false)

[1] The individuals who ordered the invasion, who planned it, who contributed in any way by fighting, making munitions, acting as doctors, and so on.

the latter is true (or false) and *vice versa*, the ontological implication is that the State is not in any way an entity over and above its members. And it seems a quite inadequate criticism if it is simply pointed out that we cannot get along in ordinary language without using such terms as 'Russia'. It is true enough. But then we want to know what is the ontological implication of this point of view. Are we to say that the State *is* something over and above its members? If not, how is the concept of the State to be clarified? In terms of individuals related in certain ways? In what ways? It may be said that these questions can be answered by looking at the ways in which terms such as 'State' are actually used. But it seems obvious that in the process of looking we shall find ourselves referring to extra-linguistic factors. Similarly, it is not sufficient to criticize the statement, say, that the world is the class of things on the ground that we cannot get along without being able to refer to 'the world'. This is true. But then we can quite sensibly ask, 'Do you mean that the world cannot properly be regarded as the class of things? If so, how do you conceive it? Your way may be better; but we want to know what it is.'

These remarks are, however, not intended as a general apologia for Russell's use of reductive analysis. For it may very well be that on examining a particular case of such analysis we find that an essential feature is left out. And in the present writer's opinion this is verified, for example, in the case of Russell's analysis of the self. There was a time, as we have seen, when he thought that the phenomenology of consciousness or awareness implies that the I-subject is uneliminable. Later on, however, he depicted the self as a logical construction out of events, thus developing the phenomenalism of Hume. But it seems to me perfectly clear that when sentences beginning with the pronoun 'I' have been translated into sentences in which only 'events' are mentioned and the word 'I' does not appear, an essential feature of the original sentence has simply been omitted, with the result that the translation is inadequate. In a sense Wittgenstein saw this clearly when he spoke in the *Tractatus* about the metaphysical subject. True, he remarked that if I wrote a book about what I found in the world, I could not mention the metaphysical subject. But it could not be mentioned simply because it is subject and not object, not one of the objects which 'I' find in the world. Empirical psychology, therefore, can carry on without the concept of the metaphysical or transcendental ego or I-subject. But for the

492 THE REVOLT AGAINST IDEALISM

phenomenology of consciousness it is uneliminable, as Wittgenstein appears to have seen. Russell, however, attempted to eliminate it by eliminating consciousness. And the present writer does not consider his attempt to have been a success. This is not, of course, an argument against reductive analysis as such. What is genuinely superfluous should doubtless be dealt with by Ockham's razor. But it by no means follows that all that Russell thought superfluous *is* superfluous. The attempt, however, to eliminate the uneliminable may have a pragmatic value, in the sense that it can serve to show what cannot be eliminated by analysis.

This may perhaps sound as though the present writer looks on reductive analysis as *the* philosophical method but disagrees with some of Russell's applications of it. This would, however, be an erroneous impression. I think that reductive analysis has its uses. I do not see how exception can be taken to it as *a* possible method. But I certainly do not think that it is the only philosophical method. For one thing, we become aware of the I-subject, the transcendental ego, by the method of transcendental reflection, not by reductive analysis. True, I have suggested that the failure of reductive analysis to eliminate the I-subject may serve to draw attention to the subject. But in actual fact the failure serves this purpose only if it stimulates a transition to phenomenology, to transcendental reflection. The failure as such simply leaves us perplexed, as it did David Hume. For another thing, if reductive analysis is assumed to be *the* philosophical method, this seems to presuppose a metaphysics, an 'atomic' metaphysics opposed to the 'monistic' metaphysics of absolute idealism. And if one's choice of method presupposes a metaphysics, it is no good claiming that this metaphysics is the only 'scientific' one, unless it is uniformly successful in accounting for experience whereas other methods are not.

To turn to another point. We have seen that Russell set out to obtain certainty. And he has said that 'philosophy arises from an unusually obstinate attempt to arrive at real knowledge'.[1] This presupposes that reality, the universe, is intelligible.[2] But a few years later we are told that 'order, unity and continuity are human inventions'.[3] In other words, the intelligibility of the universe is imposed by man, by the human mind. And this enables Russell to

[1] *An Outline of Philosophy*, p. 1.
[2] It is worth noting that inquiry also presupposes a value-judgment, about the value of truth as a goal for the human mind.
[3] *The Scientific Outlook*, p. 101.

dispose, for example, of the claim of Sir James Jeans, the astronomer, that the world should be conceived as the expressed thought of a divine mathematician. For the fact that the world can be interpreted in terms of mathematical physics is to be attributed to the skill of the physicist in imposing a network. It may be said, of course, that even if the original attempt to understand the world presupposes its intelligibility, this presupposition is simply an hypothesis, and that Russell afterwards comes to the conclusion that the hypothesis is not verified. But the refutation of the hypothesis is the result of an examination of the world, an analysis which itself presupposes the intelligibility of what is examined and analyzed. And in any case, if order, unity and continuity are human inventions, what becomes of the claim that science provides definite knowledge? It seems that what is provided is knowledge simply of the human mind and of its operations. And the very same thing might be said, of course, of the results of Russell's reductive analysis. But in any case can we really believe that science does not provide us with any objective knowledge of the extra-mental world? Nobody would deny that science 'works', that it has pragmatic value. In this case, however, the question immediately arises whether the world must not have certain intelligible characteristics for science to possess this pragmatic value. And if the intelligibility of reality is once admitted, the door is again opened to metaphysical questions which Russell is inclined to dismiss in a cavalier manner.

To conclude. Russell's total literary achievements, ranging from abstract mathematical logic to fiction,[1] is extremely impressive. In the history of mathematical logic his place is obviously assured. In general philosophy his development of empiricism with the aid of logical analysis, together with his recognition of the limitations of empiricism as a theory of knowledge, constitutes an important phase in modern British philosophical thought. As for his popular writings in the fields of ethics, politics and social theory, these obviously cannot be put on the same level as, say, *Human Knowledge*, much less *Principia Mathematica*. Yet they reveal, of course, a personality of interest, a humanist who has said, for example, that his intellect leads him to the conclusion that there is nothing in the universe which is higher than man, though his emotions violently rebel. He admits that he has always desired to

[1] Russell published a book of short stories, *Satan in the Suburbs*, in 1953 and *Nightmares of Eminent Persons* in 1954.

find in philosophy some justification for the 'impersonal emotions'. And even if he has failed to find it, 'those who attempt to make a religion of humanism, which recognizes nothing greater than man, do not satisfy my emotions'.[1] Russell may be the great patron of non-religious humanism in Great Britain in the present century; but he has his reservations, at least on the emotive level.

It is thus difficult to classify Russell in an unambiguous manner, for example as an 'empiricist' or as a 'scientific humanist'. But why should we wish to do so? After all, he is Bertrand Russell, a distinct individual and not simply a member of a class. And if in his old age he has become, as it were, a national institution, this is due not simply to his philosophical writing but also to his complex and forceful personality, aristocrat, philosopher, democrat and campaigner for causes in one. It is indeed natural that those of us who hold firm beliefs which are very different from his and which he has attacked, should deplore certain aspects of his influence. But this should not blind one to the fact that Russell is one of the most remarkable Englishmen of the century.

[1] *The Philosophy of Bertrand Russell*, edited by P. A. Schilpp, p. 19.

EPILOGUE

WE have seen that though Bertrand Russell has often expressed very sceptical views about the philosopher's ability to provide us with definite knowledge about the world and though he has certainly little sympathy with any philosopher who claims that his particular system represents final and definitive truth, he has always looked on philosophy as motivated by the desire to understand the world and man's relation to it. Even if in practice philosophy can provide only 'a way of looking at the results of empirical inquiry, a frame-work, as it were, to gather the findings of science into some sort of order',[1] this idea, as put forward by Russell, presupposes that science has given us new ways of seeing the world, new concepts which the philosopher has to take as a point of departure. The scope of his achievement may be limited, but it is the world with which he is ultimately concerned.

In an important sense G. E. Moore was much closer to being a revolutionary. He did not indeed lay down any restrictive dogmas about the nature and scope of philosophy. But, as we have seen, he devoted himself in practice exclusively to analysis as he understood it. And the effect of his example was to encourage the belief that philosophy is primarily concerned with analysis of meaning, that is, with language. True, Russell developed logical analysis and was often concerned with language; but he was concerned with much else besides. Both men, of course, directed attention, in their different ways, to analysis. But it was Moore rather than Russell who seems to us, on looking back, to be the herald, by force of example rather than by explicit theory, of the view that the primary task of the philosopher is the analysis of ordinary language.

For an explicit dogmatic statement about the nature and scope of philosophy we have, however, to turn to Ludwig Wittgenstein. We have noted that it was Wittgenstein who converted Russell to the view that the propositions of logic and pure mathematics are 'tautologies'. In the *Tractatus Logico-Philosophicus*[2] Wittgenstein

---

[1] *Wisdom of the West*, p. 311.

[2] The original version of this work appeared in 1921 in Ostwald's *Annalen der Philosophie*. The work was published for the first time as a book, with facing German and English texts, in 1922 (reprint with a few corrections, 1923). An edition with a new translation by D. F. Pears and B. P. McGuiness was published in 1961.

explained that what he meant by a tautology was a proposition which is true for all possible states of affairs and which therefore has as its opposite a contradiction, which is true for no possible state of affairs. A tautology, therefore, gives us no information about the world, in the sense of saying that things are one way when they could be another way. A 'proposition', however, as distinct from a tautology, is a picture or representation of a possible fact or state of affairs in the world. A proposition in this sense is either true or false; but we cannot know by inspecting its meaning (*Sinn*) whether it is true or false. To know this we have to compare it, as it were, with reality, with the empirical facts.[1] On the one hand therefore we have the tautologies of logic and pure mathematics which are necessarily true but give us no factual information about the world, while on the other hand there are propositions, empirical statements, which say something about how things are in the world but which are never necessarily true.

Now, propositions, in Wittgenstein's technical use of the term in the *Tractatus*, are identified by him with the propositions of the natural sciences.[2] This identification seems to be unduly restrictive. For there is no good reason, on Wittgenstein's premises that is to say, why an ordinary empirical statement, which would not normally be called a scientific statement, should be excluded from the class of propositions. But Wittgenstein would presumably admit this, in spite of the identification of the totality of propositions with the totality of the natural sciences. In any case the important point is that propositions are not philosophical. A scientific statement is not a philosophical proposition. Nor, of course, is a statement such as 'the dog is under the table'. Nor are tautologies philosophical propositions. Mathematics is no more philosophy than is natural science. It follows therefore that there is no room in Wittgenstein's scheme for philosophical propositions. In fact there are no such things.[3] And if there are no such things, it

---

[1] A complex proposition is for Wittgenstein a truth-function of elementary propositions. For example, proposition X, let us suppose, is true if propositions a, b and c are true. In such a case it is not necessary to verify X directly in order to know whether it is true or false. But at some point there must be verification, a confrontation of a proposition or of propositions with empirical facts.

[2] *Tractatus*, 4.11. Empirical psychology is included among the natural sciences.

[3] If one were to say to Wittgenstein that 'the continuum has no actual parts' is a philosophical proposition, he would doubtless reply that it is in fact a tautology or a definition, giving the meaning, or part of it, of the word 'continuum'. If, however, it were understood as asserting that there are in the world actual examples of a continuum, it would be an ordinary empirical statement.

obviously cannot be the business of philosophy to enunciate them.[1]

What, then, is the function of philosophy? It is said to consist in the clarification of propositions.[2] And the propositions to be clarified are obviously not philosophical ones. Indeed, if we take literally Wittgenstein's identification of propositions with those of the natural sciences, it follows logically that the business of philosophy is to clarify scientific propositions. But it is by no means immediately clear how and in what sense the philosopher can do this. Further, though the logical positivists of the Vienna Circle certainly attributed to philosophy a modest positive function as a kind of handmaid of science,[3] from what Wittgenstein says elsewhere in the *Tractatus*[4] he appears to be thinking primarily of a sort of linguistic therapeutic, designed to clear up logical confusion. For example, as Russell pointed out, in ordinary or colloquial language the grammatical form of a sentence often disguises the logical form. Hence there can arise for the philosopher the temptation to make 'metaphysical' statements (for instance, that 'the golden mountain' must have some peculiar kind of ontological status half-way between actual existence and nonentity) which are the result of not understanding the logic of our language. The philosopher who sees this can clear up the confusion in his colleague's mind by restating the misleading sentence so as to exhibit its logical form, on the lines of Russell's theory of descriptions. Again, if someone tries to say something 'metaphysical', it can be pointed out to him that he has failed to give any definite meaning (*Bedeutung*, reference) to one or more terms. An example actually given by Wittgenstein, who is extremely sparing of examples in the *Tractatus*, is 'Socrates is identical'. For the word 'identical' has no meaning when used in *this* way as an adjective. But what Wittgenstein has to say would doubtless apply, under certain conditions, to a question such as 'what is the cause of the world?' For if we assume that causality signifies a relation *between* phenomena, it makes no sense to ask for the

---

[1] The *Tractatus* is, of course, a philosophical work and contains 'philosophical propositions'. But with admirable consistency Wittgenstein does not hesitate to embrace the paradoxical conclusion that the propositions which enable one to understand his theory are themselves nonsensical (*unsinnig*, 6.54).

[2] *Tractatus*, 4.112.

[3] For example, the logical positivists of the Vienna Circle envisaged the philosopher as concerned with the language of science and as trying to construct a common language which would serve to unify the particular sciences, such as physics and psychology.

[4] Cf. 4.002–4.0031, 5.473, 5.4733 and 6.53.

cause of *all* phenomena. Further, on Wittgenstein's premisses, we cannot talk about the world as a totality.[1]

Wittgenstein's *Tractatus* was one of the writings which exercised an influence on the Vienna Circle, the group of logical positivists who more or less recognized as their leader Moritz Schlick (1882–1936), professor of philosophy in the University of Vienna.[2] And there are certainly points of agreement between the doctrine of the *Tractatus* and logical positivism. Both are agreed, for example, about the logical status of the propositions of logic and pure mathematics and about the fact that no empirical statement is necessarily true.[3] Further, both the *Tractatus* and logical positivism exclude metaphysical propositions, that is, if considered as providing, or as capable or providing, information about the world, which is either true or false. But while in the *Tractatus* this exclusion follows from Wittgenstein's definition of the proposition and his identification of the totality of propositions with the totality of scientific propositions, in logical positivism it follows from a certain criterion of meaning, namely that the meaning of a 'proposition' or factually informative statement is identical with the mode of its verification, verification being understood in terms of possible sense-experiences. And it is at any rate disputable whether this criterion of meaning is necessarily implied by what Wittgenstein has to say in the *Tractatus*. To be sure, if a proposition asserts or denies a possible state of affairs, we cannot be said to know what it means unless we have sufficient knowledge of the state of affairs which would make it true to be able to distinguish between this state of affairs and the state of affairs which would make it false. In this sense we must know what would verify the proposition. But it by no means necessarily follows that the meaning of the proposition or factually informative statement is identical with the mode of its verification, if 'mode of verification' signifies what we or anyone else could *do* to verify the statement.

In any case, even if those are right who think that the logical

---

[1] Such talk is obviously excluded if every proposition is a picture or representation of a possible state of affairs *in* the world. True, Wittgenstein himself speaks about the world as a whole. But he is perfectly ready to admit that to do so is to attempt to say what cannot be said.

[2] The Vienna Circle was not a group of 'disciples' of Schlick but rather a group of like-minded persons, some of them philosophers, others scientists or mathematicians, who agreed on a common general programme.

[3] These two points, if taken alone, do not constitute logical positivism. Taken alone, they would admit, for example, the possibility of an inductive metaphysics which proposed its theories as provisional hypotheses.

positivist criterion of meaning is implicitly contained in the *Tractatus*, there seems to be a considerable difference of atmosphere between this work and the typical attitude of the logical positivists in the heyday of their early enthusiasm. The positivists admitted indeed that metaphysical statements could possess an emotive-evocative significance;[1] but some of them at least made it clear that in their opinion metaphysics was a pack of nonsense in the popular, and not simply in a technical, sense. If, however, we consider what Wittgenstein has to say about the metaphysical subject,[2] we can discern a certain seriousness and profundity of thought. To attempt to say something about the metaphysical subject, the I-subject as a pole of consciousness, is inevitably to reduce it to the status of an object. All statements about the metaphysical subject are thus attempts to say what cannot be said. At the same time in a real sense the metaphysical subject shows itself as the limit of 'my world', as the correlative of the object. Strictly speaking, not even this can be said. None the less attempts to do so can facilitate our in some sense 'seeing' what cannot be *said*. But the 'mysticism' which makes an occasional appearance in the *Tractatus* was not congenial to the logical positivists.

To all intents and purposes logical positivism was introduced into England by the publication in 1936 of *Language, Truth and Logic*[3] by A. J. Ayer (b. 1910). This book, with its drastic and lively attack on metaphysics and theology, enjoyed a *succès de scandale*; and it remains as probably the clearest exposition of dogmatic logical positivism. But though logical positivism, as mediated by this work, certainly attracted a great deal of attention, it can hardly be said to have won a notable degree of acceptance among professional philosophers in Great Britain.[4] For the matter of that, Professor Ayer himself has considerably modified his views, as can be seen from his later writings.[5] And it

---

[1] A statement is said to possess emotive-evocative significance if it expresses an emotive attitude and is designed, not so much by conscious intention as by its nature, to evoke a similar emotive attitude in others.

[2] Cf. *Tractatus*, 5.62–5.641. Cf. also *Notebooks, 1914–1916* (Oxford, 1961), pp. 79–80, where a certain influence by Schopenhauer is evident.

[3] Second edition, 1946.

[4] We can note in passing that Professor R. B. Braithwaite of Cambridge has made a much-discussed attempt to reconcile his logical positivism with his adherence to Christianity. See, for example, his lecture, *An Empiricist's View of the Nature of Religious Belief*, Cambridge, 1955.

[5] These include *The Foundations of Empirical Knowledge* (1940), *Thinking and Meaning* (1947), *Philosophical Essays* (1954), *The Concept of a Person and Other Essays* (1963).

is now generally recognized that logical positivism constituted an interlude in the development of modern British philosophy.[1]

Meanwhile Wittgenstein was engaged in changing his views.[2] In the *Tractatus* he had tried to exhibit the 'essence' of the proposition. And the effect of his definition had been to place descriptive language in a privileged position. For it was only descriptive statements which were recognized as possessing meaning (*Sinn*). He came, however, to see more clearly the complexity of language, the fact that there are many kinds of propositions, descriptive statements forming only one class. In other words, Wittgenstein came to have a clearer view of actual language as a complex vital phenomenon, as something which in the context of human life has many functions or uses. And this understanding was accompanied by a radical change in Wittgenstein's conception of meaning. Meaning became use or function and was no longer dentical with 'picturing'.

If we apply these ideas to logical positivism, the result is the dethronement of the language of science from the position of a uniquely privileged language. For logical positivism meant in effect the selection of the language of science as the model language. Its criterion of meaning, as applied to synthetic propositions in general, was the result of an extension or extrapolation of a certain analysis of the scientific statement, namely as a prediction of certain possible sensible experiences. And, apart from the question whether or not this analysis of the scientific statement is tenable, the dethronement of scientific language as the model language involved the abandonment of the logical positivist criterion of meaning, if considered as a general criterion. Hence, whatever one may think of the precise relation between the *Tractatus* and logical positivism, Wittgenstein's later ideas about language were certainly incompatible with dogmatic logical positivism.

At the same time Wittgenstein had no intention of resuscitating the idea of the philosopher which was excluded by the *Tractatus*, the idea, that is to say, of the philosopher as capable of extending our factual knowledge of the world by pure thought or philosophical reflection. The difference between the concept of the

[1] This is not always recognized by continental philosophers, some of whom still seem to be under the impression that practically all British philosophers are logical positivists.
[2] These are represented by posthumously published writings. *The Blue and Brown Books* (Oxford, 1958), contains notes dictated to pupils in the period 1933–5. *Philosophical Investigations* (Oxford, 1953) represents Wittgenstein's later ideas.

function of philosophy offered in the *Tractatus* and that offered in *Philosophical Investigations* is not one between a revolutionary concept and a traditional concept. Wittgenstein sees himself as having attempted in the *Tractatus* to reform language, to interfere with its actual use, by, for example, equating the proposition with the descriptive statement, and indeed, if we take literally his identification of the totality of propositions with the totality of the natural sciences, with the scientific statement. In *Philosophical Investigations*, however, we are told that 'philosophy may in no way interfere with the actual use of language; it can in the end only describe it'.[1] Negatively, philosophy uncovers examples of nonsense resulting from our not understanding the limits of language;[2] positively, it has the function of describing the actual use of language.

The sort of thing that Wittgenstein has in mind can be explained with the aid of his own analogy of games.[3] Suppose that someone asks me what a game is. And suppose that I reply in this way: 'Well, tennis, football, cricket, chess, bridge, golf, racquets, baseball are all games. And then there are others too, playing at Red Indians, for example, or hide-and-seek.' The other man might retort impatiently: 'I am perfectly well aware of all this. But I did not ask you what activities are customarily called "games": I asked you what a game is, that is to say, I wanted to know the definition of a game, what is the essence of "game". You are as bad as Socrates' young friends who, when asked what beauty is, started mentioning beautiful things or people.' To this I might reply: 'Oh, I see. You imagine that because we use one word "game", it must signify one meaning, one single essence. But this is a mistake. There are only games. There are indeed resemblances, of various sorts. Some games are played with a ball, for example. But chess is not. And even in the case of games which are played with a ball the balls are of different kinds. Consider football, cricket, golf, tennis. True games have some sort of rules, explicit or implicit. But the rules differ with different games. And in any case a definition of "game" in terms of rules would hardly be adequate. There are rules of conduct in criminal courts, but the processes of law are not generally recognized as games. In other words, the only proper answer to your original question is to remind you how the word "game" is used in actual language. You

---

[1] I, s. 124.   [2] I, s. 119.
[3] Cf. *Philosophical Investigations*, I, ss. 66–9, 75.

may not be satisfied. But in this case you are evidently still labouring under the mistaken idea that there must be a single meaning, a single essence, corresponding to each common word. If you insist that we must find such a meaning or essence, you are really insisting on a reform of or interference with language.'

In using this sort of analogy Wittgenstein is clearly thinking primarily of his own attempt in the *Tractatus* to give the essence of the proposition, whereas in point of fact there are many kinds of propositions, many kinds of sentences, descriptive statements, commands, prayers, and so on.[1] But his point of view possesses a wider field of application. Suppose, for example, that a philosopher identifies the 'I' or self with the pure subject or, alternatively, with the body in the sense in which we commonly use the term 'body'. Has he given the essence of 'I', of the self or ego? Wittgenstein might point out that neither interpretation of the pronoun 'I' is compatible with the actual use of language. For example, the identification of the 'I' with the metaphysical subject is not compatible with such a sentence as 'I go for a walk'. Nor is the identification of the 'I' with the body in the ordinary sense compatible with such a sentence as 'I consider Tolstoy a greater writer than Ethel M. Dell'.

This way of disposing of exaggerated philosophical theories, interpreted as attempts to 'reform' language, is described by Wittgenstein as bringing words 'back from their metaphysical to their everyday usage'.[2] And it obviously presupposes that actual language is all right as it is. Consequently, it is all the more necessary to understand that Wittgenstein is not excluding, for example, the technical language which has been developed in order to express man's growing scientific knowledge and new scientific concepts and hypotheses. What he is opposed to is the belief that the philosopher is capable of digging out, as it were, or revealing hidden meanings, hidden essences. And the only reform of language which he allows the philosopher is the restatement which may be required in order to clear up those confusions and misunderstandings which give rise to what Wittgenstein considers to be bogus philosophical problems and theories. Reform of this kind, however, is simply designed to bring out the real logic of actual language. Philosophy can thus be said to aim at the elimination of difficulties, perplexities, problems, which arise from our not understanding the actual use of language. In spite,

---

[1] Cf. *Philosophical Investigations*, I, s. 23.   [2] *Ibid.*, I, s. 116.

therefore, of the change in Wittgenstein's view of language, his general idea of philosophy as a kind of linguistic therapeutic remains the same in broad outline.

Though, however, Wittgenstein himself did not hesitate to dogmatize about the nature and function of philosophy, those philosophers who either have been influenced by his post-*Tractatus* line of reflection or have thought much the same thoughts for themselves, have, generally speaking, refrained from dogmatic pronouncements of this sort. For example, in his 1931 paper on 'Systematically Misleading Expressions'[1] Professor Gilbert Ryle of Oxford (b. 1900), while announcing that he had come to the conclusion that the business of philosophy was at least, and might be no more than, the detection in linguistic idioms of recurrent misconstructions and absurd theories, added that his conversion to this view was reluctant and that he would like to be able to think that philosophy had a more sublime task. In any case if one looks at the writings of those British philosophers who sympathize with Wittgenstein's later ideas, one can see that they have devoted themselves to the implementation of the positive programme of 'describing' the actual use of language rather than simply to the rather negative task of eliminating puzzles or difficulties.

The implementation of the positive programme can take various forms. That is to say, the emphasis can be differently placed. It is possible, for example, to concentrate on exhibiting the peculiar characteristics of different types of language in the sense in which the language of science, the language of morals, the language of the religious consciousness and aesthetic language constitute different types; and one can compare one type of language with another. When the logical positivists turned scientific language into a model language, they tended to lump together a number of other different kinds of propositions as possessing only emotive-evocative significance. The dethronement, however, of scientific language from the position of the model language, except, of course, for specific purposes, naturally encouraged a more careful examination of other types of language, taken separately. And a great deal of work has been done on the language of morals.[2] Again, there has been an appreciable amount

---

[1] Originally published in the *Proceedings of the Aristotelian Society*, this paper was reprinted in *Logic and Language*, Vol. I (Oxford, 1951), edited by A. G. N. Flew.

[2] Cf., for example, *The Language of Morals* (Oxford, 1952) and *Freedom and Reason* (Oxford, 1963), by R. M. Hare.

of discussion of the language of religion. If, for instance, we wish to determine the range of meaning of the term 'God', it is not of much use to say that it is 'meaningless' because it is not a scientific term. We have to examine its uses and functions in the language which, as Wittgenstein puts it, is 'its native home'.[1] Further, one can compare the use of images and analogies in religious language with their use in, say, the language of poetry. It is indeed probably true to say that in the discussion of religious language in recent British philosophy the factor which has attracted the most public attention has been the contention of some philosophers that this or that religious statement really says nothing because it excludes nothing.[2] But it must be remembered that the discussion as a whole brought once more into prominence the subject of analogical language, a theme which was treated by a number of medieval thinkers but which, with some exceptions, was little treated by later philosophers.[3]

It is also possible to concentrate not so much on different general types of language in the sense mentioned above as on the different kinds of sentences in ordinary colloquial language and on the distinctions made in or implied by such language. This kind of mapping-out of ordinary language was characteristic of the late Professor J. L. Austin (1911–60) of Oxford, who distinguished himself by his meticulous care in differentiating between types of 'speech-acts'[4] and showed by actual analysis how inadequate was the logical positivist classification of propositions, and how much more complex and subtle ordinary language is than one might think.

Not unnaturally a good deal of criticism has been levelled against this concentration on ordinary language. For at first sight it looks as though philosophy were being reduced to a trivial occupation or a practically useless game played for its own sake by a number of university professors and lecturers. But though the practitioners of the analysis of ordinary language, notably Austin, have deliberately chosen examples of sentences which make those

[1] *Philosophical Investigations*, I, s. 116.
[2] See, for instance, the discussion on 'Theology and Falsification' which was reprinted in *New Essays in Philosophical Theology*, edited by A. G. N. Flew and A. MacIntyre (London, 1955).
[3] Berkeley has something to say on the matter. Kant refers to symbolic language in a theological context. And Hegel, of course, discusses the 'pictorial' language of religion in its relation to aesthetics on the one hand and philosophy on the other.
[4] See, for example, Austin's posthumously published *Philosophical Papers* (Oxford, 1961) and *How to do Things with Words* (Oxford, 1962).

who are accustomed to talk about Being raise their eyebrows, in the opinion of the present writer such analysis is by no means useless. For example, in the development of language in response to experience human beings have expressed in a concrete way a multitude of distinctions between varying degrees of responsibility. And the activity of reflecting on and mapping out these distinctions can be of considerable use. On the one hand it serves the purpose of drawing our attention to factors which have to be taken into account in any adequate discussion of moral responsibility. On the other hand it sets us on our guard when confronted with philosophical theories which ride roughshod, in one direction or another, over the distinctions which human experience has found it necessary to express. It may indeed be objected that ordinary language is not an infallible criterion by which to judge philosophical theories. But Austin did not say that it was. He may have tended to act as though he thought this. But in word at least he disclaimed any such dogmatism, simply observing that in a conflict between theory and ordinary language the latter was more likely to be right than the former, and that in any case philosophers, when constructing their theories, neglected ordinary language at their peril.[1] In any case, even if we consider that the importance of ordinary language has been exaggerated, it does not necessarily follow that we have to consider examination of such language useless or irrelevant to philosophy.

The point can be made clearer perhaps by reference to Professor G. Ryle's celebrated book, *The Concept of Mind* (London, 1949). From one point of view it is a dissolution of the theory of 'the ghost in the machine', the dualistic theory attributed to Descartes, by means of an examination of what we are accustomed to say about man and his mental activities in ordinary language. But from another point of view it might be considered as an attempt to exhibit the concept of mind, and indeed of the nature of man, which finds concrete expression in the sentences of ordinary language. And such an attempt is undoubtedly useful and relevant to philosophy.[2] Obviously, if one works backwards, as it were, from a philosophical theory to a view implicit in ordinary language, one is returning to a point antecedent to the raising of

---

[1] In *Sense and Sensibilia* (Oxford, 1962), a posthumous work representing courses of lectures, Austin tries to dispose of a particular philosophical theory, namely the sense-datum theory.

[2] Whether Professor Ryle's attempt is successful or unsuccessful and how far it embodies the author's own theories, are not questions which need detain us here.

philosophical problems. And the only valid reason for stopping there would be the belief that any real problems which then arise are not philosophical in character but psychological or physiological or both, belonging, that is to say, to science and not to philosophy. At the same time it is useful to remind oneself and obtain a clear view of what we ordinarily say about man. For ordinary language certainly favours a view of man as a unity; and in so far as this view can be considered as expressing man's experience of himself, it has to be taken into account.

And yet, of course, it is a great mistake to oppose ordinary language to theory, as though the former were entirely free of the latter. Apart from the fact that theories and beliefs of one kind or another leave their deposits, as it were, in ordinary language, our language is not in any case a simple photograph of bare facts. It expresses interpretation. Hence it cannot be used as a touchstone of truth. And philosophy cannot be simply uncritical of so-called ordinary language. Nor can it be critical without indulging in theory.

Needless to say, this is not a discovery of the present writer. It is a matter of common recognition.[1] Hence it is only to be expected that in recent years the concept of philosophy should have tended to broaden, even within the analytic movement itself. One expression of this process, in certain circles at least, has been the displacement of the dogmatic restriction of the nature and scope of philosophy, which was characteristic of Wittgenstein, by an attitude of tolerance which is willing to give a hearing even to the avowed metaphysician, provided, of course, that he is prepared to explain why he says what he does. But it is not simply a matter of toleration, of the growth of a more 'ecumenical' spirit. There have also been signs of a developing conviction that analysis is not enough. For example, in *Thought and Action*,[2] Professor Stuart Hampshire observed that the language of ethics cannot be adequately treated unless it is examined in the light of the function of such language in human life. Hence the need for a philosophical anthropology.

The concentration on ordinary language, however, which is in harmony with the ideas expounded by Wittgenstein in *Philosophical Investigations*, represents only one tendency, even if a prominent one, in the analytic movement as a whole. For it has

[1] See, for instance, Professor A. J. Ayer's inaugural lecture at Oxford, which forms the first chapter in his book, *The Concept of a Person*.
[2] London, 1959.

long been recognized that a great deal of what was popularly called 'linguistic analysis' would be far better described as 'conceptual analysis'. And the idea of conceptual analysis can open up wide vistas. For instance, in his well-known book *Individuals: An Essay in Descriptive Metaphysics*[1] Mr. P. F. Strawson of Oxford spoke of descriptive metaphysics as exploring and describing the actual structure of our thought about the world, that is, as describing the most general features of our conceptual structure, whereas revisionary metaphysics is concerned with changing our conceptual structure, with making us see the world in a new light. Revisionary metaphysics was not condemned, but descriptive metaphysics, in the sense explained, was said to need no further justification than that of inquiry in general.

In so far as generalization in this matter is legitimate, it seems safe to say that the following remarks represent an attitude towards metaphysics which is not uncommonly adopted by contemporary British philosophers. To describe metaphysics as meaningless, as the logical positivists did, is to pass over the obvious fact that the great metaphysical systems of the past often expressed visions of the world which can be stimulating and, in their several ways, illuminating. Further, in the context of logical positivism to say that metaphysical propositions are meaningless is really to say that they are different from scientific propositions.[2] This is true enough; but it contributes little to an understanding of metaphysics as an historical phenomenon. To obtain this understanding we have to examine actual metaphysical systems with a view to sorting out the various types of metaphysics and the different kinds of arguments employed.[3] For it is a mistake to suppose that they all conform to one invariable pattern. Again, we cannot legitimately take it for granted that metaphysics is simply an attempt to answer questions which arise out of 'the bewitchment of our intelligence by means of language'.[4] This is a matter for detailed examination. Moreover, it is clear that the

---

[1] London, 1959.
[2] That is to say, this is the essential factual content of the description. A judgment of value may also, of course, be included or implied.
[3] *The Nature of Metaphysics* (edited by D. F. Pears, London, 1957) represents a series of broadcast talks by different philosophers, including Professor Ryle. The general attitude to metaphysics is critical but comparatively sympathetic. A considerably more extensive examination of metaphysics is undertaken by Professor W. H. Walsh of Edinburgh University in *Metaphysics* (London, 1963).
[4] *Philosophical Investigations*, I, s. 109. The fact that some writers have appealed to psycho-analysis as perhaps capable of explaining the recurrence of a particular type of metaphysics, such as monism, shows at any rate that they consider metaphysics to have roots which go deeper than linguistic or logical confusion.

impulse to develop a unified interpretation of the world in terms of a set of concepts and categories is not something intrinsically improper or blameworthy. True, since the time of Kant we cannot accept the idea that the philosopher is capable of deducing the existence of any entity in an *a priori* manner. Further, before attempting to construct large-scale syntheses it would be wiser to do more spade-work by tackling precise questions separately. At the same time philosophical problems tend to interlock; and in any case it would be absurd to attempt to ban metaphysical synthesis. The construction of a world-view or *Weltanschauung* is indeed a somewhat different activity from that of trying to answer particular questions to which, in principle, quite definite answers can be given. But while the demand that philosophers who are interested in pursuing the second sort of activity should devote themselves to synthesis instead is unjustified, a wholesale condemnation of metaphysical synthesis is also unreasonable.

As far as it goes, this growth of a more tolerant attitude towards forms of philosophy other than the microscopic analysis which has been a conspicuous feature of recent British thought is something to be welcomed. Taken by itself, however, it leaves a good many questions unanswered. Suppose, for the sake of argument, that we accept the restriction of philosophy to the clarification of propositions which are not philosophical propositions, the restriction which is made in the *Tractatus*. The presupposition is clear enough, namely that philosophy is not a discipline with a special subject-matter of its own, alongside the particular sciences.[1] The philosopher cannot enunciate philosophical propositions which increase our knowledge of the world. If, however, we drop the dogmatic restriction of the nature and scope of philosophy and show ourselves prepared to regard metaphysics, at least in some recognizable form, as a legitimate philosophical activity, we can reasonably be expected to explain what change in the concept of philosophy is implied by this concession. It is really not sufficient to say that we do not undertake to reform language, and that the word 'philosophy', as actually used, certainly covers metaphysics, whereas it no longer covers physics or biology. For the following question can always be asked: 'When you say that you have no wish to prohibit metaphysics, do you mean simply that if some people feel the urge to develop theories which are akin to poetic and imaginative visions

[1] This is explicitly stated in the *Tractatus*, 4.111.

of reality, and which cannot legitimately lay claim to represent or increase knowledge, you have no desire to interfere with them? Or are you seriously prepared to admit the possibility that metaphysics is capable in some sense of increasing our knowledge? If so, in what sense? And what do you think that metaphysical knowledge is or could be about or of?'

The analytic philosophers might, of course, reply that it is simply a question of their being prepared to give the metaphysician a hearing instead of barring the way in advance to all dialogue and mutual understanding. It is the metaphysician's business to explain what he is about. When he has done so, his own account of his activities can be examined.

Though, however, this line of reply is reasonable up to a point, it seems to neglect two facts. First, if we repudiate a dogmatic restrictive definition of philosophy, this repudiation has implications. And it is not unreasonable if we are invited to make them explicit. Secondly, as the analytic philosophers like to point out, they do not constitute a completely 'homogeneous' school. On the contrary, several rather different tendencies are discernible; and it is obvious enough from an examination of their writings that a number of philosophers who would popularly be classed as 'analysts' are doing something very different from what could accurately be described as 'linguistic analysis'. It is all very well for them to say that they are doing 'philosophy'. No doubt they are. But what is philosophy in this wide sense? What precisely is its nature, function and scope? It is in regard to their British colleagues' view on such general issues that the continental philosopher of a different tradition is apt to find himself hopelessly at sea.

The conclusion to be drawn is perhaps that the so-called revolution in philosophy has lost any clearly defined shape, and that no clear concept of the nature of philosophy has yet taken the place of the various restrictive definitions proposed by the logical positivists, by the *Tractatus* and then again by *Philosophical Investigations*. This obviously does not prevent British philosophers from doing valuable work on particular themes. But it means that the external observer may well be left wondering what particular game is being played, and why. What is the relevance of philosophy to life? And why is it thought necessary to have chairs of philosophy in universities? Such questions may be naïve, but they require an answer.

APPENDIX A
JOHN HENRY NEWMAN

Introductory remarks—Newman's approach to the problem of religious belief in his university sermons—The approach in The Grammar of Assent—*Conscience and God—The convergence of probabilities and the illative sense—Final remarks.*

1. To say that we are concerned here with John Henry Newman (1801–90) simply as a philosopher is perhaps somewhat misleading. For it might be understood as suggesting that in addition to his many other interests and activities Newman devoted himself to philosophical problems for their own sake, for their intrinsic interest as theoretical puzzles. And this would be far from the truth. Newman's approach to the philosophical topics which he discussed was that of a Christian apologist. That is to say, he wrote from the point of view of a Christian believer who asks himself to what extent, and in what way, his faith can be shown to be reasonable. Newman made no pretence of temporarily discarding his faith, as it were, in order to give the impression of starting all over again from scratch. He tried, of course, to understand other people's points of view. But his discussion of religious belief was conducted, as it might be expressed, within the area of faith. That is to say, it was a question of faith seeking understanding of itself rather than of an unbelieving mind wondering whether there was any rational justification for making an act of faith. At the same time the attempt to show that Christian belief is in fact reasonable led Newman to develop philosophical ideas. To put the matter in another way, his attempt to exhibit the insufficiency of contemporary rationalism and to convey a sense of the Christian vision of human existence led him to delineate lines of thought which, while certainly not intended to present the content of Christian belief as a set of conclusions logically deduced from self-evident principles, were meant to show to those who had eyes to see that religious faith was not the expression of an irrational attitude or a purely arbitrary assumption. And even if it involves a certain mutilation of his thought as a whole, we can pick out for brief consideration here some of the lines of thought which can reasonably be described as philosophical.

Now there have been apologists who concerned themselves not so much with the reasons people actually have for believing as with developing arguments which, in their opinion, should convince the minds of any unbelievers capable of understanding the terms used, though the ordinary believer may never have thought of these arguments at all and might even be incapable of understanding and appreciating them if they were presented to him. Newman, however, is more concerned with showing the reasonableness of faith as it actually exists in the great mass of believers, most of whom know nothing of abstract philosophical arguments. And he tries to make explicit what seems to him to be the chief ground which he himself and other people have for a living belief in God.[1] In other words, he tries to outline a phenomenological analysis of the spontaneous movement of the mind culminating in assent to the existence of God as a present reality. At the same time he obviously does not intend to write simply as a psychologist who may describe various reasons why people believe in God, even if some or all these reasons appear to him unable to justify assent to God's existence. On the contrary, Newman argues that the main empirical ground on which belief rests is a sufficient ground.

An analogy may clarify the point. We all have a practical belief in the objective existence of external objects independently of their being perceived by us. And there is clearly a difference between making explicit the grounds which people actually have for this belief and trying, as some philosophers have done, to justify the belief by excogitating philosophical arguments which are thought to provide better and sounder grounds for belief than those which people actually have, even if they are not reflectively aware of them. Indeed, it is arguable that the philosopher is not in a position to provide better grounds for the belief in question than those on which our belief actually, if implicitly, rests. Analogously, Newman is very conscious of the difference between showing that religious belief, as it actually exists, is reasonable and showing that it would be reasonable if people had other grounds for believing than those which they in fact have.

There is a further point which is worth noticing. When Newman talks about belief in God, he is thinking of what we might call a living belief, a belief which involves an element of personal commitment to a personal being apprehended as a present reality and which tends to influence conduct, not about a mere notional assent to an abstract proposition. Hence when he is reflecting on grounds for belief in God, he tends to neglect impersonal metaphysical arguments addressed simply to the intellect and to concentrate on the movement of the mind which, in his opinion, brings a man up against God as a present reality, as manifested in the voice of conscience. His line of thought is therefore addressed to the man who has a lively sense of moral obligation. Similarly, when dealing with the evidences for the truth of Christianity he is speaking primarily to the genuine and open-minded

---

[1] Newman does not, of course, exclude the role of grace. But he prescinds from it when he is trying to show that a sufficient ground for belief in God is available to all.

inquirer, particularly to the man who already believes in God, and who has, as Newman puts it, a presentiment of the possibility of revelation. In both cases he presupposes certain subjective conditions, including moral conditions, in his reader. He does not profess to provide demonstrations modelled on those of mathematics.

Given this approach, it is not surprising that the name of Newman has often been linked with that of Pascal. Both men were concerned with Christian apologetics, and both fixed their attention on effective belief and on the way in which people actually think and reason in concrete issues rather than on a mathematical model of demonstration. The 'spirit of geometry' was alien to both minds. And both emphasized the moral conditions for appreciating the force of arguments in favour of Christianity. If therefore someone excludes Pascal from the class of philosophers on the ground that he was a special pleader, he is likely to treat Newman in the same way. Conversely, if someone recognizes Pascal as a philosopher, he is likely to accord a similar recognition to Newman.[1]

Newman's philosophical background was, however, very different from that of Pascal. For it was constituted to a large extent by British philosophy. As a student Newman acquired some knowledge of Aristotle. And though nobody would call him an Aristotelian, the Greek philosopher certainly exercised some influence on his mind. As for Platonism, which in certain respects he found congenial, Newman's knowledge of it seems to have been obtained mainly from certain early Christian writers and the Fathers. Of British philosophers he certainly studied Francis Bacon, and he knew something of Hume, whom he considered acute but dangerous; but in the *Apologia* he states that he never studied Berkeley. For Locke, however, he felt a profound respect. He tells us explicitly that he felt this respect 'both for the character and the ability of Locke, for his manly simplicity of mind and his outspoken candour';[2] and he adds that 'there is so much in his remarks upon reasoning and proof in which I fully concur, that I feel no pleasure in considering him in the light of an opponent to views which I myself have ever cherished as true'.[3] Besides Locke we must mention Bishop Butler,[4] who exercised an obvious and admitted influence on Newman's mind.

Later on Newman studied the writings of Dean Mansel (1820–71),

[1] It is as well to remember that the constructors of original metaphysical systems have often employed argument to commend views of reality already present to their minds, at least in outline. Yet this fact does not by itself show that a given argument is devoid of force. Analogously, the fact that Newman writes as a Christian believer does not necessarily entail the conclusion that his philosophical reflections are valueless.
[2] *An Essay in Aid of a Grammar of Assent* (3rd edition, 1870), p. 155. This work will be referred to as *GA*.
[3] *Ibid.*
[4] For Bishop Joseph Butler (1692–1752), see Vol. V of this *History*, pp. 165–70 and 184–91.

of some of the Scottish philosophers and the *Logic* of J. S. Mill. Further, in spite of a disclaimer on his part, it can be shown that he had some acquaintance with Coleridge. Of German thought, however, Newman appears to have known little, particularly at first-hand. If therefore we leave the early study of Aristotle out of account, we can say that his philosophical ideas were formed in the climate of British empiricism and of the influence of Butler. Newman's varied interests and activities left him indeed little time and energy for serious philosophical reading, even if he had had the inclination to read widely in this field. But in any case what he did read was simply a stimulus for forming his own ideas. He was never what would be called a disciple of any philosopher.

As for Scholastic philosophy, Newman knew little about it. In later years he at any rate possessed some writings by pioneers in the revival of Scholasticism. And when Leo XIII published his Encyclical *Aeterni Patris* in 1870, urging the study of St. Thomas, Newman composed, even if he did not send, an appreciative letter to the Pope. But it is fairly evident from the letter that what he had in mind was a revival of intellectual life in the Church, in continuity with the thought of the Fathers and Doctors, rather than of Thomism in particular. And in any case the old-fashioned textbook Thomism would hardly have been congenial to Newman's mind. It is true that since his death a number of Scholastic philosophers have adopted or adapted lines of thought suggested by his writings and have used them to supplement traditional arguments. But it scarcely needs saying that this fact provides no adequate reason for making out that Newman was 'really' a Scholastic. His approach was quite different, though he was quite willing to admit that other approaches might have their uses.

2. In a university sermon which he preached at Oxford in 1839 Newman insists that faith 'is certainly an exercise of Reason'[1]. For the exercise of reason lies 'in asserting one thing, because of some other thing.'[2] It can be seen in the extension of our knowledge beyond the immediate objects of sense-perception and of introspection;[3] and it can be seen also in religious belief or faith, inasmuch as this is 'an acceptance of things as real, which the senses do not convey, upon certain previous grounds'.[4] In other words, as Newman does not postulate any faculty of intuiting God (or indeed any external immaterial being), he must admit that in some sense at least the existence of God is inferred.

Reasoning, however, is not necessarily correct: there can be faulty reasoning. And Newman is well aware that for the rationalist any

---

[1] *Oxford University Sermons* (*Fifteen sermons preached before the University of Oxford*) (3rd edition, 1872), p. 207. This work will be referred to as *OUS*. Newman obviously means that faith presupposes an exercise of reason.
[2] *Ibid.*
[3] We can see here a reflection of the empiricist point of view.
[4] *OUS*, p. 207.

process of reasoning or inference presupposed by religious faith is invalid. According to the popular or common idea of reason and its exercise we should exclude the influence of all prejudices, preconceptions and temperamental differences and proceed simply according to 'certain scientific rules and fixed standards for weighing testimony and examining facts'[1], admitting only such conclusions 'as can produce their reasons'.[2] It is evident, however, that most believers are unable to produce reasons for their belief. And even when they are, it by no means follows that they began to believe for this reason or that they will cease believing if the reasons are challenged or placed in doubt. Further, 'faith is a principle of action, and action does not allow time for minute and finished investigations'.[3] Faith does not demand unquestionable demonstration; and it is influenced by antecedent probabilities and presumptions. True, this is frequently verified in the case of non-religious belief. For example, we frequently believe what we read in the newspapers, without any examination of the evidence. But though this behaviour is undoubtedly necessary for life, the fact remains that what appears probable or credible to one man may appear in quite a different light to someone else. 'It is scarcely necessary to point out how much our inclinations have to do with our belief.'[4] It is thus easy to understand the rationalist depreciation of faith as the expression of wishful thinking.

In a real sense, of course, unbelief or scepticism is in the same boat as faith. For unbelief 'really goes upon presumptions and prejudices as much as Faith does, only presumptions of an opposite nature. . . . It considers a religious system so improbable, that it will not listen to the evidence of it; or, if it listens, it employs itself in doing what a believer could do, if he chose, quite as well . . .; viz., in showing that the evidence might be more complete and unexceptionable than it is.'[5] Sceptics do not really decide according to the evidence; for they make up their minds first and then admit or reject evidence according to their initial assumption. Hume provides a signal example of this when he suggests that the impossibility of miracles is sufficient refutation of the testimony of witnesses. 'That is, the antecedent improbability is a sufficient refutation of the evidence.'[6]

Newman seems to be quite justified in suggesting that unbelievers often proceed according to assumptions, and that they are as open as anyone else to the influence of inclination and temperament. But though this is a polemical point of some value, it obviously does not show that faith, considered as what Newman calls an exercise of reason, measures up to the standard demanded by the rationalist, if this standard is understood as that of strict logical demonstration from self-evident principles. Newman, however, has no intention of pretending

---

[1] *OUS*, p. 229.   [2] *Ibid.*, p. 230.   [3] *Ibid.*, p. 188.
[4] *Ibid.*, p. 189.   [5] *Ibid.*, p. 230.   [6] *Ibid.*, p. 231.

that it does. He argues instead that the rationalist conception of reasoning is far too narrow and does not square with the way in which people actually, and legitimately, think and reason in concrete issues. It must be remembered that his contention is that faith is reasonable, not that its content is logically deducible according to the model of mathematical demonstration.

It is no valid argument against the reasonableness of religious faith to say that it assumes what are judged to be antecedent probabilities. For we all find ourselves under the necessity of making assumptions, if we are to live at all. We cannot live simply by what is logically demonstrable. For example, we cannot demonstrate that our senses are trustworthy, and that there is an objective external world with which they put us in contact. Nor can we demonstrate the validity of memory. Yet in spite of our being sometimes deceived, to express the matter in a popular way, we assume and cannot help assuming that our senses are fundamentally trustworthy, and that there is an objective external world. Indeed, nobody but the sceptic questions scientific inference as such, though the scientist does not prove the existence of a public physical world but assumes it. Again, we do not allow our mistakes and slips to destroy all belief in the validity of memory. Further, unless we try to adopt a position of complete scepticism, a position which we cannot maintain in practice, we necessarily assume the possibility of valid reasoning. We cannot demonstrate it *a priori*; for any attempt at demonstration presupposes what we are trying to demonstrate. In fine, 'whether we consider processes of Faith or other exercise of Reason, men advance forward on grounds which they do not, or cannot produce, or if they could, yet could not prove to be true, on latent or antecedent grounds which they take for granted'[1].

We can note in passing that in Newman's readiness to say that the existence of a public external world is an unprovable assumption we can perhaps discern an echo of his impression at an early age, an impression recorded in the first chapter of the *Apologia*, that there were only two luminously self-evident beings, himself and his Creator. But we are also reminded of Hume's contention that though we cannot prove the existence of bodies apart from our perceptions, Nature has placed us under the necessity of believing in it. A philosopher can indulge in sceptical reflections in his study; but in ordinary life he, like the rest of mankind, has a natural belief in the continued objective existence of bodies even when they are not perceived. Reason cannot demonstrate the truth of this belief. But the belief is none the less reasonable. The unreasonable man would be the one who tried to live as a sceptic and not to act on any assumption which could not be proved.

It is indeed obviously true that men cannot help believing in the

[1] *Ibid.*, pp. 212–13.

existence of an external, public world,[1] and that it would be unreasonable to attempt to act on any other assumption. If we refused to
act on anything but logically demonstrated conclusions, we could not
live at all. As Locke aptly remarked, if we refused to eat until it had
been demonstrated that the food would nourish us, we should not eat
at all. But it can be objected that belief in God is not a natural belief
comparable to that in the existence of an external world. We cannot
help believing in practice that bodies exist independently of our
perception; but there does not seem to be any such practical necessity
to believe in God.

Newman's line of argument is that there is something, namely
conscience, which belongs to human nature as much as do the powers
of perceiving and of reasoning, and which predisposes to belief in God,
in the sense that it carries with it a 'presentiment' of the divine
existence. A belief in God which is based on conscience is thus not
grounded simply on the temperamental idiosyncrasy of certain
individuals, but rather on a factor in human nature as such or at least
on a factor in every human nature which is not morally stunted or
maimed. The voice of conscience does not indeed carry with it any
proof of its own credentials. In this sense it is an 'assumption'. But it
manifests the presence of a transcendent God; and assent to the
existence of the God so manifested is reasonable.

Before, however, we consider Newman's argument from conscience
to the existence of God a little more closely, we can turn our attention to his approach to the problem of religious belief as outlined in
his much later work, *The Grammar of Assent*, which was published in
1870.[2]

3. Assent, as Newman uses the term, is given to a proposition and is
expressed by assertion. But I cannot properly be said to assent to a
proposition unless I understand its meaning. This understanding is
called by Newman apprehension. Hence we can say that assent presupposes apprehension.

There are, however, two types of apprehension, corresponding to two
types of propositions. 'The terms of a proposition do or do not stand
for things. If they do, then they are singular terms, for all things that
are, are units. But if they do not stand for things they must stand for
notions, and are common terms. Singular nouns come from experience,

---

[1] The present writer has no intention of committing himself to the view that
we cannot properly be said to know that there is an external world. Of course, if
we so define knowledge that only the propositions of logic and mathematics can
be said to be known to be true, it follows that we do not know that things exist
when we are not perceiving them. But as the word 'know' is used in ordinary
language, we can perfectly well be said to know it.

[2] It would be misleading to describe *The Grammar of Assent* as a philosophical
work, for in the long run it is concerned with 'the arguments adducible for
Christianity' (*GA*, p. 484). But these arguments are placed in a general logical and
epistemological context.

common from abstraction. The apprehension of the former I call real, and of the latter notional.'[1]

Exception might be taken to some of the expressions and statements in this quotation. But the general thesis seems to be reasonably clear. Apprehension or understanding of a term which stands for a thing or person is called real, while apprehension of an abstract idea or universal concept is called notional. If we apply this distinction to propositions, apprehension of, for example, a proposition in geometry would be notional, while the apprehension of the statement 'William is the father of James' would be real.

It follows from this that we must also distinguish between two types of assent. Assent given to a proposition apprehended as notional, as concerned with abstract ideas or universal terms, is notional assent, while that which is given to propositions apprehended as real, as concerned directly with things or persons, is real assent.

Now Newman takes it that things and persons, whether objects of actual experience or presented imaginatively in memory, strike the mind much more forcibly and vividly than do abstract notions. Real apprehension therefore is 'stronger than notional, because things, which are its objects, are confessedly more impressive and effective than notions, which are the object of notional [apprehension]. Experiences and their images strike and occupy the mind, as abstractions and their combinations do not.'[2] Similarly, although, according to Newman, all assent is alike in being unconditional,[3] acts of assent 'are elicited more heartily and forcibly, when they are made upon real apprehension which has things for its objects, than when they are made in favour of notions and with a notional apprehension'.[4] Further, real assent, though it does not necessarily affect conduct, tends to do so in a way in which purely notional assent does not.[5]

Real assent is also called belief by Newman. And it is obvious that the belief in God with which he is primarily concerned as a Christian apologist is a real assent to God as a present reality, and an assent which influences life or conduct, not simply a notional assent to a proposition about the idea of God. True, if assent is given to propositions, real assent will in this case be given to the proposition 'God exists' or 'there is a God'. But it will be given to the proposition apprehended as real, the term 'God' being understood as signifying a present reality, a present personal being. And from this it follows that Newman is not, and cannot be, primarily interested in a formal demonstrative inference to God's existence. For in his view, which recalls that of Hume, demonstration exhibits the logical relations between notions or ideas. That is to say, it derives conclusions from

---

[1] *GA*, pp. 20–1. [2] *Ibid.*, p. 35.
[3] So-called doubtful assent is for Newman unconditional assent to the statement that the truth of a given proposition is doubtful.
[4] *GA*, p. 17. [5] Cf. *ibid.*, p. 87.

premisses, the terms of which stand for abstract or general ideas. Thus the assent given to the conclusion is notional and lacks that element of personal commitment which Newman associates with real assent to the existence of God.

As has already been mentioned, however, Newman does not postulate in man any power of intuiting God directly. Hence some sort of inference is required, some movement of the mind from what is given in experience to what transcends immediate experience or perception. At the same time it must not be the type of inference which leads to notional rather than to real assent. Thus the following questions arise: 'Can I attain to any more vivid assent to the Being of a God, than that which is given merely to notions of the intellect? . . . Can I believe as if I saw?' Since such a high assent requires a present experience or memory of the fact, at first sight it would seem as if the answer must be in the negative; for how can I assent as if I saw, unless I have seen? But no one in this life can see God. Yet I conceive a real assent is possible, and I proceed to show how.'[1] Newman's attempt to show how this real assent is possible will be considered in the next section.

4. We have seen that according to Newman even our non-religious beliefs rest on at any rate latent assumptions.[2] Something is taken for granted, whether explicitly or implicitly. There is some point of departure which is taken as given, without proof. In the case of belief in God this point of departure, the given basis of the movement of the mind, is conscience. Conscience is as much a factor in human nature, in the complex of mental acts, 'as the action of memory, of reasoning, of imagination, or as the sense of the beautiful'.[3] And it is 'the essential principle and sanction of Religion in the mind'.[4]

Conscience, however, can be considered under two aspects which, though not separate in fact, are none the less distinguishable. In the first place we can consider it as a rule of right conduct, as judging about the rightness or wrongness of particular actions. And it is an empirical fact that different people have made different ethical judgments. Some societies, for example, have approved conduct which other societies have condemned. In the second place we can consider conscience simply as the voice of authority, that is, as imposing obligation. And the sense of obligation is essentially the same in all who possess a conscience. Even if A thinks that he ought to act in one way while B

---

[1] *GA*, p. 99.

[2] As for formal demonstrative inference, this, Newman insists, is conditional. That is to say, the truth of the conclusion is asserted on the condition of the premisses being true. And though Newman himself does not deny that there are self-evident principles, he points out that what seems self-evident to one man does not necessarily seem self-evident to another. In any case the possibility of valid reasoning is assumed. If we try to prove everything and to make no assumptions whatsoever, we shall never get anywhere.

[3] *GA*, p. 102.   [4] *Ibid.*, p. 18.

thinks that he ought to act in another way, the consciousness of obligation, considered in itself, is similar in both men.

Considered under this second aspect, as the voice of internal authority,
conscience 'vaguely reaches forward to something beyond self, and
dimly discerns a sanction higher than self for its decisions, as evidenced
in that keen sense of obligation and responsibility which informs
them'.[1] The inward law of conscience does not indeed carry with it any
proof of its own validity, but it 'commands attention to it on its own
authority'.[2] The more this inward law is respected and followed, the
clearer become its dictates, and at the same time the clearer becomes
the presentiment or vague awareness of a transcendent God, 'a supreme
Power, claiming our habitual obedience'.[3]

A lively sense of obligation thus carries the mind forward to the
thought of something beyond the human self. Further, conscience
possesses an emotive aspect, on which Newman lays considerable
emphasis. Conscience produces 'reverence and awe, hope and fear,
especially fear, a feeling which is foreign for the most part, not only to
Taste, but even to the Moral Sense, except in consequence of accidental
associations'.[4] And Newman argues that there is an intimate connection
between affections and emotions on the one hand and persons on the
other. 'Inanimate things cannot stir our affections; these are correlative
with persons.'[5] Hence 'the phenomena of Conscience, as a dictate, avail
to impress the imagination with the picture of a Supreme Governor, a
Judge, holy, just, powerful, all-seeing, retributive'.[6] In other words,
conscience can produce that 'imaginative' awareness of God which is
required for the vivid assent to which reference has already been made.

What Newman says on this matter was doubtless verified in his own
case. When he spoke of the mind of a child who recognizes obligation
and who has been preserved from influences destructive of his 'religious
instincts'[7] as reaching forward 'with a strong presentiment of the
thought of a Moral Governor, sovereign over him, mindful and just',[8]
we may well discern a generalization from his own experience. Further,
if we consider what he has to say as a descriptive account of the basis
of real assent to God, it is doubtless verified in many other cases. For
it is certainly arguable that with many believers respect for the dictates
of conscience is a powerful influence in keeping alive the consciousness
of God as a present reality. True, it is possible to neglect and disobey
the dictates of conscience and still believe in God. But it is also probably
true that if one habitually turns a deaf ear to the voice of conscience,
so that it becomes dim or obscured, belief in God, if retained, tends to

[1] *Ibid.*, p. 104.   [2] *OUS*, p. 19.   [3] *Ibid.*
[4] *GA*, pp. 104–5. By Taste Newman means the aesthetic sense, considered as
the sense of the beautiful, while by Moral Sense he means in this context a sense
of the fittingness or deformity of actions, involving moral approval or disapproval.
[5] *Ibid.*, p. 106.   [6] *Ibid.*, p. 107.   [7] *Ibid.*, p. 109.
[8] *Ibid.*

degenerate into what Newman would call a purely notional assent. In other words, from the phenomenological point of view Newman's account of the relation between conscience and belief in or real assent to God has an indubitable value. There are indeed other factors which have to be considered in a phenomenological analysis of belief in God. But Newman certainly illustrates one aspect of the matter.

At the same time Newman is not concerned simply with describing the way in which, in his opinion, people come to believe in God, as though the belief were or could be on the same level as a belief, say, in the existence of elves and fairies. He wishes to show that belief in God is reasonable, and in some sense or other he intends to indicate the outlines of a 'proof' of God's existence. For instance, he says explicitly that the argument from conscience is 'my own chosen proof of that fundamental doctrine [God's existence] for thirty years past'.[1] And elsewhere he remarks that while he does not intend to prove 'here' the existence of a God, 'yet I have found it impossible to avoid saying where I look for the proof of it'.[2]

But what sort of a proof is it? In a sermon preached in 1830 Newman says that 'Conscience implies a relation between the soul and a something exterior, and that, moreover, superior to itself; a relation to an excellence which it does not possess, and to a tribunal over which it has no power'.[3] In spite, however, of the use of the word 'imply', he can hardly mean that the idea of conscience implies the idea of God in such a way that to assert the existence of conscience and deny the existence of God constitutes a logical contradiction. Moreover, elsewhere Newman uses phrases which suggest a causal inference. For instance, he says of conscience that 'from the nature of the case, its very existence carries on our minds to a Being exterior to ourselves; for else whence did it come?'[4] And we have already noted his remark, when speaking of the emotive aspect of conscience, that 'inanimate things cannot stir our affections; these are correlative with persons'.[5] But Newman is, of course, aware that by no means all philosophers would agree that we can legitimately infer the existence of God from the sense of obligation. And if he skates lightly over views different from his own, it is fairly evident that he is really concerned not so much with a causal inference to an explanatory hypothesis, analogous to causal inference in science, as with inviting his hearers or readers to enter into themselves and to reflect on the question whether they are not in some sense aware of God as manifested in the voice of conscience.

In other words, Newman seems to be primarily concerned with

[1] From the 'Proof of Theism', a paper published for the first time in Dr. A. J. Boekraad's The Argument from Conscience to the Existence of God according to J. H. Newman (Louvain, 1961), p. 121.
[2] GA, p. 101. [3] OUS, p. 18.
[4] Sermons Preached on Various Occasions (2nd edition, 1858), p. 86.
[5] GA, p. 106.

personal insight into the 'significance' or 'implications' of the awareness of obligation in a sense of these terms which it is difficult to define. And his line of thought appears to bear more resemblance to the phenomenological analyses performed in our own day by Gabriel Marcel than to metaphysical arguments of the traditional type. Newman admits indeed that a generalized inductive argument is possible. Just as from sense-impressions 'we go on to draw the general conclusion that there is a vast external world',[1] so by induction from particular instances of awareness of an inner imperative, an awareness which opens the mind to the thought of God, we can conclude to 'the Ubiquitous Presence of One Supreme Master'.[2] But assent to the conclusion of a generalized inductive argument will be, for Newman, a notional assent. Hence an argument of this kind appears to fall into the same class as arguments from Nature to God, of which he says in one place that while he has no intention of questioning their beauty and cogency, he certainly does question 'whether in matter of fact they make or keep men Christians'.[3] For such an argument to be 'effective', yielding real assent, we have to 'apply our general knowledge to a particular instance of that knowledge'.[4] That is to say, for assent to the conclusion of a generalized moral argument to become a living belief and the basis of religion, I have to enter within myself and hear the voice of God manifesting itself in the voice of conscience.[5] It is the personal appropriation of the truth which counts for Newman, not a mere intellectual assent to an abstract proposition.

In other words, Newman really wants to make us 'see' something for ourselves in the context of our personal experience rather than to argue that one proposition follows logically from another. After all, he says himself that he does not intend to deal 'with controversialists'.[6] In a real sense he wishes to make us see what we are. Without conscience a man is not really a man. And unless conscience leads us to belief in God by bringing us, so to speak, up against God as a present reality manifested in the sense of obligation, it remains stunted. Human nature expands, as it were, in faith. It is from the start open to God. And in Newman's view this potential openness is realized, basically, through personal insight into the 'phenomenon' of conscience. It is thus probably a mistake to interpret his argument from conscience to God as a public proof of the existence of God. True, the phenomenological analysis is public in the sense that it is a written explicitation of what Newman regards as the spontaneous movement of the unspoiled mind. But the public analysis cannot possibly do what Newman wishes it to do, to

---

[1] *Ibid.*, pp. 60–1. [2] *Ibid.*, p. 61.
[3] *Sermons Preached on Various Occasions*, p. 98. [4] *GA*, p. 61.
[5] It should be noted that Newman did not hold that the moral law depends on the arbitrary *fiat* of God. He maintained that in recognizing our obligation to obey the moral law we implicitly recognize God as Father and Judge.
[6] *GA*, p. 420.

facilitate real assent, unless it is interiorized, applied, as he puts it, to the particular instance.

5. We cannot examine here Newman's discussion of the evidences for the truth of Christianity. But there is a logical point connected with the discussion which is worth mentioning.

Formal demonstrative inference can, of course, be employed within theology, to exhibit the implications of statements. But when we are considering the evidences for Christianity in the first place, we are largely concerned, Newman takes it, with historical matters, with matters of fact. And at once a difficulty arises. On the one hand in reasoning about matters of fact rather than about the relations between abstract ideas our conclusions enjoy some degree of probability, perhaps a very high degree, but still only probability. On the other hand all assent, Newman insists, is unconditional. How then can we be justified in giving unconditional assent, such as is demanded of the Christian, to a proposition which is only probably true?

To answer this objection Newman makes use of ideas found in Pascal, Locke and Butler and argues that an accumulation of independent probabilities, converging towards a common conclusion, can render this conclusion certain. In his own words, where there is a 'cumulation of probabilities, independent of each other, arising out of the nature and circumstances of the case which is under review; probabilities too fine to avail separately, too subtle and circuitous to be convertible into syllogisms, too numerous and various for such conversion, even were they convertible',[1] but which all, taken together, converge on a certain conclusion, this conclusion can be certain.

It can doubtless be admitted that we do in fact often take a convergence of probabilities as sufficient proof of the truth of a proposition. But it can still be objected against Newman that no definite rule can be given for determining when the truth of a certain conclusion is the only possible rational explanation of a given convergence. Hence though we may be perfectly justified in assuming the truth of the conclusion for all practical purposes, an unconditional or unqualified assent is unjustified. For any hypothesis remains revisible in principle. It is all very well for Newman to say that in the case of religious inquiry we are 'bound in conscience to seek truth and to look for certainty by modes of proof, which, when reduced to the shape of formal propositions, fail to satisfy the severe requisitions of science'.[2] The fact remains that if unconditional assent to a proposition is taken to exclude the possibility of the proposition turning out to be false, it cannot legitimately be given to a conclusion drawn from a convergence unless we are able to show that at some point probability is transferred into certainty.

Obviously, Newman can hardly mean by unconditional assent one which excludes all possibility of the relevant proposition turning out to

[1] *GA*, p. 281.   [2] *Ibid.*, p. 407.

be false. For if all assent is unconditional, it must include assent to propositions which we very well know might turn out to be false. In its most general form the statement that all assent is unconditional can hardly mean more than that assent is assent. However, in the case of adherence to Christianity Newman clearly has in mind an absolute self-commitment, an unqualified assent in the fullest sense. And though he would doubtless admit that there is no infallible abstract rule for determining when a convergence of possibilities is such that the conclusion is certain, he argues that man possesses a 'faculty' of the mind, analogous to the Aristotelian *phronesis*, which is susceptible of different degrees of development and which is in principle capable of discerning the point at which the convergence of probabilities amounts to conclusive proof. This is the illative sense. 'In no class of concrete reasonings, whether in experimental science, historical research, or theology, is there any ultimate test of truth and error in our inferences besides the trustworthiness of the Illative Sense that gives them its sanction.'[1] We either 'see' or we do not see that a given inference is valid. Similarly, we either see or we do not see that the only rational explanation of a given accumulation of converging independent probabilities is the truth of the conclusion on which they converge. By the nature of the case there can be no further criterion of judgment than the mind's estimate of the evidence in a particular case.

It may seem that Newman places the emphasis on subjective or psychological states. He says, for example, that 'certitude is a mental state: certainty is a quality of propositions. Those propositions I call certain, which are such that I am certain of them.'[2] And this may give the impression that in his opinion any proposition is certainly true if it causes the feeling of being certain in a human being. But he goes on to say that in concrete questions certitude is not a 'passive impression made upon the mind from without . . . but . . . an active recognition of propositions as true. . . .'[3] And as 'everyone who reasons is his own centre',[4] there can be no further criterion of evidence or of the validity of inference in concrete matters of fact than seeing that the evidence is sufficient or that the inference is valid. Newman has no intention of denying the objectivity of truth. He means rather that if we think that a man's reasoning in questions of fact is faulty, we can only ask him to look again at the evidence and at his process of reasoning. If it is objected that there can be a 'logic of words',[5] the sort of deduction which can be performed by a machine, Newman does not deny this. But he insists that a distinction must be made between the logic of words and reasoning about matters of fact. The former leads to purely notional assent; and this does not interest him when he is writing as a

[1] *Ibid.*, p. 352. The illative sense is 'the power of judging about truth and error in concrete matters' (*ibid.*, p. 346).
[2] *Ibid.*, p. 337.   [3] *Ibid.*   [4] *Ibid.*, p. 338.   [5] *Ibid.*

Christian apologist who wishes to justify real assent. He does not set out to argue that reasoning about Christian evidences can be reduced to the logic of words, to formal demonstrative inference. What he wishes to show is rather that in all concrete issues of fact we have to employ inference which is not so reducible, and that the believer's assent to the conclusion of reasoning about the evidences for Christianity cannot therefore be justifiably described as a mere leap or as the result of wishful thinking because it does not conform to a pattern of demonstration which certainly has its uses but which is inappropriate outside a certain limited field.

6. We have already had occasion to refer to a certain affinity between Newman's reflections on conscience and Gabriel Marcel's phenomenological analyses. But the intellectual antecedents and formations of the two men were, needless to say, very different; and whereas Newman was out to prove something, to show that Christian belief is reasonable, the apologetic motive is much less obvious with Marcel. Indeed, Marcel's philosophical reflections helped to bring him to Christianity, whereas Newman's philosophical reflections presuppose the Christian faith, in the sense that it is a case of faith reflecting on itself. At the same time there are certain limited affinities.

Similarly, in spite of the great differences between the two men Newman's preoccupation with the personal appropriation of truth as a basis for life and with personal self-commitment may put us in mind of Kierkegaard,[1] whose span of life (1813–55) fell entirely within that of Newman. This is not to suggest, of course, that Newman knew anything at all about the Danish thinker, or even of his existence. But though Newman certainly did not go so far as Kierkegaard in describing truth as subjectivity, there is none the less a certain degree of spiritual affinity between the two men.

As for Newman's insistence on the moral conditions for the fruitful pursuit of truth in religious inquiry, this has become a commonplace of the newer apologetics, as has indeed Newman's approach from within the soul rather than from external Nature. In other words, there is at any rate some affinity between Newman's approach to apologetics and that associated in modern times with the name of Maurice Blondel (1861–1949).

The point of these remarks is this. If we take Newman simply as he stands, there are a good many questions which modern British logicians and philosophers would wish to ask, and objections which they would feel inclined to make. But it seems safe to say that Newman is not now regarded, except possibly by a few devotees, as a philosopher whose thought one either accepts or rejects, as the case may be. By saying that he is not 'now' regarded I do not mean to imply that he was ever looked on in this light. I mean rather that the growth of interest in his

[1] For Kierkegaard see ch. 17 of Vol. VII of this *History*.

philosophical thought and in his style of apologetics has coincided with the spread of movements in philosophy and in apologetics which, on our looking back, are seen to have certain affinities with elements in Newman's reflections. Hence those who take an interest in his philosophical reflections tend to look on them as a source of stimulus and inspiration rather than as a rigid, systematic doctrine, which, of course, Newman himself never intended them to be. And in this case detailed criticism of particular points necessarily seems pedantic and appears, to those who value Newman's general approach, as more or less irrelevant.

APPENDIX B

A SHORT BIBLIOGRAPHY

General Works

For the sake of brevity titles of general histories of philosophy mentioned in the first section of the Bibliography in Volume VII of this *History* have not been repeated here. Nor have I attempted to supply bibliographies for all the philosophers mentioned in the text of the present volume. In the case of a considerable number of philosophers works are mentioned in the text or in footnotes, which have not been listed here.

Adams, G. P. and Montague, W. P. (editors). *Contemporary American Philosophy.* 2 vols. New York, 1930. (Personal Statements.)

Anderson, P. R. and Fisch, M. H. *Philosophy in America.* New York, 1939.

Blau, J. L. *Men and Movements in American Philosophy.* New York, 1939.

Bochenski, I. M. *Contemporary European Philosophy,* translated by D. Nicholl and K. Aschenbrenner. London and Berkeley, 1956.

Brinton, Crane. *English Political Thought in the Nineteenth Century.* Cambridge (Mass.), 1949.

Deledalle, G. *Histoire de la philosophie américaine de la guerre de sécession à la seconde guerre mondiale.* Paris, 1955.

Lamanna, A. P. *La filosofia del novecento.* Florence, 1964.

Merz, J. T. *History of European Thought in the Nineteenth Century.* 4 vols. London, 1896–1914.

Metz, R. *A Hundred Years of British Philosophy,* translated by J. W. Harvey, T. E. Jessop and H. Sturt. London, 1938. (An account of British philosophy from about the middle of the nineteenth century onwards.)

Muelder, W. E. and Sears, L. *The Development of American Philosophy.* Boston, 1940.

Muirhead, J. H. (editor). *Contemporary British Philosophy: Personal Statements.* 2 vols. London, 1924–5. (The first volume includes statements by, for example, Bosanquet, McTaggart, Bertrand Russell and Schiller, the second by James Ward and G. E. Moore.)

Passmore, J. *A Hundred Years of Philosophy.* London, 1957. (A useful account of philosophy, mainly but not exclusively British, from J. S. Mill, with a concluding chapter on existentialism.)

Riley, I. W. *American Thought from Puritanism to Pragmatism and Beyond.* New York, 1923 (2nd edition).

Schneider, H. W. *A History of American Philosophy*. New York, 1946,
Seth (Pringle-Pattison), A. *English Philosophers and Schools of Philo-
sophy*. London, 1912. (From Francis Bacon to F. H. Bradley.)
Warnock, G. J. *English Philosophy Since 1900*. London, 1958. (A clear
and succinct account of the development of the modern analytic
movement.)
Warnock, M. *Ethics Since 1900*. London, 1960.
Werkmeister, W. H. *A History of Philosophical Ideas in America*. New
York, 1949.

Part I: Chapters I–V

1. *General Works Relating to the Utilitarian Movement.*
Albee, E. *A History of English Utilitarianism*. London, 1902.
Davidson, W. L. *Political Thought in England: Bentham to J. S. Mill*.
London, 1950.
Guyau, J. M. *La morale anglaise contemporaine*. Paris, 1904 (5th ed.).
Halévy, E. *The Growth of Philosophic Radicalism*, translated by M.
Morris, with a preface by A. D. Lindsay. London, 1928.
Laski, H. J. *The Rise of European Liberalism*. London, 1936.
Leslie, S. W. *Political Thought in England. The Utilitarians from
Bentham to Mill*. London and New York, 1947.
Mondolfo, R. *Saggi per la storia della morale utilitaria*. 2 vols. Verona
and Padua, 1903–4.
Plamentaz, J. *The English Utilitarians*. Oxford, 1949.
Stephen, L. *The English Utilitarians*. 3 vols. London, 1900. (The
volumes are devoted respectively to Bentham, James Mill and
J. S. Mill.)

2. *Bentham*
Texts
The Works of Jeremy Bentham, edited by John Bowring. 11 vols.
Edinburgh, 1838–43.
Benthamiana, Select Extracts from the Works of Jeremy Bentham,
edited by J. H. Burton. Edinburgh, 1843.
Oeuvres de Jérémie Bentham, translated by E. Dumont. 3 vols.
Brussels, 1829–30.
Colección de obras del célebre Jeremias Bentham, compiled by E.
Dumont with commentaries by B. Anduaga y Espinosa. 14 vols.
Madrid, 1841–3.
An Introduction to the Principles of Morals and Legislation, edited by
L. Lafleur. New York, 1948. (The 1876 Oxford edition is a
reprint of the 1823 edition.)
Theory of Legislation, translated from the French of E. Dumont by
R. Hildreth. London, 1896.

Bentham's Theory of Legislation, edited by C. K. Ogden. London, 1950.

A Fragment on Government, edited by F. C. Montague. London, 1891.

Bentham's Theory of Fictions, edited by C. K. Ogden. London, 1932.

Bentham's Handbook of Political Fallacies, edited by H. A. Larrabee. Baltimore, 1952.

Deontology, or the Science of Morality, edited by J. Bowring. 2 vols. London, 1834.

The Limits of Jurisprudence Defined, edited by C. W. Everett. New York, 1945.

Jeremy Bentham's Economic Writings, Critical Edition based on his Printed Works and Unprinted Manuscripts, edited by W. Stark. 3 vols. London, 1952–4. (Each volume contains an introductory essay. The second appendix, contained in the third volume, is a systematic survey of the surviving Bentham manuscripts.)

Catalogue of the Manuscripts of Jeremy Bentham in the Library of University College, London, edited by A. T. Milne. London, 1937.

Studies

Atkinson, C. M. *Jeremy Bentham, His Life and Work.* London, 1905.

Baumgardt, D. *Bentham and the Ethics of Today.* Princeton (U.S.A.) and London, 1952.

Busch, J. *Die moralische und soziale Ethik Benthams.* Neisse, 1938.

Everett, C. W. *The Education of Jeremy Bentham.* New York, 1931.

Jones, W. T. *Masters of Political Thought: From Machiavelli to Bentham.* London, 1947.

Keeton, G. W. and Schwarzenberger, G. (editors). *Jeremy Bentham and the Law.* London, 1948.

Laski, H. J. *Political Thought in England: Locke to Bentham.* London, 1950.

Mack, M. P. *Jeremy Bentham: An Odyssey of Ideas, 1748–1792.* London, 1962.

Mill, J. S. *Mill on Bentham and Coleridge,* edited by F. R. Leavis. London, 1950.

Quintodamo, N. *La morale utilitaristica del Bentham e sua evoluzione nel diritto penale.* Naples, 1936.

Stephen, L. *The English Utilitarians: Vol. I, Jeremy Bentham.* London, 1900.

3. *James Mill*

Texts

History of India. 3 vols. London, 1817. (4th edition, 9 vols., 1848; 5th edition, with continuation by M. H. Wilson, 10 vols., 1858.)

Elements of Political Economy. London, 1821 (3rd and revised edition, 1826).

Analysis of the Phenomena of the Human Mind, edited by J. S. Mill, with notes by A. Bain, A. Findlater and G. Grote. 2 vols. London, 1869.
A Fragment on Mackintosh. London, 1835.

Studies

Bain, A. *James Mill, A Biography*. London 1882.
Bower, G. S. *Hartley and James Mill*. London, 1881.
Hamburger, J. *James Mill and the Art of Revolution*. Yale, 1964.
Ressler, A. *Die Beiden Mill*. Cologne, 1929.
Stephen, L. *The English Utilitarians: Vol. II, James Mill*. London, 1900.

4. *J. S. Mill*
Texts

Collected Works of John Stuart Mill, general editor F. E. L. Priestley. Toronto and London. Vols. XII–XIII, *The Earlier Letters, 1812–1848*, edited by F. E. Mineka, 1963; vols. II–III, *The Principles of Political Economy*, with an introduction by V. W. Bladen, edited by J. M. Robson, 1965.
Autobiography, edited by H. J. Laski. London, 1952. (Among other editions there is the one edited by J. J. Cross, New York, 1924.)
The Early Draft of J. S. Mill's Autobiography, edited by J. Stillinger. Urbana (Ill.), 1961.
Mill's Utilitarianism reprinted with a Study of the English Utilitarians, by J. Plamentaz. Oxford, 1949.
On Liberty, Considerations on Representative Government, edited with an introduction by R. B. McCallum. Oxford, 1946.
Considerations on Representative Government, edited with an introduction by C. V. Shields. New York, 1958.
A System of Logic. London, 1949 (reprint).
Examination of Sir William Hamilton's Philosophy. London, 1865.
John Stuart Mill's Philosophy of Scientific Method, edited by E. Nagel. New York, 1950. (Selections, with introductory material, from the *Logic* and the *Examination*.)
Dissertations and Discussions. 5 vols. Boston (U.S.A.), 1865–75.
Mill on Bentham and Coleridge, edited by F. R. Leavis. London, 1950.
Auguste Comte and Positivism. London, 1865.
Inaugural Address at St. Andrews. London, 1867.
Three Essays on Religion. London, 1874. (*Theism*, edited by R. Taylor. New York, 1957.)
John Stuart Mill and Harriet Taylor: Their Friendship and Subsequent Marriage, edited by F. A. Hayek. Chicago, 1951. (Contains the Mill–Taylor correspondence.)

Lettres inédites de John Stuart Mill à Auguste Comte, publiées avec les résponses de Comte, edited by L. Lévy-Bruhl. Paris, 1899.

Bibliography of the Published Works of John Stuart Mill, edited by N. MacMinn, J. R. Hinds and J. M. McCrimmon. London, 1945.

Studies

Anschutz, R. P. *The Philosophy of J. S. Mill.* Oxford, 1953. (Illustrates very well the different tendencies in Mill's thought.)

Bain, A. *John Stuart Mill: A Criticism with Personal Recollections.* London, 1882.

Borchard, R. *John Stuart Mill, the Man.* London, 1957.

Britton, K. *John Stuart Mill.* Penguin Books, 1953.

Casellato, S. *Giovanni St. Mill e l'utilitarismo inglese.* Padua, 1951.

Castell, A. *Mill's Logic of the Moral Sciences: A Study of the Impact of Newtonism on Early Nineteenth-Century Social Thought.* Chicago, 1936.

Courtney, W. L. *The Metaphysics of John Stuart Mill.* London, 1879.

Cowling, M. *Mill and Liberalism.* Cambridge, 1963.

Douglas, C. *J. S. Mill: A Study of His Philosophy.* London, 1895.
 Ethics of John Stuart Mill. Edinburgh, 1897.

Grude-Oettli, N. *John Stuart Mill zwischen Liberalismus und Sozialismus.* Zürich, 1936.

Hippler, F. *Staat und Gesellschaft bei Mill, Marx, Lagarde.* Berlin, 1934.

Jackson, R. *An Examination of the Deductive Logic of John Stuart Mill.* London, 1941.

Kantzer, E. M. *La religion de John Stuart Mill.* Caen, 1914.

Kennedy, G. *The Psychological Empiricism of John Stuart Mill.* Amsterdam, 1928.

Kubitz, O. A. *The Development of John Stuart Mill's System of Logic.* Urbana (Ill.), 1932.

McCosh, J. *An Examination of Mr. J. S. Mill's Philosophy.* New York, 1890 (2nd edition).

Mueller, I. W. *John Stuart Mill and French Thought.* Urbana (Ill.), 1956.

Packe, M. St. John. *The Life of John Stuart Mill.* New York, 1954.

Pradines, M. *Les postulats métaphysiques de l'utilitarisme de Stuart Mill et Spencer.* Paris, 1909.

Ray, J. *La méthode de l'économie politique d'après John Stuart Mill.* Paris, 1914.

Roerig, F. *Die Wandlungen in der geistigen Grundhaltung John Stuart Mills.* Cologne, 1930.

Russell, Bertrand. *John Stuart Mill.* London, 1956. (Bristol Academy Lecture.)

Saenger, S. *John Stuart Mill, Sein Leben und Lebenswerk*. Stuttgart, 1901.

Schauchet, P. *Individualistische und sozialistische Gedanken im Leben John Stuart Mills*. Giessen, 1926.

Stephen, L. *The English Utilitarians:* vol. III, *John Stuart Mill*. London, 1900.

Towney, G. A. *John Stuart Mill's Theory of Inductive Logic*. Cincinnati, 1909.

Watson, J. *Comte, Mill and Spencer*. Glasgow, 1895.

Zuccante, G. *La morale utilitaristica dello Stuart Mill*. Milan, 1899. *Giovanni S. Mill e l'utilitarismo*. Florence, 1922.

5. Herbert Spencer
Texts

A System of Synthetic Philosophy. 10 vols. London, 1862–93. (For some detailed information about the various editions of the books comprising the *System* see pp. 240–1.)

Epitome of the Synthetic Philosophy, by F. H. Collins. London, 1889 (5th edition, 1901).

Essays, Scientific, Political and Speculative. 3 vols. London, 1891. (Two volumes of *Essays, Scientific, Political and Speculative* appeared at London in 1857 and 1863 respectively and one volume of *Essays. Moral, Political and Aesthetic* at New York in 1865.)

Education, Intellectual, Moral, Physical. London, 1861.

The Man versus The State. London, 1884.

The Nature and Reality of Religion. London, 1885.

Various Fragments. London, 1897.

Facts and Comments. London, 1902.

Autobiography. 2 vols. New York, 1904.

Studies

Allievo, G. *La psicologia di Herbert Spencer*. Turin, 1914 (2nd edition).

Ardigò, R. *L'Inconoscibile di Spencer e il noumeno di Kant*. Padua, 1901.

Asirvatham, E. *Spencer's Theory of Social Justice*. New York, 1936.

Carus, P. *Kant and Spencer*. Chicago, 1889.

Diaconide, E. *Étude critique sur la sociologie de Herbert Spencer*. Paris, 1938.

Duncan, D. *The Life and Letters of Herbert Spencer*. London, 1912.

Elliott, H. *Herbert Spencer*. London, 1917.

Ensor, R. C. *Some Reflections on Spencer's Doctrine that Progress is Differentiation*. Oxford, 1947.

Fiske, J. *Outlines of Cosmic Philosophy*. 2 vols. London, 1874. (These lectures are critical as well as expository of Spencer's thought.)

Gaupp, O. *Herbert Spencer*. Stuttgart, 1897.

Guthmann, J. *Entwicklung und Selbstentfaltung bei Spencer*. Ochsenfurt, 1931.

Häberlin, P. *Herbert Spencers Grundlagen der Philosophie*. Leipzig, 1908.

Hudson, W. H. *Introduction to the Philosophy of Herbert Spencer*. London, 1909.

Jarger, M. *Herbert Spencers Prinzipien der Ethik*. Hamburg, 1922.

Macpherson, H. *Herbert Spencer, The Man and His Work*. London, 1900.

Parisot, E. *Herbert Spencer*. Paris, 1911.

Parker-Bowne, B. *Kant and Spencer*. New York, 1922.

Ramlow, L. A. *Riehl und Spencer*. Berlin, 1933.

Royce, J. *Herbert Spencer: An Estimate and Review with a chapter of Personal Reminiscences by J. Collier*. New York, 1904.

Rumney, J. *Herbert Spencer's Sociology: A Study in the History of Social Theory*. London, 1934.

Sergi, G. *La sociologia di Herbert Spencer*. Rome, 1903.

Sidgwick, H. *Lectures on the Ethics of T. H. Green, Mr. Herbert Spencer, and J. Martineau*. London, 1902.

Solari, G. *L'opera filosofica di Herbert Spencer*. Bergamo, 1904.

Stadler, A. *Herbert Spencers Ethik*. Leipzig, 1913.

Thompson, J. A. *Herbert Spencer*. London, 1906.

Tillett, A. W. *Spencer's Synthetic Philosophy: What It is All About. An Introduction to Justice, 'The Most Important Part'*. London, 1914.

Part II: Chapters VI–X

1. *General Works Relating to British Idealism*

Abbagnano, N. *L'idealismo inglese e americano*. Naples, 1926.

Cunningham, G. W. *The Idealistic Argument in Recent British and American Philosophy*. New York, 1933.

Dockhorn, K. *Die Staatsphilosophie des englischen Idealismus, ihre Lehre und Wirkung*. Pöppinghaus, 1937.

Haldar, H. *Neo-Hegelianism*. London, 1927.

Milne, A. J. M. *The Social Philosophy of English Idealism*. London, 1962.

Muirhead, J. M. *The Platonic Tradition in Anglo-Saxon Philosophy*. London, 1931.

Pucelle, J. *L'idéalisme en Angleterre de Coleridge à Bradley*. Neuchatel and Paris, 1955. (Can be highly recommended.)

2. *Coleridge*
Texts

Works, edited by W. G. T. Shedd. 7 vols. New York, 1884.
The Friend. 3 vols. London, 1812. (2 vols, 1837).
Biographia Literaria. London, 1817. (Everyman Library, 1906 and reprints.)
Aids to Reflection. 2 vols. London, 1824–5 (with addition of the *Essay on Faith*, 1890).
On the Constitution of Church and State, edited by H. N. Coleridge. London, 1839.
Confessions of an Inquiring Spirit, edited by H. N. Coleridge. London, 1840.
Treatise on Method. London, 1849 (3rd edition).
Essays on His Own Times. 3 vols. London, 1850.
Anima Poetae, edited by E. H. Coleridge. London, 1895.
Letters, edited by E. H. Coleridge. London, 1895.
Unpublished Letters. London, 1932.
The Political Thought of Coleridge, selected by R. J. White. London, 1938.
The Philosophical Lectures of S. T. Coleridge, Hitherto Unpublished, edited by K. Coburn. London, 1949.
The Notebooks of S. T. Coleridge, edited by K. Coburn. 2 vols. London, 1957–62.

Studies

Blunden, E. and Griggs, E. L. (editors). *Coleridge Studies*. London, 1934.
Campbell J. D. *Life of S. T. Coleridge*. London, 1894.
Chambers, E. K. *S. T. Coleridge: A Biographical Study*. Oxford, 1938.
Chinol, E. *Il pensiero di S. T. Coleridge*. Venice, 1953.
Coburn, K. *Inquiring Spirit. A New Presentation of Coleridge* (from published and unpublished writings). London, 1931.
Ferrando, G. *Coleridge*. Florence, 1925.
Green, J. H. *Spiritual Philosophy, Founded on the Teaching of the late S. T. Coleridge*. 2 vols. London, 1865.
Hanson, L. *Life of S. T. Coleridge Early Years*. London, 1938.
Kagey, R. *Coleridge: Studies in the History of Ideas*. New York, 1935.
Lowes, J. L. *The Road to Xanadu: A Study in Ways of the Imagination*. London, 1927 (revised edition 1930).
Muirhead, J. H. *Coleridge as Philosopher*. London, 1930.
Richards, I. A. *Coleridge on Imagination*. London, 1934.
Snyder, A. D. *Coleridge on Logic and Learning*. New Haven, 1929.
Wellek, R. *Immanuel Kant in England*. Princeton, 1931. (Only partly on Coleridge.)

Winkelmann, E. *Coleridge und die kantische Philosophie.* Leipzig, 1933.

Wunsche, W. *Die Staatsauffassung S. T. Coleridge's.* Leipzig, 1934.

3. Carlyle

Texts

Works, edited by H. D. Traill. 31 vols. London, 1897–1901.

Sartor Resartus. London, 1841, and subsequent editions.

On Heroes, Hero-Worship and the Heroic in History. London, 1841.

Correspondence of Carlyle and R. W. Emerson. 2 vols. London, 1883.

Letters of Carlyle to J. S. Mill, J. Sterling and R. Browning, edited by A. Carlyle. London, 1923.

Studies

Baumgarten, O. *Carlyle und Goethe.* Tübingen, 1906.

Fermi, L. *Carlyle.* Messina, 1939.

Garnett, R. *Life of Carlyle.* London, 1887.

Harrold, C. F. *Carlyle and German Thought, 1819–34.* New Haven, 1934.

Hensel, P. *Thomas Carlyle.* Stuttgart, 1901.

Lammond, D. *Carlyle.* London, 1934.

Lea, F. *Carlyle, Prophet of Today.* London, 1944.

Lehman, B. H. *Carlyle's Theory of the Hero.* Duke, 1939.

Neff, E. *Carlyle and Mill: Mystic and Utilitarian.* New York, 1924. *Carlyle.* New York, 1932.

Seillière, E. *L'actualité de Carlyle.* Paris, 1929.

Storrs, M. *The Relation of Carlyle to Kant and Fichte.* Bryn Mawr, 1929.

Taylor, A. C. *Carlyle et la pensée latine.* Paris, 1937.

Wilson, D. A. *Carlyle.* 6 vols. London, 1923–34.

4. T. H. Green

Texts

Works, edited by R. L. Nettleship, 3 vols. London, 1885–8. (Contains Green's *Introductions to Hume's Treatise,* lectures on Kant, on Logic and on *The Principles of Political Obligation,* together with a memoir of the philosopher by Nettleship.)

Introductions to Hume's Treatise in vols. 1 and 2 of the *Philosophical Works of David Hume* edited by T. H. Green and T. M. Grose. London, 1874.

Prolegomena to Ethics, edited by A. C. Bradley. London, 1883.

Principles of Political Obligation. London, 1895.

Studies

Günther, O. *Das Verhältnis der Ethik Greens zu der Kants.* Leipzig, 1915.

Fairbrother, W. H. *The Philosophy of T. H. Green.* London, 1896.
Fusai, M. *Il pensiero morale di T. H. Green.* Florence, 1943.
Lamont, W. D. *Introduction to Green's Moral Philosophy.* New York, 1934.
Muirhead, J. H. *The Service of the State: Four lectures on the Political Teaching of Green.* London, 1908.
Pucelle, J. *La nature et l'esprit dans la philosophie de T. H. Green. I, Métaphysique–Morale.* Louvain, 1961. (A thorough and sympathetic study.)

5. *E. Caird*
Texts
   A Critical Account of the Philosophy of Kant. Glasgow, 1877. (Revised edition in 2 vols. with the title *The Critical Philosophy of Kant*, Glasgow, 1889.)
   Hegel. Edinburgh, 1883.
   The Social Philosophy and Religion of Comte. Glasgow, 1885.
   Essays on Literature and Philosophy. 2 vols. Glasgow, 1892.
   The Evolution of Religion. 2 vols. Glasgow, 1893.
   The Evolution of Theology in the Greek Philosophers, 2 vols. Glasgow, 1904.

Studies
   Jones, H. and Muirhead, J. H. *The Life and Philosophy of Edward Caird.* London, 1921.

6. *Bradley*
Texts
   The Presuppositions of Critical History. London, 1874.
   Ethical Studies. London, 1876 (2nd edition, 1927).
   Mr. Sidgwick's Hedonism. London, 1877.
   The Principles of Logic. London, 1883 (2nd edition with Terminal Essays in 2 vols, 1922.)
   Appearance and Reality. London, 1893 (2nd edition with Appendix, 1897).
   Essays on Truth and Reality. London, 1914.
   Aphorisms. Oxford, 1930.
   Collected Essays. 2 vols. Oxford, 1935. (This work includes *The Presuppositions of Critical History.*)

Studies
   Antonelli, M. A. *La metafisica di F. H. Bradley.* Milan, 1952.
   Campbell, C. A. *Scepticism and Construction. Bradley's Sceptical Principle as the Basis of Constructive Philosophy.* London, 1931.
   Chappuis, A. *Der theoretische Weg Bradleys.* Paris, 1934.

Church, R. W. *Bradley's Dialectic*. London, 1942.

De Marneffe, J. *La preuve de l'Absolu chez Bradley. Analyse et critique de la méthode*. Paris, 1961.

Kagey, R. *The Growth of Bradley's Logic*. London, 1931.

Keeling, S. V. *La nature de l'expérience chez Kant et chez Bradley*. Montpellier, 1925.

Lomba, R. M. *Bradley and Bergson*. Lucknow, 1937.

Lofthouse, W. F. *F. H. Bradley*. London, 1949.

Mack, R. D. *The Appeal to Immediate Experience. Philosophic Method in Bradley, Whitehead and Dewey*. New York, 1945.

Ross, G. R. *Scepticism and Dogma: A Study in the Philosophy of F. H. Bradley*. New York, 1940.

Schüring, H.-J. *Studie zur Philosophie von F. H. Bradley*. Meisenheim am Glan, 1963.

Segerstedt, T. T. *Value and Reality in Bradley's Philosophy*. Lund, 1934.

Taylor, A. E. *F. H. Bradley*. London, 1924. (British Academy lecture.)

Wollheim, R. *F. H. Bradley*. Penguin Books, 1959.

In *Mind* for 1925 there are articles on Bradley by G. D. Hicks, J. H. Muirhead, G. F. Stout, F. C. S. Schiller, A. E. Taylor and J. Ward.

7. *Bosanquet*
Texts

Knowledge and Reality. London, 1885.

Logic, or the Morphology of Knowledge. 2 vols. London, 1888.

Essays and Addresses. London, 1889.

A History of Aesthetic. London, 1892.

The Civilization of Christendom and Other Studies. London, 1893.

Aspects of the Social Problem. London, 1895.

The Essentials of Logic. London, 1895.

Companion to Plato's Republic. London, 1895.

Rousseau's Social Contract. London, 1895.

Psychology of the Moral Self. London, 1897.

The Philosophical Theory of the State. London, 1899.

The Principle of Individuality and Value. London, 1912.

The Value and Destiny of the Individual. London, 1913.

The Distinction between Mind and Its Objects. London, 1913.

Three Lectures on Aesthetics. London, 1915.

Social and International Ideals. London, 1917.

Some Suggestions in Ethics. London, 1918.

Implication and Linear Inference. London, 1920.

What Religion Is. London, 1920.

The Meeting of Extremes in Contemporary Philosophy. London, 1921.

Three Chapters on the Nature of Mind. London, 1923.
Science and Philosophy and Other Essays, edited by J. H. Muirhead
and R. C. Bosanquet. London, 1927.

Studies

Bosanquet, H. *Bernard Bosanquet.* London, 1924.
Houang, F. *La néo-hégelianisme en Angleterre: la philosophie de
Bernard Bosanquet.* Paris, 1954.
      *De l'humanisme à l'absolutisme. L'évolution de la pensée
      religieuse du néo-hégelien anglais Bernard Bosanquet.*
      Paris, 1954.
Muirhead, J. H. (editor). *Bosanquet and His Friends: Letters Illus-
trating Sources and Development of His Philosophical Opinions.*
London, 1935.
Pfannenstil, B. *Bernard Bosanquet's Philosophy of the State.* Lund,
1936.

8. *McTaggart*
Texts

Studies in the Hegelian Dialectic. Cambridge, 1896 (2nd edition 1922).
Studies in the Hegelian Cosmology. Cambridge, 1901 (2nd edition,
1918).
Some Dogmas of Religion. London, 1906, (2nd edition, with bio-
graphical introduction by C. D. Broad, 1930).
A Commentary on Hegel's Logic. Cambridge, 1910 (new edition, 1931).
The Nature of Existence. 2 vols. Cambridge, 1921–7. (The second vol.
is edited by C. D. Broad.)
Philosophical Studies, edited, with an introduction by S. V. Keeling,
London, 1934. (Mainly a collection of published articles, includ-
ing that on the unreality of time.)

Studies

Broad, C. D. *Examination of McTaggart's Philosophy.* 2 vols. Cambridge, 1933–8.
Dickinson, G. Lowes. *McTaggart, a Memoir.* Cambridge, 1931.

Part III: Chapters XI–XIII

1. *General Works Relating to Idealism in America*
Abbagnano, N. *L'idealismo inglese e americano.* Naples, 1926.
Adams, G. P. *Idealism and the Modern Age.* New Haven, 1919.
Barrett, C. and Others. *Contemporary Idealism in America.* New
York, 1932.

Cunningham, G. W. *The Idealistic Argument in Recent British and American Philosophy.* New York, 1933.

Frothingham, O. B. *Transcendentalism in New England.* New York, 1876.

Jones, A. L. *Early American Philosophers.* New York, 1898.

Miller, P. *The New England Mind: The Seventeenth Century.* New York, 1939.

Parrington, V. L. *Main Currents of American Thought.* New York, 1927.

Riley, I. W. *American Philosophy: The Early Schools.* New York, 1907.

Rogers, A. K. *English and American Philosophy Since 1800.* New York, 1922.

Royce, J. *Lectures on Modern Idealism.* New Haven, 1919.

Schneider, H. W. *The Puritan Mind.* New York, 1930.
   A History of American Philosophy. New York, 1946.

Stovall, F. *American Idealism.* Oklahoma, 1943.

2. Emerson

Texts

The Complete Works of Ralph Waldo Emerson, edited by E. W. Emerson. 12 vols. Boston, 1903–4. (Fireside edition, Boston, 1909.)

Works, 5 vols. London, 1882–3.
   6 vols., edited by J. Morley, London, 1883–4.

The Journals of Ralph Waldo Emerson, edited by E. W. Emerson and W. F. Forbes. 10 vols. Boston, 1909–14.

The Letters of Ralph Waldo Emerson, edited by R. L. Rusk. New York, 1939.

Studies

Alcot, A. B. *R. W. Emerson, Philosopher and Seer.* Boston, 1882.

Bishop, J. *Emerson on the Soul.* Cambridge (Mass.), and London, 1965.

Cabot, J. E. *A Memoir of R. W. Emerson.* 2 vols. London, 1887.

Cameron, K. W. *Emerson the Essayist: An Outline of His Philosophical Development through 1836.* 2 vols. Raleigh (N.C.), 1945.

Carpenter, F. I. *Emerson and Asia.* Cambridge (Mass.), 1930.
   Emerson Handbook. New York, 1953.

Christy, A. *The Orient in American Transcendentalism.* New York, 1932.

Firkins, O. W. *R. W. Emerson.* Boston, 1915.

Garnett, R. *Life of Emerson.* London, 1888.

Gray, H. D. *Emerson: A Statement of New England Transcendentalism as Expressed in the Philosophy of Its Chief Exponent.* Palo Alto (Calif.), 1917.

Hopkins, V. C. *Spires of Form: A Study of Emerson's Aesthetic Theory*. Cambridge (Mass.), 1951.
James, W. *Memories and Studies*. New York, 1911. (Includes an address on Emerson.)
Masters, E. L. *The Living Thoughts of Emerson*. London, 1948.
Matthiessen, F. O. *American Renaissance: Art and Expression in the Age of Emerson and Whitman*. London and New York, 1941.
Michaud, R. *Autour d'Emerson*. Paris, 1924.
  La vie inspirée d'Emerson. Paris, 1930.
Mohrdieck, M. *Demokratie bei Emerson*. Berlin, 1943.
Paul, S. *Emerson's Angle of Vision*. Cambridge (Mass.), 1952.
Perry, B. *Emerson Today*. New York, 1931.
Reaver, J. R. *Emerson as Myth-Maker*. Gainesville (Flor.), 1954.
Rusk, R. L. *The Life of Ralph Waldo Emerson*. New York, 1949.
Sahmann, P. *Emersons Geisteswelt*. Stuttgart, 1927.
Sanborn, F. B. (editor). *The Genius and Character of Emerson*. Boston, 1885.
Simon, J. *R. W. Emerson in Deutschland*. Berlin, 1937.
Whicher, S. B. *Freedom and Fate: An Inner Life of Ralph Waldo Emerson*. Philadelphia, 1953.

3. *Royce*
Texts

The Religious Aspect of Philosophy. Boston, 1885.
California: A Study of American Character. Boston, 1886.
The Spirit of Modern Philosophy. Boston, 1892.
The Conception of God: A Philosophical Discussion concerning the Nature of the Divine Idea as a Demonstrable Reality. New York, 1897. (This work, by several authors, includes Royce's intervention at a philosophical discussion in 1895.)
Studies of Good and Evil. New York, 1898.
The World and the Individual. 2 vols. New York, 1900–1.
The Conception of Immortality. Boston, 1900.
The Philosophy of Loyalty. New York, 1908.
Race Questions, Provincialisms and Other American Problems. New York and London, 1908.
William James and Other Essays on the Philosophy of Life. New York, 1911.
The Sources of Religious Insight. Edinburgh, 1912.
The Problem of Christianity. 2 vols. New York, 1913.
War and Insurance. New York, 1914.
Lectures on Modern Idealism. New Haven, 1919. (Edition by J. E. Smith, New York and London, 1964.)
Royce's Logical Essays, edited by D. S. Robinson. Dubuque (Iowa), 1951.

Josiah Royce's Seminar 1913-14, as recorded in the notebooks of H. Costello, edited by G. Smith. New Brunswick, 1963.

Studies

Albeggiani, F. *Il sistema filosofico di Josiah Royce*. Palermo, 1930.

Amoroso, M. L. *La filosofia morale di Josiah Royce*. Naples, 1929.

Aronson, M. J. *La philosophie morale de Josiah Royce*. Paris, 1927.

Cotton, J. H. *Royce on the Human Self*. Cambridge (Mass.), 1954.

Creighton, J. E. (editor). *Papers in Honor of Josiah Royce on His Sixtieth Birthday*. New York, 1916.

De Nier, M. *Royce*. Brescia, 1950.

Dykhuizen, G. *The Conception of God in the Philosophy of Josiah Royce*. Chicago, 1936.

Fuss, P. *The Moral Philosophy of Josiah Royce*. Cambridge (Mass.), 1965.

Galgano, M. *Il pensiero filosofico di Josiah Royce*. Rome, 1921.

Humbach, K. T. *Einzelperson und Gemeinschaft nach Josiah Royce*. Heidelberg, 1962.

Loewenberg, J. *Royce's Synoptic Vision*. Baltimore, 1955.

Marcel, G. *La métaphysique de Royce*. Paris, 1945.

Olgiati, F. *Un pensatore americano: Josiah Royce*. Milan, 1917.

Smith, J. E. *Royce's Social Infinite*. New York, 1950.

Part IV: Chapters XIV–XVI

1. General Works Relating to Pragmatism

Baumgarten, E. *Der Pragmatismus: R. W. Emerson, W. James, J. Dewey*. Frankfurt, 1938.

Bawden, H. H. *Pragmatism*. New York, 1909.

Berthelot, R. *Un romantisme utilitaire*. 3 vols. Paris, 1911-13.

Childs, J. L. *American Pragmatism and Education: An Interpretation and Analysis*. New York, 1956.

Chiocchetti, E. *Il pragmatismo*. Milan, 1926.

Hook, S. *The Metaphysics of Pragmatism*. Chicago, 1927.

Kennedy, G. (editor). *Pragmatism and American Culture*. Boston, 1950.

Lamanna, E. P. *Il pragmatismo anglo-americano*. Florence, 1952.

Leroux, E. *Le pragmatisme américain et anglais*. Paris, 1922.

Mead, G. H. *The Philosophy of the Present*. Chicago, 1932.

Moore, A. W. *Pragmatism and Its Critics*. Chicago, 1910.

Moore, E. C. *American Pragmatism: Peirce, James and Dewey*. New York, 1961.

Morris, C. W. *Six Theories of Mind*. Chicago, 1932.

Murray, D. L. *Pragmatism*. London, 1912.

Perry, R. B. *Present Philosophical Tendencies*. New York, 1912.
Pratt, J. B. *What is Pragmatism?* New York, 1909.
Simon, P. *Der Pragmatismus in der modernen französischen Philosophie*. Paderborn, 1920.
Spirito, U. *Il pragmatismo nella filosofia contemporanea*. Florence, 1921.
Stebbing, L. S. *Pragmatism and French Voluntarism*. Cambridge, 1914.
Sturt, H. (editor). *Personal Idealism*. London, 1902.
Van Wessep, H. B. *Seven Sages: The Story of American Philosophy*. New York, 1960. (Includes Chapters on James, Dewey and Peirce.)
Wahl, J. A. *Les philosophies pluralistes d'Angleterre et d'Amérique*. Paris, 1920.
Wiener, P. P. *Evolution and the Founders of Pragmatism*. Cambridge (Mass.), 1949.

2. Peirce
Texts

Collected Papers of Charles Sanders Peirce. 8 vols. Cambridge, Mass. Volumes I–VI, edited by C. Hartshorne and P. Weiss and first published 1931–5, have been re-issued in 1960 as three volumes. Volumes VII–VIII, edited by A. W. Burke, were published in 1958.
There are also some books of selections, such as:
Chance, Love and Logic, edited by M. R. Cohen, with a supplementary essay by J. Dewey, New York, 1923.
The Philosophy of Peirce. Selected Writings, edited by J. Buchler. London, 1940 (reprint, New York, 1955).
Essays in the Philosophy of Science, edited by V. Tomas. New York, 1957.
Values in a Universe of Chance, edited by P. P. Wiener. Stanford and London, 1958.

Studies

Boler, J. F. *Charles Peirce and Scholastic Realism. A Study of Peirce's Relation to John Duns Scotus*. Seattle, 1963.
Buchler, J. *Charles Peirce's Empiricism*. London, 1939.
Carpenter, F. I. *American Literature and the Dream*. New York, 1955. (Includes a chapter on Peirce.)
Feibleman, J. K. *An Introduction to Peirce's Philosophy Interpreted as a System*. New York, 1946; London, 1960.
Freeman, E. *The Categories of Charles Peirce*. La Salle (Ill.), 1934.
Gallie, W. B. *Peirce and Pragmatism*. Penguin Books, 1952.
Goudge, T. A. *The Thought of C. S. Peirce*. Toronto and London, 1950.

Guccione Monroy, A. *Peirce e il pragmatismo americano.* Palermo, 1959.
Kempski, J. V. C. A. *Peirce und der Pragmatismus.* Stuttgart and Cologne, 1952.
Mullin, A. A. *Philosophical Comments on the Philosophies of C. S. Peirce and L. Wittgenstein.* Urbana (Ill.), 1961.
Murphey, M. G. *The Development of Peirce's Philosophy.* Cambridge (Mass.), 1961.
Thompson, M. *The Pragmatic Philosophy of C. S. Peirce.* Chicago and London, 1953.
Wennerberg, H. *The Pragmatism of C. S. Peirce.* Lund, 1963.
Wiener, P. P. and Young F. H. (editors). *Studies in the Philosophy of Charles Sanders Peirce.* Cambridge (Mass.), 1952.

3. James
Texts

The Principles of Psychology. New York, 1890.
The Will to Believe and Other Essays. New York and London, 1897 (reprint New York, 1956).
The Varieties of Religious Experience. New York and London, 1902.
Pragmatism. New York and London, 1907.
The Meaning of Truth. New York and London, 1909.
A Pluralistic Universe. New York and London, 1909.
Some Problems of Philosophy. New York and London, 1911.
Memories and Studies. New York and London, 1911.
Essays in Radical Empiricism. New York and London, 1912.
Collected Essays and Reviews. New York and London, 1920.
The Letters of William James, edited by H. James. 2 vols. Boston, 1926.
Annotated Bibliography of the Writings of William James, edited by R. B. Perry. New York, 1920.

Studies

Bixler, J. S. *Religion in the Philosophy of William James.* Boston, 1926.
Blau, T. *William James: sa théorie de la connaissance et de la verité.* Paris, 1933.
Boutroux, E. *William James.* Paris, 1911. (English translation by A. and B. Henderson, London, 1912.)
Bovet, P. *William James psychologue: l'intérêt de son oeuvre pour les éducateurs.* Saint Blaise, 1911.
Busch, K. A. *William James als Religionsphilosoph.* Göttingen, 1911.
Carpio, A. P. *Origen y desarrollo de la filosofía norteamericana. William James y el pragmatismo.* Buenos Aires, 1951.
Castiglioni, G. *William James.* Brescia, 1946.

Compton, C. H. (compiler). *William James: Philosopher and Man.* New York, 1957. (Quotations and References in 652 books.)

Cugini, U. *L'empirismo radicale di W. James.* Naples, 1925.

Kallen, H. M. *William James and Henri Bergson.* Chicago, 1914.

Knight, M. *William James.* Penguin Books, 1950.

Knox, H. V. *The Philosophy of William James.* London, 1914.

Le Breton, M. *La personnalité de William James.* Paris, 1929.

Maire, G. *William James et le pragmatisme religieux.* Paris, 1934.

Menard, A. *Analyse et critique des 'Principes de la Psychologie' de William James.* Paris, 1911.

Morris, L. *William James.* New York, 1950.

Nassauer, K. *Die Rechtsphilosophie von William James.* Bremen, 1943.

Perry, R. B. *The Thought and Character of William James.* 2 vols. Boston, 1935. (This is the standard biography.)
The Thought and Character of William James. Briefer Version. New York, 1954.
In the Spirit of William James. New Haven, 1938.

Reverdin, H. *La notion d'expérience d'après William James.* Geneva, 1913.

Roback, A. A. *William James, His Marginalia, Personality and Contribution.* Cambridge (Mass.), 1942.

Royce, J. *William James and Other Essays on the Philosophy of Life.* New York, 1911.

Sabin, E. E. *William James and Pragmatism.* Lancaster (Pa.), 1916.

Schmidt, H. *Der Begriff der Erfahrungskontinuität bei William James und seine Bedeutung für den amerikanischen Pragmatismus.* Heidelberg, 1959.

Switalski, W. *Der Wahrheitsbegriff des Pragmatismus nach William James.* Braunsberg, 1910.

Turner, J. E. *Examination of William James' Philosophy.* New York, 1919.

There are several collections of essays by various authors such as:
Essays Philosophical and Psychological in Honor of William James. New York, 1908.
In Commemoration of William James, 1842–1942. New York, 1942.
William James, the Man and the Thinker. Madison (Wis.), 1942.

4. Schiller
Texts

Riddles of the Sphinx. First published anonymously (by 'a Troglodyte') at London in 1891, then with the author's name at New York in 1894.
New edition, with sub-title *A Study in the Philosophy of Humanism.* London, 1910.

Axioms as Postulates, in *Personal Idealism,* edited by H. Sturt, London, 1902.

Humanism, Philosophical Essays. London, 1903 (2nd edition, 1912).

Studies in Humanism. London, 1907 (2nd edition, 1912).

Plato or Protagoras? London, 1908.

Formal Logic: A Scientific and Social Problem. London, 1912 (2nd edition, 1931).

Problems of Belief. London, 1924.

Why Humanism?, in *Contemporary British Philosophy,* First Series, edited by J. H. Muirhead. London, 1924.

Tantalus, or The Future of Man. London, 1924.

Eugenics and Politics. London, 1926.

Pragmatism, in *Encyclopædia Britannica,* 14th edition, 1929.

Logic for Use: An Introduction to the Voluntarist Theory of Knowledge. London, 1929.

Social Decay and Eugenical Reform. London, 1932.

Must Philosophers Disagree? and Other Essays in Popular Philosophy. London, 1934.

Studies

Abel, R. *The Pragmatic Humanism of F. C. S. Schiller.* New York and London, 1955.

Marett, R. *Ferdinand Canning Scott Schiller.* London, 1938. (British Academy lecture.)

White, S. S. *A Comparison of the Philosophies of F. C. S. Schiller and John Dewey.* Chicago, 1940.

5. Dewey

Texts

Psychology. New York, 1887 (3rd revised edition, 1891).

Leibniz's New Essays Concerning the Human Understanding. A Critical Exposition. Chicago, 1888.

The Ethics of Democracy. Ann Arbor, 1888.

Applied Psychology. Boston, 1889.

Outlines of a Critical Theory of Ethics. Ann Arbor, 1891.

The Study of Ethics: A Syllabus. Ann Arbor, 1894.

The Psychology of Number and Its Applications to Methods of Teaching Arithmetic (with J. A. McLellan). New York, 1895.

The Significance of the Problem of Knowledge. Chicago, 1897.

My Pedagogic Creed. New York, 1897.

Psychology and Philosophic Method. Berkeley, 1899.

The School of Society. Chicago, 1900 (revised edition, 1915).

The Child and the Curriculum. Chicago, 1902.

The Educational Situation. Chicago, 1902.

Studies in Logical Theory (with Others). Chicago, 1903

Logical Conditions of a Scientific Treatment of Morality. Chicago, 1903.
Ethics (with J. H. Tufts). New York, 1908.
How We Think. New York, 1910.
The Influence of Darwin on Philosophy and Other Essays in Contemporary Thought. New York, 1910.
Educational Essays, edited by J. J. Findlay. London, 1910.
Interest and Effort in Education. Boston, 1913.
German Philosophy and Politics. New York, 1915 (revised edition, 1942).
Schools of Tomorrow (with E. Dewey). New York, 1915.
Democracy and Education. New York, 1916.
Essays in Experimental Logic. Chicago, 1916.
Reconstruction in Philosophy. New York, 1920 (enlarged edition, 1948).
Letters from China and Japan (with A. C. Dewey, edited by E. Dewey. New York, 1920).
Human Nature and Conduct: An Introduction to Social Psychology. New York, 1922.
Experience and Nature. Chicago, 1925 (revised edition, 1929).
The Public and Its Problems. New York, 1927 (2nd edition, 1946).
Characters and Events. Popular Essays in Social and Political Philosophy, edited by J. Ratner. 2 vols. New York, 1929.
Impressions of Soviet Russia and the Revolutionary World, Mexico, China, Turkey. New York, 1929.
The Quest for Certainty. New York, 1929.
Individualism, Old and New (reprinted articles), New York, 1930.
Philosophy and Civilization. New York, 1931.
Art as Experience. New York, 1934.
A Common Faith. New Haven, 1934.
Education and The Social Order. New York, 1934.
Liberalism and Social Action. New York, 1935.
The Teacher and Society (with Others). New York, 1937.
Experience and Education. New York, 1938.
Logic: The Theory of Inquiry. New York, 1938.
Intelligence in the Modern World: John Dewey's Philosophy, edited by J. Ratner. New York, 1939. (Mostly selections from published writings.)
Theory of Valuation. Chicago, 1939.
Freedom and Culture. New York, 1939.
Education Today, edited by J. Ratner. New York, 1940.
Knowing and the Known (with A. F. Bentley). Boston, 1949.
There are several books of selections and compilations based on Dewey's writings, such as:
Intelligence in the Modern World: John Dewey's Philosophy, edited by J. Ratner. New York, 1939.

Dictionary of Education, edited by R. B. Winn. New York, 1959.
Dewey on Education, selected with an introduction and notes by M. S. Dworkin. New York, 1959.
For fuller bibliographies see:
A Bibliography of John Dewey, 1882–1939, by M. H. Thomas and H. W. Schneider, with an introduction by H. W. Schneider. New York, 1939.
The Philosophy of John Dewey, edited by P. A. Schilpp. New York, 1951 (2nd edition).

Studies

Baker, M. *Foundation of John Dewey's Educational Theory*. New York, 1955.
Baumgarten, E. *Der Pragmatismus: R. W. Emerson, W. James, J. Dewey*. Frankfurt, 1938.
Bausola, A. *L'etica di John Dewey*. Milan, 1960.
Brancatisano, F. *La posizione di John Dewey nella filosofia moderna*. Turin, 1953.
Buswell, J. O. *The Philosophies of F. R. Tennant and J. Dewey*. New York, 1950.
Child, A. *Making and Knowing in Hobbes, Vico and Dewey*. Berkeley, 1953.
Corallo, G. *La pedagogia di Giovanni Dewey*. Turin, 1950.
Crosser, P. K. *The Nihilism of John Dewey*. New York, 1955.
Edman, I. *John Dewey, His Contribution to the American Tradition*. Indianopolis (Ind.), 1955.
Feldman, W. T. *The Philosophy of John Dewey. A Critical Analysis*. Baltimore, 1934.
Fleckenstein, N. J. *A Critique of John Dewey's Theory of the Nature and the Knowledge of Reality in the Light of the Principles of Thomism*. Washington, 1954.
Geiger, G. R. *John Dewey in Perspective*. London and New York, 1938.
Gillio-Tos, M. T. *Il pensiero di John Dewey*. Naples, 1938.
Grana, G. *John Dewey e la metodologia americana*. Rome, 1955.
Gutzke, M. G. *John Dewey's Thought and Its Implications for Christian Education*. New York, 1956.
Handlin, O. *John Dewey's Challenge to Education: Historical Perspectives on the Cultural Context*. New York, 1959.
Hook, S. *John Dewey: An Intellectual Portrait*. New York, 1939.
Leander, F. *The Philosophy of John Dewey. A Critical Study*. Göteborg, 1939.
Levitt, M. *Freud and Dewey on the Nature of Man*. New York, 1960.
Mack, R. D. *The Appeal to Immediate Experience. Philosophic Method in Bradley, Whitehead and Dewey*. New York, 1945.
Mataix, A. (S.J.), *La norma moral en John Dewey*. Madrid, 1964.

Nathanson, J. *John Dewey*. New York, 1951.
Roth, R. J., (S.J.). *John Dewey and Self-Realization*. Englewood Cliffs (N.J.), 1963.
Thayer, H. S. *The Logic of Pragmatism: An Examination of John Dewey's Logic*. New York and London, 1952.
White, M. G. *The Origin of Dewey's Instrumentalism*. New York, 1943.
White, S. S. *A Comparison of the Philosophies of F. C. S. Schiller and John Dewey*. Chicago, 1940.

Symposia on Dewey:
John Dewey, The Man and His Philosophy, edited by S. S. White. Cambridge (Mass.), 1930. (Discourses in honour of Dewey's seventieth birthday.)
The Philosopher of the Common Man, edited by S. S. White. New York, 1940. (Essays in celebration of Dewey's eightieth birthday.)
The Philosophy of John Dewey, edited by P. A. Schilpp. New York, 1951 (2nd edition).
John Dewey: Philosopher of Science and Freedom, edited by S. Hook. New York, 1950.
John Dewey and the Experimental Spirit in Philosophy, edited by C. W. Hendel. New York, 1959.
John Dewey: Master Educator, edited by W. W. Brickman and S. Lehrer. New York, 1959.
Dialogue on John Dewey, edited by C. Lamont. New York, 1959.
John Dewey: His Thought and Influence, edited by J. Blewett. New York, 1960.

Part V: Chapters XVII–XXI[1]

1. *Some general works describing or illustrating recent philosophy, especially in Great Britain.*

Adams, G. P. and Montague, W. P. (editors). *Contemporary American Philosophy*. 2 vols. New York, 1930.
Ayer, A. J. and Others. *The Revolution in Philosophy*. London, 1956. (Broadcast Talks.)
Black, M. *Language and Philosophy*. Ithaca and London, 1949.
        Problems of Analysis: Philosophical Essays. Ithaca and London, 1954.
Blanshard, B. *Reason and Analysis*. London and New York, 1962. (A critical discussion of linguistic philosophy.)
Boman, L. *Criticism and Construction in the Philosophy of the American New Realism*. Stockholm, 1955.

[1] No bibliography has been supplied for Wittgenstein, as his philosophical ideas have been mentioned only in general discussion or incidentally.

Charlesworth, M. *Philosophy and Linguistic Analysis*. Pittsburgh and Louvain, 1959. (Critical as well as historical.)

Drake, D. and Others. *Essays in Critical Realism*. New York and London, 1921.

Flew, A. G. N. (editor). *Logic and Language* (first series). Oxford, 1951.
  Logic and Language (second series). Oxford, 1955.
  Essays in Conceptual Analysis. Oxford, 1953.
  New Essays in Philosophical Theology. London, 1955.

Gellner, E. *Words and Things*. London, 1959. (A very critical treatment of linguistic philosophy in England.)

Ginestier, P. *La pensée anglo-saxonne depuis 1900*. Paris, 1956.

Holt, E. B. and Others. *The New Realism*. New York, 1912.

Kremer, R. P. *Le néo-realisme américain*. Louvain, 1920.
  La théorie de la connaissance chez les néo-realistes anglais. Louvain, 1928.

Lewis, H. D. (editor). *Contemporary British Philosophy* (third series). London, 1956.

Linsky, L. (editor). *Semantics and the Philosophy of Language*. Urbana (Ill.), 1952.

Mace, C. A. (editor). *British Philosophy in the Mid-Century*. London, 1957.

MacIntyre, A. (editor). *Metaphysical Beliefs*. London, 1957.

Muirhead, J. H. *Rule and End in Morals*. London, 1932. (Discusses the ethical issues treated by Prichard, Carritt, Ross, Joseph, and others.)

Pears, D. F. (editor). *The Nature of Metaphysics*. London, 1957. (Broadcast Talks.)

Sellars, R. W. and Others. *Essays in Critical Realism*. New York and London, 1920.

Urmson, J. O. *Philosophical Analysis. Its Development between the Two World Wars*. Oxford, 1956.

Warnock, G. J. *English Philosophy Since 1900*. (A clear account of the development of the analytic movement.)

Warnock, M. *Ethics Since 1900*. London, 1960. (Mainly on the development of English ethical theory from Bradley. But discusses the ideas of the American philosopher C. L. Stevenson and contains a chapter on Sartre.)

2. G. E. Moore
Texts

Principia Ethica. Cambridge, 1903 (2nd edition, 1922; new edition, 1960).

Ethics. London, 1912 (and reprints).
Philosophical Studies. London, 1922 (new edition, 1960). (This work includes 'The Refutation of Idealism' from *Mind*, 1903.)
Some Main Problems of Philosophy. London, 1953. (This volume includes some hitherto unpublished lectures delivered in the winter of 1910–11.)
Philosophical Papers. London, 1959. (This volume includes 'A Defence of Common Sense' from *Contemporary British Philosophy*, Second Series, 1925.)
Commonplace Book, 1919–1953, edited by C. Lewy. London, 1962.

Studies

Braithwaite, R. B. *George Edward Moore, 1873–1958*. London, 1963. (British Academy lecture.)
Schilpp, P. A. (editor). *The Philosophy of G. E. Moore*. New York, 1952.
White, A. R. *G. E. Moore: A Critical Exposition*. Oxford, 1958.

3. *Russell*
Texts

German Social Democracy. London and New York, 1896.
An Essay on the Foundations of Geometry. Cambridge, 1897.
A Critical Exposition of the Philosophy of Leibniz. Cambridge, 1900.
The Principles of Mathematics. Cambridge, 1903.
Principia Mathematica (with A. N. Whitehead). 3 vols. Cambridge, 1910–13 (2nd edition, 1927–35).
Philosophical Essays (reprinted articles). London and New York, 1910.
The Problems of Philosophy. London and New York, 1912.
Our Knowledge of the External World as a Field for Scientific Method in Philosophy. London and Chicago, 1914 (revised edition, 1929).
The Philosophy of Bergson (controversy with Professor H. W. Carr). London, Glasgow and Cambridge, 1914.
Scientific Method in Philosophy. Oxford, 1914.
War, the Offspring of Fear (pamphlet). London, 1915.
Principles of Social Reconstruction. London, 1916 (2nd edition, 1920).
Policy of the Entente, 1904–1914: A Reply to Professor Gilbert Murray (booklet). Manchester and London, 1916.
Justice in War-Time. London and Chicago, 1916 (2nd edition, 1924).
Political Ideals. New York, 1917.
Mysticism and Logic and Other Essays (reprinted essays). London and New York, 1918.
Roads to Freedom: Socialism, Anarchism and Syndicalism. London, 1918.

Introduction to Mathematical Philosophy. London and New York, 1919.
The Practice and Theory of Bolshevism. London and New York, 1920 (2nd edition, 1949).
The Analysis of Mind. London, 1921, New York, 1924.
The Problem of China. London and New York, 1922.
Free Thought and Official Propaganda (lecture). London and New York, 1922.
The Prospects of Industrial Civilization (with D. Russell). London and New York, 1923.
The ABC of Atoms. London and New York, 1923.
Icarus, or the Future of Science (booklet). London and New York, 1924.
How To Be Free and Happy (lecture). New York, 1924.
The ABC of Relativity. London and New York, 1925 (revised edition, 1958).
On Education, Especially in Early Childhood. London and New York, 1926. (In America with the title *Education and the Good Life.*)
The Analysis of Matter. London and New York, 1927 (reprint, 1954).
An Outline of Philosophy. London and New York, 1927. (In America with the title *Philosophy.*)
Selected Papers of Bertrand Russell (selected and introduced by Russell). New York, 1927.
Sceptical Essays (largely reprints). London and New York, 1928.
Marriage and Morals. London and New York, 1929.
The Conquest of Happiness. London and New York, 1930.
The Scientific Outlook. New York, 1931.
Education and the Social Order. London and New York, 1932. (In America with the title *Education and the Modern World.*)
Freedom and Organization, 1814–1914. London and New York, 1934. (In America with the title *Freedom versus Organization.*)
In Praise of Idleness and Other Essays. New York, 1935.
Religion and Science. London and New York, 1935.
Which Way to Peace? London, 1936.
The Amberley Papers (with P. Russell.) 2 vols. London and New York, 1937.
Power: A New Social Analysis. London and New York, 1938.
An Inquiry into Meaning and Truth. London and New York, 1940.
Let the People Think (essays). London, 1941.
A History of Western Philosophy: Its Connection with Political and Social Circumstances from the Earliest Times to the Present Day. London and New York, 1945 (2nd edition, 1961).
Human Knowledge: Its Scope and Limits. London and New York, 1948.

Authority and the Individual. London and New York, 1949.

Unpopular Essays (largely reprints). London and New York, 1950.

The Impact of Science on Society (lectures). New York, 1951.

New Hopes for a Changing World. London, 1951.

Human Society in Ethics and Politics. London and New York, 1954.

Logic and Knowledge: Essays, 1901–1950, edited by R. C. Marsh. London and New York, 1956. (This volume includes Russell's 1918 lectures on the philosophy of logical atomism, also the article on logical atomism written for *Contemporary British Philosophy*, First Series, 1924.)

Why I am not a Christian, and Other Essays. London and New York, 1957.

My Philosophical Development. London and New York, 1959.

Wisdom of the West. London, 1959.

Has Man a Future? Penguin Books, 1961.

Fact and Fiction. London, 1961.

Studies

Clark, C. H. D. *Christianity and Bertrand Russell*. London, 1958.

Dorward, A. *Bertrand Russell*. London, 1951. (A booklet written for the British Council and the National Book League.)

Feibleman, J. K. *Inside the Great Mirror. A Critical Examination of the Philosophy of Russell, Wittgenstein and their Followers*. The Hague, 1958.

Fritz, C. A. *Bertrand Russell's Construction of the External World*. New York and London, 1952.

Götlind, E. *Bertrand Russell's Theories of Causation*. Upsala, 1952.

Jourdain, P. E. B. *The Philosophy of Mr. Bertrand Russell* (satire). London and Chicago, 1918.

Leggett, H. W. *Bertrand Russell* (pictorial biography). London, 1949.

Lovejoy, A. O. *The Revolt Against Dualism*. Chicago, 1930. (Chapters 6–7 treat of Russell's theory of mind.)

McCarthy, D. G. *Bertrand Russell's Informal Freedom*. Louvain, 1960 (doctorate dissertation).

Riveroso, E. *Il pensiero di Bertrand Russell*. Naples, 1958.

Santayana, G. *Winds of Doctrine*. London, 1913. (Includes a study of Russell's philosophy.)

Schilpp, P. A. (editor). *The Philosophy of Bertrand Russell*. New York, 1946 (2nd edition).

Urmson, J. O. *Philosophical Analysis. Its Development between the Two World Wars*. Oxford, 1956. (Includes a critical discussion of Russell's reductive analysis. Russell's reply, together with replies to criticisms by G. J. Warnock and P. F. Strawson, is reprinted in chapter 18 of *My Philosophical Development*.)

Wood, A. *Bertrand Russell, The Passionate Sceptic* (biographical). London, 1957.

        Russell's Philosophy: A Study of Its Development (an unfinished essay printed at the end of Russell's *My Philosophical Development*).

Wood, M. G. *Why Mr. Bertrand Russell is not a Christian.* London, 1928.

There are, of course, many articles on particular points or aspects of Russell's thought in *Mind, Analysis, The Proceedings of the Aristotelian Society, The Philosophical Review,* and other periodicals. But they cannot possibly be listed here.

INDEX

(The principal references are in heavy type. Asterisked numbers refer to bibliographical information.)

Voltaire, François Marie Arouet de (1694–1778) 482

wages 23, 42–3
Wallace, Alfred Russel (1823–1913) 102
Wallace, William (1844–97) 185
Walsh, William Henry (b. 1913) 507 n. 3
war 133 *and see* nuclear disarmament
Ward, James (1843–1925) 96, 202 n. 1, **247-50**, 251–3, 403
Warnock, Geoffrey J. (b. 1923) 399 n. 1
Warnock, M. 386 n. 1
wealth, distribution of 24, 42
Weitz, Morris 443 n. 1
welfare state 42
what of things, the 270, 273
Whateley, Richard (1787–1863) 50–1, 66
Whewell, William (1794–1866) 27, 52, 59–60, 77
Whitehead, Alfred North (1861–1947) 328–9, 399–401, 436–7, 439
whole, infinite 195
Wilberforce, Samuel (1805–73) 107
will: 21, 93, 95, 152, 155, 208, 224, 238, 276, 302
   absolute W. 288
   general W., the 226–9, 230, 232
   good W., the 192–4
   infinite W. 278, 293
   moral W. 153, 268
   universal W. 192, 194
   will of all, the 227
   See also freedom of the will, volition

will to believe 337–8
Willich, A. F. M. 149
Wittgenstein, Ludwig (1889–1951) ix–x, 17, 151, 402, 418, 430, 438, 444–9, 462 n. 2, 468, 491–2, **495-504**, 507
Wollaston, William (1689–1724) 258
words:
   bringing back W. to everyday usage 502
   logical W. 462
   object-words *see* object-words *above*
Wordsworth, William (1770–1850) 26 n. 1, 155
world, the:
   and beginning in time 481
   as expression of absolute system of ideas 278
   as necessary to God 299
   as plastic 350
   as totality 497–8
   common W. 221–2
   construction of 220–1
   'my' W. 276, 278, 499
   private W. 221
   See also reality, universe
world-government 471, 480
world-state 229
world-views 327, 333, 340, 342, 344, 376–7, 379, 393–4, 396, 399, 507–9
Wright, Chauncey 304 n. 1
wrong actions *see* right actions
Wundt, Wilhelm (1832–1920) 247

Yeomans, Professor 123

A
HISTORY OF PHILOSOPHY

VOLUME IX
MAINE DE BIRAN TO SARTRE

BY
FREDERICK COPLESTON, S.J.

A

HISTORY OF PHILOSOPHY

Volume IX
MAINE DE BIRAN TO SARTRE

by

FREDERICK COPLESTON, S.J.

CONTENTS

CONTENTS

VIII. THE SPIRITUALIST MOVEMENT 155

The term 'spiritualism'—The philosophy of Ravaisson—
J. Lachelier and the bases of induction—Boutroux and contingency—A. Fouillée on *idées-forces*—M. J. Guyau and the philosophy of life.

IX. HENRI BERGSON (1) 178

Life and works—Bergson's idea of philosophy—Time and freedom—Memory and perception: the relation between spirit and matter—Instinct, intelligence and intuition in the context of the theory of evolution.

X. HENRI BERGSON (2) 202

Introductory remarks—Closed morality—Open morality: the interpretation of the two types—Static religion as a defence against the dissolvent power of intelligence—Dynamic religion and mysticism—Comments.

PART III

FROM BERGSON TO SARTRE

XI. PHILOSOPHY AND CHRISTIAN APOLOGETICS 216

Ollé-Laprune on moral certitude—Blondel and the way of immanence—Laberthonnière and Christian philosophy—Some remarks on modernism.

XII. THOMISM IN FRANCE 250

Introductory remarks: D. J. Mercier—Garrigou-Lagrange and Sertillanges—J. Maritain—E. Gilson—P. Rousselot and A. Forest—J. Maréchal.

XIII. PHILOSOPHY OF SCIENCE 271

H. Poincaré—P. Duhem—G. Milhaud—E. Meyerson—A. Lalande—G. Bachelard.

XIV. PHILOSOPHY OF VALUES, METAPHYSICS, PERSONALISM 293

General remarks—R. Polin—Metaphysics of values: R. Le Senne and the philosophy of spirit—R. Ruyer and J. Pucelle—L. Lavelle and the philosophy of act—The personalism of E. Mounier.

XV. TWO RELIGIOUS THINKERS 318

Teilhard de Chardin—G. Marcel—Differences in outlook.

XVI. THE EXISTENTIALISM OF SARTRE (1) . . . 340

Life and writings—Pre-reflective and reflexive consciousness: the imagining and the emotive consciousness—Phenomenal being and being in itself—Being for itself—The freedom of being for itself—Consciousness of others—Atheism and values.

CONTENTS

PREFACE

THE seventh and eighth volumes of this work were originally intended to cover nineteenth-century philosophy in Germany and in Great Britain respectively. The seventh volume conforms to this plan, inasmuch as it ends with a treatment of Nietzsche who died in 1900 and whose period of literary activity falls entirely within the nineteenth century. The eighth volume however includes treatments of G. E. Moore, Bertrand Russell and the American philosopher John Dewey. All three were born in the nineteenth century; and both Dewey and Russell had published before the turn of the century. But all were active well on into the twentieth century. Indeed, Russell was still alive when the volume was published and was able to make an appreciative comment in a letter to the author. The present ninth volume carries even further this tendency to go beyond the limits of nineteenth-century thought. It was originally intended to cover French philosophy between the revolution and the death of Henri Bergson. In point of fact it includes a fairly extensive treatment of Jean-Paul Sartre, a briefer outline of some of Merleau-Ponty's ideas and some remarks on the structuralism of Lévi-Strauss.

This extension of the account of French philosophy after the revolution to include a number of thinkers whose literary activity falls within the twentieth century and some of whom at any rate are still alive has meant that I have been unable to fulfil my original plan of including within the present volume treatments of nineteenth-century thought in Italy, Spain and Russia. Reference has been made to one or two Belgian thinkers, such as Joseph Maréchal; but otherwise I have restricted the area to France. Indeed, it is more accurate to say that I have treated of French philosophers than of philosophy in France as a geographical area. For example, Nikolai Berdyaev settled at Paris in 1924 and pursued a vigorous literary activity on French soil. But it seems to me improper to annex him for France. He belongs to the religious tradition in Russian thought. There may indeed be more reason for annexing Berdyaev for French philosophy than there would be for counting Karl Marx as a British philosopher on the ground that he spent his last years in London and worked in the British Museum. At the same time the Russian

vii

writers who lived and wrote in exile in France remained Russian thinkers.

If we leave foreign exiles out of account, France is in any case rich in philosophical writers, both professional philosophers and literary figures whose writings can be described as having philosophical significance. Unless however the historian proposes to write a complete comprehensive survey, which would amount to little more than a list of names or require several tomes, he cannot include them all. There are of course philosophers who obviously have to be included in any account of French philosophy since the revolution. Maine de Biran, Auguste Comte and Henri Bergson are examples. It is also clear that discussion of a given movement of thought entails reference to its leading representatives. Whatever may be one's estimate of Victor Cousin's merits as a thinker, it would be absurd to write about eclecticism in France without saying something about its chief representative, especially in view of the position which he occupied for a time in the academic life of his country. Similarly, an account of neo-criticism involves some discussion of Renouvier's thought. Though however there is a considerable number of philosophers whom the historian would rightly be expected to include, either because of their intrinsic interest and their reputation, contemporary or posthumous, or as representatives of a given movement of thought, there are plenty of others among whom he has to make a selection. And any selection is open to criticism on some ground or other. Thus in regard to the present volume some readers may be inclined to think that space has been allotted to cloudy metaphysicians and idealists which might have been more profitably devoted to philosophy of education or to aesthetics, or to a more extended treatment of social philosophy. Again, if a religious thinker such as Teilhard de Chardin is to be given prominence, why is there no mention of Simone Weil, a very different sort of writer, it is true, but one who has been widely read? Further, in view of the fact that the volume includes a treatment not only of nineteenth-century French political thinkers but also of Sartre's version of Marxism, why is nothing said, for example, about Bertrand de Jouvenel and Raymond Aron?

In the cases of some philosophers it may be relevant to point out that reputation and influence in their own country may very well justify their inclusion, in spite of the fact that in a country with a different philosophical tradition they are little known or

read. The reader presumably wishes to hear something about
thinkers who have enjoyed some prominence in France, even if
they are pretty well unknown in England. Indeed, if their names
are little known in England, this could be advanced as an excellent reason for including them. The thought of Louis Lavelle, for
instance, would doubtless have left G. E. Moore in a state of
mystification; and it would hardly have commended itself to
J. L. Austin. But this is no more a reason for omitting Lavelle
from an account of recent French philosophy than the lack of
sympathy which many French philosophers would probably
have with J. L. Austin's preoccupation with ordinary language
would constitute a valid reason for omitting Austin's name
from an account of recent philosophical thought in Great
Britain.

At the same time it must be admitted that there are gaps in the
present volume. This is partly due of course to considerations of
space. But it is only honest to add that it is partly due to the
circumstances in which this volume has been written. If one is
Principal of a School of the University of London, one's time for
reading and research is inevitably very limited. And one has to use
for writing such intervals as may occur. I have doubtless tended
to write about philosophers of whom I already knew something
and have omitted thinkers who might well have been included.
This might be considered a very sound reason for postponing
completion of the work. As however I have already indicated, I
wish to use the time which retirement may put at my disposal for
a rather different sort of volume.

Even when one has decided, for good or ill, on the philosophers
about whom one intends to write, there may well be problems of
classification or labelling. For example, in the present work Jules
Lachelier has been considered in the chapter devoted to what is
customarily described as the spiritualist movement. Though
however there is precedent for doing this, Lachelier's best-known
work is a treatise on the foundations of induction; and it might
thus be thought more appropriate to put his ideas under the heading of philosophy of science. At the same time he develops his
ideas in such a way as to outline a philosophy which would qualify
him for classification as an idealist. Again, while Meyerson has
been considered in the text as a philosopher of science, his theory
of identity might equally well be treated as a speculative philosophy of the idealist type.

Talk about problems of classification may appear to be the
expression of a misguided desire to fit all philosophers into neatly
labelled pigeon-holes or of a failure to appreciate the complexities
of human life and thought. Or it may seem that one has fallen
victim to the bewitching influence of language, imagining that one
enjoys conceptual mastery over what one has named. The matter
is not however quite so simple. For hesitation in regard to labelling may express not so much a passion for pigeon-holing as a real
difficulty in deciding which aspect or aspects of a man's thought
are to be regarded as the most significant. The question arises of
course: significant in what respect? Consider the case of Berkeley
in British philosophy. If an historian is intent on tracing the
development of classical British empiricism, he is likely to emphasize those aspects of Berkeley's thought which make it plausible
to regard it as a link between Locke and Hume. This has been a
common enough procedure. If however the historian is more concerned with Berkeley's declared interests and with the bishop's
own estimation of the significance of his philosophy, stress will be
laid on the metaphysical aspects of Berkeley's thought and on its
religious bearing. Similarly, if an historian is concerned with
exhibiting a movement of thought leading up to the philosophy
of Bergson, he is likely to label as a 'spiritualist' a writer such as
Lachelier, whose thought, considered by itself, might well be
given a different label. Again, in the present volume Brunschvicg's
philosophy has been treated under the general heading of idealism.
But if one thought that idealism was undeserving of attention,
one might include Brunschvicg among philosophers of science.
For he certainly had something to say on the subject.

Classificatory problems might indeed be avoided by treating the
development of philosophical thought in terms of problems and
themes, as Windelband did, rather than by taking philosophers in
succession and treating the thought of each as one block. This
procedure might seem to be especially appropriate in the case of
French philosophers, who have frequently had wide-ranging
interests and have written on a variety of topics. Though however
this procedure has much to commend it, it also has disadvan-
tages for the reader who wishes to devote his uninterrupted attention to a particular philosopher but is unable to find his thought
considered as a whole. In any case, in this ninth volume I did
not wish to change the procedure which has been followed, for
good or ill, in the preceding volumes. There will be scope

for a different approach in the projected tenth and final volume.

Reference has been made above to cloudy metaphysicians. This remark should not of course be understood as a judgment on French philosophy. The present writer is not indeed quite so impressed as some people seem to be by the common assertion that French thought is conspicuous for its logical structure and clarity. This may apply to Descartes, the foremost French philosopher; and the writers of the Enlightenment were doubtless clear. But some more recent thinkers seem to have done their best to rival the obscure language which we tend to associate with German philosophy since Kant. It is not that they are unable to write clearly. For they often do. But in their professional philosophical writings they seem to prefer to express their ideas in turgid jargon. Sartre is a case in point. And as for the metaphysicians, talk about *l'être* is not necessarily more illuminating than talk about *das Sein*. At the same time it would be quite wrong to imply that French philosophy is predominantly concerned with metaphysical obscurities. A concern with man is a much more conspicuous feature. The first notable philosopher to be treated in this volume, Maine de Biran, approached philosophy by way of psychology; and it was reflection on man's inner life which led him to metaphysics. The last philosopher to be discussed at some length, Jean-Paul Sartre, is a thinker who has concentrated on man as a free agent and whose personal commitment in the social and political area is well known.

Obviously, philosophers can be concerned with man in different ways. Some have focussed their attention on man's spontaneous activity and freedom, as with Maine de Biran and in what is commonly described at the spiritualist movement in French philosophy, while others, such as Le Senne, have emphasized man's recognition of values and his transcending of the empirically given. Other philosophers have dwelt more on the life of thought and on man's reflection on the mind's activity as manifested in history. Brunschvicg is a case in point. These various approaches have tended to broaden out into general interpretations of reality. Ravaisson, for example, started with reflection on habit and ended with a general view of the world, while Bergson reflected on man's experiences of duration and of voluntary activity and developed a religiously oriented philosophy of the universe. In the case of those who concentrated their attention on the mind's self-criticism and its reflection on its own activity, as manifested in various spheres, the resulting general view has tended to be of an idealist type. With other thinkers the emphasis has been laid on man in society. This can of course take the form of objective and dispassionate inquiry, as in, for example, the sociology of Émile Durkheim or the structuralist anthropology of Lévi-Strauss. Reflection on man in society can also be pursued in a spirit of commitment, with a view to promoting action or change rather than simply with the aim of understanding. This was naturally the case in the aftermath of the revolution. In the first chapter of this volume attention is paid to a group of thinkers who were deeply concerned with the reconstruction of society and who believed that it could not be effected except through the reassertion of certain threatened traditions. In the fourth chapter another group of thinkers are briefly considered who were convinced that while the revolution had overthrown the old régime, its ideals had still to be realized in positive social construction and development. For the matter of that, Auguste Comte, the high priest of positivism, was profoundly concerned with the organization of society, even if he had a rather naïve faith in the perfecting of society through the development of scientific knowledge. At a later period we find a similar spirit of commitment, manifested in a desire to transform society either through Marxist-inspired revolution, as with Sartre, or through the development of a more personalist socialism, as with Emmanuel Mounier.

Such distinguishable lines of thought are not of course all mutually exclusive. They can be found in varying degrees of combination. The thought of Sartre is an obvious example. On the one hand he has laid great emphasis on human freedom and on the individual's choice of his own values and on the way in which the individual gives meaning to his life. On the other hand he has emphasized self-commitment in the social–political sphere and the need for the transformation of society. The effort to combine the two lines of thought, individualistic and social, has led to his attempt to present a version of Marxism which incorporates in itself an existentialist insistence on human freedom. It is no matter for surprise if he has found difficulty in combining his conviction that it is man who both makes history and gives it meaning with the Marxist tendency to depict history as a dialectical and teleological process, or in combining his existentialism, with its 'every man is an island' atmosphere, with a Marxist emphasis on the social group. The point is however that in the thought of Sartre the emphasis on human freedom which was characteristic of the line of thought stemming from Maine de Biran has met the line of thought which lays stress on man in society and regards the French revolution as simply one stage in an unfinished process of social transformation.

To claim that concern with man has been a conspicuous feature of French philosophy is not of course to assert that philosophy in France has been concerned simply with man. Such an assertion would be clearly untrue. If however we compare recent philosophical thought in France with recent British philosophy, it is evident that what Georges-André Malraux has described as 'the human condition' occupies a place in the former which it certainly does not occupy in the latter. And themes which have been treated by, for example, Gabriel Marcel and Vladimir Jankélévitch hardly appear at all in British philosophy. As for social and political thought, British philosophers are accustomed to follow a policy of neutrality which would be clearly unacceptable to a writer such as Sartre. In general, French philosophical thought gives an impression of relevance to man and society which is not given by the recently prevailing line of thought in Great Britain.

Such remarks do not necessarily imply a comparative judgment of value. How one evaluates the situation depends to a great extent on one's concept of the nature and functions of philosophy. Bertrand Russell did not hesitate to commit himself on moral and political issues; but he did not regard the writings in which he did so as belonging to philosophy in a strict sense. If one believes that the philosopher's function is to reflect on the language of morals and politics, and that if he commits himself on substantive issues he does so as a man and a citizen rather than as a philosopher, one will obviously not regard it as a failure or a fault on the part of philosophers if they maintain in their writings a predominantly detached and analytic approach. It is not the intention of the present author to follow Bertrand Russell in endorsing the sustained attack on leading British philosophers which was made by Professor Ernest Gellner in his provocative and amusing, even if exaggeratedly polemical book, *Words and Things*. This does not however alter the fact that there is a difference in philosophical atmosphere, so to speak, between the two countries. In England philosophy has become a highly specialized pursuit, with a great care for clarity and precision of expression and a marked distaste for emotively charged and ambiguous language and for slovenly argumentation. In France there are much closer interconnections between philosophy, literature and art. Obviously, one can find philosophical specialization and what some people regard as ivory-tower philosophy in France as elsewhere. But the area in which philosophy and literature are inter-related seems to be considerably more extended in France than in England. Perhaps the fact that in the French educational system students are introduced to philosophy while still at the lycée has something to do with this. As for political commitment, there are clearly historical and socio-political reasons why, for example, since the second world war there has been a preoccupation with Marxism which is not to be found in England, certainly not to the same extent.

The claim, advanced above, that man has been a conspicuous theme in French philosophy was made with a view to counterbalancing any impression which might be given by the passages in this volume on metaphysicians such as Lavelle and idealists such as Hamelin that philosophy has been predominantly concerned with 'metaphysical obscurities'. Though however man would commonly be considered a more concrete and relevant theme than *l'être* or *das Sein*, it must be admitted that talk about man is no guarantee of clarity and precision. In the opinion of the present writer it is much easier to understand Bergson's general view of the world than it is to grasp the meaning of certain more recent French writers on, say, the phenomenology of human consciousness. I am not thinking of Sartre. His jargon is simply irritating. If what he says sometimes seems to be extremely obscure, this is not because what he is saying is unintelligible, but because he has chosen to express in difficult language something which could have been said much more plainly. There are however certain other philosophers whose writing seems to be so impressionistic and vague that the author of this volume saw little prospect of being able to summarize their lines of thought in a manner suitable for presentation in a history of philosophy. One can of course retort, 'so much the worse for histories of philosophy'. This may be fair comment. But it is noticeable that in the case of some philosophers available expositions of their thought are even less illuminating than the original texts. Merleau-Ponty is of course quite right in saying that philosophers should not hesitate to pursue exploratory inquiries which require fresh concepts and expression. To demand that nothing should be said except what can be precisely handled with already available tools would be to demand an abandonment of creative thought and a petrification of philosophy. But this does not alter the fact that what is in process of coming to birth and has not yet acquired shape is hardly apt material for the historian of philosophy.

PART I

FROM THE REVOLUTION TO AUGUSTE COMTE

CHAPTER I

THE TRADITIONALIST REACTION TO THE REVOLUTION

Introductory remarks—De Maistre—De Bonald—Chateaubriand—Lamennais—Traditionalism and the Church.

1. To us the French revolution is an historical event, the causes and development and effects of which can be investigated in a dispassionate manner. At the time judgments were obviously accompanied and often affected by strong feelings. To many people the revolution naturally appeared not only as a national liberation and a regenerating force in French society but also as a movement destined to bring light and freedom to other nations as well. The Terror might of course be deplored, or perhaps excused; but the ideals of the revolution were approved and welcomed as an assertion of human freedom, and sometimes as a long-awaited extension of the religious Reformation into the political and social spheres. Equally naturally however there were others to whom the revolution appeared as a disastrous event which threatened the foundations of society, substituted an anarchic individualism for social stability, was wantonly destructive of the traditions of France and expressed a rejection of the religious basis of morals, education and social cohesion. Obviously, hostility to the revolution could be prompted to a large extent by selfish motives; but so could support of it. And just as idealism could be enlisted on the side of the revolution, so could there be an opposition to the revolutionary spirit which expressed a sincere conviction about its destructive and impious character.

A thought-out opposition to the revolution on the philosophical plane was expressed by the so-called Traditionalists. Both supporters and opponents of the revolution were inclined to regard it as the fruit of the Enlightenment, though they obviously differed sharply in their respective evaluations of and attitudes to the Enlightenment. It is of course easy to dismiss the Traditionalists as reactionaries filled with nostalgia for the past and blind to the movement of history.[1] But however myopic they may have been in certain respects, they were eminent and influential writers and cannot simply be passed over in an account of French thought in the early decades of the nineteenth century.

2. The first writer of whom mention must be made is the famous royalist and ultramontanist Count Joseph de Maistre (1753–1821). Born at Chambéry in Savoy, he studied law at Turin and became a senator of Savoy. When the French invaded his country, he took refuge first in Aosta and then at Lausanne, where he wrote his *Considerations on France* (*Considérations sur la France*, 1796). De Maistre had once had some liberal sympathies; but in this work he made clear his opposition to the revolution and his desire for a restoration of the French monarchy.

In 1802 de Maistre was appointed minister-plenipotentiary of the King of Sardinia to the Russian court at St. Petersburg. He remained in Russia for fourteen years, and it was there that he wrote his *Essay on the Generative Principle of Political Constitutions* (*Essai sur le principe générateur des constitutions politiques*, 1814). He also occupied himself with the composition of his work *On the Pope* (*Du Pape*), which was finished at Turin and published in 1819, and the *Evenings at St. Petersburg* (*Soirées de Saint-Pétersbourg*) which appeared in 1821. His *Examination of the Philosophy of Bacon* (*Examen de la philosophie de Bacon*) was published posthumously in 1836.

In his earlier years de Maistre had been associated with a masonic circle at Lyons which derived some inspiration from the ideas of Louis-Claude de Saint-Martin (1743–1803), who had himself been stimulated by the writings of Jakob Boehme.[2] The circle was opposed to the philosophy of the Enlightenment and turned to metaphysical and mystical doctrines representing a fusion of Christian and Neoplatonist beliefs. And Saint-Martin saw in history the unfolding of divine providence. History was for him a continuous process linked throughout to God, the One.

It is perhaps not unreasonable to discern some echoes at any rate of such ideas in de Maistre's *Considerations on France*. True,

---

[1] This phrase is ambiguous. If the movement of history means the succession of events, the Traditionalists were obviously not blind to it. If the phrase implies that change and progress (in an evaluative sense) are synonymous terms, this identification presupposes a philosophy of history which cannot be simply taken for granted. It is however doubtless possible to fail to appreciate the fact that the emergence of new forces and ideas exclude the successful restoration and revivification of a previously existing structure.

[2] See Vol. III of this *History*, pp. 270–3.

he is horrified by the revolution, the act of regicide, the attack on the Church and the Terror; but at the same time his concept of history stands in the way of an exclusively negative evaluation of the revolution. He regards Robespierre and the other leaders as scoundrels and criminals, but he also sees them as the unwitting instruments of divine providence. Men 'act at the same time voluntarily and necessarily'.[1] They act as they will to act, but in doing so they further the designs of providence. The leaders of the revolution thought that they were in control of it; but they were instruments to be used and thrown aside, while the revolution itself was God's instrument to punish sin: 'Never had the divinity shown itself so clearly in any human event. If it employs the vilest instruments, it is a case of punishing in order to regenerate.'[2] If the factions involved in the revolution sought to attain the destruction of Christianity and of the monarchy, 'it follows that all their efforts will result only in the exaltation of Christianity and of the monarchy.'[3] For there is a 'secret force'[4] which works in history.

De Maistre's idea of history as exhibiting the operation of divine providence and of individuals as instruments was not in itself a novelty, though he applied it to a very recent event or series of events. The idea is obviously open to objections. Apart from any difficulty in reconciling human freedom with the unfailing realization of the divine purpose, the concept of revolutions and wars as divine punishments gives rise to the reflection that it is by no means only the guilty (or those who may seem to human eyes to be guilty) who suffer from such cataclysms. De Maistre tries however to meet such objections by a theory of the solidarity of the nation, and indeed of the human race, as constituting an organic unity. It is this theory which he opposes to what he regards as the erroneous and pernicious individualism of the Enlightenment.

Political society, de Maistre insists, is certainly not a collection of individuals united through a social compact or contract. Nor can a viable constitution be thought out *a priori* by the human reason in abstraction from national traditions and the institutions which have developed through the centuries. 'One of the great errors of a century which professed all errors was to believe that a political constitution could be written and created *a priori*,

---

[1] *Considérations sur la France* (Brussels, 1838), p. 2.
[2] *Ibid.*, p. 21.   [3] *Ibid.*, p. 127.   [4] *Ibid.*, p. 128.

whereas reason and experience are united in showing that a
constitution is a divine work, and that it is precisely what is most
fundamental and essentially constitutional in the laws of a nation
which could not be written.'[1] If we look at the English constitution, we can see that it is the result of a vast number of contributing factors and circumstances which served as the instruments of
providence. A constitution of this kind, which was certainly not
constructed in an *a priori* manner, is always allied with religion
and takes a monarchic form. It is not surprising therefore if
revolutionaries, who wish to establish a constitution by decree,
attack both religion and the monarchy.

In general terms de Maistre is violently opposed to the
rationalism of the eighteenth century which he sees as treating of
abstractions and as disregarding traditions which, in his opinion,
exhibit the operation of divine providence. The abstract human
being of *les philosophes*, who is not essentially a Frenchman or an
Englishman or a member of some other organic unity, is a fiction.
So is the State when interpreted as the product of a contract or
convention. When de Maistre makes a complimentary remark
about an Enlightenment thinker, it is because he regards him as
transcending the spirit of *a priori* rationalism. For example,
Hume is commended for his attack on the artificiality of the social
contract theory. If de Maistre goes back beyond the Enlightenment and attacks Francis Bacon, the reason is that in his view
'modern philosophy is entirely the daughter of Bacon'.[2]

Another rationalist fiction, according to de Maistre, is natural
religion, if the term is taken to mean a purely philosophical
religion, a deliberate construction of the human reason. In reality
belief in God is handed down from a primitive revelation to mankind, Christianity being a fuller revelation. In other words ,there
is only one revealed religion; and man can no more construct a
religion *a priori* than he can construct a constitution *a priori*.
'The philosophy of the last century, which will form in the eyes of
posterity one of the most shameful epochs of the human spirit . . .
was in fact nothing but a veritable system of practical atheism.'[3]

According to de Maistre the philosophy of the eighteenth
century has found expression in the theory of the sovereignty of

[1] *Essai sur le principe générateur des constitutions politiques*, p. IX. The page
reference is to the essay as printed in the same volume as the *Considérations sur la
France* (Brussels, 1838).
[2] *Examen de la philosophie de Bacon*, II, p. 231 (Paris, 1836).
[3] *Soirées de Saint-Pétersbourg*, p. 258 (Brussels, 1838).

the people and in democracy. The theory of the sovereignty of the people is however groundless, and the fruits of democracy are disorder and anarchy. The remedy for these evils is a return to historically grounded and providentially constituted authority. In the political sphere this means the restoration of the Christian monarchy, while in the religious sphere it means acceptance of the supreme and unique sovereignty of the infallible pope. Human beings are such that government is necessary; and absolute power is the only real alternative to anarchy.[1] 'I have never said that absolute power, in whatever form it may exist in the world, does not involve great inconveniences. On the contrary, I expressly acknowledged the fact, and I have no thought of attenuating these inconveniences. I said only that we find ourselves placed between two abysses.'[2] In actual practice the exercise of absolute power is inevitably restricted by a variety of factors. And in any case political sovereigns are, or ought to be, subject to the jurisdiction of the pope, in the sense that he has the right to judge their actions from the religious and moral points of view.

De Maistre is best known for his ultramontanism and his insistence on papal infallibility a considerable time before this doctrine was defined at the first Vatican Council. This insistence however was by no means acceptable to all those who shared his hostility to the revolution and sympathized with his desire for the restoration of the monarchy. Some of his reflections on political constitutions and the values of tradition were similar to those of Edmund Burke (1729–97). But it is very much as the author of *Du Pape* that he is remembered.

3. A more impressive figure from the philosophical point of view was Louis Gabriel Ambroise, Vicomte de Bonald (1754–1840). A former officer of the royal guard, he was a member of the Constituent Assembly in 1790; but in 1791 he emigrated and lived in poverty. In 1796 he published at Constance his *Theory of Political and Religious Power in Civil Society (Théorie du pouvoir politique et religieux dans la société civile)*. On his return to France he supported Napoleon, in whom he saw the instrument for the political and religious unification of Europe. But after the restoration he gave his support to the monarchy. In 1800 he published an *Analytical Essay on the Natural Laws of Social Order (Essai analytique sur les lois naturelles de l'ordre social)*. This was followed

---

[1] De Maistre makes an exception, though with reservations, for England.
[2] *Du Pape*, p. 172 (Brussels, 1838).

in 1802 by *Primitive Legislation* (*La législation primitive*). His other writings include *Philosophical Studies on the Primary Objects of the Moral Sciences* (*Recherches philosophiques sur les premiers objets des connaissances morales*, 1818) and a *Philosophical Demonstration of the Constitutive Principle of Society* (*Démonstration philosophique du principe constitutif de la société*, 1827).

It has sometimes been said that de Bonald rejects all philosophy. The statement however is inaccurate. It is true that he emphasizes the necessity for a religious basis of society, and that he contrasts this necessity with the insufficiency of philosophy as a social foundation. In his view a union between religious and political society is 'as necessary for constituting the civil or social body as simultaneity of *will* and *action* is necessary for constituting the human *ego*',[1] whereas philosophy lacks the authority to dictate laws and impose sanctions. It is also true that he dwells on the succession of conflicting systems and concludes that 'Europe . . . is still awaiting a *philosophy*'.[2] At the same time he shows an evident admiration for some philosophers. He speaks, for instance, of Leibniz as 'perhaps the most comprehensive (*vaste*) genius who has appeared among men'.[3] Further, he distinguishes between the men of ideas or concepts, from Plato onwards, 'who have enlightened the world',[4] and the men of imagination, such as Bayle, Voltaire, Diderot, Condillac, Helvétius and Rousseau, who have led people astray. The description of writers such as Bayle and Diderot as men of imagination may seem odd; but de Bonald is not referring to poetically inclined thinkers. He is referring primarily to those who derive all ideas from sense-experience. When, for example, Condillac talks about 'transformed sensations', the phrase may appeal to the imagination which can picture to itself at will transformations and changes. 'But this transformation, when applied to the operations of the mind, is nothing but a word which is void of meaning; and Condillac himself would have been very embarrassed at having to give it a satisfactory application.'[5]

In general the men of imagination, as de Bonald understands the term, are sensationalists, empiricists and materialists. The men of ideas or concepts are primarily those who believe in innate

---

[1] *Essai analytique*, p. 23 (Paris, 1812). *Oeuvres*, v. p. 10 (Paris, 7 vols., 1854).
[2] *Recherches philosophiques*, I, p. 2, *Oeuvres*, iv, p. 1.
[3] *Essai analytique*, p. 36, *Oeuvres*, v, p. 16.
[4] *Ibid.*, p. 20, *Oeuvres*, v, p. 9.
[5] *Recherches philosophiques*, I, pp. 33–4. *Oeuvres*, iv, p. 16.

ideas and ascribe them to their ultimate source. Thus Plato 'proclaimed *innate ideas* or universal ideas, imprinted in our minds by the supreme intelligence',[1] whereas Aristotle 'humiliated the human intelligence by rejecting innate ideas and by representing ideas as coming to the mind only by the mediation of the senses'.[2] 'The reformer of philosophy in France was Descartes.'[3]

It is indeed true that de Bonald refers to the absence of philosophy among the Jews of Old Testament times and among other vigorous nations, such as the early Romans and the Spartans, and that he concludes from the history of philosophy that philosophers have been unable to find any secure basis for their speculations. He refuses however to admit that we ought therefore to despair of philosophy and reject it altogether. On the contary, we must look for 'an absolutely primitive fact'[4] which can serve as a secure point of departure.

It hardly needs saying that de Bonald was not the first man to look for one secure basis for philosophy. Nor was he the last. It is interesting however to read that he finds his 'primitive fact' in language. Philosophy in general is 'the science of God, of man and of society'.[5] The primitive fact which is being sought must therefore lie at the foundation of man and society. And this is language. It may seem that language cannot be a primitive fact. But according to de Bonald man could not have invented language to express his thoughts, as thought itself, involving general concepts, presupposes language of some kind. In other words, to express his thoughts man must be already a language-using being. Language is required for man to be man. Again, human society presupposes language and could not exist without it.

In looking on symbolic expression as an essential characteristic of man de Bonald is not saying anything which is likely to cause astonishment nowadays, even if there are various puzzling questions which can be asked. He goes on however to argue that man received the gift of language at the same time that he received existence, and that consequently 'there must necessarily have existed, before the human species, a first cause of this marvellous effect (i.e. language), a being superior to man in intelligence, superior to anything that we can know or even imagine, from

---

[1] *Ibid.*, p. 12. *Oeuvres*, iv, p. 6.   [2] *Ibid.*, p. 13, *Ibid.*
[3] *Ibid.*, p. 35. *Oeuvres*, p. 17.
[4] *Recherches philosophiques*, I, p. 85. *Oeuvres* iv, p. 40.
[5] *Ibid.*, p. 80. *Oeuvres*, p. 37.

whom man has positively received the gift of thought, the gift of the word . . . .'[1] In other words, if, as noticed by Rousseau,[2] man needs speech in order to learn to think but could not have constructed speech unless he could think, he cannot have invented language; and this fact serves as the basis of a proof of God's existence.

There is no need of course to accuse de Bonald of overlooking the multiplicity of languages, nor the fact that we can and do invent linguistic expressions. His contention is that we cannot reasonably depict man as first developing thought and then sitting down, as it were, to invent language to express this thought. For actual thinking already involves symbolic expression, even if no words are uttered aloud.[3] De Bonald certainly makes a good point by refusing to divide thought and language with a hatchet.[4] Whether his account of the relation between thought and language can serve as a basis for a proof of the existence of God is another question. He assumes that while our ideas of particular objects in the world depend on sense-experience, there are certain basic concepts (of God, for instance) and certain fundamental principles or truths which represent a primitive revelation by God to man. As this revelation could not be grasped or appropriated in the first instance without language, and as man cannot himself have invented language, it (language) must be a primitive gift of God to man at his creation. De Bonald is obviously thinking of man as having been directly created by God as a language-using being, whereas we probably think within the framework of an evolutionary theory.

The social philosophy of de Bonald is triadic in the sense that, according to him, 'there are three *persons* in every society.'[5] In the religious society there are God, his ministers and the people whose salvation is the aim of the relation between God and his ministers. In the domestic society or family we have father, mother and the child or children. In political society there are the head of the

---

[1] *Ibid.*, p. 98. *Oeuvres*, p. 46.

[2] Rousseau makes this remark in the first part of his *Discourse on the Origin of Inequality*.

[3] It is arguable that thinking 'to oneself' presupposes language as a social phenomenon.

[4] Some distinction must obviously be made. Otherwise it becomes very difficult to account for our ability to translate. But we might represent the distinction as analogous to Aristotle's distinction between 'form' and 'matter', thought being analogous to 'forms' which do not exist apart from all matter but can inform different matter.

[5] *Législation primitive*, I, p. 134 (Paris, 1817). *Oeuvres*, iii, p. 49.

State (representing power), his officers of various kinds and the people or general body of citizens.

Now if we ask whether in the family power belongs to the father as the result of an agreement or compact, the answer, for de Bonald, must be negative. The power belongs naturally to the father and is derived ultimately from God. Similarly, in political society sovereignty belongs to the monarch, not the people, and it belongs to him by nature. 'The establishment of the public power was neither voluntary nor forced; it was *necessary*, in conformity, that is to say, with the nature of beings in society. And its causes and origins were all natural.'[1] This idea can be applied even in the case of Napoleon. The revolution was both the culmination of a long sickness and an effort made by society to return to order. That someone capable of bringing order out of anarchy should assume power was necessary and therefore natural. Napoleon was the man.

Like de Maistre, de Bonald insists on the unity of power or sovereignty. Sovereignty must be one, independent and definitive or absolute.[2] It must also be lasting, from which premise de Bonald concludes to the need for hereditary monarchy. The peculiar characteristic of his thought however is his theory about the origin of language and of the transmission, by means of language, of a primitive divine revelation which lies at the basis of religious belief, morality and society. It is perhaps none too clear how this theory of the transmission of a primitive revelation squares with de Bonald's enthusiasm for the theory of innate ideas. But presumably he thinks of innate ideas as required for the appropriation of revelation.

4. Both de Maistre and de Bonald were obviously traditionalists in the sense that they upheld the old political and religious traditions of France against the revolutionary spirit. Further, de Bonald in particular was a traditionalist in the technical sense of one who defends the idea of the tradition or handing-on of a primitive revelation. Both men attacked the philosophy of the Enlightenment, though of the two de Maistre was the more sweeping and indiscriminate in his condemnation. In one sense of the word 'rationalism' they were both anti-rationalists. Neither however can properly be said to represent simply irrationalism. For both men offered reasoned defences of their positions and

---

[1] *Démonstration philosophique*, p. 108 (Paris, 1830). *Oeuvres*, iv, p. 448.
[2] Absolute power is distinguished from the tyrannical or arbitrary use of power.

appealed to reason in their attacks on the thought of the eighteenth century.

When however we turn to François-René, Vicomte de Chateaubriand (1768–1848), we find a rather different emphasis. Educated in the philosophy of the Encyclopaedists, Chateaubriand went into exile at the revolution, and it was in London that he wrote his *Historical, Political and Moral Essay on Revolution (Essai historique, politique et moral sur les révolutions*, 1797). In this work he accepted the force of the objections brought by eighteenth-century philosophers against Christianity, with its doctrines of providence and immortality, and went on to maintain a cyclic theory of history. In the cycles of history events substantially repeat themselves, though the human beings involved and the circumstances are of course different. It is idle therefore to look on the French revolution as a completely fresh start which will bring permanent gains. It repeats substantially the revolutions of former times. The dogma of progress is an illusion.

Later on Chateaubriand was to say, doubtless rightly, that in spite of his onetime rejection of Christianity he still retained a religious nature. In any case he was drawn to the Christian religion, and in 1802 he published his famous work *The Genius of Christianity (Génie du Christianisme)*. The subtitle of the work, 'Beauties of the Christian Religion' (*Beautés de la religion chrétienne*), expresses well the spirit of the work, in which the author appeals above all to the aesthetic qualities of Christianity. 'All the other kinds of apologies are exhausted, and perhaps they would even be useless today. Who would now read a theological work? Some pious men who have no need to be convinced, some true Christians who are already persuaded.'[1] In place of some old-style apologetics one ought to try to show that 'the Christian religion is the most poetic, the most human, the most favourable to liberty, to the arts and to letters, of all the religions which ever existed.'[2]

This sounds as though Chateaubriand intended to argue that the Christian religion must be true because it is beautiful, because its beliefs are consoling and because some of the greatest artists and poets have been Christians. And apart from the fact that some minds might not agree about the beauty of Christianity, this point of view lies open to the objection that the aesthetic and consoling qualities of Christianity do not prove its truth. If Dante and

---

[1] *Génie du christianisme*, I, p. 13 (Paris, 1803).   [2] *Ibid.*, p. 12.

Michelangelo were Christians, what does this show, except something about Dante and Michelangelo? If the doctrines of the resurrection and heaven are a source of consolation to many people, does it follow that they are true? It is understandable that Chateaubriand has been accused of irrationalism or of substituting appeals to aesthetic satisfaction for rational argument.

It is true that with Chateaubriand traditional philosophical arguments to show the credibility of the Christian religion are relegated to a completely subordinate position, and that appeal is made chiefly to aesthetic considerations, to sentiment and to reasons of the heart. At the same time we have to remember that he has in mind those opponents of Christianity who argue that Christian doctrine is repellent, that the Christian religion impedes the development of the moral consciousness, that it is inimical to human freedom and anti-cultural, and that, in general, it has a cramping and stifling effect on the human spirit. He makes it clear that he is not writing for 'sophists' who 'are never searching for the truth in good faith',[1] but for those who have been seduced by the sophists into believing that Christianity is, for instance, the enemy of art and literature, and that it is a barbarous and cruel religion, detrimental to human happiness. His work can be regarded as an *argumentum ad hominem* which aims at showing that Christianity is not what these people think that it is.

5. A more interesting figure is Félicité Robert de Lamennais (1782–1854). Born at St. Malo, Lamennais was in youth a follower of Rousseau, though he soon returned to Christian belief. When de Bonald's *Primitive Legislation* appeared in 1802, Lamennais was profoundly impressed by it. In 1809 he published *Reflections on the State of the Church in France during the Eighteenth Century and on its Actual Situation*, in which he made suggestions for the Church's renewal. Ordained a priest at Vannes in 1816, he published in the following year the first volume of his *Essay on Indifference in Matters of Religion* (*Essai sur l'indifférence en matière de religion*, 1817–23), a work which brought him immediate fame as an apologist for the Christian religion.

In the first volume of this work Lamennais insists that in religion, morals and politics, no doctrines are matters of indifference. 'Indifference, considered as a permanent state of soul, is opposed to the nature of man and destructive of his being.'[2] This

---

[1] *Ibid.*, p. 11. The 'sophists' are presumably *les philosophes*.
[2] *Essai sur l'indifférence*, I, p. 37 (Paris, 1823).

thesis is based on the premises that man cannot develop himself as man without religion, that religion is necessary for society, inasmuch as it is in the basis of morals, and that without it society degenerates into a group of persons each of whom is intent on furthering his own particular interests. In other words, Lamennais insists on the social necessity of religion and rejects the belief which spread in the eighteenth century that ethics can stand on its own feet, apart from religion, and that there could be a satisfactory human society without religion. Given this point of view, Lamennais argues that indifference towards religion is disastrous for man. It might of course be maintained that even if indifference in general is undesirable, it does not necessarily follow that all points of traditional religious belief possess social importance and relevance. According to Lamennais however heresy prepares the way for deism, deism for atheism, and atheism for complete indifference. It is therefore a case of a package deal.

It may appear that Lamennais is attaching an exclusively pragmatic value to religion, as though the only justification for religious belief was its social utility. This is not however an adequate account of his attitude. He explicitly rejects the point of view of those who see in religion nothing but a socially and politically useful institution and conclude that it is necessary for the common people. In his opinion the Christian doctrines are not only useful but true. Indeed, they are useful because they are true. This is the reason why, for Lamennais, there is no justification for picking and choosing, for heresy in other words.

The difficulty is to see how Lamennais proposes to show that Christian doctrines are true, in a sense of 'true' which goes beyond a purely pragmatist understanding of the term. For in his opinion our reasoning is so subject to a variety of influences which can operate even 'without our knowing it'[1] that it cannot yield certainty. It is all very well to claim that we can deduce conclusions from self-evidently true axioms or basic principles. The fact of the matter is that what seems self-evidently true to one man may not seem so to another man. In this case we can well understand Lamennais' rejection of any attempt to reduce religion to 'natural' or philosophical religion. But the question remains, how does he propose to exhibit the truth of revealed religion?

The remedy for scepticism, Lamennais maintains, is to trust not one's own private reasoning but the common consent of mankind.

[1] *Ibid.*, II, p. 137.

For it is this common consent or *sentiment commun* which is the basis of certitude. Atheism is the fruit of false philosophy and of following one's private judgment. If we look at this history of mankind, we find a spontaneous belief in God, common to all nations.

Passing over the question whether the historical facts are as Lamennais claims them to be, we can note that he would be involved in inconsistency if he meant that most human beings, each by his own reasoning, conclude that there is a God. If, that is to say, the alleged common consent were equivalent to a collection of conclusions arrived at by individuals, Lamennais could be challenged to show that it possessed any greater degree of certainty than that attaching to the result of the individual's process of inference. In point of fact however Lamennais has recourse to a traditionalist theory. For example, we know the meaning of the word 'God' because it belongs to the language which we have learned; and this language is ultimately of divine origin. 'It must be then that the first man who has transmitted them (i.e. certain words or concepts) to us, received them himself from the mouth of the Creator. Thus we find in the infallible word of God the origin of religion and of the tradition which preserves it.'[1]

To say this is to say in effect that it is on authority that we know the truth of religious belief, and that there is in reality only revealed religion. What has been called natural religion is really revealed religion, and it has been commonly accepted because human beings, when unspoiled and not led astray by false reasoning, see that 'man is always obliged to obey the greatest authority which it is possible for him to know'.[2] The common consent of mankind about the existence of God expresses acceptance of a primitive revelation;[3] and belief in the teaching of the Catholic Church expresses acceptance of God's further revelation in and through Christ.

This theory gives rise to a number of awkward questions which cannot however be discussed here. We must pass instead to Lamennais' political attitude. Given his insistence on authority in the religious sphere, one might expect him to emphasize the role of monarchy in the manner of de Maistre and de Bonald. But this is not in fact the case. Lamennais is still a monarchist,

---

[1] *Ibid.*, III, p. 14   [2] *Ibid.*, II, p. 382.
[3] Obviously, on this view it is necessary to interpret polytheism as representing a process of degeneration of an original monotheism.

but he shows a realistic attitude. Thus in his work *On Religion Considered in its Relations with the Political and Civil Order* (*De la religion considérée dans ses rapports avec l'ordre politique et civil*, 1825–6) he remarks that the restored monarchy is 'a venerable souvenir of the past'[1] while France is in reality a democracy. True, 'the democracy of our times . . . rests on the atheist dogma of the primitive and absolute sovereignty of the people.'[2] But Lamennais' reflections on this state of affairs led him in the direction of ultramontanism within the Church rather than to a hankering after absolute monarchy. In contemporary France the Church is tolerated and even supported financially; but this patronage by the State constitutes a great danger to the Church, as it tends to make of the Church a department of the State and to hamper the former's freedom to penetrate and christianize the life of the nation. It is only emphasis on the supreme authority of the pope which can prevent the subordination of the Church to the State and make it clear that the Church has a universal mission. As for the monarchy, Lamennais has misgivings. In his work *On the Progress of the Revolution and of the War against the Church* (*Du progrès de la révolution et de la guerre contre l'église*, 1829) he remarks that 'towards the end of the monarchy human power had become, thanks to Gallicanism, the object of a real idolatry'.[3] Lamennais still thinks of the revolution as dissolving the social order and as the enemy of Christianity; but he has come to believe that the trouble started with the rise of absolute monarchy. It was Louis XIV who 'made despotism the fundamental law of the State'.[4] The French monarchy sapped the life of the Church by subordinating it to the State. And it would be disastrous if in their desire for the apparent security of State patronage and protection the clergy were to acquiesce in a similar subordination to the post-revolutionary and post-Napoleonic State. A clear recognition of papal authority in the Church is required as a safeguard.

In spite of his continued attack on political liberalism and individualism Lamennais had come to believe that liberalism contained a valuable element, 'the invincible desire of freedom which is inherent in the Christian nations which cannot put up with an arbitrary or purely human power'.[5] And the revolution of 1830 convinced him that no reliance could be placed on monarchs

[1] *De la religion*, p. 33 (Paris, 1826).   [2] *Ibid.*, p. 95.
[3] *Du progrès de la révolution*, p. 58 (Paris, 1829).   [4] *Ibid.*, p. 7.
[5] *Ibid.*, p. 256.

for the regeneration of society. It was necessary to accept the democratic State as it was, to secure a complete separation of the Church from the State, and, within the Church, to insist on the supreme authority of the infallible pope. In other words, Lamennais combined acceptance of the idea of a democratic and religiously non-affiliated State with insistence on ultramontanism within the Church. He hoped of course that the Church would succeed in christianizing society; but he had come to believe that this end could not be attained unless the Church renounced all State patronage and any privileged status.

In 1830 Lamennais founded the newspaper *Avenir* which stood for the authority and infallibility of the pope, acceptance of the French political system of the time, and separation between Church and State. The paper enjoyed the support of some eminent men, such as the Comte de Montalembert (1810–70) and the famous Dominican preacher Henri-Dominique Lacordaire (1802–61); but the views propounded were by no means acceptable to all Catholics. Lamennais tried to secure the approval of Pope Gregory XVI; but in 1832 the pope issued an encyclical letter (*Mirari vos*) in which he censured indifferentism, liberty of conscience and the doctrine that Church and State should be separated. Lamennais was not named in the letter. While however the pope's condemnation of indifferentism could be taken as an endorsement of Lamennais' early *Essai sur l'indifférence*, the editor of *Avenir* was clearly affected by the encyclical.

In 1834 Lamennais published *Words of a Believer (Paroles d'un croyant)* in which he supported all oppressed and suffering peoples and groups and advocated complete freedom of conscience for all. In point of fact he endorsed the ideals of the revolution, liberty, equality and fraternity, as interpreted in a religious setting. The book was censured by Pope Gregory XVI in June 1834 in a letter addressed to the French bishops; but by then Lamennais was pretty well detached from the Church. And two years later, in *Affairs of Rome (Affaires de Rome)*, he rejected the idea of achieving social order either through monarchs or through the pope. He had become a believer in the sovereignty of the people.

In later writings Lamennais argued that Christianity, in its organized forms, had outlived its usefulness; but he continued to maintain the validity of religion, considered as a development of a divine element in man which unites him with God and with his fellows. In 1840 he published a brochure directed against the government and police and underwent a year's imprisonment as a result. After the 1848 revolution he was elected a deputy for the department of the Seine. But when Napoleon III assumed power, Lamennais retired from politics. He died in 1854 without any formal reconciliation with the Church.

6. In a very general or broad sense of the term we can describe as traditionalists all those who saw the French revolution as a disastrous attack on the valuable political, social and religious traditions of their country and who advocated a return to these traditions. In the technical sense of the term however, the sense, that is to say, in which it is used in recounting the history of ideas in the decades following the revolution, traditionalism means the theory that certain basic beliefs, necessary for man's spiritual and cultural development and well-being, are not the result simply of human reasoning but have been derived from a primitive revelation by God and have been handed on from generation to generation through the medium of language. Obviously, traditionalism in the broad sense does not exclude traditionalism in the narrower sense. But it does not entail it. It hardly needs saying that a Frenchman could quite well support the restoration of the monarchy without the theory of a primitive revelation and without placing restrictions on the range of philosophical proof. Again, it was possible to adopt traditionalist theories in the technical sense and yet not to demand a restoration of the *ancien régime*. The two could go together; but they were not inseparable.

It may appear at first sight that traditionalism in the technical sense, with its attack on the philosophy of the Enlightenment, its insistence on divine revelation and its tendency to ultra-montanism would be highly acceptable to ecclesiastical authority. But though ultramontanist tendencies were naturally pleasing to Rome, the traditionalist philosophy brought upon itself ecclesiastical censures. To attack this or that eighteenth-century philosophy on the ground that its premises were unwarranted or its arguments unsound was all very well. In fact it was a commendable activity. But to attack the thought of the Enlightenment on the ground that the human reason in unable to attain certain truth was quite another matter. If the existence of God could be known only on authority, how did one know that the authority was trustworthy? For the matter of that, how did the first man know that what he took to be revelation was revelation? And if the human reason was as powerless as the more extreme traditionalists made it out to be,[1] how could one show that the voice of Christ was the voice of God? It is understandable that ecclesiastical authority, while sympathizing with attacks on the Enlightenment and the revolution, was not enthusiastic about theories which left its claims without any rational support save questionable appeals to the consent of mankind.

To take one example. The second volume of Lamennais' *Essai sur l'indifférence* exercised a considerable influence on Augustin Bonnetty (1798–1879), founder of the *Annales de philosophie chrétienne*. In an article in this periodical Bonnetty wrote that people were beginning to understand that the whole of religion rested on tradition and not on reasoning. His general thesis was that revelation was the only source of religious truth, and he drew the conclusion that the scholasticism which prevailed in seminaries was an expression of a pagan rationalism which had corrupted Christian thought and had eventually born fruit in the destructive philosophy of the Enlightenment. In 1855 Bonnetty was required by the Congregation of the Index to subscribe to a number of theses, such as that the human reason can prove with certainty the existence of God, the spirituality of the soul and human freedom, that reasoning leads to faith, and that the method used by St. Thomas Aquinas, St. Bonaventure and the Scholastics does not lead to rationalism. A series of similar propositions had already been subscribed to in 1840 by Louis-Eugène–Marie Bautain (1796–1867).

It may very well occur to the reader that imposition by ecclesiastical authority of the thesis that the existence of God can be philosophically proved contributes little to showing how this is done. However it is clear that the Church came down on the side of what Bonnetty regarded as rationalism. And definitive pronouncements on this matter were made at the first Vatican Council in 1870, the Council which also marked the triumph of ultramontanism. As for the general idea that France could be regenerated only through a return to the monarchy in alliance with the Church, this idea was to find a fresh lease of life with the *Action française* movement, founded by Charles Maurras (1868–1952). But Maurras himself was, like some of his closer associates,

---

[1] Some traditionalists maintained that while reason divorced from tradition (in effect, revelation) could not prove God's existence, once man had the concept of God as handed on in society he could discern reasons for belief. But others seemed to imply that metaphysics should be rejected altogether.

an atheist,[1] not a believer such as de Maistre or de Bonald. And it is not altogether surprising if his cynical attempt to use Catholicism for political ends led eventually to a condemnation by Pope Pius XI. Incidentally, in his *Essai sur l'indifférence* Lamennais had included among 'systems of indifference' the view of religion as being simply a politically and socially useful instrument.

[1] Maurras, condemned to life imprisonment in 1945 for collaboration with the Vichy régime, was reconciled with the Church shortly before his death. But for most of his life he was an admitted atheist. As for his philosophy, this was not of course traditionalism in the technical sense.

CHAPTER II

THE IDEOLOGISTS AND MAINE DE BIRAN

The ideologists—Maine de Biran: life and writings—Philosophical development—Psychology and knowledge—Levels of human life.

1. As we have seen, the Traditionalists attacked the spirit and thought of the Enlightenment, which they regarded as largely responsible for the revolution. Those who welcomed the revolution tended to take a similar view of the relation between eighteenth-century thought and the revolution. To attribute the revolution simply to the influence of *les philosophes* would be of course an obvious exaggeration and too flattering a compliment to the power of philosophy. Though however the philosophers of the eighteenth century aimed not at violence, bloodshed and terror but at the spread of knowledge and, through the diffusion of knowledge, at social reform, they helped to prepare the way for the overthrow of the *ancien régime*; and it hardly needs saying that the influence of the Enlightenment was prolonged beyond the revolution. Once conditions became sufficiently settled, the scientific work associated with a man such as d'Alembert (1717–83)[1] began to develop and flourish. The demands of a Condorcet (1743–94)[2] for an educational system based on a secular ethics and free from theological presuppositions and ecclesiastical influences were eventually fulfilled in the programme of public education in France. And though Condorcet was himself to become a victim of the revolution,[3] his vision of man's perfectibility and of history as a process of intellectual and moral advance, together with the interpretation of history expounded by Turgot (1727–81),[4] prepared the way for the philosophy of Auguste Comte, which will be considered in due course.

The immediate inheritors of the spirit of the Enlightenment, and in particular of the influence of Condillac (1715–80)[5] were the so-called ideologists (*les idéologues*). In 1801 Destutt de Tracy (1754–1836) published the first volume of his *Elements of Ideology*

---

[1] On d'Alembert see Vol. VI of this *History*, pp. 43–7.
[2] See Vol. VI of this *History*, pp. 168–71.
[3] He committed suicide when under arrest.
[4] See Vol. VI of this *History*, pp. 56–8.   [5] See *ibid.*, pp. 28–35.

(*Éléments d'idéologie*); and it was from this work that the label 'ideologist' was taken. The members of the group included, besides de Tracy, the Comte de Volney (1757–1820), and Cabanis (1757–1808).[1] The group had two principal centres, the *École Normale* and the *Institut National*, both of which were established in 1795. It was not long however before the ideologists aroused the suspicions of Napoleon. Though for the most part they had been favourable to his rise, they soon came to the conclusion that he had failed to preserve and implement the ideals of the revolution. In particular they resented and opposed his restoration of religion. On his side the emperor came to attribute to what he regarded as the 'obscure metaphysics' of the ideologists all the evils from which France was suffering; and he held them responsible for a conspiracy against himself in 1812.

As used by Destutt de Tracy, the term 'ideology' should not be understood in the sense in which we are accustomed to speak of ideologies. It would be nearer the mark to think of the term as meaning a study of the origin of ideas, of their expression in language and of their combination in reasoning. In point of fact however de Tracy was more concerned with the study of human faculties and their operations. He regarded this as a basic study contributing the foundation of such sciences as logic, ethics and economics. We can say therefore that he was concerned with developing a science of human nature.

Mention has been made of the influence of Condillac. It is important however to understand that de Tracy rejected the reductive analysis expounded by Condillac. We can recall that the latter tried to show that all mental operations, such as judging and willing, could be exhibited as what he called transformed sensations. In other words, Condillac tried to improve on Locke by reducing all mental operations in the long run to elementary sensations and by arguing that the human faculties can be reconstructed, as it were, from sensation alone. In de Tracy's view however this was an artificial process of analysis and reconstruction, an ingenious account of how things might have been, without any attention being paid to what we might describe as the phenomenology of consciousness. In his view Condillac sometimes confused what ought to be distinguished and at other times separated what ought to be united. In any case de Tracy was more concerned with discovering the basic human faculties as

[1] See *ibid.*, pp. 50–1.

revealed to immediate and concrete observation than with the genesis of ideas, with arguing that they were all derivable from sensations.

The basic faculties for de Tracy are feeling, remembering, judging and willing. The operation of judging can be seen as the foundation of both grammar (considered as the study of signs as used in discourse) and logic, which is concerned with the ways of attaining certainty in judgment.[1] Reflection on the effects of the will grounds ethics, considered mainly as the study of the origins of our desires and of their conformity or lack of it with our nature, and economics which is looked on as an enquiry into the consequences of our actions in regard to meeting our needs.

Passing over the details of ideology we can notice the following two points. First, when laying down the fundamental notions of ideology de Tracy turned from the reductive analysis of Condillac to immediate self-observation, from hypothetical reconstruction of man's psychical life out of its basis in elementary sensation to reflection on what we actually perceive to take place when we think and speak and act voluntarily. Secondly, de Tracy maintained that if Condillac's psychology, which laid all the emphasis on receptivity, was true, we could never know that there was an external world. We should be left with the insoluble problem of Hume. In point of fact the real ground of our knowledge of the external world is our activity, our motion, our voluntary action which meets with resistance.

If we bear these points in mind, it is easier to understand how de Tracy could exercise an influence on Maine de Biran, the forerunner of what is called the spiritualist movement in nineteenth-century French philosophy. The ideologists helped to turn his mind away from the empiricism of Locke and Condillac and stimulated him to set out on a path of his own.

It is worth noticing that Thomas Jefferson (1743–1826), who had a high opinion of the French ideologists, maintained a correspondence with Destutt de Tracy from 1806 until 1826. In 1811 Jefferson published a translation of de Tracy's commentary on Montesquieu's De l'esprit des lois. And he also published an edition of de Tracy's Treatise on Political Economy (1818).

2. François-Pierre Maine de Biran (1766–1824) was born at

---

[1] In logic de Tracy lays emphasis on the relation by which one idea contains another. He therefore plays down the role of logical rules and stresses the need for direct examination of the ideas which one employs to see whether in point of fact a contains or implies b.

Bergerac and educated at Périgueux. At the age of eighteen he went to Paris and enrolled in the royal guard. He was wounded in 1789, and not long after the dissolution of the guard in 1791 he retired to the castle of Grateloup near Bergerac and devoted his time to study and reflection. In 1795 he was appointed administrator of the department of the Dordogne, and in 1797 he was elected a member of the Council of Five Hundred. In 1810, under Napoleon, he was nominated a member of the *Corps législatif*, but at the close of 1813 he was associated with a group which publicly expressed opposition to the emperor. After the restoration of the monarchy he was re-elected a deputy for the department of the Dordogne. In 1816 he acted as a councillor of State, and he served on various committees.

In 1802 Maine de Biran published an essay, though without the author's name, on the *Influence of Habit on the Faculty of Thinking (Influence de l'habitude sur la faculté de penser)* which won for him a prize from the Institute of France. This essay was a revised version of one which he had submitted to the Institute in 1800 and which, while not winning the prize, had aroused the attention of the ideologists Destutt de Tracy and Cabanis. In 1805 he won another prize from the Institute for an essay on the analysis of thought *(Mémoire sur la décomposition de la pensée)* and was elected a member of the Institute. In 1812 he won a prize from the Academy of Copenhagen for an *Essay on the Relations of Physics and Morals in Man (Mémoire sur les rapports du physique et du moral de l'homme)*. Neither of these essays was published by Maine de Biran himself; but in 1817 he published, again without giving his name, an *Examination of the Lectures on Philosophy of M. Laromiguière (Examen des leçons de philosophie de M. Laromiguière)*. And in 1819 he wrote an article on Leibniz *(Exposition de la doctrine philosophique de Leibniz)* for the *Biographie universelle*.

It will be seen from what has been said above that Maine de Biran published very little himself, the essay of 1802, the *Examination* (both anonymously), and the article on Leibniz. In addition he published a number of papers, mainly on political topics. But he wrote copiously; and it appears that up to the end of his life he planned to produce one major work, a science of human nature or a philosophical anthropology, incorporating revised versions of early essays. This major work was never completed; but a good deal of the manuscript material[1] seems to represent various phases

[1] Some of the manuscript material was lost, but a great deal was preserved.

in the attempt to realize the project. For example, the *Essay on the Foundations of Psychology* (*Essai sur les fondements de la psychologie*), at which de Biran was working in the years 1811–12, represents one phase in the writing of the unfinished work.[1]

In 1841 Victor Cousin published an (incomplete) edition of Maine de Biran's writings in four volumes.[2] In 1859 E. Naville and M. Debrit brought out three volumes of the unpublished works (*Oeuvres inédites de Maine de Biran*). In 1920 P. Tisserand began publication of the *Works* in fourteen volumes (*Oeuvres de Maine de Biran accompagnées de notes et de d'appendices*). Tisserand actually published twelve volumes (1920–39). The last two volumes were brought out by Professor Henri Gouhier in 1949. Gouhier has also published an edition of Maine de Biran's journal in three volumes (*Journal intime*, 1954–7).

3. By temperament Maine de Biran was strongly inclined to introspection and self-communing. And in his youth, during the period of retirement at the castle of Grateloup, he was powerfully influenced by Rousseau, considered more as the author of the *Confessions*, the *Rêveries du promeneur solitaire* and the *Profession de foi du vicaire savoyard* than as the expounder of the social contract theory. 'Rousseau speaks to my heart, but sometimes his errors afflict me.'[3] For example, while Maine de Biran sympathized with Rousseau's idea of the inner sense or feeling as prompting belief in God and immortality, he rejcted decisively the modest natural theology proposed by the *vicaire savoyard*. As far as reasoning was concerned, agnosticism was the only proper attitude.[4]

Another point on which Maine de Biran finds fault with Rousseau is the latter's view of man as essentially good, good by nature. It does not follow that Maine de Biran looks on man as essentially bad or as having become prone to evil through a Fall. In his view man has a natural impulse to seek after happiness, and virtue is a condition of happiness. This by no means entails the conclusion however that man is naturally virtuous. He has the power to become either virtuous or vicious. And it is reason alone

---

[1] This *Essay*, as published by E. Naville, was a compilation made from several manuscripts.

[2] The fourth volume was a reprint of a volume which Cousin had already published in 1834.

[3] *Oeuvres*, I, p. 63. References to *Oeuvres* are to the Tisserand–Gouhier edition mentioned above.

[4] At this time Maine de Biran was also strongly anti-clerical, and he had no use for theologians' claims to possess knowledge of God and his will.

which can discover the nature of virtue and the principles of
morals. In other words, the reason why Maine de Biran criticizes
Rousseau's theory of man's natural goodness is that he looks on
it as involving the doctrine of innate ideas. In point of fact 'all our
ideas are acquisitions.'[1] There are no innate ideas of right and
wrong, good and bad. Ethics can however be established by
reason, by a process of reasoning or reflection, that is to say, based
on observation or experience. This can be done without any
dependence on religious belief.

Given his idea of reason, it was natural that when it was a
question of developing a science of man Maine de Biran should
turn to contemporary 'scientific' psychology, which professed to
be based on the empirical facts. In addition to Locke, the natural
writers to turn to were Condillac and Charles Bonnet (1720–93).
But it required very little time for Maine de Biran to see the extreme artificiality of Condillac's reduction of men's psychical life
to externally caused sensations and of his notion of reconstructing
man's mental operations from this basis. For one thing, Condillac
passed over the evident fact that externally caused sensation
affects a subject endowed with appetite and instinct. In other
words, Condillac was a theorist who constructed or invented a
psychology according to a quasi-mathematical method and was
quite prepared to ride roughshod over the evident fact that there
is much in man which cannot be accounted for in terms of what
comes from without.[2] As for Bonnet, de Biran at first thought
highly of him; and a quotation from Bonnet was placed at the
beginning of his essay on the *Influence of Habit*.[3] But, as in the
case of Condillac, de Biran came to look on Bonnet as the con-
structor of a theory which was insufficiently based on empirical
evidence. After all, Bonnet had never observed the movements
of the brain and their connections with mental operations.

From Condillac and Bonnet, Maine de Biran turned to Cabanis
and Destutt de Tracy. True, Cabanis was the author of some
pretty crude materialist statements, such as his famous assertion
that the brain secretes thought as the liver secretes bile. But he

---

[1] *Oeuvres*, I, p. 185.
[2] Condillac refused to admit any difference between philosophical and mathematical analysis.
[3] 'What are the movements of the soul except movements and repetitions of
movements?' Bonnet emphasized the relation between mental operations and
movements in the brain. But the quotation gives a very inadequate idea of
Bonnet's anthropology. He believed, for instance, that the soul survives the death
of the body.

saw that Condillac's picture of the statue gradually endowed with one sense-organ after another represented an extremely inadequate and one-sided theory of the genesis of man's mental life. For Cabanis the nervous system, interior or organic sensations, the inherited physiological constitution and other factors belonging to the 'statue' itself were of great importance. Cabanis was indeed a reductionist, in the sense that he tried to find physiological bases for all men's mental operations. But he studied carefully the available empirical data, and he tried to account for human activity, which could hardly be explained in terms of Condillac's statue model. As for de Tracy, Maine de Biran remarks in the introduction to his essay on the *Influence of Habit* that 'I distinguish all our impressions into *active* and *passive*',[1] and in a note he pays tribute to de Tracy for being the first writer to have seen clearly the importance of man's faculty of moving or 'motility' (*motilité*), as de Tracy called it. For example, de Tracy saw that the judgment about the real existence of a thing, or of our knowledge of external reality, could not be accounted for without experience of resistance, which itself presupposed 'motility'.

In fine, Maine de Biran reacted against the psychology of Condillac by insisting on human activity. 'It is *I* who move or who *will* to move, and it is also *I* who am moved. Here are the two terms of the relation which are required to ground the first simple judgment of personality *I am*.'[2] In a real sense Maine de Biran is re-echoing the conviction of Rousseau who in the first part of his *Discourse on the Origin of Inequality* asserted roundly that man differs from the animals by being a free agent. But among the physiological psychologists de Biran has found his stimulus in the writings of the ideologists. And it was natural that when he submitted the revised version of his first prize-winning essay, Cabanis and de Tracy, who were among the judges, should have given both it and him a warm welcome.

Though however the ideologists regarded Maine de Biran as one of themselves, he soon came to the conclusion that Destutt de Tracy had failed to exploit his own addition to the psychology of Condillac, namely the idea of the active power in man. He may at first have regarded himself as correcting the ideas of the ideologists where they tended to fall back into the Condillacian psychology, but he was gradually moving away from the reductionist

---

[1] *Oeuvres*, II, (1954), p. 20. The reference to de Tracy is on p. 22, note 1.
[2] *Ibid.*, p. 22.

tradition to which the ideologists really belonged, in spite of the improvements which they introduced. In his *Mémoire sur la décomposition de la pensée*, which won a prize in 1805, he is still writing as an ideologist; but he asks whether a distinction should not be made between objective and subjective ideology. An objective ideology would be based chiefly 'on the relations which link the sensitive being to external things, in regard to which it finds itself placed in a relation of essential dependence, both in regard to the affective impressions which it receives from them and in regard to the images which it *forms* of them.'[1] Subjective ideology, 'enclosing itself in the consciousness of the *thinking* subject, would endeavour to penetrate the intimate relations which it has with itself in the free exercise of its intellectual acts.'[2] De Biran does not deny the importance of physiological psychology. He has no intention of rejecting Cabanis and all his works. But he is convinced that something more is required, something which we can describe as the phenomenology of consciousness. The self experiences itself in its operations; and we can envisage a reflection in which knower and known are one.

This may sound as though Maine de Biran were engaged in reintroducing the metaphysical concept of the self as a substance, the thinking substance of Descartes. He insists however that he is doing nothing of the kind. Muscular effort, willed effort that is to say, is a primitive fact. And the real existence of the ego or I is to be found 'in the apperception of the effort of which it feels itself subject or cause'.[3] To be sure, we can hardly think or speak about the ego or self without distinguishing it from the willed effort or action as cause from effect. But we should not allow ourselves to be misled with the metaphysician into postulating a self as a *thing*, a soul which 'exists before acting and which can act without knowing its acts, without knowing itself'.[4] With willed effort apperception or consciousness arises in the human being, and with consciousness *personal* existence as distinct from the existence of a merely sensing being. 'The fact of a power of action and of *will*, proper to the thinking being, is certainly as evident to him as the very fact of his own existence; the one does not differ from the other.'[5] Again, 'here is the sensitive being without *I*; there begins an identical *personality*, and with it all the faculties of the intelligent and moral being.'[6] In other words, consciousness cannot be

---

[1] *Oeuvres*, III, 1, p. 41.   [2] *Ibid.*, pp. 40-1.   [3] *Ibid.*, p. 216.
[4] *Ibid.*, p. 127.   [5] *Ibid.*, p. 178.   [6] *Ibid.*

explained simply in terms of 'transformed sensations' as understood by Condillac. It must be related to willed effort, to human activity meeting with resistance. If it is asked why in this case personality is not intermittent, present only at the moment when we are engaged in willed effort, de Biran's reply is that it is a mistake to suppose that such efforts occur only occasionally or now and again. In some form or another it continues during waking existence and lies at the basis of perception and knowledge.

Perhaps we can say that through the process of reflection first on the psychology of Condillac and Bonnet, then on that of Cabanis and de Tracy, Maine de Biran arrives at a reassertion of Rousseau's statement that man differs from the animals by being a free agent. We must add however that the reflection on contemporary psychology is always carried out in the light of the facts, the phenomena, as de Biran sees them. In his view the ideologists have seen facts to which Condillac was blind, or at any rate the significance of which he did not understand properly. And he refers to Cabanis and de Tracy as agreeing that the ego or I resides exclusively in the will.[1] But it by no means follows that Maine de Biran feels himself at one with the ideologists. For while becoming reflectively aware of the distance which now separates him from Condillac, he has reluctantly arrived at the conclusion that de Tracy, so far from exploiting or developing his own insights, has been retreating backwards. Maine de Biran may look on himself as the heir of the ideologists. But his letters testify to his growing conviction that their paths are diverging.

4. The ideas which found expression in the *Essay on the Decomposition of Thought* were taken up again and reconsidered in the manuscript of the *Essay on the Foundations of Psychology* which Maine de Biran brought with him to Paris in 1812. In this essay metaphysics, in the sense in which it is acceptable to the author, is really the same as reflexive psychology. If we understand by metaphysics a study of things in themselves (of noumena, to use Kantian terminology), apart from their appearance in consciousness, it is excluded. This means that philosophy cannot provide knowledge of the soul as an 'absolute' substance, existing apart from consciousness. If however metaphysics is understood as the science of 'interior phenomena'[2] or as the science of the primitive data of the interior sense (*sens intime*), it is not only possible but also required. Metaphysics in this sense

[1] *Ibid.*, p. 180.   [2] *Oeuvres*, VIII, p. 270.

reveals the existence of the subject as the active ego or I in the relation of willed effort encountering resistance. Further, the subject perceives itself as one power or active force encountering a succession of resistances; and it perceives itself as self-identical inasmuch as it is one subject in relation to the same organism. It may appear that Maine de Biran is in effect claiming that the ego intuitively perceives itself as a substance. His actual claim however is that the ego is aware of itself as cause. 'On the basis of the primitive fact of interior sense, one can assure oneself that every phenomenon relative to consciousness, every mode in which the *I* participates or unites itself in any manner, includes necessarily the idea of a *cause*. This cause is *I* if the mode is active and perceived as the actual result of a willed effort; It is *not-I* if it is a passive impression, felt as opposed to this effort or as independent of every exercise of the will.'[1] In other words, awareness of the ego or *I* as a causal agent is fundamental. The concept of the soul as an 'absolute' substance existing apart from self-consciousness is an abstraction. At the same time de Biran tries to include awareness of personal identity within the intuition of causal efficacy.

Part of the *Essay on the Foundations of Psychology* seems to have been ready for publication when Maine de Biran came to Paris in 1812. But conversation and correspondence with his friends such as Ampère,[2] Dégerando[3] and Royer-Collard,[4] convinced him that he ought to devote further attention to the development of his ideas. And the result was that he never completed and published the work.

If the existence of the ego or subject as active cause is given in intuition, it is natural to think of this cause as persisting, at any rate as a virtual cause, even when it is not actually conscious of its causal efficacy in willed effort. And in this case it is natural to think of it as a substance, provided at least that the concept of substance is interpreted in terms of active force or causality and not as the idea of an inert substratum. So it is not altogether surprising to find Maine de Biran writing to Dégerando that he 'believes' in the metaphenomenal subject or ego. 'If you ask me

---

[1] *Oeuvres*, IX, p. 335.
[2] André-Marie Ampère (1775–1836), physicist and mathematician, was the author of a *Mathematical Theory of Electromagnetic Phenomena, deduced solely from Experience* (1827) and of an *Essay on the Philosophy of the Sciences* (1834).
[3] Marie-Joseph Dégerando (1772–1842) was a member of the group of ideologists and author of a *Theory of Signs* (1800).
[4] Further reference to Pierre-Paul Royer-Collard, professor of the Sorbonne, will be made in the next chapter.

why and on what ground I *believe* it, I reply that I am made in this way, that it is impossible for me not to have this belief, and that it would be necessary to change my nature for me to cease to have it.'[1] In other words, we *perceive* or intuit the ego or I as an active cause or force in actual concrete relations, and we have a natural and irresistible tendency to *believe* in its metaphenomenal or noumenal existence as a permanent substantial force which exists apart from actual apperception. The phenomenal is the object of intuition, while the noumenal or 'absolute' is the object of belief. To put the matter in another way, the subject or I which reveals itself in willed effort is 'the phenomenal manner in which my soul manifests itself to the interior vision'.[2]

In the *Essay on the Foundations of Psychology* Maine de Biran conceived metaphysics as the science of principles, the principles being sought and found in the primitive facts or basic data of intuition. Now he is seeking principles outside the objects of intuition. For the ego or I of consciousness is regarded as the phenomenal manifestation of a noumenal and substantial soul, the 'absolute' which appears in the relation of consciousness as the active subject. The question arises therefore whether the existence of the noumenal self, which is the object of belief, not of knowledge, is inferred. In point of fact de Biran does sometimes speak of induction and also of deduction in this context. But what he seems to be claiming is that this belief is the result of a spontaneous movement of the mind rather than of a deliberately performed inferential operation. 'The spirit of man, which cannot know or conceive anything except under certain relations, always aspires to the absolute and the unconditional.'[3] This aspiration may appear to constitute a leap beyond the frontiers of knowledge into the sphere of the unknowable. But de Biran also asks himself whether 'from the fact that one cannot conceive an act or its phenomenal result without conceiving a being in itself by which the act is produced, it does not follow necessarily that the relation of causality comprises the notion of substance.'[4] In any case metaphysics seem to extend beyond a study of the primitive facts or data of intuition or the interior sense to include reflection on the metaphenomenal conditions of these facts.

In arriving at his new ideas Maine de Biran was stimulated not only by conversation and correspondence with his friends but also

[1] *Oeuvres*, X, p. 26.   [2] *Ibid.*, pp. 312–13.
[3] *Oeuvres*, X, p. 95, note 1.   [4] *Oeuvres*, XI, p. 272.

by reflection on eminent philosophers such as Descartes, Leibniz and Kant. As we have seen, his philosophizing was first situated for a time in the tradition of Francis Bacon, Locke, Condillac and Bonnet. And he had little use for the defenders of the theory of innate ideas or those who tried to prove the existence of meta-phenomenal realities. In the course of time however he came to believe that there was more in Descartes and Leibniz than he had imagined; and though he seems to have had no first-hand know-ledge of Kant's writings, he obtained some acquaintance of the German philosopher's thought from secondary sources, and he was clearly influenced by his reading.

In so far as the *Cogito, ergo sum* (I think, therefore I am) of Descartes could be taken as expressing not an inferential opera-tion but an intuitive apprehension of a primitive fact or datum of consciousness, Maine de Biran came to appreciate Descartes' insight. De Biran naturally preferred the formula *Volo, ergo sum* (I will, therefore I am), inasmuch as it was in the expression of willed effort encountering resistance that, in his opinion, the I of consciousness arose. But he certainly thought of the existence of the ego as given in its appearing to consciousness as a causal agent. The existence of the subject or ego which was given as a phenomenal reality was however precisely its existence 'for itself', as active subject, that is to say, within consciousness or apperception. Descartes' great mistake, in de Biran's opinion, was that he confused the phenomenal self with the noumenal or substantial self. For from the *Cogito, ergo sum* Descartes draws conclusions about the ego or I 'in itself', thus going beyond the sphere of objects of knowledge. Kant however avoids the confu-sion by his distinction between the I of apperception, the pheno-menal ego or the ego appearing to itself and existing 'for itself', and the noumenal, substantial principle. Not that Maine de Biran's position is precisely the same as that of Kant. For instance, whereas for Kant the free agent presupposed by moral choice in the light of the concept of obligation was the noumenal self, for Maine de Biran freedom is, to use Bergsonian language, an immediate datum of consciousness, and the phenomenal ego is the free causal agent. This does not alter the fact however that de Biran sees some affinity between his idea of the permanent soul as the object of belief rather than of knowledge and Kant's idea of the noumenal self. He states, for example, that 'the relative supposes something which pre-exists absolutely, but as this absolute ceases to be such and necessarily assumes the character of the relative directly we come to know it, a contradiction is implied in saying that we have any positive knowledge or idea of the *absolute*, although we cannot prevent ourselves from believing that it exists or admitting it as a primary datum inseparable from our mind, pre-existing before all *knowledge*.'[1] To say this is to come down on the side of Kant rather than on that of Descartes.

Maine de Biran is not however content with postulating an 'absolute' as existing independently of actual consciousness and claiming that nothing further can be said about it than that it is or that we believe that it is. After all, how can we assert the existence of something when we are unable to say *what* is supposed to exist? Here Leibniz comes to de Biran's aid. Provided that the concept of substance is rethought in terms of force, it becomes easier to claim that the substantial soul manifests itself within consciousness, namely as the active subject in the relation of consciousness, and that the concept required for thinking the soul, the concept of substance that is to say, is included in the explicitation of the inner experience of causal activity or efficacy. The area of 'metaphysics' is thus extended, and Maine de Biran can state that 'Kant is wrong in refusing to the understanding the power of conceiving anything beyond *sensible* objects, outside, that is to say, the qualities which constitute these sensible objects, and in asserting that things in themselves are unknowable by the understanding.'[2]

5. The idea of seeing in the phenomenal ego the self-manifestation of an 'absolute' or substantial soul may suggest the idea of seeing all phenomena as manifesting the Absolute or God as their ultimate ground or as the cause of their existence. Though however Maine de Biran did come to regard all phenomena as related to God, it seems unlikely that he would have arrived at this position, had it not been for his meditative and religiously oriented nature and for a felt need for God. To *argue*, in the manner of traditional metaphysics, from internal phenomena to the noumenal self and from external phenomena, or from all phenomena, to the Absolute or Unconditional was really foreign to his mind.[3] It was much

---

[1] *Oeuvres*, X, p. 124.   [2] *Oeuvres*, XI, p. 284.
[3] Maine de Biran did indeed say at an early date that he believed that the world was governed by a divine intelligence. But this was a matter of spontaneous conviction or of the interior sense (*sens intime*) rather than of any cosmological argument in the traditional style.

more a question of a broadening of de Biran's idea of man's inner life. Just as he came to see in the I (*moi*) of consciousness the substantial soul manifesting itself in a relation and thus to knowledge, so did he come to see in certain aspects of man's life a manifestation of the divine reality. As he grew older, Maine de Biran developed a deeply religious philosophy. But he remained a philosopher of man's inner life. And the change in his philosophical outlook expressed a change in his reflections on this life, not a sudden conversion to traditional metaphysics.

Reference has already been made to de Biran's insistence, while in retirement at Grateloup, that belief in God is not required to lead a moral life, but that man has it within his own power to live morally. An atheist can perfectly well recognise moral values and try to realize them through his actions. De Biran was influenced by Stoicism and admired the Stoic heroes, such as Marcus Aurelius; but he naturally brought his ethical ideas into connection with his psychology, so far as this was possible. The end or goal is happiness; and a condition of attaining it is that harmony and balance should be achieved in man's powers or faculties. This means in effect that the active thinking subject of consciousness should rule over or govern the appetites and impulses of the part of man's nature which is presupposed by the life of consciousness. In other words, reason should rule over the impulses of sense. To give content however to the ideas of virtue and vice we have to consider man in his social relations, man as acting on others and as being acted on by society. 'From the feeling of free and spontaneous action which, of itself, would not have any limits, there derive what we call *rights*. From the necessary social reaction which follows the individual's action and which does not exactly conform to it (seeing that men are not like material things which react without acting or originating action) and which often anticipate it, forcing the individual to coordinate his action with that of society, there arise duties. The feeling of obligation (duty) is the feeling of this social *coercion* from which every individual knows well that he cannot free himself.'[1]

Maine de Biran became however more and more conscious of the limitations of the human reason and will, when left to themselves. 'This Stoic morality, sublime as it is, is contrary to the nature of man inasmuch as it tends to bring under the dominion

---

[1] *Journal* (H. Gouhier), I, p. 87. The interpretation of the feeling of obligation in terms of social pressure reappears in Bergson's theory of the 'closed morality'.

of the will affections, feelings or causes of excitation which do not depend on it in any way, and inasmuch as it annihilates a part of man from which he cannot become detached. Reason alone is powerless to provide the will with the motives or principles of action. It is necessary that these principles should come from a higher source.'[1] To the two levels of human life which he has already distinguished, the life of man as animal, as a sensitive being, and the life of man precisely as man, the life, that is to say, of consciousness, of the thinking and free subject, Maine de Biran is thus led to add a third level or dimension, the life of the spirit, characterized by love communicated by the divine Spirit.[2]

The concept of the three levels of human life can be expressed in this way. It is possible for man to allow his personality and liberty to be submerged in abandonment 'to all the appetites, to all the impulses of the flesh'.[3] Man as man then becomes passive, yielding to his animal nature. It is possible for him to maintain, or at least try to maintain, the level on which 'he exercises all the faculties of his nature, where he develops his moral force, by fighting against the unruly appetites of his animal nature. . . .'[4] And it is possible for him to rise to the level of 'absorption in God',[5] the level at which God is for him all in all. 'The *I* (le *moi*) is between these two terms.'[6] That is to say, the level of personal and self-sufficient existence lies between the level of the passivity of self-abandonment to the impulse of sense and the level of the passivity involved in living in God and under his influence. The second level is however ordered to the third, the divinization of man.

If one considers first of all the psychology expounded in the *Essay on the Influence of Habit* and then the ideas presented in de Biran's *Journal* from 1815 onwards or in works such as *New Essays in Anthropology*, one is likely to receive the impression that a revolution has taken place in the author's outlook and that the ideologist, strongly influenced by the thought of the Enlightenment, has been transformed into a Platonist and religious mystic. To a certain extent the impression would be justified. A series of

---

[1] *Journal*, II, p. 67.
[2] The three levels are discussed in the *Journal* (in for example, the entries for December 1818, II, p. 188, and for October 1823, II, pp. 389 f., and in the *New Essays in Anthropology* (*Oeuvres*, XIV) where the third part is devoted to the life of the spirit.
[3] *Oeuvres*, XIV, p. 369.
[4] *Ibid.*, p. 370.
[5] *Ibid.*, p. 369.
[6] *Journal*, II, p. 188.

changes certainly occurred.[1] At the same time it is important to understand that when Maine de Biran conceived and developed the idea of the life of the spirit, he did not so much reject as add to his former psychological theories. For instance, he did not reject his theory of consciousness as relational, nor his view of the life of the free and active subject of consciousness as that which is peculiar to man and as the level on which personal existence arises. He came to believe that as there is a passivity which is presupposed by the life of consciousness, so is there a receptivity above the level of personal self-sufficient existence, a receptivity in relation to the divine influence which manifests itself, for example, both in mystical experience and in the attraction exercised by the great ideals of the good and the beautiful of which Plato speaks and which constitute ways in which the divine Absolute manifests itself.

To be sure, if we speak of an 'addition', we must recognize that the addition brings about a marked change in perspective. For the life of the autonomous subject, which for the eighteenth-century *philosophe* was the highest life for man, is now subordinated to the life of the spirit in which man is dependent on the divine action within him.[2] Obviously de Biran is quite aware of the change of perspective. Thus in a frequently quoted passage he remarks that he spent his youth in studying 'individual existence and the faculties of the *self* (*moi*) and the relations, grounded in pure *consciousness*, of this self to external or internal sensations, ideas and all that is *given* to the soul or to sensibility and received by the organs, the different senses etc.'[3] He then adds that he now accords 'the primacy of importance to man's relations with God and with the society of his fellows'.[4]

In the same entry in the *Journal* however Maine de Biran says that he still believes that a 'thorough knowledge of the relations between the *ego* (*moi*) or the soul of man with the entire human being (the concrete person) should precede in the order of *time* or of study all the theoretical or practical inquiries into the two first

---

[1] The changes are admirably presented in *Les conversions de Maine de Biran* (Paris, 1948) by Professor H. Gouhier, who is also at pains to illustrate the elements of continuity in de Biran's thought.

[2] Maine de Biran writes of the self's absorption in God, of the ego's self-consciousness being swallowed up in the awareness of God or of the divine influence. But he makes it clear that he is referring to a mystical absorption in a *psychological* sense, and that he is not asserting an ontological identification of the substantial soul with God.

[3] *Journal*, II, p. 376.   [4] *Ibid.*

relations.'¹ Further, 'it is experimental *psychology* or a science at first purely reflexive which should lead us in due order to determine our moral relations to the beings like ourselves and our religious relations to the infinite superior being, whence our soul issues and to which it tends to return through the exercise of the sublimest faculties of our nature.'² In other words, the psychological study of the self constitutes the basis for reflection in the ethical and religious spheres, and the method to be employed throughout is that of what de Biran calls 'experimental psychology', though 'reflexive psychology' would be preferable. Throughout phenomena of man's inner life constitute the point of departure. Referring to the life of the spirit, de Biran asserts that 'the third division, the most important of all, is that which philosophy has hitherto felt obliged to leave to the speculations of mysticism, although it can also be reduced to facts of observation, drawn, it is true, from a nature lifted above the senses but not one which is at all alien to the *spirit* which knows God and itself. This division will therefore comprise the facts or the modes and acts of this spiritual life. . . .'³ We can say perhaps that under the label 'experimental psychology' de Biran includes a psychological approach to the phenomenal effects or influence of what theologians have called divine grace.

It has been claimed that de Biran turned from Stoicism to Platonism rather than to Christianity, and that though meditation on literature such as the *Imitation of Christ* and writings by Fénelon certainly brought him closer to Christianity, he was attracted by the idea of the Holy Spirit much more than by that of Christ as son of God in a unique sense. There seems to be a good deal of truth in this contention. However, de Biran's later writings express the conviction that the Christian religion 'alone reveals to man a third life, superior to that of the sensibility and to that of the reason or of the human will. No other system of philosophy has risen so high.'⁴ In any case the onetime agnostic of Grateloup died as a Catholic, even if his religion had been a Platonizing Christianity.

Maine de Biran was not a systematic thinker in the sense of one who creates a developed philosophical system. But he exercised a very considerable seminal or stimulating influence in psychology and on the philosophical movement, passing through Ravaisson

¹ *Ibid.*, pp. 376–7. The two first relations are those to our fellows and to God.
² *Ibid.*, p. 377.   ³ *Oeuvres*, XIV, p. 223.   ⁴ *Ibid.*, p. 373.

and Fouillée and culminating in Bergson, which is known as the spiritualist movement or current of thought.[1] In the religious sphere the type of apologetics 'from within' which was represented, for example, by Ollé-Laprune and afterwards by Blondel owed something to de Biran. His influence however, being more by way of stimulus to personal reflection in this or that field (such as psychology of volition, phenomenology of consciousness, the concept of causality and religious experience) than by the creation of disciples, is so widely diffused and so mixed with other influences that specialist studies are required to disentangle it.

[1] Spiritualism in this sense has nothing to do with spiritualism in the ordinary English sense of the term.

CHAPTER III

ECLECTICISM

The label—Royer-Collard—Cousin—Jouffroy

1. MAINE de Biran derived stimulus from a variety of sources. He was well aware of the fact, and at one period at any rate he defended what he described as a policy of electicism. When however reference is made to the eclectics in French philosophy during the first half of the nineteenth century, it is primarily to Royer-Collard and Cousin, rather than to Maine de Biran. It is true that de Biran was a friend of Royer-Collard and that Cousin published an edition of his writings. It is also true that Royer-Collard and Cousin can be regarded as representatives of the spiritualist movement of which de Biran was the initiator in French philosophy after the revolution. But de Biran's influence was chiefly felt at a later date, in the fields of psychology and phenomenology, whereas Cousin developed an explicitly eclectic philosophy which constituted for a time a kind of official academic system and then suffered a demise. During his lifetime Cousin enjoyed an incomparably greater fame than de Biran had ever enjoyed; but his reputation had declined when de Biran's began to increase. And while Royer-Collard and Cousin are known specifically for their eclecticism, de Biran is known for his reflection on human consciousness.

To give a precise definition of eclecticism is not an easy task. The root-meaning is indeed clear enough. The term is derived from a Greek verb (*eklegein*) meaning to pick out or choose out; and, in general, the eclectic philosophers are those who select from different schools or systems the doctrines of which they approve and then combine them. The presupposition of this procedure is obviously that every philosophical system expresses or is likely to express some truth or truths or some aspect of reality or some perspective or way of looking at the world or human life which needs to be taken into account in any overall synthesis.[1] The

---

[1] Leibniz expressed this idea by suggesting that every system was right in what it asserted but wrong in what it denied. In other words, original philosophers have seen something which was there to be seen, but what each saw was not all that there was to be seen.

implications however of this presupposition may or may not be fully grasped. At one extreme there are the philosophers who are lacking in the power of original thought and who pursue a policy of syncretism, combining or juxtaposing logically compatible (one hopes) doctrines from various schools or traditions but without having any very clear idea of the criteria which are being employed and without creating an organic unity. Such philosophers can be described appropriately as eclectics. At the other extreme are those philosophers, such as Aristotle and Hegel, who see the historical development of philosophy as the process whereby the most adequate philosophy up to date, namely their own systems, comes into being, subsuming in itself the insights of past thinkers. To describe such philosophers as eclectics would be to misdescribe them. If a thinker derives stimulus from a variety of sources, this does not, by itself, make him an eclectic. Or, if it does, the meaning of the term becomes too extended to be of much use. It is probably best reserved for those philosophers who combine or juxtapose doctrines taken from various sources without creating an organic unity. For if a philosopher does create an organic unity, through the consistent overall use of basic principles or fundamental pervasive ideas, he has created a recognizable system which is more than a collection of juxtaposed doctrines.

Obviously, there can be borderline cases. For example, a man might select from various systems the elements which in his opinion possessed truth-value and think that he had welded them together into an organic unity, whereas his critics might be convinced that his claim was unjustified and that he was nothing but an eclectic. The critics would however be giving to the term 'eclecticism' the meaning which we have proposed above as the appropriate meaning. Cousin indeed proclaimed himself an eclectic and then tried to distinguish between eclecticism, as he understood it, and a mere juxtaposition of ideas taken from different systems. But even if he tried to create a unified system, his claims to have done so have met with persistent criticism.

It has often been said that French eclecticism represented or at any rate was closely connected with a political attitude. This statement is not simply the expression of a general tendency to interpret philosophical movements in terms of political categories. There is more to it than that. The leading eclectics were actively engaged in politics. And they believed in the desirability of a constitution which would combine in itself the valuable elements

ECLECTICISM   39

in monarchy, aristocracy and democracy. In other words, they
supported constitutional monarchy. On the one hand they were
opposed not only to any hankering after the return of absolute
monarchy but also to the rule of Napoleon as emperor. On the
other hand they were opposed to those who believed that the
revolution had not gone far enough and needed to be renewed and
extended. It has been said of them that they represented a spirit
of bourgeois compromise. They themselves thought of their
political theory as expressing a sane eclecticism, an ability to
discern the valuable elements in conflicting systems and to combine them in a viable political and social structure.

We can find a similar attitude in the religious sphere. The
eclectics were opponents of materialism and atheism and of the
sensationalism of Condillac. At the same time, while believing in
religious freedom and having no wish to see the Church subjected
to persecution, they certainly did not admit the Church's claim
to be the sole guardian of truth in the religious and moral spheres;
nor had they any sympathy with the idea of an ecclesiastically
inspired and controlled system of education. They aimed at
promoting a philosophically-based religion, existing alongside
official organized religion and working with it in important ways
but not subject to ecclesiastical authority and destined perhaps
to take the place of Catholicism as then known.

In fine, while Traditionalists such as de Maistre dreamed of a
return to a strong monarchy and preached ultramontanism, and
while the social theorists who will be mentioned later demanded
the extension of the revolution,[1] the eclectics tried to steer a
middle course between two extremes, claiming to effect a combination of the different valuable elements in conflicting positions.
To what extent political attitudes influenced philosophical positions and to what extent philosophical ideas exercised an influence
on political convictions is obviously open to discussion. It is not
in any case a question which can be answered purely abstractly,
without consideration of individual thinkers. What seems to be
clear however is that what was described as eclecticism expressed
an attitude which manifested itself outside the sphere of academic
philosophy.

[1] The reference is not of course to an extension of the Terror. Rather was it a
case of believing that while the revolution had destroyed the old régime it had
failed to implement its ideals in a genuine social reform. For one thing, its progress
had been hampered by the rise to power of Napoleon and the arrest of any
movement towards socialism.

2. Paul Royer-Collard (1763–1845) was born at Sompuis in the department of the Marne. In 1792 he was a member of the Commune of Paris and in 1797 of the Council of the Five Hundred. Though his philosophical training was meagre, he became a professor of philosophy at the Sorbonne in 1811 and retained the post until 1814. He had no liking for Napoleon; but the emperor highly approved of the inaugural lecture in which Royer-Collard attacked Condillac. In Napoleon's eyes Royer-Collard's thought would be an instrument for discomfiting and routing the ideologists. After the emperor's final overthrow Royer-Collard became a deputy for the department of the Marne and a leading figure among the so-called *doctrinaires*, who believed that their political theories could be deduced from purely rational principles.

Apart from a lecture delivered to inaugurate his course on the history of philosophy, we possess only the fragments of Royer-Collard's philosophizing which were collected by Jouffroy. He is best known for his introduction into France of the philosophy of common sense of Thomas Reid.[1] In 1768 a French translation of Reid's *Inquiry* had been published at Amsterdam; but it received little attention. Royer-Collard introduced his hearers to the work and then went on to develop some ideas of his own, though the main object of his criticism was Condillac, whereas Reid had been concerned with attacking the scepticism of Hume.

Reid's reply to Hume was not very well thought out. But one of the distinctions which he made was between Locke's simple ideas and Hume's impressions on the one hand and perception on the other. For Reid the former were not the positive data on which knowledge is grounded, but rather postulates arrived at through an analysis of what actually is given in experience, namely perception. Perception always carries with it a judgment or natural belief, about, for example, the existence of the thing perceived. If we insist on starting with subjective impressions, we remain shut up in the sphere of subjectivism. Perception however comprises within itself a judgment about external reality. This judgment stands in need of no proof[2] and is natural to all mankind, thus belonging to the principles of 'common sense'.

---

[1] For Thomas Reid (1710–96) see Vol. 5 of this *History*, pp. 364–73.

[2] Besides tending to forget that Hume himself had insisted on the force of natural beliefs, Reid leaves his readers in some doubt about the precise logical status to be attributed to the judgment. He speaks of self-evidently true principles; but as the judgment that what we perceive really exists is said to be a contingent truth, it seems that its self-evidence can be interpreted in terms of a natural propensity to believe it.

Royer-Collard utilizes Reid's distinction in his attack on the sensationalism of Condillac. Descartes started the trouble by taking a self-enclosed ego as his point of departure and then trying to prove the real existence of physical objects and other persons. But Condillac completed the development of 'idealism' by reducing everything to fleeting sensations, which are of their nature subjective. On his premises he was unable to explain our ability to judge, an ability which shows clearly the activity of the mind. Judgment is involved in perception, inasmuch as the perceiver naturally judges both that there is a permanent and causally active self and that the object of externally directed perception really exists. By sensations Royer-Collard understands feelings of pleasure and pain. These are clearly subjective experiences. But perception gives us objects existing independently of sensation. The armchair sceptic may entertain doubts about the existence of a permanent self and of physical objects, reducing everything to sensation; but he, like everyone else, acts in accordance with the primitive and natural judgments that there is a causally active permanent self and that there are really existing physical objects. Such judgments belong to the sphere of common sense, and they constitute the basis for the further work of reason, which can develop inductive science and which can argue to the existence of God as ultimate cause. There is no need for any supernatural authority to reveal to man the basic principles of religion and morality. Common sense and reason are sufficient guides. In other words, rejection of the sensationalism of Condillac does not entail recours to Traditionalism or to an authoritarian Church. There is a middle way.

The thought of Royer-Collard has some interest as associating a middle way in philosophy with a middle way in politics. To judge however by the fragments of his philosophizing his theories stand in need of a clarification which they do not receive. For example, in his view the self and its causal activity are given immediately to consciousness or to internal perception. Thus in the phenomenon of deliberate attention I am immediately aware of myself as a causal agent. We might expect therefore that Royer-Collard would also claim that we enjoy intuitive knowledge of the existence of perceived objects and an immediate awareness of causal relations in the world. We are told however that each sensation is a 'natural sign'[1] which in some mysterious way

[1] *Les fragments philosophiques de Royer-Collard*, edited by A. Schimberg, p. 22 (Paris, 1913).

suggests not only the idea of an external existent but also the irresistible persuasion of its reality. Royer-Collard also implies that we are led irresistibly by an awareness of the self as a causal agent to find (non-voluntary) causal activity in the external world. As critics have pointed out, Hume explicitly admitted that we have a natural and, in practice, irresistible belief in the real existence of bodies independently of our impressions or perceptions. He could therefore quite well have said that this belief was a matter of common sense. But though Hume thought that the validity of the belief could not be proved, he at any rate inquired into its genesis, whereas Royer-Collard finds such inquiries uncongenial and leaves his hearers in some doubt about precisely what he is claiming. It is indeed clear that he rejects the reduction of the self and the external world to sensations and the attempt to reconstruct them on this basis. It is also clear that he lays emphasis on the idea of perception as distinct from sensation and as a means of overcoming subjectivism. But his treatment of the way in which perception establishes the existence of the external world is ambiguous. He seems to wish to find room for an inductive inference which leads to a conclusion which is certainly, and not simply probably true. But the point is not developed.

3. Victor Cousin (1792–1867) came of a family of poor artisans in Paris. It is related that in 1803, when playing in the gutter, he intervened to rescue a pupil of the Lycée Charlemagne from a gang of pursuing schoolmates, and that in gratitude the boy's mother undertook to provide for Cousin's education.[1] At the Lycée Charlemagne Cousin carried off the prizes, and on leaving the school he gained entry to the École Normale. As soon as he had finished his course of studies he was appointed assistant professor of Greek, being then twenty years old. In 1815 he lectured at the Sorbonne as a substitute for Royer-Collard on the Scottish philosophy of common sense. At the École Normale he had indeed attended lectures by Laromiguière[2] and Royer-Collard; but his knowledge of philosophy was at the time pretty limited. For the matter of that, so was Royer-Collard's.

Cousin then applied himself to learning something about Kant

---

[1] For such details see *Victor Cousin* (London, 1888) by Jules Simon, who had been a pupil of Cousin.

[2] Pierre Laromiguière (1756–1837) accepted the general method of Condillac, but he adopted a twofold point of departure by adding the motive power of attention to the receptivity of sensation. It has been already noted that Maine de Biran wrote on Laromiguière's *Lectures* (*Leçons*).

whose doctrine he soon mastered, in his own opinion at least if not in that of posterity. In 1817 he went to Germany to make the acquaintance of the post-Kantian philosophers. On this visit he met Hegel, while on a subsequent visit in 1818 he came to know Schelling and Jacobi. On a third visit to Germany in 1824 Cousin had an opportunity to widen his knowledge of German philosophy while in prison for six months, suspected by the Prussian police of being a conspirator.

In 1820 the École Normale was closed, and Cousin lost his chair. He then set about editing the works of Descartes and of Proclus and started translating Plato. In 1828 he was restored to his chair, and with the accession to the throne of Louis-Philippe his day had come at last. In 1830 he became a councillor of State, in 1832 a member of the Royal Council and director of the École Normale, in 1833 a peer of France and in 1840 minister of public instruction. In the years of his glory he was to all intents and purposes not only the official philosopher of France but also a philosophical dictator who described the French philosophers of philosophy as his 'regiment' and excluded from the teaching staff of the Sorbonne those of whom he disapproved, such as Comte and Renouvier. The revolution of 1848 however brought Cousin's philosophical dictatorship to an end, and he retired into private life. At the accession to power of Louis Napoleon he became a professor emeritus with a pension.

Cousin described the sensationalist theory of Condillac and his associates as 'sensualism'. Hence the title of his work *Sensualist Philosophy in the Eighteenth Century* (*Philosophie sensualiste au XVIIIe siècle*, 1819). Among other writings one can mention *Philosophical Fragments* (*Fragments philosophiques*, 1826). *On the True, Beautiful and the Good* (*Du vrai, du beau et du bien*, 1837), a *Course of the History of Modern Philosophy* (*Cours de l'histoire de la philosophie moderne*, 5 volumes, 1841) and *Studies on Pascal* (*Études sur Pascal*, 1842).

It was Cousin's conviction that the nineteenth century stood in need of eclecticism. It needed it in the political sphere, in the sense that monarchy, aristocracy and democracy should function as component elements in the constitution. In the philosophical sphere the time had arrived for a systematic policy of eclecticism, for a welding together of the valuable elements contained in different systems. Man himself is a composite being, and just as in man an harmonious integration of different powers and activities is a desirable goal, so in philosophy do we require an integration of different ideas, each of which is apt to be over-emphasized by one or other philosophical system.

According to Cousin, reflection on the history of philosophy reveals that there are four basic types of system, which are 'the fundamental elements of all philosophy'.[1] In the first place there is sensualism, the philosophy 'which relies exclusively on the senses'.[2] Then there is idealism, which finds reality in the realm of thought. Thirdly there is the philosophy of common sense. And in the fourth place there is mysticism, which turns its back on the senses and takes refuge in interiority. Each of these systems or types of system contains some truth, but no one of them contains the whole truth or is uniquely true. For example, the philosophy of sensation must obviously express some truth, as sensibility is a real aspect of man. It is not however the whole of man. In regard therefore to the basic kinds of system we have to be careful 'not to reject any one, and not to be the dupe of any of them'.[3] We have to combine the true elements. To do so is to practise eclecticism.

Eclecticism is presented by Cousin as the culmination of an historical process. 'The philosophy of a century arises from all the elements of which this century is composed.'[4] In other words, philosophy is the product of the complex factors which compose a civilization, even though, once arisen, it takes on a life of its own and can exercise an influence. At the close of the Middle Ages, according to Cousin, the new spirit which arose first took the form of an attack on the dominant medieval power, the Church, and so of a religious revolution. A political revolution came second. 'The English revolution is the great event of the end of the seventeenth century.'[5] Both revolutions expressed the spirit of freedom, which was then manifested in the science and philosophy of the eighteenth century. The spirit of freedom or liberty led indeed to the excesses of the French revolution; but subsequently it was given a balanced expression in a political system combining the elements of monarchy, aristocracy and democracy, in constitutional monarchy that is to say. It follows that the philosophy required by the nineteenth century is an eclecticism which combines independence of the Church with a rejection of materialism and atheism. In fine, an eclectic spiritualism is required which transcends the philosophy of sensation of the eighteenth century

---

[1] *Cours de philosophie. Histoire de la philosophie*, I, p. 141 (Brussels, 1840).
[2] *Ibid.*, p. 118.   [3] *Ibid.*, p. 141.   [4] *Ibid.*, p. 8.   [5] *Ibid.*, p. 11.

but does not fall back into subservience to ecclesiastical dogma and tutelage.

It would not be fair to Cousin to suggest that he is blind to the fact that this sort of interpretation of the history of development presupposes a philosophy, a definite stand in regard to criteria of truth and falsehood. He may speak on occasion as though he were an impartial observer, judging philosophy from outside; but he also admits explicitly that we cannot separate truth from error in philosophical systems without criteria which are the result of previous philosophical reflection, and that for this reason eclecticism 'assumes a system, starts from a system'.[1]

Cousin's rejection of the sensationalism of Condillac by no means entails a rejection of the method of observation and experiment in philosophy, nor indeed of starting with psychology. In his view Condillac's use of observation was deficient. As was seen by Laromiguière, observation gives us phenomena such as active attention which cannot be reduced to passively received impressions. And Maine de Biran threw light, by means of observation, on the active role of the self. If Condillac rightly asserted the existence and importance of human sensibility, de Biran rightly asserted the existence and importance of the human will, of voluntary activity. Observation however, Cousin insists, will take us further than this. For it reveals to us the faculty of reason, which is reducible neither to sensation nor to will and which sees the necessary truth of certain basic principles, such as the principle of causality, that are implicitly recognized by common sense. Psychology therefore reveals the presence of three faculties in man, namely sensibility, will and reason. And philosophical problems fall into three corresponding groups, concerned respectively with the beautiful, the good and the true.

To develop a philosophy of reality we have of course to go beyond the purely psychological sphere. It is the faculty of reason which enables us to do this. For with the aid of the principles of substance and causality it enables us to refer the interior phenomena of willed effort to the self or ego and passively received impressions to an external world or Nature. These two realities, the ego and the non-ego, limit one another, as Fichte held, and cannot constitute the ultimate reality. Both must be ascribed to the creative activity of God. It is thus reason which enables us to emerge from the subjective sphere and to develop an ontology in

[1] *Fragments philosophiques* (1838 edition), I, p. 41.

which the self and the not-self are seen as related to the causal activity of God.

The Traditionalists emphasized the impotence of the human reason in the metaphysical and religious spheres, when working independently of revelation. The Catholic Church eventually took a stand against this attitude; and it may thus appear that it should have been gratified by Cousin's metaphysics. But what Cousin was driving at was a middle way between Catholicism on the one hand and eighteenth-century atheism and agnosticism on the other. It is understandable therefore that his point of view was not altogether acceptable to those who believed that the bosom of the Church was the only viable and proper alternative to infidelity. Further, Cousin was accused of pantheism on the ground that he represented the world as a necessary actualization of the divine life. That is to say, he thought of God as necessarily manifesting himself in the physical world and in the sphere of finite selves. The world, in his opinion, was as necessary to God as God to the world; and he spoke of God as returning to himself in human consciousness.[1] Cousin denied that such ways of speaking entailed pantheism; but little weight was attached to his denial by critics who were convinced of the inherently irreligious tendencies of philosophy. To be sure, he advised philosophers to steer clear of talking about religion, by which he meant primarily Catholicism. But he certainly talked about God; and to his religious critics his way of speaking seemed to be at variance with what they believed to be true religion and to confirm their suspicions of philosophy.

As an exponent of a middle way, of a policy of compromise, Cousin was naturally faced with criticism from two sides. His metaphysics was acceptable neither to materialists and atheists nor to the Traditionalists. His political theories satisfied neither the republicans and the socialistically minded nor the authoritarian royalists. His more academic critics have objected that the transition which he makes from psychology to ontology is unjustified. In particular, Cousin gives no clear explanation how principles of universal and necessary validity, capable of grounding an ontology and a metaphysics, can be derived from inspection of the data of consciousness. He asserts that 'as is the method of a

---

[1] Cousin's ideas on this subject obviously show the influence of German metaphysical idealism. It was however his general habit to minimize foreign influence in his thought. He even went so far as to represent electicism as a specifically French contribution to philosophical thought.

philosopher, so will be his system', and that 'the adoption of a
method decides the destiny of a philosophy'.[1] Those critics who
find Cousin's eclecticism incoherent may be inclined to agree,
adding that in his case a clearly defined method was conspicuous
by its absence.

Though however Cousin's thought has been submitted to a good
deal of patronizing or even contemptuous criticism, he made a
considerable contribution to the development of academic
philosophy in France, especially perhaps in the field of the history
of philosophy. His view that there was truth in all systems
naturally encouraged study of them; and he set an example by
his historical writings. It is easy to write him off as a man who
gave theoretical expression to the reign of Louis-Philippe. The
fact remains that he left his mark on university philosophy in
France.

4. Among the pupils of Cousin was Théodore Simon Jouffroy
(1796–1842). He entered the École Normale in 1814 and after his
studies became a lecturer there until his appointment in 1833 as
professor of ancient philosophy at the Collège de France.[2] From
1833 he also served as a deputy in the Chamber. His writings include two sets of philosophical essays (*Mélanges philosophiques*,
1833, and *Nouveaux mélanges philosophiques*, 1842) and two
courses, one on natural law (*Cours de droit naturel*, 2 volumes, 1834–
42) and one on aesthetics (*Cours d'esthétique*, 1843). The second
course, published posthumously, consists of notes of his lectures
taken by a hearer.

In regard to philosophy, or at any rate to philosophical systems,
Jouffroy shows a marked scepticism. In 1813 he realized that he
had lost his Christian faith. That is to say, he found that the
answers provided by Christian dogmas to problems about human
life and destiny were no longer valid for him. In his view philosophy would or at least might one day take the place of Christian
dogmas and solve the problems which could no longer be answered
by the authoritative pronouncements of a religion claiming to
embody divine revelation.[3] In this matter Jouffroy was more
outspoken than Cousin who, whatever he may have thought,
tended to emphasize the co-existence of philosophy and religion

---

[1] *Elements of Psychology*, translated by C. S. Henry, p. 28 (London, 1851).
[2] Previously to his nomination to this chair Jouffroy had lectured at the Sorbonne as well as at the École Normale.
[3] In 1825 Jouffroy published an article on the end of dogmas and their eventual
replacement by philosophy.

rather than the replacement of the latter by the former.[1] Though however Jouffroy remained convinced that each individual had in fact a vocation, a task in life, he did not believe that anyone could know with certainty what his vocation was, nor that philosophy as it existed could provide definite answers to problems of this kind. In his opinion philosophical systems reflected the outlook, ideas, historical and social circumstances and needs of their times. Systems, in other words, express relative, not absolute truth. Like religion, they can have pragmatic value; but a final philosophical system is a remote ideal, not an actuality.

Jouffroy combined this partial scepticism in regard to philosophical systems with belief in principles of common sense which are prior to explicit philosophy and express the collective wisdom of the human race. Royer-Collard and Cousin aroused in him an interest in the Scottish philosophy of common sense, an interest which bore fruit in his translation into French of Dugald Stewart's[2] *Outlines of Moral Philosophy* and of Reid's works. Reflecting on the Scottish philosophy Jouffroy came to the conclusion that there are principles of common sense which possess a degree of truth and certainty which is not enjoyed by the philosophical theories of individuals.[3] To be sure, these theories cannot be simply the product of individuals, if philosophies express the spirit of their times. But the principles of common sense represent something more permanent, the collective wisdom of mankind or the human race, to which appeal can be made against the one-sidedness of a philosophical system. One philosopher, for example, may expound a materialist system, while another regards spirit as the sole reality. Common sense however recognizes the existence of both matter and spirit. Presumably therefore any adequate or universally true philosophy would be basically an explication of common sense, of the wisdom of mankind, rather than of the ideas, outlook, circumstances and needs of a particular society.

There are of course some pretty obvious objections to any sharp division between individual opinions and theories on the one hand

---

[1] As a kind of philosophical dictator, the official mouthpiece of philosophy in France, Cousin was anxious not to antagonize potentially hostile groups but to harmonize different points of view. As we have noted, his policy of compromise was not particularly successful. The point is however that his position encouraged adoption of a policy which a man such as Jouffroy, who did not share Cousin's ambitions, had much less interest in pursuing.

[2] For Dugald Stewart see Vol. 5 of this *History*, pp. 375–83.

[3] On this subject see Jouffroy's essay on philosophy and common sense in *Mélanges philosophiques*.

and the collective wisdom of mankind on the other. For example, common sense is said to express itself in self-evidently true propositions which lie at the basis of logics and ethics. But the truth of such principles is grasped by individual minds. And in his psychological reflections, where he treats of human faculties, their development and cooperation, Jouffroy certainly depicts reason as capable of apprehending truth. To a certain extent perhaps the tension between individualism and what we may perhaps, for want of a better word, call collectivism can be overcome by representing the fully developed human being as participating in the common mind or wisdom. But the tension in Jouffroy's thought remains. For instance, his view of common sense as expressing human solidarity might be expected, as historians have pointed out, to influence his political ideas in the direction of socialism, whereas in fact he spoke on occasion of society as a collection of individuals. Perhaps however Jouffroy would maintain that the integration of the common and the individual is an ideal towards which mankind moves. In the case of philosophy at any rate he believed that the divergence between one-sided systems and common sense would one day be overcome. And he seems also to have thought that nationalism was in process of giving way to internationalism as an expression of human fraternity.

We have seen that Cousin tried to base ontology on psychology. Jouffroy did not follow him here. He insisted that psychology should be kept free from metaphysics and studied with the same scientific detachment that we find in the physicist. At the same time he emphasized the distinction between psychology and physical science.[1] When the physicist observes a series or set of phenomena, he is not simultaneously presented with their cause or causes. Further inquiry is required. In inner observation or perception however the cause, namely the self, is a datum. This may sound like an excursion into metaphysics; but Jouffroy seems to be referring, in a manner reminiscent of Maine de Biran, to the ego which is aware of itself in consciousness or apperception rather than to a substantial soul.

In his lectures on natural law Jouffroy devoted his attention very largely to ethical themes. In a sense good and evil are relative. For every man has his own particular vocation in life, his life-task; and good actions are those which contribute to the

[1] See Jouffroy's essay on the legitimacy of the distinction between psychology and physiology in *Nouveaux mélanges philosophiques.*

fulfilment of this vocation, while evil actions are those which are incompatible with its fulfilment. We can say therefore that good and evil are relative to the individual's self-realization. But this is not all that can be said. Underlying all ethical codes and systems of law are the basic principles which belong to common sense. Further Jouffroy seems to regard all individual vocations as contributing to the development of a common moral order. And if a unified moral ideal cannot be fully realized in this life, it may perhaps be the case that it will be realized in another.

CHAPTER IV

SOCIAL PHILOSOPHY IN FRANCE

General remarks—The utopianism of Fourier—Saint-Simon and the development of society—Proudhon, anarchism and syndicalism—Marx on the French socialists.

1. THE Traditionalists, as we have seen, were concerned with what they regarded as the breakdown of social order exhibited in and consequent on the revolution, the revolution itself being attributed in large measure to the thought and influence of the eighteenth-century philosophers. To depict the Traditionalists as being reactionaries to such an extent as to envisage the restoration of the pre-revolutionary régime together with all the abuses which rendered change inevitable would be to do them an injustice. But they certainly believed that social reconstruction on a firm basis demanded a reassertion of traditional principles of religion and of monarchic government. In this sense they looked backwards, though a writer such as de Maistre was, as we have noted, a strong upholder of ultramontanism and no friend of the tradition of Gallicanism.

The ideologists, regarded by Napoleon as pestilential 'metaphysicians', were not much given to political pronouncements. But their methods had implications in the social field. For example, they insisted on careful analysis of empirical phenomena and on education through discussion. The emperor doubtless thought that the ideologists were concerned with trivialities and useless or unprofitable inquiries; but the fact of the matter is that they were opposed to the idea of moulding the youth to a pattern and to the educational system as envisaged by Napoleon, as well as to his restoration of the Catholic religion in France.

The eclectics favoured constitutional monarchy and a compromise policy, acceptable to the bourgeoisie. They were themselves active in political life; and they can be said to have represented a class which gained in status through the revolution and which did not desire further drastic experiments, whether imperialistic conquests or socialist programmes of change.

It is only to be expected however that there should have been other thinkers who were convinced that the revolution ought to be carried further, not indeed in the sense of a renewal of bloodshed but in the sense that the ideals of the revolution needed to be realized in a reformation of the structure of society. Liberty might have been achieved by the revolution; but the realization of equality and fraternity was by no means so conspicuous. These would-be social reformers who were convinced that the work of the revolution needed to be extended, were idealists,[1] and their positive proposals have often been described as utopian, especially by Marx and his followers. In some cases at any rate the description has an obvious foundation in fact. If the Traditionalists had their dreams, so had their opposite numbers. To admit this patent fact does not however entail the conclusion that Marxism is scientific as opposed to utopian socialism.[2] In any case a sharp distinction tends to conceal the fact that the ideas of the French social reformers in the first half of the nineteenth century contributed to the development of political theory on socialist lines.

2. It must be admitted that Karl Marx's view of François Marie Charles Fourier (1772–1837) as a well-meaning and myth-creating utopian socialist was not unjustified. For while Fourier certainly drew attention to a real problem, his solution contained elements which now and then bordered on the fantastic. His views were often eccentric; and some of his prophecies, as about the functions which animals might or would come to fulfil, amounted to highly imaginative science fiction. But he was a kindly man and was inspired by a genuine desire for the regeneration of society.

A native of Besançon, where he received his schooling from the Jesuits, Fourier was the son of a merchant and gained his livelihood in the world of trade. Apart from this occupation he devoted himself to the propagation of his views on human society. His writings include a *Theory of the Four Movements and of General Destinies* (*Théorie des quatres mouvements et des destinées générales,* 1808), a *Theory of Universal Unity* (*Théorie de l'unité universelle,* 1822) and a work entitled *The New Industrial and Social World*

---

[1] There is of course no reference to idealism in any technical philosophical sense.

[2] It is arguable at any rate that a more helpful distinction can be made between pragmatic socialism, which is of course inspired by at least implicit socio-ethical ideals but is comparatively free from ideological dogmatism, and doctrinaire socialism in which the interests of individuals and groups here and now may very well be sacrificed in the name of the society of the future, the advent of which is regarded either as the inevitable result of an historical process or as so overwhelmingly desirable that the measures supposed to be required for its attainment must take precedence over the correction of present abuses and evils.

(*Le nouveau monde industriel et sociétaire*, 1829). Except for his secondary schooling at Besançon he was a self-taught man who possessed plenty of intelligence, a lively imagination and a smattering of knowledge on a variety of topics.

Fourier was an uncompromising and outspoken critic of established society as he knew it. More accurately, he followed Rousseau in blaming civilization for the ills of mankind. Everywhere in civilized society, according to Fourier, we can see selfishness and self-interest masquerading as service to humanity. For example, doctors thrive on the spread of ailments among their fellow citizens, and the clergy desire the deaths of their wealthier parishioners in order to receive substantial fees for performing the funeral rites.[1] Moreover, civilized society is afflicted with hordes of parasites. Women and children, for instance, are domestic parasites, while soldiers and traders are social parasites. Obviously, not even Fourier's eccentricity goes so far as to suggest that women and children should be eliminated. What he means is that in civilized society women and children lead unproductive lives. In his opinion, women should be emancipated and free to take part in productive work, while children, he quaintly suggests, who love playing in the gutter, might well be employed in cleaning up the streets. As things are, only a comparatively small section of the population is engaged in productive work. Armies are engaged in destruction, not production; and in times of peace they are parasites on society. As for traders and merchants, 'commerce is the natural enemy of the producer.'[2] It by no means follows however that the producers are either happy or free from the prevailing selfishness. Their conditions of life are often deplorable, and 'each worker is at war with the mass and bears ill will towards it from personal interest'.[3] In fine, civilized society is infected thoughout with selfishness, discord and disharmony.

What is the origin of the evils of civilized society? According to Fourier it is the repression of the passions, for which civilization is

---

[1] Fourier evidently gives one-sided pictures or caricatures of the motives and outlooks of groups and classes. Caricature apart however, he is certainly quick to detect evidence of what he believes to be sham and humbug and to draw inferences from behaviour to motives of which the agents may not be consciously aware. In other words, his picture of society, though doubtless one-sided, exhibits some psychological insight. In the case of politicians, for example, claims to be concerned exclusively with the public welfare often arouse sceptical thoughts in minds which have never heard of Fourier.

[2] *Four Movements*, p. 332; *Universal Unity*, II, p. 217.

[3] *Four Movements*, p. 29.

responsible. The world was created by a good God who implanted in man certain passions which must therefore be good in themselves. Among the thirteen passions implanted by God Fourier includes, for example, the five senses, social passions such as love and family feeling, distributive passions such as that for variety (the 'butterfly' passion), and the crowning passion for harmony which unites or synthesizes the others.[1] Civilization has repressed these passions in such a way as to render harmony impossible. What is required therefore is a reorganization of society which will secure the release of the passions and, consequently, both the development of individuals and the attainment of concord or harmony between them.

The social organization to which Fourier pinned his hopes was what he called a 'phalanx', a group of men, women and children amounting in number to between one and a half and two thousand people.[2] The members of a phalanx would be persons of different temperaments, abilities and tastes. They would be grouped according to occupation or type of work; but no member would be given work for which he was unsuited or which he would find repugnant. If his tastes changed or he felt the need for other work, he could satisfy the 'butterfly' passion.[3] Thus each member of a phalanx would have full opportunity to develop his talents and passions to the full; and he would understand the significance of his particular work in the general scheme. There would be competition between sub-groups; but harmony would reign. Indeed, if only one phalanx was successfully established, the evident harmony, happiness and prosperity of its members would inevitably stimulate imitation. Relations between different phalanxes would be loose, though there would have to be provision for groups of workers to perform special temporary tasks in different phalanxes. There would not of course be any wars. Their place would be taken by gastronomic contests or competitions.[4]

Some of Fourier's ideas strike most readers as odd or bizarre. Thus he believed that human social regeneration would have remarkable effects not only in the animal kingdom but even among

[1] It is hardly necessary to say that by passion Fourier does not mean something excessive and disordered, as when we say of someone that he flew into a passion or that he was carried away by ungovernable passion.
[2] The ideal number, according to Fourier, would be 1620, as this would facilitate all combinations of the thirteen basic passions.
[3] The family would be retained in the phalanx. But release of the 'butterfly' passion would mean abolition of tabus in regard to conjugal fidelity.
[4] Fourier laid stress on 'gastrosophy'.

the heavenly bodies. But the oddity of some of his ideas does not alter the fact that he saw a real problem which is acute enough today, namely that of humánizing industrial society and labour and overcoming what is described as alienation. His solution obviously suffers from the defects of utopianism, such as the notion that there is only one ideal form of social organization. At the same time it had its points. To a certain extent it was a socialist solution; but Fourier did not envisage the abolition of private property, which he believed to be necessary for the development of the human personality. What he was suggesting was an experi- mental cooperative society with shareholders, the shares being allotted in stated proportion to labour, capital and talent, and the highest interest going to those who held the least stock.

Fourier himself never succeeded in realizing his project. But after his death a disciple called Godin founded a 'phalanstery' in France, while another disciple, Victor Considérant, experimented on Fourierist lines in Texas. Fourier's doctrines, trimmed of their more bizarre features, attracted a number of adherents both in France and America; but their effect was understandably limited and passing. He regarded himself as the Newton of social thought, the discoverer of the laws of social development and, in particular, of the transition from 'civilization' to the harmonious and perfect society which would realize the divine plan. His own estimate of himself has not been accepted. But while it is understandable that his ideas should be regarded as being to a large extent an historical curiosity, he was by no means devoid of perspicacity. Such problems as how to organize social and industrial structures in the service of man and how to harmonize individual and collec- tive needs are obviously still with us.

3. A more influential precursor of socialism was Claude-Henri de Rouvroy, Comte de Saint-Simon (1760–1825). Scion of a noble though by no means wealthy family Saint-Simon received his education from private tutors, one of whom was the philosopher and scientist d'Alembert.[1] It was doubtless d'Alembert who stimulated in Saint-Simon's mind his faith in science as the source of enlightenment. At the age of seventeen Saint-Simon became an officer in the army and took part in the American war of indepen- dence. When the revolution broke out, he supported it up to a point, though his cooperation seems to have consisted mainly in buying confiscated property cheaply. In 1793 he was arrested,

[1] For d'Alembert see vol. 6 of this *History*, pp. 39–47.

under the name which he had adopted for his profitable enterprises, but was subsequently released. He was politically active under the Directory but eventually·gave himself entirely to the development and publicization of his social ideas, at times in a position of very considerable hardship.[1] In 1807–8 he published his *Introduction to the Scientific Works of the Nineteenth Century* (*Introduction aux travaux scientifiques de XIXe siècle*), and in 1813 his *Essay on the Science of Man* and *Work on Universal Gravitation* (*Mémoire sur la science de l'homme* and *Travail sur la gravitation universelle*). From 1814 until 1817 he worked in collaboration with Augustin Thierry; and the work entitled *Reorganisation of European Society* (*Réorganisation de la société européenne*, 1814) appeared under both names. From 1818 Auguste Comte acted as his secretary and collaborator until the two men quarrelled in 1824, the year before Saint-Simon's death. Comte owed a considerable debt to Saint-Simon and he could on occasion acknowledge the fact; but, in general, he preferred not to.

Saint-Simon described the philosophy of the eighteenth century as critical and revolutionary, whereas the philosophy of the nineteenth century was destined to be inventive and organizational. 'The philosophers of the eighteenth century made an Encyclopaedia to overthrow the theological and feudal system. The philosophers of the nineteenth century should also make an Encyclopaedia to bring into being the industrial and scientific system.'[2] That is to say, the thinkers of the eighteenth century subjected the old régime and the beliefs on which it rested to destructive criticism. If, in Saint-Simon's opinion, the last kings of France had had the good sense to ally themselves with the rising industrial class instead of with the nobility, the transition to a new system could have been affected peaceably. In point of fact however the old régime was swept away in a violent revolution. At the same time a political system cannot disappear entirely, unless a new system, capable of taking its place, is waiting, so to speak, in the wings. In the case of the French revolution the new system, destined to take the place of the old, was not ready. It is no matter for surprise therefore if after a time the monarchy was restored. The nineteenth century however was destined to be a period of new social construction and organization. And in the fulfilment of this task the nineteenth-century thinkers had an

---

[1] In 1823 Saint-Simon attempted suicide.
[2] *Oeuvres complètes de Saint-Simon et Enfantin* (Paris, 1865–76), X, pp. 104–5.

important role to play, the thinkers, that is to say, who, like Saint-Simon himself, could point out the lines which the process of constructive organization should take.

Though however Saint-Simon emphasized the critical and destructive aspects of the philosophy of the eighteenth-century Enlightenment, there was another aspect of it which he regarded as providing the basis for later construction. This was its exaltation of the rational and scientific spirit. In Saint-Simon's opinion, it was science which had undermined the authority of the Church and the credibility of theological dogmas. At the same time it was the extension of the scientific approach from physics and astronomy to man himself which provided the basis for social reorganization. 'Knowledge of man is the one thing which can lead to the discovery of the ways of reconciling the interests of people.'[1] And knowledge of man can be attained only by treating man as a part of nature and by developing the idea, already prepared by certain writers of the Enlightenment and by Cabanis, of psychology as a department of physiology. Psychology however must also include study of the social organism. In other words, a new science is needed, described by Saint-Simon as social physiology.[2] Society and politics or, more generally, man in society can then be studied no less scientifically than the movements of the heavenly bodies. In fine, the application of Newtonian science to man himself, his psychology, his moral behaviour and his politics, is an indispensable basis for solving the social problems of Europe.

The sciences of astronomy, physics and chemistry have already been placed on a 'positive basis',[3] that is to say on observation and experiment.[4] The time has now come to place the science of man on a similar basis.[5] This will bring about the unification of the sciences and the realization of the ideal which inspired the *Encyclopaedia*. It is true that a completely unified and final scientific knowledge of the world remains an ideal towards which the human mind can approximate but which it cannot fully attain, inasmuch as advance in scientific knowledge is always possible.

---

[1] *Ibid.*, XI, p. 40.

[2] The term 'sociology' derives from Comte rather than from Saint-Simon.

[3] *Oeuvres*, XI, p. 17.

[4] Saint-Simon emphasizes the role of observation and experiment. Obviously, experimentation, in the sense in which we speak of experiments in chemistry, is hardly possible in astronomy. But the term can be understood in a wide sense. And nowadays the situation has altered from what it was in Saint-Simon's time.

[5] We are reminded of the famous passage in Hume's introduction to the *Treatise*, in which he envisages placing the science of man on a solid foundation of experience and observation.

At the same time Saint-Simon thinks in terms of the extension of the approach and method of classical physics, considered as definitive in its main lines, to the study of man. And he believes that this extension will complete the transition from the stage of human thought in which theology and metaphysics passed as knowledge to the stage of positive or scientific knowledge.

Some writers have seen a discrepancy between Saint-Simon's ideal of the unification of the sciences and his later insistence on the superior dignity of the science of man. It has been argued, that is to say, that the ideal in question implies that all sciences are on the same level, whereas to ascribe a higher dignity to the science of man is to assume that there is a qualitative difference between man and other beings and to fall back on the medieval notion that the dignity of a science depends on its subject-matter or 'formal object'.[1]

This may be the case. But it does not seem necessary to postulate any radical change in Saint-Simon's position. He does indeed come to hold that social physiology has a special subject-matter, namely the social organism, which is more than a collection of individuals. But he demands that society should be studied by means of the same sort of method which is employed in other sciences. And if he adds a value-judgment, this does not necessarily involve him in a radical shift of position, not at any rate if we interpret him as referring to the importance of the science of man rather than as implying that man is qualitatively different from other things to an extent which precludes scientific study of human society. This implication was obviously not intended.

Saint-Simon does not of course treat society in a purely abstract manner. Social and political institutions develop and change; and Saint-Simon assumes that there must be a law which governs such changes. To study human society scientifically involves therefore discovery of the law or laws of social evolution. If we take it that any such law can be discovered only inductively, by investigating and reflecting on the historical phenomena, it is obvious that a survey of the widest possible field is desirable. Or, if a preliminary statement of the law of social change is based on an inquiry into a limited field, inquiry into other fields is required in order to see whether the hypothesis is confirmed or falsified. Though however

---

[1] See, for example, what is said by E. Bréhier in the sixth volume of his *History of Philosophy* (*The Nineteenth Century: Period of Systems, 1800–1850*, translated by Wade Baskin, Chicago and London, 1968, p. 267).

Saint-Simon does make general remarks about historical stages in the process of social evolution, what really interests him is the transition from medieval to modern civilization, apart from what he has to say about the future.

In his general views of the transition from theological beliefs and metaphysical speculation to the era of positive or scientific knowledge, of the need for a science of human society, and of historical changes as law-governed, Saint-Simon obviously anticipates the positivism of Auguste Comte. The latter's disciples were inclined to belittle the former's influence; and some even tried to make out that it was Saint-Simon who was influenced by Comte rather than the other way round. But this contention cannot be defended successfully. To be sure, both men had their precursors in the eighteenth century, writers such as Turgot and Condorcet.[1] And during their period of collaboration Saint-Simon doubtless derived stimulus from Comte. The point is however that Saint-Simon arrived at his basic ideas well before the period of his association with Comte. And whatever some of his disciples may have said, Comte could bring himself on occasion, at any rate in correspondence, to recognize his debt to Saint-Simon. True, Comte worked out his ideas in his own way. But it is a question of deriving stimulus from Saint-Simon and being influenced by him in important respects rather than of slavish appropriation of ideas. In view of Comte's reputation as the founder of classical positivism it is as well to draw attention to the important role played by Saint-Simon.

In his account of social change Saint-Simon lays great emphasis on the basic importance of ideas. For example, the beliefs and ideas of the Middle Ages exercised a determining influence on the social and political institutions of the time,[2] while the development of the sciences and the transition to the stage of positive knowledge demands and leads to the creation of new social and political structures. In thus emphasizing the basic role played by ideas he is linked with Comte rather than with Marx. At the same time Saint-Simon also stresses the importance of man's economic life by what he has to say about the rise of the class of merchants and artisans. In his opinion the feudal society of the Middle Ages reached its culminating point in the eleventh century. After

---

[1] For Turgot and Condorcet, see Vol. 6 of this *History*, pp. 56–8 and pp. 168–71.
[2] Saint-Simon regards the medieval period as a necessary stage in historical development and has thus little sympathy with the eighteenth-century tendency to dismiss the Middle Ages as a period of darkness.

this time there emerged within it two factors which were the remote augurs of its dissolution. One was the introduction of scientific ideas from the Islamic world, while the other was the emergence of the communes, representing a class of producers in a sense in which the Church and the feudal nobility were not producers.[1] Within the medieval period itself neither factor became strong enough to constitute a real threat to existing authority. In the sixteenth century however the power of the Church was weakened by the challenge of the reformers; and it allied itself with, or subordinated itself to the monarchy instead of being, as in the Middle Ages, a rival to the temporal power. Scientific knowledge grew and threatened theological beliefs, eventually leading intellectuals at any rate to question all established authority and ideas. Further, as the French monarchs foolishly associated themselves with the nobility, once it had been reduced to a condition of submission, rather with the interests of the rising class of producers, violent revolution became in the end inevitable. The French revolution was simply the outcome of a process which had been going on 'for more than six centuries'.[2] It set the rising class free and rendered possible the transition to industrial society.

Saint-Simon looked on contemporary society as being in an intermediary phase, intermediate, that is to say, between the old régime and the establishment of a new society based on scientific knowledge and on industry. The conditions for a new society were already there. It would not matter if France were to lose the monarchy, the bishops and the landowners; but it would certainly matter if it lost the only really useful class, the producers or workmen. (The scientists must also be included of course as an indispensable element in society.) It by no means follows however that Saint-Simon demanded the development of social democracy or concerned himself with extension of the franchise to all citizens or with their participation in government. What he does look forward to is the rule of scientists and of captains of industry. In *L'Organisation* (1819) he envisaged three chambers of experts.

---

[1] It does not follow that Saint-Simon regarded the Church and the feudal nobility as parasites on medieval society. For him medieval society was 'organic', and he looked on the feudal nobility and the Church as performing useful functions within this society. He did not, for instance, regard religion simply as harmful superstition, but rather as an historical necessity, even though religious beliefs were destined to be supplanted by scientific knowledge.

[2] *Oeuvres*, V. p. 78.

The first, the chamber of invention, consisting of engineers and artists, would draw up plans or projects which would then be examined by the second chamber, consisting of mathematicians, physicists and physiologists.[1] The third chamber would be responsible for putting into execution projects proposed by the first chamber and examined and approved by the second. Saint-Simon called the third body the chamber of deputies. It would consist of elected representatives of agriculture and industry; but the electorate would consist only of producers.

There is no need to lay a great deal of emphasis on these proposals. In his work *On the Industrial System* (*Du système industriel*, 1821–22) Saint-Simon more or less contented himself with demanding that finances should be put into the hands of a chamber of industry and that the Institute of France should take over the role in education which had once been played by the Church. In any case, the concrete proposals express a number of general presuppositions. For example, it is presupposed that the scientists have become the intellectual élite and that they can be trusted to make and approve plans beneficial to society. Again, it is presupposed that in contemporary society the interests which bind men together and which call for common deliberation and action are no longer theological or military but economic. Government, when understood as coercive and as associated with military adventures is on its way to being transformed into a managerial administration concerned with promoting the real interests of society.

Industrial society, according to Saint-Simon, would be a peaceful society, at any rate when fully developed and given the appropriate form of government or administration. What he calls the industrial class includes not only captains of industry but also the workmen. And Saint-Simon assumes that their interests coincide or harmonize with one another. Further, the industrial class in, say, France has much more in common with the parallel class in England than it has with the French nobility. The rise of the industrial class therefore provides the basis for human solidarity and for overcoming national enmities. True, governments as they actually exist represent a prolongation of the old régime, a hangover, as one might express it, from an outmoded social structure. The transition however to a form of adminstration appropriate to the

---

[1] The term 'physiologist' must obviously be understood in Saint-Simon's sense as referring to specialists in the science of man. This second chamber would have also the function of controlling education.

new industrial society and devoted to its interests will justify confidence in international peace. This goal cannot be attained by alliance between or conferences between governments which do not properly represent the interests of the productive and naturally peaceful class. A fuller development of industrial society is first required.

Karl Marx showed considerable respect for Saint-Simon. But he obviously disagreed with the latter's assumption that the real or true interests of the captains of industry coincided with those of the workmen. From Marx's point of view Saint-Simon, while seeing the importance of man's economic life, had failed to understand the clash of interests between the bourgeoisie and the proletariat and the connection between bourgeois society and war. In brief, Saint-Simon was a utopian. We may indeed be inclined to think that in his own way Marx himself was a utopian, and that people living in glass houses would be well advised to refrain from throwing stones. But it can hardly be denied that Saint-Simon was over-optimistic in regard to the inherently peaceful nature of industrial society.

To do Saint-Simon justice however, he came to see that ignorance is not the only bar to progress, and that the spread of scientific knowledge and government by experts was not sufficient to secure realization of the ideal of human brotherhood, the ideal of *fraternité*. There was man's self-seeking and egoism to reckon with. And selfishness could not be overcome without an appropriate morality or ethics. In his *New Christianity* (*Nouveau Christianisme*, 1824) Saint-Simon found this morality in the Christian ethics of love. He was not recommending a return to the Christian system of dogmas which, in his view, had been superseded by positive scientific knowledge of the world. He was however convinced that the Christian ideal of fraternal love, which had been obscured by the Church's power-structure and by the policy of religious intolerance and persecution, possessed permanent value and relevance. The Catholic system was outmoded, while Lutheranism had emphasized an interiority divorced from political life. What was needed was the realization of the message of the Christian gospel in the social-political sphere.

As Saint-Simon's insistence on ethico-religious motivation was expressed in a work which appeared in the year preceding that of his death, it has sometimes been thought that it represented a radical change in his thought and pretty well a recantation of positivism. But this view is inaccurate. Saint-Simon does not appear to have ever been a complete positivist, if we understand the term as implying rejection of all belief in God. He seems to have believed in an impersonal immanent Deity, pantheistically conceived, and to have thought this belief quite compatible with his positivism. Further, he always regarded Christianity with respect. To be sure, he did not accept Christian dogmas. But he looked on the theological outlook of the Middle Ages not as deplorable superstition but as an historical necessity. And though the theological stage of thought had, in his opinion, been superseded by the scientific stage, he did not think of this transition as entailing abandonment of all Christian moral values. He did indeed become convinced that the new society needed a new religion, to overcome both individual and national egoism and to recreate in a new form the 'organic' society of the Middle Ages. But the new religion was for him the old religion, in regard, that is to say, to what he considered to be the essential and permanently valuable element in the old religion. We can say perhaps that Saint-Simon envisaged a 'secularized' Christianity. The 'new Christianity' was Christianity as relevant to the age of the industrial society and of positive science.

Saint-Simon was not a systematic thinker. He advanced numerous lines of thought but tended to leave them only partly developed and did not make any prolonged effort to combine them in a systematic manner. His ideas however aroused widespread interest; and after his death some of his disciples founded the journal *Le producteur* to propagate these ideas. In 1830 a newspaper entitled *Le globe* also became an organ of Saint-Simonianism. Saint-Amand Bazard (1791–1832), one of Saint-Simon's principal disciples, tried to present his master's doctrine in a systematic way, paying special attention to its religious aspects. His lectures on Saint-Simon attracted a good deal of attention. Shortly before his death however he quarrelled with the other founding father, Barthélemy Prosper Enfantin (1796–1864), who pretty well turned Saint-Simonianism into a religious sect, though not an austere one, as Enfantin advocated generous ideas in regard to love between men and women. Bazard had been much more of a logical thinker; Enfantin was both an impassioned publicist and inclined to take up one particular project or cause after another. In spite however of his activity the Saint-Simonian school started to decline after the split between himself and Bazard.

The influence of Saint-Simon was not confined to those who can be classified as disciples. Outside their ranks the two most important thinkers who derived stimulus from his thought were doubtless Auguste Comte and Karl Marx. Both Marx and Engels admired Saint-Simon. It is true that Marx criticized him, as we have already noted, for failing to understand the class antagonism between capitalists and workers and for concentrating, in Marx's opinion, on glorifying bourgeois society in comparison with feudalism. At the same time Marx thought that in *The New Christianity* Saint-Simon had spoken up for the emancipation of the proletariat. We know from Engels that Marx was generally accustomed to express his esteem for Saint-Simon, whereas he regarded Comte as a reactionary and a thinker of little value.

4. Fourier and Saint-Simon were at one with the Traditionalists in believing that after the overthrow of the old régime at the revolution a reorganization of society was required. Obviously the two groups had different ideas about the form which such reorganization should take. The Traditionalists looked back, in the sense that they insisted on the permanent validity and value of certain traditional beliefs and institutions, whereas Fourier and Saint-Simon looked forward to the creation of those new forms of social organization which they believed to be demanded by the march of history. Both groups however emphasized the need for social reorganization. It may appear therefore that Proudhon, as a professed anarchist, should be sharply differentiated from both Traditionalists and socialists, inasmuch as the term anarchy suggests an absence, or rather a rejection, of social organization. Though however Proudhon accepted the label 'anarchist' in 1840, he did not understand by anarchism a general social chaos, anarchy in the popular sense of the term, but rather the absence of centralized authoritarian government. What he desired was social organization without government. In Marxist terminology, he envisaged the withering away of the State. Up to a point therefore there was an affinity between Proudhon and Saint-Simon, inasmuch as the latter looked for the transformation of 'government' into 'administration'. At the same time Proudhon went further than Saint-Simon. For he hoped that the form of social organization which he considered desirable would render centralized administration unnecessary.

Pierre-Joseph Proudhon (1809–1865) was born at Besançon. After a short period of school education he became an apprentice in the local diocesan printing press[1] and later a partner in a firm of printers. Though however he had to leave school for work, he continued to educate himself, and in 1838 he obtained a scholarship which enabled him to go to Paris. In 1840 he published his essay *What is Property?* (*Qu'est-ce que la propriété?*), in which he made his famous statement that property is theft. This was followed by two further essays on the subject (1841 and 1842), the second of which was regarded as inflammatory propaganda by the civil authorities.[2]

In 1843 Proudhon published a work *On the Creation of Order in Humanity* (*De la création de l'ordre dans l'humanité*). In it he maintained that the human mind progresses through the two successive stages of religion and philosophy to the scientific stage. At this third stage it becomes possible for man to discover the serial laws operating in the world, both infra-human and human. The science which shows how man should apply his knowledge of these laws in society is called by Proudhon 'serial dialectic'. In maintaining that there are ascertainable laws governing social development Proudhon is obviously at one with Saint-Simon and, for the matter of that, with Montesquieu.[3]

For a time Proudhon worked at Lyons, with visits to Paris. At Lyons he consorted with socialists, while at Paris he made the acquaintance of Marx, Bakunin and Herzen. Introduced to the ideas of Hegel, he undertook to apply the Hegelian dialectic in the sphere of economics.[4] The result was his *System of Economic Contradictions or the Philosophy of Poverty* (*Système des contradictions économiques ou Philosophie de la misère*, 1846). The contradiction or antithesis between the system of equality-destroying property on the one hand and independence-destroying socialism (communism) on the other is resolved in 'mutualism' (or 'anarchy'), a society of producers united by means of free contracts. Marx, who had hailed Proudhon's first essay on poverty as representing 'scientific socialism',[5] hastened to attack this new work in his

---

[1] At this time Proudhon read widely in theology and learned Greek and Hebrew. Later he was to say that it is a duty of the thinking and free man to expel the idea of God from his mind.

[2] Proudhon's ideas were found difficult to follow, and he was acquitted.

[3] For Montesquieu see Vol. 6 of this *History*, pp. 9–15.

[4] Proudhon's knowledge of Hegel was never profound. And there is little point in discussing his degree of fidelity to Hegel's thought. Proudhon simply derived some stimulus from what he had read and from what he had been told by left-wing Hegelians.

[5] It is possible that Marx took over this phrase from Proudhon himself.

Poverty of Philosophy (*Misère de la philosophie*, 1847). The split between the two men is in no way surprising. For Proudhon was never a communist, and in Marx's eyes he expressed the interests of the *petite bourgeoisie*.

When the monarchy was overthrown in February of 1848 Proudhon gave only a very qualified support to the revolution.[1] However he showed activity in a variety of ways, by campaigning for the establishment of a People's Bank, by making popular speeches, and by founding an anarchist paper *The Representative of the People* (*Le représentant de peuple*). In June of 1848 he was elected to the National Assembly. But an attack in his paper on Louis Napoleon, then president, led to his being sentenced to imprisonment for three years.[2] In 1849 he wrote *Confessions of a Revolutionary* (*Les confessions d'un révolutionnaire*), and in 1851 he published his *General Idea of Revolution in the Nineteenth Century* (*Idée générale de la révolution au XIXe siècle*), in which he expounded his vision of the ideal free society.

At the end of 1851 Louis Napoleon made himself emperor; and when Proudhon was released from prison in 1852, he was subjected to police supervision. In 1853 he published his *Philosophy of Progress* (*Philosophie du progrès*) in which he denied the existence of any absolutes and of any permanence and asserted a theory of universal movement or change both in the universe at large and in particular spheres such as morals, politics and religion. When however he published *Justice in the Revolution and the Church* (*De la justice dans la révolution et dans l'église*, 1858), he got into trouble. This was not of course because Proudhon now rejected the idea of the resolution of thesis and antithesis in a synthesis and substituted an expression of belief in continuing antinomies which produce a dynamic, though unstable, equilibrium of forces or factors. He was charged with attacking religion, morality and the law. To escape further imprisonment he went to Belgium, remaining there even after he had been pardoned in 1860. While in Brussels he wrote several works, for example *War and Peace* (*La guerre et la paix*).

Returning to Paris in 1862, Proudhon published his work *On the Federal Principle* (*Du principe fédératif*, 1863) and wrote the *Theory of Property* (*Théorie de la propriété*), a revision of his

[1] Proudhon was no great believer in political revolutions. He wanted economic changes.
[2] The imprisonment was not particularly stringent. Proudhon was sometimes allowed out on parole. And he was able to write.

thoughts on this subject. This revision was published posthumously, as was also *On the Political Capacity of the Working Classes* (*De la capacité politique des classes ouvrières*, 1865).

Proudhon came of a family of peasant stock, and he remained always on the side of the small producer, whether peasant or artisan. When he said that property was theft,[1] he was not suggesting that a peasant who owned and worked a plot of land and lived by the fruit of his labours or that a man who lived by making and selling chairs and claimed ownership of the tools of his trade was a thief. By 'property' Proudhon really meant what he regarded as an abuse, what he called the right of escheat or *aubaine*. For example, the landowner who did not himself work the land but none the less took the profits derived from the labours of others was a thief. In Proudhon's language there could be a right of 'possession', of exclusive *use*; but there was no right of 'property' as this would mean a right to exploit other people. 'Possession' means a right to make use of an object, whether it be land or tools. As 'property' means the *misuse* of objects (as means to exploitation), there can be no right to it. It involves theft.

It is important to understand that when Proudhon denounced property, he was not simply denouncing exploitation by individual landowners and capitalists. He believed that for the maintenance of human independence and dignity peasants and artisans should 'possess' the land which they worked on or the tools which they used and that they should receive the fruit of their labours. And he was therefore opposed to any system of collective ownership which meant that the State would take the place of the non-productive landowner or capitalist. When referring later to his rejection of property in the essay of 1840 he remarks that 'I rejected it for both the group and the individual, the nation and the citizen, and thus I am not advocating either communism or State ownership.'[2]

If we bear this point in mind, it becomes easier to understand how in his *System of Economic Contradictions* Proudhon could retain the idea of property as theft and at the same time offer a new definition of it as liberty. There is the constant possibility of abuse, of exploitation, which spells theft. At the same time property is a spontaneous creation of society and a bulwark against the ever-encroaching power of the State. Proudhon came to doubt whether his previous distinction between property and possession

[1] *What is Property?*, p. 131.   [2] *Theory of Property*, p. 16.

was as useful as he had once thought it. He came to the conclusion that 'property is the only power which can act as a counterweight to the State.'[1] It is understandable that Marx, who in his analysis of capitalism made use of Proudhon's idea of theft, later attacked the French writer as an upholder of the interests of the *petite bourgeoisie*. But though Proudhon may have changed his terminology, he had always been on the side of the small producer; and he was a consistent enemy of communist theories.

Revolution, the product of the conflict between opposed forces or factors, obviously has a negative side, in the sense that a revolution negates or destroys or overthrows something. This however is only one aspect of revolution. If revolution negates, it must also affirm. The French revolution asserted the ideals of liberty, fraternity and equality; but on the positive side it was incomplete, a partial failure. It produced a measure of political liberty and equality, but it failed to produce liberty and equality in the economic sphere. 'Society should afterwards have been organized in terms of labour and not in those of politics and war';[2] but this is not what happened. The task of the revolution, to establish 'an egalitarian industrial régime',[3] was not fulfilled. And Proudhon's social and economic theorizing is designed to contribute to this fulfilment. For Marx, needless to say, he is a utopian. And one can see why Marx says this. It is however relevant to notice that Proudhon does not believe in permanent solutions to social problems. Industrial democracy, as he puts it, must succeed industrial feudalism.[4] But no blueprint for the organization of society can be absolute and definitive truth. For oppositions of some sort are always latent in human society, and their emergence involves further change.

Property (or 'possession'), duly distributed, safeguards independence and equality. But human society obviously cannot exist without some form or forms of organization. Such organization may be imposed from above, by the authority of the State as represented by the government. But what Proudhon envisages is a transition from political to economic organization, when the economic organization or forms of association are not dictated from above but are produced by agreements or contracts freely made by producers. This is what he calls 'anarchy'. The centralized government State will, he hopes, wither away, its place

---

[1] *Ibid.*, p. 144.   [2] *General Idea of the Revolution*, p. 125.
[3] *Ibid.*   [4] *Manuel du spéculateur à la Bourse*, 1857, p. 499.

being taken by a social order arising out of associations freely
entered into for economic reasons, such as the demands of production, the needs of consumption and the security of the producers. 'The notion of *anarchy* in politics is just as rational and
positive as any other. It means that once industrial functions have
taken over from political functions, then business transactions
and exchange alone produce the social order.'[1] Writing towards
the end of his life Proudhon remarks that he has always had 'a
particular horror of regimentation'.[2] In his opinion, freedom can
flourish only when associations and federations of associations are
based on free contracts, contract being 'the dominant idea in
politics'.[3] As he puts it, commutative justice or rule by contract
must take the place of the old systems of distributive justice,
associated with the rule of law and a centralized governmental
régime.

In so far as Proudhon envisages the existence and self-main-
tenance of a coherent and stable industrial society in the form of a
loosely knit system of producers' associations, with contracts
instead of laws and industrial companies instead of armies, he can
not unfairly be described as a Utopian. For he sees all citizens as
cooperating harmoniously, inasmuch as private and collective
interests will be identical, and as behaving in the manner which he
considers rational. It must be remembered however that Proudhon's great slogan is progress, continual change. He does not
claim that any form of social organization is free from all antimonies or tensions and can be considered as the final goal, one
which will be fully attained and, when attained, will represent
perfection. He is quite ready to admit that 'what we call anarchy
and others fraternity'[4] is a more or less mythical symbol, a spur to
stimulate men to realize the revolutionary ideal of fraternity
which, in Proudhon's opinion, can be realized only through
transformation of the intermediary régime consequent on the
revolution into an industrial society of the kind which he envisages. He desires a more just society; but just as humanity itself
changes and develops, so is the ideal of justice 'changing all the
time'.[5] 'We cannot see beyond the antithesis which is suggested
to us by the present.'[6] Proudhon's utopianism and his idea of laws
of social change are balanced by a conviction that there are no

[1] *The Federal Principle*, p. 278.   [2] *Theory of Property*, p. 28.
[3] *The Federal Principle*, p. 315.   [4] *Correspondence*, IV, p. 157.
[5] *Justice*, I, p. 233.   [6] *Correspondence*, IV, p. 158.

absolutes and that we cannot make infallible judgments about
the future.

Whatever we may think about the viability of the kind of
industrial society envisaged by Proudhon, some of his ideas are
clearly sensible enough. For example, his proposals about the
education of workers, to overcome the sharp division between the
literate and illiterate classes and to facilitate the profitable use of
leisure, and about apprentices being taught a variety of skills in
order to diminish the monotony of the slavish repetition of one
particular task were not without point. Nor indeed were his ideas
about a credit system and a People's Bank. As for influence,
during his last years at Paris he had a considerable following
among the workers; and in 1871 a large section of the Paris Commune consisted of Proudhonians. Subsequently Marxist communism came to the fore; but Proudhon's ideas, or some of them
at any rate, continued to exercise an influence on the minds of a
number of French socialists and syndicalists. Further, through
Michael Bakunin (1814–1876) Proudhon can be said to have
influenced the anarchist movement.

5. Obviously, if we were to take Proudhon's plans for a People's
Bank and Fourier's proposals about the establishment of phalanxes
by themselves, they would not justify our describing these two
thinkers as philosophers. Both men however had general theories
about history and historical progress, even if Proudhon's ideas
were vaguer than Fourier's.[1] It may well be true that it is possible
to consider Fourier's concrete proposals without reference to his
theory of the stages through which mankind must pass. But the
theory is there; and if we interpret the word 'philosophy' in a
broad sense, Fourier can be said to have outlined a philosophical
anthropology and a philosophy of history. As for Proudhon, his
denial of any absolutes presumably counts as a philosophical
theory. To be sure, both fall short of the standards of preciseness
and close argument which philosophers might be expected to aim
at. The point is however that to classify them simply as sociologists or as political scientists or as economists would be somewhat misleading. In other words, it does not seem altogether unreasonable to include mention of them in a history of philosophy,

---

[1] If we consider Proudhon's writings as a whole, it seems that he sometimes
implies the inevitability of historical progress, while at other times he says pretty
clearly that it is not inevitable. But it is arguable that it is a case not so much of
inconsistency as of his changing his mind and of coming to emphasize man's
freedom to solve his social problems when he understands them.

not at any rate if we are prepared to include political and social theory as part of philosophy.

It must be admitted however that Saint-Simon's theory of historical and social change is more impressive than Fourier's, not to speak of Proudhon's. Further, as writers on early French socialism have noted,[1] his view of the way in which society should be changed is connected with his conception of the law-governed movement of history. In other words, of the three writers Saint-Simon gives the most coherent and developed general view of the pattern of historical and social change. And we naturally think of him as a predecessor of Auguste Comte and Karl Marx.

Mention has been made more than once of the fact that Marx and Engels describe the early French socialists as utopians. The word 'utopian' naturally suggests the idea of an unrealistic or unpractical reformer, someone who proposes as a solution for man's social and political problems some ideal state of affairs which seems to us an impracticable and perhaps fantastic solution. In this sense the word may well apply to Fourier and Proudhon, but it might obviously be applied also to Marx himself, even if Marx was much less inclined than Fourier to provide any detailed account of the future utopia. Though however this sort of meaning may have been part of the meaning which Marx and Engels attached to the word, it was not the element on which they laid the most emphasis. When they described the French socialists as utopians, what they had primarily in mind was the French writers' failure to understand the nature of class-antagonism and the irreconcilable nature of class-interests. Though the early socialists certainly believed that the ideals which had found expression in the French revolution had only been partially and very imperfectly realized and that a further transformation of society was required, they tended to think that this transformation could be brought about in a peaceful manner, by men coming to understand the problems and needs of society and the appropriate way of solving the problems and meeting the needs. Marx and Engels however were convinced that the desired transformation of society could be achieved only by revolution, by, that is to say, a class-war in which the proletariat, led by the enlightened, would seize power. In their view it was simply an expression of 'utopianism' if anyone thought that the interests of the ruling class or classes and those of the exploited could be peacefully

[1] See, for example J. Plamenatz's *Man and Society*, Vol. 2, p. 42.

reconciled through a spread of knowledge or understanding. For the interest of the dominant class was precisely the preservation of the actual state of affairs, whereas it was in the interest of the exploited class that the actual state of affairs should be radically changed. To call for a transformation of society while failing to see that it could be achieved only through a proletarian revolution was unrealistic and utopian.

For the proletarian revolution envisaged by Marx and Engels to take place it was a pre-requisite that there should be men who understood the movement of history and who could turn the exploited class into a self-conscious united whole, a class not only 'in itself' but also 'for itself'. They thus had a considerable respect for Saint-Simon, not only because he conceived of history as law-governed (Fourier too had this concept) but also because in his case there was a much closer connection than in the case of Fourier between his theory of history and his idea of the desirable transformation of society. Moreover Saint-Simon, with his notion of social physiology, could be said to have expounded a 'materialist' interpretation of man. At the same time, if we bear in mind the role attributed by Saint-Simon to captains of industry in the transformation of society, it is clear that he too would be guilty of utopianism in the eyes of Marx and Engels. For though captains of industry might agree to changes within the existing social framework, it would not be in their interest to contribute to the radical transformation which was required.

In view of the great historical importance of Marxism it is natural enough to think of the early French socialists in terms of their relations to Marx and Engels. But though this approach is easily understandable, it is a rather one-sided approach if we insist on looking at them simply as predecessors of Marx. In any case they realized clearly enough that while the revolution had destroyed the old régime, it had failed to bring peace and harmony between individuals, groups and nations. So of course did the Traditionalists. But whereas the Traditionalists adopted a negative attitude towards the Enlightenment and the revolution, the socialists looked for a prolongation and more satisfactory applica-tion of the ideals which inspired these movements. Obviously, if we assume with Saint-Simon that the course of history is governed by laws, in a sense at any rate which makes historical progress inevitable and social changes predictable in principle, even if in fact only very wide or vague predictions are feasible, there arises the problem of harmonizing this view of history with the emphasis on the role of human initiative and action which we would expect to find in the writings of any social reformer. But this is a problem which arises in the case of Marx and Engels as well. If we consider simply the French socialists' ideas of desirable changes, it is clear that they disliked the idea of the centralized bureaucratic State. It is true that Saint-Simon saw the need for economic planning; but he envisaged the transformation of 'government' into managerial 'administration' and in this sense can be said to have anticipated the doctrine of the withering away of the State. As for Fourier and Proudhon, it is clear that they both mistrusted and disliked the increasing power of the State, the centralized political authority. In actual fact of course control by State bureaucracy has vastly increased in modern society. And it is ironic that it should be such a conspicuous feature of Soviet communism. In spite however of the rather fantastic ideas of Fourier and Proudhon, we can see in the French socialists a respect for the individual and a marked dislike of violence. Marx of course thought that they were over-optimistic in their conviction that radical changes could be brought about without revolutionary violence. But it is an optimism with which many people would sympathize, irrespective of the concrete proposals made by the French writers.

CHAPTER V

AUGUSTE COMTE

*Life and writings—The three stages in human development—
The classification and methodology of the sciences—Tasks of
the philosopher in the positive area—The science of man; social
statics and social dynamics—The Great Being and the religion
of humanity.*

1. THE impact of the development of natural science on philosophy was felt in the seventeenth century and became more
marked in the eighteenth. As we have seen, in the eighteenth
century the call was raised, as by Hume in England and by some
of the French philosophers, for an extension of the 'experimental'
method to the study of man, his conduct and his social life, while
in the last decades of the century Kant maintained that reflection
on the contrast between the solid and increasing knowledge
achieved in the scientific area on the one hand and the conflicting systems of metaphysics on the other led inevitably to a
radical questioning of the claim of traditional metaphysics to
provide anything which could properly be described as knowledge
of reality. It was of course possible for science to coexist with
theological beliefs and with metaphysical speculation, as it did in
the mind of Newton. But with the growth of a stronger sense of
historical development it was natural enough that the idea of
successive stages in human thought should be proposed, the idea,
that is to say, of a progressive development in which theological
beliefs and metaphysical speculation are succeeded by scientific
explanation and positive knowledge. This sort of idea had been
proposed by Turgot and Condorcet in the eighteenth century; and
in the last chapter attention was drawn to Saint-Simon's theory
of historical stages or epochs. It is however with the name of
Auguste Comte (1798–1857), the foremost exponent and representative of classical positivism[1] that the theory of the human
mind's development from a theological through a metaphysical
phase to that of positive scientific knowledge has become traditionally associated.

[1] 'Classical' in distinction from the neo-positivism or logical positivism of the
twentieth century.

Born at Montpellier, Comte was brought up as a Catholic and a royalist. At the age of fourteen however he declared that he was no longer a Catholic, and it seems that at the same age he became a republican. From 1814 until 1816 he was a pupil at the École Polytechnique, where he studied under the guidance of leading scientists. It was doubtless during this period that he formed the conviction that society should be organized by a scientific élite.

In 1816 Comte was expelled from the École Polytechnique which had been given a royalist reorientation. He remained in Paris however and continued his studies, which included the thought of the ideologists, such as Destutt de Tracy and Cabanis, and the writings both of political economists and of historians such as Hume and Condorcet. Then in the summer of 1817 he became secretary to Saint-Simon. The association between the two men lasted for seven years; and while the extent of Comte's debt to Saint-Simon is a matter of dispute, there can be no doubt of the important part played by their collaboration in the formation and development of Comte's thought. It is clear that Saint-Simon was the first to propose certain ideas which reappeared in Comte's philosophy. At the same time Comte developed these ideas in his own way. For example, while Saint-Simon tended to think in terms of one overall scientific method and of the application of this method in the development of a new science of man, Comte regarded each science as developing its own method in the historical process of its emergence and advance.[1] Both men however looked for a reorganization of society with the aid of a new science of human behaviour and of man's social relations.

An acrimonious quarrel, leading to the severance of relations, arose between the two men, when Comte came to the conclusion that he had good reasons for believing that Saint-Simon intended to publish a paper by Comte as the concluding part of a work of his own and without proper acknowledgement on the title-page. In 1826 Comte began lecturing on his positivist philosophy to a private audience. The course of lectures was however interrupted by a breakdown induced by overwork and by the strain consequent on an unfortunate marriage. Indeed, Comte made an unsuccessful attempt at suicide. In 1829 Comte was able to resume the course, and the lectures formed the basis of his *Course of Positive Philosophy* (*Cours de philosophie positive*, six volumes, 1830–42). The basis had already been provided by a *Plan of the Scientific*

---

[1] For the necessary qualifications to this statement see pp. 85–6.

Researches Necessary for Reorganizing Society,[1] which he wrote in 1822. The title of this sketch or outline of the positive philosophy gives clear expression to Comte's basic social concern.

In the *Discourse on the Positivist Outlook (Discours sur l'esprit positif,* 1844) and the *Discourse on Postitivism as a Whole (Discours sur l'ensemble du positivisme,* 1848) Comte's idea of the religion of humanity made its appearance. Some biographers see in this development the influence of Comte's religious upbringing, with the difference that Humanity is substituted for God as the object of devotion. Others however have seen it, perhaps rather fancifully, as an extension to the human race of the philosopher's attachment to Madame Clothilde de Vaux, whose husband had disappeared to avoid a prosecution for embezzlement and with whom Comte fell in love in 1844.[2]

Comte never occupied a university chair, and for some time he had to support himself by doing tutorial work for students of the École Polytechnique. In 1851–4 he published his four-volume *System of Positive Policy (Système de politique positive)* and in 1852 his *Positivist Catechism (Catéchisme positiviste).* In this period he was trying to bring together the scientific and religious aspects of his thought. In 1856 he produced the first volume of a *Synthesis or Universal System of Concepts Proper to the Normal State of Humanity (Synthèse subjective ou système universel des conceptions propres à l'état normal de l'humanité).* But this attempt at a synthesis of all the sciences in terms of their relations to normal human needs was brought to an end by Comte's death in 1867. He had been living mainly on funds provided by his own devoted followers.

2. In a preface to his *Course of Positive Philosophy* Comte remarks that the expression 'positive philosophy' is constantly used in his lectures 'in a rigorously invariable sense',[3] and that it is therefore superfluous to give a definition other than that contained in his uniform use of the term. He goes on however to explain that by 'philosophy' he understands what the ancients, and in particular Aristotle, understood by the word, namely 'the general system

---

[1] This *Plan des travaux scientifiques nécessaires pour réorganiser la société* is included in *Opuscules de philosophie sociale,* 1819–28, published in 1883.

[2] It is clear enough from what Comte himself says that his love for Madame de Vaux influenced his idea of the religion of humanity. But it does not necessarily follow that Humanity, as an object of devotion, is simply Madame de Vaux writ large. Though rejecting traditional theological beliefs, Comte admired the so-called Age of Faith, and he wished to give humanism a religious dimension.

[3] *Cours de philosophie positive* (second edition, Paris, 1864), I, p. 5. This edition will be referred to in footnotes as C.P.P.

of human concepts',[1] while by 'positive' he understands the idea
of theories as having for their aim 'the coordination of observed
facts'.[2] Comte's statement, however, if taken by itself, is somewhat misleading. For in his view it is the sciences which subsume
phenomena or observed facts under general laws which are
descriptive and not explanatory, while philosophy examines the
nature of scientific methods and effects a systematic synthesis of
the various particular sciences. But his statement can stand if we
take it as meaning that philosophy coordinates observed facts
indirectly, inasmuch as it aims at a general synthesis of the partial
coordinations achieved in the sciences.

Positive knowledge is restricted by Comte to knowledge of
observed facts or phenomena and to the coordinating and descriptive laws of phenomena. Use of the word 'phenomena' does indeed
express Comte's conviction that we know reality only as appearing
to us, but it should not be taken to imply that for him the human
mind knows only subjective impressions. On occasion he refers to
Hume with respect; but Humean scepticism is really foreign to
Comte's mind, except in regard to theological beliefs and to the
claims of metaphysics to provide us with knowledge of what
transcends the phenomenal level. He stands closer to his
eighteenth-century French predecessors than to Humean empiricism. That is to say, Comte insists that genuine philosophy
takes the form of a systematic extension of the use of what
d'Holbach described as 'good sense' or 'natural ideas'.[3] And for
him this means that only what can stand up to empirical testing
can count as knowledge. The formulation of general laws enables us
to predict, and so to test. That this is the way to attain real knowledge is for Comte a matter of common sense or 'popular good
sense'.[4] It is this good sense which dismisses 'absurd metaphysical
doubts'[5] about ,say, the existence of physical objects external to
the mind. Comte has little patience with speculations of this kind.
His 'positive philosophy' is not a sceptical philosophy in the sense
of suggesting that our knowledge is confined to sense-data.

The positive spirit or outlook presupposes of course the birth
and advance of the natural sciences and is the result of an historical development of the human mind. In Comte's view this
process depends on man's nature and is thus necessary. In its

---

[1] *Ibid.,*   [2] *Ibid.,*
[3] D'Holbach's work *Le bon sens, ou idées naturelles opposées aux idées sur-
naturelles* appeared in 1772 at Amsterdam.
[4] See Comte's *Discours sur l'esprit positif,* section 34.   [5] *Ibid.,* section 10.

historical development through the centuries the human mind passes through three main stages or phases, the theological, the metaphysical and the positive. These three stages in the intellectual development of mankind have their analogues however in the life of the individual man as he passes from infancy through adolescence to manhood. 'When contemplating his own history does not each of us recollect that he has been successively . . . *theologian* in his infancy, *metaphysician* in his youth, and *physicist* in his maturity?'[1] Unless he dies prematurely, the individual normally passes from infancy to maturity by way of adolescence. And these three phases are reflected in the intellectual development of mankind as a whole. If the race continues to exist, the phases or stages of mental growth succeed one another in a certain pattern because man is what he is. In this sense it is necessary, hypothetically necessary, we might say.

It is indeed obvious enough that unless a person dies or unless some factor intervenes to prevent the natural course of development, the individual passes from infancy through adolescence to adulthood. But though Comte may have seen himself as a theologian in infancy and a metaphysician in adolescence, it is by no means everyone who would interpret his or her mental development in this way. Comte's theory of stages becomes much more plausible when applied to the general intellectual development of mankind. Indeed, it is clear that reflection on human history is the chief influence which leads Comte to formulate his theory,[2] even if he goes on to connect the stages with phases in the life of the individual and to see these phases writ large in history. In any case consideration of Comte's account of the three main stages in the history of mankind is a simple way of approaching his positivist philosophy.

The first stage, the theological, is understood by Comte as being that phase of man's mental development in which he seeks the ultimate causes of events and finds them in the wills of personal, superhuman beings or in the will of one such being. It is, in general, the age of the gods or of God. Subdivision is however required. In the infancy of the race man instinctively tried to explain phenomena, the real causes of which were unknown, by ascribing to objects passions and affects analogous to those of

---

[1] *CPP*, I, p. 11.
[2] It is not intended to imply that the theory was brand new. Attention has already been drawn to Comte's predecessors.

human beings. In other words, man endowed physical objects with life, passions and will, in a vague manner. This animistic mentality represented what Comte describes as the stage of fetishism. In the course of time however the animating forces immanent in objects were projected externally in the form of the gods and goddesses of polytheism. Later on the deities of polytheistic religion were fused in the concept of the one God of monotheism. These three successive sub-stages of fetishism, polytheism and monotheism constitute together the theological stage.

The second general stage is described by Comte as the metaphysical stage. The description however is apt to give rise to misunderstanding. For what Comte has in mind is the transformation of personal deities or of God into metaphysical abstractions, not, for instance, the theistic metaphysics of medieval thinkers such as Aquinas or, later, of Bishop Berkeley. In the metaphysical stage, that is to say, instead of explaining phenomena in terms of the activity of a divine will the mind has recourse to such fictional ideas as ether, vital principles, and so on. The transition from the theological to the metaphysical stage takes place when the concept of a supernatural and personal Deity is succeeded by the concept of all-inclusive Nature and when explanations are sought in terms of abstract entities of one kind or another, such as force, attraction and repulsion.[1]

The third stage is the positive stage, namely that of the mature scientific outlook or mentality. Here there is no attempt to find ultimate explanatory causes or to discuss the 'real' but unobservable inner essence of things. The mind concerns itself with phenomena or observed facts, which it subsumes under general descriptive laws, such as the law of gravitation. These coordinating descriptive laws make prediction possible. Indeed, the mark of real positive knowledge is precisely the ability to predict and so, within limits, to control. Positive knowledge is real, certain and useful.

Though however Comte describes positive knowledge as certain, he also insists that it is in a sense relative. For we do not know the

[1] In his *De Motu* Berkeley attacked the idea that there are realities or entities corresponding to abstract terms such as 'attraction', 'force' or 'gravity'. The terms, Berkeley maintained, had their uses as 'mathematical hypotheses'; but it was a mistake to think that they stood for corresponding abstract entities. The view which Berkeley attacked is a good example of what Comte meant by metaphysics, when he spoke of the metaphysical stage in the development of human thought.

whole universe. We know it only as appearing to us. Positive knowledge is knowledge of our world, and the extent of our world, the world as appearing to us, is not something fixed and determined once and for all. Positive knowledge is also relative in the sense that the search for absolutes is abandoned. Even if there are ultimate causes, we cannot know them. What we know are phenomena. Hence the mind which appreciates the nature and function of positive knowledge will not waste time in profitless theological and metaphysical speculation.

The theory of the three stages as just summarized may seem to have little connection with a concern for the reorganization of society. In point of fact however each stage is associated by Comte with a distinct form of social organization. The theological stage is associated with belief in absolute authority and the divine right of kings and with a militaristic social order. That is to say, social order is maintained by the imposition of authority from above, and the warrior class is pre-eminent. In the metaphysical stage the former régime is subjected to radical criticism; belief in abstract rights and in popular sovereignty comes to the fore; and royal and priestly authority is replaced by the reign of law. Finally, the positive stage is associated with the development of industrial society. Man's economic life becomes the centre of attention; and there arises a scientific élite, whose vocation it is to organize and regulate industrial society in a rational manner. This type of society is regarded by Comte, as by some contemporaries, as naturally peaceful.[1] But for its proper development a new science is required, namely sociology. Natural science enables man to control, within limits, his physical environment. The science of man will enable him to organize a peaceful industrial society. The emergence of the positive spirit or mentality will thus be accompanied by a reorganization of society.

For Comte the ancient world and the Middle Ages represented the theological outlook or mentality, while the Enlightenment represented the metaphysical stage. In his own world he saw the beginning of the positive stage. Further, just as he regarded adolescence as a period of transition between childhood and maturity, so did he look on the metaphysical stage as a period of transition in which the beliefs and institutions of the theological stage were

---

[1] The idea that industrial society would be a peace-loving society was not confirmed to French socialists. In the second half of the nineteenth century Herbert Spencer defended the same point of view.

subjected to criticism and the way was being prepared for the development of the positive mentality.

If we confine ourselves to sweeping impressions, Comte's theory of the three stages can obviously appear plausible. That is to say, if we consider simply the dominant position of theology among the subjects studied in the Middle Ages, certain aspects of thought in the eighteenth-century Enlightenment and the subsequent development of a conviction that science is the only reliable way of increasing our knowledge of the world, it may seem perfectly reasonable to divide up European history into the theological, metaphysical and positive stages. When however we begin to look at European history in more detail, it at once becomes clear that if Comte's divisions are pressed in a rigid way, they cannot accommodate the facts. For instance, philosophy flourished in ancient Greece; and mathematics too underwent development. Again, natural science had made striking progress long before the end of what Comte describes as the metaphysical period.

It is hardly necessary to say that Comte is aware of such facts. And he does his best to accommodate them within his general scheme. For example, he recognizes that in the Middle Ages theology was accompanied by metaphysics, but he regards this metaphysics as tailored to the theological mentality and as really forming part of it. Again, Comte does not claim that science began only with the positive stage. He is perfectly well aware that mathematics was cultivated by the Greeks. But he maintains that in the development of science there was a progression from the most abstract science, mathematics, to the most concrete science, sociology, which is the peculiar contribution of the positive stage. As for physics, it certainly started to develop well before the positive stage; but at one time it expressed the metaphysical mentality by postulating abstract entities as explanatory causes. It is only with the beginning of the positive stage that the real nature of physical science and of its concepts and laws comes to be understood.

Comte is therefore quite prepared to recognize a measure of overlapping between the stages. 'Thus we shall have to regard, for example, the theological epoch as still existing to the extent in which moral and political ideas have retained an essentially theological character, despite the transition of other intellectual categories to the purely metaphysical stage, and even when the genuinely positive stage has already begun in regard to the simplest of such categories. Similarly, it will be necessary to prolong the metaphysical epoch, properly speaking, into the beginning of positivism. . . . By this manner of procedure, the essential aspect of each epoch will remain as pronounced as possible, while the spontaneous preparation of the following epoch is clearly brought out.'[1] In the case of a given individual, psychological features belonging to an earlier stage of growth may persist in the grown man and co-exist with features characteristic of maturity. Analogously, expressions of the mentality of a previous historical epoch may be discernible at a later stage. 'Even in our days what in reality, for a positive mind, is this cloudy pantheism in which so many profound metaphysicians, especially in Germany, take such pride but fetishism generalized and systematized?'[2]

Some of Comte's remarks, taken by themselves, are sensible enough. But the overall impression is that of a man intent on fitting facts into a general interpretative scheme, based on a certain initial vision of European history. Comte is of course perfectly entitled to approach European history with a general framework of interpretation and see how the facts fit it. But the more the adjustments which he has to make, so much the more fluid does the division into stages or epochs become. Further, if the succession of stages is understood as representing progress, in the intellectual and social spheres, a judgment of value or a set of value-judgments is clearly presupposed. In other words, Comte reads European history from the point of a view of a convinced positivist. This is not indeed a crime. But the result is not simply a neutral description, but rather a reconstruction from a certain point of view. In other words, the truth of positivism seems to be a presupposition of Comte's interpretation of history. He was not prepared to consider the possibility of a post-positivist stage of intellectual development. To be sure, Comte tried to support his theory of historical stages by a psychological account of the unfolding of man's mental life in the process of growth towards maturity. But it seems pretty clear that this account too presupposes the truth of positivism, in the sense that it is governed by the assumption that the mature mind and the scientific mentality as Comte understands it are one and the same thing.

Before we turn to Comte's classification of the sciences, we can

[1] *CPP*, V, p. 24.   [2] *Ibid.*, p. 33.

note two points. The first relates to religious belief. The natural way of understanding Comte is to interpret him as maintaining that just as man sheds belief in elves and fairies when he understands that there is no good reason for thinking that there are such beings, so does he progressively shed belief in a transcendent God, not because God's non-existence has been demonstrated, but because there is no positive reason for believing that there is a transcendent God. In other words, the spread of atheism is a feature of the mind's advance into maturity, not the result of a philosophical proof of God's non-existence. Though however this is a natural way of interpreting Comte's theory of the three stages, what he actually insists on as being progressively shed by the wayside is recourse to God as an hypothesis to explain phenomena. That is to say, the more man comes to look for scientific 'explanations' of events, the less does he seek a supernatural explanation. And when the mature mind is ignorant of the scientific explanation of an event, it expects one and looks for it, instead of having recourse to God to fill a gap. At the same time Comte does not assert atheism. In his opinion, theism and atheism are concerned with problems which cannot be solved. For no empirical test is possible. There may be an ultimate cause or ultimate causes. But whether this is the case or not, we do not and cannot know.

The second point relates to the way in which Comte correlates three main types of social organization with the three main stages of man's intellectual development. He is perfectly ready to admit that man's intellectual advance can outrun his social progress, and that the positivist spirit, for example, can make its appearance before the corresponding form of social organization has developed. Apart from any other consideration, Comte's insistence on the need for social planning by a scientific élite compels him to recognize the fact that mental advance can outrun social progress. At the same time he wishes to preserve the idea of the correlation of two aspects, cognitive and social, of one historical movement. He therefore insists that even when man's intellectual progress outruns his social progress, we can none the less discern the preparatory stages of the emergence of a new form of social organization. Further, once the transition to a properly organized industrial society has taken place, this will strengthen and consolidate the positivist outlook.

3. Progress in knowledge is for Comte progress in scientific knowledge. Science however takes the form of the particular

sciences. They are all concerned with the coordination of phenomena, but they treat either of different classes of phenomena or of different aspects of things, having, as the Scholastics would say, different 'formal objects'. Further, they have their 'characteristic procedures'[1] or methods. There is thus a certain fragmentation of science. And it is one of the philosopher's main tasks to achieve a synthesis, not by obliterating differences by means of a systematic classification.

If such a classification is to be made, the first requirement is to ascertain the basic or fundamental sciences. To do so, we ought to consider 'only scientific theories and in no way their application'[2]. That is to say, the use made of scientific theory in the field of technology should be left out of account. Further, attention should be paid to the more general or abstract sciences rather than to those which really constitute branches or particular applications of the former. For example, the general laws of physics belong to abstract physics, whereas study of the earth in particular is a concrete science and involves consideration of factors other than the abstract laws of physics. Similarly, it pertains to abstract science to formulate the general laws of life, whereas a science such as botany is concerned with a particular kind or level of life.

In his *Course of Positive Philosophy* Comte discovers six basic sciences, namely mathematics, astronomy, physics, chemistry, physiology and biology, and social physics or sociology. It will be noted that psychology does not appear in the list. The explanation is that on the one hand Comte rejects introspective psychology, while on the other he is writing before the period in which empirical psychology underwent real development. Psychology as he understands it is therefore divided between physiology and sociology. In assigning to physiology, or biology, the study of man as an individual Comte is walking in the footsteps of Condillac and Cabanis. The study of human nature and behaviour as social phenomena is assigned to social physiology, as Saint-Simon called it, or sociology.

In later writings Comte found room for ethics as an additional science. Ethics however meant for him not a normative science concerned with determining values and moral rules but rather social psychology, a study of man's overt social behaviour with a

---

[1] *CPP*, i, p. 83. For example, chemistry lays stress on experiment, whereas astronomy relies more on observation. It is not possible to remove a heavenly body in order to discover the effect of this action.
[2] *Ibid.*, p. 56.

view to the formulation of laws enabling us to predict and to pursue social planning.

For the purpose of systematic classification, Comte insists, we should start with what is simplest and most general or abstract and proceed according to the logical order of dependence to the more complex and less general. Mathematics, for example, is more abstract than astronomy; and astronomy depends on mathematics in the sense that the former presupposes the latter. Similarly, physiology or biology, dealing with the general laws of life, is more abstract than sociology which treats specifically of man in society. If we proceed on these lines, we end with the hierarchy of basic sciences mentioned above, arranged in an order in which the mind starts with what is most abstract and most removed from specifically human phenomena, with mathematics that is to say, and ends with sociology, which is concerned with such phenomena to a greater degree than any of the other sciences.

Mention has already been made of the fact that whereas Saint-Simon tended to think in terms of one overall scientific method, Comte regarded each science as developing its own method. This statement however stands in need of qualification. If we have in mind Comte's use of the word 'method', he recognizes only one scientific method. 'For every *science* consists in the coordination of facts; if the different observations were entirely isolated, there would be no science.'[1] If therefore we mean by method the observation of facts or phenomena and their coordination through the formulation of laws, there is one method common to all the sciences. If however we have in mind what Comte calls 'procedures', it is true to say, in his view, that in the process of its development each science perfects its own procedure or technique, its own way of coping with the data. There are indeed procedures which are not restricted to any one particular science. The use of hypothesis, deduction and testing is a case in point. At the same time experiment plays a role in, say, chemistry which it cannot play in astronomy, while in sociology use has to be made of an historical approach.

A further qualification is required to the statement that Comte recognizes a plurality of methods. When classifying the basic sciences, Comte insists on a logical order being followed, each successive science in the hierarchy logically presupposing its predecessor. At the same time he is convinced that 'one does not

[1] *CPP*, 1, p. 99.

know a science completely as long as one does not know its history'.[1] A science, that is to say, reveals its real nature in proportion as it is developed or perfected rather than in its origins[2]. For example, mathematics has as its original data phenomena considered under their quantitative aspects, and it sets out to determine the relations between given quantities. But in its development mathematics becomes progressively more abstract until it is 'completely independent of the nature of the objects examined and bears only on the numerical relations which they present'.[3] As it becomes 'purely logical, rational',[4] consisting of 'a more or less prolonged series of rational deductions',[5] it is transformed into what Comte describes as the science of the calculus. And in this form it constitutes 'the true rational basis of the entire system of our positive knowledge'.[6] In this purely abstract form mathematics enables us to coordinate phenomena in other sciences in a way which would not otherwise be possible. It is true of course that we cannot convert biology, for example, into pure mathematics. But biology becomes a real science in proportion as the relations between biological phenomena are mathematically determined.

Further, in its developed or perfected state mathematics is a purely deductive science and Comte regards it as the model of scientific method.[7] Physics, for instance, grows in perfection in proportion as the deductive method preponderates. If therefore we look at the sciences from this particular point of view, we might say that there is one model scientific method, exemplified at its purest in mathematics. Comte does not claim however that every basic science can be transformed into a purely deductive science. The further we move away from pure mathematics in the hierarchy of the sciences, the less possible does such a transformation become. For one thing, the phenomena become even more complex. In practice therefore each science, as it advances, develops its own 'procedure', though it makes use, when possible, of mathematics with a view to obtaining greater precision. Sociology cannot be simply converted into mathematics. Nor can it proceed purely deductively. But it will make use of mathematics when it can.

4. We have noted that for Comte one of the main functions of

---

[1] *Ibid.*, p. 65.   [2] This is evidently an Aristotelian point of view.
[3] *CPP*, i, p. 103. Comte tries to combine his view that all science is concerned with phenomena with a recognition of the abstract nature of mathematics.
[4] *Ibid.*, p. 104.   [5] *Ibid.*   [6] *Ibid.*, p. 109.   [7] *Ibid.*, p. 122.

philosophy is to achieve a unification or synthesis of the sciences. Part of this task is fulfilled in the systematic classification of the sciences treated of in the last section. But Comte also speaks of a doctrinal synthesis or of a unification of scientific knowledge. And the question arises, how is this doctrinal synthesis to be understood?

The aim of a science is to coordinate phenomena of a given type through the formulation of descriptive laws, such as the law of gravitation in Newtonian physics. At first sight therefore it may seem to follow that the aim of philosophy in the positive stage of its development must be to coordinate *all* phenomena in terms of one single law. That is to say, it may seem to follow that positive philosophy should aim at exhibiting the most general laws of the particular sciences as derivable from or as presupposing one all-embracing law. Comte however explicitly rejects this concept of the function of philosophy. 'According to my profound personal conviction I consider these attempts to achieve the universal explanation of all phenomena by one unique law as eminently chimerical, even when they are made by the most competent minds. I believe that the means at the disposal of the human mind are too feeble and the universe too complex for such a scientific perfection to be ever open to us. . . .'[1] We can unify the sciences in the sense that we can find a method which lies at the basis of their different procedures; but we cannot achieve a doctrinal unification in the sense just mentioned.

This means in effect that we cannot achieve a doctrinal synthesis by following an 'objective' method, by extending the process of coordinating phenomena, which is common to all the sciences, to the point of reducing all laws to one law. We can however achieve a doctrinal synthesis by means of a 'subjective' method, by viewing the sciences, that is to say, in their relations to humanity, to the needs of man as a social being. This means that the synthesizing principle must be looked for in sociology. Once the science of man has arisen, we can look back and see the development of science as a progress from consideration of non-human to consideration of human phenomena, as a movement from the external world to man himself. We can then unify the sciences from the point of view of the subject, when the subject is humanity in general rather than the individual subject of epistemology.

[1] *CPP*, 1, p. 44.

Comte is not of course suggesting that sociology should or could absorb all the other sciences. He is suggesting that sociology, having as its subject-matter man in society, offers the organizing principle for the unification of scientific knowledge, namely the idea of humanity and its needs. From the historical point of view sociology was the last science to appear on the scene. Once however sociological theory has been freed from theological beliefs and ethical assumptions and has reached the positive stage of its development, we are entitled to invert, as it were, the historical order and give supremacy to the human or 'subjective' point of view. If objective scientific knowledge was to be attained, the subjective point of view had to be disregarded. But when the basic sciences, sociology included, have been firmly established as scientific disciplines, we can follow the policy of unifying them in terms of their several relations to human needs without impairing their scientific objectivity, whereas at an earlier stage this policy would have been detrimental to the advance of the sciences.

The positive philosophy however does not aim simply at effecting a theoretical unification of the sciences. It has also a practical aim. Comte refers to 'the immense social revolution in the midst of which we are living and to which the totality of preceding revolutions has really contributed only a necessary preliminary.'[1] A reorganization of society is called for. This task cannot however be performed without a knowledge of the laws of society as formulated in sociology. Without knowledge of the laws which coordinate the phenomena of Nature man cannot effectively control or mould his external natural environment. Similarly, without knowledge of the laws relating to man in society we cannot effectively promote and achieve social renovation and progress. It is this social reorganization which is the practical goal of the 'subjective' synthesis of the sciences, their unification in terms of their relations to humanity and its needs.

5. Sociology or social physics is regarded by Comte as presupposing the other basic sciences, as the culmination of the development of science and as the special contribution of the positive stage to man's intellectual advance. It is divided by him into social statics and social dynamics. Social statics studies the general laws of existence common to human societies, the essential conditions, that is to say, of social solidarity. Social dynamics studies the laws of the movement or development of societies, the laws of social

progress. In Comte's view social statics 'forms the direct link between the final science and the totality of the preliminary sciences, above all biology, from which it appears to be inseparable.'[1] It is itself presupposed by and looks forward to social dynamics, the laws of which are said to apply above all to politics, whereas those of social statics 'belong rather to morals'.[2] Sociology as a whole, comprising, that is to say, both social statics and social dynamics, conceives 'progress as the gradual development of order',[3] while it also 'represents order as manifested by progress'.[4]

Social statics finds the basis of society in man's nature as a social being and shows how in any society there must be both division of labour and coordination of human effort with a view to realizing a common purpose. It also exhibits the necessity and basic nature of government. Social statics is thus primarily concerned with the element of order which is essential to any society; and in this field Aristotle made a notable contribution to thought. Though however order is essential to any society, the result of canonizing a given form of social organization is petrifaction. It was the great fault of utopians such as Plato that they represented one possible form of social organization as the one ideal form of order. Indeed, even 'the most powerful mind of all antiquity, the great Aristotle, was so dominated by his century that he was unable even to conceive a society which was not necessarily founded on slavery. . . .'[5]

The idea of order is thus insufficient. The idea of progress is also required. And this is studied in social dynamics. Comte insists however on the intimate connection between social statics and social dynamics. Order without progress or development results in petrifaction or in decay; but change without order would spell anarchy. We have to see in progress the actualization of the inherent dynamic tendency of social order. 'Progress remains always the simple development of order';[6] and this means that social order assumes successively different forms. Progress is 'oscillatory',[7] in the sense that it covers cases of retardation or even of retrogression as moments in a general movement of advance.

---

[1] *Système de politique positive* (1825), II, p. 1. This work will be referred to in footnotes as *Pol.*
[2] *Ibid.*, p. 2. [3] *Ibid.*, p. 2. [4] *Ibid.*, p. 2.
[5] *CPP*, IV, p. 37. [6] *Pol.*, III, p. 72. [7] *Ibid.*

We have noted that Comte praises Aristotle's contribution to social statics. In the field of social dynamics he pays tribute to Montesquieu. 'It is to Montesquieu that we must attribute the first great direct effort to treat politics as a science of facts and not of dogmas.'[1] But just as Aristotle had his shortcomings, so had Montesquieu. The latter did not succeed in freeing his thought from metaphysics; he did not properly understand the necessary succession of different political organizations; and he ascribed an exaggerated importance to forms of government. To find a real advance we must turn to Condorcet who was the first to see clearly that 'civilization is subject to a progressive advance, the stages of which are rigorously linked to one another by natural laws which philosophical observation of the past can reveal. . . .'[2] Not even Condorcet however understood properly the natures of the successive stages or epochs. It was Comte himself who contributed this understanding[3].

According to Comte, 'the fundamental characteristic of the positive philosophy is to regard all phenomena as subject to invariable natural *laws*.'[4] The phrase 'all phenomena' includes of course human phenomena. Comte does not claim that the coordination of human phenomena by the formulation of laws has reached the same degree of development in sociology which it has reached in some other sciences. None the less he maintains that the philosopher should regard human phenomena as capable of being subsumed under laws. This means in effect that the successive forms of social-political organization must be correlated with the successive stages of man's intellectual development. As we have seen, Comte's view is that in the theological epoch society was necessarily a military society, organized for conquest, industry being simply such as was required for the maintenance of human life. In the metaphysical stage, which was a period of transition, society was also in a state of transition, 'no longer frankly military, and not yet frankly industrial.'[5] In the positive stage society is organized with a view to production, and it is by nature a peaceful society, aiming at the common good. In fine, the three successive modes of human activity, 'conquest, defence and labour',[6] 'correspond exactly with the three states of intelligence, fiction, abstraction and demonstration. From this basic correla-

---

[1] *Ibid.*, IV, p. 106 (of the General Appendix).   [2] *Ibid.*, p. 109.
[3] Obviously, Saint-Simon is not accorded due recognition.
[4] *CPP*, I, p. 16.   [5] *Pol.*, IV, p. 112 (of the General Appendix).
[6] *Ibid.*, III, p. 63.

tion there results at once the general explanation of the three natural ages of humanity.'[1]

Man is not however simply an intellectual and active being. He is also characterized by feeling. 'In every normal existence affection constantly dominates speculation and action, though their intervention is indispensable for it to be able to undergo and modify external impressions.'[2] Man has, for example, a social instinct or sentiment. In antiquity it was directed to the city (the *polis*), while in the Middle Ages it found expression in corporations of various kinds. In the positive or industrial epoch the social instinct tends, under the influence of the unifying factors of science and industry, to take the form of love of humanity in general. This idea provides Comte with a ground for claiming that the third basic form of social organization is inherently peaceful.

It is hardly necessary to say that just as Comte tries to reconcile his theory of the three stages of man's intellectual development with facts which seem to tell against the theory, so does he attempt to reconcile with his account of the correlated forms of social organization those historical facts which might be cited as evidence against the truth of this account. For example, if evidence is cited to show that even the more highly industrialized nations can indulge in aggressive military action, Comte replies that the process of industrialization begins and develops while ways of thought and feeling characteristic of earlier epochs are still influential. He does not claim that no society in which industrialization is developing ever manifests an aggressive spirit or goes to war. What he claims is that as industrial society grows to maturity, the unification of mankind, promoted by common scientific knowledge and by industrialization, will result, under the guidance of a scientic élite, in a peaceful society in which differences will be settled by rational discussion.

There is of course no reason why Comte should not try to accommodate facts within the framework of an hypothesis, provided that he is ready to revise or even abandon the hypothesis if it proves to be incompatible with the facts. But it is none too clear why an increase in scientific knowledge must lead to the moral improvement of mankind or why an industrial society must be more peaceful than a non-industrialized society. After all, Comte is not simply saying what, in his opinion, *ought* to happen, from

[1] *Ibid.*   [1] *Ibid.*, p. 67.

an ethical point of view. He is saying what *will* happen, in virtue of the law or laws governing man's development. And it is difficult to avoid the impression that the law of the three stages tends to become for Comte not so much a falsifiable hypothesis as the expression of a faith or of a teleological philosophy of history in the light of which the historical data have to be interpreted.

If the historical process is governed by law and the future is predictable, at any rate in principle, the question arises whether any room is left for social planning. What, for example, can a scientific élite do to influence society and the course of history? From one point of view perhaps there is no particular problem. As we have seen, Comte insists that while all science coordinates phenomena by subsuming them under laws, these laws are purely descriptive. If we found that man could produce effects in the physical world which were incompatible with hitherto accepted physical laws, we would obviously revise the laws in question. The laws, as descriptive generalizations, are revisible in principle. Similarly, as far as his professed theory of scientific laws is concerned, Comte could perfectly well maintain that the laws of sociology are subject to falsification and so revisible in principle. A law might be falsified by human action. When however it is a question of the law of the three stages, Comte tends to speak as though it were inviolable, and as though society will develop in the way indicated by this law whatever man may do. The question therefore inevitably arises whether it makes any sense to call for social planning by a scientific élite.

Comte is quite well aware of the need to answer this question. And he argues that there is no incompatibility between the idea of all phenomena being subject to laws and the idea of human planning and control. On the contrary, man's power to modify phenomena of any sort can be exercised only if there is 'a real knowledge of their respective natural laws'.[1] To take an example from the modern world, a knowledge of the relevant physical laws is an essential condition of successful space-exploration. Similarly, a knowledge of the laws of human behaviour is an essential condition of intelligent and effective social planning. According to Comte, social phenomena are more complex than physical phenomena; and this means that the laws formulated in sociology are less precise than physical laws, less amenable than

[1] *CPP*, IV, p. 220.

physical laws to mathematical formulation. None the less, the
formulation of laws in sociology permits prediction. For social
phenomena are 'as susceptible of prediction as all the other kinds
of phenomena, within the limits of precision which are compatible with their greater complexity.'[1] And so far from being
incompatible with social planning, this predictability is an essential condition of it.

This may seem sensible enough. But it does not quite answer
the question, to what extent can human action affect the course
of history? Comte replies by making a distinction. Man cannot
change the order of the successive stages of historical development. But human action or inaction can accelerate or retard this
development. The emergence of the positive stage of thought and
of the correlated form of society is necessary, man being what he
is. But the development of industrial society can be accelerated by
intelligent planning. For social phenomena are 'by their nature at
the same time the most modifiable of all and the ones which have
the most need of being usefully modified according to the rational
indications of science.'[2] This modifiability of social phenomena
permits effective planning; but what can be actually achieved is
limited by what is evidently taken to be the working out of an
unalterable law. Social development is modifiable 'in its speed,
within certain limits, by a number of physical and moral causes. . . .
Political combinations belong to the number of these causes. This
is the sole sense in which it is given to man to influence the march
of his own civilization.'[3] Comte certainly wishes to allow room for
human initiative and action. But the space allowed is limited by
his interpretation of human history as governed by a law which
man can no more alter than he can alter physical laws. And
Comte is quite sure that he knows the law governing the development of human history.[4]

6. It was Comte's firm conviction that society should be
organized by those who possessed real knowledge. On this matter
he agreed with Plato. Comte had little use for democracy, if this
is taken to imply that the will of the people, whatever it may happen to be, should prevail. He favoured paternalist government for
the common good. Just as in the Middle Ages men were expected

---

[1] *Ibid.*, p. 226.   [2] *Ibid.*, p. 249.
[3] *Pol.*, IV, p. 93 (of the General Appendix).
[4] We find of course an analogous situation in Marxist philosophy. Room is left
for revolutionary activity and social planning. But revolutionary activity can
only accelerate the coming of what will come in any case.

to accept the teaching of the Church whether or not they understood the doctrines and the reasons for them, so would the citizens of the 'positive polity' be expected to accept the principles
laid down by the positivist élite, namely the scientists and positivist philosophers. In Comte's society of the future this élite
would control education and form public opinion. It would be in
fact the modern equivalent of the medieval spiritual power, while
the government, drawn from the managerial class, would be the
modern equivalent of the medieval temporal power. In the
exercise of its functions the government would (or rather 'will',
given the law of the three stages) consult the positivist élite, the
high priests of science. Though he thought of the medieval period
as succeeded by the metaphysical and then the positivist eras,
Comte was by no means a despiser of the Middle Ages. The
scientists and positivist philosophers would take the place of the
pope and bishops, while members of the managerial class would
exercise the functions of medieval monarchs and nobles.

Comte saw of course the French revolution as dissolving an
outdated régime which would have been quite unable to meet the
needs of the nascent society. But he had scant sympathy with
liberal insistence on the alleged natural rights of individuals. The
notion that individuals had natural rights independently of, and
even against society, was foreign to his mind. In his view this
notion was based on a failure to understand the fact that the basic
reality is humanity rather than the individual. Man as an individual is an abstraction. And the regeneration of society 'consists
above all in substituting duties for rights, in order better to
subordinate personality to sociability.'[1] 'The word *right* should be
as much erased from the true language of politics as the word
cause from the true language of philosophy. . . . In other words,
nobody possesses any other right than that of always doing his
duty. It is only in this way that politics can at last be subordinated to morals, in accordance with the admirable programme of
the Middle Ages.'[2] In the positive epoch society will indeed
guarantee certain 'rights' to the individual, as this is required for
the common good. But these rights do not exist independently
of society.

Comte is not of course suggesting that the positive society will
be characterized by governmental oppression of individuals.
His contention is that as the new society develops, the idea of

[1] *Pol.*, I, p. 361.   [2] *Ibid.*, p. 361.

performing one's duties to society and of serving the interests of humanity will prevail over the concept of society as existing to serve the interests of individuals. In other words, he is confident that the development of industrial society, when properly organized, will be accompanied by a moral regeneration involving the substitution of concern with the welfare of humanity for concern with the individual's private interests. We may well think that he is somewhat over-optimistic. But the trouble is not that he hopes for moral regeneration but rather his confidence that this regeneration will inevitably accompany the development of a society based on science and industry. It is difficult to see why this should be the case.

However this may be, the highest form of the moral life consists for Comte in the love and service of humanity. In the positive phase of thought humanity takes the place occupied by God in theological thought; and the object of positivist worship is the 'Great Being' (le Grand Être), Humanity with a capital letter. To be sure, humanity does not possess all the attributes once predicated of God. Whereas, for example, the world was conceived as God's creation and as dependent on him, humanity is 'always subject to the totality of the natural order, of which it constitutes only the noblest element'.[1] The Great Being's 'necessary dependence' does not however affect its relative superiority. And Comte works out a religious system based on the Catholicism in which he was brought up. Positivism will have its saints (the great benefactors of mankind), its temples, its statues, its commination of the principal enemies of mankind, its commemoration of the dead, its social sacraments, and so on.

John Stuart Mill, who sympathized with Comte's general positivist attitude, criticized sharply the way in which Comte aspired to subject people to the straitjacket of a dogmatic religion expounded by positivist philosophers.[2] Mill also maintained that Comte's positivist religion had no organic connection with his genuinely philosophical thought but was a superfluous, and indeed repugnant, addition. These two contentions are of course separable. That is to say, we can quite well regard as repugnant what T. H. Huxley described as Comte's Catholicism without Christianity without necessarily subscribing to Mill's view that it had no

---

[1] Ibid., II, p. 65.
[2] For Mill's views on Auguste Comte see his Auguste Comte and Positivism (1865). His own concept of the religion of humanity can be found in Three Essays on Religion (1874). Mill's correspondence with Comte has been edited.

organic connection with positivism. And this view has in fact been challenged. In spite of what Mill's critics say, there is an important sense in which his contention seems to be fully justified. For the idea that theology and metaphysics have been succeeded by science, which alone gives us genuine and useful knowledge, does not entail the elevation of humanity into an object of religious worship, nor the establishment of an elaborate religious cult. Comte's positivist religion, which influenced a number of his disciples and led to the establishment of a positivist Church,[1] is not a logical consequence of a positivist theory of knowledge. At the same time it is certainly arguable that there is a psychological connection between Comte's positivist philosophy and his religion of humanity. It seems true to say that Comte was at one with the Traditionalists in believing that a moral and religious regeneration of society was required. Believing however that God was a fiction, he had to look elsewhere for an object of devotion. And thinking, as he did, that the basic social reality was humanity rather than separate individuals and that individuals could transcend egoism only by devoting themselves to the service of humanity, it is understandable that in his 'Great Being' he found a substitute for the focus of devotion and worship in the Middle Ages. An emphasis on the service of humanity does not indeed entail the establishment of a religious cult. But Comte evidently thought that in modern society the unifying and elevating function once performed by belief in God could be fulfilled only by a religious devotion to humanity. While therefore Mill is undoubtedly right in maintaining that a positivist theory of knowledge does not entail the religion of humanity, it is relevant to remember that Comte was concerned not only with a theory of knowledge but also with social regeneration, and that his positivist religion, bizarre though it may seem, was for him an integral part of this regeneration.

A pertinent question however is whether in his talk about the Great Being Comte does not relapse into the metaphysical stage of thought as he conceived it. To be sure, he is ready to admit that the Great Being acts only through individuals. But it seems clear that to be considered as a proper object of worship by individuals humanity has to be hypostatized, to be conceived as a totality

---

[1] Reference will be made in the next chapter to Comte's followers in France. For a brief mention of his disciples in England see Volume VIII of this *History*, pp. 113 f.

which is more than the succession of individual human beings. Indeed, Comte refers to 'one immense and eternal Being, Humanity'.[1] Perhaps such statements should not be taken too seriously. They might be understood as expressing a hope that humanity will not in fact be destroyed by the 'cosmological fatalities'[2] which might extinguish it. At the same time it is clear that humanity as an object of common worship becomes an hypostatized abstraction and thus an example of the metaphysical stage of thought as described by Comte. This aspect of the matter is illustrated by what Comte has to say about immortality. Sometimes he speaks of continued existence 'in the heart and mind of others'[3]; but when he speaks of our nature needing 'to be purified by death'[4] and of man becoming 'an organ of humanity'[5] in the second life, he seems to be regarding humanity as a persistent entity which is irreducible to the succession of human beings living in the world.

The matter can be put in this way. In the classical positivism of Comte, as distinct from the logical positivism of the twentieth century, the notion of meaninglessness does not function prominently. As we have seen, Comte was anxious to defend positivism against the charge of atheism. He did not assert dogmatically that there was no God. The thesis which he generally adopted was that the idea of God has become more and more of an unverified hypothesis, in proportion, that is to say, as man has substituted scientific for theological explanations of phenomena. At the same time it might be inferred from some of the things which he says that an unverifiable hypothesis would lack any clear meaning. And occasionally this view is explicitly stated. Comte asserts, for example, that 'any proposition which is not ultimately reducible to the simple enunciation of a fact, whether particular or general, would not present (*ne saurait offrir*) any real intelligible sense.'[6] If such utterances were pressed, it would seem difficult to maintain that the concept of the 'Great Being' (Humanity), considered as an object of worship and religious devotion, had any clearly intelligible meaning. For if the Great Being is reducible to phenomena and the relations between them, the religion of humanity becomes an extremely odd affair. Comte's

---

[1] *The Catechism of Positive Religion*, translated by R. Congreve (3rd edition, 1891), p. 45.
[2] *Ibid.*, p. 45.   [3] *Ibid.*, p. 55.   [4] *Pol.*, IV, p. 35.   [5] *Ibid.*, II, p. 60.
[6] *CPP*, VI, p. 600. Comte is here quoting himself from an earlier writing.

positivist religion requires that the Great Being should be regarded as a reality which is irreducible to a collection of individual men and women. Hence in proposing his religion he seems to slip back into the mentality of the metaphysical, if not the theological stage.[1]

[1] According to Comte, however, it is 'our metaphysicians' who reduce Humanity to individuals, considered in abstraction from the whole.

PART II

FROM AUGUSTE COMTE TO HENRI BERGSON

CHAPTER VI

POSITIVISM IN FRANCE

E. Littré and his criticism of Comte—C. Bernard and the experimental method—E. Renan; positivism and religion—H. Taine and the possibility of metaphysics—E. Durkheim and the development of sociology—L. Lévy-Bruhl and morals.

1. AUGUSTE Comte, the most famous French positivist of the nineteenth century, had his faithful disciples who accepted the master's thought as a whole, including his religion of humanity. Foremost among them was Pierre Lafitte (1825–1903) who became a professor of the Collège de France in 1892 and who was recognized as their leader by the London Positivist Committee which was founded in 1881 with J. H. Bridges (1832–1906) as its president.[1] There were however philosophers who accepted positivism as an epistemological theory but who had little use for it as a religious cult and who regarded Comte's political ideas and his teleological interpretation of human history as constituting a departure from the genuine spirit of positivism. An eminent representative of this line of thought was Émile Littré (1801–1881).

Littré studied medicine for a time[2]; but he is best known for his dictionary of the French language.[3] In 1863 his candidature for election to the French Academy was vehemently opposed by Bishop Dupanloup of Orléans, who was himself a member of the Academy; but in 1871 Littré was at last elected. In the same year he became a deputy, and in 1875 he was made a senator for life. It is with his philosophical thought that we are concerned here.

When Littré came to read Comte's *Course of Positive Philosophy* he had already shed theological beliefs and rejected metaphysics. The *Course* provided him with something positive and

---

[1] The London Committee broke away from the original group of English Comtists, led by Richard Congreve (1818–99). The two groups were later reunited.

[2] His *Dictionnaire de médecine* appeared in 1855.

[3] *Dictionnaire de la langue française* (4 volumes, 1863–72).

definite to hold on to. 'It was in 1840 that I came to know M. Comte. A common friend lent me his system of positive philosophy; M. Comte, on learning that I was reading the book, sent me a copy of it. . . . His book conquered me. . . . I became from then on a disciple of the positive philosophy, and such I have remained, without other changes than those imposed on me by the increasing effort to carry out, in the midst of other obligatory labours, the corrections and enlargements which it allows of.'[1] In 1845 Littré reprinted a number of articles as a book with the title *On the Positive Philosophy* (*De la philosophie positive*).

In 1852 Littré broke with Comte; but his disagreements with the high priest of positivism did not affect his adherence to the philosophical outlook expounded in the *Course*. And in 1863 he published *Auguste Comte and the Positive Philosophy* (*Auguste Comte et la philosophie positive*) in which he warmly defended what he regarded as the main and valuable ideas of Comte, while also expressing some criticism of points on which he disagreed. Further, in 1864 he wrote a preface[2] for the second edition of Comte's *Course*, while in 1866 he tried to defend Comte against J. S. Mill. In 1873 Littré published *Science from the Philosophical Point of View* (*La science au point de vue philosophique*), which included a number of articles which had appeared in the *Revue de philosophie positive*. In 1879 he brought out a second edition of his *Conservation, Revolution and Positivisme* (*Conservation, révolution et positivisme*) in which he revised some of the ideas expressed in the first edition of the work (1852).

In Littré's opinion, Comte filled a vacuum. On the one hand the mind seeks a general or overall view; and this was just what metaphysics provided. The trouble was however that the metaphysician developed his theories *a priori*, and that these theories lacked a solid empirical basis. On the other hand the particular sciences, while proposing empirically testable hypotheses, inevitably lacked the generality which was characteristic of metaphysics. In other words, the discrediting of metaphysics left a gap which could be filled only by the creation of a new philosophy. And it was Comte who met this need. 'M. Comte is the founder of the positive philosophy.'[3] Saint-Simon did not possess the necessary scientific knowledge. Further, by trying to reduce the

---

[1] *Auguste Comte et la philosophie positive*, p. 1 (preface). This work will be referred to in footnotes as *AC*.
[2] It bore the title *Préface d'un disciple*.   [3] *AC*, p. 38.

forces of nature to one ultimate force, namely gravitation, he relapsed into the metaphysical mentality.[1] Comte however 'has constructed what nobody before him had constructed, the philosophy of the six fundamental sciences'[2] and has exhibited the relations between them. 'By discussing the interconnection of the sciences and their hierarchic system (Comte) discovered at the same time the positive philosophy.'[3] Comte also showed how and why the sciences developed historically in a certain order from mathematics to sociology. Metaphysicians may reproach other philosophers with neglecting consideration of man, the subject of knowledge; but this reproach does not affect Comte, who established the science of man, namely sociology, on a sound basis. Moreover by excluding all 'absolute' questions[4] and by giving philosophy a firm scientific basis, Comte at last made philosophy capable of directing 'minds in research, men in their conduct and societies in their development'[5]. Theology and metaphysics tried to do this; but as they treated of questions which transcended human knowledge, they were necessarily ineffective.

The positive philosophy, Littré asserts, regards the world as consisting of matter and the forces immanent in matter. 'Beyond these two terms, matter and force, positive science knows nothing.'[6] We do not know either the origin of matter or its essence. The positive philosophy is not concerned with absolutes or with knowledge of things in themselves. It is concerned simply with reality as accessible to human knowledge. If therefore it is claimed that phenomena can be accounted for in terms of matter and its immanent forces, this is not equivalent to a dogmatic materialism, which professes, for example, to tell us what matter is in itself or to 'explain' the development of life or thought. The positive philosophy shows, for instance, how psychology presupposes biology, and biology other sciences; but it steers clear of questions about the ultimate cause of life or about what thought is in itself, apart from our scientific knowledge of it.

Though however Littré is keen on differentiating between positivism and materialism, it is not at all clear that he is successful in this attempt. As mentioned above, he maintains that the

---

[1] Littré minimized Saint-Simon's influence on Comte. And he denied that Comte was ever in a real sense Saint-Simon's disciple.
[2] *AC*, p. 105.   [3] *Ibid.*, p. 106.
[4] *AC*, p. 107. Littré is referring to such questions as those about the ultimate origin and end or purpose of things.
[5] *Ibid.*, p. 107.   [6] *CPP*, I, p. ix (Préface d'un disciple).

positive philosophy recognizes nothing beyond matter and the forces immanent in matter. It is true of course that this thesis is expressed in terms of an assertion about scientific knowledge, and not as an assertion about ultimate reality or about what is 'really real'. At the same time Littré finds fault with J. S. Mill for leaving the existence of a supernatural reality an open question; and he criticizes Herbert Spencer's attempt to reconcile science and religion by means of his doctrine of the Unknowable. Perhaps we can say that two lines of thought are discernible in Littré's mind. On the one hand there is the tendency to insist that the positive philosophy simply abstains from questions relating to realities the existence of which cannot be verified by sense-experience. In this case there is no reason why such questions should not be left open, even if they are considered unanswerable[1]. On the other hand there is a tendency to regard assertions about alleged realities which transcend the sphere of the scientifically verifiable as nonsensical. In this case of course it makes no sense to ask whether or not such realities exist. The questions cannot then be regarded as open questions, and Littré's criticism of Mill becomes understandable.

Though however Littré was and remained in substantial agreement with the ideas expressed by Comte in his *Course of Positive Philosophy*, he believed that in later writings Comte had pretty well betrayed the positivist outlook. For example, Littré had no use for the 'subjective method', in which human needs constitute the synthesizing principle,[2] as advocated by Comte in his *System of Positive Polity* and the one completed volume of the *Subjective Synthesis*. By the subjective method Littré understood a process of reasoning which set out from premises asserted *a priori* and arrived at conclusions which were warranted only by their formal logical connections with the premises. In his opinion, this was the method followed in metaphysics; and it had no place in positive philosophy. What Comte did was to introduce a confusion between the subjective method as followed by metaphysicians and the deductive method as developed in the scientific era. The deductive method in the second sense 'is subject to the twofold condition of having experimentally acquired points

---

[1] Bertrand Russell, we may note, maintained, on occasion at any rate, that it was one of the jobs of philosophy to keep alive an awareness of certain important problems which were yet, in his opinion, insoluble.

[2] The needs, that is to say, of social man or the human collectivity rather than of the individual as such.

of departure and experimentally verified conclusions'.[1] By reintroducing the subjective method, which deals with the logical connection between ideas or propositions without any real attention being paid to empirical verification, Comte 'let himself be conquered by the Middle Ages'.[2]

Among the particular points criticized by Littré are Comte's identification of mathematics with logic and his subordination of the mind to the heart or to the affective aspect of man. It is one thing to emphasize the cooperating role of feeling in human activity, and it is quite another thing to suggest, as Comte does, that the heart should dominate the intelligence or dictate to it. This suggestion, Littré insists, is quite incompatible with the positivist mentality. As for the religion of humanity, to a very limited extent Littré is prepared to agree with Comte on the need for religion, as distinct from theology. 'In my opinion, M. Comte followed a legitimate deduction by investing the positive philosophy of which he is the author with a role equivalent to that of religions.'[3] That is to say, if we mean by religion a general world-view, the positivist conception of the world can be described as a religion. Comte however goes very much further than this. For he postulates a collective being, humanity, and proposes it as an object of cult. Love of humanity is indeed a noble and admirable sentiment; but 'there is no justification for selecting for adoration either humanity or any other fraction of the whole or the great whole itself'.[4] What Comte does in effect is to relapse into the theological mentality. And 'for all this the subjective method is responsible'.[5]

As for ethics or morals, Littré blames Comte for having added morals to the list of sciences as a seventh member. This was a mistake; for 'morals does not at all belong, as do the six sciences, to the objective order'.[6] Rather oddly, Littré goes on to say, practically immediately, that there is need of a science of morals.[7] The apparent contradiction would indeed be eliminated if we were justified in interpreting Littré as finding fault with Comte for thinking that a normative ethics could be a science or have an integral place in positive philosophy and as himself maintaining that a purely descriptive study of ethical phenomena or of man's moral behaviour was needed. And he does indeed speak elsewhere

[1] AC, p. 536. [2] AC, p. 562. [3] Ibid., p. 524.
[4] Ibid., Littré had no use for pantheism.
[5] AC, p. 579. [6] Ibid., p. 677. [7] Ibid., p. 677.

about 'the observation of the phenomena of the moral order as revealed whether by psychology or by history and political economy',[1] as serving as a foundation for the scientific knowledge of human nature. But he also refers to human progress, conceived in positivist terms, as 'the source of profound convictions, obligatory for conscience'.[2]

We can reasonably conclude that Littré did not work out his ideas on ethics in a clear and consistent manner. It is however evident enough that his general quarrel with Comte's later writings is that they show serious departures from the positivist conviction that the only genuine knowledge of the world or of man is empirically verified knowledge. Or perhaps it might be better to say that in Littré's opinion Comte came to introduce into the positive philosophy ideas which had no legitimate place there and thus created a state of confusion. It was therefore necessary to return to the pure positivism of which Comte himself had been the great expounder.

3. The conviction that experimental science alone is the source of knowledge about the world was shared by the famous French physiologist, Claude Bernard (1813–78), professor of physiology at the Sorbonne and of medicine at the Collège de France. His best known work is his *Introduction to the Study of Experimental Medicine* (*Introduction à l'étude de la médecine expérimentale*), which he published in 1865. Three years later he was elected to the French Academy; and in 1869 he became a senator.

To include mention of Claude Bernard in a chapter devoted to positivism may seem to be quite inappropriate. For not only did he say that the best philosophical system is not to have one but he also explicitly condemned the positivist philosophy for being a system[3]. He wished to make medicine more scientific; and the better to promote this cause he undertook an investigation into the nature of scientific method. He was not concerned with creating a philosophical system, nor with defending an already existing one. At the same time Bernard insisted that the experimental method was the only one which could yield objective knowledge of reality. He did indeed speak of 'subjective truths' as absolute truths; but he was referring to mathematics, the truths of which are formal, independent, that is to say, of what is the case in the world.

---

[1] *CPP*, VI, '. xxxiv (Préface d'un disciple).
[2] *Ibid.*, p. xlviii.   [3] *Introduction*, p. 387.

By the experimental method Bernard meant the construction and empirical testing of verifiable hypotheses, an objective method which eliminated, as far as possible, the influence of subjective factors such as the desire that X rather than Y should be the case. Theologians and metaphysicians claimed that their unverified ideal constructions represented absolute or definitive truth. Unverifiable hypotheses however do not represent knowledge. Positive knowledge of the world, which is knowledge of the laws of phenomena, can be obtained only through the use of scientific method. And this yields results which are provisional, revisible in principle that is to say.

It is true that Bernard asserts that there is an 'absolute principle of science',[1] the principle of determinism, which states that a given set of conditions (together constituting a 'cause') infallibly produce a certain phenomenon or effect. Bernard's contention however is that this principle is 'absolute' simply in the sense that it is a necessary working assumption of science. The scientist necessarily assumes a regular causal order in the world. The principle is not 'absolute' in the sense of being an *a priori* metaphysical truth or a philosophical dogma. It is not equivalent, Bernard maintains, to fatalism. He does indeed sometimes write as though the principle of determinism were in fact an absolute truth which is known *a priori*. But though a measure of inconsistency may be discernible in his various utterances, his official position, so to speak, is that the determinism in question is methodological, involved, that is to say, in the scientific approach to the world, rather than a philosophical doctrine.

We have seen that Bernard refuses to recognize theology and metaphysics as sources of knowledge about reality. In this matter his attitude is clearly positivistic. At the same time he also refuses to rule out what are sometimes described as ultimate questions on the ground that they are meaningless or that they should not be asked. And though he was not himself a religious believer, he insisted on leaving a place for belief as well as knowledge. The two should not be confused; but belief of some sort is natural to man, and religious belief is quite compatible with scientific integrity, provided that it is recognized that articles of belief are not empirically verified hypotheses. Bernard is therefore critical of Comte's doctrine of the three stages. Theological beliefs and metaphysics cannot legitimately be regarded simply

[1] *Introduction*, p. 69.

as *past* stages of human thought. There are questions of importance to man which transcend the scope of science, and so the field in which knowledge is possible; but belief in certain answers is legitimate, provided that they are not proposed as assured truths about reality, and that there is no attempt to impose them on others.

If therefore the question is raised whether Bernard was or was not a positivist, we have to make a distinction. His idea of what constituted positive knowledge of reality was in line with the ideas of Comte. We can quite well speak of Bernard's positivist outlook. At the same time he rejected positivism as a dogmatic philosophical system, though he had no wish to substitute for it any other philosophical system. To be sure, anyone who writes, as Bernard did, on human knowledge, its scope and limits, is bound to make philosophical statements or statements which have philosophical implications. But Bernard tried to avoid the temptation to expound a philosophy in the name of science. Hence his insistence that his principle of determinism should not be regarded as a philosophical dogma. Again, while he was prepared to speak of the organism which functions in virtue of its physico-chemical elements, he also admitted that the physiologist must look on the living organism as an individual unity, the development of which is directed by a 'creative idea' or 'vital force'[1]. This may sound like a contradiction. But Bernard tried, whether successfully or not, to steer clear of any philosophical assertion either that there is or is not a vital principle in the organism. His point was that though physicists and chemists must describe the organism in physico-chemical terms, the physiologist cannot help recognising the fact that the organism functions as a living unity and not simply as a collection of distinct chemical elements. Bernard tried at any rate to distinguish between thinking of the organism in a certain way and making a metaphysical assertion about entelechies.

4. Joseph Ernest Renan (1823-92) is best known for his *Life of Jesus* (*La vie de Jésus*, 1863). In 1862 he was appointed professor of Hebrew at the Collège de France[2]; and his two main publications were his *History of the Origins of Christianity* (*Histoire des origines du christianisme*, 1863-83) and his *History of the People of*

---

[1] *Introduction*, p. 151.
[2] Renan's lecturing activity at the Collège de France was soon suspended, as a consequence of his clear denial of the divinity of Christ. But he resumed his teaching after 1870, and in 1878 he was elected to the French Academy.

Israel (*Histoire du peuple d'Israël*, 1887–93). He also wrote on the Semitic languages and published French versions, with critical introductions, of certain books of the Old Testament. It may seem therefore that he is a most unsuitable person for mention in a history of philosophy. Though however he was not a professional philosopher and was far from being a consistent thinker,[1] he published some philosophical writings, such as *The Future of Science* (*L'avenir de la science*, written in 1848–49, though not published until 1890), *Essays on Morals and Criticism* (*Essais de morale et de critique*, 1859), and *Philosophical Dialogues and Fragments* (*Dialogues et fragments philosophiques*, 1876). His philosophical thought was a curious amalgam of positivism and religiosity, ending in scepticism. It is with his relation to positivism that we are concerned here.

When Renan left the seminary of Saint-Sulpice in 1845, he became a friend of Marcelin Pierre Eugène Berthelot (1827–1907), who was to become professor of organic chemistry at the Collège de France and subsequently minister of education. Like Comte, Berthelot believed in the triumph of scientific knowledge over theology and metaphysics. And Renan, who had lost his faith in the supernatural (in, that is to say, the existence of a transcendent and personal God), shared this belief up to a point. In his *Memoirs of Childhood and Youth* he remarked that from the first months of 1846 'the clear scientific vision of a universe in which there is no perceptible action of a free will superior to that of man'[2] became for Berthelot and himself an immovable anchor. Similarly, in the preface to the thirteenth edition (1866) of the *Life of Jesus* Renan asserted that he had rejected the supernatural for the very same reason for which he rejected belief in centaurs, namely that they had never been seen. In other words, knowledge of reality is obtained through observation and the verification of empirical hypotheses. This was the view expressed in *The Future of Science*. The scientific view of the world did not indeed mean for Renan simply the natural scientist's view. He emphasized (naturally enough, given his own intellectual interests) the importance and role of history and philology. But positive knowledge of reality, he insisted, must have an experimental basis. This is

---

[1] Renan tended to take pride in this lack of consistency, on the ground that it was only by trying out different hypotheses that one could hope to see the truth once in one's life.

[2] *Souvenirs d'enfance et de jeunesse* (2nd edition, 1883) p. 337.

why the enlightened man cannot believe in God. 'A being who does not reveal himself by any act is for science a being which does not exist.'[1]

If this were all, we would know where we were. But it is far from being all that Renan has to say. He rejects the idea of a personal God who intervenes in history. The occurrence of divine interventions has never been proved. And events which seemed to past generations to be divine acts have been explained in other ways. But to reject the personal transcendent Deity is not to embrace atheism. From one point of view God is the developing totality of existence, the divine being which becomes, God *in fieri*. From another point of view God, considered as perfect and eternal, exists only in the ideal order, as the ideal end of the whole process of development. 'What reveals the true God, is the moral sentiment. If humanity were simply intelligent, it would be atheist; but the great races have found in themselves a divine instinct. 'Duty, devotion, sacrifice, all of them things of which history is full, are inexplicable without God.'[2] True, all statements about God are simply symbolic. But the divine none the less reveals itself to the moral consciousness. 'To love God, to know God, is to love what is beautiful and good, to know what is true.'[3]

To give a precise account of Renan's concept of God is probably something which exceeds human capacity. We can discern the general influence, to a certain extent, of German idealism. More basic however is Renan's own religiosity or religious feeling which expresses itself in a variety of ways, not always mutually consistent, and which makes him quite incapable of being a positivist in the style of Littré. Obviously, there is no reason why a positivist should not have moral ideals. And if he wishes to interpret religion as a matter of sentiment or of the heart[4] and religious belief as the expression of feeling, not of knowledge, he can combine religion with a positivist theory of knowledge. But if he introduces the idea of the Absolute, as Renan does in his letter to Berthelot of August 1863,[5] he clearly goes beyond the limits of what can reasonably be described as positivism without the term being deprived of definite meaning.

In view of what has been said above it is hardly surprising to

---

[1] *Dialogues* (1876), p. 246.   [2] *Ibid.*, pp. 321–22.   [3] *Ibid.*, p. 326.
[4] In a letter of August 1862, addressed to Adolphe Guéroult, Renan said that to believe in the living God he needs only 'to listen in silence to the imperative revelation of my heart' (*Dialogues*, p. 251), a statement reminiscent of Rousseau.
[5] This letter is included in *Dialogues*, pp. 153–91.

find that Renan's attitude to metaphysics is complex. In an essay on metaphysics and its future, which he wrote in reply to a work entitled *Metaphysics and Science* (*La métaphysique et la science*, 2 volumes, 1858) by Étienne Vacherot,[1] he insisted that man had both the power and the right 'to rise above facts'[2] and to pursue speculation about the universe. He also made it clear however that he regarded such speculation as akin to poetry or even to dreaming. What he denied was not the right to indulge in metaphysical speculation but the view of metaphysics as the first and fundamental science 'containing the principles of all the others, a science which can by itself alone, and by abstract reasonings, lead us to the truth about God, the world and man'.[3] For 'all that we know, we know by the study of nature or of history'.[4]

Provided that positivism is not understood as entailing the claim that all metaphysical questions are nonsensical or meaningless, this view of metaphysics is doubtless compatible with the positivist thesis that all knowledge of reality comes through the sciences. So perhaps is Renan's assertion that while he denies that metaphysics is a 'progressive' science, in the sense that it can increase our knowledge, he does not reject it if it is considered as a science 'of the eternal'.[5] For he is referring not to an eternal reality but rather to an analysis of concepts. In his view logic, pure mathematics and metaphysics do not tell us anything about reality (about what is the case) but analyse what one already knows. To be sure, an equation of metaphysics with conceptual analysis is not the same as an assimilation of it to poetry or dreams. For in the first case it can reasonably be described as scientific, while in the second it cannot be so described. But Renan might of course reply that the word 'metaphysics' can bear both senses, and that he rejects neither of them. In other words, metaphysics can be a science provided that it is regarded simply as conceptual analysis. But if it professes to treat of existing realities, such as God, which transcend the spheres of natural science and of history, it is not and cannot be a science. One is entitled to speculate, but such speculation no more increases our knowledge of reality than do poetry and dreaming.

Given these two views of metaphysics, it is rather disconcerting to find Renan saying that philosophy is 'the general result of all

---

[1] Vacherot (1809–97) maintained the view that metaphysics could be made into a science. Renan's reply is reprinted in *Dialogues*.
[2] *Dialogues*, p. 282.   [3] *Ibid.*, p. 283.   [4] *Ibid.*, p. 284.   [5] *Ibid.*, p. 175.

the sciences'.[1] Taken by itself, this statement might be understood in a Comtean sense. But Renan adds that 'to philosophize is to know the Universe,'[2] and that 'the study of nature and of humanity is then the whole of philosophy'.[3] It is true that he uses the word 'philosophy', not the word 'metaphysics'. But philosophy considered as 'the science of the whole'[4] is, one would have thought, one of the meanings not uncommonly ascribed to 'metaphysics'. In other words, philosophy as the general result of all the sciences tends to mean metaphysics, though the precise status attributed by Renan to philosophy in this sense is by no means clear.

Renan was obviously a man who believed that positive knowledge about the world could be obtained only through the natural sciences and through historical and philological inquiries. In other words, science, in a broad sense of the word,[5] had taken the place of theology and metaphysics as a science of information about existing reality. In Renan's view, belief in the transcendent personal God of Jewish and Christian faith had been deprived of any rational ground by the development of science. That is to say, such belief was incapable of being confirmed experimentally. As for metaphysics, whether it was regarded as speculation about problems which were scientifically unanswerable or as some form of conceptual analysis, it could not increase man's knowledge of what is the case in the world. In one aspect of his thought therefore Renan was clearly on the side of the positivists. At the same time he was unable to rid himself of the conviction that through his moral consciousness and his recognition of ideals man entered, in some real sense, into a sphere transcending that of empirical science. Nor could he rid himself of the conviction that there was in fact a divine reality, even if all attempts at definite description were symbolic and open to criticism.[6] It is evident that he wished to combine a religious outlook with the positivist elements in his thought. But he was not enough of a systematic thinker to achieve a coherent and consistent synthesis. Further, it was hardly possible in any case to harmonize all his various beliefs, not at any rate in the forms in which he expressed them. How,

---

[1] *Ibid.*, p. 290.   [2] *Ibid.*, p. 292.   [3] *Ibid.*, p. 292.   [4] *Ibid.*, p. 304.

[5] Renan uses the word 'science' in several senses. Sometimes it just means knowledge, while sometimes it means natural sciences and sometimes it includes the historical sciences.

[6] For example, 'every phrase applied to an infinite object is a myth' (*Dialogues*, p. 323).

for example, could one reconcile the view that experimental or empirical verification is required to justify the assertion that something exists with the following claim? 'Nature is only an appearance; man is only a phenomenon. There is the eternal ground (*fond*), there is the infinite substance, the absolute, the ideal . . . there is . . . *he who is*'.[1] Empirical verification, in any ordinary sense, of the existence of the Absolute seems to be excluded. It is therefore not altogether surprising if in the last years of his life Renan showed a marked tendency to scepticism in the religious sphere. We cannot *know* the infinite or even that there is an infinite, nor can we establish that there are absolute objective values. True, we can act as if there were objective values and as if there were a God. But such matters lie outside the range of any positive knowledge. To claim therefore that Renan abandoned positivism would be inaccurate, though it is evident that it did not satisfy him.

5. If Renan's thought contains different elements, so does that of Hippolyte-Adolphe Taine (1828–93). Neither of the two thinkers can be adequately described by labelling him as a positivist. But whereas with Renan the obvious feature of his thought as a whole is his attempt to revise religion in such a way that it can be combined with his positivist ideas, in the case of Taine the salient characteristic of his thought is his attempt to combine positivist convictions with a marked inclination to metaphysics, an inclination stimulated by study of Spinoza and Hegel. Further, while the interests of neither Renan nor Taine are confined to the area of philosophy, their main extra-philosophical activities are somewhat different. Renan, as we have noted, is well known for his works on the history of the people of Israel and on the origins of Christianity, whereas Taine is celebrated for his work in psychology. He also wrote on art, literary history and the development of modern French society. Both men however were influenced by the positivist outlook.

Taine was attracted to philosophy at an early age; but at the time when he was studying at the École Normale at Paris, philosophical studies were more or less dominated by the thought of Victor Cousin, with which Taine had little sympathy. For a time he turned to teaching in schools and to literature. In 1853 he published his *Essay on the Fables of La Fontaine* (*Essai sur les fables de La Fontaine*) and in 1856 an *Essay on Livy* (*Essai sur*

[1] *Dialogues*, p. 252.

Tite-Live). These writings were followed by *Essays in Criticism and History* (*Essais de critique et d'histoire*, 1858) and the four-volume *History of English Literature* (*Histoire de la littérature anglaise*).[1] In the philosophical field Taine published *The French Philosophers of the Nineteenth Century* (*Les philosophes français du dix-neuvième siècle*) in 1857. But philosophical ideas also found expressions in the prefaces to Taine's other writings.

In 1864 Taine obtained a chair at the École des Beaux-Arts, and his *Philosophy of Art*[2] was the result of his lectures on aesthetics. In 1870 Taine published his *De l'intelligence* in two volumes.[3] He planned to write another work on the will; but he was too occupied with his five-volume work on *The Origins of Contemporary France* (*Les origines de la France contemporaine*, 1875–93), in which he treated of the old régime, the revolution and the later development of French society. Another volume of essays on criticism and history appeared in 1894. Taine also published some travel books.

Taine was brought up a Christian but lost his faith at the age of fifteen. Doubt and scepticism were not however to his taste. He looked for knowledge that was certain; and he hankered after comprehensive knowledge, knowledge of the totality. Science, developed through the empirical verification of hypotheses, seemed to be the only road to secure knowledge of the world. At the same time Taine believed that the continuation of a metaphysical worldview, a view of the totality as a necessary system, was not only a legitimate but also a necessary enterprise. And his persistent problem was that of combining his conviction that there was nothing in the world but events or phenomena and the relations between them with his conviction that a metaphysics was possible which would go beyond the results of the particular sciences and achieve a synthesis. From the chronological point of view the attraction which he felt for the philosophies of Spinoza and Hegel preceded the development of his positivist ideas. But it was not a case of positivism arriving on the scene and driving out metaphysics. Taine reasserted his belief in metaphysics and endeavoured to reconcile the two tendencies in his thought. Whether he was

---

[1] 1863–4. There is an English translation by H. van Laun (Edinburgh, 1873).
[2] *Philosophie de l'art* (1865) was published in New York in an English translation by J. Durand. An enlarged French edition appeared in 1880.
[3] In 1871 an English translation, *Intelligence*, by T. D. Hayes was published in London.

successful, and indeed whether he could have been successful,[1] is disputable. But there can be no doubt about what he was trying to do.

The general nature of this attempt is made clear by Taine himself in his work on the French philosophers of the nineteenth century,[2] in his study of John Stuart Mill (*Le positivisme anglais. Étude sur Stuart Mill*, 1864) and in his history of English literature. The English empiricists, in Taine's opinion, regard the world as a collection of facts. To be sure, they concern themselves with the relations between phenomena or facts; but these relations are for them purely contingent. For Mill, who represents the culmination of a line of thought starting with Francis Bacon, the causal relation is simply one of factually regular sequence. Indeed, 'the law which attributes a cause to every event has for him no other basis, no other value and no other bearing than an experience. . . . It simply gathers together a sum of observations'.[3] By confining himself simply to experience and its immediate data Mill 'has described the English mind while believing that he was describing the human mind'.[4] The German metaphysical idealists however have had the vision of the totality. They have seen the universe as the expression of ultimate causes and laws, as a necessary system, not as a collection of facts or of phenomena which are related in a purely contingent manner. At the same time, in their enthusiasm for the vision of the totality they have neglected the limitations of the human mind and have tried to proceed in a purely *a priori* manner. They have tried to reconstruct the world of experience by pure thought.[5] In point of fact they have constructed imposing edifices which presently collapse in ruins. There is thus room for a middle way, a combination of what is true and valuable in both English empiricism and German metaphysics. The achievement of this synthesis is reserved for the French mind. 'If there is a place between the two nations, it is

---

[1] If we mean by positivism a philosophy which explicitly excludes metaphysics, it is evident that any attempt to combine positivism with metaphysics is excluded by definition, even if we think that positivism implies a metaphysics in the sense of a theory of being (say, *esse est percipi vel percipi posse*). But Taine himself did not of course look on the empiricist tendencies in his thought as excluding from the start the sort of metaphysics which he envisaged.

[2] This work was later entitled *The Classical Philosophers* (*Les philosophes classiques*).

[3] *Le positivisme anglais*, p. 102.   [4] *Ibid.*, p. 110.

[5] Taine apparently thinks of Hegel as trying to deduce even particulars, a task which the German philosopher in fact disclaimed, in spite of his remarks about the planets.

ours'.[1] It is the French mind which is called to correct the faults of both English positivism and German metaphysics, to synthesize the corrected outlooks, 'to express them in a style which everyone understands and thus to make of them the universal mind'.[2] The English excel in the discovery of facts, the Germans in the construction of theories. Fact and theory need to be brought together by the French, if possible by Taine.

One's mind may well boggle at the thought of combining English empiricism with German idealism, Mill with Hegel. But Taine is not concerned simply with stating an ideal which doubtless seems to many minds unrealizable and perhaps even silly. He indicates what he considers to be the ground on which a synthesis can be constructed, namely man's power of abstraction. Taine's use of the word 'abstraction' stands however in need of some explanation.

In the first place Taine does not mean to imply that we are entitled to assume that abstract terms refer to corresponding abstract entities. On the contrary, he attacks not only Cousin and the eclectics but also Spinoza and Hegel for making precisely this assumption. Words such as 'substance', 'force' and 'power' are convenient ways of grouping similar phenomena, but to think, for example, that the word 'force' signifies an abstract entity is to be misled by language. 'We believe that there are no substances, but only systems of facts. We regard the idea of substance as a psychological illusion. We consider substances, force and all the metaphysical beings of the moderns as a relic of Scholastic entities. We think that there is nothing in the world but facts and laws, that is to say events and their relations; and like you we recognize that all knowledge consists in the first instance in linking or in adding facts.'[3] In his work on intelligence Taine insists that there are no entities corresponding to words such as 'faculty', 'power', 'self'. Psychology is the study of facts; and in the self or ego we find no facts except 'the series of events',[4] which are all reducible to sensations. Even positivists have been guilty of the reification of abstract terms. A signal example of this is provided by Herbert Spencer's theory of the Unknowable, considered as absolute Force.[5]

In this line of thought, considered by itself, Taine goes as far as any empiricist could wish. 'We think that there are neither minds

---

[1] *Le positivisme anglais*, p. 147.   [2] *Ibid.*, p. 148.   [3] *Ibid.*, p. 114.
[4] *De l'intelligence*, I, p. 6.   [5] *Derniers essais de critique et d'histoire*, p. 199.

nor bodies, but simply groups of movements present or possible, and groups of thoughts present or possible'.[1] And it is interesting to observe Taine's insistence on the bewitching power of language, which induces philosophers to postulate unreal entities that 'vanish when one scrupulously examines the meaning of the words'.[2] His empiricism also shows itself in his rejection of the *a priori* method of Spinoza, a method which can do more than reveal ideal possibilities. Any knowledge of existing reality must be based on and result from experience.

By abstraction therefore Taine does not mean the formation of abstract terms or concepts which are then mistakenly thought to stand for abstract entities. But what does he mean by it? He describes it as 'the power of isolating the elements of facts and considering them separately'.[3] The assumption is that what is given in experience is complex and that it is analyzable into constituent elements which can be considered separately or in abstraction. The natural way of understanding this is in terms of reductive analysis as practised by Condillac in the eighteenth century or by Bertrand Russell in the twentieth. Analysis (*décomposition*) is said to give us the nature or essence of what is analyzed. But Taine takes it that among the constituent elements which form 'the interior of a being'[4] there can be found causes, forces and laws. 'They are not a new fact added to the first; they are a portion of it, an extract; they are contained in them, they are nothing else but the facts themselves.'[5] For example, proof of the statement that Tom is mortal does not consist in arguing from the premise that all men die (which, as Mill maintained, begs the question), nor in appealing to the fact that we do not know of any human being who has not eventually died, but rather by showing that 'mortality is joined to the quality of being a man',[6] inasmuch as the human body is an unstable chemical compound. To find out whether Tom will die or not, there is no need to multiply examples of men who have died. What is required is abstraction, which enables us to formulate a law. Every single example contains the cause of human mortality; but it has of course to be isolated by the mind, picked out or extracted from complex phenomena, and formulated in an abstract manner. To prove a fact, as Aristotle said, is to show its cause. This cause is comprised within the fact.

[1] *Le positivisme anglais*, p. 114. Taine agrees with Mill on the need for introducing the idea of possible sensations.
[2] *De l'intelligence*, I, p. 339.   [3] *Le positivisme anglais*, p. 115.
[4] *Ibid.*, p. 116.   [5] *Ibid.*, p. 116.   [1] *Ibid.*, p. 124.

And when we have abstracted it, we can argue 'from the abstract to the concrete, that is to say from cause to effect'.[1] We can however go further than this. We can practise the operation of analysis on groups or sets of laws and, in principle at any rate, arrive at the most primitive and basic elements of the universe. There are 'simple elements from which derive the most general laws, and from these the particular laws, and from these laws the facts which we observe'.[2] If these simple or unanalyzable elements can be known, metaphysics is possible. For metaphysics is the search for first causes. And, according to Taine, the first causes are knowable, inasmuch as they are everywhere exemplified, in all facts. It is not as though we had to transcend the world in order to know its first cause or causes. They are everywhere present and operative; and all that the human mind has to do is to extract or abstract them.

Given his insistence that the ultimate causes of empirical facts are contained within the facts themselves and so within experience, Taine can think of himself as correcting and enlarging British empiricism, not as contradicting it flatly. As far as he is concerned, metaphysics is really continuous with science, though it has a higher degree of generality. It is however evident that he starts with the assumption that the universe is one rational or law-ordered system. The notion that laws are convenient or practically useful fictions of the mind is quite alien to his thought. He assumes that 'there is a reason for everything, that every fact has its law; that every composite is reducible to simple elements; that every product implies causes (*facteurs*); that every quality and every existence must be deducible from some superior and anterior term'.[3] Taine assumes too that cause and effect are really the same thing under two 'appearances'. These assumptions are obviously derived not from empiricism but from the influence on his mind of Spinoza and Hegel. When he envisages one ultimate cause, one 'eternal axiom' and 'creative formula',[4] he is clearly speaking under the influence of a metaphysical vision of the totality as a necessary system which exhibits in innumerable ways the creative activity of an ultimate (though purely immanent) cause.

As we have noted, Taine criticizes the German idealists for having tried to deduce *a priori* such 'particular cases' as the

[1] *Ibid.*, p. 125.   [2] *Le positivisme anglais*, p. 137.   [3] *Ibid.*, p. 138.
[4] *The French Philosophers of the Nineteenth Century*, p. 371.

planetary system and the laws of physics and chemistry. But he appears to be objecting not to the idea of deducibility as such, deducibility in principle that is to say, but rather to the assumption that the human mind is able to perform the deduction, even when it has ascertained the primitive laws or ultimate causes. Between, so to speak, the primitive laws and a particular exemplification in the world as given in experience, there is an infinite series, criscrossed, so to speak, by innumerable cooperating or counterbalancing causal influences. And the human mind is too limited to be able to take in the whole pattern of the universe. But if Taine admits, as he seems to do, deducibility in principle, this admission obviously expresses a general vision of the universe which he has derived not from empiricism but from Spinoza and Hegel. This vision includes in its scope not only the physical universe but also human history. In his view history cannot become a science in the proper sense until causes and laws have been 'abstracted' from the facts or historical data.[1]

Talk about a metaphysical 'vision' may seem to be simply a case of employing the philosophical jargon which was fashionable some years ago among those who rejected the claim of metaphysics to be able to increase our positive knowledge of reality but who were not prepared to write off metaphysical systems as sheer nonsense. The term 'vision' however has a special appositeness in Taine's case. For he never developed a metaphysical system. He is best known for his contribution to empirical psychology. In psychopathology he tried to show how the constituent elements of what is *prima facie* a simple state or phenomenon can be dissociated; and he also made use of neural physiology to exhibit the mechanism which underlies mental phenomena. In general, he gave a powerful impetus to that development of psychology in France which is associated with such names as Théodule Armand Ribot (1859–1916), Alfred Binet (1857–1911) and Pierre Janet (1859–1947). In the fields of literary, artistic and social-political history Taine is known for his hypothesis of the formative influence on human nature of the three factors of race, environment and time and for his insistence, when dealing with the origins of contemporary France, on the effects of excessive centralization as manifested in different ways in the old régime, in the republic and under the empire. Throughout his work however Taine had, as he

[1] See, for example, *Essais de critique et d'histoire*, p. xxiv.

put it, 'a certain idea of causes',[1] an idea which was not that of the empiricists. In his view the eclectic spiritualists, such as Cousin, located causes outside the effects, and the ultimate cause outside the world. But the positivists banished causality from science.[2] Taine's idea of causality was obviously inspired by a general view of the universe as a rational and deterministic system. This vision remained a vision, in the sense that while he looked on his idea of causality as demanding and making possible a metaphysics, he did not himself attempt to develop a metaphysical system which would exhibit the 'first causes' and their operation in the universe. What he insisted on was the possibility of and the need for such a system. And while he could and did speak in an empiricist way of the scientific method of 'abstraction, hypothesis, verification'[3] for the ascertaining of causes, it is pretty clear that he meant more by 'cause' than would be meant by the empiricist or positivist.

6. Auguste Comte gave a powerful impetus to the development of sociology, an impetus which bore fruit in the later decades of the nineteenth century. To say this is certainly not to claim that French sociologists such as Durkheim were devoted disciples of the high priest of positivism. But by insisting on the irreducibility of each of his basic sciences to the particular science or sciences which it presupposed in the hierarchy and by emphasizing the nature of sociology as the scientific study of social phenomena Comte put sociology on the map. To be sure, the beginnings of sociology can be traced back well beyond Comte to Montesquieu, for example, and to Condorcet, not to speak of Saint-Simon, Comte's immediate predecessor. But Comte's clear recognition of sociology as a particular science, with a character of its own, justified Durkheim in regarding him as the father or founder of this science,[4] in spite of the fact that Durkheim did not accept the law of the three stages and criticized Comte's approach to sociology.

Émile Durkheim (1858–1917) studied in Paris at the École

[1] *Les philosophes français du dix-neuvième siècle*, p. x.
[2] The positivists would claim of course that it was a question of interpreting the causal relation rather than of banishing causality from science. Taine's view of the matter was obviously the expression of a non-empiricist view of the causal relation.
[3] *Les philosophes français*, p. 363.
[4] Durkheim regarded sociology as having been developed mainly in France. He had a low opinion of J. S. Mill's originality in this field, but he valued the contribution of Herbert Spencer, though with certain reservations, as will be indicated in the text.

Normale Supérieure and then taught philosophy in various schools. In 1887 he started to lecture in the University of Bordeaux, where he was appointed to the chair of social science in 1896. Two years later he founded *L'année sociologique*, a periodical of which he became editor. In 1902 he moved to Paris, where he was appointed professor of education in 1906 and then, in 1913, of education and sociology. In 1893 he published *De la division du travail social*[1] and in 1895 *Les règles de la méthode sociologique*.[2] Further writings included *Le suicide*[3] and *Les formes élémentaires de la vie religieuse*,[4] which appeared respectively in 1897 and 1912. Posthumously published writings, representing ideas expressed in lecture-courses, include *Sociologie et philosophie*,[5] *L'éducation morale*[6] and *Leçons de sociologie: physique des moeurs et du droit*.[7] These works appeared respectively in 1924, 1925 and 1950.

Sociology was for Durkheim the empirically based study of what he described as social phenomena or social facts. A social fact meant for him a general feature of a given society at a given stage of its development, a feature or general way of acting which could be regarded as exercising a constraint on individuals.[8] A condition of the possibility of sociology as a science is that there should be in any given society 'phenomena which would not exist if this society did not exist and which are what they are only because this society is constituted in the way it is'.[9] And it is the business of the sociologist to study these social phenomena in the same objective manner in which the physical scientist studies physical phenomena. Generalization must result from a clear perception of social phenomena or facts and their interrelations. It should not precede

---

[1] Translated as *The Division of Labour in Society* by G. Simpson (Glencoe, Illinois, 1952).
[2] Translated as *The Rules of Sociological Method* by S. A. Solovay and J. H. Mueller (Glencoe, Illinois, 1950).
[3] Translated as *Suicide* by J. A. Spaulding and G. Simpson (Glencoe, Illinois, 1951).
[4] Translated as *The Elementary Forms of the Religious Life* by J. W. Swain (London, 1915).
[5] Translated as *Sociology and Philosophy* by D. F. Pocock (London and Glencoe, Illinois, 1953).
[6] Translated as *Moral Education* by H. Schnurer and E. K. Wilson (Glencoe, Illinois, 1961).
[7] Translated as *Professional Ethics and Civic Morals* by C. Brookfield (London, 1957).
[8] See, for example, the first chapter (*What is a Social Fact?*) of *The Rules of Sociological Method*.
[9] From *La Sociologia ed il suo dominio scientifico* (1900). Quoted from the English translation by K. H. Wolff in *Essays on Sociology and Philosophy*, edited by K. H. Wolff (New York, 1960), p. 363.

such perception or constitute an *a priori* framework of interpretation in such a way that the sociologist is studying not the social facts themselves but his ideas of them.

From a philosophical point of view it is difficult to make a clear distinction between a fact and one's idea of it. For one cannot study anything at all without conceiving it. But there is no great difficulty in understanding the sort of procedure to which Durkheim objects. For example, while he gives credit to Auguste Comte for seeing that social phenomena are objective realities which fall within the natural world and can be studied scientifically, he finds fault with Comte for approaching sociology with a preconceived philosophical theory of history as a continual process of the perfecting of human nature. In his sociology Comte finds what he wants to find, namely what will fit into his philosophical theory. It is thus not so much the facts as his idea of the facts which Comte studies. Similarly, Herbert Spencer was concerned not so much with studying social facts in and for themselves as with showing how they verify his general evolutionary hypothesis. In Durkheim's opinion, Spencer pursued sociology as a philosopher, to prove a theory, rather than by letting the social facts speak for themselves.

We have seen above that Durkheim relates a social fact to a given society. And he laid great emphasis on the plurality of human societies, each of which has to be studied first of all in itself. On this matter he saw a difference between Comte and Spencer. Comte assumed that there was one human society which developed through successive stages, each of which was correlated with and in a sense dependent on the corresponding stage of man's intellectual advance. His philosophy of history made him myopic in regard to the particular questions which arise out of the careful study of given different societies. Further, by incorporating sociology into a philosophical system Comte really ensured that his sociology would make no progress in the hands of his disciples. For development to be possible the law of the three stages had to be jettisoned.[1] In the case of Herbert Spencer however the situation is rather different. For he recognized the plurality of societies and tried to classify them according to their types. Further, he discerned the operation of obscure forces beneath the level of

---

[1] In an article published in 1915, in *La science française*, Durkheim refers to Comte's law of the three stages as possessing 'only an historical interest'. See *Essays on Sociology and Philosophy* (cf. note 83), p. 378.

thought and reason and avoided the exaggerated emphasis placed by Comte on man's scientific advance. At the same time in his *Principles of Sociology* Spencer started out with a definition of society which was an expression of his own *a priori* concept rather than the result of meticulous study of the relevant data or facts.[1]

These social facts are for Durkheim *sui generis*. It is the business of the sociologist to study these facts as he finds them and not to reduce them to some other kind of fact. When a new science is beginning to develop, one has to take models from already existing developed sciences. But a new science becomes a science only in so far as it attains independence. And this involves having its own subject-matter and its own set of concepts formed through reflection on this subject-matter. Durkheim is thus no reductionist. At the same time he believes that for sociology to make real progress it must, like previously developed sciences, emancipate itself from philosophy. This does not mean simply liberating itself from subordination to a philosophical system such as that of Comte. It also means that the sociologist should not allow himself to become entangled in philosophical disputes, such as the dispute between determinists and upholders of free will. All that sociology requires is that the principle of causality should be applied to social phenomena, and then only as an empirical postulate, not as a necessary *a priori* truth.[2] Whether it is in fact possible to avoid all philosophical presuppositions, as Durkheim supposes, is debatable. But he is not of course saying that philosophers should not discuss such topics as freedom of the will, if they wish to do so. He is saying that there is no need for the sociologist to do so, and that the development of sociology requires that he should in fact abstain from such discussion.

The subject-matter of sociology is provided by what Durkheim calls social phenomena or social facts. And reference has been made above to his idea of social facts as exercising constraint on the individual. Social facts in this sense include, for example, the morality and the religion of a given society. Use of the term 'constraint' need not therefore imply coercion in the sense of the use of force. In the process of upbringing a child is initiated into a set of valuations which come from the society to which he belongs rather than from himself; and his mind can be said to be

---

[1] In *The Rules of Sociological Method* (pp. 20 f.) Durkheim refers to Spencer's use of the idea of co-operation as a basis for classifying societies.
[2] See, for example, the conclusion to *The Rules of Sociological Method*.

'constrained' by his society's moral code. Even if he rebels against the code, it is there, so to speak, as that against which he rebels and so as governing his reaction. There is no great difficulty in understanding this sort of idea. But Durkheim speaks of social phenomena such as morality and religion as expressions of the social or collective consciousness or of the common spirit or mind. And something has to be said about this topic, as use of a term such as 'collective consciousness' can easily be misunderstood.

In his essay on 'Individual and Collective Representations' Durkheim blames individualistic sociology for trying to explain the whole by reducing it to its parts.[1] And elsewhere he says that 'It is the whole that, in a large measure, produces the part.'[2] If such passages were isolated and considered simply by themselves, it would be natural to conclude that according to Durkheim the collective consciousness was a kind of universal substance from which individualistic consciousnesses proceed in a manner analogous to that in which plurality was said to emanate from the Neoplatonist One. It would then be somewhat disconcerting to find Durkheim stating that the parts cannot be derived from the whole. 'For the whole is nothing without the parts which form it.'[3]

The term 'collective consciousness' is apt to mislead and is therefore unfortunate. What Durkheim is trying to say however is reasonably clear. When he speaks of a collective consciousness or of a common spirit or mind, he is not postulating a substance existing apart from individual minds. A society does not exist apart from the individuals which compose it; and the system of a society's beliefs and value-judgments is borne, as it were, by individual minds. But it is borne by them in so far as they have come to participate in something which is not confined to any given set of individuals but persists as a social reality. Individuals have their own sensory experiences, their own tastes, and so on. But when the individual learns to speak, he comes to participate, through language, in a whole system of categories, beliefs and value-judgments, in what Durkheim describes as a social consciousness. We can thus distinguish between individual and collective 'representations', between what is peculiar to an individual as such and what he owes to or derives from the society to which he belongs. In so far as these collective 'representations'

---

[1] This essay, which was first published in the *Revue de Métaphysique et de Morale* in 1898, is included in *Sociology and Philosophy*, pp. 1–34).
[2] *Essays on Sociology and Philosophy* (see note 83), p. 325.   [3] *Ibid.*, p. 29.

affect the individual consciousness, we can speak of the parts as derived from or explained by the whole. That is to say, it makes sense to speak of the social 'mind' as causally affecting the individual mind, as affecting it, as it were, from without. According to Durkheim, it is by participating in civilization, the totality of 'intellectual and moral goods'[1] that man becomes specifically human. In this sense the part depends on the whole. At the same time civilization could not exist without individual human beings. And in this sense the whole is nothing without the parts which constitute it. The social facts or phenomena, which for Durkheim constitute the data of the sociologist's reflection, are social institutions of one kind or another which are the products of man in society and which, when once constituted, causally affect the individual consciousness. For instance, the outlook of a Hindu is formed not only by his private sensory experience but also by the religion of his society and by the institutions connected with it. The religion however could not exist as a social reality without any Hindus.

The constraint exercised by 'collective representations' or by the collective consciousness can be seen clearly, according to Durkheim, in the field of morals. There are indeed moral facts, but they exist only in a social context. 'Let all social life disappear, and moral life will disappear with it. . . . Morality, in all its forms, is never met with except in society. It never varies except in relation to social conditions.'[2] Morality, in other words, does not originate in the individual considered precisely as such. It originates in society and is a social phenomenon; and it bears upon the individual. In the sense of obligation, for example, it is the voice of society which speaks. It is society which imposes obligatory rules of conduct, their obligatory character being marked by the attachment of sanctions to the infringement of such rules. For the individual as such the voice of society, speaking through the sense of obligation, comes, as it were, from without. And it is this relationship of externality (of the whole functioning as a social reality in regard to the part) which makes it possible to regard the voice of conscience as the voice of God. For Durkheim however religion is basically the expression of a 'collective ideal';[3] and God is an hypostatization of the collective consciousness. It is quite

[1] *Ibid.*, p. 325.
[2] *The Division of Labour in Society*, translated by G. Simpson, p. 399.
[3] *The Elementary Forms of the Religious Life*, translated by J. W. Swain, p. 423.

true that in relation to the individual consciousness moral precepts and the sense of obligation to obey them possess an *a priori*
character, imposing themselves, as it were, from without. But the
religiously minded person's voice of God speaking through conscience and Kant's Practical Reason are really simply the voice of
society; and the sense of obligation is due to the participation
of the individual in the collective consciousness. If we are thinking
simply of the individual consciousness considered purely as such,
society speaks from without. But it also speaks from within,
inasmuch as the individual is a member of society and participates in the common consciousness or spirit.

It is obviously true that society is constantly exercising pressure
on individuals in a variety of ways. But even if it is an incontestable rule of conduct, emanating from the social consciousness,
that we should 'realize in ourselves the essential traits of the
collective type',[1] many people are likely to think that there is a
middle way between thoroughly anti-social behaviour and conformity to a common type, and that society is enriched by the
development of the individual personality. Further, many people
would be prepared to envisage cases in which the individual could
justifiably protest against the voice of society in the name of a
higher ideal. Indeed, how else can moral progress be realized?

While Durkheim insists that morality is a social phenomenon,
he does not of course see this theory as entailing social conformism
in a sense which would exclude the development of individual
personality. His view is that with the development of civilization
the collective type of ideal becomes more abstract and so admits
of a much greater degree of variety within the framework of what
is demanded by society. In a primitive society the essential traits
of the collective type are defined in a very concrete manner. The
man is expected to act according to a definite traditional pattern
of behaviour; and so is the woman. In more advanced societies
however the likenesses which are demanded between members of
the society are less than in the more homogeneous primitive tribe
or class. And if the collective type or ideal becomes that of
humanity in general, it is so abstract and general that there is
plenty of room for the development of the individual personality.
The area of personal freedom thus tends to grow as society
becomes more advanced. At the same time, if a modern industrial
society does not impose all the obligations imposed by a primitive

[1] *The Division of Labour in Society*, p. 396.

tribe, this does not alter the fact that in every case it is society which imposes the obligation.

A point which needs to be mentioned is that 'society' for Durkheim does not necessarily mean simply the State or political society, at any rate not as a completely adequate source of an ethical code. For example, in modern society a large part of human life is passed in the industrial and commercial world where ethical rules are lacking. In economically advanced societies therefore, with their highly developed specialization or division of labour, there is need for what Durkheim calls occupational ethics. 'Functional diversity induces a moral diversity that nothing can prevent.'[1] In all cases however the individual as such is subject to social pressure to act or not to act in certain ways.

It is hardly necessary to say that Durkheim is trying to turn ethics into an empirical science, treating of social facts or phenomena of a particular kind. In his view both the utilitarians and the Kantians reconstruct morality as they think it ought to be or as they would wish it to be, instead of observing carefully what it is. According to Durkheim, if we look closely at the facts, we see that social pressure or constraint exercised by the collective consciousness in regard to the individual is the chief constituent of morality. Though however he insists that the approach of the utilitarians and the Kantians is wrong, the attempt, that is to say, to find a basic principle of morality and then to proceed deductively, he also makes an effort to show that his own ethical theory comprises in itself the elements of truth contained in the theories which he attacks. For example, morality does as a matter of fact serve useful purposes within the framework of society. And its utility can be examined and ascertained. At the same time the chief characteristic of the moral consciousness is the sense of obligation which is felt as a 'categorical imperative'. The rule, imposed by society, has to be obeyed simply because it is a rule.[2] We can thus find a place for Kant's idea of duty for duty's sake, though we can also find a place for the utilitarian's concept of usefulness to society. Morality exists because society needs it; but it takes the form of the voice of society demanding obedience because it is the voice of society.

One obvious comment is that whereas Kant's idea of the

[1] *Ibid.*, p. 361.
[2] See, for example, a review-article by Durkheim in *L'année sociologique* Vol. X (1905–6), in which he discusses works by Fouillée, Belot and Landry.

categorical imperative as issuing from the practical reason provides a basis for criticizing existing moral codes, Durkheim's theory provides no such basis. If moral rules are relative to given societies, expressing the collective consciousness of a particular society, and if moral obligation means that the individual is obliged to obey the voice of society, how can the individual ever be justified in questioning the moral code or the value-judgments of the society to which he belongs? Does it not follow that moral reformers must be condemned as subversive elements? If this is not the case, how can we reasonably equate morality with the moral codes of particular societies? For the reformer appeals against such a code to something which seems to him higher or more universal.

Durkheim is not of course blind to this line of objection. He sees that he can be accused of holding that the individual must accept passively the dictates of society, whatever they may be, without ever having the right to rebel.[1] And as he has no wish to push the demand for social conformism to this point, he looks to the idea of utility to provide him with a reply. 'No fact relating to life—and this applies to moral facts—can endure if it is not of some use, if it does not answer some need.'[2] A rule which once fulfilled a useful social function may lose its usefulness as society changes and develops. Individuals who are aware of this are justified in drawing general attention to the fact. Indeed, it may not be simply a question of a particular rule of conduct. Social changes may be taking place on such a scale that what amounts to a new morality is demanded by these changes and begins to make its appearance. If then society as a whole persists in clinging to the traditional and outmoded order of morality, those who understand the process of development and its needs are justified in challenging the old dictates of society. 'We are not therefore obliged to bow to the force of moral opinion. In certain cases we are justified even in rebelling against it. ... The best way of doing so may appear to be to oppose these ideas not only theoretically but also in action.'[3]

This line of reply may be ingenious, but it is hardly adequate. If it is society which imposes obligation, obedience to the actual dictates of any given society is presumably obligatory. If however, as Durkheim allows, there can be situations in which individuals

---

[1] See, for example *Sociology and Philosophy*, translated by D. F. Pocock, pp. 59f.
[2] *The Division of Labour*, p. 35.   [3] *Sociology and Philosophy*, p. 61.

are justified in questioning, or even in rebelling against, the dictates of society, some moral criterion other than the voice of society is required. The moral reformer, it may be said, appeals from the actual voice of society, as embodied in traditional formulas, to the 'real' voice of society. But what is the criterion for assessing the 'real' voice of society, what society ought to demand as distinct from what it does demand? If it is utility, a society's real interests, one should presumably adopt utilitarianism. One is then faced however with the task of supplying a criterion for assessing a society's real interests. Referring to the possibility that a modern society might lose sight of the rights of the individual, Durkheim suggests that the society could be reminded that the denial of rights to the individual would be to deny 'the most essential interests of society itself'.[1] He might claim that this refers simply to the interests of modern European society as it has in fact developed, and not, for instance, to a closely-knit primitive clan. But even in this case one would be appealing from the actual voice of society to what one believed ought to be its voice. And it is difficult to see how normative judgments of this kind can be included in a purely descriptive study of moral phenomena.

Like morality, religion is for Durkheim essentially a social phenomenon. In one place he asserts that 'a religion is a unified system of beliefs and practices relative to sacred things, that is to say, things set apart and forbidden—beliefs and practices which unite into one single moral community, called a Church, all those who adhere to them.'[2] When Durkheim insists that 'we do not find a single religion without a Church'[3] and that 'religion is inseparable from the idea of a Church',[4] he does not mean simply a Christian Church. He means a community of persons who represent the sacred and its relation to the profane in the same way, and who translate these beliefs and ideas into common practice. Obviously, there are different beliefs and different symbols in different religions. But 'one must know how to go underneath the symbol to the reality which it represents and which gives it its meaning'.[5] We then find that religion is 'the primary form of the *collective consciousness*'.[6] Indeed, 'I see in the divinity only society transfigured and symbolically expressed'.[7]

[1] *Ibid.*, p. 60.   [2] *The Elementary Forms of the Religious Life*, p. 47.
[3] *Ibid.*, p. 44.   [4] *Ibid.*, p. 45.   [5] *Ibid.*, p. 2.
[6] *The Division of Labour in Society*, p. 285.   [7] *Sociology and Philosophy*, p. 52.

In primitive or undeveloped societies, according to Durkheim, morality was essentially religious, in the sense that man's most important and numerous duties were those towards his gods.[1] In the course of time morality has become progressively separated from religious belief, partly through the influence of Christianity with its insistence on love between human beings. The area of the sacred has diminished, and the process of secularization has advanced. Religion 'tends to embrace a smaller and smaller sector of social life'.[2] At the same time there is a sense in which religion will always persist. For society always needs to represent to itself 'the collective sentiments and the collective ideas which make its unity and its personality'.[3] If however a new faith arises, we cannot foresee the symbols which will be used to express it.

It is of course in the light of his theory of the essential nature of religion that we have to understand Durkheim's assertion that 'in reality there are no religions which are false. All are true in their own fashion; all answer, though in different ways, to the given conditions of human existence'.[4] Obviously, Durkheim does not mean to imply that all religious beliefs, if considered as statements about reality, are equally true. He is thinking of different religions as all expressing, each in its own way, a social reality. One religion can be described as superior to another if, for example, it is 'richer in ideas and sentiments' and contains 'more concepts with fewer sensations and images'.[5] But no religion can properly be described as being simply false. For even the most barbarous rites and the most fantastic myths 'translate some human need, some aspect of life, either individual or social'.[6] This is not to say that a religion is true in so far as it proves useful. It is true in so far as it expresses or represents, in its own fashion, a social reality.

Durkheim obviously considers religion from a purely sociological and external point of view. Moreover, he assumes that if we wish to ascertain the essential features of religion, we have to examine primitive or elementary religion. And this assumption is open to criticism, quite apart from the fact that some of Durkheim's theories about the origins of religion are highly disputable. For unless we assume from the start that religion is essentially

[1] See L'éducation morale, p. 6.
[2] On the Division of Labour in Society, p. 143.
[3] The Elementary Forms of the Religious Life, p. 427.
[4] Ibid., p. 3.   [5] Ibid., p. 3.   [6] Ibid., p. 2.

a primitive phenomenon, why should not its nature be better manifested in the course of its development than in its origins? Durkheim could of course argue that in primitive society religion played a much greater part in social life than it does today, and that as it is a receding phenomenon, it is only reasonable to look for its essential features at a period when it was most notably a living force. But this line of argument, though reasonable up to a point, seems to presuppose a certain idea of religion, Durkheim's idea, which represents it as the expression of the collective consciousness. Further, just as in his treatment of morality Durkheim concentrates on what Bergson describes as 'closed' morality, so in his treatment of religion does he concentrate on what Bergson describes as 'static' religion. But this is a theme which is best left to the relevant chapter on the philosophy of Bergson.

7. Though Durkheim recognized successive distinguishable mentalities and outlooks, he did not make such a sharp dichotomy between the primitive and later mentalities as to exclude a theory of the development of the former into the latter. He saw the category of causality, for example, as being first developed and employed in an essentially religious context and outlook and then as being later detached from the framework. It was Lucien Lévy-Bruhl (1857–1939) who expounded the theory that the mentality of primitive peoples was pre-logical in character.[1] He maintained, for example, that the primitive mind did not recognize the principle of non-contradiction but operated according to an implicit idea of 'participation' which allowed a thing to be itself and at the same time something other than itself. 'Primitive mentality considers and at the same time feels all beings and objects to be homogeneous, that is, it regards them all as participating in the same essential nature, or in the same ensemble of qualities.'[2] Again, the primitive mind was indifferent to empirical verification. It credited things with qualities and powers when the presence in things of these qualities and powers was in no way verified by experience. In fine, Lévy-Bruhl found a sharp distinction between the primitive mentality, which for him was essentially

---

[1] This view was expressed in *Les fonctions fondamentales dans les sociétés inférieures* (1910). Other writings in the anthropological field were *La mentalité primitive* (1921) and *L'âme primitive* (1927). Though best known as an anthropologist, Lévy-Bruhl was in fact a professor of philosophy at the Sorbonne from 1899 until 1927.
[2] *The 'Soul' of the Primitive* (*L'âme primitive*), translated by L. A. Clare (London, 1928), p. 19.

religious and even mystical, and the logical and scientific mentality. If considered in its pure state at any rate, in primitive
man that is to say, and not as surviving in co-existence with a
different emerging outlook, the former was different in kind from
the latter.

Nowadays it would be generally agreed that Durkheim was
justified in criticizing this dichotomy and Lévy-Bruhl's charac-
terization of primitive mentality as 'pre-logical'. In many ways
the world of primitive man was doubtless very different from ours,
and he had many beliefs which we do not share. But it does not
follow that his natural logic was entirely heterogeneous from
ours, as Lévy-Bruhl at first asserted.

In 1903 Lévy-Bruhl published *La morale et la science des
moeurs*.[1] Like Durkheim, he aimed at contributing to the development of a science of morals, something which had to be carefully
distinguished from morals itself. Morality is a social fact and needs
no philosopher to bring it into being. But the philosopher can
examine this social fact. He then finds that it is a case of facts
rather than of a fact. That is to say, in every society there is a set
of moral rules, an ethical code, relative to that society. A theoretical and abstract system, elaborated by a philosopher, bears
as little resemblance to the actual ethical phenomena as does an
abstract philosophical religion to the historic religions of mankind. If a philosopher works out an abstract ethical system and
describes it as 'natural ethics', the ethics of man as such, this is a
misnomer. 'The idea of a "natural ethics", ought to give way to
the idea that all existing ethics are natural.'[2] What we need to do
first is to ascertain the historical data in the field of morals. It
should then be possible, on the basis of positive knowledge so
gained, to develop some guidelines for the future. But the result
would be an empirically based art rather than an abstract or ideal
system of ethics as conceived by some philosophers in the past.

The task of collecting historical data is hardly the business of
the philosopher as such. And it is arguable that the task of seeing
what practical use can be made of the knowledge obtained in this
way can perfectly well be performed by the sociologist. It might
therefore be suggested that if Lévy-Bruhl rejected, as he did, the
idea of elaborating an abstract ethical system, he might have done
well, if he wished to act as a philosopher, to concentrate on the

---

[1] Translated as *Ethics and Moral Science* by E. Lee (London, 1905).
[2] *Ethics and Moral Science*, p. 160.

analysis of ethical concepts and language. To a certain extent both he and Durkheim provided such analyses. But the analyses really consisted in giving a naturalistic interpretation of ethical terms. Lévy-Bruhl occupied a chair of philosophy; but he was primarily an anthropologist and a sociologist.

CHAPTER VII

NEO-CRITICISM AND IDEALISM

Cournot and inquiry into basic concepts—The neo-criticism and personalism of Renouvier—Hamelin and idealist metaphysics—Brunschvicg and the mind's reflection on its own activity.

1. It would be misleading to refer to thinkers such as Cournot and Renouvier as representing a neo-Kantian movement in nineteenth-century philosophical thought in France. For this way of speaking would imply a closer connection with and a greater dependence on the thought of Kant than was actually present. Renouvier, it is true, liked to regard himself as Kant's true successor and described his own thought as neo-criticism. But he attacked some of Kant's cherished theories; and though there were indeed features of his thought which justified its description as neo-criticism, there were other features which would make personalism a more appropriate label. As for Cournot, he did indeed conduct a critical inquiry into the role of reason and into certain basic concepts and has been described as a critical rationalist; but he rejected Kant's Copernican revolution and has therefore been sometimes described as a critical realist. To perpetrate a tautology, Cournot was Cournot. He was neither a Kantian nor a Comtean.

Antoine Augustin Cournot (1801–77) was a distinguished mathematician and economist who was also a philosopher. After preliminary studies, partly at a school in his native town of Gray near Dijon and partly alone, he entered the École Normale Supérieure at Paris with a view to continuing his studies in mathematics. In 1823 he became secretary to Marshal Saint-Cyr and tutor to the latter's son. After the Marshal's death Cournot held a post at Paris until he was appointed professor of analysis and mechanics at Lyon. Shortly afterwards however he was appointed head of the Academy at Grenoble, a post which he combined with that of inspector general of public education, until confirmation in this second post led to his taking up his abode in Paris in 1838. His published writings were in the fields of mathematics, mechanics, economics, education and philosophy. He contributed to the application of mathematics to economics. In the philosophical area he published in 1843 an *Exposition de la théorie des chances et des probabilités* (*Exposition of the Theory of Chance and of Probability*). This was followed in 1851 by his *Essai sur les fondements de nos connaissances et sur les caractères de la critique philosophique*.[1] In 1861 Cournot published a *Traité de l'enchaînement des idées fondamentales dans les sciences et dans l'histoire* (*Treatise on the Connection between the Fundamental Ideas of the Sciences and of History*). In 1872 there appeared his *Considérations sur la marche des idées et des événements dans les temps modernes* (*Reflections on the Movement of Ideas and Events in Modern Times*) and in 1875 *Matérialisme, vitalisme, rationalisme: Études sur l'emploi des données de la science en philosophie* (*Materialism, Vitalism, Rationalism: Studies on the Use of the Data of Science in Philosophy*).

Cournot was not at all the man to think that philosophy could profitably pursue an isolated path of its own, without reference to the development of the sciences. 'Philosophy without science soon loses sight of our real relations with the Universe.'[2] Philosophy needs to feed, so to speak, on science. At the same time Cournot resolutely refused to regard philosophy either as a particular science or as a synthesis of the sciences. In his view science and philosophy were interrelated in a variety of ways; they were none the less distinguishable. And because they were distinct lines of inquiry, there was no good reason for thinking that the progress of science entailed the gradual disappearance of philosophy.

While recognizing that 'innumerable meanings'[3] have been given to the term 'philosophy' in popular usage and by philosophers themselves, Cournot regards philosophy as having two essential functions, 'on the one hand the study and investigation of the reason of things and, on the other hand, the study of the forms of thought and of the general laws and processes of the human mind'.[4] By the reason of things Cournot means, in general, rational or intelligible interconnection; and he makes a distinction between reason and cause. Consider, for example, the Russian revolution. Obviously, a multitude of causal actions were involved. But to understand the Russian revolution we have to find an intelligible structure connecting all these causes and events. And if we decide that the reason for the revolution was the unyielding

---

[1] Translated by M. M. Moore as *An Essay on the Foundations of Our Knowledge* (New York, 1956). As the work is divided into consecutively numbered sections, references will be given as *Essai* followed by the number of the relevant section.
[2] *Essai*, section 323.   [3] *Ibid.*, section 325.   [4] *Ibid.*, section 325.

autocratic constitution or régime, we are not talking about an efficient cause in the sense in which, for instance, a certain action by one man is the efficient cause of injury to another. The reason explains the series of causes. It answers the question 'why did these events take place'? The reason of things is thus akin to Leibniz's sufficient reason, though Cournot, who greatly admired Leibniz, remarks that the word 'sufficient' is superfluous. An insufficient reason would not be the reason of things.

When Cournot says that 'the search for the explanation and the reason of things is what characterizes philosophical curiosity, no matter what the order of facts to which it is applied',[1] he is thinking of an objective reason, of something which is there to be discovered. But it is of course the human reason, subjective reason, which seeks to grasp the objective reason. And subjective reason can reflect on its own activity. It can be concerned with 'the evaluation of certain regulative and fundamental ideas or with criticism of their representative value'.[2] Critical inquiry of this sort is the second function of philosophy. But the two functions are closely interrelated. For example, the human reason, according to Cournot, is regulated by the idea of order, in the sense that order is what reason seeks to find and what it can recognize when found. In fact, reason is guided by the idea of the perfection of order, inasmuch as it compares possible arrangements of phenomena and prefers that which best satisfies its idea of what constitutes order. At the same time the mind does not simply impose order on phenomena: it discovers it. And it is in the light of such discovery that reason can evaluate its own regulative idea. Cournot likes to quote Bossuet to the effect that only reason can introduce order into things, and that order can be understood only by reason. When the two sides, the subjective and the objective, are in accord, there is knowledge.

Cournot is therefore not prepared to accept the theory that the mind simply imposes order on what is in itself without order or that it simply projects into things their 'reasons'.[3] There is a marked element of realism in his thought. He insists, for example, that whatever Kant may have said Newtonian physics 'implies the existence of time, space and geometrical relations outside the

---

[1] *Ibid.*, section 26.   [2] *Ibid.*, section 325.
[3] The ideas of order and of the reason of things are for Cournot closely related. Indeed, the two ideas are 'the same idea under two different aspects'. *Essai*, section 396.

mind'.[1] At the same time he maintains both that what we know are the relations between phenomena, and that our knowledge of these relations is never absolute but always revisible in principle. When the astronomer, for example, tries to determine the movements of the heavenly bodies, he is certainly concerned with objective knowledge; but the knowledge which he obtains is relative in several ways. For instance, the movements which he establishes are relative to a certain system; and he cannot determine absolute points of reference in space. The astronomer's knowledge is real and relative at the same time. It is subject to revision. Our hypotheses can possess varying degrees of probability; but they do not amount to absolute knowledge, even when they produce the subjective feeling of certainty.

The concept of probability is, like that of order, one of the basic ideas discussed by Cournot. He makes a distinction between mathematical probability and probability in a general sense or what he calls philosophical probability. The former is concerned with objective possibility and is described as 'the limit of *physical possibility*',[2] whereas in the case of the latter the grounds of our preference are not amenable to precise mathematical formulation. Suppose that we are confronted with three *prima facie* explanations of a phenomenon or set of phenomena. It may be that we can rule out one of them as mathematically impossible. In deciding however between the other two we introduce criteria which are not amenable to exact mathematical treatment. Moreover, even if we succeed in falsifying empirically one of the hypotheses and therefore feel subjectively certain about the truth of the other, it may be that further developments in scientific knowledge will demand revision. Apart from matters of purely logical or mathematical demonstration, we have to rely on 'variable, subjective probability'.[3] In formulating a law of phenomena, for example, reason refers to certain criteria, such as simplicity, and the mind may feel certain that it has found the law. But this feeling of certainty does not alter the fact that what we judge to be more probable depends on the limited extent of our present knowledge and thus on a variable factor.

According to Cournot therefore reason seeks and finds order in the world, even if its knowledge of the order or reason of things is not absolute. Cournot's world however also contains fortuitous events, the result of the operation of chance. And this idea needs

[1] *Ibid.*, section 142. [2] *Ibid.*, section 35. [3] *Ibid.*, section 51.

some explanation. By a chance event Cournot does not mean a rare or surprising event. It might of course be rare or surprising, but these characteristics are not included in the meaning of the term. Nor does Cournot mean a causeless event. 'Everything that we call an event must have a cause.'[1] A chance event is one which is brought about by the conjunction of other events which belong to independent series.[2] A simple example given by Cournot himself is that of a Parisian who takes a train to a destination in the country. There is a railway accident, and the Parisian is among the victims. The accident has of course its cause or causes; but the operation of these causes has nothing to do with the presence of the particular Parisian on the train. The accident would have occurred even if he had decided at the last moment to stay in the city instead of going to the country. In this sense his being killed or injured is a fortuitous event, resulting from the conjunction of two series of causes which were originally independent of each other.

Chance in this sense is for Cournot an objective or real feature of the world. That is to say, it is not something which is simply dependent on and relative to the limitations of our knowledge.[3] 'It is not accurate to say, as Hume does, that "chance is only our ignorance of real causes".'[4] In principle the mind, by using the calculus of probabilities, could foretell possible conjunctions of independent series of causes. And a superhuman intelligence could do so to a greater extent than we can. This does not show however that chance events are law-governed, or that it would be possible to foretell with certainty actual events due to the conjunction of independent series of causes. In other words, for Cournot, as for Boutroux after him, contingency is a metaphysical reality, in the sense that there is in the universe an irreducible element of indeterminacy. Not even in principle could estimation of the probability of possible events in the future be converted into complete objective certitude.

Though Cournot argues that there are certain basic concepts, such as order, which are common to the sciences, he also insists that actual examination of and reflection on the sciences shows us

---

[1] *Ibid.*, section 29.

[2] It is for Cournot a matter of common sense that there are independent or only externally related series of events. *Ibid.*, section 30.

[3] The idea of chance as an objective factor in the universe is found also in the philosophy of C. S. Peirce in America. See Vol. 8 of this *History*, pp. 323 f.

[4] *Essai*, section 36.

that different sciences have to introduce different basic concepts. It is therefore impossible to reduce all sciences to one science, such as physics. For example, it is the behaviour of the living organism which excludes the possibility of accounting for it simply in terms of the physico-chemical elements of the constituent parts or elements, and which forces us to introduce the idea of a vital energy or plastic force. This concept and its implications are not indeed altogether clear. We cannot suppose that life precedes organic structure and produces it. But neither can we suppose that organic-structure precedes life. We have to assume that 'in organic and living beings organic structure and life play simultaneously the roles of cause and effect through a reciprocity of relations',[1] which is *sui generis*. And though a term such as vital or plastic force 'does not give the mind an idea which can be clearly defined',[2] it expresses a recognition of the irreducibility of the living to the non-living.

This irreducibility implies of course that in the process of evolution there is emergence of what is new, of what cannot be described simply in terms of that out of which it emerges. It does not follow however that evolution is for Cournot a continuous process, in the sense that it takes the form of a linear series of ascending levels of perfection. In Cournot's view evolution takes the form of distinct creative impulses or movements, in accordance with a kind of rhythm of relative activity and rest; and in his *Traité* he anticipates Bergson's idea of divergent paths or directions of development. As however he is sharply opposed, like Bergson after him, to any purely mechanistic interpretation of evolution, he regards it as legitimate for the philosopher to think in terms of finality and of a creative divine intelligence. This does not mean that after asserting the reality of chance as a factor in the Universe Cournot then goes on to reject this idea and to represent the universe as rational through and through. We have seen that for him the concept of order which regulates the mind's inquiries is not simply a subjective form of thought which reason imposes on phenomena but also represents what the mind discovers. Both order and chance are real factors in the universe. And reason is justified in extending the concept of order into the sphere of 'trans-rationalism', provided that it is not used in such a way as to be incompatible with the idea of chance. In Cournot's view the reality of chance 'is not in conflict with the generally

---

[1] *Essai*, section 129.   [2] *Ibid.*, section 130.

accepted idea of a supreme and providential direction',[1] not at
any rate if we avoid implying that all events are caused by God.
Cournot's positive contribution to philosophical thought consists primarily in his critical inquiry into basic concepts, whether
those which he regards as common to the sciences or those which
particular sciences find it necessary to introduce if they are to
develop and to handle their subject-matter satisfactorily. It is
this aspect of his thought which justifies treatment of it under the
general heading of critical philosophy or 'neo-criticism'. But
though he approaches this theme through an inquiry into the
sciences, we have seen that he insists on the distinction between
science and philosophy. For one thing, 'the intuitions of the philosophers precede the organization of positive science.'[2] For another
thing, the mind can let itself be guided by 'the presentiment of a
perfection and harmony in the works of nature'[3] which is superior
to anything discovered by the sciences. The mind can thus pass
into the field of speculative philosophy, a field in which it crosses
the boundaries of formal demonstration and of scientific testing
and in which it has to rely on 'philosophical' probability which is
not amenable to mathematical treatment. This field of trans-
rationalism is not excluded by science; and though it goes beyond
science, we have to remember that scientific hypotheses themselves cannot be more than probably true.

2. In comparison with his contribution in the field of economics
Cournot's philosophical writing was at first largely neglected.
He worked patiently at a number of problems, avoiding extreme
positions and not allowing himself to be distracted by temporarily
fashionable lines of thought. Moreover, though he rejected the
positivist exclusion of metaphysics, he did not himself present
any striking metaphysical vision of the universe. He hinted, it is
true, at possible lines of thought; but it was left to other philosophers, such as Bergson, to develop them in a manner which aroused
general interest. Nowadays Cournot is respected for his careful
critical analysis; but it is easy to understand how Renouvier,
who was influenced to a certain extent by Cournot, came to make
a greater impression on his contemporaries.

Charles Bernard Renouvier (1815–1903) was born at Montpellier, the birthplace of Auguste Comte, and when he entered the
Ecole Polytechnique at Paris he found Comte there acting as
instructor in mathematics. Renouvier never occupied an academic

---

[1] *Ibid.*, section 36.   [2] *Traité*, I, section 226.   [3] *Essai*, section 71.

position, but he was a prolific writer. He began by publishing several manuals, on modern and ancient philosophy in 1842 and 1844 respectively[1] and in 1848 a *Republican Handbook on Man and the Citizen*.[2] At this time Renouvier was strongly influenced by the ideas of Saint-Simon and other French socialists, and the last named work was intended for schoolteachers. His republican convictions suffered a severe blow when Napoleon III made himself emperor, and he gave himself to philosophical reflection and writing. In 1872 however Renouvier started a periodical entitled *Critique philosophique*, and in its first years it included a good many articles of a political nature, aimed at supporting the restored republic. Later this periodical became *L'année philosophique*, edited in collaboration with F. Pillon.

Renouvier's first major philosophical publication was his four-volume *Essais de critique générale* (1854–64). This work impressed William James, who remained an admirer of Renouvier and contributed a number of philosophical articles to his periodical. In 1869 Renouvier wrote a two-volume work on the science of morals, *La science de la morale*, and in 1876 a sketch of what might have been, but was not, the historical development of European civilization, to which he gave the title *Uchronie*.[3] In 1866 there appeared a two-volume *Esquisse d'une classification systématique des doctrines philosophiques* (*Outline of a Systematic Classification of Philosophical Doctrines*), and in 1901 two works on metaphysics, *Les dilemmes de la métaphysique pure* and *Histoire et solution des problèmes métaphysiques*.[4] Renouvier's book on personalism[5] was published in 1903, and his well known work on Kant, *Critique de la doctrine de Kant*, was brought out in 1906 by his friend Louis Prat.

In the preface to his *Essais de critique générale* Renouvier announced his acceptance of one basic principle of positivism, namely the restriction of knowledge to the laws of phenomena. Though however he was prepared to assert his agreement with Comte on this point, the philosophy which he developed was certainly not positivism. As has already been mentioned, Renouvier liked to describe it as 'neo-criticism'. But while he clearly

---

[1] *Manuel de philosophie moderne* and *Manuel de philosophie ancienne*.
[2] *Manuel républicain de l'homme et du citoyen*.
[3] The full title is *Uchronie, l'utopie dans l'histoire. Esquisse historique du développement de la civilisation européenne, tel qu'il n'a pas été, tel qu'il aurait pu être*.
[4] *The Dilemmas of Pure Metaphysics* and *History and Solution of Metaphysical Problems*.
[5] *Le personnalisme, suivi d'une étude sur la perception externe et sur la force*.

derived stimulus from Kant, in the introduction to his work on the
German philosopher he roundly stated that he was concerned
primarily not with exposition but with 'a critique of the Kantian
Critique.'[1] The fact of the matter is that he used Kant's thought
in developing his own personalist philosophy.

In Renouvier's eyes one of the most objectionable features of
Kant's philosophy was the theory of the thing-in-itself. Kant
assumed that the phenomenon was the appearance of something
other than itself. But as this something other was on Kant's own
view unknowable, it was simply a superfluous fiction, like Locke's
substance.[2] It does not follow however that because phenomena
are not appearances of unknowable things-in-themselves, they are
for Renouvier simply subjective impressions. They are all that we
can perceive and all about which we can make judgments. In
other words, the phenomenal and the real are the same.[3]

Another feature of the Kantian philosophy attacked by Renouvier is the theory of antimonies.[4] Kant believed, for example,
that it could be both proved and disproved that the world had a
beginning in time and that space is limited or finite. Renouvier
saw in this thesis a flagrant disregard of the principle of non-
contradiction. This verdict rather misses the point. For Kant was
not concerned with denying the principle of non-contradiction. He
was concerned with arguing that if the human mind pursued the
path of 'dogmatic' metaphysics and claimed to know the world as
a whole, it became involved in antimonies which showed that the
claim was bogus and that metaphysics of the traditional kind was
a pseudo-science. Renouvier however was not prepared to accept
Kant's dismissal of metaphysics. And in regard to the particular
points at issue he maintained that it could be proved that an
infinite series of phenomena was impossible, on the ground that it
involved the contradictory idea of an infinite number,[5] that space
must be limited or finite, and that the contrary theses could be

---

[1] *Doctrine de Kant*, p. 3.
[2] Renouvier collaborated with F. Pillon in translating Hume's *Treatise of
Human Nature* into French; and he thought that Hume was right in eliminating
the concept of substance as expounded by Locke.
[3] The word 'phenomenon' tends to suggest, as Renouvier admits, the idea of
the appearance of a reality which does not itself appear. But for Renouvier the
phenomenon is simply the thing as appearing or as capable of appearing.
[4] See Vol. VI of this *History*, pp. 286 f.
[5] If we like to look back to medieval philosophy ,we can say that Renouvier
was at one with St. Bonaventure, who maintained that the impossibility of an
infinite series could be demonstrated. See Vol. II of this *History*, pp. 262–5 and
366–7.

decisively disproved. In other words, no antimony arose, as only one of the opposed theses could be proved, not both as Kant thought.

Though however Renouvier criticizes Kant pretty sharply in regard to important features of the latter's philosophy, he associates his own doctrine of categories with Kant's, at any rate to the extent that he offers his own doctrine as an improvement on that of the German philosopher. For Renouvier the basic and most general or abstract of all categories is that of relation, inasmuch as nothing at all can be known except as related. Renouvier then proceeds to add the categories of number, position, succession, quality, becoming, causality, finality or purposiveness and personality, the movement being from the most abstract to the most concrete. It is evident that Renouvier's list of categories differs from Kant's. Further, no attempt is made to deduce the categories *a priori* by a transcendental method. As with Cournot, Renouvier's categories are based on or derived from experience. The connection with Kant is thus pretty loose. But this does not alter the fact that Renouvier derived some stimulus from Kant and liked to think of himself as Kant's true successor.

Similarly, we can see a connection between Kant's theory of faith as based on the practical reason or moral will and Renouvier's idea of the role played by the will in belief, an idea which appealed to William James. Here again however the connection is a loose one, being a matter of stimulus rather than of Renouvier actually adopting a Kantian doctrine. Kant made a sharp distinction between the sphere of theoretical knowledge and that of practical or moral faith; and this distinction presupposed that between the phenomenon and the noumenon. As Renouvier rejected this second distinction, it is not surprising that he refused to admit any sharp division between knowledge and belief. 'The Kantian separation between the speculative reason and the practical reason is an illusion.'[1] In the second *Essai* Renouvier insisted that certitude always involves an element of belief, and that belief involves the will to believe. This is applicable even to the *Cogito, ergo sum* of Descartes. For an act of the will is required to unite the I-subject and the me-object in the assertion of personal existence.

What Renouvier does is to extend the scope of Kant's account

---

[1] *Doctrine de Kant*, p. 164.

of practical faith beyond the sphere to which Kant confines it. The objection then arises that nothing much is being said. For example, suppose that I maintain that the will to believe enters even into science. And suppose that I then go on to explain that what I mean is that the scientist's activity rests on an act of choice, that he wills to embrace the hypothesis which seems to him most probable or most likely to prove fruitful in a scientific context, and that the actual decision to adopt an hypothesis which is in principle revisible involves an act of the will. The comment might be made that what I say is true, but that it has little to do with the will to believe in the sense in which this idea has given rise to objections. When however Renouvier rejects Kant's sharp division between the theoretical and practical uses of reason, he is claiming that in all knowledge there is a personal element, an intervention of the will. In other words, he is developing a theory of knowledge in the light of a personalist philosophy. We have seen that for him personality is the most concrete of the basic categories. And he insists that in the activity of the human person no absolute dichotomy between reason and will can legitimately be made, though in this or that sphere of activity there may be of course a predominance of reason or of will or of feeling. In the ethical field this personalist approach shows itself in Renouvier's disapproval of Kant's tendency to think that an action has moral worth in proportion as it is performed simply and solely out of a sense of obligation and without regard to inclination and feeling. As moral action is the expression of the whole person, duty and feeling, for Renouvier, should ideally accompany one another.

Sometimes Renouvier refers to phenomena in a quite general way, as when he maintains that phenomena and the relations between them constitute the objects of human knowledge. At the same time he insists that there are irreducible levels of reality, culminating in the level of personality. Man can of course try to interpret himself exclusively in terms of categories or concepts which are applicable at a non-human level. This attempt is possible because, while the mind cannot conceive any phenomenon except in terms of the basic category of relation, there is room for choice in the selection of more determinate categories. Though possible however, attempts at reductionism are bound to fail. For example, freedom is a datum of consciousness. While rejecting Kant's notion of man as noumenally free and phenomenally determined and insisting that man is free as a phenomenon,[1] Renouvier agrees with Kant in associating awareness of freedom with the moral consciousness. The possibilities of choice and action are of course limited in various ways. The moral agent, 'capable of contraries, does not cease from being circumscribed within a static or dynamic order of relations.'[2] But though the area of freedom should not be exaggerated, morality cannot be understood unless we conceive freedom as an attribute of the human person. Freedom is indeed a datum of the moral consciousness rather than something which can be demonstrated. For Renouvier however determinism cannot be held without the determinist involving himself in the absurdity of claiming that the man who asserts freedom is determined to assert that he sees himself to be free.

When Renouvier talks about the free moral agent, it is of course the individual person of whom he is speaking.[3] In the philosophical area he has no use for Spinozism or for theories of the Absolute as found in post-Kantian German idealism or, in general, for any philosophical theory which represents individuals as moments in the life of the One. His dislike for such theories extends to any form of positivism which represents history as a necessary process subject to a law or laws and, in the theological sphere, to beliefs which seem to him to make human beings puppets of a divine universal causality. In the political field Renouvier is vehemently opposed to any political theory which depicts the State as a subsistent entity over and above its members He is not indeed an anarchist. But the desirable society is for him one which is founded on respect for the individual person as a free moral agent. The State is not itself a person or a moral agent: it is a name for individuals organized in certain ways and acting collectively. In his work on the science of morals Renouvier lays emphasis on the fictional character of such concepts as 'the nation'[4] and he insists that if the State is regarded as a subsistent entity,

---

[1] In Renouvier's opinion this attempt to have things both ways is another example of Kant's neglect of the principle of non-contradiction. As for Renouvier's insistence that man is free as a phenomenon, it must be remembered that by this he means that man as we experience him is free. He is not of course thinking in terms of the Kantian distinction between phenomenon and thing-in-itself, which, as we have seen, he rejects.

[2] *Essais*, II, p. 466.

[3] Like Leibniz, Renouvier had an acute sense of differentiation. And in 1899 he published, in collaboration with L. Prat, a work entitled *The New Monadology* (*La nouvelle monadologie*).

[4] *La science de la morale*, II, chapter 96.

the conclusion will be drawn either that there is one morality for the State and another for the individual or that the State stands above the ethical sphere. The moral order can be built up only by persons acting together or in concert; but it is by individual persons that it is constructed and maintained, not by a fictional super-person.

As the title of his work *La science de la morale* clearly implies, Renouvier believes that there can be a science of ethics. For this to be possible there must of course be moral phenomena. And inasmuch as science is concerned with relations between phenomena, we might perhaps expect that he would confine the sphere of morality to relations between different persons. But this is not in fact the case. In Renouvier's opinion the concept of rights has meaning only within a social context. Rights as a moral phenomenon arise only in society. But though a man has rights only in relation to his fellows, and though in a social context rights and duties are correlative, the concept of duty is for Renouvier more fundamental than that of rights. It would be absurd to speak of an entirely isolated individual as possessing rights; but he would have moral duties. For in every individual there is a relation between what he is and his higher or ideal self, and he is under an obligation to realize this higher self in his character and conduct. Renouvier thus agrees with Kant that obligation is the basic moral phenomenon; but he distinguishes various aspects of obligation. There is obligation on the part of the will to be in conformity with the ideal (*devoir-être*); there is obligation on the part of persons to perform their duty (*devoir-faire*); and one can also say that certain things ought to be (*devoir-être*), through human agency that is to say.[1] In society the concept of justice arises and becomes effective; and justice demands respect for the value and rights of other persons who, as Kant maintained, should not be used simply as means to the attainment of one's own ends.

As Renouvier insisted on personality as the highest category and on the value of the human person, it is natural that he should be opposed not only to any exaltation of the State but also to dogmatism and authoritarianism in the religious sphere. He was a strong anti-clerical and a supporter of secular education;[2] and for a time he published an anti-Catholic supplement (*La critique*

---

[1] *La science de la morale*, I, p. 10.
[2] In 1879 Renouvier published a *Little Treatise on Morals for the Secular Schools* (*Petit traité de morale pour les écoles laïques*).

religieuse) to his philosophical periodical. Renouvier was not however an atheist. He regarded reflection on the moral consciousness as opening the way to and as rendering legitimate, thought not as logically entailing, belief in God. And he insisted that God must be conceived in terms of man's highest category, and so as personal. At the same time Renouvier's conviction that recognition of the existence of evil was incompatible with belief in an infinitely good, omnipotent and omniscient Deity led him to conceive of God as finite or limited. It was only this concept, he believed, which could allow for man's creative freedom and responsibility.

It has been said of Renouvier that he was the philosopher of radicalism and that he combined the outlook of the Enlightenment and the revolution's ideal of liberty with themes which reappeared in the spiritualist movement in French thought, while employing the Kantian philosophy to sever the link between these themes and traditional metaphysics. And there is doubtless truth in this view. It is significant however that the last work which he himself published was entitled *Personalism*. As has already been noted, Renouvier described his philosophy as neocriticism. And in the posthumously published *Last Conversations* he is recorded as referring to a study of the categories as being the key to everything. But it is arguable that what most attracted Renouvier in Kant's thought were its personalist elements. And it was his own personalism which determined his attitude to German metaphysical idealism,[1] to Comte's idea of history as governed by a law, to determinism, to traditional theology, to the Catholic Church as he saw it, to deification of the State on the one hand and to communist ideas and projects on the other.

3. It is customary to describe Octave Hamelin (1856–1907) as a disciple of Renouvier. Indeed, this was the way in which he described himself. He dedicated his main work, an *Essay on the Principal Elements of Representation* (*Essai sur les éléments principaux de la représentation*, 1907) to Renouvier; and in his posthumously published book *The System of Renouvier*[2] he asserted that this system had been for him 'the object of long meditations'.[3] Though however Renouvier's neo-criticism certainly exercised a considerable influence on Hamelin, the latter,

---

[1] The reference is of course to doctrines of the Absolute.
[2] *Le système de Renouvier*, edited by P. Mouy (1927).
[3] *Le système de Renouvier*, p. 2.

who became a professor at the Sorbonne, used Renouvier's thought as a point of departure for his own thinking. He was not a disciple in the sense of someone who simply adopts, continues and defends the master's system. For the matter of that, Hamelin was influenced by other thinkers too, such as Jules Lachelier (1832–1918), whose philosophy will be considered in connection with the so-called spiritualist movement in French thought.

It would be untrue to say that in his theory of categories Renouvier simply juxtaposed a number of basic concepts without any serious attempt to exhibit their mutual relations. For he tried to show that the other categories, culminating in that of personality, were progressively more concrete specifications of the most abstract and universal category, namely relation. Further, he represented each category as a synthesis between a thesis and an antithesis. Number, for example, was said to be a synthesis of unity and plurality. In other words, Renouvier attempted a dialectical deduction of the categories. In Hamelin's opinion however Renouvier's procedure was insufficiently systematic. What was needed was to develop a systematic dialectical construction of the categories in such a way that they would together constitute a complete system. In this way 'M. Renouvier's table of categories would develop into a completely rational system'.[1] The more systematic thought becomes, the more complete it is.

Like Renouvier, Hamelin begins with the category of relation, which he tries to establish in this way. It is a primitive fact of thought that 'everything *posited* excludes an *opposited*, that every *thesis* leaves outside itself an *antithesis*, and that the two opposed factors have meaning only in so far as they are mutually exclusive.'[2] To this primitive fact however we must add another which completes it. As the opposed factors receive their meaning precisely through their mutual opposition, they form two parts of one whole. This synthesis is a relation. 'Thesis, antithesis and synthesis, here is the simplest law of things in its three phases. We shall call it by the single word *relation*.'[3]

Having established, to his satisfaction, the basic category of relation, Hamelin proceeds to deduce that of number. In what he describes as relation the two opposed factors, the thesis and antithesis, exist in mutual opposition. It can therefore be said that the one needs the other in order to exist. At the same time the inability of the one to exist without the other implies that in some way

---

[1] *Système de Renouvier*, p. 114.   [2] *Essai*, p. 1.   [3] *Ibid.*, p. 2.

(*en quelque façon*) the one must exist without the other, in the manner, that is to say, which is compatible with, or indeed necessitated by, their mutual opposition. And 'number is the relation in which one posits that the one is without the other'.[1] We cannot follow Hamelin through his whole deduction of the categories. Nor indeed would it be very profitable to do so. The list or table differs somewhat from Renouvier's. For example, the category of time is deduced before that of space. Both men however begin with relation and end with personality. According to Hamelin the category of personality is the synthesis of causality (efficient causality that is to say) and of finality, the synthesis taking the form of being existing for itself. To exist for oneself is to be conscious. 'The for-itself or consciousness: such is the synthesis to which we aspired.'[2] Inasmuch as all the other categories are progressively more concrete specifications of the most abstract category of relation, the final category must be itself a relation. Further, as final it must be a relation which does not give rise to or demand any further category. These conditions are fulfilled in consciousness, which is 'the synthesis of the ego and the non-ego, the reality outside which the one and the other possess existence only in an abstract sense'.[3]

Hamelin's approach to the deduction of the categories is, as he intended, much more *a priori* and rationalistic than Renouvier's. And the influence of German idealism is clear. Hamelin presents us with a series of categories which are supposed to constitute a complete and self-contained system in which, in a real sense, beginning and end coincide. 'The two extremes of the hierarchy are doubtless demonstrated the one by the other, but not in the same manner. The more simple derives from the more complex by a series of analyses: the more complex superimposes itself necessarily on the more simple by a series of syntheses.'[4] In other words, it is possible to start with self-consciousness or personality and proceed backwards, so to speak, by a process of analysis from the more complex and concrete to the more simple and abstract. And it is also possible to start with the most abstract and simple category and let the system develop itself towards the more complex and concrete through the dialectical process of thesis, antithesis and synthesis.

The question arises whether Hamelin regards himself as concerned simply with the deduction of human forms of representation,

[1] *Ibid.*, p. 31.   [2] *Ibid.*, p. 266.   [3] *Ibid.*, p. 267.   [4] *Ibid.*, p. 15.

with human ways of conceiving things-in-themselves which
are independent of consciousness. The answer is in the negative.
'The thing-in-itself can only be a fiction, because the idea of it is
self-contradictory.'[1] The non-ego exists only in relation to the ego,
for consciousness that is to say. If it seems to follow from this
view that the world consists of relations, this does not deter
Hamelin. 'The world is a hierarchy of relations. . . .'[2] it is constituted 'not of things but of relations'.[3] Representation is not a
mirror. It 'does not reflect an object and a subject which would
exist without it; it is object and subject, it is reality itself. Representation is being, and being is representation.'[4] In other words,
mind or spirit is the Absolute. This last term would indeed be
inappropriate, if it were understood as referring to an ultimate
reality beyond all relations. 'But if by absolute one understands
that which contains in itself all relations, we must say that Mind
is the absolute.'[5]

Hamelin does not of course intend to assert that the whole
world is the content of my consciousness, in the sense that it
exists solely in relation to myself as this particular subject. Some
might wish to argue that from a logical point of view idealism of
this kind cannot avoid solipsism. For him the subject-object relation falls within the Absolute. What he is claiming is that reality
is the dialectical unfolding of thought or consciousness through a
hierarchy of grades. And his insistence that the dialectical advance
from the more simple and abstract to the more complex and concrete is 'synthetic' rather than purely 'analytic' leaves room for a
theory of creative emergent evolution, provided that the process
is interpreted in an idealist sense, as the development of consciousness. Hamelin therefore denies that consciousness must
always mean clear consciousness, 'that of which the psychologists
ordinarily speak.'[6] We must allow for 'an indefinite extension of
consciousness'.[7] As Leibniz maintained, every being perceives or
mirrors the whole; 'and this sort of consciousness suffices.'[8]
Reflective consciousness represents a level which is reached only
through the progressive development of mind or spirit.[9]

This may sound as though Hamelin is simply claiming that we
can look on reality as a unified process whereby potential con-

[1] *Système de Renouvier*, p. 50.   [2] *Essai, p.* 15.   [3] *Ibid.*, p. 272.
[4] *Ibid.*, p. 279.   [5] *Ibid.*, p. 363.   [6] *Ibid.*, p. 269.
[7] *Ibid.*, p. 269.   [8] *Ibid.*, p. 269.
[9] Like the German term *Geist*, the French term *esprit* is difficult to translate.
Both 'mind' and 'spirit' have their drawbacks.

sciousness is progressively actualized. In point of fact however he tries to combine his idealism with theism. 'God, it goes without saying, is the spirit in which we have not hesitated to recognize the absolute.'[1] In other words, the Absolute is personal. In Leibnizian language, the existence of God, as absolute spirit, is a truth of reason; but the divine goodness, according to Hamelin, is a truth of fact. That is to say, 'it was not, it could not be necessary that the absolute spirit should become absolute goodness. . . . In the field of possibility there was offered to the spirit, besides absolute goodness, the vista (*perspective*) of some erroneous perversity such as that which pessimism torments itself by imagining.'[2] Like Schelling, Hamelin thinks of God as willing goodness freely, and of the divine freedom being reflected in man's capacity to choose good or evil.[3]

In some respects Hamelin's idealism has an obvious affinity with that of Hegel. But he does not seem to have made any prolonged study of Hegel's philosophy; and he appears to have regarded the Hegelian Absolute in much the same way as Hegel himself had regarded Schelling's theory of the Absolute in his so-called 'system of identity'. That is to say, Hamelin interpreted Hegel as maintaining that no positive terms could be predicated of the Absolute, with the result that, as far as our knowledge was concerned, the Absolute would be a void, the night in which all cows are black as Hegel sarcastically remarked with reference to Schelling's theory of the Absolute as the vanishing-point of all differences. Hamelin's interpretation of Hegel is clearly disputable. But it is understandable that Hamelin insists on the personal character of the Absolute. For he follows Renouvier in regarding personality as the highest category and as the developed form of the abstract category of relation. On Hamelin's premises, if the Absolute is the totality, the all-embracing relation, it must be personal. At any rate this description is entailed by his premises even if it is difficult to see what precisely is meant by it. For one thing, if we start with the human subject or ego as standing to the non-ego in a reciprocal relationship, it is none too easy to see how we can detach the world, considered as object for a subject, from the human subject and attach it to a divine subject. Indeed, it is difficult to see how solipsism can be successfully evaded, except

---

[1] *Essai*, p. 269.   [2] *Ibid.*, p. 370.
[3] Freedom is defined by Hamelin as 'the synthesis of necessity and contingency'; and a free action is said to be 'the same thing as a motivated action' *Ibid.*, p. 310.

by recourse to the demands of common sense. For another thing, while identification of God with reality as a whole has the advantage of making unnecessary any proof of God's existence, it is none too clear that this identification can be properly described as theism. In other words, Hamelin's idealist metaphysics seems to stand in need of a good deal of rethinking. But the philosopher was only fifty-one years old when he died in an attempt to save two persons from drowning. And it is obviously impossible to know what modifications, if any, he would have made in his system, had he lived longer.

4. To treat here of Léon Brunschvicg (1869–1944) is open to objection on the ground that reference should be made to him after discussion of Bergson and not before. But though the objection is doubtless valid on chronological grounds, it is convenient to include him in the chapter devoted to the critical philosophy in France. Brunschvicg was first and foremost a philosopher who reflected on the nature of mind or spirit as it reveals itself historically in its activity in various fields. And his reflections on mathematics and science have to be seen in this light.

Born at Paris, Brunschvicg studied first at the Lycée Condorcet and then at the École Normale where in 1891 he received the licentiate in both letters and science. In 1897 he published his doctoral thesis on *The Modality of Judgment*.[1] In 1909 he was appointed to a chair of philosophy at the Sorbonne. In 1940 he retired to the south of France. His publications included *Les étapes de la philosophie des mathématiques* (1912, *Stages in the Philosophy of Mathematics*), *L'expérience humaine et la causalité physique* (1922, *Human Experience and Physical Causality*), *Le progrès de la conscience dans la philosophie occidentale* (1927, *The Progress of Consciousness in Western Philosophy*) and *La philosophie de l'esprit* (1949, *The Philosophy of Mind*). Brunschvicg also wrote on Spinoza and Pascal, besides publishing a well known edition of the latter's *Pensées* in 1897.

In his work on the modality of judgment Brunschvicg asserts his idealist standpoint clearly enough. From the properly philosophical point of view 'knowledge is no longer an accident which is added from without to being, without altering it . . .; knowledge constitutes a world which is for us the world. Beyond it there is

---

[1] The second edition of *La modalité du jugement* appeared in 1934. The third edition, amplified by a French translation of the Latin thesis on the metaphysical force of the syllogism according to Aristotle, was published at Paris in 1964.

nothing. A thing which was beyond knowledge would be by
definition inaccessible, non-determinable. That is to say, for us it
would be equivalent to nothing.'[1] In philosophy the mind 'seeks
to grasp itself in its movement, in its activity. ... Intellectual
activity coming to consciousness of itself, this is the integral study
of integral knowledge, this is philosophy.'[2] In other words, from
the point of view of naïve common sense the object of knowledge
is something external and fixed, something which, in itself, lies
outside knowledge but which comes to be known. We make the
transition to the philosophical point of view when we see that the
distinction between subject and object arises within the sphere
of reason, of the mind's activity. According to Brunschvicg therefore his own (or contemporary) idealism should not be confused
with a subjective idealism which is opposed to a metaphysical
realism. Critical or 'rational idealism'[3] does not entail a denial of
any distinction between subject and object or between man and
his environment. What it entails is the assertion that this distinction arises within consciousness, and that something beyond
consciousness and knowledge would be for us nothing at all.

Brunschvicg's idea of philosophy as the mind's activity in
coming to reflective consciousness of itself naturally recalls the
transcendental philosophy of Kant. Though however Brunschvicg
is perfectly well aware of Kant's influence on the development of
idealism, he insists that the philosophy which he has in mind does
not consist in an *a priori* deduction of supposedly unchangeable
categories. He sees the mind as coming to know itself through
reflection on its activity as manifested historically in, for example,
the development of science. And through this reflection the mind
sees that its categories change: it sees its own inventiveness and
creativity and is open to new categories and ways of thought. The
Kantian attitude leads to a sterile idealism. Genuine idealism is
'a doctrine of the living mind. ... All progress in the knowledge
and determination of the mind is linked to the progress of science.'[4]
It is not however simply a question of science. In the sphere of
morals too genuine idealism remains open to a fresh understanding
of moral principles in the light of social progress. As has been
mentioned, Brunschvicg published a work on the progress of
consciousness in western philosophy. The word *conscience* can
mean conscience as well as consciousness. And just as Brunschvicg

[1] *La modalité du jugement* (1964 edition), p. 2.   [2] *Ibid.*, p. 4.
[3] *L'idéalisme contemporain* (1905), p. 5.   [4] *Ibid.*, p. 176.

rejects an *a priori* deduction of categories which would exclude any radical changes in scientific theory, so does he reject any *a priori* deduction of moral principles which would exclude advances in moral insight. The mind or spirit comes to know itself in its activity, but its activity has not ceased at any given point at which it reflects on itself. Science is capable of change and progress; so is society; and so is man's moral life. The mind may aspire to a comprehensive and final synthesis; but it cannot attain it. For the mind or spirit remains inventive and creative. It creates new forms and comes to know itself in and through its own creations.

Metaphysics, for Brunschvicg, is reducible to the theory of knowledge; the constitutive act of knowledge is the judgment; and judgment is characterized by the affirmation of being.[1] But what is affirmed or posited as being can be affirmed in two ways. In the first place it can be affirmed simply in the sphere of intelligibility, under the form of 'interiority'. That is to say, the being which is posited is constituted simply by an intelligible relation. An arithmetical judgment is of this type. The being of the copula is purely logical. In the second place the being affirmed can be that of existence, the judgment being the expression of the mind's recognition of a 'shock', of its being constrained or limited, as it were, by something external to itself and of its own activity in giving content to this experience of constraint.[2] We are not however faced with an irreducible dualism between purely formal judgments on the one hand and discrete judgments of perception on the other. For the mind or intellect seeks intelligibility, unity that is to say. The judgments which in the first instance belong to the purely intelligible sphere of interiority are applied, and the relations affirmed in the sphere of exteriority are subjected to the conditions or demands of intelligibility. In brief, the world of mathematical physics is constructed. This creation of the mind's activity cannot however be given the form of pure mathematics, an exclusively deductive form. There is a constant tension between 'interiority' and 'exteriority'. The scientist deduces; but he must also test empirically, having recourse to experience. In the area of pure mathematics necessity rules; in that of science probability holds sway. The world of science is the creation of the

---

[1] *La modalité du jugement*, p. 40.
[2] It is intelligence, according to Brunschvicg, which determines the object. That which is given in the 'shock' is completely undetermined. Any judgment of perception involves both interiority and exteriority.

human spirit;[1] but it is a creation which never reaches a final and absolutely irreformable state.

In his treatment of the moral sphere, that of the practical judgment, Brunschvicg again emphasizes the human spirit's movement towards unification. He sees human beings as moving towards assimilation through participation in the activity of consciousness as it creates values which transcend self-centredness. In the theoretical sphere reason creates a network of coherent relations, as it moves towards the ideal limit of an all-encompassing coherent system. In the sphere of the moral life too the human spirit moves towards the interrelations of justice and love. As for religion, there is no question with Brunschvicg of a personal God transcending the sphere of human consciousness. He uses the word 'God', it is true; but with him it signifies reason as transcending the individual as such, though immanent in him, and as moving towards unification. 'Man participates in the divinity inasmuch as he is *particeps rationis*.'[2] And human life has a religious dimension in so far as it overcomes the barriers between man and man.

Brunschvicg is better described as an idealist than as a philosopher of science. It would not however be fair to him, if one were to represent him simply as forcing science into an idealist framework of thought. He does indeed start with idealist presuppositions; and it is undeniable that they influence his interpretation of science. At the same time he insists that the nature of mind or spirit can be seen only by studying its activity. And though his idealism influences his interpretation of science, his reflection on science in its actual development influences his idealist philosophy. For example, he sees clearly enough that science militates against the idea that the process of arriving at knowledge can be represented as a purely deductive process. He also sees however that the scientist's inventiveness and creativity rules out pure empiricism. And it is perhaps worth noting that in Einstein's relativity theory he saw a confirmation of his view of science as revealing the mutual interdependence of reason and experience. He also saw in it of course a justification of his rejection of fixed categories and of space and time as realities which are antecedent to and independent of the activity of the mind. 'In all domains,

---

[1] So of course is the world of common sense or of the pre-scientific consciousness. Both are real.

[2] *Le progrès de la conscience*, p. 796. In 1939 Brunschvicg published *La raison et la religion* (*Reason and Religion*).

from the analysis of Cauchy or of Georg Cantor to the physics of M. Planck or of M. Einstein the decisive discoveries have been made in the opposite direction to the schema which was predetermined by the doctrine of forms and categories. Instead of applying unchangeable principles to new matter, progress has consisted on the one hand in looking back to the classical principles in order to question their apodictic truth and on the other hand in bringing to birth novel and unforeseeable relations.'[1] Whatever we may think of the Fichtean elements in Brunschvicg's thought (his attempt, for example, to derive externality from the activity of reason), he certainly did not try to canonize certain scientific theories in the name of philosophy. For it was precisely changes in scientific theory which he saw as revealing the inventiveness and creativity of the mind, a creativity which he also saw in the ethical sphere.

[1] *Ibid.*, p. 705.

CHAPTER VIII

THE SPIRITUALIST MOVEMENT

The term 'spiritualism'—The philosophy of Ravaisson—
J. Lachelier and the bases of induction—Boutroux and con-
tingency—A. Fouillée on idées-forces—*M. J. Guyau and the*
philosophy of life.

1. It hardly needs saying that when the term 'spiritualism' is
used as a philosophical label in the context of nineteenth-century
thought in France, it has nothing to do with the belief that the
living can communicate with departed spirits by means of practices which are thought appropriate for the purpose. To give to
the term a precise positive definition is however none too easy.
Victor Cousin used it to refer to his own eclecticism. And in his
Letter on Apologetics Maurice Blondel remarked that the label
should be relegated to the lumber-room, inasmuch as it shared the
discredit into which eclecticism had fallen.[1] In spite of Blondel
however Cousin's philosophy is still sometimes referred to as
'eclectic spiritualism' or 'spiritualist eclecticism'. And if by
'spiritualism' we mean a rejection of materialism and determinism
and an assertion of the ontological priority of spirit to matter, this
description of Cousin's philosophy is doubtless justified. But if the
term is understood in this wide sense, it covers all theistic philosophies and the various forms of absolute idealism, such as the
thought of Hamelin. It would then lack any specific reference to
modern French philosophy and could be used to describe the
philosophies of, say, Aquinas, Descartes, Berkeley, Schelling,
Hegel, Rosmini and Berdyaev.

Perhaps the best policy is to abandon any attempt to give a
precise abstract definition and to say simply that in the present
context the word 'spiritualism' is used to signify the current of
thought which recognizes Maine de Biran as a fountainhead and
which runs from Ravaisson through Lachelier, Fouillée and others
to Bergson. In other words, the term is used to signify a movement
in which Maine de Biran's insistence on the spontaneity of the
human will and his reflection on the human spirit's activity as a

---

[1] See the *Letter* as translated by A. Dru and I. Trethowan, p. 150 (London,
1964).

key to the nature of reality are seen as a counterblast to the
materialism and determinism of some of the thinkers of the
Enlightenment and as a return to what are regarded as the genuine
traditions of French philosophy. Cousin's thought then qualifies
for being described as spiritualist to the extent in which he
derives stimulus from Maine de Biran or from ideas similar to
those of de Biran. It must be added however that as the movement
develops Maine de Biran's psychological approach and his emphasis on the spontaneity and freedom of the will come to take the
form of a general philosophy of life. This is obvious enough in the
case of Bergson. Indeed, though Bergson acknowledged an
indebtedness to Maine de Biran and Ravaisson, it is arguable that
in some respects Blondel stands closer than Bergson to de Biran,
in spite of Blondel's recommendation that use of the term
'spiritualism' should be abandoned.

2. Jean Gaspard Félix Ravaisson-Mollien (1813–1900), commonly known simply as Ravaisson, was born at Namur and after
studies at Paris attended Schelling's lectures at Munich. In 1835
he presented to the Academy of Moral and Political Sciences a
prize essay on the metaphysics of Aristotle, which was published
in a revised form in 1837 under the title *Essai sur la métaphysique
d'Aristote*. A second volume was added in 1846. In 1838 Ravaisson
presented two theses for the doctorate at Paris, a Latin thesis on
Speusippus and a French thesis on habit, *De l'habitude*. He taught
philosophy for a short while at Rennes; but differences with Victor
Cousin, who was then pretty well dictator of philosophical studies
in the universities, stood in the way of his pursuing an academic
career at Paris. In 1840 he was appointed inspector general of
libraries, and in 1859 he became inspector general of higher
education. Ravaisson was interested not only in philosophy but
also in art, especially painting, and in classical antiquities. He was
elected to membership both of the Academy of Moral and Political
Sciences and of the Academy of Inscriptions and Fine Arts. In
1870 he was appointed curator of classical antiquities at the
Louvre.

In 1867 Ravaisson published, at the request of the government,
a Report on *Philosophy in France in the Nineteenth Century*
(*Rapport sur la philosophie en France au XIXe siècle*) in which he
provided both a source of information about a large number of
philosophers and a programmatic defence of the metaphysical
tradition of spiritualist realism, which he saw as going back beyond

the nineteenth century and as having been reasserted by Maine de Biran. Ravaisson took the opportunity of attacking not only positivism but also the eclecticism of Cousin, of which he took a dim view, regarding it as a pitiable mixture of the Scottish philosophy of common sense with some misunderstood ideas derived from Maine de Biran. In effect it was made pretty clear that de Biran's true successor was Ravaisson himself. His *Philosophical Testament and Fragments* was published posthumously in 1901 in the *Revue des deux mondes*.[1]

As the title indicates, Ravaisson's *De l'habitude* is devoted to a special topic; but his treatment of the theme exhibits a general philosophical outlook. Reflection on our habit-forming, according to the author, shows that in habit voluntary movement, which encounters resistance and is accompanied by the feeling of effort, is transformed into instinctive movement, the conscious tending to become unconscious. In habit the spontaneous activity of life submits, as it were, to its material conditions, to the sphere of mechanism, and in so doing provides a basis for the further activity of will, of the voluntary movement and effort of which, as Maine de Biran argued, we are conscious in ourselves. This can be seen in the formation of physical habits, which form the foundation and background of purposeful action. To take a simple example, if I decide to walk to a friend's house to visit him, the carrying out of my purpose presupposes the formation of physical habits such as those of walking. And we can see an analogous situation in the ethical sphere, where, according to Ravaisson, virtuous activity is at first achieved only by deliberate effort but can become habitual, thus forming a 'second nature' and providing a basis for the further pursuit of ideals.

More generally, Ravaisson sees in the world two basic factors, space as the condition of permanence or stability, time as the condition of change. To these two factors there correspond respectively matter and life. The former is the sphere of necessity and mechanism, the latter of the spontaneous activity which is manifested in living organisms and which in man rises to the level of 'freedom of the understanding'.[2] The point of intersection between the two spheres is habit, which combines in itself the mechanism of matter and the dynamic finality of life. If however habit presupposes voluntary movement and effort[1] and is, so to speak, intelligence which has gone to sleep or has entered an infra-conscious state, and if it provides the basis for further activity by the will, this shows the priority, from the finalistic point of view, of the upward movement of life. Between the lowest limit of Nature and 'the highest point of reflective freedom there is an infinity of degrees which measure the development of one and the same power'.[2] Habit 'redescends' the line of descent and can be described as an intuition in which the real and the ideal are one.

In the emphasis which Ravaisson places on voluntary movement and effort and in his tendency to look within man for the key to the secret of the world we see of course the inspiration of Maine de Biran. In his theory of habit we can also see evidence of the influence of Schelling, for example in talk about the unity of the ideal and the real.[3] Looking forward, we can see a clear anticipation of Bergsonian themes. In the commemorative discourse which Bergson delivered on succeeding Ravaisson as a member of the Academy of Moral and Political Sciences he referred to *De l'habitude* and made the following comment. 'Thus habit gives us the living demonstration of this truth, that mechanism is not self-sufficient: it would be only, so to speak, the fossilized residue of a spiritual activity.'[4] In other words, Bergson sees in Ravaisson's thought an anticipation of his own theory of the *élan vital* and of Nature as obscured consciousness or dormant volition.

Ravaisson's theory of habit expresses his conviction that the lower has to be explained through reference to the higher. And this is indeed a basic element in his general philosophical outlook. Thus in his *Report* he finds fault with those philosophers who attempt to explain mental activity either in terms of physico-chemical processes or, as in phenomenalism, by reduction to impressions or in terms of abstract categories. The analytic intelligence or understanding tends by its very nature to explain phenomena by reduction to ultimate constituent elements. But though this procedure certainly has its legitimate role in natural science, Ravaisson insists that we cannot understand spiritual phenomena in this way. They have to be viewed in the light of

---

[1] In Ravaisson's view there can be no habits, properly speaking, in the inorganic sphere.

[2] *De l'habitude*, p. 34.

[3] On some points of course the influence of Aristotle can be discerned pretty clearly.

[4] *La pensée et le mouvant. Essais et conférences*, p. 296, (3rd edition, 1934).

their finality, of the goal-directed upward movement of life, both at the infra-conscious and conscious levels. This movement is grasped by a kind of intuition which apprehends it first of all in our inner experience of goal-directed effort. It is in inner experience that we can see the will as seeking the Good, which manifests itself in art as Beauty. The Good and Beauty, the ideal goals of the will, are God, or at any rate symbols of God. And in the light of this truth we can interpret the material world, considered as the sphere of necessity and mechanism, as the effect of the self-diffusion of the divine Good and as the setting for the upward movement of light.

It has been said of Ravaisson[1] that he combines the psychology of Maine de Biran with the metaphysics of Schelling, whereas in the discourse to which reference has been made above Bergson remarks that Schelling's influence on Ravaisson should not be exaggerated[2] and that the vision of the universe as the manifestation of an ultimate reality which gives of itself in liberality was to be found among the Greek philosophers.[3] Bergson prefers to emphasize the influence of the development of biological studies in nineteenth-century science.[4] Though however there is doubtless a good deal of truth in what Bergson says, the influence of Schelling cannot be discounted. Ravaisson's view of Nature clearly has some affinity with Schelling's picture of Nature as slumbering spirit, even if in his *Report* he refers more to contemporary psychological ideas and theories. Further, Ravaisson's tendency to regard creation as a kind of cosmic Fall and his emphasis on the idea of a return to God justifies reference to the influence of the German philosopher. In any case we can see in Ravaisson's distinction between the activity of the analytic intelligence on the one hand and, on the other, an intuitive grasp of the movement of life an anticipation of central themes in the philosophy of Bergson.

3. Though Ravaisson was never a professor at Paris, he none the less exercised a considerable influence. It was he who divined the philosophical capacity of Jules Lachelier (1832–1918), when the latter was a student of the École Normale, and who did his best to promote Lachelier's career. In his years as a professor at the École Normale (1864–1875) Lachelier was himself to have a powerful stimulative effect on the minds of students of philosophy. He was not however a prolific writer. In 1871 he published a work

---

[1] By R. Berthelot.   [2] *La pensée et le mouvant*, p. 291.
[3] *Ibid.*, p. 317.   [4] *Ibid.*, p. 303.

on induction, *Du fondement de l'induction*, which was his French thesis for the doctorate, the Latin thesis being on the syllogism.[1] He also published a number of essays, the best known of which deal with psychology and metaphysics (*Psychologie et méta-physique*, 1885) and with Pascal's wager (*Notes sur le pari de Pascal*, 1901). But his *Works*, which include inverventions during discussions at the French Society of Philosophy and annotations on draft entries for Lalande's *Vocabulaire*, form only two modest volumes.[2] When Lachelier retired from the École Normale in 1875, he was appointed inspector of the Academy of Paris; and in 1879 he became inspector general of public education. In 1896 he was elected a member of the Academy of Moral and Political Sciences.

There would be ample justification for considering the thought of Lachelier in the chapter on neo-criticism and idealism. For in his main work, that on induction, he approaches his theme in a Kantian manner, by inquiring into the necessary conditions of our experience of the world. And on this basis he outlines an idealist philosophy which makes him a predecessor of Hamelin. At the same time there are elements in his thought which exercised an influence on the spiritualist movement; and though Bergson was not actually a pupil of Lachelier, as a student he read the work on induction and regarded its author as his teacher. Further, Lachelier referred to his own thought as a form of spiritualism.

By induction Lachelier understands 'the operation by which we pass from the knowledge of facts to that of the laws which govern them'.[3] Nobody doubts that this process actually takes place in science. But it gives rise to a problem. On the one hand experience gives us only a certain number of observed cases of practical connections between phenomena; but it does not tell us that they must be always so connected. On the other hand in inductive reasoning we do not hesitate to draw a universal conclusion, applying to unobserved and future connections; and, according to Lachelier, this implies that we are confident of the reign of necessity in Nature. He does not intend to assert that induction is in practice always correct. 'In fact, induction is always subject to error.'[4] But the revisibility of scientific laws does not alter the fact that our attempts to formulate them rest on and express a confidence that there are necessary connections to be found. And

---

[1] *De natura syllogismi* (1871).   [2] *Oeuvres de Jules Lachelier* (Paris, 1933).
[3] *Oeuvres*, I, p. 21.   [4] *Ibid.*, p. 25.

the question arises, can this confidence be theoretically justified? Or, as Lachelier puts it, what is the principle in virtue of which we add to the data of experience the elements of universality and necessity?

In the first place induction implies that phenomena are organized in series of mechanically related members. To put the matter in another way, phenomena are intelligible only if they are subject to the law of efficient causality. But the principle of causality does not by itself provide a sufficient basis for induction. For inductive reasoning presupposes not only mechanically related series of phenomena but also complex and recurring groups of phenomena, functioning as wholes, each whole being of such a kind that it determines the existence of its parts. A whole of this kind is what we call a final cause. The concept of laws of nature, 'with the exception of a small number of elementary laws, seems therefore to be based on two distinct principles: the one in virtue of which phenomena form series in which the existence of the preceding (member) determines that of the following; the other in virtue of which these series form in their turn systems, in which the idea of the whole determines the existence of the parts.'[1] In a nutshell, 'the possibility of induction rests on the double principle of efficient causes and of final causes.'[2]

It is one thing however to claim that inductive reasoning rests on a certain principle (or, more accurately, on two principles), and it is another thing to validate or justify this principle. Lachelier is not prepared to follow the Scottish School and Royer-Collard in appealing to common sense. Nor does he wish to claim simply that the principle is a self-evident indemonstrable truth. But though he commends J. S. Mill for trying to justify induction, he does not believe that the attempt was, or indeed could be successful, given Mill's empiricist premises. Further, he sees that if a solution is offered simply in terms of the human mind's imposing its *a priori* categories or concepts, necessitated by its own nature or structure, on phenomena which are appearances of things-in-themselves, the question can be raised whether the result of this imposition can properly be described as knowledge. In other words, Lachelier wishes to show that the principles of efficient causality and of final causes are not *a priori* simply and solely in a subjective sense, but that they govern both thought and the object of thought. This involves showing not only that, in general,

---

[1] *Ibid.*, p. 27.   [2] *Ibid.*, p. 27.

'the conditions of the existence of phenomena are the very conditions of the possibility of thought.'[1] but also, in particular, that the two principles on which induction rests are conditions of the possibility of thought.

In regard to the first principle, that of efficient causality, Lachelier tries to show that the serial linking of phenomena through causal relations is necessarily involved by the unity of the world, which is itself a condition of the possibility of thought. His line of argument is somewhat difficult to follow; but it proceeds on these lines. Thought would not be possible without the existence of a subject which distinguishes itself from each sensation and which remains one despite the diversity of sensations, simultaneous and successive. Here however there arises a problem. On the one hand knowledge does not consist in the activity of a subject shut up in itself and cut off from or external to its sensations. Lachelier tries to solve this problem by seeking the required unity in relations between the sensations, the subject or self being regarded not as something over and above and cut off from its sensations but rather as the 'form' of diverse sensations. But natural relations between our sensations cannot be different from relations between the corresponding phenomena. 'The question of knowing how all our sensations are united in one single thought is then precisely the same as that of knowing how all phenomena compose one single universe.'[2] For Lachelier at any rate a condition of phenomena constituting one world is that they should be causally related. Mere succession would locate phenomena in space and time; but for a real link between phenomena the causal relation is necessary. As therefore things exist for us only in so far as they are objects of thought, the condition of phenomena forming one world and the condition of the unity of thought are one and the same, namely the principle of efficient causality.

This point of view gives us only what Lachelier describes as 'a sort of idealist materialism'.[3] The world which it presents is a world in relation to thought, but it is a world of mechanical causality, of the reign of necessity. To complete the picture we have to consider the second principle of induction, namely final causality. Induction, according to Lachelier, presupposes something more than mechanically related series of discrete phenomena. It also presupposes complex and recurring groups of phenomena,

[1] *Ibid.*, p. 48.   [2] *Ibid.*, p. 51.   [3] *Ibid.*, p. 68.

functioning as wholes. And we cannot account for these wholes, existing at various levels, without introducing the regulative idea of immanent finality. The most obvious example of the sort of thing which Lachelier has in mind is obviously the living organism, in the case of which the 'reason' of the whole complex phenomenon is found in itself, in an immanent final cause which governs the behaviour of the parts. But it is not only of living organisms that Lachelier is thinking. He has in mind all complex groups of phenomena which function as unities. Indeed, he sees every phenomenon as the manifestation of a force which expresses a spontaneous tendency towards an end. Further, it is this idea of force which explains the varying intensity of our sensations and which lies at the basis of our conviction that the world is not reducible to our sensations considered as purely subjective. Final causality may be a regulative idea; but it is required for induction which presupposes an intelligible world, one that is penetrable by thought and so reveals in itself the functioning of unconscious thought as seen in the development of recurrent unities functioning as wholes. It is not a question of final causality simply replacing or annulling mechanical causality. The latter forms a basis for the former. But once we introduce the idea of final causality as penetrating the world of mechanical causality and subordinating the latter to itself, our concept of the world changes. Materialist idealism (or idealist materialism, as Lachelier also describes it) is transformed into 'a spiritualist realism, in the eyes of which every being is a force, and every force a thought which tends to a more and more complete consciousness of itself.'[1]

The concept of spiritualist realism is developed in the essay on psychology and metaphysics. Psychology is said to have as its demesne 'sensible consciousness' (la conscience sensible), whereas metaphysics is described as 'the science of thought in itself, of the light at its source'.[2] This statement may give the impression that for Lachelier metaphysics is really part of psychology. For how can we exclude from psychology the study of thought? Lachelier does not mean however that the psychologist's attention must be confined to the study of sensation and perception and feeling without any reference at all to thought or will.[3] What he insists on is that psychology is concerned with thought in so far as

---

[1] *Ibid.*, p. 92.   [2] *Ibid.*, p. 219.
[3] In the study of 'sensible consciousness' physiology has its own field, which, according to Lachelier, consists of the laws governing the succession of states.

thought becomes a datum of consciousness, an objectifiable factor in, for example, perception. Similarly, psychology is concerned with will in so far as it is manifested in man's perceptive and affective life. Philosophy or metaphysics is concerned with thought itself, pure thought, which is also pure liberty or freedom, the thought which works unconsciously in Nature, at successive levels, and which comes to think itself in and through man. Metaphysics is thus equivalent to what Lachelier elsewhere describes as the profounder spiritual realism. In the comments which he makes on the entry 'spiritualism' for Lalande's *Vocabulary* he remarks that every doctrine that recognizes the independence and primacy of spirit, in the sense of conscious thought, or that regards spirit as above Nature and irreducible to physical pressures can be described as spiritualist. He then goes on to claim that there is a profounder spiritualism which consists in seeking in spirit the explanation of Nature and in believing that the thought which operates unconsciously in Nature is the same as the thought which becomes conscious in man. 'It is this second spiritualism which was, as it seems to me, that of M. Ravaisson.'[1] Evidently, this 'second spiritualism' is metaphysics as Lachelier understands the term.

The thought which Lachelier has in mind is clearly absolute thought, the thought which 'posits *a priori* the conditions of all existence'.[2] And we might well feel inclined to comment that 'idealism' would be a more appropriate word than 'realism'. But by 'idealism' Lachelier tends to mean subjective idealism, in the sense of the theory that the world consists of *my* representations, actual and possible. A philosophy which recognizes a plurality of subjects and for which '*my* world' has become '*the* world' can be described as realism. At the same time Lachelier insists that in so far as different subjects attain universal truth this thought is to be considered as one, as the manifestation of the thought which operates unconsciously in Nature and consciously in man. And this point of view is generally described as objective idealism. Lachelier does indeed assert that the object of thought is other than thought itself, and that 'thought could not produce it (the object) out of itself'.[3] But he adds that this is because thought is not what it ought to be, namely intuitive in a sense which would make the object immanent to thought, so that the two would be

---

[1] *Ibid.*, II, p. 221.   [2] *Ibid.*, I, p. 218.   [3] *Ibid.*, II, p. 210.

one. He is presumably saying that human thinking cannot coincide entirely with absolute thought and so retains a realist outlook, even if it recognizes that the whole world is the self-manifestation of absolute thought or spirit.

Lachelier does indeed endorse Aristotle's definition of first philosophy or metaphysics as the science of being as being; but he interprets this in the sense of the science of thought in itself and in things. As this thought is the one ultimate reality or being, which, as we have seen, operates unconsciously in Nature and comes to self-awareness in and through man, Lachelier is quite prepared to admit that 'pure philosophy is essentially pantheistic'.[1] He goes on however to say that one can *believe* in a divine reality transcending the world. And at the close of his notes on Pascal's wager he remarks that 'the sublimest question of philosophy, but perhaps more religious than philosophical, is the transition from the formal absolute to the real and living absolute, from the idea of God to God.'[2] This transition is the transition from philosophy to religion. At the end of the essay on induction Lachelier asserts that spiritual realism, so far as he has presented it, is 'independent of all religion',[3] though the subordination of mechanism to finality prepares the way for an act of moral faith which transcends the limits of Nature and of thought. By 'thought' in this context he doubtless means philosophy. Religion goes beyond not only science but also philosophy. And though Brunschvicg tells us that Lachelier was a practising Catholic,[4] the latter's discussion with Durkheim makes it clear that for him religion has no intrinsic relation to a group but is 'an interior effort and consequently solitary'.[5] From the historical point of view Durkheim is justified in protesting against this rather narrow concept of religion. But Lachelier is evidently convinced that religion is essentially the individual's act of faith by which the abstract Absolute of philosophy becomes the living God.

4. Among Lachelier's pupils at the École Normale was Émile Boutroux (1845–1921). After finishing his studies at Paris Boutroux taught for a while in a lycée at Caen; but after he had received the doctorate he was given a University post, first at Montpellier, then at Nancy. From 1877 until 1886 he lectured at the École Normale at Paris, and from 1886 until 1902 he occupied a chair of philosophy at the Sorbonne. His best known work is his

---

[1] *Ibid.*, p. 201.　　[2] *Ibid.*, p. 56.　　[3] *Ibid.*, I, p. 92.
[4] *Ibid.*, I, p. xvi.　　[5] *Ibid.*, II, p. 171.

doctorate thesis *La contingence des lois de la nature*[1] which appeared in 1874, three years after the publication of Lachelier's work on induction. The ideas which Boutroux had expressed in his thesis were developed in a work which he published in 1895, *De l'idée de loi naturelle dans la science et la philosophie contemporaines*.[2] Other writings include *La science et la religion dans la philosophie contemporaine*,[3] which appeared in 1908, and, in the historical field, *Études d'histoire de la philosophie*.[4] The posthumously published collection of essays *La nature et l'esprit* (1926) includes the programme for Boutroux's Gifford Lectures on *Nature and Spirit* which were delivered at Glasgow in 1903–04 and 1904–05.

In his preface to the English translation of *De la contingence de lois de la nature* Boutroux remarks that philosophical systems seem to him to belong to three main types, 'the idealist, the materialist and the dualist or parallelist types.'[5] All three have a common feature, namely that they represent the laws of nature as necessary. In rationalist systems of philosophy the mind tries to reconstruct reality by means of a logical deduction of its structure from what it takes to be self-evidently true propositions. When the mind abandons this dream and turns to phenomena known through sense-perception in order to ascertain their laws, it imports the idea of logical necessity into that of natural law and depicts the world as 'an endless variety of facts, linked together by necessary and immutable bonds'.[6] The question arises however whether the concept of a necessary relation is actually exemplified in the relations between phenomena; and Boutroux proposes to argue that natural laws are contingent and that they are 'bases which enable us constantly to rise towards a higher life'.[7]

Boutroux starts, very properly, by inquiring what is meant in this context by a necessary relation. Absolute necessity, the necessity, that is to say, which eliminates all conditions and is reducible to the principle of identity ($A = A$), can be left out of account. For the laws of nature are not simply tautologies. What

---

[1] Translated by F. Rothwell as *The Contingency of the Laws of Nature* (London, 1916).
[2] Translated by F. Rothwell as *Natural Law in Science and Philosophy* (London, 1914).
[3] Translated by J. Nield as *Science and Religion in Contemporary Philosophy*, (London, 1909).
[4] Originally published in 1897, this work was translated by F. Rothwell as *Historical Studies in Philosophy* (London, 1912).
[5] *The Contingency of the Laws of Nature*, p. vi.
[6] *Ibid.*, p. 4.   [7] *Ibid.*, p. vii.

we are concerned with is not absolute but relative necessity, 'the existence of a necessary relation between two things.'[1] In other words, when we inquire into the alleged necessity of the laws of nature, we are looking not for purely analytic truth, but for necessarily true synthetic propositions. But here again we must make a distinction. If the laws of nature are necessarily true synthetic propositions, they cannot be *a posteriori* propositions. For while experience can reveal to us constant relations, it does not by itself reveal necessity. Nor can it do so. Hence the aim of our inquiry is to discover whether the laws of nature can properly be described as *a priori* synthetic propositions. If they can, then they must assert necessary causal relations.[2] The question therefore comes down to this. Are there *a priori* causal syntheses?

It will be noted that Boutroux's use of terminology is based on that of Kant. Moreover, he does not deny that the principle of causality can be stated in such a form that it is necessarily true. At the same time he maintains that this is not the sense in which the principle is actually used in the sciences. 'In reality, the word "cause", when used scientifically means "immediate condition".'[3] For scientific purposes it is quite sufficient, for the formulation of laws, that 'relatively invariable relations exist between the phenomena'.[4] The idea of necessity is not required. In other words, the principle of causality, as actually employed in science, is derived from experience, not imposed *a priori* by the mind. It is a very general and abstract expression of observed relations; and we do not observe necessity, though we can of course observe regular sequences. True, if we restrict our attention simply and solely to quantity, to the measurable aspects of phenomena, it may be in conformity with experience to assert an absolute equivalence between cause and effect. In point of fact however we find qualitative changes, a qualitative heterogeneity, which excludes the possibility of showing that the cause (immediate condition) must contain all that is required to produce the effect. And if the effect can be disproportionate to the cause from the qualitative point of view, it follows that 'nowhere in the real concrete world can the principle of causality be rigidly applied'.[5] To be sure, it can serve as a practical maxim for the scientist.

---

[1] *Ibid.*, p. 7.
[2] Boutroux rejects the idea that any end must necessarily be realized or that, given an end, the means are determined necessarily. He therefore restricts the field of inquiry to relations of efficient causality.
[3] *Ibid.*, p. 23.   [4] *Ibid.*, p. 24.   [5] *Ibid.*, p. 30.

But the development of the sciences themselves suggest that the laws of nature do not express objectively *necessary* relations and that they are not irreformable or unrevisible in principle. Our scientific laws enable us to deal successfully with a changing reality. It would be absurd to question their utility. But they are not definitive.

In his later work, *De l'idée de loi naturelle*, Boutroux carried the matter further. In pure mathematics there are of course necessary relations, depending on certain postulates. But pure mathematics is a formal science. It is obviously true that a natural science such as astronomy makes use of mathematics and could not have advanced without it. Indeed in certain sciences we can see clearly enough the attempt to fit Nature, as it were, to mathematics and to formulate the relations between phenomena in a mathematical manner. But there always remains a gap between Nature as it exists and mathematics; and this gap becomes more manifest as we shift our attention from the inorganic sphere to that of life. The scientist is justified in emphasizing the connection between biological and even mental phenomena on the one hand and physico-chemical processes on the other. But if we assume the reducibility of the laws governing biological evolution to the more general laws of physics and chemistry, it becomes impossible to explain the appearance of novelty. Despite their admitted utility, all natural laws are of the nature of compromises, approximations to an equation between reality and mathematics; and the more we proceed from the very general laws of physics to the spheres of biology, psychology and sociology, the clearer does this characteristic of approximation become. For we have to allow for creativeness and the emergence of novelty. For the matter of that, it is not certain that even on the purely physical level there is no variability, no breach in determinism.

Nowadays the idea that the structure of reality can be deduced *a priori* from basic propositions which are indemonstrable but self-evidently true can hardly be described as fashionable. And while we could not reasonably claim that there is universal agreement about the proper use of the term 'law of nature' or about the logical status of scientific laws, it is at any rate a common enough view that scientific laws are descriptive generalizations with predictive force and that they are synthetic propositions and therefore contingent. Further, we are all aware of the claim, based on Heisenberg's principle of uncertainty, that universal determinism has been disproved on the sub-atomic level. To be sure, it is not everyone who would admit that all propositions which are informative about reality are contingent.[1] Nor would everyone agree that universal determinism has in fact been disproved. The relevant point however is that a good deal of what Boutroux says about the contingency of the laws of nature represents lines of thought which are common enough today. For the matter of that, his anti-reductionism and his claim that there are qualitatively different kinds or levels of being do not appear startling. Obviously, talk about lower and higher levels of being is likely to elicit the comment that judgments of value are being made. But when Boutroux maintains that science takes the form of the sciences and that we cannot reduce all the other sciences to mathematical physics, most people would agree with him.

Boutroux is not however concerned simply with philosophy of science for its own sake. When, for example, he insists on the contingent character of the laws of nature and maintains that they cannot be reduced to and derived from an absolutely necessary truth, he is not simply pursuing an inquiry into the logical status of scientific laws. He is doing this of course; but he is also illustrating what for him are the limitations of science, with a view to arguing that there is room for a religious metaphysics which satisfies reason's demand for a unified and harmonious world-outlook. In the programme for the Gifford Lectures he remarks that 'in a general manner, science is a system of symbols with the task of providing us with a convenient and usable representation of realities which we cannot know directly. Now the existence and properties of these symbols can be explained only in terms of the original activity of the spirit.'[2] Similarly, in *Science and Religion* Boutroux asserts that science, so far from being something stamped by things on a passive intelligence, is 'an *ensemble* of symbols imagined by the mind in order to interpret things by means of pre-existent notions . . .'.[3] Science in its developed state does not presuppose a metaphysics;[4] but it does presuppose the creative activity of the mind or spirit or reason. The life of the spirit takes

---

[1] It would be claimed by some that there can be and are what, in Kantian terminology, would be classified as synthetic *a priori* propositions.
[2] *La nature et l'esprit*, p. 27. The words 'destiné à nous procurer' have been translated as 'having the task of providing us'.
[3] *Science and Religion in Contemporary Philosophy*, translated by J. Nield (London, 1909), p. 249.
[4] Cf. *La nature et l'esprit*, p. 15.

the form of scientific reason; but this is not the only form which it takes. The life of the spirit is something much wider, including morality, art and religion. The development therefore of the scientific use of reason, which 'seeks to systematize things from an impersonal standpoint',[1] does not exclude a 'subjective systematization',[2] based on the concept of the value of the person and on reflection on the life of the spirit in its various forms, a reflection which produces its own symbolic expression.

As Boutroux was a pupil of Lachelier, it is not surprising if we can see in his ideas about the limitations of science a certain measure of Kantian influence. His view of metaphysics however seems to have some affinity with that of Maine de Biran. For example, while allowing of course for psychology as a science, he suggests that 'it is impossible to find real frontiers between psychology and metaphysics'.[3] Similarly, 'metaphysics, to be legitimate and fruitful, must proceed not from outside to the inside, but from within outwards.'[4] He does not mean that metaphysics, 'an original activity of spirit,'[5] is science, whether psychology or otherwise, transformed into metaphysics. For a science which tries to convert itself into metaphysics is unfaithful to its own nature and aims. Boutroux means that metaphysics is spirit's reflection on its own life, which is considered in psychology from a scientific point of view but which overflows, as it were, the limits placed by this point of view.

In his general view of the universe Boutroux sees the world as a series of levels of being. A higher level is not deducible from a lower level: there is the emergence of novelty, of qualitative difference. At the same time heterogeneity and discontinuity are not the only features of the world. There is also continuity. For we can see a creative teleological process at work, a striving upwards towards an ideal. Thus Boutroux does not assert a rigid distinction between the inanimate and animate levels. There is spontaneity even at the level of so-called 'dead matter'. Moreover, in a manner reminiscent of Ravaisson, Boutroux suggests that 'animal instinct, life, physical and mechanical forces are, as it were, habits that have penetrated more and more deeply into the spontaneity of being. Hence these habits have become almost unconquerable. Seen from without, they appear as necessary laws.'[6]

[1] *Science and Religion*, p. 365.   [2] *Ibid.*, p. 365.
[3] *La nature et l'esprit*, p. 15.   [4] *Ibid.*, p. 37.   [5] *Ibid.*, p. 37.
[6] *The Contingency of the Laws of Nature*, p. 192.

At the human level we find conscious love and pursuit of the ideal, a love which is at the same time a drawing or attracting by the divine ideal which in this way manifests its existence. Religion, 'a synthesis—or, rather, a close and spiritual union—of instinct and intellect,'[1] offers man 'a richer and deeper life'[2] than the life of mere instinct or routine or imitation or the life of the abstract intellect. It is not so much a case of reconciling science and religion, considered as sets of theories or doctrines, as of reconciling the scientific and the religious spirits. For even if we can show that religious doctrines do not contradict scientific laws or hypotheses, this may leave unaffected the impression of an irreconcilable conflict between the scientific and religious spirits and attitudes. Reason however can strive to bring them together and to fashion, from their union, a being richer and more harmonious than either of them taken apart.[3] This union remains an ideal goal; but we can see that the religious life which, in its intense form, is always mysticism, has a positive value inasmuch as it lies 'at the heart of all the great religious, moral, political and social movements of humanity'.[4]

Bergson was a student for a while at the École Normale at Paris while Boutroux was teaching there. And the latter's *Contingency of the Laws of Nature* certainly exercised an influence on his mind, even if the degrèe of influence should not be exaggerated. In any case it is clear that Bergson carried on and developed some of Boutroux's ideas, though it does not necessarily follow of course that he actually derived them directly from this source.

5. Boutroux was clearly a resolute opponent not of course of science but of scientism and of positivist naturalism. When we turn to Alfred Fouillée (1838–1912), who lectured at the École Normale at Paris from 1872 to 1875,[5] we find him adopting a more eclectic attitude and envisaging a harmonization between the valuable and true ideas in the positivist and naturalist line of thought on the one hand and the idealist and spiritualist traditions on the other. The conclusions to which Fouillée came place him definitely within the spiritualist movement; but his intention was to effect a reconciliation between different currents of thought.

---

[1] *Science and Religion*, p. 378.   [2] *Ibid.*, p. 378.   [3] *Ibid.*, p. 400.
[4] *Ibid.*, p. 397. Boutroux is referring to active mysticism', not to what he describes as 'an abstract and barren form of mysticism' (*ibid.*).
[5] Before joining the staff of the École Normale Fouillée had been a professor in schools (*lycées*) at Douai and Montpellier and at the University of Bordeaux. He retired from the École Normale for reasons of health.

In spite of this ecumenical attitude, recalling Leibniz's notion that all systems were right in what they affirmed and wrong in what they denied, Fouillée was polemically inclined. In particular he attacked the philosophy of evolution as presented by Herbert Spencer and the epiphenomenalist theory of consciousness defended by T. H. Huxley.[1] Fouillée did not attack the idea of evolution as such. On the contrary, he accepted it. What he objected to was Spencer's attempt to account for the movement of evolution in purely mechanistic terms, which seemed to him a very limited and one-sided view of the matter. For the mechanistic conception of the world was, in Fouillée's opinion, a human construction; and the concept of force on which Spencer laid such emphasis was a projection of man's inner experience of effort and volitional activity. As for the epiphenomenalist theory of consciousness, this was irreconcilable with the active power of the mind and the evident fact of its ability to initiate movement and action. It was not necessary to follow the idealists in regarding thought as the one reality in order to see that in the process of evolution consciousness had to be taken into account as an effective contributing factor. It was *sui generis* and irreducible to physical processes.

In defence and explanation of his insistence on the effective causal activity of consciousness Fouillée proposed the theory which is especially associated with his name, namely the theory of what he called *idée-force* or thought-force. Every idea[2] is a tendency to action or the beginning of an action.[3] It tends to self-realization or self-actualization and is thus a cause. Even if it is itself caused, it is also a cause which can initiate movement and through physical action affect the external world. We are thus not faced with the problem of finding an additional link between the world of ideas and the world of physical objects. For an idea is itself a link, in the sense that it has the active tendency to self-realization. It is a mistake to regard ideas simply as representations or reflections of external things. They have a creative aspect. And as they are of course mental phenomena, to say that they exercise causal force is to say that the mind

---

[1] T. H. Huxley certainly proposed an epiphenomalist theory of consciousness. But he insisted that he had no intention of identifying mental activity with the physical processes on which it was dependent; and he rejected the label 'materialist'. Cf. Volume 8 of this *History*, pp. 104–7.

[2] For Fouillée an idea is a consciously conceived idea.

[3] We can compare this thesis with Josiah Royce's notion of the 'internal meaning' of an idea, described by him as 'the partial fulfilment of a purpose'. See Volume 8 of this *History*, pp. 270–3.

exercises causal activity. In this case it cannot be a mere epiphenomenon, passively dependent on physical organization and
processes.

In his work on freedom and determinism (*La liberté et le déterminisme*, 1872) he uses the theory of *idées-forces* in an attempt to
effect a reconciliation between the partisans of freedom and the
determinists. At first he gives the impression of allying himself
with the determinists, inasmuch as he subjects to criticism the
views defended by such defenders of human liberty as Cournot,
Renouvier and Lachelier. He rejects liberty of indifference as a
misguided notion, refuses to associate freedom with the idea of
chance, dismisses Renouvier's contention that determinism
implies the human being's passivity, and expresses agreement
with Taine's questioning of the theory that determinism deprives
moral values of all significance. In Fouillée's opinion determinism
does not necessarily imply that because something is all that it can
be, it is 'thereby all that it should be'.[1]

Though however Fouillée is not prepared to make the sort of
forthright attack on determinism which was characteristic of the
spiritualist current of thought, he points out that even determinists have to find room for the idea of freedom. He then proceeds to argue that though a psychological explanation of the idea
of freedom can be offered, this idea is an *idée-force* and thus tends
to realize itself. The idea of freedom is certainly effective in life;
and the stronger it becomes, the freer we are. In other words,
even if the genesis of the *idée-force* can be explained on determinist lines, once it is formed it exercises a directive power or
causal activity. It can obviously be objected that Fouillée reconciles determinism with libertarianism by the simple expedient of
equating freedom with the idea or feeling of freedom. And he does
indeed speak as though the two were the same. But he seems to
mean that when we act in the consciousness of freedom, for
example, in striving after the realization of moral ideals, our
actions express our personalities as human beings, and that this is
the real significance of freedom. With the idea of freedom we act
in a specific way; and there can be no doubt that such action can
be effective.

Fouillée developed his theory of *idées-forces* in works such as
The Evolution of Thought-Forces (*L'évolutionisme des idées-forces*,
1890), *The Psychology of Thought-Forces* (*La psychologie des*

[1] *La liberté et le déterminisme* (4th edition), p. 51.

idées-forces, 2 volumes, 1893) and *The Ethics of Thought-Forces* (*La morale des idées-forces*, 1908). This last-named book elicited praise from Bergson, not least because in it Fouillée argued that consciousness of one's own existence is inseparable from consciousness of the existence of others, and that the attribution of value to oneself implies the attribution of value to other persons. Fouillée's ethical theory was characterized by a conviction in the attractive power of ideals, especially those of love and fraternity or brotherhood, and by belief in the growth of an inter-personal consciousness with common ideals as a principle of action.

It is interesting to note that Fouillée claimed to have anticipated Bergson (and Nietzsche) in holding that movement is real. In his opinion the associationist psychologists, for example, were deceived by the artifice of language and broke up movement into successive discrete states, which might be compared to instantaneous photographs of waves.[1] In Fouillée's terminology, they retained the terms but omitted the relations and so failed to grasp the current of life, of which we have the feeling in, say, the experiences of enjoyment, suffering and wishing. Though however Fouillée was prepared to speak of the grasping or consciousness of duration, he was not prepared to accept Bergson's theory of an intuition of pure duration. In a letter to Augustin Guyau he remarked that in his opinion pure duration was a limiting concept and not an object of intuition.

6. Augustin Guyau was the son of Fouillée's stepson, Marie Jean Guyau (1854–88), who was a professor at the Lycée Condorcet for a short while during the period when Bergson was a pupil at the school. As his dates show, M. J. Guyau's life was a short one; but he made his mark by a series of publications. His first two works were *La morale d'Épicure et ses rapports avec les doctrines contemporaines* (*The Ethics of Epicurus and Its Relations to Contemporary Doctrines*) and *La morale anglaise contemporaine* (*Contemporary English Ethics*), which appeared respectively in 1878 and 1879. He also wrote on aesthetics in *Problèmes de l'esthétique contemporaine* (1884, *Problems of Contemporary Aesthetics*) and in the posthumously published (1889) *L'art au point de vue sociologique* (*Art from the Sociological Point of View*). He is best known however for his *Esquisse d'une morale sans obligation ni sanction*[2] and

---

[1] *La psychologie des idées-forces*, II, p. 85.
[2] Translated by G. Kapteyn as *A Sketch of Morality Independent of Obligation or Sanction* (London, 1898).

L'irréligion de l'avenir.[1] Published respectively in 1885 and 1887 these books were known and esteemed by Nietzsche. *Education et hérédité*[2] was published posthumously in 1889, while *La genèse de l'idée de temps* (*The Origin of the Idea of Time*) appeared in 1890 and was reviewed by Bergson.[3] To a certain extent M. J. Guyau agrees with his stepfather's theory of *idées-forces*. Thought is directed to action, and it is through action that 'those problems to which abstract thought gives rise'[4] are solved, in part even if not completely. But the relation of thought to action expresses something deeper and more universal, namely the creative movement of life. This idea should not indeed be understood in a theistic sense. The background of Guyau's philosophy was formed by the concept of an evolving universe, without any doctrine of a supernatural cause or creator of the universe. He looked on evolution however as the process by which life comes into being and in its creative activity brings forth successively higher forms. Consciousness is simply 'a luminous point in the great obscure sphere of life'.[5] It presupposes intuitive action, which expresses an infra-conscious will-to-live. If therefore we mean by 'ideas' ideas at the level of consciousness, their relation to action is the form taken at a particular level by the dynamism of life, its creative activity. 'Life is fecundity';[6] but it has no end save its own maintenance and intensification. The Bergsonian emphasis on becoming, life and the *élan vital* are already present in Guyau's thought, but without that belief in a creative God which was to become, eventually at any rate, a marked feature of Bergson's philosophy.

It is in terms of the concept of life that Guyau develops his ethical theory. In his opinion attempts to give morality a firm theoretical basis have been unsuccessful. We cannot find the required basis simply in the abstract concept of obligation. For this by itself provides us with little guidance. Further, people have felt under a moral obligation to pursue lines of conduct which we at any rate regard as immoral or as irrational. If however the Kantian type of morality will not do, neither will hedonism or utilitarianism. It is of course an empirical fact that human beings

---

[1] Translated as *The Non-Religion of the Future* (London, 1897) and reprinted at New York in 1962.
[2] Translated by W. J. Greenstreet as *Education and Heredity* (London, 1891).
[3] Guyau's essay on time first appeared in 1885 in the *Revue philosophique*. The posthumous republication (of an extended manuscript) by A. Fouillée was reviewed by Bergson in the *Revue philosophique* for 1891.
[4] *Esquisse*, p. 250.   [5] *Ibid.*, p. 10.   [6] *Ibid.*, p. 24.

tend to pursue what they have found to be pleasurable activities and to avoid what they have experienced as painful. But a much more fundamental tendency or urge is that of life to expand and intensify itself, a tendency which operates not only at the conscious but also at the infra-conscious and instinctive level. 'The end which in fact determines all conscious action is also the cause which produces all unconscious action; it is life itself. . . .'[1] Life, which by its nature strives to maintain, intensify and expand itself, is both the cause and the end of all action, whether instinctive or conscious. And ethics should be concerned with the means to the intensification and self-expansion of life.

The expansion of life is interpreted by Guyau largely in social terms. That is to say, the moral ideal is to be found in human cooperation, altruism, love and brotherhood, not in self-isolation and egoism. To be as social as one can is the authentic moral imperative. It is true that the idea of the intensification and expansion of life, when taken by itself, may appear to authorize, and indeed does authorize, actions which according to conventional moral standards are regarded as immoral. But for Guyau an important factor in human progress is the pursuit of truth and intellectual advance, and in his opinion intellectual development tends to inhibit purely instinctive and animal-like behaviour. The pursuit of truth however should go hand in hand with pursuit both of the good, especially in the form of human brotherhood, and of the beautiful. It can be added that the pleasures accompanying man's higher activities are precisely those which can most be shared in common. My enjoyment, for example, of a work of art does not deprive anyone else of a similar enjoyment.

Not only morality but also religion is interpreted by Guyau in terms of the concept of life. Religion as an historical phenomenon was largely social in character; and the idea of God was a projection of man's social consciousness and life. As man's moral consciousness developed, his concept of God changed too, from that of a capricious despot to that of a loving Father. But religion was throughout clearly linked with man's social life, expressing it and contributing to maintain it. Though however Guyau regards the idea of God as mythical, the title of his book *L'irréligion de l'avenir* is somewhat misleading. By 'religion' he means primarily acceptance of unverifiable dogmas imposed by religious organizations. A religion means for him an organized religious system.

_____
[1] *Ibid.*, p. 87.

In his view religion in this sense is disappearing and ought to disappear, inasmuch as it inhibits the intensification and expansion of life, intellectual life for example. But he does not envisage the disappearance of religious feeling, nor of the ethical idealism which was a feature of the higher religions. For the matter of that, Guyau does not call for the rooting out of all religious beliefs in the ordinary sense. The attempt to destroy all religious belief is for him as misguided and fanatical as the attempt to impose such beliefs. Even if ethical idealism is in itself sufficient, there are likely to be in the future as in the past people with definite religious beliefs. If such beliefs are the spontaneous expression, as it were, of the personalities of those who accept them and are embraced as hypotheses which seem reasonable to the believer, well and good, provided that no attempt is made to impose such beliefs on others. In other words, the religion of the future will be a purely personal matter, something distinct from the transformation of 'religion' into freely embraced and commonly recognized ethical values.

Guyau has been compared with Nietzsche. He has also been described as a positivist. As for the first point, there is obviously some affinity between the two philosophers, inasmuch as each expounds a philosophy of the intensification of life and of ascending life. Equally obviously however, there are important differences. Guyau's insistence on human solidarity and brotherhood is markedly different from Nietzsche's insistence on rank and diversification. As for positivism, there are certainly positivist and naturalistic features in Guyau's thought. But his ethical idealism comes to occupy the centre of the stage. In any case, even if it may seem odd, from some points of view, to include Guyau among representatives of the 'spiritualist' movement, he has in common with them a firm belief in human liberty and in the emergence of what is new in the process of evolution; and his philosophy of life clearly has a place in the line of thought of which Bergson is the best known exponent.[1]

---

[1] The precise relationship between Guyau and Bergson is none too clear. For instance, though Guyau's treatment of time is psychological and less metaphysical than Bergson's, there are certain phrases which appear also in pretty well the same form in Bergson's writings. Bergson however maintained that when Fouillée prepared Guyau's work for posthumous publication, he introduced phrases taken from his own (Bergson's) *Time and Free Will.*

CHAPTER IX

HENRI BERGSON (1)

Life and works—Bergson's idea of philosophy—Time and freedom—Memory and perception: the relation between spirit and matter—Instinct, intelligence and intuition in the context of the theory of evolution.

1. HENRI Bergson (1859–1941) was born at Paris and studied at the Lycée Condorcet. He was attracted, as he himself relates, both to mathematics and to letters; and when he finally opted for the latter, his professor of mathematics visited his parents to expostulate. On leaving the lycée in 1878 Bergson became a student of the École Normale. During the period 1881–97 he taught successively in lycées at Angers, Clermont-Ferrand[1] and Paris. From 1897 until 1900 he was a professor at the École Normale, and from 1900 until 1924[2] at the Collège de France, where his lectures attracted hearers even from the non-academic and fashionable world of Paris.[3] Already a member of the Institute and of the Academy of Moral and Political Sciences, he was elected to the French Academy in 1914 and received the Nobel prize for literature in 1928.

After the first world war Bergson was active in the work of promoting international understanding, and for a time he was chairman of the committee for intellectual cooperation established by the League of Nations, until bad health forced him to retire. In the final year of his life Bergson came very close to the Catholic Church, and in his testament he said that he would have become a Catholic, had it not been for his desire not to separate himself from his fellow-Jews during their persecution by the Nazis.[4]

---

[1] At Clermont-Ferrand Bergson also lectured in the University.
[2] In 1921 reasons of health compelled Bergson to consign his lecturing work to Édouard Le Roy, who succeeded formally to Bergson's chair in 1924. In 1891 Bergson had married a cousin of Marcel Proust, Louise Neuberger.
[3] It is said that in order to attend Bergson's lectures hearers found themselves driven to sit through the preceding lecture.
[4] In point of fact Bergson's name appears to have been included in the list of eminent Frenchmen who were not to be molested on the German occupation of France.

Bergson's first well known work was his *Essai sur les données immédiates de la conscience*, which appeared in 1889. Its subject-matter is perhaps better indicated by the title given to the English translation, *Time and Free Will*.[1] This work was followed in 1896 by *Matière et mémoire*[2] which gave Bergson the occasion for a more general treatment of the relation between mind and body. In 1900 Bergson published *Le rire*,[3] and in 1903 his *Introduction à la métaphysique* appeared in the *Revue de la métaphysique et de morale*.[4] His most famous work *L'évolution créatrice*[5] appeared in 1907, and this was followed by *L'énergie spirituelle*[6] in 1910 and *Durée et simultanéité*.[7] In 1932 Bergson published his notable work on morals and religion, *Les deux sources de la morale et de la religion*.[8] A collection of essays entitled *La pensée et le mouvant*[9] followed in 1934. Three volumes of *Écrits et paroles* were edited by R. M. Mossé-Bastide and published at Paris in 1957–59, with a preface by Édouard Le Roy. The centenary edition of Bergson's works appeared in 1959.

2. Although Bergson once had a great name, his use of imagery and metaphor, his sometimes rather high-flown or rhapsodic style, and a certain lack of precision in his thought have contributed to his being depreciated as a philosopher by those who equate philosophy with logical or conceptual analysis and who attach great value to precision of thought and language. Obviously, this is true in the first place of countries in which the analytic movement has prevailed, and where the tendency has been to look on Bergson as more of a poet or even a mystic than as a serious philosopher. In some other countries, including his own, he has fallen into neglect for another reason, namely the eclipse of the philosophy of life by existentialism and phenomenology.

---

[1] Translated by F. L. Pogson (London and New York, 1910).
[2] Translated by N. M. Paul and W. S. Palmer as *Matter and Memory* (London and New York, 1911).
[3] Translated by G. C. Brereton and F. Rothwell as *Laughter, An Essay on the Meaning of the Comic* (New York, 1910).
[4] Translated by T. E. Hulme as *An Introduction to Metaphysics* (London and New York, 1912).
[5] Translated by A. Mitchell as *Creative Evolution* (London and New York, 1911).
[6] Translated by H. Wildon Carr as *Mind-Energy* (London and New York, 1910).
[7] Second edition, with three appendices, 1923.
[8] Translated by R. A. Audra and C. Brereton, with the assistance of W. Horsfall-Carter, as *The Two Sources of Morality and Religion* (London and New York, 1935).
[9] Translated by M. L. Andison as *The Creative Mind* (New York, 1946).

It may be true to say that in recent years the stir caused by the writings of Teilhard de Chardin has led to some revival of interest in Bergson, in view of the affinities between the two thinkers. But though the vogue enjoyed by Teilhard de Chardin and recognition of the relationship between him and his predecessor Bergson may have tended to make the latter's thought seem more actual and relevant, they do little to mitigate the force of objections brought by logical or conceptual analysts against Bergson's style of philosophizing. For similar objections can obviously be levelled against Teilhard de Chardin.

The accusations brought against Bergson's way of philosophizing are certainly not groundless. At the same time it is only fair to him to emphasize the fact that he was not trying to accomplish the sort of task to which logical analysts devote themselves, but failing signally to do so. He had his own idea of the nature and function of philosophy; and his way of philosophizing, and even his style, were connected with this idea. It is thus appropriate to begin by giving a brief explanation of his concept of philosophy.

In an essay which he wrote specially for the collection entitled *La pensée et le mouvant* Bergson began by asserting, perhaps somewhat surprisingly, that 'what has been most wanting in philosophy, is precision'.[1] What he had in mind were the shortcomings, as he saw them, of philosophical systems, which are 'not tailored to the reality in which we live'[2] but which are so abstract and vast as to try to comprise everything, the actual, the possible 'and even the impossible'[3]. It seemed to him at first that the philosophy of Herbert Spencer was an exception, inasmuch as, in spite of some vague generalities, it bore the imprint of the actual world and was modelled on the facts. At the same time Spencer had not delved deeply enough into the basic ideas of mechanics; and Bergson resolved to complete this work. In the course however of trying to do so he found himself brought to consider the subject of time. He was impelled to distinguish between the mathematical time of the scientist, in which time is broken up into moments and conceived in a spatial manner, and 'real' time, pure duration, continuity, which we can grasp in inner experience but can conceptualize only with difficulty.

Bergson therefore comes to conceive of philosophy or metaphysics as based on intuition, which he contrasts with analysis.

---

[1] *La pensée et le mouvant*, p. 7 (3rd edition, 1934).
[2] *Ibid.*, p. 7.   [3] *Ibid.*, p. 7.

By analysis he means the reduction of the complex to its simple constituents, as when a physical object is reduced to molecules, to atoms and finally to sub-atomic 'particles' or as when a new idea is explained in terms of a new arrangement of ideas which we already possess. By intuition he means the 'immediate consciousness'[1] or direct awareness of a reality. Bergson also contrasts the symbolization which is required by analytic thought with intuitive freedom from symbolization.[2] Even if however the intuitive perception of a reality may, in itself, be unexpressed in linguistic symbols, there can obviously be no philosophy without conceptualization and language. Bergson is of course well aware of this fact. An effort of reflection[3] is required to grasp the content of an intuition and to appreciate its significance and illuminative bearing. The idea which expresses an intuition seemes at first to be obscure rather than clear; and though appropriate terms, such as 'real duration', can be employed, the linguistic expression will not really be understood unless one participates in the intuition. The philosopher should indeed strive after clarity; but he cannot achieve this unless intuition and expression go, as it were, hand in hand or unless symbolization is checked by a return to intuitive awareness of what the philosopher is speaking about. Further, images may have a useful role to play by suggesting the content of an intuition and facilitating a participation in it[4].

It is all very well to say that philosophy is based on intuition. What is the object of such intuition? A general answer might be that it is movement, becoming, duration, that which can be known only through immediate or intuitive awareness, and not through a reductive analysis which distorts it or destroys its continuity. To say this is to say (within the framework of Bergson's thought) that the object of intuition is reality. For in the second of his Oxford Conferences he makes the often quoted statement that 'there are changes, but there are not, under the change, things

---

[1] *La pensée et le mouvant*, p. 35.   [2] Cf. *ibid.*, p. 206.

[2] When replying to critics who interpret intuition as consisting in hunches or feelings, Bergson says that 'our intuition is reflection' (*Ibid.*, p. 109). At first hearing at any rate this sounds like a contradiction in terms. But he may be thinking in part of the 'reflection' of Maine de Biran, the immediate awareness by the self of its inner life, reflexive psychology in other words. In any case, even if intuition itself is not reflection, Bergson certainly thinks of the philosopher's mind as appropriating the intuition, so to speak, through a process of reflection which tries to keep as close as possible to the intuition.

[4] In the case of exceptional intuitions, such as those enjoyed by the mystics, the use of imagery may be the most appropriate way of trying to convey some idea of the intuitions or experiences.

which change: change has no need of a support. There are movements, but there is no inert, invariable object which moves: movement does not imply a *mobile*.'[1] In the first instance however the object of intuition is, as with Maine de Biran, the inner life of the self, of the spirit. Bergson remarks, for example, that existence is only given in experience. He then goes on to say that 'this experience will be called sight or contact, exterior perception in general, if it is a question of a material object: it will have the name "intuition" when it bears on the spirit'.[2] It is true that according to Bergson his first concern is with real duration. But he finds this in the life of the self, in 'the direct vision of the spirit by the spirit',[3] in the interior life.

Bergson can thus maintain that while positive science is concerned with the material world, metaphysics 'reserves for itself the spirit'.[4] This may seem to be patently untrue, given the existence of psychology. For Bergson however psychology as a science treats the spirit or mind as if it were material. That is to say, it analyses the life of the mind in such a way as to represent it on an analogy with spatial and material objects. The empirical psychologist does not necessarily assert that mental phenomena are material. But he extends reductive analysis from physical objects to the mind and considers it as something over against himself. The metaphysician however takes as his point of departure an intuitive or immediate awareness of the inner life of the spirit as it is lived; and he tries to prolong this intuition in his reflection.

Science and metaphysics therefore have different objects or subject-matters according to Bergson. He assigns 'matter to science and spirit to metaphysics'.[5] It is thus clear enough that he does not regard philosophy as a synthesis of the particular sciences. There is no question of claiming that philosophy can 'go beyond science in the generalization of the same facts'.[6] Philosophy 'is not a synthesis of the particular sciences'.[7] The objects of science and philosophy are different. So too are their methods.

---

[1] *La pensée et le mouvant*, p. 185. Bergson does not mean that there is no existing reality. His contention is that reality is a becoming, the past persisting in the present, and the present being carried into the future, the whole process being continuous throughout and divisible only through the artificial separation effected by the intelligence for its own purposes.

[2] *Ibid.*, p. 61.   [3] *Ibid.*, p. 35.

[4] *Ibid.*, p. 50. Bergson's use of the word 'metaphysics' in this context recalls to mind the use made of the term by Maine de Biran.

[5] *Ibid.*, p. 54.   [6] *Ibid.*, p. 155.   [7] *Ibid.*, p. 156.

For science is the work of the intelligence and works by analysis, whereas metaphysics is, or is based on and draws its life from, intuition. To say however that science and metaphysics differ from one another in subject-matter and method is by no means the whole of the story. For in Bergson's view reality is change or becoming, real duration or the life of the spirit; and the material world of the physicist is regarded, by an extension of Ravaisson's theory of habit, as a kind of deposit made by the movement of life in its creative advance. If therefore we ask whether it is science or metaphysics which reveals reality to us, the answer must be that it is metaphysics. For it is only in intuition that the mind can have direct awareness of the actual movement of life.

Bergson endeavours to show that he is not concerned with depreciating science, nor with suggesting that the philosopher can profitably dismiss the findings of the scientist. He explains, for example, that when he insists on the difference between the positive sciences and philosophy he is concerned with the purification of science from 'scientism', from a metaphysics, that is to say, which masquerades as positive scientific knowledge, and with freeing philosophy from any misconception of itself as a super-science, capable of doing the scientist's work for him or of providing generalizations from the data of science which the scientist is unable to provide. Referring to accusations against him of being an opponent of science, Bergson remarks 'once again, we wanted a philosophy which would submit itself to the control of science and which could also contribute to its (science's) advance.'[1] The work of the intelligence is necessary for action; and science, the product of the intelligence, is required if man is to have conceptual and practical control of his environment. Moreover, science, Bergson suggests rather vaguely, can provide verification for metaphysics,[2] while metaphysics, as it is based on intuition of truth, can help science to correct its errors. While therefore they remain distinct, science and philosophy can cooperate; and neither of them should be depreciated. As they differ in subject-matter and method, disputes about relative dignity are otiose.

Obviously, Bergson is justified in emphasizing the need for the work of the intelligence, and so of science. To be sure, Bergson's ideas are by no means always clear and unambiguous. Sometimes, for example, he speaks as though the world of individual things,

[1] *Ibid.*, p. 82.   [2] *Ibid.*, p. 83.

of substances which change, is a fiction or fabrication of the intelligence. At other times he implies that in its individualizing activity the intelligence makes objectively grounded distinctions. His precise meaning is left obscure. At the same time it is obvious that we could not possibly live, in any recognizable sense of 'live', simply with the consciousness of a continuous flow of becoming. We could not live and act without a world of distinct things. And we could not understand and control this world without science. Hence Bergson is quite justified in claiming that he has no intention of attacking science as a superfluity. When all this is said however, it remains true that for him it is intuition, not intelligence, and metaphysics rather than science, which reveals to us the nature of reality, underlying the constructed, even if necessarily constructed, world of the scientist. And when Bergson speaks about metaphysics submitting itself to the control of science, he really means that in his view modern science is developing in such a way as to confirm rather than to falsify his philosophical theories. In other words, if we assume the truth of Bergson's position, it seems to follow that in important respects metaphysics must be superior to science, however much Bergson may have tried to disclaim such judgments of value.

Reference has already been made to Bergson's negative attitude to philosophical systems. It is hardly necessary to say that he has no liking for attempts to deduce the structure of reality *a priori* from allegedly self-evidently true propositions. A man who believes that 'philosophy has never frankly admitted this continuous creation of unforeseeable novelty'[1] is obviously not disposed to look with favour on any system of a Spinozistic type. Indeed, Bergson explicitly disclaims the intention of constructing any sort of comprehensive system. What he does is to consider distinct questions in succession, reflecting on the data in various areas.[2] Some of the questions which have seemed of great importance to metaphysical philosophers are dismissed by Bergson as pseudo-problems. 'Why is there something rather than nothing?' and 'Why is there order rather than disorder?' are given as examples of pseudo-problems or at any rate of badly formulated questions.[3] In view of his reputation for high-flown poetry or imaginative

---

[1] *Ibid.*, p. 132.
[2] In an interview (*Mercure de France*, 1914, p. 397) Bergson asserted that he did not know in advance to what conclusions his premises would lead.
[3] *La pensée et le mouvant*, pp. 121 f.

and imprecise language, it is only fair to Bergson to emphasize the fact that he intends to be as concrete and as faithful as possible to reality as experienced. It is true that a more or less unified world-outlook emerges from his successive writings. But this is due to a convergence of his various lines of thought rather than to any deliberate attempt to construct a comprehensive system. There are of course certain recurrent and pervasive key-ideas, such as intuition and duration; but they are not postulated in advance like the premises of a deductive system.

When Bergson is treating of the mental life, there is no great difficulty in understanding what he means by intuition, even if one does not care for the term. It is equivalent to the immediate consciousness of Maine de Biran. When however Bergson turns to a general theory of evolution, as in *L'évolution créatrice*, it is not so easy to see how this theory can be said to be based on intuition. Even if we are immediately aware of a vital impetus or *élan vital* in ourselves, a good deal of extrapolation is required in order to make this intuition the basis for a general view of evolution. The philosophy of *l'esprit* becomes very much wider in its scope than any kind of reflexive psychology. However there is not much point in trying to discuss such matters in advance of a treatment of Bergson's successive lines of inquiry.

3. In the preface to *Time and Free Will* Bergson announces his intention of trying to establish that 'every discussion between determinists and their opponents implies a previous confusion of duration with extension, of succession with simultaneity, of quality with quantity.'[1] Once this confusion has been cleared up, one may perhaps find that objections against freedom vanish, together with the definitions which have been given to it, and, 'in a certain sense, the very problem of free will'.[2] In this case Bergson has of course to explain the nature of the alleged confusion before going on to show how its dissipation affects determinism.

We conceive of physical objects, according to Bergson, as existing and occupying positions in 'an empty homogeneous medium',[3] namely space. And it is the concept of space which determines our ordinary idea of time, the concept of time as

---

[1] *Time and Free Will*, pp. xix–xx. References to this work are given to the English translation, for the convenience of the reader. But as I have myself translated from the French, there are slightly different wordings in places.
[2] *Ibid.*, p. xx.   [3] *Ibid.*, p. 95.

employed in the natural sciences and for purposes of practical
life. That is to say, we conceive time according to the analogy of an
unbounded line composed of units or moments which are external
to one another. This idea gives rise to the sort of puzzles raised
centuries ago by Zeno.[1] But it enables us to measure time and to
fix the occurrence of events, as simultaneous or as successive,
within the time-medium, which is itself empty and homogeneous,
like space. This concept of time is in fact the spatialized or mathe-
maticized idea of duration. Pure duration, of which we can become
intuitively or immediately aware in consciousness of our own
inner mental life, when, that is to say, we enter into it in depth, is
a series of qualitative changes melting into and permeating one
another, so that each 'element' represents the whole, like a musical
phrase, and is an isolated unit not in reality but only through
intellectual abstraction. Pure duration is a continuity of movement, with qualitative but not quantitative differentiations. It
can thus be described as heterogeneous, not as homogeneous.
Language however 'demands that we should establish between our
ideas the same clear and precise distinctions, the same discontinuity, as between material objects'.[2] Discursive thought and
language require that we should break up the uninterrupted flow
of consciousness[3] into distinct and numerable states, succeeding
one another in time, represented as a homogeneous medium. This
concept of time however is 'only the ghost of space haunting the
reflective consciousness',[4] whereas pure duration is 'the form taken
by the succession of our states of consciousness when our ego lets
itself live, when it abstains from making a separation between its
present and preceding states'.[5] We can say in effect that the idea of
pure duration expresses the nature of the life of the deeper self,
while the concept of the self as a succession of states represents
the superficial self, created by the spatializing intelligence. Pure
duration is grasped in intuition, in which the self is coincident
with its own life, whereas the self of analytic psychology is the
result of our looking at ourselves as external spectators, as though
we were looking at physical objects outside us.

Now suppose that we conceive the self as a succession of distinct

[1] As the individual units, which are conceived as constituting time in their
succession, are 'virtual stoppages of time' (*La pensée et le mouvant*, p. 9).
[2] *Time and Free Will*, p. xix.
[3] To what extent Bergson was influenced by other writers, such as William
James, is a matter of dispute.
[4] *Time and Freewill*, p. 99.   [5] *Ibid.*, p. 100.

states in spatialized time. It is then natural to think of a preceding state as causing the succeeding state. Further, feelings and motives will be regarded as distinct entities which cause or determine successive entities. This may sound far-fetched. But that this is not the case can be seen by reflecting on talk about motives determining choices. In such language motives are clearly hypostatized and given a substantial existence of their own. Bergson thus asserts a close link between determinism and the associationist psychology. And in his view no answer to determinism is possible, if the adequacy of this psychology is once assumed. For it makes little sense to picture one state of consciousness as oscillating between making two mutually exclusive choices and then opting for one choice when it might have opted for the other. If we once accept the associationist psychology as adequate, it is a waste of time to look for answers to determinism. We cannot refute the determinists on their own selected ground. What is needed is to challenge their whole concept of the self and its life. And, as Bergson sees things, this means setting the idea of pure duration against the spatialized or geometric concept of time. If time is assimilated to space and states of consciousness are conceived on an analogy with material objects, determinism is inevitable. If however the life of the self is seen in its continuity, its uninterrupted flow, it can also be seen that some acts spring from the totality, the whole personality; and these acts are free. 'We are free when our acts flow from our whole personality, when they express it, when they have with it that indefinable resemblance which one sometimes finds between the artist and his work.'[1]

Bergson thus carries on that insistence on human freedom which we find among his predecessors in the spiritualist movement. A good deal of what he has to say, especially by way of criticism or attack, is sensible enough. It is pretty clear, for example, that talk about a man's choices being determined by his motives is misleading, inasmuch as it suggests that a motive is a substantial entity which pushes a man, as though from without, into a certain course of action. Again, while character-determinism, as portrayed by writers such as J. S. Mill, can be made extremely plausible, talk about a man's actions being determined by his character implies that to the noun 'character' there corresponds a block-entity which exercises a one-way causal activity on the

[1] *Ibid.*, p. 172.

will. In general, Bergson's contention that the determinists, especially those who presuppose the associationist psychology, are held captive by a spatial picture is well argued.

It does not follow of course that Bergson is an upholder of 'liberty of indifference'. For as he conceives this theory, it involves the same sort of misleading picture which can be found with the determinists.[1] In Bergson's view 'any definition of freedom will ensure the victory of determinism'.[2] For a definition is the result of analysis, and analysis involves the transformation of a process into a thing and of duration into extension. Freedom is the indefinable 'relation of the concrete self to the act which it performs'.[3] It is something of which we are immediately aware, but it is not something which can be proved. For the attempt to prove it involves taking the very point of view which leads to determinism, the point of view from which time is identified with space or at any rate is interpreted in spatial terms.

Bergson does not of course maintain that all the actions performed by a human being are free actions. He distinguishes between 'two different selves, one of which is, as it were, the external projection of the other, its spatial and, so to speak, social representation'.[4] We are reminded here of Kant's distinction between the phenomenal and the noumenal self; but Kant is found fault with by Bergson for his account of time. For Bergson free acts are those which proceed from the self considered as pure duration. 'To act freely, is to regain possession of oneself, to get back into pure duration.'[5] But a great part of our lives is lived at the level of the superficial self, the level at which we are acted upon, by social pressure for instance, rather than act ourselves. And this is why we are rarely free.'[6] This theory may seem to enable Bergson to evade the awkward position of Kant, the notion, that is to say, that the same actions are determined from one point of view and free from another. Even for Bergson of course a free act, springing from the 'deeper' self or the whole personality, appears as determined if it is located, so to speak, in homogeneous and

[1] It implies, according to Bergson, the picture of the ego as traversing a number of distinct states and then as oscillating between two ready-made paths lying before it.
[2] *Time and Free Will*, p. 220.
[3] *Ibid.*, p. 219.
[4] *Ibid.*, p. 231.
[5] *Ibid.*, pp. 231–2.
[6] *Ibid.*, p. 231.

spatialized time. But he regards this point of view as erroneous, even if it is required for practical, social and scientific purposes. What Bergson has to say about the two levels of the self recalls to mind not only the Kantian philosophy but also the later existentialist distinction between authentic and inauthentic existence. There are of course considerable differences between the philosophy of Bergson and existentialism, as there are too between the various brands of existentialism. But it is not a question of representing existentialism as an historical development of the Bergsonian philosophy of life. Rather is it a matter of affinities. In the spiritualist movement and in existentialism too we can see an attack on 'scientism', showing itself in an insistence on human freedom and in an interpretation of freedom in terms of the idea of a deeper self of some kind. If we consider the philosophy of Karl Jaspers, we can see that his contention that if we adopt the position of external spectators, of the objectifying scientist, we cannot avoid an at any rate methodological determinism, whereas freedom is something of which the agent, as agent, is aware, is akin to the position of Bergson. The fact that the influences on Jaspers' thought were Kant, Kierkegaard and Nietzsche rather than Bergson does not alter the fact that there is some affinity between their lines of thought.

4. In *Matière et mémoire* Bergson tackles the problem of the relation between mind and body. In his introduction he says that the book asserts the reality of both spirit and matter, and that his position is thus frankly dualistic. It is true that he speaks of matter as an aggregate of images. But by using the word 'image' he does not mean to imply that a physical object exists only in the human mind. He means that an object is what we perceive it to be and not something entirely different. In the case of a red object, for instance, it is the object which is red. Redness is not something subjective. In fine, a physical object is 'an image, but an image which exists in itself'.[1] Among such physical objects there is one which I know not only by perception but also 'from within by affections. It is my body.'[2] What is the relation between my body and my mind? In particular, are mental processes identifiable with physical processes in the brain, so that talk about the former and talk about the latter are simply two languages or ways of

---

[1] *Matter and Memory*, p. viii. Page-references are given to the English translation, even when my own translation differs slightly.
[2] *Ibid.*, p. 1.

speaking which refer to the same thing? Or is the mind an epiphenomenon of the cerebral organism, so that it is completely and
throughout dependent on the brain? To put the matter in another
way, is the relation between mind and the brain of such a kind that
anyone who had a complete knowledge of what was going on in
the brain would thereby have a detailed knowledge of what was
proceeding in consciousness?

Bergson remarks that 'the truth is that there would be one way,
and one only, of refuting materialism, that of establishing that
matter is absolutely what it appears to be.'[1] For if matter is
nothing but what it appears to be, there is no reason for ascribing it to occult capacities such as thought. This is one reason
why Bergson dwells at some length on the nature of matter.
However, though what Bergson takes to be the position of
common sense should suffice, philosophical reflection requires
something more. And Bergson tackles his problem by means of a
study of memory, on the ground that memory, as representing
'precisely the point of interaction between mind and matter',[2]
seems to provide the strongest support for materialism and
epiphenomenalism. A study of memory however involves also a
study of perception, as perception is 'wholly impregnated with
memory-images which complete it while interpreting it'.[3]

To cut a long story short, Bergson makes a distinction between
two kinds of memory. In the first place there is the kind of memory
which consists in motor-mechanisms which resemble or are
habits. Thus one can learn by heart, as we say, a certain
series of words, a lesson or a poem. And when the appropriate
stimulus is provided, the mechanism starts to function. There is
'a closed system of automatic movements which succeed one
another in the same order and occupy the same time'.[4] Memory in
this sense of mechanical repetition is a bodily habit, like walking;
considered precisely as such, it does not include mental representation of the past but is rather a bodily aptitude, an organic
disposition to respond in a certain way to a certain stimulus.
Memory in this sense is not confined to human beings. A parrot,
for example, can be trained to respond to a stimulus by uttering
certain words in succession. This kind of memory is different from
what Bergson calls 'pure memory', which is representation and
records 'all the events of our daily life',[5] neglecting no detail.

---

[1] *Ibid.*, p. 80.   [2] *Ibid.*, p. xii.   [3] *Ibid.*, p. 170.
[4] *Ibid.*, p. 90.   [5] *Ibid.*, p. 92.

Memory in this sense is spiritual, and to admit its existence is obviously to admit that part of the mind is infra-conscious. If the whole of my past is stored, as it were, in my mind in the form of memory-images, it is clear that only a few of these images are even recalled to consciousness at a given time. They must then be stored in the infra-conscious area of the mind. Indeed, if the whole of my past, including every detail, were present to my consciousness at once, action would become impossible. And here we have the key to the relation between the brain and pure memory. That is to say, the function of the brain, according to Bergson, is to inhibit the invasion of consciousness by the pure memory and to admit only those recollections which are related in some way to contemplated or required action. In itself pure memory is spiritual; but its contents are filtered, as it were, by the brain. Pure memory and memory as habit come together of course in practice, as in, for example, the intelligent repetition of something learned. But they should not be confused. For it is this confusion which leads support to materialism.

The concept of pure memory is linked by Bergson with that of pure duration. And he argues, with the help of a study of pathological phenomena such as aphasia, that there is no cogent evidence of memories being spatially located in the brain. In his view the brain is not a storehouse of memories but plays a role analogous to that of a telephone-exchange. If one could penetrate into the brain and see clearly all the processes taking place in it, all that one would find would probably be 'sketched-out or prepared movements'.[1] That is to say, the cerebral state represents only a small part of the mental state, namely 'that part which is capable of translating itself into movements of locomotion'.[2] In other words, Bergson tries to refute psycho-physical or psycho-neural parallelism by arguing that the state of the brain indicates that of the mind only in so far as the psychic life is turned towards action and is the remote beginning of or at least the preparation for action.

Perception, Bergson insists, is different in kind from recollection. In perception the perceived object is present as object of an intuition of the real, whereas in recollection an absent object is remembered. Though however perception is an intuition of the real, it is a mistake to suppose that perception as such is directed towards pure knowledge. On the contrary, it is 'entirely oriented

---

[1] *Ibid.*, p. xiii.   [2] *Ibid.*, p. xiii.

towards action'.[1] That is to say, perception is basically selective with a view to possible action or reaction. It is utilitarian in character. At root, it concentrates on what can answer to a need or tendency. And we can assume that with animals perception is generally just this.[2] As we ascend the stages of the evolution of organic life, moving into the sphere of consciousness and freedom, the area of possible action and of the subjectivity of perception grows. But perception in itself, 'pure perception', is oriented to action. And it is not the same thing as memory. If our perceptions were all 'pure', simple intuitions of objects, the function of consciousness would be to unite them by means of memory. But this would not convert them into memories or acts of recollection.

In point of fact however pure perception is pretty well a limiting concept. 'Perception is never a simple contact of the mind with the present object. It is wholly impregnated with memory-images which complete it while interpreting it.'[3] Pure memory manifests itself in images; and these images enter into our perceptions. In theory we can distinguish between pure memory and pure perception. And for Bergson it is important that the distinction should be made. Otherwise, for instance, recollection will be interpreted as a weakened form of perception, when it is in fact different in kind and not simply in intensity. In practice however recollection and perception interpenetrate each other. In other words, perception in its concrete or actual form is a synthesis of pure memory and pure perception, and so 'of mind (*esprit*) and matter'.[4] In concrete perception the mind contributes memory-images which confer on the object of perception a completed and meaningful form. In Bergson's view this theory helps to overcome the opposition between idealism and realism and also throws light on the relation between mind or spirit and body. 'Mind (or spirit) borrows from matter the perceptions from which it draws its nourishment and restores them to matter in the form of movement on which it has stamped its own freedom.'[5] Pure perception

---

[1] *Ibid.*, p. 21.

[2] It may be objected that in the case of animals reference should be made to sensation rather than to perception. But Bergson is not prepared to regard sensation as more fundamental than perception. 'Our sensations are to our perceptions what the real action of our body is to its possible or virtual action' (*Ibid.*, p. 58). Virtual action precedes real action. A body's real action is manifested within itself in the form of affective sensations. A herbivorous animal, for instance, perceives grass. The nearer the grass is, the more does the virtual action prefigured in perception tend to become real action. Real action is of course accompanied by sensation.

[3] *Ibid.*, p. 170.   [4] *Ibid.*, p. 325.   [5] *Ibid.*, p. 332.

which, as a limiting concept, is the coincidence of subject and object, belongs to the side of matter. Pure memory, which exhibits real duration, belongs to the side of spirit. But memory, as a 'synthesis of the past and the present in view of the future',[1] brings together or unites the successive phases of matter to use them and to manifest itself by the actions which constitute the reason for the soul's union with the body. In Bergson's opinion spirit and matter, soul and body, are united for action; and this union is to be understood not in spatial terms[2] but in terms of duration.

As in the case of Bergson's other writings most readers of *Matière et mémoire* often find it difficult to make out his precise meaning. And they may well suspect that if they fail to find it, this is not their fault. However Bergson's general position can be summarized in this way. The body is 'an instrument of action, and of action only'.[3] Pure perception is virtual action, at any rate in the sense that it detaches from the field of objects the object which interests from the point of view of possible bodily action. 'The virtual action of things on our body and of our body on things is our perception itself.'[4] And the state of the brain corresponds exactly to the perception. Actual perception however is not 'pure perception' but is enriched and interpreted by memory which is in itself, as 'pure memory', 'something other than a function of the brain'.[5] Perception as we actually experience it therefore (impregnated, that is to say, with memory-images) is a point where spirit and matter, soul and body, intersect dynamically, in an orientation to action.[6] And while the 'pure perception' element corresponds exactly to the state of the brain or to processes in the brain, the 'pure memory' element does not. Spirit or mind is not in itself a function of the brain, nor an epiphenomenon; but as turned to action it depends on the body, the instrument of action, and virtual action, prefiguring or sketching out and preparing real action, is dependent on the brain. Damage to the brain may inhibit action; but it should not be thought of as destroying the mind or spirit in itself.[7]

---

[1] *Ibid.*, p. 294.
[2] This is said to be the mistake of 'ordinary dualism' (*ibid.*).
[3] *Ibid.*, p. 299.   [4] *Ibid.*, p. 309.   [5] *Ibid.*, p. 315.
[6] As mentioned above, memory is stated by Bergson to be the point of intersection. But we are speaking here of concrete and conscious perception, in which memory-images are always present, not of the limiting concept of pure perception.
[7] Bergson looks on this view not so much as a proof of immortality as removing a major obstacle to belief in it.

5. In *Time and Free Will* and *Matter and Memory* Bergson introduces his readers, in the contexts of particular problems, to his ideas of mathematical or spatialized time on the one hand and of pure duration on the other, of the analytical intelligence, dominated by the concept of space, on the one hand and of intuition on the other, of matter as the sphere of mechanism and of spirit as the sphere of creative freedom, of man as an agent rather than as a spectator and of the intelligence as serving the needs of action, even if man, through intuition, is capable of grasping the nature of becoming as manifested in his own inner life. In *Creative Evolution* he exhibits such ideas in a wider context.

The year of Bergson's birth, 1859, was the year in which *The Origin of Species* was published. Though however the theory of evolution in general permeated Bergson's thought, he found himself unable to accept any mechanistic interpretation of it, including Darwinism. The theory of 'natural selection', for example, in virtue of chance or random variations which adapt the organism for survival seemed to him quite inadequate. In the process of evolution we can see a development of complexity. But a higher degree of complexity involves a greater degree of risk. If survival-value were the only factor, one might expect evolution to stop with the simplest types of organism. As for chance or random variations, if these occurred in a part of a whole (such as the eye), the functioning of the whole might well be impeded. For the effective functioning of the whole there must be coordination or coadaptation; and to attribute this simply to 'chance' is to make too great a demand on credulity. At the same time an explanation of evolution in terms of finality seemed to Bergson unacceptable, if the idea of finality were taken to mean that the process of evolution was simply the working out or realization of a predetermined end. For this sort of theory eliminated all novelty and creativity and in some important respects resembled mechanism. It added of course the idea of a preconceived or predetermined end; but neither in the case of a mechanistic acconunt or in that of a teleological account[1] was any room left for the emergence of novelty.

In Bergson's view we are justified in looking to man's inner life

---

[1] The expression 'a teleological account' must be understood in the sense of an account of evolution which represents it as the progressive realization of a preconceived plan, the working out of a blueprint. Bergson is far from denying an immanent teleology in the organism. Nor does he exclude a general teleology which allows for the emergence of what is novel.

for the key to the evolution of life in general. In ourselves we are aware, or rather can be aware, of a vital impetus, an *élan vital*, manifested in the continuity of our own becoming or duration. As a speculative hypothesis at any rate we are justified in extrapolating this idea and postulating 'an *original impetus* of life, passing from one generation of germs to the following generation of germs by way of the developed organisms which form the uniting link between the generations of germs.'[1] This impetus is regarded by Bergson as the cause of variations, at any rate of those which are passed on, accumulate and produce new species.[2] Its mode of operation should not be regarded as analogous to that of the manufacturers who assemble ready-made parts to form a whole but rather as an organizing action[3] which proceeds from a centre outwards, effecting differentiation in the process. The *élan vital* encounters resistance from inert matter; and in its effort to overcome this resistance it tries fresh paths. In fact it is the meeting between the 'explosive' activity of the vital impetus and the resistance of matter which leads to the development of different lines and levels of evolution. In its creative energizing the vital impetus transcends the stage of organization which it has reached. Hence Bergson's comparison of the movement of evolution to the fragmentation of an exploding shell, provided that we imagine the fragments as being themselves shells which explode in turn.[4] When the vital impetus organizes matter successfully at a certain level, the impetus is continued at this level in the successions of individual members of the species in question. The creative energy of the *élan vital* is not however exhausted at a particular level but expresses itself anew.

The movement of evolution is seen by Bergson as following three main directions, that of plant life, that of instinctive life and that of intelligent or rational life. He does not mean to deny that the different forms of life had a common origin in more primitive and hardly differentiated organisms. Nor does he intend to imply that they have nothing in common. But they have not simply succeeded one another. Plant life, for example has not been

---

[1] *Creative Evolution*, p. 92. Page-references are to the English edition, though I have, once again, translated from the French.
[2] *Ibid.*, p. 92.
[3] Bergson admits that the term 'organization' suggests the assembling of parts to form a whole. But he insists that in philosophy the term must be given a sense other than that which it bears in the contest of manufacture and in a scientific context.
[4] Cf. *Creative Evolution*, p. 103.

superseded by animal life. Bergson thinks therefore that it is more reasonable to regard the three levels as fulfilling three divergent tendencies of an activity which has split up in the course of its development than as three successive degrees of one and the same tendency. The world of plants is marked by the predominance of the features of fixity or stability and of insensibility, whereas in the world of animals we find mobility and consciousness (in some degree) as predominating characteristics. Further, in the animal world we can distinguish between those species in which intuitive life has become the dominant characteristic, as in the case of insects such as bees and ants, and the vertebrate species in which intelligent life has emerged and developed.

Bergson is at pains to point out that his theory of the three divergent tendencies in evolution necessitates, for the purpose of discussion, the making of more clear-cut distinctions that can actually be found. 'There is scarcely any manifestation of life which does not contain in a rudimentary state, whether latent or virtual, the essential characteristics of the majority of other manifestations. The difference lies in the proportions.'[1] The group should thus be defined not by its simple possession of certain characteristics but rather by its tendency to accentuate them. For example, in actual fact intuitive life and intelligent life interpenetrate in varying degrees and proportions. But they are none the less different in kind, and it is important to consider them separately.

Both instinct and intelligence are defined by Bergson with reference to the making and using of instruments. Instinct is 'a faculty of using and constructing organized instruments',[2] instruments, that is to say, which are parts of the organism itself. Intelligence is 'the faculty of making and using unorganized instruments',[3] artificial instruments, that is to say, or tools. Psychical activity as such tends to act on the material world. And it can do so either directly or indirectly. If therefore we assume that a choice has to be made, we can say that 'instinct and intelligence represent two divergent solutions, equally elegant, of one and the same problem.'[4]

If therefore man is regarded historically, he should be described, according to Bergson, not as *homo sapiens* but as *homo faber*, man the worker, in terms of the construction of tools with a view to

[1] *Ibid.*, p. 112.   [3] *Ibid.*, p. 147.
[2] *Ibid.*, p. 147.   [4] *Ibid.*, p. 150.

acting on the material environment. For man is intelligent, and 'intelligence, considered in what appears to be its original application, is the faculty of fabricating artificial objects, in particular of tools to make tools, and of varying their manufacture indefinitely.'[1] Whatever intelligence may have become in the course of human history and of man's scientific advance, its essential feature is its practical orientation. It is, like instinct, at the service of life.

Inasmuch as the human intellect is primarily oriented to construction, to acting on man's material environment by means of the instruments which it creates, it is concerned first and foremost with inorganic solids, with physical objects external to and distinct from other physical objects, and, in such objects, with parts considered as such, clearly and distinctly. In other words, the human intellect has as its chief object what is discontinuous and stable or immobile; and it has the power of reducing an object to its constituent elements and of reassembling them. It can of course concern itself with organic living beings, but it tends to treat them in the same way as inorganic objects. The scientist, for example, will reduce the living thing to its physical and chemical components and try to reconstitute it theoretically from these elements. To put the matter negatively 'the intellect is characterized by a natural inability to comprehend life'.[2] It cannot grasp becoming, continuity and pure duration as such. It tries to force the continuous into its own moulds or categories, introducing sharp and clear-cut conceptual distinctions which are inadequate to the object. It is unable to think pure duration without transforming it into a spatialized, geometric concept of time. It takes, as it were, a series of static photographs of a continuous creative movement which eludes its grasp. In fine, the intellect, though admirably adapted for action and for making possible control of the environment (and of man himself, in so far as he can be turned into a scientific object), is not fitted for grasping the movement of evolution, of   life, 'the continuity of a change which is pure mobility'.[3] It breaks up the continuous becoming into a series of states, each of which is immobilized. Moreover, as the analytic understanding strives to reduce becoming to given elements and to reconstitute it from these elements, it cannot allow for the creation of what is novel and unforeseeable. The movement of evolution, the creative activity of the *élan vital*, is represented either as a mechanical process or as the progressive

---

[1] *Ibid.*, p. 146.   [2] *Ibid.*, p. 174.   [3] *Ibid.*, p. 171.

realization of a preconceived plan. In neither case is there room for creativity.

If we assume with Bergson that evolution is the creative activity of a vital impulse which uses and, so to speak, lights up matter in its onward continuous movement,[1] and if, as Bergson claims, the human intellect or intelligence is unable to grasp this movement as it really is, it follows that the intellect is unable to understand reality, or at any rate that it can apprehend it only by distorting it and producing a caricature. Bergson is thus far from holding that the primary function of the intellect is to know Reality with a capital letter and that its functions of scientific analysis and of technological invention are secondary or even low-grade employments. On the contrary, the intellect has developed primarily for action and for purposes of practical control of the environment, and its logical and scientific uses are natural to it, whereas it is unfitted by nature to grasp Reality. Man, as already remarked, is *homo faber* rather than *homo sapiens*, as far at any rate as his original nature is concerned.

In this case the question obviously arises whether we can know the nature of reality at all, as it is in itself that is to say. For what other means have we of knowing but the intellect? Instinct may be closer to life. It may be, as Bergson claims, a prolongation of life. But it is not reflective. To return to instinct would be to leave the sphere of what would ordinarily be called knowledge. If therefore conceptual thought is incapable of grasping the true nature of the real, of creative becoming, it seems to follow that we can never know it but that we are condemned to live simply with our own fictional representations of reality.

It should hardly be necessary to say that Bergson raises this sort of question himself, and that he attempts to answer it. His main line of thought can indeed be inferred from what has already been said. But in *L'évolution créatrice* it is set in the wide context of evolutionary theory and linked with the idea of divergent directions or tendencies in the process of evolution. Intelligence is concerned with matter, and 'by means of science, which is its work, will reveal to us more and more completely the secret of physical operations.'[2] It can however grasp life only by translating it in terms of inertia. Instinct is turned towards life, but it is without

---

[1] The vital impetus does not, for Bergson, actually create matter. It explodes creatively through matter and uses matter.

[2] *Creative Evolution*, p. 186.

reflective consciousness. If however instinct, which is a prolongation of life itself,[1] could extend its object and also reflect upon
itself, 'it would give us the key to vital operations'.[2] And this idea
is verified in intuition, which is 'instinct become disinterested,
conscious of itself, capable of reflecting on its object and of
enlarging it indefinitely'.[3] Intuition presupposes the development
of intelligence. Without this development instinct would have
remained riveted to objects of practical interest with a view to
physical movements. In other words, intuition presupposes the
emergence of reflective consciousness, which then splits up into
intelligence and intuition, corresponding respectively to matter
and life. 'This doubling of consciousness is thus related to the
twofold form of the real, and the theory of knowledge must be
dependent on metaphysics.'[4]

Let us assume with Bergson that intelligence is oriented to
matter, intuition to life. Let us also assume that developed intelligence creates the natural sciences. The obvious implication is
that philosophy, treating of life, is based on intuition. Indeed,
Bergson tells us that if intuition could be prolonged beyond a few
instants, philosophers would be in agreement.[5] The trouble is
however that intuition cannot be prolonged in such a way as to
make rival systems of philosophy immediately disappear. In
practice there has to be interchange between intuition and intelligence. Intelligence has to apply itself to the content of intuition;
and what intelligence makes of this content has to be checked and
corrected by reference to intuition. We have to make do, so to
speak, with the instruments at hand; and philosophy can hardly
attain the degree of purity which is attained by positive science
in proportion as it frees itself from metaphysical assumptions and
prejudices. Without intuition however philosophy is blind.

Bergson used the intuition of our own freedom, our own free
creative activity, as a key to the nature of the Universe. 'The
universe is not made, but is being made continually.'[6] More precisely, there is both making and unmaking. Bergson uses the
metaphor of a jet of steam issuing at high pressure from a vessel,
with drops condensing and falling back. 'So, from an immense
reservoir of life jets must be leaping out without ceasing, each of
which, falling back, is a world.'[7] Matter represents the falling

[1] Bergson describes instinct as 'sympathy' (cf. *ibid.*, 186).
[2] *Ibid.*, p. 186.   [3] *Ibid.*, p. 186.   [4] *Ibid.*, p. 188.
[5] *Ibid.*, p. 252.   [6] *Ibid.*, p. 255.   [7] *Ibid.*, p. 261.

back, the process of unmaking, while the movement of life in the world represents what remains of the direct upward movement in the inverted movement. The creation of living species is due to the creative activity of life; but from another point of view the self-perpetuating species represents a falling back. 'Matter or mind, reality has appeared to us as a perpetual becoming. It makes itself or it unmakes itself, but it is never something (simply) made.'[1]

What, we may ask, is Bergson's justification for this extrapolation of an experience of free creative activity in ourselves? Or does he claim that we can have an intuition of becoming in general, of the cosmic *élan vital?* In his *Introduction to Metaphysics* he asks the following question. 'If metaphysics should proceed by intuition, if intuition has for its object the mobility of duration, and if duration is psychological in essence, are we not going to shut up the philosopher in the exclusive contemplation of himself?'[2] Bergson replies that the coincidence, in intuition, with our own duration puts us in contact with a whole continuity of durations and so enables us to transcend ourselves. But it seems that this can be the case only if the experience of our own duration is an intuition of the creative activity of the cosmic vital impulse. And this is what Bergson appears to imply when he refers to a 'coincidence of the human consciousness with the living principle from which it emanates, a contact with the creative effort.'[3] Elsewhere he asserts that 'the matter and life which fill the world are also in us; the forces which work in all things, we feel them in ourselves; whatever the intimate essence of that which is and of that which makes itself may be, we participate in it.'[4] So presumably it is our participation in the *élan vital* or its operation in us which enables Bergson to base a general philosophical theory on an intuition which, in the first instance, is of duration in man himself.

The concept of the *élan vital* bears some resemblance at any rate to that of the soul of the world as found in ancient philosophy and in some modern philosophers such as Schelling. Bergson also speaks of the vital impulse as 'supra-consciousness'[5] and likens it to a rocket, the extinguished fragments of which fall back as

---

[1] *Ibid.*, p. 287.   [2] *La pensée et le mouvant*, p. 233.
[3] *Creative Evolution*, p. 391. Bergson is speaking of the intuition which, he claims, is the basis of philosophy and enables the philosopher to treat of becoming in general.
[4] *La pensée et le mouvant*, p. 157.   [5] *Creative Evolution*, p. 275.

matter. In addition he uses the word 'God', God being described as 'a continuity of leaping out'[1] or, more conventionally, as 'unceasing life, action, freedom'.[2] In *Creative Evolution* therefore the concept of God is introduced simply in the context of evolutionary theory, as signifying an immanent cosmic vital impulse which is not creator in the Judaeo-Christian traditional sense but uses matter as the instrument of the creation of fresh forms of life. However Bergson's ideas of God and religion are much better left to the next chapter, where his work on the subject will be considered.

Reference has already been made to Bergson's lack of linguistic precision. But if conceptual thought cannot grasp reality as it is in itself, we can hardly expect a high degree of precision. 'Comparisons and metaphors will suggest here what one does not succeed in expressing. ... As soon as we begin to treat of the spiritual world, the image, even if it aims only at suggesting, can give us the direct vision, while the abstract term, which is of spatial origin and which claims to express, leaves us on most occasions with metaphor.'[3] As there does not seem much that can usefully be said on this matter, in view, that is to say, of Bergson's premises, we can go on to remark that in this chapter we have made no attempt to assess the influences on Bergson's thought. There can be little doubt, for example, that he was influenced by Ravaisson's idea of the inverse movement of matter and of mechanism as a kind of relapse of freedom into habit. But though Bergson refers to some eminent philosophers of the past, such as Plato, Aristotle, Spinoza, Leibniz and Kant, and, among the moderns, to Herbert Spencer and to a number of scientists and psychologists, he makes very little reference to his immediate predecessors. He acknowledged some debt to Plotinus, to Maine de Biran and to Ravaisson; but even if it can be shown, despite his disclaimers, that he had probably read some essay or book by an immediate predecessor or a contemporary,[4] it does not necessarily follow that he simply borrowed the idea in question. Disputes about his originality or lack of it are apt to be inconclusive. Nor is the matter of any great importance. Wherever they may have originated, the ideas appropriated by Bergson are part of his philosophy.

---

[1] *Ibid.*, p. 262.   [2] *Ibid.*, p. 262.   [3] *La pensée et le mouvant*, p. 52.
[4] Though Bergson was not actually a pupil of Lachelier, he read the latter's book on induction while he was a student, and he liked to regard Lachelier as one of his teachers.

CHAPTER X

HENRI BERGSON (2)

Introductory remarks—Closed morality—Open morality: the interpretation of the two types—Static religion as a defence against the dissolvent power of intelligence—Dynamic religion and mysticism—Comments.

1. BERGSON's general procedure or way of going about things has been illustrated in the last chapter by reference to *Time and Free Will, Matter and Memory* and *Creative Evolution*. He selects certain sets of empirical data which interest him and arrest his attention and tries to interpret them in terms of some coordinating hypothesis or basic concept. For example, if the immediate data of consciousness suggest the mind's transcendence of matter while scientific research seems to point in the direction of epiphenomenalism, the question of the relation between mind and body (or between soul and body) presents itself once more and calls for the development of a theory which will accommodate both sets of data. While however Bergson is often certain that a given theory is inadequate or erroneous, he is not given to the dogmatic proclamation of his own theories as the definitive and finally proved truth. He shows us a picture which in his opinion is a better portrayal of the landscape than other pictures and provides persuasive arguments to show that this is the case; but he often shows himself conscious of the tentative and speculative character of his explanatory hypotheses.

In his last main work *The Two Sources of Morality and Religion* Bergson follows his customary procedure by taking as his point of departure sets of empirical data relevant to man's moral and religious life. In the field of morals, for example, he sees that there are facts exhibiting connections between codes of conduct and particular societies. At the same time he sees the part played in the development of ethical ideas and convictions by individuals who have risen above the standards of their societies. Similarly, in the area of religion Bergson sees the sociological aspects of religion and its social functions in history, while he is also aware of the personal and deeper levels of the religious consciousness. True, for information about the empirical data he relies to a considerable extent on the writings of the sociologists such as Durkheim and Lévy-Bruhl and, in regard to the mystical aspects of religion, on writers such as Henri Delacroix and Evelyn Underhill. The point is however that his theory of *two* sources of morality and religion is based on his conviction that there are distinguishable sets of empirical data which cannot be accounted for without a complex theory or explanation of this kind.

Bergson does not begin his treatment of morals by formulating explicitly certain problems or questions. But the nature of his questions emerges more or less clearly from his reflection on the data. One way of formulating his question would be to ask, what is the part played by reason in morality? He has of course to assign some role to reason; but it is not that of being a source. In his view there are two sources of morality, one infra-rational, the other supra-rational. Given his treatment of instinct, intelligence and intuition in *Creative Evolution*, this position is what might have been expected. In other words, the convictions which Bergson has already formed certainly (and naturally) influence his reflections on the data relevant to man's moral and religious life. At the same time his religious ideas are developed in the *Two Sources* well beyond anything that was said in *Creative Evolution*. In fine, the Bergsonian general world-outlook, as has already been stated, emerges from or is built up by a series of particular inquiries or lines of thought which are linked together through the pervasive presence of certain key-concepts, such as duration, becoming, creativity and intuition.

2. Bergson begins his treatment of morals with reflection on man's sense of obligation. He is far from agreeing with Kant's derivation of morality from the practical reason. Nor is he prepared to give to the concept of obligation the pre-eminent position which it occupies in Kantian ethics. At the same time Bergson recognizes of course that the sense of obligation is a prominent feature of the moral consciousness. Further, he agrees with Kant that obligation presupposes freedom. 'A being does not feel itself obliged unless it is free, and every obligation, taken separately, implies freedom.'[1] It is not possible to disobey laws of nature. For they are statements of the way in which things actually behave; and if we find that some things act in a manner contrary to an alleged law we reformulate the law in such a way as to cover the

---

[1] *The Two Sources*, p. 19. Page-references are to the English translation, though the wording of my translation from the French sometimes differs slightly.

exceptions. But it is quite possible to disobey a moral law or rule. It is thus a case not of necessity but of obligation. Talk about obeying the laws of nature should not be taken literally. For such laws are not prescriptive but descriptive.[1] Obedience and disobedience to moral prescriptions however are familiar phenomena. The question which Bergson raises concerns the cause or source of obligation. And the answer which he gives is that society is the source. That is to say, the sense of obligation is a sense of social pressure. The voice of duty is not something mysterious, coming from another world; it is the voice of society. The social imperative bears on the individual as such. This is why he feels obliged. But the individual human being is also a member of society. Hence for a great part of the time we observe social rules without reflection and without experiencing any resistance in ourselves. It is only when we do experience such resistance that we are actually aware of a sense of obligation. And as such cases are infrequent in comparison with the number of times in which we obey pretty well automatically, it is a mistake to interpret the moral life in terms of doing violence to oneself, of overcoming inclination, and so on. As man has his 'social self', his social aspect, he is generally inclined to conform to social pressure. 'Each of us belongs to society as much as to himself.'[2] The further we delve into the personality, the more incommensurable it becomes. But the plain fact of the matter is that on the surface of life, where we mainly dwell, there is a social solidarity which inclines us to conform to social pressure without resistance.

Bergson is at pains to argue that this sort of view does not imply that an individual living alone would be aware of no duties, no sense of obligation. For wherever he goes, even to a desert island, he carries with him his 'social ego'. He is still joined in spirit to society which continues to speak to him in his thinking and language, which have been formed by society. 'Generally, the verdict of conscience is that which would be given by the social self.'[3]

We can now ask two questions. First, what does Bergson mean by 'society'? Secondly, what does he mean by 'obligation'? The first question is answered fairly easily. By society Bergson means in the context any 'closed society', as he expresses it. This may be

---

[1] Bergson did not think of the laws of nature as necessary in the absolute sense. But the scientist would not speak of a law of nature unless he conceived it as exemplified in every member of a class of phenomena.
[2] *The Two Sources*, p. 6.   [3] *Ibid.*, p. 8.

a primitive tribe or a modern State. Provided that it is a particular
society which is conscious of itself as *this* society, distinct from
other social groups, it is, in Bergson's language, a closed society.
It is from society in this sense that obligation emanates; and the
function of the social pressure which gives rise to the sense of
obligation in individual members of the society is to maintain the
society's cohesion and life.

The second question is more difficult to answer. Sometimes he
seems to mean by obligation the feeling or sense of obligation. We
can then say that, for him, an empirical fact, namely social pressure, is the cause of a specifically ethical feeling. Sometimes
however Bergson speaks as though the awareness of obligation
were the awareness of social pressure as such. In this case obligation seems to be identified with a non-moral empirical fact. To
complicate matters, Bergson introduces the idea of the essence of
social pressure, which he also describes as the totality of obligation
and defines as the 'concentrated extract, the quintessence of the
thousand special habits which we have contracted of obeying the
thousand particular demands of social life.'[1] It is perhaps natural
to understand this as referring to a generalization from particular
obligations, so that 'the totality of obligation' would be logically
posterior to particular obligations. But this interpretation can
hardly be accepted. For the totality of obligation is also described
as 'the habit of contracting habits';[2] and though this is said to be
the aggregate of habits, it is also the necessity or need for contracting habits and a necessary condition for the existence of
societies. In this case it is presumably logically prior to social
rules.

Though however Bergson uses the word 'obligation' in a
lamentably loose manner, in several senses that is to say, it is at
any rate clear that for him the efficient cause of obligation is the
pressure exercised on its members by a closed society, and that its
final cause is the maintenance of the society's cohesion and life.
Obligation is thus relative to the closed society and has a social
function. Further, its origin is infra-intellectual. In a society such
as those of bees and ants instinct takes care of social cohesion and
service of the community. If however we imagine a bee or an ant
becoming self-conscious and capable of intellectual reflection, we
can picture it asking why it should continue to act as it has
been hitherto acting by instinct. At this point we can see social

[1] *Ibid.*, p. 13.   [2] *Ibid.*, p. 17.

pressure making itself felt through the insect's social self, the awareness of this pressure being a sense of obligation. If therefore we personify Nature, as Bergson is inclined to do, we can say that social pressure and obligation are the means used by Nature to secure society's cohesion and preservation when man emerges in the process of creative evolution. The morality of obligation is thus of infra-intellectual origin in the sense that it is the form taken in human society by the instinctive activity of members of infra-human societies.

Preservation of a society's cohesion is obviously not secured simply by pressure to observe rules which would be classified as moral rules by members of an advanced society, accustomed to differentiate between social conventions and ethical norms. A primitive society, when looked at from one point of view, extends the coverage of moral obligation to rules of conduct which we would be unlikely to classify as moral norms. As experience widens and civilization progresses, the human reason starts to discriminate between rules of conduct which are still necessary or genuinely useful to society and those which are no longer necessary or useful. It also begins to discriminate between rules which are seen to be required for the cohesion and maintenance of any tolerable society and conventions which differ from society to society. Further, when a traditional code of conduct has once been subjected to radical questioning by human intelligence, the mind will look for reasons to support the code. There is thus plenty of scope for reason in the ethical field. But this does not alter the fact that the ethics of obligation as such as of infra-intellectual origin. Reason does not originate it. It gets to work on what is already there, clarifying, discriminating, tidying up and defending.

3. The morality of obligation, relative to the closed society, is not regarded by Bergson as coterminous with the whole field of morality. He is well aware that the moral idealism of those individuals who have embodied in their own lives values and standards higher and more universal in their effect than the current ethical codes of the societies to which they belonged cannot be easily explained in terms of the social pressure of a closed group. He therefore asserts the existence of a second type of morality which is different in kind from the morality of obligation, which is characterized by appeal and aspiration, and which relates to man as man or to the ideal society of all human beings rather than to the closed group in any of its forms. Consider, for example, an

historical figure who not only proclaims the ideal of universal love but also embodies it in his own personality and life. The ideal, so embodied, acts by way of attraction and appeal rather than by way of social pressure; and those who respond to the ideal are drawn by example rather than impelled by the sense of obligation which expresses the pressure of a closed group.

This open and dynamic morality[1] is, for Bergson, of supra-rational origin. The morality of obligation is, as we have seen, of infra-intellectual origin, being the analogue at the human level of the constant and never failing pressure of instinct in infra-human societies. The open morality however originates in a contact between the great moral idealists and prophets and the creative source of life itself. It is, in effect, the result of a mystical union with God, which expresses itself in universal love. 'It is the mystical souls which have drawn and continue to draw civilized societies in their wake.'[2]

There is a natural inclination to think that it is all a question of degree, and that love of the tribe can become love of the nation and love of the nation love of all men. Bergson however rejects this view. The closed and open moralities are for him different in kind and not simply in degree. Though the open morality does in fact involve the ideal of universal love, it is essentially characterised not so much by its content (which, taken in itself, could logically be an extension of the content of closed morality) as by a vital impetus in the will which is quite different from social pressure or obligation. This vital impetus, also described by Bergson as 'emotion', is of supra-rational origin. In terms of the theory of evolution it expresses the creative movement of ascending life, whereas the closed morality represents rather a certain fixed deposit of this movement.

As Bergson insists on the difference between the two types of morality, he naturally treats them successively. Though however he thinks of primitive human society as dominated by the closed mentality, he recognizes of course that in society as we know it the two types not only coexist but interpenetrate. In a Christian nation, for example, we can find both types showing themselves. Just as we can consider pure memory and pure perception separately though

---

[1] 'Open' in the sense that it is essentially universal, aspiring to union between all human beings; 'dynamic' in the sense that it strives to change society, not simply to preserve it as it is.
[2] *The Two Sources*, p. 68.

they interpenetrate in concrete perception, so we can and ought to distinguish and consider separately the closed and open moralities, though in our actual world they coexist and mingle. An important factor in the bringing together of the two types of morality is the human reason or intelligence. Both the infra-intellectual drive of social pressure and the supra-intellectual appeal are projected, as it were, onto the plane of reason in the form of representations or ideas. Reason, acting as an intermediary, tends to introduce universality into the closed morality and obligation into the open morality. The ideals presented by the open morality become effective in society only in so far as they are interpreted by the reason and harmonized with the morality of obligation, while the closed morality receives an influx of life from the open morality. In its actual concrete form therefore morality includes both 'a system of *orders* dictated by *impersonal* social demands and a group of *appeals* made to the conscience of each one of us by *persons* who represent the best that there is in humanity.'[1]

Though the closed and open moralities intermingle with one another, there remains a tension between them. The open morality tries to infuse fresh life and new vistas into the closed morality, but the latter tends to bring down, as it were, the latter by turning what is essentially appeal and aspiration into a fixed code and by minimizing or whittling away ideals. We can however envisage the possibility of man's moral advance. In the final chapter of *The Two Sources* Bergson remarks that modern technology has made possible the unification of man in one society. This might of course be brought about by the triumph of an imperialism which would simply represent the closed mentality writ large. But we can also imagine a truly human society in which man's free response to the highest ideals would be the uniting factor rather than the tyrannical force and power of a world-imperialism. In such a society obligation would not disappear, but it would be transformed by man's response to ideals which are ultimately the expression of an influx of divine life as mediated to society by persons who have opened themselves to the divine life.

4. We have already had occasion to refer to a religious theme, mysticism, in connection with open morality. Bergson however distinguishes, as one might expect, between two types of religion,

---

[1] *Ibid.*, p. 68.

described respectively as static and dynamic. They correspond of course to the two types of morality, static religion being infra-intellectual in origin and dynamic supra-intellectual.

Let us once more imagine a bee or an ant suddenly endowed with intelligence and self-consciousness. The insect will naturally tend to pursue its private interests instead of serving the community. In other words, intelligence, when it emerges in the course of evolution, is a potentially dissolving power in regard to the maintenance of social cohesion. Reason is critical and questioning; it enables man to use his initiative and so endangers social unity and discipline.[1] Nature however is not at a loss what to do. What Bergson calls the myth-making faculty gets to work; and the protective deity of the tribe or the city appears 'to forbid, threaten, punish'.[2] In primitive society morality and custom are the same; and the sphere of religion is coterminous with that of social custom. The god protects the structure of custom by ordering the observance of the customs and punishing disobedience, even if the infringement is not known by a man's fellows.

Again, though the vital impulse turns animals away from the image of death and though there is no reason for supposing that any animal can argue to the inevitability of its own death, man is certainly able to conceive the fact that he will inevitably die. What does Nature do? 'To the idea that death is inevitable she opposes the image of continuation of life after death; this image, thrown by her into the field of intelligence, puts things in order again.'[3] Nature thus attains two ends. She protects the individual against the depressing thought of the inevitability of death; and she protects society. For a primitive society requires the presence and continuing authority of the ancestors.

Once more, as primitive man is extremely limited in his power to influence and control his environment, and as he is being constantly confronted with and reminded of the gap between the actions which he takes and the results for which he hopes, Nature or the vital impulse conjures up in him the image of and belief in

---

[1] Bergson remarks that though reason can convince a person that by promoting the happiness of others he promotes his own, it took centuries of culture to produce J. S. Mill, and he 'has not convinced all philosophers, let alone the mass of mankind' (*ibid.*, p. 101).

[2] *Ibid.*, p. 101. Bergson also discusses tabu and magic; but we cannot follow him into this discussion. We confine our remarks to polytheism.

[3] *Ibid.*, p. 109. Bergson explains that he is not denying immortality as such but maintaining that primitive man's image of life after death is 'hallucinatory'.

friendly powers interested in his success, to whom he can pray and who will help him.[1]

In general therefore static religion can be defined as 'a defensive reaction of nature against what could be depressing for the individual and dissolvent for society in the exercise of intelligence'.[2] It attaches man to life and the individual to society by means of myths. In the first instance it is found with primitive man, in some form or other; but it does not follow of course that it ceased with primitive man. On the contrary, it continued to flourish. But to say this is to say that the primitive mentality survived in civilization. Indeed it still survives, though the development of natural science has of course contributed powerfully to discrediting the religious myths. In Bergson's view, if in a modern war both parties express confidence that God is on their side, the mentality of static religion is showing itself. For though both sides may profess to be invoking the same God, the God of all mankind, each tends to treat him in practice as a national deity. Again, religious persecution was an expression of the primitive mentality and of static religion. For universal belief by a society was a criterion of its truth. Hence unbelief could not be regarded with equanimity. Common belief was considered a necessary ingredient of social solidarity or cohesion.

5. As for dynamic religion, its essence is mysticism, the ultimate end of which is 'a contact, and consequently a partial coincidence, with the creative effort of which life is the manifestation. The effort is of God, if it is not God himself. The great mystic is an individual who transcends the limits assigned to the species by its material nature and who thus continues and prolongs the divine action. Such is our definition.'[3] For Bergson therefore complete mysticism means not only a movement upwards and inwards which culminates in a contact with the divine life but also a complementary movement downwards or outwards by which a fresh impulse from the divine life is communicated through the mystic to mankind. In other words, Bergson thinks of what he describes as complete mysticism as issuing in activity in the world. He therefore regards a mysticism which concentrates simply on turning away from this world to the divine centre or which results in an intellectual grasp of the unity of all things, coloured by

---

[1] Bergson adds that a logical consequence of belief in friendly powers is a belief in unfriendly or antagonistic powers. But this second belief is, he maintains, derivative and even degenerate, as the vital impulse is optimistic (*ibid.*, p. 117).
[2] *Ibid.*, p. 175.   [3] *Ibid.*, p. 188.

sympathy or compassion but not by dynamic activity, as incomplete. And he finds a mysticism of this sort represented especially, though not exclusively, in the East, whereas 'complete mysticism is in effect that of the great Christian mystics'.[1]

We cannot undertake to discuss here Bergson's views on oriental and western mysticism. But there are one or two points worth noticing. In the first place Bergson raises the question whether mysticism provides us with an experimental approach to problems about the existence and nature of God. 'Generally speaking, we judge that an existing object is one which is perceived or which could be perceived. It is therefore given in a real or possible experience.'[2] Bergson is aware of the difficulties, or at any rate some of them, involved in proving that a given experience is an experience of *God*. But he suggests that reflection on mysticism can serve as confirmation of a position already reached. If, that is to say, the truth of creative evolution has been established, and if we can envisage the possibility of an intuitive experience of the principle of all life, reflection on the data of mysticism can add probability to the thesis that there is a transcendent creative activity. In any case mysticism, according to Bergson, can throw light on the divine nature. 'God is love, and he is object of love: this is the whole contribution of mysticism.'[3] Bergson writes, as usual, in an impressionistic manner; and he is far from tackling the logical difficulties in a professional way. His general position however is clearly that while reflection on evolution can bring us to the conviction that there is an immanent creative energy operative in the world, reflection on 'dynamic religion' or mysticism sheds further light on the nature of this principle of life, revealing it as love.[4]

In the second place, if 'the creative energy must be defined as love',[5] we are entitled to conclude that creation is the process whereby God brings into being 'creators, in order to have, beside himself, beings worthy of his love.'[6] In other words, creation appears as having an end or goal, the coming into being of man and his transformation through love. In the final chapter of *The Two Sources* Bergson sees the advance of technology as the progressive construction of what one might describe as one body (the

---

[1] *Ibid.*, p. 194.   [2] *Ibid.*, p. 206.   [3] *Ibid.*, p. 216.
[4] Needless to say, it was largely Bergson's reflections on mysticism which brought him to the point of contemplating formal adherence to Catholicism.
[5] *The Two Sources*, p. 220.   [6] *Ibid.*, p. 218.

unification of mankind on the levels of material civilization and of science), and the function of mystical religion as that of infusing a soul into this body. The universe thus appears as 'a machine for the making of gods',[1] a deified humanity, as transformed through an influx of divine love. Objections based on man's physical insignificance are rejected. The existence of man presupposes conditions, and these conditions other conditions. The world is the condition for man's existence. This teleological conception of creation may seem to contradict Bergson's previous attack on any interpretation of evolution in finalistic terms. But he was then thinking of course of the sort of finalistic scheme which would entail determinism.

In the third place Bergson sees mysticism as shedding light on the problem of survival. For in mystical experience we can see a participation in a life which is capable of indefinite progress. If it has already been established that the life of the mind cannot in any case be properly described in purely epiphenomenalistic terms, the occurrence of mysticism, which 'is presumably a participation in the divine essence',[2] adds probability to belief in the soul's survival after bodily death.

Just as Bergson sees the closed and open types of morality inter-penetrating one another in man's moral life as it actually exists, so does he see actual religion as a mingling of various degrees of static and dynamic religions. For example, in historical Christianity we can see the impulse of dynamic religion recurrently manifesting itself; but we can also discern plenty of evidence of the mentality characteristic of static religion. The ideal is that static religion should be transformed by dynamic religion; but, apart from limiting cases, the two intermingle in practice.

6. If anyone asks what Bergson means by closed and open morality, static and dynamic reality, there is no great difficulty in mentioning examples of the sets of phenomena to which these terms refer. It does not necessarily follow that Bergson's interpretation of the historical or empirical data has to be accepted. It is clear that he interprets the data within the framework of the conclusions to which he has already come about evolution in general and about the roles of instinct, intelligence and intuition in particular. The picture which he already has in his mind predisposes him to split up morality and religion into distinct types, different in kind. Obviously, his reflections on ethical and religious

_____
[1] _Ibid._, p. 275.   [2] _Ibid._, p. 227.

data seem to him to confirm his previously embraced conclusions; and the picture which he forms of man's moral and religious life reacts on the concept of the world which he already has in his mind. At the same time it is possible to admit the facts which Bergson mentions (facts, for example, about the relation between different codes of conduct and different societies) but to accommodate them in a different interpretative scheme or overall picture. It is not of course a question of blaming Bergson for painting an overall picture. It is simply a question of pointing out that other pictures are possible, which do not involve the Bergsonian dualism.

How far however we to press this theme of dualism? That Bergson asserts a psychological dualism of soul and body is clear enough. It is also clear that in his theory of morals and religion there is a dualism of origin. That is to say, closed morality and static religion are said to be of infra-intellectual origin, while open morality and dynamic religion are said to be of supra-intellectual origin.[1] But Bergson attempts to bring together soul and body by means of the concept of human action. And in his theory of morals and religion the different types of morality and religion are all ultimately explained in terms of the divine creative activity and purpose. In spite therefore of the dualistic features of his philosophy Bergson provides the material for a line of thought, such as that of Teilhard de Chardin, which is more 'monistic' in character.

In any case it is really the overall picture, the painting as a whole, which counts. It is possible of course to take particular points for consideration, such as Bergson's account of moral obligation. And then it is easy to criticize his sometimes inconsistent and often imprecise use of language and his failure to carry through a sustained and careful analysis. It is also possible to dwell on the influence exerted by particular views, such as the vital or biological primary function of intelligence. But it is probably true to say that Bergson's widest influence was exercised by his general picture,[2] which offered an alternative to mechanistic and positivist pictures.

[1] In theological terms one might perhaps say that they are, for Bergson, of natural and supernatural origin respectively.

[2] By the general picture, that is to say, conveyed by his writings up to and including *Creative Evolution*. Between 1907, when this work was published, and 1932, when *The Two Sources* appeared, there was a considerable gap. The climate of thought had changed a good deal in the meantime. Further, *The Two Sources* showed how Bergson's mind had been moving closer to Christianity than anyone might have expected from *Creative Evolution*.

In other words, this picture exercised a liberating influence on many minds. For it offered a positive and to many people appealing interpretation of the world, an interpretation which was neither confined to criticism of and attack on other views nor a return to past ways of thought. It did not seem to be a philosophy thought out by someone fighting a rearguard action but rather the expression of an outlook for the future. It was capable of arousing excitement and enthusiasm, as something new and inspiring,[1] and as putting the theory of evolution in a fresh light.

Bergson had some disciples, such as Édouard Le Roy (1870–1954), who succeeded him in his chair at the Collège de France.[2] But there was no Bergsonian school in any strict sense. Rather was it a question of a diffused influence, which it is often difficult to pin down. For example, William James hailed the appearance of *Creative Evolution* as marking a new era in thought; and he was doubtless influenced to some extent by Bergson. At the same time Bergson has been accused of basing his idea of real duration on James's theory of the stream of consciousness. (Bergson denied this, while paying tribute to James and recognizing similarities in thought.) Again, there are ideas, such as the originally biological or practical function of intelligence, which were certainly features of Bergson's philosophy but which could also have been derived from German philosophy, the writings of Schopenhauer for example.[3] If we pass over learned research into the particular ways in which Bergson influenced or may have influenced other philosophers in France and in other countries, it is sufficient to say that in his heyday Bergson appeared as the spearhead of the vitalist current of thought or philosophy of life and that, as such, he exercised a wide but not easily definable influence. It is worth adding however that this influence was felt outside the ranks of professional philosophers, as by the well known French writer Charles Pierre Péguy (1873–1914) and the revolutionary social

---

[1] One can of course find anticipations of a large number of Bergson's ideas in previous French philosophers. And some writers have challenged Bergson's originality. But this is really a matter for historians. As far as the general public are concerned, Bergson's thought was novel.

[2] Le Roy interpreted scientific theories and laws as useful fictions, making possible effective action to meet human needs. In *Dogma and Criticism* (*Dogme et critique*, 1906) he gave a pragmatist interpretation of religious dogmas, interpreting them as directives for moral action.

[3] How far Bergson himself was influenced by nineteenth-century German philosophers, such as Schopenhauer and Eduard von Hartmann, has been matter for dispute. It seems probable however that any influence was indirect, by way of French thought, rather than direct.

and political theorist Georges Sorel (1847–1922). Before he became a Thomist, Jacques Maritain was a disciple of Bergson; and though he criticized the Bergsonian philosophy, he retained a profound respect for his onetime master. Finally, as has already been mentioned, Pierre Teilhard de Chardin (1881–1955) had obvious affinities with Bergson and can be regarded as having continued his way of thinking into the contemporary world, provided at any rate that one does not give the erroneous impression that Teilhard simply borrowed his ideas from Bergson or Le Roy.

PART III
FROM BERGSON TO SARTRE
CHAPTER XI
PHILOSOPHY AND CHRISTIAN APOLOGETICS

Ollé-Laprune on moral certitude—Blondel and the way of immanence—Laberthonnière and Christian philosophy—Some remarks on modernism.

1. DURING the eighteenth-century Enlightenment Christian apologetics tended to follow a rationalistic pattern. The arguments of atheists were countered by philosophical proofs of the existence of God as cause of the world and as responsible for order in the universe, while the deists' attacks on revealed religion were met by arguments to prove the trustworthiness of the New Testament accounts of the life of Christ, including the accounts of miracles, and the fact of revelation. In the Age of Reason, that is to say, the arguments of rationalists, whether atheists or deists, had as their counterpart a kind of Christian rationalism.

After the revolution apologetics in France underwent a change. The general influence of the romantic movement showed itself in a turning away from rationalistic philosophy of the Cartesian type and in an emphasis on the way in which the Christian religion fulfilled the needs of man and society. As we have seen, Chateaubriand explicitly stated the need for a new type of apologetics and appealed to the beauty or aesthetic qualities of Christianity, maintaining that it is the intrinsic excellence of Christianity which shows that it comes from God rather than that it must be judged excellent because it has been proved to have come from God. The Traditionalists, such as de Maistre and de Bonald, appealed to the transmission of a primitive divine revelation rather than to metaphysical arguments for the existence of God. Lamennais, while making some use of traditional apologetics, insisted that religious faith requires a free consent of the will and is far from being simply an intellectual assent to the conclusion of a deductive inference. He also laid emphasis on the benefits conferred by religion on individuals and societies as evidence for its truth. The Dominican preacher Henri-Dominique Lacordaire (1802–61), who was for a time associated with Lamennais, tried to show the truth of Christianity by exhibiting the content and implications of the Christian faith itself and showing how it fulfils man's needs and the legitimate demands of human society.

It was obviously a strong point in the new line of apologetics in France in the first half of the nineteenth century that it tried to show the relevance of Christian faith by relating it to man's needs and aspirations both as an individual and as a member of society, rather than by proceeding simply on the plane of abstract metaphysical proofs and historical arguments. At the same time appeals to aesthetic considerations, as with Chateaubriand, or to the actual or possible beneficial social effects of Christianity could easily give the impression of attempts to stimulate the will to believe. That is to say, in so far as persuasive arguments were substituted for the traditional proofs, the substitution might be seen as expressing a tacit admission that religious faith rested on the will rather than on the reason.

Unless however Christian faith was to be regarded as being of the same nature as intellectual assent to the conclusion of a mathematical demonstration, some role had to be attributed to the will. After all, even those who were convinced of the demonstrative character of traditional metaphysical and apologetic arguments could hardly maintain that the unbeliever's withholding of his assent was always and exclusively due to his failure to understand them. It was natural therefore that the role of the will in religious belief should be explored, and that an attempt should be made to combine recognition of this role with avoidance of a purely pragmatic or voluntarist interpretation of Christian faith. Thus the question was raised, can there be a legitimate certitude, legitimate from the rational point of view, in which the will plays an effective role?

The name which first comes to mind in connection with this question is that of Léon Ollé-Laprune (1839–98). After completing his studies at the École Normale at Paris, Ollé-Laprune taught philosophy in lycées until he was given a post at the École Normale in 1875. In 1870 he published a work on Malebranche, *La Philosophie de Malebranche*, and in 1880 a book on moral certitude, *De la certitude morale*. An essay on the ethics of Aristotle, *Essai sur la morale d'Aristote*, appeared in 1881,[1] while *La philosophie*

---

[1] A Latin version had already been presented as one of the dissertations for the doctorate.

et le temps présent and a work on the value of life, *Le prix de la vie,* were published respectively in 1890 and 1894. Among other writings are two posthumously published works, *La raison et le rationalisme* (1906) and *Croyance religieuse et croyance intellectuelle* (1908, *Religious Belief and Intellectual Belief*).

It was a firm conviction of Ollé-Laprune that the will had a role to play in all intellectual activity. And there is of course a sense in which this is obviously true. Even in mathematical reasoning attention is required; and intention implies a decision to attend. It is also clear that there are areas of inquiry where there is room for the influence of prejudice of one sort or another and where the effort to be open-minded is required. Though however Ollé-Laprune liked to lay emphasis, in a general way, on thinking as a form of life, of action, he was particularly concerned with the search for truth in the religious and moral spheres. Here above all there was need for thinking 'with the whole soul, with the whole of oneself'.[1] In arriving at this conviction Ollé-Laprune was influenced by the thought of Pascal[2] and by Newman's *Grammar of Assent*,[3] as well as by Ravaisson and by Alphonse Gratry (1805–72). Gratry was a priest who maintained in his writings that though Christian faith could not be attained simply by human effort, it none the less satisfied man's deepest aspirations and that the way to it could be prepared if a man sought truth with his whole being and if he tried to live in accordance with moral ideals.

In his work on moral certitude Ollé-Laprune begins by examining the nature of assent and of certitude in general. As one would expect in the case of a French philosopher, there are frequent references to Descartes. A prominent feature however of Ollé-Laprune's reflections is the stimulus derived from Newman's *Grammar of Assent*. For example, he agrees with Newman that assent itself is always unconditional;[4] and he also accepts Newman's distinction between real and notional assent, though he expresses it as a distinction between two types of certitude. 'There is then a certitude which one can call *real* and another which one can call *abstract*. The latter is related to *notions*, the former to *things*.'[5] Ollé-Laprune also distinguishes between implicit certitude, preceding reflection, and actual or explicit certitude, which arises as a result of a reflective appropriation of

---

[1] *La philosophie et le temps présent*, p. 264.
[2] See Volume 4 of this *History*, pp. 153–173.
[3] For Newman see Appendix A to Volume 8 of this *History*.
[4] *De la certitude morale* (3rd edition, 1898), p. 22.   [5] *Ibid.*, p. 23.

implicit knowledge. As for the role played by the will, no truth can be perceived without attention; and attention is a voluntary act. Further, when it is not a question of assent to self-evidently true 'first principles' but a matter of reasoning, of the discursive activity of the mind, an effort of the will is obviously required to sustain this activity. But Ollé-Laprune is not prepared to accept the view of Descartes that judgment, in the form of affirmation or of denial, is in itself an act of the will. In the case of legitimate certitude it is the light of the evidence which determines assent, not an arbitrary choice by the will between affirmation and denial. At the same time truth may, for example, be displeasing, as when I hear a critical statement about myself, the truth of which I do not want to accept. An act of the will is then required to 'consent' to what I really perceive to be the truth. Consent (*consentement*) must however be distinguished from assent (*assentiment*), even if the two are often intermingled. '*Assent* is involuntary, but the *consent* which is added to it, or rather which is present as by way of implication, is voluntary.'[1] It is true that the intervention of the will may be required to overcome hesitation in giving assent; but this intervention is legitimate only when the hesitation is judged to be unreasonable. In other words, Ollé-Laprune wishes to avoid any implication that truth and falsity depend on the will and at the same time to attribute to the will an effective role in man's intellectual life.

This general treatment of assent and certitude constitutes a basis for reflection on man's assent to moral truths. A moral truth in the strict sense is an ethical truth. But Ollé-Laprune extends the range of meaning of the term to include metaphysical truths which, in his view, are closely connected with ethical truth. The moral life is defined as any exercise of human activity which implies the idea of obligation; and a truth of the moral order is 'any truth which appears as a *law* or a *condition* of the moral life'.[2] Thus 'all together, moral truths in the proper sense and metaphysical truths, form what one may call the order of moral things (*choses*), the moral order. One can also say that it is the religious order, if we abstract from positive religion.'[3] Moral truths can be summed up under four main headings: the moral law, liberty, the existence of God, and the future life.[4]

[1] *Ibid.*, p. 65. [2] *Ibid.*, p. 4.
[3] *Ibid.*, p. 3. Ollé-Laprune means that he is abstracting from revelation.
[4] *Ibid.*, p. 98.

The influence of Kant can be seen not only in the close connection which Ollé-Laprune makes between man's moral life and his religious belief, but also in particular lines of thought. For example, Ollé-Laprune agrees with Kant that moral obligation implies freedom; and he approaches belief in the future life by arguing that recognition of the moral law and of a moral order warrants conviction that this order will triumph, and that its triumph demands human immortality. Though however Ollé-Laprune often refers appreciatively to Kant, he has no intention of accepting that Kantian position that religious beliefs are objects not of theoretical knowledge but solely of practical faith. And he criticizes at length the views of philosophers, such as Kant, Pascal, Maine de Biran, Cournot, Hamilton, Mansel and Spencer, who either deny or severely restrict the mind's power to prove moral truths. To put the matter in another way, the title of the work, *On Moral Certitude*, can be misleading. The word 'moral' refers to the moral dispositions which, according to Ollé-Laprune, are required for the full recognition of truths in the moral order. But it is not intended to indicate that in the case of moral truths a firm assent is given to a more or less probable hypothesis, still less that it is given simply because one wants the relevant propositions to be true. Ollé-Laprune can therefore claim of his book that it establishes, as against the fideists, that truth is 'independent of our will and of our thought, and that we have to recognize it, not create it.'[1]

The fact of the matter is that Ollé-Laprune was a devout Catholic whose sense of orthodoxy prevented any substitution of the will to believe for the perception of adequate rational grounds for assent. When therefore he undertakes to show, as against the *'dry rationalists* who admit only a kind of logical mechanism',[2] that in regard to the recognition of moral truths the will has a particular role to play, he has to stop short of any view which would entail the conclusion that these truths cannot be known to be true. At one end, so to speak, he can maintain that effective recognition of such truths requires personal dispositions of a moral nature which are not required for recognition of the truth of, say, mathematical propositions. For example, a man may refuse to recognize a moral obligation which entails consequences that, for lack of the requisite dispositions, he is reluctant or unwilling

---

[1] *Ibid.*, p. vii.   [2] *Ibid.*, p. vii.

to accept. And an effort of will is required to overcome this aversion to the truth. At the other end Ollé-Laprune can maintain that a purely intellectual assent to the conclusion of a proof of God's existence cannot become 'consent' and be transformed into a living faith without a personal commitment of the whole man, including the will. 'Complete certitude is *personal*: it is the total act of the soul itself embracing by a free choice, no less than by a firm judgment, the truth which is present to it. . . .'[1] Ollé-Laprune can also admit that in the case of moral truths an effort of the will may be required to overcome the hesitation occasioned by 'obscurities' which are not present in the case of purely formal truths, such as mathematical propositions. If, for instance, a man contemplates only 'the ordinary course of nature',[2] appearances seem to tell against immortality; and the man may therefore hesitate to assent to any argument in favour of human survival. Ollé-Laprune insists however that though an intervention of the will is required to overcome such hesitation, this intervention derives its justification not simply from the desire to believe but rather from recognition of the fact that hesitation to give assent is unreasonable and therefore ought to be overcome.

It is understandable that to some minds Ollé-Laprune should have appeared as a pragmatist or as a pioneer of modernism, in spite of his efforts to safeguard the objective truth of religious beliefs. But even the most orthodox theologian could hardly object to the claim that it is not simply by a process of reasoning that philosophy passes into religion, and that for a living faith what Ollé-Laprune describes as *consentement* is required. Moreover, from the theological point of view it is considerably easier to see how room is left for the activity of divine grace in Ollé-Laprune's account of religious belief than it is in the case of the purely rationalist apologetics which he criticizes. To be sure, Ollé-Laprune writes from the standpoint of a convinced believer; and what appear to some people as adequate grounds for not believing are presented by him as occasions for doubts and hesitations which the genuine seeker after truth can see that he is morally obliged to overcome. But though the arguments which he presents to establish the truth of the beliefs which he judges of importance for human life may appear unconvincing to many minds, he himself regards them as possessing a force which, for the man of good will, should outweigh the force of contrary

[1] *Ibid.*, p. 79.   [2] *Ibid.*, p. 107.

appearances. In other words, he has no intention of expounding a pragmatist theory of truth.

2. Mention has been made of the fact that Ollé-Laprune regarded thought as a form of action. But this theme is best considered in connection with his pupil Maurice Blondel (1861–1949), author of *L'action*.

Blondel was born at Dijon; and after studying at the local lycée he entered the École Normale at Paris, where he had Ollé-Laprune and Boutroux as his teachers and Victor Delbos as his fellow-student.[1] Blondel experienced considerable difficulty in getting action accepted as the subject for a thesis, though he eventually succeeded.[2] After two failures he obtained the *agrégation* in 1886 and was appointed to teach philosophy in the lycée at Montauban. In the same year he was transferred to Aix-en-Provence. In 1893 his thesis, *L'Action*, was submitted to the Sorbonne. His application for a university post was at first refused, on the ground that his thought was not properly philosophical. He was then offered a chair of history. But in 1894 the then minister of education, Raymond Poincaré, appointed him professor of philosophy in the University of Aix-en-Provence. Blondel held this post until 1927, when he retired because of failing eyesight.

The original edition of *L'Action* appeared in 1893.[3] This was also the date of Blondel's Latin thesis on Leibniz.[4] What is generally known as Blondel's *Trilogy* appeared in 1934–7. It consisted of *Thought (La Pensée*, 2 vols., 1934), *Being and Beings (L'être et les êtres*, 1935) and *Action* (2 vols., 1936–7). This last-mentioned work should not be confused with the original *L'Action*, which was reprinted in 1950 as the first volume of Blondel's *Premiers écrits (First Writings)*. *La philosophie et l'esprit chrétien (Philosophy and the Christian Spirit)* was published in two volumes in 1944–6, and *Exigences philosophiques du christianisme (Philosophical Requirements of Christianity)* appeared posthumously in 1950.

---

[1] Victor Delbos (1862–1916) became a professor of the Sorbonne and published studies on Spinoza, Kant and German idealism. He was a friend and correspondent of Blondel.

[2] Blondel's preliminary reflections can be found in *Carnets intimes*.

[3] *L'Action. Essai d'une critique de la vie et d'une science de la pratique*. There were three versions, the thesis itself, a printed version and a version revised and added to by Blondel.

[4] *De vinculo substantiali et de substantia composita apud Leibnitium*. A French version, *Une énigme historique: le 'Vinculum substantiale' d'après Leibniz*, appeared in 1930.

In addition Blondel published a considerable number of essays, such as his Letter on the *Requirements of Contemporary Thought in the Matter of Apologetics* and *History and Dogma*.[1] The correspondence between Blondel and the Jesuit philosopher Auguste Valensin (1879–1953) was published in three volumes at Paris in 1957–65, while Blondel's *Philosophical Correspondence* with Laberthonnière, edited by C. Tresmontant, appeared in 1962. There is also a collection of philosophical letters written by Blondel to Boutroux, Delbos, Brunschvicg and others (Paris, 1961).

Blondel has often been described as a Catholic apologist. So indeed he was, and so he saw himself. In the project for his thesis *L'Action*, he referred to the work as philosophical apologetics. In a letter to Delbos he stated that for him philosophy and apologetics were basically one.[2] From the start he was convinced of the need for a Christian philosophy. But in his opinion 'there has never yet been, strictly speaking, any Christian philosophy.'[3] Blondel aspired to meet this need, or at any rate to point out the way to do so. Further, he spoke of trying to do 'for the Catholic form of thought what Germany has long since done, and continues to do for the Protestant form'.[4] But there is no need to multiply references to justify the description of Blondel as a Catholic apologist.

Though however the description is justifiable, it can be extremely misleading. For it suggests the idea of a heteronomous philosophy, a philosophy, that is to say, which is used to support certain theological positions or to prove certain preconceived conclusions which are considered to be both philosophically demonstrable and an essential propaedeutic to or theoretical basis for Christian belief. In other words, the description of a philosophy as Christian apologetics suggests the idea of philosophy as a handmaid or servant of theology. And in so far as the business of Christian philosophy is conceived to be that of proving certain theses dictated by theology or by ecclesiastical authority, the

---

[1] These two long essays, published respectively in 1896 and 1904, have appeared in English translation, with an introduction, by Alexander Dru and Illtyd Trethowan (London, 1964).

[2] *Lettres philosophiques*, p. 71.

[3] *Lettre sur les exigences* (1956), p. 54. (*Letter on Apologetics*, English translation, p. 171).

[4] *Lettres philosophiques*, p. 34. Blondel's interest in German thought was stimulated by the lectures of Boutroux and by the studies of his friend Delbos, as well as by his own reading.

conclusion is likely to be drawn that Christian philosophy is not philosophy at all but theology in disguise.

Blondel recognized of course that philosophical concepts could be used in the explicitation of the content of Christian faith. But he insisted, rightly, that this process was internal to theology.[1] Philosophy itself, he was convinced, should be autonomous, in fact and not simply in theory. Christian philosophy too should therefore be autonomous. But an autonomous Christian philosophy did not, in his opinion, exist. It was something to be created. It would be Christian in the sense that it would exhibit man's lack of self-sufficiency and his opening to the Transcendent. In the process it would exhibit its own limitations as human thought and its lack of omnicompetence. Blondel was convinced that autonomous philosophical reflection, consistently and rigorously pursued, would in fact reveal in man an exigency for the supernatural, for that which is inaccessible to human effort alone. It would open the horizon of the human spirit to the free self-communication of the divine, which answers indeed to a profound need in man but which cannot be given through philosophy.[2] In brief, Blondel envisaged a philosophy which would be autonomous in its reflection but, through this reflection, self-limiting, in the sense that it pointed to what lay beyond itself. He was considerably influenced by Pascal, but he had a greater confidence in systematic philosophy. Perhaps we can say that Blondel aimed at creating the philosophy which was demanded by the thought of Pascal. But it must be philosophy. Thus in one place Blondel asserts that 'apologetical philosophy ought not to become a philosophical apologetics'.[3] That is to say, philosophy ought to be a process of autonomous rational reflection, not simply a means to an extra-philosophical end.

Blondel therefore wished to create something new or at any rate to make a substantial contribution to its creation. But he was not of course thinking of creation out of nothing, of bringing into existence, that is to say, a novelty without relation to past

---

[1] Mathematics, for example, is an autonomous discipline. But mathematical concepts might be used by a theologian. And if he uses such concepts, this does not convert theology into mathematics.

[2] Blondel was of course concerned, as was Augustine, with man in the concrete, who, from the point of view of Christian faith, is called to a supernatural end. For Blondel man as he is exhibits the need for the supernatural, for what transcends his own powers but towards which he reaches out.

[3] From the letter to Charles Denis, editor of *Annales de philosophie chrétienne* (*Lettre sur les exigences*, p. 3).

thought. We cannot enter here into any detailed discussion of the influence exercised upon his mind by particular movements and individual thinkers.[1] But a general, even if very sketchy account of the sort of way in which he interpreted the development of western philosophy seems to be required for the elucidation of his aims.

In Aristotelianism Blondel saw a remarkable expression of rationalism, of the tendency of reason, that is to say, to assert its omnicompetence and to absorb religion into itself. With Aristotle thought was divinized, and theoretical speculation was represented as man's highest activity and end. In the Middle Ages Aristotelianism was of course harmonized with Christian theology in a way which limited the scope of philosophy. But the harmonization was a conjunction of two factors, one of which, left to itself, would aspire to absorb the other; and the limitation of philosophy was imposed from outside. Philosophy may have been autonomous in theory; but in practice it was heteronomous. When the external control weakened or was lifted, rationalistic philosophy once more asserted its omnicompetence.[2] At the same time new lines of thought came into being. For example, whereas medieval realism had concentrated on objects of knowledge, Spinoza, though one of the great rationalists, started with the active subject and the problems of human existence and man's destiny. To this extent he pursued the way of 'immanence'; but he also understood that man can find his true fulfilment only in the Absolute which transcends himself.[3]

A step forward was made by Kant, with whom we see philosophy becoming self-critical and self-limiting. It is not, as in the Middle Ages, a question of limitations imposed from outside. The limitations are self-imposed as the result of self-criticism. The act of limiting is therefore compatible with the autonomous character of philosophy. At the same time Kant drove a wedge

---

[1] There are several books on aspects of this subject. For example, *The Blondelian Synthesis* by J. J. McNeil (Leiden, 1966) deals with Blondel's relation to Spinoza, Kant and the great German idealists, while *Hegel and Blondel* by P. Henrici (Munich, 1958) deals with his relation to Hegel in particular. For remarks by Blondel himself see *L'itinéraire philosophique de Maurice Blondel*, edited by F. Lefèvre (Paris, 1928).

[2] Blondel saw Luther's hostility to rationalism and his separation between philosophy and theology as having the practical effect of encouraging philosophy to assert its independence and to invade the sphere of theology.

[3] Blondel was fully conscious of course of Spinoza's pantheism and of his intellectualist interpretation of love and union with God. But when referring to past philosophers Blondel is more concerned with their significance for him than with exegesis.

between thought and being and between theory and practice or action, whereas Spinoza had aimed at overcoming the gulf between thought and being. Syntheses were attempted by the great German idealists, from whom the philosopher has much to learn.[1] But with Hegel especially we see a tendency to divinize reason, to identify human and absolute thought, and to absorb religion into philosophy. As a counterweight we can turn to the tradition from Pascal through Maine de Biran up to Ollé-Laprune and others which starts with the concrete active subject and reflects on the exigencies of its activity. What is wanting in this tradition however is a method which will make possible the construction of a philosophy of immanence which at the same time leads or points to transcendence.

From what has been said it should be clear that Blondel was no supporter of the 'Back to Aquinas' movement.[2] In his opinion the Christian thinker, concerned with the development of philosophy of religion, should not attempt to go back but rather to enter into the development of modern philosophy and to go beyond it from within. One great contribution of modern thought, he was convinced, was the concept of autonomous but self-limiting philosophy. This rendered possible for the first time a philosophy which would both point to the Transcendent and refrain, through its own critical self-limitation, from trying to capture the Transcendent in a rationalistic network. It would thus leave room for the divine self-revelation. Another contribution of modern philosophy (though foreshadowed in earlier thought) was the approach to being by way of the active subject's reflection on its own dynamism of thought and will, the method of immanence in other words. In Blondel's opinion it was only by means of this approach that a philosophy of religion could be developed which would mean

---

[1] For example, Blondel had considerable sympathy with Schelling's later philosophy of religion, though he regarded the division between negative and positive philosophy (or between philosophy of essence and philosophy of existence) as something which needed to be overcome.

[2] In earlier writings, such as the *Letter on Apologetics*, Blondel made some pretty sharp comments about Thomists and Scholasticism. As several writers have pointed out, what he had in mind was a form of Thomism which held aloof from modern thought or mentioned it only to criticize it, often caricaturing it in the process, and which suspected heresy in any Catholic philosopher who did not follow the party-line. Blondel's remarks about pseudo-philosophizing would not apply, for example, to Maréchal who tried to do one of the very things which Blondel thought necessary, to develop a Kantian line of thought beyond the position reached by Kant himself. Later Blondel devoted some more study to Aquinas himself and became more sympathetic. The Thomists whom Blondel castigated obviously paid little attention to the *spirit* of Aquinas.

something to modern man. For God to become a reality for him and not simply an object of thought or of speculation, man must rediscover God from within, not indeed as an object which can be found by introspection but by coming to see that the Transcendent is the goal of his thought and will.

If however Blondel was convinced that Catholic philosophers should throw themselves into the stream of modern thought, he did not mean to imply that modern philosophers had solved all the major problems which they raised. For example, whereas Aristotle in the ancient world had exalted thought to the detriment of practice or action, Kant in the modern world had emphasized the moral will at the expense of the theoretical reason, doing away with reason, as he put it, to make way for faith. The problem remained of uniting thought and will, thought and action or practice. Again, the *method* of immanence, the approach to being through critical reflection on the subject, could easily be converted and had in fact been converted, into a *doctrine* of immanence, asserting that nothing exists outside human consciousness or that the statement that anything so exists is devoid of meaning. There remained therefore the problem of pursuing the method of immanence while avoiding the doctrine or principle of immanence.

To be sure, some of Blondel's critics accused him of immanentism, in the sense that they attributed to him the principle or doctrine of immanence and concluded that on his premises man could never emerge from the prison-house of subjective impressions and ideas and assert the existence of any reality except as a content of human consciousness. Though however they were able to select certain passages in support of this interpretation, it is evident that he had no intention of proposing any doctrine which would entail subjective idealism. It is indeed true that he derived stimulus from a number of philosophers who enclosed all reality within the realm of thought.[1] But one of his aims was to close the gap between thought and being (considered as object of thought) without reducing being to thought. And though he was obviously

---

[1] In the case of a philosopher such as Hegel it was not of course a question of enclosing all reality within the realm of human thought as such. Hegel was not a subjective idealist. Reality was for him the self-expression of absolute thought, in which the human mind participates, at any rate at certain levels. In Blondel's opinion however Hegelianism was in fact an apotheosis of the human reason. And Blondel wished to open man's mind to the Transcendent, not to divinize the human reason.

aware of the fact that God cannot be conceived except through consciousness, he had no intention of suggesting that God is identifiable with man's idea of him. He wished to pursue a method of immanence which would lead to an affirmation of the Transcendent as an objective reality, in the sense of a reality which was not dependent on human consciousness.

For the solution of his problems Blondel looked to a philosophy of action. The term 'action' naturally suggests the idea of something which may be preceded by thought or accompanied by it but is not itself thought. But as Blondel uses the term, thought itself is a form of action. There are of course thoughts, ideas and representations which we tend to conceive as contents of consciousness and possible objects of thought. More fundamental however is the act of thinking which produces and sustains thought. And thought as activity or action is itself the expression of the movement of life, the dynamism of the subject or of the whole person. 'There is nothing in the properly subjective life which is not act. That which is properly subjective is not only what is conscious and known from within . . .; it is what causes the fact of consciousness to be.'[1] Action might perhaps be described as the dynamism of the subject, the aspiration and movement of the person seeking self-fulfilment. It is the life of the subject considered as integrating or synthesizing pre-conscious potentialities and tendencies, as expressing itself in thought and knowledge, and as reaching out towards further goals.

Blondel makes a distinction between what he calls 'the will-willing' (la volonté voulante) and 'the will-willed' (la volonté voulue). The latter consists of distinct acts of volition. One wills first this, then that. The former, the will-willing, is 'the movement which is common to every will'.[2] Blondel does not of course mean to imply that there are in man two wills. His contention is that there is in man a basic aspiration or movement (la volonté voulante) which expresses itself in willing distinct finite objects or ends but which can never be satisfied with any of them but reaches out beyond them. It is not itself the object of psychological introspection but rather the condition of all volitions or acts of will and at the same time that which lives and expresses itself in them and passes beyond them, as they are inadequate to it. Moreover, it is the operation of the basic will which leads to thought and knowledge. 'Knowledge is nothing more than the middle term, the fruit of

---

[1] L'Action, p. 99.   [2] Ibid., p. xxi.

action and the seed of action.'[1] Thus even mathematics can be seen as 'a form of the development of the will'.[2] It does not follow that truth is simply what we decide that it is to be. What Blondel means is that man's life of thought and knowledge, whether in the sciences or in philosophy, is rooted in man's basic activity and must be seen in relation to it. In his view the genesis and the meaning or end of science and philosophy can be properly understood only in terms of the subject's fundamental and dynamic orientation.

It hardly needs saying that in his insistence on the basically dynamic character of the subject or ego Blondel stands within the general current of thought to which Maine de Biran gave such a powerful stimulus. But he also derived inspiration from his reflection on the thought of the German philosophers, as he understood it. Though, for example, he wished to overcome the Kantian dichotomies between theoretical and practical reason, the noumenal and phenomenal selves, and the spheres of freedom and necessity, he was certainly influenced by Kant's emphasis on the primacy of the practical reason or moral will. Again, we can find links between Blondel's concept of *la volonté voulante*, Fichte's idea of the pure ego as activity and Schelling's theory of a basic act of will or primitive choice which expresses itself in particular choices. But it is a question not of Blondel's taking or borrowing this idea from one philosopher and that idea from another philosopher but rather of his developing his own ideas in dialogue with the ideas of other thinkers either as expressed directly in their writings or as conveyed to him through the works of his friend Delbos. And we cannot discuss this process of dialogue here.

The philosophy of action can be described as a systematic inquiry into the conditions and dialectic of the dynamism of the subject, or as critical reflection on the *a priori* structure of the will-willing, seen as determining or expressing itself in man's thought and action, or perhaps as critical reflection on the basic orientation of the active subject as manifested in the genesis of morality, science and philosophy. The word 'subject' should not be understood in the narrow sense of the Cartesian ego or of the transcendental ego of German idealism. For action is the life of the 'human composite, the synthesis "of body and soul".'[3] But it is the basic orientation of the person as aiming at a goal with which Blondel

---

[1] *Lettres philosophiques*, p. 84.   [2] *L'Action*, p. 55, n. 1.
[3] *Lettres philosophiques*, p. 82.

is concerned. In other words, he is using the method of immanence to solve what he sees as the problem of human destiny.

To take an example, Blondel tries to show that the idea of liberty or freedom arises on the basis of the determinism of nature. The will is subject to desires and tendencies, but in its potential infinity it transcends the factual order and reaches out towards ideal ends. On the basis of a determinism of nature the subject becomes aware of its freedom. But at the same time it substitutes for the determinism of nature that of reason and obligation. Obligation is 'a necessary postulate of the will'[1] and a synthesis of the ideal and the real. Morality or the moral order does not represent therefore an imposition from without: it arises in the dialectical self-unfolding of the dynamism of the subject. But the feeling of obligation, the awareness of a moral imperative, can arise only through the subject transcending the factual, in the sense that it learns to find the motive of its behaviour in the ideal. In other words, the moral consciousness involves an implicit metaphysics, an implicit recognition of the natural or factual order as related to a metaphysical or ideal sphere of reality.

As one might expect, Blondel proceeds to argue that the total activity of the human subject cannot be understood except in terms of an orientation to a transcendent Absolute, to the infinite as final end of the will. This does not mean of course that the Transcendent can be discovered as an object, whether internal or external. Rather is it a question of the subject becoming aware of its dynamic orientation to the Transcendent and of being faced with an option, the choice between asserting and denying the reality of God. Philosophical reflection, that is to say, gives rise to the idea of God; but precisely because God is transcendent, man can either affirm or deny the reality of God. Blondel sees man as beset by what an existentialist might call 'anxiety', as seeking an adequation between the will-willed and the will-willing. In his view the adequation cannot be attained except through God. But the method of immanence can lead only to the necessity of an option. As Sartre was to say after him, Blondel tells us that 'man aspires to be God'.[2] This means however that he is faced with the choice between substituting his own will for the divine will, thus choosing against God with the idea of God,[3] and becoming God (united with God) only through God. Ultimately, what a man

[1] *L'Action*, p. 302.   [2] *L'Action*, p. 356.
[3] As Nietzsche may be said to have done.

becomes depends on his will. Is his will to live sufficient, to speak paradoxically, to die 'by consenting to be supplanted by God',[1] his will being united with the divine will? Or will he seek to be self-sufficient and autonomous without God? The choice is man's. At a point in the dialectic of man's basic movement or aspiration the idea of God as a reality necessarily arises. But it still remains open to man to affirm or to deny God as a reality.

Blondel's theory of the option was understood by some critics as implying that in his view the existence of God was incapable of proof, and that assertion of it was simply the result of an act of the will, of the will to believe that is to say. In point of fact however Blondel did not reject all proofs of God's existence. He regarded the philosophy of action as itself constituting a proof, inasmuch as the way of immanence showed the necessity of the idea of God. It was not a question of rejecting, for example, the argument from contingency as worthless but rather of interiorizing it and trying to show how the idea of the necessary being arises through the subject's reflection on its own orientation or movement and aspiration. As for the option, Blondel regards this as necessary if God is to be a reality 'for us'.[2] Speculative knowledge may precede the option; but without the option, without the subject's free self-relating to God, there can be no *effective* knowledge. 'The living thought which we have of him (God) is and remains living only if it turns towards practice, if one lives by it and if one's action is nourished by it.'[3] This however demands a voluntary act of self-relating not to the idea of God but to God as being.

Catholic critics also understood Blondel as claiming that supernatural revelation and life were not gratuitous but necessary, fulfilling, that is to say, a demand in the nature of man, a demand which man's creator had to satisfy. Though however Blondel's statements sometimes provided ground for this interpretation, it is clear that 'the supernatural' which is demanded by the method of immanence is simply the 'undetermined supernatural', in the sense that the philosophy of action shows, for Blondel, that man should accept and surrender himself to the Transcendent. Christian revelation is the positively determined form of the supernatural; and man should accept it, if it is true. But the method of immanence cannot prove that it is true. At the same time nobody could accept the positively determined supernatural, unless there were something in him to which it answered and responded.

[1] *L'Action*, p. 354. [2] *L'Action*, p. 426. [3] *Ibid.*, p. 354.

Otherwise it would be irrelevant. And the method of immanence shows that this something, a dynamic orientation to the Transcendent, is really there.[1]

Of course, if we say, as we have said above, that the philosophy of action reveals the necessity of the idea of 'God', the impression can easily be given that Blondel regards the method of immanence as leading to the specifically Christian belief in God. Looking back however on modern philosophy Blondel sees some systems as resolutely trying to exclude the Transcendent and others as trying to take the Transcendent by storm, as it were, and producing only an idol or caricature. In his view the method of immanence, as pursued in the philosophy of action, opens man's mind and will to the Transcendent, while leaving room for God's self-revelation. In this sense a truly critical philosophy is a Christian philosophy and a Christian apologetics, not in the sense that it tries to prove the truth of Christian doctrines but rather in the sense that it leads man to the point at which he is open to God's self-revelation and to the divine action. 'Philosophy cannot directly demonstrate or procure (for us) the supernatural'.[2] But it can proceed indirectly by eliminating incomplete solutions to the problem of human destiny and showing us 'what we inevitably have and what is necessarily lacking to us.'[3] Philosophy can show the insufficiency of the natural order for providing the goal of the dynamic orientation of the human spirit. At the same time philosophy's self-criticism reveals its own incompetence to provide man with the beatitude to which he aspires. It thus points beyond itself.

Though Blondel made it clear enough that he had no intention of identifying God with the immanent idea of God, and though he was opposed to the historicism of the modernists, to anyone who is aware of the situation in the Catholic Church during the modernist crisis it is not surprising that Blondel came under suspicion and was thought by some to have been involved in the condemnation of 'religious immanentism' in the encyclical *Pascendi* which Pope Pius X issued in 1907. Matters were not improved by Blondel's opposition to the *Action Française* movement, which he regarded as an unholy alliance between positivist sociology and a reactionary Catholicism. For though Charles

---

[1] For a discussion of Blondel's position in regard to the supernatural see *Blondel et le christianisme* by Henri Bouillard (Paris, 1961).
[2] *Lettre sur les exigences*, p. 85 (*Letter on Apologetics*, p. 198).   [3] *Ibid.*, p. 85.

Maurras was an atheist who endeavoured to make use of the Church for his own ends, the movement was supported by a number of distinguished but very traditional theologians and Thomists who disliked Blondel's originality and independence, considered him corrupted by German thought, and did not hesitate to accuse him of modernism. In point of fact Blondel's ideas were never condemned by Rome, in spite of efforts in this direction. But it is probably fortunate for him that he had not become a priest, as he had once thought of doing. It must be added however that he did not indulge in the kind of ardent polemics carried on by his friend Laberthonnière. And the obscurity of his style or, if preferred, the fact that he was a highly professional philosopher and not a popularizer may well have contributed some protection.

In any case Blondel weathered the years of controversy and criticism and, as has already been mentioned, he at length produced his trilogy (*La Pensée*, *L'Être et les êtres* and the second *L'Action*), followed by *Philosophy and The Christian Spirit*. Some writers on Blondel have pretty well neglected the later works, perhaps regarding them as an expression of second thoughts under the pressure of criticism and as being tamer and more traditional than the original *L'Action*. Other writers have insisted that the trilogy represents the philosopher's mature thought, sometimes adding that the emphasis placed in it on ontological and metaphysical themes shows that it is a mistake to describe him as an apologist on the basis of the first *L'Action* and the *Letter on Apologetics*. In some instances they have been glad of the opportunity to assimilate his thought to the metaphysical tradition passing through St. Thomas Aquinas.[1] Though however the trilogy obviously does represent Blondel's mature thought and though he did indeed come to have a greater respect for Aquinas, Blondel continued to be concerned with developing an autonomous philosophy which would be at the same time open to Christianity. In this sense he remained an apologist, even if in his later writings he emphasized the ontological implications and presuppositions of his thought as previously presented.

In *La Pensée* Blondel inquires into the antecedent conditions of human thought and defends the theory of 'cosmic thought' (*la pensée cosmique*). In his view we cannot justifiably make a sharp

[1] See, for example, *Introduction à la métaphysique de Maurice Blondel* by Claude Tresmontant (Paris, 1963).

dichotomy between human beings as thinking subjects on the one hand and Nature as mindless matter on the other. On the contrary, Leibniz was right in maintaining that the material always has its psychical aspect. Indeed, the intelligible organic universe can be described as 'a subsistent thought',[1] not of course conscious thought but thought 'in search of itself'.[2] In the process of the world's development conscious thought arises on the basis of a hierarchy of levels, each successive level prerequiring the antecedent levels, introducing something new and creating problems, as it were, the solution of which demands a higher level. In man the spontaneous, concrete thought present in Nature persists; but there also arises abstract analytic thought which deals with symbols.[3] The tension between them had been noted by some previous philosophers. The Scholastics spoke of 'reason' (*ratio*) and 'intellect' (*intellectus*), Spinoza of degrees of knowledge, Newman of notional and real assent. Together with advertence to the distinction between different types of thought there has gone the vision of a synthesis at a higher level, as with the Scholastics and Spinoza in their several ways. The condition of any such synthesis, of the self-perfecting of thought, is participation in the life of absolute thought, in a union with God in which vision and love are one. But the attainment of this goal of the dialectic of thought lies beyond the competence of philosophy and of human effort in general.

In *L'Être et les êtres* Blondel turns from thought to being and interrogates, as it were, different kinds of things to discover whether they merit being described as beings. Matter fails to pass the test. It is not a being. It is 'less a thing than the common condition of the resistances, which all things oppose to us and which we oppose to ourselves.'[4] It is indeed, to use the language of Aristotelianism, the principle of individuation and multiplicity, and it thus provides a good ground for the rejection of monism, but it is not itself substantial being. The living organism, with its specific unity, its spontaneity and relative autonomy, presents a better claim; but though it transmits an *élan vital*, its activity is counterbalanced by passivity, and it lacks both real autonomy and immortality. As for human persons, they present a still better claim. At the same time their lack of self-sufficiency can be shown

---

[1] *La Pensée*, I, p. 4.   [2] *Ibid.*, p. 6.
[3] Blondel adds to his distinction between will-willing and will-willed a distinction between *cogitatio ut natura* (*La Pensée*, I, p. 495) and thought-thought.
[4] *L'Être*, p. 80.

in many ways. It may seem therefore that it is the universe in its totality which alone merits the name of being. But the universe is becoming rather than being. It participates in being; but it is not being itself.

In these reflections Blondel obviously takes it that there is in man an implicit and real idea of 'Being in itself',[1] which is found not to be fully instantiated in matter, organisms, persons or even in the universe considered as a developing totality. But he does not claim that this implicit idea is able to provide a basis for the ontological argument of St. Anselm. Hence he is bound to ask whether there is justification for asserting that the idea refers to a reality. While not rejecting arguments of a traditional nature from the world to God, Blondel maintains that 'our idea of God has its source, not in a light which belongs to us, but in the illuminating action of God in us.'[2] 'The fundamental and congenital aptitude of the spirit for knowing and desiring God is the initial and supreme cause of the whole movement of nature and thought, so that our certainty of being is thus grounded on Being itself.'[3]

In the second *Action* Blondel says that in the original work of this name he had deliberately left on one side 'the redoubtable metaphysical difficulties of the problem of secondary causes'[4] and had considered action only in man and with a view to a study of human destiny. In the second *Action* however he widens his horizon to include action in general, and he includes themes which had been passed over in the first version. He argues, for example, that the pure and complete concept of action is verified only in God, who is absolute activity (*l'Agir absolu*) and who is the productive course of all finite things. At the same time there are graded approximations, so to speak, to the absolute divine activity; and the question arises, how is it possible for God to create finite beings as free and responsible moral agents? Blondel tries to combine recognition of man's creative activity and moral responsibility with the belief in divine creation and with his theory of the basic orientation of the human spirit to the Transcendent and of the perfecting of human nature through the union of the human will with the divine.

This broadening of horizons to cover wide-ranging ontological and metaphysical themes undoubtedly gives to the trilogy a different flavour, as it were, from that of the original *L'Action* and

---

[1] *Ibid.*, p. 156.   [2] *Ibid.*, p. 163.   [3] *Ibid.*, p. 167.
[4] *L'Action* (trilogy), I, p. 298.

the *Letter on Apologetics*. But though the trilogy widens the scope of reflection, it does not constitute a repudation of the first *L'Action*. Blondel remains profoundly convinced of the basic dynamic orientation of the human spirit to God; and the widening of horizons can be seen as a covering of problems implicit in his original line of thought. The change in Blondel's ways of expressing his thought and the respectful attitude which he often shows to Aquinas can be misleading. For instance, though in *La Pensée* Blondel is careful to allow for the role of traditional-type proofs of God's existence, he makes it clear that if they are taken in isolation and as exercises in theoretical metaphysics, they lead to an *idea* of God, and that for God to be a living reality for man, the God of the religious consciousness, something more is required. He may avoid use of the word 'option'; but the fundamental idea remains. Blondel will not allow that there is a final and unbridgeable dichotomy between 'the God of the philosophers' and 'the God of religion'. The difference arises because there are different types of thought in man; but the ideal is an integration of conflicting tendencies within man. And this ideal was obviously present in the original *L'Action*.

It is difficult to see how Blondel can ever be a popular writer. He writes for philosophers rather than for the general public. Moreover, a good many readers, even if they are philosophers, are probably often left wondering precisely what he means. But he is notable as a Catholic thinker who developed his ideas in dialogue with modern philosophy in its spiritualist, idealist and positivist movements. He did not call simply for a return to the medieval past, when brought into line with modern science. Nor did he adopt an attitude of discipleship in regard to any given thinker. We can of course discern lines of thought which link him with Augustine and Bonaventure, just as we can see affinities with Leibniz, Kant, Maine de Biran and others. But he was throughout an original thinker. And the general idea of a philosophy which should be intrinsically autonomous but at the same time self-critical and self-limiting and open to Christian revelation is presumably acceptable in principle to all Catholic thinkers who have any use for metaphysical philosophy.[1] Some may of course believe that the approach to metaphysics 'from within', by way of reflection on the active subject, which was characteristic of

[1] How far Blondel's philosophy really is 'autonomous' is of course open to discussion.

Maine de Biran and which is especially noticeable in the first *Action*, smacks of subjectivism. In this case they will welcome the widening of horizons in the trilogy as equivalent to an acknowledgement of the inadequacy of the way of immanence. But Blondel's approach does at any rate have the merit of trying to exhibit the relevance of religion. And he recognized the fact, also seen by the so-called transcendental Thomists, that the traditional proofs of God's existence, based on the external world, rest on presuppositions which can be justified only by systematic reflection on the activity of the subject in thought and volition.

3. Among Blondel's correspondents was Lucien Laberthonnière (1860–1932).[1] After studying in a seminary at Bourges Laberthonnière became an Oratorian in 1886 and taught philosophy in the Oratorian school at Juilly and then at a school in Paris. In 1900 he returned to Juilly as rector of the College; but when the Combes government had passed its legislation against religious orders and congregations in 1902, he went to live in Paris. In 1903 he published *Essays in Religious Philosophy* (*Essais de philosophie religieuse*) and in 1904 *Christian Realism and Greek Idealism* (*Le réalisme chrétien et l'idéalisme grec*). In 1905 Blondel made him editor of the *Annales de philosophie chrétienne*. In the following year however two of his writings were placed on the Index. In 1911 he published *Positivism and Catholicism* (*Positivisme et catholicisme*); but in 1913 he was prohibited by the ecclesiastical authorities from further publication. In this period of enforced silence one or two writings of Laberthonnière were published under the name of friends.[2] But the bulk had to await posthumous publication. In 1935 Louis Canet started to publish these works at Paris under the general title *Oeuvres de Laberthonnière*.

In spite of the treatment which he received Laberthonnière never broke with the Church. Still less did he abandon his deep Christian faith. It is indeed both probable and natural that the placing of two of his books on the Index and the later veto on further publication increased his hostility not only to authoritarianism but also to Aristotelianism and Thomism.[3] But this hostility certainly did not originate in reaction to the measures taken by ecclesiastical authority. It was a reasoned attitude,

---

[1] This correspondence has been edited by C. Tresmontant, *Correspondance philosophique, Maurice Blondel–Lucien Laberthonnière* (Paris, 1961).
[2] For example, P. Sanson's *L'inquiétude humaine* was really written by Laberthonnière.
[3] Laberthonnière was much more polemically inclined than Blondel.

based on his view of human life, of the nature of philosophy and of the Christian religion. If it had not been for his reduction to silence, his ideas might have made a much greater impression. As it was, other philosophers were coming to the fore by the time when his works were at length published. One must add however that whereas Blondel concentrated on expounding his own thought, Laberthonnière tended to work out and exhibit his ideas while discussing those of other thinkers, sometimes in a markedly polemical manner. Thus the first volumes of the *Works* as published by Louis Canet contain Laberthonnière's *Studies on Descartes* (*Études sur Descartes*, 1935) and his *Studies in Cartesian Philosophy* (*Études de philosophie cartésienne*, 1938) while the *Outline of a Personalist Philosophy* (*Esquisse d'une philosophie personnaliste*, 1942) presents a philosophical outlook which is developed, in large measure, by way of critical discussion of the ideas of other philosophers, such as Renouvier, Bergson and Brunschvicg. One part, for example, is entitled 'the pseudo-personalism of Charles Renouvier'. It does not follow of course that Laberthonnière's ideas are not of value. Moreover, Blondel too developed his thought through a process of dialogue with other philosophers. At the same time in the original *L'Action* and in the trilogy the reader is much less distracted from the author's own line of thought by polemical and historical excursions than in the case of Laberthonnière's main works.

In the notes which form the preface to his *Studies on Descartes* Laberthonnière asserts that 'every philosophical doctrine has as 'ts end to give a meaning to life, to human existence'.[1] Every philosophy has a moral motivation, even if the philosopher gives to his thought a quasi-mathematical form. This can be seen even in the case of Spinoza, in whose thought the geometrical structure is really subordinate to the underlying aim and motivation. Further, the test of a philosophy's truth is its viability, its capacity for being lived. Laberthonnière is actually referring to the need for detecting the animating principle, the underlying and pervasive moral motivation, in any philosophy studied. But what he has to say expresses of course his own idea of what philosophy should be. 'There is only one problem, the problem of ourselves, from which all the others derive.'[2] What are we? And what ought we to be?

---

[1] *Études sur Descartes*, I, p. 1.
[2] *Études de philosophie cartésienne* (1938), p. 1.

The animal, Laberthonnière asserts, is certainly not a machine; but it does not enjoy the self-consciousness which is required for raising problems in regard to the world and itself. For the matter of that, the human will-to-live is in origin akin to that of the animal. That is to say, the human will-to-live is oriented first of all to 'the things of time and space'.[1] The living organism, impelled by the will-to-live, learns empirically to seek for some things as satisfying desires and needs and to shun other things as causing suffering or menacing its existence. With the awakening of self-consciousness however the situation changes. Man becomes conscious of himself not as something already made and complete but rather as something which is to be and ought to be. In fact, according to Laberthonnière we are carried, as it were out of or beyond ourselves by the aspiration to possess the plenitude of being. Here however several paths lie open to man.

In the first place man finds himself in a world of things, which self-consciousness sets over against him. On the one hand he can make of this world of things a spectacle, an object of theoretical or aesthetic contemplation, possessing things, so to speak, without being possessed by them. This is the attitude exemplified in Aristotle's idea of contemplation. On the other hand man can strive to discover the properties of things and the laws governing the succession of phenomena in order to obtain mastery over things, to use them and to produce or destroy phenomena as he wills. Both attitudes can be described as pertaining to physics. But in the first case we have a physics of contemplation, while in the second case we have a physics of exploitation, such as has been practised from the time of Descartes onwards.

In the second place however man does not find himself simply in a world of things. He is not simply an isolated individual face to face with a material and non-self-conscious environment. He finds himself also in a world of persons who, like him, can say 'I' or 'I am'. This world of persons forms already a certain unity. We live and feel and thnk and will in a social world. Within however this material unity human beings can obviously experience hostility to one another. Beyond the basic natural unity there is a moral unity which is something to be achieved rather than something given. In this field the aspiration to possess the plenitude of being takes the form of the sense of obligation to become one with others, to achieve a moral unity of persons. Laberthonnière

[1] *Ibid.*, p. 2.

distinguishes between 'things' and 'beings', reserving the word 'being' for the self-conscious subject, who is characterized by an interiority which the 'thing' does not possess. This self-conscious subject aspires to possess the plenitude of being through union with other subjects.

How is this unity to be achieved? It is of course possible to attempt to achieve it by means of an authority, of whatever kind, which dictates what men should think and say and do, treating human beings as animals which have to be trained. But this procedure can produce no more than an external unity which, according to Laberthonnière, simply transfers conflict from the external to the internal spheres. The only efficacious way of achieving unity between beings which exist in and for themselves is by each person overcoming his egoism and giving himself by setting himself at the service of others, so that the unification is the fruit of an expansion from within, so to speak, and not imposed from without. There is of course a place for authority, but for an authority which maintains a common ideal and tries to help persons to develop themselves as persons rather than to mould them by coercion or to reduce them to the level of sheep.

What Laberthonnière has to say on this matter obviously has its implications both in the political and in the ecclesiastical sphere. For example, when referring in one place to what he regards as the wrong use of authority, he mentions 'Caesarist or Fascist'[1] domination. It does not follow however that emphasis on Fascist totalitarianism is accompanied by a blindness to the possible shortcomings of democracy. For instance, in a note he speaks of democracy which 'instead of being a dynamic movement (*élan*) towards the ideal through the spiritualization of human life has become a stampede towards the goods of the earth through a systematic materialization of life'.[2] In other words, modern western democracy, though animated originally by an impulse directed to ideal goals, has become materialistic and cannot therefore simply be contrasted with political authoritarianism as the good is contrasted with the bad. As for the ecclesiastical sphere, it is obvious that Laberthonnière was opposed to the policy of trying to impose uniformity from above and to the sort of methods from which he personally was to suffer. He had, as it were, a post-Vatican II mentality long before the second Vatican Council. The same kind of ideas about the development of persons as

---

[1] *Ibid.*, p. 5.   [2] *Ibid.*, p. 5n.

persons and of their union through personally willed acceptance of common ideals came out in his theory of education. According to Laberthonnière therefore there is a natural unity. 'All men constitute one humanity by nature.'[1] There is also a unity which remains to be achieved, as a willed ideal. This shows that we have a common origin and a common goal. Beings (self-conscious subjects, that is to say) proceed from God and can attain their end only through union with the divine will. God is not so much a problem as 'the solution of the problem which we are for ourselves'.[2] Without reference to God we cannot answer such questions as 'what are we?' and 'what ought we to be?'. Or, rather, in attempting to answer these questions we are inevitably led into the sphere of religious belief.

Laberthonnière was influenced by Maine de Biran and Boutroux, and also by Blondel. Philosophy was for him the science of life, human life; and its point of departure was *'ourselves* as interior and spiritual realities having consciousness of ourselves'.[3] The word 'science' however must not be misunderstood. Science in the ordinary sense is a science of things, a physics of some kind, even if it takes human beings in their phenomenal reality into consideration. But metaphysics, to have a meaning for us, must illuminate the problems of life; and it must be livable. Biology deals with life and psychology with mind; and they have of course their value. But metaphysics is concerned with the self-conscious active subject as oriented to an ideal and a goal; and it is a science of life in the sense that it illuminates the nature and goal of the life of this subject (or of the person) considered as such.

There is no great difficulty in understanding Laberthonnière's hostility to Aristotelianism and traditional Thomism, an hostility which led him to take a dim view of what he regarded as the weak concessions made by Blondel to Aquinas and the Thomists. In Laberthonnière's opinion Aristotelianism was a physics rather than a metaphysics, even if part of it was labelled 'metaphysics'. And the God of Aristotle, wrapped up in himself, bore little resemblance to the living and active God of religion. As for Spinoza and other monists, they denied to all intents and purposes the irreducible distinctness of persons, while the positivists cut off the goal of unity-in-distinction from its ultimate transcendent and at the same time immanent foundation.

---

[1] *Ibid.*, p. 11.   [2] *Ibid.*, p. 11.
[3] *Esquisse d'une philosophie personnaliste* (1942), p. 7.

The reader is likely to conclude that Laberthonnière's idea of philosophy and his critical discussions of other philosophers, such as Aristotle, Descartes, Spinoza and Bergson, were influenced by his Christian belief. This conclusion would be obviously correct. But in the case of Laberthonnière all was out in the open; there was no attempt at concealment. In his view it was wrong to suppose that Christianity could be superimposed on a philosophy which had already been constructed or which was developed independently of Christian faith. For Christianity is 'itself *the* philosophy in the etymological sense of the word, that is to say wisdom, the science of life which explains what we are and, on the basis of what we are, what we ought to be.'[1] The question whether or not there can be a Christian philosophy rests on a false assumption if one is thinking of a philosophy worked out independently of Christian belief and which would serve as a 'natural' basis on which Christianity could be superimposed as a 'supernatural' superstructure. This is the sort of idea which followed in the wake of the invasion of Aristotelianism in the Middle Ages. Christianity is itself the true philosophy. And by the very fact that it is the true philosophy it excludes every other system. For 'every philosophy which deserves this name . . . presents itself, if not as exhaustive, at least as exclusive of what is not itself.'[2]

Laberthonnière obviously does not mean to imply that a man who is not a Christian is unable to raise and reflect on metaphysical problems. For it is clear that human life or existence can give rise to problems in anyone's mind, whether he is a Christian or not. Laberthonnière's thesis is rather that it is Christianity which provides the most adequate solution available to man. Or, better, Christianity is for him the saving wisdom, the true 'science of life', by which man can live. As he explicitly recognizes, Laberthonnière thus returns to the point of view of St. Augustine and other early Christian writers who looked on Christianity as being itself the true and genuine philosophy which fulfilled and supplanted the philosophies of the ancient world. The separation and subsequent conflict between philosophy and theology was a disaster. St. Thomas Aquinas did not baptize Aristotle; he aristotelianized Christianity, introducing into it 'the pagan conception of the world and of life'.[3] To be sure, if we once make a sharp separation between philosophy and theology, it appears inappropriate to describe Christianity as a philosophy,

[1] *Ibid.*, p. 13.   [2] *Ibid.*, p. 13.   [3] *Ibid.*, p. 643.

even as the true philosophy. But there is no compelling reason
to make the separation. It may seem that philosophy is the work
of 'pure reason' and belongs to the natural level, whereas theology
is the fruit of revelation proceeding from the supernatural sphere.
But according to Laberthonnière it is a mistake to look on the
natural and the supernatural as two worlds, of which the latter is
superimposed on the former. The terms 'natural' and 'supernatural' should be understood not in terms of a metaphysical
dualism but as referring to 'two opposed manners of being and
acting, of which one corresponds to what we are, to what we think
and to what we do in virtue of our innate egocentricism, while the
other corresponds to what we have the obligation of being, of
thinking and of doing through willed generosity.'[1] If therefore
metaphysical philosophy is regarded as dealing with the problems of what we are and what we ought to be, it is in no way
derogatory to Christianity to describe it as the true philosophy.
For it is precisely on these problems that it throws light, with a
view to enabling man to become what he ought to be.

Given this point of view, it is natural enough that Laberthonnière should emphasize the close connection between truth and
life. 'One does not demonstrate that God exists, no more than one
demonstrates any existence. One finds him in seeking him. But
one seeks only because one has already found him, only because
he is present and active in the consciousness which we have of
ourselves.'[2] In regard to Christian dogmas too Laberthonnière
thoroughly dislikes the idea of them as pieces of information, so to
speak, which come from a supernatural world and which we simply
have to accept on authority. He certainly rejects a purely relativistic view of Christian dogmas, but he looks on them from the
point of view of their capacity to illuminate human problems and
to be guides for life. Without relevance for human life they would
have no real meaning for us. It is not, Laberthonnière insists, a
case of making man the measure of all truth, including revealed
truth. For by considering truth in relation to ourselves and our
lives we thereby measure ourselves by the truth rather than the
other way round. If we understand the term 'pragmatism' as
covering the view that truth in the religious sphere becomes 'our
truth' when we see its relevance to our lives, we can of course

[1] *Ibid.*, p. 15. The distinction, Laberthonnière remarks, is really the same as
that between St. Paul's carnal and spiritual man.
[2] *Ibid.*, p. 19. This is basically Augustinian doctrine.

describe Laberthonnière as a pragmatist. But if we understand pragmatism as implying, for example, that the assertion of God's existence is true only in the sense that it is useful for man to make this assertion, he was certainly not a pragmatist. For he believed that we cannot know ourselves properly without recognizing the *reality* of God.

From one point of view Laberthonnière's view of the nature of philosophy and metaphysics is a matter of terminology. That is to say, if we decide to mean by 'metaphysics' the saving wisdom, it is clear that for the Christian Christianity itself must be '*the* metaphysics'.[1] And if Laberthonnière were accused of reducing the Christian religion to the level of a philosophy, he could reply that the accusation rested on a misunderstanding of his use of the word 'philosophy'. At the same time, when he says that metaphysics, identified with Christian doctrine as 'the science of our life',[2] has *ourselves* as its point of departure, one can understand theologians suspecting him of pure immanentism, especially if they take such propositions out of the context in which he is distinguishing between what he means by metaphysics and what Aristotle meant.

It may seem that Laberthonnière has really no place in a history of philosophy. But this judgment obviously presupposes a concept of philosophy which he rejects. In any case his thought is of some interest. It continues the approach to metaphysics from within which was characteristic of Maine de Biran, but in its concept of the relation between metaphysics and Christianity it goes back to St. Augustine. By his attitude to Aquinas's attempt to incorporate Aristotelianism into a comprehensive theological-philosophical world-vision Laberthonnière recalls to our minds the reaction which produced and followed on the condemnations of 1277. But his hostility to Aristotle and Aquinas is motivated not so much by veneration for the *sancti* and for tradition as such as by his own personalist and, to a certain extent, existentialist approach. For instance, his attack on the Aristotelian theory of matter as the principle of individuation is made in the name of a spiritualist personalism. He is in a real sense a modern Augustinian who develops his thought through dialogue with other philosophers such as Descartes, Bergson and Brunschvicg. His insistence on Christian doctrines becoming truths for us, *our* truths, in proportion as we discern and appropriate their relevance to human life

[1] *Ibid.*, p. 7.   [2] *Ibid.*, p. 7.

may assimilate him to the modernists. But he combines this insistence with a genuine attempt to avoid a relativism which would exclude the claim that there are objective and abiding Christian truths.

4. The term 'modernism' was first used in the early years of the twentieth century and seems to have been coined by opponents of the movement, though it was also used by writers such as Buonaiuti, who published *The Programme of the Modernists* (*Il programma dei modernisti*) in 1907. It is easy enough to mention names of persons who are universally classified as modernists. In France there is Alfred Loisy (1857–1940), in Italy Ernesto Buonaiuti (1881–1946) and in Great Britain George Tyrrell (1861–1909). But it is a great deal more difficult to give a clear account of the content of modernism, and still more difficult to define it. Perhaps the easiest way of coping with the matter is to give an historical account, as proper attention can then be paid to differences in interests and lines of thought.[1] One can of course attempt to delineate modernism as a system, in an abstract manner; but one then exposes oneself to the pertinent objection that modernism as a clearly defined system was created not by the modernists themselves but by the ecclesiastical documents condemning them, such as the decree *Lamentabili* and, much more, the encyclical *Pascendi*, both of which appeared in 1907.[2] It would however be quite out of place to attempt to give a history of the modernist movement in this chapter. And the primary purpose of the following remarks is to show why thinkers such as Blondel and Laberthonnière were suspected of modernism, and how the thought of Blondel at any rate differed from modernism in the sense in which modernism was condemned by Rome.

The term 'modernism', taken by itself, might be understood in terms of modernization, in the sense of an attempt to bring Roman Catholic thought into line with contemporary scholarship and intellectual developments. In view of his positive attitude towards the greatly increased knowledge of Aristotelianism which

---

[1] Among general works on the subject mention can be made of *Le modernisme dans l'église* by J. Rivière (Paris, 1929), *The Modernist Movement in the Roman Church* by A. R. Vidler (London, 1934) and *Histoire, dogme et critique dans la crise moderniste* by E. Poulat (Paris, 1962).

[2] In the papal encyclical *Pascendi* it is explicitly stated that the document gathers together views which are expressed separately in the writings of the modernists and arranges them in a systematic manner, so that their presuppositions and implications can be clearly seen. In other words, the document undertakes to make explicit what is regarded as an implicit system.

was creating a stir in the thirteenth century, St. Thomas Aquinas has been spoken of as a modernist.[1] Again, Catholic scholars such as Louis Duchesne (1843–1922), who were concerned with applying to the origins of Christianity the methods of historical criticism which had developed in liberal Protestantism, especially in Germany, can be described as modernist in this general sense of the term. So of course can writers such as Blondel who insisted on the need for a more positive appreciation of modern philosophy.

As used however with reference to a current of thought in the Catholic Church at the end of the nineteenth century and in the first decade of the present century, the term 'modernism' is obviously more specific than modernization or *aggiornamento* in a general sense. In the case of Loisy, for example, it refers to his conclusions about what was required or implied by the updating of historical and biblical studies. For instance, Loisy believed that Jesus as the Son of God was the creation of Christian faith reflecting on and transforming the man Jesus of Nazareth. This transformation involved also a deformation inasmuch as, for example, it involved attributing to the man Jesus miraculous actions the acceptance of which as historical events was ruled out by modern thought and knowledge. The task of historical criticism was to rediscover the historical figure hidden beneath the veils which faith had woven about it. In brief, Loisy maintained in effect that the historian of Christianity must approach his subject as he would approach any other historical theme, and that this approach demanded a purely naturalistic account of Christ himself and of the origins and rise of the Christian Church. We may of course wish to distinguish between historical inquiry in itself and 'higher criticism' as it developed in liberal Protestantism and then influenced some Catholic thinkers, but it is understandable that Loisy's ideas did not commend themselves to the authorities of the Church. For these ideas pretty well undermined the Church's claims.

Loisy was not a professional philosopher and was quite prepared to admit that philosophy was not his speciality.[2] At the same time

---

[1] Étienne Gilson suggested that St. Thomas's 'modernism' was the only one which had proved successful. Laberthonnière retorted, 'successful in what?'. In Laberthonnière's view the success consisted in Aristotelian Thomism eventually receiving an official blessing from ecclesiastical authority, a result which was a matter for regret rather than for rejoicing.

[2] Loisy makes this admission in his *Simple Reflections* on *Lamentabili* and *Pascendi* (*Simples réflexions sur le décret du Saint-Office 'Lamentabili sane exitu' et sur l'encyclique 'Pascendi dominici gregis'*, Paris, 1908, p. 198). Buonaiuti was more given to philosophy than was Loisy.

in his remarks about belief in God he can be said to assume that the human mind cannot attain knowledge of the Transcendent. God is really the Unknowable of Spencer, that which transcends the reach of what Kant described as theoretical knowledge. We think of God in terms of symbols, and from a practical point of view we are warranted in acting as though there were a personal divine will having a claim on the human will. But in the moral and religious sphere we cannot prove the absolute truth of any belief. In this sphere truth, as related to man's good, is as subject to change as man himself. There are no absolutely true and immutable revealed truths. What is called revelation is man's interpretation of his experience; and both experience and interpretation are subject to change.

Later on Loisy approached the position of Auguste Comte. That is to say, he saw in the history of religion an expression of the experience not of the individual but of the community. Christianity had promoted the ideal of a united humanity and was passing into the religion of humanity. Finally, Loisy seems to have returned to the idea of a transcendent God, not however to any belief in revelation or in the Church as custodian of revelation. For present purposes however we can emphasize simply his relativistic and pragmatist view of truth in the ethico-religious sphere.

In general, the modernists tended to assume that modern philosophy had shown that the human mind cannot transcend the sphere of consciousness. In one sense of course this is a truism, in so far, that is to say, as it means that we cannot be conscious of anything without being conscious of it or think of anything without thinking of it. But immanentism was understood as excluding any proof of God's existence by, for example, a causal argument. What is given in man is a need for the divine which, rising into consciousness, takes the form of a religious feeling or sense which is equivalent to faith. Revelation is man's interpretation of his religious experience. This interpretation is expressed of course in conceptual or intellectual forms. But these can become antiquated and stifling, so that new forms of expression have to be sought. Revelation in a general sense can be considered as the work of God, even if from another point of view it is man's work. But the idea of God revealing absolute truths from outside, as it were, truths which are promulgated by the Church in the form of unchangeable statements of unchanging truths is incompatible with the concept of evolution, when applied to man's cultural and religious life, and with the accompanying relativistic view of religious truth.

The foregoing remarks are of course a partial summary of views expressed in writings by different authors.[1] But they may suffice to show how Catholic philosophers such as Blondel and Édouard Le Roy could be accused of modernism or of modernist leanings. For Blondel, as we have seen, pursued what he called the method of immanence and approached God in terms of the human spirit's basic orientation as manifested in its activity, while Le Roy, through his acceptance and application of the Bergsonian views of intelligence and intuition, appeared to attribute to religious dogmas a purely pragmatic value. Blondel however never accepted immanentism as a doctrine. Nor could he, as he tried, by means of the method of immanence, to open the mind to the transcendent divine reality and lead it to the stage at which there was a point of insertion, so to speak, for God's self-revelation. As for Le Roy, he certainly expounded a pragmatic interpretation of scientific truth and applied it also to religious dogmas. But he defended his position and was never separated from the Church, either by his own action or by that of ecclesiastical authority. According to Laberthonnière, who was given to such remarks, what Le Roy did was to reduce not Christianity to Bergsonism but Bergsonism to Christianity.

The main theme of this chapter has been philosophy as apologetics. The new approach in apologetics was represented by Ollé-Laprune, Blondel and Laberthonnière. Their thought had indeed some points in common with views expressed by the modernists. But they were primarily concerned with philosophical approaches to Christianity, whereas the modernists were primarily concerned with reconciling Catholic faith and beliefs with freedom in historical, biblical and scientific research. While therefore Blondel, as a professional philosopher, was careful not only to stop short of pronouncements about revelation but also to justify this stopping short in terms of his own concept of the nature and

---

[1] Tyrrell spoke of revelation as being man's statements about his spiritual experiences rather than God's statements to man. But he did not deny that in and through these experiences man encounters God. According to Tyrrell God is known only in and through his effects. These effects are divine impulses in man, which man interprets in his own categories and language. And the test of the interpretations is their spiritual fruitfulness. Tyrrell certainly felt at times a strong inclination or temptation to agnosticism. But he tried to hold on to belief in God as a reality.

scope of philosophy, the modernists were naturally compelled to reconsider the nature of revelation and of Catholic dogma. In other words, they occupied themselves with theological topics in a way in which Blondel did not. And as their idea of what was demanded by modern historical and biblical research was a radical one, they naturally fell foul of ecclesiastical authorities who were convinced that the modernists were undermining the Christian faith. Looking back, we may think that the authorities were so much concerned with the conclusions at which the modernists arrived that they failed to consider whether or not the modernistic movement expressed recognition of genuine problems. But we have to see things in their historical perspective. Given the actual situation, including the attitude of the authorities on the one hand and the concept of 'modern' scholarship and knowledge on the other hand, one could hardly expect events to be other than what they were. Moreover, from the philosophical point of view the thought of Blondel is of considerably more value than the ideas of the modernists.

CHAPTER XII

THOMISM IN FRANCE

Introductory remarks; D. J. Mercier — Garrigou-Lagrange and Sertillanges — J. Maritain — E. Gilson — P. Rousselot and A. Forest—J. Maréchal.

1. It would be incorrect to say that the Thomist revival in the nineteenth century originated with the publication in 1879 of Pope Leo XIII's encyclical letter *Aeterni Patris*. But papal assertion of the permanent value of Thomism and the encyclical's exhortation to Catholic philosophers to draw their inspiration from Aquinas while developing his thought to meet modern intellectual needs certainly gave a powerful impetus to an already existing movement. Papal endorsement of Thomism had of course several effects. On the one hand it encouraged the formation, especially in clerical circles and in ecclesiastical seminaries and academic institutions, of what one might describe as a party-line, a kind of philosophical orthodoxy. In other words, it could be used in support of the subordination of philosophy to theological interests and of the activities of the rigid and narrow-minded Thomists who were suspicious of and hostile to the more original and independent-minded Catholic thinkers, such as Maurice Blondel. On the other hand the call to look back to the thought of an outstanding thinker of the Middle Ages and to apply the principles of his thought to problems arising in the modern cultural situation undoubtedly helped to promote a great deal of serious philosophical reflection. Whatever one may think about the perennial value of Aquinas's thought, there was a lot to be said in favour of approaching philosophy by way of the system of an outstanding thinker and of thinking on systematic lines, in terms, that is to say, of certain basic philosophical principles and of their application instead of following the rather wishy-washy eclecticism which had tended to prevail in ecclesiastical academic institutions.

Exaggeration should be avoided. Official approval of a certain line of thought could and did produce a party-spirit which was narrow and polemical. At no time indeed was Thomism as such imposed on Catholic philosophers in a way which would imply that it was part of the Catholic faith. In theory the autonomy of philosophy was upheld. It is however undeniable that in some circles there was a marked tendency to depict Thomism as the only line of philosophical thought which really fitted in with Catholic theology. The theory was of course that it fitted in because it was true rather than it must be thought of as true because it fitted in. But one can hardly shut one's eyes to the fact that in many ecclesiastical institutions Thomism, or what was considered such, came to be taught in a dogmatic manner analogous to that in which Marxism-Leninism is taught in Communist-dominated education. At the same time the 'back to Aquinas' movement could obviously stimulate more able minds to endeavour to recapture the spirit of Aquinas and to create a synthesis in the light of the contemporary cultural situation. And there certainly have been Thomist philosophers who have embraced Thomist principles not because they were taught to do so but because they came to believe in their validity, and who have tried to apply these principles in a constructive way to modern problems. To this positive development of Thomist thought France has made a signal contribution; and it is with this contribution that we are concerned here.

In its earlier days the Thomist revival owed a great deal to Désiré Joseph Mercier (1851–1926) and to his collaborators at Louvain. After having taught philosophy in the seminary at Malines Mercier was appointed professor of Thomist philosophy in the University of Louvain in 1882. In 1888 he founded the Philosophical Society of Louvain, and in 1889 he became the first president of the newly established Institute of Philosophy of the University. The *Revue néo-scolastique* (now the *Revue philosophique de Louvain*) was started by the Philosophical Society under Mercier's editorship. In his years as a professor Mercier laboured strenuously to develop Thomism in the light of modern problems and of modern philosophy. Among his writings are two volumes on psychology (1892), a work on logic (1894), a book on general metaphysics or ontology (1894) and a work on the theory of knowledge, *Critériologie générale* (1899). In general, Mercier concerned himself with developing a realist metaphysics in critical dialogue with empiricism, positivism and the philosophy of Kant. But he was also particularly insistent on the need for a first-hand knowledge of science and for a positive relation between philosophy and the sciences. He himself wrote on experimental psychology, and through the Institute of Philosophy he encouraged the formation of a band not only of philosophers but also of scientists, such as the experimental psychologist Albert-Édouard Michotte (1881–1965) who had studied in Germany with Wundt and Külpe. Nowadays Mercier's philosophical writings may seem rather old-fashioned; but there can be no doubt of his real contribution to bringing Thomism into closer touch with contemporary philosophical and scientific thought and with making it intellectually respectable. In 1906 he was appointed archbishop of Malines, and in the following year he was made a Cardinal.

Though Mercier admired Kant in some respects, he criticized at length what seemed to him to be Kant's subjectivism and his restriction of the scope of metaphysics. For a considerable time Kant was one of the principal bogeymen of the Scholastics. At a later date however another Belgian, Joseph Maréchal, of whom more will be said later, adopted a much more positive approach, trying to appropriate Kant, as it were, and then to go beyond him. Some people doubt whether the so-called transcendental Thomism which stems from Maréchal can properly be described as Thomism. But at any rate its development is one expression of the marked change in the attitude of Thomists to other currents of thought in modern philosophy. Nowadays the orthodox Thomist of the type of Jacques Maritain has become comparatively rare.

The relaxing of polemical attitudes on the part of Thomist philosophers through a genuine effort to enter into, understand and evaluate other currents of thought has been accompanied in recent years by a notable diminution in the Church's attempt to encourage and promote a philosophical party-line. For example, the second Vatican Council was careful not to make pronouncements in the philosophical area. Besides, a number of Catholic theologians are understandably anxious to emphasize the independence of faith from any philosophical system, including Thomism, while others prefer to look for a philosophical basis in, say, the anthropology of Martin Heidegger. Again, certain developments in theological thought have tended to weaken the idea that Christian beliefs need to be expressed in categories borrowed from a particular philosophical tradition. It is indeed questionable whether theologians can get along without philosophy quite as easily as some of them seem to assume. The point is however that the 'handmaid of theology' situation, to which reference was made above, has greatly changed.

Given the changed situation, it is arguable that the impetus of the Thomist revival is spent. With diminished official backing and with the development of tendencies in theology which are hostile to the use of metaphysics for apologetic purposes, if not to metaphysics as such, it is natural that there should be a marked reaction against Thomism. There may of course be a renewal of interest in the spirit and ways of thought of Aquinas. The present writer is however happily not called upon to indulge in hazardous prophecies. His task is to make some remarks about Thomism in France.

2. France has made a signal contribution to the development of Thomism in the modern world. Among the pioneers Réginald Garrigou-Lagrange (1877–1964), a well known Dominican philosopher and theologian, has indeed appeared to a good many people as a rather narrow representative of neo-Thomism, intent on maintaining and promoting an orthodox party line. But despite his rather limited outlook[1] he contributed by his writings to raising the standard of thought in Thomist circles. An opponent of modernism, in 1909 he published *Le sens commun, la philosophie de l'être et les formules dogmatiques* (*Common Sense, the Philosophy of Being and Dogmatic Formulas*). His well known book on natural theology, *Dieu, son existence et sa nature*, appeared in 1915.[2] In 1932 he published *Le réalisme du principe de finalité* (*The Realism of the Principle of Finality*), and in 1946 *La synthèse thomiste*.[3] He also published theological works and books on Christian spirituality and mysticism, a number of which have been translated into English.

Another name which should be mentioned is that of Antonin-Dalmace Sertillanges (1863–1948), also a Dominican. Sertillanges was a prolific writer, who tried to exhibit the applicability and fruitfulness of Thomist principles in a variety of spheres and who devoted special attention to the relation between philosophy and Christianity. His best known work is probably his two-volume study of St. Thomas, *S. Thomas d'Aquin*, the first edition of which appeared in 1910.[4] Other publications on Aquinas include a study of his ethics, *La philosophie morale de S. Thomas*

---

[1] Garrigou-Lagrange would claim of course that if his outlook was limited, it was limited by a perception of the truth of perennial philosophical principles on the one hand and by divine revelation on the other.
[2] An English translation by B. Rose appeared in two volumes in 1934, *God, His Existence and His Nature*.
[3] There is an English translation by P. Cummings, *Reality. A Synthesis of Thomist Thought* (London, 1950).
[4] It was later entitled *La philosophie de S. Thomas d'Aquin*.

d'Aquin (1914, later edition 1942) and *Les grandes thèses de la philosophie thomiste*[1] which appeared in 1928. A two-volume work on the relation between philosophy and Christianity, *Le christianisme et les philosophies* appeared in 1939–41, and another two-volume work on the problem of evil, *Le problème du mal*, in 1949–51. Among other writings we can mention a book on socialism and Christianity, *Socialisme et christianisme* (1905), and one on the thought of Claude Bernard, *La philosophie de Claude Bernard* (1944).

3. The two names however which are most associated with putting Thomism on the map, with, that is to say, bringing it out of a rather narrow and predominantly ecclesiastical circle and making it respectable in the eyes of the academic world, are Jacques Maritain and Étienne Gilson. Professor Gilson of course is widely known for his historical studies which have won him respect even among those who are not particularly sympathetic to Thomism. Maritain is first and foremost a theoretical philosopher. Gilson, as befits an historian, has concerned himself with exhibiting the thought of Aquinas in its historical setting and therefore in its theological context. Maritain has been more concerned with exhibiting Thomism as an autonomous philosophy which can enter into dialogue with other philosophies without appealing to revelation and the principles of which are relevant to the solution of modern problems. Given the suspicion of metaphysics which is not infrequently encountered among theologians, including Catholic theologians, and given the natural reaction in Catholic colleges and seminaries to past indoctrination in what amounted to a Thomist party line, it is understandable if Maritain in particular is commonly regarded as old-fashioned and if his writings no longer have the vogue which they once enjoyed.[2] But this does not alter the fact that his was probably the greatest single contribution to the Thomist revival to which impetus was given by the encyclical letter *Aeterni Patris* in 1879.

Jacques Maritain was born at Paris in 1882. When he went to the Sorbonne as a student, he looked to science to solve all problems; but he was liberated from scientism by the influence of the lectures of Henri Bergson. In 1904 Maritain married Raissa

---

[1] There is an English translation by G. Anstruther under the title *The Foundations of Thomistic Philosophy* (London, 1931).
[2] This is applicable more to Maritain than to Gilson, as the value of Gilson's historical studies does not depend on one's attitude to Thomism as a philosophy for today.

Oumansoff, a fellow student, and in 1906 they were converted to Catholicism under the influence of Léon Bloy (1846–1917), the famous French Catholic writer and vigorous opponent of bourgeois society and religion. In 1907–08 Maritain studied biology at Heidelberg with Hans Driesch, the neovitalist.[1] He then devoted himself to studying the works of Aquinas and became an ardent disciple. In 1913 he delivered a series of conferences on the philosophy of Bergson;[2] and in 1914 he was appointed to lecture on modern philosophy at the Institut Catholique at Paris. He has also taught at the Pontifical Institute of Medieval Studies at Toronto, at Columbia University and at Notre Dame, where a centre was set up in 1958 to encourage studies on the lines of his thought. After the second world war Maritain was French ambassador to the Holy See from 1945 until 1948 and then taught at Princeton University. Later he lived in retirement in France. He died in 1973.

It has sometimes been said that whereas Gilson rules out the so-called critical problem as a pseudo-problem, Maritain admits it. This statement is however misleading, if taken by itself, for it suggests that Maritain starts his philosophizing either with trying to prove, abstractly, that we can have knowledge or with following Descartes in taking self-consciousness as undeniable and then attempting to justify our natural belief that we have knowledge of objects external to the self or that there are things corresponding to our ideas of them. If the critical problem is understood in this sort of way, Maritain excludes it just as much as Gilson does. He does not try to prove a priori that knowledge is possible. And he sees clearly that if we once shut ourselves up in the circle of our ideas, there we remain. He is a realist, and he has always insisted that when I know Tom, it is Tom that I know, not my idea of Tom.[3] At the same time Maritain certainly admits the critical problem, if by this is meant reflection by the mind on its pre-reflexive knowledge with a view to answering the question, what is knowledge? To ask in an abstract manner whether there can be knowledge and to attempt to answer this question in a

---

[1] See Vol. 6 of this *History*, pp. 383–4.
[2] Published as *La philosophie bergsonienne* (1914). English translation, *Bergsonian Philosophy and Thomism*, by M. L. Andison and J. G. Andison (N.Y., 1955).
[3] Obviously, objections can be raised. But Maritain has clung tenaciously to the view that though from a psychological point of view ideas are mental modifications, the intentional object, considered precisely as such, is not different from the object referred to. In scholastic language, he has always refused to transform the *medium quo* into a *medium quod*.

purely *a priori* manner is to enter a blind alley. The only way out
is the way we came in. But there can perfectly well be an inquiry
leading to knowledge of knowledge, the result of the mind's
reflecting on its own activity in knowing something.

The question, 'what is knowledge'? suggests however that there
is only one kind of knowledge, whereas Maritain's concern has
been with inquiring into distinguishable ways of knowing reality.
He has written a good deal in the field of theory of knowledge;
but his best known work on the topic is probably *Distinguer pour
unir, ou Les degrés du savoir*, the first edition of which appeared in
1932.[1] One of his preoccupations, here and elsewhere, is to
interpret knowledge in such a way that it does count as knowledge
of the world but yet not only leaves room for but also demands
philosophy of Nature in particular and metaphysics in general.
In *The Degrees of Knowledge* Maritain expresses his agreement
with Meyerson that a concern with ontology, with causal explanation that is to say, is not foreign to science as it actually exists (as
distinct from what may be said about it); but he argues that the
mathematical nature of modern physics has resulted in the continuation of a world which is so remote from the world of ordinary
experience as to be practically unimaginable. He is not of course
objecting to the mathematicization of physics. 'To be experimental
(in its matter) and deductive (in its form, but above all in regard
to the laws of the variations of the quantities involved), such is the
ideal proper to modern science.'[2] But in Maritain's view 'the
encounter of the law of causality, which is immanent in our
reason, and of the mathematical conception of Nature has as a
result the construction in theoretical physics of more and more
geometrized universes in which fictional causal entities with a
basis in reality (*entia rationis cum fundamento in re*), the function
of which is to serve as support for mathematical deduction, come
to include a very detailed account of empirically determined real
causes or conditions.'[3] Theoretical physics certainly provides
scientific knowledge, in the sense that it enables us to predict and
to master Nature. But the functions of its hypotheses are pragmatic. They do not provide certain knowledge of the *being* of
things, their ontological structure. And in *The Range of Reason*
Maritain commends the views on science advanced by the Vienna
Circle. As one would expect, he rejects the thesis that 'whatever

[1] English translation, *The Degrees of Knowledge*, by G. B. Phelan (N.Y., 1959).
[2] *Les degrés du savoir* (1932 edition), p. 90.   [3] *Ibid.*, p. 87.

has no meaning *for the scientist* has no meaning *at all'*.[1] But in regard to the logical structure of science itself and in regard to what has meaning for the scientist as such, 'the analysis of the School of Vienna is, I believe, generally accurate and well-founded'.[2] Maritain is still convinced however that though science constructs *entia rationis* possessing pragmatic value, it is inspired by a desire for a knowledge of reality, and that science itself gives rise to 'problems which go beyond the mathematical analysis of sensory phenomena'.[3]

Theoretical physics for Maritain is therefore a cross, as it were, between purely observational or empirical science on the one hand and pure mathematics on the other. It is 'a mathematicization of the sensible'.[4] Philosophy of Nature however is concerned with the essence of 'mobile being as such and the ontological principles which account for its mutability'.[5] It deals with the nature of the continuum, of quantity, of space, motion, time, corporal substance, vegetative and sensitive life, and so on. Metaphysics is concerned not with mobile being as such but simply with being as being. It therefore has a wider range and, according to Maritain, goes deeper. All this is set in the framework of a theory of degrees of abstraction based on Aristotle and Aquinas. The philosophy of Nature, just like science, abstracts from matter as the individuating principle (that is to say, it is not concerned with particular things as such); but it is still concerned with the material thing as that which can neither exist without matter nor be conceived without it. Mathematics is largely concerned with quantity and quantitative relations *conceived* in abstraction from matter, though quantity cannot *exist* without matter. Finally, metaphysics includes knowledge of that which not only can be conceived without matter but can also exist without it. It is 'at the purest degree of abstraction because it is furthest removed from the senses: it opens up on the immaterial, on a world of realities which exist or can exist in separation from matter.'[6]

It is hardly necessary to say that Maritain is reasserting the concept of the hierarchy of the sciences derived from Aristotle and Aquinas. He has of course to fit modern science into this scheme;

[1] *The Range of Reason*, p. 6.　　[2] *Ibid.*, p. 6.　　[3] *Ibid.*, p. 4.
[4] *Les degrés du savoir*, pp. 269–70.　　[5] *Ibid.*, p. 346.
[6] *Ibid.*, pp. 11–12. Maritain does not mean to imply that metaphysics (the 'first philosophy' of Aristotle) treats solely of what transcends sensible reality. Its subject-matter is being as being. But as it abstracts from materiality, it can proceed to the sphere of spiritual reality.

for physical science as it has developed since the Renaissance is not the same as what Aristotle called 'physics'.[1] Basically however the scheme is the same, though, like Aquinas, Maritain leaves room at the apex of the sciences for Christian theology, based on revealed premises. Theology apart, metaphysics is the highest of the sciences, science being conceived in Aristotelian fashion as knowledge of things through their causes. Nobody could accuse Maritain of lacking the courage to express his convictions. He admits of course that metaphysics is 'useless', in the sense that it is contemplative, not experimental, and that from the point of view of one who wishes to make empirical discoveries or to increase our mastery of Nature metaphysics cuts a very poor figure in comparison with the particular sciences. But he insists that metaphysics is an end, not a means, that it reveals to man 'authentic values and their hierarchy',[2] that it provides a centre for ethics, and that it introduces us to the eternal and absolute.

Maritain insists that if he adopts the principles of Aristotle and Aquinas, this is because the principles are true, not because they come from these venerable figures. As however his metaphysics is substantially that of Aquinas, at any rate when separated from Christian theology, it would be inappropriate to outline the content here.[3] It is sufficient to say that Aquinas, with his emphasis on *esse* (being in the sense of existence) is represented as the genuine 'existentialist', though Maritain is not the man to despise 'essences', which he thinks of as grasped within the existent, though the mind considers them in abstraction. Rather than attempting to recapitulate Thomist metaphysics it is preferable to draw attention to the two following points.

In the first place, though Maritain is the last man to despise the activity of the discursive reason and though he criticizes what he regards as Bergson's exaggerated depreciation of the intelligence and of the cognitive value of concepts, he has always been ready to recognize other ways of knowing than those exemplified in the 'sciences'. For example, he claims that there can be a non-

---

[1] What Aristotle called physics corresponds more with Maritain's philosophy of Nature.

[2] *Les degrés du savoir*, p. 10.

[3] See, for example, *Sept leçons sur l'être* (1934) (translated as *A Preface to Metaphysics: Seven Lectures on Being*, London and N.Y., 1939) and *Court Traité de l'existence et de l'existent*, (1947) (translated as *Existence and the Existent* by L. Galantière and G. B. Phelan, N.Y., 1948). But Maritain's books on knowledge, such as *The Degrees of Knowledge*, also treat of metaphysics. For knowledge and metaphysics are for him closely related.

conceptual, pre-reflective knowledge. Thus there can be an implicit knowledge of God which is not recognized by the person who has it as knowledge of God. In virtue of the internal dynamism of the will choice of the good, as against evil, involves an implicit affirmation of God, the Good itself, as the ultimate goal of human existence. This is 'a purely practical, non-conceptual and non-conscious knowledge of God which can co-exist with a theoretical ignorance of God.'[1] Again, Maritain has written about what he calls 'knowledge by connaturality'. This is found, for example, in religious mysticism. But it also plays a part in our knowledge of persons. And another form of it, distinct from mysticism, is 'poetic knowledge', arising 'through the instrumentality of emotion, which, received in the preconscious life of the intellect, becomes intentional and intuitive',[2] and tends by its nature to expression and creation. Knowledge by connaturality is also prominent in moral experience. For though moral philosophy[3] belongs to the conceptual, discursive, rational use of reason, it by no means follows that a man actually arrives at his moral convictions in this way. On the contrary, moral philosophy presupposes moral judgments which express a knowledge by connaturality, a conformity between the practical reason and the essential inclinations of human nature.

In the second place Maritain has tried to develop Thomist social and political philosophy, applying its principles to modern problems. If Aquinas had lived in the time of Galileo and Descartes, he would, according to Maritain, have freed Christian philosophy from the mechanics and astronomy of Aristotle, while remaining faithful to the principles of Aristotelian metaphysics. If he were living in the modern world, he would free Christian thought from 'the images and fantasies of the *sacrum imperium*'[4]

---

[1] *The Range of Reason*, p. 70. Obviously, this view is relevant to Maritain's assessment of atheism. In addition to 'practical atheists' (who believe that they believe in God but deny him by their conduct) and 'absolute atheists' he admits a class of 'pseudo-atheists' (who believe that they do *not* believe in God but who in fact believe in him unconsciously). Cf. *Ibid.*, pp. 103 ff.

[2] See also *Art et scolastique*, first published in 1920. *Art and Scholasticism and The Frontiers of Poetry*, translated by J. W. Evans (N.Y., 1962) contains also an English version of *Frontières de la poésie* (1935). See also *Creative Intuition in Art and Poetry* (N.Y., 1953).

[3] Maritain's writings on this subject include *Neuf leçons sur les notions premières de la philosophie morale* (*Nine lectures on the First Notions of Moral Philosophy*) published in 1951, and *La philosophie morale*, vol. 1, which appeared in 1960 (English translation, *Moral Philosophy*, by M. Suther and others, 1964).

[4] *Humanisme intégral* (1936), p. 224. There is an English translation, *True Humanism*, by M. R. Adamson (London, 1938).

and from worn-out temporal systems. In outlining a philosophical basis for the fulfilment of such a task Maritain has recourse to the distinction, also encountered in the personalism of Mounier, between 'individual' and 'person'. Accepting the Aristotelian-Thomist theory of matter as the principle of individuation, he describes individuality as 'that which excludes from oneself all other men' and as 'the narrowness of the ego, foreover threatened and forever eager to grasp for itself'.[1] Personality is the subsistence of the spiritual soul as communicated to the composite human being and as characterized by self-giving in freedom and love. In the concrete human being individuality and personality are of course combined, as man is a unity. But there can be societies which disregard man as a person and consider him simply as an individual. They emphasize individuals precisely as distinct particulars, neglecting the universal, as in bourgeois individualism, which corresponds, philosophically, to nominalism. Or they may emphasize the universal to such an extent that the particulars are completely subordinated to it. This happens in totalitarian societies of various kinds, which correspond, philosophically, to ultra-realism, for which the universal is a subsistent reality. The 'moderate realism' of St. Thomas would be expressed, in the social-political sphere, in a society of persons, which would indeed satisfy the needs of human beings as biological individuals but would at the same time be grounded on respect for the human person as transcending the biological level and, indeed, any temporal society. 'Man is by no means for the State. The State is for man.'[2] It may be added that during the Spanish Civil War Maritain supported the Republic and thus incurred a good deal of opprobrium in certain circles. Politically speaking, he has been on the left rather than on the right.

4. Étienne Henri Gilson was born at Paris in 1884 and did his university studies at the Sorbonne. After the first world war, in which he served as an officer, he was appointed professor of philosophy at Strasbourg. In 1921 however he accepted the chair of history of medieval philosophy at the Sorbonne, a post which he held until he was appointed to a similar chair at the Collège de France in 1932. He founded and directed the *Archives d'histoire doctrinale et littéraire du moyen âge* and also the series *Études de*

[1] *The Person and the Common Good*, p. 27 (English translation, 1947, of *La Personne et le bien commun*).
[2] *Man and the State* (Chicago, 1951), p. 13.

philosophie médiévale. In 1929 he cooperated in founding the Institute of Medieval Studies at Toronto, and after the second world war he acted as its director. In 1947 he was elected a member of the French Academy. On the advice of Lévy-Bruhl Gilson studied the relations between Descartes and Scholasticism. His main doctorate thesis was on freedom in Descartes (*La liberté chez Descartes et la théologie,* 1913) while the minor thesis was entitled *Index scolastico-cartesien* (1913). But the main fruit of the research suggested by Lévy-Bruhl was Gilson's *Études sur le rôle de la pensée médiévale dans la formation du système cartésien* (*Studies on the Role of Medieval Thought in the Formation of the Cartesian System*), which appeared in 1930. Meanwhile Gilson had studied Aquinas, and in 1919 he published the first edition of *Le thomisme. Introduction à l'étude de S. Thomas d'Aquin.*[1] The first edition of *La philosophie au moyen âge* was published in 1922.[2] Works followed on St. Bonaventure,[3] St. Augustine,[4] St. Bernard,[5] Dante[6] and Duns Scotus.[7] Gilson has also collaborated in the production of volumes on modern philosophy.

Despite his astonishing productivity in the historical field, which is not confined to the writings mentioned above, Gilson has also published works in which he presents personal philosophical positions, even if his views are often developed in an historical setting or context.[8] One of the features of his philosophical outlook is his rejection of the primacy of the so-called critical problem. If we cancel out, as it were, all our actual knowledge and then try to decide *a priori* whether knowledge is possible, we create for

[1] There have been a number of editions. There is a version in English, *The Christian Philosophy of St. Thomas Aquinas* (N.Y., 1951).
[2] The 1944 edition was practically a new work. And the English *History of Christian Philosophy in the Middle Ages* (London, 1955) is also a work on its own.
[3] *La philosophie de S. Bonaventure* (1924). The English translation, *The Philosophy of St. Bonaventure*, appeared in 1938. There was a second French edition in 1943.
[4] *Introduction à l'étude de S. Augustin* (1929 and subsequent editions). There is an English translation, *The Christian Philosophy of St. Augustine*, by L. E. M. Lynch (London, 1961).
[5] *La Théologie mystique de S. Bernard* (1934, 2nd edition 1947).
[6] *Dante et la philosophie* (1939; 2nd edition 1953).
[7] *Jean Duns Scotus. Introduction à ses positions fondamentales* (1952).
[8] We can mention, for example, *The Unity of Philosophical Experience* (N.Y., 1937; London, 1938), *Being and Some Philosophers* (Toronto 1949, an English version of *L'être et l'essence*, 1948 and 1962), *Painting and Reality* (N.Y., 1958), *Elements of Christian Philosophy* (N.Y., 1960), *Le philosophe et la théologie* (Paris, 1960; English version, *The Philosopher and Theology*, N.Y., 1962), and *Introduction aux arts du beau* (Paris, 1963).

ourselves a pseudo-problem. For we could not even raise the question unless we knew what knowledge is. And we know this through actually knowing something. In other words, it is in and through the act of knowing something that the mind becomes aware of its capacity to know. In Gilson's opinion Aquinas's attitude on this matter was far superior to that of those modern philosophers who have believed that the proper way of starting philosophy was to wrestle with the question whether we can know anything at all outside the subjective contents of our own minds.

Gilson's realism is also evident in his criticism of what he describes as 'essentialist' philosophy. If we try to reduce reality to clear and distinct concepts, universal by their nature, we omit the act of existence which is an act of singular or individual things. According to Gilson, this act is not conceptualizable, as existence is not an essence but the act by which an essence exists. It can be grasped only in and through essence, as its act, and it is affirmed in the existential judgment, which must be distinguished from the descriptive judgment. Thomism, as concerned with existing reality, is the authentic 'existentialism'. It does not, like the philosophies which are nowadays described as existentialist, interpret 'existence' narrowly, in the sense of something peculiar to man. Nor does it exclude essence. But it is primarily concerned with reality as existing and with the relation between received or participated existence and the infinite act in which essence and existence are indentical. One of the chief representatives of essentialist philosophy, in Gilson's eyes, was Christian Wolff; but he traces the origin of this line of thought back into the Middle Ages, where Aquinas is for him the chief exponent of existential philosophy.

Another feature of Gilson's thought is his refusal to extract a purely self-contained Thomist philosophy from the total thought of Aquinas. He does not indeed deny that the distinction made by St. Thomas between philosophy and theology is a valid distinction. But he insists on the artificiality of tearing from its theological setting a philosophy in which the selection and ordering of themes is determined by theological ends or by their theological context. Further, it seems clear to Gilson that theological beliefs, in free divine creation for example, have had a great influence on philosophical speculation, and that whatever some Thomists may say, they do in fact philosophize in the light of their Christian beliefs, though it by no means follows that their philosophical reasoning must be invalid or that they have to appeal to theological premises. In other words, Gilson has maintained that there can be a Christian philosophy which is genuinely philosophical. Its Christian character would not indeed be ascertainable simply by inspecting its logical arguments. For if this were the case, it would be theology rather than philosophy. But comparison between philosophies shows that there can be a philosophy which, while remaining genuinely philosophical, does not deprive itself of the light afforded by revelation. This point of view has given rise to a good deal of discussion and controversy. Some writers have maintained that to speak of a Christian philosophy is as inappropriate as to speak of a Christian mathematics. But Gilson has persisted in maintaining his thesis. In so far as this is the historical judgment of a scholar who sees clearly the influence exercised on philosophy by Christian belief, especially in the patristic and medieval periods, there is no difficulty in accepting it. For it can hardly be denied that under the influence of Christian belief concepts derived from Greek thought were often given a new stamp or character, fresh themes were suggested, and philosophy, pursued for the most part by theologians, was used to extend a general Christian world-vision. Whereas however many people would claim that philosophy became adult only through separation from Christian theology and the attainment of complete autonomy, Gilson insists that there is still room for genuine philosophy pursued not simply by Christians but by philosophers *as Christians*. He is doubtless justified in rejecting the claim that Christians who develop natural theology, for example, are in no way influenced by their antecedent beliefs. But some would conclude that it is then a case of apologetics, not of authentic philosophy. The retort might be made that the complete autonomy of philosophy is a myth, and that if it is not the handmaid of theology, it is the handmaid of something else, being always 'parasitic'. However, the question whether philosophizing pursued in the interests of the development of a comprehensive Christian world-view is genuine philosophizing or not, is probably best answered by inspecting examples.

From the titles of books mentioned above it will be seen that Gilson, like Maritain, has written on aesthetics. In a general sense his point of view is Thomist. Art is regarded as a making or production of beautiful objects which cause contemplative enjoyment or pleasure. Gilson however derives from this view of art as creative the conclusion that it is a great mistake to think that imitation belongs to its essence or nature. Abstract art as such needs no special justification. Whether a given picture, for example, is or is not a genuine work of art is clearly not a question which can be settled by philosophical reasoning. But if art is creative, there can be no good reason for regarding non-representational works as deficient, still less as disqualified from counting as works of art.

5. Mention has been made of Garrigou-Lagrange, Sertillanges, Maritain and Gilson. It is neither possible nor desirable to list all French Thomists here. In view of his influence however mention should be made of Pierre Rousselot (1878–1915), a Jesuit theologian and philosopher who was killed on service in the first world war. In theological circles he is known for his views on the analysis of faith; but his main publication is L'intellectualisme de S. Thomas d'Aquin[1] in which he argues that the movement of the intellect to Being is the expression of a dynamism of the will, of love that is to say, which can find its goal only in God. In other words, he tries to dispose of the view that Aquinas was an arid intellectualist by revealing the dynamic orientation of the human spirit which underlies and gives rise to the movement of the mind in philosophical reflection.

Sime similar ideas can be found in the writings of Aimé Forest (b. 1898), who was appointed professor of philosophy at Montpellier in 1943. Author of works on Aquinas,[2] he is best known for his development of the idea of 'consent' to being,[3] in which he shows the influence of modern French philosophers. In the first place consent to being means consent to a movement of the human spirit whereby it does not stop short at empirical reality but transcends it towards the ultimate ground of all finite being. As the mind can stop short, or attempt to stop short, at the empirically given, consent or option is required to recognize the realm of values and to pass beyond to God, who alone makes empirical reality intelligible. In the second place consent to being involves regarding finite existence as a gift, arousing a response in the human spirit. In other words, with Forest the metaphysics of being assumes a religious and also ethical character.

---

[1] This work, published in 1908, was translated into English by F. James as *The Intellectualism of St. Thomas* (London, 1935).

[2] *S. Thomas d'Aquin* (1933) and *La structure métaphysique du concret selon S. Thomas d'Aquin* (1931, 2nd edition, 1956).

[3] *Du consentement à l'être* (1936, *On Consent to Being*) and *Consentement et création* (1943, *Consent and Creation*).

6. Garrigou-Lagrange obviously looked on most modern philosophers as 'adversaries', as defending positions which were to a greater or lesser degree opposed to the truth as represented by St. Thomas Aquinas. With Maritain and Gilson we find indeed intelligent discussions of the development and currents of modern philosophical thought; but their realism was such that they could not but regard the procedures of, say, Descartes and Kant as aberrations. It by no means follows, for example, that Gilson is unable to appreciate the achievement of Kant, given the latter's premises. But it is clear that for Gilson the premises should be avoided in the first place. An outstanding thinker doubtless shows his talent in the way in which he develops the implications of his premises and steers clear of any patchwork eclecticism which tries to combine elements which do not really fit together. But constructive talent of this kind does not entail the validity of the premises.

A much more positive attitude to modern philosophy, especially in regard to Kant, was shown by Joseph Maréchal (1878–1944), a Belgian Jesuit who was a professor of philosophy in the Jesuit house of studies at Louvain from 1919 until 1935. A doctor of science of the University of Louvain, he had also studied experimental psychology and psychotherapy in Germany; and his interest in the psychology of religion found expression in the two volumes of his *Études sur la psychologie des mystiques*[1] which appeared respectively in 1924 and 1937. He is best known however for his *Point de départ de la métaphysique*,[2] particularly for the fifth Cahier or volume on Thomism in confrontation with the critical philosophy of Kant (*Le Thomisme devant la philosophie critique*). Maréchal is not of course so foolish as to claim that St. Thomas Aquinas in the thirteenth century provided in advance all the solutions to problems raised centuries later by Immanuel Kant in a different historical context. He does however claim that the Kantian antimony between understanding and pure reason, with its implications for metaphysics, can be overcome by developing a synthesis in terms of an idea of intellectual dynamism which is virtually present, in his opinion, in the thought of St. Thomas

---

[1] There is a partial translation, *Studies in the Psychology of the Mystics*, by A. Thorold (London, 1927).
[2] The first, second, third and fifth Cahiers were published in 1922–6. The fourth Cahier, on idealism in Kant and the post-Kantians, was published posthumously (from notes) in 1947. There was to have been a sixth Cahier which, Maréchal remarked, would have clarified his personal position.

and to which Kant, given his view of the mind's activity, should have devoted greater attention. In other words, Maréchal does not simply confront the Kantian philosophy as it stands with traditional Thomism and then argue that the latter is superior. He uses an idea which he believes to be basic in the thought of St. Thomas to develop the critical philosophy in such a way that the antimony between understanding and pure reason is overcome and the Kantian agnosticism is transcended.

The fifth Cahier contains two complementary parts. Both have as their point of departure the immanent object, immanent, that is to say, in consciousness. The first part is devóted to what Maréchal describes as a metaphysical critique of the object, and the second to a transcendental critique. In the first critique the object is regarded as strictly intentional and so as having ontological reference, while in the second the object is taken as a phenomenon. But we cannot enter into details. To cut a long story short, Maréchal enters by Kant's door and inquires into the *a priori* conditions of knowledge or of the possibility of objectification. It his view the most important *a priori* condition, overlooked by Kant, is the intellectual dynamism of the subject as oriented to absolute Being. No more than Kant does Maréchal postulate an intellectual intuition of the Absolute or of God in himself. But he sees the act of judgment, which sets the subject over against the object, as a partial realization of the intellect's dynamic orientation and as pointing beyond itself. In other words, every judgment implicitly affirms the Absolute, which reveals itself not as the direct object of an intellectual intuition but as the *a priori* condition of all objectification and the ultimate goal of the movement of the intellect. Affirmation of the existence of God is thus a speculative necessity, and not simply a practical postulate.

It has been objected against Maréchal that he assumes illegitimately that the Kantian method of transcendental reflection is 'neutral', in the sense that it can be used to enable us to reach conclusions which go beyond anything contemplated by Kant, in particular to establish the existence of God. If, it is contended, we once adopt the Kantian point of departure and method, we shall try in vain to overcome the Kantian agnosticism. It has also been objected that Maréchal confuses the intellect with a natural appetite or pre-reflexive volitional tendency. Maréchal's thesis however is that we cannot justifiably make a dichotomy between the formally cognitive function of the intellect and its dynamic tendency. The former has to be interpreted in the light of the latter. Further, the fact that Kant recognized the activity of the mind shows that he ought to have reflected on the intellect's dynamism as an *a priori* condition of knowledge. For Maréchal at any rate his development of Kant does not contradict the exigencies of the critical approach.

We are entitled to regard Maréchal as initiating the movement of thought which is customarily described as transcendental Thomism. To say this is not to deny that there were other antecedent influences, the thought of Blondel for example. But Maréchal regarded Blondel as inclining too much to voluntarism; and he himself emphasized an intellectual dynamism which he believed to be implicit in the philosophy of Aquinas and which, if developed, would enable Thomism to satisfy the demand of modern philosophy, as represented by Kant and Fichte, for the 'transcendental turn', as it is sometimes described, and at the same time to overcome the agnosticism which had made Kant the bogeyman of the neo-Scholastics. For, as we have seen, he was convinced that use of the method whereby thought reflects on its own object-oriented activity would show that absolute Being is an *a priori* condition of the possibility of this activity. Instead of rejecting the critical philosophy as a pernicious influence, he thought that it was necessary to adopt the transcendental method and at the same time to bring to light a condition of the possibility of the mind's intentional acts to which Kant himself had failed to do justice. As however Maréchal believed that use of the transcendental method was a justifiable development of what was virtually present in the thought of Aquinas and that it could show the legitimacy of a metaphysics which Kant rejected, he regarded himself as a Thomist. He thus prepared the way for the development of transcendental Thomism.[1] But it would be misleading to describe the transcendental Thomists as Maréchal's 'disciples'. In the case of writers in German, such as J. B. Lotz and

---

[1] The objection has been raised that transcendental Thomism is Thomist only in the sense that a method derived from Kant and German idealism, supported in some cases by strong doses of phenomenology and of Heidegger's existentialist philosophy, is used to reach Thomist conclusions or at any rate conclusions which are in agreement with Thomism. (See, for example, the second Appendix to Leslie Dewart's *The Foundations of Belief*, London 1969). The retort can be made however that whatever traditional Thomists may say, the philosophy of Aquinas makes presuppositions which the transcendental Thomists try to make explicit and to justify in a systematic manner.

E. Coreth (an Austrian), the contributory influence of other factors, notably the thought of Martin Heidegger,[1] is clear enough. And in France the influence of other French philosophers, such as Blondel, has to be taken into account. Still, Maréchal is the patron saint, so to speak, of the movement. Maréchal, as we have seen, was concerned in a special way with Kant. That is to say, it was the critical philosophy of Kant, at any rate when regarded in the light of subsequent idealist developments, which provided the setting or context for Maréchal's approach to transcendental philosophy. And in his fifth Cahier Maréchal was particularly concerned with the problem set by Kant's antimony between the understanding and pure reason and his rejection of traditional metaphysics. Some of the transcendental Thomists however have used the transcendental method to outline at any rate a general system of thought without noticeable emphasis on or preoccupation with Immanuel Kant. It would be inappropriate here to speak of non-French representatives of the movement. But a very brief mention can be made of André Marc (1892–1961), a French Jesuit who was a professor of philosophy first at Jesuit houses of study and then at the Institut Catholique at Paris. In his *Psychologie réflexive*[2] he used the method whereby thought takes itself in act as object of reflection to start with language as revelatory of the nature of man and then to develop a philosophical anthropology. In doing so he also deduced 'from our act of knowledge and its structure, as well as from the structure of its object, the diversification of the sciences, at any rate in outline.'[3] In a subsequent volume, *Dialectique de l'affirmation*, which has as its subtitle *Essai de métaphysique réflexive*, Marc developed a metaphysics, employing the 'reflexive method', thought's reflections on its own acts, to study 'the laws of being as such'.[4] In another volume, *Dialectique de l'agir* (Paris-Lyon, 1954) Marc devoted his attention to the development of an ethics, defining the moral destiny or vocation of man in the light of his theories of man's metaphysical nature and of the structure

---

[1] The writings of B. Lonergan, the Canadian Thomist, seem to be free of Heideggerian influence. As for Coreth, the influence of Heidegger is clear enough. But so is that of Fichte, by whom Maréchal himself was influenced.
[2] Two volumes, Paris, 1948–9.
[3] *Dialectique de l'affirmation* (Paris, 1952), p. 17.
[4] *Ibid.*, p. 43. The method involves reductive analysis, to get back to the proper point of departure, followed by a deductive and dialectical process of reflection.

of being. Other writings dealt with the possibility and conditions of an acceptance of Christian revelation.[1]

There are of course other French thinkers who have been influenced to some extent by Maréchal, such as Jacques Édouard Joseph de Finance (b. 1904), a professor of philosophy at the Gregorian University in Rome, who has given special attention to freedom and man's moral vision and action. But instead of making further brief and inadequate remarks about individuals we can conclude this section by suggesting one or two general features of transcendental Thomism. In the first place the transcendental Thomists seem intent on developing a presuppositionless philosophy or at any rate going back to an unquestionable point of departure. This can be seen in the first moment or phase of the transcendental method, the reductive or analytic phase. In the second place they seem intent on developing metaphysics as a deductive science, systematically deduced, that is to say, from the point of departure.[2] And in the third place they try to develop philosophy as the conscious subject's reflection on its own activity. It can hardly be claimed that this procedure is in accordance with the traditional presentation of Thomism. This does not of course show that the procedure is misguided. But it provides some ground for the critics' claim that 'Thomism' as a misnomer, and for the suggestion that harmony between the results or conclusions of transcendental Thomism and traditional Thomism is due as much to common religious beliefs and preoccupations as to any factor intrinsic to purely philosophical argumentation. This is not however a question which can be settled by dogmatic *a priori* pronouncements on either side. Instead we can remark that several philosophers have tried to make philosophy properly scientific by taking as a point of departure an unquestionable datum or proposition. Descartes was one of them, Husserl another. And the transcendental Thomists join the company. Even if however it is allowed that the attempt to develop a presuppositionless philosophy is legitimate, the question arises whether idealism does not result if the subject is taken as the basis of all philosophical reflection. Needless to say, the transcendental Thomists

---

[1] For example, *L'être et l'esprit* (Paris-Louvain, 1958) and *Raison et conversion chrétienne* (Paris, 1961).

[2] The transcendental Thomists are not all in agreement about the proper point of departure. For example, whereas Lotz starts with analysis of the judgment as an act of absolute affirmation, Coreth thinks that the philosopher must go further back, to what he calls the question.

do not believe that this is the case. Indeed, they would claim to have demonstrated that it is not the case. The more old-fashioned Thomists however remain unconvinced. What Aquinas himself would have said about the matter, whether he would have approved of Maritain or preferred Maréchal, we obviously cannot know.

CHAPTER XIII

PHILOSOPHY OF SCIENCE

H. Poincaré — P. Duhem — G. Milhaud — E. Meyerson —
A. Lalande — G. Bachelard.

1. Mention has already been made of a number of philosophers
who concerned themselves with reflection on the natural sciences.
Reference has been made for example, to Comte and to writers
belonging more or less to the positivist line of thought, such as
Bernard and Taine, to the neo-critical philosophers Cournot and
Renouvier, and to thinkers such as Ravaisson, Lachelier and
Boutroux, who belong to the spiritualist movement. We can now
take a brief glance at the ideas of a few writers who can more
easily be described as philosophers of science.

A well known name in this group is that of Jules Henri Poincaré
(1854–1912)[1]. Born at Nancy, he studied mining engineering; but
from an early age he was interested in mathematics, and in 1879
he started to teach mathematical analysis at Caen. In 1881 he
went to the University of Paris where he lectured on mathematics,
physics and astronomy. In 1887 he was elected a member of the
Académie des Sciences and in 1908 of the Académie Française.
In 1902 he published *La science et l'hypothèse*,[2] in 1905 *La valeur* de
la science[3] and in 1908 *Science et méthode*.[4] His *Dernières Pensées*
appeared in 1912.[5]

The best known feature of Poincaré's philosophy of mathematics and science is probably the element of conventionalism
which it contains. When referring, for example, to geometry, he
remarks that geometrical axioms are neither synthetic *a priori*
intuitions nor experimental facts. 'They are conventions.'[6] And
this means that they are definitions in disguise'.[7] It does not follow,
Poincaré insists, that the axioms are decided purely arbitrarily.
For though our choice is free and limited only by the need to

---

[1] Raymond Poincaré, who became President of the Republic, was a cousin.
[2] Translated by W. J. Greenstreet as *Science and Hypothesis* (London, 1905;
New York, Dover Publications, 1952).
[3] Translated by G. B. Halsted as *The Value of Science* (London, 1907).
[4] Translated by F. Maitland as *Science and Method* (London, 1914).
[5] Translated by J. W. Bolduc as *Mathematics and Science: Last Essays* (New
York, 1963).
[6] *Science and Hypothesis*, p. 50.   [7] *Ibid.*, p. 50.

avoid any contradiction, by the demands of logical consistency that is to say, it is also guided by the experimental facts. One system of geometry is not in itself truer than any other system. But it can be more convenient than another system or more suitable for a specific purpose. We cannot justifiably claim that Euclidean geometry is truer than the non-Euclidean geometries. We might just as well claim that a decimal coinage is truer than a non-decimal coinage. But a decimal coinage may be the more convenient. And for most purposes, though not for all, Euclidean geometry is the most convenient system.

Such conventions or disguised definitions play a role in physical science too. A proposition can start as an empirical generalization or hypothesis and end as a convention, inasmuch as this is what the physicist makes it to be. For example, 'it is *by definition* that force is equal to the product of the mass and the acceleration; this is a principle which is henceforth beyond the reach of any future experiment. Thus it is by definition that action and reaction are equal and opposite.'[1] Science begins with observation and experiment; but with the development of mathematical physics the role played by conventions grows too.

It would however be a great mistake to think that according to Poincaré science consists entirely of conventions in the sense of disguised definitions. This is a view which he describes as nominalism, attributes to Édouard Le Roy and attacks. For Le Roy 'science consists only of conventions and it is solely to this circumstance that it owes its apparent certainty. . . . Science cannot teach us the truth, it can serve us only as a rule for action.'[2] To this theory Poincaré objects that scientific laws are not simply like the rules of a game which can be altered by common agreement in such a way that the new rules serve as well as the old ones. One might of course construct a set of rules which would not serve their purpose because they were mutually incompatible. But, this point apart, we cannot properly speak of the rules of a game as being verified or falsified, whereas the empirical laws of science are rules of action in so far as they predict, and the predictions are open to falsification. In other words, empirical hypotheses are not simply conventions or disguised definitions: they have a cognitive value. And even though absolute certainty is not attainable, inasmuch as an empirical generalization is always revisable in principle, in some cases at any rate science attains a high degree

[1] *Ibid.*, p. 104. [2] *La valeur de la science*, p. 214.

of probability. In mathematical physics conventions have a part to play; and, as we have seen, what was originally an empirical generalization may be so interpreted that it is transformed into a disguised definition which is not open to falsification, as it is not allowed, so to speak, to be falsifiable. But this does not alter the fact that science aims at knowledge of the relations between things, that it predicts, and that some predictions are verified, even if not conclusively, while others are falsified. It cannot therefore be legitimately claimed that science consists entirely of conventions, and that, given internal consistency, any scientific system would serve as well as any other.

Poincaré's use of language is sometimes open to question. For example, when distinguishing between different kinds of hypotheses he includes the disguised definitions which, he tells us, are to be found especially in mathematics and mathematical physics.[1] And it is obviously arguable that he ought to reserve the name 'hypotheses' for empirical hypotheses which are open to falsification. However this may be, it is perfectly clear that for Poincaré the natural sciences can increase our knowledge, and that this increase is attained by testing empirical generalizations which permit prediction. It is true that he regards some empirical statements of natural science as resoluble into a principle or convention and a provisional law, an empirical hypothesis, that is to say, which is revisible in principle. But the mere fact that he makes this distinction shows that he does not regard science as consisting simply of principles in the sense of conventions or disguised definitions. Conventionalism therefore is only one element in his philosophy of science.

Science, for Poincaré, aims at attaining truth about the world. It rests indeed on presuppositions or assumptions, the basic ones being the unity and the simplicity of Nature. That is to say, it is presupposed that the parts of the Universe are interrelated in a manner analogous to that in which the organs of the living body are interrelated. And the simplicity of Nature is presupposed in the sense at any rate that if two or more generalizations are possible, so that we have to choose between them, 'the choice can only be guided by considerations of simplicity.'[2] Though however science rests on presuppositions, it none the less aims at truth.

---

[1] *Science and Hypothesis*, pp. xxii–xxiii.
[2] *Ibid.*, p. 146. Poincaré also talks about 'simple facts'. Cf. *Science et méthode*, pp. 10 f.

'In my eyes it is knowledge which is the end, and action which is the means.'[1]

What however is it that science enables us to know? It is certainly not the essences of things. 'When a scientific theory claims to tell us what heat is, or what electricity is, or what life is, it is condemned in advance: all that it can give us is a rough image.'[2] The knowledge which we obtain through science is knowledge of the relations between things. Poincaré sometimes uses a sensationalist language and maintains that what we can know are the relations between sensations.[3] But he does not wish to assert that there is nothing of which our sensations are the reflection. And it is simpler to say that for him science tells us the relations between things rather than the inner natures of things. For example, a theory of light tells us the relations between the sensible phenomena of light rather than what light is in itself. Indeed, Poincaré is prepared to claim that 'the only objective reality is the relations between things, from which the universal harmony derives. Without doubt these relations, this harmony, could not be conceived apart from a mind which conceives or perceives them. But they are none the less objective inasmuch as they are, will be or will remain common to all thinking beings.'[4]

The impression may perhaps have been given that while Poincaré certainly did not regard all scientific laws as conventional, he looked on pure mathematics as dependent entirely on conventions. This is not however the case. For while he was quite ready to see certain axioms as disguised definitions, he believed that mathematics also comprised certain synthetic *a priori* propositions, the truth of which was discerned intuitively. He was thus not prepared to accept the view that Kant's view of mathematics had been simply exploded. Nor was Poincaré favourably disposed to the thesis, as maintained, for example, by Bertrand Russell, that mathematics is reducible to formal logic. On the contrary, he criticized the 'new logics', 'of which the most interesting is that of M. Russell.'[5]

In his sensationalism Poincaré was influenced by the thought of Ernst Mach,[6] while his view of mechanics seems to have been influenced by Heinrich Rudolf Hertz (1857–94).

---

[1] *La valeur de la science*, p. 220.   [2] *Ibid.*, p. 267.
[3] Sensations, Poincaré says, are non-transmissible. 'But it is not the same with relations between sensations'. *Ibid.*, p. 263.
[4] *Ibid.*, p. 271.   [5] *Science et méthode*, p. 172. See also *Dernières pensées*.
[6] For some brief remarks on Mach see Volume VII of this *History*, p. 359.

2. We have seen that according to Poincaré science is concerned not with the nature of things in themselves but with the relations between things as appearing to us or between sensations. The same sort of view was advanced by Pierre Maurice Marie Duhem (1861–1916), who was both a theoretical physicist and a philosopher and distinguished historian of science. In 1886 Duhem published at Paris a work on thermodynamics,[1] and in the following year he began to lecture in the Faculty of Science at Lille. In 1893 he went to Rennes, and in 1895 he was appointed to a chair in the University of Bordeaux. His most important theoretical publication was *La Théorie physique, son objet et sa structure*, the first edition of which appeared at Paris in 1906.[2] Duhem also published several works on the history of science,[3] the best known being *Le système du monde. Histoire des doctrines cosmologiques de Platon à Copernic (The System of the World. A History of Cosmological Doctrines from Plato to Copernicus)*, consisting of eight volumes (Paris, 1913–1958). In Duhem's opinion study of the history of science was not simply a learned luxury, so to speak, which could be neglected without any detriment to one's study of actual scientific problems. As he saw the matter, one could not fully understand a scientific theory or concept without knowledge of its origins and development and of the problems which it was designed to solve.

One of Duhem's principal aims is to make a clear theoretical separation between physics and metaphysics. The metaphysician, in Duhem's view, is concerned with explanation, to explain being, 'to strip reality of the appearances covering it like a veil, in order to see the bare reality itself.'[4] But it is only metaphysics which raises the question whether there is a reality underlying or distinct from sensible appearances. As far as physics is concerned, phenomena or sensible appearances are all that there is. Hence it cannot aim at explanation in the sense mentioned. 'A physical theory is not an explanation. It is a system of mathematical propositions, deduced from a small number of principles, which aim at

---

[1] *Le potentiel thermodynamique et ses applications à la mécanique chimique et à la théorie des phénomènes électriques.*
[2] The second edition has been translated by P. P. Wiener as *The Aim and Structure of Physical Theory* (Princeton, 1954). This work will be referred to as *Physical Theory*.
[3] These include *L'évolution de la mécanique* (Paris, 1903), *Les origines de la statique* (Paris, 1905–6) and studies on Leonardo da Vinci (*Études sur Léonard da Vinci*, Paris, 1906–13).
[4] *Physical Theory*, p. 7.

representing as simply, as completely and as exactly as possible a set of experimental laws.'[1] A theory however is not exclusively a representation of experimental laws: it is also a classification of them. That is to say, by deductive reasoning it exhibits these laws as consequences of certain basic hypotheses or 'principles'. And the test of a theory, a theory of light for example, is its agreement or disagreement with the experimental laws which themselves represent relations between phenomena or sensible appearances. 'Agreement with experiment is the sole criterion of truth for a physical theory.'[2] A physical theory does not explain the laws, though it coordinates them systematically. Nor do the laws explain reality. Duhem is at one with Poincaré in insisting that what we know are the relations between sensible phenomena. He adds indeed that we cannot avoid the feeling or conviction that observed relations correspond to something in things apart from their sensible appearances to us. But he insists that this is a matter of natural faith or belief and not something which can be proved in physics.

Duhem is aware of course that scientific theories permit prediction. We can 'draw some consequences which do not correspond to any of the experimental laws previously known and which simply represent possible experimental laws'.[3] Some of these consequences are empirically testable. And if they are verified, the value of the theory is increased. If however a prediction which represents a legitimate conclusion from a theory is falsified, this shows that the theory must be modified, if not abandoned altogether. In other words, if we assume the truth of a given hypothesis and then deduce that on this assumption a certain event should occur in certain circumstances, the actual occurrence of the event in these circumstances does not prove the truth of the hypothesis. For the same conclusion, namely that in certain circumstances a certain event should occur, might also be deducible from a different hypothesis. If however the event which ought to occur does not occur, this shows that the hypothesis is false or that it stands in need of revision. If therefore we leave out of account other reasons for changing or modifying theories, such as considerations of greater simplicity or economy, we can say that science advances through the elimination of hypotheses rather than through verification in a strong sense. A scientific hypothesis can be conclusively falsified and so eliminated, but

[1] *Ibid.*, p. 19.   [2] *Ibid.*, p. 21.   [3] *Ibid.*, p. 28.

it cannot be conclusively proved. There is not and cannot be a 'crucial experiment' in Francis Bacon's sense of the phrase. For the physicist can never be sure that there is not another conceivable hypothesis which would cover the phenomena in question.[1] 'The truth of a physical theory is not decided by heads or tails.'[2]

Though Duhem agrees with Poincaré on a number of issues, he refuses to admit that there are scientific hypotheses which are beyond the reach of experimental refutation and must be regarded as definitions which remain unaffected by empirical testing. There are indeed hypotheses which, if taken in isolation, have no 'experimental meaning'[3] and which cannot therefore be directly confirmed or falsified by experiment. But these hypotheses do not in fact exist in isolation. They constitute foundations of wide-ranging theories or physical systems; and it always remains possible that the consequences of the system taken as a whole will be subjected to experimental refutation on such a scale that the whole system will crumble, together with those basic hypotheses which, if considered in isolation, cannot be directly refuted.

According to Duhem his interpretation of physics is 'positivist in its conclusions as well as in its origins'.[4] Physical theories, as he sees them, have nothing to do with metaphysical doctrines or with religious dogmas; and it is a mistake to attempt to use them for apologetic purposes. For example, the attempt to prove the creation of the world from thermodynamics (the law of entropy) is misguided. But it by no means follows that Duhem is a positivist in the sense that he rejects metaphysics. He is concerned with making a sharp distinction between physics and metaphysics, not with condemning the latter. Whether we can in fact make such a rigid distinction as Duhem has in mind is doubtless open to dispute. But it is obviously true that science has progressively developed its autonomy; and it is also arguable that those writers who have tried to base metaphysical or religious doctrines on revisible physical theories have been misguided. In any case Duhem is not an anti-metaphysician. As for religion, 'I believe

---

[1] Duhem makes his point clear by considering two different hypotheses. But he insists that what a physicist actually subjects to experimental testing is a group of hypotheses, not an isolated one. (We have seen that for him a physical theory combines and coordinates a set of hypotheses.) Falsification of a prediction therefore indicates that some member of the group must be modified or changed. But if the prediction is the result of a deduction based on the set or group, its non-fulfilment does not by itself indicate which member of the group should be revised.

[2] *Physical Theory*, p. 190.   [3] *Ibid.*, p. 215.   [4] *Ibid.*, p. 275.

with all my soul in the truths which God has revealed to us and which he has taught us through his Church.'[1]

3. A certain measure of affinity with the ideas of Poincaré and Duhem is evident in the philosophy of science of Gaston Milhaud (1858–1918), who after having been professor of philosophy at Montpellier[2] went to Paris in 1909 to occupy a newly created chair in the history of philosophy in its relationship to the sciences.[3] For example, in his *Essay on the Conditions and Limits of Logical Certitude (Essai sur les conditions et les limites de la certitude logique*, 1894, second edition 1897), Milhaud asserts that what we know of things are the sensations which they arouse in us.[4] At the same time he is at one with Poincaré and Duhem in emphasizing the mind's activity in reflection on experience and in the development of scientific hypotheses. Milhaud is less inclined to talk about 'conventions'; but he insists, as in his work *The Rational (Le rationnel*, 1898) on the spontaneity of the human reason.

While however Duhem was anxious to claim that his idea of science was positivistic, with the aim of making a sharp distinction between natural science and metaphysics, Milhaud draws attention to the shortcomings of positivism, by which he meant the ideas of Auguste Comte in particular. For example, in the introduction to his work on *The Geometer-Philosophers of Greece (Les philosophes géomètres de la Grèce*, 1900) he alludes to the naïvely confident way in which Comte undertook to assign the precise limits at which knowledge could arrive and in which he rejected in advance any attempt to effect a radical change in accepted scientific theories. Comte wanted 'to attribute to the system of already acquired scientific knowledge the power of immediately organizing society on unshakable foundations, or, once society was organized, to prescribe the submission of all to him or to those who would have in their hands the rational direction of mankind.'[5] The dogmatism of Comte was thus in opposition not simply to scepticism but even 'to the spirit of free inquiry'.[6] It is true that Comte believed in progress; but he thought of progress as an advance towards a determinate goal or limit, the point at which science could constitute the basis for the sort

---

[1] *Ibid.*, p. 273.
[2] Before becoming a professor in the University of Montpellier, Milhaud taught mathematics at a school in the same town.
[3] Milhaud published several works on the history of Greek and modern science in its relationship to philosophy.
[4] *Essai*, p. 2.   [5] *Les philosophes géomètres*, p. 4 (second edition, 1934).
[6] *Ibid.*, p. 4.

of society which he considered desirable. Comte therefore had no use for the dreams of never-ending progress indulged in by eighteenth-century thinkers. In his view science had already arrived 'if not at the final term of its advance, at any rate at the state of consolidation in which no further radical transformations were to be foreseen, in which the fundamental concepts were definitely fixed, and in which new concepts could not differ much from the old ones.'[1] We cannot however set bounds in this way to the creativity of the human mind.

At first Milhaud made a sharp distinction between pure mathematics, which rests on the principle of non-contradiction, and empirical science. But he soon came to emphasize the element of rational decision which is present in all branches of science. He had indeed no intention of suggesting that scientific hypotheses are purely arbitrary constructions. He saw them as based on or suggested by experience and as constructed in such a way as to satisfy logical demands of consistency and also practical and aesthetic requirements. But he refused to admit that scientific theories were necessitated either by logic or by experience. They express the creativity of the human mind, though this creative activity is guided in science by rational decision and not by caprice. Further, we can never say that scientific knowledge has attained its final form. We cannot exclude radical transformations in advance. There is indeed an ideal goal, but it is an ever-receding goal, even though progress is real. If we think of Comtean positivism are representing the third stage of human thought, we must add that this stage has to be transcended, as it constitutes an obstacle to the mind's creative activity.[2]

4. We have seen that Duhem made a sharp distinction between science on the one hand and metaphysics or ontology on the other. A rather different view of the nature of science was taken by Émile Meyerson (1859–1933). Born at Lublin of Jewish parentage, he studied classics and then chemistry in Germany.[3] In 1882 he took up his abode at Paris, and later, after the 1914–18 war, he became a naturalized French citizen. He never occupied any official academic post, but he was an influential thinker. In 1908 he published at Paris his well known book *Identité et réalité*[4] and in

[1] *Études sur la pensée scientifiques chez les grecs et chez les modernes* (1906), p. 230.
[2] See *Le positivisme et le progrès de l'esprit* (*1902*).
[3] Meyerson's chemical studies were pursued under R. W. Bunsen.
[4] Translated by K. Loewenberg as *Identity and Reality* (London and New York, 1930).

1921 a two-volume work on explanation in the sciences (*De l'explication dans les sciences*). These publications were followed by a book on relativity theory (*La déduction relativiste*, 1925), a three-volume work on the ways of thought (*Du cheminement de la pensée*, 1931) and a small book on quantum theory (*Réel et déterminisme dans la physique quantique*, 1933). A collection of essays (*Essais*) appeared posthumously in 1936.

In the first place Meyerson is strongly opposed to a positivist view of science as concerned simply with prediction and control or action. According to the positivist science formulates laws which represent the relations between phenomena or sensible appearances, laws which enable us to predict and so serve action and our control of phenomena. Though however Meyerson has no wish to deny that science does in fact enable us to predict and extend the area of control, he refuses to admit that this is the primary goal or operative ideal of science. 'It is not accurate to say that science has action as its sole end, nor that it is governed solely by the desire of economy in this action. Science seeks also to make us *understand* Nature. It tends in fact, as M. Le Roy expresses it, to the 'progressive rationalization of the real'.[1] Science rests on the presupposition that reality is intelligible; and it hopes that this intelligibility will become ever more manifest. The mind's drive towards understanding lies at the basis of all scientific inquiry and research. It is therefore a mistake to follow Francis Bacon, Hobbes and Comte in defining the goal of science simply in terms of prediction with a view to action. 'The positivist theory rests at bottom on a palpable error in psychology.'[2]

If science rests on the presupposition that Nature is intelligible and seeks to discover its intelligible character, we cannot legitimately maintain that scientific hypotheses and theories are simply intellectual constructions which are devoid of ontological import. 'Ontology is joined to science itself and cannot be separated from it.'[3] It is all very well to claim that science should be stripped of all ontology and metaphysics. The fact of the matter is that this very claim involves a metaphysics or theory about being. In particular, science cannot get away from the concept of things or substances. A positivist may claim that science is concerned simply with formulating laws and that the concept of things or substances

---

[1] *Identité et realité*, p. 438 (my translation); English version, p. 384.
[2] *De l'explication dans les sciences* (1927), p. 45. This work will be referred to as *Explication*.
[3] *Identité et realité*, p. 439; English version, p. 384.

which are independent of the mind can be thrown overboard; but the idea of law as expressing relations presupposes the idea of related things. If it is objected that the concept of things, existing independently of consciousness, belongs to the sphere of naïve common sense and must be abandoned at the level of science, the reply can be made that 'the hypothetical beings of science are really more *things* than the things of common sense'.[1] That is to say, atoms or electrons, for example, are not direct objects of sense or sense-data; and they thus exemplify the concept of a thing (as existing independently of sensation) more clearly than the sensible objects of the level of common sense. Science has its point of departure in the world of common sense; and when it transforms or abandons common sense concepts, 'what it adopts is as ontological as what it abandons.'[2] According to Meyerson, those who think otherwise fail to grasp the nature of science at work, in its actual reality; and they themselves produce theories about science which have ontological implications of which they seem to be blissfully unaware. The positivist idea of separating science from all ontology 'corresponds neither with science today nor with that which humanity has known in any epoch of its development'.[3]

Reference has been made to common sense. One of Meyerson's strongest convictions is that science is 'only a prolongation of common sense'.[4] We ordinarily assume that our perception of objects is something simple and primitive. If we analyze perception, we arrive in the long run at states of consciousness or sensations. To build up perception out of primitive subjective data, we have to introduce memory. Otherwise we could not account for our belief in permanent possibilities of sensation. But in the construction of the world of common sense we go further than this. We use, though not of course explicitly or with conscious reflection, the principle of causality to construct the concept of permanent physical objects. Common sense is thus shot through with ontology or metaphysics. We explain our sensations in terms of physical objects as causes of our sensations. On the level of common sense we hypostatize our sensations as far as we can, attributing, for example, colour and other qualities to objects, whereas science transforms the objects. But science has its point of

---

[1] *Explication*, pp. 39–40.   [2] *Ibid.*, p. 39.
[3] *Identité et realité*, p. 439; English version, p. 384.
[4] *Ibid.*, p. 402; English version, p. 354.

departure in common sense, and it prolongs our use of the causal principle. The entities postulated by the scientist may differ from those of common sense; but physics can no more get along without the concept of things or substances or without causal explanation than common sense can. The concept of law, establishing relations between phenomena, is not enough by itself. Given this point of view, it is understandable that Meyerson insists that science is explanatory and not simply descriptive. Comte and others may have tried to expel explanation and explanatory theories from science; but 'the existence of explanatory science is a *fact*',[1] a fact which cannot be got over by ingenious accounts of what the scientist is about. A phenomenon is explained in so far as it is deduced from antecedents which can be described as the cause of the phenomenon or, to use Leibnizian terminology, as its sufficient reason, sufficient, that is to say, to produce the phenomenon in question. 'The cause can be defined as the point of departure of a deduction of which the phenomenon is the point of arrival.'[2] It is true, according to Meyerson, that in science we do not actually find deductions corresponding fully with an abstract concept of what deductive explanation should be. But though this shows that in science, as elsewhere, man pursues a goal which transcends his grasp, it does not show that the pursuit does not exist. The drive to explain phenomena involves the presupposition that reality is intelligible or rational. The attempt to understand reality meets with resistance, in the form of the irrational, of that which cannot be rendered fully intelligible. But this does not affect the fact that science aims at explanation.

It is clear that Meyerson assimilates the causal relation to that of logical implication. Indeed, he regards causal explanation as a process of identification. In so far as a phenomenon is explained by deducing it from its antecedents, it is identified with these antecedents. 'The principle of causality is simply the principle of identity applied to the existence of objects in time.'[3] That the mind seeks persistence through motion and time can be seen, for example, in its formulation of principles such as those of inertia, of conservation of matter and conservation of energy. When pushed however to the limit the demand for causal explanation is a demand for an identification of cause and effect such that the two would coincide, time would be eliminated and nothing would

¹ *Explication*, p. 57.   ² *Ibid.*, p. 66.
³ *Identité et realité*, p. 38; English version, p. 43.

happen. In other words, the reason aspires after an Eleatic world,
'a universe eternally immutable,'[1] a universe in which, paradoxically, there is no causality and nothing ever happens. As a limiting
concept, the world which would fully satisfy the will to identification would be one in which distinct bodies had been eliminated
by their reduction to space, and so to nonentity. For that which
does not act and is not the cause of anything is as if it were not.
Meyerson has not of course taken complete leave of his senses.
He does not in fact believe that science will ever arrive at acosmism
as a final conclusion. He is known indeed as a philosopher of
science; but in the first instance he is an epistemologist, in the
sense that he is interested in developing a critique of reason. He
wishes, that is to say, to discover the principles governing human
thought.[2] To achieve this task he turns neither to introspection
nor to a priori reflection but to an 'a posteriori analysis of expressed
thought'.[3] In other words, he examines the products of thought.
And his attention is focussed for the most part, though not
exclusively, on physical science. In this area he finds that the
mind aims at understanding phenomena through causal explanation, that the principle of causality, in its pure form so to speak,
is the principle of identity applied to objects in time, and that the
a priori drive of the reason is thus to identification. The mind in
its activity is governed by the principle of identity. He proceeds
to show what sort of universe, in his opinion, would satisfy this
will to identification, if it were able to proceed unchecked and
without encountering any resistance. In point of fact however it
does not proceed unchecked; and it does encounter resistance. We
cannot get over the irreversibility of time and the reality of
becoming or change. 'Identity is the eternal framework of our
mind';[4] but science has come to be increasingly dominated by
empirical elements which militate against the will to identification. The universe as presented to us by science is thus not a
Parmenidean universe. This remains a limiting concept, a projected goal of the mind's inborn or a priori drive to identification,
if we suppose that it encounters no resistance.

Perhaps the matter can be expressed in this way. Whatever
the positivists may have asserted, science is explanatory. It

[1] Ibid., p. 256; English version, p. 230.
[2] As Meyerson puts it, using a Leibnizian term, he seeks to know the nature
of 'the intellect itself' (intellectus ipse). Needless to say, he is aware of the affinity
between his inquiry and Kant's; but his approach and method are different.
[3] Essais, p. 107.   [4] Identité et realité, p. 322; English version, p. 284.

exemplifies a drive to understanding by means of causal explanation, a drive which belongs to the human mind as such and is already present and operative on the level of common sense. This approach presupposes that reality is intelligible or rational. And as, according to Meyerson, the search for causal explanation is governed by the principle of identity, reality, if completely rational, would be one self-identical being, the cause of itself, or *causa sui*. But the completely self-identical being would be equivalent to not-being. Science cannot arrive at a *causa sui*. Further, reality is in any case not fully rational in the sense mentioned. In modern science we have become more and more aware of the irreversibility of time and of the emergence of novelty. Reality, as constructed by science, will not fit into the schema of rationalism. It does not follow from this that science is not explanatory. That is to say, it always embodies the drive to understanding by means of causal explanation. But science can never find a final resting-place. The 'irrational', in the sense of what is unforseen and unforeseeable, breaks in, as in quantum physics. The behaviour of living things cannot be simply deduced from what we know of the behaviour of inorganic bodies. And even if some apparently irrational phenomena come to be explained, there is no guarantee whatever that the scientist will not be faced with new ones, or that new theories will not supplant or profoundly modify their predecessors. We have had an Einstein. There may be others. 'We shall never be able really to *deduce* Nature, . . . We shall always have need of new experiences and these will always give rise to new problems, will cause new contradictions to break out (*éclater*), according to Duhem's term, between our theories and our observations.'[1] The drive or impulse of reason remains the same. 'Everyone, always and in every circumstance, has reasoned and reasons still in an essentially invariable way.'[2] But reason cannot attain its ideal goal. It has to adapt itself to empirical reality. And science as it exists exemplifies the dialectic between the drive of reason, which postulates the completely rational character of reality, and the obstacles which it constantly encounters.

Meyerson was interested in philosophical systems and applied his ideas to, for example, Hegel's philosophy of Nature. Hegel tried to subject what he regarded as the irrational to the dominion of reason. And we cannot legitimately object to the attempt to understand and explain. For 'reason must tend to subject to itself all that does not come from it; it is its proper function, for it is this which we call *reasoning*. We have seen moreover, in our previous book, that explanatory science is nothing but an operation pursued entirely according to this pattern.'[1] But the fact of the matter is that reality cannot be taken by storm in the manner envisaged by those who construct comprehensive deductive systems. They are sure to meet with a check. And this check constitutes precisely a demonstration of the fact that the 'irrational' cannot be totally mastered by the deductive reason.

Evidently, in a certain sense Meyerson sympathizes fully with the mathematical deductive ideal of knowledge. This is what, in his view, reason strives after and will always strive after. But Nature exists independently of us, even though it becomes known only through our sensations, through the sensible appearances of things. We cannot simply reconstruct Nature deductively. We have to have recourse to experience. The ways of Nature can be different from those of pure reason. And this fact sets limits to our power of conceptual mastery. The philosopher who produces a comprehensive deductive system tries to subject Nature completely to the demands of reason. But Nature is refractory; it takes its revenge. Hence science as it exists must be both deductive and empirical. It advances in the process of understanding; but it must always be ready for shocks and for the revision of its theories. Reason seeks an ideal goal, which is set by the essence or nature of reason; but the attainment of the goal is an ever-receding limit of aspiration. In one sense reason suffers frustration. But in another sense it does not. For if the goal were completely attained, there would be no science.

5. According to Meyerson, as we have just seen, reason, governed in its operation by the principle of identity, seeks a Parmenidean One, a *causa sui* in which diversity is overcome and complete self-identity is realized. To be sure, this limiting goal can never be attained. For novelty and the unforeseeable break in and prevent reason coming to any final rest. But the ideal limit remains, that of a complete explanation of all events or phenomena through identification with their ultimate cause. In Kantian language this ideal limit is a regulative idea of the reason.

We can perhaps see some affinity at any rate between Meyerson's idea of reason and that of André Lalande (1867–1964), the editor of the well known *Vocabulaire technique et critique de la*

---

[1] *Explication*, p. 402.

philosophie.[1] With Lalande the Eleatic overtones are missing, but he lays emphasis on a movement towards homogeneity and unification and of the role played by reason in this movement as found in human life. In 1899 he published a thesis in which he opposed Herbert Spencer's contention that the movement in evolution is one of differentiation, a movement from homogeneity to heterogeneity.[2] Lalande did not of course deny that there is a process of differentiation; but in his view the movement of what he called 'dissolution' or 'involution'[3] was of wider significance. In Nature this movement can be seen in entropy, in the increasing unavailability of thermal energy and the tendency towards an equilibrium which would result in a kind of thermal death.[4] In the organic sphere we do indeed find a process of differentiation, a movement from the homogeneous to the heterogeneous; but the movement of life can be likened to that of an object thrown into the air. The vital energy or impetus is finally spent, and living things relapse in the end into inanimate matter. In the long run it is homogeneity which prevails over heterogeneity, assimilation over differentiation.

In point of fact Herbert Spencer, in his general theory of evolution, allowed for an alternation of differentiation and dissolution or, as Lalande would say, involution.[5] But as a resolute champion of individual liberty and a strong opponent of the organic theory of the State,[6] Spencer clearly regarded increasing differentiation, increasing heterogeneity, as the desirable goal in the development of human society and as the mark of progress. Here Lalande parts company with him. He does not regard processes in Nature as proper objects of moral judgments. But in the sphere of human life he looks on the movement towards homogeneity as desirable and as constituting progress. In other words, Lalande sees man's biological nature and tendencies as impelling him to self-centredness and egoism, as separating human beings. The desirable

---

[1] Lalande began publishing his *Technical and Critical Vocabulary of Philosophy* in 1902. In 1904 he was appointed to a philosophical chair at Paris.

[2] *L'idée directrice de la dissolution opposée à celle de l'évolution.* A revised edition appeared in 1930 with the title *Les illusions évolutionistes* (*Evolutionist Illusions*).

[3] The word 'involution' was substituted for 'dissolution' in the revised version of the thesis

[4] Extension of the second law of thermodynamics from a closed thermal system to the universe is now commonly regarded as illegitimate.

[5] For Herbert Spencer see Vol. 8 of this *History*, chapter V.

[6] By the organic theory of the State I mean the theory of the State as an organism which is more than the sum of its members.

movement is the one which tends to make men not more unlike but more like one another, not indeed through an imposed uniformity or one which would eliminate our human freedom, but rather through a common participation in the realm of reason, morality and art. The movement of biological life is differentiating, divisive. Reason tends to unify and to assimilate.

In science the unifying function of reason is obvious. Particulars are grouped under universals, in classes that is to say; and the tendency is towards the coordination of phenomena under ever fewer and more general laws. In the spheres of logical thought and of scientific inquiry reason assimilates in the sense that it tends to make people think alike, even if they feel differently. Obviously, feeling can influence thought; but the point is that in so far as reason triumphs, it unites men rather than divides them. It may seem that the more science is given a technological application, the more individuals are identified with their functions, becoming simply members of a social organism. But according to Lalande the growth of technology serves to liberate the individual. It is true that in modern society men and women tend to become more alike, and that a certain uniformity is produced; but in this very process they are liberated from ancient tyrannies, such as that of the patriarchal family, and increasing specialization sets people free to enjoy common cultural values, such as aesthetic values. The assimilating tendency of modern society, with the breakdown of old hierarchies, is at the same time a process of liberation for the individual. Man becomes free to enter more fully into his common cultural heritage.

As we are all aware, some writers have seen in the development of modern society a process of levelling-out which tends to produce a uniform mediocrity prejudicial to the individual personality, while others have emphasized the identification, as they interpret it, of the individual with his social function. The growth of homogeneity can be interpreted as equivalent to the growth of what Nietzsche described as the 'Cold Monster' or as leading in the direction of a totalitarian society. Lalande proposes a different point of view, seeing modern society as potentially liberating the individual for his self-enrichment by entering into the common cultural world of reason and art. Biological urges are divisive; reason and morals and aesthetics are unifying factors. It is therefore not surprising that in a work on *Reason and Norms* (*La raison et les normes*), which appeared in 1948, he criticized

phenomenologists and existentialists. For example, while phenomenologists emphasized the origins of the concepts of space and
time in the experience of the individual as a being in the world,
Lalande emphasized the common space and time of mathematicians and physicists, in which he saw the unifying work of reason.
Lalande did indeed write specifically about the philosophy of
science. Thus in 1893 he published the first of the numerous
editions of *Lectures sur la philosophie des sciences* (*Readings in the
Philosophy of the Sciences*) and in 1929 *Les théories de l'induction
et de l'expérimentation* (*Theories of Induction and Experimentation*).
But his thought was much wider than what could usefully be
described as philosophy of science. For his concern was with
emphasizing the movement of 'involution' and the role played in it
by what he called 'constituting reason'. Science is one field in which
reason unifies. But morals is another, where reason is capable of
promoting agreement and producing a lay or secular ethics. In
general, reason fosters mutual understanding and cooperation
between human beings. The effort devoted by Lalande to editing
and re-editing his *Vocabulary* was based on this assumption.

6. Meyerson and Brunschvicg both emphasized the impulse to
unification which is manifested in science. This was natural
enough, not only because this emphasis fitted into or was demanded
by their general philosophies but also because unification of
phenomena clearly constitutes a real aspect of science. It is not
necessary to talk about identification or to follow Meyerson in
introducing Parmenidean themes in order to see that when the
mind is faced with a plurality of phenomena conceptual unification forms a real aspect of understanding. Conceptual mastery
cannot be obtained without unification. Or, rather, it is a process
of unification. At the same time it is possible to emphasize the
pluralism in science, the elements of discontinuity and the plurality of theories. Brunschvicg, as we have seen, allowed for this
aspect. But there is a difference between finding room for the facts
within the framework of an idealist philosophy which emphasizes
the nature of mind or spirit as a unity and singling out and laying
emphasis on aspects of the history of science which it is not so easy
to harmonize with the general idea of reason as progressively
imposing its own unity and homogeneity on phenomena.

Emphasis on plurality and discontinuity was characteristic of
the philosophy of science of Gaston Bachelard (1884–1962). After
having been employed in the postal service he obtained a degree

in mathematics and science and then taught physics and chemistry in his home town, Bar-sur-Aube. In 1930 he was appointed professor of philosophy in the university of Dijon,[1] and after ten years he went to Paris as professor of the history and philosophy of science. He published a considerable number of works, in 1928 an *Essai sur la connaissance approchée* (*Essay on Approximative Knowledge*), in 1932 *Le pluralisme cohérent de la chimie moderne* (*The Coherent Pluralism of Modern Chemistry*), in 1933 *Les intuitions atomistiques* (*Atomistic Intuitions*), in 1937 *La continuité et la multiplicité temporelles* (*Temporal Continuity and Multiplicity*) and *L'expérience de l'espace dans la physique contemporaine* (*The Experience of Space in Contemporary Physics*), in 1938 *La formation de l'esprit scientifique* (*The Formation of the Scientific Mind*), in 1940 *La philosophie du non* (*The Philosophy of No*), in 1949 *La rationalisme appliqué* (*Applied Rationalism*), in 1951 *L'activité rationaliste de la physique contemporaine* (*The Rationalist Activity of Contemporary Physics*), and in 1953 *Le matérialisme rationnel* (*Rational Materialism*). Bachelard was also interested in the relation between the activity of the mind in science and its activity in poetic imagination. In this field he published a number of works, such as *La psychoanalyse du feu* (1938, *The Psychoanalysis of Fire*), *L'eau et les rêves* (1942, *Water and Dreams*), *L'air et les songes* (1943, *Air and Dreams*), *La terre et les rêveries de la volonté* (1948, *Earth and the Reveries of the Will*), *La poétique de l'espace* (1957, *The Poetics of Space*) and *La flamme d'une chandelle* (1961, *The Flame of a Candle*).

In Bachelard's view existentialist talk about the absurdity or meaninglessness of the world is an illegitimate exaggeration. It is indeed true that scientific hypotheses and theories are the creation of mind; but experiment or empirical testing is necessary to science, and the interplay of reason and experience in the development of scientific knowledge does not support the view that the world is completely unintelligible in itself and that intelligibility is nothing but a mental imposition. When however we consider the nature and course of this interplay of reason and experience, we find that scientific progress cannot properly be regarded as a continuous advance in which reason simply adds to the coherent system of knowledge already attained. It is all very well for some philosophers to lay down first principles and then to interpret reality as exemplifying them and as filling in the preconceived

[1] Bachelard received the doctorate in 1927.

outline of a picture. They can always regard refractory material as of little significance or as illustrating the contingent or even irrational nature of the given. Their philosophy remains 'a philosopher's philosophy'[1] and has little to do with science. In the growth of scientific knowledge discontinuity is an essential feature. That is to say, new experiences force us to say 'no' to old theories; and for an old model of interpretation we may have to substitute a new one. Indeed, we may have to change concepts or principles which have seemed basic. The genuinely scientific mind is open. It will not do, for example, to reject quantum mechanics, with its recognition of a measure of indeterminism, simply because it will not fit into a sacrosanct framework. Conceptual frameworks may have to be negated in favour of new ones, though these too of course are themselves open to negation in the future. The philosophy of science must itself be pluralistic, open to a variety of perspectives. The old rationalistic deductive ideal of Descartes and others is untenable and discredited. Reason has to follow science. That is to say, it must learn the various forms of reasoning from seeing them at work in the sciences.[2] 'The traditional doctrine of an absolute and changeless reason is only a philosophy. It is a philosophy which has perished.'[3]

In his *Philosophie du non* Bachelard does not of course understand by 'no' a mere negation. The new physics, for example, does not simply deny or cancel out the classical physics. Classical concepts are given fresh meanings in a new framework. The negation is dialectical rather than pure rejection. At the same time the emphasis is laid by Bachelard on discontinuity, on rupture in thought and on 'transcendence' of previous levels. For instance, the world as represented in science transcends the pre-scientific world. There is a rupture between the naïve consciousness and the scientific consciousness. But within science itself there are ruptures. Science, for example, was once a kind of organized common sense, treating either of concrete objects or of objects which sufficiently resembled the concrete things of common sense for them to be imaginable. With the advent however of non-Euclidean geometries, of theories of the world which can be expressed only mathematically and of concepts of 'objects' which are not imaginable things like those of common sense, science has become

---

[1] *La philosophie du non*, p. 8 (5th edition, 1970).
[2] Here Bachelard says much the same as Brunschvicg.
[3] *La philosophie du non*, p. 145.

concerned, according to Bachelard, with relationships rather than with things. It looks beyond things and immediate objects to mathematically formulable relationships. And there has thus taken place a 'dematerialization of materialism'.[1] Thought tends to become fossilized in a realistic outlook; but the crisis of discovery forces it forward into the process of abstraction which is made possible by mathematics. There arises therefore a scientific world which is not communicable to the non-scientific mind and which is far removed not only from the world of naïve consciousness but also from that of the imaginable world of earlier science.

The creative activity of the mind is exemplified, Bachelard insists, both in the work of scientific reason and in the poetic imagination, their roots being, in his view, discoverable by psychoanalysis. Though however both science and poetry (or art in general) manifest the creative activity of the mind, they take different directions. In art man projects his dream, the product of the imagination, on things, while in modern science the mind transcends both subject and object towards mathematically formulable relationships. In regard to this sphere of the scientific reason Bachelard obviously agrees with Brunschvicg both in the rejection of fixed categories and models and in the view that reason comes to know its nature through reflection on its actual work, on its historical development. For Bachelard the nature of reason is thus revealed as pluriform and as plastic or changing. But if we ask why reason in its creative activity constructs the world of science, the answer, even if it is not clearly given by Bachelard, must presumably be similar to that given by Brunschvicg, namely that the mind pursues unification. Emphasis on discontinuity, on revisibility and on the non-final character of scientific concepts, models and theories does not really affect the issue. For Brunschvicg himself did not envisage a complete and final unification or assimilation as actually attainable. To be sure, the obviously idealist presuppositions and ideas of Brunschvicg are absent from Bachelard's thought. But the latter's view of modern man as projecting or creating an extremely abstract world of relationships, in which materialism is left behind or at any rate transformed, might perhaps be given an idealist setting, if one wished to do so.

We have noted the lively interest shown by recent French philosophers of science in epistemological themes. In this field the

[1] *Le nouvel esprit scientifique*, p. 67.

philosophers mentioned above manifested a strong reaction to positivism on the one hand and to the Cartesian ideal of knowledge on the other. They emphasized the inventiveness and creativity of the mind and the approximating and revisible character of its interpretation of reality. Duhem was something of an exception. For though he agreed, in large measure, with the conventionalism of Poincaré, he was concerned with separating science from ontology and metaphysics. Generally speaking however the sciences were looked on as embodying the mind's urge to understand the world through the unification of phenomena. And the ideas of the inventiveness and creativity of the mind and of the essentially revisible character of scientific hypotheses and theories were obviously grounded in reflection on the history of science. In other words, it was science in its actuality which prompted the conclusion that both the purely rationalistic and deductive picture of the mind's operation and Comte's rather naïve conception of positive knowledge were alike discredited. Again, philosophers such as Brunschvicg and Bachelard saw clearly that neither pure rationalism nor pure empiricism could provide a satisfactory account of science as it existed. We may of course be inclined to think that the French philosophers of science were too 'philosophical'. But at any rate they tried to make their philosophical positions clear and explicit, even if their success was not always conspicuous.

CHAPTER XIV

PHILOSOPHY OF VALUES, METAPHYSICS, PERSONALISM

*General remarks — R. Polin — Metaphysics of values: R. Le Senne
and the philosophy of spirit — R. Ruyer and J. Pucelle —
L. Lavelle and the philosophy of act — The personalism of
E. Mounier.*

1. It hardly needs saying that moral philosophy in one form or
another has been a prominent feature of French thought from the
time of the Renaissance. Even Descartes, whose name is primarily
associated with methodology, metaphysics and the view of the
world as a machine, emphasized the practical value of philosophy
and envisaged a science of ethics as its crown. The philosophers
of the eighteenth-century Enlightenment were concerned with
setting ethics on its own feet, separating it, that is to say, from
theology and metaphysics. In the nineteenth century ethical
themes were prominent in the writings of positivists such as
Durkheim, of spiritualists such as Guyau and Bergson[1] and of
thinkers such as Renouvier who belonged to the neo-critical
movement. In spite however of this tradition of ethical thought
the philosophy of values was a comparative latecomer on the
French scene, in comparison with Germany that is to say; and it
met at first with some suspicion and resistance. Obviously the
concept of the good and of desirable ends had been familiar enough,
and philosophers had discussed moral ideals as well as truth and
beauty. In a sense ethical discussion had always included discussion of values. At the same time the French moral philosophers
had tended to focus their attention on ethical phenomena as an
empirical or given point of departure for reflection; and there
was some doubt about the utility of the abstract analysis of
values, especially as this sort of language suggested the idea of
subsistent essences 'out there'. Besides, the explicit philosophy of
values as practised by Max Scheler and Nicolai Hartmann was
connected with phenomenology, which developed in Germany and

---

[1] Bergson's ethical writing belongs of course to the twentieth century. But his
philosophy was the culmination of a movement which began and developed in the
nineteenth century.

at first had little impact in France.[1] There was of course Nietzsche's discussion of values. But for a considerable time Nietzsche was regarded in France more as a poet than a philosopher. From a phenomenological point of view it can reasonably be argued that values are recognized or discovered. Consider, for example, the case of someone who judges that love is a value, something to be valued, whereas hatred is not. It is clearly arguable that his attitude is one of recognizing or seeing love as a value and hatred as a disvalue. Whatever his theory of values may be, it can be argued that as far as his immediate consciousness is concerned, love imposes itself on his mind as a value. Similarly, from the phenomenological point of view it is reasonable to use the language of recognition or discovery in regard to truth and beauty considered as values. In other words, our experience of values provides a ground or basis for the idea of values as objective and as transcendent, in the sense that they do not depend simply on one's own choice of them. To be sure, one has to find room for different and even incompatible value-judgments. But we can always refer, as some phenomenologists have done, to the possibility of a blindness to values and of varying degrees of insight into the field of values. And these ideas can be applied both to societies and to individuals.

From an ontological or metaphysical point of view however it seems absurd, to most people at any rate, to conceive values as existing in some ethereal world of their own. We can of course substitute the word 'subsist' for the word 'exist'; but it is doubtful if this verbal change really improves the situation. If therefore we wish to assert the objectivity of values, and if at the same time we wish to avoid committing ourselves to the view that universals such as love or truth or beauty can exist or 'subsist' in a Platonic world of their own, we can either regard values as objective qualities of things and actions in addition to other qualities, or we can try to work out some general metaphysics which will permit us to talk about the objectivity of values without committing ourselves to the concept of a realm of subsistent universal essences.

If may of course seem very much simpler to deny the objectivity of values, if this is taken to imply that values have an ontological status of their own, whether as ethereal substances or as objective qualities of things, persons and actions. That is to say, it may seem

---

[1] In Germany there was also of course the Neo-Kantian School of Baden. See Vol. 7 of this *History*, pp. 364–6.

much simpler, and also more sensible, to throw all the weight on the value-judgment or on the act of valuation and to maintain, for example, that to assert that beauty is a value is to express the act of attributing value to beautiful things or persons. We can maintain, in other words, that it is through the act of attributing value that human beings create values. Values depend on and are relative to the human will and choice.

If we adopt this line of thought, we have of course to account in some way for the feeling of recognizing or discovering values. For this seems to be a datum of consciousness. We can try to explain this feeling by referring it to the bearing of the collective consciousness, as conceived by Durkheim, on the individual consciousness. Or, if we wish to speak only in terms of individuals, we might adopt a line of thought represented by Sartre and see the individuals' particular value-judgments as determined by an original *projet* or a basic operative ideal.

Leaving aside for the moment not only the existentialism of Sartre, which will be discussed later, but also those who have tried to give a metaphysical foundation to values, we can turn first to a philosopher, Raymond Polin, who has discussed a variety of axiological theories and attitudes and who himself comes down on the anti-objectivist side.

2. Raymond Polin was born in 1910. After studying at the École Normale and obtaining the doctorate in letters, he taught philosophy first in several lycées, such as the Lycée Condorcet at Paris, and then as professor of ethics in the university of Lille. In 1961 he became a professor at the Sorbonne. His publications include *La création des valeurs* (1944, *The Creation of Values*), *La compréhension des valeurs* (1945, *The Understanding of Values*), *Du laid, du mal, du faux* (1948, *On the Ugly, the Evil and the False*) and *Éthique et politique* (1968, *Ethics and Politics*). Polin has also published works on Hobbes and Locke.[1]

Phenomenology, Polin asserts, seems to offer 'the most adequate method for the study of values',[2] inasmuch as for the consciousness which thinks or conceives them values coincide with their meaning (*signification*). He envisages two steps, first a phenomenological reduction giving access to the pure axiological consciousness (the consciousness of value) with a view to defining the

---

[1] *Philosophie et politique chez Thomas Hobbes* (1953) and *La politique morale de John Locke* (1960).
[2] *La création des valeurs*, p. 1.

essence of values, and secondly a movement of liberation, freeing the mind, that is to say, both from the pressure exercised by received values and from the influence of all existing theories of value. In other words, he wishes to take a fresh and unprejudiced view of the matter. The mind should place itself in a position of neutrality in regard to any determinate hierarchy of values and in regard to all existing theories. It should prescind from all authority, including that of society.

As Polin refers frequently to 'values', using the noun that is to say, one may be tempted to conclude that for him there is a realm of essences which have some sort of existence of their own or which have to be given an ontological or metaphysical foundation. Indeed, the subtitle of his work on the creation of values is *Recherches sur le fondement de l'objectivité axiologique (Inquiries into the Foundation of Axiological Objectivity)*. We have already noted however that for him a value coincides with its meaning for the consciousness which thinks it. It thus has intentional objectivity, in the sense that the act of thinking or conceiving a value-meaning is a reality. But a value does not exist as an object 'out there', independently of the subject which thinks it. As for finding a foundation for values, other than the act of evaluating, this would have to be different from the values themselves (if it were to serve as a foundation) and at the same time to stand in an intelligible and necessary relation to the values which it founded. But how can there be a necessary relation between what is not a value and a value? Or to express the matter in a different and more familiar way, how can a factual statement entail a value-judgment?

In point of fact Polin's talk about values is somewhat misleading. He is really concerned with the act of evaluation, by which values are constituted. In his view evaluation cannot be understood apart from the concept of human action. 'Phenomenological inquiry into the essence of values is vain and futile unless it constitutes the introduction to a philosophy of action.'[1] Human action presupposes and expresses evaluation, which is an act of the free subject. The free subject outruns or transcends the empirically given, creating its own values with a view to action. The values created have of course a certain exteriority, in the sense that they are the objects of an intentional and teleological consciousness. But it is a mistake to think that there is an axiological reality or

[1] *Ibid.*, p. 3.

realm of values apart from the consciousness which creates them. The only given reality is empirical reality; but this is evaluated in relation to action. Values are grounded in the self-transcending creative subject. And this is the only foundation which they have or require.

According to Polin therefore values are not real objects 'out there' waiting to be known. On the contrary, there is an irreducible distinction between knowledge of things, in which the 'noetic' consciousness is absorbed in the object, and the axiological consciousness which transcends what is given and creates the 'unreal'. In other words, we must not confuse truth and value. 'Truth is not a value,'[1] and we ought not to speak of the truth of values. But there is a truth of action. That is to say, while theoretical truth is attained through the conformity of thought with reality, truth in action is attained through the conformity produced in the reality (work) created by action 'with the axiological project and intention'.[2] We know a fact when our thought is conformed to an objective state of affairs. In the sphere of action however truth consists in the conformity between what we achieve or bring about and our value-laden intention. But this is not all there is to be said. For through his action a man creates not simply his work but also himself. 'This is why the truth of action embraces the totality of the work and its creator. It is at the same time the work and the man who accomplishes the work.'[3]

In his insistence that it is man who feely creates values Polin stands in the Nietzschean line of thought. And in this and some other respects, such as his view that through the process of evaluation and action man creates himself, he obviously stands close to Sartre. But what, we may ask, does Polin make of the social aspect of morality? In his view, 'action is social by its essence, by its object, by its conditions; it is inconceivable without the presence of the other.'[4] This means that vlaues, as the expression of a creative will, tend to become norms; and norms, as universalizable, are essentially social. Moreover, whereas values (valuations) are personal and cannot be imposed, norms can be imposed by others. A society or group, for example, can accept certain norms and try to enforce or impose acceptance on its individual members or on another group. Norms then become values rendered static; and they can be accepted servilely or because people are looking for a secure foothold or a refuge from personal decision which is always

[1] Ibid., p. 296.   [2] Ibid., p. 296.   [3] Ibid., p. 297.   [4] Ibid., p. 259.

a venture, as it means going beyond or transcending the given. At the same time values can also present themselves not as constraining norms or rules or commandments but as attracting or exercising an appeal. To their creator values can appear as attracting ideals and ends; and they can appear in the same way to others. 'The commandment is replaced by an appeal.'[1] The creator then 'owes his domination over others simply to the influence of the values which he creates'.[2] In this line of thought we can see perhaps a resumption of Bergson's theme of the closed and open moralities.

In his analysis of 'axiological attitudes' Polin begins by examining what he describes as the contemplative attitude. Here the subject conceives transcendence not in the form of creative human action but in that of 'a static and given being: the transcendent'.[3] Values are conceived not as 'unreal' entities which are realized only through human action but as realities existing independently of man. Polin admits that values, as so conceived, can provide a 'model of a perfect human activity';[4] but, as objects of contemplation, they do not, in his view, 'give rise to any efficacious *action*'.[5] A value is not, as it were, a moment in the total process or cycle of human action, but rather a detached object of contemplation which exists, or if preferred, subsists, independently of human consciousness.

Polin does not of course share this axiological attitude. And most of us would probably find it difficult to accept a theory which postulated a world of subsistent value-essences, which would really be subsistent universals, in addition to particular individual things. At the same time it is arguable, as has already been noted, that from the phenomenological point of view there is such an experience as recognizing or discovering values. That is to say, there is an experience which seems to demand the use of such terms. And even if one is determined to avoid the literal implication of a term such as 'discovery', namely the implication that there is a pre-existing reality waiting to be discovered, any adequate theory of values must at any rate allow for the type of experience which prompts the use of terms which are potentially misleading. Hence it is perfectly understandable that some philosophers are not content with any theory which interprets values simply as free creations of the individual subject. And even if

---

[1] *La compréhension des valeurs*, p. 134.   [2] *Ibid.*, p. 134.
[3] *Ibid.*, p. 58.   [4] *Ibid.*, p. 58.   [5] *Ibid.*, p. 58.

in some cases it involves retracing our steps from the chronological point of view we can consider briefly two or three French philosophers who have tried to link up a theory of values with a general metaphysics.

3. A name which comes at once to mind in this connection is that of René Le Senne (1882–1954). A pupil of Hamelin at the École Normale, Le Senne taught in lycées at Chambéry, Marseilles and then Paris, becoming a professor of moral philosophy at the Sorbonne in 1942. Together with his friend Louis Lavelle he founded and edited the series entitled *Philosophie de l'esprit* (*Philosophy of Spirit*), published by Aubier at Paris. Among his works we can mention his *Introduction to Philosophy* (*Introduction à la philosophie*, 1925, revised and enlarged edition 1939), his doctorate thesis entitled *Duty* (*Le Devoir*, 1930, second edition 1950), *Obstacle and Value* (*Obstacle et valeur*, 1934), a general treatise on ethics (*Traité de morale générale*, 1942), a work on characterology (*Traité de caractérologie*, 1945), *Personal Destiny* (*La destinée personnelle*, 1951), and the posthumously published work *The Discovery of God* (*La découverte de Dieu*, 1955).

In an essay entitled *La philosophie de l'esprit*[1] Le Senne remarks that to follow the development of French philosophy from Descartes to Hamelin, or even to Bergson, is to understand the fecundity of Cartesianism.[2] From one point of view this may seem to be an odd assertion. Is there not, we may ask, a very great difference between the rationalism of Descartes, with his mathematical model of reasoning, and his appeal to clear and distinct concepts, and Bergson's appeal to intuition and his philosophy of duration and of the movement of life? It hardly needs saying however that Le Senne is perfectly well aware of the differences. When he refers to the continuity between the thought of Descartes on the one hand and the spiritualist and idealist movements in nineteenth-century French philosophy on the other, he is thinking not of Descartes' mathematical model nor of his view of the material world as a machine but of the emphasis placed by Descartes on the thinking and active self or ego and of the relation which is asserted between the self and God. Le Senne is thinking,

---

[1] *Philosophic Thought in France and the United States*, edited by Marvin Farber (Buffalo, N.Y., 1950), pp. 103–20. The fact that in the American version of the work the title of Le Senne's essay is given in French is perhaps significant. The word *esprit* can indeed be translated as 'mind'. But though mind is included in its range of meaning, *esprit* has, in the context, metaphysical and religious connotations which favour use of the word 'spirit'.

[2] *Ibid.*, p. 103.

in other words, of elements in Cartesianism which were preserved and developed in the movement of thought from Maine de Biran onwards, but which were menaced by positivism in its various forms and by certain aspects of technological civilization. Obviously, Le Senne makes a judgment of value about what constitutes authentic philosophy.

And one characteristic of authentic philosophy, in his view, is that it transcends the initial empiricist attitude of common sense, which 'leads to *realism* and even to *materialism*',[1] and discovers the self as that which thinks the objective world and is conscious of itself. In this movement of thought however there is a dialectic or dialogue between intellectualism or idealist rationalism on the one hand and, on the other, opposition to the reduction of existence to thought. 'As against Descartes, Pascal, Malebranche combines in his philosophy the demands of Cartesianism with the Augustinian inspiration. From Condillac comes Biran, but the latter reacts against the former. At the beginning of this century the dialogue is continued between Hamelin and Bergson.'[2] These two philosophers 'have maintained with the same fidelity the ideal of a knowledge which seeks the reason or the one and indivisible source of all that is and is thought'.[3] As for French existentialism, Le Senne sees, as one would expect, a great difference between the religiously oriented and 'optimistic' philosophy of thinkers such as Marcel and the 'negative' and 'pessimistic' existentialism of Sartre.[4]

As one would expect of a philosopher influenced by Hamelin, there are evident idealist elements in Le Senne's thought. He asserts, for example, that 'the celebrated formula of Berkeley *Esse est percipi vel percipere* (to be is to be perceived or to perceive) is false only inasmuch as it is too narrow. To perceive, to think abstractly, to feel, to will, to love, to have a presentiment of, to regret, and so on indefinitely, so that no experience of the spirit is omitted, this is reality and the whole of reality.'[5] Le Senne adds however a note to explain that while he denies that matter is a thing in itself, in the sense that it exists independently of any spirit, he does not intend to imply that matter has no reality at all. It exists only in relation to spirit, but in this relation it is real and functions 'sometimes as obstacle, sometimes as a support, in

---

[1] *Introduction à la philosophie* (2nd edition, 1947), p. 7.
[2] *Ibid.*, p. 134.   [3] *Ibid.*, p. 135.
[4] We cannot discuss here the use of the words 'existentialism' and 'existentialist'. This must be left until we come to treat explicitly of Marcel and Sartre.
[5] *Introduction à la philosophie*, p. 250.

regard both to action and to contemplation.'[1] In other words, matter exists only in relation to spirit; and in regard to the human spirit it can function either as an obstacle or a help in spirit's fufillment of its vocation. The question arises of course, what does Le Senne mean by spirit? Let us begin with the human spirit. 'When I affirm that I am a spirit, I mean that I distinguish myself from things by the consciousness which I have correlatively of them and of myself, that the multiplicity of determinations and qualities with which I furnish space and time are accessible to me only by reason of an envelopment of which I am the centre.'[2] This enveloping is however an active synthesis. 'I will say therefore of spirit, as I grasp it in myself, that it is a dynamic unity of linking together (*liaison*), in the widest sense of the last term, according to which to distinguish and to exclude is still to link together.'[3] But what I grasp in myself, according to Le Senne, is simply a finite reflection of spirit in itself, which can be defined as 'the operative unity of an active relation (*une relation en exercice*), interior to itself, between itself as infinite Spirit and the multitude of finite spirits.'[4] In other words, absolute Spirit is one and many. One can conceive it as 'the relation between itself as one and therefore as unlimited and itself as many, in short as the union of God ... and of finite consciousnesses.'[5] By distinguishing itself from the non-self and from other selves the finite spirit experiences limits and obstacles. It cannot achieve an all-embracing synthesis. This is realized only in and through infinite Spirit, which is at the same time other than and immanent in and inseparable from the finite spirit. Spirit in the most general sense is the relation between the two terms, God and the finite self.

In Le Senne's philosophy of spirit there seems to be a certain tension between absolute idealism and the theism which he certainly accepts. However this may be, his spiritualist metaphysics forms the setting for his theory of values. He sees the human spirit as oriented to value. '*That which is worthy of being sought after* is what everyone calls value.'[6] The statement that value is that which *is* worthy of being sought after indicates that for Le Senne value is not simply the creation of the human will. At the same time a value which was not a value for anyone would not be a value. '*If it does not exist through the subject, it is for the*

[1] *Ibid.*, p. 252.   [2] *Ibid.*, p. 254.   [3] *Ibid.*, p. 254.   [4] *Ibid.*, p. 257.
[5] *Ibid.*, p. 258.   [6] *Traité de morale générale* (3rd edition, 1949), p. 693.

subject.'[1] Recognition of value unites persons, and value 'can have meaning only for them'.[2] It does not follow of course that everyone makes the same value-judgments, nor that all human beings give precedence to the same value or values. One man may regard the aesthetic value of beauty as taking precedence, when another man gives the precedence to truth or to moral value. But the search for value plays a central role in the constitution of personality; and human beings are united by a common recognition of values. This is obvious, for example, in regard to both truth and love. Such recognition implies the transcendence of values, in the sense that they do not depend simply on man's arbitrary decree; but they are for man, in the sense that they are not values unless they can be appropriated, so to speak, in experience and realized in life.

Le Senne admits therefore that there is a plurality of values. Moral value, which he links with the idea of acting in accordance with duty or moral obligation, is not the only value. Truth, beauty and love are also values. Consider, for example, a mother who performed those actions in regard to her child which love would prompt but who did so simply and solely out of a sense of moral obligation. She 'would be a moral mother; but it would be false to say that she loved her child.'[3] For love involves the heart. No value can be identified with a particular thing. The aesthetic value of beauty, for example, cannot be identified with this or that empirical reality of which we say that it is beautiful. But this does not alter the fact that there are distinct values, irreducible to one another or to one particular 'cardinal' value, such as moral value or truth or beauty.

Though positive, values have also a negative aspect. A particular value exists only in opposition to a correlative non-value. Thus love is opposed to hatred; courage has meaning only in opposition to cowardice; truth is correlative to falsity; and so on. Further, one particular value can exclude another, so that precedence has to be given to one or the other. Le Senne does not however try to unify values in terms of a systematically graded hierarchy of particular values.[4] He seeks the principle of unity in

---

[1] *Introduction à la philosophie*, p. 365. The original text is *si elle n'est pas par lui, elle est pour lui. Lui* refers to *le sujet.*
[2] *Obstacle et valeur*, p. 192.
[3] *Introduction à la philosophie*, p. 381.
[4] For some summary lines of objection to this procedure see *Traité de moral générale*, p. 698.

absolute value, 'one and infinite'.[1] All particular values are for him relative and phenomenal. They are the ways in which pure or absolute value appears to the human consciousness or mediates itself to us. Absolute value is not the highest member of a hierarchy. It transcends and at the same time grounds all particular values. These constitute for us the phenomena or appearances of the Absolute, which is their source and is yet immanent in them.[2] Man's destiny or vocation is *an exploration* oriented to value, which is identical with the absolute'.[3] He experiences value 'in a given historical situation';[4] but he can transcend the determinate situation and conceive the value abstractly. He can also transcend particular values towards absolute value; but he discovers it only in and through its appearances, so that value is essentially 'a relational unification between its source, which is independent of the self, and the self.'[5] By realizing particular values, such as truth or love, in his life man attains authentic personality and participates in absolute value, inasmuch as the latter is at the heart of every relative value.

In one place Le Senne asserts that 'value is the knowledge of the Absolute'.[6] Elsewhere he speaks of the Absolute as being itself pure and infinite value. And as infinite value must comprise, in an eminent way, the value of personality, the Absolute 'must be called God'.[7] Hence Le Senne can give to the eighth chapter of his *Introduction to Philosophy* the heading 'Value or God', which implies that the two terms are synonymous. Whether these various ways of speaking can be harmonized is open to discussion. We have indeed noted Le Senne's statement that a value which was completely self-enclosed and incapable of being a value *for* anyone would not be a value. So it is understandable if he speaks of value, even of absolute value, in terms of a relation. But this way of speaking seems to fit in better with the view of the Absolute itself as relational, as comprising the two related terms of infinite spirit and finite spirit, than with the theory of the divine transcendence which is also defended by Le Senne.

Le Senne's theory of value calls Platonism to mind, at any rate if we are prepared to identify the absolute Good of the *Republic* with the Beauty in itself of the *Symposium* and the *One* of the

[1] *Obstacle et valeur*, p. 180.
[2] Le Senne refers to Bradley's theory of the Absolute.
[3] *Introduction à la philosophie*, p. 265.   [4] *Traité de moral générale*, p. 694.
[5] *La destinée personelle*, p. 210.   [6] *Obstacle et valeur*, p. 181.
[7] *Traité de morale générale*, p. 693.

Parmenides, the difference being that Le Senne's absolute value is identified with the personal God of the Christian religion. And unless we are inclined to write off all metaphysics as so much nonsense, we can presumably form some idea of what he means. For example, he claims that there is a transcendent divine reality which reveals itself not simply in the physical world as experienced by man but also in the axiological world or world of values, which constitutes a constituent element in experience. Though however Le Senne's theory of values is doubtless religiously edifying, and though we can have a general impression of its meaning, there are a good many questions to which no very clear answers are provided. For example, how would Le Senne analyze the value-judgment? It is indeed clear that he would not accept an analysis which interpreted it simply as expressing man's feelings or emotive attitudes or desires. For in his view value is neither simply psychological nor simply metaphysical but psycho-metaphysical.[1] Perhaps he would claim, for instance, that to say of something that it is beautiful is to say that it participates in beauty and, by implication, that it reflects the Absolute in a limited and finite way. But the metaphysics of participation itself gives rise to questions, as Plato was well aware.

4. There are of course other attempts in recent French philosophy to integrate a theory of values into a general world-view. We can just mention, for instance, Raymond Ruyer,[2] whose work *La conscience et le corps* (1937, *Consciousness and Body*) expressed an abandonment of his former mechanistic outlook and the development of a theory according to which every being manifests a teleological activity. That is to say, subjectivity or consciousness is present in all beings, though it is only at a certain level that the distinction between subject and object emerges. In the case of every being therefore its activity in the spatio-temporal sphere[3] is directed to an end, though it is only at the level of man that there is actual awareness of values belonging to an axiological realm which transcends space and time. The meaning of the activity of any being cannot be understood without reference to the realm of

---

[1] *Ibid.*, p. 697.
[2] Born in 1902, Ruyer was appointed a professor of the university of Nancy in 1945. In 1946 he published *Éléments de psycho-biologie* (*Elements of Psychobiology*), in 1952 *Néo-finalisme* (*Neo-finalism*) and in 1958 *La genèse de formes vivantes* (*The Genesis of Living Forms*).
[3] Objectivity, the spatio-temporal sphere, is conceived by Ruyer as phenomenal. All genuine activity is rooted in and proceeds from subjectivity.

values; but it is only at the level of man that such reflective understanding arises.

Ruyer has devoted special studies to the theory of values, *Le monde des valeurs* (1948, *The World of Values*) and *Philosophie de la valeur* (1952, *Philosophy of Value*). The unification of the phenomenal world of space and time and the world of subjectivity and of values is sought in the idea of God, conceived both as the ultimate source of all activity in the world and as the perfect qualitative unity of all values, their point of convergence.

The philosophy of Ruyer is to some extent a revival of lines of thought expounded by Leibniz. When we turn to Jean Pucelle, who is a professor in the University of Poitiers,[1] we find an approach to the subject of values which seems to represent both a reaction to the existentialist theory of values as the creation of the individual[2] and a desire to avoid any objectivist theory which postulates values as entities existing out there, independently of consciousness. Further, Pucelle is concerned with integrating the concepts of value and norm, instead of separating them sharply in the manner of those who tend to regard norms as static hindrances to liberty. It is true that norms belong to the juridical sphere, and that if human behaviour were dictated simply by norms and rules, it would degenerate into legalism. At the same time norms arise out of the recognition of values and serve as a condition or matrix for the exercise of creative liberty.

Pucelle allows that we can distinguish between the judgment of fact and the judgment of value. But he insists that 'it is only by abstraction that one distinguishes them'.[3] In his view, that is to say, no concrete factual judgment is entirely free of valuational elements. He traces back the value-judgment to the subject-object relation, in the sense that it presupposes both desire of an object and a distantiation (*détachement*) of the self from the object, whereby one transforms the actually desired into the desirable. At the same time the transition from felt desire to the value-judgment, by detaching, as it were, the self from the object, opens up the field of evaluation. And ideal values arise on the plane of intersubjectivity. Recognition of the value of love, for example, presupposes actual love between persons. The ideal value is

---

[1] Pucelle's publications include *La source des valeurs* (1957, *The Source of Values*) and *Le règne des fins* (1959, *The Kingdom of Ends*).
[2] The reference is of course to the Sartrian type of existentialism.
[3] *La source des valeurs*, p. 34.

clearly not a thing out there; but it is objectified for consciousness in the value-judgment. We have to avoid the extremes of pure subjectivism on the one hand and a reifying objectivism on the other and recognize that values are relational. 'Truth is a privileged relation *between* terms *for* at least one mind,'[1] though we can go on to argue that truth has meaning only in the context of intersubjectivity.

In Pucelle's opinion 'intersubjective relations are the source of all values'.[2] He extends this idea to cover 'the appeal of God and man's response'[3] in the Judaeo-Christian ethical tradition. He also insists that axiology has to be set within an ontology and introduces the idea of the presence of Being and of man's consent to Being. Here he seems to come close to Le Senne by seeing the ultimate foundation of values in a 'theandric' relation. For example, it is because value is a relation between Being and beings that every existence has value. And it is because the presence of Being can be sought or unknown or ignored by man that the field of one's valuational vision can be very restricted.

When the word 'Being' with a capital letter is introduced and there is talk of the presence of Being and of consent to Being, some philosophers are inclined to give up.[4] This point apart however, it might perhaps be asked whether, given Pucelle's initial interpretation of the value-judgment, it is really necessary to look for a metaphysical foundation of values. Or is it a case not so much of being compelled to look for a foundation outside the world of human persons in their relationship to one another and their environment as of fitting the recognition of values into a pre-existing religious world-outlook? One might perhaps reply that reflection on an experience of values naturally suggests a religiously metaphysical complement or framework, unless one rejects such a framework on other grounds. But we cannot prolong discussion of such issues.

The work by Pucelle from which we have quoted above is

---

[1] *Ibid.*, p. 155.
[2] *Ibid.*, p. 164. Though Pucelle begins by considering the subject-object relation in the individual, he does not intend to imply that we can make a complete distinction between private and inter-subjective consciousness.
[3] *Ibid.*, p. 165.
[4] It might be simpler to use the word 'God', if this is what is meant. Being of course sounds more metaphysical or ontological; but a religious person at any rate can more easily find meaning in talk about the presence of God and response to God than about the presence of and consent to Being. The reply might be made however that the concept of God (as personal) is a determination of the concept of Being.

dedicated to the memory of Louis Lavelle and René Le Senne, the co-founders and editors of the series *The Philosophy of Spirit*. Something has already been said about Le Senne as a philosopher of values. We can now turn briefly to a consideration of the metaphysics of Lavelle.

5. Louis Lavelle (1883–1951) was a pupil at Lyons of Arthur Hannequin (1856–1905), author of a well known thesis on the atomic hypothesis[1] in which he maintained that science knows only what it creates and in which he looked to metaphysics to overcome the agnosticism implied by this Kantian-inspired view and to reveal the nature of reality. Later Lavelle came under the influence of Hamelin's writings. Indeed, he combined in his own thought a considerable variety of influences. That of the French spiritualist tradition was prominent; but Lavelle was also open to the problems raised by existentialists, though he tried to solve them in a different manner from philosophers such as Sartre. In 1932 Lavelle was appointed to a chair of philosophy at the Sorbonne. From 1941 he was a professor at the Collège de France. He was a prolific writer.[2]

In a sense Lavelle goes back to Descartes and builds his metaphysics on the foundation of the *Cogito, ergo sum*, on consciousness of the self. Consciousness is an act, and by this act I give myself being. That is to say, the act of consciousness is the genesis of the self. It is not a question of my coming through consciousness to contemplate a self which is already there. Rather is it a question of bringing the I to birth in and through consciousness, by opposing it to the non-self. In other words, the ego grasps itself as activity, an activity which first creates itself. This may seem to be absurd. How, we may ask, can the ego bring itself into being? Lavelle however insists that we cannot distinguish between an ego which confers consciousness and an ego on whom consciousness is conferred. Being and act are identical. This identity, revealing the nature of being, is thus discovered in self-consciousness. And it follows that the proper approach to metaphysics is through subjectivity, through, that is to say, reflection on the self as activity rather than through reflection on the multiplicity of phenomena which the ego opposes to itself under the form of externality. We have to retreat inwards, so to speak, rather than outwards, when 'outwards' refers to the external world. 'Metaphysics rests on

---

[1] *Essai Critique sur l'hypothèse des atomes dans la science contemporaine* (1895).
[2] For Lavelle's works see the Bibliography.

a privileged experience which is that of the act which makes me be.'[1]

It is in the act of consciousness that I become aware of being. But I am certainly not the plenitude of being. 'Being overflows the self and at the same time sustains it.'[2] There is not and cannot be anything outside Being, whether selves or external objects. Being is the whole in which I participate. The word Being with a capital letter, taken by itself, suggests the idea of a Parmenidean One; and Lavelle's insistence in De l'être on the universal and univocal character of Being tends to support this idea. But we have seen that in De l'acte he argues that in self-consciousness I grasp being as act, which is the 'interiority' of being. Being with a capital letter therefore, the Whole from which I derive my existence and in which I participate, must be pure and infinite Act. 'Being does not exist in front of me as a motionless object which I seek to attain. It is in me by the operation which makes me give being to myself.'[3] Being is infinite Act, infinite Spirit; but it is at the same time the *immanent* cause of all finite selves, giving them the act by which they constitute themselves. As for the non-self, external reality or the world, this must ultimately be correlative to pure Act as the infinite self. But the world comes to be for me, my world arises, only in correlation with myself as active subject. To be sure, I find myself in a world, which is for me something given. Indeed, it is the condition of there being a plurality of selves. The self comes into being only in correlation with a world, to which it gives meaning in terms of its ideas, its evaluations, its activity. But to say this is to say that in giving me the act by which I came to be a self pure Act also gives me the world as a datum. In other words, the world, for Lavelle, must be correlative to an active self. There is no world which is independent of all consciousness whatsoever. It does not follow however that the world is a mere phantom. It is at the same time the condition for the plurality of finite selves, the field of their activity, and the instrument of mediation between consciousnesses, and thus the basis of human society. It is also the 'interval' between pure Act and participated act. It is by transcending the limits and obstacles posited by the world that the human person fulfils its destiny or vocation and tends to realize on the level of consciousness its oneness with infinite Act.

---

[1] *De l'acte* (*On Act*), p. 11. This work is the second volume of Lavelle's *La dialectique de l'éternel présent*, the first being *De l'être* (*On Being*).
[2] *Ibid.*, p. 59.   [3] *Ibid.*, p. 72.

Any reader who is well acquainted with German idealism is likely to be struck by the resemblances between much of what Lavelle has to say and the philosophy of Fichte. For example, Fichte's theories of the pure or absolute ego as activity, of the positing of the limited ego and non-ego, of the world as the field for and instrument of man's moral vocation and of the world as the appearance to us of absolute Being, are all present in some form in Lavelle's thought. It does not follow however that Lavelle borrowed his ideas from German idealism. It is a question of noting certain similarities rather than of asserting direct influence.

Mention has already been made of Lavelle's insistence in *De l'être* on the universal and univocal character of Being. This view is repeated in *De l'acte*. 'To say that Being is universal and univocal is to say that we all form part of the same Whole and that it is the same Whole which gives us the same being which belongs to it and outside which there is nothing.'[1] This combination of the theory of Being as univocal, whether considered in itself or in its creations, with the whole-and-part language obviously suggests a monistic pantheism. But Lavelle uses the doctrine of the univocal character of the concept of Being to support the conclusion that the Absolute is not only the source of personal existence but also itself personal, indeed a person 'which must be distinguished from all other persons'.[2] In other words, he has no intention of simply throwing theism overboard. He wishes to maintain that God, considered in himself, is not in any way diminished through creation of finite selves and the world. and he has recourse to a theory of participation. 'Participation obliges me therefore to admit that there are at the same time homogeneity and heterogeneity not only between the participant and the participated, but also between the participated and the participable.'[3] And this theory of participation is regarded as implying a distinction between Act and Being, between, that is to say, the divine Act and the totality of Being. 'The totality is the very unity of Act considered as being the unique and indivisible source of all the particular modes, which seem to be always contained eminently, and, so to speak, by way of excess, in the very impulse (*élan*) which produces them and in which all beings participate according to their power.'[4] The totality of Being, in other words, is not something achieved, accomplished, static. There is a creative process of totalization, which is the expression

[1] *Ibid.*, p. 78.   [2] *Ibid.*, p. 140.   [3] *Ibid.*, p. 72.   [4] *Ibid.*, p. 80.

of pure Act, the source and immanent cause of all finite beings but at the same time distinguishable from them.

Lavelle's philosophy is of course an example of the tendency in religiously oriented metaphysics to get away from pictorial or imaginative theism, with its concept of a God 'out there' or 'up there', without however relapsing into Spinozism or into a monism which would exclude the concept of a personal God. This tendency to a panentheism designed to avoid two extremes is perfectly understandable. But it is very difficult to state this sort of theory in any satisfactorily consistent and coherent manner. Ferdinand Alquié,[1] a redoubtable opponent of monism in all its forms and of the objectivation of Being, may be unfair in interpreting Lavelle in a monistic sense. But the latter certainly speaks of Being as the totality, even if the whole is conceived in an Hegelian rather than in a Parmenidean way. And though Lavelle tries to save the situation, from a theistic point of view, by making a distinction between pure Act and the totality of Being, regarding the former as the creative inwardness or interiority of the latter, it is obviously open to dispute whether his various assertions are in fact compatible. It can be claimed of course that language is bound to reveal its inadequacy when we try to talk about the Absolute and the relation of particulars to the Absolute. But the retort might be made that in this case silence would be the best policy. Indeed, according to Alquié Being as such remains inaccessible to us. For though it grounds all that is given in experience, it cannot itself be a datum.

6. Although in the philosophy of spirit as represented by Le Senne and Lavelle there is a strong dose of metaphysics, there is also a prominent emphasis on the idea of the destiny or vocation of the human person. Indeed Le Senne published a book with the title *La destinée personelle* and Lavelle one entitled *Le moi et son destin*. Further, Lavelle, as we have seen, starts with the act which in his view brings the human person into being. Again, it is clear that those philosophers who have been generally labelled existentialists have also been concerned with the person. Marcel, for example, talks a great deal about personal relationships, while Sartre has laid emphasis on man's creative freedom. Thomists

---

[1] Ferdinand Alquié, born in 1906, was a professor in the university of Montpellier from 1947 until 1952 and was appointed to a chair in the Sorbonne. Among his works are *La nostalgie de l'être* (1950, *The Nostalgia of Being*), *Philosophie du surréalisme* (1955, *Philosophy of Surrealism*), *Descartes, l'homme et l'oeuvre* (1956, *Descartes, the Man and his Work*) and *L'expérience* (1957, *Experience*).

too, such as Jacques Maritain, have stressed the personalist elements in their own thought. To go further back in time, Renouvier, who influenced William James, entitled his last work *Le personnalisme*. In other words, emphasis on the nature and value of the human person and on the idea of the human person as relevant to our general interpretation of reality has not been confined to any one School or group in recent French philosophy. One can find the roots of personalism in the spiritualist tradition in French philosophy; and one can connect the fairly widespread emphasis on the person in recent French thought with a shared reaction to both intellectual and social-political tendencies which appear to treat man simply as an object of scientific study or to reduce him to his function in the economic sphere or in the social-political totality. In some cases of course, as with Le Senne and Lavelle as also with such different thinkers as Marcel and Maritain, there is also a strong religious motivation. The human person is seen as oriented by nature to a super-empirical end or goal.

When however reference is made to personalism in recent French philosophy, it may be primarily to the thought of Emmanuel Mounier (1905–50), editor of *Esprit*, and of certain other writers such as Denis de Rougemont, a Swiss Protestant, and Maurice Nédoncelle, a French priest. It is in this restricted use of the term that personalism will be understood in this section. And it is therefore important to emphasize the fact that the restriction should not be interpreted as implying that the writers mentioned here are the only French philosophers who have expressed characteristically personalist ideas. The point is rather that Mounier conducted a specific campaign in support of personalism as such, whereas with other thinkers personalist ideas have often formed part, even if an important part, of a philosophy to which another label has been attached, such as philosophy of spirit or existentialism or Thomism.

Emmanuel Mounier was born at Grenoble and studied philosophy first in his home town and then at Paris. He was influenced by the writings of Charles Péguy (1873–1914), and in 1931 he published, in collaboration, a book on Péguy's thought.[1] He was also influenced by the famous Russian philosopher, Nikolai Berdyaev (1874–1948), who had settled in Paris in 1924. Mounier taught philosophy in schools for some years; and in 1932 he

[1] *La pensée de Charles Péguy* (*The Thought of Charles Péguy*).

undertook the editorship of the newly founded periodical *Esprit*, which continued publication until 1941 when it was banned by the Vichy government.[1] After the war he revived *Esprit* as an organ of personalism.

In 1935 Mounier published *Révolution personnaliste et communautaire* (*Personalist and Communal Revolution*), in 1936 a work entitled *De la propriété capitaliste à la propriété humaine* (*From Capitalist Property to Human Property*) and a personalist manifesto, *Manifesto au service du personnalisme*. In some Catholic circles his writings won him the reputation of being pretty well a Marxist. In 1946 he published an introduction to the existentialist philosophies, *Introduction aux existentialismes*,[2] and a work on character, *Traité du caractère*. Among other post-war publications we can mention *Qu'est-ce que le personalisme?* (1947, *What is Personalism?*) and *Le personnalisme* (1950, Personalism).

At the beginning of his work on the existentialist philosophies Mounier remarks that in very general terms the existentialist movement might be described as 'a reaction of the philosophy of man against the excesses of the philosophy of ideas and the philosophy of things'.[2] By the philosophy of ideas in this context he means the type of philosophizing which concentrates on abstract universal concepts and devotes itself to classification in terms of ever more comprehensive categories to such an extent that particulars are given a subordinate place and are regarded as objects of philosophical reflection only in so far as they can be subsumed under universal ideas and deprived of their singularity and, in the case of man, of freedom. This line of thought, starting in ancient Greece, is looked on as reaching its culmination in the absolute idealism of Hegel, at any rate as interpreted by Kierkegaard. The philosophy of things means the kind of philosophical thought which assimilates itself to natural science and regards man purely 'objectively', as an object among other objects in the physical universe. Mounier recognizes that rationalism on the one hand and positivism on the other have involved 'excesses'. But in his opinion the existentialist reaction, especially in its atheistic form, has also been guilty of exaggeration. In a general way personalism is for him akin to existentialism, as expressing a reaction against systems such as those of Spinoza and Hegel on

---

[1] Mounier himself was arrested in 1942 and spent some months in prison before being released. He was an active member of the Resistance.
[2] *Existentialist Philosophies*, translated by E. Blow (London, 1948), p. 2.

the one hand and positivism, materialism and beheaviourism on the other. But he also sees in existentialism 'a dual tendency to solipsism and pessimism, which separates it radically from personalism as we understand it'.[1]

Personalism, Mounier insists, is 'not a system'.[2] For its central assertion is the existence of free and creative persons, and it thus introduces 'a principle of unpredictability'[3] which resists definitive systematization. By a 'system' Mounier evidently understands a philosophy which tries to understand all events, including human actions, as necessary implications of certain first principles or as necessary effects of ultimate causes. A 'system' excludes all creative freedom in human persons. To say however that personalism is not a system is not the same thing as saying that it is not a philosophy and cannot be expressed in terms of ideas, or that it is simply an attitude of mind. There is such a thing as a personalist universe, seen from the perspective of man as a free and creative person; and there is such a thing as a personalist philosophy. More accurately, there can be different personalist philosophies. For there can be an agnostic personalism, whereas Mounier's personalism is religious and Christian. But they could not be appropriately described as personalist philosophies, unless they had some basic idea in common. This idea however is also a call to action. And Mounier himself was always a campaigner, a fighter. In the foreword to his *Traité de caractère* he states explicitly that his science is 'a fighting science'.[4] In being a campaigner Mounier resembles Bertrand Russell. But while Russell made a sharp distinction between his activity as a campaigner and his role as a professional philosopher, Mounier regarded his philosophical convictions as expressing themselves by their very nature in the sphere of action.

In its view of man the personalism of Mounier is of course opposed to materialism and the reduction of the human being simply to a complicated material object. But it is also opposed both to any form of idealism which reduces matter, including the human body, to a mere reflection of spirit or to appearance and to psycho-physical parallelism. Man is not simply a material object; but it does not follow either that he is pure spirit or that he can

---

[1] *Be Not Afraid*, translated by C. Rowland (London, 1951), p. 184. This volume contains two of Mounier's publications; and the quotation comes from the second part, which is a translation of *Qu'est-ce que le personalisme?*
[2] *Personalism*, translated by P. Mairet (London, 1952), p. vii.
[3] *Ibid.*, p. viii.   [4] *Une science combattante; Traité de caractère*, p. 7.

be neatly divided into two substances or two sets of experiences. Man is 'wholly body and wholly spirit',[1] and subjective existence and bodily existence belong to the same experience. Man's existence is embodied existence; he belongs to Nature. But he can also transcend Nature in the sense that he can progressively master it or subdue it. This mastery of Nature can of course be understood simply in terms of exploitation. But for the personalist Nature presents man with the opportunity of fulfilling his own moral and spiritual vocation and of humanizing or personalizing the world. 'The relation of the person to Nature is not purely exterior but a dialectic of exchange and of ascension.'[2]

Personalism can thus be seen as man's reassertion of himself against the tyranny of Nature, represented on the intellectual plane by materialism. And it can also be seen as a reassertion by the person of his own creative freedom against any totalitarianism which would reduce the human being to a mere cell in the social organism or would identify him with his economic function. But it by no means follows that personalism and individualism are the same thing. The individual, in the pejorative sense in which personalists are inclined to use the term, is the egocentric man, the atomistic individual in abstraction from society. The term also signifies man as devoid of a sense of moral vocation. Thus Denis de Rougemont describes the individual as 'a man without destiny, a man without vocation or reason for existing, a man from whom the world demands nothing.'[3] The individual is man centralized in himself. For Mounier this egocentricism represents a degeneration of or a falling away from the idea of the person. 'The first condition of personalism is his (man's) decentralization,'[4] that he may give himself to others and be available for them in communication or communion. The person exists only in a social relationship, as a member of the 'we'. It is only as a member of a community of persons that man has a moral vocation. De Rougemont interprets the idea of vocation in a frankly Christian manner. Person and vocation are possible 'only in their unique act of obedience to the order of God which is called the love of the neighbour ... Act, presence and commitment, these three words define the person, but also what Jesus Christ commands us to be: the neighbour.'[5] Mounier is no less Christian in his outlook.[6] But

---

[1] *Personalism*, p. 3   [2] *Ibid.*, p. 13.   [3] *Politique de la personne*, p. 56.
[4] *Personalism*, p. 19.   [5] *Politique de la personne*, pp. 52–3.
[6] See, for example, *Personnalisme et Christianisme* (*Personalism and Christianity*), reprinted in *Liberté sans conditions* (1946).

he gives a more general and 'sufficient' statement of the personalist point of view, 'that the significance of every person is such that he is irreplaceable in the position which he occupies in the world of persons'.[1] In other words, every human being has his or her vocation in life, in response to recognized values; but this vocation presupposes the world of persons and of interpersonal relations. If we prescind from the religious aspect of vocation (the response to the divine appeal), man's vocation, the exercise of his creative freedom in the realization of values, is his unique contribution, as it were, to the building-up of the world of persons and the humanization or personalization of the world.

In his personalist *Manifesto*, which appeared in *Esprit* in October 1936, Mounier, while maintaining that no strict definition of the concept of person could be given, offered the following definition or description as passing muster. 'A person is a spiritual being constituted as such by a manner of subsistence and of independence in being; it maintains this subsistence by its adhesion to a hierarchy of values, freely adopted, assimilated and lived, by a responsible self-commitment and by a constant conversion; it thus unifies all its activity in liberty and develops, moreover, by means of creative acts, its own unique vocation.' The concept of constant conversion is presumably more or less equivalent to Kierkegaard's idea of repetition and Marcel's idea of fidelity or faithfulness. As for self-commitment, Mounier regarded personalism as having implications in the social and political spheres; and it has already been noted that he looked on it not simply as an exercise in theoretical understanding but also as a call to action.

We have remarked above that personalism can be regarded as a reaction against collectivism or totalitarianism. This description is however one-sided and inadequate, as Mounier himself is not slow to point out. To be sure, personalism is opposed to the reduction of the human person to a mere cell in the social organism and to the complete subordination of man to the State. 'The State is meant for man, not man for the State.'[2] In totalitarianism the value of the person is overlooked. Indeed, the 'person' is reduced to the 'individual', even if the individual is regarded on an analogy with the cell in an organic whole. But it by no means follows that Mounier is prepared to defend bourgeois capitalist democracy. It is not simply a question of flagrant abuses which can be and to a certain extent have been overcome within the

---

[1] *Personalism*, p. 41.   [2] *Personalism*, p. 112.

capitalist system. Mounier sees the developing capitalist system
as containing within itself factors which point to and demand
the transition to socialism. It is all very well to propose idealistic
schemes according to which political authority and all constraint
would be suppressed in favour of personal relations. Anarchism
may be idealistic, but it is also unrealistic. It does not understand
that the links which bind together persons as persons must find
expression in political structures and authority. Personalism
aims at a social reorganization which will meet the requirements
of economic life as it has developed but which will at the same
time be grounded on recognition of the nature and rights of the
human person. In important respects capitalism is inhuman. But
so is totalitarianism. And anarchism is no solution. In brief,
personalism demands the rethinking of our social and political
structures with a view to the development of a personalized
socialism.

Mounier does not of course confine himself simply to generalities.
But we cannot discuss his more concrete suggestions here. It must
suffice to point out that he is well aware of attempts to exploit
personalism (the defence of the person) in the interests of 'the
narrowest form of social conservation'[1] or in the service of bourgeois democracy. He emphasizes the inadequacy of simply using
words such as 'person' and 'community'. To preserve the revolutionary edge of personalism we must also say, 'the end of western
bourgeois society, the introduction of socialist structures, the
proletarian role of initiative.'[2] At the same time Mounier is very
conscious of the tendency of all societies, political or religious, to
become closed societies or groups and so to stand in the way of
advance towards the unification of mankind which is demanded by
the nature which, despite Sartre, human beings have in common.
Moreover, although in his analysis of capitalism Mounier tends to
think in a manner similar to that of Marx, he does not of course
regard man's vocation or destiny as realizable simply in a terrestrial society, even an ideal one. His Christian faith is always there.
But he refuses to use it as an excuse for passivity or for neglect of
tasks in the social-political sphere. And if he had lived longer, he
would most probably have sympathized with attempts to develop
dialogue between Christians and Marxists on the themes of man
and humanism.

With Maurice Nédoncelle we find a much more contemplative

---

[1] *Personalism*, p. 187.   [2] *Ibid.*, p. 186.

attitude. Personalism takes the form of a phenomenology and metaphysics of the person, special attention being paid to the basic structure of human consciousness as expressed in the I–thou relationship (consciousness of the I or self is inseparable from consciousness of the other) and in its religious bearing and significance.[1] Though however Nédoncelle's view of man is in basic agreement with that of Mounier, he has expressed his hesitation in speaking of the political and social implications of personalism. He admits that in a general sense personalism has social implications. For example, any form of social organization which denies the rights of the person as person or devalues the person is to this extent incompatible with the personalist outlook. But he will not allow that personalism can legitimately be used in support of 'any party';[2] and he shows a measure of pessimism, doubtless often justified, in regard to hopes of solving social and political problems by revolution or by the hasty realization of some ideal scheme. It is wise 'not to expect too much from collective life'.[3] In Nédoncelle's view 'it is perhaps in *religious philosophy* that the repercussions of personalism are the most considerable'.[4] Obviously, his attitude differs somewhat from that of Mounier.[5]

---

[1] See especially *La réciprocité des consciences. Essai sur la nature de la personne.* (*The Reciprocity of Consciousness. An Essay on the Nature of the Person*), 1942.
[2] *Vers une philosophie de l'amour et de la personne* (*Towards a Philosophy of Love and of the Person*), 1957, p. 267.
[3] *Ibid.*, p. 266.   [4] *Ibid.*, p. 259.
[5] I do not mean to imply that Mounier was a blind optimist. He was not. But he was definitely committed in the social–political field.

CHAPTER XV

TWO RELIGIOUS THINKERS

Teilhard de Chardin — G. Marcel — Differences in outlook.

1. ONE of the more surprising phenomena of recent years has been the very widespread interest in the thought of a Jesuit priest, Pierre Teilhard de Chardin (1881–1955). The interest is surprising in the sense that though there have been distinguished Jesuit astronomers and scholars, one does not normally expect from this source a world-view of a sufficiently original and striking nature as to win attention not only from readers belonging to different Christian traditions but also from people who profess no religious beliefs in the ordinary sense of the term. It is true that Teilhard de Chardin was unable to obtain permission from his ecclesiastical superiors to publish the writings with which his name is chiefly associated. But it would be absurd to attribute his fame to the difficulties which he experienced in the matter of publication. The interest taken in the writings which have appeared after his death has been due to the content of his world-vision. This assumes an evolutionary view of the world and of man, not grudgingly or apologetically but enthusiastically, and extends this view in the form of a world-vision which is not only metaphysical but also Christological. This mingling of scientific theory with philosophical speculation and Christian themes is understandably uncongenial, if for different reasons, to a number of scientists, philosophers and theologians, especially perhaps as the whole is presented as a persuasive world-vision rather than in the form of conclusions to closely reasoned arguments. But a world-vision of this kind, which synthesizes in itself science, a metaphysics of the universe and Christian belief and is at the same time markedly optimistic, is just the sort of thing which many people have looked and hoped for and have not found elsewhere. And it has been able to appeal even to some, such as Sir Julian Huxley, who feel themselves unable to go all the way with Teilhard de Chardin. Teilhard's new-style apologetics may not fare as well when the prolonged attention of the coldly analytic reason is directed to it; but there can be no doubt of its meeting a felt need.

Teilhard de Chardin was born in the Auvergne, not far from

Clermont-Ferrand. Educated at a Jesuit school, he entered the Society of Jesus as a novice in 1898. Ordained priest in 1911, he served in the first world war in the medical corps of the French army. Interested in geology from an early age, he had developed an enthusiasm for palaeontology during a period when he was teaching in a Jesuit school in Cairo before beginning his theological studies at Ore Place near Hastings;[1] and in 1908 he published an article on the eocene strata of the region of Minieh (*L'éocène des environs de Minieh*). After the war Teilhard studied natural science at the Sorbonne, and in 1922 he successfully defended his doctorate thesis on the mammals of the Lower Eocene period in France and their strata. In 1923-4 Teilhard was a member of a palaeontological team in China. By this time he had already formed his idea of cosmogenesis, his view, that is to say of the world as a dynamic evolutionary movement in which any dualism between matter and spirit is dissolved.[2] Matter is not simply the opposite of spirit; but spirit emerges from matter, and the movement of the world is towards the further development of spirit.[3] For Teilhard man naturally came to occupy a central place in the evolutionary movement; and the profound Christian faith which he possessed from youth led him to the notion of the cosmic Christ, evolution being placed in a Christocentric setting.

In 1920 Teilhard started teaching in the Institut Catholique at Paris, and he returned there after his first visit to China. But as a result of excursions outside the field of science, such as attempts to harmonize the doctrine of original sin with his evolutionary outlook, he was asked by his religious superiors to leave Paris and to confine his writing to scientific topics. From 1926 until 1927 he was in China, and then, after a brief interlude in France, he went to Ethiopia and thence back again to China, where he continued geological and palaeontological research. Apart from visits to France, America, England, India and some other eastern countries, he remained in China until 1946. In 1926 he wrote *Le milieu divin*,[4] a religious meditation in which the Christocentric character

[1] In 1902 the French Jesuits left France for English territory, as the result of the laws passed under the anticlerical government of Combes; and Teilhard did his earlier studies as a Jesuit on the island of Jersey.
[2] Teilhard read and was influenced by Bergson. But he did not accept Bergson's idea of divergent paths of evolution. He opted for the idea of convergence.
[3] It seems that it was in about 1925 that Teilhard conveived the idea of the 'noosphere', a term which was adopted by his friend Édouard Le Roy, then a professor at the Collège de France.
[4] An English translation by Bernard Wall appeared in 1957 with the title *Le Milieu Divin. An Essay on the Interior Life.*

of his world-vision comes out clearly, while *Le phénomène humain*[1] was begun in 1938 and completed in 1940; but he was not permitted to publish his major works in the non-scientific field. Indeed, in 1947 he was told to keep off philosophy.

From 1946 until 1951 Teilhard was in Paris. In 1948 he was offered a chair at the Collège de France, as successor to the Abbé Breuil; but he was directed by his religious superiors to decline the offer. However, in 1947 he had been elected a member of the Académie des Sciences, and in 1950 he was elected a member of the Institut de France. In 1951 Teilhard left France for a visit to South Africa, after which he went to New York where he remained until his death, apart from a second visit to Africa, under the auspices of the Wenner Gren Foundation, various trips in the United States and a visit to France in 1954. He died of a heart attack on Easter Sunday, 1955. He had taken the advice of a French Jesuit friend to leave the manuscripts of his unpublished works in safe hands, and publication began in the year of his death.

The statement that Teilhard de Chardin starts with the world as represented in scientific theory and that he extends what he considers to be the scientific view of the world into the spheres of metaphysical speculation and religious belief is doubtless true; but it is a partial truth and can be misleading. For from the beginning the world presents itself to him as the totality of which we are members and as having value. We can of course ask precisely what is meant by claiming that the world has value; and it is difficult to find an answer which would satisfy an analytic philosopher. But there is no doubt that for Teilhard the world is not simply a complex system of interrelated phenomena, a system which just happens to be there, but rather the totality which has value and significance. In the first instance the world presents itself in experience as a complex of phenomena of varied types. From one point of view science breaks up the things of experience into smaller centres of energy, as in the atomic theory; but at the same time it exhibits their interrelations and shows them as unified through the transformation of energy and as constituting one complex network or system. The world thus forms not simply a collection but a totality, one whole. Further, this totality is not static but developing. For Teilhard evolution is not simply a

---

[1] This work has been published in an English translation by Bernard Wall, with an introduction by Sir Julian Huxley, under the title *The Phenomenon of Man* (London, 1959).

theory about the origin of living species, a biological theory; it is a
concept which applies to the world or universe as a whole. Natural
science obviously presupposes consciousness. For without consciousness there could be no science. But science has tended to
discount consciousness as much as possible and to concentrate
on the quantitative and measurable, so that the sphere of mind,
consciousness, spirit, appears as something over against the
material world or as an epiphenomenon. For Teilhard life and
consciousness are potentially there, in matter, from the beginning. As Leibniz saw, there is nothing which does not possess a
psychic aspect, an inner force, so to speak. The world thus appears as a totality, a whole, which is developing towards an end,
an increasing actualization of spirit. Human beings are members
of an evolving organic whole, the universe, which possesses
spiritual value and appears as a manifestation of the divine.
According to Teilhard, humanity has been spontaneously converted 'to a kind of religion of the world'.[1] And he can say that he
believes in matter or that he believes in the world, when belief
obviously means much more than belief in the existence of matter
or of the world.

Teilhard does not of course present us simply with this very
general sketchy vision of the world. He distinguishes, for example,
two components in energy, tangential energy, linking one element
or particle with others of the same degree of complexity in the
universe, and radial energy, drawing the element or particle
towards increasing complexity and 'continuity' or consciousness.' Again, he argues that if we resolve what he describes as
'the stuff of the universe' into a dust of particles, in this 'pre-vital'
stage the 'within' of things corresponded point by point with
their 'without', with their external aspect or force, so that a
mechanistic science of matter is not excluded by the view that all
elements of the universe have their internal or vital aspect. From
the outside point of view it is only with the emergence of the cell
that the biosphere or sphere of life begins. And Teilhard opts for
the hypothesis that the genesis of life on earth was a unique and,
once it had happened, unrepeatable event. In other words, it is a

[1] *Science et Christ*, p. 151. The quotation comes originally from a paper published in 1933.
[2] See *The Phenomenon of Man* (English translation), pp. 63–6, where Teilhard
offers a line of solution in regard to the problem of reconciling his view of increasing energy (especially 'radial' energy) in the universe with the laws of thermodynamics.

moment in a process of evolution which is moving towards a goal. Teilhard is of course perfectly well aware that many or most scientists would deny, or would see no reason for asserting, that the process of evolution in general, or of life in particular, is directed to any goal. But he is convinced that he can trace within the natural history of living things a movement towards the emergence of consciousness and thought. With the appearance of consciousness and thought there is born the noosphere, in embryo indeed but moving through personalization towards a hyper-personal focus of union which Teilhard calls 'Omega Point', the union of the personal and the collective on the planes of thought and love. Indications of this convergence towards Omega Point are to be seen, for example, in the increasing intellectual unification of mankind, as in science, and in the pressures which make for social unification.

A good many writers have noted the affinity between the thought of Teilhard de Chardin and the philosophy of Hegel. When Teilhard says, for example, that man is evolution becoming conscious of itself[1] and proposes the concept of the noosphere, the sphere of universal thought and knowledge which exists not as a separate entity but in and through individual consciousnesses, unifying them and forming a one-in-many, we are reminded of Hegel's doctrine of the self-development of Spirit. To be sure, Hegel himself lived before Darwin and did not regard the evolutionary hypothesis, with its idea of temporal succession, as relevant to the logical dialectic of his philosophy of Nature. As far as biological evolution is concerned, Teilhard obviously stands much closer to Bergson than to Hegel. Moreover, Teilhard thought of Hegel as expounding an *a priori* logical dialectic which was very different from his own scientifically-based concept of evolution. But this does not alter the fact that Teilhard's general idea of the developing world or universe as coming to self-consciousness in and through the human mind, of the noosphere as presupposing the biosphere and the biosphere as presupposing a stage which makes mechanistic physics a possibility bears a striking resemblance to Hegel's vision of self-actualizing Spirit. The historical contexts of the two philosophers are of course different. Hegelianism has to be seen in the context of the development of post-Kantian German idealism, a context which is evidently not that of the thought of Teilhard de Chardin. But the degree of

[1] *The Phenomenon of Man*, p. 221.

difference which we find between the two lines of thought depends
to a certain extent on our interpretation of Hegel. If we interpret
Hegel as postulating the pre-existence, so to speak, of a logical
Idea which actualizes itself with dialectical necessity in cosmic
and human history, we are likely to emphasize the difference
between Hegel's approach and that of Teilhard, with his point of
departure in empirical science. If however we believe that Hegel
has been unjustly represented as a despiser of empirical science,
and if we bear in mind the fact that for both men the process of
'cosmogenesis' is a teleological or goal-directed process, we are
likely to emphasize the resemblances between them. For if
Teilhard seriously thinks of evolution as directed towards a goal,
Omega Point, the process must presumably be in some sense the
working-out of an Idea. There is no question of course of claiming
that Teilhard borrowed the framework of his thought from Hegel.
He seems to have known little of Hegel and, in regard to what
little he did know, to have emphasized differences rather than
resemblances. But similarity can exist between the general lines
of thought of two thinkers without any borrowing having taken
place. One can perfectly well deny that X borrowed from Y and
at the same time assert the existence of similarities between their
lines of thought.

Even if however there are some similarities between the thought
of Teilhard de Chardin and the philosophy of Hegel, it is essential
to add that Teilhard is not really concerned with developing a
metaphysical system.[1] As a Christian believer he is anxious to
show that Christianity has not become too small and too dated to
be able to meet the needs of modern man's world-consciousness.
He wishes to integrate his interpretation of cosmic evolution with
his Christian beliefs or, better, to show how Christian belief is able
to subsume in itself and enrich a view of the world attained by
what he describes as 'phenomenology', a reflective interpretation
of the significance of man as appearing to himself in his experience
and science.[2] To some admirers of Teilhard the specifically
Christian themes in his thought naturally tend to appear as an
extra, the expression of a personal faith which they feel themselves

[1] Referring to Plato, Spinoza and Hegel, Teilhard says that while they developed views which compete in breadth with the perspectives opened up by belief
in the incarnation, 'none of these metaphysical systems advanced beyond the
limits of an ideology' (The Phenomenon of Man, p. 295).
[2] Obviously, Teilhard uses the term 'phenomenology' in a different sense from
that in which it was used by Husserl.

unable to share. Though however Teilhard is aware that in introducing belief in the incarnation and in the cosmic role of Christ he is going 'beyond the plane of phenomenology',[1] his Christocentricism is for him an integral feature of his total world-vision, the vision which he tries to communicate in his writings taken as a whole.

Teilhard's way of thinking was of course opposed not only to any sharp dualism between matter and mind or spirit but also to any bifurcation of reality into natural and supernatural spheres cut off from one another or so related that the supernatural is simply superimposed on the natural. And his mind was so filled with the idea of the organic unity of the developing universe, of its convergence on man and of human consciousness and knowledge of the world as the world's self-reflection in and through man as part of the totality that some of the lyrical passages in which he praised or exalted the universe gave to some readers the impression that for him the universe was itself divine and that he denied the divine transcendence. In spite however of his reverential feeling for the material world as pregnant with spirit and as evolving creatively towards a goal he insisted that the source of the whole process and the centre of unification 'must be conceived as pre-existing and transcendent'.[2] Further, as a Christian he believed that God had become incarnate in Christ, and he thought of the risen Christ as the centre and consummation of the movement towards Omega Point. He saw Christ as progressively uniting all men in love, and in the light of his Christian belief he interpreted Omega Point as the point at which, in St. Paul's words, God becomes 'all in all'.[3] For Teilhard, 'evolution has come to infuse new blood, so to speak, into the perspectives and aspirations of Christianity. In return, is not the Christian faith predestined, is it not preparing, to save and even to take the place of evolution?'[4] Evolution in the widest sense of the term becomes a process not simply of 'hominization' but also of divinization in and through the risen Christ.

This optimistic vision of the cosmic process constitutes a form of apologetics, not indeed in the old sense of apologetic arguments designed to serve as external buttresses or supports to an act of faith in revealed truths but rather in the sense that Teilhard hopes to make people *see* what he sees, the relevance of

---

[1] *The Phenomenon of Man*, p. 308, *n* 2.   [2] *Ibid.*, p. 309.
[3] 1 *Corinthians*, xv, 28.   [4] *The Phenomenon of Man*, p. 297.

Christianity to an evolutionary view of the world and the significance conferred on the process of evolution when the process is
conceived in the context of Christian belief. In a sense Teilhard's
world-vision renews the ancient idea of the 'emanation' from God
and the return to God. But with him the return does not take the
form of the individual turning his back on an alien world and
seeking an ecstatic union with the One, Plotinus's 'flight of the
alone to the Alone'. The evolutionary process is itself the process of
return, and individuals are envisaged as becoming a one-in-many
in and through Christ. Nietzsche refused to admit that man as he
existed was the peak-point of evolution and proclaimed the idea of
Superman, a higher form of man.[1] Teilhard sees man as attaining
a higher form of existence through following the lines of evolution
converging to the point at which the person, while remaining a
person, is united with all other persons in a whole which is greater
than himself. And this point turns out to be what we might
perhaps describe as the 'Christosphere'. From one point of view
the universe is seen as interiorizing itself, as taking more and more
the form of self-reflection (through man) in the noosphere. From
the point of view of Christian faith this process of cosmogenesis is
seen as a process of Christogenesis, the total Christ that is to say,
Christ in his mystical body.

It is of course easy enough to find objections against Teilhard's
world-vision. It can be objected, for example, that though the
theory of evolution is accepted by practically all scientists, it
remains an hypothesis, and that in any case the scientific hypothesis is insufficient to bear the weight of the edifice which Teilhard builds on it. Again, it can be objected that a distinction must
be made between the scientific hypothesis of evolution and the
optimistic idea of progress for which Teilhard opts and which is
clearly connected with his religious beliefs. Further, the objection
can be made that in outlining his optimistic world-vision Teilhard
devotes too little attention to the negative side, to the facts of
evil and suffering and to the possibility of shipwreck and failure.
Some have complained that Teilhard mixes up science, metaphysics and Christian faith, and that he sometimes presents
as conclusions of a scientist ideas which are due rather to free

[1] By saying this I do not intend to imply that Nietzsche believed that Superman would necessarily emerge as a product of inevitable evolution. He does indeed
talk about evolution; but it seems evident to me that the concept of Superman is
intended much more as a spur and goal to the human will than as a prediction of
something which will come to pass through an inevitable process of evolution.

metaphysical speculation or to personal religious convictions. In general it can be, and often has been objected that he presents us with vague impressions and concepts which are not clearly defined. The whole thing, it may be said, is a mixture of science, poetry and religious faith, which impresses only those who are unable or unwilling to respect ideals of preciseness of thought and clarity of language. The Teilhardian world-vision may thus appear as at best elevating and hope-inspiring poetry and at worst as a large-scale confidence-trick which tries to put across under the guise of science a world-view which has really little to do with science.

It would take an ardent disciple to claim that such objections are completely groundless. But as the expression of the outlook of a man who was both a scientist and a convinced Christian and who tried not simply to reconcile but rather to integrate what he regarded as a scientific world-view with a Christocentric faith, Teilhard's vision of reality has an indubitable sweep and grandeur which tend to make the objections appear as pedantic or irrelevant. It may be said that he was a visionary or seer who presented in broad and sometimes vague and ambiguous outlines a prophetic programme, so to speak, which others are called upon to investigate in detail, to clarify, render more precise and justify with sustained argument. There is indeed the possibility that an original world-vision will be drained of its life and power when it is submitted to this sort of treatment.[1] Hegel towers above Hegelians, Nietzsche above Nietzscheans. But Teilhard's bold extension of the concept of evolution into a profoundly religious world-view, not by way of mere additions or superimpositions but rather through a process of broadening out so as to include distinguishable dimensions in an integrated and comprehensive vision, can of course provide an inspiring programme for further reflection. Some have thought the scientific hypothesis of evolution irreconcilable with Christian orthodoxy. Others have found it reconcilable but with certain reservations. Teilhard is not really bothered with 'reconciling', except when criticism by others drives him to it. The concept of evolution is taken as the perspective

---

[1] I am not referring of course to Teilhardian scholarship. Like Aristotelian or Kantian scholarship, this can command respect, even when it is not particularly exciting. I am referring to devoted disciples who are concerned with propagating the master's views but who lack his power of vision and who 'scholastize' his theories. What they say may of course be reasonable enough; but it is apt to be much more pedestrian than the original, at any rate if the disciples are not really caught in the grip of the problems which stimulated the master's intellectual activity.

from which modern man must see the world, if he is to see it rightly. And Teilhard tries to show how this way of seeing the world broadens out, or can broaden out, to take the form of a Christocentric vision of the world and of human existence. In so doing he gives hostages to fortune, in the sense that the scientific theories on which he bases his world-vision are, from the logical point of view, revisable in principle. But it would be a mistake to think of him as claiming that religious faith is logically dependent on the truth of certain scientific hypotheses. He is concerned with showing that a marriage, so to speak, between the evolutionary view of man and Christian belief bears fruit in a general world-vision in which Christianity is seen neither as something parochial and outdated nor as despising this world and concentrating on another but as a world-affirming faith and as the religion for present and future man. It is sometimes said that the idea that science and religion are incompatible is dead. For with some exceptions Christians do not now interpret Biblical texts in a manner which produces a clash with science. But even if there is no logical incompatibility between religion and science, there can obviously be divergent mentalities or outlooks. For example, belief in God can appear not as logically incompatible with science but as superfluous and irrelevant. Teilhard, with his firm belief in the value of scientific knowledge and theory and his deep religious faith, tries to display their interrelations in one unified outlook.

2. When we turn to Gabriel Marcel, we are turning to a very different kind of thinker. Teilhard de Chardin did indeed lay great emphasis on man; but he did so in the context of the general process of cosmogenesis. His eyes were fixed on the universe, the world. Gabriel Marcel explores a different kind of world. To say that he is concerned with an inner world would be misleading. For it suggests the notion of self-concentration or introspection, whereas interpersonal relationships constitute a central datum for Marcel's reflection. Science hardly figures in his thought. Whereas Teilhard asserts enthusiastically his belief in science,[1] Marcel is much more likely to assert his belief in the value and significance of personal relationships. A comparison between Teilhard and thinkers such as Hegel, Bergson and Whitehead makes sense at any rate. But in

---

[1] It might of course be questioned whether to say 'I believe in science' is a sensible way of speaking. But Teilhard obviously means in particular that he believes firmly in the truth and the wider significance of the theory of evolution, and, in general, that he accepts the scientific view of the world as a point of departure.

the case of Marcel it would be a matter of pointing out radical differences rather than of drawing attention to similarities.[1] Further, even if Teilhard is often vague and impressionistic in his utterances, it is possible to say, in outline, 'what he holds', whereas Marcel's thought is so elusive that to ask what his 'doctrines' are would be pretty well tantamount to inviting either silence or the reply that the question should not be put, as it rests on a false assumption.

Gabriel Marcel has often been classified (by Sartre among many others) as a Catholic existentialist. But as he himself has repudiated the label, it is best abandoned.[2] It is doubtless natural enough to look for a label of some sort, but there is no general label which really fits. Marcel has sometimes been described as an empiricist. But though he certainly bases his reflections on experience and does not try to deduce a system of ideas *a priori*, the word 'empiricism' is too much associated with the reductive analysis of Hume and others for it to be anything but thoroughly misleading if applied to the thought of Marcel. Again, though Marcel certainly develops what can be described as phenomenological analyses, he is no disciple of Husserl, or indeed of anyone else. He has gone his own way and cannot be treated as a member of any definite school. He tells us however that a pupil once suggested that his philosophy was a kind of neo-Socratism. And on reflection Marcel concluded that the term might be the least inexact which could be applied, provided that his questioning or interrogating attitude was not understood as implying scepticism.[3]

Marcel was born at Paris in 1889. His father, a Catholic turned agnostic, was for a time French minister to Sweden and later director of the Bibliothèque Nationale and of the Musées Nationaux. His mother, who came of a Jewish family, died while

---

[1] One might perhaps compare some of Marcel's reflections with parts of Hegel's *Phenomenology of Spirit*. But Marcel's philosophy in general bears little resemblance to absolute idealism.

[2] There was a time when Marcel at any rate tolerated the label 'existentialist', even if he did not care for the addition of 'Christian', on the ground that people who did not regard themselves as Christians could adhere to existentialism as he understood it. Indeed, in an autobiographical essay he referred to 'my first existentialist statements' (*The Philosophy of Existence*, translated by Manya Harari, London, 1948, p. 89). However, Marcel has indeed definitely repudiated the label 'existentialist', probably largely to avoid confusion with the philosophy of Sartre. And in this case it is better not to use it.

[3] See Marcel's preface to the English translation of his *Metaphysical Journal* (translated by B. Wall, London, 1952).

he was a small child; and he was brought up by his aunt, a convert to Protestantism[1] and a woman of strong ethical convictions. When he was eight, Marcel spent a year with his father at Stockholm; and not long after his return to Paris he was sent to the Lycée Carnot. He was a brilliant pupil, but he loathed the educational system to which he was subjected and took refuge in the world of music and of the imagination. Thus he started writing plays at an early age. After his studies at the lycée he went to the Sorbonne, and in 1910 he obtained the Agrégation in philosophy. Attracted for a time by idealism, especially by the thought of Schelling, he soon turned against it. Fichte irritated him, and he mistrusted Hegel, while admiring him. For F. H. Bradley he had a profound regard; and much later he was to publish a book on Josiah Royce. But idealism did not seem to him to come to terms with concrete existence; and the first part of his *Metaphysical Journal* expresses his criticism of idealist ways of thought from a point of view which was still influenced by idealism. His experience with the French Red Cross in the first world war[2] confirmed him in his conviction of the remoteness of abstract philosophy from concrete human existence. For a few years Marcel taught philosophy in various lycées; but for most of his life he was a freelance writer, publishing philosophical works and plays and acting as a literary, dramatic and musical critic. In 1948 he received the Grand Prix de Littérature of the French Academy, in 1956 the Goethe Prize and in 1958 the Grand Prix National des Lettres. In 1949–50 Marcel gave the Gifford lectures at Aberdeen. He was elected a member of the Institut de France. He died in 1973.

If we understand by a philosophical system a philosophy which is developed by a process of deduction from a point of departure which is taken as certain, there is no such thing as Gabriel Marcel's system. He has no use for systems in this sense. What he does is to develop a series of 'concrete approaches'. These approaches are of course convergent, in the sense that they are not incompatible and that they can be regarded as contributing towards a general interpretation of human experience. But it would be a great mistake to think that Marcel regards these 'concrete approaches' as providing a series of results or conclusions or solutions to

---

[1] Marcel's aunt does not appear to have had much more belief in Protestant doctrines than his father had in Catholic ones.

[2] Marcel's state of health disqualified him from serving as a soldier. He was employed in obtaining news for families of wounded soldiers and in trying to locate the missing.

problems, which can be put together to constitute a set of proved theses. To use one of his analogies,[1] if a chemist invents a certain product, it can then, let us suppose, be bought by anyone in a shop. Once made, the product can be sold and bought without reference to the means by which it was first discovered. In this sense the result is separable from the means whereby the result was obtained. But for Marcel this is certainly not the case in philosophy. The result, if one may use the word, is inseparable from the process of research or inquiry leading to it. Inquiry must of course start somewhere, with some dis-ease or exigence or situation which gives rise to the inquiry. But a philosophical exploration is for Marcel something intensely personal; and we cannot simply separate the result from the exploration and pass it on as an impersonal truth. Communication is possible. But this is really a matter of participation in the actual process of philosophizing. And if it is objected that in this case philosophy involves a repeated starting again and that there can be no set of proved or verified results which can serve as a foundation for further reflection, Marcel's reply is 'this perpetual beginning again ... is an inevitable part of all genuinely philosophical work'.[2]

There are of course pervasive themes in Marcel's philosophizing. And we can try to indicate one or two of them. If however it is the actual process of reflection which counts, rather than results or conclusions, any attempt at summarizing Marcel's thought in a brief review of it is bound to be inadequate and unsatisfactory. When referring to someone who asked him to express the essence of his philosophy in a couple of sentences, Marcel remarked that the question was silly and could really only be answered by a shrug of the shoulders.[3] If however an historian is writing about recent French philosophy, he can hardly omit the thought of one of the best known thinkers. So he just has to reconcile himself to his remarks being inadequate.

There is however one point which should be clarified in advance. Reference has already been made to the description of Marcel as a 'Christian existentialist'. And he is well known as a devout Catholic. The conclusion may therefore be drawn that his philosophy is dependent on his Catholic faith. But it would be mistaken.

[1] The Mystery of Being. I, Reflection and Mystery, translated by G. S. Fraser, London, 1950, pp. 4 f.
[2] The Philosophy of Existence, p. 93.   [3] Reflection and Mystery, p. 2.

Marcel's *Journal Métaphysique* was published in 1927, and its entries date from the beginning of 1914 until the spring of 1923. He became a Catholic in 1929; and it is much truer to say that his conversion was part of the general development of his thought than that his philosophy was the result of his conversion. Indeed the second statement is patently false. His adherence to Catholicism has doubtless confirmed his conviction that the philosopher should pay attention to certain themes, but reflection on religious faith is a prominent feature of the first part of his *Journal.*

In 1933 Marcel published a play with the title *The Broken World* (*Le Monde cassé*). As a philosophical postscript he wrote an essay on 'the ontological mystery'[1], in which the broken world is described as the functionalized world. 'The individual tends to appear both to himself and to others as an agglomeration of functions.'[2] There are the vital functions, and there are the social functions, such as those of the consumer, the producer, the citizen, the ticket-collector, the commuter, the retired civil servant, and so on. Man is, as it were, fragmented, now a churchgoer, now a clerk, now a family man. The individual is medically overhauled from time to time, as though he were a machine; and death is written off as a total loss. This world of functionalization is, for Marcel, an empty or devitalized world; and in it 'the two processes of atomization and collectivization, far from excluding each other as a superficial logic might be led to suppose, go hand in hand and are two essentially inseparable aspects of the same process of devitalization.'[3] In such a world there is of course room for problems, technological problems for example. But there is a blindness to what Marcel describes as 'mysteries'. For they are correlative to the person; and in a broken world the person becomes the fragmented individual.

This brings us to Marcel's distinction, which he regards as very important, between problem and mystery. He admits that no clear line of demarcation can be drawn, as reflection on a mystery and the attempt to state it inevitably tend to transform it into a problem. But it would obviously be futile to use the two terms unless it were possible to give some indication of the difference in meaning. And we must try to give such an indication. Happily, Marcel supplies some examples.

---

[1] *Positions et approches concrètes du mystère ontologique,* an English translation is included in *Philosophy and Existence.*
[2] *Philosophy and Existence,* p. 1.   [3] *Reflection and Mystery,* p. 27.

A problem, in Marcel's use of the term, is a question which can be answered purely objectively, without the questioner himself being involved. Consider a problem in mathematics. I may of course be interested in the problem, perhaps intensely so. Solving it may be for me a matter of importance, as it would be, for instance, if I were tackling an examination and success was essential to my career. But in my attempt to solve the problem I hold it over against me, as it were, considering it purely objectively and leaving myself out of the picture. I am the subject, the problem the object. And I do not enter into the object. It is true of course that the solving is done by me. But it could be done in principle not only by anyone else but also by a machine. And the solution, once attained, can be handed on. The problem moves, so to speak, purely on the plane of objectivity. If it is a question of solving problems relevant to putting a man into space and bringing him back again safely, it is clear that the more the people concerned tackle the problems purely objectively and leave themselves outside, so much the better will it be for everybody.

The term 'mystery' can be misleading. It does not refer to mysteries in the sense in which theologians have used the word, namely truths revealed by God which cannot be proved by reason alone and which transcend the comprehension of the human mind. Nor does the term mean the unknowable. In the essay referred to above Marcel describes a mystery as 'a problem which encroaches upon its own data, invading them, as it were, and thereby transcending itself as a simple problem.'[1] Elsewhere, in Être et avoir, he gives the same description and adds that 'a mystery is something in which I am myself involved, and which is therefore thinkable only as a sphere where the distinction between what is in me and what is before me loses its significance and its initial validity.'[2] Suppose, for example, that I ask 'what am I?' and that I answer that I am a soul or a mind which has a body. To answer in this way is to objectify my body as something over against me, something which I can have or possess, as I might have an umbrella. It is then quite impossible to reconstitute the unity of the human person. I *am* my body. But I am obviously not identifiable with the body in the sense which the term 'body' bears when it has been distinguished from 'soul' and objectified as a

[1] *Philosophy of Existence*, p. 8.
[2] *Être et avoir*, p. 169 (*Being and Having*, translated by K. Farrer, London, 1949, p. 117).

thing which I can consider, as it were, from outside. To grasp the unity of the human person I have to return to the lived experience of unity which precedes the mental separation into two data or factors. If, in other words, I separate myself into soul and body, objectify them as data for the solution of a problem and try to link them together, I shall never be able to do so. I can grasp the unity of myself only from within. One has to try to explore on the level of second reflection 'that massive, indistinct sense of one's total existence'[1] which is presupposed by the dualism produced by primary reflection.

We have just alluded to primary and secondary reflection. The distinction can perhaps be elucidated in this way. John and Mary love one another. They think of one another, but they do not, let us suppose, think of love in an abstract way and raise problems about it. There is simply the concrete unity or communion of mutual loving in which both John and Mary are involved. Let us then suppose that John stands back, as it were, from the actual experience or activity of loving, objectifies it as an object or phenomenon before him and asks, 'what is love?'. Perhaps he tries to analyse love into constituent elements; or he interprets it as something else, in terms, for instance, of the will to power. This analytic process is an example of first reflection, and love is considered as setting a problem to be solved, the problem of the nature of love, which is solved by means of reductive analysis of some kind. Let us further suppose that John comes to see the remoteness of this analysis from the actual experience of loving or from love as a lived communion between persons. He returns to the actual togetherness of love, the communion or unity which was presupposed by primary reflection, and he tries to grasp it in reflection but as from within, as a lived personal relationship. This is an example of second reflection.

Bradley, it may be remembered, postulated an original experience of the unity of reality, of the One, on the level of feeling or immediacy, a unity which analytic reflection breaks up or fragments but which metaphysics tries to restore, to recapture on the level of thought. Marcel is not of course an absolute idealist; but the project of grasping in reflection what is first present in feeling, on the level of immediacy, and is then distorted or broken up by analytic thought is a basic feature of his philosophy as it is of Bradley's. For example, my relation to my body, a relation

---

[1] *Reflection and Mystery*, p. 93.

which is *sui generis* and irreducible, is experienced on the level of 'feeling'. On the level of first reflection the unity of this feeling-experience is broken up by analytic thought. That which is in itself irreducible is subjected to reductive analysis and thus distorted. It by no means follows that first reflection is devoid of value. It can serve practical ends.[1] But in order to grasp the *sui generis* relation between myself and my body it is necessary to return to the original feeling-experience at the level of second reflection.

The general idea of recuperating a lost unity at a higher level is understandable. It is rather like the idea of recovering a primitive innocence at a higher level which presupposes its loss and recovery.[2] Implementation of the project however presents some difficulty. For it may well appear that reflection or mediation cannot be combined with immediacy, but that the latter is necessarily transformed by the former. In other words, is not second reflection a dream? John, it may be said, is either involved in the immediacy of loving or committed to playing the part of a spectator and objectifying love as an object of reflection. He cannot combine the two at a higher level, however much he may dream of doing so.

Marcel is aware of the difficulty. He admits that second reflection can easily degenerate into first reflection. At the same time he envisages second reflection as an exploration of the metaphysical significance of experience. For example, he sees love as an act of transcendence on the part of the human person and as a participation in Being. And he asks, what does this experience reveal to me of myself as a human person and of Being? Marcel's use of the term 'Being' is somewhat perplexing. He insists that Being is not and cannot be made into an object, a direct object of intuition for instance. It can only be alluded to indirectly. However, it is clear that he sees in personal relationships such as love and in experiences such as hope keys to the nature of reality which are not available on the level of objectifying scientific thought. John loves Mary, but Mary has died, and science offers no assurance of her continued existence or of her reunion with

---

[1] Bradley recognized of course that science was not possible without analytic thought, though he regarded science as manifesting a drive towards unification which could not fully attain its goal on the level of science.

[2] We can note that at the end of *Être et avoir* Marcel includes an essay on Peter Wust (1884–1940), the German philosopher who wrote about the second 'naïvety' or piety which is a recuperation of the first religious faith subsequent to the work of the critical intelligence.

John.[1] For love and hope in union however there remains a communion, a 'we', which enables John to transcend the level of empirical evidence and to be confident in Mary's continued existence and of their future reunion. From the point of view of common sense this act of transcendence is simply an instance of wishful thinking. For Marcel it is grounded in a mysterious presence which is a participation in Being. On the level of first reflection an object cannot be described as present to me, unless it is locatable, according to specifiable criteria, in space and time. On the level of intersubjectivity and personal communion another person can be present to me, even after his or her bodily death, as a 'thou'. The bond is broken on the physical plane. But on the metaphysical plane it persists for 'creative fidelity', which is 'the active perpetuation of presence'.[2]

It hardly needs saying that Marcel is not prepared to regard God as an object, the existence of which is asserted as a conclusion that solves a problem. Faith is a matter not of believing *that* but of believing *in*; and God is for Marcel, as for Kierkegaard,[3] the absolute thou.[4] He is thus encountered rather than proved. The human being, according to Marcel, has an exigence of Being, which in religious language is an orientation to the absolute Thou. But there are various ways in which the orientation to God can be appropriated. That is to say, there are various concrete approaches to God. God is 'absolute presence', and he can be approached through the intersubjective relationships, such as love and creative fidelity, which are sustained by and point to him. Or a man can encounter God in worship and prayer, in invocation and response. The various ways are not of course mutually exclusive. They are ways of coming to experience the divine presence. But man can shut his eyes to this presence. In discussing personal relationships Marcel makes much of the concept of availability (*disponibilité*). If I am available to another, I thereby transcend my egoism; and

---

[1] It should be added perhaps that Marcel has had a continuing interest in meta-psychical experiences; but his metaphysic of hope does not rest on parapsychology. For a definition of hope see the end of Marcel's essay on a metaphysic of hope, which is included in *Homo Viator* (translated by E. Craufurd, London, 1951).
[2] *The Philosophy of Existence*, p. 22.
[3] Marcel's ideas on this subject were formed before he read Kierkegaard. On reading him he recognized of course certain points of similarity. We can also draw attention to the affinity between Marcel and Martin Buber, in regard to the I–Thou relationship.
[4] In his *Metaphysical Journal* (p. 281) Marcel raises the question, how is it possible to conceive a *thou* which is not also a *he* (in the sense of an object)?

the other is present to me on the plane of intersubjectivity. If I am not available for or open to a person, I shut the person out, so to speak, and he or she is not present to me except perhaps in a purely physical sense. It is also possible for me to shut out God and deny him, refusing invocation. This is, for Marcel, an option, an act of the will.

For some readers Marcel is undoubtedly a disconcerting writer. When looked at under certain aspects his thought gives the impression of being thoroughly realistic and down to earth. For example, with him there is no question of starting with a self-enclosed ego and then trying to prove the existence of an external world and of other people. Man is essentially 'incarnate', embodied, in the world. He finds himself in a situation, in the world; and his self-consciousness grows correlatively to his awareness of others. But for many readers Marcel becomes progressively elusive. We find him taking familiar terms, such as 'have', 'presence', 'love', 'hope', 'testimony', and proceeding to inquire into their meaning. And we are prepared, if not for exercises in linguistic analysis, at any rate for phenomenological analyses. The analyses however open up into what seems to be a peculiarly elusive form of metaphysics, in regard to which we may be left wondering not only whether we have really grasped what has been said but also whether in fact anything intelligible has been said. And it is understandable if some readers are tempted to regard Marcel's philosophizing as a kind of poetry or as highly personal meditations, rather than as public-property philosophy.

That Marcel's thought is elusive and also highly personal can hardly be denied. His own value-judgments reveal themselves clearly enough. It is important however to realize that he is not trying to explore what transcends all human experience. He is concerned throughout with human experience. What he tries to do is to reveal or to draw attention to the metaphysical significance hidden in the familiar, to the pointers to eternity which are present, as he sees it, in the personal relationships to which he attaches great positive value and to an all-pervading and unifying presence. His philosophy centres round personal relationships and the relationship to God. This doubtless tells us a good deal about Marcel. But if his philosophizing has no further significance for us than an indication of what he himself most values in life, he might comment that our outlook has obviously been so conditioned by this 'broken world' that we are unable, or at least find it extremely difficult, to discern the metaphysical dimensions of experience. Heidegger has written about Hölderlin. Marcel has written about Rilke as a witness to the spiritual.[1] He is aware of course of Rilke's increasing opposition to Christianity and refers to it. But he sees the poet as open to and perceptive of dimensions of our being and world which are hidden from many eyes. And we can look on Marcel's essays in 'second reflection' as attempts to facilitate our perception of these dimensions.

3. Teilhard de Chardin and Gabriel Marcel are both Christian thinkers. But there are obvious differences between them. Teilhard's attention is focussed on the evolving universe. Nothing is for him completely lifeless. Matter is pregnant with life and with spirit, the spirit which comes to birth in man and which develops towards a hyper-personal consciousness. The whole process is teleological, oriented to Omega Point when the world reaches its fulfilment in the union of all men in the cosmic Christ. Modern science and our modern technological civilization are preparing the way for a higher consciousness in which man as we know him will be surpassed. In brief, Teilhard's world-vision is thoroughly optimistic. With Gabriel Marcel however we hear little about the universe in Teilhard's sense of the word. To be sure, Marcel insists, like Teilhard, on man's situation as a being in the world. But it is not the material changing world on which he focusses his intention. When speaking of man as a traveller, he remarks that anything connected with evolution must be eliminated from the discussion.[2] Evolution, that is to say, is quite irrelevant to his 'second reflection', and to his exploration of 'mysteries'. The act of transcendence is for him an entering into communion with other people and with God, not the movement from the biosphere to the noosphere and so to Omega Point. Attention is directed, to speak paradoxically, to the beyond within, to the revelatory significance and metaphysical dimensions of the relationships which are possible for actual persons at any time. Marcel shows a great sensitivity to uniting relations between human beings; but we can hardly imagine him hymning the world or the universe in the way that Teilhard did. And while some readers of Teilhard have found difficulty in distinguishing between the world and God, such an impression would scarcely be possible in the case of Marcel, for whom God is the absolute Thou. Moreover, though it

---

[1] The two lectures on Rilke are included in *Homo Viator*.
[2] *Homo Viator*, p. 7.

would be wrong to describe Marcel as a pessimist, he is very conscious of the precariousness of what he values and of the ease with which depersonalization can take place. To regard the other person as an object and to treat him as such is common enough both in private relationships and in wider social contexts. For Marcel our world is 'essentially broken';[1] and he seems to see in our modern civilization an increasing depersonalization. In any case the idea that the world is inevitably proceeding from good to better is certainly not his. In 1947 he discussed with Teilhard the question, to what degree does the material organization of humanity lead man to spiritual maturity? While Teilhard of course maintained an optimistic view, Marcel was sceptical. He saw in collectivization and in our technological society a Promethean spirit expressing itself in a refusal of God. Marcel believes indeed in the eschatological triumph of goodness; and he admits that an optimistic view can be maintained on religious grounds, in the light of faith, that is to say. But for him invocation and refusal have always been two possibilities for men and always will be. And the dogma of progress is 'a completely arbitrary postulate'.[2] In other words, while Teilhard can reasonably be regarded as trying to capture the Hegelian and Marxist views of history for Christianity (or to interpret Christianity in such a way as to assimilate and transcend them), Marcel will have nothing to do with a point of view which, in his opinion, obscures human freedom, is oblivious, in theological language, of the effects of the Fall, and fails to take real account of evil and suffering.

The differences in outlook between the two men should not of course be exaggerated. For example, Marcel's position does not entail rejection of the scientific hypothesis of evolution, an hypothesis which stands or falls according to the strength or weakness of the empirical evidence. He regards the scientific theory as irrelevant to philosophy as he conceives it; and what he objects to is the inflation of a scientific hypothesis into a metaphysical world-view which incorporates a doctrine of progress which he regards as unwarranted. Again, there is no question of suggesting that Teilhard attached no value to those personal relationships in which Marcel sees the expression of genuine human personality. In his private life he set great store by such relationships; and in a real sense the movement of cosmogenesis was for him a movement from exteriority to interiority, to the full actualization of spirit.

---

[1] *Reflection and Mystery*, p. 34.   [2] *Faith and Reality*, p. 183.

At the same time the perspectives of the two men are clearly different, despite their common religious allegiance. And they appeal to different types of mind. One can see this in their respective attitudes to notable thinkers such as Marx and Bergson. Neither Teilhard nor Marcel is a Marxist; but their respective evaluations of Marxism are understandably different. As for Bergson, it is natural to think of Teilhard as continuing his general line of thought. Though however Marcel pays tribute to Bergson's distinction between the 'closed' and the 'open', he then gives to the idea of 'openness' an application which fits in with his own perspective and interests. If we mentally associate Teilhard with Bergson, we associate Marcel with thinkers such as Kierkegaard and Jaspers, though Marcel did not derive his ideas from the former and though he had considerable reservations in regard to the latter's philosophy. What unites Teilhard and Marcel is their Christian faith and their regard for man. But whereas Teilhard takes an optimistic view of man's future,[1] seeing it in the light of his philosophy of evolution, Marcel is much more conscious, as Pascal was, of ambiguity, fragility and precariousness.

[1] Teilhard was prepared to say that he had no intention of stating dogmatically that the future *must* be rosy. At the same time he obviously came down decisively on the side of optimism.

CHAPTER XVI

THE EXISTENTIALISM OF SARTRE (1)

Life and writings — Pre-reflexive and reflexive consciousness: the imagining and the emotive consciousness — Phenomenal being and being in itself — Being for itself — The freedom of being for itself—Awareness of others—Atheism and values.

1. IN his popular lecture *Existentialism and Humanism* Sartre informs his audience that there are two kinds of existentialists, Christian and atheist. As representatives of Christian existentialism he mentions 'Jaspers and Gabriel Marcel, of the Catholic confession',[1] while as representatives of atheist existentialism he mentions Heidegger and himself. In point of fact Karl Jaspers was not a Catholic and, moreover, came to prefer a descriptive label for his philosophy other than 'philosophy of existence' (*Existenzphilosophie*). Gabriel Marcel is indeed a Catholic; but, as we have noted, he eventually repudiated the label 'existentialist'. As for Heidegger, he has explicitly dissociated himself from Sartre; and, though he is certainly not a Christian, he does not like being described as an atheist. Though therefore books on existentialism generally include treatments of all the philosophers named by Sartre, and often of others as well, as far as definite acceptance of the label 'existentialist' is concerned we seem to be left with Sartre, who has described himself in this way and has expounded what he considers to be the essential tenet of existentialism.

It may thus appear somewhat disconcerting when we find Sartre telling us in recent years that Marxism is the one living philosophy of our time. It does not follow however that Sartre has definitely turned his back on existentialism and adopted Marxism instead. As will be explained in the next chapter, he looks for a fusion of the two, a rejuvenation of ossified Marxism through an injection of existentialism. The present chapter will be devoted to an exposition of Sartrian existentialism as such, as developed in *Being and Nothingness* and other writings before he turned his hand to the task of a systematic fusion of existentialism and Marxism.

[1] *L'existentialisme est un humanisme*, p. 17 (Paris, 1946). English translation by P. Mairet, *Existentialism and Humanism*, p. 26 (London, 1948).

There are fashions in the world of philosophy as elsewhere; and the vogue of existentialism has declined. Further, as Sartre has published a considerable number of novels and plays which have made his name well known by many people who would be disinclined to tackle his philosophical works, there is a not unnatural tendency to regard him as a literary figure rather than as a serious philosopher. Indeed, it has sometimes been said, though unfairly, that he derives all his philosophical ideas from other thinkers, especially German ones. And his long-standing flirtation with Marxism, culminating in his attempt to combine it with existentialism, has perhaps encouraged this impression. But while Sartre as a philosopher may have been overvalued by his fervent admirers in the past, he can also be undervalued. The fact that he is a novelist, a dramatist and a campaigner for social and political causes does not entail the conclusion that he is not an able and serious thinker. He may have written in Parisian cafés; but he is an extremely intelligent man, and his philosophy is certainly not without significance, even if it is no longer as fashionable in France as it once was. We are concerned here with Sartre as a philosopher, not as a dramatist or novelist.

Jean-Paul Sartre was born at Paris in 1905.[1] His higher studies were done at the École Normale from 1924 until 1928. After obtaining the *agrégation* in philosophy he taught philosophy at lycées in Le Havre, Laon and then Paris. From 1933 until 1935 he was a research student first at Berlin and then at the University of Freiburg, after which he taught in the Lycée Condorcet at Paris. In 1939 he joined the French army and was captured in 1940. Released in 1941, he returned to teaching philosophy and was also an active participant in the Resistance movement. Sartre has never occupied a University chair.

Sartre started writing before the war. In 1936 he published an essay on the ego or self[2] and a work on the imagination, *L'imagination. Étude critique*,[3] while in 1938 he published his famous novel *La nausée*.[4] In 1939 there appeared a work on the emotions,

---

[1] Sartre's reminiscences of his childhood, *Les mots*, appeared in 1964. There is an English translation, *Words*, by I. Clephane (London, 1965). Simone de Beauvoir's memoirs contain other biographical material.

[2] *La transcendance de l'égo: esquisse d'une description phénoménologique*, translated into English by F. Williams and R. Kirkpatrick as *The Transcendence of the Ego* (New York, 1957).

[3] There is an English translation by F. Williams, *Imagination: A Psychological Critique* (Ann Arbor, Michigan, 1962).

[4] Translated by Robert Baldick as *Nausea* (Harmondsworth, 1965).

Esquisse d'une théorie des émotions[1] and several stories under the title *Le Mur*.[2] During the war, in 1940, Sartre published a second book on the imagination, *L'imaginaire: psychologie phénoménologique de l'imagination*,[3] and his main philosophical tome, *L'être et le néant: essai d'une ontologie phénoménologique* appeared in 1943.[4] His play *Les mouches*[5] was performed in the same year. The first two volumes of the novel *Les chemins de la liberté* appeared in 1945,[6] and also the well known play *Huis clos*.[7] Two other plays appeared in 1946, the year of publication of the lecture to which reference has been made above[8] and also of *Réflexions sur la question juive*.[9]

In subsequent years Sartre has published a considerable number of plays, while collections of essays under the title *Situations* have appeared in 1947, 1948, 1949 and 1964.[10] Sartre was one of the founders in 1945 of the review *Les temps modernes*, and some of his writings have appeared in it, such as the 1952 articles on Communism. His attempt to combine existentialism and Marxism has led to the production in 1960 of the first volume of the *Critique de la raison dialectique*.[11] Sartre has also published an introduction to the works of Jean Genet, *Saint Genet: comédien et martyr*.[12]

2. In one of his essays Sartre remarks that for three centuries Frenchmen have been living by 'Cartesian freedom', with, that is to say, a Cartesian intellectualist idea of the nature of freedom.[13]

---

[1] There are two English translations, one by P. Mairet under the title *Sketch for a Theory of Emotions* (London, 1962).

[2] An English translation by Lloyd Alexander, *Intimacy*, is available in paperback in Panther Books. It appeared originally at London in 1949.

[3] *The Psychology of the Imagination*, translated by B. Frechtman (London, 1949).

[4] *Being and Nothingness*, translated by H. Barnes (New York, 1956; London, 1957).

[5] *The Flies*, translated by S. Gilbert, is contained in *Two Plays* (London, 1946).

[6] The first two volumes, *L'âge de la raison* and *Le sursis*, have been translated by E. Sutton as *The Age of Reason* and *The Reprieve* (London, 1947). The third volume, *La mort dans l'âme* (1949) has been translated by G. Hopkins as *Iron in the Soul* (London, 1950).

[7] Translated by S. Gilbert as *In Camera* and included in *Two Plays* (London, 1946).

[8] See note 1.

[9] There are two translations, one by E. de Mauny, *Portrait of an Anti-Semite* (London, 1948).

[10] Some of these essays have been translated by A. Michelson as *Literary and Philosophical Essays* (London, 1955).

[11] The first section of this volume has been translated by H. Barnes as *Search for a Method* (New York, 1963; London, 1964).

[12] Translated by B. Frechtman as *Saint Genet* (New York, 1963).

[13] *Literary and Philosophical Essays*, p. 169.

However this may be, it is hardly an exaggeration to say that the shadow of Descartes lies across French philosophy, not of course in the sense that all French philosophers are Cartesians but in the sense that in many cases personal philosophizing begins through a process of reflection in which positions are adopted for or against the ideas of the foremost French philosopher. We can see this sort of influence at work in the case of Sartre. But he has also been strongly influenced by Hegel, Husserl and Heidegger. Here again he is no more a disciple of any German philosopher than he is of Descartes or his successors. The influence of Heidegger, for example, is shown clearly enough in *Being and Nothingness*, even if the German philosopher is often criticized by Sartre and has himself repudiated association with Sartrian existentialism. From an academic point of view[1] Sartre's thought has developed partly though reflection on the methods and ideas of Descartes, Hegel, Husserl and Heidegger, whereas British empiricism hardly enters his field of vision,[2] and materialism, in its non-Marxist forms at any rate, is not a philosophy for which he seems to have much use.

The influence of the background formed by Cartesianism and phenomenology shows itself not only in Sartre's essay of 1936 on the ego but also in his works on imagination and emotion and in the attention given to consciousness in the introduction to *Being and Nothingness*. At the same time Sartre makes clear the differences between his position and those of Descartes and Husserl. For Sartre the basic datum is what he calls the pre-reflexive consciousness, awareness, for example, of this table, this book or that tree. What Descartes starts with however in his *Cogito, ergo sum* is not the pre-reflexive but the reflexive consciousness, which expresses an act whereby the self is constituted as object. He thus involves himself in the problem of passing from the self-enclosed ego, as object of consciousness, to a warranted assertion of the existence of external objects and of other persons. This problem does not arise if we go behind the reflexive consciousness to the pre-reflexive consciousness, which is 'transcendent', in the sense that it posits its object as transcending itself, as that

---

[1] As distinct, that is to say, from his own experience of and reflections on life and the world.

[2] In *Being and Nothingness* there is some discussion of Berkeley's *esse est percipi*, and Hume is mentioned twice. The philosophers whose names appear most frequently are Descartes, Hegel, Heidegger, Husserl, Kant and Spinoza. In *L'imaginaire* Sartre does however quote from Hume on ideas as images, but only to dismiss his theory as illusion. See *L'imaginaire*, p. 17 (English translation, pp. 12–13).

towards which it reaches.[1] 'All consciousness, as Husserl has shown, is consciousness *of* something. This means that there is no consciousness which is not the *positing* of a transcendent object, or, if one prefers, that consciousness has no "content".'[2] Suppose, for example, that I am aware of this table. The table is not *in* my consciousness as a content. It is in space, near a window or near the door or wherever it may be. And when I 'intend' it, I posit it as transcending, and not as immanent in consciousness. In this case of course Husserl's policy of bracketing existence, of treating all the objects of consciousness as purely immanent and suspending judgment, as a matter of principle, about their objective reference, is misguided. As far as perception is concerned, the object of consciousness is posited as transcendent and as existent. When I perceive this table, the table itself, and not a mental representation of it, is the object of the intentional act; and it is posited as existing. Sartre therefore follows Heidegger in rejecting Husserl's claim that the bracketing of existence is essential to phenomenology.[3]

Sartre is not of course claiming that we never make mistakes about the nature of the object. Suppose, for example, that in the twilight I think that I see a man in the wood, and that it turns out to be the stump of a tree. I have obviously made a mistake. But the mistake does not consist in my having confused a real thing, namely the stump of a tree, with a mental content, the representation of a man, which was the object of consciousness. I perceived an object, positing it as transcendent; but I misread or misinterpreted its nature. That is to say, I made an erroneous judgment about a real object.

What then of images and imagination? Imagination, as a form of consciousness, is intentional. It has its own characteristics. 'Every consciousness posits its object, but each does so in its own way.[4] Perception posits its object as existent; but the imagining consciousness, which manifests the mind's freedom, can do so in several ways. For example, it can posit its object as non-existent.

---

[1] In this context words such as 'transcendence' and 'transcend' should obviously not be understood as referring to what transcends the world or the limits of human experience. To say that consciousness is transcendent is to say that it is not confined to purely immanent objects, subjective ideas or images or copies of external things.

[2] *L'être et le néant*, p. 17 (English translation, p. 11).

[3] Husserl's approach led him eventually into the development of an idealist philosophy.

[4] *L'imaginaire*, p. 24 (English translation, p. 20).

Sartre is more concerned however with arguing that just as perception intends an object posited as transcendent and not a mental content which stands in place of the extramental object, so does the imagining consciousness intend an object other than the image as image. One can of course reflect on the first-order imagining consciousness and say, whether felicitously or not, 'I have an image'. But in the first-order imagining consciousness itself the image is not the intended object but a relation between consciousness and its object. What Sartre means is seen most easily in a case such as my imagining Peter as present, when Peter is a real but absent friend. The object of consciousness is Peter himself, the real Peter; but I imagine him as present, the image or picture being simply a way in which I relate myself to Peter or make him present to me. Reflection of course can distinguish between image and reality; but the actual first-order imagining consciousness intends or has as its object Peter himself. It is 'the imaginative consciousness of Peter.'[1] It may be objected that though this line of interpretation holds good in cases such as the one just mentioned, it is hardly applicable to cases in which the imagining consciousness freely creates an unreal anti-world, as Sartre puts it, of phantom objects, which represents an escape from the real world, a negation of it.[2] In such cases does not consciousness intend the image or images? For Sartre at any rate it is the reflexive consciousness which, through reflection, constitutes the image as such. For the actual imagining consciousness the image is the way in which consciousness posits an unreal object as non-existing. It does not posit the image as an image (this is what reflection does); it posits unreal objects. Sartre is prepared to say that this unreal 'world' exists 'as unreal, as inactive';[3] but that which is posited as non-existent obviously 'exists' only as posited. If we consider a work of fiction, we can see that its unreal world 'exists' only through and in the act of positing; but in first-order consciousness attention is directed to this world, to the saying and doings of imagined persons, not to images as images, as, that is to say, psychical entities in the mind.[4]

---

[1] *Ibid.*, p. 17 (English, p. 14).

[2] For Sartre negation is involved in imagination. When, for instance, I imagine the absent Peter as present, I do not deny that he is absent (for I posit him as real but absent); but I try to overcome or negate the absence by imagining him as present.

[3] *L'imaginaire*, p. 180 (English, p. 157). Elsewhere (p. 17, *n* 1; English, p. 15, *n* 1), Sartre remarks that the chimera exists neither as an image nor otherwise.

[4] In *L'imaginaire* Sartre writes at some length about the pathology of the imagination and about dreams. But we cannot pursue these themes here.

In his book on the emotions Sartre insists on the intentionality of the emotive or emotional consciousness. 'Emotional consciousness is at first consciousness *of* the world.'[1] Like the imagining consciousness, it has its own characteristics. For example, the emotive way of apprehending the world is 'a transformation of the world',[2] the substitution, though not of course an effective substitution, of a magical world for the world of deterministic causality. But it is always intentional. A man who is afraid is afraid *of* something or someone. Other people may think that there is no real objective ground for his fear. And the man himself may say in subsequent reflection, 'there was nothing to be afraid of after all.' But if he genuinely felt fear, his first-order emotive or affective consciousness certainly intended something or someone, even if vaguely conceived. 'Emotion is a certain way of apprehending the world';[3] and the fact that one may clothe objects or persons with qualities which they do not possess or read a malign significance into a person's expression or words or actions does not alter this fact. The projection of emotive significance on a thing or person clearly involves intending the thing or person as object of consciousness. In *L'imaginaire* Sartre repeats the same basic point. To feel hate towards Paul is 'the consciousness *of* Paul as hateful';[4] it is not consciousness of hatred, which pertains to the reflexive consciousness. The theme of emotion is also pursued in several sections of *Being and Nothingness*.

We have seen that Sartre insists on the distinction between the pre-reflexive and the reflexive consciousness. To love Peter, for example, is not the same act as to think of myself as loving Peter. In the first case Peter himself is the intentional object, whereas in the second case myself-loving-Peter is the intentional object. The question arises therefore whether or not Sartre confines self-consciousness to the level of reflection, so that first-order or pre-reflexive consciousness is regarded as unaccompanied by self-consciousness. To answer this question we can turn to the 1936 essay on the transcendence of the ego.

In this essay Sartre asserts that 'the mode of existence of consciousness is to be conscious of itself'.[5] And if we take this statement by itself, it may seem to follow that self-consciousness

---

[1] *Esquisse d'une théorie des emotions*, p. 29 (Frechtman's translation, p. 51).
[2] *Ibid.*, p. 33 (English, p. 58).   [3] *Ibid.*, p. 30 (English, p. 52).
[4] *L'imaginaire*, p. 93 (English, p. 82).
[5] *The Transcendence of the Ego*, p. 40.

belongs to the pre-reflexive consciousness. But Sartre adds immediately that consciousness is consciousness of itself insofar as it is consciousness of a transcendent object. In the case of pre-reflexive consciousness this means that consciousness of, say, a table is indeed inseparably accompanied by consciousness of itself (it is and must be, so to speak, conscious consciousness); but the 'self-consciousness' which is an essential feature of pre-reflexive consciousness is, in Sartre's jargon, non-positional or non-thetic in regard to the ego. An example may clarify the matter. Let us suppose that I am absorbed in contemplating a particularly splendid sunset. Consciousness is directed wholly to the intentional object; there is no place in this consciousness for the ego. In the ordinary sense of the term therefore there is no self-consciousness, inasmuch as the ego is not posited as an object. Only the sunset is posited as an object. The positing of the ego arises on the level of reflection. When I turn consciousness of the sunset into an intentional object, the ego is posited. That is to say, the 'me' arises as an object for (reflexive) consciousness.

For phenomenology therefore the basic datum for Sartre is the pre-reflexive consciousness, in which the ego of reflexive consciousness does not appear. But we cannot of course think or talk about pre-reflexive consciousness without objectifying it, turning it into an intentional obect. And in this reflexive consciousness the ego and the world are posited as correlative to one another. The ego is the 'me', posited as the unity to which all my states of consciousness, experience and actions are ascribed, and posited also as the subject of consciousness, as in 'myself imagining Peter' or 'myself loving Mary'. The world is posited as the ideal unity of all objects of consciousness. Husserl's transcendental ego is excluded or suppressed; and Sartre thinks that in this way he can avoid following Husserl into idealism.[1] His line of thought also enables him to avoid Descartes's problem of proving the existence of the external world. For reflexive consciousness the ego and the world arise in correlation, as the subject in relation to its transcendent object. To isolate the subject and treat it as though it were a datum given in isolation is a mistake. We have

---

[1] Sartre distinguishes between the 'I' and the 'me' as two aspects or functions of the ego. But in *The Transcendence of the Ego* he represents the ego and the world as objects of 'absolute consciousness' which, according to him, is impersonal and without a subject. It is rather as though one adopted Fichte's theory of the constitution of the limited or finite subject and its object while omitting the transcendental ego.

not got to infer the world from the self, nor the self from the world: they arise together in correlation.

All this may seem very remote from anything that we ordinarily associate with existentialism. But it provides Sartre with a realist basis, the self in relation to its transcendent object. Further, though the self is not created by its object, any more than the object is created by the self (for they are posited together in correlation), the self is derivative, appearing only for reflexive consciousness, for consciousness, that is to say, which reflects on pre-reflexive consciousness. The self emerges or is made to appear from the background of first-order consciousness, as one pole of consciousness. The way thus lies open for Sartre's analysis of the self as derivative and fugitive. Further, as the ego is posited as the point of unity and the source of all one's experiences, states and actions, it is possible for man to try to conceal from himself the boundless freedom or spontaneity of consciousness and to take refuge in the idea of a stable self which ensures regular patterns of conduct. Afraid of boundless freedom, man can attempt to avoid his responsibility by attributing his actions to the determining causality of the past as precipitated, so to speak, in the self or ego. He is then in 'bad faith', a theme on which Sartre likes to dwell.

These ideas however are best considered in the context of Sartre's analysis of the self-conscious subject and of Being in *Being and Nothingness*. The analysis is indeed involved. But given the fact that Sartre is well known as a dramatist and novelist, it is desirable to make it clear that he is a serious and systematic philosopher and not simply a dilettante. He is not of course the creator of a system such as that of Spinoza, a system formed on a mathematical model. At the same time his existentialist philosophy can be seen as the systematic development of certain basic ideas. It is certainly not a mere juxtaposition of impressionistic views.

3. Consciousness, as we have seen, is for Sartre consciousness *of* something, something other than itself and in this sense transcendent. The transcendent object appears to or for consciousness, and it can thus be described as a phenomenon. It would however be a mistake to interpret this description as meaning that the phenomenal object is the appearance of an underlying reality or essence which does not appear. The table of which I am now aware as I sit before it is not the appearance of a hidden noumenon or of a

reality distinct from itself. 'The phenomenal being manifests itself, it manifests its essence as well as its existence.'[1] At the same time the table is obviously more than what appears to me here and now in a given act of awareness or consciousness. If there is no hidden and non-appearing reality of which the phenomenal table is the appearance, and if at the same time the table cannot be simply equated with one individual appearance or manifestation, it must be identified with the series of its manifestations. But we can assign no finite number to the series of possible appearances. In other words, even if we reject the dualism between appearance and reality and identify a thing with the totality of its appearances, we cannot simply say with Berkeley that to be is to be perceived. 'The being of that which *appears* does not exist *only* in so far as it appears.'[2] It surpasses the knowledge which we have of it and is thus transphenomenal. And according to Sartre the way thus lies open for inquiry into the transphenomenal being of the phenomenon.

If we ask what being in itself is, as revealing itself to consciousness, Sartre's answer recalls to our minds the philosophy of Parmenides: 'Being is. Being is in itself. Being is what it is.'[3] Being is opaque, massive: it simply is. As the foundation of the existent, it cannot be denied. Such remarks, taken by themselves, are perhaps somewhat baffling. Consider however a table. It stands out from other things as being a table and not something else, as being suitable for this purpose and not for that, and so on. But it appears for consciousness as a table precisely because human beings give it a certain meaning. That is to say, consciousness makes it appear as a table. If I wish to spread out my books and papers on it or to set a meal, it obviously appears primarily as a table, an instrument for the fulfilment of certain purposes. In other circumstances it might appear for consciousness (be made by consciousness to appear) as primarily firewood or a battering-ram or a solid object to hide under or an obstacle in my flight from an attacker or as a beautiful or an ugly object. It has a certain meaning or significance in its relation to consciousness. It does not follow however that consciousness creates the object. It indubitably is or exists. And it is what it is. But it acquires an instrumentalist meaning, standing out from its background as this sort of thing and not another, only in relation to consciousness.

---

[1] *L'être et le néant*, p. 12 (English, p. xlvi).
[2] *Ibid.*, p. 29 (English, p. lxii).   [3] *Ibid.*, p. 34 (English, p. lxvi).

In general, the world considered as a system of interrelated things with instrumental significance is made to appear for consciousness. In his theory of the conferring of meaning on things in terms of perspectives and purposes Sartre derives stimulus from Martin Heidegger. And in developing his theory of the way in which this is done he discusses Hegel's dialectic of being and not-being. For Sartre being in itself is logically prior to not-being and cannot be identified with it; but the table, for example, is constituted as a table through a negation. It is a table and not something else. All differentiation within being is due to consciousness, which makes something to appear by differentiating it from its background and in this sense negating the background. The same sort of thing can be said about spatial and temporal relations. A thing appears as 'near' or as 'far away' in relation to a consciousness which compares and relates. Similarly, it is for consciousness that this event appears as happening 'after' that event. Again, the Aristotelian distinction between potency and act arises only through and for consciousness. It is in relation to consciousness, for example, that the table is potentially firewood. Apart from consciousness, it simply is what it is.

In fine, it is for consciousness that the world appears as an intelligible system of distinct and interrelated things. If we think away all that is due to the activity of consciousness in making the world appear, we are left with being in itself (*l'en-soi*, the in-itself), opaque, massive, undifferentiated, the nebulous background, as it were, out of which the world is made to appear. This being in itself, Sartre tells us, is ultimate, simply there. It is 'without reason, without cause and without necessity'.[1] It does not follow that being is its own cause (*causa sui*). For this is a meaningless notion. Being simply is. In this sense being is gratuitous or *de trop*, as Sartre puts it in his novel *Nausea*.[2] In this work Roquentin, sitting in the municipal garden at Bounville, has an impression of the gratuitous or superfluous character of the being of the things about him and of himself. That is to say, there is no reason for their being. 'To exist is simply *to be there*.'[3] Being in itself is contingent, and this contingency is not an 'outward show', in the sense that it can be overcome by explaining it with

---

[1] *Ibid.*, p. 713 (English, p. 619).
[2] *Being and Nothingness* presents in systematic form the point of view expressed in *Nausea*.
[3] *La nausée*, p. 171 (English, Penguin edition, p. 188).

reference to a necessary being. Being is not derivable or reducible. It simply is. Contingency is 'the absolute itself and consequently perfectly gratuitous'.[1] 'Uncreated, without reason for being, without any relation to another being, being-in-itself is gratuitous for all eternity.'[2]

It is clear enough that there are different perspectives and that things can appear differently to different people. And we can make sense of the statement that it is consciousness which makes things to appear in certain ways or under certain aspects. To the climber or would-be climber a mountain appears as possessing certain characteristics, while to someone else who has no intention of trying to climb it but who is contemplating it aesthetically from a distance other characteristics stand out. And if one wishes to speak of each consciousness as making the object appear in a certain way or under certain aspects by negating other aspects or relegating them to a foggy background, this way of speaking is understandable, even if it is somewhat pretentious. Again, in so far as human beings have common interests and purposes, things appear to them in similar ways. It is not unreasonable to speak of human beings as conferring meanings on things, especially when it is a case of instrumental meaning. But Sartre carries this line of thought beyond the limit to which many people would be prepared to accompany him. For example, we have noted that in his view distinctions between things are due to consciousness, inasmuch as they are due to the act of distinguishing (of negation, in Sartrian terminology, or of denying that this is that). This is obviously true in a sense. Without consciousness there can be no distinguishing. At the same time most people would probably wish to claim that the mind is not confined to designating distinctions in what is in itself without distinction, but that it can recognize objective distinctions. And if Sartre disagrees, it is difficult to avoid the impression that he is carrying his line of thought as far as he can, without falling into what he would recognize as idealism, in order to be able to present being in itself in the way that he does. To be sure, there is no need to deny that the sort of impression or experience which Roquentin is represented as having in the gardens of Bouville can occur. But it by no means follows that Sartre is justified in drawing from this sort of impression the ontological conclusions which he in fact draws. He does indeed argue in *Being and Nothingness* that to

---

[1] *Ibid.*, p. 171.   [2] *L'être et le néant*, p. 34 (English, p. lxvi).

ask why there is being is to ask a question devoid of meaning, as it presupposes being.[1] But when making this statement he obviously cannot be referring to beings. For he has already said that it is consciousness which makes beings appear as such, as distinct that is to say. He is presumably arguing that it is meaningless to ask why there is being, inasmuch as being is what he has declared it to be, *de trop*, 'just there'. He might of course have raised difficulties in regard to the presuppositions involved in the use of the word 'why'. But what he actually does is to disallow the question 'why is there being'? on the ground that it presupposes being. And it is difficult to see how the question can be excluded on this ground, unless the being referred to is understood in the sense of transphenomenal and ultimate being, the Absolute. Sartre does indeed argue against other views. Something will be said later about his criticism of theism. But his own view seems to be the result of thinking away or abstracting from all in the object that he considers to be due to consciousness and then declaring the residue to be the Absolute, *l'en-soi* opaque and, in itself, unintelligible.

4. The concept of 'the in-itself' (*l'en-soi*) is one of the two key concepts of *Being and Nothingness*. The other key concept is that of consciousness, 'the for-itself' (*le pour-soi*). And it is hardly surprising if most of the work is devoted to this second theme. For if being in itself is opaque, massive, self-identical, there is obviously little that can be said about it. Besides, as an existentialist Sartre is primarily interested in man or, as he likes to put it, the human reality. He insists on human freedom, which is essential to his philosophy; and his theory of freedom is based on his analysis of 'the for-itself'.

Once more, all consciousness is consciousness *of* something. Of what? Of being as it appears. In this case it seems to follow that consciousness must be other than being, not-being that is to say, and that it must arise through a negation or nihilation of being in itself. Sartre is explicit about this. Being in itself is dense, massive, full. The in-itself harbours no nothingness. Consciousness is that whereby negation or nihilation is introduced. By its very nature consciousness involves or is distantiation or separation from being, though if it is asked what separates it from being, the answer can only be 'nothing'. For there is no intervening or separating entity. Consciousness is itself not-being, and its activity, according to Sartre, is a process of nihilation. When I am

[1] *Ibid.*, p. 713 (English, p. 619).

aware of this piece of paper, I distantiate myself from it, deny that I am the paper; and I make the paper appear, stand out from its background, by denying that it is anything else, by nihilating other phenomena. 'The being by which nothingness comes into the world is a being in which, in its own being, there is question of the nothingness of its being: *the being by which nothingness comes into the world must be its own nothingness.*'[1] 'Man is the being through whom nothingness comes into the world.'[2]

The language employed by Sartre is clearly objectionable. Consciousness is said to be its own nothingness; but it is also referred to as a being, as indeed it must be if it is to be described as exercising the activity attributed to it. Of course, one can see easily enough what Sartre means by ascribing to consciousness a process of nihilation. If I fix my attention on a particular picture in a gallery, I relegate the others to an indeterminate background. But one might emphasize equally well, or perhaps better, the positive activity involved in the intentional act.[3] Still, if we assume that being in itself is what Sartre says that it is, and if being is made to appear as the object of consciousness, consciousness of being must presumably involve the distantiation or separation of which he speaks, and in this sense not-being. If we object to the language, as well we may, we had better examine the premises which lead to its employment.

How does consciousness arise? It is difficult to see how being in itself, if it is as Sartre describes it, could give rise to anything at all, even to its own negation. It is equally difficult, if not more so, to see how consciousness could originate itself, as *causa sui*. As for the ego-subject, this arises, as we have seen, not on the level of pre-reflexive consciousness but on that of reflexive consciousness. It comes into being through the reflection of consciousness on itself; and it is thus made to appear as object. In this case there is no transcendental ego which could originate consciousness. However, that consciousness has arisen is an indubitable fact. And Sarte depicts it as rising through the occurrence of a fissure or rupture in being, resulting in the distantiation which is essential to consciousness.

It does not seem to the present writer that Sartre offers any really clear account of the origin of consciousness. However, as it

---

[1] *Ibid.*, p. 59 (English, p. 23).   [2] *Ibid.*, p. 60 (English, p. 24).
[3] So-called nihilation is itself a positive activity of course. But I am referring to the actual focussing of attention.

arises through the occurrence of a fissure or gap in being in itself, it must presumably come in some way or other out of being, even if by a process of negation, and so be derivative. As we have seen, Sartre excludes the question 'why is there being'? But he allows the question 'why is there consciousness'? True, he relegates explanatory hypotheses to the sphere of 'metaphysics' and says that phenomenological 'ontology' cannot answer the question. But he ventures the suggestion that *everything takes place as if* the in-itself, in a project to ground itself, gave itself the modification of the for-itself'.[1] How the in-itself could have such a project is none too clear. But the picture is that of the Absolute, being in itself, undergoing a process or performing an act of self-diremption whereby consciousness arises. It is as though being in itself tries to take the form of consciousness while remaining being. But this goal cannot be achieved. For consciousness exists only through a continuous separation or distantiation from being, a continuous secretion of the nothing which separates it from its object. Being in itself and consciousness cannot be united in one. They can be united only by the for-itself relapsing into the in-itself and ceasing to be for-itself. Consciousness exists only through a process of negation or nihilation. It is a relation to being, but it is other than being. Arising out of being in itself through a process of self-diremption in being it makes beings (a world) to appear.

5. Being in itself, massive, opaque and without consciousness, is obviously not free. The for-itself however, as separated from being (even if by nothing), cannot be determined by being. It escapes the determination of being in itself and is essentially free. Freedom, according to Sartre, is not a property of human nature or essence. It belongs to the structure of the conscious being. 'What we call freedom is thus impossible to distinguish from the *being* of the 'human reality.'[2] Indeed, in contrast with other things man first exists and then makes his essence. 'Human freedom precedes the essence of man and makes it possible.'[3] Here we have the belief which, Sartre tells us, is common to all existentialists, namely that 'existence precedes essence'.[4] Man is the not-already-made. He makes himself. His course is not predetermined: he does not proceed, as it were, along a pair of rails from which he cannot diverge. He makes himself, not of course in the

---

[1] *L'être et le néant*, p. 715 (English, p. 621).
[2] *Ibid.*, p. 61 (English, p. 25).   [3] *Ibid.*, p. 61 (English, p. 25).
[4] *L'existentialisme est un humanisme*, p. 17 (English, Mairet, p. 26).

sense that he creates himself out of nothing but in the sense that what he becomes depends on himself, on his own choice. It is not necessary to hold a theory of occult essences, hidden away inside things, in order to find difficulty in the notion of man's existence preceding his essence. In his lecture on existentialism and humanism Sartre explains that in his view there is no God who creates man according to some idea of human nature, so that each human being exemplifies human essence. Well and good, all atheists would obviously agree. But we are concerned here with man himself, not with the question whether or not he was created by God. Quite irrespective of man's relation to God, Sartre maintains that in man existence precedes essence. What then exists in the first instance? The answer is presumably a reality capable of making itself, of defining its own essence. But has this reality no characteristics other than freedom? Whether there is a human nature or essence which is fixed, immutable, static, non-plastic, is another question. The point is that it is very difficult to suppose that there is no human nature in any sense, distinguishable from the natures of lions or roses. Indeed, even if we take literally what Sartre says, it is clear that human beings have a certain common essence or nature, namely that they are the beings which make themselves to be what they become. After all, Sartre can talk about the 'human reality' or about human beings with the conviction that people will recognize what he is talking about. However, we need not really worry very much about Sartre's pronouncements taken in a literal sense. His main contention is clearly that man is wholly free, that whatever he does is the result of free choice, and that what he becomes depends entirely on himself.

At first sight this appears highly implausible. Sartre is not of course talking about reflex acts, which cannot be counted as human actions in the proper sense. But even if we confine our attention to acts which can be ascribed to the for-itself, to consciousness, the contention that we are totally or absolutely free may seem to be quite incompatible with facts. Quite apart from determinist theory, it may be said, our freedom is surely limited by all sorts of internal and external factors. What about the limiting, if not determining influence of physiological and psychological factors, of environment, upbringing, education, of a social pressure which is exercised continuously and generally without our being reflectively aware of it? Again, even if we reject determinism and admit freedom, must we not recognize the fact that people tend to act in accordance with their characters, and that we often believe that we can predict how they will act or react in a given set of circumstances? True, people sometimes act in un-expected ways. But do we not then tend to conclude that we did not know them as well as we thought, and that if we had known them better, we would have made more accurate predictions? The thesis that the human being is totally or absolutely free is surely at variance with the empirical facts and with our ordinary ways of thinking and speaking.

It is hardly necessary to say that Sartre is well aware of such lines of objection and has his answer ready. He sees the for-itself as projecting its own ideal goal and striving to attain it. In the light of this project certain things appear as obstacles. But it depends entirely on my choice whether they appear as obstacles to be overcome, as stepping-stones, so to speak, on the path of my exercise of freedom or whether they appear as insurmountable obstacles in the way. To take a simple example of a kind used by Sartre himself. I desire to take a holiday in Japan. But I lack the money to do so, and consequently cannot go. My lack of money appears to me an insurmountable obstacle only because I have freely formed the project of taking my holiday in Japan. If I freely choose to go to Brighton instead, for which I have the money, my financial situation no longer appears as an obstacle at all, let alone an insurmountable one. Or suppose that I have strong inclinations to act in ways which are incompatible with the ideal which I have projected for myself and my conduct. It is I myself who make these inclinations appear in this or that way. In themselves they constitute a kind of in-itself, a datum, the meaning or bearing of which is constituted by myself. If I give way to them completely, this is because I have chosen to regard them as insurmountable obstacles. And this choice shows in turn that my real project, my actually operative ideal, is not what I told myself that it was, deceiving myself. A man's actually operative ideal is revealed in his actions. It is all very well for Garcin in the play *Huis Clos* (*In Camera*) to claim that he was not actually a coward. As Inez says, it is what one does that reveals what one is, what one has chosen to be. In Sartre's opinion, to be 'overcome' by a passion or emotion, such as fear, is simply a way of choosing, though it is obviously a comparatively unreflective way of reacting to a given situation. Similar remarks can be made about, say, the influence of environment. It is consciousness itself which gives meaning to the environment. To one man it appears as an opportunity, to another as something which, as it were, sucks him down and absorbs him. In both cases it is the man himself who makes his environment appear in a certain way.

Sartre is not of course blind to the fact that we are often unable to alter external factors, in the sense of physically removing them or of removing oneself from them. Practically speaking, I may not be able to alter my place and environmental situation. And even though I can do so in theory and perhaps also in practice, I must be in some place and in some environmental situation. Sartre's contention is that the meaning which such factors have for me is chosen by myself, even if I fail or decline to recognize the fact. Similarly, I cannot alter the past in the sense of bringing it about that what I have done should not have been done. If I betrayed my country, this fact has become frozen, as it were, unalterable. It belongs to myself as *facticité*, as something already made. But, as we have seen, being in itself is not, for Sartre, temporal. It makes no sense to speak of being in itself as comprising succession. Temporality is 'the mode of being peculiar to being-for-itself'.[1] That is to say, the for-itself is a perpetual flight from what it was towards what it will be, from itself as something made towards itself as something to be made. In reflection this flight grounds the concepts of past, present (as present to being) and future. In other words, the self is beyond its past, what it has made of itself, surpassing it. If it is asked what separates the self in its flight from itself as already made, as its past, the answer is 'nothing'. To say this however is to say that the self negates itself as made and so surpasses it and is beyond it. The self as already made relapses into the condition of the in-itself. And one day, at death, the for-itself becomes wholly something already made and can be regarded purely objectively, as by the psychologist or the historian. But as long as it is the for-itself, it is ahead of itself as past and so cannot be determined by itself as past, as essence.[2] As has been noted, the self cannot alter its past, in the sense of bringing it about that what happened did not happen or that actions

---

[1] *L'être et le néant*, p. 188 (English, p. 142). Temporality is discussed at length in chapter two of the second part of the work. See also the following chapter, on transcendence. Sartre is strongly influenced by Heidegger; but he dismisses and criticizes the views of some other philosophers too.

[2] Sartre makes play with Hegel's saying *Wesen ist, was gewesen ist* (Essence is what has been).

performed were not performed; but it depends on its own choice what meaning the self gives to its past. And it follows that any influence exercised by the past is exercised because one chooses that it should. One cannot be determined by one's past, by oneself as already made.

According to Sartre therefore freedom belongs to the very structure of the for-itself. In this sense one is 'condemned' to be free. We cannot choose to be free or not: we simply are free by the fact that we are consciousnesses. We can however choose to try to deceive ourselves. Man is totally free; he cannot but choose and commit himself in some way; and in whatever way he commits himself, he ideally commits everyone else.[1] The responsibility is entirely his. Awareness of this total freedom and responsibility is accompanied by 'anguish' (*angoisse*), akin to the state of mind experienced by a man standing on a precipice who feels both attracted and repelled by the abyss. Man may therefore try to deceive himself by embracing some form of determinism, by throwing the responsibility on to something apart from his own choice, God or heredity or his upbringing and environment or what not. If however he does so, he is in bad faith. That is to say, the structure of the for-itself is such that a man can be, as it were, in a state of knowing and not-knowing at the same time. Radically, he is aware of his freedom; but he can see himself, for example, as being what he is not (his past), and he then draws a veil over, or masks for himself, the total freedom which gives rise to *angoisse* as a kind of vertigo.[2]

This may sound as though for Sartre all human actions are absolutely unpredictable, as though no intelligible pattern can be found in a man's life. That this is not at all what he means can be seen by recalling what he says in his lecture on existentialism and humanism about the young man who during the second world war asked for advice whether he should remain in France to look after his mother, who was estranged from his collaborating father and whose other son had been killed in 1940, or whether he should attempt to get to England in order to join the Free French forces. Sartre refused to give an answer. And when, in the discussion after

---

[1] If I commit myself to Communism, for example, I choose ideally for others too.

[2] Bad faith is not, for Sartre, the same thing as lying. One can lie to other people, telling them what one knows perfectly well to be untrue. In bad faith or self-deception there is a mixture of knowing and not-knowing, the possibility of which is based on the fact that the for-itself is not what it is (its past) and is what it is not (its possibilities or future).

the lecture, M. Naville said that advice should have been given, Sartre replied not only that the decision was up to the young man and could not be made for him but also that 'I knew moreover what he was going to do, and that is what he did'.[1] In Sartre's opinion the for-itself makes an original or primitive choice, projecting its ideal self, a projection implying a set of values; and particular choices are informed, as it were, by this basic free projection. A man's operative ideal way of course may be different from his professed ideal, from what he says is his ideal. But it is revealed in his actions. The original project *can* be changed, though this demands a radical conversion or change. Apart however from this radical change a man's particular actions implement and reveal his original choice or *projet*. A man's actions are thus free, inasmuch as they are contained in his original free choice; but the more clearly the external observer sees a man's basic *projet* revealed in his actions, so much the more can the observer predict how the man will act in a given situation. Besides, if someone asks advice from a particular man, whose ideas and attitudes are known to him, he has in effect already decided. For he has chosen to hear what he wants to hear.

What we have said about the possibility of conversion obviously implies that different people can have different projects, which reveal themselves in their actions. Underlying all such projects however, there is, according to Sartre, a basic project which belongs to the very structure of *le pour-soi*. The for-itself is, as we have seen, a flight from the past into the future, from itself as something already made towards its possibilities, towards the being which it will be. It is thus a flight from being to being. But the being which it seeks and strives after is not simply *l'en-soi*, devoid of consciousness. For it seeks to preserve itself, the for-itself that is to say. In fine, man reaches out to the ideal project of becoming the in-itself-for-itself, being and consciousness in one. This ideal however corresponds with the concept of God, self-grounded conscious being. We can say therefore that 'to be man is to strive towards being God; or, if one prefers, man is fundamentally the desire to be God.'[2] 'Thus my freedom is the choice of being God, and all my acts, all my projects, translate this choice and reflect it in a thousand and one ways, for there is an infinity of ways of being and of having.'[3] Unfortunately, the idea of God is

---

[1] *L'existentialisme est un humanisme*, p. 141 (English, Mairet, p. 70).
[2] *L'être et le néant*, pp. 653–4 (English, p. 566).   [3] *Ibid.*, p. 689 (English, p. 599).

contradictory. For consciousness is precisely the negation of being. Sartre therefore draws the somewhat pessimistic conclusion that 'man is a useless striving'.[1] The for-itself aspires after Deity; but it inevitably relapses into the opacity of *l'en-soi*. Its flight is terminated not in realization of its basic project but in death.

6. So far we have paid little attention to the plurality of consciousnesses. We cannot follow Sartre into his discussion of the theories of other philosophers, such as Hegel, Husserl and Heidegger,[2] about our knowledge of the existence of other persons. But something at any rate should be said about his own line of thought. And we can draw attention at once to his rejection of the idea that the existence of other minds or consciousnesses is simply inferred from observation of bodies and their movements. If I see a body walking in the street and infer that there is in it a consciousness similar to my own, this is simply conjecture on my part.[3] If the other self lies right outside my experience, I can never prove that what I take to be a human being is not in fact a robot. At best I might claim that whereas my own existence is certain (*Cogito, ergo sum*), the existence of the Other is probable. And this is not a position which Sartre considers tenable. He wishes to show that there is a real sense in which the *Cogito* reveals to me 'the concrete and indubitable presence of this or that concrete Other'.[4] He is not looking for reasons for believing that there are other selves but for the revelation of the Other as a subject. He wishes to show that I encounter the Other directly as a subject which is not myself. And this involves exhibiting a relation between my consciousness and that of the Other, a relation in which the Other is given to me not as an object but as a subject.

It is therefore not a question of deducing the existence of other selves in an *a priori* manner, but of giving a phenomenological analysis of the sort of experience in which the Other is revealed to me as subject. And Sartre's line of thought is perhaps best illustrated by summarizing one of the examples which he actually gives. Complaints are sometimes made that Sartre does not offer proofs of what he asserts. Even if however such complaints are sometimes justified, it should be remembered that in a context

---

[1] *Une passion inutile. Ibid.*, p. 708 (English, p. 615).
[2] In Sartre's opinion Husserl cannot escape solipsism, and Hegel's theory, though chronologically prior, is much superior. Heidegger made further progress.
[3] There is indeed the possibility of embracing behaviourism. But this is not a solution to whch Sartre is prepared to give favourable consideration.
[4] *L'être et le néant*, p. 308 (English, p. 251).

such as the present one it is in his view sufficient 'proof' if attention is drawn to situations in which the Other is clearly revealed as a subject to one's consciousness, within one's experience. If it is said that other people are always objects for oneself and never subjects, Sartre tries to refute the statement by giving examples of situations in which it is falsified. Whether he is successful or not, there does not seem to be anything disreputable in this procedure, except perhaps in the eyes of those who think that philosophers should assert only what they have deduced *a priori* from some unquestionable point of departure.

Let us imagine that I am squatting down in the corridor of a hotel looking through a keyhole. I am not thinking of myself at all; my attention is absorbed in what is going on inside a room. I am in a state of pre-reflexive consciousness. Suddenly I become aware that an employee or a fellow guest of the hotel is standing and watching me. I am at once ashamed. The *cogito* arises, in the sense that I become reflexively aware of myself as object, as object, that is to say, of another consciousness as subject. The other's field of consciousness, so to speak, invades mine, reducing me to an object. I experience the Other as a free conscious subject through his look (*regard*), whereby he makes me an object for another. The reason why common sense opposes an unshakable resistance to solipsism is that the Other is given to me as an evident presence which I cannot derive from myself and which cannot seriously be doubted. The consciousness of the Other is not of course given to me in the sense that it is mine; but the fact of the Other is given in an incontestable manner in the reduction of myself to an object for a transcendence which is not mine.

In view of the way in which Sartre tackles the subject of one's encounter with the Other it is not surprising to find him saying that 'conflict is the original meaning of being-for-others'.[1] If the Other's look reduces me to an object, I can try either to absorb the Other's freedom while leaving it intact or to reduce the Other to an object. The first project can be seen in love, which expresses a desire 'to possess a freedom as freedom',[2] whereas the second can be seen in, for example, indifference, sexual desire and, in an extreme form, sadism. Both projects are however doomed to failure. I cannot absorb another person's freedom while leaving it intact; he or she always eludes me, as the other self necessarily transcends myself, and the look which reduces me to objectivity

[1] *Ibid.*, p. 431 (English, p. 364).   [2] *Ibid.*, p. 434 (English, p. 367).

is always reborn.[1] As for the reduction of the Other to an object, this can be completely achieved through destruction, killing; but this is a frustration of the project of reducing a subject as such to the condition of an object. As long as there is another for-itself, the reduction cannot be carried through; and if it is carried through, there is no longer a for-itself.

Sartre's preoccupation with the existential analysis of phenomena such as masochism and sadism naturally gives the impression that he regards love as doomed to frustration and that he is not prepared to recognize genuine community, the we-consciousness. He does not however intend to deny that there is such a thing as an experience of 'we'. For example, during a theatrical performance or a football match there is or can be what Sartre describes as a non-thetic we-consciousness. That is to say, though each consciousness is absorbed in the object (the spectacle), the spectators at a cup final, for instance, are certainly co-spectators, even though they are not reflecting on the we-subject. The non-thetic we-consciousness shows itself clearly enough in a spontaneous outburst of applause.

On the level of the reflexive consciousness however the emphasis is laid by Sartre on the we-subject as arising in confrontation with Others. Consider, for example, the situation of an oppressed class. It experiences itself or can come to experience itself as an Us-object for the oppressors, as an object of the look of a They. If subsequently the oppressed class becomes a self conscious revolutionary class, the We-subject arises, which turns the tables on the oppressors by transforming them into an object. There can therefore perfectly well be a we-consciousness in which one group confronts another.

What however about humanity as a whole? According to Sartre, as one would indeed expect, the human race as a whole cannot become conscious of itself as an Us-object without postulating the existence of a being which is the subject of a look comprising all members of the race. Humanity can become an Us-object only in the posited presence of the being who looks at but can never be looked at. 'Thus the limiting concept of humanity (as the totality of the Us-object) and the limiting concept of God imply one another and are correlative.'[2] As for the experience of a

---

[1] In connection with this project Sartre examines devious ways, such as masochism, of wooing, as it were, another's freedom.
[2] *L'être et le néant*, p. 495 (English, p. 423).

universal We-subject, Sartre insists that this is a purely psychological or subjective event in a single consciousness. One can indeed conceive the ideal of a We-subject representing all humanity; but this ideal is conceived by a single consciousness or by a plurality of consciousnesses which remain separate. The actual constitution of a self-conscious intersubjective totality remains a dream. Sartre can therefore conclude that 'The essence of the relations between consciousnesses is not the *Mitsein*; it is conflict.'[1] The for-itself cannot do away with the basic dilemma. It must attempt to turn the Other into an object or allow itself to be objectified by the Other. As neither of these projects can be really successful, it can hardly be claimed that *Being and Nothingness* provides a promising basis for any such concept as Teilhard de Chardin's theory of a hyper-personal consciousness.

7. We have noted that according to Sartre humanity as a whole can become for itself an Us-object only if the existence of an omnipotent and all-seeing God is posited. And if there were a God, humanity could become a we-subject, in striving, for instance, to master the world in defiance of God. But Sartre does not believe that there is a God. In fact he is convinced that there cannot be a God, if by 'God' we mean an infinite self-conscious Being.[2] He does indeed represent belief in God as the result of an hypostatizing of 'the look' (*le regard*), a point of view which finds expression in *Les mots*[3] and in the account in *The Reprieve* of Daniel's conversion, as well as in *Being and Nothingness*, where Sartre refers to Kafka's *The Trial* and remarks that 'God is here only the concept of the Other pushed to the limit'.[4] This account of the origin of man's idea of God, if taken simply by itself, would leave open the possibility of there being a God. For all we know, there might be an all-embracing 'look'. But Sartre also argues, as we have already noted, that the concept of God is self-contradictory, inasmuch as it tries to unite two mutually exclusive concepts, that of being in itself (*l'en-soi*) and that of the for-itself

---

[1] *Ibid.*, p. 502 (English, p. 429). *Mitsein*, to be with or being with. Sartre's contention is that Heidegger's *Mitsein* is a psychological experience which does not reveal a basic ontological relation between consciousnesses.

[2] It is sometimes said that Sartre denies the existence of God only as conceived by theists. But such remarks are not so important as the people who make them seem to think that they are. If, for example, we care to call *l'en-soi* God, then of course Sartre does not deny the existence of God. But given the ordinary use of terms in the West, it would be extremely misleading or confusing to say that Sartre believes in God because he postulates the existence of *l'en-soi*.

[3] *Words* (Penguin edition), p. 65.

[4] *L'être et le néant*, p. 324 (English, p. 266). Cf. *ibid.*, p. 341 (p. 281).

(le pour-soi). It is indeed pretty obvious that if consciousness is
the negation of being in itself, there cannot be a self-grounded
and non-derived consciousness, and that the concept *l'en-soi-
pour-soi* is self-contradictory.

It is hardly necessary to say that the validity of this logical
demonstration of atheism depends on the validity of Sartre's
analysis of his two basic concepts. And here there is a formidable
difficulty. For the more he assigns to consciousness the active role
of conferring meanings on things and constituting an intelligible
world, so much the less plausible does it become to represent
consciousness as a negation of being. It is true of course that
being in itself is depicted as self-identical in a sense which excludes
consciousness, so that the rise of consciousness can be represented as a negation of being. But the contention that being as so
depicted is the Absolute, in so far as there is an Absolute, depends
for its validity on the further contention that *le pour-soi* not
only involves a negation or 'nihilation' of being as depicted by
Sartre but is also in itself a negation, not-being. And it is very
difficult to see how this position can be maintained, if consciousness is as active as Sartre says that it is. In other words, the force
of his demonstration of the self-contradictory nature of theism
seems to depend on the assumption that being in itself must be
without consciousness, an assumption which requires, if it is to be
justified, a proof that consciousness is not-being. And this cannot
be proved in terms of the assumption which it is used to justify.
In the long run Sartre appears simply to assume or to assert that
infra-conscious being, when stripped of all the intelligibility
conferred on it by consciousness, is absolute being.

However this may be, what role does atheism play in the
philosophy of Sartre? Sometimes he says that it does not make any
difference whether God exists or not. But what he seems to mean
by this is that in either case man is free, inasmuch as he *is* his
freedom. For freedom belongs to the very structure of the for-
itself. In *The Flies* (*Les mouches*) therefore, when Zeus says that he
created Orestes free in order that he might serve him (Zeus),
Orestes replies that once he had been created free, he ceased to
belong to Zeus and becme independent, able to defy the god if he
so wished. In this sense it makes no difference, according to
Sartre, whether God does or does not exist. But it by no means
follows that atheism plays no important role in Sartrian existentialism. Indeed, Sartre himself has explicitly stated that it does.

In his lecture on existentialism and humanism he asserts that 'existentialism is nothing else but an attempt to draw all the conclusions from a coherent atheist position'.[1] A conclusion which he mentions is that if God does not exist, values depend entirely on man and are his creation. 'Dostoievsky wrote, "if God did not exist, everything would be permitted". This is the point of departure of existentialism.'[2] Sartre could of course refer also to Nietzsche, who had no use for the idea that one could reject belief in God and still maintain belief in absolute values or in a universally obligatory moral law.

Sartre's position can be expressed in this way. Man is free; and this means that it depends on man what he makes of himself. He cannot however avoid making something of himself.[3] And what he makes of himself implies an operative ideal, a basic project, which he has freely chosen or projected for himself. It is not therefore a question of man being under an *a priori* moral obligation to choose his values. For he does so in any case. Even if he endorses, so to speak, a set of values or of ethical norms which he receives from society, this endorsement is an act of choice. The values become *his* values only through his own act. This would apply to acceptance of commands and prohibitions which the religious believer conceived as emanating from God. God could indeed punish a man for disobedience; but if man is free, it depends on him whether or not he accepts the divine commands as his ethical norms. From this point of view therefore we can say that it makes no difference whether there is a God or not. Even if God existed, man would still have to pursue goals which he had chosen. At the same time, if there is no God, there can obviously be no foreordained divine plan. There can be no one common ideal of human nature which man has been created to realize through his actions. He is thrown back entirely on himself, and he cannot justify his choice of an ideal by appealing to a divine plan for the human race. In this sense the existence or non-existence of God does make a difference. It is true that if a man accepts the ethical norms which he believes to have been promulgated by God, this implies that he has freely projected his ideal as that of a God-fearing man. The point is however that if in fact there is no God who has created man for a purpose, to attain a determinate end or

---

[1] *L'existentialisme est un humanisme*, p. 94 (English, Mairet, p. 56).
[2] *Ibid.*, p. 36 (English, p. 33).
[3] Even if a man commits suicide, he has made something of himself.

goal, there is no given moral order to which man can appeal to justify his choice. The notion that there are absolute values subsisting in some celestial realm of their own, apart from a divine mind, is quite unacceptable to Sartre. It may indeed be the case that he could have approached the matter in a simpler way by interpreting 'values' simply in terms of the act of evaluation. But he would still insist of course that if there is no God, there is no possibility of justifying man's act of evaluation, say as 'rational', by appealing to a divinely determined ideal of human nature which is the measure of self-fulfilment or self-realization. To be sure, Sartre himself sees man as striving after the realization of a basic project, that of becoming *l'en-soi-pour-soi* or God. But he adds that the project is doomed to frustration, inasmuch as the concept of the unity of being in itself and consciousness is a self-contradictory concept. And in this sense the (necessary) non-existence of God makes a difference.

Sartre is anxious to dissipate the impression that he is concerned with promoting moral anarchy or encouraging a purely capricious choice of values and ethical norms. He argues therefore that to choose between x and y is to assert the value of what we choose (that x, for example, is better than y), and that 'nothing can be good for us without being good for all'.[1] That is to say, in choosing a value one chooses ideally for all. If I project a certain image of myself as I choose to be, I am projecting an ideal image of man as such. If I will my own freedom, I must will the freedom of all other men. In other words, the judgment of value is intrinsically universal, not of course in the sense that other people necessarily accept my judgment but in the sense that to assert a value is to assert it ideally as a value for everyone. Sartre can therefore claim that he is not encouraging irresponsible choice. For in choosing values and deciding on ethical norms 'I am responsible for myself and for all'.[2]

The validity of the contention that in choosing a value one chooses ideally for all men is perhaps not so clear as Sartre seems to think that it is. Is it logically inadmissible for me to commit myself to a course of action without claiming that anyone else in the same situation ought to commit himself in the same way? It may be so; but further discussion would be appropriate. Indeed, a philosophical ethics would have to consist, on Sartre's premises,

---

[1] *L'existentialisme est un humanisme*, pp. 25-6 (English, p. 29).
[2] *Ibid.*, p. 27 (English, p. 30).

in an analysis of the judgment of value and of the moral judgment as such. It is true of course that within the frame of reference of his personally chosen values Sartre could develop a moral philosophy with concrete content. And within this frame of reference he can pass judgment on other people's attitudes and actions. But his personally chosen system of ethics could not legitimately be presented as entailed by existentialism, not, that is to say, if existentialism illuminates possibilities of choice while leaving the actual choice entirely to the individual. It has indeed appeared to some readers that Sartre really regards freedom as an absolute value, and that the outline of an ethical system could be deduced from existentialist premises. In this case however existentialism would stand in need of some revision. The idea of there being a common human nature would reappear.[1] And it is perhaps not surprising that Sartre denies that he looks on freedom as an absolute value. Freedom makes possible the creation or choice of values; but it is not itself a value. It can hardly be claimed however that Sartre successfully avoids making statements which imply that recognition by the for-itself of its total freedom and realization of this freedom in action are intrinsically valuable.

[1] It appears in any case of course, given Sartre's analysis of the common basic structure of the for-itself. His attempt to admit a universality of condition (such as being-in-the-world) while denying a universal human nature is not conspicuously successful.

CHAPTER XVII

THE EXISTENTIALISM OF SARTRE (2)

Sartre and Marxism — The aims of the Critique *— Individual praxis — The anti-dialectic and the domination of the practico-inert — The group and its fate — Critical comments.*

1. SARTRIAN existentialism as outlined in the last chapter by no means excludes personal self-commitment in a given historical situation. Provided therefore that Sartre did not claim that the values which he was defending were absolute in a metaphysical sense, there was no incompatibility between his existentialist philosophy and his support of the Resistance in the second world war. In regard however to his support of Marxism the situation is more complex. If it were simply a question of collaborating with a political Party with a view to realizing certain social ends which were considered desirable, such collaboration would hardly be incompatible with existentialism from a logical point of view, even if we felt inclined to question the wisdom of a champion of human freedom making common cause with a Party whose dictatorial ways are notorious. Marxism however is a philosophy with doctrines, not to say dogmas, which cannot be reconciled with Sartrian existentialism. For example, whereas Sartre represents the for-itself as the source of all meaning, Marxism depicts history as being in itself an intelligible process, a process which can be discerned by the human mind and which, when stated in the form of dialectical materialism, represents scientific knowledge rather than metaphysical speculation. The question arises therefore to what extent Sartre has come to accept Marxism as a philosophy, and, if he accepts it, whether he has abandoned existentialism or tries to combine it with Marxism.

In 1946 Sartre published in *Les temps modernes* a long article on materialism and revolution.[1] In it he accepts Marx's view of man as self-alienated and of the need for revolution if this alienation is to be overcome. He objects however to Marxist materialism. He is indeed prepared to admit that, historically speaking, materialism

[1] Reprinted in *Situations III* (1949). An English translation is included in *Literary and Philosophical Essays.*

has been 'bound up with the revolutionary attitude',[1] and that from the short-term view of the politician or the political activist it is 'the *only myth* which suits revolutionary requirements'.[2] At the same time Sartre insists that this is precisely what materialism is, namely a myth and not the expression of scientific knowledge or of absolute truth. Further, dogmatic materialism makes it impossible to understand man as the free self-transcending subject. To be sure, the Marxists protest that their materialism is dialectical and different from old-fashioned materialism. And in practice they obviously call for and rely on man's free activity. This simply shows however that even if materialism has a temporary pragmatic value, a genuine philosophy of revolution must discard this myth. For such a philosophy must be able to accommodate and explain the movement of transcendence, in the sense of the human subject transcending the present social order towards a society which does not yet exist, which is therefore not clearly perceived, and which man seeks to create but which will not come about automatically or · inevitably. This possibility of transcending a given situation and grasping it in a perspective which unites understanding and action 'is precisely what we call freedom'.[3] And it is this which materialism is incapable of explaining.

The article to which we have been referring certainly reads like a sustained attack on Marxism and, by implication at any rate, as a defence of existentialism. Sartre asserts however that 'the Communist Party is the only revolutionary party',[4] and in a subsequently added note he explains that his criticism was directed not so much against Marx himself as against 'the Marxist scholasticism of 1949'.[5] In other words, Sartre looks on the Communist Party as the spearhead of social revolution and as the organ of man's transcendence in a given situation. And in his articles on the Communists and peace in *Les temps modernes* (1952 f.) he defends the Party and exhorts workers to join it. He has not himself joined it however, and he has continued to believe that Marxism has become a dogmatism which stands in need of rejuvenation through a rediscovery of man as the free active subject. As long as dialectical materialism retains its present form, existentialism must continue to exist as a distinct line of thought. If however

---

[1] *Literary and Philosophical Essays*, p. 207. The implication is that theism, for example, is linked with a conservative outlook.
[2] *Ibid.*, p. 208.   [3] *Ibid.*, p. 220.   [4] *Ibid.*, p. 238.   [5] *Ibid.*, p. 185, n 1.

Marxism were rejuvenated by basing itself on man rather than on
Nature, existentialism would cease to exist as a distinct philosophy.
This point of view finds expression in Sartre's *Question de
méthode*,[1] which is prefaced to the first volume of his *Critique de la
raison dialectique*.[2] In no age, according to Sartre, is there more
than one living philosophy, a living philosophy being the means
by which the ascending class comes to consciousness of itself in an
historical situation, whether clearly or obscurely, directly or
indirectly.[3] Between the seventeenth and twentieth centuries
Sartre finds only three epochs of real philosophical creation.
'There is the "moment" of Descartes and of Locke, that of Kant
and of Hegel, finally that of Marx.'[4] The philosophy of Marx is
thus the living philosophy of our time; and it cannot be surpassed
as long as the situation out of which it arose remains unsurpassed.[5]
Unfortunately, the philosophy of Marx has ceased to grow and is
affected with sclerosis. 'The open concepts of Marxism have
become closed; they are no more *keys*, interpretative schemata;
they are asserted in themselves, as already achieved knowledge.'[6]
In Kantian terminology, regulative ideas have been transformed
into constitutive ideas; and heuristic schemes have become dogmas imposed by authority. This has meant that the Marxists have
misrepresented historical events, such as the Hungarian revolution
of 1956, by forcing them into a rigid theoretical framework,[7]
while the heuristic principle of seeking the universal in its particulars has been converted into the terrorist principle 'liquidate
particularity',[8] a liquidation which under Stalin at any rate
assumed an obviously physical form.

A living philosophy is for Sartre a process of 'totalization'.
That is to say, it is not a totality or finished whole, like a fully
constructed machine, but rather a unifying or synthesizing process,

---

[1] Translated by H. Barnes as *Search for a Method* (New York, 1963).
[2] Paris, 1960. This work will be referred to in footnotes as *C.R.D.*
[3] For example, the consciousness of the bourgeoisie is said to have been expressed obscurely 'in the image of universal man proposed by Kantianism'
(*C.R.D.*, p. 15).
[4] *C.R.D.*, p. 17.
[5] According to Sartre, any attempt to go beyond Marxism is in effect a return
to a pre-Marxist position.
[6] *C.R.D.*, p. 28.
[7] It is of course true that events such as the Hungarian revolution and the
liberalization of the régime in Czechoslovakia under Dubcek were misrepresented
by theoreticians and publicists of the Soviet Union. But it is also pretty obvious
that the actions of the Soviet authorities were influenced by other factors besides
ideological blinkers.
[8] *C.R.D.*, p. 28.

bringing together past and present and oriented to a future which is not determined in advance. The philosopher is within an ongoing process, and he cannot take the place of God and see all history as a totality. This is however precisely what the Marxists try to do when they speak of the future as assured and of the inevitable march of history towards a certain goal. Moreover, they thus make nonsense of human freedom and creativity, even though their political activism demands and presupposes human freedom.

A natural conclusion to draw from Sartre's criticism is that Marxism is certainly not the living philosophy of our time, even if it is the official ideology of a powerful social-political movement. Sartre however will not allow that the sclerosis of Marxism is the result of senility. 'Marxism is still young, almost in infancy; it has hardly begun to develop. It remains therefore the philosophy of our time.'[1] The original inspiration of Marxism has indeed been forgotten by theoreticians of the Communist Party. And if the Marxist follows Engels in finding the dialectic at work in Nature itself, quite independently of man, and regards human history as the prolongation of natural processes which develop inevitably, man is reduced to the condition of a passive instrument of an hypostatized dialectic. Though however Marxism has been distorted, it is capable of rediscovering its original inspiration and its basic humanism. Sartre quotes the well known statement by Engels in a letter to Marx that it is human beings themselves who make their history, though they do so in a situation which conditions their activity.[2] He uses texts of this kind to support his contention that Marxism can rediscover within itself the idea of man as defined by his project, by his movement of transcendence towards his possibilities, towards a future which, though conditioned by the present, can be realized only through man's free action.

If Marxism returns to its original inspiration and rediscovers the human dimension within itself, 'existentialism will no longer have any reason to exist.'[3] That is to say, it will cease to be a distinct line of thought and will be absorbed, preserved and surpassed in 'the totalizing movement of philosophy',[4] in the one living and developing philosophy of our time. Marxism is the only philosophy which really expresses the consciousness of man living in a world of 'scarcity' (rareté), in a world in which there is an unequal distribution of material goods and which is therefore

[1] Ibid., p. 29.   [2] Ibid., p. 60.   [3] Ibid., p. 111.   [4] Ibid., p. 111.

characterized by conflict and class antagonism. And a humanized
Marxism (an existentialized Marxism, one might say) would be
the only genuine philosophy of revolution. If however the social
revolution were to be realized and a society were to come into
being from which scarcity and class antagonism were absent,
Marxism would have fulfilled its destiny and would be succeeded
by another 'totalizing' philosophy, a philosophy of freedom.[1]
In other words, to say that Marxism is the one living philosophy
of our time is not to say that it is the final philosophy for all future
time.

2. We have been referring to the essay on method (*Question
de méthode*), which was originally entitled *Existentialism and
Marxism*. Sartre tells us[2] that though this essay was written
before the *Critique of Dialectical Reason* and has been used as an
introduction to it, the *Critique* is prior from the logical point of
view, inasmuch as it provides the critical foundations of the essay
on method. This does not alter the fact that the essay is considerably easier to read than the *Critique* itself, which is long,
rambling and turgid.

In the *Critique* Sartre is concerned with dialectical thinking as
the only way of understanding history. He makes a distinction
between analytical and dialectical rationalism. The analytical
reason, represented by eighteenth-century rationalism and by
positivism, adopts the position of a spectator, of an external
judge. Further, it tries to explain new facts by reducing them to
old facts; and it is thus incapable of understanding the emergence
of novelty. The dialectical reason however, which moves through
thesis, antithesis or negation, and the negation of the negation,
does not reduce the new to the old; nor does it attempt to explain
the whole by reducing it to its constituent parts. It expresses an
irreversible movement, oriented to the emergence of novelty. It
can be described, Sartre tells us, as 'the absolute intelligibility of
an irreducible novelty *in so far* as it is an irreducible novelty'.[3]
It understands the 'parts', such as particular historical situations
and social groups, not in the light of a totality, in the sense of a
finished or complete whole, but in terms of an ongoing process of
totalization, oriented to the new.

Sartre agrees therefore with the Marxists that the movement of

---

[1] Sartre is referring of course to freedom from the slavery of material production as hitherto experienced, not to freedom as the structure of *le pour-soi*. For the
latter is an ever-present reality.
[2] *C.R.D.*, p. 9.   [3] *Ibid.*, p. 147.

history can be understood only by dialectical thinking. He finds fault with them however for not grounding the dialectical method in an *a priori* manner. He himself proposes to establish *a priori* 'the heuristic value of the dialectical method, when it is applied to the sciences of man, and the necessity, whatever may be the fact envisaged, provided that it is *human*, of setting it in the ongoing totalization (*dans la totalisation en cours*) and of understanding it in this context.'[1] For example, Sartre wishes to grasp, in and through the real alienations of concrete history, alienation as an '*a priori* possibility of human *praxis*'.[2] In the first volume of the *Critique* he is not concerned with adding to our knowledge of historical facts, nor with playing the part of a sociologist by studying the development of particular societies or groups. Rather is he concerned with asking 'on what conditions is the knowledge of *a history* possible? Within what limits can the connections which are brought to light be *necessary*? What is dialectical rationality, what are its limits and its foundations'?[3] Sartre therefore entitles his work a *Critique* of the dialectical reason, the term being obviously suggested by Kant's use of the term *Kritik*. Indeed, in one place Sartre remarks that, to 'parody' Kant, his aim might be described as that of laying the foundations of a 'Prolegomena for every future anthropology'.[4]

Mention of Kant can however be misleading. For though Sartre is concerned with the conditions of possibility for history being an intelligible but not determined process, he does not regard his inquiry as purely formal, as a reflection by the mind on a pattern of thought which it imposes on a process which is not itself dialectical in structure. The word 'dialectic', he remarks, can be used in two ways, as meaning either a method, a movement of thought, or a movement in the object of thought. He claims however that the two meanings are simply two aspects of one process. The dialectical reason has indeed to reflect on itself. For it 'can be criticized, in the sense in which Kant understood the term',[5] only by itself. But to grasp the basic structures of dialectical thought is also to grasp the basic structures of the movement of history. The dialectical reason's reflection on itself can thus be seen as history becoming conscious of itself.

What Sartre tries to do in the first volume of the *Critique* is to

---

[1] *Ibid.*, p. 153.
[2] *Ibid.*, p. 154. By *praxis* Sartre means human action. Philosophy as oriented to the future, is itself a form of action and can thus be subsumed under *praxis*.
[3] *Ibid.*, p. 135.   [4] *Ibid.*, p. 153.   [5] *Ibid.*, p. 120.

reconcile the thesis that it is man who makes history, and so the
dialectic, with recognition of the fact that human activity is
subject to and limited by antecedent conditions to such an extent
that he can appear to be 'undergoing' the dialectic rather than
making it. To put the matter in another way, Sartre is determined
to preserve his existentialist view of man as a free agent, defined
by his project, while he is also determined to adopt and justify the
Marxist interpretation of history as a dialectical process. His
determination to make human freedom the basic factor in history
means that he cannot accept any mechanistic interpretation of
history which would imply that human beings are simply puppets
or instruments of a dialectical law which operates in Nature apart
from man and continues to govern human history. In the *Critique*
he does not seem prepared to state roundly that talk about a
dialectical process in Nature in itself, apart from man, is nonsensical. But he makes it clear that the claim that there is such a
process is for him no more than an unverified hypothesis which
should be disregarded. And he confines his attention to human
history, insisting that it is made by man, whereas Nature 'in
itself' is obviously not man's creation. At the same time Sartre's
determination to do justice to the contention of Marx and Engels
that human activity is subject to antecedent conditions means
that he has to place a greater emphasis than in *Being and Nothingness* on the influence of man's situation. Man exists, for example,
in a material environment; and though he works on the environment, the environment (or Nature not 'in itself' but in relation to
man) acts on him and conditions his activity. Within limits man
can change his environment; but then the changed environment
constitutes a new objectivity, a new set of antecedent conditions
which influence and limit human activity. In other words, the
relationship between man and Nature is a changing dialectical
relationship. And analogous remarks can be made about the
relationship between man and his social environment. Societies
and groups are created by man; but every human being is born
into a social environment, and the fact of social pressure is undeniable, even though man is capable of transcending a given
social situation in view of a projected goal which, if realized, constitutes a new objectivity or set of antecedent conditions.

The reconciliation of the two theses, that man makes history
and that his activity is subject to and limited by antecedent
conditions, can be found, according to Sartre, only by discovering

the roots of the whole dialectical process of history in human *praxis* or action. Sartre tells us that in the first volume of the *Critique* he looks 'exclusively for the intelligible foundations of a structural anthropology, in so far, it is understood, as these synthetic structures constitute the very condition of an ongoing totalization which is perpetually oriented.'[1] He treats first of what he calls the constituting dialectic. This is grasped in and through reflection on the individual's *praxis*, on his productive work; and it is in fact the dialectic of the worker, considered as an individual. Sartre then tries to show how the constituting dialectic gives rise to its negation, the anti-dialectic, in which man becomes a prisoner of his own product, of the 'practico-inert'. This is of course the sphere of alienation, the sphere in which human beings are united in 'collections', like the individuals who are brought together by being concerned with the maintenance and running of a certain machine. Thirdly, the transition from the negation to the negation of the negation is effected by the constitution of the 'group', in which human beings are united by sharing a common end or project and transcend their given situation towards possibilities to be realized through concerted free action. The third phase therefore, described as the constituted dialectic, is in effect the dialectic of the group. The whole process, in all its phases, is rooted in human *praxis*, in man's productive action. And if we can say that in the dialectical reason's self-reflection history becomes conscious of itself, this means that human *praxis* becomes conscious of itself and of its dialectical developments as free activity which presupposes antecedent conditions.

In the first volume of the *Critique* therefore Sartre pursues what he describes as a regressive method, working back to the underlying dialectical structure of the relations between man and Nature and between human beings. He inquires into the fundamental structures which make it possible to claim with truth that it is men who make history but that they do so as the basis of antecedent conditions. It is clear however that human action can have results which are different from those envisaged by the agents. A group may carry out concerted action which appears as successful to the members of the group, though the long-term result, the 'diachronic' effect as Sartre puts it, may be different from what the group intended or extended. To take a simple example, 'the victory of 1918 creates in the common field of

[1] *Ibid.*, p. 156.

Europe the possibility of the defeat of 1940.'[1] It may thus appear that in the long run it is not so much a question of men freely making history as of their suffering or undergoing a necessity which is beyond their control. There is need therefore for use of the method of 'synthetic progression' to unify the multiplicity of human actions or, rather, to show how they ceaselessly 'totalize' themselves in an intelligible but open-ended historical process. And Sartre informs us that in the promised second volume of the *Critique* he 'will try to establish that there is *one* human history, with *one* truth and *one* intelligibility'.[2]

The development of an overall philosophy of history is not quite what one would expect from the author of *Being and Nothingness*. But critical comment is best left until we have outlined, in an inevitably brief and sketchy manner, some of the lines of thought contained in the one published volume of the *Critique*. For the moment it is sufficient to note that Sartre is determined to prove a thesis, to justify the view that Marxism is the one living philosophy of our time, even if it needs rejuvenation through an injection of existentialism.

3. As we have already indicated, Sartre begins by considering the action or *praxis* of the individual. For if it is men who make history, and if history is a dialectical totalization of the actions of individuals, it is essential to show that human action possesses an inherently dialectical structure. '*The whole of the historical dialectic rests on individual praxis which is already dialectical*, that is to say in the measure in which action is in itself a negating transcendence of a contradiction, a determination of a present totalization in the name of a future totality, a real and efficacious working of matter.'[3]

This tiresome jargon is used to refer to quite ordinary situations. Sartre assumes the existence of man as a living organism. That is to say, the organic negates the inorganic. Man however experiences need (*besoin*). He needs food, for example. And this need is said to be a negation of the negation, in the sense that the organism transcends itself towards its material environment. By doing so it totalizes its environment as the field of possibilities, as the field, that is to say, in which it seeks to find satisfaction of its needs and so to conserve itself as an organic totality in the future. The action proceeding from the need is a working of matter.

By totalizing his environment in this way man constitutes it as

---

[1] *Ibid.*, p. 635.   [2] *Ibid.*, p. 635.   [3] *Ibid.*, pp. 165–6.

a passive totality. 'Matter revealed as a passive totality by an organic being which endeavours to find therein its being, here is Nature in its first form.'[1] Nature however, as so constituted, reacts on man by revealing itself as a menace to the life of the human organism, as an obstacle and threat of possible death. In this sense Nature negates man. Sartre preserves the point of view maintained in *Being and Nothingness* that it is consciousness which confers meaning on being-in-itself. For it is the organism's transcending towards its natural environment which reveals this environment as threatening or menacing. Nature's negating of man is thus due to man himself. This does not however alter the fact that Nature does appear as a menace or a threat of destruction. And to protect himself man has, according to Sartre, to make himself 'inert matter'. That is to say he has to act on matter by means of a tool, whether it is a tool in the ordinary sense or his own body treated as a tool. This action however is inspired by a *projet* and thus has a mediating function between present and future, in the sense that man's acting on his material environment is directed to his own conservation, as a present totality, in the future. 'Praxis is at first nothing else but the relation of the organism as an exterior future to the present organism as a threatened totality.'[2] It is therefore through his productive labour, and so through the mediation of Nature, that man totalizes himself, linking himself as a present totality to himself as a future possibility, as the goal of his movement of transcendence. According to Sartre the relations between man and his material environment thus take the form of 'dialectical circularity',[3] man being 'mediated' by things to the extent in which things are 'mediated' by man.

Even on the level of individual praxis however there are obviously relations between individuals, though the genuine group does not belong to this phase of the dialectic. Consider, for example, two workers who agree on an exchange of products. Each voluntarily becomes a means for the other, in and through his product. And we can say that each recognizes the other's *praxis* and project. But unity does not go further than this. In a world of scarcity of course one man represents a menace or threat to the other. But this situation leads to conflict rather than to genuine unity, even if one man succeeds in compelling another to serve as an instrument for the attainment of his own end. In Sartre's view

[1] *Ibid.*, p. 167.   [2] *Ibid.*, p. 168.   [3] *Ibid.*, p. 165.

'unity comes from outside',[1] a theme already familiar from *Being and Nothingness*. In some cases unification is affected simply in the consciousness of the third party. One of the examples given by Sartre is that of a bourgeois on holiday, who watches from a window two workers, one working on a road, the other in a garden. The watcher negates them by differentiating himself, as a bourgeois on holiday, from the two workers, but by doing so he unites them in terms of their praxis. This unification has of course a foundation in fact, inasmuch as the two men are actually workers; but the unification takes place in the mind of the watcher, not in the minds of the labourers who are *ex hypothesi* unaware of one another. In other cases however the unification (or totalization) is effected in a plurality of consciousnesses through the mediation of a third party. For example, in the presence of the exploiting boss a we-consciousness, that of the exploited, can arise in the minds of the workmen.

As has been noted, explicit treatment of such themes as exploitation does not really belong to consideration of the first phase of the dialectic. For individual praxis as such does not involve either exploitation or the formation of a group. At the same time the possibility of such developments is prefigured in individual praxis. And this is the point which Sartre wishes to make. He is arguing that the conditions of possibility of the dialectic of history, interpreted of course on Marxian lines, are present from the start in individual praxis, so that human action is the foundation of the whole dialectic. To put the matter in another way, he wishes to maintain the position of *le pour-soi* in *Being and Nothingness* as the giver of meaning. For example, Sartre argues that in Nature in itself there is no scarcity. Scarcity is present in Nature only through the mediation of man, in relation, that is to say, to human needs. Once present in the material environment, making Nature appear as a threat to man's life, scarcity then rebounds, so to speak, onto man himself, making his fellow men appear to the individual as a threat. This situation in turn makes possible not only conflict, violence[2] and exploitation but also the forming of genuine groups. Thus while he finds room for Marx's concept of man as standing in a dialectical relationship to his environment before the development of conflict and class antagonism, at any rate in a logical sense of 'before', Sartre can also assert that the conditions of possibility of the whole dialectic of history are

---

[1] *Ibid.*, p. 197.   [2] For Sartre violence is interiorized scarcity.

precontained in man's free action, and that history is thus made by man.

4. When speaking of scarcity Sartre refers to scarcity of products, scarcity of tools, scarcity of workers, scarcity of consumers. The basic reference however is to shortage of the goods required for the maintenance of human life. Scarcity in this sense grounds the possibility of social division into haves and have-nots or at any rate into consumers and sub-consumers, and so of class division. Such division can of course take place as the result of war, when one population is compelled to work for another. But what is inevitable is that in a world of scarcity there should be class divisions of some kind. As for determinate social relations and structures, Sartre accepts the Marxian doctrine that they depend on the mode of production. 'The essential discovery of Marxism is that work as an historical reality and as the utilization of determinate tools in an already determinate social and material milieu is the real basis of the organization of social relations. This discovery *can no more* be questioned. . . . In the milieu of scarcity all the structures of a determinate society rests on its mode of production.'[1] At the same time Sartre tries to go back behind social division and struggle, the negation of man by man, 'the negation of man by matter considered as the organization of his being outside himself in Nature.'[2]

The point of view which finds expression in this typical spcimen of Sartrian jargon can be illustrated in the following way. To overcome scarcity man acts on his material environment and invents tools to do so. But then matter worked on by man (*matière œuvrée*) turns against man, becoming 'counter-man'. Thus the Chinese peasants won arable soil 'against Nature'[3] by pursuing a policy of deforestation. The result of this was a series of inundations against which there was no protection. Nature exhibited a 'contra-finality' and affected human praxis and social relations. Again, the invention of machines and the development of industrialization was intended to overcome scarcity but in fact produced a further negation of man by making human beings the slaves of machines. Man thus falls under the domination of the 'practico-inert' which he himself has created. Man makes the machine; but the machine then reacts on man, reducing him to the level of the practico-inert, to what can be manipulated. To be sure, man remains the *for-itself*, and so free. At the same time hs becomes subject to the

---

[1] *Ibid.*, pp. 224–5, notes.   [2] *Ibid.*, p. 223.   [3] *Ibid.*, p. 232.

domination of the worked matter (*matière œuvrée*) which he himself has made and which represents man as outside himself, as objectified in matter. Man is thus alienated or estranged from himself. Sartre lays great emphasis on the power of worked matter to affect social relations. 'It is the object and the object alone which *combines* human efforts in its inhuman unity.'[1] For example, it is the demands of the machine which differentiate workers into skilled and unskilled. It is also the practico-inert which determines the stratification of classes, a class being for Sartre a collective or collection. In the collection human beings are united by something outside themselves in the way that a number of people waiting for an already crowded bus are united. They constitute a 'series', not in the sense that they are all standing in a line but in the sense that each member is a unit, interested in his getting a place in the bus, a unit for which other members of the series are potential rivals or enemies. Similarly, each worker in a factory is intent on gaining his livelihood; and what brings the workers together in this particular collection is the machine or set of machines. Again, it is worked matter or the practico-inert which lies at the basis of class-division. To use an Hegelian term, Sartre is speaking of the class 'in itself', not of the class 'for itself'. And he accepts the Marxist view that the mode of production determines the nature of class division.

This domination of man by matter represents the sphere of what Sartre describes as the anti-dialectic.[2] And he lays such emphasis on it that some writers have seen in his attitude an almost Manichaean view of matter as evil or at any rate as the source of evil. However this may be, it should be remembered that worked matter is for Sartre man exteriorized and that man's subjection to the practico-inert is in a sense subjection to himself, though in a form which involves self-estrangement or self-alienation. Though enslaved to his creation, man remains free. And just as the constituting dialectic contains within itself the possibility of an anti-dialectic, so does the anti-dialectic contain within itself the possibility of the constituted dialectic. Thus the class in itself can

---

[1] *Ibid.*, p. 350.
[2] The sphere or phase of the anti-dialectic is associated by Sartre with the analytical reason, the mode of thought characteristic of the bourgeoisie. This is one reason why Sartre describes the bourgeois intellectuals who discovered the dialectical reason as 'traitors' to their class. Obviously, the word 'traitor' is used descriptively, and not in a condemnatory sense.

become the class for itself, and the series can be transformed into the group.

5. This transition is not for Sartre inevitable or automatic but depends on human freedom, on individuals negating the domination of the practico-inert and transcending the social situation created by this domination towards a new social form, with a view to constituting or making it 'on the basis of the anti-dialectic'.[1] The unification of the workers as a genuine group, taking concerted action in view of a common end, must come from within. The transformation of the series into a group or of the class in itself into the class in and for itself comes about through a synthesis, a marriage as it were, of the original freedom which expresses itself in individual praxis, in the constituting dialectic, with the externally produced totalization in a series which pertains to the phase of the anti-dialectic.

The original constitution of the group expresses an upsurge of freedom. But Sartre is under no illusion about the group's stability. Once its immediate aim is attained, the storming of the Bastille for example, it tends to fragment or fall apart. The threat of atomization is met, if it is met, by 'the oath' (le serment), a term which should be understood not in the sense of a formal oath or of a social contract but rather in that of the will to preserve the group. This will however is inevitably accompanied by the exercise of constraint on members of the group whose actions tend to disintegrate it. In other words, the preservation of a group is accompanied by the development of authority and institutionalism. There then arises the temptation on the part of the leader or leaders of the group to represent his or their will as the 'real' will of all, considered as constituting an organic totality. But Sartre refuses to admit that the group is or can be an organic entity over and above its interrelated members. It is true that the leader may succeed not only in imposing his will but also in getting it accepted by the other members as their will. But the individual member is then reduced to the status of a quasi-inorganic entity, while 'the group is the machine which the sovereign makes to function perinde ac cadaver'.[2] The group can thus come to resemble an inorganic entity, a machine; but when constraint is removed, its members tend to break apart, thus manifesting the fact that while they are individual organic entities, the group is not.

---

[1] C.R.D., p. 376.
[2] Ibid., p. 601. Perinde ac cadaver, like a corpse.

The State is for Sartre the group of organizers and administrators to which the other groups composing a given society have conceded authority, probably more out of impotence than because they positively willed to do so. It is true that the organized State is required for the protection of groups; but it is not an organic entity with some sacred status. And its legitimacy consists in its ability to combine and manipulate other collections and groups. 'The idea of a diffused popular sovereignty which embodies itself in the sovereign is a mystification. There is no diffused sovereignty. The legitimacy of the sovereign is simply one of empirical fact, the ability to govern. 'I obey because I *cannot* do otherwise.'[2]

Sartre rejects therefore any deification of the State. And, as one would expect, he accepts the Marxist view that in the class struggle the State acts as 'the organ of the exploiting class (or classes)'.[3] At the same time he recognizes that even if the State acts as the organ of a dominant class, it none the less claims to represent the national interest and that it may conceive a 'totalizing' view of the common good and impose its mediating policy even on the dominant class. To say this however is to say that the group which constitutes the State tries to maintain itself as the accepted legitimate sovereign 'by serving the interests of the class from which it proceeds, and, *if needed, against its interests*.'[4] In plain English, a government composed of people from a particular class may take a wider view than that which would be suggested by the *prima facie* interests or advantage of the class in question. If so, this is to be interpreted in Marxist terms as a subtle way of preserving the position of the dominant class, which might otherwise be threatened.

To do him justice, Sartre is quite prepared to extend his rather cynical view of the State to the Communist State. In his opinion it is in the interest of the dominant group in the State to reduce other groups to collections or series and at the same time to condition the members of these series in such a way that they have the illusion of belonging to a genuine totality. This was what the Nazi government tried to do. And it can also be seen in the case of the so-called dictatorship of the proletariat. Talk about the proletariat exercising a dictatorship is for Sartre 'mystification'. The plain fact is that the dominant group takes good care to see that no other genuine groups arise and combines coercion with

---

[1] *Ibid.*, p. 609.   [2] *Ibid.*, p. 609.   [3] *Ibid.*, p. 610.   [4] *Ibid.*, p. 612.

conditioning to preserve the illusion that its own interest is that of the totality.

6. There is an obvious difference in atmosphere between *Being and Nothingness* on the one hand and the *Critique of Dialectical Reason* on the other. In the earlier work it is the totally free individual who stands in the centre of the picture, the individual who chooses his own values and is constantly transcending himself towards his future possibilities in the light of his freely chosen basic operative ideal, until at death he relapses into the facticity of *l'en-soi*, the in-itself. In spite of topical examples, the work can be looked on as an abstract analysis of the two fundamental concepts of the for-itself and the in-itself and as applying to man at all times. In the later work, the *Critique*, the general movement of history comes to the fore, and a much greater emphasis is laid on the group and concerted action by a group as it transcends a given social situation towards the realization of a new society. Again, though in the earlier work Sartre certainly recognizes the fact that every human being exists and acts in a given historical situation, and the fact that the exercise of human freedom is influenced by a variety of factors, environmental, physiological, and psychological, he is chiefly intent on arguing that limitations on human freedom are limitations only because the individual confers on them this significance. In the *Critique* this point of view does indeed reappear; but there is clearly a much greater emphasis on the constraining pressure of antecedent conditions on human activity. 'Above all, let no one proceed to interpret us as saying that man is free in all situations, as the Stoics claimed. We want to say exactly the contrary, namely that all men are slaves in so far as their experience of life develops in the field of the practico-inert and in the precise measure in which this field is originally conditioned by scarcity.'[1]

To draw attention to differences between *Being and Nothingness* and the *Critique of the Dialectical Reason* is not however to deny that there is any discernible continuity. In the earlier work, we can say, there is a dialectical relationship between the for-itself and the in-itself, between consciousness and being. The former arises through a negation of the latter; and it thus presupposes and depends on being in itself. At the same time being in itself requires consciousness in order to possess meaning and to be revealed as a world. In the *Critique* this dialectical relationship

[1] *Ibid.*, p. 369.

takes the form of that between man and his material environment. Man presupposes a material environment and acts on it; but the environment is revealed as Nature only through the mediation of man. Again, in *Being and Nothingness* there is a dialectical relationship between distinct consciousnesses, inasmuch as the for-itself is said to negate and yet to require the Other. The Other's 'look' both threatens the self and reveals it to itself. In the *Critique* the threat represented by the Other is described in terms of the concept of scarcity rather than in that of the look; but the basic dialectical relationship remains. Moreover, in spite of the prominence which Sartre gives to the idea of the group, his account of the genesis, nature and disintegration of the group shows clearly enough that for him the individual free agent is still the basic factor. And even though in the *Critique* a much greater emphasis is placed on the constraining influence of antecedent conditions, the domination of man by matter is represented as man's subjection to himself as exteriorized, as a self-estrangement which can be freely transcended.

As Sartre has not simply abandoned existentialism for Marxism but has tried to combine the two by re-interpreting Marxism in the light of an existentialist anthropology, it is only to be expected that we should find in his thought elements both of continuity and of discontinuity. It does not necessarily follow however that his existentialized Marxism is free of all ambiguity. As we have seen, he tries to combine two positions. On the one hand there is the thesis that it is man himself who makes history, and that he does so in a sense which excludes the claim that a certain social situation in the future is assured, as, that is to say, the inevitable result of the working out of a dialectical law which governs the historical process. On the other hand there is the thesis that the dialectical pattern is not simply imposed on history by the human mind but that history possesses a dialectical structure of such a kind that it makes sense to speak of man undergoing or suffering the dialectic. Sartre wishes to retain the concept of man as the free agent and at the same time to make room for the idea of man as the slave of the practico-inert. He wishes to say on the one hand that it is man who freely makes the dialectical movement of history, while on the other hand he proposes the view that history is one intelligible open-ended process. If by claiming that history is intelligible Sartre meant simply that historians can write intelligible accounts of historical events and movements, there would be no difficulty, other than the puzzles which the philosopher can propose about the relation between, for instance, an historian's reconstruction in the present and a past which no longer exists. But when Sartre claims that history is intelligible, he obviously does not mean simply that historiography is possible. He is claiming that history as a whole, though an unfinished whole, a process of 'totalization', embodies one intelligible movement. And the more this claim is pressed, the closer does Sartre come to a teleological view of history which implies the very conclusion which he wishes to avoid, namely that history is governed by a dialectical law of which man is the instrument.

Sartre can reply, for example, that the statement that it is man who makes history and thus its dialectical pattern is not incompatible with the statement that man does not simply impose the pattern but finds or recognizes it. For man finds what he has made. If he finds in history his own self-alienation and his enslavement to the practico-inert, he is recognizing in reflection what he himself has brought about. It does not follow that man deliberately caused his enslavement. The fact of the matter is that man's activity is conditioned from the start by an antecedent or given situation. He acts freely, but not in a vacuum. His action has results which constitute antecedent conditions for the actions of others. And so on. Given man's basic situation, the course of his history is what one might expect. But it is none the less the story of the activity of free agents. History should not be represented as an entity over and above human action and as determining it. It is human action, as subject to the constraining pressure of antecedent conditions. And this pressure can amount to enslavement, though it does not destroy man's basic freedom and his ability to transcend his enslavement.

Though however Sartre can make a good job of reconciling positions which may appear at first sight to be incompatible, it is difficult to feel satisfied. As we have noted, Sartre looks in man himself for the conditions of possibility of the dialectic of history. This enables him to claim that it is man himself who makes history and its dialectical pattern and that there is no impersonal dialectical law working independently and using man as an instrument. As however man acts in a situation, we may well be inclined to draw the conclusion that the movement of history is simply the unfolding or development of the original or basic dialectical relationship between man and his environment. In other words,

Sartre's grounding of the dialectic in man himself is not free from ambiguity. It might imply that man happens to have chosen to act in a certain way, when he could have acted in another way. Or it might imply that the dialectical movement of history is the development of a basic situation, a development which is predictable in principle. In this second case it would seem reasonable to speak of the operation of a law, even if the law were a law of man's nature as existing in a certain environment. As the second volume of the *Critique* has not yet appeared, it is obviously difficult to know how precisely Sartre proposes to develop his view of human history as possessing '*one* truth and *one* intelligibility'[1] without implying that the historical process is necessary. It would not be surprising however if he found the task rather difficult and was driven to talk about the analytical reason's inability to grasp the movement of dialectical thought.

The foregoing remarks relate of course simply to certain difficulties which arise if a philosopher tries to fuse Sartrian existentialism with Marxism. But we can very well go on to ask why Sartre or anyone else should make this attempt. It is not sufficient to answer that Marxism has become fossilized and that it needs an injection of humanism. This may very well be the case. But why choose Marxism in particular for rejuvenation? As we have seen, Sartre's reply is that Marxism is the one living philosophy of our time. Why however does he think this? He assumes of course that history can be divided up into epochs, and that in each epoch there is only one living philosophy. And even if we are prepared to grant the first assumption or at any rate to pass over it in silence, the second assumption is clearly questionable. There are other philosophies besides Marxism which are alive today. What makes Marxism more living than the others? It can hardly be because Marxism has practical implications, whereas so-called linguistic analysis, for example, is not practically oriented. For Sartre tells us that 'every philosophy is practical, even that which appears at first to be the most contemplative'.[2]

The answer is of course simple enough. Sartre assumes that in every epoch there is one ascending class. And the living philosophy of an epoch is for him the philosophy which brings to explicit expression the needs, interests, aspirations and goal of this class. It need not be thought out by members of the class in question. Marx and Engels were members of the bourgeoisie. But they

[1] *Ibid.*, p. 635.   [2] *Ibid.*, p. 16.

developed the philosophy which turned the proletariat from a class in itself into a class in and for itself and transformed it, or part of it, from a series of collections into a group. Marxism brings to explicit expression the consciousness of the ascending class and enables it to transcend the existing social situation towards a future to be realized by concerted revolutionary action. It is the one genuine revolutionary philosophy of our time, and it is therefore the one living philosophy of our time.

It is true that Sartre sometimes speaks of philosophy in what appears at first sight to be a different way. For example, he tells his readers that philosophy 'must present itself as the totalization of contemporary knowledge. The philosopher achieves the unification of all branches of knowledge.'[1] Taken by itself, this statement of the function of philosophy sounds like a reintroduction of the concept of a synthesis of the sciences as found in classical positivism. Sartre goes on however to say that the philosopher unifies contemporary knowledge by means of directive schemata which express 'the attitudes and the techniques of the ascending class in relation to its epoch and to the world'.[2] So the living philosophy is still the philosophy of the ascending class, in spite of talk about unification of the sciences.

It may well be true to say that every statement of the nature of philosophy expresses a philosophical stance, unless perhaps it is a case of a statement simply about linguistic usage. However this may be, it seems pretty clear that Sartre's concept of living philosophy expresses a previous acceptance of Marxism. For the matter of that, it is a previous acceptance of a Marxist point of view which governs his selection of historical examples and even his definition or description of man as 'a practical organism living with a multiplicity of organisms in a field of scarcity'.[3] Man is doubtless what Sartre says that he is, even if this is not all that he is. But the selection of certain aspects of man and his situation for particular emphasis is clearly governed by a previous conviction that Marxism is the one living philosophy of our time. In the long run we can hardly avoid the conclusion that it is Sartre's personal social and political commitment which is basically responsible for his choice of Marxism as the philosophy which he proposes to rejuvenate.

If the living philosophy of an epoch represents the self-consciousness and aspirations of the ascending class, the natural conclusion to draw is that it is true only in a relative sense. For

[1] *Ibid.*, p. 15.   [2] *Ibid.*, p. 15.   [3] *Ibid.*, p. 688.

there have been other epochs, with other ascending classes and other living philosophies. Sartre however does not wish to tie Marxism in an exclusive manner to the rising class. In the *Critique* he insists that Marxism is the philosophy of alienated man, not simply of the alienated worker. And, as we have seen, he tries to give Marxism a foundation in an anthropology or doctrine of man which exhibits the possibility of man's enslavement but is none the less logically prior to the emergence of the class struggle, inasmuch as it goes back to the basic situation of man as such. When looked at under this aspect, Marxism seems to be presented not simply as the philosophy of a particular class but rather as the true philosophy of man and of his history. To a certain extent a harmonization of the two points of view is perhaps possible. For it may be claimed, as the Marxist would doubtless claim, that the triumph of the proletariat will bring with it, sooner or later, the liberation of man in general. The salvation of man will be achieved through the proletarian revolution. But in this case Marxism would seem to be not simply the living philosophy of our time, in the sense mentioned above, but the one true philosophy, which would have been true at any time. Perhaps in the second volume of the *Critique* Sartre will devote some careful reflection to the question of precisely what truth-claims he wishes to make on behalf of his rejuvenated Marxism. As things stand, he does not seem to have made the matter very clear.

To many people however criticism of this kind has little value. Those who can swallow the contention that Marxism is the living philosophy of our time will regard such criticism as just the sort of tiresome exhibition which one might expect from an obscurantist bourgeois philosopher. Those however who believe that Marxism has life and power only because it has become the official ideology of a powerful, self-perpetuating and authoritarian Party and that, left to itself, it would go the way of other notable systems, may be impatient for another reason. They may think that Sartre has devoted his very considerable talents to pouring new wine into old skins, and that there are more valuable occupations than pointing out inconsistencies or ambiguities in his attempt to rejuvenate a philosophy which belongs to the nineteenth century rather than to the second half of the twentieth century. Perhaps so. But Marxism still has a powerful appeal. It possesses an obvious importance, even today. This however is compatible with its being a powerful myth, powerful, that is to say, when it is believed. It is arguable that Sartre has become fascinated by this myth because he sees in it the expression and instrument of a cause to which he has committed himself. At the same time it is a myth which can be misused and turned into the instrument of an oppressive group intent on the preservation of its power. Hence the attempt to rejuvenate the myth and to give it fresh life as a revolutionary call to the creation of a new society.

CHAPTER XVIII

THE PHENOMENOLOGY OF MERLEAU-PONTY

A. Camus; the absurd and the philosophy of revolt — Merleau-Ponty; the body-subject and its world — Merleau-Ponty and Marxism — Lévi-Strauss and man.

1. IF a philosopher wishes to discuss such themes as human freedom, authenticity, self-commitment and personal relationships, his treatment is inevitably abstract and expressed in terms of general or universal concepts. Karl Jaspers, for instance, made a sharp distinction between the scientific objectification of man and the philosopher's endeavour to illuminate man's inner awareness of his freedom with a view to clarifying for man his basic possibilities of self-transcendence.[1] But even Jaspers had to write *about* man, employing universal concepts, even if he insisted on the need for special categories for this purpose. It is therefore understandable if in addition to their more professional philosophical writings certain thinkers, such as Sartre and Marcel, have published plays and, in Sartre's case, novels too, in which they have been able to exhibit 'problems of life' in terms of the actions, predicaments, options and relationships of individuals. Such works may give concrete and dramatic expression to themes which have already been treated in a more abstract way, or, as in Marcel's case, they may precede the more abstract and philosophical expression. In both cases however the two kinds of works have a recognizable relationship to one another which is lacking in cases in which a writer sets his philosophy aside and produces popular detective stories to augment his income.

If however the thought of Sartre is discussed in accounts of French philosophy, it is because of the writings which profess to be and are philosophical works, not on account of plays such as *The Flies* or *In Camera*, even if the latter stand in a recognizable relationship to the former. And the question arises whether one is

---

[1] Jaspers' point of view might be expressed in this manner. Considered as an object of scientific study, man is something already made, and individuals are classifiable in various ways by physiologists, psychologists and so on. For the philosophers of 'existence' (*Existenz*) man is the free agent who makes himself: he is always 'possible existence'. And each individual is unique, a unique possibility of self-transcendence.

justified in including mention of literary figures who are commonly thought of as having philosophical significance but who not only did not publish philosophical works in the academic sense but also refrained from making any claim to be philosophers. It is difficult to determine rules to which no exception can reasonably be taken. If we think of philosophy as a science which is concerned with proving that certain propositions are true, we shall be unlikely, for example, to include a treatment of Dostoievsky in a history of Russian philosophy. And though mention of his name occurs fairly frequently in, for instance, the work by N. O. Lossky,[1] he is mentioned incidentally and not listed among Russian philosophers. At the same time it is possible to take a wider view of philosophically significant writing; and no great surprise would have been caused if aspects of Dostoievsky's thought had been considered. In fact, the *Encyclopedia of Philosophy* edited by Paul Edwards contains an article devoted to the great Russian novelist.

In regard to recent French thought similar questions can be raised in regard to A. Camus.[2] He was not indeed a professional philosopher, nor did he ever claim to be. But in view of the themes of which he wrote he has been commonly mentioned in accounts of existentialism in France, even though he denied that he was an existentialist. And the insertion of some remarks about him seems defensible, though not obligatory.

Albert Camus (1913–60) was born and educated in Algeria. In 1940 he went to Paris, where he participated actively in the Resistance. In 1942 he published his novel *L'étranger*[3] and a well known essay entitled *Le mythe de Sisyphe*.[4] After the war he continued to be involved in political activity, and a number of his political essays, which originally appeared in the newspaper *Combat* and elsewhere, have been reprinted in the three volumes of *Actuelles*.[5] Camus' famous novel *La Peste* appeared in 1947,[6]

---

[1] *History of Russian Philosophy* (New York, 1951).

[2] There are of course a good many French literary figures whose writings possess philosophical significance but who cannot be all discussed in a history of philosophy. Georges Bataille, author of *L'expérience intérieure* (1943), *Sur Nietzsche* (1945) and other works is a case in point.

[3] Translated by S. Gilbert as *The Outsider* (London, 1946) and *The Stranger* (New York, 1946).

[4] Translated as *The Myth of Sisyphus and Other Essays* by J. O'Brien (New York and London, 1955).

[5] Paris, 1950–8. A selection of these articles have been published in an English translation by J. O'Brien entitled *Resistance, Rebellion and Death* (New York and London, 1961).

[6] Translated as *The Plague*, by S. Gilbert (London and New York, 1948).

and in 1951 he published *L'homme revolté*,[1] an essay which led to a breach in relations between himself and Sartre. The novel entitled *La chute*[2] appeared in 1956. In the following year Camus received the Nobel prize for literature. But in 1960 he was killed in a motor accident. His *Notebooks* (*Carnets*) have been translated into English[3] and also some of his plays.[4]

Camus is well known for his statement that 'there is only one really serious philosophical problem, that of suicide. To judge that life is or is not worth the trouble of being lived, this is to reply to the fundamental question of philosophy.'[5] On the face of it this may seem a very eccentric view of philosophy. The presupposition however is that man seeks a meaning in the world and in human life and history which would ground and support his ideals and values. Man wants to be assured that reality is an intelligible teleological process, comprising an objective moral order. To put the matter in another way, man desires metaphysical assurance that his life is part of an intelligible process directed to an ideal goal, and that in striving after his personal ideals he has the backing and support, so to speak, of the universe or of reality as a whole. The great religious leaders and creators of metaphysical systems and world-views have tried to supply this need. But their interpretations of the world cannot stand up to criticism. In the end the world is revealed, to the clear-sighted man, as without any determinate purpose or meaning. The world is not rational. Hence arises the feeling of the absurd (*le sentiment de l'absurde*). Strictly speaking, the world is not absurd in itself: it simply is. 'The absurd arises from this confrontation between man's appeal and the irrational silence of the world. . . . The irrational, human nostalgia and the absurd which arises from their confrontation, those are the three personages of the drama . . .'[6] The feeling of the absurd can arise in a variety of ways, through, for example, the perception of Nature's indifference to man's values and ideals, through recognition of the finality of death, or through the shock caused by the

---

[1] Translated as *The Rebel* by A. Bower (London, 1953; revised version, New York, 1956).

[2] Translated as *The Fall* by J. O'Brien (London and New York, 1957).

[3] *Notebooks 1935–42*, translated by P. Thody (New York and London, 1963). *Notebooks 1942–51*, translated by J. O'Brien (New York, 1965).

[4] *Caligula and Three Other Plays*, translated by S. Gilbert (London and New York, 1958).

[5] *Le mythe de Sisyphe* (new French edition, Paris, 1942), p. 15.

[6] *Ibid.*, p. 45. Camus distinguishes between the feeling of the absurd and the idea or conviction (the clear consciousness) of the absurd.

sudden perception of the pointlessness of life's routine. Some thinkers understand the absurd but then pursue a policy of escapism. Thus Karl Jaspers leaps from the 'shipwreck' of human longings to the Transcendent, while Leo Chestov makes a similar leap to a God who is beyond reason. But the man who, like Nietzsche, is able to look the absurdity of human existence in the face sees the meaning of the world disappear. Hence the problem of suicide. For 'to see the meaning of this life dissipated, to see our reason for existing disappear, that is what is unbearable. One cannot live without meaning.'[1]

Suicide is not however the action recommended by Camus. In his opinion suicide means surrender to the absurd, capitulation. Human pride and greatness are shown neither in surrender nor in the sort of escapism indulged in by the existential philosophers (*les philosophes existentiels*, such as Jaspers) but in living in the consciousness of the absurd and yet revolting against it by man's committing himself and living in the fullest manner possible. There are indeed no absolute standards which permit us to dictate to a man how he should live. As Ivan Karamazov says, all is permitted. But it does not follow that the absurd 'recommends crime. This would be puerile. . . . If all experiences are indifferent, that of duty is as legitimate as any other. One can be virtuous by caprice.'[2] The man of the absurd (*l'homme absurde*) can take various forms. The Don Juan who enjoys to the full, as long as he is able, experiences of a certain type, while conscious that none of them possesses any ultimate significance, is one form. So is the man who recognizes the meaninglessness of history and the ultimate futility of human action but who none the less commits himself to a social or political cause in his historical situation. So is the creative artist who sees clearly enough that both he and his works are doomed to extinction but who none the less devotes his life to artistic production. And in *La peste* Camus raises the question whether there can be an atheist saint. The man of the absurd lives without God. But it by no means follows that he cannot devote himself in a self-sacrificing manner to the welfare of his fellow men. Indeed, if he does so without hope of reward and conscious that in the long run it makes no difference how he acts, he exhibits the greatness of man precisely by this combination of recognition of ultimate futility with a life of self-sacrificing love. It is possible to be a saint without illusion.

---

[1] From the play *Caligula*.   [2] *Le mythe de Sisyphe*, p. 94.

In maintaining the meaninglessness of the world and of human history (in the sense that they have no goal or purpose which is given independently of man) Camus is substantially at one with Sartre, though the latter does not dwell so much as the former on the theme of 'the absurd'. Sartre is not however the source of Camus' assumption. We should not of course speak as though an original writer such as Camus simply borrowed his ideas from a predecessor. But it is clear that it was Nietzsche who provided a stimulating influence. Camus believed that Nietzsche had rightly seen the advent and rise of nihilism; and, like the German philosopher, he looked to man as the only being capable of overcoming nihilism. At the same time it does not follow that Camus can be properly described as a Nietzschean. For one thing, Camus came to be more and more concerned with injustice and oppression in human society in a manner in which Nietzsche was not. Camus did not indeed renounce his belief 'that this world has no ultimate meaning';[1] but he came to lay more and more stress on revolt against injustice, oppression and cruelty rather than on revolt against the human condition as such. Indeed, he became convinced that the feeling of the absurd, taken by itself, can be used to justify anything, murder included. 'If one believes in nothing, if nothing makes sense, if we can assert no value whatsoever, everything is permissible and nothing is important. ... One is free to stoke the crematory fires or to give one's life to the care of lepers.'[2] In point of fact revolt presupposes the assertion of values. True, they are man's creation. But this does not alter the fact that if I revolt against oppression or injustice, I assert the values of freedom and justice. With Camus, in other words, cosmic absurdity, so to speak, tends to retreat into the background; and a moral idealism comes to the fore, a moral idealism which did not call for the production of an élite, an aristocracy of higher men, at the expense of the herd, but which insisted on freedom and justice for all, real freedom and justice moreover, not oppression or enslavement masquerading under these honoured names.

Camus was no admirer of bourgeois society. But he became acutely aware of the way in which revolt against the existing order can end with the imposition of slavery. 'The great event of the twentieth century was the forsaking of the values of freedom by the revolutionary movement, the progressive retreat of socialism based on freedom before the attacks of a Caesarian and military

[1] *Resistance, Rebellion and Death*, p. 21.   [2] *The Rebel*, p. 13.

socialism.'[1] Man cannot play the part of a spectator of history as a whole; and no historical enterprise can be more than a risk or adventure for which some degree of rational justification can be offered. It follows that no historical enterprise can rightly be used to justify 'any excess or any ruthless and absolutist position'.[2] For example, killing and oppression in the name of the movement of history or of a terrestrial paradise to be attained at some indefinite future date are unjustified. If absolute nihilism can be used to justify anything, so can absolute rationalism, in which God is replaced by history. In regard to their consequences, 'there is no difference between the two attitudes. From the moment that they are accepted, the earth becomes a desert.'[3] We have to get away from absolutes and turn to moderation and limitation. 'Absolute freedom is the right of the strongest to dominate'[4] and thus prolongs injustice. 'Absolute justice is achieved by the suppression of all contradiction: therefore it destroys freedom.'[5] It is on behalf of living human beings not on behalf of history or of man in some future age that we are called upon to rebel against existing injustice and oppression, wherever it may be found. 'Real generosity towards the future lies in giving all to the present.'[6]

As has already been noted, the publication of *The Rebel* (*L'homme revolté*) led to a breach of relations between Camus and Sartre.[7] The latter had been coming closer to Communism, though without joining the Party, and he was already engaged in the project of combining existentialism and Marxism. Camus, while disclaiming the label 'existentialist', was convinced that the two were incompatible, and that Marxism, with its secularization of Christianity and substitution of the movement of history for God, led straight to the death of freedom and the horrors of Stalinism. As for bourgeois democracy, which replaced eternal divine truths by abstract principles of reason, the trouble has been, according to Camus, that the principles have not been applied. In the name of freedom bourgeois society has condoned exploitation and social injustice; and it has sanctioned violence. What then does Camus wish to put in the place of Communism, Fascism, Nazism and bourgeois democracy? Apart from some

---

[1] *Resistance, Rebellion and Death*, p. 67.   [2] *The Rebel*, p. 253.
[3] *Ibid.*, p. 253.   [4] *Ibid.*, p. 251.   [5] *Ibid.*, p. 252.   [6] *Ibid.*, p. 268.
[7] A critical review of the work was published by Francis Jeanson. Camus replied in the form of a letter addressed to the editor, Sartre himself. And this elicited a combative counterblast from Sartre.

remarks about the benefits to man which have been obtained through trade unionism, he gives no clear picture. And Sartre of course sees him as criticizing various movements but offering only vague and abstract ideas. Camus however has no intention of offering a blueprint. His philosophy of revolt is mainly concerned with moral values and the development of moral responsibility; and he insists that though the rebel must act because he believes that it is right to do so, he must also act with the recognition that he might be wrong. The Communist will not entertain the idea that he might be wrong. Hence his ruthlessness. The only hope for the future is an open society, in which the passion of revolt and the spirit of moderation are in constant tension.[1]

It does not follow however that Camus is an optimist with unbounded faith in man, provided that unjust institutions can be overthrown. In *The Fall* he makes his central character, Clamence, refer to 'the basic duplicity of the human being',[2] as though he located the root of evil in man himself. This is not indeed incompatible with what he has to say about social institutions. For they are made by man. At the same time there seems to be a shift of emphasis in his thought from the absurdity which arises in the confrontation between man and the world to social evils, and from social evils to the evil in the heart of man. How his thought would have developed if it had not been for his untimely death, it is obviously impossible to say.

Camus was a man who found himself unable to accept Christian belief but who not only had high moral ideals but was also passionately concerned with human freedom, social justice, peace and the elimination of violence. He was not anti-Christian in the sense in which this term would be ordinarily understood. What he objected to was not so much Christianity as such (he had Christian friends whom he admired) but the compromise and ambiguous attitude in regard to social and political evils which he regarded as a betrayal of the original Christian inspiration. 'When man submits God to moral judgment, he kills him in his own heart.'[3] The question then arises, what is the basis of morality? If we deny God in the name of justice, 'can the idea of justice be understood without the idea of God?'[4] Camus was not sufficiently interested

---

[1] Camus laid great emphasis on the reduction of violence. This included for him the elimination of capital punishment. See his 'Reflections on the Guillotine' in *Resistance, Rebellion and Death*.
[2] *The Collected Fiction of Albert Camus* (London, 1960), p. 282.
[3] *The Rebel*, p. 57.   [4] *Ibid.*, p. 57.

in professional philosophy to devote time and energy to prolonged reflection on such problems. He was convinced however that man cannot live without values. If he chooses to live, by that very fact he asserts a value, that life is good or worth living or should be made worth living. Man as man can revolt against exploitation, oppression, injustice and violence, and by the very fact that he revolts he asserts the values in the name of which he revolts. A philosophy of revolt has therefore a moral basis; and if this basis is denied, whether explicitly or in the name of some abstraction such as the movement of history or through a policy of expediency, what began with revolt, with the expression of freedom, turns into tyranny and the suppression of freedom. Camus tended to leave his assertions without any developed theoretical support; but he undoubtedly threw light, as the citation asserted when he was awarded the Nobel Prize, on the problems of human conscience in our times. He was genuinely and deeply concerned with these problems, and in treating of them he displayed, as writers on him have noticed, a combination of commitment and detachment. He was certainly committed; but at the same time he preserved the measure of detachment which enabled him to avoid the lamentable but not uncommon tendency to fulminate against the evils of one political system while excusing similar or even worse evils in another system or country. In other words, Camus' commitment was basically moral rather than political in character.

2. In turning from Albert Camus to Maurice Merleau-Ponty (1908–61) we turn from a socially and politically committed essayist, novelist and dramatist to a professional philosopher. Not that Merleau-Ponty can be described as uncommitted. For he believed that ethics cannot be divorced from political action; and up to a point he supported the Marxists, even if he had little use for Marxist dogmatism. Whereas however we cannot consider Camus' thought apart from his social and political commitment, there are large areas of Merleau-Ponty's philosophy which can be treated on a purely theoretical level.

After studying at the École Normale in Paris and taking his agrégation in philosophy, Merleau-Ponty taught in a lycée and then at the École Normale. After the war, during which he served as an officer, he became a professor first at the University of Lyon and then at the Sorbonne. In 1952 he was appointed to the chair of philosophy at the Collège de France. Merleau-Ponty was one of the founders of *Les temps modernes* and a co-editor, along with

Sartre. He has sometimes been described as an existentialist;[1] but though there is indeed ground for associating him with atheist existentialism, he is better described as a phenomenologist. This label helps at any rate to differentiate him from Sartre. It is true of course that Sartre has developed phenomenological analyses. The point is however that the label 'existentialist', together with the fact that Merleau-Ponty was for a time associated with Sartre, tends to give the impression that the former was a junior partner or even disciple of the latter, whereas he was really an independent and original thinker.

Merleau-Ponty's first main publication was *La structure du comportement*,[2] which appeared at Paris in 1942. This was followed in 1945 by *Phénoménologie de la perception*.[3] In 1947 Merleau-Ponty published *Humanisme et terreur, essai sur le problème communiste*, in which he examined the problem of the use of terror by the Communists. A collection of essays, entitled *Sens et non-sens*, appeared in 1948.[4] The inaugural lecture given by Merleau-Ponty at the Collège de France was published in 1953 under the title *L'éloge de la philosophie*.[5] In 1955 he published *Les aventures de la dialectique*, which includes a criticism of Sartre, and this was followed in 1960 by *Signes*.[6] Before his death Merleau-Ponty had started on a new work, *Le visible et l'invisible*, intended as a fresh statement of his philosophy. The part of the work which he had written was published in 1964, together with notes for the projected parts.

In a lecture which he gave at Geneva in 1951 Merleau-Ponty asserts that the twentieth century has erased the dividing line between body and mind and 'sees human life as through and through mental and corporeal, always based upon the body and always (even in its most carnal modes) interested in relationships between persons'.[1] This statement refers of course to the overcoming of dualism on the one hand and of a reductive materialism on the other. And the reader may wonder whether it is not perhaps

---

[1] For example, there is one excellent work on his thought by A. de Waehlens entitled *Une philosophie de l'ambiguité: l'existentialisme de Maurice Merleau-Ponty* (Louvain, 1951).

[2] Translated by A. L. Fisher as *The Structure of Behaviour* (Boston, 1963).

[3] Translated by C. Smith as *Phenomenology of Perception* (London and New York, 1962).

[4] Translated by H. L. and P. A. Dreyfus as *Sense and Nonsense* (Evanston, Ill., 1964).

[5] Translated by J. Wild and J. M. Edie as *In Praise of Philosophy* (Evanston, Ill., 1963).

[6] Translated by R. C. McCleary as *Signs* (Evanston, Ill., 1964).

too sweeping. Sartre, for example, is certainly a twentieth-century writer; but as far as his analysis of the concepts of 'the in-itself' and 'the for-itself' is concerned, the distinction between the two seems to be sharpened into an antithesis, a pretty obvious dualism. Merleau-Ponty is however quite well aware of this fact. When he refers to twentieth-century thought, he is clearly referring to what he considers its most significant and valid trend, a more adequate self-awareness by man, an awareness which is expressed in, though not confined to, Merleau-Ponty's own philosophy. He sees the line of thought which he sums up in his concept of the 'body-subject' as triumphing over dualism on the one hand and materialism and behaviourism on the other and, to put the matter in another way, as going beyond the antithesis between idealism and materialism. In existentialism man is indeed conceived as essentially a being in the world, dialectically related to it in the sense that man cannot be understood apart from the world, apart from his situation, while what we call 'the world' cannot be understood apart from the meanings conferred on it by man. This sort of idea is of course present in Sartre and expresses the trend of thought to which Merleau-Ponty refers. But Sartre also presses the distinction between consciousness and its object in such a way as to give new life to a version of the Cartesian dualism against which Merleau-Ponty vigorously reacts.

By dualism Merleau-Ponty understands the view of man as a composite of body and spirit or mind, the former being considered as a thing among things, subject to the same causal relations which are found between other material objects, while the latter is looked on as the source of all knowledge, freedom and openness to others or, to use Merleau-Ponty's term, as 'existence'. Obviously, Merleau-Ponty does not deny that the body can be treated as an object and considered as such in scientific inquiry and research. But in his view this possibility presupposes the human body as being itself a subject, in dialogue with the world and with other persons. It is not a question of maintaining that there is in the body a distinct soul or spirit, in virtue of which the composite being can be described as a subject. It is the body which is subject. This view obviously entails understanding body in a sense rather different from that in which it would be understood within a dualistic framework of thought, namely as opposed to mind or spirit. It is precisely this opposition which Merleau-Ponty wishes

[1] *Signs*, pp. 226–7.

to overcome and thinks that he has overcome through his concept of body-subject. If we start with dualism and then try to overcome it by making the one or other factor primary, we either reduce mind to body or identify the real man with an incorporeal soul or spirit. Merleau-Ponty however rejects such reductionism and insists that the human body is one reality which is at the same time material and spiritual. He is of course aware that there are factors in the situation which provide an at any rate *prima facie* ground for dualism; and he is aware of the very great difficulty which we encounter if we try to avoid language which implies dualism. In other words, he admits that the concept of the body-subject is difficult to express, and that one has to look for a new language to express it. He is convinced however that this is precisely what philosophers ought to try to do, and that they should not tamely let themselves remain imprisoned in old linguistic and conceptual fetters.

It may seem that Merleau-Ponty's project bears a marked similarity to that of Gilbert Ryle in his work *The Concept of Mind*. So it does in some respects. Both philosophers are opponents of dualism, but neither wishes to reduce man to a machine. For each of them the human being is one single 'incarnate' reality which lives, desires, thinks, acts, and so on. At the same time there is also a clear dissimilarity. One of Ryle's contentions is that all mental operations should be understood in terms of public or witnessable activities.[1] It is natural therefore that he should devote his attention to the mental phenomena of which we are easily aware; and as a counterblast to dualism he constantly cites examples of what we are accustomed to say in ordinary language, to expressions which militate against the idea of purely private and occult mental activities, and so against the notion of 'the ghost in the machine'. Merleau-Ponty however is intent on showing that mental activities, in the sense of activities at the level of more or less clear consciousness, do not constitute a mental life which accrues to a body that is itself without subjectivity, but that they presuppose the body-subject. He is not trying to reduce psychical to physical processes. He argues that already at a preconscious level the body is subject. In other words, he wishes to explore a territory which underlies and is presupposed by the various activities that give rise to the dualistic expressions of

---

[1] It is this aspect of his thought which has given rise to the accusation of behaviourism, the validity of which Ryle rejects.

ordinary language. It is understandable therefore that he insists on the need for fresh concepts and modes of expression. The field specially chosen for investigation by Merleau-Ponty is perception. In a paper which he wrote in connection with his candidacy for a chair at the Collège de France he says that his 'first two works sought to restore the world of perception'.[1] If we simply state however that Merleau-Ponty develops a phenomenology of perception, the statement is apt to mislead. For the word 'perception' may suggest the activity of describing the essential structure of this conscious activity when it has been turned into an object of reflection. Merleau-Ponty however is concerned with perception as the mode of existence of the body-subject at a pre-conscious level, with, that is to say, the dialogue between the body, as subject, and its world at a level which is presupposed by consciousness. In this case of course the phenomenological method, as employed by him in this context, cannot take the form of a faithful description of an immediate datum of reflective awareness or consciousness. It is a case of delving into the region of obscurity; and Merleau-Ponty admits that any complete illumination of this obscure field is unattainable. One can only feel one's way, grope, and try to let in as much light as one can. He believes however that it is important to make the effort. For 'the perceived world is the always presupposed foundation of all rationality, all value and all existence'.[2] It is not a case of maintaining that thought, for example, consists of transformed sensations. It is a case of trying to penetrate to the presupposed foundation of thought and of all conscious activity and trying to elucidate its structure. The philosopher, as Merleau-Ponty conceives him, is very much an explorer.

In his first main work, La structure du comportement (The Structure of Behaviour) Merleau-Ponty approaches the theme of the relations between man and his environment through an examination of certain modern physiological and psychological theories, such as behaviourism and the Gestalt psychology. In other words, he places himself on the level of scientific theories and confronts these theories with what he believes to be the facts of man's perceptual behaviour. He argues, for example, that we cannot account for the facts by interpreting the relation between

[1] The Primacy of Perception and Other Essays, edited by J. M. Edie (Northwestern University Press, 1964), p. 3.
[2] Ibid., p. 13.

the human body and its environment in terms which imply that
the body is a machine with pre-established mechanisms which are
set in motion simply by reaction to external stimuluses. 'The true
stimulus is not the one defined by physics and chemistry; the
reaction is not this or that particular series of movements; and the
connection between the two is not the simple coincidence of two
successive events'.[1] Science, for its own purposes, can legitimately
consider the body as a thing among things; but the scientific point
of view is formed through a process of abstraction from a level of
real behaviour at which the organism exhibits a kind of prospective activity, behaving as though it were oriented towards certain
meanings or goals. The organism's capacity for meaningful
response can be exercised of course only within limits and in
dependence on conditions in its environment. It is not however
a question simply of a 'blind' response. The organism exhibits
'subjectivity', though at a pre-conscious level.

Merleau-Ponty's line of thought can be expressed in this way.
The relation between the human organism and its environment
cannot be expressed simply in terms of mechanistic reciprocal
causality. That is to say, we cannot reduce the reciprocal action
between the terms of the relation 'to a series of uni-directional
determinations'.[2] There is indeed causal interaction. For example,
food acts on the organism, and the organism acts on the food by
assimilating it. But the food is *food* only in virtue of the structure,
needs and activity of the organism. The effect produced by *x*
cannot be understood simply in terms of *x*. There is a complex
dialectical relationship. And subjectivity is present when for
one of the factors in the relationship all other factors constitute a
world. Merleau-Ponty does not mean to imply that the perceived
world (at the level of experience under consideration) is consciously
perceived by the body-subject as a world. But he insists that on
the level of perceptual behaviour there is already a global environment or milieu as a term in a dialectical relationship, correlative
to the aptitudes (the 'can' or ability) of the subject. As we ascend
the levels of experience and consciousness, the environment takes
on new forms or shapes, in correlation with the meaning-confer-
ring activity of the subject. But these presuppose a pre-conscious
level on which the human organism unconsciously confers meaning and constitutes a milieu or environment. It does not of course
confer meaning on nothing; nor does it create the things about it.

---

[1] *The Structure of Behaviour*, p. 99.   [2] *Ibid.*, p. 161.

But if we can talk about the ego and its world at the level of consciousness, we can also talk about the body-subject and its world or milieu at the pre-conscious level. The epistemological distinction between subject and object is not yet there. But there is none the less a *lived* dialectical relationship, which forms the constantly presupposed basis for higher levels of experience, though a higher level differs qualitatively from a lower level.

To assert that there is a dialectical relationship between man and his environment is to assert that man is from the beginning a being in the world, and that both terms of the relationship are real. In this sense Merleau-Ponty is a realist. At the level of reflective consciousness it becomes possible for philosophers to advance theories which subordinate the object to the subject, idealist theories that is to say; but this sort of theory distorts the original and basic relationship between man and his environment which is presupposed by every level of behaviour and experience. At the same time to say that this relationship is dialectical or that it is a continual dialogue between man and his environment is to say, among other things, that the meanings of things are determined not only by the object but also by the subject. To take a simple example, if that tree appears as far away, it is for me, in relation to myself, that it appears as far off. I am the centre in relation to which one tree appears as near, another as far. On the scientific level of course one can freely adopt the frame of reference which suits one's purpose; but on the level of perceptual behaviour spatial relations 'appear' within the dialogue between the human organism and its environment. Similarly, colours are neither purely objective nor purely subjective; they appear in the lived dialogue between the body-subject and the world. Obviously, the environment or situation changes. So does the subject, not simply as an effect of external stimuli but also through its own active responses which contribute to determining the meanings of the stimuli. The dialectical relationship is not static; the active dialogue is perpetual, as long as the subject exists. But it is within the dialogue between the body-subject and its environment that 'the world' comes to appear, though its appearances change.

In *La structure du comportement* Merleau-Ponty considers, as we have already mentioned, certain modern psychological theories. He tries to show that the facts discovered by these psychologists are at variance with and do not fit their presuppositions and implied ontological perspectives. On the contrary, the facts demand neither the reduction of the subject to a thing or object nor an idealist theory of a consciousness which creates the object but rather a recognition of the basic situation of an 'incarnate' subject involved in the world and in constant dialogue with it. In other words, Merleau-Ponty takes certain theories and tries to delve into the obscure region which is presupposed by all thought and knowledge. In his subsequent work *Phénoménologie de la perception* (*Phenomenology of Perception*) he instals himself from the first in perceptual behaviour 'in order to pursue the analysis of this exceptional relation between the subject and its body and its world'.[1] We cannot however reproduce the contents of this remarkable work. It must suffice to draw attention to a few points.

It may well have occurred to the reader that inasmuch as the passage just quoted makes a distinction between subject and body, it is hardly compatible with what we have been saying about Merleau-Ponty's concept of the body-subject as one single reality. But it is necessary to make some distinctions. We can of course consider the body purely objectively, and then we naturally distinguish between the body as object and the subject. However, 'the objective body is not the truth of the phenomenal body, the truth, that is to say, of the body as we live it. It is only an impoverished image thereof, and the problem of the relations between soul and body do not concern the objective body, which has only a conceptual existence, but the phenomenal body.'[2] The body considered as a purely physical object distinct from the subject is an abstraction, legitimate enough for a variety of purposes but not an expression of the body as lived or experienced. The latter is the body-subject. At the same time the body-subject is temporal: it transcends itself, and there are distinguishable levels. For example, the body considered as a group of habits can be considered as 'my body' by the subject or 'I' as it transcends the already given. 'We do not say that . . . the subject *thinks itself* as inseparable from the idea of the body.'[3] Indeed, Merleau-Ponty sometimes speaks of 'the soul', as a higher level of the subject's self-organization. But he insists that such distinctions refer to distinguishable aspects of one reality, and that they should not be understood in a dualistic sense. All such distinctions are made within a unity, the body-subject.

Merleau-Ponty's rejection of any dualistic interpretation of the

[1] *The Primacy of Perception*, pp. 4–5.
[2] *Phénoménologie de la perception*, p. 493.   [3] *Ibid.*, p. 467.

human being is naturally accompanied, or followed, by a rejection of any real distinction between language and thought. It is true of course that when linguistic expressions have once been created and have become the common possession of a given society, with meanings determined by convention, they can be repeated and handed on from generation to generation. The 'spoken word',[1] language as already constituted, thus forms a datum which human beings appropriate in the course of education. And as, given this datum, it is possible for writers to invent new expressions to express new concepts, thus adding 'the speaking word'[2] to the 'spoken word', there is a natural inclination to regard thought as an inner activity which is distinct from language. One thinks and then gives verbal expression to the thought. Merleau-Ponty however regards this as a mistaken interpretation of the situation. In the case of the 'speaking word' the meaning is indeed in a state of coming to be; but it by no means follows that it comes to be *before* its symbolic or linguistic expression. We may talk, for example, of the poet seeking words to express his thoughts but the thought takes shape in and through its expression. He does not first have his poem 'in his mind' in an unexpressed state and then express it. For if he has it in his mind, he has already expressed it. Whether he has written it down or spoken it aloud is irrelevant. If the poem can be said to be present in his mind, it is present as expressed. It is precisely in the case of the 'speaking word' that the relation between thought and language becomes most clearly apparent. They are two aspects of one reality. If we separate them, words become mere physical occurrences, *flatus vocis*, to use a medieval term.

The general view maintained by Merleau-Ponty of the relation between thought and language is of course in harmony with that of the so-called 'linguistic analysts', who are opposed to the idea of a separation or real distinction between an occult activity, thought, on the one hand and the public phenomenon of language on the other. Like Gilbert Ryle, Merleau-Ponty recognizes the absurdity of complaining that we have only the words of a philosopher of the past, such as Plato or Hegel, and do not enjoy access to his thoughts or to his mind. For the philosopher's thoughts are expressed in his writings; and access to his words is access to his mind. The philosophers of ordinary language however are principally concerned with what Merleau-Ponty calls

---

[1] *Ibid.*, p. 229, *La parole parlée.*   [2] *Ibid.*, *La parole parlante.*

'the spoken word'. Inasmuch as they do not exclude in principle either the revision of ordinary language or the invention of fresh terms, they leave room for the 'speaking word'. At the same time the emphasis is laid on the 'spoken word', whereas Merleau-Ponty lays emphasis rather on 'the speaking word'. For he is intent on exhibiting the connections between his theory of language and his theory of the body-subject. He recognizes a kind of pre-linguistic understanding by the body of its world, a 'practognosis' as he calls it,[1] which is not distinct from the bodily behaviour in question. But thought in any proper sense of the word comes to exist in and through linguistic expression. The social aspects of the subject are of course manifested in the 'spoken word'. The human subject however is capable of transcending the already given or acquired; and this aspect is exhibited in the 'speaking word', in the creativity of scientists, poets and philosophers. But even with them thought and expression go together; and this shows that thought is anchored, so to speak, in the body-subject. There are successive levels of subjectivity; but the subject is always the 'incarnate' subject which, as it develops its potentialities, gives new meanings to the world. Thought represents one aspect of the body-subject, its subjectivity, while language represents another aspect, its corporeality. But just as the body-subject is one single reality, even if there are distinguishable aspects, so are thought and language one reality.

We have spoken of man's dialogue with his environment. This environment is not however simply the physical world of things or objects. Man is born into an historical and cultural situation. 'I do not have only a physical world, I do not live only in the milieu of the earth, air and water, I have around me roads, plantations, villages, streets, churches, utensils, a bell, a spoon, a pipe. Each of these objects bears stamped on it the mark of the human action for which it serves.'[2] Though however the human being is born into a world of cultural objects, it is obviously not a question of inferring the existence of other persons from such objects. This would give us at best an anonymous One. 'In the cultural object I experience the near presence of the Other under a veil of anonymity.'[3] Must we then say that we infer the existence of other persons from their overt behaviour, from their bodily movements? It is difficult to see what else one could say, if the

[1] *Ibid.*, p. 164. *Praktognosie* is the word coined by Merleau-Ponty.
[2] *Ibid.*, p. 399.   [3] *Ibid.*, p. 400.

body were understood in the sense required by dualism. But if the subject is not something hidden away in a body but the body itself, the body-subject, we can see that the existence of other subjects is experienced in man's pre-reflective dialogue with the world. The small child does not *infer* the existence of its mother from the smile which it sees on her face or from the movements of her hands. It has a pre-reflective perception of its mother in the dialogue of their behaviours. We have indeed to admit that a conflict can arise between different subjects, and that one subject can try to reduce another to the level of an object. But such conflicts obviously presuppose awareness of the existence of other persons. It may be objected that it is only as appearing for me or to me that other persons come to exist in my world. But it does not follow that they do not appear for me as other subjects. Certainly, I cannot *be* the other subject. Communication cannot be total and complete: the self is always involved in a certain solitude. But the solitude of real life is not that of solipsism. 'Solitude and communication ought not to be regarded as the two terms of an alternative, but as two moments of a single phenomenon, since, in fact, other people exist for me.'[1] To exist is to exist in a world which includes a social dimension; and the theoretical puzzles which can be raised on the level of reflection in regard to our knowledge of others presuppose an experienced or lived dialogue with other subjects.

In the *Phenomenology of Perception* Merleau-Ponty has some sensible remarks to make on the subject of freedom. He begins by recapitulating briefly the theory of Sartre in *Being and Nothingness*. For Sartre freedom is absolute. Our decisions are not determined by motives. For 'the alleged motive does not exercise weight on my decision; on the contrary, it is my decision which gives the motive its force.'[2] Again, it depends on me whether I see human being as things or as human beings, as objects or as free subjects; and it depends on my will to climb it that a rock appears to me as unclimbable or as a difficult obstacle. Merleau-Ponty objects that if freedom is said to be absolute and without limits, the word 'freedom' is deprived of all definite meaning. 'If, in effect, freedom is equal in all our actions and even in our passions . . . one cannot say that there is any *free action*. . . . It (freedom) is everywhere, if you like, but it is also nowhere.'[3] It is obviously true that it is I who give to

[1] *Ibid.*, p. 412.   [2] *Phénoménologie de la perception*, p. 497.
[3] *Ibid.*, p. 499.

this precipice the meaning of being an 'obstacle' to the ascent of the mountain which I envisage; but my dialogue with the world, in which this meaning arises, *is* a dialogue, not a monologue. The relation between the precipice and my body does not depend simply on me. When I give the precipice the significance of being an obstacle, I am already in a situation. Similarly, my past behaviour and the habits which I have formed constitute a situation. It does not follow that my present choice is determined. What follows is that freedom is never absolute but always 'situated'. This does not mean that a free action is divisible, as it were, into a part which is free and a part which is determined. It means that man is not a pure consciousness, but that the level of consciousness and freedom is conditioned by a pre-conscious level. To take an example given by Merleau-Ponty,[1] the bourgeois intellectual who breaks with his class and identifies himself with the proletarian revolutionary movement does so freely; but he reaches his decision not as a pure consciousness, existing apart from all social classes, but as one who is already situated by birth and upbringing. His decision, though free, is the decision of a bourgeois intellectual; he chooses precisely as such, and though in the end he may succeed in closing the gap between bourgeois intellectual and member of the proletarian class, he cannot do so through one initial decision to break with his own class and espouse the cause of another. His exercise of freedom is conditioned by a pre-existing situation.

Merleau-Ponty did not claim to have provided definitive solutions of the problems which he considered. His thought was exploratory; and he regarded himself as making a contribution which opened the way to further reflection. In general, he was faced with the problem of harmonizing belief that man, the existing subject, confers meanings on his world with the evident fact that, as conscious beings, we find ourselves in a world already clothed with meaning. His treatment of perception and perceptual behaviour at a pre-conscious level was a contribution to the solution of this problem. But Merleau-Ponty never intended to imply that all levels of experience could be reduced to pre-conscious experience, or that the structures characteristic of higher levels could be described or analyzed simply in terms of the structures characteristic of the level of perception. The realm of perception, the 'life-world', constituted for him the basis of other

---

[1] *Ibid.*, pp. 509–10.

levels. We all continue to live in the realm of perception. At the same time the higher levels require individual treatment; and Merleau-Ponty planned to follow up *The Structure of Behaviour* and the *Phenomenology of Perception* with works on such subjects as the origin of truth and the sociological significance of prose literature. In point of fact the planned volumes were not written; but he developed ideas on a number of subjects in important essays. An example is his paper on the phenomenology of language (1951) in which he maintains that 'when I speak or understand, I experience that presence of others in myself or of myself in others which is the stumbling-block of the theory of intersubjectivity.'[1] Another example is the notable essay *L'oeil et l'esprit* (*Eye and Mind*), which appeared in 1961.[2] This was the last piece of writing which Merleau-Ponty himself published. In it he expressed his view of operational science as having lost touch with the 'real world' and of art as drawing on the fabric of meaning which modern science 'would prefer to ignore'.[3] Reflection on art is used to support the basic idea of the body-subject as a perceiving and perceptible reality, the reality in the world through which Being becomes partially visible or is revealed. The author refers to music as representing 'certain outlines of Being—its ebb and flow, its growth, its upheavals, its turbulence';[4] but he concentrates his attention on painting as giving direct expression to concrete realities. Merleau-Ponty is not of course suggesting that science is useless or that it should be done away with. He is suggesting that it cuts itself off from the real world to which the artist has direct access.

What does Merleau-Ponty mean by Being? In his last writings, particularly in the part of *The Visible and the Invisible* which he was able to finish before his death, his phenomenology takes a more metaphysical turn, and the theme of an ultimate or basic reality comes to the fore. Man is a perceptible reality, and as such he belongs to Nature or the world. He is also a perceiving reality, in dialogue with the world. But it does not follow that as subject man is a consciousness apart from or outside the world. What follows is that in his act of vision the world becomes visible to itself, in and through man. To put the matter in another way, man's awareness of Nature is Nature's awareness of itself,

---

[1] *Signs*, p. 97.
[2] An English translation is included in *The Primacy of Perception*.
[3] *The Primacy of Perception*, p. 161.
[4] *Ibid.*, p. 161.

inasmuch as man belongs to Nature and is rooted in it. This is the metaphysical significance, so to speak, of the statement that man is both a perceiving and a perceptible reality. Though however man as perceiving constitutes his world (not in the sense that he creates it but in the sense that he makes structures appear), reality is more than becomes visible or perceptible. And that which becomes visible and which underlies the distinction between subject and object is Being. Being in itself is invisible. To speak paradoxically, it manifests itself as the non-appearing foundation of that which appears in the dialogue between the body-subject and its environment. It is not itself a perceptible structure but the field of all structures. Being becomes visible to itself in and through man, but only in the form of perceptible structures. What Merleau-Ponty calls 'the flesh of the world' grounds both subject and object and thus logically precedes them. It manifests itself both in perceptible structures and to thought (in the sense that man can become intellectually aware of its reality); but, considered in itself, it remains hidden.

It is perfectly reasonable to see in this theory of Being a significant development in Merleau-Ponty's thought. And it is understandable if some of those who admire him as a philosopher but who are distressed by his earlier exclusion of such concepts as the Absolute and God like to dwell on a metaphysical development which recalls Schelling's idea of Nature coming to know itself in and through man and of Being as hidden in itself but as grounding both subject and object. At the same time we should not read too much into Merleau-Ponty's concept of Being. Being is for him the invisible dimension of the visible. It is indeed the ultimate reality, in the sense that it becomes visible in the structures of the world; but it is not the God of theism. And even if this metaphysical turn in his thought would make it easier for him to find an opening to religious belief, there is no real justification for trying to annex Merleau-Ponty for Christianity.

3. What we have said hitherto may have given the impression that Merleau-Ponty stood aloof from social and political issues and confined himself to abstract philosophy. In point of fact he was strongly attracted by Marxism. One reason for this was obviously the emphasis laid by Marx on the basic situation of man as a being in the world and on man's dialogue with his environment. Merleau-Ponty may have tended to interpret Marx in terms of his own philosophy; but he was genuinely impressed by the

close connection made by Marxism between ideals and social realities and between ethics and politics. He was never the man to accept an ideology on authority or to submit his mind to the requirements of a Party line, and he had little use for a deterministic view of history. But in *Humanisme et terreur* he asserted that Marxism was 'the simple statement of those conditions without which there would be neither any humanism . . . nor any rationality in history',[1] and that as a criticism of existing society and of other humanist theories it could not be surpassed. Though however in this work Merleau-Ponty did his best to understand sympathetically the use of terror in the Soviet Union and the purges instituted by Stalin, he later became not only highly critical of Soviet policy and of Communist orthodoxy but also prepared to admit that Communist practice was the logical consequence of Marx's adoption of a theory of history which enabled the Communist leaders to lay claim to scientific knowledge of the movement and demands of history and to justify their actions and dictatorial and repressive behaviour in a manner analogous to that in which the Inquisitors would have justified their actions in the name of their knowledge of divine truth and of the divine will.[2] Merleau-Ponty never lost his admiration for Marx as a thinker; but he had little use for the idea of a philosophy which had become science and could be used to justify dictatorship. He was certainly not an upholder of capitalism. But neither was he a Communist. And it seems reasonable to claim that at no time was he really a Marxist. What attracted him to the thought of Marx were the elements which fitted in with his own philosophy. And whereas he at first tried to dissociate Marx himself from the developments in Communism which he disliked, he later came to think that the origins of these developments could be found in Marx's later ideas.

In an essay Merleau-Ponty remarks that ever since Nietzsche the humblest student would flatly reject a philosophy which did not teach him to live fully.[3] The context of the remark is provided by the statement that we do not accuse painters of escapism, whereas philosophers are liable to be reproached in this way. Context apart however, would Merleau-Ponty's philosophy serve as a guide to life? It is difficult to say, when it remained incomplete. As it stands, it can be seen as demanding reciprocal

---

[1] *Humanisme et terreur*, p. 165.   [2] See *Les aventures de la dialectique*.
[3] *The Primacy of Perception*, p. 161 (in the essay, *The Eye and the Mind*).

412 FROM BERGSON TO SARTRE

recognition among human beings, a respect for human freedom and a self-commitment to the cause of social liberation without the claim to absolute knowledge and to the right to coerce human beings in the name of this alleged knowledge. In other words, Merleau-Ponty's philosophy can be regarded as a form of humanism. But if he is remembered, it will presumably be for his phenomenological inquiries. And these, we may suppose, will be considered not as definitive treatments (which Merleau-Ponty never claimed that they were) but as stimulating explorations, as points of departure.

4. One of Merleau-Ponty's essays is entitled *From Mauss to Claude Lévi-Strauss*,[1] and Lévi-Strauss dedicated his work *La pensée sauvage*[2] to the memory of Maurice Merleau-Ponty, his colleague at the Collège de France. Lévi-Strauss was born in the same year (1908) as Merleau-Ponty, and after his studies he taught philosophy for a time in secondary schools (*lycées*). But in 1935 he accepted the chair of sociology at the University of Sao Paulo in Brazil, where he remained until 1939. After the war he acted as cultural attaché to the French ambassador in Washington; but in 1947 he returned to France, He became Director of Studies at the École des Hautes Études at Paris, and in 1959 he was appointed to the chair of social anthropology at the Collège de France. He is first and foremost an anthropologist;[3] but his ideas have, or have been given, philosophical implications. Structuralism has been presented as embodying or implying a view of man rather different from the existentialist view. Indeed, it has been represented by Michel Foucault[4] as completing Nietzsche's 'death of God' by the 'death of man'. Though therefore the present writer would not be competent to discuss anthropological themes, even if considerations of space permitted such discussion, we can hardly leave French philosophy without some remarks, however inadequate, about the structuralist movement in recent French thought.

In the first and last chapters of his *Structural Anthropology* Lévi-Strauss discusses the use of such terms as ethnography,

[1] *Signs*, pp. 114–125.
[2] Translated as *The Savage Mind* (London, 1962).
[3] Lévi-Strauss discusses the use of terms such as ethnology, social and cultural anthropology, and sociology in chapter XVII of his *Anthropologie structurale* (1958; English translation by C. Jacobson and B. G. Schoerf, *Structural Anthropology*, New York and London, 1963).
[4] Author of *Les mots et les choses* (Paris, 1966).

ethnology, physical anthropology, social anthropology and cultural anthropology. In his view ethnography, ethnology and anthropology do not constitute three different disciplines but rather 'three stages, or three moments of time, in the same line of investigation'.[1] Ethnography, for example, 'aims at recording as accurately as possible the respective modes of life of various groups';[2] it is concerned with observation and description. The movement of the mind is then one of synthesis, in which ethnology forms a stage. Synthesis however is concerned primarily with the relations between social phenomena; and anthropology aims at establishing basic structural relations underlying man's whole social life and organization. The sociologist, as Lévi-Strauss sees him, is concerned with the observer's own society or with societies of the same type, whereas the anthropologist seeks to formulate theories which are applicable 'not only to his own fellow countrymen and contemporaries, but to the most distant native population'.[3] Further, the anthropologist, while not of course neglecting man's conscious processes, should include also his unconscious processes, with a view to bringing to formulation the basic structures of which all social and cultural institutions are projections or manifestations. In other words, anthropology is concerned with what Marcel Mauss described as the total social phenomenon. While however it is not indifferent to highly developed societies which express man's conscious endeavour or to the historical processes which led to their development, its aim is to go behind the sphere of conscious ideas and purposes and that of historical processes to 'the complete range of unconscious possibilities'.[4] These possibilities, according to Lévi-Strauss, are limited in number. If therefore the anthropologist can determine the relations of compatibility and incompatibility between these different possibilities or potentials, he can formulate a logical framework for all historical-social developments. Lévi-Strauss quotes the statement of Marx that while men make their own history, they do not know that they are making it; and he comments that while the first part of the statement justifies history, the second part justifies anthropology.

In coming to his idea of structural analysis in anthropology Lévi-Strauss was influenced by linguistics which, in his view, was the social science which had made the most notable progress.

[1] *Structural Anthropology*, p. 356. [2] *Ibid.*, p. 2.
[3] *Ibid.*, p. 363. [4] *Ibid.*, p. 23.

This progress was achieved through the development of structural linguistics by N. Troubetzkoy and others. In his *Psychologie du langage*[1] Troubetzkoy assigned four basic operations to structural linguistics: the study of the unconscious infrastructure of linguistic phenomena, concentration on the relations between terms, exhibition of the structures of phonemic systems (systems of vocal sounds), and the discovery of general laws which would formulate basic necessary relationships. Lévi-Strauss does not claim that the method of structural linguistics can be simply abstracted and then applied literally in anthropology. For the anthropologist concerns himself with human behaviour and attitudes which cannot be reduced to systems of terminology or shown to be nothing but expressions of language. While he interprets society in terms of a theory of communication, Lévi-Strauss does not restrict communication to language. Nor does he regard all other forms of communication as derivatives of language. At the same time he insists on collaboration between linguistics and anthropology and on their mutual relations, and the method of structural linguistics has served him as a model in formulating a method of anthropology. He looks on the relations between social phenomena as providing the material for the construction of abstract models[2] which should make the observed facts intelligible. The anthropologist will endeavour to go behind (or beneath) conscious models to unconscious models and, by studying the relations between types of models, to bring to light the necessary relationships which govern man's mental, affective, artistic and social life. Further, while not claiming that all social phenomena must be susceptible of numerical measurement, Lévi-Strauss envisages the possibility of the use of mathematics as a tool in anthropological analysis.

The matter can be clarified somewhat in this way. In *La pensée sauvage* Lévi-Strauss rejects the distinction, made, for example, by Lévy-Bruhl, between the logical mentality of civilized man and the prelogical mentality of primitive man. 'The savage mind is logical in the same sense and the same fashion as ours, though as ours is only when it is applied to knowledge of a universe

---

[1] Paris, 1933.
[2] A structural model, we are told, must have the characteristics of a system, in the sense that none of its elements should be able to undergo a change without changes being effected in other elements. Further, it should be possible, in the case of any given model, to state a series of transformations which result in a group of models of the same type.

in which it recognizes physical and semantic properties simultaneously.'[1] In this case of course there must be a logic in myths. And when writing about mythology in *Le cru et le cuit* (1964) Lévi-Strauss argues that there is no arbitrary disorder or mere fantasy in the choice of images or in the ways in which they are associated, opposed or limited. The reason is that the myths express unconscious mental structures which are the same for all. These structures however are purely formal in character. That is to say, they do not provide content, like the archetypes of Jung, but rather the formal structures or patterns which condition all forms of mental life. In spite of the obvious differences between myths and science, the same formal structures are expressed in both. In a sense the basic structures correspond to the *a priori* categories of Kant. But they are not referred to any transcendental subject or ego. They belong to the sphere of the unconscious, and Lévi-Strauss evidently thinks of them as having their origin behind man, not in a metaphysical but in a naturalistic sense.

Lévi-Strauss has written on a number of particular themes, such as kinship structures (*Les structures élémentaires de la parenté*, 1949), totemism (*Le totémisme aujourd'hui*, 1962, and *La pensée sauvage*, 1962) and, as we have seen, on mythology. He has utilized both the relevant anthropological literature and his own field work; and he naturally, and rightly, regards himself as an anthropologist, not as a philosopher. Moreover, philosophies seem to be for him phenomena which, like myths, provide material for the anthropologist's inquiry and research, inasmuch as they embody the formal structures which express themselves in the whole of human life and culture. At the same time the scope of anthropology, as dealing with the total social phenomenon and as concerned with discovering the formal bases of man's mental life, becomes so wide that it is difficult to draw any clear line of demarcation between anthropology as a social science[2] and philosophical anthropology. Further, the fact that Lévi-Strauss does not claim to be a philosopher does not necessarily prove that he has no personal philosophical point of view which is implied by and sometimes finds more or less explicit expression in his anthropological writings.

[1] *The Savage Mind*, p. 268.
[2] Lévi-Strauss allows that anthropology can be described as a social science. But he rejects any tendency to consider it as an isolated discipline. Through physical anthropology it is linked with the natural sciences, and it is also linked to humanistic studies through, for example, linguistics and archaeology.

A philosophy of man is clearly implied by some remarks made by Lévi-Strauss in the ninth chapter of *La pensée sauvage*. When discussing Sartre's concept of the dialectical reason, he admits that in Sartre's terminology he can be described as 'a transcendental materialist and aesthete'.[1] He is a 'transcendental materialist' inasmuch as he regards dialectical reason not as something other than analytical reason but as something additional within analytical reason. 'Sartre calls analytical reason reason in repose; I call the same reason dialectical when it is raised to action, tensed by its efforts to transcend itself.'[2] Reason's effort to transcend itself is not however an effort to grasp the Transcendent but the effort to find the ultimate bases of language, society and thought or, to express the matter more provocatively, 'to undertake the resolution of the human into the non-human'.[3] As for the term 'aesthete', Lévi-Strauss says that it applies to himself inasmuch as Sartre uses it to describe anyone who studies men as if they were ants. Indeed, the ultimate goal of the human sciences is 'not to constitute, but to dissolve man'.[4]

It is hardly necessary to say that Lévi-Strauss has no intention of denying that there are human beings. Man is the subject of his study. The word 'dissolve' is to be understood in terms of reduction. But Lévi-Strauss insists that he does not mean by this the reduction of a 'higher' to a 'lower' level. The level which is to be reduced must be conceived in all its distinctive characteristics and qualities; and if it is reduced to another level, some of its richness will be communicated retroactively to this other level. For example, if we were to succeed in understanding life as a function of inert matter, we would find that 'the latter has properties very different from those previously attributed to it'.[5] It is not a question of reducing the complex to the simple, but of replacing a less intelligible complexity by one which is more intelligible. Thus to reduce man's mental, social and affective life to unconscious formal structures or patterns is not to deny that the former is what it is: it is to make the complexity of the forms of social and cultural phenomena intelligible in the light of a complex structure which is expressed in and unifies the phenomena but from which the phenomena cannot simply be deduced *a priori*. For we have also to take into account the dialectic between man and his environment and between man and man.

---

[1] *The Savage Mind*, p. 246.　　　　[2] *Ibid.*, p. 246.
[3] *Ibid.*, p. 246.　　　[4] *Ibid.*, p. 247.　　　[5] *Ibid.*, p. 248.

Lévi-Strauss doubtless believes that these ideas fall within the scope of anthropology, and that it is a mistake to represent them as philosophical theories. While however he does not develop them as a philosophy, it seems clear enough that they imply a naturalism which is different from the crude reductionism of some eighteenth-century *philosophes*. If Lévi-Strauss is prepared to accept the Sartrian label 'transcendental materialist', his materialism is of the somewhat ambiguous type represented by dialectical materialism, which has indeed exercised a certain influence on his thought. In any case he opposes a view which reintegrates man into Nature to the Sartrian dichotomy between the for-itself and the in-itself, and a conditioning of man's thought and activity by formal structures which underlie consciousness to the absolute freedom proclaimed by the author of *Being and Nothingness*.

Structuralism has its antecedents in, for example, structural psychology and, more recently, structural linguistics, as well of course as in the theories of Durkheim and Mauss. Its principal field of application is the human sciences, where it concentrates on the relations and supposedly invariant laws of combination between the relevant phenomena. It does not neglect historical development, the 'diachronic' element; but it concentrates on the 'synchronic' element, the basic formal structures which are believed to be independent of historical change. This approach has been applied in a variety of fields, such as literary criticism, art, psychology and the interpretation of Marxism; and in so far as it is a question of a heuristic method, there can obviously be no cogent objection to experimenting with it and evaluating the results. The method however is connected with hypotheses which can reasonably be seen as implying a naturalistic philosophy which differs from both existentialism and Marxism, even if elements from both sources are incorporated. Given the emphasis on heuristic method, it is doubtless an exaggeration to speak of a system of structuralist philosophy. Equally, given the wide area of application of the method in the human sciences, one can justifiably speak of a current of thought which differs from both existentialism and Marxism and which can perhaps be described as a new naturalism, based on reflection in the field of social and cultural anthropology.

A SHORT BIBLIOGRAPHY

In the bibliography at the end of Volume VII of this work a number of general histories of philosophy were mentioned, the titles of which have not been repeated here. Encyclopaedias have not been listed, except for the two mentioned under General Works below. Nor have bibliographies been provided for all the philosophers whose names appear in the text of this volume.

General Works

Balodi, N. *Les constantes de la pensée française.* Paris, 1948.

Benrubi, J. *Contemporary Thought of France.* London, 1926. *Les sources et les courants de la philosophie contemporaine en France.* 2 vols. Paris, 1933.

Boas, G. *French Philosophies of the Romantic Period.* New York, 1925, reissued 1964. *Dominant Themes of Modern Philosophy.* New York, 1957.

Bréhier, E. *Histoire de la philosophie. La philosophie moderne. Tome 2; deuxième partie, XIXe et XXe siècles.* Paris, 1944. *The History of Philosophy. Vol. VI, The Nineteenth Century, Period of Systems, 1800–1850,* translated by W. Baskin. Chicago, 1968.

Charlton, D. G. *Positivist Thought in France during the Second Empire, 1852–1870.* Oxford, 1959.

Collins, J. *A History of Modern European Philosophy.* Milwaukee, 1954. (includes chapters, with bibliographies, on Comte and Bergson).

Cruickshank, J. (editor). *The Novelist as Philosopher. Studies in French Fiction, 1935–60.* London 1962.

Edwards, P. (editor). *The Encyclopedia of Philosophy.* 8 vols. New York and London, 1967. (Besides a general article on French philosophy there are articles on distinct movements and on a considerable number of individual philosophers.)

Enciclopedia Filosofica. Second edition, 6 vols. Florence, 1967.

Farber, M. (editor). *Philosophic Thought in France and the United States. Essays representing Major Trends in Contemporary French and American Philosophy.* Buffalo, N.Y., 1950.

Gouhier, H. *Les grandes avenues de la pensée philosophique en France depuis Descartes.* Paris, 1966.

Gunn, J. Alexander. *Modern French Philosophy. A study of the Development since Comte.* London 1922.

Lavelle, L. *La philosophie française entre les deux guerres.* Paris, 1942.

Lévy-Bruhl, L. *A History of Modern Philosophy in France.* Translated by G. Coblence. London and Chicago, 1899.

Mandelbaum, M. *History, Man and Reason. A Study in Nineteenth-Century Thought.* Baltimore and London, 1971. (A general study, but includes a treatment of several French philosophers.)

Parodi, D. *La philosophie contemporaine en France.* Paris, 1919.

Pierce, R. *Contemporary French Political Thought.* London, 1966.

Plamenatz, J. *Man and Society. A Critical Examination of Some Important Social and Political Theories from Machiavelli to Marx.* Vol. 2, London, 1963. (This volume is devoted mainly to Hegel and Marx, but it includes a treatment of the early French socialists.)

Randall, J. H., Jr. *The Career of Philosophy: Vol. 2, From the German Enlightenment to the Age of Darwin.* New York and London, 1965. (Includes a brief treatment of French philosophy from the Revolution up to Comte.)

Ravaisson, F. *La Philosophie en France au XIXᵉ siècle.* Paris 1868.

Simpson, W. J. S. *Religious Thought in France in the Nineteenth Century.* London, 1935.

Smith, C. *Contemporary French Philosophy. A Study in Norms and Values.* London, 1964.

Soltan, R. *French Political Thought in the Nineteenth Century.* New Haven, 1931.

Trotignon, P. *Les philosophes français d'aujourd'hui.* Paris, 1967.

Wahl, J. *Tableaux de la philosophie française.* Paris, 1946.

Chapter I

1. General Works relating to Traditionalism

Boas, G. *French Philosophies of the Romantic Period.* New York, 1925, reissued 1964.

Ferraz, M. *Histoire de la philosophie en France au XIXᵉ siècle: Traditionalisme et ultramontanisme.* Paris, 1880.

Foucher, L. *La philosophie catholique en France au XIXᵉ siècle.* Paris, 1955. (First four chapters.)

Hocedez, E. *Histoire de la théologie au XIXᵉ siècle*, I–II. Brussels and Paris, 1948–52.

Hötzel, N. *Die Uroffenbarung im französischen Traditionalismus.* Munich, 1962.

Lacroix, J. *Vocation personnelle et tradition nationale.* Paris, 1942.

Laski, N. *Authority in the Modern State.* New Haven, 1919.

Roche, A. V. *Les idées traditionalistes en France.* Urbana, 1937.

Menzer, B. (editor). *Catholic Political Thought (1789–1848).* Westminster, Maryland, 1952.

2. De Maistre

Texts

Oeuvres complètes. 14 vols. 1884–7.

The Works of Joseph de Maistre (Selections), translated by J. Lively. New York, 1965.
Considérations sur la France. Neuchâtel, 1796.
Essai sur le principe générateur des constitutions politiques. Paris, 1814 (and Lyons, 1929).
Du Pape. 2 vols. Lyons, 1819.
Soirées de Saint-Pétersbourg. 2 vols. Paris, 1821.
Examen de la philosophie de Bacon. Paris, 1836.

Studies

Bayle, F. *Les idées politiques de Joseph de Maistre.* Paris, 1945.
Brunello, B. *Joseph de Maistre, politico e filosofo.* Bologna, 1967.
Gianturco, E. *Joseph de Maistre and Giambattista Vico.* Washington, DC, 1937.
Goyau, G. *La pensée religieuse de Joseph de Maistre.* Paris, 1921.
Huber, M. *Die Staatsphilosophie von Joseph de Maistre im Lichte des Thomismus.* Basel and Stuttgart, 1958.
Lecigne, C. *Joseph de Maistre.* Paris, 1914.
Rhoden, P. R. *Joseph de Maistre als politischer Theoretiker.* Munich, 1929.

2. De Bonald

Texts

Oeuvres complètes. 7 vols. Paris, 1857–75 (3rd edition).
Oeuvres, edited by J. P. Migne. 3 vols. Paris, 1859.
Théorie du pouvoir politique et religieux dans la société civile. 3 vols. Constance, 1796. There is an edition by C. Capitan, Paris, 1965.
Essai analytique sur les lois naturelles de l'ordre social. Paris, 1800.
La législation primitive. 3 vols. Paris, 1802.
Recherches philosophiques sur les premiers objets des connaissances morales. 2 vols. Paris, 1818.
Démonstration philosophique du principe constitutif de la société. Paris, 1827.

Studies

Adams, A. *Die Philosophie de Bonalds.* Münster, 1923.
Faguet, E. *Politiques et moralistes du XIXᵉ siècle.* Series 1, Paris, 1891.
Moulinié, H. *De Bonald.* Paris, 1915.
Quinlan, M. H. *The Historical Thought of the Vicomte de Bonald.* Washington, DC, 1953.
Reinerz, H. W. *Bonald als Politiker, Philosoph und Mensch.* Leipzig, 1940.
Soreil, A. *Le Vicomte de Bonald.* Brussels, 1942.

3. *Chateaubriand*

Texts

Oeuvres complètes. 20 vols. Paris, 1858–61.
Essai historique, politique et moral sur les révolutions. London, 1797.
Génie du christianisme. 5 vols. Paris, 1802.

Studies

Bertrin, G. *La sincérité religieuse de Chateaubriand.* Paris, 1899.
Döhner, K. *Zeit und Ewigkeit bei Chateaubriand.* Ghent, 1931.
Giraud, V. *Le christianisme de Chateaubriand.* 2 vols. Paris, 1925–8.
Lemaître, J. *Chateaubriand.* Paris, 1912.
Maurois, A. *Chateaubriand.* Paris, 1938.
Sainte-Beuve, C. A. *Chateaubriand et son groupe littéraire sous l'Empire.* Paris, 1869.

4. *Lamennais*

Texts

Oeuvres complètes. 12 vols. Paris, 1836–7.
Oeuvres choisies et philosophiques. 10 vols. Paris, 1837–41.
Oeuvres posthumes, edited by E. D. Forgues. 6 vols. Paris, 1855–9.
Oeuvres inédites, edited by A. Blaize. 2 vols. Paris, 1866.
Essai sur l'indifférence en matière de religion. 4 vols. Paris, 1817–1824.
Défense de l'Essai sur l'indifférence. Paris, 1821.
Paroles d'un croyant. Paris, 1834.
Esquisse d'une philosophie. 4 vols. Paris, 1841–6.

Studies

Boutard, C. *Lamennais, sa vie et ses doctrines.* 3 vols. 1905–13.
Derré, J. R. *La Mennais, ses amis et le mouvement des idées à l'époque romantique (1824–34).* Paris, 1962.
Duine, M. *La Mennais, sa vie, ses idées, ses ouvrages.* Evreux, 1922.
Gibson, W. *The Abbé de Lamennais and the Liberal Catholic Movement in France.* London and New York, 1896.
Janet, P. *La philosophie de Lamennais.* Paris, 1890.
Le Guillon, L. *L'évolution de la pensée religieuse de Félicité Lamennais.* Paris, 1966.
Mourre, M. *Lamennais, ou l'hérésie des temps modernes.* Paris, 1955.
Roe, W. G. *Lamennais and England. The Reception of Lamennais' Religious Ideas in England in the Nineteenth Century.* Oxford, 1966.
Verucci, G. F. *Lamennais. Dal cattolicesimo autoritario al radicalismo democratico.* Naples, 1963.

Chapter II

1. *The Ideologists*

Texts

Destutt de Tracy. *Éléments d'idéologie.* 4 vols. Paris, 1801–15.
 Traité de la volonté et de ses effets. Paris 1805.
 Commentaire sur l'esprit des lois de Montesquieu.
 Liège, 1817. Translated by Thomas Jefferson as
 *A Commentary and Review of Montesquieu's
 Spirit of Laws.* Philadelphia, 1811.

Studies

Cailliet, E. *La tradition littéraire des idéologues.* Philadelphia, 1943.
Chinard, J. *Jefferson et les idéologues.* Baltimore, 1925.
Picavet, F. *Les idéologues.* Paris, 1891. (The standard work).
Riverso, E. *I problemi della conoscenza et del metodo nel sensismo
 degli ideologi.* Naples, 1962.
Van Duzen, C. *The Contributions of the Idéologues to French Revolu-
 tionary Thought.* Baltimore, 1935.

2. *Maine de Biran*

Texts

Oeuvres de Maine de Biran, edited by P. Tisserand and H. Gouhier.
 14 vols. Paris, 1920–9. (This edition entirely supersedes Victor
 Cousin's four-volume edition of de Biran's *Oeuvres Philoso-
 phiques.* Paris, 1841.)
Journal intime, edited by H. Gouhier. Paris, 1954–7.
The *Mémoire sur l'habitude* (1802) has been translated by M. Boehm
 as *The Influence of Habit on the Faculty of Thinking.* Baltimore,
 1929.
De l'apperception immédiate. Mémoire de Berlin 1807, edited by
 J. Echeverría, Paris, 1963.

Studies

Ambrosetti, G. *La filosofia sociale di Maine de Biran.* Verona, 1953.
Antonelli, M. T. *Maine de Biran.* Brescia, 1947.
Buol, J. *Die Anthropologie Maine de Birans.* Winterthur, 1961.
Cresson, A. *Maine de Biran.* Paris, 1950.
De la Valette Monbrun, A. *Maine de Biran. Essai de biographie
 historique et psychologique.* Paris, 1914.
Delbos, V. *Maine de Biran et son œuvre philosophique.* Paris, 1931.
Drevet, A. *Maine de Biran.* Paris, 1968.
Ghio, M. *Maine de Biran e la tradizione biraniana in Francia.* Turin,
 1962.
Fessard, P. *La méthode de réflexion chez Maine de Biran.* Paris, 1938.

Funke, H. *Maine de Biran. Philosophisches und politisches Denken zwischen Ancien Régime und Bürgerkönigtum in Frankreich.* Bonn, 1947.

Gouhier, H. *Les conversions de Maine de Biran.* Paris, 1947. (Highly recommended.)

Hallie, P. P. *Maine de Biran, Reformer of Empiricism.* Cambridge (Mass.), 1959.

Henry, M. *Philosophie et phénoménologie du corps. Essai sur l'ontologie biranienne.* Paris, 1965.

Lacroze, R. *Maine de Biran.* Paris, 1970.

Lassaigne, J. *Maine de Biran, homme politique.* Paris, 1958.

Lemay, P. *Maine de Biran.* Paris, 1946.

Le Roy, G. *L'expérience de l'effort et de la grâce chez Maine de Biran.* Paris, 1937.

Madinier, G. *Conscience et mouvement.* Paris, 1939.

Monette, A. *La théorie des premiers principes selon Maine de Biran.* Montreal and Paris, 1945.

Moore, F. C. T. *The Psychology of Maine de Biran.* Oxford, 1970.

Paliard, J. *La raisonnement selon Maine de Biran.* Paris, 1925.

Robef, I. *Leibniz et Maine de Biran.* Paris, 1927.

Thibaud, M. *L'effort chez Maine de Biran et Bergson.* Grenoble, 1939.

Tisserand, P. *L'anthropologie de Maine de Biran, ou la science de l'homme intérieur.* Paris, 1909.

Voutsinas, D. *La psychologie de Maine de Biran.* Paris, 1964.

There are some collections of articles, such as those in the number of the *Revue internationale de Philosophie* dedicated to Maine de Biran on the occasion of the second centenary of his birth (Brussels, 1966).

Chapter III

1. *Royer-Collard*

Texts

Les fragments philosophiques de Royer-Collard, edited by A Schimberg. Paris, 1913.

Studies

De Barante, A. *La vie politique de M. Royer-Collard, ses discours et ses écrits.* 2 vols. Paris, 1878 (3rd edition).

Nesmesdesmarets, R. *Les doctrines politiques de Royer-Collard.* Montpellier, 1908.

Spuller, E. *Royer-Collard.* Paris, 1895.

2. *Cousin*

Texts

Philosophie sensualiste au XVIIIᵉ siècle. Paris, 1819.

Fragments philosophiques. Paris, 1826.

Cours de l'histoire de la philosophie. 3 vols. Paris, 1829.
De la métaphysique d'Aristote. Paris, 1835.
Du vrai, du beau et du bien. Paris, 1837.
Cours de l'histoire de la Philosophie moderne. 5 vols. Paris, 1841.
Études sur Pascal. Paris, 1842.
Justice et charité. Paris, 1848.

Studies

Cornelius, A. *Die Geschichtslehre Victor Cousins.* Geneva, 1958.
Dubois, P. F. *Cousin, Jouffroy, Damiron, souvenirs publiés avec une introduction par Adolphe Lair.* Paris, 1902.
Janet, P. *Victor Cousin et son œuvre.* Paris, 1885.
Mastellone, S. *Victor Cousin e il risorgimento italiano.* Florence, 1955.
Saint-Hilaire, J. B. *Victor Cousin, sa vie, sa correspondance.* 3 vols. Paris, 1895.
Simon, J. *Victor Cousin.* Paris, 1887. There is an English translation by M. B. and E. P. Anderson, Chicago, 1888.

3. *Jouffroy*

Texts

Mélanges philosophiques. Paris, 1833.
Nouveaux mélanges philosophiques, edited by F. Damiron. Paris, 1842.
Cours de droit naturel. 2 vols. Paris, 1834–42.
Cours d'esthétique. Paris, 1843.

Studies

Lambert, L. *Der Begriff des Schönen in der Ästhetik Jouffroys.* Giessen, 1909.
Ollé-Laprune, L. *Théodore Jouffroy.* Paris, 1899.

Chapter IV

1. *Fourier*

Texts

Oeuvres complètes. 6 vols. Paris, 1841–5.
Théorie des quatre mouvements et des destinées générales. 2 vols. Lyons, 1808.
Théorie de l'unité universelle. 2 vols. Paris, 1822.
Le nouveau monde industriel et sociétaire. Besançon, 1829.
La fausse industrie morcelée, répugnante, mensongère, et l'antidote: l'industrie naturelle, combinée, attrayante, véridique, donnant quadruple produit. 2 vols. Paris, 1835–6.
(For manuscript work see *Les cahiers manuscrits de Fourier* by E. Poulat, Paris, 1957.)

Studies

Bourgin, H. Fourier, *Contribution à l'étude du socialisme français.*
Paris, 1905.
Lehouck, E. *Fourier aujourd'hui.* Paris, 1966.
Manuel, F. E. *The Prophets of Paris.* Cambridge (Mass.), 1962.
Tosi, V. *Fourier e il suo falansterio.* Savona, 1921.
Vergez, A. *Fourier.* Paris, 1969.

2. Saint-Simon

Texts

Oeuvres complètes de Saint-Simon et Enfantin. 47 vols. Paris, 1865–76.
Oeuvres. 6 vols. Paris, 1966.
Textes choisis, edited by J. Dautry. Paris, 1951.
Selected Writings, translated with an introduction by F. M. H.
Markham. Oxford, 1942.
Lettres d'un habitant de Genève à ses contemporains. Geneva, 1802–03.
Edited by A. Pereire, Paris, 1925.
Introduction aux travaux scientifiques du XIXe siècle. 2 vols. Paris,
1807–08.
Esquisse d'une nouvelle Encyclopédie. Paris, 1810.
Mémoire sur la science de l'homme. Paris, 1813.
Travail sur la gravitation universelle. Paris, 1813.
De la réorganisation de la société européenne. Paris, 1814. (In collabo-
ration with A. Thierry.)
L'industrie. Paris, 1818.
La politique. Paris, 1819.
L'organisation. Paris, 1819–20.
Catéchisme des industriels. Paris, 1824.

Studies

Charléty, S. *Essai sur l'histoire du saint-simonisme.* Paris, 1896.
Dondo, M. M. *The French Faust, Henri de Saint-Simon.* New York,
1955.
Durkheim, E. *Le socialisme, sa définition, ses débuts. La doctrine
saint-simonienne.* Edited by M. Mauss. Paris, 1928. Translated
into English by C. Sattler as *Socialism and Saint-Simon,* Yellow
Springs (Ohio), 1958.
Fazio, M. F. *Linea di sviluppo del pensiero di Saint-Simon.* Palermo,
1942.
Gurvitch, G. *Les fondateurs français de la scociologie contemporaine:
Saint-Simon et P.-J. Proudhon.* Paris, 1955.
Leroy, M. *La vie véritable du comte de Saint-Simon.* Paris, 1925.
Manuel, F. E. *The New World of Henri de Saint-Simon.* Cambridge
(Mass.), 1956.

Muckle, F. *Henri de Saint-Simon, Persönlichkeit und Werk.* Jena, 1908.

Vidal, E. *Saint-Simon e la scienza politica.* Milan, 1959.

3. Proudhon

Texts

Oeuvres complètes. 26 vols. Paris, 1867–71.

Correspondance. 14 vols. Paris, 1875.

Oeuvres complètes, edited by C. Bouglé and H. Moysset. 11 vols. Paris, 1920–39 (incomplete).

Selected Writings of Pierre-Joseph Proudhon, edited with an introduction by S. Edwards and translated by E. Fraser. London, 1970.

Qu'est-ce que la propriété? Paris, 1840. Translated by B. Tucker as *What is Property?* Princeton, 1876.

De la création de l'ordre dans l'humanité. Paris, 1843.

Système des contradictions économiques ou Philosophie de la misère. Paris, 1846. Translated by B. Tucker as *System of Economic Contradictions.* Boston, 1888.

Idée générale de la révolution du XIXᵉ siècle. Paris, 1851. Translated by J. B. Robinson as *General Idea of the Revolution in the Nineteenth Century,* London, 1923.

La justice dans la révolution et dans l'église. Paris, 1858.

La guerre et la paix. Paris, 1861.

Du principe féderatif et de la nécessité de reconstituer le parti de la révolution. Paris, 1863.

De la capacité des classes ouvrières. Paris, 1865.

Studies

Ansart, P. *Sociologie de Proudhon.* Paris, 1967.

Brogan, C. *Proudhon.* London, 1936.

De Lubac, H. *Proudhon et le christianisme.* Paris, 1945. Translated by R. E. Scantlebury as *The Un-Marxian Socialist: A Study of Proudhon.* 2 vols. Paris, 1896.

Diehl, C. *P.-J. Proudhon, seine Lehre und sein Leben.* 3 vols. Jena, 1888–96.

Dolléans, E. *Proudhon.* Paris, 1948 (4th edition).

Gröndahl, B. *P.-J. Proudhon.* Stockholm, 1959.

Heintz, P. *Die Autoritätsproblematik bei Proudhon. Versuch einer immanenten Kritik.* Cologne, 1957.

Jackson, J. H. *Marx, Proudhon and European Socialism.* New York, 1962.

Lu, S. V. *The Political Theories of P.-J. Proudhon.* New York, 1922.

Prion, G. *Proudhon et syndicalisme révolutionnaire.* Paris, 1910.

Saint-Beuve, C. A. *Proudhon, sa vie et sa correspondance.* Paris, 1870.

Woodcock, G. *Pierre-Joseph Proudhon: A Biography*. London, 1956. (Highly recommended.)

Chapters on Proudhon can be found in, for example, *The Anarchists* by J. Joll (London, 1964), *A History of Socialist Thought*, Vol. 1 by G. D. H. Cole (London, 1953) and *Anarchism* by G. Woodcock (London, 1963).

Chapter V

Comte

Texts

Cours de philosophie positive. 6 vols. Paris, 1830–42. There is a loose English version (approved by Comte) by H. Martineau, *Cours, The Positive Philosophy of Auguste Comte*. 2 vols, London 1853.

Discours sur l'esprit positif. Paris, 1849. (This was originally prefixed to the *Traité philosophique d'astronomie populaire*.) Translated by Fr. S. Beesly as *A Discourse on the Positive Spirit*. London, 1903.

Discours sur l'ensemble du positivisme. Paris, 1848.

Calendrier positiviste. Paris, 1849.

Système de politique positive. 4 vols. 1851–54. Translated by J. H. Bridges and F. Harrison as *The System of Positive Polity*, 4 vols., London, 1857–77.

Catéchisme positiviste. Paris, 1852. Translated by R. Congreve as *The Catechism of Positive Religion*. London, 1858.

Appel aux conservateurs. Paris, 1855.

Synthèse subjective, ou Système universel des conceptions propres à l'état normal de l'humanité. Vol. 1, Paris, 1856.

Rather oddly, there is no complete and critical selection of Comte's works. H. Gouhier however has published *Oeuvres choisies d'Auguste Comte*, Paris, 1943, while C. Le Verrier has published in two volumes the first two lectures of the *Cours de philosophie positive* and the *Discours sur l'esprit positif*, Paris, 1943.

There are several collections of letters. *Lettres d'Auguste Comte à John Stuart Mill*, 1841–6 (Paris 1877), *Lettres à des positivistes anglais* (Paris, 1889), *Correspondance inédite d'Auguste Comte* (4 vols., Paris, 1903–04), *Nouvelles lettres inédites* (Paris, 1939).

Studies

Arbousse-Bastide, P. *La doctrine de l'éducation universelle dans la philosophie d'Auguste Comte*. 2 vols. Paris, 1957.

    Auguste Comte. Paris, 1968.

Caird, E. *The Social Philosophy and Religion of Comte*. Glasgow, 1885.

Cresson, A. *Auguste Comte, sa vie, son oeuvre*. Paris, 1941.

Defourny, G. *La sociologie positiviste d'Auguste Comte*. Louvain, 1902.

De Lubac, H. *Le drame de l'humanisme athée.* Paris, 1944. Translated by E. M. Riley as *The Drama of Atheist Humanism.* London, 1950. (Comte is one of the philosophers considered in this work.)

Devolvé, J. *Réflexions sur la pensée comtienne.* Paris, 1932.

Ducassé, P. *Méthode et intuition chez Auguste Comte.* Paris, 1939.

Dumas, G. *Psychologie de deux Messies positivistes: Saint-Simon et Auguste Comte.* Paris, 1905.

Gouhier, H. *La vie d'Auguste Comte.* Paris, 1931.
      La jeunesse d'Auguste Comte et la formation du positivisme. 3 vols. Paris, 1933–41. (Highly recommended.)

Gould, F. J. *Auguste Comte.* London, 1920.

Gruber, H. *Comte, der Begründer des Positivismus.* Freiburg i/B., 1889.

Hawkins, R. L. *Auguste Comte and the United States (1816–53).* Cambridge (Mass.), 1936.

Lacroix, J. *La sociologie d'Auguste Comte.* Paris, 1956.

Lévy-Bruhl, L. *La philosophie d'Auguste Comte.* Paris, 1900. Translated by K. de Beaumont-Klein as *The Philosophy of Auguste Comte.* New York, 1903.

Littré, E. *Auguste Comte et la philosophie positive.* Paris, 1863.
      Auguste Comte et Stuart Mill. Paris, 1867.

Marvin, F. S. *Comte: The Founder of Sociology.* London, 1936.

Mill, J. S. *Auguste Comte and Positivism.* London, 1865.

Moschetti, A. M. *Auguste Comte e la pedagogia positiva.* Milan, 1953.

Negt, O. *Strukturbeziehungen zwischen den Gesellschaftslehren Comtes und Hegels.* Frankfort, 1964.

Peter, J. *Auguste Comte. Bild vom Menschen.* Stuttgart, 1936.

Whittaker, T. *Comte and Mill.* London, 1908.

Part II: Chapter VI

1. *Littré*

Texts

De la philosophie positive. Paris, 1845.

Application de la philosophie positive au gouvernement des sociétés. Paris, 1849.

Conservation, révolution et positivisme. Paris, 1852 (2nd edition, 1879).

Paroles de philosophie positive. Paris, 1859 (2nd edition, 1863).

Auguste Comte et la philosophie positive. Paris, 1863.

Auguste Comte et Stuart Mill. Paris, 1867.

Principes de philosophie positive. Paris, 1868.

La science au point de vue philosophique. Paris, 1873.

Fragments de philosophie positive et de sociologie contemporaine. Paris 1876. (The articles published in *De la philosophie positive* are reprinted in this work.)

Studies

Aquarone, S. *The Life and Works of Emile Littré.* Leyden, 1958.
Caro, E. *Littré et le positivisme.* Paris, 1883.
Charlton, D. G. See under General Works.
Six, L. *Littré devant Dieu.* Paris, 1962.

2. *Bernard*

Texts

Introduction à la médecine expérimentale. Paris, 1865. Translated by
  N. C. Green as *An Introduction to the Study of Experimental
  Medicine.* New York, 1927.
La science expérimentale. Paris, 1878.
Pensées. Notes détachées, edited by L. Delhoume. Paris, 1937.
Philosophie, edited by J. Chevalier. Paris, 1938.
*Leçons sur les phénomènes de la vie communs aux animaux et aux
  végétaux.* Paris, 1966.

Studies

Clarke, R. *Claude Bernard et la médecine expérimentale.* Paris, 1961.
Cotard, H. *La pensée de Claude Bernard.* Grenoble, 1945.
Foulquié, P. *Claude Bernard.* Paris (undated).
Lamy, P. *Claude Bernard et le matérialisme.* Paris, 1939.
Mauriac, P. *Claude Bernard.* Paris, 1941 (2nd edition 1954).
Olmsted, J. M. D. and E. H. *Claude Bernard and the Experimental
  Method in Medicine.* New York, 1952.
Sertillanges, A. D. *La philosophie de Claude Bernard.* Paris, 1944.
Virtanen, R. *Claude Bernard and his Place in the History of Ideas.*
  Lincoln (Nebraska), 1960.
Various Authors. *Philosophie et méthodologie scientifique de Claude
  Bernard.* Paris, 1966.

3. *Taine*

Texts

Les philosophes français du dix-neuvième siècle. Paris, 1857.
Essais de critique et d'histoire. Paris, 1858.
Histoire de la littérature anglaise. 4 vols. Paris, 1863–4. Translated by
  H. van Laun as *History of English Literature,* 2 vols, Edinburgh,
  1873.
Nouveaux essais de critique et d'histoire. Paris, 1865.
Philosophie de l'art. Paris, 1865. Translated by J. Durand as *The
  Philosophy of Art.* New York, 1865. (Second French edition
  1880.)
De l'intelligence. 2 vols. Paris, 1870. Translated by T. D. Hayes as
  Intelligence. London 1871.

Les origines de la France contemporaine. 5 vols. Paris, 1875–93.
Derniers essais de critique et d'histoire. Paris, 1894.

Studies

Aulard, A. *Taine, historien de la révolution française.* Paris, 1907.
Barzelotti, G. *Ippolito Taine.* Rome, 1896.
Boosten, J. P. *Taine et Renan et l'idée de Dieu.* Maastricht, 1936.
Castiglioni, G. *Taine.* Brescia. 1945.
Cresson, A. *Hippolyte Taine.* Paris, 1951.
Giraud, V. *Essai sur Taine: son œuvre et son influence.* Paris, 1901.
   Hippolyte Taine: Études et documents. Paris, 1928.
Ippolito, F. G. *Taine e la filosofia dell'arte.* Roma, 1911.
Kahn, S. J. *Science and Aesthetic Judgment: A Study in Taine's Critical Method.* New York, 1953.
Lacombe, P. *La Psychologie des individus et des sociétés chez Taine.* Paris, 1906.
   Taine, historien et sociologue. Paris, 1909.
La Ferla, G. *Ippolito Taine.* Rome, 1937.
Mongardini, C. *Storia e sociologia nell'opera di Hippolyte Taine.* Milan, 1965.
Relevant aspects of Taine's thought are discussed in such works as Benedetto Croce's *Estetica* and *Teoria e storia della storiografia* and H. Sée's *Science et philosophie de l'histoire* (2nd edition, Paris, 1933).

4. Durkheim

Texts

De la division du travail social. Paris, 1893. Translated by G. Simpson as *The Division of Labour in Society,* New York, 1952.
Les règles de la méthode sociologique. Paris, 1895. Translated by S. A. Solovay and J. H. Mueller as *The Rules of Sociological Method,* Chicago, 1938 (republished at Glencoe, Illinois, 1950).
Le suicide. Étude de sociologie. Paris, 1897. Translated by J. A. Spaulding and G. Simpson as *Suicide: A Study in Sociology,* Glencoe, Illinois, 1951).
Les formes élémentaires de la vie religieuse: le système totémique en Australie. Paris, 1912. Translated by J. W. Swain as *The Elementary Forms of the Religious Life: A Study in Religious Sociology,* London and New York, 1915.
Éducation et sociologie. Paris, 1922. Translated by J. D. Fox as *Education and Sociology,* Glencoe, Illinois, 1956.
Sociologie et philosophie. Paris, 1924. Translated by D. F. Pocock as *Sociology and Philosophy,* London and Glencoe, Illinois, 1953.

L'éducation morale. Paris, 1925, Translated by E. K. Wilson and H. Schnurer as *Moral Education: A Study in the Theory and Application of the Sociology of Education*, New York, 1961.

Le socialisme. Paris, 1928.

L'évolution pédagogique en France. France, 1938.

Leçons de sociologie: physique des mœurs et du droit. Paris, 1950. Translated by C. Brookfield as *Professional Ethics and Civic Morals*, London, 1957.

Montesquieu et Rousseau, précurseurs de la sociologie. Paris, 1953.

La science sociale et l'action. Introduction et présentation de J. C. Filloux. Paris, 1970.

There are various collections of articles by Durkheim, such as *Journal sociologique*, edited by J. Duvignaud, Paris, 1969. In English there is *Émile Durkheim, 1858–1917: A Collection of Essays, with Translations and a Bibliography*, edited by K. H. Wolff, Columbus, Ohio, 1960. This work also contains essays on Durkheim by various authors.

Studies

Aimard, G. *Durkheim et la science économique.* Paris, 1962.

Alpert, H. *Émile Durkheim and His Sociology.* New York, 1939.

Bierstedt, R. *Émile Durkheim.* New York and London, 1966.

Coser, L. A. *Masters of Sociological Thought.* New York, 1971. (Contains a chapter on Durkheim.)

Davy, G. *Durkheim, choix de textes avec étude du système sociologique.* Paris, 1911.

Duvignard, J. *Durkheim: sa vie, son œuvre, avec un exposé de sa philosophie.* Paris, 1965.

Fletcher, R. *The Making of Sociology*, Vol. 2. London, 1971.

Gehlke, C. E. *Émile Durkheim's Contributions to Sociological Theory.* New York, 1915.

La Capra, D. *Émile Durkheim: Sociologist and Philosopher.* Ithaca and London, 1972.

Lukes, S. *Émile Durkheim. His Life and Work. A Historical and Critical Study.* London, 1973. (Highly recommended. Includes a comprehensive bibliography.)

Nisbet, R. A. *Émile Durkheim.* Englewood Cliffs, N.J., 1965.

Parsons, T. *The Structure of Social Action.* New York, 1937, and Glencoe, Illinois, 1949.

Seger, I. *Durkheim and his Critics on the Sociology of Religion.* New York, 1957.

Vialatoux, J. *De Durkheim á Bergson.* Paris, 1939.

Wolff, K. H. (editor). See above under Texts.

5. *Lévy-Bruhl*

Texts

Histoire de la philosophie moderne en France. Paris. Translated by
G. Coblence, London and Chicago, 1899.

La Philosophie de Jacobi. Paris, 1894.

La philosophie d' Auguste Comte. Paris, 1900. Translated by K. de
Beaumont-Klein as *The Philosophy of Auguste Comte*, London,
1903.

Les fonctions fondamentales dans les sociétés inférieures. Paris, 1910.
Translated by L. A. Clare as *How Natives Think*, London and
New York, 1923.

La mentalité primitive. Paris, 1921. Translated by L. A. Clare as
Primitive Mentality, London, 1928.

L'âme primitive. Paris, 1921. Translated by L. A. Clare as *The
'Soul' of the Primitive*, London, 1928.

Le surnaturel et la nature dans la mentalité primitive. Paris, 1931.
Translated by L. A. Clare as *Primitives and the Supernatural*,
London, 1936.

*La mythologie primitive. Le monde mythique des Australiens et des
Papous.* Paris, 1935.

L'expérience mystique et les symboles chez les primitifs. Paris, 1938.

Les carnets de Lucien Lévy-Bruhl. Paris, 1949.

Studies

Cailliet, E. *Mysticisme et 'mentalité mystique'. Étude d'un problème
posé par les travaux de M. Lévy-Bruhl sur la mentalité primitive.*
Paris, 1938.

Cazeneuve, J. *Lévy-Bruhl. Sa vie, son œuvre, avec un exposé de sa
philosophie.* Paris, 1963.

Evans-Pritchard, E. *Lévy-Bruhl's Theory of Primitive Mentality.*
Oxford, 1934.

Leroy, O. *La raison primitive. Essai de réfutation de la théorie du
prélogisme.* Paris, 1927.

Chapter VII

1. *Cournot*

Texts

Recherches sur les principes mathématiques de la théorie des richesses.
Paris, 1938. Translated by N. I. Bacon as *Researches into the
Mathematical Principles of the Theory of Wealth*, London, 1877.

Exposition de la théorie des chances et des probabilités, Paris, 1843.

*Essai sur les fondements de nos connaissances et sur les caractères de la
critique philosophique.* 2 vols. Paris, 1851. Translated by M. H.
Moore as *An Essay on the Foundations of all Knowledge*, New
York, 1956.

Traité de l'enchaînement dans les idées fondamentales dans les sciences et dans l'histoire. 2 vols. Paris, 1861. (The 2nd and 3rd editions, 1911 and 1922, are each comprised in one volume.)

Principes de la théorie des richesses. Paris, 1863.

Des institutions d'instruction publique en France. Paris, 1864.

Considérations sur la marche des idées et des événements dans les temps modernes. 2 vols. Paris, 1872. (Reissued Paris, 1934).

Matérialisme, vitalisme, nationalisme: Études sur l'emploi des données de la science en philosophie. Paris, 1875.

Souvenirs: 1760 à 1860, edited by E. P. Bottinelli. Paris, 1913.

There are some other writings in the fields of mathematics and economics which are not mentioned above.

Studies

Bottinelli, E. P. *A. Cournot, métaphysicien de la connaissance.* Paris, 1913.

Caizzi, B. *La filosofia di A. Cournot.* Bari, 1942.

Callot, E. *La philosophie biologique de Cournot.* Paris, 1959.

Darbon, A. *Le concept du hasard dans la philosophie de Cournot.* Paris, 1911.

De la Harpe, J. *De l'ordre et du hasard. Le réalisme critique d'Antoine Augustin Cournot.* Neuchatel, 1936.

Mentré, F. *Cournot et la renaissance du probabilisme au XIXᵉ siècle.* Paris, 1908.

Milhaud, G. *Études sur Cournot.* Paris, 1927.

Ruyer, R. *L'humanité de l'avenir d'après Cournot.* Paris, 1930.

Segond, J. *Cournot et la psychologie vitaliste.* Paris, 1911.

An issue of the *Revue de métaphysique et de morale* (1905, vol. 13, is devoted to articles on Cournot by various authors.

2. *Renouvier*

Texts

Manuel de philosophie moderne. Paris, 1842.

Manuel de philosophie ancienne. Paris, 1844.

Manuel républicain de l'homme et du citoyen. Paris, 1848.

Essais de critique générale. 4 vols. Paris, 1854–64. (The four volumes treat respectively of logic, national psychology, the principles of Nature, and philosophy of history.)

La science de la morale. 2 vols. Paris, 1869.

Uchronie, l'utopie dans l'histoire. Esquisse historique du développement de la civilisation européenne, tel qu'il n'a pas été, tel qu'il aurait pu être. Paris, 1876.

Esquisse d'une classification systématique des systèmes philosophiques. 2 vols. Paris, 1885–6.

La philosophie analytique de l'histoire,. 4 vols. Paris, 1896–7.

Les dilemmes de la métaphysique pure. Paris, 1901.
Histoire et solution des problèmes métaphysiques. Paris, 1901.
Le personnalisme. Paris, 1903.
Les derniers entretiens, edited by L. Prat. Paris, 1904.
La critique de la doctrine de Kant, edited by L. Prat. Paris, 1906.

Studies

Foucher, L. *La jeunesse de Renouvier et sa première philosophie.* Paris, 1927.
Galli, G. *Prime linee di un idealismo critico e due studi sul Renouvier.* Turin, 1943.
Hamelin, O. *Le système de Renouvier.* Paris, 1927.
Lombardi, V. *Lo sviluppo del pensiero di Charles Renouvier.* Naples, 1932.
Méry, M. *La critique du christianisme chez Renouvier.* 2 vols. Paris, 1953.
Milhaud, G. *La philosophie de Charles Renouvier.* Paris, 1972.
Mouy, P. *L'idée de progrès dans la philosophie de Renouvier.* Paris, 1972.
Prat, L. *Charles Renouvier, philosophe.* Ariège, 1973.
Séailles, G. *La philosophie de Charles Renouvier.* Paris, 1905.
Verneaux, R. *L'idéalisme de Renouvier.* Paris, 1945. *Esquisse d'une théorie de la connaissance. Critique du néocriticisme.* Paris, 1954.

3. Hamelin

Texts

Essai sur les éléments principaux de la représentation. Paris, 1907.
Le système de Descartes, edited by L. Robin. Paris, 1910.
Le système d'Aristote, edited by L. Robin. Paris, 1920.
Le système de Renouvier, edited by P. Mary. Paris, 1927.
La théorie de l'intellect d'après Aristote et ses commentateurs, edited by E. Barbotin. Paris, 1953.
Le système du savoir, selections edited by L. Millet. Paris, 1956.

Studies

Beck, L. J. *La méthode synthétique de Hamelin.* Paris, 1935.
Carbonara, C. *L'idealismo di Octave Hamelin.* Naples, 1927.
Deregibus, A. *La metafisica critica di Octave Hamelin.* Turin, 1968.
Sesmat, A. *Dialectique. Hamelin et la philosophie chrétienne.* Paris, 1955.

4. Brunschvicg

Texts

Spinoza. Paris, 1894. (Later edition, with additional material, *Spinoza et ses contemporains,* Paris, 1923.)

La modalité du jugement. Paris, 1897. (Third edition, with a French translation of Brunschvicg's 1897 Latin thesis, Paris, 1964.)
L'idéalisme contemporain. Paris, 1905.
Les étapes de la philosophie des mathématiques. Paris, 1912.
Introduction à la vie de l'esprit. Paris, 1920.
L'expérience humaine et la causalité physique. Paris, 1922.
Le progrès de la conscience dans la philosophie occidentale. 2 vols. Paris, 1927.
La raison et la religion. Paris, 1939.
Descartes et Pascal, lecteurs de Montaigne. Neuchâtel, 1942.
Héritage de mots, héritage d'idées. Paris, 1945.
Écrits philosophiques, edited by A. R. Weill-Brunschvicg and C. Lehec. 3 vols. Paris, 1951–8.

Studies

Boriel, R. *Brunschvicg.* Paris, 1964.
Carbonara, C. *Léon Brunschvicg.* Naples, 1931.
Centineo, E. *La filosofia dello spirito di Léon Brunschvicg.* Palermo, 1950.
Cochet, M. A. *Commentaire sur la conversion spirituelle dans la philosophie de Léon Brunschvicg.* Brussels, 1937.
Deschoux, M. *La philosophie de Léon Brunschvicg.* Paris, 1949. (includes a full bibliography.)
Mersaut, J. *La philosophie de Léon Brunschvicg.* Paris, 1938.

Chapter VIII

1. *Ravaisson*

Texts

Essai sur la métaphysique d'Aristote. 2 vols. Paris, 1837–46.
L'habitude. Paris, 1839. (With an introduction by J. Baruzi, Paris, 1957.)
Rapport sur la philosophie en France au XIXe siècle. Paris, 1867.
Testament philosophique et fragments, edited by C. Devivaise, Paris, 1932.

Studies

Bergson, H. *Notice sur la vie et les œuvres de M. Félix Ravisson-Mollien.* Reprinted in Bergson's *La pensée et le mouvant* (Paris, 1934) from *Comptes-rendus de l'Académie des sciences morales et politiques* (Paris, 1904). Also contained in *Testament philosophique et fragments.*
Dopp, J. *Félix Ravaisson, la formation de sa pensée d'après des documents inédits.* Louvain, 1933.

Valerio, C. *Ravaisson et l'idealismo romantico in Francia*. Naples, 1936.

2. Lachelier

Texts

Oeuvres. 2 vols. Paris, 1933.
De nature syllogismi. Paris, 1871.
Du fondement de l'induction. Paris, 1871. (The second edition, 1896, includes *Psychologie et métaphysique*, while the 1901 *Notes sur le pari de Pascal* are added in the fifth edition.)
Études sur le syllogisme. Paris, 1907.
Lachelier, la nature, l'esprit, Dieu, edited by L. Millet. Paris, 1955.
The Philosophy of Jules Lachelier, edited by E. G. Ballard. The Hague, 1960. This work contains translations of *Du fondement de l'induction*, *Psychologie et métaphysique* and *Pari de Pascal*, with an introduction by the editor.

Studies

Agosti, V. *La filosofia di Jules Lachelier*. Turin 1952.
Giglio, P. *L'ideale della libertà nella filosofia di Lachelier*. Rome, 1946.
Jolivet, R. *De Rosmini à Lachelier*. Paris, 1953.
Mauchassat, G. *L'idéalisme de Lachelier*. Paris, 1961.
Millet, L. *Le symbolisme dans la philosophie de Jules Lachelier*. Paris, 1959.
Séailles, G. *La philosophie de Jules Lachelier*. Paris, 1921.
Mention can also be made of G. Devivaise's article *La philosophie religieuse de Jules Lachelier* in the *Revue des sciences philosophiques et théologiques* (139, pp. 435–64).

3. Boutroux

Texts

De la contingence des lois de la nature. Paris, 1874. Translated by F. Rothwell as *The Contingency of the Laws of Nature*, London and Chicago, 1916.
De l'idée de loi naturelle dans la science et la philosophie contemporaines. Paris, 1895. Translated by F. Rothwell as *Natural Law in Science and Philosophy*, London, 1914.
Études d'histoire de la philosophie. Paris, 1897. Translated by F. Rothwell as *Historical Studies in Philosophy*, London, 1912.
La science et la religion dans la philosophie contemporaine. Paris, 1908. Translated by J. Nield as *Science and Religion in Contemporary Philosophy*, London, 1909.
La nature et l'esprit. Paris, 1926. (This posthumous publication includes the programme for Boutroux's Gifford Lectures.)

Studies

Baillot, A. *Émile Boutroux et la pensée religieuse.* Paris, 1958.
Crawford, L. S. *The Philosophy of Émile Boutroux.* New York, 1929.
La Fontaine, A. P. *La philosophie d'Émile Boutroux.* Paris, 1921.
Ranzoli, C. *Boutroux. La vita, il pensiero filosofico.* Milan, 1924.
Schyns, M. *La philosophie d'Émile Boutroux.* Paris, 1924.

4. Fouillée

Texts

La philosophie de Platon. Paris, 1869.
La liberté et le déterminisme. Paris, 1872.
La philosophie de Socrate. Paris, 1874.
La science sociale contemporaine. Paris, 1880.
Critique des systèmes de morale contemporains. Paris, 1883.
L'avenir de la métaphysique. Paris, 1889
L'évolutionnisme des idées-forces. Paris, 1890.
Psychologie des idées-forces. 2 vols. Paris, 1893.
Le mouvement idéaliste et la réaction contre la science positive. Paris, 1896.
Les éléments sociologiques de la morale. Paris, 1905.
Morale des idées-forces. Paris, 1908.
La pensée et les nouvelles écoles anti-intellectualistes. Paris, 1911.
Esquisse d'une interprétation du monde. Paris, 1913.

Studies

Ganne de Beaucoudrey, E. *La psychologie et la métaphysique des idées-forces chez Alfred Fouillée.* Paris, 1936.
Guyau, A. *La philosophie et la sociologie d'Alfred Fouillée.* Paris, 1913.
Moretti Costanzi, T. *Il pensiero di Alfred Fouillée.* Naples, 1936.
Pawlicky, A. *Alfred Fouillée's neue Theorie der Ideenkräfte.* Vienna, 1893.

5. Guyau

Texts

La morale d'Épicure et ses rapports avec les doctrines contemporaines. Paris, 1878.
La morale anglaise contemporaine. Paris, 1879.
Les problèmes de l'esthétique contemporaine. Paris, 1884.
Esquisse d'une morale sans obligation ni sanction. Paris, 1885. Translated by G. Kapteyn as *A Sketch of Morality Independent of Obligation or Sanction,* London, 1898.
L'irréligion de l'avenir. Paris, 1887. Translated at *The Non-Religion of the Future,* London, 1897 (reprinted at New York, 1962).

L'art au point de vue sociologique. Paris, 1889.
Éducation et hérédité. Paris, 1889. Translated by W. J. Greenstreet as *Education and Heredity*, London, 1891.
La genèse de l'idée de temps. Paris, 1890.

Studies

Aslan, G. *La morale selon Guyau.* Paris, 1906.
Fouillée, A. *La morale, l'art et la religion d'après Guyau.* Paris, 1889 (new edition 1901).
Royce, J. 'J. M. Guyau' in *Studies of Good and Evil.* New York, 1925.
Tisbe, A. *L'arte, la morale, la religione nel J.-M. Guyau.* Rome, 1938.

Chapters IX–X

Bergson

Texts

Oeuvres. Édition du centenaire. Paris, 1959. Introduction by H. Gouhier, with notes by A. Robinet.
Quid Aristoteles de loco senserit. Paris, 1889. (Doctorate thesis, translated by R. Mossé-Bastide as *L'Idée de lieu chez Aristote* and published in *Les études Bergsoniennes*, Vol. 2, Paris, 1949.)
Essai sur les données immédiates de la conscience. Paris, 1889. Translated by F. L. Pogson as *Time and Free Will: an Essay on the Immediate Data of Consciousness*, London and New York, 1910.
Matière et mémoire. Paris, 1896. Translated by N. M. Paul and W. S Palmer as *Matter and Memory*, London and New York, 1911.
Le rire. Paris, 1900. Translated by G. C. Brereton and F. Rothwell as *Laughter, An Essay on the Meaning of the Comic*, New York, 1910.
Introduction à la métaphysique. Paris, 1903 (in the *Revue de la métaphysique. et de morale*, Vol. 11). Translated by T. E. Hulme as *An Introduction to Metaphysics*, London and New York, 1912.
L'évolution créatrice. Paris, 1907. Translated by A. Mitchell as *Creative Evolution*, London and New York, 1911.
L'énergie spirituelle. Paris, 1919. Translated by H. Wildon Carr as *Mind-Energy*, London and New York, 1935.
Durée et simultanéité. Paris, 1922. (Second edition, with three appendices, Paris, 1923.)
Les deux sources de la morale et de la religion. Paris, 1932. Translated by R. A. Audra and C. Brereton, with the assistance of W. Horsfall-Carter, as *The Two Sources of Morality and Religion*, London and New York, 1935.

La pensée et le mouvant. Paris, 1934. Translated by M. L. Andison as *The Creative Mind,* New York, 1946.
Écrits et paroles, edited by R. M. Mossé-Bastide. 3 vols. Paris, 1957–9.

Studies

Adolphe, L. *La philosophie religieuse de Bergson.* Paris, 1946.
La dialectique des images chez Bergson. Paris, 1951.
Alexander, I. W. *Bergson: Philosopher of Reflection.* London, 1957.
Barthelemy-Madaule, M. *Bergson.* Paris, 1968.
Benda, J. *Le bergsonisme.* Paris, 1912.
Sur le succès du bergsonisme. Paris, 1914.
Carr, H. W. *The Philosophy of Change.* London and New York, 1912.
Chevalier, A. *Bergson.* Paris, 1926. Translated by L. A. Clare as *Henri Bergson,* New York, 1928. (New French edition, revised by Bergson himself, Paris, 1948.)
Entretiens avec Bergson. Paris, 1959.
Copleston, F. C. *Bergson and Morality.* London, 1955. (Proceedings of the British Academy, vol. 41.)
Cresson, A. *Bergson.* Paris, 1955.
Cunningham, G. W. *A Study in the Philosophy of Bergson.* New York, 1916.
Delhomme, J. *Vie et conscience de la vie: Essai sur Bergson.* Paris, 1954.
Fabris, M. *La filosofia sociale di Henri Bergson.* Bari, 1966.
Fressin, A. *La perception chez Bergson et chez Merleau-Ponty.* Paris, 1967.
Giusso, L. *Bergson.* Milan, 1949.
Gouhier, H. *Bergson et le Christ des évangiles.* Paris, 1961.
Guitton, J. *La vocation de Bergson.* Paris, 1960.
Hanna, T. (editor). *The Bergsonian Heritage.* New York and London, 1962. (Articles by various authors.)
Heidsieck, F. *Henri Bergson et la notion d'espace.* Paris, 1961.
Husson, L. *L'intellectualisme de Bergson.* Paris, 1947.
Jankélévitch, V. *Henri Bergson.* Paris, 1959.
Lacombe, R. E. *La psychologie Bergsonienne.* Paris, 1933.
Le Roy, E. *Une philosophie nouvelle: Henri Bergson.* Paris, 1912. Translated by V. Benson as *The New Philosophy of Henri Bergson.* New York, 1913.
Lindsay, A. D. *The Philosophy of Henri Bergson.* London, 1911.
McKellan Stewart, J. *A Critical Exposition of Bergson's Philosophy.* London, 1911.
Marietti, A. *Les formes du mouvement chez Bergson.* Paris, 1953.
Maritain, J. *La philosophie bergsonienne.* Paris, 1930.
Mathieu, V. *Bergson: 'Il profondo e la sua espressione.'* Turin, 1954.

Metz, A. *Bergson et le bergsonisme*. Paris, 1933.
Mossé-Bastide, R. M. *Bergson, éducateur*. Paris, 1955.
Moore, J. M. *Theories of Religious Experience, with special reference to James, Otto and Bergson*. New York, 1938.
Mousélos, G. *Bergson et les niveaux de réalité*. Paris, 1964.
Olgiate, F. *La filosofia di Enrico Bergson*. Turin, 1914. (second edition, 1922.)
Pflug, G. *Henri Bergson. Quellen und Konsequenzen einer induktiven Metaphysik*. Berlin, 1959.
Rideau, E. *Les rapports de la matière et de l'esprit dans le bergsonisme*. Paris, 1932.
Ruhe, A. *Henri Bergson*. London, 1914.
Russell, B. *The Philosophy of Bergson*. London, 1914.
Scharfstein, B. A. *Roots of Bergson's Philosophy*. New York, 1943.
Segond, J. *L'intuition bergsonienne*. Paris, 1913.
Sertillanges, A. D. *Henri Bergson et le Catholicisme*. Paris, 1941.
Stallknecht, N. P. *Studies in the Philosophy of Creation, with especial reference to Bergson and Whitehead*. Princeton, 1934.
Stephen, K. *The Misuse of Mind. A Study of Bergson's Attack on Intellectualism*. London, 1922.
Sundin, H. *La théorie bergsonienne de la religion*. Paris, 1948.
Thibaudet, A. *Le bergsonisme*. 2 vols. Paris, 1924.
Trotignon, P. *L'idée de vie chez Bergson et la critique de la métaphysique*. Paris, 1968.
There are several collections of articles by various authors. Mention should be made of *Etudes bergsoniennes*, 6 vols., Paris, 1948–61, which also contain some writings of Bergson himself. Another collection is *Pour le centenaire de Bergson*, Paris, 1959. Also *Bergson et nous*, 2 vols., Paris, 1959–60, and *Hommage à Henri Bergson*, Brussels, 1959.

Chapter XI

1. *Ollé-Laprune*

Texts

La philosophie de Malebranche. Paris, 1870.
De la certitude morale. Paris, 1880.
Essai sur la morale d'Aristote. Paris, 1881.
La philosophie et le temps présent. Paris, 1890.
Les sources de la paix intellectuelle. Paris, 1892.
Le Prix de la vie. Paris, 1894.
La vitalité chrétienne. Paris, 1901.
La raison et le rationalisme. Paris, 1906.
Croyance religieuse et croyance intellectuelle. Paris, 1908.

Studies

Acutis, G. *Un grande maestro: Ollé-Laprune.* Turin, 1947.
Blondel, M. *Ollé-Laprune.* Paris, 1925.
Crippa, R. *Il pensiero di Léon Ollé-Laprune.* Brescia, 1947.
Fonsegrive, G. *Léon Ollé-Laprune. L'homme et le penseur.* Paris, 1912.
There is an article on Ollé-Laprune by E. Boutroux in the *Revue philosophique* for 1903. See also G. Goyau's introduction (*Un philosophe chrétien*) to *La vitalité chrétienne.*

2. Blondel

Texts

L'Action. Essai d'une critique de la vie et d'une science de la pratique. Paris, 1893. (Revised edition, Paris, 1950, in *Premiers écrits.*)
De vinculo substantiali et de substantia composita apud Leibnitium. Paris, 1893. (A French version, *Une énigme historique: le 'Vinculum substantiale' d'après Leibniz,* was published at Paris in 1930.)
La pensée. 2 vols. Paris, 1934.
L'être et les êtres. Paris, 1935.
Action. 2 vols. Paris, 1936–7. (Not to be confused with the original *L'Action.*)
La philosophie et l'esprit chrétien. 2 vols. Paris, 1944–6.
Exigences philosophiques du christianisme. Paris, 1950.
Premiers écrits. Paris, 1956.
Carnets intimes. 2 vols. Paris, 1901–66.
Blondel published a considerable number of essays. His *Lettre sur les exigences de la pensée contemporaine en matière d'apologétique* (1896, and included in *Premiers écrits*) and his *Histoire et dogme* (1904, also in *Premiers écrits*) have been translated into English, with an introduction, by A. Dru and I. Trethowan as *Maurice Blondel: The Letter on Apologetics and History and Dogma.* London, 1914.
As for letters, *Lettres philosophiques* appeared at Paris in 1961, while Blondel's correspondence with Auguste Valensin was published in three volumes at Paris, 1957–65, and his *Correspondance philosophique avec Laberthonnière* appeared at Paris in 1962.
Études blondéliennes has been published from time to time, from 1951, by the *Société des amis de Maurice Blondel.*

Studies

Archambault, P. *Vers un réalisme intégral. L'œuvre philosophique de Maurice Blondel.* Paris, 1928.
   Initiation à la philosophie blondélienne, en forme de court traité de métaphysique. Paris, 1946.

(Archambault and Others). *Hommage à Maurice Blondel*. Paris, 1946.
Bouillard, H. *Bergson et le christianisme*. Paris, 1961.
Buonaiuti, E. *Blondel*. Milan, 1926.
Cartier, A. *Existence et vérité. Philosophie blondélienne de l'action et problématique existentielle*. Paris, 1955.
Cramer, T. *Le problème religieux dans la philosophie de l'Action*. Paris, 1912.
Crippa, R. *Il realismo integrale di Maurice Blondel*. Milan, 1954.
Duméry, H. *La philosophie de l'action. Essai sur l'intellectualisme blondélien*. Paris, 1948.
    Raison et religion dans la philosophie de l'action. Paris, 1963.
École, J. *La métaphysique dans la philosophie de Blondel*. Paris and Louvain, 1959.
Giordano, V. *La scienza della practica in Maurice Blondel*. Palermo, 1955.
Hayen, A. *Bibliographie blondélienne (1888-1951)*. Paris and Louvain, 1953.
Henrici, P. *Hegel und Blondel. Eine Untersuchung über Form und Sinn der Dialektik in der 'Phänomenologie des Geistes' und der ersten 'Action'* Pullach (Munich), 1958.
Lacroix, J. *Maurice Blondel. Sa vie, son oeuvre*. Paris, 1963.
La Via, V. *Blondel e la logica dell'azione*. Catania, 1964.
Lefèvre, F. *L'itinéraire philosophique de Maurice Blondel*. Paris, 1928.
McNeill, J. J. *The Blondelian Synthesis. A Study of the Influence of German Philosophical Sources on the Formation of Blondel's Method and Thought*. Leiden, 1966.
Paliard, J. *Maurice Blondel, ou le dépassement chrétien*. Paris, 1950.
Polato, F. *Blondel e il problema della filosofia come scienza*. Bologna, 1965.
Renault, M. *Déterminisme et liberté dans 'l'Action' de Maurice Blondel*. Lyons, 1965.
Romeyer, B. *La philosophie religieuse de Maurice Blondel. Origine, évolution, maturité et son achèvement*. Paris, 1943.
Saint-Jean, R. *Genèse de l'Action, 1882-93*. Paris, 1965.
Sartori, L. *Blondel e il cristianesimo*. Padua, 1953.
Sciacca, M. F. *Dialogo con Maurice Blondel*. Milan, 1962.
Somerville, J. M. *Total Commitment. Blondel's L'Action*. Washington, D.C., 1968.
Tayman's d'Eypermon, F. *Le blondélisme*. Louvain, 1935.
Tresmontant, C. *Introduction à la métaphysique de Maurice Blondel*. Paris, 1963.
Valensin, A. (with Y. de Montcheuil). *Maurice Blondel*. Paris, 1934.
Valori, P. *Maurice Blondel e il problema d'una filosofia cattolica*. Rome, 1950.

3. *Laberthonnière*

Texts

Oeuvres. 2 vols. Paris, 1948–55.
Essais de philosophie religieuse. Paris, 1903.
Le réalisme chrétien et l'idéalisme grec. Paris, 1904.
Positivisme et catholicisme. Paris, 1911.
Le témoignage des martyrs. Paris, 1912.
Sur le chemin du catholicisme. Paris, 1913.
As stated in the text, in 1913 Laberthonnière was prohibited from publishing. One or two works, pretty well written by him, were published by friends. But the bulk of his writings had to await posthumous publication, edited by L. Canet. Among these are:
Études sur Descartes. 2 vols. Paris, 1935.
Études de philosophie cartésienne et premiers écrits philosophiques. Paris, 1938.
Esquisse d'une philosophie personnaliste. Paris, 1942.
A volume of philosophical correspondence between Blondel and Laberthonnière appeared at Paris in 1961, edited by C. Tresmontant.

Studies

Abauzit, F. *La pensée du père Laberthonnière.* Paris, 1934.
Ballarò, R. *La filosofia di Lucien Laberthonnière.* Rome, 1927.
Bonafede, G. *Lucien Laberthonnière, studio critico con pagine scelte.* Palermo, 1958.
Castelli, F. *Laberthonnière.* Milan, 1927.
D'Hendercourt, M. M. *Essai sur la philosophie du père Laberthonnière.* Paris, 1948.
Golinas, J. P. *La restauration du Thomisme sous Léon XIII et les philosophies nouvelles. Études de la pensée de M. Blondel et du père Laberthonnière.* Washington, D.C., 1959.

Chapter XII

1. *Maritain*

Texts

La philosophie bergsonienne. Paris, 1914 (3rd edition 1948). Translated by M. L. and J. G. Andison as *Bergsonian Philosophy and Thomism,* New York, 1955.
Art et scolastique. Paris, 1920 (and subsequent editions). Translated by J. F. Scanlan as *Art and Scholasticism,* with Other Essays, London, 1930.
Éléments de philosophie. I, *Introduction générale à la philosophie.* Paris, 1920. II, *L'ordre des concepts.* Paris, 1923.

Théonas. Paris, 1921. Translated by F. J. Sheed as *Theonas: Conversations of a Sage*, London and New York, 1933.

Introduction à la philosophie. Paris, 1925. Translated as *Introduction to Philosophy*, London, 1930.

Trois réformateurs. Paris, 1925. Translated as *Three Reformers: Luther, Descartes, Rousseau*, London, 1928.

Réflexions sur l'intelligence et sur sa vie propre. Paris, 1924.

La primauté du spirituel. Paris, 1927. Translated by J. F. Scanlan as *The Things That are not Caesar's*, London, 1930.

Le Docteur angélique. Paris, 1929. Translated by J. F. Scanlan as *St Thomas Aquinas, Angel of the Schools*, London, 1942.

Distinguer pour unir, ou les degrés du savoir. Paris, 1932 (4th edition, Paris, 1946). Translated by G. B. Phelan as *The Degrees of Knowledge*, New York and London, 1959.

Le songe de Descartes. Paris, 1932. Translated by M. L. Andison as *The Dream of Descartes*, New York, 1944, and London, 1946.

De la philosophie chrétienne. Paris, 1933. Translated by E. H. Flannery as *An Essay on Christian Philosophy*, New York, 1955.

Du régime temporel et de la liberté. Paris, 1933. Translated by R. O'Sullivan as *Freedom in the Modern World*, London, 1935.

Sept leçons sur l'être et les premiers principes de la raison spéculative. Paris, 1934. Translated as *A Preface to Metaphysics: Seven Lectures on Being*, London and New York, 1939.

Frontières de la poésie et autres essais. Paris, 1935. Translated by J. W. Evans as *Art and Scholasticism and the Frontiers of Poetry*, New York, 1962. (The earlier translation, mentioned above, of *Art et scolastique* also contains a translation of the essay on the frontiers of poetry.)

Science et sagesse. Paris, 1935. Translated by B. Wall as *Science and Wisdom*, London and New York, 1940.

Humanisme intégral. Paris, 1936. Translated by M. R. Adamson as *True Humanism*, London and New York, 1938.

Situation de la poésie. Paris, 1938. Translated by M. Suther as *The Situation of Poetry*, New York, 1955.

Scholasticism and Politics, edited by M. J. Adler. London, 1940.

Les droits de l'homme et la loi naturelle. New York, 1942.

Christianisme et démocratie. New York, 1943.

Redeeming the Time. Various essays translated by H. L. Binsse. London, 1943.

Education at the Crossroads. New Haven, 1943.

De Bergson à Thomas d'Aquin. New York, 1944, and Paris, 1947.

Court traité de l'existence et de l'existant. Paris, 1947. Translated by L. Galantière and G. B. Phelan as *Existence and the Existent*, New York, 1948.

La personne et le bien commun. Paris, 1947. Translated by J. J. Fitzgerald as *The Person and the Common Good*, London, 1948.

Neuf leçons sur les notions premières de la philosophie morale. Paris, 1951.

Man and The State. Chicago, 1951.

The Range of Reason. New York, 1952.

Approches de Dieu. Paris, 1953. Translated by P. O'Reilly as *Approaches to God*, New York, 1954.

Creative Intuition in Art and Poetry. New York, 1953.

On the Philosophy of History. New York, 1957, London, 1959.

La philosophie morale: Vol. 1, Examen historique et critique des grands systèmes. Paris, 1960. Translated by M. Suther and Others as *Moral Philosophy: An Historical and Critical Survey of the Great Systems*, London, 1964.

The Responsibility of the Artist. New York, 1960.

Dieu et la permission du mal. Paris, 1963. Translated by J. W. Evans as *God and the Permission of Evil*, Milwaukee, 1966.

Carnet de Notes. Paris, 1964.

For a fuller bibliography see *The Achievement of Jacques and Raïssa Maritain: A Bibliography, 1906–61* by D. and I. Gallagher. New York, 1962.

Studies

Bars, H. *Maritain en notre temps.* Paris, 1959.
  La politique selon Jacques Maritain. Paris, 1961.

Cassata, M. L. *La pedagogia di Jacques Maritain.* Palermo, 1953.

Croteau, J. *Les fondements thomistes du personnalisme de Maritain.* Ottawa, 1955.

Evans, J. W. (editor). *Jacques Maritain: The Man and his Achievement.* New York, 1965.

Fecher, C. A. *The Philosophy of Jacques Maritain.* Westminster, Maryland, 1953.

Forni, G. *La filosofia della storia nel pensiero politico di Jacques Maritain.* Bologna, 1965.

Lundgaard Simonsen, V. *L'esthétique de Jacques Maritain.* Paris, 1956.

Maritain, Raïssa. *Les grandes amitiés.* 2 vols. New York 1941. Translated by J. Kernan as (Vol. 1) *We have been Friends Together* and (Vol. 2) *Adventures in Grace*, New York, 1942 and 1945.

Michener, N. W. *Maritain on the Nature of Man in a Christian Democracy.* Hull (Canada), 1955.

A SHORT BIBLIOGRAPHY 447

Pavan, A. *La formazione del pensiero di Jacques Maritain.* Padua, 1967.

Phelan, G. B. *Jacques Maritain.* New York, 1937.

Timosaitis, A. *Church and State in Maritain's Thought.* Chicago, 1959. Volume V of *The Thomist* (1943), devoted to the thought of Maritain, has been published separately as *The Maritain Volume of the Thomist,* New York, 1943.

2. Gilson

Texts

Index scolastico-cartésien. Paris, 1913.

La liberté chez Descartes et la théologie. Paris, 1913.

Le Thomisme. Introduction à l'étude de S. Thomas d'Aquin. Strasbourg, 1919. There have been a number of revised and enlarged editions. The English version, *The Christian Philosophy of St Thomas Aquinas* (New York, 1956) is really a work on its own.

La philosophie au moyen-âge. Paris, 1922. A revised and enlarged edition appeared at Paris in 1944.

La philosophie de S. Bonaventure. Paris, 1924. Translated by I. Trethowan as *The Philosophy of St Bonaventure,* London, 1938. Second French edition, Paris, 1943.

Introduction à l'étude de S. Augustin. Paris, 1929. Second edition, Paris, 1943. Translated by L. E. M. Lynch as *The Christian Philosophy of Saint Augustin,* New York, 1960; London, 1961.

Études sur le rôle de la pensée médiévale dans la formation du système cartésien. Paris, 1930.

L'esprit de la philosophie médiévale. 2 vols. Paris, 1932. Second edition, Paris, 1944: in one volume, 1948. Translated by A. H. C. Downes as *The Spirit of Medieval Philosophy,* London, 1950.

La théologie mystique de S. Bernard. Paris, 1934. Translated by A. H. C. Downes as *The Mystical Theology of St Bernard,* London, 1940. Second French edition, Paris, 1947.

Héloïse et Abélard. Paris, 1938 (new edition, 1964). Translated by L. K. Shook as *Heloise and Abelard,* London, 1953.

Dante et la philosophie. Paris, 1939. Translated by D. Moore as *Dante the Philosopher,* New York, 1949. Second French edition, Paris, 1953.

The Unity of Philosophical Experience. New York, 1937; London, 1955.

Réalisme thomiste et critique de la connaissance. Paris, 1939.

L'être et l'essence. Paris, 1948. English revision, *Being and Some Philosophers,* Toronto, 1949. Second French edition, Paris, 1962.

Les métamorphoses de la Cité de Dieu. Louvain, 1952.

Jean Duns Scot. Introduction à ses positions fondamentales. Paris, 1952.
Christian Philosophy in the Middle Ages. London, 1955.
Peinture et réalité. Paris, 1958. English version, *Painting and Reality*, New York, 1958.
Éléments de philosophie chrétienne. Paris, 1960. English version, *Elements of Christian Philosophy*, New York, 1960.
Le philosophe et la théologie. Paris, 1960. Translated by E. Gilson as *The Philosopher and Theology*, New York, 1962.
Modern Philosophy, Descartes to Kant. New York, 1962. (In collaboration with T. Langan.)
Introduction aux arts de beau. Paris, 1963.
The Spirit of Thomism. New York, 1964.
Recent Philosophy, Hegel to the Present. New York, 1966. (In collaboration with A. Maurer.)

Studies

Edie, C. J. (editor). *Mélanges offerts à Étienne Gilson.* Paris and Toronto, 1959. (This volume includes a bibliography of books and articles by Gilson up to the date of printing.)
Quinn, J. M. *The Thomism of Étienne Gilson: A Critical Study*, Villanova, Pa., 1971.

3. Maréchal

Texts

Le point de départ de la métaphysique. Leçons sur le développement historique et théorique du problème de la connaissance. 5 vols. Vols. 1, 2 and 3, Bruges and Paris, 1922–3; Vol. 4, Brussels, 1947; Vol. 5, Louvain and Paris, 1926.
Études sur la psychologie des mystiques. 2 vols. Vol. 1, Bruges and Paris, 1924; Vol. 2, Brussels, 1937. Translated (in part) by A. Thorold as *Studies in the Psychology of the Mystics*, London, 1927.
Précis d'histoire de la philosophie moderne. Vol. 1, *De la Renaissance à Kant.* Louvain, 1933. (This is the only volume.)
Mélanges Maréchal. Vol. 1, Oeuvres. Brussels, 1950. (A collection of articles, with a bibliography.)

Studies

Casula, M. *Maréchal e Kant.* Rome, 1955.
Mélanges Maréchal, Vol. 2. Paris, 1950.
Muck, O. *Die transzendentale Methode in der scholastischen Philosophie der Gegenwart.* Innsbruck, 1964. Translated by W. J. Seidensticker as *The Transcendental Method*, New York, 1968.

Chapter XIII
1. *Poincaré*

Texts

Oeuvres de Jules Henri Poincaré. 11 vols. Paris, 1928–56. (Vol. 2 contains a biography by G. Darboux, while Vol. 11 contains centenary lectures on Poincaré.)
La science et l'hypothèse. Paris, 1902. Translated by W. J. Greenstreet as *Science and Hypothesis*, London, 1905; New York, Dover Publications, 1952.
La valeur de la science. Paris, 1905. Translated by G. B. Halsted as *The Value of Science*, London, 1907.
Science et méthode. Paris, 1908. Translated by F. Maitland as *Science and Method*, London, 1914.
Dernières Pensées. Paris, 1912. Translated by J. W. Bolduc as *Mathematics and Science: Last Essays*, New York, 1963.

Studies

Bellivier, A. *Henri Poincaré, ou la vocation souveraine.* Paris, 1956.
Frank, P. *Modern Science and Its Philosophy.* Cambridge, Mass., 1949.
Hadamard, J. S. *The Early Scientific Work of Henri Poincaré.* Houston, Texas, 1922.
  The Later Scientific Work of Henri Poincaré. Houston, Texas, 1933.
(Both of the above are Rice Institute Pamphlets.)
Popper, K. R. *The Logic of Scientific Discovery.* London, 1959.
Revue de métaphysique et de morale. Vol. 211 (1913), pp. 585–718.

2. *Duhem*

Texts

Le potentiel thermodynamique et ses applications à la mécanique chimique et à la théorie des phénomènes électriques. Paris, 1886.
Le mixte et la combination chimique. Essai sur l'évolution d'une idée. Paris, 1902.
Les théories électriques de J. Clerk Maxwell. Étude historique et critique. Paris, 1902.
L'évolution de la mécanique. Paris, 1903.
Les origines de la statique. 2 vols. Paris, 1905–06.
La théorie physique, son objet et sa structure. Paris, 1906. The second edition (1914) has been translated by P. P. Wiener as *The Aim and Structure of Physical Theory*, Princeton, 1954.
Études sur Léonard de Vinci; ceux qu'il a lus et ceux qui l'ont lu. 3 vols. Paris, 1906–13.

Essai sur la notion de théorie physique de Platon à Galilée. Paris, 1908.

Le système du monde. Histoire des doctrines cosmologiques de Platon à Copernic. 8 vols. Paris, 1913-58.

Studies

Duhem, H. P. *Un savant français: P. Duhem.* Paris, 1936.
Frank, P. *Modern Science and its Philosophy.* Cambridge, Mass., 1949.
Humbert, P. *Pierre Duhem.* Paris, 1923.
Mieli, A. *L'opera di Pierre Duhem come storico della scienza.* Grottaferrata, 1917.
Picard, E. *La vie et l'œuvre de Pierre Duhem.* Paris, 1922.
Popper, K. R. *The Logic of Scientific Discovery.* London, 1959.
There are several notable articles on Duhem, such as "La philosophie-scientifiquede M. Duhem" by A. Rey in the *Revue de métaphysiquede et morale* (vol. 12, 1904, pp. 699-744) and 'Duhem versus Galilée" in *The British Journal for the Philosophy of Science* (1957, pp. 237-248).

3. Milhaud

Texts

Leçons sur l'origine de la science grecque. Paris, 1893.
Essai sur les conditions et les limites de la certitude logique. Paris, 1894.
Le rationnel. Paris, 1898.
Les philosophes-géomètres de la Grèce. Platon et ses prédécesseurs. Paris, 1900.
Le positivisme et le progrès de l'esprit. Etude critique sur Auguste Comte. Paris, 1902.
Études sur la pensée scientifique chez les Grecs et chez les modernes. Paris, 1906.
Nouvelles études sur l'histoire de la pensée scientifique. Paris, 1911.
Descartes, savant. Paris, 1923.
Études sur Carnot. Paris, 1927.
La philosophie de Charles Renouvier. Paris, 1927.
(The last three works were published posthumously.)

Studies

Nadal, A. *Gaston Milhaud* in *Revue d'histoire des sciences* (Vol. 12, 1959, pp. 1-14).
See also the *Bulletin de la société française de philosophie* of 1961 for articles by various authors on *Emile Meyerson and Gaston Milhaud.*

4. *Meyerson*

Texts

Identité et réalité. Paris, 1908. Translated by K. Loewenberg as *Identity and Reality*, London and New York, 1930.
De l'explication dans les sciences. 2 vols. Paris, 1921.
La déduction relativiste. Paris, 1925.
Du cheminement de la pensée. 3 vols. Paris, 1931.
Réel et déterminisme dans la physique quantique. Paris, 1933.
Essais. (posthumous.) Paris, 1936.

Studies

Abbagnano, N. *La filosofia di Émile Meyerson e la logica dell'identità*. Naples, 1929.
Boas, G. *A Critical Analysis of the Philosophy of Émile Meyerson*. Baltimore, 1930.
Kelly, T. R. *Explanation and Reality in the Philosophy of Émile Meyerson*. Princeton, N.J., 1937.
La Lumia, J. *The Ways of Reason: A Critical Study of the Ideas of Émile Meyerson*. London, 1967.
Metz, A. *Meyerson, une nouvelle philosophie de la connaissance*. Paris, 1932; 2nd edition, 1934.
Stumpfer, S. *L'explication scientifique selon Émile Meyerson*. Luxembourg, 1929.
See also the essays by various authors under the general title *Émile Meyerson et Gaston Milhaud* in the *Bulletin de la société française de philosophie* for 1961.

5. *Lalande*

Texts

Lectures sur la philosophie des sciences. Paris ,1893.
L'idée directrice de la dissolution opposée à celle de l'évolution dans la méthode des sciences physiques et morales. Paris, 1898. A revised edition appeared in 1930 with the title *Les illusions évolutionistes*.
Quid de mathematica vel rationali vel naturali senserit Baconus Verulamius. Paris, 1899. (Lalande's Latin thesis.)
Précis raisonné de morale pratique. Paris, 1907.
Vocabulaire technique et critique de la philosophie. 2 vols. Paris, 1926. Publication of this work was begun in 1902 in the *Bulletin de la société française de la philosophie*. The work was published in one volume.
Précis raisonné de morale pratique. Paris, 1907.

Vocabulaire technique et critique de la philosophie. 2 vols. Paris, 1926. (This work, which originally appeared in fascicules of the *Bulletin de la société française de philosophie,* from 1902 onwards, was later published in one volume, as in the 8th edition, 1962.)

Les théories de l'induction et de l'expérimentation. Paris, 1929.

La psychologie des jugements de valeur. Cairo, 1929.

La raison et les normes. Essai sur le principe et sur la logique des jugements de valeur. Paris, 1948.

Studies

Bertoni, I. *Il neo-illuminismo etico di André Lalande.* Milan, 1965.

Lacroix, J. *L'épistémologie de l'identité d'André Lalande.* In *Panorama de la philosophie française contemporaine,* pp. 185–191. Paris, 1966.

Lalande, W. (editor). *André Lalande par lui-même.* Paris, 1967. (With a bibliography.)

6. *Bachelard*

Texts

Essai sur la connaissance approchée. Paris, 1928.

L'intuition de l'instant. Paris, 1932.

Le pluralisme cohérent de la chimie moderne. Paris, 1932.

Les intuitions atomistiques. Paris, 1933.

Le nouvel esprit scientifique. Paris, 1934.

La continuité et la multiplicité temporelles. Paris, 1937.

L'expérience de l'espace dans la physique contemporaine. Paris, 1973.

La formation de l'esprit scientifique. Paris, 1938.

Le psychanalyse du feu. Paris, 1938.

La philosophie du non. Essai d'une philosophie du nouvel esprit scientifique. Paris, 1940.

L'eau et les rêves. Essai sur l'imagination de la matière. Paris, 1942.

L'air et les songes. Paris, 1943.

La terre et les rêveries de la volonté. Paris, 1945.

La terre et les rêveries du repos. Paris, 1945.

Le rationalisme appliqué. Paris, 1949.

L'activité rationaliste de la physique contemporaine. Paris, 1951.

Le matérialisme rationnel. Paris, 1953.

La poétique de l'espace. Paris, 1957.

La poétique de la rêverie. Paris, 1960.

La flamme d'une chandelle. Paris, 1961.

Studies

Hommage à Gaston Bachelard. Paris, 1957.

Dagognet, F. *Gaston Bachelard. Sa vie, son œuvre, avec un exposé de sa philosophie.* Paris, 1965.

Quillet, P. *Gaston Bachelard.* Paris, 1964.
The *Revue internationale de philosophie* (Vol. 19, 1964) contains a
bibliography of Bachelard's works and of articles on him.

Chapter XIV

1. *Polin*

Texts

La création des valeurs. Paris, 1944.
La compréhension des valeurs. Paris, 1945.
Du laid, du mal, du faux. Paris, 1948.
Philosophie et politique chez Thomas Hobbes. Paris, 1953.
La politique morale de John Locke. Paris, 1960.
Le bonheur considéré comme l'un des beaux-arts. Paris, 1965.
Éthique et politique. Paris, 1968.

2. *Le Senne*

Texts

Introduction à la philosophie. Paris, 1925 (revised editions, 1939 and
     1947.)
Le devoir. Paris, 1930.
Le mensonge et le caractère. Paris, 1930.
Obstacle et valeur. Paris, 1934.
Traité de morale générale. Paris, 1942.
Traité de caractérologie. Paris, 1945.
La destinée personnelle. Paris, 1951.
La découverte de Dieu. Paris, 1955.

Studies

Berger, G. *Notice sur la vie et les travaux de René Le Senne.* Paris, 1956.
Centineo, E. *René Le Senne.* Palermo, 1953.
          Caratterologia e vita morale. La caratterologia del
     Le Senne. Bologna, 1955.
Gutierrez, M. *Estudio del carácter según Le Senne.* Madrid, 1964.
Guzzo, A. and Others. *René Le Senne.* Turin, 1951.
Paumen, J. *Le spiritualisme existentiel de René Le Senne.* Paris, 1949.
Pirlot, J. *Destinée et valeur. La philosophie de René Le Senne.* Namur,
     1953.
The third numbers of *Études philosophiques* and of the *Giornale di
     metafisica* for 1955 contain articles on Le Senne by various
     authors.

3. *Ruyer*

Texts

Esquisse d'une philosophie de la structure. Paris, 1930.

La conscience et le corps. Paris, 1937.
Éléments de psycho-biologie. Paris, 1946.
Le monde de valeurs. Paris, 1948.
Néo-finalisme. Paris, 1952.
Philosophie de la valeur. Paris, 1952.
La cybernétique et l'origine de l'information. Paris, 1954.
La genèse des formes vivantes. Paris, 1958.

4. Pucelle

Texts

L'idéalisme en Angleterre. Neuchâtel, 1955.
Le Temps. Paris, 1955.
La source des valeurs. Paris, 1957.
Le règne des fins. Paris, 1959.
La nature et l'esprit dans la philosophie de T. H. Green. I, Métaphysique-Morale. Louvain, 1961.

5. Lavelle

Texts

La dialectique du monde sensible. Strasbourg, 1921.
La perception visuelle de la profondeur. Strasbourg, 1921.
La dialectique de l'éternel présent. 3 vols, Paris. Vol. 1, *De l'être,* 1928; Vol. 2, *De l'acte,* 1937; Vol. 3, *Du temps et de l'éternité,* 1945.
La conscience de soi. Paris, 1933.
La présence totale. Paris, 1934.
Le moi et son destin. Paris, 1936.
L'erreur de Narcisse. Paris, 1939. Translated by William Gairdner as *The Dilemma of Narcissus.* London, 1973.
Les puissances du moi. Paris, 1939.
Le mal et la souffrance. Paris, 1940.
La philosophie française entre les deux guerres. Paris, 1942.
La parole et l'écriture.
Introduction à l'ontologie. Paris, 1947.
Traité des valeurs. 2 vols., Paris. Vol. 1, *Théorie générale de la valeur,* 1951; Vol. 2, *Le système de différentes valeurs,* 1955.
L'intimité spirituelle. Paris, 1955.
Conduite à l'égard d'autrui. Paris, 1957.
Manuel de méthodologie dialectique. Paris, 1962.

Studies

Andrés, M. *El problema del assoluto-relativo en la filosofia de Louis Lavelle.* Buenos Aires, 1957.
Beschin, G. *Il tempo e la libertà in Louis Lavelle.* Milan, 1964.

Centineo, E. *Il. problema della persona nella filosofia di Lavelle.* Palermo, 1944.
D'Ainval, C. *Une doctrine de la présence spirituelle. La philosophie de Louis Lavelle.* Louvain and Paris, 1967.
Delfgaauw, B. M. I. *Het spiritualistiche Existentialisme van Louis Lavelle.* Amsterdam, 1947.
École, J. *La métaphysique de l'être dans la philosophie de Louis Lavelle.* Louvain and Paris, 1957.
Grasso, P. G. *Louis Lavelle.* Brescia. 1948.
Nobile, O. M. *La filosofia di Louis Lavelle.* Florence, 1943.
Sargi, B. *La participation à l'être dans la philosophie de Louis Lavelle.* Paris, 1957.
Truc, G. *De Jean-Paul Sartre à Louis Lavelle, ou désagrégation et réintégration.* Paris, 1946.

6. Mounier

Texts

Oeuvres, edited by P. Mounier, 4 vols. Paris, 1961-3.
La pensée de Charles Péguy. Paris, 1931. (Written in collaboration with M. Péguy and G. Izard.)
Révolution personnaliste et communautaire. Paris, 1935.
De la propriété capitaliste à la propriété humaine. Paris, 1936.
Manifesto au service du personnalisme. Paris, 1936.
L'affrontement chrétien. Paris, 1944.
Liberté sous conditions. Paris, 1946.
Traité du caractère. Paris, 1946. Translated by C. Rowland as *The Character of Man.* London, 1956.
Introduction aux existentialismes. Paris, 1946. Translated by E. Blow as *Existentalist Philosophies*, London, 1948.
Qu'est-ce que le personnalisme? Paris, 1947. Translated by C. Rowland in *Be Not Afraid*, London, 1951.
La petite peur du XXe siècle. Paris and Neuchâtel, 1948. Translated by C. Rowland in *Be Not Afraid*, London, 1951.
Le personnalisme. Paris, 1949. Translated by C. Mairet as *Personalism*, London, 1952.
Carnets de route. 3 vols. Paris, 1950-3.
Les certitudes difficiles. Paris, 1951.
Communisme, anarchie et personnalisme. Paris, 1966. (Published by the *Bulletin des amis d'Emmanuel Mounier.*)

Studies

Amato, C. *Il personalismo rivoluzionario di E. Mounier.* Messina, 1966.
Campanini, G. *La rivoluzione cristiana. Il pensiero politico di Emmanuel Mounier.* Brescia, 1967.

Carpentreau, J. and L. Rocher. *L'esthétique personnaliste d'Emmanuel Mounier*. Paris, 1966.

Conihl, J. *Emmanuel Mounier: sa vie, son œuvre, avec un exposé de sa philosophie*. Paris, 1966.

Guissard, L. *Mounier*. Paris, 1962.

Moix, C. *La pensée d'Emmanuel Mounier*. Paris, 1960.

Rigobello, A. *Il contributo filosofico di Emmanuel Mounier*. Rome, 1955.

Esprit for December 1950 is devoted to Mounier. See also the Bulletin published by the Association des amis d'Emmanuel Mounier.

Chapter XV

1. Teilhard de Chardin

Texts

Oeuvres, edited by C. Cuénot. 10 vols. (to date). Paris, 1955– .

Le phénomène humain. Paris, 1955. Translated by B. Wall, with a preface by Sir Julian Huxley, as *The Phenomenon of Man*, London and New York, 1959.

L'apparition de l'homme. Paris, 1956. Translated by J. M. Cohen as *The Appearance of Man*, London, 1965.

Le groupe zoologique humain. *Paris*, 1956. Later editions entitled *La place de l'homme dans la nature*. Translated by R. Hague as *Man's Place in Nature. The Human Zoological Group*, London and New York, 1966.

Le milieu divin. Paris, 1957. Translated by B. Wall and Others as *Le Milieu Divin: An Essay on the Interior Life*, London, 1960.

La vision du passé. Paris, 1957. Translated by J. M. Cohen as *The Vision of the Past*, London, 1966.

L'avenir de l'homme. Paris, 1959. Translated by N. Denny as *The Future of Man*, London, 1964.

Hymne de l'univers. Paris, 1961. Translated by G. Vann as *Hymn of the Universe*, London, 1965.

L'énergie humaine. Paris, 1962. Translated by J. M. Cohen as *Human Energy*, London, 1969.

L'activation de l'énergie. Paris, 1963.

Science et Christ. Paris, 1965. Translated by R. Hague as *Science and Christ*, London, 1968.

Comment je crois. Paris, 1969. The essay with the title translated by R. Hague as *How I believe*, London and New York, 1969. The other essays translated as *Christianity and Evolution*, London, 1971.

Of the various volumes of correspondence which have been published
some are available in English translations. For example, *Lettres
de voyages* (Paris, 1956) has been translated by R.
Hague and
Others as *Letters from a Traveller* (London, 1962), while the
correspondence with Blondel, with commentary by H. de
Lubac (Paris, 1965) has been translated by W. Whitman
(New York, 1967).
From 1958 the Fondation Teilhard de Chardin has published at
Paris a number of Cahiers containing hitherto unpublished
material.
For futher bibliographical material see C. Cuénot's *Teilhard de
Chardin* (as mentioned below) and the *Internationale Teilhard-
Bibliographie, 1955–1965* edited by L. Polgar (Munich, 1965).
For an annual list of publications of more recent date see the
Archivum Historicum Societatis Jesu, published at Rome.

Studies

Barjon, L. and Leroy, P. *La carrière scientifique de Pierre Teilhard
de Chardin*. Monaco, 1964.
Barral, L. *Eléments du bâti scientifique teilhardien*. Monaco, 1964.
Barthélemy-Madaule, M. *Bergson et Teilhard de Chardin*. Paris, 1963.
       La personne et le drame humain chez Teilhard de Chardin.
       Paris, 1967.
Blanchard, J. P. *Méthode et principes du père Teilhard de Chardin*.
       Paris, 1961.
Chauchard, P. *Man and Cosmos. Scientific Phenomenology in Teilhard
de Chardin*. New York, 1965.
Cognet, L. *Le père Teilhard de Chardin et la pensée contemporaine*.
       Paris, 1952.
Corbishley, T. *The Spirituality of Teilhard de Chardin*. London, 1971.
Corte, N. *La vie et l'âme de Teilhard de Chardin*. Paris, 1957. Trans-
lated by M. Jarrett-Kerr as *Pierre Teilhard de Chardin: his Life
and Spirit*, London, 1960.
Crespy, C. *La pensée théologique de Teilhard de Chardin*. Paris, 1961.
Cuénot, C. *Pierre Teilhard de Chardin: les grandes étapes de son
évolution*. Paris, 1958 (second edition, 1962). Translated by V.
Colimore and edited by R. Hague as *Teilhard de Chardin: A
Biographical Study*, Baltimore and London, 1965. (This work
includes a complete bibliography of Teilhard's writings.)
Delfgaauw, B. *Teilhard de Chardin*, Baarn, 1961. Translated by H.
Hoskins as *Evolution: The Theory of Teilhard de Chardin*,
London and New York, 1969.
De Lubac, H. *La pensée religeuse du père Teilhard de Chardin*. Paris,
1962. Translated by R. Hague as *The Religion of Teilhard de
Chardin*, London, 1967.

458 APPENDIX

La prière du père Teilhard de Chardin. Paris, 1964.
Translated by R. Hague as *The Faith of Teilhard de
Chardin,* London, 1965.
Teilhard, missionnaire et apologiste. Toulouse, 1966.
Translated by A. Buono as *Teilhard Explained,*
New York, 1968.
L'éternel féminin. Paris, 1968. Translated by R. Hague
as *The Eternal Feminine,* London, 1971.
De Terra, H. *Mein Weg mit Teilhard de Chardin.* Munich, 1962.
Translated by J. Maxwell Brownjohn as *Memories of Teilhard
de Chardin,* London and New York, 1969.
D'Ouince, R. *Un prophète en procès: Teilhard de Chardin dans
l'église de son temps.* Paris, 1970.
Francoeur, R. T. (editor). *The World of Teilhard.* Baltimore, 1961.
Frenaud, G. and Others. *Gli errori di Teilhard de Chardin.* Turin,
1963.
Grenet, P. B. *Pierre Teilhard de Chardin, ou le philosophe malgré lui.*
Paris, 1960.
Haguette, A. *Panthéisme, action, Oméga chez Teilhard de Chardin.*
Paris, 1967.
Hanson, A. (editor). *Teilhard Reassessed.* London, 1970.
Monestier, A. *Teilhard ou Marx?* Paris, 1965.
Müller, A. *Das Naturphilosophische Werk Teilhard de Chardins.
Seine naturwissenschaftlichen Grundlagen und seine Bedeutung
für eine natürliche Offenbarung.* Munich, 1964.
North, R. *Teilhard de Chardin and the Creation of the Soul.* Milwaukee,
1967.
Philippe de la Trinité. *Teilhard et teilhardisme.* Rome, 1962.
Rabut, O. *Dialogue avec Teilhard de Chardin.* Translated as *Dialogue
with Teilhard de Chardin.* London and New York, 1961.
Raven, C. E. *Teilhard de Chardin: Scientist and Seer.* London, 1962.
Rideau, E. *La pensée du père Teilhard de Chardin.* Paris, 1965.
Translated by R. Hague as *Teilhard de Chardin: A Guide to His
Thought,* London, 1967.
Smulders, P. *La vision de Teilhard de Chardin. Essai de réflexion
théologique.* Paris, 1964.
Soucy, C. *Pensée logique et pensée politique chez Teilhard de Chardin.*
Paris, 1967.
Speaight, R. *Teilhard de Chardin. A Biography.* London, 1967.
Thys, A. *Conscience, réflexion, collectivisation chez Teilhard.* Paris,
1964.
Towers, B. *Teilhard de Chardin.* London, 1966.
Tresmontant, C. *Introduction à la pensée de Teilhard de Chardin.*
Paris, 1956.
Vernet, M. *La grande illusion de Teilhard de Chardin.* Paris, 1964.

Vigorelli, G. *Il gesuita proibito. Vita e opere del Padre Teilhard de Chardin*. Milan, 1963.

Wildiers, N. M. *Teilhard de Chardin*. Paris, 1960 (revised edition, 1964). Translated by H. Hoskins as *An Introduction to Teilhard de Chardin*, London and New York, 1968.

Zaehner, R. C. *Evolution in Religion. A Study in Sri Aurobindo and Pierre Teilhard de Chardin*. Oxford, 1971.

Of the books listed above some are concerned with showing the religious orthodoxy of Teilhard de Chardin, while a few (such as those listed under Frenaud, Philippe and Vernet) are frankly polemical. For a much more extensive bibliography of writing on Teilhard see the work by J. E. Jarque: *Bibliographie générale des œuvres et articles sur le père Teilhard de Chardin, parus jusqu'à fin décembre 1969*. Fribourg (Switzerland), 1970.

2. Marcel

Texts

Journal métaphysique. Paris, 1927. Translated by B. Wall as *Metaphysical Journal*, London and Chicago, 1952.

Être et avoir. Paris, 1935. Translated by K. Farrer as *Being and Having*, London, 1949.

Du refus à l'invocation. Paris, 1940. Translated by R. Rosthal as *Creative Fidelity*, New York, 1964.

Homo Viator. Paris, 1945. Translated by E. Craufurd, London and Chicago, 1951.

La métaphysique de Royce. Paris, 1945. Translated by V. and G. Ringer as *Royce's Metaphysics*, Chicago, 1956.

Positions et approches concrètes du mystère ontologique. Louvain and Paris, 1949 (with an introduction by M. De Corte). This essay was originally published with the play *Le Monde cassé* (Paris, 1933). An English translation by M. Harari is included in *Philosophy of Existence*, London, 1948; New York, 1949. This collection of essays was republished at New York in 1961 under the title *Philosophy of Existentialism*.

The Mystery of Being. 2 vols. I, *Reflection and Mystery*, translated by G. S. Fraser, London and Chicago, 1950; II, *Faith and Reality*, translated by R. Hague, London and Chicago, 1951. This work consists of Marcel's Gifford Lectures. The French version, *Le mystère de l'être*, was published in two volumes at Paris in 1951.

Les hommes contre l'humain. Paris, 1951. Translated by G. S. Fraser as *Man against Humanity*, London, 1952, and *Man against Mass Society*, Chicago, 1952. (This work consists of articles and lectures, 1945–50.)

Le déclin de la sagesse. Paris, 1954. Translated by M. Harari as *The Decline of Wisdom*, London, 1954; Chicago, 1955.

L'homme problématique. Paris, 1955. Translated by B. Thompson as *Problematic Man*, New York, 1967.

Présence et immortalité. Paris, 1959. Translated by M. A. Machado (and revised by A. J. Koren) as *Presence and Immortality*, Pittsburgh, 1967.

Fragments philosophiques, 1909–14. Louvain, 1962.

The Existential Background of Human Dignity. Cambridge, Mass., 1963. This volume contains Marcel's Williams James Lectures for 1961. The French version, *La dignité humaine et ses assises existentielles*, was published at Paris in 1964.

(Marcel's plays have not been listed above, exept for the incidental reference to *Le monde cassé.*)

Studies

Ariotti, A. M. *L'"homo viator' nel pensiero di Gabriel Marcel.* Turin, 1966.

Bagot, J. P. *Connaissance et amour: Essai sur la philosophie de Gabriel Marcel.* Paris, 1958.

Bernard, M. *La philosophie religieuse de Gabriel Marcel* (with an appendix by Marcel). Paris, 1952.

Cain, *Gabriel Marcel.* London and New York, 1963.

Chaigne, L. *Vies et œuvres d'écrivains. Tome 4.* Paris, 1954.

Chenu, J. *Le théâtre de Gabriel Marcel et sa signification métaphysique.* Paris, 1948.

Davy, M. M. *Un philosophie itinérant; Gabriel Marcel.* Paris, 1959.

De Corte, M. *La philosophie de Gabriel Marcel.* Paris, 1938. (Compare De Corte's introduction to *Positions et approches*, as mentioned above.)

Fessard, G. *Théâtre et mystère.* (Introduction to Marcel's play *La soif*, Paris, 1938.)

Gallagher, K. T. *The Philosophy of Gabriel Marcel* (with a Foreword by Marcel). New York, 1962.

Hoefeld, F. *Der christliche Existenzialismus Gabriel Marcels.* Zürich, 1956.

O'Malley, J. B. *The Fellowship of Being. An Essay on the Concept of Person in the Philosophy of Gabriel Marcel.* The Hague, 1966.

Parainvial, J. *Gabriel Marcel.* Paris, 1966.

Prini, P. *Gabriel Marcel et la méthodologie de l'invérifiable.* Paris, 1953.

Ralston, Z. T. *Gabriel Marcel's Paradoxical Expression of Mystery.* Washington, 1961.

Rebollo Pena, A. *Crítica de la objectividad en el existencialismo de Gabriel Marcel.* Burgos, 1954.

Ricoeur, P. *Gabriel Marcel et Karl Jaspers*. Paris, 1947.
Schaldenbrand, M. A. *Phenomenologies of Freedom. An Essay on the Philosophies of J. P. Sartre and Gabriel Marcel*. Washington, 1960.
Scivoletto, A. *L'esistenzialismo di Marcel*. Bologna, 1951.
Sottiaux, E. *Gabriel Marcel, philosophe et dramaturge*. Louvain, 1956.
Troisfontaines, R. *De l'existence à l'être*. 2 vols. Paris, 1953. (With a preface by Marcel. Contains a bibliography up to 1953.)
Widmer, C. *Gabriel Marcel et le théisme existentiel*. Paris, 1971.

Chapters XVI–XVII

Sartre

Texts

La transcendance de l'égo. Esquisse d'une description phénoménologique. Paris, *Recherches philosophiques*, (6, pp. 85–123), 1936–37. Translated by F. Williams and R. Kirkpatrick as *The Transcendence of the Ego*, New York, 1957.
L'imagination. Étude critique. Paris, 1936. Translated by F. Williams as *Imagination: A Psychological Critique*, Ann Arbor, Mich., 1962.
La Nausée. Paris, 1938. Translated by L. Alexander as *The Diary of Antoine Roquentin*, London, 1949, and as *Nausea*, New York, 1949. Translated by R. Baldick as *Nausea*, Harmondsworth, 1965.
Esquisse d'une théorie des émotions. Paris, 1939. Translated by B. Frechtman as *Outline of a theory of the Emotions*, New York, 1948, and by P. Mairet as *Sketch for a Theory of the Emotions*, London, 1962.
Le Mur. Paris, 1939. Translated by L. Alexander as *Intimacy*, London, 1949; New York, 1952. (Panther Books edition, London, 1960.)
L'imaginaire. Psychologie phénoménologique de l'imagination. Paris, 1940. Translated by B. Frechtman as *The Psychology of the Imagination*, London, 1949.
L'Être et le néant. Essai d'ontologie phénoménologique. Paris, 1943. Translated by H. Barnes as *Being and Nothingness*, New York, 1956; London, 1957.
Les Mouches. Paris, 1943. Translated by S. Gilbert as *The Flies* in *Two Plays*, London, 1946.
Les chemins de la liberté; I. *L'Âge de raison*. Paris, 1945. Translated by E. Sutton as *The Age of Reason*, London, 1947. The second volume, *Le Sursis* (Paris, 1945), was translated by E. Sutton as *The Reprieve*, London, 1947. And the third volume, *La mort dans l'âme* (Paris, 1949), was translated by G. Hopkins as *Iron in the Soul*, London, 1950.

Huis Clos. Paris, 1945. Translated by S. Gilbert as *In Camera* in *Two Plays*, London, 1946.

L'existentialisme est un humanisme. Paris, 1946. Translated by B. Frechtman as *Existentialism*, New York, 1947 and by P. Mairet as *Existentialism and Humanism*, London, 1948.

Réflexions sur la question juive. Paris, 1946 (reissued, Paris, 1954). Translated by E. de Mauny as *Portrait of the Anti-Semite*, London, 1948; and by J. Becker as *Anti-Semite and Jew*, New York, 1948.

Baudelaire. Paris, 1947. Translated by M. Turnell as *Baudelaire*, London, 1949.

Situations: 1, Paris, 1947; 2, Paris, 1948; 3, Paris, 1949; 4–5, Paris, 1964. These are collections of essays. Some of the essays contained in *Situations* 1–3 have been translated by A. Michelson as *Literary and Philosophical Essays*, London, 1955. An essay from *Situations* 2 has been translated by B. Frechtman as *What is Literature?* New York, 1949, and London, 1951.

Entretiens sur la politique (with D. Rousset and G. Rosenthal). Paris, 1949.

Saint Genet: comédien et martyr. (Vol. 1 of the *Oeuvres complètes* of Jean Genet.) Translated by B. Frechtman as *Saint Genet*, New York, 1963.

Critique de la raison dialectique. Tome 1: Théorie des ensembles pratiques. Paris, 1960. The *Question de méthode*, which forms the first part of this volume, has been translated by H. Barnes as *Search for a Method*, New York, 1963.

Les Mots. Paris, 1964. Translated by I. Clephane as *Words. Reminiscences* of Jean-Paul Sartre, London, 1964, and by B. Frechtman as *The Words: The Autobiography of Jean-Paul Sartre*, New York, 1964.

The Philosophy of Jean-Paul Sartre, edited by R. D. Cumming (London, 1968), contains extensive selections in English from Sartre's writings.

Only those plays and stories by Sartre which are mentioned in the text of this volume have been listed above. And no attempt has been made to list the multitudinous essays which Sartre has published, especially in *Les Temps Modernes*. For details of Sartre's life during the period not covered by *Words* see the three volumes of Simone de Beauvoir's memoirs which have been published at London in English translations in 1959, 1960 and 1965 (Deutsch, Weidenfeld and Nicolson).

Studies

Albérès, R. M. *Jean-Paul Sartre.* Paris, 1953.
Ayer, A. J. 'Novelist-Philosophers: J. P. Sartre' in *Horizon*, vol. 12 (1945).

Campbell, R. *Jean-Paul Sartre, ou une Littérature philosophique,* Paris, 1945.

Cera, G. *Sartre tra ideologia e storia.* Brescia, 1972.

Champigny, R. *Stages on Sartre's Way.* Bloomington, Indiana, 1959.

Chiodi, P. *Sartre e il marxismo.* Milan, 1965.

Contat, M. and Rybalka, M. *Les écrits de Sartre.* Paris, 1970.

Cranston, M. *Sartre.* London, 1962.

Dempsey, P. J. R. *The Psychology of Sartre.* Cork and Oxford, 1950.

Desan, W. *The Tragic Finale. An Essay on the Philosophy of Jean-Paul Sartre.* Cambridge, Mass., 1954.
   The Marxism of Jean-Paul Sartre. New York, 1965.
   (Both these books are careful and critical expositions.)

Fell, J. P. III. *Emotion in the Thought of Sartre.* New York and London, 1965.

Greene, N. N. *Jean-Paul Sartre: The Existentialist Ethic.* Ann Arbor, Mich., 1960.

Green, M. *Dreadful Freedom.* London and Chicago, 1948.

Hartman, K. *Grundzüge der Ontologie Sartre's.* Berlin, 1963.

Haug, W. F. *Jean-Paul Sartre und die Konstruktion des Absurden.* Frankfurt, 1967.
   Sartre's Sozialphilosophie. Eine Untersuchung zur 'Critique de la raison dialectique'. Berlin, 1966.

Holz, H. H. *Jean-Paul Sartre: Darstellung und Kritik seiner Philosophie.* Meisenheim, 1951.

Jameson, F. R. Sartre. *The Origins of a Style.* New Haven, 1961.

Jeanson, F. *Le problème morale et la pensée de Sartre.* Paris, 1947. (With a preface by Sartre.)
   Sartre par lui-même. Paris, 1958.

Jolivet, R. *Sartre ou la théologie de l'absurde.* Paris, 1965.

Kuhn, H. *Encounter with Nothingness.* Hinsdale, Illinois, 1949.

Lafarge, R. *La philosophie de Jean-Paul Sartre.* Toulouse, 1967.

Laing, R. D. and Cooper, D. G. *Reason and Violence: A Decade of Sartre's Philosophy, 1950–1960.* London, 1964. (This work includes a treatment of the *Critique de la raison dialectique.* There is a Foreword by Sartre.)

Manno, A. *L'esistenzialismo di Jean-Paul Sartre.* Naples, 1958.

Manser, A. *Sartre: A Philosophic Study.* London, 1966. (Examines Sartre's thought as expressed in his writings as a whole.)

Möller, J. *Absurdes Sein? Eine Auseinandersetzung mit der Ontologie Jean-Paul Sartres.* Stuttgart, 1959.

Murdoch, I. *Sartre: Romantic Rationalist.* Cambridge and New Haven, 1953.

Natanson, M. A. *A Critique of Jean-Paul Sartre's Ontology.* Lincoln, Nebraska, 1951.

Palumbo, G. *La filosofia esistenziale di Jean-Paul Sartre.* Palermo, 1953.

Pressault, J. *L'être-pour-autrui dans la philosophie de Jean-Paul Sartre.* Rome, 1969. (Dissertation.)

Schaldenbrand, M. A. *Phenomenologies of Freedom. An Essay on the Philosophies of Jean-Paul Sartre and Gabriel Marcel.* Washington, 1960.

Spiegelberg, H. *The Phenomenological Movement.* 2 vols. The Hague, 1960. (Ch. 10 of Vol. 2 is devoted to Sartre.)

Stern, A. *Sartre: His Philosophy and Psychoanalysis.* New York, 1953.

Streller, J. *Jean-Paul Sartre: To Freedom Condemned.* New York, 1960.

Thody, P. *Jean-Paul Sartre: A Literary and Political Study.* London, 1960.

Troisfontaines, R. *Le choix de Jean-Paul Sartre.* Paris, 1945.

Truc, G. *De Jean-Paul Sartre à Louis Lavelle, ou désagrégation et réintégration.* Paris, 1946.

Varet, G. *L'ontologie de Sartre.* Paris, 1948.

Warnock, M. *The Philosophy of Sartre.* London, 1965.

All general studies of existentialism include a treatment of Sartre. Among such studies by French philosophers we can mention the following:

Jolivet, R. *Les doctrines existentialistes de Kierkegaard à Jean-Paul Sartre.* Paris, 1948.

Mounier, E. *Introduction aux existentialismes.* Paris, 1946. Translated by E. Blow as *Existentialist Philosophies.* London, 1948.

Wahl, J. *Les philosophies de l'existence.* Paris, 1959. Translated by F. M. Lory as *Philosophies of Existence. An Introduction to the Basic Thought of Kierkegaard, Heidegger, Jaspers, Marcel and Sartre,* London, 1969.

Chapter XVIII

1. *Camus*

Texts

Oeuvres Complètes. 6 vols. Paris, 1962.

L'étranger. Paris, 1942. Translated by S. Gilbert as *The Stranger,* New York, 1946; London, 1946, *The Outsider.*

Le Mythe de Sisyphe. Paris, 1942. Translated by J. O'Brien as *The Myth of Sisyphus and Other Essays,* New York and London, 1955.

Lettres à un ami allemand. Paris, 1945. Translated by J. O'Brien in *Resistance, Rebellion and Death,* New York and London, 1961.

La Peste. Paris, 1947. Translated by S. Gilbert as *The Plague*, London, 1948.

Actuelles. 3 vols. Paris, 1950-58. A selection of the articles collected in these volumes have been published in English translation in *Resistance, Rebellion and Death* (see above).

L'homme révolté. Paris, 1951. Translated by A. Bower as *The Rebel*, London, 1953. (Revised version, New York, 1956.)

La chute. Paris, 1956. Translated by J. O'Brien as *The Fall*, London and New York, 1957.

L'exil et le royaume. Paris, 1957. Translated by J. O'Brien as *Exile and the Kingdom*, London and New York, 1957.

Réflexions sur la peine capitale. Paris, 1960. Translated as 'Reflections on the Guillotine' in *Resistance, Rebellion and Death* (see above).

Carnets. Paris, 1962. Translated by P. Thody, as *Notebooks 1935-42* and by J. O'Brien as *Notebooks 1942-51*, New York and London, 1963 and 1965.

R. Ruillot has edited Camus' published writings in two volumes: *Théâtre, récits, nouvelles* (Paris, 1962) and *Essais* (Paris. 1965).

The Collected Fiction of Albert Camus (London, 1960) contains *The Outsider (L'Étranger)*, *The Plague*, *The Fall*, and *Exile and the Kingdom*.

Caligula and Three Other Plays (New York, 1958) contains translations of Camus' plays translated by S. Gilbert.

Studies

Bonnier, H. *Albert Camus ou la force d'être.* Lyons, 1959.

Brée, G. *Camus.* New Brunswick, 1961.
　　　　(editor). *Camus: A Collection of Critical Essays.* Englewood Cliffs, N.J., 1962.

Brisville, J. C. *Camus.* Paris, 1959.

Cruickshank, J. *Albert Camus and the Literature of Revolt.* London, 1959.

Durand, A. *Le cas Albert Camus.* Paris, 1961.

Gélinas, G. P. *La liberté dans la pensée de Camus.* Fribourg, 1965.

Ginestier, P. *Pour connaître la pensée de Camus.* Paris, 1964.

Hanna, T. *The Thought and Art of Albert Camus.* Chicago, 1958.

Hourdin, G. *Camus le juste.* Paris, 1960.

Lebesque, M. *Camus par lui-même.* Paris, 1963.

Majault, J. *Camus.* Paris, 1965.

Nicolas, A. *Une philosophie de l'existence; Albert Camus.* Paris, 1964.

Onimus, J. *Camus.* Paris, 1965. Translated by E. Parker as *Albert Camus and Christianity*, Dublin and London, 1970.

Papamalamis, D. *Albert Camus et la pensée grecque.* Nancy, 1965.

Passeri Pignoni, V. *Albert Camus, uomo in rivolta.* Bologna, 1965.

Parker, E. *Albert Camus: The Artist in the Arena*. Madison, Wisc., 1965.

Quillot, R. *La mer et les prisons*. Paris, 1956 (revised edition, 1970.)

Rigobello, A. *Albert Camus*. Naples, 1963.

Roeming, R. F. *Camus: A Bibliography*. Madison, Wisc., 1968. (Complete bibliography of writings by and on Camus.)

Sarocchi, J. *Camus*. Paris, 1968.

Schaub, K. *Albert Camus und der Tod*. Zürich, 1968.

Simon, P. H. *Présence de Camus*. Paris, 1962.

Stuby, G. *Recht und Solidarität im Denken von Albert Camus*. Frankfurt, 1965.

Thody, P. *Albert Camus: A Study of His Work*. London, 1957.

Albert Camus, 1913–1960. London and New York, 1961.

Van-Huy, N. P. *La métaphysique du bonheur chez Albert Camus*. Neuchâtel, 1964.

In 1960 special numbers of *La table ronde* (February), of *La nouvelle revue française* (March) and of *Yale French Studies* (Spring) were devoted to Camus.

2. Merleau-Ponty

Texts

- *La structure du comportement*. Paris, 1942 (2nd edition, 1949). Translated by A. L. Fisher as *The Structure of Behaviour*, Boston, 1963; London, 1965.

Phénoménologie de la perception. Paris, 1945. Translated by C. Smith as *Phenomenology of Perception*, London and New York, 1962.

Humanisme et terreur. Paris, 1947. Translated in part by N. Metzel and J. Flodstrom in *The Primacy of Perception and Other Essays*, edited by J. M. Edie, Evanston, Illinois, 1964.

Sens et non-sens. Paris, 1948. Translated by H. L. and P. A. Dreyfus as *Sense and Nonsense*, Evanston, Illinois, 1964.

Les relations avec autrui chez l'enfant. Paris, 1951. Translated by W. Cobb in *The Primacy of Perception* (see above).

Les sciences de l'homme et la phénoménologie: Introduction. Paris, 1951. Translated by J. Wild in *The Primacy of Perception* (see above).

Éloge de la philosophie. Paris, 1953. Translated by J. M. Edie and J. Wild as *In Praise of Philosophy*, Evanston, Illinois, 1963.

Les aventures de la dialectique. Paris, 1955. Translated in part by N. Metzel and J. Flodstrom in *The Primacy of Perception* (see above).

Signes. Paris, 1960. Translated by R. C. McCleary as *Signs*, Evanston, Illinois, 1964.

L'œil et l'esprit. Paris, 1961. Translated by C. Dallery in *The Primacy of Perception* (see above).
Le visible et l'invisible suivi de notes de travail. Paris, 1964. This work, edited by C. Lefort, contains the part of a book which Merleau-Ponty had written before his death, together with notes for the projected parts.
For a list of the writings of Merleau-Ponty, including articles, see A. Rabil's work, listed below.

Studies

Barral, M. E. *Merleau-Ponty: The Role of the Body—Subject in Interpersonal Relations.* Pittsburgh and Louvain, 1965.
Centineo, E. *Una fenomenologia della storia. L'esistenzialismo di Merleau-Ponty.* Palermo, 1959.
Derossi, G. *Maurice Merleau-Ponty.* Turin, 1965.
De Waehlens, A. *Une philosophie de l'ambiguïté: l'existentialisme de Maurice Merleau-Ponty.* Louvain, 1951 (2nd edition, 1967).
Fressin, A. *La perception chez Bergson et chez Merleau-Ponty.* Paris, 1969.
Halda, B. *Merleau-Ponty ou la philosophie de l'ambiguïté.* Paris, 1966.
Heidsieck, F. *L'ontologie de Merleau-Ponty.* Paris, 1971.
Hyppolite, J. *Sens et existence. La philosophie de Maurice Merleau-Ponty.* Oxford, 1963 (Zaharoff Lecture).
Kaelin, E. *An Existentialist Aesthetic: The Theories of Sartre and Merleau-Ponty.* Madison, Wisc., 1962.
Kwant, R. C. *The Phenomenological Philosophy of Merleau-Ponty.* Pittsburgh and Louvain, 1963.
          From Phenomenology to Metaphysics. An Inquiry into the Last Period of Merleau-Ponty's Philosophical Life. Pittsburgh and Louvain, 1966.
Langan, T. *Merleau-Ponty's Critique of Reason.* New Haven and London, 1966.
Maier, W. *Das problem der Leiblichkeit bei Jean-Paul Sartre und Maurice Merleau-Ponty.* Tübingen, 1964.
Rabil, A., Jr. *Merleau-Ponty: Existentialist of the Social World.* New York and London, 1967. (With bibliographies.)
Robinet, A. *Merleau-Ponty: Sa vie, son œuvre, avec un exposé de sa philosophie.* Paris, 1963.
Semerari, G. *Da Schelling a Merleau-Ponty. Studi sulla filosofia contemporanea.* Bologna, 1962.
Speigelberg, H. *The Phenomenological Movement: A Historical Introduction.* 2 vols. The Hague, 1960. (Ch. 11 of Vol. 2 is devoted to Merleau-Ponty.)
Strasser ,S. *Phenomenology and the Human Sciences.* Translated by H. J. Koren, Pittsburgh, 1963.

Tilliette, X. *Philosophes contemporains* (pp. 49–86). Paris, 1962.
    *Le corps et le temps dans la 'Phénoménologie de la per-
    ception'*. Basle, 1964.
Touron del Pie, E. *El hombre, el mundo en la fenomenologia de
    Merleau-Ponty*. Madrid, 1961.
See also *Maurice Merleau-Ponty*, a volume of articles by various
    authors, Paris, 1961.

INDEX

(When there are several references, the principal ones are in heavy type. A small *n* indicates that the reference is to a note. There are entries for both Marx and Marxism. Otherwise references to theories, such as Cartesian, are generally included in the entries for the relevant philosophers. The Index does not include references to the Bibliography.)

INDEX

473

474 INDEX